Greece

written and researched by

Marc Dubin, Mark Ellingham,
John Fisher and Natania Jansz

with additional contributions by

Andrew Benson, John Bozman, Lance Chilton,
Nick Edwards, Geoff Garvey and Samantha Stenzel

ROUGH
GUIDES

www.roughguides.com

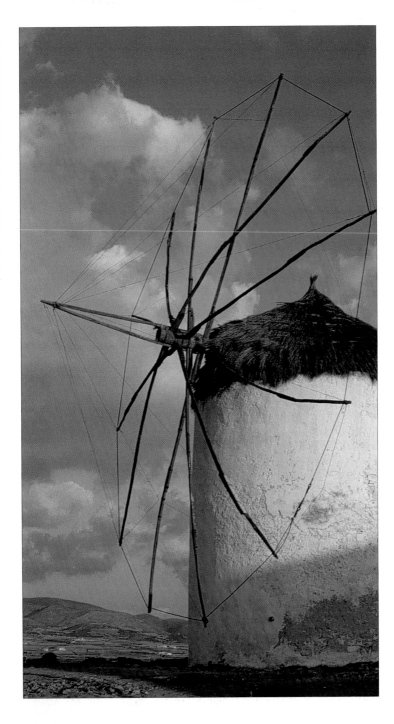

Introduction to

Greece

With well over a hundred inhabited islands and a territory that stretches from the south Aegean to the Balkan countries, Greece offers enough to fill months of travel. The historic sites span four millennia, encompassing both the legendary and the obscure, where a visit can still seem like a personal discovery. Beaches are parcelled out along a convoluted coastline equal to France's in length, and islands range from backwaters where the boat calls twice a week to resorts as cosmopolitan as any in the Mediterranean.

Modern Greece is the result of extraordinarily diverse **influences**. Romans, Arabs, Latin Crusaders, Venetians, Slavs, Albanians, Turks, Italians, not to mention the Byzantine Empire, have been and gone since the time of Alexander the Great. All have left their mark: the Byzantines in countless churches and monasteries; the Venetians in impregnable fortifications in the Peloponnese; and other Latin powers, such as the Knights of Saint John and the Genoese, in imposing castles across the northeastern Aegean. Most obvious is the heritage of four centuries of Ottoman Turkish rule which, while universally derided, contributed substantially to Greek music, cuisine, language and way of life. Significant, and still-existing, minorities – Vlachs, Muslims, Catholics, Jews, Gypsies – have also helped to forge the hard-to-define but resilient **Hellenic identity**, which has kept alive the people's sense of themselves throughout their turbulent history. With no local ruling class or formal Renaissance period to impose superior models of taste or patronize the arts, medieval Greek peasants, fishermen and shepherds created a vigorous and truly popular culture, which found expression in the songs and dances,

iii

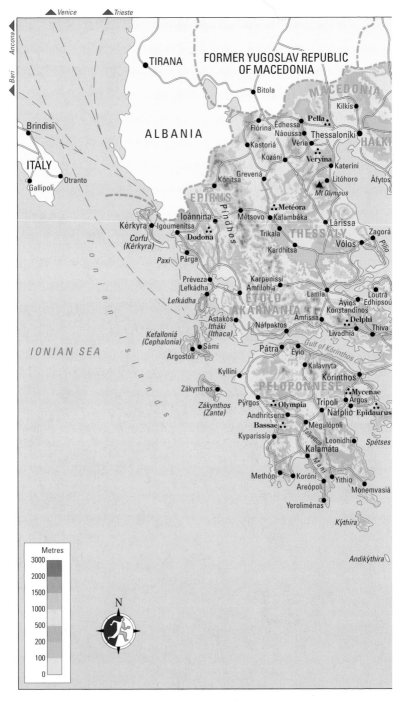

Venice Trieste

Ancona

Bari

TIRANA

FORMER YUGOSLAV REPUBLIC OF MACEDONIA

Bitola

MACEDONIA

Kilkís

Brindisi

ALBANIA

Flórina Édhessa **Pella**
Náoussa Thessaloníki
Kastoriá Véria

HALKI

ITALY

Kozáni **Veryína** Kateríni

Otranto

Grevená Kónitsa Litóhoro Áfytos

Gallipoli

Mt Olympus

EPIRUS **Metéora**

Kérkyra Ioánnina Métsovo Kalambáka Lárissa

Corfu (Kérkyra) Igoumenítsa **Dodóna** Trikala THESSALY Zagorá

P|lío

Paxí Párga Kardhítsa Vólos

Préveza Karpeníssi

Lefkádha Amfilohía

Lefkádha ÉTOLO Lamía Loutrá

AKARNANÍA Áyios Edhipsoú
Konstandínos

Astakós Amfissa **Delphi**

Itháki Náfpaktos Thíva
(Ithaca) Livadhiá

Kefalloniá (Cephalonia) Sámi Gulf of Kórinthos

IONIAN SEA Pátra Éyio

Argostóli Kalávryta

Kyllíni Kórinthos

Zákynthos PELOPONNESE **Mycenae**

Zákynthos (Zante) Pýrgos **Olympia** Trípoli Árgos
Andhrítsena Náfplio Epidaurus
Bassae Megalópoli
Kyparissía Leonídhio *Spétses*
Kalamáta

Methóni Koróni Yíthio
Aréopoli Monemvasiá

Yeroliménas

Kýthira

Andikýthira

Metres
3000
2000
1500
1000
500
200
100
0

N

BULGARIA

TURKEY

Istanbul

Sea of Marmara

Bursa

Edirne
Kastaniés
Dhráma
Sérres
Xánthi
Komotiní
THRACE
Kípi
Philíppi
Kavála
Liménas
Alexandhroúpoli
Thássos
Samothráki
DHIKÍ
Ierissós
Políyiros
Ouranoúpoli
Sithonía
Mt Athos
The North Aegean
Kassándhra

Límnos
Mýrina

Balıkesir

AEGEAN SEA

Áyios Efstrátios

Mólyvos
Ayvalık
Mytilíni

TURKEY

Skiáthos
The Sporades
Alónissos
Skópelos
Skýros

Lésvos

Manisa

Kými
Halkídha
Évvia

Psará
Inoússes
Híos
Híos
Çeşme

İzmir

ATTICA
ATHENS

Ándhros

The East
Aegean

Vathý
Sámos

Kuşadası

Pireás
Éyina
Póros
Sounion
Kéa
Tínos
Ikaría
Foúrni
Lipsí

The Argo-
Saronic
Idhra
Kýthnos
Sýros
Delos
Mýkonos
The Cyclades
Pátmos
Léros

Bodrum

Marmaris

Sérifos
Páros
Dhonoússa
Kálymnos
Kós

Sífnos
Andíparos
Náxos
Amorgós
Kós
Nissyros
Sými

Ródhos

Síkinos
Íos
Astypálea
Tílos
Hálki

Kameiros

Mílos
Folégandhros
Anáfi
The
Dodecanese
Líndhos

Thíra
(Santoríni)
Rhodes
(Ródhos)

Kárpathos

Haniá
Kástelli
Lefká
Óri
Réthymnon
Knossós
Áyios
Nikólaos
Sitía
Kássos

Paleohóra
Iráklion
Psilorítis
Zákros

Gortys
Ierápetra
Crete (Kríti)

Kastellórizo, Cyprus & Israel

Haifa

0   150 km

Fact file

● Greece is currently the easternmost member of the EU, with a **surface area** of 131,957 square kilometres (50,949 square miles) divided into 51 provinces. No other country, with the obvious exceptions of Indonesia and the Philippines, has so much of its territory in the form of islands. The **population** is overwhelmingly **Greek-speaking** and 96 percent are **Greek Orthodox** in religious affiliation, though there are noticeable Catholic, Sunni Muslim, Jewish and evangelical Christian minorities, plus pockets of Turkish-, Romany- and Macedonian-speakers. Well over half the population live in urban areas.

● Per "native" population of roughly 10.4 million, Greece has the highest proportion of **immigrants** in Europe – estimated at 800,000 to 1.1 million, most of these Albanian.

● Since 1974 Greece has been a **parliamentary republic**, with the president as head of state, and a 300-seat, single-chamber parliament led by a prime minister. At present PASOK, the (approximately) social-democratic ruling party, is enjoying its third consecutive term in office, something unheard of in the perennially unstable – and historically rightist – Greek political world.

● **Tourism** is the country's main foreign-currency earner. **Shipping**, which used to occupy second place, is in crisis and has been replaced by **agricultural products**, in particular olive oil and olives, citrus, raisins and wine.

Not to be missed are Greece's great ancient sites and medieval castles

costumes, embroidery, carved furniture and the white Cubist houses of popular imagination. During the last few decades much of this has disappeared under the impact of Western consumer values, relegated to museums at best, but recently the country's architectural and musical heritage in particular have undergone a renaissance, with buildings rescued from dereliction and performers reviving, to varying degrees, half-forgotten musical traditions.

Of course there are formal cultural activities as well: **museums** that shouldn't be missed, magnificent medieval mansions and **castles**, as well as the great **ancient sites** dating from the Neolithic, Bronze Age, Minoan, Classical, Hellenistic, Roman and Byzantine eras. Greece hosts some excellent summer **festivals** too, bringing international theatre, dance and musical groups to perform in ancient theatres, as well as castle courtyards and more contemporary venues in coastal and island resorts.

But the call to cultural duty will never be too overwhelming on a Greek holiday. The **hedonistic pleasures** of languor and warmth – going lightly dressed, swimming in balmy seas at dusk, talking and drinking under the stars – are just as appealing. And despite recent improvements to the tourism "product", Greece is still essentially a land for adaptable sybarites, not for those who crave orthopedic mattresses, faultless plumbing, Cordon-Bleu cuisine and attentive service. Except at the growing number of luxury facilities in new or restored buildings, hotel and pension rooms can be box-like, campsites offer the minimum of facilities, and the food at its best is fresh and uncomplicated.

The Greek People

To attempt an understanding of the Greek people, it's useful to realize just how recent and traumatic were the events that created the modern state and **national character** – the latter a complex blend of extroversion and pessimism, which cannot be accounted for merely by Greece's position as a natural bridge between Europe and the Middle East. Until the early decades of the twentieth century many parts of Greece were in Ottoman (or in the case of the Dodecanese, Italian) hands. Meanwhile, numerous Greek Orthodox lived in Asia Minor, Egypt, western Europe and in the northern Balkans. The Balkan Wars of 1912–13, Greece's 1917–18 World War I involvement, the Greco–Turkish war of 1919–22 and the organized **population exchanges** – essentially regulated ethnic cleansing – which followed each of these conflicts had sudden, profound effects. Worse was to come during World War II, and its aftermath of civil war between the Communists and the UK- and US-backed Nationalist government forces. The viciousness of this period found a later echo in nearly seven years of military dictatorship under the colonels' junta between 1967 and 1974.

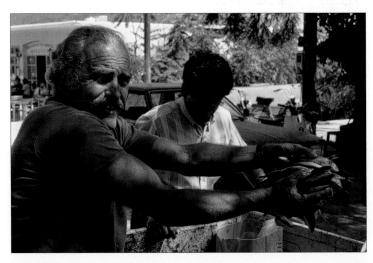

The Evil Eye

Belief in the Evil Eye (in Greek, simply *to Máti* or "the Eye") is pan-Mediterranean and goes at least as far back as Roman times, but nowhere has it hung on so tenaciously as in Greece (and neighbouring coastal Turkey). In a nutshell, whenever something attractive, valuable or unusual – an infant, a new car, a prized animal – becomes suddenly, inexplicably indisposed, it is assumed to be *matisméno* or "eyed". Blue-eyed individuals are thought most capable of casting this spell, always unintentionally or at least unconsciously (unlike *máyia* or willful black magic). The diagnosis is confirmed by discreet referral to a "wise woman", who is also versed in the proper counter-spell. But prevention is always better than cure, and this involves two main strategies. When admiring something or someone, the admirer – blue-eyed or otherwise – must mock-spit ("*phtoo, phtoo, phtoo!*") to counteract any stirrings of envy which, according to anthropologists, are the root-cause of the Eye. And the proud owners or parents will protect the object of admiration in advance with a blue amulet, hung about the baby's/animal's neck or the car's rear-view mirror, or even painted directly onto a boat-bow.

Such memories of misrule, diaspora and catastrophe (including frequent devastating earthquakes) remain uncomfortably close for many Greeks, despite nearly three decades of democratic stability and the country's integration into the EU. The poverty of, and enduring paucity of opportunity in, their homeland long frustrated talented and resourceful Greeks, many of whom **emigrated**. Those who stayed were lulled, until the late 1980s, by a civil-service-driven full-employment policy which resulted in the lowest jobless rate in western Europe. The downside of this was an occasionally staggering lack of worker initiative, but official attempts to impose a more austere economic line are still often met by waves of strikes. Since the early 1990s, Greece has become fully integrated into the Western economy, privatization and competition have demolished state monopolies, and inevitably growing disparities in wealth have appeared.

Outside the public sector, the meticulousness of Greek craftworkers is legendary, even if their values and skills took a back seat to the demands of crisis and profiteering when the evacuation of Asia Minor and the rapid 1950s depopulation of rural villages prompted the graceless **urbanization** of Athens and other cities. Amidst the often superficial sophistication that resulted, it's easy to forget the nearness of the village past and stubbornly lingering Third World attributes. You may find, for example, that buses operate with Germanic efficiency, but ferries sail with an unpredictability little changed since the time of Odysseus.

Social attitudes, too, are in transition as Greece adapts to mass tourism and the modern world. The encounter has been painful and at times destructive, as the values of a rural, conservative society have been irrevocably lost. Though younger Greeks are adaptable and cash registers ring happily, at least in tourist areas, visitors still need to be sensitive in their behaviour towards the older generation. The mind boggles imagining the reaction of black-clad elders to nudism, or even scanty clothing, in a country where the Orthodox Church remains an all-but-established faith and the self-appointed guardian of national identity. Although senior clerics have recently depleted a huge reservoir of respect with regressive stances on a number of issues, even the most worldly young Greeks, who never otherwise set foot in a church, are still likely to be married, buried and have their children baptized with Orthodox rites.

Where to go

S prawling, polluted **Athens** is an obligatory, almost unavoidable introduction to Greece: home to over a third of the population, on first acquaintance a nightmare for many, but also, as Greeks themselves often joke, *to megálo horió* – the largest "village" in the country. It also offers the widest range of cultural diversions, from museums to concerts, the best-stocked shops and some of the most accomplished restaurants. **Thessaloníki**, the metropolis of the North, after years of playing provincial second fiddle to the capital, has emerged in its own right as a stimulating, cutting-edge place with restaurants and nightlife to match Athens', Byzantine monuments compensating for a lack of "ancient" ones, and – among the inhabitants – a tremendous capacity for enjoying life. In all honesty, there are no other "world class" cities in Greece. The mainland shows its best side in the well-preserved ruins of **Corinth**, **Olympia** and **Delphi** (plus the Athenian **Parthenon**), the frescoed and mosaiced Byzantine churches and monasteries at **Mount Athos**, **Metéora**, **Ósios Loukás**, **Kastoriá** and **Mystra**, the massive fortified towns of **Monemvasiá**, **Náfplio**, **Koróni** and **Methóni**, the distinctive architecture of **Zagóri**, **Pílio** and the **Máni**, and the long, sandy **beaches** on the Peloponnesian and Epirot west coast. Perhaps more surprisingly, the mainland mountains offer some of the best and least-exploited hiking, rafting, canyoning and skiing in Europe.

Out in the Aegean or Ionian seas, you're even more spoilt for choice. Perhaps the best strategy for initial visits is to sample assorted islands from contiguous archipelagos – Crete, the Dodecanese, the Cyclades and the northeast Aegean are all reasonably well connected with each other, though the Sporades, Argo-Saronic and Ionian groups offer limited (or no) possibilities for island-hopping. If time and money are short, the best place to head for is well-preserved **Ídhra** in the Argo-Saronic, just a short ride from Pireás (the main port of Athens), but an utterly different place once the day-cruises have gone. Among the Cyclades, cataclysmically volcanic **Thíra (Santoríni)** and **Mýkonos** with its perfectly preserved harbour town rank as must-see spectacles, but fertile, mountainous **Náxos**, dramatically cliff-girt **Amorgós** or gently rolling **Sífnos** have life more independent of cruise-ship tourism and seem more amenable to long stays. **Crete** could (and does) fill an entire Rough Guide to itself, but the highlights have to be **Knossós** and the nearby **archeological museum** in Iráklion, the other Minoan palaces at **Festós** and **Ayía Triádha**, and the west in general – the proud city of **Haniá**, with its hinterland extending to the relatively unspoiled southwest coast, reachable via the fabled **Samarian gorge**.

> ## The mainland mountains offer some of the best hiking, rafting and skiing in Europe

Rhodes, with its unique old town, is capital of the Dodecanese, but picturesque, Neoclassical **Sými** opposite, and austere **Pátmos**, the island of Revelations, are far more manageable. It's easy to continue north via **Híos**, with its striking medieval architecture, to balmy, olive-cloaked **Lésvos**, perhaps the most traditional of all islands in way of life. The Ionian islands are, probably more than any other spot except Crete and Rhodes, package-holiday territory, but if you're exiting Greece towards Italy by all means stop off at **Corfu** to at least savour the Venetian-style main town, which along with neighbouring **Paxí** islet survived severe 1953 earthquake damage.

When to go

Most places and people are far more agreeable, and resolutely Greek, outside the **peak period** of early July to the end of August, when soaring temperatures, plus crowds of foreigners and locals alike, can be overpowering. You won't miss out on **warm weather** if you come in **June** or **September**, excellent times almost everywhere but particularly in the islands. An exception to this pattern, however, is the north-mainland coast – notably the Halkidhikí peninsula – and the islands of Samothráki and Thássos, which only really cater to visitors during **July** and **August**. In **October** you will almost certainly hit a stormy spell, especially in western Greece or in the mountains, but for most of that month the "summer of Áyios Dhimítrios" (the

Wayside shrines

Throughout Greece you'll see, by the side of the road, small shrines or *ikonostáses* which usually hold a saint's icon, an oil lamp, a few floatable wicks and a box of matches. Unlike in Latin America, they don't necessarily mark the spot where someone met their end in a motoring accident (though just occasionally they do); typically they were erected by one family or even one individual in fulfilment of a vow or *támma* to a particular saint to reciprocate for any favours granted. *Ikonostáses* come in various sizes and designs, from spindly, derrick-like metal constructions to sumptuous, gaily painted models of small cathedrals in marble and plaster which you can practically walk into. Often they indicate the presence of a larger but less convenient (and often locked) church off in the countryside nearby, dedicated to the same saint, and act as a substitute shrine where the devout wayfarer can reverence the icon it contains.

The períptero

The *períptero* or pavement kiosk is a quintessentially Greek institution. They originally began as a government-employment scheme for wounded veterans of the Balkan Wars and World War I, and the concessions are jealously guarded by their descendants or sold on for tidy sums. Positioned on *platíes* and strategic thoroughfares all over Greece, they keep long hours and contribute considerably to the air of public street-safety after dark. If you are lost the *períptero* is typically the first place to go for directions, and they usually know what you're looking for. Their stock in trade is predictable: sweets, bagged nuts, tissues, newspapers, bus tickets, shaving needs, key-rings with football-team logos, cigarettes, pens and pencils, (often heat-damaged) photo film, plus cold drinks and yogurts. Most of them used to have at least one telephone, with a queue of customers waiting their turn to shout down a crackly line, either across town or across the globe. Now, few kiosks sport even a card-phone, but they're still one of the best places to buy a top-up card for your Greek pay-as-you-go mobile.

Greek equivalent of Indian summer) prevails, and the southerly Dodecanese and Crete are extremely pleasant. Autumn in general is beautiful; the light is softer, the sea often balmier than the air, and the colours subtler.

December to **March** are the coldest and least reliable months, though even then there are many crystal-clear, fine days, and the glorious lowland flowers begin to bloom very early in spring. The more northerly latitudes and high altitudes of course endure far colder and wetter conditions, with the mountains themselves under snow from November to May. The mildest **winter climate** is to be found on Rhodes, or in the southeastern parts of Crete. As spring slowly warms up, **April** is still uncertain, though superb for wild flowers, green landscapes and photography; by **May** the weather is more generally predictable, and Crete, the Peloponnese, the Ionian islands and the Cyclades are perhaps at their best, even if the sea is still a little cool for swimming. Note, however, that these are the historical patterns as observed until the early 1990s; thanks to global warming, recent years have seen erratic climate, with unusually cold Mays, warm Octobers, little (and late) rain, plus very early spring flowering.

Other factors that affect the timing of your Greek travels have to do with the level of tourism and the amenities provided. Service standards, particularly in tavernas, slip under peak-season pressure, and room rates top out from July to September (as well as during Easter or Christmas week). If you can only visit during midsummer, reserve a package well in advance, or plan your itinerary off the beaten track: you might for example explore the less obvious parts of the Peloponnese or the northern mainland, or island-hop with an eye for the remoter places.

Out of season, especially between late October and late April, you have to contend with reduced ferry services to the islands (and nonexistent hydrofoils or catamarans), plus fairly skeletal facilities when you arrive. You will, however, find reasonable service on all main routes and at least one hotel and taverna open in the port or main town of all but the tiniest isles. On the mainland, winter travel poses no special difficulties except, of course, in mountain villages either cut off by snow or (at weekends especially) monopolized by avid Greek skiers.

Average temperatures (°F) and rainfall

	Jan °F Max	Jan Min	Jan Rain Days	Mar °F Max	Mar Min	Mar Rain Days	May °F Max	May Min	May Rain Days	July °F Max	July Min	July Rain Days	Sept °F Max	Sept Min	Sept Rain Days	Nov °F Max	Nov Min	Nov Rain Days
Athens	54	44	13	60	46	10	76	60	9	90	72	2	84	66	4	65	52	12
Crete (Haniá)	60	46	17	64	48	11	76	56	5	86	68	0	82	64	3	70	54	10
Cyclades (Mýkonos)	58	50	14	62	52	8	72	62	5	82	72	0.5	78	68	1	66	58	9
North Greece (Halkidhíki)	50	36	7	59	44	9	77	58	10	90	70	4	83	64	5	60	47	9
Ionian (Corfu)	56	44	13	62	46	10	74	58	6	88	70	2	82	64	5	66	52	12
Dodecanese (Rhodes)	58	50	15	62	48	7	74	58	2	86	70	0	82	72	1	68	60	7
Sporades (Skiáthos)	55	45	12	58	47	10	71	58	3	82	71	0	75	64	8	62	53	12
East Aegean (Lésvos)	54	42	11	60	46	7	76	60	6	88	70	2	82	66	2	64	50	9

42

things not to miss

It's not possible to see everything that Greece has to offer in one trip – and we don't suggest you try. What follows is a selective taste of the country's highlights: outstanding buildings and ancient sites, natural wonders and colourful festivals. They're arranged in five colour-coded categories, which you can browse through to find the very best things to see, and experience. All highlights have a page reference to take you straight into the guide, where you can find out more.

01 Acropolis Page **118** • Dominating Athens, the Acropolis is one of the archetypal images of Western civilization.

02 Kolonáki
Page **134** •
Superbly sited on the slopes of Lykavitós Hill, Athens' well-heeled Kolonáki district brims with fashionable shops and pavement cafés.

03 Herodes Atticus theatre
Page **116** • The ancient Roman Herodes Atticus theatre is a major venue for classical music concerts during the Hellenic summer festival.

04 Poseidon temple, Cape Sounion
Page **166** • The dramatically sited Poseidon temple is a familiar landmark to boats at sea.

05 Dhiakoftó railway Page **297** •
A ride on the Dhiakoftó rack-
and-pinion railway through the
Vouraïkós gorge makes for an
unforgettable journey.

06 Ósios Loukás, mosaics
Page **315** • Decorated with vivid
mosaics, Ósios Loukás ranks as one of
Greece's finest Byzantine buildings.

07 Melissáni Cave, Kefalloniá Page **972** • Take a
boat trip to the underwater Melissáni cave,
and admire the rock formations and play of
light on the cave walls.

08 Delphi: theatre and Temple of Apollo Page
317 • Delphi, site of the famous oracle, was
believed by the ancient Greeks to be the
centre of the earth.

09 Mount Pílio Page **346** • Mount Pílio peninsula has it all: lush countryside,
excellent beaches, characterful villages and some superb hiking trails.

10 **Tower house in the Máni** Page **229** • Designed for pitched battles at close quarters, these medieval tower houses are a relic of internecine warfare in Greece's deep South.

11 **Koróni town and port** Page **268** • Beautiful Koróni town commands sweeping views across the Messenian gulf.

12 **Mystra** Page **245** • The Byzantine town of Mystra is the most exciting and dramatic site in the Peloponnese.

13 Fortifications of Acrocorinth
Page **184** • Acrocorinth is a huge, barren rock crowned by a great medieval fortress.

14 Náfplio: café on Platía Syndágmatos Page **199** • Platía Syndágmatos is the main square of one of the Peloponnese's most elegant towns.

15 Monemvasiá: old town and fortress Page **215** • The heavily fortified medieval town of Monemvasiá rises spectacularly from its island-like rock.

16 Lion Gate, Mycenae Page **192** • Imposing relief lions guard the main entrance to the Citadel of Mycenae.

17 **Windsurfing off Vassilikí, Lefkádha** Page **966** • Located in a vast, cliff-flanked bay, Vassilikí is one of Europe's biggest windsurf centres.

18 **Dovecotes on Tínos** Page **604** • Distinctive, ornate dovecotes, introduced by the Venetians, punctuate the island of Tínos.

19 **"Paradise" beach, Mýkonos** Page **613** • The golden sand of "Paradise" beach attracts numerous holiday-makers in summer.

20 **View over Firá** Page **654** • The island capital of Firá is one of several villages that teeter at the edge of Thíra's (Santoríni's) caldera cliff.

21 Mólyvos, Lésvos

Page **876** • The castle-crowned village of Mólyvos ranks as one of the most beautiful on Lésvos.

22 Monastery of Saint John, Pátmos

Page **818** • Built in honour of Saint John the Divine, this huge monastery is a warren of interconnecting courtyards, chapels, stairways, arcades, galleries and roof terraces.

23 Volcano floor, Níssyros

Page **787** • No stay on Níssyros would be complete without a visit to the island's dormant volcano.

24 Knossós palace, Crete

Page **681** • The most restored, vividly coloured and ultimately the most exciting of Crete's Minoan palaces.

25 **Metéora** Page **370** • The exquisite Byzantine monasteries of Metéora perched atop pinnacles of rock are arguably mainland Greece's most extraordinary sight.

26 **Zagóri: Víkos gorge** Page **404** • A hike through or around the Víkos gorge is likely to be one of the highlights of a visit to the Zagóri region.

27 **Loggerhead sea turtle** Page **987** • The Ionian islands harbour one of the Mediterranean's main concentrations of the endangered loggerhead sea turtle.

28 **Thessaloníki: fish stall at Modhiáno market** Page **462** • The Modhiáno market is Thessaloníki's central meat, fish and produce market and an atmospheric place for a meal.

29 **Mount Olympus: trekkers on the way to Stefáni Peak** Page **476** • Believed by the ancient Greeks to be the home of the gods, Mount Olympus is Greece's highest and most magical mountain.

30 **Gorge of Samariá, Crete** Page **730** ● The magnificent Gorge of Samariá is the longest in Europe.

31 **Haniá old town waterfront, Crete** Page **719** ● Haniá displays haunting vestiges of its Venetian and Ottoman past.

32 **Skýros** Page **919** ● Only "discovered" by tourism in the early 1990s, Skýros remains one of the most traditional islands in the Aegean.

33 **Kárpathos: view south from Ólymbos village** Page **749** ● The view south from windswept, remote Ólymbos gives a good idea of the rugged coast of unspoilt northern Kárpathos.

34 **Préspa lakes** Page **492** ● The eerily beautiful Préspa lakes are a haven for birds and other wildlife.

35 **Sorting mastic and vegetables, Pyrgí, Híos** Page **856** ● The architecturally unique *mastihohoriá* (mastic villages) in southern Híos were built with the wealth generated by the export of mastic resin, here being sorted and cleaned.

36 **Ayíou Pávlou monastery, Mount Áthos** Page **523** ● Ayíou Pávlou is one of twenty monasteries in the "monks' republic" of Mount Áthos.

37 **Kérkyra (Corfu) old town** Page **941** ● With its elegant Venetian architecture and fine museums, Corfu's capital is the cultural heart of the Ionians.

38 **Ídhra** Page **565** ● Ídhra's perfect horsehoe-shaped harbour is surrounded by grand eighteenth-century mansions.

39 Lindos acropolis, Rhodes Page **761**
• From the Hellenistic acropolis of Lindos, high above the modern village, you look north along the length of Rhodes island.

40 Vái beach, Crete Page **706** • A superb beach, fringed with palm trees – claimed to be Europe's only indigenous wild date-palm grove.

41 Sámos: mountain vineyards Page **829** • Despite recent fires, Sámos remains arguably the most verdant and beautiful of the east Aegean islands.

42 Harbour, Sými Page **774** • The mansions of Sými's picturesque harbour, built with wealth from the sponge trade, are part of an architecturally protected area.

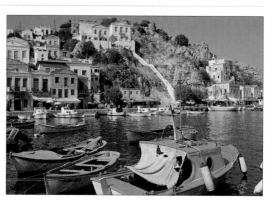

contents

Using the Rough Guide

We've tried to make this Rough Guide a good read and easy to use. The book is divided into five main sections, and you should be able to find whatever you want in one of them.

front section

The front colour section offers a quick tour of Greece. The **introduction** aims to give you a feel for the place, with suggestions on where to go. We also tell you what the weather is like and include a basic country fact file. Next, our authors round up their favourite aspects of Greece in the **things not to miss** section – whether it's great food, amazing sights or a special hotel. Right after this comes the Rough Guide's **contents** list.

basics

You've decided to go and the basics section covers all the **pre-departure** nitty-gritty to help you plan your trip. This is where to find out which airlines fly to your destination, what paperwork you'll need, what to do about money and insurance, about internet access, food, security, public transport, car rental – in fact just about every piece of **general practical information** you might need.

guide

This is the heart of the Rough Guide, divided into user-friendly chapters, each of which covers a specific region. Every chapter starts with a list of **highlights** and an **introduction** that helps you to decide where to go, depending on your time and budget. Likewise, introductions to the various towns and smaller regions within each chapter should help you plan your itinerary. We start most town accounts with information on arrival and accommodation, followed by a tour of the sights, and finally reviews of places to eat and drink, and details of nightlife. Longer accounts also have a directory of practical listings. Each chapter concludes with **public transport** details for the area covered.

contexts

Read contexts to get a deeper understanding of how Greece ticks. We include a brief **history**, articles about **wildlife** and **music**, together with a detailed further-reading section that reviews dozens of **books** relating to the country.

index + small print

Apart from a **full index**, which includes maps as well as places, this section covers publishing information, credits and acknowledgements, and also has our contact details in case you want to send in updates and corrections to the book – or suggestions as to how we might improve it.

contents ▶

basics ▶

guide ▶

contexts ▶

language ▶

index ▶

chapter map of **Greece**

contents

colour section

basics

8–86

guide: the mainland

87–548

guide: the islands · 549–572

contexts · 991–1091

language · 1093–1107

5

map symbols

symbols
maps are listed in the full index using coloured text

-------	International boundary		⊌	Marshland
-----	Chapter division boundary		⇃	Waterfall
▬▬▬	Motorway		⩗	Spring/spa
═══	Major paved road		◓	Cave
═══	Minor paved road		⊙	Statue/memorial
───	Unpaved road		⚡	Ski area
··········	Road under construction		♙	Refuge
▬▬▬	Pedestrianized street		⛺	Campsite
------	Footpath		◉	Accommodation
‖‖‖‖	Steps		■	Restaurant
━━━	Railway		✗	Airport
─ ─ ─	Ferry route		🅿	Parking
═══	Waterway		Ⓜ	Metro station
⛫	Mosque		★	Bus/taxi stop
✡	Synagogue		🛉	Lighthouse
⚱	Church		ⓘ	Information office
�	Monastery or convent		⊠	Post office
∴	Archeological site		ℰ	Telephone
♥	Castle		▮	Building
⋰	Hill		➕	Church
▲	Peak		⊹	Christian cemetery
⋀⋀	Mountains		▦	Park
⋭	Viewpoint		⬚	Beach

basics

basics

Getting there

It's 2000 miles (or more) from the UK and Ireland to Athens, so for most north European visitors flying is the only viable option. There are direct flights to a variety of Greek destinations from all the major British airports; flying time is three and a half to four and a half hours, depending on your start point and Greek destination. Road or rail alternatives from the UK take a minimum of three days, and are only worth considering if you plan to visit Greece as part of an extended trip through Europe. The most popular route is down through Italy, then across to Greece by ferry. The old overland route through former Yugoslavia will remain impractical for the foreseeable future, but a much longer route via Hungary, Romania and Bulgaria is still possible.

Only two carriers currently fly direct to Greece from North America, so most North Americans travel to a gateway European city, and pick up an onward connecting flight with an associated airline. You may discover that it's cheaper to arrange the final Greece-bound leg of the journey yourself, in which case your only criterion will be finding a suitable, good-value North America–Europe flight; such onward flights from the UK are detailed on pp.11–13.

It's fairly easy to track down flights from Australia to Athens, less so from New Zealand. But given most people's travel plans, you might be better off with a Round-the-World (RTW) ticket that includes Greece. If London is your first destination in Europe, and you've picked up a reasonably good deal on a flight there, it's probably best to wait until you reach the UK before arranging your onward travel to Greece.

Airfares to Greece from Europe and North America always depend on the **season**, with the highest in effect from June to August (plus Easter week), when the weather is best; fares drop during the "shoulder" seasons – April/May and September/October – and you'll get the best prices during the low season, November to March (excluding Christmas and New Year weeks when prices are hiked up and seats are at a premium). Note also that flying on weekends from North America ordinarily adds $50 or so to the round-trip fare; price ranges quoted below assume midweek travel. Australian and New Zealand fares have their low season from mid-January to the end of February and October/November; high season is mid-

May to August, plus December to mid-January; and shoulder season the rest of the year.

You can often cut costs by going through a **specialist flight agent** – either a consolidator, who buys up blocks of tickets from the airlines and sells them at a discount, or a **discount agent**, who in addition to dealing with discounted flights may also offer special student and youth fares and a range of other travel-related services such as travel insurance, rail passes, car rentals, tours and the like. Some UK agents specialize in **charter flights**, which may be cheaper than anything available on a scheduled flight, but again departure dates are fixed and withdrawal penalties are high. For Greece, you may even find it more cost-effective (especially from the UK) to pick up a **package deal**, with accommodation included, from one of the tour operators listed below.

Booking flights online

Many airlines and discount travel websites offer you the opportunity to book your tickets online, cutting out the costs of agents and middlemen. Good deals can often be found through discount or auction sites, as well as through the airlines' own websites. Even if you don't end up actually buying your ticket online, the websites are worth a visit to clue you up on what the prevailing published economy fares are; however, these sites often don't have the really inexpensive, transient deals. The cheapest of the airlines' published fares is an APEX (Advance Purchase Excursion) ticket, which has certain restrictions. You may be expected to book – and pay – at least 14–21 days before departure, keep to a minimum/maximum limit on your stay (typically 30 or 60 days), and be liable to penalties (including total loss of ticket value) if you change your schedule. Some airlines also issue "student" tickets to those under 26, often extending the maximum stay to a year. There is also a number of "Senior" or "Golden" fares available for those over 60. When exploring a quoted fare on a website, always click the "Rules" link – all conditions will be spelled out in small print. Any reputable site will have a secure, encrypted facility for making credit-card payments – if it doesn't, you're probably better off not using the site to purchase.

Online booking agents and general travel sites

Ⓦ www.etn.nl/discount.htm A hub of consolidator and discount agent web links, maintained by the nonprofit European Travel Network.

Ⓦ www.princeton.edu/Main/air800.html Has an extensive list of airline toll-free numbers and websites.

Ⓦ www.flynow.com Online air travel info and reservations site.

Ⓦ www.smilinjack.com/airlines.htm Lists an up-to-date compilation of airline website addresses.

Ⓦ http://travel.yahoo.com Incorporates a lot of Rough Guide material in its coverage of destination countries and cities across the world, with information about places to eat and sleep etc.

Ⓦ www.cheaptickets.com or www.cheaptickets.co.uk Discount flight specialists.

Ⓦ www.cheapflights.com Flight deals, travel agents, plus links to other travel sites.

Ⓦ www.lastminute.com Offers good last-minute holiday package and flight-only deals.

Ⓦ www.deckchair.com Bob Geldof's online venture, drawing on a wide range of airlines.

Ⓦ www.expedia.com or www.expedia.co.uk Discount airfares, all-airline search engine and daily deals.

Ⓦ www.travelocity.co.uk Destination guides, hot web fares and best deals for car rental, accommodation and lodging as well as fares. Provides access to the travel agent system SABRE, the most comprehensive central reservations system in the US.

Ⓦ www.travelselect.com Useful, fairly easy-to-use site without most of the guff and banner adverts of the better-known sites. Linked to walk-in travel agency in the UK (London storefront) and

---

Surviving Athens airport

Athens' **new airport**, Eleftherios Venizelos, opened March 28, 2001, replacing the old, cramped but undeniably convenient one at Ellinikó, south of town. The new terminal has made itself widely unpopular with travellers for its distance east of Athens (26km), its (thus far) indirect public transport connections into town, its battery-farm architecture and its enormous size (claimed third largest in the world), this last factor making **missed connections** a distinct possibility. Poor marking makes mad dashes down nightmarishly endless concourses and up escalators (there are a few lifts for luggage trolleys) doubly stressful.

Printed airport rules stipulate a **minimum of 55 minutes** between your incoming flight's arrival and onward flight's departure, but some airlines – for example Olympic – are insisting on a minimum leeway of **90 minutes**. Given Olympic's habitual lateness, the presence of security checks even for transfer passengers and the fact that all aircraft for domestic flights are parked a very long shuttle-coach-ride distant on the runway, prudence would dictate observing this rule when buying fares. Some, but not all, ticketing systems won't let you book an itinerary if the layover is too short.

Now, the good news: the departure concourse **shops are excellent** (you can even find a few Rough Guides in the bookstore), and eating opportunities are fairly abundant, though seats are in short supply (as they are in all departure lounges). Best of all – and the only conspicuous advantage of the new unified terminal – you can have your **luggage checked through to your final domestic destination**, even if your international- and domestic-leg airlines are different. Do this at the outset as a precaution, and even if your inbound flight is hideously late, you stand a good chance of getting yourself and your carry-on to the end of your itinerary as planned, even if your baggage only shows up the next day.

the US (two premises) if you want to talk to a human.

@www.hotwire.com Bookings from the US only. Last-minute savings of up to forty percent on regular published fares. Travellers must be at least 18 and there are no refunds, transfers or changes allowed. Log-in required.

@www.priceline.com or www.priceline.co.uk Bookings from the US/UK only. Name-your-own-price website that has deals at around forty percent off standard fares. You cannot specify flight times (although you do specify dates) and the tickets are nonrefundable, nontransferable and nonchangeable.

@www.skyauction.com Bookings from the US only. Auctions tickets and travel packages using a "second bid" scheme. The best strategy is to bid the maximum you're willing to pay, since if you win you'll pay just enough to beat the runner-up regardless of your maximum bid.

@ www.travel.com.au Australian website with a good range of discounted airfares; no-nonsense, easy to use and interpret.

@www.travelshop.com.au Australian website offering discounted flights, packages, insurance and online bookings.

Domestic airlines

Aegean-Cronus City Centre ☏010/99 44 444, 99 88 414 or countrywide ☏0801/20 000; airport ☏010/35 34 294 or 35 30 101.
Axon City Centre ☏010/68 00 063; airport: ☏010/35 32 533.
Olympic Airways City Centre ☏010/96 66 666 or countrywide ☏0801/44 444; airport ☏010/93 65 529.

Flights from the UK and Ireland

Most of the cheaper flights from Britain and Ireland to Greece are **charters**, which are sold either with a package holiday or (less commonly) as a flight-only option. The flights have fixed and unchangeable outward and return dates, and usually a maximum stay of four weeks.

For longer stays or more flexibility, or if you're travelling out of season (when few charters are available), you'll need a **scheduled flight**. As with charters, these are

offered under a wide variety of fares, and are again often sold off at a discount by agents. Useful advertisements for discounted flights are found in the weekend-supplement travel sections of newspapers like *The Independent*, *The Guardian*, *The Observer* and *The Sunday Times*, as well as weekly listings magazines such as *Time Out*.

Although **Athens** remains the prime destination for cheap fares, there are also direct flights from Britain to **Thessaloníki**, **Kalamáta**, **Kavála** and **Préveza (Áktio)** on the Greek mainland, and to the islands of **Crete**, **Rhodes**, **Kós**, **Corfu**, **Mýkonos**, **Zákynthos**, **Kefalloniá**, **Skiáthos**, **Sámos**, **Lésvos** and **Límnos**. And with any flight to Athens, you can buy a **domestic connecting flight** (on the national carrier, Olympic, or its rivals Axon and Cronus-Aegean) to one of three dozen or so additional Greek mainland and island airports.

Charter flights

Travel agents throughout Britain sell **charter flights** to Greece, which usually operate from late April or May to late October or mid-November (depending on destination); late-night departures and early-morning arrivals are common, though you may have a choice of more civilized hours. Even the high-street chains frequently promote "flight-only" deals, or discount all-inclusive holidays, when their parent companies need to offload their seat allocations. Charter airlines include Air 2000, Flying Colours, Britannia, JMC and Monarch, but you can only book tickets on these through their designated agents (see pp.13–14), and you may find that flight-only deals are rare indeed at peak season.

Charter flights to Athens are reasonable – **sample return fares** to Athens from London in midsummer start from around £160 (Manchester £180, Glasgow £200), but there are always bargains to be had. You generally pay dearly for the convenience of a direct flight to the holiday island of your choice, skipping Athens: sample high-season fares range from £210 (Gatwick to Rhodes or Corfu) up to a hefty £300 (Manchester to Zákynthos or Kefalloniá). Sámos is particularly outrageous at around £350 – you may well find scheduled services via Athens are cheaper.

The greatest variety of **flight destinations**

tends to be from London (Heathrow/Gatwick) and Manchester. In summer, if you book in advance, you should have a choice of most of the Greek regional airports listed above. Flying from elsewhere in Britain (Birmingham, Bristol, Cardiff, East Midlands, Luton, Stansted, Glasgow or Newcastle), or looking for last-minute discounts, you'll find options more limited, most commonly to Athens, Corfu, Rhodes, Kós and Crete.

Summer charters operate **from Dublin and Belfast** to Athens and there are additional services to Mýkonos, Rhodes, Crete and Corfu. A high-season charter from Dublin to Athens costs upwards of €317 return, while a week's package on one of the above islands costs from €635 per person for two weeks.

It's worth noting that **non-EU nationals** who buy charter tickets to Greece must buy a round-trip ticket, to return after no fewer than three days and no more than four weeks, and must accompany it with an accommodation voucher for at least the first few nights of their stay – check that the ticket satisfies these conditions or you could be refused entry. In practice, the "accommodation voucher" has become a formality; it has to name an existing hotel, but you're not expected to use it (and probably won't be able to if you try).

The other important condition regards **travel to Turkey** (or any other neighbouring country). If you travel to Greece on a charter flight, you may visit another country only as a day-trip; if you stay overnight, you will possibly invalidate your ticket. This rule is justified by the Greek authorities because they subsidize charter airline landing fees, and are therefore reluctant to see tourists spending their money outside Greece. Whether you go along with that rationale or not, there is no way around it, since the Turkish authorities clearly stamp all passports, and the Greeks usually check them. We have, however, had reports of charter-flight-only patrons flying to Kós, happily spending a week in Turkish Bodrum, and then returning without incident, but it would be wise to double-check if the rule is still in effect.

Student/youth charters can be sold as one-way flights only. By combining two one-way charters you can, therefore, stay for over a month. Student/youth charter tickets are available to anyone under 26, and to all card-carrying full-time students under 32.

Finally, remember that **reconfirmation** of return charter flights is vital and should be done at least 72 hours before departure. If you've travelled out with a package company, this service will usually be included as part of the rep's duties, but you should not assume that it has been done. Personal visits to the airline's representative office are best, as phone numbers given on ticket wallets are typically engaged.

Scheduled flights

The advantages of **scheduled flights** are that they can be booked well in advance, have longer ticket validities (30, 60, 90 or even 180 days), involve fewer or none of the typical restrictions applicable to charters, and often leave at more social hours. However, many of the cheaper, shorter-duration fares do have advance-purchase and/or minimum-stay requirements, and also severe restrictions on date changes or refunds. As with charters, discount fares on scheduled flights are available from most high-street travel agents, as well as from a number of specialist flight and student/youth agencies – though it's always well worth contacting the airlines direct, using the telephone numbers below. Like charters, they must be reconfirmed within 72 hours of the return leg (in practice, 36 hours is usually enough).

Scheduled airlines

Aer Lingus in Republic of Ireland ☎01/705 3333 or 844 4777, ✆www.aerlingus.ie.

British Airways ☎0845/773 3377, in Republic of Ireland ☎1-800/626 747, ✆www.britishairways.com.

British Midland ☎0870/607 0555, in Northern Ireland ☎0845/755 4554, in Republic of Ireland ☎01/283 8833, ✆www.flybmi.com.

Cronus Airlines ☎020/7580 3500, ✆www.cronus.gr.

easyJet ☎0870/600 0000, ✆www.easyjet.com.

Olympic Airways ☎0870/606 0460, in Republic of Ireland ☎01/608 0090, ✆www.olympic-airways.gr.

Ryanair ☎0870/156 9569, in Republic of Ireland ☎01/609 7800, ✆www.ryanair.com.

The widest choice of scheduled flights from the **UK to Greece** is with the Greek national carrier **Olympic Airways** and with **British Airways**, who both fly from London Heathrow to Athens (twice daily on BA, three times daily on Olympic), mostly direct, but on Olympic stopping four times weekly in Thessaloníki. In addition, Olympic has three weekly flights to Athens from Manchester. BA also offers one daily Athens service from Gatwick, but nothing to Thessaloníki. Both airlines have a range of special fares, and even in July and August, discount flight agents or websites can come up with deals, valid for sixty days away, for as low as £200 return, including tax; more realistically, you'll pay around £250 return during high season from London, £300 from Manchester. It may be worth avoiding absolutely rock-bottom fares, as Olympic in particular no longer allows changes to your return date on tickets of under ninety-days' validity. In the spring or autumn, return fares to Athens run to about £180 including taxes, and in winter dip to about £150. As this route is common-rated between these airlines, you'll also be able to book onward connections simultaneously to domestic Greek airports, though discounts will apply only if using Olympic on all legs of the journey.

Cronus Airlines, so far the only private Greek airline to challenge Olympic on international routes to Britain, offers daily late-evening services to Athens from London Heathrow, arriving at dawn the next day. Any advertised fares to Thessaloníki all currently go via Athens, with a two-hour layover; direct services have yet to consistently materialize. Fares to either city weigh in at about £170 low season, tax included, or £250 high season.

Note that flights from British regional airports route through Heathrow in the first instance, with a supplement applicable. Olympic has a code-sharing partnership with British Midland, which should ease the pain (and possibly the cost) of connections from Scotland and the north of England in particular.

Potentially the cheapest, no-frills service is provided by **easyJet**, out of London Luton to Athens only; fares vary from £49 to £159 one way, tax included, with the exact amount depending on the season, how far in advance you book and availability for the particular flight – a last-minute booking for three weeks from the end of August will probably result in a combined return fare of £210. Departures also vary with time of year, but typically there are two flights daily, in the early afternoon and quite late in the evening. The cheaper tickets are obviously very restrictive, and there's no on-board meal service. On the plus side, easyJet usually offers special train fares from central London (Waterloo, West Hampstead, King's Cross) to Luton Parkway (free shuttle bus thence to airport) in co-operation with Thameslink.

Irish travellers will find year-round scheduled services with Aer Lingus and British Airways operating from both **Dublin** and **Belfast via Heathrow** to Athens, or from Dublin via Heathrow on British Midland and Olympic, but you'll find them pricey compared to charters. Youth and student fares are offered by usit NOW (see overleaf for address).

Travelling to London and buying a separate ticket there is an alternative if direct flights from Ireland are in short supply, and may sometimes save you a little money, but on the whole it's rarely worth the time and effort. For the record, budget flights to London are offered by British Midland, Aer Lingus and Ryanair.

Flight and travel agents in the UK and Republic of Ireland

Air 2000 ☏0870/750 0001, ⊛www.firstchoice.co.uk. Flight-only division (charters) of First Choice Holidays.

Aran Travel International Galway ☏091/562595, 🖷564581, ⊛www.iol.ie/~aran/aranmain.htm. Good-value flights to all parts of the world.

Argo Holidays 100 Wigmore St, London W1H 9DR ☏020/7331 7000. Designated consolidator for Olympic, BA and Virgin Atlantic; consistently does some of the lowest fares, and offers better service than the airlines concerned.

Avro Vantage House, 1 Weir Rd, London SW19 8UX ☏020/8715 4440, ⊛www.avro.co.uk. Seat-only sales of all Monarch charter flights to Athens, Corfu, Iráklion (Crete) and Rhodes from a selection amongst Gatwick, Luton, Manchester and Glasgow.

CIE Tours International Dublin ☏01/703 1888, ⊛www.cietours.ie. General flight and tour agent.

Co-op Travel Care Belfast ☏028/9047 1717, 🖷9047 1339. Flights and holidays around the world.

Cosmos ☏0870/908 4299, ⊛www.cosmos-holidays.co.uk. Offers flight-only arrangements on Monarch from Manchester, Gatwick and Birmingham to a variety of holiday islands.

Greece & Cyprus Travel Centre 44 Birmingham Rd, Sutton Coldfield, West Midlands B72 1QQ ☎0121/355 6955, ⊛www.greece-cyprus.co.uk. Flight consolidator and general Greek packages specialist.

JMC ☎0870/758 0194, ⊛www.jmc.com. Good selection of flights only to Kefalloniá, Zákynthos, Áktio (Préveza-Lefkádha), Kós, Skiáthos, Sámos and Rhodes from a half-dozen UK airports.

Joe Walsh Tours Dublin ☎01/872 2555 or 676 3053, Cork ☎021/427 7959, ⊛www.joewalshtours.ie. General budget fares agent.

Lee Travel Cork ☎021/427 7111; ⊛www.leetravel.ie. Flights and holidays worldwide.

Liffey Travel Dublin ☎01/878 8322 or 878 8063. Package-tour specialists.

The London Flight Centre ☎020/7244 6411, ⊛www.topdecktravel.co.uk. Long-established agent dealing in discount flights.

Mondial Travel 8 Moscow Rd, London W2 4BT ☎020/7792 3333. Good consolidator agent for scheduled flights to Greece; can nearly match easyJet prices on the major airlines.

North South Travel Moulsham Mill Centre, Parkway, Chelmsford, Essex CM2 7PX ☎01245/608291, ⊛www.nstravel.demon.uk. Friendly, competitive flight agency, offering discounted fares worldwide – profits are used to support projects in the developing world, especially the promotion of sustainable tourism.

Rosetta Travel Belfast ☎028/9064 4996, ⊛www.rosettatravel.com. Flight and holiday agent.

STA Travel ☎0870/160 6070, ⊛www.statravel.co.uk. Worldwide specialists in low-cost flights and tours for students and under-26s, though other customers welcome. A dozen branches across England, especially on or near university campuses.

Student & Group Travel Dublin ☎01/677 7834. Student and group specialists, mostly to Europe.

Sunset Air Fares Sunset Business Centre, Manchester Rd, Bolton BL4 8RT ☎0870/607 5085. Flight-only and fly-drive deals from regional airports to Kalamáta, Áktio (Préveza-Lefkádha) and Kavála (for Thássos) in addition to the usual destinations; typically on Flying Colours.

Thomson ☎0870/550 2555, ⊛www.thomson-holidays.com. Limited flight-only deals on Britannia to Corfu, Rhodes, Iráklion (Crete), Thessaloníki, Zákynthos, Kós, Sámos, Kefalloniá, Skiáthos and

Kavála (for Thássos) on Britannia Airways.

Trailfinders ☎020/7628 7628, in Republic of Ireland ☎01/677 7888, ⊛www.trailfinders.com. One of the best-informed and most efficient agents for independent travellers; for scheduled flights only; all branches (there's at least one in all the UK's largest cities, plus Dublin) open daily until 6pm, Thurs until 7pm.

usit CAMPUS ☎0870/240 1010, ⊛www.usitcampus.co.uk. Student/youth travel specialists, offering discount flights, with town branches in London, Birmingham, Bristol, Cambridge, Edinburgh, Manchester and Oxford, as well as a presence in all YHA shops and many university campuses across Britain.

usit NOW Belfast ☎028/9032 7111, Dublin ☎01/602 1777 or 677 8117, Cork ☎021/427 0900, Derry ☎028/7137 1888, ⊛www.usitnow.ie. Student and youth specialists for flights and trains.

Packages and tours

Virtually every British **tour operator** includes Greece in its programme, though with many of the larger, cheap-and-cheerful outfits you'll find choices limited to the established resorts – notably the islands of Rhodes, Kós, Crete, Skiáthos, Zákynthos and Corfu, plus Tólo and the Halkidhikí peninsula on the mainland. If you buy one of these at a last-minute discount, especially in spring or autumn, you may find it costs little more than a flight – and you can use the accommodation included as much or as little as you want.

For a more low-key and genuinely "Greek" resort, however, it's better to book your holiday through one of the **specialist agencies** listed opposite. Most of these are fairly small-scale operations, providing competitively priced packages with flights (unless otherwise stated) and often more traditional village-based accommodation. They also make an effort to offer islands and corners of the mainland without overdeveloped tourist resorts. Such agencies tend to divide into two types: those which, like the major chains, contract a block of accommodation and flight seats (or even their own plane) for a full season, and an increasing number of bespoke agencies which tailor holidays at your request, making all transport and accommodation arrangements on the spot. These can work out somewhat more expensive, but the quality of flights and lodging is often correspondingly higher.

The **walking** holiday operators listed overleaf either run trekking groups of ten to fifteen people plus an experienced guide, or provide customers with a printed, self-guiding itinerary, and arranged accommodation at the end of each day. Walks tend to be day-long hikes from one or more bases, or point-to-point treks staying in village accommodation en route. Camping out is not usually involved.

Sailing holidays usually involve small flotillas of four- to eight-berth yachts, taking in different anchorages each night, or are shore-based, with instruction in small-craft handling. All levels of experience are catered for. Prices start at around £520 per person, flights included, in a group of four on a two-week flotilla. Alternatively, confident sailors can simply arrange to charter a yacht from a broker; the Greek National Tourist Organization has lists of companies.

Specialist package operators

VILLA OR VILLAGE ACCOMMODATION
Argo Holidays 100 Wigmore St, London W1H 9DR ☎020/7331 7070, ⓦwww.argo-holidays.com. Packages to luxury hotels and top villas on about twenty islands; special strengths are the Argo-Saronic, northeast Aegean and Dodecanese (including "Winter Sun" on Rhodes).
Cachet Travel First Floor, Coomb House, 7 St Johns Rd, Isleworth, Middlesex TW7 6NH ☎020/8768 1818, ⓦwww.cachet-travel.co.uk. Attractive range of villas and apartments, in the more unspoilt south and west of Crete.
CV Travel 43 Cadogan St, London SW3 2PR ☎0870/606 0013, ⓦwww.cvtravel.co.uk. Quality villas, mostly on Corfu and Paxí but also Itháki, Spétses, Pátmos, Alónissos, Crete and Thíra.
Direct Greece Granite House, 31–33 Stockwell St, Glasgow G1 4RY ☎0141/559 7111; Manchester ☎0161/236 2838; London ☎020/8785 4000; ⓕ0141/553 1752. Moderately priced villas, apartments and restored houses on Rhodes, Hálki, Kálymnos, Kefalloniá, Lésvos, Corfu, and Crete, plus (on the mainland) Párga and the outer Máni.
Elysian Holidays 16 High St, Tenterden, Kent TN30 6AP ☎01580/766599, ⓦwww.elysianholidays.co.uk. Began as Híos restored-house specialists, now have a wide programme of quality premises on a dozen islands, including Páros, Sýros, Spétses, Mýkonos, Pátmos and the Candili Estate on Évvia.
Filoxenia Sourdock Hill, Barkisland, Halifax, West Yorkshire HX4 0AG ☎01422/375999,

ⓦwww.filoxenia.co.uk. Tailor-made itineraries and bespoke packages to unspoiled areas of the mainland such as the Peloponnese and Epirus, also special-interest holidays and a few islands offered; flight arrangements on scheduled or charter airlines.
Greek Islands Club 10–12 Upper Square, Old Isleworth, Middlesex TW7 7BJ ☎020/8232 9780, ⓦwww.greekislandsclub.com. Extremely high-quality villas throughout the Ionian and Sporades islands; also Pátmos, Thíra and Crete.
Greek Sun Holidays 1 Bank St, Sevenoaks, Kent TN13 1UW ☎01732/740317, ⓦwww.greeksun.co.uk. Good-value package holidays, including some fly-drive options, in the Dodecanese, northeast Aegean, Cyclades and on the Peloponnese or Mount Pílio; also tailor-made island-hopping itineraries.
Hidden Greece ☎020/7839 2553 ⓕ7839 4327 ⓔhiddengreece@ntours.co.uk. A bespoke agency running for forty-plus years now, arranging accommodation on and transport to thirty less-visited islands, mostly in the Cyclades and Dodecanese.
Houses of Pelion ☎01963/210667 (calls are forwarded automatically to the proprietors, who live full-time on the peninsula – ☎04230/65471 in Greece; or ⓦwww.pelion.co.uk.) Longest-running operator for the area, offering an excellent collection of inland cottages and coastal apartments.
Island Wandering 51a London Rd, Hurst Green, Sussex TN19 7QP ☎01580/860733, ⓦwww.islandwandering.com. Tailor-made island-hopping itineraries between most Greek archipelagos; deals range from prebooked accommodation only (this tends to be on the basic side) to minitours, with local ferry or air transfers arranged.
Laskarina Holidays St Marys Gate, Wirksworth, Derbyshire DE4 4DQ ☎01629/822203, ⓦwww.laskarina.co.uk. Top-end villas, quality hotels and restored houses on Spétses, Skópelos, Alónissos, Hálki, Sými, Tílos, Kálymnos, Télendhos, Léros, Lipsí, Pátmos, Ikaría and Sámos; scores consistently high marks for customer service.
Pure Crete 79 George St, Croydon CR10 1LD ☎020/8760 0879, ⓦwww.pure.crete.com. Characterful, converted cottages and farmhouses in western Crete.
Simply Simon Holidays 1/45 Nevern Square, London SW5 9PF ☎020/7373 1933, ⓦwww.simplysimon.co.uk. Cyclades specialist, focusing on small hotels and studios; direct charters to Mýkonos.
Simply Travel Kings House, Wood St, Kingston-

upon-Thames, Surrey KT1 1UG, ⓦwww.simply-travel.com. Administers three separate programmes: Simply Greece ⓣ020/8541 2277 for the mainland, Thíra, Sámos and Pátmos; Simply Ionian ⓣ020/8541 2202 for the entire Ionian island chain; and Simply Crete ⓣ020/8541 2201. Offers high-quality apartments, villas and small hotels for each area.

Sunvil Holidays Sunvil House, 7–8 Upper Square, Old Isleworth, Middlesex TW7 7BJ ⓣ020/8568 4499, ⓦwww.sunvil.co.uk/greece. Durable and consistently high-quality outfit specializing in upmarket hotels and villas in the Ionian islands, the Sporades, select Cyclades, western Crete, Límnos, Sámos, Ikaría, Pátmos, the Peloponnese, the Pílio, Párga and Sývota. Also mainland fly-drives.

Tapestry Holidays 24 Chiswick High Rd, London W4 1TE ⓣ020/8235 7788, ⓦwww.tapestryholidays.com. Top-rated Turkey specialists now branched out into quality villas, hotels and restoration inns on Kefalloniá and Pílio.

Travel à la Carte First Floor, 32 High St, Thatcham, Berks RG19 3JD ⓣ01635/863030, ⓦwww.travelalacarte.co.uk. Established Corfu specialist, now branched out to beach and rural villas on Alónissos, Hálki, Paxí, Skiáthos, Skópelos and Sými as well.

Travelux 40 High St, Tenterden, Kent TN30 6AR ⓣ01580/765000, ⓦwww.travelux.co.uk. Long-established Lefkádha villa specialists; also the only operator to Zagóri, with the best hotels there and a range of activity holidays (such as hiking, painting, photography, Alexander technique).

WALKING AND HORSE-RIDING HOLIDAYS

ATG Oxford ⓣ01865/315678, ⓦwww.atg-oxford.co.uk. Somewhat pricey but high-standard guided walks on Ándhros, Náxos and select mainland destinations like the Mánia and parts of Epirus.

Equitour 40–41 South Parade, Summertown, Oxford OX2 7JP ⓣ01865/511642, ⓦwww.peregrine.holidays.com. Horse-riding holidays on the Pílio peninsula.

Exodus 9 Weir Rd, London SW12 0LT ⓣ020/8675 5550, ⓦwww.exodus.co.uk. One-week treks on Évvia/Skýros, or the White Mountains of Crete; also sail-walk two-week tours through the Cyclades.

Explore Worldwide 1 Frederick St, Aldershot, Hampshire GU11 1LQ ⓣ01252/760 1000, ⓦwww.exploreworldwide.com. Treks on Crete and in Zagóri; also island-wanderer trips, mostly in the Cyclades, mixing kaïki-sailing with light walking ashore.

Headwater 146 London Rd, Northwich, Cheshire CW9 5HH ⓣ01606/813367, ⓦwww.headwater-holidays.co.uk. Treks on Mount Taïyettos, the Máni and Amorgós island; "Best of Ionian" eight-day holiday taking in Itháki and Kefalloniá; self-guiding routes in Zagóri and Pílio.

Ramblers Holidays Longcroft House, Fretherne Rd, Welwyn Garden City, Herts AL8 6PQ ⓣ01707/331133, ⓦwww.ramblersholidays.co.uk. An outfit which has shed its former fusty image, actively courts a younger clientele and now offers fairly challenging treks in Crete and the Máni; also easier outings on Sámos, Pátmos, Náxos, Sérifos, Kýthnos and Amorgós.

Sherpa Expeditions 131a Heston Rd, Hounslow, Middlesex TW5 0RD ⓣ020/8577 2717, ⓦwww.sherpa-walking-holidays.co.uk. Good range of more difficult mainland treks on Mount Olympus and in the Píndhos, though some of these may be self-guiding.

Waymark Holidays 44 Windsor Rd, Slough SL1 2EJ ⓣ01753/516477, ⓦwww.waymarkholidays.co.uk Spring and autumn walking holidays (10–14 days) on Sámos, Mílos and Crete's White Mountains.

NATURE AND WILDLIFE

Limosa ⓣ01263/578143. Springtime birding on Lésvos, and in the wetlands and forests of Thrace.

Marengo Guided Walks 17 Bernard Crescent, Hunstanton PE36 6ER ⓣ01485/532710, ⓦwww.marengo.supanet.com. Annually changing programme of easy walks guided by ace botanist Lance Chilton; past one-week offerings have included Sámos, Sými, northern Lésvos, Crete, the Párga area, southern Peloponnese and Thássos.

Naturetrek Cheriton Mill, Cheriton, Alresford, Hampshire SO24 0NG ⓣ01962/733051, ⓦwww.naturetrek.co.uk. Fairly pricey but expertly led two-week natural history tour of the Víkos Gorge, Mt Gamíla and Mt Smólikas.

Peregrine Holidays 40–41 South Parade, Summertown, Oxford OX2 7JP ⓣ01865/559988, ⓦwww.peregrineholidays.com. Does at least one yearly natural history tour, typically springtime in the Peloponnese.

SAILING HOLIDAYS

The Moorings Bradstowe House, Middle Wall, Whitstable, Kent CT5 1BF ⓣ01227/776677, ⓦwww.moorings.com. Operates bareboat charters out of Athens, Corfu, Skiáthos and Kós Town.

Nautilus Yachting 4 Church St, Edenbridge,

Kent TN8 5BD ☎01732/867445,
🌐www.nautilus-yachting.co.uk Bareboat yacht
charter out of Athens, Corfu, Lefkádha, Kós,
Rhodes and Skiáthos; also flotilla holidays from
Lefkádha and Póros.
Seafarer Cruising & Sailing Albatross House,
14 New Hythe Lane, Larkfield, Kent ME20 6AB
☎01732/229900, 🌐www.seafarercruises.com.
UK agent for Vernicos Yachts (Greece), with
shareboat/flotillas out of Póros and bareboats out
of Athens, Rhodes, Corfu, Skiáthos, Kós, Sámos
and Mýkonos.
Setsail Holidays ☎01737/764443,
🌐www.setsail.co.uk. Bareboat charters from
Póros, flotillas around the Peloponnese, and
sail/land-stay combinations.
Sportif ☎01273/844919, 🌐www.sportif-
uk.com. Windsurfing packages on Kós, Rhodes,
Kárpathos, Lefkádha and Náxos. Instruction
clinics in conjunction with nearby
accommodation.
Sunsail The Port House, Port Solent, Portsmouth,
Hampshire PO6 4TH ☎023/9222 2222,
🌐www.sunsail.com. Resort-based tuition in
dinghy sailing, yachting and win dsurfing at five
locations in Greece, including southern Pílio; one-
or two-week flotilla sailings northwards out of
Kós Town, Lefkádha, Kefalloniá and the Sporades.
Good facilities for nonsailing children.

MIND AND BODY

Skyros Centre 92 Prince of Wales Rd, London
NW5 3NE ☎020/7267 4424, 🌐www.skyros.com.
Holistic health, fitness, crafts and "personal
growth" holidays at two centres on the island of
Skýros, as well as prestigious writers' workshops
tutored by big names.

By rail from the UK, Ireland and the rest of Europe

Travelling **by train** from Britain or Ireland to
Greece takes three and a half to four and a
half days and fares work out much more
expensive than flights. However, with a reg-
ular ticket, stopovers are possible – in
France, Switzerland and Italy – while with an
InterRail or Eurail pass you can take in
Greece as part of a wider train trip around
Europe.

Routes

The most practical route from Britain crosses
France, Switzerland and Italy before embark-

ing on the ferry from Bari or Brindisi to Pátra
(Patras). Book seats well in advance, especially in summer (for ferry information, see
the box on pp.20–21).

Until 1990, the route through **former
Yugoslavia** was the most popular; for obvious reasons this is a non-starter for the foreseeable future, recent developments in
Serbia notwithstanding. A more roundabout
alternative from Budapest runs via
Bucharest and **Sofia** to **Thessaloníki**,
which is advised as your first Greek stop,
since Athens is six to seven hours further on
the train.

Standard tickets

Regular train tickets from Britain to Greece
are not good value; London to Athens costs
at least £400 return, undiscounted second-
class. If you are under 26, you can get a
youth ticket, discounting these fares by
around 25 percent; these are available
through usit CAMPUS and Connex. Both
regular and youth tickets have two-months'
return validity, or can be purchased as one-
ways, and the Italy routes include the ferry
crossing. The tickets also allow for
stopovers, so long as you stick to the route
prescribed.

Rail passes

Better value by far is to buy an **InterRail
pass**, which offers unlimited travel (except
for express-train supplements and reservation fees) on a zonal basis with 28 European
rail networks. These passes are only available to **European residents**, and you will be
asked to provide proof of residency before
being allowed to purchase one. The passes
come in over-26 and (cheaper) under-26
versions; they're available for 22 days (one
zone only), or one month, and you can purchase up to three zones, or a global pass
covering all zones. You may save a bit by
booking via the InterRail website
🌐www.inter-rail.co.uk

To reach Greece from the UK you'll need a
pass valid for at least two zones; Greece
falls in Zone G, together with Italy, Turkey
and Slovenia, plus most of the
Brindisi–Igoumenítsa ferries. To reach Italy
from Britain, you'll need to purchase a Zone

E pass to cross France; to reach northern Greece via central Europe, you'll need so many other zones (C, D and H) that you'll be obliged to buy an all-zone pass. InterRail passes do not allow free travel between Britain and the continent, although InterRail Pass holders are eligible for discounts on rail travel in Britain and Northern Ireland, the cross-Channel ferries, and the London–Paris Eurostar service.

Finally, anyone over 60 and holding a British Rail Senior Citizen Railcard, can buy a **Rail Europe Senior Card** (£5 for a year). This gives up to thirty percent reductions on rail fares throughout Europe and thirty percent off sea crossings.

For **North Americans, Australians and New Zealanders, a Eurail Pass** is not likely to pay for itself if you're planning to stick to Greece. This pass, which must be purchased before arrival in Europe, allows unlimited free first-class train travel in Greece and sixteen other countries, and is available in increments of fifteen days, 21 days, one month, two months and three months. If you're under 26, you can save money with a Eurail Youthpass, which is valid for second-class travel or, if you're travelling with one to four other companions, a joint Eurail Saverpass, both of which are available in the same increments as the Eurail Pass. You stand a better chance of getting your money's worth out of a Eurail Flexipass, which is good for ten- or fifteen-days' travel within a two-month period. This, too, comes in first-class, under-26/second-class (Eurorail Youth Flexipass) and group (Eurail Saver Flexipass) versions.

In addition, a scaled-down version of the Flexipass, the **Europass**, is available which allows first-class and youth (second-class) travel in France, Germany, Italy, Spain and Switzerland for any five, six, eight, ten- or fifteen-days within two months. Up to four "associate" countries (Austria/Hungary, Benelux, Greece, Portugal) can be included for an additional fee. The Europass Saverpass is a version of the Europass for people travelling in groups of two or more that offers a saving of fifteen percent per person on the regular fare. Details of prices for all these passes can be found on Ⓦ www.raileurope.com, and the passes can be purchased from one of the agents listed below.

Rail contacts

In the UK and Ireland

Connex ☎ 0870/001 0174. International enquiries and reservations.
Iarnród Éireann Dublin ☎ 01/836 6222, Ⓦ www.irishrail.ie.
Northern Ireland Railways ☎ 028/9089 9411, Ⓦ www.nirailways.co.uk.
Rail Europe (SNCF French Railways) ☎ 0870/584 8848, Ⓦ www.raileurope.co.uk.
Standard as well as discounted rail fares for under-26s on a variety of European routes; also agents for InterRail, Eurostar and Eurodomino.
usit CAMPUS ☎ 0870/240 1010, Ⓦ www.usitcampus.co.uk. Books student/youth discount train tickets and sells passes.

In North America

CIT Rail ☎ 1-800/223-7987, 1-800/CIT-TOUR or 212/730-2400, in Canada ☎ 1-800/361-7799, Ⓦ www.fs-on-line.com. Eurail and Europass.
DER Travel ☎ 1-888/337-7350, Ⓦ www.dertravel.com/Rail. Eurail, Europass and many individual country passes.
European Rail Services Canada ☎ 1-800/205-5800 or 416/695-1211, Ⓦ www.europeanrailservices.com. Eurail, Europass and many individual country passes.
Europrail International Inc Canada ☎ 1-888/667-9734, Ⓦ www.europrail.net. Eurail, Europass and many individual country passes.
Online Travel ☎ 1-800/660-5300 or 847/318-8890, Ⓦ www.eurorail.com. Eurail Pass, Europass and individual country passes for Austria, Britain, Bulgaria, Czech Republic, Germany, Greece, Holland, Italy, Norway and Spain.
Rail Europe ☎ 1-800/438-7245, Canada ☎ 1-800/361-7245, Ⓦ www.raileurope.com/us. Official North American Eurail Pass agent; also sells Europass, multinational passes and most single-country passes.

In Australia and New Zealand

CIT World Travel Australia ☎ 02/9267 1255, Ⓦ www.cittravel.com.au. Eurail, Europass and Italian rail passes.
Rail Plus Australia ☎ 1300/555 003 or 03/9642 8644, ⓔ info@railplus.com.au; New Zealand ☎ 09/303 2484. Sells Eurail and Europass.
Trailfinders Australia ☎ 02/9247 7666, Ⓦ www.trailfinder.com.au. All European passes.

By car from the UK and Ireland

If you have the time and inclination, **driving to Greece** can be a pleasant proposition. Realistically, though, it's really only worth considering if you have at least a month to spare, are going to stay in Greece for an extended period, or want to take advantage of various stopovers en route. The most popular **route** is down through France and Italy to catch one of the Adriatic ferries. A longer alternative through eastern Europe (Hungary, Romania and Bulgaria) is just about feasible.

The fastest way to get across **to the continent** is the **Eurotunnel** service via the Channel Tunnel; the alternative is one of the time-honoured **ferry** crossings (see below). Eurotunnel operates shuttle trains 24 hours a day, for cars, motorcycles, buses and their passengers. The service runs continuously between Folkestone and Coquelles, near Calais, with up to four departures per hour (only one per hour midnight–6am) and takes 35min (45min for some night departure times), though you must arrive at least 30min before departure. It is possible to turn up and buy your ticket at the toll booths (after exiting the M20 at junction 11a), though at busy times booking is advisable. **Rates** depend on the time of year, time of day and length of stay; it's cheaper to travel between 10pm and 6am, while the highest fares are reserved for weekend departures and returns in July and August. For current information, contact the **Eurotunnel Customer Services Centre** at ℡0870/ 535 3535, ⓦ www.eurotunnel.com.

The traditional cross-Channel options for most travellers are the **ferry or hovercraft** links between Dover and Calais or Boulogne (the quickest and cheapest routes), Ramsgate and Dunkerque, or Newhaven and Dieppe. Irish drivers will prefer routes bypassing Britain, direct to Roscoff or Cherbourg, or from the southwest of England to St-Malo or Caen.

Ferry **prices** vary according to the time of year and, for motorists, the size of your car. The Dover–Calais/Boulogne runs, for example, start at about £245–340 open return for a car with up to five passengers, though this range can nearly double in peak season.

Ferries crossing the Channel and the Irish Sea

Brittany Ferries ℡0870/901 2400, Republic of Ireland ℡021/277705, ℱ277262, ⓦ www.brittanyferries.co.uk. Poole to Cherbourg; Portsmouth to Caen and St Malo; Plymouth to Roscoff (March–Nov/Dec); Cork to Roscoff (March–Oct only).

Hoverspeed ℡0870/524 0241, ⓦ www. hoverspeed.co.uk. Twenty-four daily departures. Dover to Calais and Ostend; Newhaven to Dieppe.

Irish Ferries ℡0870/517 1717, Republic of Ireland ℡1890/313 131, ⓦ www.irishferries.com. Dublin to Holyhead; Rosslare to Pembroke, Cherbourg and Roscoff. Continental services March to end Sept.

P&O European Ferries ℡0870/242 4999, ⓦ www.poportsmouth.com. Portsmouth to Cherbourg and Le Havre.

P&O Irish Sea ℡0870/242 4777, Republic of Ireland ℡01/800 409 049, ⓦ www.poirishsea.com. Larne to Cairnryan or Fleetwood; Dublin to Liverpool.

P&O Stena Line ℡0870/600 0600, ⓦ www.posl.com. Dover to Calais.

Sea France ℡0870/571 1711, ⓦ www.seafrance.com. Dover to Calais.

Stena Line ℡0870/570 7070, Republic of Ireland ℡01/204 7777, ⓦ www.stenaline.co.uk. Rosslare to Fishguard; Dun Laoghaire or Dublin to Holyhead; Belfast to Stranraer.

Via Italy

For motorists heading for western Greece or the Ionian islands, it has always made most sense to drive **via Italy** – and whatever your final destination, taking a ferry on the final leg makes for a more relaxed journey. Initial routes down to Italy through **France** and **Switzerland** are very much a question of personal taste. One of the most direct is Calais–Reims–Geneva–Milan and then down the Adriatic coast to the Italian port of your choice. Even on the quickest autoroutes (with their accompanying tolls), the journey will involve two overnight stops.

Once in **Italy**, you've a choice of five **ports**. Regular car and passenger ferries link **Ancona**, **Bari** and **Brindisi** with **Igoumenítsa** (the port of Epirus in western Greece) and/or **Pátra** (at the northwest tip of the Peloponnese and the closest port to Athens). Most sail via the island of **Corfu**, and a bare handful of companies link other

Note: all timings are approximate.

From Ancona ANEK and Minoan to Pátra (24–26hr), usually via Igoumenítsa (16–19hr); 5 weekly Jan–May, 6 weekly May–Oct with ANEK; 6 weekly year-round on Minoan except mid-Jan to mid-Feb. Blue Star daily Oct–March to Igoumenítsa (15hr) and Pátra (21hr). Also Superfast direct to Igoumenítsa (15hr) or Pátra (19hr) almost daily year round. Most sailings at 7–10pm, but there are a number of early-afternoon departures on ANEK and Blue Star.

From Bari Ventouris to Pátra direct (17hr 30min), 3–4 weekly June–Dec; Igoumenítsa (11hr 30min) via Corfu (10hr), 3 weekly April–June & mid-Sept to Dec, 6 weekly July to mid-Sept; Marlines to Igoumenítsa (12hr) 4 weekly late June to mid-Oct, July–Sept calls at Corfu once weekly; Superfast heads almost daily year-round for Igoumenítsa (9hr 30min) and Pátra (15hr 30min). Most sailings at 7–10pm.

From Brindisi Agoudimos to Igoumenítsa at least 4 weekly April–Dec, daily late June to early Sept (9hr). Blue Star almost daily year-round to Corfu (7hr) and Igoumenítsa (8hr 30min). Fragline to Corfu/Igoumenítsa (9hr) almost daily late March to early Oct. Med Link Lines, daily year-round to Pátra (10hr direct); via Kefalloniá (11hr) 4–6 weekly mid-July to mid-Aug, via Igoumenítsa sporadically mid-June to mid-Aug. Minoan, almost daily late May to late Sept to Corfu (7hr) and Igoumenítsa (8hr 30min). Ventouris, conventional ferry 6 weekly to Corfu (7hr) and Igoumenítsa (8hr 30min) late June to early Sept; high-speed craft daily late April to mid-Sept to Corfu (3hr) and Igoumenítsa (4hr), 3 daily Fri–Sun late June to mid-Sept, calling at Paxí (5hr) once daily late July to early Sept.

There's a fairly even division between late-morning and -evening departures, with high-speed craft doing daytime crossings. Agoudimos, Fragline, Med Link and Ventouris in August all depart 7–9.30pm, while Minoan and Ventouris in other months leave at 11am. The Ventouris high-speed craft departs at 3pm in spring, and in summer at 8.30am, 2pm and 7pm; Blue Star leaves at 10.30am all year.

From Trieste ANEK to Igoumenítsa (24hr), 5 weekly Jan–April, daily April–Oct; most days continues to Pátra (31hr). Usually departs 2pm.

From Venice Blue Star, 4 weekly year-round to Igoumenítsa (26hr) and Pátra (33hr); Minoan daily April–Oct to the same ports (25hr and 35hr respectively), also stopping at Corfu. Departures at about 7pm.

Sample fares

Prices below are one-way high/low season fares; port taxes (€5–8 per person and per car in each direction) are not included. Substantial reductions apply on many lines for both InterRail or Eurail pass-holders, and for those under 26. Discounts of 30–50 percent are usually available on return tickets, even in peak season. Many companies allow you to sleep in your van on board, sparing you the cost of a cabin berth; ask about reduced "camping" fares.

Ionian islands such as **Paxí** or **Kefalloniá** en route to Pátra from mid-July (eastbound) to mid-September (westbound) only; you can stop over at no extra charge if you get these halts specified on your ticket. Generally, these ferries run year round, but services are greatly reduced out of season. Ferries also sail regularly from **Venice** and less frequently from **Trieste**. For more details see the box above.

The crossing to Igoumenítsa is usually, but not always, substantially cheaper than to Pátra; the **cheapest** of all the crossings is from Brindisi to Igoumenítsa. However, drivers will discover that the extra cost in Italian motorway tolls and fuel offsets the Brindisi or Bari route's savings over those from Ancona, Trieste or Venice; the shipping companies are well aware of this and set their prices accordingly.

In summer, it is essential to **book tickets** a few days ahead, especially in the peak July–August season. During the winter you can usually just turn up at the main ports (Brindisi, Trieste and Venice have the most reliable departures at that time of year), but

Igoumenítsa from Bari or Brindisi: deck class €40–47/€22–32; car from €46–51/€26–32. Superfast fares are €51/42 (deck) and €58/39 (car), also valid all the way to Pátra. The Ventouris high-speed craft work out at €65/56 for a seat, €59/35 per car to Igoumenítsa or Corfu; Paxí is a considerably dearer destination.

Pátra from Ancona: conventional ferry deck class €63/37; car from €86/47. Superfast fares to Igoumenítsa or Ancona are €78/56 (deck) and €104/71 (car). Blue Star is cheaper for comparable speed at €62/41 deck, €85/52 car.

Pátra from Brindisi: deck class €44/29; car from €47/28.

Pátra from Trieste: deck class €71/54; car from €103/66.

Pátra from Venice: deck class €62–72/43–57; car from €103–106/55–67.

Italian agents

The dialling code for Italy is ☎ 39.

Agoudimos c/o Hellas Ferry Lines, Corso Garibaldi 81, Brindisi ☎ 0831/529 091, Ⓕ 529 217.

ANEK Ancona: Stazione Marittima ☎ 0710/205 959; Trieste, Stazione Marittima ☎ 040/322 0604, Ⓕ 322 0142.

Blue Star Brindisi: ☎ 0831/548 115; Ancona: Stazione Marittima ☎ 071/207 1068, Ⓕ 207 0874; Venice: Stazione Marittima 103 ☎ 041/277 0559, Ⓕ 277 0367.

Fragline Via Spalato 31, Brindisi ☎ 0831/548 534, Ⓕ 540 147.

Marlines c/o Pier Paolo Santelia, Stazione Marittima, Bari ☎ 080/523 1824, Ⓕ 523 0287.

Med Link Lines c/o Discovery Shipping, Costa Morena, Brindisi ☎ & Ⓕ 0831/548 116.

Minoan Lines Ancona: Via Astagno 1 ☎ 071/201 708, Ⓕ 201 933; Brindisi, c/o Euromare, Corso Garibaldi 102–104 ☎ 0831/562 936, Ⓕ 562 952; Venice, Santa Marta (San Basilio) Magazzino 17 ☎ 041/271 2345, Ⓕ 521 2929.

Superfast Ferries Ancona: Via XXIX Settembre 2/0 ☎ 071/202 033, Ⓕ 202 219; Bari, Corso A. de Tullio 6 ☎ 080/521 1416, Ⓕ 572 0427.

Ventouris Bari: c/o P. Lorusso & Co, Stazione Marittima Booths 18–20 ☎ 080/521 7609, Ⓕ 521 7734; Brindisi, c/o Venmare, Corso Garibaldi 56 ☎ 0831/521 614; Ⓕ 521 654.

Ferries on the internet

All of the shipping companies have websites, as given below. Viamare Travel Ltd (☎ 020/7431 4560, Ⓦ www.viamare.com) is the UK agent for most of these companies.

Agoudimos Lines Ⓦ www.agoudimos-lines.com

ANEK Ⓦ www.anek.gr

Blue Star Ⓦ www.bluestarferries.com

Fragline Ⓦ www.fragline.gr

Marlines Ⓦ www.marlines.com

Med Link Lines Ⓦ www.mll.gr

Minoan Lines Ⓦ www.minoan.gr

Superfast Ⓦ www.superfast.com

Ventouris Ⓦ www.ventouris.gr

---

it's still wise to book in advance, certainly if you are taking a car or want a cabin. A few phone calls or internet searches before leaving home are, in any case, advisable, as the range of fares and operators (from Brindisi especially) is considerable; if you do just turn up at the port, it's worth spending some time shopping around the agencies.

Via Hungary, Romania and Bulgaria

Avoiding former Yugoslavia involves a pretty substantial diversion through Hungary, Romania and Bulgaria. Too exhausting and too problematic at the best of times, this is not a drive to contemplate unless you actively want to see some of the countries en route. However, it's all simpler than it was, with visas easier to obtain at the borders, if you haven't fixed them in advance.

From **Budapest**, the quickest route **through Romania** is via Timişoara, then on towards Sofia in Bulgaria and across the Rila mountains to the border at Kulata. Once at the Greek border, you have a three- to four-hour drive to Thessaloníki or Kavála. Bear in mind that road conditions are often poor and border formalities extensive. Contact the relevant embassies and the AA for more advice.

Flights from North America

The Greek national airline, Olympic Airways, flies out of New York (JFK), Boston, Montréal and Toronto. The airline – and also its domestic competitors Axon and Cronus-Aegean – can offer reasonably priced add-on flights within Greece, especially to the Greek islands. Delta is the only North American carrier currently offering any direct service to Athens, though American Airlines, TWA and USAir have code-sharing agreements with Olympic, and in conjunction with Olympic they quote through fares to/from Chicago, Dallas/Fort Worth, Denver, LA, Miami, Ottawa, Quebec, SF, Seattle, Tampa, Vancouver and Washington DC.

Another option to consider is picking up any suitable flight to Europe and making your way to Greece by train, in which case a Eurail Pass makes a reasonable investment – details are given on p.17.

Useful airlines in North America

Air Canada ☎1-888/247–2262, ⓦwww.aircanada.ca.
Air France ☎1-800/237-2747, in Canada ☎1-800/667-2747, ⓦwww.airfrance.com.
Alitalia ☎1-800/223-5730, in Canada ☎1-800/361-8336, ⓦwww.alitalia.com.
American Airlines ☎1-800/433-7300, ⓦwww.aa.com.
British Airways ☎1-800/247-9297, ⓦwww.british-airways.com.
Canadian Airlines ☎1-888/247-2262, ⓦwww.aircanada.ca.
Continental Airlines domestic ☎1-800/523-3273, international ☎1-800/231-0856, ⓦwww.continental.com.
Delta Air Lines domestic ☎1-800/221-1212, international ☎1-800/241-4141, ⓦwww.delta.com.
Iberia ☎1-800/772-4642, ⓦwww.iberia.com.
KLM/Northwest US domestic ☎1-800/225-2525, international ☎1-800/447-4747, in Canada ☎514/397-0775, ⓦwww.klm.com.
Lufthansa ☎1-800/645-3880, in Canada ☎1-800/563-5954, ⓦwww.lufthansa-ca.com.
Olympic Airways ☎1-800/223-1226 or 212/735-0200, ⓦwww.olympic-airways.gr.

Swissair ☎1-800/221-4750, ⓦwww.swissair.com.
TWA domestic ☎1-800/221-2000, international ☎1-800/892-4141, ⓦwww.twa.com.
US Airways domestic ☎1-800/428-4322, international ☎1-800/622-1015, ⓦwww.usairways.com.
Virgin Atlantic Airways ☎1-800/862-8621, ⓦwww.virgin-atlantic.com.

Discount travel companies

Air Brokers International ☎1-800/883-3273 or 415/397-1383, ⓦwww.airbrokers.com. Consolidator and specialist in RTW and Circle-Pacific tickets.
Airhitch ☎1-800/326-2009 or 212/864-2000, ⓦwww.airhitch.org. Standby seat broker: for a set price, they guarantee to get you on a flight as close to your preferred Western European destination as possible, within a week. Costs are currently $165 (plus taxes and a $29 processing fee) from or to the East Coast region; $233 (plus tax and $29 reg. fee) from/to the West Coast or (when available) the Pacific Northwest; $199 (plus tax and $29 reg. fee) from/to the Midwest; and $177 (plus tax and $29 reg. fee) from/to the southeast. (Taxes for all Europe itineraries are $16 eastbound and $46 westbound.)
Airtech ☎212/219-7000, ⓦwww.airtech.com. Standby seat broker; also deals in consolidator fares and courier flights.
Council Travel ☎1-800/226-8624 or 617/528-2091, ⓦwww.counciltravel.com. Nationwide (sixty branches) organization that mostly, but by no means exclusively, specializes in student/budget travel.
Educational Travel Center ☎1-800/747-5551 or 608/256-5551, ⓦwww.edtrav.com. Student/youth discount agent.
High Adventure Travel ☎1-800/350-0612 or 415/912-5600, ⓦwww.airtreks.com. RTW and Circle-Pacific tickets. The website features an interactive database that lets you build and price your own RTW itinerary.
New Frontiers/Nouvelles Frontières ☎1-800/677-0720 or 212/986-6006, ⓦwww.NewFrontiers.com. French discount-travel firm. Other branches in LA, San Francisco and Québec City.
Skylink US ☎1-800/AIR-ONLY or 212/573-8980, Canada ☎1-800/SKY-LINK. Consolidator.
STA Travel ☎1-800/777-0112 or 781-4040, ⓦwww.sta-travel.com. Worldwide specialists in independent travel; also student IDs, travel insurance, car rental, rail passes, etc.

Student Flights ☎1-800/255-8000 or 480/951-1177, ⓦwww.isecard.com. Student/youth fares, student IDs.

TFI Tours International ☎1-800/745-8000 or 212/736-1140. Consolidator.

Travac ☎1-800/872-8800, ⓦwww.thetravelsite.com. Consolidator and charter broker, with another office in Orlando.

Travel Avenue ☎1-800/333-3335, ⓦwww.travelavenue.com. Full-service travel agent that offers discounts in the form of rebates.

Travel Cuts in Canada ☎1-800/667-2887, in US ☎416/979-2406, ⓦwww.travelcuts.com. Canadian student-travel organization.

Worldtek Travel ☎1-800/243-1723, ⓦwww.worldtek.com. Discount travel agency for worldwide travel.

Worldwide Discount Travel Club ☎305/534-2642. Discount travel club.

Flights from the US and Canada

The daily nonstop flights **to Athens out of New York-JFK and Boston** (one stop) on Olympic start at around US$700 round trip in winter, rising to around $1400 in summer for a maximum thirty-day stay with seven-day advance purchase. Delta has several weekly direct services from New York-JFK to Athens, but high-season published discount fares are vastly overpriced at close to $2000; you can save a bit by changing in Paris to Axon Airlines for the final leg. In general, one-stop flights are less expensive; at the time of writing, Alitalia was offering the cheapest summer fares New York–Athens (via Rome) at just over $1000, less than half that in winter. Travelling during the May and October "shoulder seasons" will also yield significant savings.

Common-rating (ie price-fixing) and marketing agreements between the various airlines means that fares to **Athens from the Midwest, Deep South or the West Coast** are little different; from Chicago, Miami, Dallas, Seattle or Los Angeles you're looking at $1700–1900 high season, $500–600 in winter, something in between at shoulder season. These tickets typically involve the use of American Airlines, Air France, Alitalia, Iberia, KLM and Swissair, via their European gateway cities. With little to distinguish these itineraries price-wise, you might examine the stopover time at their respective European hubs, as these can sometimes be overnight. You may be better off getting a domestic

add-on to New York and heading directly to Athens from there.

As with the US, airfares **from Canada to Athens** vary depending on where you start your journey, and whether you take a direct service. Olympic flies nonstop out of Montréal and Toronto four times weekly for a scheduled return fare of about CDN$1400 in winter, climbing to nearly CDN$3000 in summer. Indirect flights on Air Canada and British Airways (both via London Heathrow), or KLM, Air France, Sabena or Swissair will cost about CDN$500 less in summer, though in winter their fares are little different from Olympic; frequencies via the European hubs are daily or nearly so. From Calgary or Vancouver, there are no direct flights; expect to pay CDN$2800–3000 during summer, on such combinations as Air Canada/Lufthansa or Air Canada/KLM.

European–Greek regional connections

There are direct scheduled flights (some summer only), mostly with Olympic or Cronus, to:

Thessaloníki from Amsterdam, Belgrade, Berlin, Brussels, Bucharest, Budapest, Dusseldorf, Frankfurt, Larnaca, London, Milan, Moscow, Munich, Paris, Prague, Stuttgart, Vienna, Zurich.

Iráklion (Crete) from Helsinki, Larnaca, Paris, Stuttgart.

Specialist tour operators: North America

Adventures Abroad Canada ☎1-800/665-3998 or 604/303-1099, ⓦwww.adventures-abroad.com. Offers a twenty-day "Poetic Greek Isles" tour in spring or autumn, about $2000 land-only.

BCT Scenic Walking ☎1-800/473-1210, ⓦwww.bctwalk.com. Offers an eight-day "Ancient Isle of Crete" tour, spring and autumn, with a mix of gorge-walking and archeological sites.

Caravan Tours ☎1-888/227-2826, ⓦwww.caravantours.com. Rather rushed eighteen-day land-and-sea tour, taking in mainland highlights and a cruise of select islands; six departures annually May–Oct.

Classic Adventures ☎1-800/935-5000, ⓦwww.classicadventures.com. Two good offerings, at about $2400 land-only: spring or autumn rural cycling tours of "classical Greece", crossing the north Peloponnese to Zákynthos in eleven days, or a pedal through the archeological sites and medieval towns of Crete, in twelve days. **Hellenic Adventures** ☎1-800/851-6349, ⓦwww.hellenicadventures.com. Small-group, human-scale tours, led by an enthusiastic Greek-American; the five hiking-and-sailing itineraries are much better than average, taking in unusual highlights such as Zagóri, Pertoúli, Pílio, Kastoriá, Ioánnina, Híos and Límnos. The website is fun and easy to use, too.

Himalayan Travel ☎1-800/225-2380 or 203/743-2349, ⓦwww.gorp.com/himtravel.htm. The widest array of Greek walking tours, self-guiding and hotel/inn-based unless otherwise indicated: Kefalloniá–Itháki (eight days, $1000); Crete's southwest coast (eight days, $1050); Zagóri/Víkos Gorge (eight days, $1000); and peaks of the Píndhos plus Mt Ólymbos (fifteen days, $1300, escorted).

IST Cultural Tours ☎1-800/833-2111, ⓦwww.ist-tours.com. Their "Historic Greece & Turkey" tour runs to sixteen days, nine of it cruising; fairly upmarket, and divided evenly between Greece and Turkey.

Samodyssey ☎ & ⓕ 773/472-2765, ⓔSamodyssey@aol.com. Twice-yearly small-group tours of about three-weeks' duration put together by Hellenophile Sam Stenzel, who lived in Athens for decades; includes a changing selection from the islands and mainland, plus the Turkish coast.

Valef Yachts ☎1-800/223-3845, ⓦwww.valefyachts.com. Offers a choice of fixed, eight-day motor-yacht cruises in the Dodecanese or the Ionian islands; a bit rushed, but affordable at $900–1150 per person. Also very expensive bareboat charter (sailing or motor yacht); pick your craft from the online brochure.

Flights from Australia and New Zealand

With the huge Greek-emigrant community in Australia, Olympic does a fair job of providing direct links to Greece, though they're seldom the cheapest option. The airline offers three weekly flights to Athens from Sydney, and two from Melbourne, via Bangkok, with onward connections to other Greek destinations. There are no direct flights from New Zealand – you'll have to get yourself to Australia, Southeast Asia or a nearby European hub for onward travel.

Tickets purchased direct from the airlines tend to be expensive; travel agents or Australia-based websites offer much better deals on fares and have the latest information on limited specials, Round-the-World fares and stopovers. Some of the best discounts are through Flight Centres, Trailfinders and STA, who can also advise on visa regulations.

If Greece is only one stop on a longer journey, you might want to consider buying a Round-the-World (RTW) fare. Some travel agents can sell you an "off-the-shelf" **RTW ticket** that will have you touching down in about half a dozen cities (Athens is on many itineraries); others will have to assemble one for you, which can be tailored to your needs but is apt to be more expensive. Figure on A$2250/2600 low/high season for a RTW ticket including Greece, on Star Alliance airlines. In the past, Qantas and British Airways have also offered RTW fares, dubbed the "Global Explorer". RTW fares from any point in Australia are usually common-rated, ie the price is the same from whichever Australian airport you commence travel. From New Zealand, allow over NZ$3500 for the same programmes.

For a **simple return fare**, you may have to buy an add-on internal flight to reach the international gateways of Sydney or Melbourne. Because of the way Australians travel, most tickets are **valid for one year**; at the time of writing, **high-season** departures could be had for A$1770 (one-stop flight on PIA and Qantas) to A$1900 on Olympic, the latter valid all the way to any domestic airport in Greece. Cheaper multi-stop fares on Egyptair (A$1500), Emirates ($A1720) or Gulf Air (A$1800) tend to be reserved for students or over-60s. Leaving at **low season** means fares of A$1460 (Olympic) to A$1520 (combination of United, Lufthansa and Singapore Airlines); students can try Egyptair (A$1360), while seniors currently have Gulf Air (A$1410). Other airlines which in the past have had advantageous fares to Greece include Aeroflot (via Singapore and Moscow) Alitalia (via Rome or Milan), Royal Jordanian (via Amman) and Thai Airways (via Bangkok).

From New Zealand, the usual routes to Athens are either westbound several times weekly via Bangkok, Sydney or Singapore, on Thai Airways, Singapore Airlines or Air New Zealand, or eastbound almost daily via Los Angeles with Air New Zealand. Published return fares are currently edging up to NZ$3500, and even discount outlet tickets close to NZ$3000, so a RTW fare as described opposite may be your best option.

Airlines

Aeroflot Australia ☎02/9262 2233, ⓦwww.aeroflot.com.

Air New Zealand Australia ☎13 2476, New Zealand ☎0800/737 000 or 09/357 3000, ⓦwww.airnz.com.

Alitalia Australia ☎02/9244 2400, New Zealand ☎09/302 1452, ⓦwww.alitalia.it.

British Airways Australia ☎02/8904 8800, New Zealand ☎09/356 8690, ⓦwww.british-airways.com.

Egyptair Australia ☎02/9267 6979, ⓦwww.egyptair.com.

Gulf Air Australia ☎02/9244 2199, New Zealand ☎09/308 3366, ⓦwww.gulfairco.com.

Lufthansa Australia ☎1300/655 727 or 02/9367 3887, New Zealand ☎09/303 1529 or 0800/945 220, ⓦwww.lufthansa.com.

Olympic Airways Australia ☎1800/221 663 or 02/9251 2044, ⓦwww.olympic-airways.com.

Qantas Australia ☎13 1313, New Zealand ☎09/357 8900 or 0800/808 767, ⓦwww.qantas.com.au.

Royal Jordanian Airlines Australia ☎02/9244 2701; New Zealand agent: Innovative Travel ☎03/365 3910; ⓦwww.rja.com.jo.

Singapore Airlines Australia ☎13 1011 or 02/9350 0262, New Zealand ☎09/303 2129 or 0800/808 909, ⓦwww.singaporeair.com.

Thai Airways Australia ☎1300/651 960, New Zealand ☎09/377 3886, ⓦwww.thaiair.com.

Travel agents

Anywhere Travel Australia ☎02/9663 0411 or 018 401 014, ⓔanywhere@ozemail.com.au.

Budget Travel New Zealand ☎09/366 0061 or 0800/808 040.

Destinations Unlimited New Zealand ☎09/373 4033.

Flight Centre Australia ☎02/9235 3522 or for nearest branch ☎13 1600, New Zealand ☎09/358 4310, ⓦwww.flightcentre.com.au.

Northern Gateway Australia ☎08/8941 1394, ⓔoztravel@norgate.com.au.

STA Travel Australia ☎13 1776 or 1300/360 960, New Zealand ☎09/309 0458 or 366 6673, ⓦwww.statravel.com.au.

Student Uni Travel Australia ☎02/9232 8444, ⓔAustralia@backpackers.net.

Thomas Cook Australia ☎13 1771 or 1800/801 002, New Zealand ☎09/379 3920, ⓦwww.thomascook.com.au.

Trailfinders Australia ☎02/9247 7666.

usit BEYOND New Zealand ☎09/379 4224 or 0800/788 336, ⓦwww.usitbeyond.co.nz.

Specialist agents and tour operators

Adventure Travel Company ☎09/379 9755, ⓔadvakl@hot.co.nz. New Zealand agent for Peregrine Adventures (see below).

Australians Studying Abroad ☎03/9509 1955 or 1800/645 755, ⓦwww.asatravinfo.com.au. Their "Hellenic Heritage" study tour takes a relatively leisurely 23 days to cover most of the major ancient/medieval sites on the mainland and islands, with Istanbul thrown in; fairly pricey at A$7000 land only.

House of Holidays Australia ☎1800/335 084, ⓦwww.houseofholidays.com.au. Offers various tours of four to fourteen days' duration; the latter "Best of Greece" package takes in Athens, assorted ruins on the mainland and finishes with a short island cruise.

Kompas Holidays Australia ☎07/3222 3333 or 1800/269 968, ⓦwww.kompasholidays.com.au. Scores for its Greek island-hopping programme, covering eleven of the better-known islands; they arrange hotels (three-day minimum stay per island) and all ferry transfers.

Peregrine Adventures Australia ☎03/9662 2700 or 1300/655 433, ⓦwww.peregrine.net.au. Exclusive antipodean reps for Exodus (UK), selling their eight-day walking expedition around Tínos.

Sun Island Tours Australia ☎02/9283 3840, ⓦwww.sunislandtours.com.au. An assortment of island-hopping, fly-drives, cruises and guided land-tour options.

Visas and red tape

UK and all other EU nationals (plus those of Norway and Iceland) need only a valid passport for entry to Greece; you are no longer stamped in on arrival or out upon departure, and in theory at least enjoy uniform civil rights with Greek citizens. US, Australian, New Zealand, Canadian and most non-EU Europeans receive mandatory entry and exit stamps in their passports and can stay, as tourists, for ninety days. Note that such nationals arriving by flight or boat from another EU state may not be stamped in routinely at minor ports, so it's best to make sure this is done in order to avoid unpleasantness on exit.

If you are planning to **travel overland**, you should check current visa requirements for Hungary, Romania and Bulgaria at their closest consulates; transit visas for most of these territories are at present issued at the borders, though at a higher price than if obtained in advance at a local consulate.

Visa extensions

If you wish to remain in Greece for longer than three months, as a non-EU/EFTA national you should officially apply for an extension. This can be done in the larger cities like Athens, Thessaloníki, Pátra, Rhodes and Iráklion through the Ypiresía Allodhapón (Aliens' Bureau); prepare yourself for concerted bureaucracy. In other locations you visit the local police station, where the staff are apt to be more co-operative.

Unless of Greek descent, visitors from **non-EU** countries are currently allowed only one six-month extension to a tourist visa, for which a hefty fee is charged – up to €150. In theory, EU nationals are allowed to stay indefinitely but, to be sure of avoiding any problems, it's best to get a resident visa and (if appropriate) a work permit – see "Finding work", p.76. In either case, the procedure should be set in motion at least four weeks before your time runs out. If you don't already have a work permit, you will be required to present pink, personalized bank **exchange receipts** totalling at least €1500 for the preceding three months, as proof that you are importing sufficient funds to support yourself without working. Possession of unexpired credit cards, a Greek **savings account passbook** or travellers' cheques can to some extent substitute for the pink receipts; the pages of the passbook in particular should be photocopied and given to the police.

Certain individuals get around the law by leaving Greece every three months and re-entering a few days later, ideally via a different frontier post, for a new, ninety-day tourist stamp. However, with the recent flood of Albanian and Eastern European refugees into the country, all looking for work, security and immigration personnel don't always look very kindly on this practice.

If you **overstay** your time and then leave under your own power – ie are not deported – you'll be hit with a huge spot fine upon departure, effectively a double-priced retroactive visa extension; no excuses will be entertained except perhaps a doctor's certificate stating you were immobilized in hospital. It cannot be overemphasized just how exigent Greek immigration officials often are on this issue.

Greek embassies abroad

Australia 9 Turrana St, Yarralumla, Canberra, ACT 2600 ☎ 02/6273 3011.
Britain 1a Holland Park, London W11 3TP ☎ 020/7221 6467, ⓦ www.greekembassy.org.uk.
Canada 80 Maclaren St, Ottawa, ON K2P 0K6 ☎ 613/238-6271.
Ireland 1 Upper Pembroke St, Dublin 2 ☎ 01/676 7254.
New Zealand 5–7 Willeston St, Wellington ☎ 04/473 7775.
USA 2221 Massachusetts Ave NW, Washington, DC 20008 ☎ 202/939-5800, ⓦ www.greekembassy.org.

Insurance

Even though EU health care privileges apply in Greece (see overleaf for details), you'd do well to take out an insurance policy before travelling to cover against theft, loss, illness or injury. Before paying for a whole new policy, however, it's worth checking whether you are already covered: some all-risks homeowners' or renters' insurance policies *may* cover your possessions when overseas, and many private medical schemes (such as BUPA or PPP in the UK) offer coverage extensions for abroad.

In Canada, provincial health plans usually provide partial cover for medical mishaps overseas, while holders of official student/teacher/youth cards in Canada and the US are entitled to meagre accident coverage and hospital inpatient benefits. **Students** will often find that their student health coverage extends during the vacations and for one term beyond the date of last enrolment. Most **credit-card issuers** also offer some sort of vacation insurance, which is often automatic if you pay for the holiday with their card. However, it's vital to check just what these policies cover – frequently only death or dismemberment in the UK.

After exhausting the possibilities above, you might want to contact a **specialist travel insurance** company, or consider the travel insurance deal we offer (see box, below). A typical travel insurance policy usually provides cover for the **loss** of baggage, tickets and – up to a certain limit – cash, cards or

cheques, as well as **cancellation** or curtailment of your journey. Most of them exclude so-called **dangerous sports** unless an extra premium is paid: in the Greek islands this means motorbiking, windsurfing and possibly sailing, and on the mainland this could mean rafting, skiing or trekking, with most visitors engaging in one or the other at some point. Many policies can be chopped and changed to exclude coverage you don't need – for example, sickness and accident benefits can often be excluded or included at will. If you do take medical coverage, ascertain whether benefits will be paid as treatment proceeds or only after return home, whether there is a **24-hour medical emergency number**, and how much the deductible is (sometimes negotiable). When securing baggage cover, make sure that the **per-article limit** – typically under £500 in the UK – will cover your most valuable possession. Travel agents and tour operators in the UK are

Rough Guide travel insurance

Rough Guides offers its own travel insurance, customized for our readers by a leading UK broker and backed by a Lloyds underwriter. It's available for anyone, of any nationality, travelling anywhere in the world.

There are two main Rough Guide insurance plans: **Essential**, for basic, no-frills cover; and **Premier** – with more generous and extensive benefits. Alternatively, you can take out **annual multitrip insurance**, which covers you for any number of trips throughout the year (with a maximum of sixty days for any one trip). Unlike many policies, the Rough Guides schemes are calculated by the day, so if you're travelling for 27 days rather than a month, that's all you pay for. If you intend to be away for the whole year, the Adventurer policy will cover you for 365 days. Each plan can be supplemented with a "Hazardous Activities Premium" if you plan to indulge in sports considered dangerous, such as skiing, scuba-diving or trekking. Rough Guides also does good deals for older travellers, and will insure you up to any age, at prices comparable to Saga's.

For a policy quote, call the Rough Guide Insurance Line toll-free on ☎0800/015 0906 (in the UK); on ☎1-866/220-5588 (in the USA); or, if you're calling from elsewhere ☎+44 1243/621046. Alternatively, get an online quote at ⊛www.roughguides.com/insurance

likely to **require travel insurance** when you book a package holiday, though after a change in the UK law in late 1998 they can no longer insist that you buy their own – however, you will be required to sign a declaration saying that you have a policy with a particular company.

If you need to make a **medical claim**, you should keep receipts for medicines and treatment, and in the event you have anything stolen or lost, you must obtain an **official statement** from the police or the airline which lost your bags. In the wake of growing numbers of fraudulent claims, most insurers won't even entertain one unless you have a police report. There is usually also a **time limit** for submitting claims after the end of your journey.

Health matters

British and other EU nationals are officially entitled to free medical care in Greece upon presentation of an E111 form, available from most post offices. "Free", however, means admittance only to the lowest grade of state hospital (known as a *yenikó nosokomío*), and does not include nursing care, special tests or the cost of medication. If you need prolonged medical care, you should make use of private treatment, which is as expensive as anywhere in western Europe – this is where your travel insurance policy (see above) comes in handy. The US, Canada, Australia and New Zealand have no formal healthcare agreements with Greece (other than allowing for free emergency trauma treatment).

There are no required **inoculations** for Greece, though it's wise to ensure that you are up to date on tetanus and polio. The **water** is safe pretty much everywhere, though you will come across shortages or brackish supplies on some of the drier and more remote islands. Bottled water is widely available if you're feeling cautious.

Specific hazards

The main health problems experienced by visitors have to do with **overexposure to the sun**, and the odd nasty from the sea. To combat the former, don't spend too long in the sun, cover up limbs, wear a hat, and drink plenty of fluids in the hot months to avoid any danger of **sunstroke**; remember that even hazy sun can burn. For sea-gear, goggles or a dive mask for swimming and footwear for walking over wet or rough rocks are useful.

Hazards of the deep

In the sea, you may have the bad luck to meet an armada of **jellyfish** (*tsoúkhtres*),

especially in late summer; they come in various colours and sizes ranging from purple "pizzas" to invisible, minute creatures. Various over-the-counter remedies for jellyfish stings are sold in resort pharmacies; baking soda or diluted ammonia also help to lessen the sting. The welts and burning usually subside of their own accord within a few hours; there are no deadly man-of-war species in Greek waters.

Less vicious but more common are black, spiky **sea urchins** (*ahíni*), which infest rocky shorelines year-round; if you step on or graze one, a sewing needle (you can crudely sterilize it by heat from a cigarette lighter) and olive oil are effective for removing spines; if you don't extract them they'll fester. You can take your revenge by eating the roe of the reddish–purple ones, which is served as a delicacy in a few seafood restaurants.

The worst maritime danger – fortunately very rare – is the **weever fish** (*dhrákena*) which buries itself in shallow-water sand with just its poisonous dorsal and gill spines protruding. If you tread on one, the sudden pain is excruciating, and the exceptionally potent venom can cause permanent paralysis of the affected area. Imperative first aid is to immerse your foot in water as hot as you can stand, which degrades the toxin and relieves the swelling of joints and attendant pain, but you should still seek medical attention as soon as possible.

Somewhat more common are **stingrays and skates** (Greek names include *platý*, *seláhi*, *vátos* or *trígona*), which mainly frequent bays with sandy bottoms where they can camouflage themselves. Though shy, they can give you a nasty lash with their tail if trodden on, so shuffle your feet a bit when entering the water.

When snorkelling in deeper water, especially around Crete, the Dodecanese, or the east Aegean, you may happen upon a brightly coloured **moray eel** (*smérna*) sliding back and forth out of its rocky lair. Keep a respectful distance – their slightly comical air and clown-colours belie an irritable temper and the ability to inflict nasty bites or even sever fingers.

Sandflies, dogs and mosquitoes

If you are sleeping on or near a **beach**, it's wise to use insect repellent, either lotion or wrist/ankle bands, and/or a tent with a screen to guard against **sandflies**. Their bites are potentially dangerous, as these flies spread leishmaniasis, a parasitic infection characterized by chronic fever, listlessness and weight loss. It's difficult to treat, requiring long courses of medication.

In Greece, the main reservoirs for leishmaniasis are **dogs**. Transmission of the disease to humans by fleas has not been proven, but it's wisest not to befriend strays as they also carry echinococcosis, a debilitating liver fluke. In humans these form nodules and cysts which can only be removed surgically.

Mosquitoes (*kounóupia*) in Greece carry nothing worse than a vicious bite, but they can be infuriating. One solution is to burn pyrethrum incense coils (*spíres* or *fidhákia*), which are widely and cheaply available, if pungently malodorous. Better, if you can get them, are the small electrical devices (trade names Vape-Net or Bay-Vap) that vaporize an odourless insecticide tablet; many accommodation proprietors supply them routinely. Insect repellents such as Autan are available from most general stores and kiosks.

Creepy-crawlies

Adders (*ohiés*) and **scorpions** (*skorpií*) are found throughout Greece; both creatures are shy, but take care when climbing over drystone walls where snakes like to sun themselves, and don't put hands or feet in places, like shoes, where you haven't looked first. The wiggly, fast-moving **centipedes** which look like a rubber toy from Hong Kong should also be treated with respect, as they pack a nasty bite.

The number of annual deaths from **snakebite** in Europe is very small. Many snakes will bite if threatened, whether they are venomous or not. If a bite injects venom, then swelling will normally occur within thirty minutes. If this happens, get medical attention; keep the bitten part still; and make sure all body movements are as gentle as possible. If medical attention is not nearby then bind the limb firmly to slow the blood circulation, but not so tightly as to stop the blood flow.

Many reptiles, including snakes, can harbour *Salmonella* bacteria, so should be handled cautiously and preferably not at all. This applies particularly to tortoises.

In addition to munching its way through a fair fraction of Greece's surviving pine forests, the **pine processionary caterpillar** – taking this name from the long, nose-to-tail convoys which individuals form at certain points in their life cycle – sports highly irritating hairs, with a poison worse than a scorpion's. If you touch one, or even a tree-trunk they've been on recently, you'll know all about it for a week, and the welts may require antihistamine to heal.

Pharmacies, drugs and contraception

For **minor complaints** it's enough to go to the local *farmakío*. Greek pharmacists are highly trained and dispense a number of medicines which elsewhere could only be prescribed by a doctor. In the larger towns and resorts there'll usually be one who speaks good English. Pharmacies are usually closed evenings and Saturday mornings, but all should have a monthly schedule (in both English and Greek) on their door showing the complete roster of night and weekend duty pharmacists in town.

Greeks are famously hypochondriac, so pharmacies are veritable Aladdin's caves of arcane drugs and sundry formulas – just about everything available in North America and northern Europe is here, and then some. **Homeopathic** and **herbal** remedies are quite widely available, too, and the largest towns have dedicated homeopathic pharmacies, identified by the characteristic green cross. There is a large homeopathic centre in Athens at Nikosthénous 8, Platía Plastíra, Pangráti ☎010/70 98 199; the Centre of Homeopathic Medicine is at Perikléous 1, Maroússi ☎010/80 52 671.

If you regularly use any form of **prescription drug**, you should bring along a copy of the prescription, together with the generic name of the drug; this will help should you need to replace it, and also avoids possible problems with customs officials. In this regard, it's worth being aware that **codeine is banned** in Greece. If you import any you might find yourself in serious trouble, so check labels carefully; it's the core ingredient of Panadeine, Veganin, Solpadeine, Codis and Empirin-Codeine, to name just a few common compounds.

Hayfever sufferers should be prepared for the early Greek pollen season, at its height from April to June. If you are taken by surprise, you'll be able to get tablets and creams at a pharmacy, but it's cheaper to come prepared. Commercial antihistamines like Triludan are difficult to find in smaller towns, and local brands can be overpriced.

Contraceptive pills are more readily available every year, but don't count on getting these – or spermicidal jelly/foam – outside of a few large island towns, over-the-counter at the larger *farmakía*; Greek women tend not to use any sort of birth control systematically, and have an average of four abortions during their adult life. **Condoms**, however, are inexpensive and ubiquitous – just ask for *profylaktiká* (the slangy terms *plastiká* or slightly vulgar *kapótes* are even better understood) at any pharmacy or corner *períptero* (kiosk).

Women's hygienic supplies are sold in pharmacies or in supermarkets near the toilet paper and diapers. Napkins ("Always" brand) are ubiquitous; tampons can be trickier to find in remoter spots, especially on the smaller islands.

Doctors and hospitals

You'll find English-speaking **doctors** in any of the bigger towns or resorts; the tourist police, hotel staff or even your consulate should be able to come up with some names if you have any difficulty.

For an **ambulance**, phone ☎166. In **emergencies** – cuts, broken bones, etc – treatment is given free in **state hospitals**, though you will only get the most basic level of nursing care. Greek families routinely take in food and bedding for relatives, so as a tourist you'll be at a severe disadvantage. Somewhat better are the ordinary state-run **outpatient clinics** (*yiatría*) attached to most public hospitals and also found in rural locales. These operate on a first-come, first-served basis, so go early; usual hours are 8am to noon, though it's sometimes possible to get seen by someone between 1 and 5pm.

Costs, money and banks

The cost of living in Greece has spiralled during the years of EU membership: the days of renting an island house for a monthly pittance are long gone, and food prices at corner shops now differ little from those of other member countries. However, outside the established resorts, travel between and around the islands remains reasonably priced, with the cost of restaurant meals, short-term accommodation and public transport still cheaper than anywhere in northern or western Europe except parts of Portugal.

Prices depend on where and when you go. Mainland cities, larger tourist resorts and the trendier small islands (such as Sými, Sífnos, Paxí and Pátmos) are more expensive, and costs everywhere increase sharply in July, August and at Christmas, New Year and Easter. **Students** with an International Student Identity Card (ISIC) can get discounted (sometimes free) admission at many archeological sites and museums; those **over 60** can rely on site-admission discounts of 25 to 30 percent, as well as similar discounts for transport. These, and other occasional discounts, tend to be more readily available to EU nationals.

Some basic costs

On most islands a **daily per-person budget** of £23–27/US$32–38 will get you basic accommodation, breakfast, picnic lunch, a short ferry or bus ride and a simple evening meal, as one of a couple. Camping would cut costs marginally. On £35–38/$49–54 a day you could be living quite well, plus sharing the cost of renting a large motorbike or small car.

Inter-island **ferries**, a main unavoidable expense, are reasonably priced, subsidized by the government in an effort to preserve remote island communities. To give you some idea of prices, the cheapest cabin for the overnight journey from Athens to Sámos, an eleven-hour trip, costs about €37, while a deck-class ticket for the four-hour trip from Rhodes to Kós costs about €11. For €4–7 you can catch a short-hop ferry to the numerous small islands that lie closer to Rhodes, Kós and Sámos, the most likely touchdown points if you're flying to the Dodecanese or east Aegean on a direct

charter; a cheap cabin from Pireás to Rhodes, one of the longest single ferry journeys in Greece, will set you back €47. Local ferries in the Cyclades are a bit pricier for the sea miles travelled; Páros or Náxos to Thíra in the Cyclades runs at about €9.

The simplest double **room** generally costs around €20.50–26.50 a night, depending on the location and the plumbing arrangements. Bona fide single rooms are rare, and cost about seventy percent of double rates. Organized **campsites** are little more than €4 per person, with similar charges per tent and perhaps 25 percent more for a camper van. With discretion you can camp for free in the more remote, rural areas.

A basic taverna **meal** with local wine can be had for around €9–10 a head. Add a better bottle of wine, seafood or more careful cooking, and it could be up to €20 a head; you'll rarely pay more than that. Sharing seafood, Greek salads and dips is a good way to keep costs down in the better restaurants, and even in the most developed of resorts, with inflated "international" menus, you'll often be able to find a more earthy but decent taverna where the locals eat.

Youth and student discounts

Various official and quasi-official **youth/student ID cards** soon pay for themselves in savings. Full-time students are eligible for the International Student ID Card (ISIC), which entitles the bearer to special air, rail and ferry fares and discounts at museums, theatres and other attractions. For Americans there's also a health benefit, providing up to $3000 in emergency medical coverage and $100 a day for 60 days in the hospital, plus a 24-hour hotline to call in the event of a medical, legal or financial emergency. The card costs $22 for Americans; CAN$16 for Canadians; A$16.50 for Australians; NZ$21 for New Zealanders; and £6 in the UK.

You only have to be 26 or younger to qualify for the **International Youth Travel Card**, which costs US$22/£7 and carries the same benefits. Teachers qualify for the **International Teacher Identity Card (ITIC)**, offering similar discounts and costing £6, US$22, CAN$16, A$16.50 and NZ$21. All these cards are available in the US from Council Travel, STA, Travel CUTS and, in Canada, Hostelling International; in Australia and New Zealand from STA or Campus Travel; and in the UK from CTS Travel (🕸www.ctstravel.co.uk).

Several other travel organizations and accommodation groups also sell their own cards, good for various discounts. A university photo ID might open some doors, but is not as easily recognizable as the ISIC cards, although the latter are often not accepted as valid proof of age.

Banks and exchange

Greek **banks** are normally open Monday to Thursday 8.30am–2pm, Friday 8.30am–1.30pm. Certain branches in the major towns or tourist centres are open extra hours in the evenings and on Saturday mornings for exchanging money. Always take your passport with you as proof of identity and be prepared for at least one long line.

Outside these times, the largest hotels and travel agencies can often provide this service, albeit sometimes with hefty commissions. On small islands with no full-service bank, "authorized" bank agents will charge yet another extra fee (1–2 percent) to cover the cost of posting a travellers' cheque to the main branch.

The safest, though most expensive, way to carry money is as **travellers' cheques**. These can be obtained from banks (even if you don't have an account) or from offices of Thomas Cook and American Express; you'll usually pay a commission of between one and two percent, though it pays to be aware of any special commission-free deals from your travel agent or your home bank. You can cash the cheques at most banks, though rarely elsewhere. Each travellers' cheque encashment in Greece will incur a minimum commission charge of €1.20–2.40 depending on the bank for amounts of up to €60 equivalent, so you won't want to make too many small-value transactions. For greater amounts, a set percentage will apply. Make sure you keep the purchase agreement and a record of cheque serial numbers safe and separate from the cheques themselves. In the event that cheques are lost or stolen, the issuing company will expect you

The euro

Greece is one of twelve European Union countries which have changed over to a single currency, the **euro** (€). The transition period, which began on January 1, 1999, was lengthy, however: euro notes and coins were not issued until January 1, 2002, with the Greek drachma (*dhrakhmí*, the oldest currency in Europe) remaining in place for cash transactions, at a fixed rate of 340.75 drachmas to 1 euro, until they were scrapped entirely on 28 February, 2002. You will be able to exchange any leftover drachma coins into euros until March 2004, and any old drachma paper notes until March 2012, at branches of the Bank of Greece. For the most up-to-date **exchange rates** of the US dollar or the pound sterling against the euro, consult the very useful currency speculators' website, 🕸www.oanda.com. Rates at the time of research are: £1 = €1.60, US$1 = €1.08, Aus$1 = €0.53. You should not be charged commission for changing euro-denomination travellers' cheques in any of the twelve countries within the euro zone (also known as "Euroland").

All local prices in this book are given in euros. Amounts were derived from the last known drachma price of late 2001, and usually rounded up – as the Greeks will almost certainly do, if the experience of decimalization in the UK is anything to go by. Also judging by past practice, Greek shopkeepers are unlikely to bother much with shortfalls of 10 cents or less, whether in their favour or yours.

Euro notes exist in denominations of 5, 10, 20, 50, 100, 200 and 500 euros, and coins in denominations of 1, 2, 5, 10, 20 and 50 cents and 1 and 2 euros.

to report the loss forthwith; most companies claim to replace lost or stolen cheques within 24 hours.

Small-denomination **foreign bank notes** are also extremely useful, and relatively unlikely to be stolen in Greece. Since the freeing up of all remaining currency controls in 1994, a number of authorized brokers for exchanging foreign cash have emerged in Athens and other major tourist centres. When changing small amounts, choose those bureaux that charge a flat percentage commission (usually one percent) rather than a high minimum. There's also a small number of 24-hour automatic **foreign-note-changing machines** in a few resorts, but again a high minimum commission tends to be deducted.

In 1998, the Greek **post office** largely abandoned the business of changing money – a nuisance, as many tiny islands have a post office but no bank. If you have a UK-based Girobank account, you may still be able to use your chequebook to get money at some remote post offices. You may also find that main post offices (in provincial capitals) are the designated receiving points for Western Union money transfers (see overleaf).

Finally, there is no need to **purchase euros** before arrival unless you're coming in at some ungodly hour to one of the remoter land or sea frontier posts, or on a Sunday. Airport arrival lounges will always have an exchange booth or cash dispenser for passengers on incoming international flights.

Credit cards and cash dispensers

Major **credit cards** are not usually accepted by cheaper tavernas or hotels, but they're almost essential for renting cars, for buying Olympic Airways tickets and for expensive souvenirs. Major travel agents may also claim to accept them, though note that a **three-percent surcharge** is often levied on the purchase of ferry (as opposed to air) tickets.

Credit/debit cards are also handy for withdrawing money from the growing network of Greek **cash dispensers** (ATMs); you'll just need to know the PIN numbers for your cards. Larger airports (such as Athens, Crete, Rhodes, Corfu and Thessaloníki) have at least one cash dispenser in the arrivals hall, and almost any

town or island with a population larger than a few thousand (or a substantial tourist traffic) also has them. The best distributed are those of the National Bank/Ethniki Trapeza, the Trapeza Pireos/Bank of Piraeus, and the Commercial Bank/Emboriki Trapeza, which happily and interchangeably accept Visa, MasterCard, Visa Electron, Plus and Cirrus cards; those of the equally widespread Alfa Trapeza/Alpha Bank and its subsidiary the Ionian Bank/Ioniki Trapeza are somewhat more restrictive, accepting only American Express and Visa-affiliated cards.

Cash-dispenser transactions with **debit cards** linked to a cheque account via the Plus/Cirrus systems attract charges of 2.25 percent on the sterling/dollar transaction value, subject to a minimum of £1.75, making them the **least expensive** way of getting money in Greece as long as you withdraw more than £80 equivalent in euros (about €130). By contrast, using **credit cards** at a cash dispenser is one of the **dearest** ways of obtaining cash: a cash advance per-transaction fee of £1.50 minimum typically applies in the UK, plus a "foreign transaction" surcharge of up to 2.75 percent on the total, depending on the card issuer.

Wiring money

All told, learning and using the PIN numbers for any debit or credit cards you have is the quickest and least expensive way of securing moderate amounts of funds from abroad. In an emergency, however, you can arrange to have more substantial amounts of **money wired** from your home **bank to a bank** in Greece. Receiving funds by SWIFT transfer takes a minimum of two working days and up to ten working days. From the UK, a bank charge of 0.03 percent, with a minimum of £17, maximum £35, is typically levied for two-day service; some building societies charge a £20 flat fee irrespective of the amount. If you choose this route, your home bank will need the address and (ideally) the branch number of the bank where you want to pick up the money. It's unwise to transfer more than the equivalent of €10,000 (currently about US$8500 or £6000); above that limit, as part of measures to combat money-laundering, the receiving Greek bank will begin asking awkward questions and imposing punitive commissions.

Having money wired from home using one of the **companies** listed below is never convenient – local affiliate offices other than the post office are thin on the ground in Greece – and is even more expensive than using a bank. However, unlike with banks, the funds should be available for collection at Amex's, Thomas Cook's or Western Union's local representative office within hours, sometimes minutes, of being sent.

Money-wiring companies

IN THE UK AND IRELAND
Moneygram ☎ 0800/018 0104,
🌐 www.moneygram.com.
Thomas Cook ☎ 01733/318922, Belfast ☎ 028/9055 0030, Dublin ☎ 01/677 1721.
Western Union Money Transfer
☎ 0800/833833, 🌐 www.westernunion.com.

IN NORTH AMERICA
American Express Moneygram ☎ 1-800/926-9400, 🌐 www.moneygram.com.
Thomas Cook US ☎ 1-800/287-7362, Canada ☎ 1-888/8234-7328,
🌐 www.us.thomascook.com.
Western Union ☎ 1-800/325-6000,
🌐 www.westernunion.com.

IN AUSTRALIA
American Express Moneygram ☎ 1800/230 100, 🌐 www.moneygram.com.
Western Union ☎ 1800/649 565,
🌐 www.westernunion.com.

IN NEW ZEALAND
American Express Moneygram ☎ 09/379 8243 or 0800/262 263, 🌐 www.moneygram.com.
Western Union ☎ 09/270 0050,
🌐 www.westernunion.com.

Information, maps and websites

The National Tourist Organization of Greece (Ellinikós Organismós Tourismoú, or EOT; GNTO abroad, 🌐 www.gnto.gr) maintains offices in most European capitals, plus major cities in North America and Australia (see opposite for addresses). It publishes an impressive array of free, glossy, regional pamphlets, which are good for getting an idea of where you want to go, even if the actual text should sometimes be taken with an occasional spoonful of salt. Also available from the EOT are a reasonable foldout map of the country and a large number of brochures on special interests and festivals.

Tourist offices

In Greece, you will find official **EOT offices** in many of the larger towns and resorts. The principal Athens office is at Amerikís 2, just up from Stadhíou. Here, in addition to the usual leaflets, you can find weekly **schedules** for the inter-island **ferries** – hardly one-hundred-percent reliable, but useful as a guideline. EOT staff should be able to advise on **bus** and **train** departures as well as current opening hours for local sites and museums, and occasionally can give assistance with accommodation – though there have been scandals in the provinces concerning certain staff taking

backhanders to steer potential clients towards particular outfits.

Where there is no EOT office, you can get information (and often a range of leaflets) from **municipally run** tourist offices, for example those in Kós and Mólyvos – these are often highly motivated and better than the EOT branches. In the absence of any of these, you can visit the **Tourist Police**, essentially a division (often just a single delegate) of the local police. They can sometimes provide you with lists of rooms to let, which they regulate, but they're really where you go if you have a **serious complaint** about an accommodation or eating establishment.

Greek national tourist offices abroad

Australia
51 Pitt St, Sydney, NSW 2000 ☎02/9241 1663,
Ⓔhto@tpg.com.au.
Canada
91 Scollard St, 2nd Floor, Toronto, ON M5R 1GR,
☎416/968-2220, Ⓔgrnto.tor@sympatico.ca.
Israel
5 Shalom Aleichem St, Tel Aviv 61262
☎03/5170501, Ⓔhellenic@netvision.net.il.
Netherlands
Kerkstraat 61, 1017 GC Amsterdam
☎20/6254212, Ⓔgnot@planet.nl.
UK
4 Conduit St, London W1R 0DJ ☎020/7734 5997,
ⒺEOT-greektouristoffice@btinternet.com.
USA
645 5th Ave, New York, NY 10022 ☎212/421-5777.

The GNTO website lists a dozen more non-English-speaking countries with full tourist offices. If your home country isn't listed there, apply to the embassy. There are no Greek tourist offices in Ireland, South Africa or New Zealand.

Maps

No authoritative, authentic maps . . . Well, isn't that as it should be? Why does anybody need maps? If an individual wants them he's a spy. If a country needs maps it's moribund. A well-mapped country is a dead country. A complete survey is a burial shroud. A life with maps is a tyranny!

This extract from Alan Sillitoe's unjustly neglected 1971 satire, *Travels in Nihilon*, pretty much sums up the prevailing attitude towards **maps** in Greece, which are an endless source of confusion and often outright misinformation. Each cartographic company seems to have its own peculiar system of transcribing Greek letters into the Roman alphabet – and these, as often as not, do not match the semi-official transliterations on the road signs.

The most reliable **general touring maps** of Greece are those published by Athens-based Road Editions (Ⓦwww.road.gr) and Emvelia Editions (Ⓦwww.emvelia.gr). Road Editions products are widely available in Greece at selected bookstores, including their own retail outlet in Athens at

Ippokrátous 39, and at a surprising number of petrol stations and general tourist shops. In Britain they are found at Stanfords (see p.37) and the Hellenic Book Service (see p.1093); in case of difficulty, contact (in Britain) Portfolio, Unit 1C, West Ealing Business Centre, Alexandria Road, London W13 0NJ (☎020/8579 7748). In the US, they're sold exclusively through Map Link (see address on p.37) or Omni Resources, PO Box 2096, Burlington, NC 27216 (☎910/227-8300, Ⓦwww.omnimap.com). Much newer Emvelia currently has just one retail outlet in Athens – Ellinoekdhotiki, at Navarínou 12 – and very sporadic sales points overseas – notably the Hellenic Book Service in London, UK – but this situation is bound to improve.

Having extensively field-tested both brands, we can give no clear answer as to **which is better**. Road Editions products are more intelligently folded and easier to read, but often lack detail; Emvelia tends to show more villages in a busier format. Both are somewhat out-of-date in the matter of current road surfaces. In short, neither is anywhere near perfect, but, based on large-scale military maps not usually available to the public, they're the best you will find, and where they go head-to-head in coverage you may want to buy both. Road Editions covers the mainland in five folding sheets at 1:250,000 scale, entitled *Thrace*, *Macedonia*, *Epiros/Thessaly*, *Central Greece*, and *Peloponnese*, as well as a 1:500,000 map encompassing the whole country. Their 1:50,000 hiking map of Mount Pílio doubles nicely as a road map. Emvelia intends to cover the mainland in six sheets at 1:250,000, entitled *Thrace*, *Makedonia*, *West Makedonia-Thessaly*, *West Greece* (*with Corfu and Lefkádha*), *Central Greece* and *Peloponnese (with Kefalloniá, Zákynthos and Kýthira)*, though as of writing only *West Greece* and *Thrace* had appeared. They also do a double-sided folding map of the whole country at 1:550,000 scale, with a useful index and fair accuracy.

Where Road and Emvelia products are unavailable, good second choices are the **GeoCenter** maps *Greece and the Islands* and *Greek Islands/Aegean Sea*, which together cover the country at a scale of 1:300,000. The single-sided foldup Freytag-Berndt 1:650,000, with an index, is very nearly as good, and easier to use when driving. Despite mid-1990s revisions and updating, Michelin #980 remains a fourth choice. All these are widely available in Britain and North America, though less easily in Greece; see the list of map outlets opposite. Freytag-Berndt also publishes a series of more detailed maps on various regions of Greece, such as the Peloponnese, the Cyclades and the northeast Aegean islands (in two sheets); these are best bought overseas from specialist outlets, though in Greece they are rejacketed and distributed by Efstathiadis.

Touring maps of **individual islands** are more easily available on the spot, and while most are wildly inaccurate or obsolete, a rare few are passably reliable and up-to-date. These include the Road Editions and Emvelia Editions products for **Crete**, plus a steadily growing number of Road titles for smaller islands, including Rhodes, Sámos, Lésvos, Kós and Corfu.

The most useful foreign-produced map of **Athens**, with a decent index, is the Falkplan, available from most specialist outlets. If you can read Greek, and plan to stay for some time in the city, the *Athina-Pireás Proastia A–Ω* street atlas, published by Kapranidhis and Fotis, is invaluable, though pricey. It has a complete index, down to the tiniest alley and also shows cinemas and most hotels. The comparable product for **Thessaloníki** is Emvelia's offering, which also includes Halkidhikí and the immediate surroundings of the city; they also do a folding map of Thessaloníki if you don't want the indexed atlas.

Hiking/topographical maps

Hiking/topographical maps are gradually improving in quality and availability, with a number of companies having a go at loosening the stranglehold which the Army has long excercised on detailed information. **Road**, in addition to their touring maps, have produced 1:50,000, GPS-compatible topographical maps for Mount Párnitha, Mount Pílio, Mount Parnassós, Mount Ólymbos and Mount Íti, usually with rudimentary route directions in English; they also have an excellent though Greek-only walking guide to the Meteóra, packaged with a useful topographical map.

The main rival to Road in this field is **Anavasi**, based at Dhragoúmi 34, 115 28 Athens (☎ & ℻ 01/72 93 541). Their GPS-compatible series is strongest on the mountains of Stereá Elládha (central Greece), with ten folding maps at scales of 1:40,000–1:55,000 covering the celebrated ranges (eg Parnassós, Karpeníssi-Proussós, Gióna) and some obscure ones visited only by Greeks (Ellikón, Krávarra, etc). They also have useful maps-with-guidelets covering Mount Taïyettos (1:25,000), the Préspa region (1:50,000) and the Zagorian Pindhós (1:50,000). Anavasi products use the same military source maps as Road, but score points for frequently better corrections of the road and path networks; there's always a useful, bilingual regional guide text bound in. They are sold in better Athens bookstores, for example Iy Folia tou Vivliou and Eleftheroudhakis (even at the airport branch), but do not as yet have much international distribution.

Between the early 1980s and mid-1990s, the Greek mountaineering magazine **Korfes** issued 1:50,000 maps of select alpine areas, with Roman-alphabet lettering appearing on a few sheets. More than eighty maps were published, issued periodically as a centrefold in the magazine – though many were revisions of previous areas. This programme appears to have ceased; to get back issues you may need to visit the magazine's office at Platía Kentrikí 16, Aharnés, Athens (ring first on ☎010/24 61 528), although the more central bookstore Iy Folia tou Vivliou (see p.155) also keeps an extensive back stock.

Compared to the Road and Anavasi titles, the *Korfes* maps are, unfortunately, unreliable in the matter of trails and new roads, but accurate enough for natural features and village position, based as they are on the older maps of the **Yeografikí Ipiresía Stratoú** (Army Geographical Service, or YIS). If you want to obtain these for islands, and mainland areas not covered by Road or *Korfes*, visit the **YIS** at Evelpídhon 4, north of Aréos Park in Athens, on Monday, Wednesday or Friday from 8am to noon only. All foreigners must leave their passport with the gate guard; EU citizens may proceed directly to the sales hall. Other nationals will probably have to go upstairs for a vetting interview; if you don't speak reasonably good Greek, it's best to have a Greek friend get them for you.

As of writing, YIS maps covering Crete, the

Dodecanese, the east Aegean, Skýros, most of Corfu and much of Epirus, Macedonia and Thrace are still off-limits to all foreigners, as well as Greeks. With matters unsettled across the Balkans, previous plans to lift such restrictions have been shelved indefinitely. A German company, **Harms**, has released a series of five maps at 1:80,000 scale which cover Crete from west to east and show, with about fifty percent accuracy, many hiking routes; despite these defects, they're invaluable until and unless the YIS declassifies this area, and they are available overseas at specialist map outlets.

Finally, for hiking in particular areas of Crete, Corfu, Sámos, Rhodes, Sými, Párga, Pílio, Thássos and Lésvos, maps-with-guide-booklets published by **Marengo Publications** in England also prove very useful. Stanfords keeps a good stock of these, or order from Marengo direct at 17 Bernard Crescent, Hunstanton PE36 6ER ☎01485/532710, ✇www.marengo.supanet .com.

Map outlets

UK and Ireland

Blackwell's Map and Travel Shop, 53 Broad St, Oxford OX1 3BQ ☎01865/792792, ✇www.bookshop.blackwell.co.uk.
Easons Bookshop, 40 O'Connell St, Dublin 1 ☎01/873 3811, ✇www.eason.ie.
Heffers Map and Travel, 20 Trinity St, Cambridge CB2 1TJ ☎01223/568568, ✇www.heffers.co.uk.
Hodges Figgis Bookshop, 56–58 Dawson St, Dublin 2 ☎01/677 4754, ✇www.hodgesfiggis.com.
James Thin Melven's Bookshop, 29 Union St, Inverness IV1 1QA ☎01463/233500, ✇www.jthin.co.uk.
John Smith and Sons, 26 Colquhoun Ave, Glasgow G52 4PJ ☎0141/552 3377, ✇www.johnsmith.co.uk.
The Map Shop, 30a Belvoir St, Leicester LE1 6QH ☎0116/247 1400.
National Map Centre, 22–24 Caxton St, London SW1H 0QU ☎020/7222 2466, ✇www.mapsnmc.co.uk.
Newcastle Map Centre, 55 Grey St, Newcastle upon Tyne NE1 6EF ☎0191/261 5622, ✇www.traveller.ltd.uk.
Ordnance Survey Service, Phoenix Park, Dublin 8 ☎01/820 6100, ✇www.irlgov.ie/osi/.

Ordnance Survey of Northern Ireland, Colby House, Stranmillis Ct, Belfast BT9 5BJ ☎028/9066 1244, ✇www.osni.gov.uk.
Stanfords, 12–14 Long Acre, London WC2E 9LP ☎020/7836 1321, ✇www.stanfords.co.uk; maps by mail or phone order are available on this number and via ✉sales@stanfords.co.uk. Other branches within British Airways offices at 156 Regent St, London W1R 5TA ☎020/7434 4744, and 29 Corn St, Bristol BS1 1HT ☎0117/929 9966.
The Travel Bookshop, 13–15 Blenheim Crescent, London W11 2EE ☎020/7229 5260, ✇www.thetravelbookshop.co.uk.

US and Canada

Adventurous Traveler Bookstore, PO Box 64769, Burlington, VT 05406 ☎1-800/282-3963, ✇www.AdventurousTraveler.com.
Book Passage, 51 Tamal Vista Blvd, Corte Madera, CA 94925 ☎415/927-0960, ✇www.bookpassage.com.
Elliot Bay Book Company, 101 S Main St, Seattle, WA 98104 ☎206/624-6600 or 1-800/962-5311, ✇www.elliotbaybook.com.
Forsyth Travel Library, 226 Westchester Ave, White Plains, NY 10604 ☎1-800/367-7984, ✇www.forsyth.com.
Globe Corner Bookstore, 28 Church St, Cambridge, MA 02138 ☎1-800/358-6013, ✇www.globecorner.com.
GORP Adventure Library online only ☎1-800/754-8229, ✇www.gorp.com.
Map Link Inc., 30 S La Patera Lane, Unit 5, Santa Barbara, CA 93117 ☎805/692-6777, ✇www.maplink.com.
Open Air Books and Maps, 25 Toronto St, Toronto, ON M5C 2R1 ☎416/363-0719.
Phileas Fogg's Travel Center, #87 Stanford Shopping Center, Palo Alto, CA 94304 ☎1-800/533-3644, ✇www.foggs.com.
Rand McNally, 444 N Michigan Ave, Chicago, IL 60611 ☎312/321-1751, ✇www.randmcnally.com; 150 E 52nd St, New York, NY 10022 ☎212/758-7488; 595 Market St, San Francisco, CA 94105 ☎415/777-3131; around thirty stores across the US – call ☎1-800/333-0136 ext 2111 or check the website for the nearest store.
Travel Books & Language Center, 4437 Wisconsin Ave, Washington, DC 20016 ☎1-800/220-2665, ✇www.bookweb.org/bookstore/travellers.
The Travel Bug Bookstore, 2667 W Broadway, Vancouver, BC V6K 2G2 ☎604/737-1122, ✇www.swifty.com/tbug.
Traveler's Choice Bookstore, 22 W 52nd St,

New York, NY 10019 ☎212/664-0995,
✉tvlchoice@aol.com.
Ulysses Travel Bookshop, 4176 St-Denis,
Montréal, PQ H2W 2M5 ☎514/843-9447,
⊕www.ulysses.ca.
World of Maps, 118 Holland Ave, Ottawa, ON K1Y
0X6 ☎613/724-6776, ⊕www.itmb.com.
World Wide Books and Maps, 1247 Granville
St, Vancouver, BC V6Z 1G3 ☎604/687-3320,
⊕www.worldofmaps.com.

Australia and New Zealand

The Map Shop, 6 Peel St, Adelaide ☎08/8231
2033, ⊕www.mapshop.net.au.
Mapland, 372 Little Bourke St, Melbourne
☎03/9670 4383, ⊕www.mapland.com.au.
Mapworld, 173 Gloucester St, Christchurch
☎03/374 5399, ℻03/374 5633,
⊕www.mapworld.co.nz.
Perth Map Centre, 1/884 Hay St, Perth
☎08/9322 5733, ⊕www.perthmap.com.au.
Specialty Maps, 46 Albert St, Auckland ☎09/307
2217, ⊕www.ubd-online.co.nz/maps.
Travel Bookshop, Shop 3, 175 Liverpool St,
Sydney ☎02/9261 8200.
Worldwide Maps & Guides, 187 George St,
Brisbane ☎07/3221 4330.

Greece on the internet

Greece is strongly represented on the **internet**, with many bilingual English–Greek websites offering information on nearly every conceivable subject. Some of it, however, is little
more than propaganda – anything to do with
Macedonia, for example, is liable to be pretty
over-the-top. Almost every well-visited island
will have its own website, though some of
these, in bizarre dialects of "Gringlish", are
barely readable, while others – mastered by
expatriate residents – are fluent enough but
rather vague on specifics so as to avoid raising local hackles. Country-wide and regional
sites recommended below are reasonably
useful, balanced and literate.

⊕**www.greektravel.com**
A subjective, North-American-oriented but highly
useful site maintained by North Carolinan Matt
Barrett, who's been visiting Greece for over three
decades. It contains lots of recommendations,
destination thumbnails, tricks and shortcuts, plus
hundreds of links to affiliated sites.

⊕**http://forecast.uoa.gr**
An excellent one-stop site for the temperature,

wind direction and rainfall countrywide, maintained
by the University of Athens physics faculty. Pick a
specific city or island for an all-parameters report;
an English option is available.

⊕**www.poseidon.ncmr.gr**
A Greek oceanographer's site maintained by the
National Centre for Marine Research which profiles
Aegean weather meticulously, including groovy
graphics of sea currents and surface winds, based
on satellite imaging. It's slowish but sophisticated,
good for yachties, and reports one topic (rain,
temperature, etc) at a time.

⊕**www.culture.gr**
The Greek Ministry of Culture's website. The best
bit is its alphabetical gazetteer to monuments,
archeological sites and museums. It's not
complete, and the opening hours are probably
unreliable, but it does have a lot of info about the
more obscure sites.

⊕**www.athensnews.gr**
The online edition of the *Athens News*, Greece's
longest-running quality English-language
newspaper, with the day's top stories. It's a bit
slow, but easy to find your way around.

⊕**www.eKathimerini.com/news/news.asp**
The online edition of the abridged English
translation of *Kathimerini*, one of Greece's most
respected dailies. It's fully archived for years back,
and has an excellent search facility.

⊕**www.hellenicbooks.com**
The website of the UK's premier Greek bookstore. It
posts full, opinionated reviews of its stock, offers
the possibility of buying online, and has witty
descriptions of every island compiled by proprietor
Stelios Jackson and his assistant Markos Stefanou.

⊕**www.ktel.org/frontpage.shtml**
Bilingual website of the KTEL, or national bus
syndicate. It posts fairly reliable schedules; the
main problem is that many provinces (including
most of the Aegean islands) are not covered.

⊕**www.ose.gr**
The Greek train network online, with an English
option. The schedule and prices pages are a bit
fiddly to work, but much more current than any
printed bumph.

⊕**www.gtp.gr**
The website of *Greek Travel Pages*, the fat (and
expensive) printed manual on every Greek travel

agent's desk. It's mostly resorted to for its ferry schedules (also kept on a separate site, ⓦwww.gtpweb.com). It was completely revamped in 2001, though is still not a hundred-percent reliable (as with anything to do with Greek shipping).

ⓦ www.west-crete.com
Cretophiles' favourite site, with all travel/cultural topics (even a naturists' page) – and not restricted to the west of the island.

ⓦ http://stigmes.gr/br
An English-summary online edition of what's claimed to be Crete's leading monthly magazine; plus it has lots of links to other Crete-related sites.

ⓦ www.kalymnos-isl.gr
The island's official website, with the English pages edited by expatriate radio journalist and author Faith Warn. The news pages are meaty and current, tourism specifics a bit anodyne.

ⓦ www.lesvos.com
An excellent overview of Lésvos, compiled by Matt Barrett (see opposite). The restaurant recommendations are particularly reliable – since he's only here a few months of the year, the author can say what he likes.

ⓦ www.symivisitor.com
Current news for aficionados, a range of accommodation, restaurant and beach profiles, presented by the publishers of the monthly island newspaper.

Getting around

The standard overland public transport in Greece is the bus. Train networks are usually slow and limited, though service on the Athens–Pátra line and the northern mainland lines is improving. Buses, however, cover just about every route on the mainland – albeit infrequently on minor roads – and provide basic connections on the islands. The best way to supplement buses is to rent a scooter, full-sized motorbike or car, especially on the islands, where in any substantial town or resort you can find a rental outlet.

Inter-island travel of course means taking **ferries**. These again are extensive, and will eventually get you to any of the 166 inhabited isles. Planes are relatively expensive, at three to four times the cost of a deck-class ferry ticket and almost twice as much as the cheapest cabin berth.

Buses

Bus services on the **major routes**, both on the mainland and islands, are highly efficient and frequent. On **secondary roads** they're less regular, with long gaps, but even the remotest villages will be connected – at least on weekdays – by a school or market bus to the provincial capital. As these often leave shortly after dawn, an alarm clock can be a useful travel aid. Coming in the opposite direction, these local buses usually leave the provincial capital at about 2pm. On the islands there are usually buses to connect the port and main town for ferry arrivals or departures.

The network is nationally run by a single syndicate known as the **KTEL** (*Kratikó Tamío Ellinikón Leoforíon*). However, even in medium-sized towns there can be several scattered terminals for services in different directions, so make sure you have the right station for your departure. Some specimen one-way fares from Athens are: Thessaloníki (€23.50), Pátra (€10.30) and Delphi (€8.40).

Buses are amazingly **prompt** as a rule, so be there in plenty of time for scheduled departures. For the major, intercity lines such as Athens–Pátra, **ticketing** is computerized, with assigned seating, and such buses often get fully booked. On smaller rural/island routes, it's generally first-come, first-served, with some standing allowed, and tickets dispensed on the spot by an *ispráktoros* or conductor. However, these tickets tend to be issued only up to the next major town, where you'll have to alight briefly and purchase an onward fare (there is always enough time for this).

Trains

The Greek railway network, run by **OSE** (*Organismós Sidherodhrómon Elládhos*), is limited to the mainland, and with a few exceptions trains are slower than the equivalent buses. However, they're also much cheaper – nearly fifty percent less on non-express services, even more if you buy a return ticket – and some of the lines are enjoyable in themselves. The best, a real treat, is the rack-and-pinion line between Diakoftó and Kalávryta in the **Peloponnese** (see p.298).

Timetables are sporadically available during May or June as small, Greek-only booklets; the best places to obtain them are the OSE offices in Athens at Sína 6, or in Thessaloníki at Aristotélous 18, or the main train stations in these cities. Always check the station schedule boards, or at information counters for photocopied addenda sheets, since which changes often crop up in the interim. Trains tend to leave promptly at the outset, though on the more circuitous lines they're invariably late by the end of the journey.

If you're starting a journey at the initial station of a run you can (at no extra cost) **reserve a seat**; a carriage and seat number

GREECE: TRAINS

0   100 km

will be written on the back of your ticket. At most intermediate points, it's first-come, first-served.

There are two basic classes: first and second. **First class** may be worth the extra money, insomuch as the wagons may be emptier and the seats more comfortable. An express category, the **Intercity** (IC on timetables), exists on certain routes between Alexandhroúpoli, Thessaloníki, Édhessa, Vólos, Kalambáka, Athens, Pátra, Kórinthos and Kalamáta. German-made rolling stock is relatively sleek, and much faster than the bus if the timetable is adhered to; accordingly, stiff supplements are charged depending on the distance travelled. There is also one nightly **sleeper** (departs between 11pm and midnight) in each direction between Athens and Thessaloníki, again with fairly hefty surcharges; interestingly, private automobiles are carried on this departure as well. Note that any kind of ticket issued on board a train carries a fifty percent surcharge.

Credit cards are accepted as payment at the midtown OSE offices of Athens, Lárissa, Vólos and Thessaloníki, as well as at the stations in Athens, Lárissa, Vólos, Thessaloníki, Alexandhroúpoli and Pátra.

InterRail and **Eurail** Pass holders (see p.17) can use their pass in Greece but must secure reservations like everyone else, and may need to pay express supplements on a few lines. InterRail passes and Eurotrain tickets are available in Greece through the International Student and Youth Travel Service (ISYTS), Níkis 11, 1st Floor, Athens, USIT Etos, Filellínon 7, Sýndagma, Athens, or at Wasteels, Mnisikléous 10a, Platía Mitropóleos, Athens.

Sea transport

Most of your sea travel is going to be to and between islands, though you may also want to make use of the hydrofoil routes between Athens and certain ports in the southeastern Peloponnese, up to Yíthio. There are four different varieties of vessel: medium-sized to large **ordinary ferries** (which operate the main services); **high-speed catamarans**, also medium-sized to large, which match hydrofoils in speed but carry a certain number of cars; **hydrofoils**, which carry only passengers; and local **kaïkia** (small boats which do short hops and excursions in season). Costs are very reasonable on the

longer journeys, though proportionately more expensive for shorter, inter-island connections. Short-haul lines with monopolies – for example Alexandhroúpoli–Samothráki and Kými–Skýros – are invariably overpriced.

We've indicated most of the **ferry, catamaran and hydrofoil connections**, both on the maps (see pp.548–549 for a general pattern) and in the "Travel Details" at the end of each chapter. Don't take our listings as exhaustive or wholly reliable, however, as schedules are notoriously erratic, and must be verified each year; details given are essentially for departures between late June and mid-September. **Out-of-season** departure frequencies are severely reduced, with many islands connected only once or twice a week. However, in spring or autumn those ferries that do operate are often compelled by the transport ministry to call at extra or unusual islands, making possible some interesting connections.

The most reliable, up-to-date information is available from the local **port police** (*limenarhío*), which maintains offices at Pireás (☏010/42 26 000) and on or near the harbours of all fair-sized islands. Smaller places may only have a *limenikós stathmós* (marine station), often just a single room with a VHF radio. Their officers rarely speak much English, but keep complete schedules posted – and, meteorological report in hand, are the final arbiters of whether a ship will sail or not in stormy weather conditions.

Few ferry companies produce regular **schedule** sheets. The only attempt at an all-inclusive Greek ferry guide is the yearly *Greek Travel Routes, Domestic Sea Schedules*, co-produced by the GNTO and the Greek travel agents' manual the GTP. The printed guide is available at GNTO/EOT offices, but you'll find a sporadically updated version at ⊛www.gtpnet.com.

Regular ferries

On most **ferry** routes, your only consideration will be getting a boat that leaves on the day, and for the island, that you want. However, when sailing from **Pireás**, the main port of Athens, to the Cyclades or Dodecanese islands, you should have a choice of at least two, often three, sailings and may want to bear in mind a few of the factors below.

Routes taken and the speed of the boats can vary enormously. A journey from Pireás

The wreck of the Express Samina – and beyond

September 27, 2000, was a sort of Judgement Day for the Greek domestic ferry industry. Around midnight in gale conditions, the *Express Samina*, the oldest ship in the domestic fleet, slammed full speed into the Pórtes rocks outside Páros harbour in the Cyclades, and sank within minutes. The bridge was unstaffed by senior officers, all of whom were elsewhere watching a football match on television. The British and Greek navies, exercising in the area, plus swarms of fishing boats from Páros, together plucked most of the 500-plus aboard from the water, including numerous foreign tourists, but 82 passengers drowned. It was the worst maritime disaster in Greece since the ferry *Iraklion* went down in December 1966, with 226 casualties.

Skipper Vassilis Yiannakis and the first mate were quickly charged with manslaughter and criminal negligence and are still in custody awaiting trial. Once the furore had died down, the pair seemed on reflection to be easy scapegoats. The boat had previously been owned by Agapitos Lines, one of several shipping companies swallowed up by Minoan Flying Dolphins in its several-year drive to acquire dominance of the Greek passenger-ferry industry and a near-monopoly on sailings to the Cyclades and the Dodecanese. In this they had been assisted by a previous merchant-marine minister in the PASOK government, who also became a focus of opprobrium, along with Minoan Flying Dolphins management (one of whom, general manager Pandelis Sfinias, committed suicide on November 30 by jumping from the sixth floor of his Pireás headquarters).

It also emerged that the 34-year-old *Express Samina* was the worst but by no means the only rust-bucket in the Greek domestic fleet well past its scrap-by date. EU regulations normally require ships to be retired after 27 years of service, but Greek shipping interests had wheedled an extension to 35 years from Brussels. With an effective monopoly and regulated fares, there was little incentive to keep boats up to date. Greek newspapers quickly tallied eighteen ferries 29 years old or older. The age of the *Express Samina* was a critical factor in her rapid sinking; newer craft have multiple airtight compartments, so that a single breach in the hull will not be fatal, but the *Express Samina* had just a single compartment, and was effectively doomed the moment the rocks tore a three-metre gash in her side (though the crew having left bulkhead doors open did not help). Most lifesaving equipment, from the ancient, cork-buoyed lifejackets to the snail-slow lifeboats, was inadequate or scarcely used at the critical hour. Only the year before, an inspection engineer had resigned in protest that his verdict on the boat as unseaworthy was being ignored by Minoan.

The government had to be seen to be doing something, and so made a show of granting some minor routes to Minoan's competitors during the weeks following the sinking, and pushed for a three-year limit on service time for boats in early 2001. It's in the medium term, however, that the fallout from the disaster has had most effect. The oldest members of the domestic fleet were instantly confined to port, pending safety inspections – which several did not pass, leaving a shortfall. Those ships which could be brought into compliance with EU standards were refitted, but clean bills of health were often issued in an arbitrary and biased manner; a loophole in the law allows substandard craft to continue operating if their destination is a non-EU country. As a result, much of 2001 saw very skeletal connections to certain remoter islands; Kastellórizo and Tílos were particularly hard hit, losing their catamaran schedule at mid-season when the boat in question switched to more lucrative ports. In the prevailing climate of protecting profits (and one's legal behind) before service, matters are likely to get worse before they get better. Only a few newly commissioned ferries – such as NEL's high-speed catamarans *Aeolos Express, Aeolos Kenderis* and *Aeolos Express II* – have taken to the water since the disaster. Investigation is still under way, and Minoan Flying Dolphins remains the target of a vast number of civil suits for wrongful death, and a criminal investigation as well – not, perhaps, unrelated to the directors' July 2001 decision to rechristen the company Hellas Flying Dolphins. Terrified of another public-relations disaster in the run-up to Greece's hosting of the 2004 Olympics, the port police have become far stricter about confining boats to port in marginal weather conditions, compounding the effect of already sparse departure frequencies.

The *Rough Guide* authors apologize, therefore, if travel details for ferry routes seem incomplete or pessimistic. Schedules only stabilized (relatively speaking) from July 2001 onward, and the route of the *Express Samina* in particular was not adequately substituted by another craft – for the first time in over half a century, there was no connection from Páros and Náxos to Sámos, and nobody was venturing any guesses as to prevailing conditions in 2002.

to Thíra (Thíra), for instance, can take anything from nine to fourteen hours. Prior to buying a ticket it's wise to establish how many stops there will be before your island, and the estimated time of arrival. Many agents act just for one specific boat (they'll blithely tell you that theirs is the only available service), so you may have to ask around to uncover alternatives. Especially in high season, early arrival is critical in getting what may be a very limited stock of accommodation.

Since the *Express Samina* disaster (see box opposite), a few of the most elderly craft have been consigned to the scrap heap or dumped overseas. Though spanking-new **boats** are still a rarity, you will more often than not be surprised to encounter a former English Channel or Scandinavian fjord ferry, rechristened and enjoying a new lease of life in the Aegean.

Regular ferry **tickets** are, in general, best bought on the day of departure, unless you need to reserve a cabin berth or space for a car. Buying tickets in advance will tie you down to a particular craft at a particular time – and innumerable factors can make you regret that. Most obviously there's bad weather, which, particularly off-season, can play havoc with the schedules, causing some small boats to remain at anchor and others to alter their routes drastically. (The ticket price is refunded if a boat fails to sail.) There are only three periods of the year – March 23–25, the week before and after Easter, and most of August – when ferries need to be booked at least a couple of days in advance.

Following cases in 1996 of captains loading ferries to double their rated capacity, **obligatory advance ticketing** was universally introduced in 1998. Staff at the gangway will bar you from embarking if you don't have a ticket, and tickets are absolutely no longer available on board. In many cases there may not even be a last-minute sales booth at the quayside. **Fares** for each route are currently set by the transport ministry and should not differ among ships or agencies. There is usually a twenty-percent discount on round-trip fares.

The cheapest class of ticket, which you'll probably automatically be sold, is **deck class**, variously called *tríti* or *gámma thési*. This gives you the run of most boats except for the upper-class restaurant and bar. On

the shorter, summer journeys the best place to be, in any case, is on deck – space best staked out as soon as you get on board. However, boats acquired recently seem, with their glaring overhead lights and moulded-plastic bucket seats, expressly designed to frustrate those attempting to sleep on deck. In such cases it's well worth the few extra euros for a **cabin bunk**, especially if you can share with friends (cabins are usually quadruple, occasionally triple or double). Class consciousness is the rule, so deck-class passengers may find themselves firmly locked out of second-class facilities at night to prevent them from crashing on the plush sofas, and may have to make do with pull-man-type seats. **First-class** cabins usually cost scarcely less than a plane flight and are not terrific value – the main difference between first and second being the presence of a bathroom in the cabin, and a better location. Most cabins, incidentally, are overheated or overchilled, and pretty airless; ask for an *exoterikí* (outer) cabin if you want a porthole (though these are always bolted shut).

All bookings are now computerized, and supposedly have accurate space allocations that preclude **overbookings**, but occasionally you may be sold a cabin berth at an intermediate port only to find that they are "full" when the boat arrives. Pursers will usually not refund you the difference between a cabin and third class. Your first- or second-class fare entitles you to a bunk, and this is clearly stated (in Greek) on the verso of your ticket. Make a scene if necessary until you are accommodated – there are often cabins in the bilge, set aside for the crew but generally unused, where you can sleep.

Motorbikes and cars get issued extra tickets, in the latter case four to five times the passenger deck-class fare, depending on size. Car fees are roughly proportionate to distance: Sámos–Ikaría is €26–29.50 depending on port and direction, while Sámos–Pireás is about €73.50. This obviously limits the number of islands you'll want to drag a car to – it's really only worth it for the larger ones like Crete, Rhodes, Híos, Lésvos, Sámos, Corfu or Kefalloniá. Even with these, unless you're planning a stay of more than four days, you may find it cheaper to leave your car on the mainland and rent another on arrival. Technically, written permission is required to take rental motorbikes and cars on ferries, though in practice few crew will bother to quiz you on this.

Some ferries sell a limited range of **food on board**, though it tends to be overpriced and mediocre. Honourable exceptions are the meals served by DANE, NEL and all ferries to Crete on their overnight sailings. On the short, daytime hops between the various islands of the Argo-Saronic, Cyclades and Sporades, it's a good idea to stock up beforehand with your own provisions; most ferries on these lines offer nothing other than biscuits, greasy, prefab pizzas, coffee and soft drinks.

Hydrofoils and catamarans

Hydrofoils – commonly known as *dhelfínia* or "Flying Dolphins" – are roughly twice as fast (and at least twice as expensive) as ordinary ferries. However, they're a useful alternative to regular ferries if you are pushed for time, and their network can also neatly fill gaps in ferry scheduling. Their main drawback (aside from frequent engine breakdowns) is that they were originally designed for cruising on placid Russian or Polish rivers, and are quite literally out of their depth on the open sea; thus they are extremely sensitive to bad weather, and even in moderate seas are not for the seasick-prone. Most of these services don't operate – or are heavily reduced – from October to June and are prone to arbitrary cancellation if not enough passengers turn up. Following the *Express Samina* sinking, hydrofoils are no longer allowed to carry scooters or bicycles as in the past.

At present, hydrofoils operate among the **Argo-Saronic** islands close to Athens, down the east coast of the **Peloponnese** to Monemvassiá, Yíthio and Kýthira, among the northern **Sporades** (Évvia, Skiáthos, Skópelos and Alónissos), between Thessaloníki and certain resorts on **Halkidhikí**, between Kavála and Thássos, between Alexandhroúpoli and **Samothráki**, among certain of the **Cyclades** (Ándros, Tínos, Mýkonos, Páros, Náxos, Amorgós, the minor islets, Íos, Thíra), and in the **Dodecanese** and east Aegean among Rhodes, Kós, Kálymnos, Léros and Pátmos, with regular forays up to Sámos, Ikaría and Foúrni, or over to Tílos and Níssyros. Services beyond Sámos to **Híos** and **Lésvos** sputter along unreliably in high sea-

son, if at all. The principal mainland ports are Zéa and Flísvos marinas in Pireás, Rafína, Vólos, Áyios Konstandínos and Thessaloníki, as well as Kavála and Alexandhroúpoli. Services in the Argo-Saronic are run by Hellas Flying Dolphins and Sea Falcon; in the Cyclades by Dolphin Sea Lines and Minoan; and in the Dodecanese or east Aegean by Kyriakoulis Maritime. You may see craft with other livery, but we have excluded them, as they are chartered by tour agencies and do not offer scheduled services controlled by the Ministry of Transport.

Around since the late 1990s, **catamarans** attempt to combine the speed of hydrofoils with the (relative) reliability and vehicle-carrying capacity of larger ferries. The fact that they are new and sleek, purpose-built in France or Scandinavia, has not prevented numerous breakdowns, since they are constantly playing catch-up to fill in weather-cancelled itineraries and thus miss necessary maintenance. **Inside** they are rather soulless: ruthlessly air-conditioned, with no deck seating to take the air and the most banal Greek TV blaring at you from numerous screens. Indeed the whole experience has been likened to **riding on a plane**, right down to the seat type. Cabins are non-existent and food facilities even more minimal than on conventional ferries – after all, you'll be at your destination within six hours, the longest trajectory at present. Car fares are normal, though passenger **tickets** are at least double a comparable ferry journey, ie similar to hydrofoil rates.

Small ferries, kaïkia and taxi boats

In season, **kaïkia** (caiques) and **small ferries** of a few hundred tonnes' displacement sail between adjacent islands and to a few of the more obscure ones. These can be extremely useful and often very pleasant, but are no cheaper than mainline services. In fact, if they're classified as tourist agency charters, and not passenger lines controlled by the transport ministry, they tend to be quite expensive, with pressure to buy return fares (one-ways are almost always available). The more consistent kaïki links are summarized in the "Travel Details" section of each chapter, though inevitably departures depend on the whims of local boat-owners, so the only firm information is to be had on the quayside. Kaïkia and small ferries, despite appearances, have a good safety record. EU regulations being what they are, however, it seems that many of these smaller boats are doomed for trivial reasons, such as not having a second lavatory. Likely to survive are the swarms of **taxi boats** which are a feature of Sými and Itháki, among other spots; these exist to shuttle clients on set routes to remote beaches or ports which can only be reached arduously, if at all, overland. Costs on these are generally reasonable, usually per person but occasionally per boat.

Motorbikes, scooters and bicycles

The cult of the **motorcycle** is highly developed in Greece, presided over by a jealous deity apparently requiring regular human sacrifice. Accidents among both foreign and local bikers are routine occurrences, with annual fatalities edging into two figures on the busier islands. Some package companies have even taken to warning clients in print against renting motorbikes (thereby making a bit extra on organized overland excursions), but with caution and common sense – and an eye to increasingly enforced regulations – riding a two-wheeler through a resort should be a lot safer than piloting one through London or New York.

Many tourists come to grief on rutted dirt tracks or astride mechanically dodgy machines. In other cases **accidents** are due to attempts to cut corners, in all senses, or by riding two to an underpowered scooter simply not designed to propel such a load. Don't be tempted by this apparent economy – you won't regret getting two separate scooters, or one powerful 100cc bike to share – and remember that you're likely to be charged an exorbitant sum for any repairs if you do have a wipeout. Also, verify that your travel insurance policy covers motorcycle accidents.

One worthwhile precaution is to wear a **crash helmet** (*kránio*); many rental outfits will offer you one, and some will make you sign a waiver of liability if you refuse it. Helmet-wearing is in fact required by law, but few riders (except army conscripts) wear them – though compliance is increasing as police set up random roadblocks to catch offenders. Reputable establishments demand a full motorcycle driving licence for

any engine over 90cc (the law actually stipulates "over 50cc"), and you will usually have to leave your passport as security. For smaller models, any driving licence will do.

Small **motor scooters** with automatic transmission, known in Greek as *papákia* (little ducks) after their characteristic noise, are good transport for all but the hilliest islands. They're available for rent on many islands and in a few of the popular mainland resorts for €11.80–17.80. This specimen rate-range can be bargained down out of peak season, or if you negotiate for a longer period of rental.

Before riding off, make sure you check the bike's **mechanical state**, since many are only cosmetically maintained. Bad brakes and worn or oil-fouled spark plugs are the most common defects; dealers often keep the front brakes far too loose, with the commendable intention of preventing you going over the handlebars. If you break down it's your responsibility to return the machine, so take down the phone number of the rental agency in case it gives out in the middle of nowhere. Better outlets often offer a free retrieval service.

There are vanishingly few true **mopeds** – motor-driven pedal-cycles – remaining in Greece; one or two models are still sold, but none is rented.

As far as **scooters** go, the Piaggio Vespa or Peugeot were always more comfortable than mopeds for long trips, but still aren't very stable on unpaved surfaces. The latest generation of these models is ultratrendy and practical enough, but thirsty on fuel; a few still don't have kick-starts as backups to the battery.Bungee cords (a *khtapódi* or "octopus" in slang) for tying down bundles are supplied on request, while capacious baskets are also often a feature.

In the family of true **motorbikes** with manual transmissions, the favourite workhorses, in descending order of reliability, are the Honda 50, Yamaha Townmate and Suzuki FB Birdie; gears are shifted with an easy-to-learn left-foot pedal action, and (very important) these can all be push-started if the starting crank fails. They can carry two, though if you have a choice, the Honda Cub 70–90cc series give more power at nominal extra cost, as does the Yamaha 80 Townmate. Best of all is the attractive, 1997-premiered Honda Astrea 100 and its rival-brand clones, very powerful but scarcely bigger than older models.

Cycling

Cycling in Greece is not such hard going as you might imagine (except in midsummer), especially on one of the mountain bikes that are rapidly supplanting the old bone-shakers at rental outfits; they rarely cost more than €6 a day. You do, however, need steady nerves, as roads are generally narrow with no verges or bike lanes (except on Kós), and many Greek drivers consider cyclists a lower form of life, on a par with the snakes regularly found run over.

If you have your own mountain or touring bike (the latter not rented in Greece), you might consider taking it along by **train** or **plane** (it's free if within your 20–23kg international air allowance). Once in Greece you should be able to take a bike for free on most of the ferries, in the guard's van on most trains (for a small fee – it goes on a later goods train otherwise), and with a little persuasion in the luggage bays of buses. Any small spare parts you might need, however, are best brought along, since specialist bike shops are only found in the provincial capitals and main cities.

Driving and car rental

Automobiles have obvious advantages for getting to the more inaccessible parts of mainland Greece, but this is one of the more expensive countries in Europe to **rent a car**. If you drive **your own vehicle** to and through Greece, via EU member states, you no longer require a Green Card. In accordance with a 1998 directive, insurance contracted in any EU member state is valid in any other, but in many cases this is only third-party cover – the statutory legal minimum. Competition in the industry is so intense, however, that many UK insurers will throw in full, pan-European cover for free or for a nominal sum, up to sixty days; shop around if necessary.

EU citizens bringing their own cars should no longer get a carnet stamp in their passport, and the car is in theory free to circulate in the country for six months, or until its home-based road tax or insurance expires, whichever comes first. In practice, drivers of **EU cars** are rarely quizzed no matter how long they've been in the country, but if you call attention to yourself, by having an accident for example, the customs has the power to impound the car immediately until or unless you can prove it's been in Greece for less than six months (the ticket for any ferry you may have arrived on from Turkey or Italy is considered sufficient). The **fines** for overstaying are horrendous, and **import duties** are likely to be around half the actual value of the vehicle. If you're resident and don't officially import your car, you're only allowed to use a car for six-month periods each year (you choose the time period).

Other nationalities will get a **non-EU** car entered in their passport; the carnet normally allows you to keep a vehicle in Greece for up to six months, exempt from road tax. It is difficult, though not impossible, to leave the country without the vehicle; the nearest customs post will seal it for you (while you fly back home for a family emergency, for example) but you must find a Greek national to act as your **guarantor**, and possibly pay storage if you don't have access to off-street parking. This person will assume ownership of the car should you ultimately abandon it; you will also need a guarantor for the single, **nine-month extension** you're allowed until the vehicle has to remain under seal for six months, as described above.

Car rental

Car rental within Greece starts at €271–291 a week in high season for the smallest, A-group vehicle from a one-off outlet or local chain, including unlimited mileage, tax and insurance. Overseas tour operators' and international chains' brochures threaten alarming rates of €353–391 for the same period but, except in August, no rental company expects to fetch that price for a car. Outside peak season, at the smaller local outfits, you can sometimes get terms of about €36 per day, all inclusive, with even better rates for three days or more. **Comparison shopping** among agencies in the larger resorts can yield a variation in quotes of up to twenty percent for the same conditions over a four-to-seven-day period; the most negotiable variable is whether or not kilometres in excess of one hundred per day (a common hidden catch) are free. Open **jeeps**, an increasingly popular extravagance, begin at about €82 per day, rising to as much as €97 at busy times and places.

Note that brochure prices in Greece almost never include tax, **collision damage waiver**

(CDW) and personal insurance. CDW in particular is absolutely vital, as the coverage included by law in the basic rental fee is generally inadequate, so check the fine print on your contract. Be careful of the hammering that cars get on dirt tracks; tyres, windshield and the underside of the vehicle are almost always excluded from even supplementary insurance policies. All agencies will want either a **credit card** or a large **cash deposit** up front; minimum age requirements vary from 21 to 23. **Driving licences** issued by any European Union state are honoured, but in theory (and increasingly, in practice) an International Driving Licence is required by all other drivers, including Australians, New Zealanders and North Americans. This must be arranged before departure, as ELPA (the Greek motoring association) no longer issues IDLs to foreign nationals.

In peak season, you may get a better price through one of the **overseas booking companies** that deal with local firms than if you negotiate for rental in Greece itself; this may also be the only way to get hold of a car, at any price, at such times. Competitive companies in Britain include Autos Abroad, Holiday Autos and Transhire. Autorent, Payless, European, Kosmos, National/ Alamo, Reliable, Eurodollar and Just are dependable Greek, or smaller international, chains with branches in many towns; all are considerably cheaper than the biggest international operators Budget, Europcar, Hertz and Avis. Specific local recommendations, mostly based on author experience, are given in the guide.

In terms of **models**, many of them unfamiliar to UK/US drivers, the more competitive companies tend to offer the Subaru M80 or Vivio, the Fiat Cinquecento or Seisento and the Suzuki Swift 1000 as A-group cars, and Opel (Vauxhall) Corsa 1.2, Fiat Uno/Punto, Peugeot 106, Hyundai Atos, Citroën Saxo, Renault Clio or Nissan Micra in the B group. Any more than two adults, with luggage, will generally require B category. The badly designed, underpowerd Suzuki Alto 600 or 800, Fiat Panda 750/900 and Seat Marbella should be avoided if at all possible as A-group cars, and indeed have been phased out by the more reputable agencies. The standard four-wheel-drive option is a Suzuki jeep (1.3- or 1.6-litre), mostly open – great for bashing down rutted tracks to remote beaches.

Car-rental agencies

In the UK and Ireland

Autos Abroad ☎0870/066 7788, ⓦwww.autosabroad.com.
Avis ☎0870/606 0100, Republic of Ireland ☎01/605 7555, ⓦwww.avisworld.com.
Budget ☎0800/181181, ⓦwww.go-budget.co.uk, Republic of Ireland ☎01/878 7814, ⓦwww.budget.ie.
Europcar ☎0845/722 2525, ⓦwww.europcar.co.uk, Republic of Ireland ☎01/614 2800, ⓦwww.europcar.ie.
Hertz ☎0870/844 8844, Republic of Ireland 01/813 3416, ⓦwww.hertz.co.uk.
Holiday Autos ☎0870/400 0000, ⓦwww.holidayautos.com, Republic of Ireland ☎01/872 9366, ⓦwww.holidayautos.ie.
National ☎0870/536 5365, ⓦwww.nationalcar.com.
Thrifty ☎01494/751600, Northern Ireland ☎028/9445 2565, ⓦwww.thrifty.co.uk.
Transhire ☎01923/834910.

In North America

Alamo ☎1-800/522-9696, ⓦwww.alamo.com.
Auto Europe US ☎1-800/223-5555, Canada ☎1-888/223-5555, ⓦwww.autoeurope.com.
Avis US ☎1-800/331-1084, Canada ☎1-800/272-5871, ⓦwww.avis.com.
Budget ☎1-800/527-0700, ⓦwww.budgetrentacar.com.
Europe by Car ☎1-800/223-1516, ⓦwww.europebycar.com.
Hertz US ☎1-800/654-3001, Canada ☎1-800/263-0600, ⓦwww.hertz.com.
Kemwel Holiday Autos ☎1-800/422-7737, ⓦwww.kemwel.com.
National ☎1-800/227-7368, ⓦwww.nationalcar.com.
Thrifty ☎1-800/367-2277, ⓦwww.thrifty.com.

In Australia

Avis ☎13 6333, ⓦwww.avis.com
Budget ☎1300/362 848, ⓦwww.budget.com
Hertz ☎1800/550 067, ⓦwww.hertz.com
National ☎13 1908.
Thrifty ☎1300/367 227, ⓦwww.thrifty.com.au.

In New Zealand

Avis ☎09/526 5231 or 0800/655 111, ⓦwww.avis.com.
Budget ☎0800/652 227 or 09/375 2270, ⓦwww.budget.com
Hertz ☎09/309 0989 or 0800/655 955,

@ www.hertz.com
National ☎ 09/537 2582.
Thrifty ☎ 09/309 0111, @ www.thrifty.com.nz.

Motoring organizations

In the UK and Ireland

AA ☎ 0800/444500, @ www.theaa.co.uk.
AA Travel Dublin ☎ 01/617 9988,
@ www.aaireland.ie.
RAC ☎ 0800/550055, @ www.rac.co.uk.

In North America

American Automobile Association (AAA) Each
state has its own branch of this club – check the
phone book for local address and phone number
(or call ☎ 1-800/222-4357, @ www.aaa.com).
Canadian Automobile Association (CAA)
☎ 613/247-0117, @ www.caa.com. Again, each
region has its own club – check the phone book
for local address and phone number.

In Australia and New Zealand

Australian Automobile Association
☎ 02/6247 7311.
New Zealand Automobile Association
☎ 09/377 4660.

Driving in Greece

Greece has the highest **accident rate** in the
European Union after Portugal, and on mainland motorways or the larger tourist islands
it's easy to see why. Driving habits amongst
locals can be atrocious: overtaking is erratic,
tailgating and barging out heedlessly from
side-roads are preferred pastimes, lane lines
and turn signals may as well not exist, and
motorbikes hog the road or weave from side
to side. **Drunk driving** is also a major problem; Sunday afternoons in rural areas are
particularly bad, and for the same reason
you should avoid driving late at night at
weekends or holidays.

Matters are made worse by poor **road
conditions**: signposting is absent or badly
placed, pavement markings are faded,
asphalt can turn into a one-lane surface or a
dirt track without warning on secondary
routes, railway crossings are rarely guarded,
and you're heavily dependent on magnifying
mirrors at blind intersections in congested
villages. Uphill drivers insist on their **right of
way**, as do those first to approach a one-

lane bridge; **flashed headlights** usually
mean the opposite of what they do in the UK
or North America, here signifying that the
other driver insists on coming through or
overtaking.

There is a limited number of **express
highways** between Pátra, Athens and
Thessaloníki, on which tolls are levied – currently €1.50–2 at each sporadically placed
gate. They're nearly twice as quick as the
old roads, and well worth using by novices
to Greek conditions. But even on these so-
called motorways, there may be no proper
far-right lane for slower traffic, which is
expected to straddle the solid white line at
the verge and allow rapid traffic to pass.

Wearing a **seatbelt** is compulsory, as is
keeping a first-aid kit in the boot (some
rental companies skimp on this), and children under the age of 10 are not allowed to
sit in the front seats. It's illegal to drive away
from any kind of accident, and you can be
held at a police station for up to 24 hours. If
this happens, you have the right to ring your
consulate immediately to summon a lawyer;
don't make a statement to anyone who
doesn't speak, and write, very good English.
In practice, once police are informed that
there was no personal injury, they rarely
come out to investigate.

Tourists with proof of AA/RAC/AAA membership are given free road assistance from
ELPA, the Greek equivalent, which runs
breakdown services on several of the larger islands; in an emergency ring their road
assistance service on ☎ 104. Many car rental
companies have an agreement with ELPA's
equally widespread competitors Hellas
Service and Express Service, which also
have three-digit nationwide numbers; however, you will always get a faster response if
you dial the local number for the province
you're stranded in (ask for these in advance).
Any breakdown service is prohibitively
expensive to summon on your own – over
€120 to enrol as an "instant member" for a
year.

Running a vehicle

Petrol/gasoline currently costs
€0.76–0.90 per litre for either regular
unleaded (*amólyvdhi*) or super unleaded;
leaded four-star will be unavailable after
January 1, 2002, with little bottles of addi-
tives available for those engines that can't

easily digest super unleaded. It is easy to run out of fuel after dark or on weekends in both rural and urban Greece; most stations close at 8pm sharp, and nearly as many are shut all day Sunday. There will always be at least one pump per district open on a rota basis, but it's not always apparent which one it is. This is not so much of a problem on the major highways, but it is a factor everywhere else. So always fill up, or insist on full rental vehicles at the outset, and if you've brought your own car, keep a full jerrycan at all times. Some stations which claim to be open around the clock are in fact automated only after-hours – you have to use bill-taking machines, which don't give change. If you fill your tank without having exhausted your credit, punch the button for a receipt and get change the next day during attended hours (assuming you're still in the area).

Petrol stations run by international companies (BP, Mobil, Shell and Texaco) often take **credit cards**; Greek chains like EKO, Mamidhakis, Jetoil, Revoil and Elinoil usually don't (except in tourist areas). The tiny, generic-petrol stations of the EP chain are always the cheapest around.

Incidentally, a few retro scooters still consume "**mix**" – a red- or green-tinted fuel dispensed from a transparent cylindrical device. This contains a minimum of three percent two-stroke oil by volume; when unavailable, you brew it up yourself by adding to supergrade fuel the necessary amount of separately bottled two-stroke oil (*ládhi dhýo trohón* in Greek). It's wise to err on the generous side – say five percent – or you risk the engine seizing up.

In terms of **maintenance**, the easiest car models to have serviced and buy parts for in Greece are VWs (including combi and Transporter vans), Mercedes, BMWs, Audis, Opels, Ladas, Skodas and virtually all French, Italian, Korean and Japanese makes. British models are a bit more difficult, but you should be fine as long as you haven't brought anything too esoteric like a Hillman Minx – the Mini is, for example, still very popular in Greece, Fords are present (though not common), and the Opel is of course the continental brand of Vauxhall.

In general, both mechanics' **workshops** and **parts retailers** are clustered at the approach and exit roads of all major towns, usually prominently signposted. For the commonest makes, emergency spares like fan belts and cables are often found at surprisingly remote service stations, so don't hesitate to ask at an unlikely-looking spot. Rural mechanics are okay for quick patch-up jobs like snapped clutch cables, but for major problems it's best to limp into the nearest sizeable town to find a mechanic who is factory-trained for your make.

Hitching

Hitching carries the usual risks and dangers, and is inadvisable for women travelling alone, but overall, Greece is one of the safer countries in which to do it. It's fairly reliable, too, as a means of getting around in remote areas, so long as you're not overly concerned about time; lifts are fairly frequent but tend to be short.

Hitching is easier on islands and in rural areas than as a means of getting out of big cities, whose suburbs tend to sprawl for miles. At its best, hitching is a useful way of picking up some Greek. While you'll often get lifts from Greeks eager to display or practise their English, there will be as many where to communicate you're forced to try the language. In the more thinly populated rural areas, you'll see numbers of elderly Greeks waving down a ride – you'll be doing a useful service by picking them up, and reciprocating in some small way for the hospitality which is still often the rule in isolated regions.

Taxis

Greek **taxis** are among the cheapest in western Europe – so long as you get an honest driver who switches the meter on (see the caveats about Athens on p.102) and doesn't use high-tech devices to doctor the reading. Use of the meter is mandatory within city or town limits, where Tariff "1" applies, while in rural areas or between midnight and 5am, Tariff "2" is in effect. On certain islands, such as Kálymnos and Léros, set rates apply on specific fixed routes for "collective" taxis – these only depart when full. Otherwise, throughout Greece the meter starts at €0.75, though the minimum fare is €1.50; any baggage not actually on your lap is charged at €0.15 apiece. Additionally, there are surcharges of €0.90 for leaving or entering an airport, and

€0.60 for leaving a harbour area. If you summon a taxi by phone on spec, there's a €1.50 charge, while a prearranged rendevous is €1.80 extra; in either case the meter starts running from the moment the driver begins heading towards you. All categories of supplemental charges must be set out on a card affixed to the dashboard. For a week or so before and after Orthodox Easter, and Christmas, a *filodhórima* or gratuity of about ten percent is levied. Any or all of these extras will legitimately bump up the basic meter reading of about €4 per ten rural kilometres.

A special warning needs to be sounded about **unlicensed taxi-drivers** who congregate outside major train stations, particularly Athens and Lárissa. These shady characters may offer to shuttle you several hundred kilometres for the same price as the train/KTEL bus, or less; upon arrival you will discover that the fare quoted is per person, not per vehicle, and that along the way stops are made to cram several more passengers in – who again do not share your fare. Moreover, the condition of the vehicles usually leaves a lot to be desired.

Domestic flights

Olympic Airways and its subsidiary Olympic Aviation (ⓦ www.olympic-airways.gr) at present operate most of the **domestic flights** within Greece. They cover a fairly wide network of islands and larger mainland towns, though most routes are to and from Athens or Thessaloníki. Airline operation has been officially deregulated in Greece since 1993, but the only private airlines to have successfully challenged the state-run carrier are the recently merged Aegean-Cronus Airlines (ⓦ www.aegeanair.com and/or ⓦ www.cronus.gr), and newcomer Axon. Aegean-Cronus has cherry-picked the high-volume, high-profit routes between Crete (Haniá and Iráklio), Thíra, Mytilíni, Rhodes, Corfu Kavála, Ioánnina, Athens and Thessaloníki; Axon, newly appeared in 2001, currently links Athens or Thessaloníki with Sámos, Mýkonos, Santórini, Rhodes and Crete (Haniá and Iráklio), though their Embraer jets are the sleekest and fastest things going domestically. **Tickets** for all three airlines are most easily obtained from travel agents (their

own high-street outlets are thin on the ground). Axon and Aegean-Cronus often undercut Olympic price-wise, and surpass it service-wise, though flight frequencies tend to be sparse. This, of course, could change drastically if financially troubled Olympic goes under, as is perennially threatened, and a successor state carrier offers inevitably reduced service.

For the moment, Olympic **schedules** can be picked up at their offices abroad (see "Getting There") or through their branch offices and representatives in Greece, which are maintained in almost every town or island of any size; English-language schedules are published twice yearly (April and Oct). Cronus-Aegean has historically produced two booklets per year, in spring and late autumn.

Fares for flights to and between the islands, including the domestic airport tax of about €10, work out around three to four times the cost of a ferry journey, but on certain inter-island hauls that are poorly served by boat (Rhodes–Kastellórizo or Kárpathos–Kássos, for example), you should consider this time well bought.

Island flights are often full in peak season; if they're an essential part of your plans, it is worth trying to make a **reservation** at least a week to ten days in advance. If a flight you've set your heart on is full, **waiting lists** exist – and are worth signing on to at the airport check-in counter; experience has shown that there are almost always one or two no-shows or cancellations. Domestic air tickets are nonrefundable, but you can change your flight, space permitting, without penalty as late as a couple of hours before your original departure.

Incidentally, the only surviving Olympic-run **shuttle buses** between the main town and the airport are on Kós, Límnos and Kastellórizo; others have long since been axed as a cost-cutting exercise. In several instances (Athens, Thessaloníki, Ioánnina, Híos, Rhodes), municipally run services have picked up the slack, but otherwise you're at the mercy of the taxi-drivers who congregate outside the arrivals gate.

Like ferries, flights are subject to **cancellation** in bad weather, since many services are on small, 50- or 68-seat ATR turbo-prop planes, or even tinier Dornier 18-seaters, none of which will fly in strong winds or (depending on the destination airport) after dark. Despite these uncertainties, a flight on a Dornier puddle-jumper is a highly recommended experience. You can watch the crew, who are often on first-name terms with passengers, flicking switches in the cockpit; virtually every seat has a view, and you fly low enough to pick out every island feature – you might even select beaches in advance.

Size restrictions also mean that the 15-kilo baggage weight limit can be fairly strictly enforced, especially on the Dorniers; if, however, you've just arrived from overseas or purchased your ticket outside Greece, you are allowed the 20–23-kilo standard international limit. All services operated on the domestic network are **non-smoking**.

Accommodation

There are huge numbers of beds for tourists in Greece, so most of the year you can rely on turning up pretty much anywhere and finding a room – if not in a hotel, then in a private house or block of rooms (the standard island accommodation). Only from early July to early September, and around Easter, the country's high season, are you likely to experience problems. At these times, if you don't have accommodation reserved well in advance, you'd be wise to keep well off the main tourist trails, turning up at each new place early in the day and taking whatever is available – you may be able to exchange it for something better later on.

Out of season, you face a slightly different problem: most private rooms – and campsites – operate only from late April or early May to October, leaving hotels your only option. During winter you may have no choice but to stay in the main towns or ports. There will often be very little life outside these places anyway, with all the seasonal beach bars and restaurants closed. On many smaller islands, you will often find just one hotel – and perhaps one taverna – staying open year-round. Be warned also that any resort or harbour hotels which do operate through the winter are likely to have a certain number of **prostitutes** as long-term guests; licensed prostitution is legal in Greece, and the management reckons this is the most painless way to keep the bills paid.

Hotels

Hotels in the larger resorts are often contracted out on a seasonal basis by foreign package-holiday companies, though there are often vacancies available (especially in spring or autumn) for walk-in trade. The tourist police set official **categories** for hotels, which range from "L" (Luxury) down to the rarely encountered "E" class; all except the top category have to keep within set price limits. There is talk, but so far only just that, of replacing the letter system with a star grading system as in other countries. While they last, letter ratings are supposed to correspond to **facilities** available, though in practice categorization often depends on location within a resort, number of rooms and "influence" with the tourism authorities – there are so-called E-class hotels with under nine rooms which are plusher than nearby C-class outfits. It is mandatory for D-class hotels to have at least some rooms with attached baths; C-class must additionally have a bar or designated breakfast area. The presence of a pool and/or tennis court will attract a B-class rating, while A-category hotels should have a restaurant, bar and extensive common areas. Often these, and the L outfits (essentially self-contained complexes), back onto a quasi-private beach.

Mainland town hotels are almost invariably poor value for money, used as they are to a business clientele on expense accounts, and thus charging the same inflated rates all year. In ski resorts and other places with significant October-to-April leisure tourism, such as Galaxídhi, Náfplio and Mount Pílio, rates are markedly higher at weekends and holidays, and generally so during winter when heating bills must be accounted for. The only exceptions to this are the Peloponnese – which has enough foreign tourism to generate some healthy competition – and to a certain extent Athens.

In terms of **food**, C-class hotels are required only to provide the most rudimentary of continental breakfasts – you may choose not to take, or pay, for it – while B-class and above will usually offer some sort of buffet breakfast including cheese, cold cuts, sausages, eggs and so on. With some outstanding exceptions, noted in the *Guide*, lunch or supper at hotel-affiliated restaurants is bland and poor value.

Hot water

A key variable in both rooms and hotels is the type of water heating. Rooftop **solar units** (*iliaká*), with their nonexistent running costs, are more popular than electric **immersion heaters** (*thermosífona*). Under typical high-season demand, however, solar-powered tanks tend to run out of hot water with the post-beach shower crunch at 6pm, with no more available until the next day. A heater, either as a backup or primary source, is more reliable; proprietors may either jealously guard the boiler controls or entrust you with its workings, which involves either a circuit breaker or a rotary switch turned to "I" for fifteen minutes. You should never shower with a *thermosífono* powered up (look for the glow-lamp indicator on the tank) – besides the risk of shock from badly earthed plumbing, it would be fairly easy to empty smaller tanks and burn out the heating element.

Private rooms

The most common island and mainland-resort accommodation is **privately let rooms** (*dhomátia*). Like hotels, these are regulated and officially divided into three classes (A down to C), according to facilities. These days the bulk of them are in new, purpose-built, low-rise buildings, but a few are still actually in people's homes, where you'll occasionally be treated to disarming hospitality.

Rooms are almost always scrupulously clean, whatever their other amenities. At their (now all-but-vanished) **simplest**, you'll get a bare, concrete-floored room, with a hook on the back of the door and toilet facilities outside in the courtyard. At the **fancier** end of the scale, they are modern, fully furnished places with an en-suite bathroom and a fully equipped kitchen shared by guests. Between these extremes there will be a choice of rooms at various prices – owners will usually show you the most expensive first. Some of the cheap places will also have more expensive rooms with en-suite facilities – and vice versa, with rare singles often tucked under stairways or in other less desirable corners of the building. Price and quality are not necessarily directly linked, so always ask to see the room before agreeing to take it.

Areas to **look for rooms**, along with recommendations of the best places, are included in the *Guide*. As often as not, however, the rooms find you: owners descend on ferry or bus arrivals to fill any space they have, sometimes waving photos of the premises. In smaller places you'll often see rooms advertised, sometimes in German (*Zimmer*); the Greek signs to look out for are "ΕΝΙΚΙΑΖΌΜΕΝΑ DHOMÁTIA" or "ΕΝΙΚΙΑΖΟΝΤΕΗ DHOMÁTIA". In the more developed island resorts, where package holiday-makers predominate, *dhomátia* owners will often require you to stay for at least three days, or even a week.

It has become standard practice for rooms proprietors, like hotel staff, to ask to keep your **passport** – ostensibly "for the tourist police", who do require customer particulars – but in reality to prevent you skipping out with an unpaid bill. Some owners may be satisfied with just taking down your details, as is done in hotels, and they'll almost always return the documents once you get to know them, or if you need them for another purpose.

If you are **stranded**, or arrive very late in a remote mountain or island village, you may very well find that there is someone with an unlicensed room prepared to earn extra money by putting you up. This should not be counted on, but things work out more often than not. Otherwise, the most polite course is to have a meal or drink at the taverna or kafenío and then, especially in summer, enquire as to the possibility of sleeping either

Accommodation price codes

Throughout the book we've categorized accommodation according to the following **price codes**, which denote the cheapest available double room in high season. All prices are for the room only, except where otherwise indicated in accounts. Many hotels, especially those in category ❹ and over, include breakfast in the price; you'll need to check this when booking. During low season, rates can drop by more than fifty percent, especially if you are staying for three or more nights. Exceptions are during the Christmas and Easter weeks when you'll pay high-season prices. Single rooms, where available, cost around seventy percent of the price of a double.

❶ Up to €24   ❸ €34–42   ❺ €59–72
❷ €24–33   ❹ €43–58   ❻ €73 and upwards

Note: Youth hostels and mountain refuges typically charge €7–9 for a dormitory bed.

in the vacant schoolhouse or in a spare room at the *kinotikó grafío* (community records office).

Old-fashioned, 1970s-vintage rooms on the remoter islets, occasionally still without private bath, tend to fall into the ❶ price category. Standard, en-suite rooms without cooking facilities weigh in at ❷; newer, well-amenitied rooms and self-catering studios occupy the top end of the ❸ niche, along with the more modest C-class hotels, the better among these edging into ❹. The top half of ❹ corresponds fairly well to the better-value B-class hotels and the humbler designer inns in popular centres like Zagória, Pílio and the trendier Cyclades, while ❺ tallies with most of B-class and the really state-of-the-art restoration projects. ❻ means A- and L-class, and the sky's the limit here – €150 is by no means unheard of these days.

Prices in any establishment should by law be displayed on the back of the door of your room, or over the reception desk. If you feel you're being overcharged at a place which is officially registered, threaten to report it to the tourist office or police, who will generally adopt your side in such cases. A hotelier is free to offer a room at any amount under the official rate, but it's an offence to charge one euro-cent over the permitted price for the **current season**. Depending on location, there are up to three of these: typically October to May (low), June to mid-July, and September (mid) and mid-July through August (high). Small amounts over the posted price may be legitimately explained by municipal tax or out-of-date forms. More commonly you will find that you have bargained so well, or arrived so far out of high season, that you

are actually paying far less than the maximum prices – which are in any case optimistically pitched for a few high-traffic days in the year.

In **winter**, officially from November 1 until early April, private rooms – except in Ródhos Old Town and the biggest towns of Crete – are closed pretty much across the board to keep the few open hotels in business. There's no point in traipsing about hoping to find exceptions; most owners obey the system very strictly. If they don't, the room-owners will find you themselves and, watching out for hotel rivals, guide you back to their place.

Villas and long-term rentals

The easiest – and usually most economical – way to arrange a **villa rental** is through one of the package-holiday companies detailed on p.15. They represent some superb places, from fairly simple to luxurious, and costs can be very reasonable, especially if shared between a few people. Several of the companies we list will arrange "**multicentre**" stays on two islands over two weeks.

On the islands, a few local travel agents arrange villa rentals, though they are often places the overseas companies gave a miss on or could not fill. **Out of season**, you can sometimes get a good deal on villa or apartment rental for a month or more by asking around locally, though in these days of EU convergence and the increasing desirability of the islands as year-round residences, "good deal" means anything under €160 per month for a large studio (*garsoniéra*) or €205 for a small one-bedroom flat.

Youth hostels

Greece is not exactly packed with **youth hostels** (*xenón neótitos* in the singular), and those that do exist tend, with few exceptions, to be pretty run-down and/or filthy, and thus a far cry from similar north European institutions. Competition from unofficial "student hostels" (see below) and inexpensive rooms means that they are not as cost-effective as elsewhere in Europe. It's best to have a valid IYHF card, but you can often buy one on the spot, or maybe just pay a little extra for your bed. Dorms tend to have three to six beds; most hostels have a curfew at 11pm or midnight, and many places only open in spring and summer.

The only surviving hostels on the **mainland** are in Athens, Mycenae and Thessaloníki. On the **islands** you'll find them on Thíra, Rhodes and Crete. Few of these are officially recognized by the IYHF.

A number of alternatives to official youth hostels exist, particularly in Athens. These inexpensive dormitory-style "student houses" are open to anyone, but can be rather insalubrious.

Monasteries

Greek **monasteries** and **convents** have a tradition of putting up travellers (of the appropriate sex). On the mainland, this is still a customary – if steadily decreasing – practice, used mostly by villagers on pilgrimage; on the islands, monastic hospitality is not so common, so you should always ask locally before heading out to a monastery or convent for the night. Also, dress modestly – shorts for men and women, and short skirts are total anathema – and try to arrive early in the evening, not later than 8pm or sunset (whichever is earlier).

For men, the most exciting monastic experience is a visit to the "Monks' Republic" of Mount Áthos (see p.512), on the Halkidhikí peninsula, near Thessaloníki. This is, however, a far from casual travel option, involving a fair amount of advance planning and the securing of a permit.

Camping

Officially recognized campsites range from ramshackle compounds on the islands to highly organized and rather soulless complexes, formerly run by EOT prior to privatization. Most places cost just under €4 a night per person, slightly less per tent and €7.50 per camper van, but at the fanciest sites, rates for two people plus a tent can add up to the price of a basic room. Generally, you don't have to worry about leaving tents or other equipment unattended at wardened campsites; Greeks are very honest. The main risk, alas, comes from other campers. The Panhellenic Camping Association publishes an annual booklet covering most officially recognized Greek campsites and the facilities they offer; it's available from many EOT offices.

Camping rough – outside authorized campsites – is such an established element of Greek travel that few people realize that it's officially illegal. Since 1977 "freelance" camping, as EOT calls it, has actually been forbidden by a law originally enacted to harass gypsies, and regulations are increasingly enforced. Another drawback is the increased prevalence of theft in rural areas, often by bands of refugees from Albania and other north Balkan states. All told, you will feel less vulnerable inside a tent, camper van or even a rock-cave – not that rain is likely during the long Greek summer, but some protection is essential from wind, sun, insects (see "Health", p.29) and stray animals raiding your food. You will always need at least a light sleeping bag, since even summer nights can get cool and damp; a foam pad is also recommended for pitching on harder ground.

If you do camp rough, it's vital to exercise sensitivity and discretion. Police will crack down on people camping (and especially littering) around popular tourist beaches, particularly when a large community of campers develops. Off the beaten track, however, nobody is very bothered, though it is always best to ask permission locally in the village taverna or café. During high season, when everything – even the authorized campsites – may be full, attitudes towards freelance camping are more relaxed, even in the most touristed places. At such times the best strategy is to find a sympathetic taverna, which in exchange for regular patronage will probably be willing to guard small valuables and let you use their facilities.

Eating and drinking

Greeks spend a lot of time socializing outside their homes, and sharing a meal is one of the chief ways of doing it. The atmosphere is always relaxed and informal, and pretensions (and expense-account prices) are rare outside of the more chi-chi parts of Athens and certain major resorts. Greeks are not prodigious drinkers – tippling is traditionally meant to accompany food – though since the mid-1990s a whole range of bars and pubs has sprung up, both in tourist resorts and as pricey music halls at the outskirts of the major towns.

Breakfasts, picnic fare and snacks

Greeks don't generally eat **breakfast**, so the only egg-and-bacon kind of places are in resorts where foreigners congregate, or where there are returned North American or Australian Greeks. Such spots can sometimes be fairly good value (€4.50–6.50 for the works, maybe even with "French" filter coffee), especially if there's competition. More indigenous alternatives are yogurts at a *galaktopolío* (milk bar), or cheese pies and pretzel rings from a bakery (see "Snacks", overpage).

Picnic fare

Picnic fare is good, cheap and easily available at bakeries and *manávika* (fruit-and-veg stalls). **Bread**, alas, is often of minimal nutritional value and inedible within a day of purchase. It's worth paying extra at the bakery (*foúrnos* or *psomádhiko*) for *olikís* (wholemeal), *sikalísio* (rye bread), *oktásporo* (eight-grain) or even *enneásporo* (nine-grain), the latter types most commonly baked where large numbers of Germans or Scandinavians are about. When buying **olives**, go for the fat Kalamáta or Ámfissa ones; they're more expensive, but tastier. However, locally gathered olives – especially the slightly shrivelled *hamádhes* or fully ripened, ground-gathered olives – often have a distinctive nutty taste, compensating for large kernels. The best **honey** is reckoned to be the pure-thyme variety from the more barren islands (such as Límnos, Náxos and Astypálea) or areas of the mainland, although it's about double the price of ordinary honeys.

Honey is an ideal topping for the famous local **yogurt**, which is not confined to the bland Fage-brand stuff of the UK supermarket. All of the larger island towns have at least one dairy shop where locally produced yogurts are sold in plastic or (better) clay containers of various sizes. Sheep-milk yogurt is richer and sweeter, scarcely requiring honey; cows-milk yogurt is tarter but more widely available. Side by side with these will be *krémes* (custards) and *ryzógala* (rice puddings) in one-serving plastic containers.

Féta cheese is ubiquitous – sometimes, ironically, imported from Holland or Denmark, though this is being clamped down on, and local brands are usually better and not much more expensive. The goat's-milk variety can be very dry and salty, so ask for a taste before buying. If you have access to a fridge, leaving the cheese overnight in a plastic container filled with water will solve both problems, though if left too long like this the cheese simply dissolves. This sampling advice goes for other indigenous cheeses as well, the most palatable of which are the expensive gruyère-type *graviéra*.

Despite membership of the EU, plus growing personal incomes and exotic tastes, Greece imports very little garden produce from abroad, aside from bananas and a few mangoes. Fruit in particular is relatively expensive and available only by season, though in the more cosmopolitan spots it is possible to find such things as avocados (light-green ones from Crete are excellent) for much of the year. Reliable picnic fruits include *yiarmádhes*, a variety of giant peach available during August and September; *krystália*, tiny, hard green pears that ripen a month or two later and are heavenly; and the *himoniátiko* melon (called casava in North America) which appears at the same time, in its yellow, puckered skin with green flecks. Greece also has a burgeoning kiwi industry, and while the first crop in October coincides with the end of the tourist season, availability carries over into the following May. Less portable, but succulent, are **figs** (*sýka*); there's a crop of large fruits in May, followed by smaller ones in August. Salad **vegetables** are more reasonably priced; besides the famous, enormous tomatoes (June to Sept), there is a bewildering variety of springtime greens, including rocket, dill, enormous spring onions and lettuces. Useful expressions for shopping are *éna tétarto* (250g) and *misó kiló* (500g).

Snacks

Traditional **snacks** can be one of the distinctive pleasures of Greek eating, though they are being increasingly edged out by an obsession with *tóst* (toasted sandwiches) and other Western junk/fast food at nationwide chains such as *Goody's* (burgers), *Everest* and *Grigoris Mikroyevmata* (assorted), *Roma Pizza* and *Theios Vanias* (baked pastries) – somewhat less insipid for being home-grown. However, independently produced kebabs (*souvlákia*) are widely available, and in most larger resorts and towns you'll find *yíros* – doner kebab with garnish in thick, doughy *píta* bread that's closer to Indian naan bread.

Other common snacks include *tyrópites* (cheese pies) and *spanokópites* (spinach pies), which can usually be found at the baker's, as can *kouloúria* (crispy pretzel rings sprinkled with sesame seeds) and *voutímata* (dark biscuits heavy on the molasses, cinnamon and butter).

Restaurants

Greek cuisine and **restaurants** are simple and straightforward. There's usually no snobbery about eating out; everyone does it regularly, and it's still reasonable – typically €9–13 per person for a substantial (non-seafood) meal with a measure of house wine. Even if the cooking is simple, you should expect it to be wholesome; Greeks are fussy about freshness and provenance and do not willingly or knowingly like to eat frozen New Zealand lamb chops, farmed fish or prefried chips.

That said, there's a lot of **lazy cooking** about – especially in resorts, where menus are dominated by pizza, spaghetti, chops and "tourist moussaká" a dish heavy with cheap potato slices, and nary a crumb of mince.

Of late you find growing numbers of what the Greeks call **"kultúra"** restaurants, often pretentious attempts at Greek nouvelle cuisine with speciality wine lists, which tend to be long on airs and graces, and (at €17.50–23.50 a head) short on value. The exceptions which succeed have been singled out in the text.

When choosing a restaurant, the usual best strategy is to go where the Greeks go. And they go late: 2pm to 3.30pm for **lunch**, 9pm to 11pm for **supper**. You can eat earlier, but you're likely to get indifferent service and cuisine if you frequent establishments catering to the tourist schedule. Chic appearance is not a reliable guide to quality; often the more ramshackle, traditional outfits represent the best value. One good omen is the waiter bringing a carafe of refrigerated water, unbidden, rather than pushing you to order bottled stuff.

In busy resort areas, it's wise to keep a wary eye on the **waiters**, who are inclined to urge you into ordering more than you want, then bring things you haven't ordered. Although cash-register receipts are required in all establishments, these are often only for the grand total, and itemized **bills** will be in totally illegible Greek script. Where prices are printed on menus, you'll be paying the right-hand (higher) of the two columns, inclusive of all taxes and usually service charge, although a small extra tip of about ten percent directly to the waiter is hugely appreciated – and usually not expected.

Bread costs extra, but consumption is not obligatory; unless it is assessed as part of the cover charge, you have the right to send it back without paying for it. You'll be considered deviant for refusing it, but so much Greek bread is inedible sawdust that there's little point in paying extra unless you actually want to use it as a scoop for dips.

Children are always welcome, day or night, at family tavernas, and Greeks don't mind in the slightest if they play tag between the tables or chase the **cats** running in mendicant packs – which you should not feed, as signs often warn you They are wild and pretty desperate, and you'll need a doctor's visit and tetanus jab if they whack at a dangled bit of food and claw your hand instead.

Estiatória

There are two basic types of restaurant: the **estiatório** and the **taverna**. Distinctions between the two are slight, though the former is more commonly found in large towns and tends to have the slightly more complicated dishes termed *mayireftá* (literally, "cooked"). With their long hours, old-fashioned-tradesmen's clientele and tiny profit margins, *estiatória* are, alas, something of a vanishing breed.

An *estiatório* will generally feature a variety of such oven-baked casserole dishes as *moussakás*, *pastítsio*, meat or game stews like *kokinistó* and *stifádho*, *yemistá* (stuffed tomatoes or peppers), the oily vegetable casseroles called *ladherá* and oven-baked meat and fish. Usually you go into the kitchen and point at the desired steam trays to choose these dishes.

Batches are cooked in the morning and then left to stand, which is why this *mayireftá* food is often **lukewarm** or even cold. Greeks don't mind this (most actually believe that hot food is bad for you), and dishes like *yemistá* are actually enhanced by being allowed to cool off and stand in their own juice. Similarly, you have to specify if you want your food with little or no oil (*horís ládhi*), but once again you will be considered a little strange since Greeks regard olive oil as essential to digestion (and indeed it is the healthiest of the vegetable oils, even in large quantities).

Desserts (*epidhórpia* in formal Greek) of the pudding-and-pie variety don't exist at *estiatória*, and yogurt or cheese only occasionally. Fruit, however, is always available in season; watermelon (often on the house), melon and grapes are the summer standards. Autumn treats worth asking after include *kydhóni* or *akhládhi stó foúrno*, baked quince or pear with some sort of syrup or nut topping. At tavernas in the northern mainland – especially in Thessaloníki – you may be offered a complementary slice of sweet semolina halva (*smigdhalísios halvás*).

Tavernas and psistariés

Tavernas range from the glitzy and fashionable to rough-and-ready ones with seating under a reed canopy, behind a beach. Really primitive ones have a very limited (often unwritten) menu, but the more established will offer some of the main *mayireftá* dishes mentioned above, as well as the standard taverna fare. This essentially means **mezédhes** (hors-d'oeuvres) or **orektiká** (appetizers) and *tís óras* (meat and fish, fried or grilled to order). A bare handful of tavernas on the mainland offer game (*kynígi*) – rabbit, venison, quail or turtle dove, especially during autumn shooting season. In the mountains of the north where there are rivers, trout, pike and freshwater crayfish are to be found in some eating places.

Psistariés or grill-houses serve spit-roasted lamb, pork or goat (generically termed *kondosoúvli*), grilled chicken (*kotópoulo skáras*) or *kokorétsi* (grilled offal roulade) – in remote mountain villages, often plonked straight on your table upon a sheet of waxed paper. They will usually have a limited selection of mezédhes and salads (*salátes*), but no *mayireftá* at all.

Since the idea of courses is foreign to Greek cuisine, starters, main dishes and salads often arrive together unless you request otherwise. The best thing is to order a selection of mezédhes and salads to share, in true Greek fashion. Waiters encourage you to take the *horiátiki saláta* – the so-called Greek **salad**, including féta cheese – because it is the most expensive. If you only want tomato, or tomato and cucumber, ask for *domatosaláta* or *angourodomáta*. *Láhano-karóto* (cabbage-carrot) and *maroúli* (lettuce) are the typical winter and spring salads respectively.

The most interesting **mezédhes** are *tzatzíki* (yogurt, garlic and cucumber dip), *melitzanosaláta* (aubergine/eggplant dip), *kolokythákia tiganitá* (courgette/zucchini slices fried in batter) or *melitzánes tiganités* (aubergine/eggplant slices fried in batter), *yígandes* (white haricot beans in vinaigrette or hot tomato sauce), *tyropitákia* or *spanakópites* (small cheese and spinach pies), *revythókeftedhes* or *pittaroúdhia* (chickpea patties similar to falafel), *okhtapódhi* (octopus) and *mavromátika* (black-eyed peas).

Among **meats**, *souvláki* (shish kebab) and *brizóles* (chops) are reliable choices, often locally produced. In both cases, pork (*hirinó*) is usually better and cheaper than veal (*moskharísio*). The best souvláki, though not often available, is lamb (*arnísio*). At *psistariés*, meaty lamb shoulder chops (*kopsídha*) are more substantial than the scrawny rib chops called *païdhákia*; roast lamb (*arní psitó*) and roast kid (*katsíki stó fournó*) are considered *estiatório* fare. *Keftédhes* (breadcrumbed meatballs), *biftékia* (similar, but meatier) and the spicy, home-made, coarse-grain sausages called *loukánika* are cheap and good. *Kotópoulo* (chicken), especially grilled, is widely available but typically battery-farmed in Ípiros or on Évvia. Other dishes worth trying are stewed goat (*gídha vrastí*) or baked goat (*katsíki stó foúrno*) – goat in general is a wonderfully healthy meat, typically free-range, undosed with antibiotics or hormones.

As in *estiatória*, traditional tavernas offer fruit rather than sticky **desserts**, though nowadays these are often available, along with coffee, in tavernas frequented by foreigners.

Fish and seafood

Seaside *psarotavérnes* offer **fish**, though for the inexperienced, ordering can be fraught with peril. Summer visitors get a relatively poor choice of fish, most of it frozen, farmed or imported from Egypt and North Africa. Drag-net-trawling is prohibited from the end of May until the beginning of October, when only lamp-lure (*grí-grí*), trident, "doughnut" trap (*kýrtos*) and multihook line (*paragádhi*) methods are allowed. During these warmer months, such few fish as are caught tend to be smaller and dry-tasting, and are served with butter sauce. Taverna owners often comply only minimally with the requirement to indicate when seafood is **frozen** (look for the abbreviation "kat.", "k" or just an asterisk on the Greek-language side of the menu).

Given these considerations, it's often best to set your sights on the **humbler**, seasonally migrating or perennially local species. The cheapest consistently available fish are *gópes* (bogue), *atherína* (sand smelts) and *marídhes* (picarel), eaten head and all, best rolled in salt and sprinkled with lemon juice. In the Dodecanese, *yermanós* (same as Australian leatherback) is a good frying fish which appears in spring; *gávros* (anchovy) and *sardhélles* (sardines) are late summer treats, at their best in the northeast Aegean. In the north Aegean or around Pílio, *pandelís* or *sykiós* (Latin *Corvina nigra*, in French "corb") is caught in early summer, and is highly esteemed since it's a rock-dweller, not

a bottom feeder – and therefore a bit pricier than the preceding. In autumn especially you may encounter *psarósoupa* (fish broth) or *kakaviá* (a bouillabaisse-like stew).

The **choicer** varieties, such as *barboúni* (red mullet), *tsipoúra* (gilt-head bream), *lavráki* (seabass) or *fangrí* (common bream), will be expensive if wild – anywhere from €26.50–41 per kilo, depending on what the market will bear. If the price seems too good to be true, it's almost certainly **farmed**. Prices are usually quoted by the kilo, and should not be much more than double the street-market rate, so if a type of bream is €14.70 a kilo at the fishmonger's, expect it to be not more than €30 at the taverna. Standard procedure is to go to the glass-fronted cooler and pick your own specimen, and have it weighed (cleaned) in your presence.

Vegetarians

If you are **vegetarian**, you may be in for a hard time, and will often have to assemble a meal from various *mezédhes*. Even the excellent standbys of yogurt with honey, *tzatzíki* and Greek salad begin to pall after a while, and many of the supposed "vegetable" dishes on menus are cooked in stock or have pieces of meat added to liven them up. Wholly or largely vegetarian restaurants, however, are slowly on the increase in touristy areas; this guide highlights them where appropriate.

Cheaper **seafood** (*thalassiná*) such as *kalamarákia* (fried baby squid, usually frozen) and *okhtapódhi* (octopus) are a summer staple of most seaside tavernas, and occasionally *mýdhia* (mussels), *kydhónia* (cockles) and *garídhes* (small prawns) will be on offer at reasonable prices. Keep an eye out, however, to freshness and season – mussels in particular are a common cause of stomach upsets or even mild poisoning.

As the more favoured species have become overfished, **unusual seafoods**, formerly the exclusive province of the poor, are putting in a greater appearance on menus. Ray or skate (variously known as *platý*, *seláhi*, *trígona* or *vátos*) can be fried or used in soup, and is even dried for decoration. Sea urchins (*ahiní*) are also a humble (and increasingly rare) favourite, being split and emptied for the sake of their (reputedly aphrodisiac) roe that's eaten raw. Only the reddish ones are gravid; special shears are sold for opening them if you don't fancy a hand full of spines. Many a quiet beach is littered with their halved carapaces, evidence of an instant Greek picnic.

Wines

Both *estiatória* and tavernas will usually offer you a choice of bottled **wines**, and many still have their own house variety: kept in barrels, sold in bulk by the quarter-, half- or full litre, and served either in glass flagons or the brightly coloured tin "monkey-cups" called *kantária*. Not as many tavernas stock their own wine as once did, but it's worth asking whether they have wine *varelísio* (barrelled) or *hýma* (in bulk). You should expect to pay €3.50–5 per litre, with smaller measures priced proportionally. Non-resinated wine is almost always more than decent. **Retsina** – pine-resinated wine, a slightly acquired taste – is also available straight from the barrel, though the bottled brands Yeoryiadhi from Thessaloníki, Malamatina from central Greece (often cut with soda water), and Cambas from near Athens, are all excellent and likely to be more consistent in quality.

Among the **bottled wines** available **nationwide**, Cambas Attikos, Boutari Lac des Roches, any white from Zítsa and the Rhodian CAIR products (especially the Moulin range) are good, inexpensive whites, while Boutari Naoussa and Kourtakis Apelia are decent, mid-range reds. If you want a better but still moderately priced red, go for the Merlot of either Boutari and Tsantali, or Averof Katoï from Epirus.

If you're travelling around **wine-producing islands**, however, you may as well go for **local bottlings**; the best available guide to the emerging Greek domaines and vintners is Nico Manessis' *The Illustrated Greek Wine Book* (see p.1082 in *Contexts* for ordering information). Almost anything produced on Límnos is decent; the Alexandrine muscat is now used for whites, the local *límnio* grape for reds and rosés. Thíra, another volcanic island, has a number of premium white products such as Ktima Arghyrou and Boutari Nykhteri, and the Gentilini Robola white of Kefalloniá is justly esteemed. Páros (Moraïtis) and Náxos also both have acceptable local vintages, while Crete is now begin-

ning to have labels superior to the bog-standard Logado, such as Economou (Sitía) and Lyrakis (Iráklio). On Rhodes, Alexandhris products from Émbonas are well thought of, as is the Emery label with its Villaré white, and CAIR's dry white "2400".

Curiously, island red wines (except for Rhodes' CAIR Moulin and Emery Cava) are almost uniformly mediocre; in this respect you're better off choosing **reds from the mainland**. Carras from Halkidhikí does the excellent Porto Carras, while Ktima Tselepou offers a very palatable Cabernet-Merlot blend. Antonopoulos Yerontoklima (Pátra), Ktima Papaïoannou Nemea (Peloponnese), and Tsantali Rapsani (Thessaly) are all superb, velvety reds – and likely to be found only in the better *kultúra* tavernas or *káves* (bottle shops). Antonopoulos, Tselepos (Mantinia domaine) and Papaïoannou also do excellent **mainland whites**.

The other **premium microwineries** on the mainland whose products have long been fashionable, in both red and white, include the vastly overrated Hatzimihali (Atalánti, central Greece); Spyropoulos (central Peloponnese), Athanasiadhi (central Greece), Skouras (Argolid) and the two rival Lazaridhi vintners (Dhráma, east Macedonia), especially their superb Merlots. For any of these you can expect to pay €7–10 per bottle in a shop, double that at a taverna.

Last but not least, CAIR on Rhodes makes its very own **"champagne"** ("naturally sparkling wine fermented en boteille", says the label), in both brut and demi-sec versions. It's not Moët & Chandon quality by any means, but at less than €6 per bottle, who's complaining...

Cafés, cake shops and bars

The Greek eating and drinking experience encompasses a variety of other places beyond restaurants. Most importantly, there is the institution of the **kafenío**, found in every town, village and hamlet in the country. In addition, you'll come across **ouzerís**, *zaharoplastía* (Greek patisseries) and *barákia*.

The kafenío

The **kafenío** (plural "kafenía") is the traditional Greek coffee shop or café. Although its main business is "Greek" (Middle Eastern) coffee – prepared *skéto* or *pikró* (unsweetened), *métrio* (medium) or *glykó* (sweet) – it also serves spirits such as oúzo (see below), brandy (usually Metaxa or Botrys brand, in three grades), beer, tea – either sage-based tea known variously as *alisfakiá* (isles) or *tsáï vounoú* (mainland), or British-style – and soft drinks. Another refreshing drink sold in cafés is *kafés frappé*, iced, jigger-shaken instant coffee with or without milk and sugar – uniquely Greek despite its French-sounding name. Like Greek coffee, it is always accompanied by a welcome glass of cold water. Standard fizzy soft drinks are also sold in all kafenía.

Usually the only **edibles** available are "spoon sweets" or *glyká koutalioú* (sticky, syrupy preserves of quince, grape, fig, citrus fruit or cherry) and the traditional, now-vanishing *ipovrýhio*, a piece of mastic submerged in a glass of water like a submarine – which is what the word means in Greek.

Like tavernas, kafenía range from the plastic, chrome and sophisticated to the old-fashioned, spit-on-the-floor or mock-retro variety, with marble or brightly painted metal tables and straw-bottomed chairs. An important institution anywhere in Greece, they form the pivot of life in the country villages. You get the impression that many men spend most of their waking hours there. Greek women are rarely to be seen in the more traditional places – and foreign women may sometimes feel uneasy or unwelcome in these establishments. Even in holiday resorts, you will find that there is at least one coffee house that the local men have reserved for themselves.

Some kafenía close at siesta time, but many remain open from early in the morning until late at night. The chief summer socializing time is 6–8pm, immediately after the siesta. This is the time to take your pre-dinner oúzo, as the sun begins to sink and the air cools down.

Oúzo, tsípouro, mezédhes, ouzerís and mezedhopolía

Oúzo and the similar *tsípouro* (north mainland) and *tsikoudhiá* (Crete), are simple spirits of up to 48 percent alcohol, distilled from grape-mash residue left over from winemaking, and then usually flavoured with herbs such as anise or fennel. There are

nearly thirty name brands of oúzo or *tsípouro*, with the best reckoned to be from Lésvos and Sámos islands, or Zítsa and Týrnavos on the mainland; inferior ones are either weak (such as the Rhodian Fokiali, at forty percent) or spiked with molasses or grain alcohol to "boost" them.

When you order, you will be served two glasses: one with the oúzo, and one full of water to be tipped into your oúzo until it turns a milky white. You can drink it straight, but the strong, burning taste is hardly refreshing if you do. It is increasingly common to add **ice cubes** (*pagáki*), a bowl of which will be provided upon request. The next measure up from a glass is a *karafáki* – a deceptively small 200ml-vial, and the favourite means of delivery for *tsípouro* – which will very rapidly render you legless if you don't alternate tippling with snacks.

A much smoother variant of oúzo is **soúma**, found chiefly on Rhodes and Sámos, but in theory anywhere grapes are grown. The smoothness is deceptive – as with *tsípouro*, two or three glasses of it and you had better not have any other firm plans for the afternoon.

Until the 1980s, every oúzo you ordered was automatically accompanied by a small plate of **mezédhes** on the house: bits of cheese, cucumber, tomato, a few olives, sometimes octopus or even a couple of small fish. Unfortunately, these days "oúzo mezédhes" is a separate, more expensive option on a price list. Often, however, they are not featured on any formal menu, but if you order a *karafáki* you will automatically be offered a small selection of snacks.

Though they are confined to the better resorts and select neighbourhoods of the larger islands and towns, one kind of drinking establishment specializes in oúzo and mezédhes. These are called **ouzerí** (same in the Greek plural, we've added 's' to the hybrid) or *tsipouradhika* (plural) in Vólos, Thessaloníki and other major centres of the north mainland. In some towns, especially in Athens, you may also come across **mezedhopolía**, basically a bigger, more upmarket kind of ouzerí. Ouzerís and *mezedhopolía* are well worth trying for the marvellous variety of mezédhes they serve (though lately numbers of mediocre tavernas have counterfeited the name). At the genuine article, several plates of mezédhes plus drinks will effectively substitute for a more involved meal at a taverna (though it usually works out more expensive if you have a healthy appetite). Faced with an often bewilderingly varied menu, you might opt for the *pikilía* (medley, assortment) available in several sizes, the largest and most expensive one usually heavy on the seafood. At other ouzerís or *tsipourádhika* the language barrier may be overcome by the waiter wielding an enormous **dhískos** or tray laden with all the current cold offerings – you pick the ones you like the look of.

Sweets, breakfast and Western coffee

Similar to the kafenío is the **zaharoplastío**, a cross between café and patisserie, serving coffee, alcohol, yogurt with honey and sticky cakes.

The better establishments offer an amazing variety of pastries, cream-and-chocolate confections, honey-soaked Greco–Turkish sweets like *baklavás*, *kataïfi* (honey-drenched "shredded wheat"), *loukoumádhes* (deep-fried batter puffs dusted with cinnamon and dipped in syrup), *galaktoboúreko* (custard pie) and so on.

If you want a stronger slant towards the dairy products and away from the pure sugar, seek out a **galaktopolío**, where you'll often find *ryzógalo* (rice pudding – rather better than the English canned variety), *kréma* (custard) and locally made *yiaoúrti* (yogurt), best if it's *próvio* (from sheep's milk).

Ice cream, sold principally at the gelaterie which have swept over Greece of late (*Dhodhoni* is the posh chain), can be very good and almost indistinguishable from Italian prototypes. A scoop (*baláki*) costs €0.90–1.30; you'll be asked if you want it in a cup (*kypelláki*) or a cone (*konáki*), and whether you want toppings like *santí* (whipped cream) or nuts. By contrast, the mass-produced brands like Delta or Evga are pretty average, with the exception of Skandalo and Nirvana labels; Häagen-Dazs is also widely available and identical to its north European profile. A sign reading "PAGOTÓ POLÍTIKO" or "KAÏMÁKI" means that the shop concerned makes its own Turkish-style ice cream – as good as or better than the usual Italian version – and the proprietors are probably of Asia Minor or Constantinopolitan descent.

Both *zaharoplastía* and *galaktopolía* are more family-oriented places than the kafenío, and many also serve a basic **continental breakfast** of *méli me voútyro* (honey poured over a pat of butter) or jam (all kinds are called *marmeládha* in Greek; ask for *portokáli* – orange – if you want proper marmalade) with fresh bread or *friganiés* (melba-toast-type slivers). You are also more likely to find proper (*evropaïkó*) tea and non-Greek coffee.

"Nes"(café) has become the generic term for all instant **coffee**, regardless of brand; it's generally pretty vile, and since the mid-1990s there's been a nationwide reaction against it. Even in the smallest provincial capital or resort there will be at least one trendy café which does a range of foreign-style coffees – filter, dubbed *fíltros* or *gallikós* (French); cappuccino; and espresso – at overseas prices.

Bars – and beer

Bars (*barákia* in the plural), once confined to towns, cities and holiday resorts, are now found all over Greece. They range from clones of Parisian cafés or Spanish bodegas to seaside cocktail bars, with music or TV running all day. At their most sophisticated, however, they are well-executed theme venues in ex-industrial premises or Neoclassical houses that can hold their own against close equivalents in Spain or London, with Western (currently techno, dub or ambient) soundtracks.

For this and other reasons, drinks are invariably more expensive than in a café. Bars are, however, most likely to stock a range of **beers**, mostly foreign labels made locally under licence at just one or two breweries on the central mainland. However, since 1996 several genuinely **local new formulae** have appeared, rapidly capturing a slice of the market: Mythos, a smooth lager in a green bottle, put out by the Boutari vintners; Veryina, brewed in Komotiní and common in eastern Macedonia and Halkidhikí; Pils Hellas, a sharp pilsner; and last but not least, the resurrected Fix, for years until its demise in 1980 Greece's only beer, though not (according to those who remember) much better the second time around than the first. Kronenberg 1664 and Kaiser are two of the more common quality **foreign-licence** varieties, with the latter available in both light and dark. Bland, inoffensive Amstel and the increasingly rare, yeasty Henninger are the two cheapies; the Dutch themselves claim that Amstel is better than the one available in Holland, and Amstel also makes a very palatable, strong (seven percent) **bock**. Heineken, still referred to as a *"prássini"* by bar and taverna staff after its green bottle, despite the advent of Mythos, is too harshly sharp for many. Since 1993 a tidal wave of even pricier, genuinely imported German beers, such as Bitburger, Fisher and Warstein (plus a few British ones), has

washed over the fancier resorts. A curiosity – confined to Corfu and Paxí – is *tsitsibýra* (ginger beer), a holdover from the nineteenth-century British occupation of the Ionian islands; cloudy, greyish-white and fizzy, it tastes vaguely of lemon and the sour beginnings of fermentation in its little bottle.

Incidentally, try not to get stuck with the one-third-litre cans, vastly more **expensive** (and more of a rubbish problem) than the returnable half-litre bottles. On ferry-boats or in remote locales you may not have a choice, however.

Communications: post, phones and internet

Postal services

Post offices are open Monday to Friday from 7.30am to 2pm, though certain main branches have hours until the evening and on Saturday morning.

Airmail letters from the mainland take three to seven days to reach the rest of Europe, five to twelve days to get to North America, and a bit longer for Australia and New Zealand. Generally, the larger the island (and the planes serving its airport), the quicker the service. Postal rates for up to 20g fall within the normal EU range: €0.60 for postcards or letters to Europe, €0.80 to North America or Australasia. For a modest fee (about €3) you can shave a day or two off delivery time to any destination by using the **express service** (*katepígonda*). **Registered** (*systiméno*) delivery is also available for a similar amount, but proves quite slow unless coupled with express service. If you are sending large purchases or excess baggage home, note that **parcels** should and often can only be handled in the main provincial or county capitals. This way, your bundle will be in Athens, and on an international flight, within a day. Always present your box open for inspection, and come prepared with tape, twine and scissors – most post offices will sell cardboard boxes, but nothing to actually close the package.

For a simple letter or card, a stamp (*grammatósimo*) can also be purchased at a *períptero* (kiosk). However, the proprietors charge ten percent commission on the cost of the stamp, and never seem to know the current international rates.

Ordinary **post boxes** are bright yellow, express boxes dark red, but it's best to use only those by the door of an actual post office, since days may pass between collections at other street-corner or wall-mounted boxes. If you are confronted by two slots, "ESOTERIKÓ" is for domestic mail, "EXOTERIKÓ" for overseas. Often there are more: one box or slot for mail into Athens and suburbs, one for your local province, one for "other" parts of Greece, and one for overseas; if in doubt, ask someone.

The **poste-restante** system is reasonably efficient, especially at the post offices of larger towns. Mail should be clearly addressed and marked "poste restante", with your surname underlined, to the main post office of whichever town you choose. It will be held for a month and you'll need your passport to collect it.

Phones

Making **telephone calls** is relatively straightforward, though the **OTE** (Organismós Tiliepikinoníon tís Elládhos, the state-run telecom) has historically provided some of the worst service in the EU. However, since the mid-1990s this has improved drastically, and rates have dropped dramatically, under the twin threats of privatization and competition from thriving local mobile networks.

All land-line exchanges are supposed to become **digital** (*psifiakó*) by the year 2002, but until this project is complete you may still encounter a few **pulse-analogue** (*palmikó*) exchanges. When ringing long-distance on such circuits, you must wait for a critical series of six electrical crunches on the line after dialling the country or Greek area code, before proceeding.

Call boxes, poorly maintained and invariably sited at the noisiest street corners, work only with phonecards; these come in four sizes – 100 units, 200 units, 500 units and 1000 units – and are available from kiosks and newsagents. Not surprisingly, the more expensive cards are the best value in terms of euros per unit. Despite numbers hopefully scribbled on the appropriate tabs, call boxes cannot be

rung back; however, green, countertop cardphones kept by many hotels can be rung.

If you won't be around long enough to use up a phonecard (the cheapest is about €3), it's probably easier to make **local calls** from a *períptero* or **street kiosk**. Here the phone may be connected to a meter (if not, there'll be a sign saying *móno topikó*, "local only"), and you pay after you have made the call. Local, one-unit calls are reasonable enough (about €0.15 for the first three minutes), but long-distance ones add up quickly.

Other options for calling include a bare handful of **counter coin-op phones** in bars, kafenía and hotel lobbies; these should take small euro coins – probably five-cent, ten-cent, twenty-cent and fifty-cent denominations – and, unlike kerbside phone boxes, can be rung back. Most of them are made in northern Europe and bear instructions in English. You'll probably want to avoid making long-distance calls **from hotel rooms**, as a minimum one-hundred-percent surcharge will be slapped on.

Useful phone codes and numbers

Phoning Greece from abroad
Dial the international access code (given below) + 30 (country code)
+ area code (minus initial 0) + number

Australia ☎0011	Canada ☎011
Ireland ☎010	New Zealand ☎00
UK ☎00	USA ☎011

Phoning abroad from Greece
Dial the country code (given below) + area code (minus any initial 0) + number

Australia ☎0061	Canada ☎001
Ireland ☎00353	New Zealand ☎0064
UK ☎0044	USA ☎001

Greek phone codes
Athens ☎010
Corfu ☎06610
Iráklion ☎0810
Kefalloniá ☎06710 (west), ☎06740 (east)
Kós ☎02420
Mýkonos ☎02890
Páros ☎02840
Pátra ☎0610
Rhodes ☎02410
Skiáthos ☎04270
Thessaloníki ☎0310
Thíra ☎02860

Zákynthos ☎06950
Local call rate (like UK's ☎0845) ☎0801
Mobiles ☎093, ☎094, ☎095, ☎097
Toll-free/Freefone ☎0800

Useful Greek telephone numbers
Ambulance ☎166
ELPA Road Service ☎104
Fire brigade, urban ☎199
Forest fire reporting ☎191
Operator ☎132 (Domestic)
Operator ☎161 (International)
Police/Emergency ☎100
Speaking clock ☎141
Tourist police ☎171 (Athens); ☎01-171 (elsewhere)

Phone charge-card operator access numbers from Greece
AT&T USA Direct ☎00 800 1311
Australia ☎00 800 6111
Australia (Optus) ☎00 800 6121
Bell Atlantic ☎00 800 1821
Bell South ☎00 800 1721
British Telecom ☎00 800 4411
Canada Direct ☎00 800 1611
MCI ☎00 800 1211
NTL (ex-Cable and Wireless) ☎00 800 4422
Sprint ☎00 800 1411

For **international** (*exoterikó*) **calls**, it's again best to use kerbside cardphones. You can no longer make metered calls from Greek telecoms offices (the OTE) themselves – most keep daytime hours only and offer at most a quieter cardphone or two. Like BT Phoneshops in the UK, they are mainly places to get Greece-based service (including OTE's own mobile network Cosmote), pay your bills, and buy one of an array of phones and fax machines for sale. **Faxes** are best sent from post offices and some travel agencies – at a price; receiving a fax may also incur a small charge.

Overseas phone calls with a 100-unit card will **cost**, approximately, €0.40 per minute to all EU countries and much of the rest of central Europe, North America and Australia – versus €0.28 per minute on a private subscriber line. There is no particular cheap rate for overseas calls to these destinations, and dialling countries with problematic phone systems like Russia, Israel or Egypt is obviously rather more. **Within Greece**, undiscounted **rates** are €0.16 per minute on a subscriber line, rather more from a cardphone; a twenty-percent discounted rate applies daily from 10pm to 8am, and from 10pm Saturday until 8am Monday.

Changes to Greek phone codes

As we go to press, we are advised that all **area codes** in Greece are set to change in early 2002, owing to the Greek telecoms running out of land lines. A "0" is to be added to the end of each area code (thus Athens will become 010, Pátra 0610, Ioánnina 06510, etc). In anticipation of this change, we have amended area codes accordingly througout the *Guide*. It is also anticipated that callers will be obliged to dial all digits (code plus subscriber number) whether they're in the same area code or not. In effect this means that, as in France, there will be no more area codes in Greece, merely ten-digit numbers, though this could not be absolutely confirmed at the time of research.

Charge-card call services from Greece back to the home country are provided in the UK by British Telecom (☎0800/345144, ⓦwww.chargecard.bt.com) and NTL (ex-Cable & Wireless, ☎0500/100505); in North America, Canada Direct, AT&T (☎0800/890

011, then 888/641 6123 when you hear the AT&T prompt to be transferred to the 24-hr Florida Call Centre), MCI and Sprint; in Australia, Optus (☎1300/300 937) or Telstra (☎1800/038 000), and in New Zealand Telecom NZ (☎04/801 9000). There are now a few local-dial numbers with some providers (given in the box overleaf) which enable you to connect to the international network for the price of a one-unit call, and then charge the call to your home number – usually cheaper than the alternatives.

Mobile phones

Mobile phones are an essential fashion accessory in Greece, which has the highest per-capita usage in Europe outside of Italy – in a population of roughly 11 million, there are claimed to be 6.5 million mobile handsets in use. There are three **networks** at present: Panafon-Vodafon, Telestet and Cosmote. Calling any of them from Britain, you will find that costs are exactly the same as calling a fixed phone – so you won't need to worry about ringing them when given as alternative numbers for accommodation – though of course such numbers are pricey when rung locally. **Coverage** countrywide is fairly good, though there is a number of "dead" zones in the shadows of mountains, or on really remote islets. **Pay-as-you-go**, contract-free plans are heavily promoted in Greece (such as Telestet B-Free and Panafon-Vodafon À La Carte), and if you're going to be around for a while – for example, studying, or working for a season in the tourist industry – an outlay of €90 or less will see you to a decent apparatus and your first calling card. This lasts up to a year – even if you use up your talk time you'll still have an incoming number, along with a voice-mail service. Top-up calling cards – predicted to be in denominations of €6, €15 and €18 depending on the network – are available at all *períptera*.

If you want to use your **home-based mobile abroad**, you'll need to check with your phone provider whether it will work. North American users will only be able to use tri-band rigs in Greece. Any GSM mobile from the UK, Australia or New Zealand should work fine in Greece.

In the UK, for all but the very top-of-the-range packages, you'll have to inform your service network before going abroad to get international access ("**roaming**") switched on. You may get charged extra for this depending on the terms of your package and where you are travelling to. You are also likely to be charged extra for **incoming calls** when abroad, as the people calling you will be paying the usual rate; discount plans are available to reduce the cost of forwarding the call to you overseas by as much as seventy percent. If you want to **retrieve messages** while you're away, you'll have to ask your provider for a new access number, as your home one (or one-stroke "mail" key) is unlikely to work abroad.

In terms of **call charges**, experience (and examining UK-based bills) has shown that the local network that you select out of the three local networks makes little difference: depending on the length of the call, chat back to the UK (including voice-mail retrieval) works out at £0.49–55 per minute; ringing land-lines within Greece is £0.23–0.26 per minute; and calling Greek mobiles ranges from £0.30 to 0.43 per minute – all significantly more than using a cardphone, but worth it to most for the convenience and privacy.

Email and internet

Email and internet use has caught on in a big way in Greece; electronic addresses or websites are given in this guide for the growing number of travel companies and hotels that have them. For your own email needs, you're best off using the various **internet cafés** which have sprung up in the larger towns – street addresses are given where appropriate. Rates tend to be about €4.50 per hour maximum, often less.

Ideally you should sign up in advance for a free **internet email address** that can be accessed from anywhere, for example YahooMail or Hotmail – accessible through Ⓦwww.yahoo.com and Ⓦwww.hotmail.com. Once you've set up an account, you can use these sites to pick up and send mail from any internet café, or hotel with internet access.

Alternatively, you can lug **your own laptop** around, not such a burden as they get progressively lighter. You will need about 2m of North American-standard cable (UK ones will *not* work), lightweight and easily purchasable in Greece, with RJ-11 male terminals at each end. The Greek **dial tone** is discontinuous and thus not recognized by most modems – instruct it to "ignore dial tone". Many newer hotel rooms have RJ-11 **sockets**, but some older ones still have their phones hard-wired into the wall. You can get around this problem with a female-female **adaptor**, either RJ-11- or 6P6C-configured, available at better electrical retailers. They weigh and cost next to nothing, so carry both (one is sure to work) for making a splice between your cable and the RJ-11 end of the cable between the wall and phone (which you simply unplug). You will usually have to dial an initial "9" or "0" to get around the hotel's central switchboard for a proper external dial tone.

Compuserve and AOL definitely have **points of presence** in Greece, but more obscure ISPs may also have a reciprocal agreement with Greek-based ISPs like forthnet.gr and otenet.gr, so ask your provider for a list of any available dial-up numbers. **Piggybacking charges** tend to be fairly high, but for a modest number of minutes per day, still work out rather less than patronizing an internet café.

The media

Although the Greek press and airwaves have been relatively free since the fall of the colonels' dictatorship in 1974, nobody would ever propose the Greek media as a paradigm of responsible or objective journalism. Papers are almost uniformly sensational, state-run radio and TV often biased in favour of the ruling party, and private channels imitative of the worst American programming. Most visitors will tune all this out, however, seeking solace in the music of private radio stations, or the limited number of English-language publications.

British **newspapers** are fairly widely available in Greece at a cost of €2–2.50 for dailies, or €3.50–4.20 for Sunday editions. You'll find one-to-two-day-old copies (same day by noon in Athens) of *The Times*, *The Telegraph*, *The Independent* and *The Guardian*'s European edition, plus a few of the tabloids, in all the resorts as well as in major towns. American and international alternatives include the turgid *USA Today* and the slightly more readable *International Herald Tribune*, the latter including as a major bonus a free though somewhat abridged English translation of the respected Greek daily *Kathimerini* (online at ⓦwww.eKathimerini .com; see also below). Among numerous foreign **magazines**, *Time* and *Newsweek* are also widely available.

There are relatively few surviving **locally produced** English-language magazines or papers. The late lamented **magazine** *The Athenian* folded in 1997 after 23 years, with a rather sloppy successor, *Atlantis*, rising less than phoenix-like from the ashes. Marginally better is the expensive, glossy *Odyssey*, produced every other month by and for wealthy diaspora Greeks, and little different from the average in-flight magazine. By far the best of the English-language **newspapers** is the four-colour *Athens News* (daily except Mon, online at ⓦwww.athens-news.gr; €1.50) in colour with good features and Balkan news, plus entertainment and arts listings on Friday, available in most resorts.

Before setting out from the **UK**, there are two **Greece-specific periodicals** well worth consulting. One is the *Anglo-Hellenic Review* (£2), published twice yearly by the Anglo-Hellenic League; it has excellent essays by renowned scholars, and good reviews of recently issued books on Greek topics. Obtain it either from the Hellenic Book Service (see p.1093) or The Hellenic Centre, 16/18 Paddington St, London W1M 4AS. The other is the Greek London Embassy's almost monthly newsletter, *Greece: Background-News-Information*. Though clearly pro-government to the point of verging on propaganda, it's well written (even humorous), giving a lively overview of events in the country over the past few weeks. To register on their mailing list (free), contact them on ☎020/7727 3071, ⓕ7727 8960 or email ⓔofficepress @compuserve.com.

Greek publications

Many papers have ties (including funding) with specific **political groups**, which bias tends to decrease the already low quality of Greek dailies. Among these, only the **centrist** *Kathemerini* – whose former proprietress Helen Vlahos attained heroic status for her defiance of the junta – approaches the standards of a major European newspaper. *Eleftherotypia*, once a PASOK mouthpiece, now aspires to more independence, and has links with Britain's *The Guardian*; *Avriani* has taken its place as the PASOK cheerleading section. *Ta Nea* is a highly popular, MOR tabloid, vaguely similar to London's *The Evening Standard* and much loved for its extensive small ads. On the far **Left**, *Avyi* is the Eurocommunist/Synaspismós forum with literary leanings, while *Rizospastis* acts as the organ of the KKE (unreconstructed Communists). *Ethnos* became notorious some years back for receiving covert funding from the KGB to act as a disinformation bulletin. At the other end of the political spectrum, *Apoyevmatini* generally supports the **centre-right** Néa Dhimokratía party, while *Estia's* no-photo format and reactionary politics are both stuck somewhere at the beginning of the twentieth century. The ultra-nationalist, lunatic fringe is staked out by paranoid *Stohos* ("Our Goal: Greater Greece; Our Capital: Constantinople").

Among **magazines** that are not merely translations of overseas titles, *Takhydhromos* is the respectable news-and-features weekly, *Ena* is more sensationalist, *Klik* a crass rip-off of Britain's *The Face*, while *To Pondiki* (The Mouse) is a satirical weekly revue in the same vein as Britain's *Private Eye*; its famous covers are spot-on and accessible to anyone with minimal Greek. More specialized niches are occupied by low-circulation titles such as *Adhesmatos Typos* (a slightly rightist, muckraking journal) and *Andi*, an intelligent biweekly somewhat in the mould of Britain's *New Statesman and Society*.

Radio

If you have a **radio** on your personal stereo, playing dial roulette can be rewarding. Greek music programmes are always accessible (if variable in quality), and since abolition of the government's former monopoly of wavelengths, regional stations have mushroomed; indeed the airwaves are now positively cluttered as every island town sets up its own studio and transmitter. The two state-run channels are ER1 (a mix of news, talk and popular music) and ER 2 (strictly popular music).

On heavily touristed islands like Rhodes, Corfu and Crete, there will usually be at least one station on the FM band trying its luck at English-moderated programming by and for foreigners. The Turkish state radio's Third Channel is also widely (if somewhat unpatriotically) listened to on border islands for its classical, jazz and blues programmes. The **BBC World Service** broadcasts on short wave throughout Greece; 6.18, 9.41, 15.07 and 12.09 MHz are the most common frequencies. However, it has been announced that short-wave services are to be phased out in many parts of the world, so if you can't live without them consult Ⓦwww.bbc.co.uk/worldservice, which lists all their global frequencies. The **Voice of America**, with its transmitters on Rhodes, can be picked up in most of the Dodecanese on medium wave.

Television

Television first appeared in Greece in 1965, but it only became dominant during the 1967–74 junta, with the ruling colonels using it as a means of social control and to purvey anodyne variety revues, sports events and so on. As in many countries, it transformed the Greeks from a nation of live performers and coffee-house habitués to introverted stay-at-homes, which dovetailed nicely with the junta's "family values".

Greece's centralized, government-controlled **TV stations**, ET1, NET and (out of Thessaloníki) ET3, nowadays lag behind private, mostly rather right-wing channels – Antenna, Star, Alpha and Makedonia TV – in the ratings. Mega is the one possible exception to the rule of private dross, recently taken on by the Boutos family and improved beyond recognition. On NET, news summaries in English are broadcast daily at 6pm. Programming on all stations has evolved little since junta days, tending to be a mix of soaps (especially Italian, Spanish and Latin American), game shows, westerns, B-movies and sports. All foreign films and serials are broadcast in their original language, with Greek subtitles. Except for the nearly-round-the-clock channels Mega, Star, Alpha and Antenna, most channels broadcast from around noon until the small hours. Numerous **cable and satellite** channels are received, including CNN, MTV, Filmnet, Euronews (in English), French TV5 and Italian Rai Due. The range available depends on the area (and hotel) you're in.

Opening hours and public holidays

It is virtually impossible to generalize about Greek opening hours, except to say that they change constantly. The traditional timetable starts at a relatively civilized hour, with shops opening between 8.30 and 9.30am, then runs through until lunchtime, when there is a long break for the hottest part of the day. Most places, except banks and government offices, may then reopen in the mid- to late afternoon.

Tourist areas tend to adopt a slightly more northern European timetable, with shops and offices, as well as the most important archeological sites and museums, usually open throughout the day.

Business and shopping hours

Most **government agencies** are open to the public on weekdays from 8am to 2pm. In general, however, you'd be optimistic to show up after 1pm expecting to be served the same day, as queues can be long. Private businesses, or anyone providing a service, frequently operate a straight 9am-to-5/6pm schedule. If someone is actually selling something, then they are more likely to follow a split shift as detailed below.

Shopping hours during the hottest months are theoretically Monday, Wednesday and Saturday from approximately 9am to 2.30pm, and Tuesday, Thursday and Friday from 8.30am to 2pm and 6 to 9pm. During the cooler months the morning schedule shifts slightly forward, the evening session a half or even a full hour back. In Athens since the mid-1990s many enterprises have taken to keeping continuous hours (*synéhies óres*) during the winter, but this is by no means universally observed, even with pressure being brought to bear by the EU. Thus, there are so many exceptions to these rules by virtue of holidays and professional idiosyncrasy that you can't count on getting anything done except from Monday to Friday, between 9.30am and 1pm. It's worth noting that **delis** and **butchers** are not allowed to sell fresh meat during summer afternoons (though some flout this rule); similarly **fishmongers** are only open in the morning until they sell out (usually by noon), as are **pharmacies**, which additionally are shut on Saturday (except for the duty pharmacist).

All of the above opening hours will be regularly thrown out of sync by the numerous public holidays and festivals – or the equally numerous strikes, which can be general or profession-specific. The most important holidays, when almost everything will be closed, are listed opposite.

Ancient sites and monasteries

All the major **ancient sites** are now fenced off and, like most **museums**, charge **admission fees** ranging from a token €1.50 to a whopping €6, with an average fee of around €2.40. At most of them reductions of 25 to thirty percent apply to senior citizens, and fifty percent to students with proper identification – students from the EU with proper ID will often get in free. In addition, entrance to all state-run sites and museums is **free** to all EU nationals on Sundays and public holidays from November to March – non-EU nationals are unlikely to be detected as such unless they go out of their way to advertise the fact.

Opening hours vary from site to site. As far as possible, individual times are quoted in the text, but bear in mind that these change with exasperating frequency, and at smaller sites may be subject to the whim of a local *fýlakas* or site guard. Unless specified, the times quoted are generally summer hours, in effect from around late May to the end of September. Reckon on similar days but later opening and earlier closing in winter. Note also that the **last admission ticket** is typically sold fifteen to twenty minutes before the cited closing time.

Along with your ticket most sites and museums will provide a little colour **folding pamphlet** prepared by the *Tamío Arheoloyikón Porón* (Archeological Receipts Fund); they usually include an accurate if potted history and site or gallery plan, and we've found them to be uniformly excellent,

Public holidays

January 1
January 6
March 25
First Monday of Lent (variable Feb/March;
see below)
Easter weekend (variable April/May; see
below)
May 1
Pentecost or Whit Monday (fifty days after
Easter; see below)
August 15
October 28
December 25 and 26

Variable religious feasts
Lenten Monday
2002   March 18
2003   March 10
Easter Sunday
2002   May 5
2003   April 27
Whit Monday
2002   June 24
2003   June 16

in stark contrast to the often miserable labelling of the sites or galleries themselves. Serious students will therefore want to invest in **site guides** or **museum catalogues**, which have often been expertly compiled by the excavating archeologists or curators.

Smaller sites generally close for a long lunch and **siesta** (even where they're not supposed to), as do **monasteries**. The latter are generally open from 9am to 1pm and 5 to 8pm (3.30 to 6.30pm in winter) for limited visits. Most monasteries impose a fairly strict **dress code** for visitors: no shorts on either sex, with women expected to cover their arms and wear skirts; the necessary wraps are sometimes provided on the spot.

It's free to take **photos** of open-air sites, though museum photography and the use of videos or tripods anywhere requires an extra fee and written permit. This usually has to be arranged in writing from the nearest Department of Antiquities (*Eforía Arheotíton*). It's also worth knowing that Classical studies students can get a free annual pass to all Greek museums and sites by presenting themselves at the office on the rear corner (Tossítsa/Bouboulínas) of the National Archeological Museum in Athens – take documentation, two passport-sized photographs and be prepared to say you're a teacher.

Festivals and cultural events

Many of the big Greek popular festivals have a religious basis, so they're observed in accordance with the Orthodox calendar. Give or take a few saints, this is similar to the regular Catholic liturgical year, except for Easter, which can fall as many as five (but usually one or two) weeks to either side of the Western festival – in 2001 the two coincided (a very rare event). Other festivals are cultural in nature, with the highlight for most people being to catch a performance of Classical drama in one of the country's ancient theatres. There's also a full programme of cinema and modern theatre, at its best in Athens, but with something on offer in even the smallest town at some point during the year.

Easter

Easter is by far the most important festival of the Greek year – infinitely more so than Christmas – and taken much more seriously than it is anywhere in western Europe, aside from Spain. From Wednesday of Holy Week until the following Monday, the state radio and TV networks are given over solely to religious programmes.

The **festival** is an excellent time to be in Greece, both for its beautiful religious ceremonies and for the days of feasting and celebration that follow. The mountainous island of **Ídhra** with its alleged 360 churches and monasteries is the prime Easter resort, but unless you plan well in advance you have no hope of finding accommodation at that time. Other famous Easter celebrations are held at Corfu, Pyrgí on Híos, Ólymbos on Kárpathos and St John's monastery on Pátmos.

The first great public ceremony takes place on **Good Friday** evening as the Descent from the Cross is lamented in church. At dusk the *Epitáfios*, Christ's funeral bier, lavishly decorated by the women of the parish (in large villages there will be more than one, from each church), leaves the sanctuary and is paraded solemnly through the streets. In many places, Crete especially, this is accompanied by the burning of effigies of Judas Iscariot.

Late **Saturday** evening sees the climax in a majestic *Anástasis* Mass to celebrate Christ's triumphant return. At the stroke of midnight all the lights in every crowded church are extinguished, and the congregation plunged into the darkness which envelops Christ as He passes through the underworld. Then there's a faint glimmer of light behind the altar screen before the priest appears, holding aloft a lighted taper and chanting "*Avtó to Fós . . .* " (This is the Light of the World). Stepping down to the level of the parishioners, he touches his flame to the unlit candles of the nearest worshippers, intoning "*Dévteh, léveteh Fós*" (Come, take the Light). Those at the front of the congregation and on the aisles do the same for their neighbours until the entire church – and the outer courtyard, standing room only for latecomers – is ablaze with burning candles and the miracle reaffirmed.

Even the most committed agnostic is likely to find this moving. The traditional greeting, as fireworks explode all around you in the street, is "*Khristós Anésti*" (Christ is risen), to which the response is "*Alithós Anésti*" (Truly He is risen). In the week up to Easter Sunday you should wish people "*Kaló Páskha*" (Happy Easter); on or after the day, you say "*Khrónia Pollá*" (Many happy returns).

Worshippers then take the burning **candles** home through the streets; they are said to bring good fortune to the house if they arrive still burning. On reaching the front door it is common practice to make the sign of the cross on the lintel with the flame, leaving a black smudge visible for the rest of the year. The forty-day **Lenten fast** – still observed by the devout and in rural areas – is traditionally broken early on Sunday morning with a meal of *mayerítsa*, a soup made from lamb tripe, rice, dill and lemon. The rest of the lamb will be roasted on a spit for Sunday lunch, and festivities often take place through the rest of the day.

The Greek equivalent of **Easter eggs** are hard-boiled eggs (painted red on Holy Thursday), which are baked into twisted, sweet bread-loaves (*tsouréki*) or distributed on Easter Sunday. People rap their eggs against their friends' eggs, and the owner of the last uncracked egg is considered lucky.

The festival calendar

Most of the other Greek festivals are celebrations of one or other of a multitude of **saints**; the most important are detailed below. A village or church bearing the saint's name is a fair guarantee of some sort of observance – sometimes right across the town or island, otherwise quiet, local and consisting of little more than a special liturgy and banners adorning the chapel in question. Saints' days are also celebrated as **name days**; if you learn that it's an acquaintance's name day, you wish them "*Khrónia Pollá*" ("Many years", as in "Many happy returns"). Also listed are a few more secular holidays, most enjoyable of which are the pre-Lenten carnivals.

In addition to the specific dates mentioned, there are literally scores of **local festivals**, or *paniyíria*, celebrating the patron saint of the main village church. With hundreds of possible name-saints' days (calendars list two or three, often obscure, for each day) you're unlikely to travel around Greece for long without stumbling on something.

It is important to remember the concept of the *paramoní*, or **eve of the festival**. Most of the events listed below are celebrated on the night before, so if you show up on the morning of the date given you will very probably have missed any music, dancing or drinking.

January 1
New Year's Day (*Protokhroniá*) in Greece is the feast day of Áyios Vassílios (Saint Basil), and is celebrated with church services and the baking of

a special loaf, the *vassilópitta*, in which a coin is baked which brings its finder good luck throughout the year. The traditional New Year greeting is "*Kalí Khroniá*".

January 6

Epiphany (*Ayía Theofánia*, or *Fóta* for short), when the *kalikántzari* (hobgoblins) who run riot on earth during the twelve days of Christmas are rebanished to the netherworld by various rites of the Church. The most important of these is the blessing of baptismal fonts and all outdoor bodies of water. At lakeside, seaside or riverside locations, the priest traditionally casts a crucifix into the deep, with local youths competing for the privilege of recovering it.

January 8

The Yinekokratía of certain villages in Thrace is a festival where Saint Domenica (Dhomníka in Greek), patroness of midwives, is celebrated by men and women reversing roles for the day: the women hold forth in the kafenía while the men do the domestic chores.

Pre-Lenten carnivals

These – known in Greek as *Apokriátika* – span three weeks, climaxing during the seventh weekend before Easter. *Katharí Dheftéra* (Lenten Monday) of the first carnival week is always seven weeks before Easter Sunday. Pátra Carnival, with a chariot parade and costume parties, is one of the largest and most outrageous in the Mediterranean; on the last Sunday before Lent there's a grand parade, with the city's large gay population in conspicuous participation. Interesting, too, are the *boúles* or masked revels which take place around Macedonia (particularly at Náoussa), Thrace (Xánthi) and the outrageous Goat Dance on Skýros in the Sporades. The Ionian islands, especially Kefalloniá, are also good for carnival, while Athenians "celebrate" by going around hitting each other on the head with plastic hammers. In Thíva, a mock shepherd wedding occurs, while most places celebrate with colourful pageants reflecting local traditions.

March 25

Independence Day and the feast of the Annunciation (*Evangelismós* in Greek) is both a religious and a national holiday, with, on the one hand, military parades and dancing to celebrate the beginning of the revolt against Turkish rule in 1821, and on the other church services to honour the news given to Mary that she was to become the Mother of Christ. There are major festivities on Tínos, Ídhra (Hydra) and any locality with a

monastery or church named Evangelístria or Evangelismós.

April 23

The feast of Áyios Yeóryios (Saint George), the patron of shepherds, is a big rural celebration, with much feasting and dancing at associated shrines and towns. Good venues include Aráhova, near Delphi, and the island of Skýros, of which George is patron saint. If April 23 falls before Easter, ie during Lent, the festivities are postponed until the Monday after Easter.

May 1

May Day (*Protomayiá*) is the great urban holiday when townspeople traditionally make for the countryside to picnic, returning with bunches of wild flowers. Wreaths are hung on their doorways or balconies until they are burnt in bonfires on Saint John's Eve (June 23). There are also large demonstrations by the Left, claiming the *Ergatikí Protomayiá* (Working-Class First of May) as their own.

May 21

The feast of Áyios Konstandínos (Saint Constantine) and his mother, Ayía Eléni (Saint Helen), the first pro-Orthodox Byzantine rulers. There are firewalking ceremonies in certain Macedonian villages; elsewhere celebrated rather more conventionally as the name day for two of the more popular Christian names in Greece.

May/June

The Monday of Áyio Pnévma (the Holy Spirit, Whit Monday in UK) marks the descent of same to the assembled disciples, fifty days after Easter. Usually a modest liturgy is celebrated at rural chapels of the Holy Spirit, gaily decked out with pennants.

June 29–30

The joint feast of Áyios Pétros and Áyios Pávlos (Saints Peter and Paul), two of the more widely celebrated name days, is on the 29th. Celebrations often run together with that for the Gathering of (all) the Holy Apostles (Áyii Apóstoli), on the 30th.

July 17

The feast of Ayía Marína: a big event in rural areas, as she's an important protector of crops. The eponymous port town on Léros will be en fête, as will Ayía Marína village on Kássos, and countless small mainland villages. Between mid-July and mid-September there are religious festivals every few days, especially in the rural areas, and what with these, the summer heat and a mass exodus from the big cities, ordinary business slows or even halts.

July 20
The feast of Profítis Ilías (the Prophet Elijah) is widely celebrated at the countless hill- or mountaintop shrines of Profítis Ilías. The most famous is on Mount Taïyettos, near Spárti, with an overnight vigil.

July 26
Ayía Paraskeví is celebrated in parishes or villages bearing that name, especially in Epirus.

August 6
Metamórfosis toú Sotíros (Transfiguration of the Saviour) provides another excuse for celebrations, particularly at Khristós Ráhon village on Ikaría, and at Plátanos on Léros. On Hálki the date is marked by messy food fights with flour, eggs and squid ink (!), so beware.

August 15
Apokímisis tís Panayías (Assumption or Dormition of the Blessed Virgin Mary). This is the day when people traditionally return to their home village, and in most places there will be no accommodation available on any terms. Even some Greeks will resort to sleeping in the streets. There is a great pilgrimage to Tínos, and major festivities at Páros, at Ayiássos on Lésvos, on Lipsí and at Ólymbos on Kárpathos.

August 29
Apokefálisis toú Prodhrómou (Beheading of John the Baptist). Popular pilgrimages and celebrations at Vrykoúnda on Kárpathos.

September 8
Yénnisis tís Panayías (Birth of the Virgin Mary) sees special services in churches dedicated to the event, and a double cause for rejoicing on Spétses where they also celebrate the anniversary of the battle of the straits of Spétses, which took place on September 8, 1822. A re-enactment of the battle takes place in the harbour, followed by fireworks and feasting well into the night. Elsewhere, a lively festival at Vourliótes, Sámos, and a pilgrimage of childless women to the monastery at Tsambíka, Rhodes.

September 14
A last major summer festival, the Ípsosis toú Stavroú (Exaltation of the Cross), keenly observed on Hálki.

September 24
The feast of Áyios Ioánnis Theológos (Saint John the Divine), observed on Níssyros and Pátmos.

October 26
The feast of Áyios Dhimítrios (Saint Demetrius), another popular name day, particularly celebrated in Thessaloníki, of which he is the patron saint. In rural areas the new wine is traditionally broached on this day, a good excuse for general inebriation.

October 28
Óhi Day, the year's major patriotic shindig – a national holiday with parades, folk-dancing and speeches to commemorate Metaxas's apocryphal one-word reply to Mussolini's 1940 ultimatum: "*Ohi!*" (No!).

November 8
Another popular name day, the feast of the Archangels Michael and Gabriel (Mihaïl and Gavríil, or *tón Taxiárhon*), marked by rites at the numerous churches named after them, particularly at the rural monastery of Taxiárhis on Sými, and the big monastery of Mandamádhos, Lésvos.

December 6
The feast of Áyios Nikólaos (Saint Nicholas), the patron of seafarers, who has many chapels dedicated to him.

December 25
A much less festive occasion than Greek Easter, Christmas (*Khristoúyenna*) is still an important religious feast celebrating the birth of Christ, and in recent years it has started to take on more of the trappings of the western Christmas, with decorations, Christmas trees and gifts. December 26 is not Boxing Day as in England but the Sýnaxis tis Panayías, or Gathering of the Virgin's Entourage.

December 31
New Year's Eve (*Paramoní Protokhroniá*), when, as on the other twelve days of Christmas, a few children still go door-to-door singing the traditional *kálanda* (carols), receiving money in return. Adults tend to sit around playing cards, often for money. The *vassilópitta* is cut at midnight (see January 1).

Cultural festivals

As well as religious festivals, Greece has a full range of **cultural festivals** – highlights of which include Classical drama in ancient theatres at Athens, Epidaurus, Dodona and Dion. A leaflet entitled *Greek Festivals*, available from GNTO offices abroad, includes details of smaller, **local festivals** of music, drama and dance, which take place on a more sporadic basis.

Major festivals

Athens: the **Hellenic Festival** (June–Sept) encompasses a wide range of performances including modern and ancient theatre, ballet, opera, jazz and classical music, held mostly at the open-air Herodes Atticus Odeion. The Athens International Jazz and Blues Festival (June) puts on big-name acts at the modern open-air theatre on Lykavitós Hill. Details and tickets for events can be obtained from the Athens Festival box office (Stadhíou 4, ☎010/32 21 459), or at Herodes Atticus itself on the day from 6 until 9pm, when most performances start. It's worth calling in very soon after you arrive in Greece, since the more prestigious events often sell out.

Epidaurus: the **Epidaurus Festival** (July–Aug) hosts strictly open-air performances of Classical drama in the ancient theatre.

Pátra: the **International Festival** (July–Sept) sees ancient drama, theatre and classical music up in the castle, as well as in the ancient odeion.

Thessaloníki: hosts the **Dhimitría Cultural Festival** (Oct) and a film festival (Nov) as well as Philoxenia, a large international trade and tourism exhibition (Nov).

Minor festivals

Itháki Music Festival (July)
Ippokrateia Festival, Kós (July–Aug)
Kassándhra Festival, Síviri and Áfytos (July–Aug)
Manolis Kalomiris Festival, Sámos (July–Aug)
Réthymnon Renaissance Festival (July–Aug)
Sými Festival (July–Sept)
Philippi/Thássos Festival, mostly at Kavála castle (early July to early Sept)
Sáni Festival, Kassándhra, Halkidhikí (early July to early Sept)
Ólympos Festival, Platamónas castle/ancient Dion (mid-July to early Sept)
Lefkádha Arts Jamboree (Aug)
Makrinítsa/Vólos Festival (Aug)
Ioánnina Folk Festival (mid-July to mid-Aug)
Iráklion Festival (early Aug)
Thíra Music Festival (Aug–Sept)
Rhodes Festival (Aug–Oct)

Cinema and theatre

Greek **cinemas** show a large number of American and British movies, always in the original soundtrack with Greek subtitles, though fly-posters tend to be Greek-only. **Indoor** screenings are highly affordable, currently €5–7 depending on location and plushness of facilities; they shut from mid-May to late September unless they have air conditioning or a roll-back roof. Accordingly in summer vast numbers of outdoor cinemas operate; an outdoor movie (marginally cheaper) is worth catching at least once for the experience alone, though it's best to opt for the early screening (about 9pm) since the sound on the 11pm show gets turned down or even off to avoid complaints of noise from adjacent residences.

Theatre gets suspended during the summer months but from late September to May there's a lot of activity; Athens alone has scores of theatres, with playbills ranging from the classics to satirical revues (all in Greek).

Sports and outdoor pursuits

The Greek seashore offers endless scope for watersports, with windsurfing-boards for rent in most resorts and, less reliably, waterskiing and parasailing facilities. On land, the greatest attraction lies in hiking, through what is one of Europe's more impressive mountain terrains. Winter also sees possibilities for skiing at one of a dozen underrated centres.

In terms of spectating, the twin Greek obsessions are **football** (soccer) and **basketball**, with **volleyball** a close third in popularity.

Watersports

The years since the mid-1980s have seen a massive growth in the popularity of **windsurfing** in Greece. The country's bays and coves are ideal for beginners, and boards can be rented in literally hundreds of resorts. Particularly good areas, with established schools, include Vassilikí on Lefkádha island, Kéfalos on Kós, Zákynthos, western Náxos, Kokkári on Sámos, several spots on Lésvos, Corfu's west coast, numerous locales on Crete (especially Paleohóra), and Methóni in the Peloponnese. You can almost always pay for an initial period of instruction, if you've not tried the sport previously. Board rental rates are very reasonable – about €10 an hour.

Waterskiing is available at a number of the larger resorts, and a fair few of the smaller ones too. By the crippling rental standards of the ritzier parts of the Mediterranean it is a bargain, with twenty-minutes' instruction often available for around €13–16. At many resorts, parasailing (*parapént* in Greek) is also possible; rates start at €18 a go.

A combination of steady winds, appealing seascapes and numerous natural harbours have long made Greece a tremendous place for **sailing**. Holiday companies offer all sorts of packaged and tailor-made cruises (see p.16 in "Getting There"). In Greece, small boats and motorized dinghies are rented out by the day at many resorts. Spring and autumn are the most pleasant and least expensive seasons; *meltémi* winds make for pretty nauseous sailing between late June

and early September, and summer rates for the same craft can be three times as high as shoulder-season prices. For more details, pick up the informative though now somewhat dated brochure *Sailing the Greek Sea* from GNTO offices, or contact the Hellenic Yachting Federation, Aktí Navárhou Koundourióti 7, 185 34 Pireás (☎010/41 37 351, ☎41 31 119).

Because of the potential for pilfering submerged antiquities, **scuba-diving** is severely restricted, its legal practice confined to certain coasts around Attica, Kálymnos, Kalamáta, Préveza, Rhodes, Skiáthos, Corfu, Zákynthos and Mýkonos. For more information and an update on new, approved sites, contact the Union of Greek Diving Centres (☎010/92 29 532 or 41 18 909), or request the sporadically available information sheet *Regulations Concerning Underwater Activities* from the nearest branch of the GNTO/EOT.

Greece also has lots of white water, especially in the Peloponnese, central mainland and Epirus, so if you're into **rafting** or **kayaking** there is much potential. Any worthwhile stretch of river will have at least one outfitter who's set up shop on the banks – keep an eye peeled locally.

Skiing

Skiing is a comparative newcomer to Greece; the first centre, on Mount Parnassós, began life in the 1950s as an R&R facility for the local bauxite miners. Especially with global warming, snow conditions have become unpredictable at the southernmost resorts, and runs remain generally short. However, there are now more than a dozen ski centres scattered about the mountains, and what they may lack in professionalism is often made up for by an easy-going and unpretentious après-ski scene. Costs are an attraction, too – much lower than in northern Europe, at around €18 a day for rental of skis and boots, plus €11.80–20.60 a day (weekdays/weekends) for a lift pass. The season generally lasts from the beginning of January to the beginning of April, with a few extra weeks possible at either end, depending on snow conditions. No foreign package operators currently feature Greece among their offerings – it's very much a local, weekender scene, with weekdays on the slopes comparatively deserted.

The most developed of the resorts is Kelariá-Fterólakkas on **Parnassós**, the legendary mountain near Delphi, offering a cable car and thirteen other lifts (six chairs), serving sixteen mostly intermediate runs. The main problem here is that the lifts are often closed owing to high winds, and this far south seasons have been very short of late. It's easily accessible from Athens; throughout the season Athenian tour operators run buses up to the resort, returning the same day. The leading operator is Klaoudhatos, a big department store on Dhimarhíou street, near Platía Omónias. In winter they devote a floor to skiing, including ski rental (though this is simpler at Parnassós itself).

Other major ski centres include **Vórras** (Mount Kaïmaktsalán), near Édhessa (2 lifts, 7 runs); **Veloúhi** (Mount Tymfristós), near Karpeníssi in central Greece (6 lifts, 10 runs); **Helmós**, near Kalávryta on the Peloponnese (7 lifts, 12 runs); and **Vérmion** (8 lifts, 21 runs), near Náoussa in Macedonia. Minor areas, at lower altitudes and thus with even shorter seasons, and where the skiing may be secondary to other local attractions, include **Pisodhéri** near Flórina, also in Macedonia (3 lifts, 4 runs); **Métsovo** in Epirus (4 lifts, 7 runs; and **Agriólefkes** on Mount Pílion (4 lifts, 4 runs).

Further details are available from the EOT, which publishes a leaflet entitled *Ski Centres and Mountaineering Shelters*.

Walking

Young urban Greeks have only recently become used to the notion that anyone should want to **walk** for pleasure, yet if you have the time and stamina it is probably the single best way to see the remoter backcountry. This guide includes descriptions of a number of the more accessible mountain hikes, as well as suggestions for more casual walking on the mainland and islands.

In addition, you may want to acquire one or more of the countrywide or regional hiking guidebooks; see p.1091 in *Contexts*. See also p.36 for details of hiking maps available, and pp.16, 23 and 25 for details of companies offering walking holidays in the mountains.

Football and basketball

Football (soccer) is far and away the most popular sport in Greece – both in terms of participating and watching. The most important (and most heavily sponsored) teams are Panathanaïkós and AEK of Athens, Olympiakós of Pireás and PAOK of Thessaloníki. Other major teams in the provinces include Lárissa and the Cretan OFÍ. If you're interested, matches (usually played on Wed nights and Sun afternoons) are easy enough to catch from September to May. In mid-autumn you might even see one of the Greek teams playing European competition. The Greek national team qualified for the 1994 World Cup in some style, and then proceeded to lose all their three games heavily and returned from the US without scoring a goal.

The nation's **basketball** team is one of the continent's strongest and won the European Championship in 1987 – cheered all the way with enormous enthusiasm. At private-club level, many of the football teams maintain basketball squads – Panathanaïkós and Olympiakós were European champions in 1996 and 1997 respectively.

Finding work

Since Greece's full accession to the European Union in early 1993, a citizen of any EU state has (in theory) the right to work in Greece. In practice, however, there are a number of bureaucratic hurdles to overcome. Formerly, the most common job for foreigners was teaching English in the numerous private cramming academies (*frondistíria*), but lately severe restrictions have been put on the availability of such positions for non-Greeks, and you'll probably have more luck finding something in the commercial or leisure-oriented trade. Similarly, that other long-standing fallback of long-haul backpackers, picking fruit or greenhouse vegetables, is now the exclusive province of Albanian males.

Short-term work

EU membership notwithstanding, short-term work in Greece is always on an unofficial basis and for this reason it will generally be where you can't be seen by the police or you're badly paid – or, more often, both. The influx, since 1990, of between 800,000 and 1.1 million (estimates vary) Albanians, Ukrainians, Bulgarians, Pakistanis, Moldavians, Russians, Somalis, Filipinos and others has resulted in a surplus of unskilled labour and severely depressed wages. **Youth hostels** are still a good source of information on temporary work – indeed a few may even offer you a job themselves, if you turn up at the right time.

Tourism-related work

Most women working casually in Greece find jobs in **bars** or **restaurants** around the main resorts. Men, unless they are "trained" chefs, will be edged out by Albanians even when it comes to washing up.

If you're waiting or serving, most of your wages will probably have to come from tips but you may well be able to get a deal that includes free food and lodging; evening-only hours can be a good shift, leaving you a lot of free time. The main drawback may be the machismo and/or chauvinist attitudes of your employer. (Ads in the local press for "girl bar staff" are certainly best ignored; see "Sexual Harassment" on p.79)

Corfu, with its big British slant, is an obvious choice for bar work; Rhodes, Kós, Crete, Skiáthos, Páros, Íos and Thíra are also promising. Start looking, if you can, around April or May; you'll get better rates at this time if you're taken on for a season.

On a similar, unofficial level you might be able to get a sales job in **tourist shops** on Corfu, Ídhra, Rhodes or Crete, or (if you've the expertise) helping out at one of the **windsurfing** schools that have sprung up all around the coast. **Yacht marinas** can also prove good hunting-grounds though less for the romantic business of crewing, than scrubbing down and repainting. Again, the best possibilities are likely to be on Rhodes, Corfu or Kálymnos; the Zéa port at Pireás is actually the biggest marina, but non-Greek owners don't tend to rest up there for long.

Perhaps the best type of tourism-related work, however, is that of courier/greeter/ group co-ordinator for a **package holiday company**. All you need is EU nationality and language proficiency compatible with the clientele, though knowledge of Greek is a big plus. English-only speakers are pretty well restricted to places with a big British package trade, namely Crete, Rhodes, Skiáthos and the Ionian islands.

Many such staff are recruited through ads in newspapers issued outside Greece, but it's by no means unheard of to be hired on the spot in April or May. A big plus, however you're taken on, is that you're usually guaranteed about six months of steady work, often with use of a car thrown in, and that if things work out you may be re-employed the following season with contract and foreign-currency wages from the home company, not from the local affiliate.

Selling and busking

You may do better by working for yourself. Travellers report rich pickings during the tourist season from **selling jewellery** on island beaches, or on boats – craftware from Asia is especially popular with Greeks. Once you've managed to get the stuff past the customs officials (who will be sceptical, for instance, that all those trinkets are presents for friends), there rarely seem to be problems with the local police, though it probably pays to be discreet.

Busking can also be quite lucrative. Playing on the Athens metro or the city's streets, it's possible to make up to €9 in a two-hour session, though in the new metro extension the practice is likely to be strictly banned.

Documentation for long-term employment

If you plan to work professionally for someone else, you first visit the nearest Department of Employment and collect two forms: one an **employment application** which you fill in, the other for the formal offer of work by your prospective employer. Once these are vetted, and revenue stamps (*hartósima*, purchased at kiosks) applied, you take them to the Aliens' Bureau (*Ypiresía Allodhapón*) or, in its absence, the central police station, to support your application for a **residence permit** (*ádhia paramonís*). For this, you will also need to bring your passport, six photographs, more *hartósima* and a stable address (not a hotel). Permits are given for terms of one year (green triptych booklets), or five years (white booklets) if they've become well acquainted with you.

You should allow four to six weeks for all the formalities to be completed; the bottleneck is usually the required **health examination** at the nearest public hospital. There you will be chest-X-rayed for signs of TB, blood-tested for hepatitis B and C, HIV and a couple of other nasties, and have a (farcical) evaluation by a neurologist or psychiatrist for signs of mental disorder; this is all done at a reasonable cost. Once you've assembled all the results, you'll have to trot these over yourself to the local public health office, where a periodic (once weekly at best) meeting of its administrative council will vet and endorse these, and issue you with a certificate of approval. Finally you take this to the local police or Aliens' Bureau, which should have your permit ready, free of charge other than for a few more *hartósima*, within three working days.

As a **self-employed professional**, you must satisfy the requirements of the Greek state with equivalent qualifications to native Greeks plying the same trade. You should also befriend a good accountant, who will advise you on which of the several varieties of incorporation are to your advantage; trading under a fictitious name is vastly more expensive tax-wise than doing business as a private person. You will need to sign on with **TEBE**, the Greek National Insurance scheme for self-employed people (analogous to Class 4 National Insurance contributions in the UK). If you are continuing to contribute to a social insurance scheme in a country which has reciprocal agreements with Greece (all EU states do), this must be proved in writing – a tedious and protracted process.

Once you're square with TEBE, visit the tax office or *eforía* to be issued a **tax number** (abbreviated "ah-fi-mi" in Greek, similar to a UK Schedule D number) which must be cited in all transactions. To be issued one of these, you need to bring a birth certificate which shows the full unmarried names of *both* your parents. You will be required to prepare receipt and invoice books with your tax number professionally printed on them, or have a rubber stamp made up for applying that number to every sheet. The tax office will also determine which rate of **VAT** (the "fi-pi-ah") you should pay for each kind of transaction; VAT returns must be filed every two months, which is where a friendly accountant comes in handy again.

The self-employed tend to be issued five-year residence permits. **EU nationals** who do not intend to work in Greece but still need a residence permit (such as second-property-owners needing to set up a bank account) will still get a "white" pass fairly easily, but must present evidence of financial solvency; personalized pink exchange receipts, travellers' cheques or credit cards are all considered valid proofs.

At present, undocumented **non-EU nationals** who wish to work in Greece do so surreptitiously, with the ever-present risk of denunciation to the police and instant deportation. Having been forced to accept large numbers of EU citizens looking for jobs in a climate of rising unemployment, Greek immigration authorities are cracking down hard on any suitable targets, be they Albanian, African, Swiss or North American. That old foreigners' standby, teaching English, is now available only to TEFL certificate-holders – preferably

Greeks, non-EU nationals of Greek descent and EU nationals in that order. If you are a non-EU foreign national of Greek descent you are termed *omólogos* (returned Greek diaspora member) and in fact have tremendous employment, taxa-tion and residence rights and privileges – you can, for example, open your very own *frondistírio* without any qualifications, something starkly evident in the often abysmal quality of language instruction in Greece.

Trouble, crime and sexual harassment

As in the past, Greece remains one of Europe's safest countries, with a low crime rate and a deserved reputation for honesty. If you leave a bag or wallet at a café, you'll most likely find it scrupulously looked after, pending your return. Similarly, Greeks are relatively relaxed about leaving possessions unlocked or unattended on the beach, in rooms or on campsites. The biggest hazards on beaches, oddly, are free-ranging goats – who will eat just about anything left accessible – and the wake of passing cruise ships or ferries, which can wash all your possessions out to sea with little or no warning.

In recent years, however, there has been a large increase in **theft** and **crimes against persons** (blamed largely on Albanian and Romanian refugees) in towns, remote vil-lages and resorts, so it's wise to lock things up and treat Greece like any other European destination. Following are also a few pointers on offences that might get you into trouble locally, and some advice on sexual harass-ment – still a lingering fact of life given the classically Mediterranean machismo of Greek culture.

Specific offences

The most common causes of a brush with authority are nude bathing or sunbathing, and camping outside an authorized site.

Nude bathing is legal on only a very few beaches (most famously on Mýkonos), and is deeply offensive to the more traditional Greeks – exercise considerable sensitivity to local feeling and the kind of place you're in. It is, for example, very bad etiquette to swim or sunbathe nude within sight of a church, of which there are many along the Greek coast. Generally, if a beach has become fairly well established as naturist, or is well secluded, it's highly unlikely that the police are going to come charging in. Where they do get both-ered is if they feel a place is turning into a "hippie beach" or nudity is getting too overt on mainstream tourist stretches. Most of the time, the only action will be a warning, but you can officially be arrested straight off – facing up to three days in jail and a stiff fine.

Topless (sun)bathing for women is tech-nically legal nationwide, but specific locales often opt out of the "liberation" by posting signs, which should be heeded.

Very similar guidelines apply to **camping rough**, which has been theoretically illegal nationwide since 1977 (see "Accommodation", p.54). Even for this you're still unlikely to incur anything more than a warning to move on. The only real risk of arrest is if you are told to clear off and fail to do so. In either of the above cases, even if the police do take any action against you, it's more likely to be a brief spell in their cells than any official prosecution.

Incidentally, any sort of **disrespect** towards the Greek state or Orthodox Church in general, or Greek civil servants in particular, may be construed as offences in the most literal sense, so it's best to keep your comments on how things are working (or not) to yourself. Every year a few foreign louts find themselves in deep trouble over a drunken indiscretion. This is a society where verbal injuries count, with a consistent backlog of court cases dealing with the alleged public utterance of *malákas* (wanker).

In the non-verbal field, ripped or soiled clothes and untucked-in shirts are considered nearly as insulting. Don't expect a uniformly civil reception if dressed in **grunge attire**, since Greeks will interpret this in one of two possible ways, neither reflecting well on you. Poverty is an uncomfortably close memory for many, and they may consider that you're making light of hard times. More to the point, the cult of *la bella figura* is developed to near-Italian levels in Greece; if you clearly have so little self-respect as to appear slovenly and dishevelled in public, why should any Greek respect you?

Drug offences are treated as major crimes, particularly since there's a mushrooming local use and addiction problem. The maximum penalty for "causing the use of drugs by someone under 18", for example, is life imprisonment and an astronomical fine. Theory is by no means practice, but foreigners caught in possession of even small amounts of grass do get long jail sentences if there's evidence that they've been supplying the drug to others. Moreover, you could be inside for well over a year awaiting a trial date, with little or no chance of bail being granted.

In an **emergency**, dial ☏ 100 for the police; ☏ 171 for the tourist police in Athens, ☏ 01-171 outside of it; ☏ 166 for an ambulance; ☏ 191 to report a forest fire; and ☏ 199 for the urban fire brigade. These calls should all be toll-free from a cardphone.

If you get arrested for any offence, you have a right to contact your **consulate**, who will arrange a lawyer for your defence. Beyond this, there is little they can, or in most cases will, do. Details of full-ranking consulates in Athens and Thessaloníki appear in their respective "Listings" sections. There are honorary British consulates on Rhodes, Crete and Corfu as well.

Sexual harassment

Thousands of women travel independently in Greece without being **harassed** or feeling intimidated. Greek machismo, however, remains strong, if less upfront than in, for example, southern Italy. With the recent sea-change in local mores – specifically, a vast increase in the "availability" of young Greek women to young local men, up to and including living together before marriage – much of the impetus for trying one's luck with foreign girls has faded. Any hassle you do get is likely to be from a dwindling minority of professionally single Greek men, known as *kamákia* (fish harpoons), who migrate in summer to the beach bars and discos of the main resorts and towns, specifically in pursuit of "liberated, fun-loving" tourists.

Indigenous Greeks, who become increasingly protective of you as you become more of a fixture in any one place, treat these outsiders with contempt; their obvious stake-outs are waterfront cafés, beach bars and dance clubs. Words worth remembering as unambiguous responses include "*pápsteh*" (stop it), "*afístemeh*" (leave me alone) and "*fíyeteh*" (go away), the latter intensified if followed by "*dhrómo!*" (road, as in "Hit the road!").

Hitching is not advisable for lone women travellers, but **camping** is generally not a problem, though away from recognized sites it is often wise to attach yourself to a local family by making arrangements to use nearby private land. In the more remote mountains and islands you may feel more uncomfortable travelling alone. The intensely traditional Greeks may have trouble understanding why you are unaccompanied, and might not welcome your presence in their exclusively male kafenía – often the only place where you can get a drink. Travelling with a man, you're more likely to be treated as a *xéni*, a word meaning both (female) stranger and guest.

Lone men need to be aware of one long-established racket in the largest mainland towns and island ports. Near Sýndagma in Athens, in particular, you may be approached by dubious gents asking the time, or your origins, and then offering to take you for a drink in a nearby bar. This is invariably staffed with hostesses (who may also be on the game), whose main job is to convince you to treat them to drinks. At the end of the night you'll be landed with an outrageous bill, some of which goes towards the hostess's "commission"; physical threats are brought to bear on reluctant payers.

Consumer protection on holiday

In a tourist industry as developed as in Greece there are inevitably a number of cowboys and shady characters amongst the taxi-drivers, hoteliers and car-rental agencies in particular. **EKPIZO**, the **Greek Consumers' Association**, has established a "Legal Information and Assistance for Tourists" programme, to be run yearly from June to September. Their main branch is in Athens ☎010/33 04 444, with offices also in Vólos, Pátra, Crete and Kavála. EKPIZO issues a pamphlet about holiday-makers' rights, available in airports and tourist offices. They are prepared to pursue serious cases, by friendly persuasion or court action if necessary.

Travellers with disabilities

It is all too easy to wax lyrical over the attractions of Greece: the stepped, narrow alleys, the ease of travel by bus and ferry, the thrill of clambering around the great archeological sites. It is almost impossible, on the other hand, for the able-bodied travel writer to see these attractions as potential hazards for anyone who has difficulty in walking, is wheelchair-bound or suffers from some other disability.

However, don't be discouraged. It is possible to enjoy an inexpensive and trauma-free holiday in Greece if some time is devoted to gathering **information** before arrival. Much existing or readily available information is out of date – you should always try to double-check. A number of addresses of contact organizations are published below. The Greek National Tourist Office is a good first step as long as you have specific questions to put to them; they publish a useful questionnaire which you could send to hotels or owners of apartment/villa accommodation.

Contacts for travellers with disabilities

In the UK and Ireland

Access Travel , 6 The Hillock, Astley, Lancashire M29 7GW ☎01942/888844, ⓦwww.access-travel.co.uk. A tour operator that can arrange flights, transfer and accommodation. This is a small business, personally checking out places before recommendation. They can guarantee accommodation standards on Rhodes in particular. ATOL bonded, established seven years.
Disability Action Group , 2 Annadale Ave, Belfast BT7 3JH ☎028/9049 1011. Provides

information about access for disabled travellers abroad.
Holiday Care , 2nd floor, Imperial Building, Victoria Rd, Horley, Surrey RH6 7PZ ☎01293/774535, Minicom ☎01293/776943,
ⓦwww.holidaycare.org.uk. Provides free lists of accessible accommodation abroad – European, American and long-haul destinations – plus a list of accessible attractions in the UK. Information on financial help for holidays available.
Irish Wheelchair Association , Blackheath Drive, Clontarf, Dublin 3 ☎01/833 8241, ⓕ833 3873, ⓔiwa@iol.ie. Useful information provided on travelling abroad with a wheelchair.
Tripscope , Alexandra House, Albany Rd, Brentford, Middlesex TW8 ONE ☎0845/758 5641, ⓦwww.justmobility.co.uk/tripscope. This registered charity provides a national telephone information service offering free advice on UK and international transport for those with a mobility problem.

In the US and Canada

Access-Able ⓦwww.access-able.com. Online resource for travellers with disabilities.
Directions Unlimited , 123 Green Lane, Bedford Hills, NY 10507 ☎1-800/533-5343 or 914/241-1700. Tour operator specializing in custom tours for people with disabilities.

Mobility International USA, 451 Broadway, Eugene, OR 97401; Voice and TDD ☎541/343-1284, ⊛www.miusa.org. Information and referral services, access guides, tours and exchange programmes. Annual membership $35 (includes quarterly newsletter).

Society for the Advancement of Travelers with Handicaps (SATH), 347 5th Ave, New York, NY 10016 ☎212/447-7284, ⊛www.sath.org. A nonprofit educational organization that has actively represented travellers with disabilities since 1976.

Travel Information Service ☎215/456-9600. Telephone-only information and referral service.

Twin Peaks Press, Box 129, Vancouver, WA 98661 ☎360/694-2462 or 1-800/637-2256, ℮twinpeak@pacifier.com. Publisher of the *Directory of Travel Agencies for the Disabled* ($19.95), listing more than 370 agencies worldwide; *Travel for the Disabled* ($19.95); the *Directory of Accessible Van Rentals* ($12.95); and *Wheelchair Vagabond* ($19.95), loaded with personal tips.

Wheels Up! ☎1-888/389-4335, ⊛www.wheelsup.com. Provides discounted airfare, tour and cruise prices for disabled travellers, also publishes a free monthly newsletter and has a comprehensive website.

In Australia and New Zealand

ACROD (Australian Council for Rehabilitation of the Disabled), PO Box 60, Curtin, ACT 2605 ☎02/6282 4333; 24 Cabarita Rd, Cabarita, NSW 2137 ☎02/9743 2699. Provides lists of travel agencies and tour operators for people with disabilities.

Disabled Persons Assembly, 4/173–175 Victoria St, Wellington, New Zealand ☎04/801 9100. Resource centre with lists of travel agencies and tour operators for people with disabilities.

Planning a holiday

There are **organized tours** and **holidays** specifically for people with disabilities; many companies in Britain will advise on the suitability of holidays or villas advertised in their brochures. If you want to be more independent, it's perfectly possible, provided that you do not leave home with the vague hope that things will turn out all right, and that "people will help out" when you need assistance. This cannot be relied on. You must either be completely confident that you can manage alone, or travel with an able-bodied friend (or two).

It's important to become an authority on where you must be self-reliant and where you may expect help, especially regarding transport and accommodation. For example, while the new Athens airport has lifts between arrivals and the departures concourse, and the Athens metro also has lifts for wheelchairs in every station, you cannot assume that every express bus between the arrivals exit and the first metro stop will be of a "kneeling" design.

It is also vital to **be honest** – with travel agencies, insurance companies, companions and, above all, with yourself. Know your limits and make sure others know them. If you do not use a wheelchair all the time but your walking capabilities are limited, remember that you are likely to need to cover greater distances while travelling (often over tougher terrain and in hotter weather) than you are used to. If you use a wheelchair, it's advisable to have it serviced before you go, and carry a repair kit.

Read your **travel insurance** small print carefully to make sure that people with a pre-existing medical condition are not excluded. And use your travel agent to make your journey simpler: **airlines** or bus companies can cope better if they are expecting you, with a wheelchair provided at airports and staff primed to help. A **medical certificate** of your fitness to travel, provided by your doctor, is also extremely useful; some airlines or insurance companies may insist on it.

Make a **list** of all the facilities that will make your life easier while you are away. You may want a ground-floor room, or access to a large elevator; you may have special dietary requirements, or need level ground to enable you to reach shops, beaches, bars and places of interest. You should also keep track of all your other special needs, making sure, for example, that you have extra supplies of drugs – carried with you if you fly – and a prescription including the generic name in case of emergency. Carry spares of any kind of drug, clothing or equipment that might be hard to find in Greece; if there's an association representing people with your disability, contact them early in the planning process.

Senior travellers

Travellers over sixty are accorded every respect in Greece; you are, for example, rather less likely to be grumbled or shouted at by the famously irate Athens bus drivers or harbour officials. Seniors are entitled to discounts at state-run attractions of twenty-five to thirty percent; long-term bus passes in the major cities are similarly discounted; and, without making much effort to publicize the fact, Olympic Airways (and quite possibly its new private competitors) also offer discounts off full fares on domestic flights. Keep proof of age to hand for all these benefits.

Contacts for senior travellers

In the UK

Saga Holidays ☎01303/771111, ⓦwww.sagaholidays.com. The country's biggest and most established specialist in tours and holidays aimed at older people.

In the US

American Association of Retired Persons, 601 E St NW, Washington, DC 20049 ☎1-800/424-3410, membership hotline ☎1-800/515-2299 or 202/434-2277, ⓦwww.aarp.org. Can provide discounts on accommodation and vehicle rental. Membership open to US and Canadian residents aged 50 or over for an annual fee of US $10 or $27 for three years. Canadian residents

only have the annual option.
Elderhostel, 75 Federal St, Boston, MA 02110 ☎1-877/426-8056, ⓦwww.elderhostel.com. Runs an extensive worldwide network of educational and activity programmes, cruises and homestays for people over 60 (companions may be younger). Programmes generally last a week or more and costs are in line with those of commercial tours.
Saga Holidays, 222 Berkeley St, Boston, MA 02116 ☎1-877/265-6862, ⓦwww.sagaholidays.com. Specializes in worldwide group travel for seniors. Saga's Smithsonian Odyssey Tours, which include Greece, have a more educational slant.
Vantage Travel ☎1-800/322-6677, ⓦwww.vantagetravel.com. Specializes in worldwide group travel for seniors.

Gay travellers

The term "Greek love" may still evoke titters from those educated in British public schools of a classicizing persuasion, but in modern Greece overtly **gay behaviour** in public remains **taboo** for men in **rural areas**. There is, however, a sizeable **gay contingent** in Athens, Thessaloníki and Pátra, plus a fairly obvious scene at **certain resorts** like Ídhra, Rhodes or Mýkonos, still the most popular European gay resort after Ibiza in Spain. Skála Eressoú on Lésvos, the birthplace of Sappho, is (appropriately) an international mecca for **lesbians**. Homosexuality is legal over the age of 17, and (male) bisexual behaviour common but rarely admitted. Greek men are terrible flirts, but cruising them is a semiotic minefield and definitely at your own risk – references in gay guides to "known" male cruising grounds should be treated sceptically. "Out" gay Greeks are rare, and "out" local lesbians rarer still; foreign same-sex couples will be regarded in the provinces with some bemusement but accorded the standard courtesy as foreigners. The gay movement in Greece is represented by Akoe Amphi, PO Box 26022, 10022 Athens ☎010/77 19 221. See also Athens "Discos and Clubs", p.151.

Contacts for gay travellers

In the UK

W www.gaytravel.co.uk Online gay and lesbian travel agent, offering good deals on all types of holiday. Also lists gay- and lesbian-friendly hotels around the world.

Dream Waves, Redcot High St, Child Okeford, Blandford DT22 8ET ☎ 01258/861149, **E** Dreamwaves@aol.com. Specializes in exclusively gay holidays, including skiing trips and summer sun packages.

Madison Travel, 118 Western Rd, Hove, East Sussex NN3 1DB ☎ 01273/202532, **W** www.madisontravel.co.uk. Established travel agents specializing in packages to gay- and lesbian-friendly mainstream destinations, and also to gay/lesbian destinations.

Respect Holidays, 74 Haverstock Hill, London NW3 2BE ☎ 020/7485 8855, **W** www.respect-holidays.co.uk. Offers exclusively gay packages to all popular European resorts.

Also check out **adverts** in the weekly papers *Boyz* and *Pink Paper*, handed out free in gay venues.

In the US and Canada

Damron Company, PO Box 422458, San Francisco, CA 94142 ☎ 1-800/462-6654 or 415/255-0404, **W** www.damron.com. Publisher of the *Men's Travel Guide*, a pocket-sized yearbook full of listings of hotels, bars, clubs and resources for gay men; the *Women's Traveler*, which provides similar listings for lesbians; and *Damron Accommodations*, which provides detailed listings of over 1000 accommodations for gays and lesbians worldwide. All of these titles are offered at a discount on the website. No specific city guides – everything is incorporated in the yearbooks.

Ferrari Publications, PO Box 37887, Phoenix, AZ 85069 ☎ 1-800/962-2912 or 602/863-2408, **W** www.ferrariguides.com. Publishes *Ferrari Gay Travel A to Z*, a worldwide gay and lesbian guide; *Inn Places*, a worldwide accommodation guide; the guides *Men's Travel in Your Pocket* and *Women's Travel in Your Pocket*; and the quarterly *Ferrari Travel Report*.

International Gay/Lesbian Travel Association, 4331 N Federal Hwy, Suite 304, Ft Lauderdale, FL 33308 ☎ 1-800/448-8550, **W** www.iglta.org. Trade group that can provide a list of gay- and lesbian-owned or friendly travel agents, accommodation and other travel businesses.

In Australia and New Zealand

Gay and Lesbian Travel **W** www.galta.com.au. Directory and links for gay and lesbian travel in Australia and worldwide.

Gay Travel **W** www.gaytravel.com. The site for trip planning, bookings and general information about international travel.

Parkside Travel, 70 Glen Osmond Rd, Parkside, SA 5063 ☎ 08/8274 1222 or 1800/888 501, **E** hwtravel@senet.com.au. Gay travel agent associated with local branch of Hervey World Travel; all aspects of gay and lesbian travel worldwide.

Pinkstay **W** www.pinkstay.com. Everything from visa information to finding accommodation and work around the world.

Silke's Travel, 263 Oxford St, Darlinghurst, NSW 2010 ☎ 02/9380 6244 or 1800/807 860, **E** silba@magna.com.au. Long-established gay and lesbian specialist, with the emphasis on women's travel.

Tearaway Travel, 52 Porter St, Prahan, VIC 3181 ☎ 03/9510 6344, **E** tearaway@bigpond.com. Gay-specific business dealing with international and domestic travel.

Travelling with children

Children are worshipped and indulged in Greece, arguably to excess, and present few problems when travelling. As elsewhere in the Mediterranean, they are not segregated from adults at meal times and early on in life are inducted into the typical late-night routine. So you'll see plenty of kids at tavernas, expected to eat (and up to their capabilities, talk) like adults. Outside of certain all-inclusive resorts, however (see "Contacts" below) there are very few amusements specifically for kids – certainly nothing like Disney World Paris.

Most ferry-boat lines and airlines in Greece offer some sort of **discount** for children, ranging from fifty to hundred percent depending on their age; hotels and rooms won't charge extra for infants, and levy a modest surcharge for "third" beds which the child occupies by him/herself.

Baby foods and nappies/diapers are ubiquitous and reasonably priced; private rooms establishments and luxury hotels are more likely to offer some kind of **babysitting** service than the mid-range, C-class hotels.

Contacts for travellers with children

In the UK and Ireland

Club Med ☎ 0700/258 2633, ⓦ www.clubmed.com. Specializes in purpose-built holiday resorts, with kids' club, entertainment and sports facilities on site; has villages in Greece near Athens (two), and on Corfu, Évvia and Kós.

Mark Warner Holidays ☎ 020/7761 7000, ⓦ www.markwarner.co.uk. Holiday villages with children's entertainment and childcare laid on.

Simply Travel ☎ 020/8541 2280, ⓦ www.simply-travel.com. Upmarket tour company offering villas and hotels in the less touristy parts of Greece. May be able to provide qualified, English-speaking nannies to come to your villa and look after the children.

In the US

Travel With Your Children, 40 5th Ave, New York, NY 10011 ☎ 212/477 5524 or 1-888/822-4388. Publish a regular newsletter, *Family Travel Times,* ⓦ www.familytraveltimes.com, as well as a series of books on travel with children including *Great Adventure Vacations With Your Kids.*

Directory

ADDRESSES In Greece streets are cited in the genitive case, usually with no tag like "Street" or "Avenue"; the number always follows. Thus something described as 36 Venizelos Avenue in Roman-alphabet letterhead comes out at Venizélou 36, and it's this convention which we've adopted throughout the book. The practice is different with **platía** (square) and **leofóros** (avenue), which always appear before the name. Postcodes are five-digit, nationwide, and precede the municipality concerned, eg 24022 Kardhamýli, in the Peloponnese.

BARGAINING This isn't a regular feature of touristic life, though you'll find it possible with private rooms and certain hotels out of season. Similarly, you should be able to negotiate discounted rates for vehicle rental, especially for longer periods. Services such as shoe, watch and camera repair don't have iron-clad rates, so use common sense when assessing charges (advance written estimates are not routine practice).

DEPARTURE TAX This is levied on all international ferries – currently €4.50–6 per person and per car or motorbike, usually (but not always) included within the quoted price of the ticket. To non-EU states (eg Turkey, Croatia and Israel) it's €11.80–14.70 per person, sometimes arbitrarily levied twice (on entry and exit). There's also an airport departure tax of £6.50 equivalent (currently €10.50) for destinations less than 750 miles away, roughly double that if it's further, but this is always included in the price of the ticket – there's no collection at the airport itself. This tax, nicknamed the *spatósima* locally, was supposedly for funding construction of the new Athens airport at Spáta, but since this opened in March 2001, it hasn't been abolished . . .

ELECTRICITY Voltage is 220 volt AC throughout the country. Wall outlets – rarely abundant enough – take double round-pin plugs as in the rest of continental Europe. Three-to-two-pin adapters should be purchased beforehand in the UK, as they can be difficult to find locally; standard 5-, 6- or 7.5-amp models permit operation of a hair dryer or travel iron. If necessary, you can change the fuse to a higher rating back in the UK; beware, they're physically smaller than the 13-amp ones popped into all three-prong plugs, and you may have to go to a specialist electrical dealer for them. Unless they're dual voltage, North American appliances will require both a step-down transformer and a plug adapter (the latter easy to find in Greece).

FILMS Fuji and Kodak print films are reasonably priced and easy to have processed – you practically trip over "One Hour Foto" places in resorts. APS film is also widely sold and processed. Kodak and Fuji slide films can be purchased, again at UK prices or better, in larger centres, but often cannot be processed there – there are E6 labs only in the main cities and provincial capitals such as Athens, Thessaloníki, Iráklion, Ioánnina and Vólos (if there's a local university, there's usually a slide processor around too).

GREEK-LANGUAGE COURSES The longest established outlet is The Athens Centre, Arhimídhous 48, Méts, 11636 Athens ⊕010/70 12 268, ⊕70 18 603, ⊜athenscr@compulink.gr. One to try on Crete is Lexis, 48 Dhaskaloyiánni, 73100 Haniá ⊕ & ⊕ 08210/55 673, ⊜lexis -glacc@cha.forthnet.gr.

LAUNDRIES *Plindíria*, as they're known in Greek, are prominent in the main resort towns; sometimes an attended service wash is available for little or no extra charge over the basic cost of €5–5.50 per wash and dry. Self-catering villas or *dhomátia* will usually be furnished with a drying line and a selection of plastic wash-tubs (*skáfes*) or a bucket (*kouvás*). In hotels, laundering should be done in a more circumspect manner; management can freak out if you use bathroom wash-basins, Greek wall-mounting being what it is, or do more than a few socks and undies. It's best to use the flat pans of showers for both washing and hanging to dry; if you haven't come with a universal flat plug, wadded-up toilet paper can be quite effective in stopping the drain hole.

PERÍPTERA These are street-corner kiosks, or sometimes a hole-in-the-wall shopfront. They sell everything from pens to disposable razors, stationery to soap, sweets to condoms, cigarettes to plastic crucifixes, yogurts to milk-in-cartons – and are often open when nothing else is.

TIME As throughout the EU, Greek summer time begins at 2am on the last Sunday in March, when the clocks go forward one hour, and ends at 2am the last Sunday in October when they go back. Be alert to this, as the change is not well publicized, leading scores of visitors to miss planes and ferries every year. Greek time is thus always two hours ahead of Britain. For North America, the difference is seven hours for Eastern Standard Time, ten hours for Pacific Standard Time, with an extra hour plus or minus for those weeks in April and October when one place is on daylight saving and the other isn't. A recorded time message (in distinctly slow Greek, 24-hour convention) is available by dialling ⊕141.

TOILETS Public toilets are usually in parks or squares, often subterranean; otherwise try a bus station. Except in areas frequented by tourists, public toilets tend to be pretty filthy – it's best to use those in restaurants and bars. Remember that throughout Greece, you drop paper in the adjacent wastebins, *not* in the bowl.

USEFUL THINGS TO BRING A high-quality, porcelain-lined canteen or drinking-water bottle; a small alarm clock for early buses and ferries; a flashlight if you're camping out; sunscreen of high SPF (25 or above, tricky to find and/or expensive in Greece); pocket knife (Swiss Army type or similar), with tweezers, mini-screwdriver and other similar accessories (these are now widely sold in Greece at hunting/fishing shops); ear plugs for noisy ferries or hotels; and good-quality tea bags.

the mainland

guide

Athens and around

CHAPTER 1   # Highlights

* **Acropolis** One of the archetypal images of Western civilization. See p.118

* **National Archeological Museum** The finest collection of Greek antiquities anywhere in the world. See p.127

* **Tower of the Winds** A graceful octagonal structure, the best-preserved and easily the most intriguing of the Roman forum ruins. See p.122

* **Pláka** A mix of Byzantine, Neoclassical and Greek-island architecture, this is one of the city's most rewarding districts for daytime wandering. See p.118

* **The bazaar** Athens' raucous and colourful street market, extending from Monástiraki district up Eoloú to the nineteenth-century covered food hall. See p.124

* **Herodes Atticus theatre** A major venue for classical music concerts during the Hellenic summer music festival. See p.116

* **Kolonáki** Superbly sited on the slopes of Lykavitós Hill, this well-heeled district brims with fashionable shops and pavement cafés. See p.134

* **Poseidon Temple, Cape Sounion** This dramatically sited temple is a familiar landmark to boats at sea. See p.166

1

Athens and around

ATHENS is not a graceful city. It looks ungainly from just about every approach, its air pollution is dire, its postwar architecture is a disaster, and traffic still clogs the streets despite the recent expansion of the metro. For many of the four million-plus visitors who pass through each year, Athens can seem a dutiful stop. Their priorities usually include visits to the Acropolis and the National Archeological Museum and an evening or two dining in the tavernas of Pláka, one of the few surviving old quarters. Most tourists then get out fast, disillusioned with such sparse evidence of the past and so little apparent charm.

Such are the basic facts – yet somehow the city has the character to transcend them. An exhausting but always stimulating mix of metropolis and backwater, First and Third World, West and East, Greater Athens has seen its population soar from 700,000 to well over four million – over a third of the nation's people – since World War II. The pace of this transformation is reflected in the city's chaotic mix of urban and rural: chickens roost in yards with state-of-the-art cars parked nearby, while eastern-style bazaars vie for space with outlets for Armani and Benetton. And the city's hectic modernity is tempered with an air of intimacy and homeness; as any Greek will tell you, Athens is merely the largest village in the country.

Once you accept this, you'll find that the **ancient sites** and the **Acropolis** – supreme monument though it is – are only the most obvious of **Athens' attractions**. There are startling views to be had from the hills of **Lykavitós**

Accommodation price codes

Throughout the book we've categorized accommodation according to the following **price codes**, which denote the cheapest available double room in high season. All prices are for the room only, except where otherwise indicated. Many hotels, especially those in category ❹ and over, include breakfast in the price; you'll need to check this when booking. During low season, rates can drop by more than fifty percent, especially if you are staying for three or more nights. Exceptions are during the Christmas and Easter weeks when you'll pay high-season prices. Single rooms, where available, cost around seventy percent of the price of a double.

❶ Up to €24
❷ €24–33
❸ €34–42
❹ €43–58
❺ €59–72
❻ €73 and upwards

Note: Youth hostels and mountain refuges typically charge €7–9 for a dormitory bed. For more accommodation details, see pp.51–54.

and **Filopáppou**; and, around the foot of the Acropolis, the **Pláka** has scattered monuments of the Byzantine and medieval town that seemed so exotic to Byron and the Romantics. As you might expect, the city also offers some of the best **eating** to be found in Greece, with a number of beautiful cafés, garden tavernas and street markets – as well as the most varied nightlife, including traditional **music and films** in the winter months, and **open-air cinema**, **concerts** and **classical drama** in summer.

Outside Athens, the emphasis shifts more exclusively to ancient sites; the beaches along the Attic coast are functional enough escapes for Athenians, but hardly priorities if you are moving on to the islands. Of the sites, the Temple of Poseidon at **Sounion** is the most popular trip, and rightly so, with its dramatic clifftop position above the cape. Lesser known and less visited are the sanctuaries at **Rhamnous** and **Brauron** (Vravróna), both rewarding ruins with beaches nearby. Dedicated Classical pilgrims might also take in the burial mound at **Marathon**, near a sandy beach, and the Sanctuary of Demeter at **Eleusis** (Elefsína).

Walkers may want to head for the **mountains – Párnitha**, most compellingly – that ring the city, where springtime hikes reveal some of the astonishing range of Greek wild flowers. Hedonists, however, will already be making escape plans for **the islands**, which are served by ferries and hydrofoils from the Athenian portsuburb (and heavy industrial centre) of **Pireás** (Piraeus) and, more selectively, from the two other Attic ferry terminals at **Rafína** and **Lávrio**. Coverage of the ports and sights of Attica starts on p.160.

Athens

For most visitors the highlight of a visit to **ATHENS** (Athína in modern Greek) is the stunning vestiges of the ancient, Classical Greek city, most famously represented by the **Acropolis** and its surrounding archeological sites. These form the first section of the guide to the city's sights in this chapter – "The Acropolis and Ancient Athens" – and, if it's your first trip to the city, they're likely to occupy a fair amount of your time. An essential accompaniment is the **National Archeological Museum**: the finest collection of Greek antiquities anywhere in the world.

Even on a brief visit, however, it is a shame to see Athens purely as the location of ancient sites and museums. Although the **neighbourhoods** may lack the style and monuments of most European capitals, they are worth at least some exploration. The old nineteenth-century quarter of **Pláka**, in particular, is a delight, with its mix of Turkish, Neoclassical and Greek-island architecture, and an array of intriguing little museums devoted to traditional arts, ceramics and music. Just to its north, the **bazaar** area, around Athinás and Eólou, retains an almost Middle Eastern atmosphere in its life and trade, while the **National Gardens**, elegant **Kolonáki** and the hill of **Lykavitós** offer respite from the maelstrom. Further afield, but still well within the limits of Greater Athens, are the monasteries of **Kessarianí** and **Dhafní**, the latter with Byzantine mosaics the equal of any in Greece.

Vólos & Thessaloníki

Malakássa

Rhamnous

Skípiza

Áyia Triádha
Pan Cave

Báfi
Refuge

Áy. Marina

Límni
Marathóna

Marathónas

Skhiniás

Phyle

Moní
Klistón

Thrakomakedhónes

Marathon

Fili

Néa Mákri

KIFISSIA

Pendhéli

Elefsína

PSYHIKO

Rafína

Dhafní
Monastery

Metro

Salamína   Pérama

Pireás   ATHENS

Peanía   Brauron
(Vravróna)

Kessarianí
Monastery

MESOYÍA

Imittós

Salamína

West (Olympic)
Terminal

East
Terminal

Márkópoulo

Pórto Ráfti

Glyfádha

Vóula

Kavoúri

Vouliagméni

Lagoníssi

Éyina

Ay. Marina

Éyina

Thoriko

Anávissos

Lávrio

N

Sounion

Makrónissos

0   20 km

Old Road to Delphi via Thíva (Thebes) & Aïgosthena
Kórinthos & the Peloponnese
Póros, Ídhra & Spétses
Évvia
The Cyclades
Kéa & Kýthnos

Some history

Athens has been inhabited continuously for over 7000 years. Its acropolis, supplied with spring water, commanding views of all seaward approaches and encircled by protective mountains on its landward side, was a natural choice for prehistoric settlement and for the Mycenaeans, who established a palace-fortress on the rock. Its development into a city-state and artistic centre continued apace under the Dorians, Phoenicians and various dynastic rulers, reaching its apotheosis in the fifth century BC. This was the **Classical period**, when the Athenians, having launched themselves into an experiment in radical democracy, celebrated their success with a flourish of art, architecture, literature and philosophy that has influenced Western culture ever since. (An account of the Classical period is given with the main sites of ancient Athens on pp.106–108; Athens' Roman history is outlined in the box on p.123.)

The discontinuity from ancient to medieval Athens was due, essentially, to the emergence of **Christianity**. Having survived with little change through years of Roman rule, the city lost its pivotal role in the Roman–Greek world after the division of the Roman Empire into Eastern and Western halves, and the establishment of Byzantium (Constantinople) as capital of the Eastern –

Byzantine – empire. There, a new Christian sensibility soon outshone the prevailing ethic of Athens, where schools of philosophy continued to teach a pagan Neoplatonism. In 529 these schools were finally closed by Justinian I, and the city's temples, including the Parthenon, were reconsecrated as churches.

Athens rarely featured in the chronicles of the time, enjoying a brief revival under the foreign powers of the Middle Ages: in the aftermath of the piratical Fourth Crusade, Athens – together with the Peloponnese and much of central Greece – passed into the hands of the **Franks**. At the Acropolis they established a ducal court (of some magnificence, according to contemporary accounts) and for a century Athens was back in the mainstream of Europe. Frankish control, however, was based on little more than a provincial aristocracy. In 1311 their forces battled **Catalan** mercenaries, who had a stronghold in Thebes, and were driven to oblivion in a swamp. The Catalans, having set up their own duchy, in turn gave way to **Florentines** and, briefly, Venetians, before the arrival in 1456 of **Sultan Mehmet II**, the Turkish conqueror of Constantinople.

Athens and its environment

The enormous and rapid population increase and attendant industrial development that characterized the postwar period had a disastrous effect on the **environment** of Athens. With a third of the Greek population, half the country's industry and over half of its cars crammed into Greater Athens, the capital has found itself with one of the world's worst **pollution** problems. A noxious brown cloud, the *néfos*, trapped by the circle of mountains and aerial inversion layers, can frequently be seen hovering over the city. Despite what your burning eyes and throat may tell you, some improvement in the situation has been registered in recent decades, though not in the critical pollutant, nitrogen dioxide. Moreover, the level of pollution still aggravates acute respiratory diseases and arguably contributed to the high death toll in the freak heatwaves or *káfsones* during the summers of 1987 and 1988. Alarmingly, the *néfos* is also gnawing away at the very fabric of the ancient city, including the Parthenon marbles. As sulphur dioxide settles on the columns and statuary, it becomes a friable coating of calcium sulphate, which is washed off by the winter rains, taking a thin layer of stone with it.

Most anti-pollution measures up until now have been aimed at restricting the use of **private cars**. Successive governments have experimented with limiting weekday use of vehicles in a central restricted zone, stipulating alternate days for odd- and even-numbered numberplates, but the government's efforts have been undermined by the fact that most shops, offices and businesses persist in closing for a three-hour summer siesta – making for four rush hours a day and double the amount of pollution and traffic problems. At least fuller integration into the EU and concomitant lowering of the once crippling import duties on private cars means that Athenians can now upgrade their vehicles more regularly, and those that use lead-free petrol are now cheaper and thus far more common.

At last, however, more far-reaching measures are being taken to help the city's **public transport** system rise to the challenge: the new airport at Spáta is open and, back in the heart of the city, virtually every landmark square has been excavated for the expansion of the metro system. The three-line metro will be complemented by a circular tram system downtown and the operation of passenger ferries between the coastal suburbs and metro stations at Pireás and Fáliro.

Furthermore, all electricity, most heating and some cooking is now fuelled by copious supplies of Russian natural gas, installed (by pipeline) in Athens in 1997. With air inversion layers prompting pollution alerts in both summer and winter, there is still a long way to go, but these policies do at least offer a ray of hope.

Turkish Athens was never much more than a garrison town. The links with the West, which had preserved a sense of continuity with the Classical and Roman city, were severed, and the flood of visitors was reduced to a trickle of French and Italian ambassadors to the Sublime Porte, and the occasional traveller or painter. The town does not seem to have been oppressed by Ottoman rule, however: the Greeks enjoyed some autonomy, and both Jesuit and Capuchin monasteries continued to thrive. Although the Acropolis became the home of the Turkish governor and the Parthenon was used as a mosque, life in the village-like quarters around the Acropolis drifted back to a semi-rural existence. Similarly, the great port of **Pireás**, still partially enclosed within its ancient walls, was left to serve just a few dozen fishing boats.

Four centuries of Ottoman occupation followed until, in 1821, in common with the inhabitants of a score of other towns across the country, the Greeks of Athens rose in **rebellion**. They occupied the Turkish quarters of the lower town – the current Pláka – and laid siege to the Acropolis. The Turks withdrew, but five years later were back to reoccupy the Acropolis fortifications, while the Greeks evacuated to the countryside. When the Ottoman garrison finally left in 1834, and the Bavarian architects of the new German-born monarchy moved in, Athens, with a population of only 5000, was at its nadir.

For all the claims of its ancient past, and despite the city's natural advantages, Athens was not the first-choice capital of modern Greece. That honour went instead to Náfplio in the Peloponnese, where the **War of Independence** was masterminded by Kapodistrias and where the first Greek National Assembly met in 1828. Had Kapodistrias not been assassinated, in 1831, the capital would most likely have remained in the Peloponnese, if not at Náfplio, then at Trípoli, Corinth or Pátra, all much more established and sizeable towns. But following Kapodistrias's death, the "Great Powers" of Western Europe intervened, inflicting on the Greeks a king of their own choosing – **Otho**, son of Ludwig I of Bavaria – and, in 1834, transferring the capital and court to Athens. The reasoning was almost purely symbolic and sentimental: Athens was not only insignificant in terms of population and physical extent but was then at the edge of the territories of the new Greek state, which had yet to include northern Thessaly, Epirus or Macedonia, or any of the islands beyond the Cyclades or Sporades.

The **nineteenth-century development** of Athens was a gradual and fairly controlled process. While the archeologists stripped away all the Turkish and Frankish embellishments from the Acropolis, a modest city took shape along the lines of the Bavarians' Neoclassical grid. **Pireás**, meanwhile, grew into a port again, though until the nineteenth century, its activities continued to be dwarfed by the main Greek shipping centres on the islands of Sýros and Ídhra (Hydra).

The first mass expansion of both municipalities came suddenly, in 1923, as the result of the tragic Greek–Turkish war in **Asia Minor**. The peace treaty that resolved the war entailed the exchange of Greek and Turkish ethnic populations, their identity being determined solely on the basis of religion. A million and a half Greeks, mostly from the age-old settlements along the Asia Minor coast, but also many Turkish-speaking peoples from the communities of inland Anatolia, arrived in Greece as refugees. Over half of them settled in Athens, Pireás and the neighbouring villages, changing at a stroke the whole make-up of the capital. Their integration and survival is one of the great events of the city's history, and has left its mark on the Athens of today. The web of suburbs that straddles the metro line from Athens to Pireás, and sprawls out into the hills, bears nostalgic names of the refugees' origins – Néa Smýrni (New Smyrna), Néa Iónia, Néa Filadhélfia – as do many streets. Originally, these neighbourhoods were basically refugee villages with populations primarily from one or another Anatolian town, built in ramshackle fashion, often with a single water source for two dozen families.

The merging of these shanty-suburbs and their populations with the established communities of Athens and Pireás dominated the years leading up to **World War II**. With the war, however, new concerns emerged. Athens was hit hard by German occupation: during the winter of 1941–2 there were an estimated 2000 deaths from starvation each day. In late 1944, when the Germans finally left (Allied policy was to tie them down in the Balkans), the capital saw the first skirmishes of **civil war**, with the British forces being ordered to fight against their former Greek allies in the Communist-dominated resistance army, ELAS. Physical evidence of the ensuing month-long battle, the *Dhekemvriatá*, can still be seen in a handful of bullet-pocked walls. From 1946 to 1949 Athens was a virtual island in the civil war, with road approaches to the Peloponnese and the north only tenuously kept open.

But during the 1950s, after the civil war, the city started to expand rapidly. A massive **industrial investment** programme – financed largely by the Americans, who had won Greece for their sphere of influence – took place, and the capital saw huge **immigration** from the war-torn, impoverished countryside. The open spaces between the old refugee suburbs began to fill and, by the late 1960s, Greater Athens covered a continuous area from the slopes of mounts Pendéli and Párnitha down to Pireás and Elefsína.

On a visual level, much of the modern city is unremittingly ugly, since old buildings were demolished wholesale in the name of quick-buck development, particularly during the colonels' junta of 1967–74 (see p.1008). Only now are planning and preservation measures being enforced – in a last-ditch attempt to rescue the city from its engulfing **pollution**. The PASOK administration of the late 1980s endowed the city with thousands of trees, shrubs, patches of garden and an ever-growing number of pedestrian-only streets – though Athens still lags far behind Paris or London in terms of open space. There is also increasing awareness of the nineteenth-century architectural heritage – what's left of it – with many old houses being restored and repainted.

Long-term solutions are proving more elusive: priorities include decanting industry and services into the provinces to ease the stresses on the city's environment (see box on p.94) and its ailing infrastructure, and creating a mass transport network capable of meeting the needs of a modern capital city.

Orientation, arrival and information

As a visitor, you're likely to spend most of your time in the central grid of Athens, a compact, walkable area. Only on arrival at, or departure from, the various far-flung stations and terminals, do you have to confront the confused urban sprawl. Once in the centre, it's a simple matter to orient yourself. There are four strategic reference points: the squares of **Sýndagma** ("Syntagma" on many English-language maps) and **Omónia** and the hills of the **Acropolis** (unmistakable with its temple crown) and (to the northeast) **Lykavitós**. Once you've established these as a mental compass you should not be lost for long – anyone will point you back in the direction of Sýndagma or Omónia.

Sýndagma (Platía Sindágmatos, "Constitution Square", to give it its full title) lies midway between the Acropolis and Lykavitós. With the Greek Parliament building – plus mammoth metro tunnelling and traffic diversions – on its uphill side, and banks and airline offices clustered around, it is to all intents and purposes the centre of the capital. Almost everything of daytime interest is within twenty to thirty minutes' walk of the square.

To the northeast, the ritzy **Kolonáki** quarter curls around the slopes of **Lykavitós**, with a funicular up the hillside to save you the final climb. To the east, behind the Parliament, the jungly **National Gardens** function as the city's chief lung and meeting place; beyond them are the 1896 Olympic stadium and the attractive neighbourhoods of **Pangráti** and **Mets**, both crammed with restaurants and bars.

To the southwest, up to the base of the **Acropolis**, spread the ramshackle but much-commercialized lanes of **Pláka**, the lone surviving area of the nineteenth-century, pre-Independence village. Beyond the Acropolis itself is **Filopáppou Hill**, an area of parkland bordered by the neighbourhoods of **Koukáki** and **Áno Petrálona**, also good choices for accommodation and meals.

Northwest of Sýndagma, two broad thoroughfares, **Stadhíou** and **Panepistimíou** (officially but ineffectually named Venizélou), run in just under a kilometre to **Omónia** (in full, Platía Omonías, "Concord Square"). This is the heart of the city for the ordinary Athenian, with department stores, computer software and discount-priced electronic goods attracting a lively trade on Saturday morning. Omónia's backstreets were not long ago compared to those around Piccadilly Circus or Times Square: more than a bit seedy, with fast-food cafés, gypsies, pickpockets and a scattering of porno shows and bordellos. This is rapidly changing, however, with the commercial success of **Psyrrí**, the entertainment district to the southwest of Omónia square. Buildings on and near Omónia have been renovated, local theatre groups have set up headquarters in old warehouses in Psyrrí and a plethora of trendy ouzerís, cafés and clubs is flourishing.

The area's popularity is spilling over into **Keramikós**, a diverse residential neighbourhood west of Psyrrí. It has a pleasantly low-key atmosphere in comparison to frenetic Psyrrí and is now home to a few chic restaurants and bars. Southwest of here is the neighbourhood of **Gázi**, named after the defunct gasworks, that once spewed out noxious fumes but has now been converted into the sleek Municipal Technopolis Centre gallery. Even further west, **Roúf**, once distinguished by its large gypsy population and produce market, has also undergone something of a renaissance. With the recent opening of a couple of very upscale restaurants, the area is being labelled the next "hotspot".

To the northeast of Omónia, beyond Panepistimíou, lies the student neighbourhood of **Exárhia**, a slightly "alternative" district, with a concentration of lively tavernas and bars there and in its extension **Neápoli**. Southeast of Omónia, stretching down to **Ermoú** street and the **Monastiráki** bazaar district on the borders of Pláka, lies the main commercial centre, crammed with offices and clusters of shops offering everything from insurance to airline tickets, machine tools to household goods.

Points of arrival

Athens' new airport – **Eleftherios Venizelos** – at Spáta, some 26km east of the city, opened in March 2001, replacing the far more convenient (if tiny) one south of town at Ellinikó. Its distance from the city, its enormous size and lack (so far) of fast, direct public transport links to the city have not particularly endeared it to travellers. On the plus side, though, it has good facilities: the arrivals hall has ample **money-changing** bureaux, including two American Express offices, plus **cash dispensers** that accept Visa, MasterCard, Cirrus and

LOCAL BUSES
◁ A Dháfni, Eléfsina
◁ B Ráfina, Soúnion, Lávrio,
       Marathón, Rhámnous
◁ C Glyfádha
◁ D #051 terminal
◁ E #091 stops
◁ F A2 terminal

War Museum
National Gallery
Cycladic Art Museum
Byzantine Museum
British Council
Presidential Palace
Benaki Museum
Parliament
National Gardens
Zappio
Olympic Stadium
Temple of Olympian Zeus
Hadrian's Arch
Theatre of Dionysios
American Express
National Bank
Flower Market
Cathedral
PLAKA
Roman Forum
Ancient Agora
ACROPOLIS
Odeion of Herodes Atticus
Areopagus
Ayii Apóstoli
Hill of the Pnyx
Ay. Dhimitrios
Prison of Sokrates
Monument of Philopappos
Thiseion
Keramikos
Hill of the Nymphs
Dora Stratou Theatre
FILOPAPPOU HILL
ANO PETRALONA
KOUKAKI
Commercial Bank
OSE
OTE
Central Market
PSYRRI
Monastiráki
First Cemetery
METS
PANGRÁTI

see Plaka map for hotels
and restaurants within inset

▶ the East Airport, Vouliagméni & Soúnion

▶ Piréas & West Airport

▶ k & 17

▶ Piréas & Tourist Police

ATHENS AND AROUND | Central Athens

CENTRAL ATHENS

0   500 m

99

Plus. **Luggage-storage** facilities are open round the clock, as are cafés, news-stands, a Sbarro food court and other fast-food restaurants. There's also a **business centre** offering internet access, fax, telephone, typing and photocopying services, though at steep prices.

Underground links from the airport the whole way into town are not fore-seen until 2003 at the earliest; for now, the best you can do is take the #**E94 express bus** (every 15min 6am–8.30pm, half-hourly 8.30pm–midnight) from outside the arrivals hall to the current last metro stop, **Ethnikí Ámyna**, and then continue into the centre. Otherwise there's the #**E95 express bus** all the way to central Sýndagma square, via the *Hilton* (every 25min 6am–7.50pm; every 35min after 7.50pm), incidentally, your only option from midnight to 6am. There is also the #**E96** express bus to **Pireás** port (every 20min 5am–7pm, half-hourly 7pm–8.30pm, every 40min 8.30pm–5am), going via the beach suburbs. All three services cost €3, but for the price you automati-cally get a "one-day" travelcard valid on all Athens public transport. Tickets should be bought from a booth beside the stops, or, if this is closed, can be pur-chased on the bus: make sure you have small change.

Getting a **taxi** is another option, though it's not necessarily the quickest way into the city; it takes an average of one hour and fifteen minutes, depending on the traffic. The fare is €11.50–14.40 to central Athens or Pireás, more expen-sive than the fare from the old airport, but a reasonable cost if split two or more ways. Before setting out in a taxi you're advised to make sure that the meter is switched on to Rate 1; overcharging of tourists can be brutal. If the driver resists or claims the meter is broken, any mention of the police should quickly change his tack. You may have fellow passengers in the cab; each drop-off will pay the full fare.

Train stations

There are two **train stations**, almost adjacent to each other, a couple of hun-dred metres northwest of Omónia, off Dheliyáni street. The **Stathmós Laríssis** handles the main lines coming from the north (Lárissa, Thessaloníki, the Balkans, western Europe and Turkey). The **Stathmós Peloponníssou** three blocks south, is the terminal for the narrow-gauge line circling the Peloponnese, including the stretch to Pátra (the main port for ferries from Italy and Corfu).

From either station you are five to fifteen minutes' walk away from the con-centration of hotels around Platía Viktorías and Exárhia, both handy for the National Archeological Museum and excellent restaurants. For hotels elsewhere, the yellow **trolleybus #1** southbound passes along Sámou, one block east of the Laríssis station (to get to it from the Peloponníssou terminal, use the giant metal overpass, then detour around the metro works); it then makes a strategic loop down through Omónia, along Stadhíou to Sýndagma, then down Filellínon to Hadrian's Arch (for Mets), and finally along Veïkoú to Koukáki (on the southeast side of Filopáppou Hill). **Bus #057** from the Peloponníssou ter-minal also passes through both central squares and down to Leofóros Syngroú.

Be wary of **taxis** (both official and unlicensed) at the train stations – some thrive on newly arrived tourists, shuttling them a couple of blocks for highly inflated fares.

Bus stations

Again, there are two principal terminals. Coming into Athens from northern Greece or the Peloponnese, you'll find yourself at **Kifissoú 100**, a ten-minute bus ride from the centre. The least expensive way into town is to take city bus #051 to the corner of Zínonos/Menándhrou, just off Omónia and only a block or two from a yellow trolleybus stop. Routes from central Greece (see chapter three for specific destinations) arrive at **Liossíon 260**, north of the train stations; to get into the centre, take the blue city bus #024 to Omónia or Sýndagma.

In addition, there are international **OSE buses**, run by the railway company, which arrive at the Stathmós Peloponníssou. Private **international bus companies** arrive at, and leave from, a variety of locations. Most will take you to the train station or to Kifissoú 100; a few drop passengers right in the city centre.

Pireás: the ferries

The simplest way to get to Athens from **Pireás** port is by **metro** to the stations at Monastiráki, Omónia or Viktorías. Trains run from 6am to midnight, with fares varying from €0.60 to €0.90 according to a zone system (you will only need to pay €0.80 if you are going up to the northern suburbs). For the airport, take express bus #E96 (see opposite). **Taxis** between Pireás and central Athens should cost around €7.20, including baggage, although rates per kilometre double at night – again, see the comments opposite. There's a full account of Pireás, together with a map of the central area, showing the metro station and harbours, on p.160.

Information

The main OTE **tourist office** (Mon–Fri 9am–4.30pm; ☎010/33 10 692 or 32 71 300) is at Amerikís 2, just up from Stadhíou; it dispenses ferry-timetable sheets (though these should be used as guidelines only), along with maps and pamphlets, and is also a source of information about the **Hellenic Festival** (see p.152).

To complement our plans and the free OTE map, the street-indexed Falkplan is a good, **large-scale map** of the city (available from the shops listed on p.155). The *Historical Map of Athens* produced by the Greek Ministry of Culture is well worth its €3.50 price. It has a good map of central Athens and, on the other side, a clear, large-scale map of Pláka. Both maps number all the sites and museums.

If you are planning a long stay, it's worth getting the **Athína-Pireás Proástia A–Ω atlas**, co-published by Kapranidhis and Fotis, and available from kiosks and bookshops. It's in Greek only, however, and is quite pricey at €20.20, but it does show absolutely everything, including cinemas and concert venues.

City transport

Athens is served by slow but wide-ranging **buses** and a fast **metro** system which is currently undergoing massive expansion; **taxis** fill in the gaps. Public transport networks operate from around 5am to midnight, with the airport buses being the only ones running in the small hours. **A daily pass** costs €3 and can be used on buses, trolleys and the metro.

Buses

The **bus network** is extensive and cheap, with a flat fare of €0.50. Tickets must be bought in advance from kiosks, certain shops and newsagents, or from the limited number of booths run by bus personnel near major stops – look for the brown, red and white logo proclaiming "Isitíria edhó" (tickets here). They're sold individually or in bundles of ten, and must be cancelled in a special machine when boarding. Fare-dodgers risk an on-the-spot fine equivalent to forty times the current fare. Cancelled tickets apply only to a particular journey and vehicle; there are no transfers. If you're staying long enough, it would be worth buying a monthly pass for €34.50, which is valid on all buses, trolleys and the metro.

Buses are very crowded at peak times, unbearably hot in summer traffic jams, and chronically plagued by strikes and slow-downs; walking is often a better option. Express services run to and from the airport – see p.100. Other **routes**, where relevant, are detailed in the text. The most straightforward are the **yellow trolleybuses**: #1 connects the Laríssis train station with Omónia, Sýndagma and Koukáki; #2, #3, #4, #5 and #12 all link Sýndagma with Omónia and the National Archeological Museum on Patissíon. In addition, there are scores of **blue city buses**, all with three-digit numbers and serving an infinity of routes out into the straggling suburbs and beyond.

The metro

The Athens **metro** has been much expanded recently, with the long-awaited addition of two new lines and a significant extension of the original Line 1 (green). The new system is designed to handle almost half a million passengers a day and is fast, quiet and user-friendly. The last stations on lines 2 and 3 are currently being completed, as well as the link between Sýndagma and Monastiráki on Line 3. It is hoped that work will be finished in time for the Olympic Games in 2004. Line 1 (€0.60) runs from Pireás in the south to Kifissiá in the north; useful stops in the centre include Thissío, Monastiráki, Omónia and Platía Viktorías. Line 2 (red) currently runs from Sýndagma to Dafní, with a useful stop at the foot of the Acropolis. Line 3 (blue) extends from Sýndagma northeast to Ethnikí Ámyna, the terminal for the airport shuttle bus. There are plans to extend this line all the way to the airport, but work has yet to start on this. The fare for Line 1 is €0.60 and slightly more for lines 2 and 3 (€0.80). Bus and metro tickets are not interchangeable.

Taxis

Athenian **taxis** are the cheapest of any EU capital – fares around the city centre will rarely run above €2.90, with the airport and Pireás only €11.50–14.40 – the exact amount determined by traffic and amount of luggage. The minimum fare is €1.50. All officially licensed cars are painted yellow and have a special red-on-white numberplate. You can wave them down on the street, pick them up at the train station, airport or the National Gardens on the corner of Sýndagma, or get your hotel to phone one for you (adding €1.20 surcharge to the fare). They are most elusive during the rush hours of 1.30–2.30pm and 7.30–8.30pm.

Make sure the **meter** is switched on when you get in, with its display visible and properly zeroed; theoretically, it's illegal to quote a flat fare for a ride within city limits – the meter must be used. If it's "not working", find another taxi. Attempts at **overcharging** tourists are particularly common with small-hours arrivals at the airport and Pireás; a threat to have hotel staff or the police adjudicate usually elicits co-operation, as they will very likely take your side and the police have the power to revoke a driver's operating permit.

Legitimate surcharges can considerably bump up the final bill from the total shown on the meter. Currently the flag falls at €0.80, there's an automatic €1.20 supplement for entering the confines of the airport, and a €0.60 surcharge for journeys involving train or ferry terminals; luggage is €0.40 extra for each bag over 10kg; the rate per kilometre almost doubles between midnight and 5am from €0.30 to €0.50; and there are Easter and Christmas bonuses which seem to extend for a week or two either side of the actual date. Every taxi must have a plastic dash-mounted placard listing regular rates and extra charges in English and Greek.

To try and make ends meet on government-regulated fare limits, taxi-drivers will often pick up a whole string of passengers along the way. There is no fare-sharing: each passenger (or group of passengers) pays the full fare for their journey. So if you're picked up by an already-occupied taxi, memorize the meter reading at once; you'll pay from that point on, plus the €0.80 minimum. When hailing an occupied taxi, call out your destination, so the driver can decide whether you suit him or not.

Accommodation

Hotels and **hostels** can be packed to the gills in midsummer – August especially – but for most of the year there are enough beds in the city to go around, and to suit most wallets and tastes. It makes sense to **phone** or if possible **email** before leaving home. If you just set out and do the rounds, you'll find somewhere, but in summer, unless you're early in the day, it's likely to be at the fourth or fifth attempt.

For cheaper places, you're on your own. Find a phone that operates on phonecards in a quiet square or side street and ring round. Almost every hotel and hostel in the city will have an English-speaking receptionist. Once you locate a vacancy, ask to see the room before booking in – standards vary greatly even within the same building, and you can avoid occasional overcharging by checking the government-regulated room prices displayed by law on the back of the door in each room.

Our listings are grouped into four main areas. The quarters of **Pláka and Sýndagma**, despite their commercialization, are highly atmospheric – and within easy walking distance of all the main sites and the Monastiráki metro station (a useful gateway for the port of Pireás). Formerly gritty and sleazy but being rapidly gentrified, the **bazaar area** is the city at its most colourful, while nearby **Thissío** is rather smarter and airier. The downside of some of the hotels in these areas is that they are subject to round-the-clock noise; if you want uninterrupted sleep, you're better off heading for one of the quieter neighbourhoods a little further out. **Koukáki** and **Pangráti** are attractive parts of the city, and though slightly out of the way – twenty-minutes' walk from Sýndagma or the heart of Pláka – compensate with excellent neighbourhood tavernas and cafés. Koukáki is easiest reached from Pireás via the #9 trolleybus, whose terminus is just outside the Petrálona metro station, while Pangráti is on the #4 or #12 trolleys from Záppio. Around **Exárhia** and **Platía Viktorías** (officially Platía Kyriákou), to the north of Omónia, you are again out of the tourist mainstream, but benefit from good-value local restaurants and the proximity of cinemas, clubs and bars. These areas now have clusters of very good-value, mid-range hotels, just a short walk away from the train stations (and metros Omónia or Viktorías).

The city's **campsites** are out in the suburbs, not especially cheap, and only worth using if you have a camper van to park; phone ahead to book space in season. Camping rough in Athens is not a good idea. Police patrol many of the parks, especially those by the train stations, and muggings are commonplace. Even the train stations are no real refuge; they close when services stop and are cleared of stragglers.

Pláka and Sýndagma

Achilleas, Lékka 21 ☏010/32 33 197, ℻32 22 412, ✉www.achilleashotel.gr. Central location on mostly quiet street. All rooms have been renovated and have a/c and TV. Breakfast served on roof terrace. ❺

Acropolis House, Kódhrou 6 ☏010/32 22 344, ℻32 44 143. A very clean, well-sited 150-year-old mansion much favoured by students and academics, who return year after year. Furnishings are eclectic and some rooms have baths across the hall. Rates include breakfast. ❹

Adonis, Kódhrou 3 ☏010/32 49 737, ℻32 31 602. A modern but unobjectionable low-rise pension across the street from *Acropolis House*, with some suites. The rooftop café has a stunning view of the Acropolis and central Athens. ❺

Arethusa, Mitropóleos 6–8 and Nikis 12 ☏010/32 29 431, ℻32 29 439 (metro Sýndagma). This modernized, surprisingly quiet hotel with a/c and TV in each room caters to independent travellers and small groups. The reception staff are lively and most helpful. Rates are quite reasonable considering the excellent location just behind the Sýndagma post office. ❹

Byron, Vironis 19 ☏010/32 53 554, ℻32 20 276. Set on a quiet side street within walking distance of the Acropolis and Pláka museums, the *Byron* is attractively renovated with a/c and TV in each room, and a few upper rooms have impressive Acropolis views. ❹

Hermes, Apollonos 19 ☏010/32 35 514, ℻32 32 073. Conveniently located near Sýndagma, with comfortable, newly painted rooms and hearty buffet breakfast included in the price. ❹

Kimon, Apollonos 27 ☏ & ℻ 010/33 14 658. Rooms are basic but clean and with a/c. A few of the upper rooms have roof-garden views of the Acropolis. ❷

Kouros, Kódhrou 11, Pláka ☏010/32 27 431 (metro Sýndagma). A slightly faded atmospheric pension, but with adequate facilities: shared baths and sinks in rooms. Some balconies overlook the pedestrianized street (the continuation of Voulís – two blocks southwest of Sýndagma). ❷

Nefeli, Iperídhou 16 ☏010/32 28 044, ℻32 25 800. Actually at Hatzimiháli 2, this newly-renovated hotel has TV and a/c in all rooms, though some of the lower rooms do suffer from some noise at night. ❸

Phaedra, Herefóndos 16 at the Adhrianoú junction ☏010/32 27 795. Old-fashioned and very plain, but clean, and quiet at night – thanks to its location at the junction of two pedestrian malls. Polite welcoming management, but only shared facilities. Half of the rooms have a/c for an extra €5.90 per night. ❷

Student Inn, Kydhathinéon 16 ☏010/32 44 808,

℻32 10 065. A former hostel, now a bona fide hotel, recently renovated and painted. Has some triple rooms, all with en-suite baths. Prone to nocturnal noise from outside, but otherwise acceptable. Small courtyard and internet facilities open to nonresidents. ❹

Thisseus Hostel, Thisséos 10 ☏010/32 45 960. You don't get much more central than this – three blocks west of Sýndagma – nor much cheaper. No frills, but clean enough, and with a kitchen for guests' use. Some three- and four-bed dorms. ❷

The Bazaar area and Thissío

Attalos, Athinás 29 ☏010/32 12 801, ℻32 43 124, ✉www.attalos.gr. Modern design, clean, comfortable rooms with a/c and TVs, and accommodating management. ❸

Cecil, Athinás 39 ☏010/32 17 079, ℻32 18 005, ✉Cecil@netsmart.gr. One of the best deals in Athens. Loving restoration of a run-down pension has re-created the charm of the 150-year-old mansion; attractively decorated rooms are larger than average and all have a/c.The location in the heart of the market district, gracious management, roof garden and hearty breakfast with Cretan jams and yogurt make this a delight. ❸

Erechthion, Flammaríou 8 ☏010/34 59 606, ℻34 62 756. A reasonable mid-range option in this lively area behind the Acropolis. All rooms with a/c and TV. ❹

Pella Inn, Ermoú 104 ☏&℻ 010/32 50 598. A family-run hotel under enthusiastic management. From the third floor up the views of the Acropolis are startling. ❹

Tembi, Eólou 29 ☏010/32 13 175, ℻32 54 179. A favourite with students and budget travellers: book exchange, drinks, fridge, plus handy affiliated travel agency. Rooms are tiny, most have shared facilities, and hot water can be sparse. But the view of the flower market at Agia Irini across the quiet pedestrian walkway is enchanting, and it's within walking distance of most central sights. ❷

Thission, Apostólou Pávlou 25 ☏010/34 67 634, ℻34 62 756. Somewhat better value than the nearby *Erechthion*, this friendly place has a/c and TV in all rooms and fine views from the roof terrace. ❸

Zinon, Keramikoú 3 and Zínonos ☏010/52 45 711, ℻52 31 548, ✉tsakiri1@otenet.gr. A comfortable and reasonably-priced Best Western hotel just off Omónia square. ❺

Koukáki and Pangráti

Acropolis View, Webster 10 ☏010/92 17 303,

℗ 92 30 705. A well-maintained small hotel on a quiet residential street whose front rooms with balconies and roof garden live up to its name. All rooms have a/c, TV, fridge, ample breakfast is included and the lobby has an amiable bar. ❻

Art Gallery, Erekhthíou 5 ☎010/92 38 376, ℗92 33 025. Original paintings on the walls of a mansion once belonging to one of the owner's family, lend this popular pension its name. Distinguished by knowledgeable and helpful staff, convenient location just a short walk from the metro and bountiful breakfast (for extra charge) served on sunny terrace with Acropolis view. ❷

Marble House, cul-de-sac off A. Zínni 35a ☎010/92 34 058, ℗92 26 461. Along with the *Art Gallery*, the best value in Koukáki, with a very helpful management. Often full, so call ahead. Rooms have been recently overhauled and eight have a/c (for extra charge). Most rooms with bath; also two self-catering studios for long stays. ❸

Youth Hostel #5, Damaréos 75, Pangráti, off map near the huge Profítis Ilías church ☎010/75 19 530. A bit out of the way but friendly, no curfew and in a decent, quiet neighbourhood; trolleys #2 and #11 from downtown stop just around the corner. Dormitory beds only. ❶

Exárhia and Platía Viktorías

Hostel Aphrodite, Inárdhou 12, cnr Mikhaïl Vódha 65 ☎010/88 39 249, ℗88 16 574. Friendly and clean, providing hot water in shared bathrooms, a safe, free storage and internet access. Open March–Sept. Dormitory bed €13, bed in double room €18.

Athenian Inn, Háritos 22 ☎010/72 38 097, ℗72 42 268. Actually in Kolonáki, adjacent to Exárhia, this mid-range hotel is small, elegant and convenient for most of the museums around the National Gardens. Rooms on lower floors pick up street noise from motorbikes and patrons of *Ratka's* next door. ❺

Elli, Heïdhen 29, Platía Viktorías ☎ & ℗ 010/88 15 876. Characterful pension in refurbished Neoclassical building on a quiet tree-lined street. TV and shower in all rooms. Best deal in the area. ❷

Exarhion, Themistokléous 55, Platía Exárhia ☎010/36 01 256, ℗38 03 296. Big 1960s highrise hotel that's surprisingly inexpensive and well placed, if a bit noisy. ❸

Feron, Férron 43, Platía Viktorías ☎010/82 32 083. A small hotel with en-suite baths in all rooms. ❷

Museum, Bouboulínas 16 ☎010/36 05 611, ℗38 00 507. Nicely placed, reasonable-value hotel, right behind the National Archeological Museum and parkland. ❷

Orion and **Dryades**, Anexartisías 5 ☎010/36 27 362, ℗38 05 193. Quiet, well-run twin hotels across from the Lófos Stréfi park – a steep uphill walk. Reception is in the cheaper *Orion*, which has shared bathrooms, a kitchen, and communal area on the roof with an amazing view of central Athens. ❷ –❸

YHA, Victor Hugo 16 ☎010/52 34 170, ℗52 34 015. Between the train station and Omónia, the only official youth hostel in Athens is friendly, informative and includes a café and left-luggage store. Membership €2.10 per day on top of bed price still makes it cheaper than other dorm deals. Annual membership €12.10.

Campsites

Athens Camping, Leofóros Athinón 198 ☎010/58 14 114. This campsite is the closest to the centre of Athens. It has a minimarket, snack bar and hot water. Take bus #A16 from Platía Eleftherias to Elefsina.

Camping Nea Kifissia ☎010/80 75 579. Located in the cool, leafy suburb of Kifissiá and has a swimming pool. Take bus #A7 from Platía Kánningos or metro to Kifissiá and transfer onto bus #528 to the terminal close to the campsite. Open all year round.

Voula Camping ☎010/89 52 712. On the beach but with swimming pool, bar and restaurant. Bus #A2 from Panepistimíou or Sýndagma square. Open all year round.

The Acropolis and ancient Athens

This section covers the **Acropolis** and the assorted Classical and Roman sites on its **slopes**; the hills of the **Pnyx** and **Philoppapus (Filopáppou)** over to the southwest; and the neighbouring **Ancient Agora** (marketplace) and **Kerameikos** (cemetery) to the northwest. This is essentially the core of the ancient, Classical Greek city, though a few further pockets and Roman extensions are covered in the Pláka section, beginning on p.118.

ANCIENT ATHENS

OMONIA

Lykavitós

Themistocles' Wall

PIREOS

STADHIOU

PANEPISTIMIOU

ATHINAS

N

Sacred Way to Eleusis

Kerameikos Cemetery
Dipylon Gate
Sacred Gate
Panathenaic Way

ERMOU

Thiseion

Agora

Roman Forum

Hadrian's Library

SINDAGMA

VAS. SOFIAS

Tower of the Winds

APOST. PAVLOU

Areopagus

Acropolis

Monument of Lysikratos

AMALIAS

Hadrian's Wall

Pnyx

Odeion of Herodes Atticus

D. AREÓPAYITOU

Theatre of Dionysos

Hadrian's Arch

Long Walls to Piraeus

Filopáppou Hill

Temple of Olympian Zeus

River Ilissós (now covered over)

Stadium

Monument of Philopappos

SINGROU

0   500 m

Classical Athens: some history

Perhaps the most startling aspect of ancient, Classical Athens is how suddenly it emerged to the power and glory for which we remember it – and how short its heyday proved to be. In the middle of the **fifth century BC**, Athens was little more than a country town in its street layout and buildings. The latter comprised a scattered jumble of single-storey houses or wattled huts, intersected by narrow lanes. Sanitary conditions were notoriously lax: human waste and rubbish were dumped outside the town with an almost suicidal disregard for plague and disease. And on the rock of the Acropolis, a site reserved for the city's most sacred monuments, stood blackened ruins – temples and sanctuaries burned to the ground during the Persian invasion of 480 BC.

There was little to suggest that the city was entering a unique phase of its history in terms of power, prestige and creativity. But following the victories over the Persians at Marathon (490 BC) and Salamis (480 BC), Athens stood unchallenged for a generation. It grew rich on the export of olive oil and of silver from the mines of Attica, but above all it benefited from its control of the **Delian League**, an alliance of Greek city-states formed as insurance against Persian resurgence. The Athenians relocated the League's treasury from the island of Delos to their own acropolis, ostensibly on the grounds of safety, and with its revenues their leader **Pericles** was able to create the so-called **golden age** of the city. Great endowments were made for monumental construction, arts in all spheres were promoted, and – most significantly – a form of **democracy** emerged.

This democracy had its beginnings in the sixth-century BC reforms of Solon, in which the political rights of the old land-owning class had been claimed by farmer- and craftsmen-soldiers. With the emergence of Pericles the political process was radically overhauled, aided in large part by the Delian League's wealth – which enabled office-holders to be paid, thereby making it possible for the poor to play a part in government. Pericles's constitution ensured that all policies of the state were to be decided by a general assembly of Athenian male citizens – six thousand constituted a quorum. The assembly, which met outside at either the **Agora** or the **Pnyx**, elected a council of five hundred members to carry out the everyday administration of the city and a board of ten *strategoi* or generals to guide it. Pericles, one of the best-known and most influential of the *strategoi*, was as vulnerable as any other to the electoral process: if sufficient numbers had cast their lot (*ostra*) against him, his citizenship would be forfeited (he would be literally ostracized); as it was, he managed to stave off such a fate and died with his popularity intact.

In line with this system of democratic participation, a new and exalted notion of the Athenian citizen emerged. This was a man who could shoulder political responsibility, take public office and play a part in the **cultural** and **religious events** of the time. The latter assumed ever-increasing importance. The city's Panathenaic festival, honouring its protectress deity Athena, was upgraded along the lines of the Olympic Games to include drama, music and athletic contests. Athenians rose easily to the challenge. The next five decades were to witness the great dramatic works of **Aeschylus**, **Sophocles** and **Euripides**, and the comedies of **Aristophanes**. Foreigners such as **Herodotus**, considered the inventor of history, and **Anaxagoras**, the philosopher, were drawn to live in the city. And they, in turn, were surpassed by native Athenians. **Thucydides** wrote *The Peloponnesian War*, a pioneering work of documentation and analysis, while **Socrates** posed the problems of philosophy that were to exercise his follower **Plato** and to shape the discipline to the present day.

But it was the great civic **building programme** that became the most visible and powerful symbol of the age. Under the patronage of Pericles and with vast public funds made available from the Delian treasury, the architects **Iktinos**, **Mnesikles** and **Kallikrates**, and the sculptor **Pheidias**, transformed the city. Their buildings, justified in part as a comprehensive job-creation scheme, included the Parthenon and Erechtheion on the Acropolis; the Hephaisteion and several *stoas* (arcades) outside the Agora; a new *odeion* (theatre) on the south slope of the Acropolis hill; and, outside the city, the temples at Sounion and Rhamnous.

Athenian culture flourished under democracy, but the system was not without its contradictions and failures. Only one in seven inhabitants of the city was an actual citizen; the political status and civil rights that they enjoyed were denied to the many thousands of women, *metics* (foreigners) and slaves. While

The sites: opening hours and fees

Summer opening hours for the **sites** and **museums** in Athens are included with some trepidation. They are notorious for changing without notice, from one season to another, or from one week to the next, owing to staff shortages.

To be sure of admission, it's best to visit between 9am and noon, and to be wary of Monday – when many museums and sites close for the whole day. Last tickets are sold at the time given for closure, although the site may be open fifteen minutes more. For (generally) reliable and up-to-the-minute details, ask at the OTE office at Amerikas 2 for their printed list of opening hours.

For many years, during the off-season (Oct–March), entrance has been free on Sundays except at the Acropolis. During the summer months some sites and museums may let students in for half-price (EU students free) and there may be a reduced price if you are over 65. The response will vary from site to site, but ask.

the lives of men became increasingly public and sociable, with meetings at the Agora or Pnyx and visits to the gymnasiums and theatres, **women**, other than *hetaera* (the educated and entertaining courtesans) and streetwalking prostitutes, were secluded in small and insanitary homes. Their subordination was in fact reinforced by a decree in 451 BC, which restricted their property rights, placing them under the control of fathers, husbands or guardians. At any one time, only forty women could be appointed priestesses – one of the few positions of female power. Aeschylus summed up the prevailing attitude when he declared that the mother does no more than foster the father's seed.

The city's democracy was also sullied by its **imperialist** designs and actions, which could be brutal and exploitive, although acts of mercy against rebellious allies were also documented. Atrocities included the wholesale massacre of the male population of Melos – and the building programme of Pericles itself relied on easy pickings from weaker neighbours and allies. In the *polis* of Athens the achievements of democracy could be overshadowed, too, with attacks on the very talents it had nurtured and celebrated: Aristophanes was impeached, Pheidias and Thucydides were exiled, Socrates was tried and executed.

But, historically, the fatal mistake of the Athenian democracy was allowing itself to be drawn into the **Peloponnesian War** against Sparta, its persistent rival, in 431 BC. Pericles, having roused the assembly to a pitch of patriotic fervour, died of the plague two years after war began, leaving Athens at the mercy of a series of far less capable leaders. In 415 BC a disastrous campaign in Sicily saw a third of the navy lost; in 405 BC defeat was finally accepted after the rest of the fleet was destroyed by Sparta in the Dardanelles. Demoralized, Athens succumbed to a brief period of oligarchy.

Through succeeding decades Athens was overshadowed by Thebes, though it recovered sufficiently to enter a new phase of democracy, the **age of Plato**. However, in 338 BC, nearly one and a half centuries after the original defeat of the Persians, Athens was again called to defend the Greek city-states, this time against the incursions of **Philip of Macedon**. Demosthenes, said to be as powerful an orator as Pericles, spurred the Athenians to fight, in alliance with the Thebans, at Chaironeia. There they were routed, in large part by the cavalry commanded by Philip's son, Alexander, and Athens fell under the control of the Macedonian empire.

The city continued to be favoured, particularly by **Alexander the Great**, a former pupil of Aristotle, who respected both Athenian culture and its democratic institutions. Following his death, however, came a more uncertain era, which saw periods of independence and Macedonian rule, until 146 BC when the **Romans** swept through southern Greece and it was incorporated into the Roman province of Macedonia.

The Acropolis

The **rock of the Acropolis** (April–Sept daily 8am–6.30pm; Oct–March Mon–Fri 8am–4.30pm, Sat & Sun 8am–4.30pm; site and museum €5.75), with the ruins of the Parthenon rising above it, is one of the archetypal images of Western culture. A first glimpse of it above the traffic is a revelation, and yet feels utterly familiar. Pericles had intended the temple to be a spectacular landmark, a "School for Hellas" and a symbol of the city's imperial confidence – as such, it was famous throughout the ancient world. Even Pericles, however, could not have anticipated that his ruined temple would come to symbolize the emergence of Western civilization – nor that, two millennia on, it would attract some three million tourists a year.

As Donald Horne points out in *The Great Museum*, it would be hard to imagine the ruins having such a wide appeal if they had retained more of their

THE ACROPOLIS
Reconstruction of missing buildings

N

Belvedere
Museum
Temple of Rome and Augustus
Parthenon
Theatre of Dionysos
Halkotheke
Asklepion
Stoa of Eumenes
Erechtheion
Old Temple of Athena
Statue of Athena Promachos
Sacred Way
Artemis Sanctuary
Propylaia
Temple of Athena Nike
Beule Gate
Odeon of Herodes Atticus

Parthenon
Erechtheion
Propylaia
Temple of Athena Nike

Based on a drawing by N. Gouvoussis

former glory: if, for example, the Parthenon "still had a roof, and no longer appealed to the modern stereotype for outline emerging from rough stone", or if "we repainted it in its original red, blue and gold and if we reinstalled the huge, gaudy cult-figure of Athena festooned in bracelets, rings and necklaces". Yet it's hard not to feel a sense of wonder as you catch glimpses of the ancient ruins from the city below. The best of these street-level **views** are along Eólou, where the Parthenon forms the focal point of the horizon. Calmer and quieter vantage points higher up include the nearby hills of **Lykavitós**, **Ardhittós** and **Filopáppou**, where you can look on, undisturbed, from among the pine groves; a walk to one of these is highly recommended.

The main **approach** to the ruins is the path that extends above Odhós Dhioskoúron, where it joins Theorías at the northwest corner of Pláka. Two alternative options – though both perhaps better as ways down from the rock – are to make your way through the ancient Agora (entrance on Adhrianoú; see p.116) or, from the south side of the slope, around the footpath beside the Odeion of Herodes Atticus.

The Propylaia and Athena Nike temple

Today, as throughout its history, the Acropolis offers but one entrance – from a terrace above the Agora. Here in Classical times the Panathenaic Way extended along a steep ramp to a massive monumental double-gatehouse, the **Propylaia**; the modern path makes a more gradual, zigzagging ascent through an arched Roman entrance, the **Beule Gate**, added in the third century AD.

The **Propylaia** were constructed by Mnesikles upon completion of the Parthenon, in 437 BC, and their axis and proportions aligned to balance the temple. They were built from the same Pentelic marble (from Mount Pendéli, northeast of the city), and in grandeur and architectural achievement are no mean rival to the Parthenon temple. In order to offset the difficulties of a sloping site, Mnesikles combined for the first time standard Doric columns with the taller and more delicate Ionic order. The ancient Athenians, awed by the fact that such wealth and craftsmanship should be used for a purely secular building, ranked this as their most prestigious monument.

The halls had a variety of uses, even in Classical times. To the left of the central hall (which before Venetian bombardment supported a great coffered roof, painted blue and gilded with stars), the Pinakotheke – currently in scaffolding – exhibited paintings of Homeric subjects by Polygnotus. Executed in the mid-fifth century BC, these were described 600 years later by Pausanias in his Roman-era *Guide to Greece*. There was to have been a similar wing-room to the right, but Mnesikles's design trespassed on ground sacred to the Goddess of Victory and the premises had to be adapted as a waiting room for her shrine – the Temple of Athena Nike.

Simple and elegant, the **Temple of Athena Nike** was begun late in the rebuilding scheme (probably due to conflict over the extent of the Propylaia's south wing) and stands on a precipitous platform overlooking the port of Pireás and the Saronic Gulf. Pausanias recounts that it was from this bastion that King Aegeus maintained a vigil for the tell-tale white sails that would indicate the safe return of his son Theseus from his mission to slay the Minotaur on Crete. Theseus, flushed with success, forgot his promise to swap the boat's black sails for white. On seeing the black sails, Aegeus assumed his son had perished and, racked with grief, threw himself to his death. The temple's frieze, with more attention to realism than triumph, depicts the Athenians' victory over the Persians at Plateia.

Amazingly, the whole temple was reconstructed, from its original blocks, in the nineteenth century; the Turks had demolished the building two hundred years previously, using it as material for a gun emplacement. Recovered in this same feat of jigsaw-puzzle archeology were the reliefs from its parapet – among them *Victory Adjusting her Sandal*, the most beautiful exhibit in the Acropolis Museum.

In front of this small temple are the scant remains of a **Sanctuary of Brauronian Artemis**. Although its function remains obscure, it is known that the precinct once housed a colossal bronze representation of the Wooden Horse of Troy. More noticeable is a nearby stretch of **Mycenaean wall** (running parallel to the Propylaia) that was incorporated into the Classical design.

The Parthenon

Seen from the Propylaia, the Acropolis is today dominated by the Parthenon, set on the rock's highest ground. In Classical times, however, only the temple's pediment could be viewed through the intervening mass of statues and buildings. The ancient focus was a ten-metre-high bronze statue of *Athena Promachos* (Athena the Champion), moved to Constantinople in Byzantine times and there destroyed by a mob who believed that its beckoning hand had directed the Crusaders to the city in 1204. The statue was created by Pheidias as a symbol of the Athenians' defiance of Persia; its spear and helmet were visible to sailors approaching from Sounion.

To the right of the statue passed the Panathenaic Way, the route of the quadrennial festival in honour of the city's patroness, the goddess Athena. Following this route up today, you can make out grooves cut for footholds in the rock and, to either side, niches for innumerable statues and offerings.

The **Parthenon** was the first great building in Pericles' scheme. Designed by Iktinos, it utilizes all the refinements available to the Doric order of architecture to achieve an extraordinary and unequalled harmony. Its proportions maintain a universal 9:4 ratio, not only in the calculations of length to width, or width to height, but in such relationships as the distances between the columns and their diameter. Additionally, any possible appearance of disproportion is corrected by meticulous mathematics and craftsmanship. All seemingly straight lines are in fact slightly curved, an optical illusion known as *entasis* (intensification). The columns (their profile bowed slightly to avoid seeming concave) are slanted inwards by 6cm, while each of the steps along the sides of the temple was made to incline just 12cm over a length of 70m.

Built on the site of earlier archaic temples, the Parthenon was intended as a new sanctuary for Athena and a home for her cult image – a colossal wooden statue of *Athena Polias* (Athena of the City) overlaid with ivory and gold plating, with precious gems as eyes and sporting an ivory gorgon death's-head on her breast. Designed by Pheidias, the statue was installed in the semi-darkness of the *cella* (cult chamber), where it remained an object of prestige and wealth, if not veneration, until at least the fifth century AD. The sculpture has been lost since ancient times but its characteristics are known through numerous later copies (including a fine Roman one in the National Archeological Museum).

The name "Parthenon" means "virgins' chamber", and initially referred only to a room at the west end of the temple occupied by the priestesses of Athena. However, the temple never rivalled the Erechtheion in sanctity and its role tended to remain that of treasury and artistic showcase, devoted rather more to the new god of the *polis* than to Athena herself. Originally its columns were painted and it was decorated with the finest frieze and pedimental sculpture of the Classsical age, depicting the Panathenaic procession, the birth of Athena and the struggles of Greeks to overcome giants, Amazons and centaurs. Of these, the best surviving examples are in the British Museum, but the greater part of the pediments, along with the central columns and the *cella*, were destroyed by the Venetian bombardment in 1687.

The Acropolis's natural setting, a craggy mass of limestone plateau, watered by springs and rising an abrupt hundred metres out of the plain of Attica, has made it a focus and nucleus during every phase of the city's development.

The site was one of the earliest settlements in Greece, its slopes inhabited by a **Neolithic** community around 5000 BC. In **Mycenaean** times it was fortified with Cyclopean walls (parts of which can still be seen), enclosing a royal palace and temples which fostered the cult of Athena. City and goddess were integrated by the **Dorians** and, with the union of Attic towns and villages in the ninth century BC, the Acropolis became the heart of the first Greek city-state, sheltering its principal public buildings. So it was to remain, save for an interval under the **Peisistratid tyrants** of the seventh and sixth centuries BC, who are-established a fortified residence on the rock. But when the last tyrant was overthrown in 510 BC, the Delphic Oracle ordered that the Acropolis should remain forever the **province of the gods**, unoccupied by humans.

It was in this context that the monuments visible today were built. Most of the substantial remains date from the **fifth century BC** or later; there are outlines of earlier temples and sanctuaries but these are hardly impressive, for they were burned to the ground when the Persians sacked Athens in 480 BC. For some decades, until Pericles promoted his grand plan, the temples were left in their ruined state as a reminder of the Persian action. But with that threat removed, in the wake of Athenian military supremacy and a peace treaty with the Persians in 449 BC, the walls were rebuilt and architects drew up plans for a reconstruction worthy of the city's cultural and political position.

Pericles' **rebuilding** plan was both magnificent and enormously expensive but it won the backing of the democracy, for many of whose citizens it must have created both wealth and work – paid for from the unfortunate Delian League's coffers. The work was under the general direction of the architect and sculptor **Pheidias** and it was completed in an incredibly short time. The Parthenon itself took only ten years to finish: "every architect," wrote Plutarch, "striving to surpass the magnificence of the design with the elegance of the execution".

Their monuments survived unaltered – save for some modest Roman tinkering – for close to a thousand years, until in the reign of Emperor Justinian the temples were converted to **Christian** worship. In subsequent years the uses became secular as well as religious, and embellishments increased, gradually obscuring the Classical designs. Fifteenth-century Italian princes held court in the Propylaia, the entrance hall to the complex, and the same quarters were later used by the **Turks** as their commander's headquarters and as a powder magazine. The Parthenon underwent similar changes from Greek to Roman temple, from Byzantine church to Frankish cathedral, before several centuries of use as a Turkish mosque. The Erechtheion, with its graceful female figures, saw service as a harem. A Venetian diplomat, Hugo Favoli, described the Acropolis in 1563 as "looming beneath a swarm of glittering golden crescents", with a minaret rising from the Parthenon. For all their changes in use, however, the buildings would have resembled – very much more than today's bare ruins – the bustling and ornate ancient Acropolis, covered in sculpture and painted in bright colours.

The Erechtheion

To the north of the Parthenon, beyond the foundations of the Old Temple of Athena, stands the **Erechtheion**, the last of the great works of Pericles to be completed. It was built over ancient sanctuaries, which in turn were predated by a Mycenaean palace. Here, in a symbolic reconciliation, both Athena and the city's old patron of Poseidon-Erechtheus were worshipped; the site, according to myth, was that on which they had contested possession of the Acropolis. The myth (which probably recalls the integration of the Mycenaeans with earlier

Sadly, such images remain only in the prints and sketches of that period: the Acropolis buildings finally fell victim to the demands of war, blown up during the successive attempts by the Venetians to oust the Turks. In 1684 the Turks demolished the temple of Athena Nike to gain a brief tactical advantage. Three years later the Venetians, laying siege to the garrison, ignited a Turkish gunpowder magazine in the Parthenon, and in the process blasted off its roof and set a **fire** that raged within its precincts for two days and nights. The apricot-tinged glow of the Parthenon marbles so admired by the Neoclassicists of the eighteenth century was one of the more aesthetic results.

Arguably surpassing this destruction, at least in the minds of modern Greeks, were the activities of Western looters at the start of the nineteenth century: the French ambassador Fauvel gathering antiquities for the Louvre, and **Lord Elgin** levering away sculptures from the Parthenon in 1801. As British Ambassador to the Porte, Elgin obtained permission from the Turks to erect scaffolding, excavate and remove stones with inscriptions. He interpreted this concession as a licence to make off with almost all of the bas-reliefs from the Parthenon's frieze, most of its pedimental structures and a caryatid from the Erechtheion – which he later sold to the British Museum. There were perhaps justifications for Elgin's action at the time – not least the Turks' tendency to use Parthenon stones in their lime kilns, and possible further ravages of war – though it was controversial even then. Byron, a more sympathetic character who roundly disparaged all this activity, visited in 1810–11, just in time to see the last of Elgin's ships loaded with the marbles. Today, however, the British Museum's continued retention of the "Elgin Marbles" (a phrase that Greek guides on the Acropolis, who portray Elgin unequivocally as a vandal, do not use) rests on legal rather than moral claims. Hopefully the British Museum will soon find a graceful pretext to back down; the long-awaited completion of the new Acropolis Museum, slated to occupy land around the Makriyánni barracks just south of the bluffs, would be a perfect opportunity, but the project – originally scheduled for completion in 1996 – seems to have stalled indefinitely.

As for the Acropolis **buildings**, their fate since the Greeks regained the Acropolis after the War of Independence has not been entirely happy. Almost immediately, Greek archeologists began clearing the Turkish village that had developed around the Parthenon-mosque; a Greek regent lamented in vain that they "would destroy all the picturesque additions of the Middle Ages in their zeal to lay bare the ancient monuments". Much of this early work was indeed destructive: the iron clamps and supports used to reinforce the marble structures were, contrary to ancient example, not sheathed in lead, so they have since rusted and warped, causing the stones to crack. Meanwhile, earthquakes have dislodged the foundations; generations of feet have slowly worn down surfaces; and, more recently, sulphur dioxide deposits, caused by vehicle and industrial pollution, have been turning the marble to dust.

Since a 1975 report predicted the collapse of the Parthenon, visitors have been barred from its actual precinct, and a major, long-term restoration scheme of the entire Acropolis embarked upon. Inevitably this has its frustrations, with many of the buildings scaffolded and the Acropolis at times taking on the appearance of a building site.

pre-Hellenic settlers) tells how an olive tree sprang from the ground at the touch of Athena's spear, while Poseidon summoned forth a seawater spring. The Olympian gods voted Athena the victor.

Pausanias wrote of seeing both olive tree and seawater in the temple, adding that "the extraordinary thing about this well is that when the wind blows south a sound of waves comes from it".

Today, in common with all buildings on the Acropolis, entrance is no longer permitted, but its series of elegant Ionic porticoes are worth close attention, particularly the north one with its fine decorated doorway and frieze of blue Eleusinian marble. On the south side is the famous **Porch of the Caryatids**, whose columns are transformed into the tunics of six tall maidens holding the entablature on their heads. The statues were long supposed to have been modelled on the widows of Karyai, a small city in the Peloponnese that was punished for its alliance with the Persians by the slaughter of its menfolk and the enslavement of the women. There is, though, little suggestion of grieving or humbled captives in the serene poses of the Caryatid women. Some authorities believe that they instead represent the Arrephoroi, young, high-born girls in the service of Athena. The ones in situ are now, sadly, replacements. Five of the originals are in the Acropolis Museum, a sixth was looted by Elgin, who also removed a column and other purely architectural features – pieces that become completely meaningless out of context in the British Museum and which are replaced here by casts in a different colour marble. The stunted olive tree growing in the precinct was planted by an American archeologist in 1917.

The Acropolis Museum

Placed discreetly on a level below that of the main monuments, the **Acropolis Museum** (April–Sept Mon 11am–6.30pm, Tues–Sun 8am–6.30pm; Oct–March Mon 10am–2.30pm, Tues–Sun 8.30am–2.30pm) contains all of the portable objects removed from the site since 1834 (with the exception of a few bronzes displayed in the National Archeological Museum). Over recent years, as increasing amounts of stone and sculptures have been removed from the ravages of environmental pollution, the collection has grown considerably. Labelling is basic at best; a supplementary guide is useful.

In the first rooms to the left of the vestibule are fragments of pedimental sculptures from the **Old Temple of Athena** (seventh to sixth century BC), whose traces of paint give a good impression of the vivid colours that were used in temple decoration. Further on is the **Moschophoros**, a painted marble statue of a young man carrying a sacrificial calf, dated 570 BC and one of the earliest examples of Greek art in marble. Room 4 displays one of the chief treasures of the building, a unique collection of **Korai**, or maidens, dedicated as votive offerings to Athena at some point in the sixth century BC. Between them they represent a shift in art and fashion, from the simply contoured Doric clothing to the more elegant and voluminous Ionic designs; the figures' smiles also change subtly, becoming increasingly loose and natural.

The pieces of the **Parthenon frieze** in Room 8 were sundered from the temple by the Venetian explosion and subsequently buried, thereby escaping the clutches of Lord Elgin. They portray scenes of Athenian citizens in the Panathenaic procession; the fact that mortals featured so prominently in the decoration of the temple indicates the immense collective self-pride of the Athenians at the height of their golden age. This room also contains a graceful and fluid sculpture, known as **Iy Sandalízoussa**, which depicts **Athena Nike** adjusting her sandal. Finally, in the last room are four authentic and semi-eroded **caryatids** from the Erechtheion, displayed behind a glass screen in a carefully rarefied atmosphere.

West and south of the Acropolis

Most visitors to the Acropolis leave by the same route they arrived – north through Pláka. For a calmer and increasingly panoramic view of the rock, it's worth taking the time to explore something of the area to the **west of the Acropolis**, punctuated by the hills of the Areopagus, Pnyx and Filopáppou, each of which had a distinct function in the life of the ancient city.

The **south slope** is rewarding, too, with its Greek and Roman theatres and the remains of *stoas* and sanctuaries. It can be approached from the Acropolis, with an entrance just above the Herodes Atticus theatre, though its main entrance is some way to the south along Leofóros Dhionissíou Areopayítou.

No less important, these sites all give access to the neighbourhoods of **Koukáki** and **Áno Petrálona**, two of the least-spoilt quarters in Athens, and with some of the city's best tavernas (see p.146).

The Areopagus, Pnyx and Filopáppou Hill

Rock-hewn stairs ascend the low hill of the **Areopagus** immediately below the entrance to the Acropolis. The "Hill of Mars" was the site of the Council of Nobles and the Judicial Court under the aristocratic rule of ancient Athens. During the Classical period the court lost its powers of government to the Assembly (held on the Pnyx) but it remained the court of criminal justice, dealing primarily with cases of homicide. Aeschylus used this setting in *The Eumenides* for the trial of Orestes, who, pursued by the Furies' demand of "a life for a life", stood accused of murdering his mother Clytemnestra.

The hill was used as a campsite by the Persians during their siege of the Acropolis in 480 BC, and in the Roman era by Saint Paul, who preached the "Sermon on an Unknown God" here, winning amongst his converts Dionysius "the Areopagite", who became the city's patron saint. Today, there are various foundation cuttings on the site, and the ruins of a church of Áyios Dhioníssios (possibly built over the court), though nothing is actually left standing. The Areopagus's historic associations apart, it is notable mainly for the views, not only of the Acropolis, but down over the Agora and towards Kerameikos – the ancient cemetery (see p.117).

Following the road or path over the flank of the Acropolis, you come out onto Leofóros Dhionissíou Areopayítou, by the Herodes Atticus theatre. Turning right, 100m or so down (and across) the avenue, a network of paths leads up **Filopáppou Hill**, also known as the "Hill of the Muses" (*Lófos Moussón*). This strategic height has played an important, if generally sorry, role in the city's history. It was from here that the shell which destroyed the roof of the Parthenon was lobbed; more recently, the colonels placed tanks on the slopes during their coup of 1967. The area is best avoided at night, as it has a reputation for rapes and muggings.

The hill's summit is capped by a somewhat grandiose monument to a Roman senator and consul, Filopappus, who is depicted driving his chariot on its frieze. Again, it is a place above all for views. To the west is the Dora Stratou Theatre (or Filopáppou Theatre) where Greek music and dance performances (see p.152) are held. Northwest, along the main path, and following a line of truncated ancient walls, is the church of **Áyios Dhimítrios**, an unsung gingerbread gem, which has kept its original Byzantine frescoes. In the cliff-face across from this to the south you can make out a kind of cave dwelling, known (more from imagination than evidence) as the **prison of Socrates**.

Further to the north, above the church, rises the **Hill of the Pnyx**, an area used in Classical Athens as the meeting place for the democratic assembly, which gathered more than forty times a year. All except the most serious political issues, such as ostracism, were aired here, the hill on the north side providing a convenient semicircular terrace from which to address the crowd. All male citizens could vote and, at least in theory, all could voice their opinions, though the assembly was harsh on inarticulate or foolish speakers. There are remains of the original walls, used to form the theatre-like court, and of *stoas* for the assembly's refreshment. The arena is today used for the *son et* *lumière* (not greatly recommended) of the Acropolis, which takes place on most summer evenings.

Beyond the Pnyx, still another hill, **Lófos Nymfón** (Hill of the Nymphs), is dominated by a nineteenth-century observatory and gardens, occasionally open to visitors.

The south slope of the Acropolis

Entrance to the **south slope of the Acropolis** (daily: summer 8am–7pm; winter 8am–2.45pm; €1.50) is on Leofóros Dhionysíou Areopayítou. The second-century Roman **Odeion of Herodes Atticus**, restored for performances of music and Classical drama during the summer festival (see p.152), dominates the south slope of the Acropolis hill. It is open only for shows, though; the main reason to come here otherwise is the earlier Greek sites to the east.

Pre-eminent among these is the **Theatre of Dionysos**, beside the main site entrance. One of the most evocative locations in the city, it was here that the masterpieces of Aeschylus, Sophocles, Euripides and Aristophanes were first performed. It was also the venue for the annual festival of tragic drama, where each Greek citizen would take his turn as member of the chorus. The ruins are impressive. Rebuilt in the fourth century BC, the theatre could hold some 17,000 spectators – considerably more than the Herodes Atticus's 5000–6000 seats; twenty of the theatre's sixty-four tiers of seats survive. Most notable are the great marble thrones in the front row, each inscribed with the name of an official of the festival or of an important priest; in the middle sat the priest of Dionysos and on his right the representative of the Delphic Oracle. At the rear of the stage along the Roman *bema* (rostrum) are reliefs of episodes in the life of Dionysos flanked by two squatting Sileni, devotees of the satyrs. Sadly, all this is roped off to protect the stage-floor **mosaic** – itself a magnificent diamond of multicoloured marble best seen from above.

Above the theatre – reached by steps, then a path to the right – looms a vast grotto, converted perhaps a millennium ago into the chapel of **Panayía Khryssospilióssissa**; it's worth a look for the setting rather than its kitsch iconography. To the west of the theatre extend the ruins of the **Asklepion**, a sanctuary devoted to the healing god Asklepios (see p.795) and built around a sacred spring. The curative centre was probably incorporated into the Byzantine church of the doctor-saints Kosmas and Damian, of which there are prominent remains. Nearer to the road lie the foundations of the Roman **Stoa of Eumenes**, a colonnade of stalls that stretched to the Herodes Atticus Odeion.

The Ancient Agora

The **Agora** or market (southeastern entrance down the path from the Areopagus; northern entrance on Adhrianoú; Tues–Sun 8.30am–3pm; €3.45), established in 3000 BC, was the nexus of ancient Athenian city life. Competing for space were the various claims of administration, commerce, market and public assembly. The result was ordered chaos. Eubolus, a fourth-century poet, observed that "you will find everything sold together in the same place at Athens: figs, witnesses to summonses, bunches of grapes, turnips, pears, apples, givers of evidence, roses, medlars . . . water clocks, laws, indictments". Women, however, were not in evidence; secluded by custom, they would delegate any business in the Agora to slaves. Before shifting location to the Pnyx, the assembly also met here, and continued to do so when discussing cases of ostracism for most of the fifth and fourth centuries BC.

Originally the Agora was a rectangle, divided diagonally by the Panathenaic Way and enclosed by temples, administrative buildings, and long porticoed *stoas* (arcades of shops) where idlers and philosophers gathered to exchange views and listen to the orators. In the centre was an open space, defined by boundary stones at the beginning of the fifth century BC; considered sacred and essential to the life of the community, those accused of homicide or other serious crimes were excluded from it by law.

The site today is an extensive jumble of ruins, dating from various stages of building between the sixth century BC and the fifth century AD. The best overview is from the Areopagus, by the southeast entrance. For some idea of what you are surveying, however, the place to head for is the **Hephaisteion**, or Temple of Hephaistos, somewhat above the general elevation, to the west. An observation point in front of it has a map, which clearly labels the various remains on the site. Because exploits of Theseus were displayed on the metopes and frieze, the Temple of Hephaistos was long thought to be dedicated to Theseus. The best preserved, though perhaps least admired, of all Doric temples, it lacks the curvature and "lightness" of the Parthenon's design. Dedicated to the patron of blacksmiths and metalworkers – hence its popular name – it was the first building of Pericles' programme, though not the first completed. Its remaining metopes depict the labours of Hercules and the exploits of Theseus, while the barrel-vaulted roof dates from the Byzantine conversion of the temple into a church of Saint George. The other bona fide church on the site – that of **Áyii Apóstoli** (the Holy Apostles), by the south entrance – is worth a glance inside for its fresco fragments, exposed during a 1950s restoration of the eleventh-century shrine.

For some background to the Agora, head for the **Museum**, housed in the reconstructed **Stoa of Attalos**. The reconstruction of the *stoa* itself was a US$1.5 million project of the American School of Archeology in Athens in 1953–56. It is, in every respect bar one, an entirely faithful reconstruction of the original. What is missing is colour: in Classical times the exterior would have been painted in bright red and blue (like the Minoan palaces of Crete). Of the displays – mostly pottery from the sixth to fourth century BC, plus some early Geometric grave offerings – highlights are the red-figure dishes depicting athletes, musicians and minor deities, together with an oil flask in the form of a kneeling boy. Particularly interesting are the *ostraka*, or shards of pottery, upon which were written the names of those people who were to be banished from Athens, considered a fate worse than death and from which the word "ostracism" is derived.

Outside the entrance to the site on the other side of Adhrianoú Street, the most prominent ruins are of the **Stoa Poikile** "Painted Stoa", where **Zeno** expounded his Stoic philosophy, and the **Basileos Stoa**, the headquarters of the Archon-king. These were unearthed in 1971 and excavations continue, so that they are not yet open to the public.

Kerameikos (Keramikós)

The **Kerameikos site** (entrance at Ermoú 148; Tues–Sun 8.30am–2.30pm; €1.50), encompassing the principal cemetery of ancient Athens, provides a fascinating and quiet retreat from the Acropolis. It is little visited and in addition has something of an oasis feel about it, with the lush Iridhanós channel, speckled with water lilies, flowing across it from east to west.

From the entrance can be seen the double line of the **Long Walls**, which ran to the port at Pireás; the inner wall was hastily cobbled together by the men, women and children of Athens while Themistocles was pretending to negotiate a mutual disarmament treaty with Sparta in 429 BC. The barriers are interrupted by the great **Dipylon Gate**, where travellers from Pireás, Eleusis and Boeotia entered the ancient city, and the **Sacred Gate**, used for the Eleusinian and Panathenaic processions. These followed the Sacred Way, once lined by colonnades and bronze statues, into the Agora. Between the two gates are the foundations of the **Pompeion**, where preparations for the processions were made and where the main vehicles were stored.

Branching off from the Sacred Way is the **Street of the Tombs**, begun in 394 BC and now excavated along a hundred or so metres. Both sides were reserved for the plots of wealthy Athenians. Some twenty, each containing numerous commemorative monuments, have been excavated, and their original stones, or replicas, reinstated. The flat vertical *stelae* were the main funerary monuments of the Classical world; the sarcophagus belonged to Hellenistic and Roman times. The sculpted crescent with the massive conglomerate base to the left of the path is the *Memorial of Dexileos*, the twenty-year-old son of Lysanias of Thorikos, who was killed in action at Corinth in 394 BC. The adjacent plot contains the *Monument of Dionysios of Kollytos*, in the shape of a pillar *stele* supporting a bull carved from Pentelic marble. As with any cemetery, however, it is the more humble monuments, such as the statue of a girl with a dog on the north side of the street, that connect past and present in the shared experience of loss. From the terrace overlooking the tombs, Pericles delivered his famous funeral oration dedicated to those who died in the first years of the Peloponnesian War. His propaganda coup inspired thousands more to enlist in a campaign during which one-third of the Athenian force was wiped out.

The **Oberlaender Museum**, named after the German-American manufacturer who financed it, contains an extensive collection of *stelae*, terracotta figures, vases and sculptures from the site. Among them, Room 1's *Ampharete Holding Her Infant Grandchild*, and *The Boxer*, with a cauliflower ear and the thongs of a glove tied around his wrist, are remarkable in their detailed execution. The terracotta figures and vases of Room 2 include some of the earliest art objects yet found in Greece.

Pláka and Monastiráki

The largely pedestrianized area of **Pláka**, with its alleys and stairs built on the Turkish plan, is the most rewarding part of the city for daytime wanderings. In addition to a scattering of Roman sites and various offbeat and enjoyable museums, it offers glimpses of an exotic past, refreshingly at odds with the concrete blocks of the metropolis. If you can, time your visit to coincide with the Sunday morning **flea market** around Monastiráki square and along that side of the Agora.

Roughly delineated by Sýndagma, Odhós Ermoú and the Acropolis, the district was basically the extent of nineteenth-century, pre-independence Athens, and provided the core of the city for the next few decades. Once away from Sýndagma, you'll find narrow winding streets lined with nineteenth-century Neoclassical houses, some grand, some humble, with gateways opening onto verdant courtyards overlooked by wooden verandas. Tiled roofs are edged with terracotta medusa-heads, goddesses and foliage designs, ornaments known collectively as *akrokerámata*; the grander facades are decorated with pilasters and capitals and wrought-iron balconies. Poor and working class for most of this century, the district has lately been extensively gentrified and renovated.

PLÁKA

Hotel Grande Bretagne

Parliament Building

National Bank

National Gardens

Russian Church

Jewish Museum

Metamorfosis

Museum of Greek Folk Art

Anglican Church

Byron Statue

Centre of Folk Art & Tradition

Ay. Andhreas

New Cathedral

Old Cathedral

Kapnikaréa

Museum of Greek Popular Musical Instruments

Ay. Ekaterini

Monument of Lysikratos

Tower of the Winds

Medresse

Roman Forum

Kanellopoulos Museum

Fethiye Tzami

Mosque (Ceramics Museum)

Hadrian's Library

FLEA MARKET

ACROPOLIS

ANAFIOTIKA

PL MONASTIRAKIOU

PLATIA SYNDAGMA

100 m

N

ACCOMMODATION

Achilleas	1
Acropolis House	4
Adonis	5
Arethusa	6
Kouros	3
Nefeli	7
Phaedra	9
Student Inn	8
Thisseus Hostel	2

RESTAURANTS

Bairaktaris/Sigalas	A
Damingos (Ta Bakaliarakia)	H
Eden	D
Iy Klimataria	E
Nefeli	F
O Platanos	C
Skholiarhio To Gerani	G
O Thanasis	B

From Sýndagma to Adhrianoú

An attractive approach to Pláka is to follow **Odhós Kydhathinéon**, a pedestrian walkway that starts near the **English and Russian churches** on Odhós
Filellínon, south of Sýndagma. It leads gently downhill, past the Greek Folk Art
Museum, on a leafy square with one of the few remaining old-time cafés on
the corner, on through café-crowded Platía Filomoússou Eterías to Hadrian's
street, **Odhós Adhrianoú**, which runs nearly the whole length of Pláka from
Hadrian's Arch past the ancient Agora.

The **Museum of Greek Folk Art** (Tues–Sun 10am–2pm; €1.45), at
Kydhathinéon 17, is one of the most enjoyable in the city. Its five floors are
mostly devoted to collections of weaving, pottery, regional costumes and
embroidery, which reveal both the sophistication and the strong Middle
Eastern influence of Greek popular arts. On the second floor, the carnival tradition of northern Greece, and the all-but-vanished shadow-puppet theatre,
are featured. The fourth floor dazzles with its exhibits of gold and silver jewellery and weaponry. Most compelling of all, on the third floor, is the reconstructed village room with a series of murals by the primitive artist
Theophilos (1873–1934). Theophilos was a rather eccentric character, dress-
ing in War of Independence outfits and painting tavernas and cafés for a meal
or a small fee. There's a museum of his work at Variá on Lésvos, and other
paintings – usually scenes from peasant life or battles during the War of
Independence – survive in situ in the Peloponnese, on Lésvos and on Mount
Pílion, though they have only in the last few decades been recognized as being
worth preserving.

More recent works of art are displayed in the newly-opened **Frissira
Museum**, Moni Asteriou 3 and 7 (Wed–Fri 11am–7pm, Sat & Sun
10am–2pm; €1.50), Greece's only modern art museum, housed in two beautifully renovated Neoclassical buildings. It has over 3000 works of art, changing exhibitions, a fine shop which also sells art works and an elegant café.

Two other museums are close by. A couple of blocks to the northwest, at
Angelikís Hatzimiháli 6, the **Centre of Folk Art and Tradition** (Tues–Fri
9am–1pm & 5–9pm, Sat & Sun 9am–1pm; closes for a moveable month during summer; free) features costumes, textiles, musical instruments and ceramic
plates in another grand Pláka mansion. A short distance to the east, at Níkis 39,
the **Jewish Museum of Greece** (Mon–Fri 9am–2.30pm, Sun 10am–2pm;
€2.90) displays art and religious artefacts from the very ancient Jewish communities scattered throughout Greece. The centrepiece is the reconstructed
synagogue of Pátra, dating from the 1920s, whose furnishings have been moved
here en bloc and remounted.

The Monument of Lysikratos and around

At the eastern end of Pláka, Odhós Lissikrátous gives onto a small, fenced-off
archeological area at one end of Odhós Tripódhon, the **Street of the Tripods**,
where winners of the ancient dramatic contests dedicated their tripod-trophies
to Dionysos. Here you can see the **Monument of Lysikratos**, a tall and
graceful stone and marble structure from 335 BC, which stands as a surprisingly complete example of these ancient exhibits. A four-metre-high stone
base supports six Corinthian columns rising up to a marble dome on which,
in a flourish of acanthus-leaf carvings, a winning tripod was placed. The
inscription on its architrave tells us that "Lysikratos of Kikyna, son of
Lysitheides was *choregos* (sponsor); the tribe of Akamantis won the victory with

a chorus of boys; Theon played the flute; Lysiades of Athens trained the chorus; Evainetos was archon." The monument was incorporated into a French Capuchin convent in 1667, and tradition asserts that Byron used the convent as a study, writing part of *Childe Harold* here; at the time Athens had no inn, and the convent was a regular lodging for European travellers.

The street beyond, **Výronos**, is named after the poet (*O Lórdhos Výronas* to Greeks). At its far end, facing you across the road, is the old Makriyánni police barracks, revered by Greek rightists for its stout resistance to Communist attack during December 1944. Part of it has been transformed into the so-called **Acropolis Study Centre** (daily 8.30am–3pm; free), flanked by the metro construction and containing little beyond plaster casts of the Elgin Marbles and models of the winning designs for the hypothetical **Acropolis Museum**.

Hadrian's Arch and the Temple of Olympian Zeus

Taking the other street at the Lysikratos monument crossroads, Odhós Lyssikrátous, you emerge at the edge of Pláka near one of the most hazardous road junctions in Athens, the meeting of Dhionyssíou Areopayítou, Amalías and Singroú. Across the way, facing Leofóros Amalías, stands **Hadrian's Arch**, erected by that emperor to mark the edge of the Classical city and the beginning of his own. On the near side its frieze is inscribed "This is Athens, the ancient city of Theseus", and on the other "This is the City of Hadrian and not of Theseus". Since there are few obvious signs of a Roman city, this makes little sense to today's visitor, but there are Roman remains south of the Temple of Olympian Zeus and recent excavations suggest that the Roman city occupied at least the Záppio area.

Directly behind the arch, the colossal pillars of the **Temple of Olympian Zeus** (Tues–Sun 8am–2.30pm; €1.50; entrance on Vasilíssis Ólgas) dominate their surroundings. The largest temple in Greece, and according to Livy, "the only temple on earth to do justice to the god", it was dedicated by Hadrian in 131 AD, some 700 years after the tyrant Peisistratos had laid its foundations. Hadrian marked the occasion by contributing a statue of Zeus and a suitably monumental one of himself, although both have since been lost. Just fifteen of the temple's original 104 Pentelic marble pillars remain erect, though the column drums of another, which fell in 1852, litter the ground, giving a startling idea of the project's size. Almost equally impressive is the fact that in the Byzantine era, a stylite made his hermitage on the temple architrave.

From the Olympian Zeus temple, a shady route up to Sýndagma or Kolonáki leads through the Záppio and the **National Gardens** (see p.132).

Anafiótika and the Kanellópoulos Museum

Continuing straight ahead from the Kydhathinéon–Adhrianoú intersection, up **Odhós Thespídhos**, you reach the edge of the Acropolis precinct. Up to the right, the whitewashed cubist houses of **Anafiótika** cheerfully proclaim an architect-free zone amid the higher slopes of the Acropolis rock. The pleasingly haphazard buildings here were erected by workers from the island of Anáfi in the southern Aegean, who were employed in the mid-nineteenth-century construction of Athens. Unable to afford land, they took advantage of a customary law to the effect that if a roof and four walls could be thrown up overnight, the premises were yours at sunrise. The houses, and the two churches that serve them, are the image of those the Cycladic islanders had left behind.

Follow Rangavá or Stratoús anticlockwise around the Acropolis rock and you will eventually emerge on Theorías, outside the eclectic **Kanellópoulos Museum** (Tues–Sun 8am–3pm; €1.50). Though there is nothing here that you won't see examples of in the bigger museums, this collection of treasures, exhibited in the topmost house under the Acropolis, has a calm appeal. The bulk of the ground-floor exhibits are icons but there is also Byzantine jewellery, bronze oil-lamps and crosses, and Roman funerary ornaments from Fayum. The top floor is given over entirely to Geometric, Classical and Hellenistic art, primarily pottery and votive figurines, generally of a high standard and distinguished by whimsical execution. The middle floor and the stairwells are devoted to Near Eastern and Cypriot art of various periods, including some exquisite Persian goldwork and flamboyantly painted "Phoenician" vials.

The Roman Forum and Tower of the Winds

The western reaches of Adhrianoú, past the Neoclassical Demotic School, is largely commercial – souvenir shops and sandals – as far as the **Roman Forum** (entrance cnr Pelopídha/Eólou; Tues–Sun 8.30am–3pm; €1.50), a large irregularly shaped excavation site bounded by railings.

The forum was built by Julius Caesar and Augustus (Octavian) as an extension of the older ancient Greek agora to its west. It has undergone substantial excavation in recent years, but the majority of it is now open to visitors. Its main entrance, on the west side, was through the relatively intact **Gate of Athena Archegetis**, which consisted of a Doric portico and four columns supporting an entablature and pediment. On the pilaster facing the Acropolis is engraved an edict of Hadrian announcing the rules and taxes on the sale of oil.

The Tower of the Winds

The best-preserved and easily the most intriguing of the forum ruins is the graceful octagonal structure known as the **Tower of the Winds** (Aéridhes in Greek). Designed in the first century BC by Andronikos of Kyrrhos, a Syrian astronomer, it served as a compass, sundial, weather vane and water clock – the latter powered by a stream from one of the Acropolis springs.

Each face of the tower is adorned with a relief of a figure floating through the air, personifying the eight winds. On the **north** side (facing Eólou) is Boreas blowing into a conch shell; **northwest**, Skiron holding a vessel of charcoal; **west**, Zephyros tossing flowers from his lap; **southwest**, Lips speeding the voyage of a ship; **south**, Notos upturning an urn to make a shower; **southeast**, Euros with his arm hidden in his mantle summoning a hurricane; **east**, Apiliotis carrying fruits and wheat; and **northeast**, Kaikias emptying a shield full of hailstones. Beneath each of these, it is still possible to make out the markings of eight sundials.

The semicircular tower attached to the south face was the reservoir from which water was channelled in a steady flow into a cylinder in the main tower; the time was read by the water level viewed through the open northwest door. On the top of the building a bronze Triton revolved with the winds. In Ottoman times, dervishes used the tower as a *tekke* or ceremonial hall, terrifying their superstitious Orthodox neighbours with their chanting, music and whirling meditation.

Roman Athens

When the **Romans** ousted Athens' Macedonian rulers and incorporated the city into the vast new province of Achaia in 146 BC, Athens continued to enjoy rare political privileges. Its status as a respected seat of learning and great artistic centre had already been firmly established throughout the ancient world: Cicero and Horace were educated here and Athenian sculptors and architects were supported by Roman commissions. Unlike Corinth, though, which became the administrative capital of the province, the city was endowed with relatively few imperial Roman **monuments**, Hadrian's Arch being perhaps the most obvious. Athenian magistrates, exercising a fair amount of local autonomy, tended to employ architects who would reflect the public taste for the simpler *propylaion*, gymnasium and old-fashioned theatre, albeit with a few Roman amendments.

The city's Roman **history** was shaped pre-eminently by its alliances, which often proved unfortunate. The first major onslaught occurred in 86 BC, when Sulla punished Athens for its allegiance to his rival Mithridates by burning its fortifications and looting its treasures. His successors were more lenient. Julius Caesar proffered a free pardon after Athens had sided with Pompey; and Octavian, who extended the old agora by building a forum, showed similar clemency when Athens harboured Brutus following the Ides of March. The most frequent visitor was the **Emperor Hadrian**, who used the occasions to bestow grandiose monuments, including his eponymous arch, a magnificent and immense library and (though it had been begun centuries before) the Temple of Olympian Zeus. A generation later **Herodes Atticus**, a Roman senator who owned extensive lands in Marathon, became the city's last major benefactor of ancient times.

Other forum ruins and Hadrian's library

The other forum ruins open to view are somewhat obscure. Among the more prominent Roman bits and pieces are a large public latrine, a number of shops and a stepped *propylaion* or entrance gate just below the Tower of the Winds. To the northwest is the oldest Ottoman mosque in Athens, the **Fethiye Tzami**, built in 1458. It was dedicated by Sultan Mehmet II, who conquered Constantinople in 1453 (*fethiye* means "conquest" in Turkish). It's now used as an archeological warehouse.

Bordering the north end of the forum site, stretching between Áreos and Eólou, stand the surviving walls of **Hadrian's Library**, an enormous building which once enclosed a cloistered court of a hundred columns. **Odhós Áreos**, alongside, signals the beginning of the Monastiráki flea market area (see overleaf). At its end, round behind the forum, are some of the quietest, prettiest and least spoiled streets in the whole of Pláka – many of them ending in steps up to the Anafiótika quarter (see p.121).

Across the street from the Tower of the Winds stands another Turkish relic – a gateway and single dome from a **medresse**, an Islamic school. During the last years of Ottoman rule and the early years of Greek independence it was used as a prison and was notorious for its bad conditions; a plane tree in the courtyard was used for hangings. The prison was closed in the 1900s and torn down.

The Museum of Greek Popular Musical Instruments

Just beside the *medresse*, at Dhioyénous 1–3, is the **Museum of Greek Popular Musical Instruments** (Tues & Thurs–Sun 10am–2pm, Wed noon–6pm; free). Superbly accommodated in the rooms of a Neoclassical building, this wonderful display traces the history and distribution of virtually everything that has ever been played in Greece, including (in the basement) some not-so-obvious festival and liturgical instruments such as triangles, strikers, livestock bells and coin garlands worn by carnival masquers. Reproductions of frescoes show the Byzantine antecedents of many instruments, and headphone sets are provided for sampling the music made by the various exhibits.

After all this plenty, it's difficult to resist the stock of the museum shop, which includes many of the recommendations in our section on music (see Contexts, p.1057), albeit at a slight mark-up.

Monastiráki: the flea market area

The northwest districts of Pláka, along Ermoú and Mitropóleos, are noisier, busier and more geared to the Greek life of the city. Neither street lays any claim to beauty, though the bottom (west) half of **Ermoú**, with its metalworkers and other craftsmen, has an attractive workaday character. The top third, from Eólou just west of the pretty Byzantine church of the Kapnikaréa east to Sýndagma Square, has been made into an attractive pedestrian mall.

Churches are also the chief feature of **Odhós Mitropóleos** (Cathedral Street). The dusty, tiny chapel of **Ayía Dhynámis** crouches surreally below the concrete piers of the Ministry of Education and Religion; the **Mitrópolis** itself, an undistinguished nineteenth-century cannibal of dozens of older buildings, carves out a square midway along; and the **cathedral** stands alongside it, a beautiful little twelfth-century church cobbled together from plain and carved blocks, some of which are as ancient as Christendom itself.

Pandhróssou, Platía Monastirakioú and the Mosque of Tzisdarákis

From the bottom corner of the pedestrianized cathedral square, **Odhós Pandhróssou** leads the way into the **Monastiráki Flea Market** – not that its name is really justified by the rich and conventional jewellery and fur shops that pack the first section. In fact, not many genuine market shops remain at all this side of Platía Monastirakioú. With the exception of a couple of specialist icon dealers, everything is geared to the tourist. Most quirky among them is the shop of Stavros Melissinos, the "poet-sandalmaker of Athens", at Pandhróssou 89. Melissinos enjoyed a sort of fame in the 1960s, hammering out sandals for the Beatles, Jackie Onassis and the like; it is said that John Lennon sought him out specifically for his poetic musings on wine and the sea, which Melissinos continues to sell alongside the footwear.

Platía Monastirakioú, full of nut sellers, lottery sellers, fruit stalls, kiosks – and currently metro-digging paraphernalia – gets its name from the little monastery church (*monastiráki*) at its centre, possibly seventeenth century in origin and badly restored in the early twentieth century. The area around has been a marketplace since Turkish times, and maintains a number of Ottoman features. On the south side of the square, rising from the walls of Hadrian's library and the shacks of Pandhróssou, is the eighteenth-century **Mosque of Tzisdarákis**, now minus minaret and home to the **Museum of Greek Folk Art Kyriazopoulos Ceramic Collection** (daily except Tues 9.30am–2pm; €1.50). Donated by a Thessaloníki professor, the well-labelled and attractively displayed collection is devoted to folk sculpture and pottery, together with some decorated household items from various points in the Hellenic world.

The mosque itself, especially its striped *mihrab* (the niche indicating the direction of Mecca) is equally interesting. Above the entrance is a calligraphic inscription recording the mosque's founder and date, and a series of niches used as extra *mihrabs* for occasions when worshippers could not fit into the main hall.

West of Platía Monastirakioú: the flea market proper

West of Monastiráki square, the **flea market** caters more and more for local needs, with clothes, iron- and copperware, tools and records in **Odhós Iféstou**; old furniture and bric-a-brac in **Platía Avyssinías**; chairs, office equipment, wood-burning stoves, mirrors, canaries and sundry other goods in **Astíngos**, **Ermoú** and nearby. Beside the church of **Ayíou Filípou**, there's a market in hopeless jumble-sale rejects, touted by a cast of eccentrics (especially on Sundays); of late this extends around the corner, along Adhrianoú, as far as Platía Thisíou.

The north entrance to the **Agora** (see p.116) is just south of Platía Avyssinías on Adhrianoú, across the cutting where the metro line for Pireás re-emerges into the open air after tunnelling under the city centre. Odhós Adhrianoú is here at its most appealing, with a couple of interesting antique shops, a shady kafenío above the metro tunnel, and good views of the Acropolis. (It is also along this stretch that the Sunday secondhand market takes place.) Following the Agora fence around to the southwest, you'll come to another good café vantage-point on busy **Apostólou Pávlou**. On the hill above is the old **Observatory**, surrounded by a last enclave of streets untroubled by tourism or redevelopment. There's nothing of particular interest here, just a pleasant wander through the very north end of Áno Petrálona, although the area is lively at night with a selection of trendy bars and cafés.

North from Pláka: the Bazaar, Omónia square and the National Archeological Museum

When the German Neoclassicists descended on Athens in the 1830s, the land between Pláka and present-day **Omónia square** was envisaged as a spacious European expansion of the Classical and medieval town. Time and the realities of Athens' status as a commercial capital have made a mockery of that grandiose vision: the main **bazaar area** is no less crowded and oriental than Monastiráki, while Omónia itself retains a certain grittiness, though there are currently attempts by the government to regenerate the area. For visitors, the focus of interest is the **National Archeological Museum**, which, with its neighbour, the **Polytekhnío**, fronts the student/alternative quarter of **Exárhia**, currently one of the city's liveliest options for nights out.

The bazaar: Ermoú to Omónia

A broad triangle of streets, delineated by Pireós (officially Tsaldhári) in the west and Stadhíou in the east, reaches north to its apex at Omónia square. Through the middle run **Athinás** and **Eólou streets** – the modern **bazaar**, whose stores, though stocked mainly with imported manufactured goods, still reflect their origins in their unaffected decor, unsophisticated packaging and, most strikingly, their specialization, similar to the Oriental *souk* system. Each street has a concentration of particular stores and wares, flouting modern marketing theory. Hence the Monastiráki end of Athinás is dedicated to tools; food stores are gathered around the central market in the middle, especially along Evripídhou; there's glass to the west; paint and brasswork to the east; and clothes in Eólou and Ayíou Márkou. Praxitélous is full of lettering merchants;

Platía Klafthmónos and Aristídhou of electrical goods; and department stores cluster around Omónia. Always raucous and teeming with shoppers, *kouloúri* (bread-ring) sellers, gypsies and other vendors, the whole area is great free entertainment. Eólou is now for pedestrians only and is much more pleasant though perhaps not so dramatic to walk along as Athinás.

The best bit is the central **meat** and **seafood** market, on the corner of Athinás and Evripídhou. The building itself is a grand nineteenth-century relic, with fretted iron awnings sheltering forests of carcasses and mounds of hearts, livers and ears – no place for the squeamish. In the middle section of the hall is the fish market, with all manner of bounty from the sea squirming and glistening on the marble slabs. Across Athinás is the fruit and vegetable bazaar arrayed around a suspended archeological dig. On the surrounding streets grocers pile their stalls high with sacks of pulses, salt cod, barrels of olives and wheels of cheese.

To the north lies the **flower market**, gathered around the church of Ayía Iríni on Eólou. This has stalls through the week but really comes alive with the crowds on a Sunday morning. An additional feature of **Eólou** is its views: walk it north to south, coming from Omónia, and your approach takes you towards the rock of the Acropolis, with the Erechtheion's slender columns and pediment peeking over the edge of the crag.

Around Omónia square

Omónia itself has little to offer in terms of aesthetics, but it is the heart of Athens for a good portion of the population. A continuous turmoil of people and cars, it is Athens at its earthiest and most urban. There are sporadically functioning escalators (the only public ones in Greece) down to the **metro**, and, at the top, *períptera* selling everything from watch straps to porn. The palms around the perimeter are replacements for their predecessors, which were cut down in the 1950s lest foreigners think Greece "too Asiatic". There are plans, however, to spruce up the square in preparation for the 2004 Olympic Games: attempts are being made to move on the prostitutes and their customers, as well as the destitute Albanian refugees who congregrate in the area. Billboards on the square are to be taken down and a large statue placed in the centre, surrounded by landscaped greenery.

To the north, just beside the National Archeological Museum on Patissíon, is the **Polytekhnío**, a Neoclassical building housing the university's school of engineering and science. It was here in late 1973 that students launched their protests against the repressive regime of the colonels' junta, occupying the building and courtyards, and broadcasting calls for mass resistance from a pirate radio transmitter. Large numbers came down to demonstrate support and hand in food and medicines. The colonels' answer came on the night of November 16. Snipers were positioned in neighbouring houses and ordered to fire indiscriminately into the courtyards while a tank broke down the entrance gate. Even today nobody knows how many of the unarmed students were killed – figures range from twenty to three hundred. Although the junta's leader, Papadhópoulos, was able publicly to congratulate the officers involved before being overthrown by secret police chief Ioannídhes, a new, more urgent sense of outrage was spreading; within a year the dictatorship was toppled.

The anniversary of the massacre is invariably commemorated by a march on the US Embassy, outpost of the colonels' greatest ally; it's a bit apathetic nowadays, but still a day out for the Left. The date is also a significant one for the shadowy terrorist group *Dhekaeftá Noemvríou* (17 November), which has operated since the early 1980s. With just two or three low-ranking members caught to date, despite the recent collaboration of Scotland Yard in the search, rumour has it that the group enjoys semi-official protection from rogue elements of the powers-that-be.

The National Archeological Museum

The National Archeological Museum (Mon 12.30–7pm, Tues–Sun 8am–7pm; €5.75), Patissíon 28, is an unrivalled treasure house of Cycladic, Minoan, Mycenaean and Classical Greek art – and an essential Athens experience. Despite inadequate labelling and generally unimaginative displays, it elbows its way into the list of the world's top ten museums. To avoid disappointment, give yourself a clear morning or afternoon for a visit; better still, take in the collection – which can be overwhelming if you delve beyond the obvious highlights – in two or more separate trips. Arriving just as the museum opens or after 5pm will usually mean you will not be competing with the tour groups for space.

The museum's main divisions are: **prehistoric**, with Mycenae predominating; **sculpture** from the Archaic (eighth century BC) to Hellenistic (third to second centuries BC) periods; and **pottery** from the Geometric period (ninth

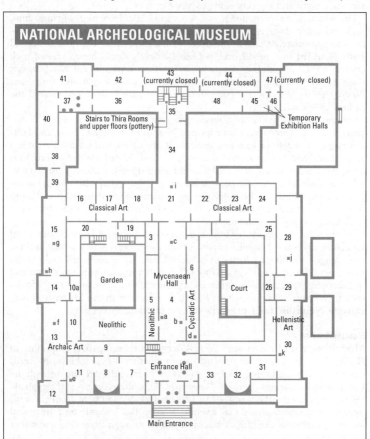

century BC) to the end of the fourth century AD. Smaller self-contained collections include **bronzes** in Rooms 36 to 40; immensely covetable **jewellery** in Room 32. Note that at the time of research, some of the rooms of sculpture and pottery were being rearranged, so the locations listed here might be incorrect when this process is finally completed. Unfortunately, the museum's entire second floor, including the brilliant Minoan-style **frescoes** from Thíra (Santoríni) upstairs in Room 48, has been closed since the 1999 Athens earthquake. The frescoes are being restored and are to be transferred to the new museum in Fira, Santoríni, specially created to house the finds from the ancient settlement of Akrotiri.

Mycenaean and Cycladic art

The biggest crowd-puller is the **Mycenaean hall**, in Room 4. Schliemann's gold finds from Grave Circle A at Mycenae (see p.191) are the big attraction; as hard to get a look at on a summer's day as the Louvre's *Mona Lisa* is the so-called funerary *Mask of Agamemnon* **[a]** in Case 3. Despite the proof offered by modern dating techniques, which indicate that it belonged to some more ancient Achaian king, crowds are still drawn by its correspondence with the Homeric myth and its compelling expression.

The Mycenaeans' consummate art was small-scale decoration of rings, cups, seals and inlaid daggers – requiring eye-tiring scrutiny of the packed showcases to appreciate. As well as the death masks, there's a superb golden-horned *Bull's Head* **[b]** in Case 18, and in Case 1 a lovely duck-shaped vase of rock crystal; in Case 3, with the "Agamemnon" mask, is a magnificent inlaid dagger. Case 8 has jewellery, daggers and a miniature golden owl and frog from Nestor's palace at Pylos; alongside, in Case 9, are baked tablets of Linear B, the earliest Greek writing.

On the left wall there are Cretan-style frescoes from Tiryns which depict chariot-borne women watching spotted hounds in pursuit of boar, and bull-vaulting reminiscent of Knossos. More finds from Tiryns, in Case 15, include a large krater with a chariot and warriors. In Case 32 **[c]** are the superb *Vafio* cups, with their scenes of wild bulls and long-tressed, narrow-waisted men, while in Case 33 an equally eye-catching cup is decorated with twining octopuses and dolphins. Further references to Homer abound: in the small Room 3 to the left there's a magnificent *Boar's Tusk Helmet* and an ivory lyre with sphinxes adorning the soundboard.

To the right of the Mycenaean hall, Room 6 houses a large collection of **Cycladic art** – pre-Mycenaean pieces from the Aegean islands. Many of these idols suggest the abstract forms of modern Cubist art – most strikingly in the much-reproduced *Man Playing a Lyre* **[d]**. Another unusual piece, at the far end of the room, is a sixteenth-century BC cylindrical vase depicting a ring of fishermen carrying fish by their tails. Room 5, to the left of the Mycenaean hall, contains **Neolithic** finds, primarily from excavations in Thessaly.

Sculpture

Most of the rest of the ground floor is occupied by **sculpture**. Beginning in Room 7, on the left of the museum's main entrance, the exhibition proceeds chronologically (and this is the best way to see it) from the Archaic through the Classical and Hellenistic periods (Rooms 7–31) to the Roman- and Egyptian-influenced periods (Rooms 41–43). The gradual development from the stiff, stylized representations of the seventh century BC towards ever freer and looser naturalism is excitingly evident as you go through these cold and rather shabby rooms.

△ Cycladic female figure from Goulandris Cycladic Museum

Early highlights include the Aristion *Stele of a Young Warrior* **[e]**, with delicately carved beard, hair and tunic-folds in Room 11, and the Croesus *kouros* (statue of an idealized youth) in Room 13 **[f]**; both are from the late sixth century BC. You need sharp eyes not to miss some of the less obvious delights. Behind the Croesus *kouros*, for instance, and quite untrumpeted, a statueless plinth is carved with reliefs showing, on one side, young men exercising in the gymnasium, on the other a group of amused friends setting a dog and cat to fight each other – a common enough sight in contemporary Greece.

Room 15, which heralds the **Classical art** collection, leaves you in rather less doubt as to its central focus. Right in the middle stands a mid-fifth-century BC bronze, *Statue of Poseidon* **[g]**, dredged from the sea off Évvia in the 1920s. The god stands poised to throw his trident – weight on the front foot, athlete's body perfectly balanced, the model of idealized male beauty. A less dramatic, though no less important, piece in the same room is the *Eleusinian Relief* **[h]**. Highly deliberate in its composition, the relief shows the goddess of fertility, accompanied by her daughter Persephone, giving to mankind an ear of corn – symbol of the knowledge of agriculture.

Other major Classical sculptures include the *Little Jockey of Artemission* (Room 21; **[i]**), the delicate bronze figure seeming too small for his galloping horse, found in the same shipwreck as the *Poseidon*; the fourth-century BC bronze *Ephebe of Antikithira* **[j]**; the bronze head of a **boxer**, burly and battered, in Room 28; and the third-century BC bronze head of a *Philosopher*, with furrowed brow and unkempt hair, in Room 30. The most reproduced of all the sculptures is also in Room 30: a first-century AD statue of a naked and indulgent *Aphrodite* **[k]** about to rap Pan's knuckles for getting too fresh – a far cry (a long fall, some would say) from the reverent, idealizing portrayals of the gods in Classical times. Room 31 has an extraordinary bronze equestrian portrait statue of the Roman *Emperor Augustus*.

Too numerous to list, but offering fascinating glimpses of everyday life and changing styles of craftsmanship and perception of the human form, are the many **stelae** or carved gravestones found in several of the Classical rooms. Also worth a mention is Room 20, where various Roman copies of the lost Pheidias *Athena*, the original centrepiece of the Parthenon, are displayed.

Exárhia and back towards Sýndagma

Exárhia, fifty-odd blocks squeezed between the National Archeological Museum and Stréfi hill, is one of the city's liveliest and most enjoyable night-time destinations. Since the early 1980s it has become home to a concentration of ouzerís, nightclubs and genuine music tavernas, many relocated from the Pláka; student budgets confronting bistro prices results in the nursing of a single drink all evening.

In the 1980s, the area was linked – in the press at least – with Athens' disaffected youth, and became synonymous with the so-called anarchists who frightened the sedate and respectable by staving in car windscreens, splattering walls with black graffiti and drug-dealing. Since then, Exárhia has been cleaned up somewhat, and the reality is not so extreme as Athenians – who like their city pretty savoury – would lead you to believe, though you still see the odd leftover punk or wasted individual.

Back towards Sýndagma

Between the counter-culturality of Exárhia and the occasional frowsiness of the bazaar, the broad busy avenues of Stadhíou, Panepistimíou and Akadhimías are lined with mainstream retailers, usually tucked into cavernous, often opulent arcades that would have gained the approval of the original Bavarian planners.

Except for the blue city buses peeling off behind on Akadhimías and the metro works along Panepistimíou, the grounds of the Neoclassical **National Library** and **University** buildings, bang in the middle of all this, are an oasis of calm. The scattered buildings, designed by the Dane, Christian Hansen, deserve a look, since their garish decoration gives an alarming impression of what the Classical monuments might have looked like when their paintwork was intact. Also worth a stop if you've time are three minor but quite enjoyable museums.

The first of these, on Platía Kolokotróni, housed the parliament from 1874 until 1935, but since 1961 has been home to the **National Historical Museum** (Tues–Sun 9am–2pm; €1.50). Its exhibits are predominantly Byzantine, though there is also a strong section on the War of Independence that includes Byron's sword and helmet.

The second, the **City of Athens Museum** (Mon, Wed Fri–Sun 9am–1.30pm; €2) is at Paparigopoúlou 7, on Platía Klafthmónos. This was the residence of the German-born King Otho in the 1830s before the new palace (now the Parliament, on Sýndagma) was completed in 1842. Exhibits – mainly prints, and still somewhat sparse – feature an interesting model of the city as it was in 1842, with just three hundred houses and a section of the ancient city walls in a basement.

The trio is completed by the **Numismatic Museum** (Tues–Sun 8am–2.30pm; €3.50), housed in a grand building at Panepistimíou 12, just up the road from the main university complex. The vast collection of over 400,000 coins, ranging from Mycenean times through Classical, Macedonian and Roman to Byzantine and the modern era, was transferred in 1998 from the National Archeological Museum.

Sýndagma, the National Gardens and south

All roads lead to Platía Syndágmatos – **Sýndagma** (Syntagma) square – so you'll find yourself there sooner or later. Catering to tourism, with a post office (extended hours), American Express, airline and travel offices grouped around – not to mention *McDonalds*, *Arby's Roast Beef* and *Wendy's* – it has convenience but not much else to recommend it.

The square

Most of the square's buildings are modern and characterless, except on the uphill (east) side where the **Voulí**, the Greek National Parliament, presides. This was built as the royal palace for Greece's first monarch, the Bavarian King Otho, who moved in in 1842. In front of it, goose-stepping **Evzónes** in tasselled caps, kilt and woolly leggings – a prettified version of traditional mountain costume – change their guard at intervals in front of the **Tomb of the Unknown Soldier**; on Sunday, at slightly before 11am, a full band and the entire corps parades from the tomb along Iródhou Attikoú to the rhythm of camera shutters. Hemingway, among others, impugned their masculinity, but they are in fact a highly trained elite corps with rigorous height and weight requirements; formerly they were recruited almost exclusively from mountain villages.

Other flanking buildings to have survived postwar development include the vast **Hotel Grande Bretagne** – Athens' grandest. In the course of one of the more nefarious episodes of British meddling in Greek affairs, it nearly became the tomb of Winston Churchill. He had arrived on Christmas Day 1944 to sort out the *Dhekemvrianá*, the "events of December", a month of serious street-fighting between British forces and the Communist-led ELAS resistance movement, whom the British were trying to disarm. ELAS saboteurs had placed an enormous explosive charge in the drains, intending to blow up various Greek and Allied VIPs; according to whom you believe, it was either discovered in time by a kitchen employee, or removed by ELAS themselves when they realized they might get Churchill as well.

"Sýndagma" means "constitution" and the name derives from the fact that Greece's first one was proclaimed by a reluctant King Otho from a palace balcony in 1843. The square is still the principal venue for mass **demonstrations**, whether trade-union protests against the government's austerity programmes or "drive-in" sabotage by taxi-drivers outraged at proposals to curtail their movements in the interest of cleaner air. In the run-up to elections, the major political parties stage their final campaign rallies here – a pretty intimidating sight, with around 100,000 singing, flag-waving Greeks packed into the square. At such times, overground city transport in the area comes to a halt.

The National Gardens

At the back of the Voulí, the **National Gardens** (sunrise to sunset; free) are the most refreshing acres in the whole city – not so much a flower garden as a luxuriant tangle of trees, whose shade and duck ponds provide palpable relief from the heat and smog of summer. They were originally the private palace gardens – a pet project of Queen Amalia in the 1840s; purportedly the main duty of the minuscule Greek navy in its early days was the fetching of rare plants, often the gifts of other royal houses, from remote corners of the globe.

Of late, however, the gardens have fallen on hard times: pond-cleaning and pruning are done only when funding permits, a botanical museum is closed more often than not, and a sorry excuse for a mini-zoo has become the target of criticism by environmental and animal-welfare groups. To add insult to injury, the metro project has requisitioned a large area of the gardens for air vents and site bungalows. The general air of dereliction is reinforced by the numerous cats abandoned here and fed only intermittently. Nonetheless, it provides a convenient refuge from the bustle of Sýndagma.

The southern extension of the gardens, open 24 hours, consists of the graceful crescent-shaped grounds of the **Záppio**. This grand Neoclassical exhibition hall, another creation of the Danish architect Hansen (he of the university), was for a period the Greek State Radio headquarters, but is now used mainly for press conferences and commercial exhibitions.

Iródhou Attikoú also fronts the **Presidential Palace**, the royal residence until Constantine's exile in 1967, where more *evzónes* stand sentry duty. The surrounding streets, with a full complement of foreign embassies and hardly a store or taverna, are very posh and heavily policed. The centre-right party, Néa Dhimokratía, has its headquarters in Odhós Rigílis nearby, as does the army's Officers' Club, scene of much anti-democratic intriguing in the past.

The Olympic Stadium

A walk to the base of Iródhou Attikoú and across busy Leofóros Ardhittoú will bring you to the **Olympic Stadium**, a nineteenth-century reconstruction on

Roman foundations, slotting tightly between the pine-covered spurs of Ardhittós hill; access is via the gate on Arhimídhous.

This site was originally marked out in the fourth century BC for the Panathenaic athletic contests, but in Roman times, as a grand gesture to mark the reign of the emperor Hadrian, it was adapted for an orgy of blood sports, with thousands of wild beasts baited and slaughtered in the arena. Herodes Atticus later undertook to refurbish the 60,000 seats of the entire stadium; his white marble gift was to provide the city with a convenient quarry through the ensuing seventeen centuries.

The stadium's reconstruction dates from the modern revival of the Olympic Games in 1896 and to the efforts of another wealthy benefactor, the Alexandrian Greek Yiorgos Averoff. Its appearance – pristine whiteness and meticulous symmetry – must be very much as it was when first restored and reopened under the Roman senator, and indeed it's still used by local athletes and as the finishing point for the Athens Marathon. Above the stadium to the south, on the secluded **Hill of Ardhittós**, are a few scant remnants of a Temple of Fortune, again constructed by Herodes Atticus.

Mets and Pangráti

South and east of Ardhittós are the only two central neighbourhoods outside Pláka to have retained something of their traditional flavour – **Mets** and **Pangráti**. Particularly in Mets, a steep hillside quarter on the southwest side of the stadium, there are still nearly intact streets of pre-World War II houses, with tiled roofs, shuttered windows, and courtyards with spiral metal staircases and potted plants. They're a sad reminder of how beautiful this out-of-control city once was, even quite recently.

Mets and the Próto Nekrotafío

More specific attractions in **Mets** are the concentration of tavernas and bars around Márkou Moussoúrou and Arhimídhous, and the Próto Nekrotafío (First Cemetery), at the top end of Anapáfseos (Eternal Rest) street, lined with florists and shops catering to the funerary trade.

The **Próto Nekrotafío** shelters the tombs of just about everybody who was anybody in nineteenth- and twentieth-century Greek public life, including Heinrich Schliemann, Melina Mercouri, actress Aliki Vouyouklaki and former prime minister Andreas Papandreas. The humbler tombs of musicians (such as *bouzouki* player Vasillis Tsitsanis), artists and writers are interspersed with ornate mausolea of soldiers, statesmen and "good" families, whose descendants come to picnic, stroll and tend the graves. One of the "unregarded wonders of Athenian life", Peter Levi called it: "the neoclassical marbles run riot, they reflower as rococo, they burst into sunblasts of baroque". The graveside statuary occasionally attains the status of high art, most notably in the works of Ianoulis Halepas, a Belle Epoque sculptor from Tínos generally acknowledged to be the greatest of a school of fellow-islanders. Halepas battled with mental illness for most of his life and died in extreme poverty in 1943; his masterpiece is the idealized **Kimiméni** (Sleeping Girl), on the right about 300m in.

Pangráti

Pangráti is the unremarkable but pleasant quarter to the north and east of the Stadium. Platía Plastíra, Platía Varnáva and Platía Pangratíou are the focal points, the first with a vast old-fashioned kafenío where you can sit for hours on a leafy terrace for the price of a coffee. Pangratíou, fringed by the local *álsos* or grove-park, is the rallying place for the neighbourhood's youthful posers. Several good tavernas are tucked away between (and on) Platía Varnáva and nearby Odhós Arhimídhous, and the latter has an impressive *laïkí agorá* – **street market** – every Friday.

More Pangráti eating places can be found down towards Leofóros Vas. Konstandínou, among the rather claustrophobic alleys opposite the **statue of Harry Truman** – repeatedly restored to his pedestal after being blown off it by leftists in reprisal for his bringing the US into the Greek civil war. The Nobel-laureate poet **George Seferis** lived not far away in Odhós Ágras, an attractive stair-street flanking the northeast wall of the Stadium.

North of Sýndagma: Kolonáki, Lykavitós and the Benáki and Cycladic Art museums

Athens is at its trendiest north of Sýndagma, and if you have money to spend, **Kolonáki** is the place to do it, catering to every Western taste from fast food to high fashion. The quarter is not especially interesting for visitors to the city – though it's a fond haunt of expatriates – but it does give access to **Lykavitós Hill**, where a funicular hauls you up for some of the best views of the city. Also close by are two fine museums: one devoted to **Cycladic Art**, the other, the **Benáki**, an assembly of just about all things Greek, from Mycenaean artefacts to twentieth-century memorabilia. Here too, what are believed to be the fourth-century BC foundations of **Aristotle's Lyceum** were recently unearthed, during routine excavation work for a new Museum of Modern Art. The discovery of the Lyceum, where Aristotle taught for thirteen years and Socrates was a frequent visitor, is of immense importance to scholars.

Kolonáki

Kolonáki is the city's most chic central address and shopping area. Although no great shakes architecturally, it enjoys a superb site on the southwest-facing slopes of Lykavitós (Lycabettus), looking out over the Acropolis and National Gardens. From its summit, on one of those increasingly rare clear days, you can see the mountains of the Peloponnese. The lower limits of Kolonáki are defined by Akadhimías and Vasilíssis Sofías streets, where in grand Neoclassical palaces Egypt, France and Italy have their embassies. The middle stretches of the quarter are taken up with shops, while the highest are purely residential.

The heart of the district is officially called Platía Filikís Eterías, but is known to all as **Kolonáki square**, after the ancient "little column" that hides in the trees on the southwest side. Other diversions include the kiosks with their stocks of foreign papers and magazines, the **British Council** on the downhill side, and numerous cafés on Patriárhou Ioakím to the east – the principal display ground for Kolonáki's well-heeled natives. Assorted cafés and pubs nearby on pedestrianized Tsakálof, Milióni and Valaorítou are better and slightly cheaper options for snacks and drinks.

Kolonáki's streets also contain an amazing density of small, classy **shops**, with the accent firmly on **fashion** and **design**. In a half-hour walk around the neighbourhood you can view the whole gamut of consumer style. Patriárhou Ioakím and Skoufá, with its cross-streets to the northwest, comprise the most promising area, along with the pedestrianized Voukourestíou–Valaorítou–Kriezótou block, just below Akadhimías.

For more random strolling, the highest tiers of Kolonáki are pleasant, with steep streets ending in long flights of steps, planted with oleander, jasmine and other flowering shrubs. The one **café** spot up here is at **Platía Dhexamenís**, a small and attractive square close to the Lykavitós loop road, where for most of the year tables are set under the trees around the **Dhexamení**, a covered reservoir begun by the emperor Hadrian.

Lykavitós Hill

Not far away from Kolonáki square, at the top of Ploutárhou, a **funicular** (Mon–Wed & Fri–Sun 8.45am–12.40am, Thurs 10.30am–12.40am, every 10min in summer, less frequent the rest of the year; €1.50) begins its ascent to the summit of **Lykavitós Hill**. For the more energetic, the principal path up the hill begins by the bus stop across from the *St George Lycabettus Hotel* above Platía Dhexamenís and rambles through woods to the top. There's a small café halfway up eyeball-to-eyeball with the Acropolis. On the summit, the chapel of **Áyios Yeóryios** dominates – a spectacular place to celebrate the saint's name-day if you're around on April 23 (or the day after Easter if Áyios Yeóryios falls during Lent.) An expensive restaurant commands the adjacent terrace facing the Acropolis and the sea. The restaurant also operates a café on the terrace facing inland.

The road up the hill goes to the open-air **Lykavitós Theatre**, which is used mainly for concerts from May to October. If you come down by the southeast slopes, you emerge near the lovely little enclave that the British and American archeological schools have created for themselves on Odhós Souidhías. Here, too, is the **Yennádhion Library**, with large collections of books on Greece and an unpublicized drawer full of Edward Lear's watercolour sketches; good-quality and reasonably priced reproductions are on sale.

The Benáki Museum

Recently reopened after a lengthy refit, the often overlooked **Benáki Museum** (Mon, Wed, Fri & Sat 9am–5pm, Thurs 9am–midnight, Sun 9am–3pm; €5.75), at Koumbári 1/cnr Vasilíssis Sofías, should not be missed. Housing a private collection given to the state by **Emmanouíl Benakis**, a collector who had grown wealthy on the Nile cotton trade, it at once surprises and fascinates, with exhibits ranging from Mycenaean jewellery, Greek costumes and folk artefacts to Byronia, and memorabilia of the Greek War of Independence. These, together with displays of jewellery from the Hélène Stathatos collection (of National Archeological Museum fame) are worth a couple of hours of anyone's time.

In the old setting the displays were jumbled and confusing, but with the reorganization, more than 20,000 items are successfully exhibited and clearly labelled in 36 rooms. Exhibits are arranged chronologically, with the ancient finds on the lower floors and the modern Greek artefacts on the upper floors. Among the more unusual items are collections of early Greek Gospels, liturgical vestments and church ornaments rescued by Greek refugees from Asia Minor in 1922; dazzling embroideries and body ornaments; and some unique historical material on the Cretan statesman Eleftherios Venizelos, Asia Minor and the Cretan Revolution.

An additional attraction, especially if you've been dodging traffic all day, is the **rooftop café**, with good snacks and views from the veranda over the nearby

National Gardens. A **shop** (Mon–Sat 9am–3pm), by the entrance, stocks a fine selection of books on Greek folk art, records of regional music and some of the best posters and postcards in the city. The nineteenth-century **Stathatos House** now functions as a wing of the museum, containing the Greek art collection of the Academy of Athens.

Goulandhrís Museum of Cycladic and Ancient Greek Art

For display, labelling, explanation and comfort, the small private **Goulandhrís Museum of Cycladic and Ancient Greek Art** (Mon & Wed–Fri 10am–4pm, Sat 10am–3pm; €3.50) on Neofýtou Dhouká, is way ahead of anything else in Athens. The collection includes objects from the Cycladic civilization (third millennium BC), pre-Minoan Bronze Age (second millennium BC) and the period from the fall of Mycenae to the beginning of historic times around 700 BC, plus a selection of Archaic, Classical and Hellenistic pottery; you learn far more about these periods than from the corresponding sections of the National Archeological Museum.

If Cycladic art seems an esoteric field, don't be put off. The distinctive marble bowls and folded-arm figurines with their sloping wedge heads are displayed in a way that highlights their supreme purity and simplicity, and elucidates their appeal to twentieth-century artists like Moore, Picasso and Brancusi. You can also see in the figurines the remote ancestry of the Archaic style that evolved into the great sculptures of the Classical period. The exact purpose of the mostly female effigies is unknown but, given their frequent discovery in grave-barrows, it has been variously surmised that they were spirit-world guides for the deceased, substitutes for the sacrifice of servants and attendants, or representations of the Earth Goddess in her role of reclaiming yet another of her children.

Much of the top floor is devoted to a collection of painted Classical bowls, often showing two unrelated scenes on opposite sides. The curators consider the one with a depiction of revellers on one face and three men in cloaks conversing on the other to be the star exhibit, but there is not one dud. Most of the more exquisite items date from the fifth century BC – not for nothing was it referred to as a "golden age". To round off the experience, there's a good **shop**, **snack bar** and shaded courtyard.

Other nearby museums

A number of other museums of somewhat more specialist interest is grouped conveniently close together near the angled intersection of Vasilíssis Sofías and Vasiléos Konstandínou, close by the Benáki and Cycladic Art museums.

Byzantine Museum

The setting of the **Byzantine Museum** (Tues–Sun 9am–9pm; €1.50) at Vasilíssis Sofías 22 is perhaps its best feature: a peaceful, courtyarded villa that once belonged to the Duchesse de Plaisance, an extravagantly eccentric French philhellene and widow of a Napoleonic general who helped fund the War of Independence. To enjoy the exhibits – almost exclusively icons, housed in two restored side galleries – requires some prior interest, best developed by a trip to the churches at Mystrás, Dhafní or Ósios Loukás. Labelling is generally Greek-only and you are told little of the development of styles, which towards the sixteenth century show an increasing post-Renaissance Italian influence, owing to the presence of the Venetians in Greece. The rear hall contains marble artefacts, plus a reconstructed basilica. An annexe is currently under construction, which will hopefully mean better exposure for artefacts previously held in storage.

War Museum

The only "cultural" endowment of the 1967–74 junta, the **war museum** (Tues–Sun 9am–2pm; free) at Vasilíssis Sofías 24, becomes predictably militaristic and right-wing as it approaches modern events: the Asia Minor campaign, the civil war, Greek forces in Korea, etc. Earlier times, however, are covered with a more scholarly concern and this gives an interesting insight into changes in warfare from Mycenae through to the Byzantines and Turks. Among an array of models is a fascinating series on the acropolises and castles of Greece, both Classical and medieval.

National Gallery of Art

The **National Gallery Alexandros Soutsos** (Tues & Thurs–Sat 9am–3pm, Mon & Wed 9am–3pm & 6–9pm, Sun 10am–2pm; €5.75) at Vasiléos Konstandínou 50, has a rather disappointing core collection of Greek art from the sixteenth century to the present. One of the few modern painters to stand out is Nikos Hatzikyriakos-Ghikas (Ghika), well represented on the ground floor. On the mezzanine is a small group of canvases by the primitive painter Theophilos (more of whose work can be seen at the Museum of Greek Folk Art in Pláka – see p.120). A recent refurbishment has created a much more prominent area for temporary exhibitions, most of them major loans from the world's best museums and definitely worth catching; keep an eye out for posters or check in the *Athens News*.

The outskirts: Dhafní, Kessarianí and Kifissiá

Athens pushes its suburbs higher and wider with each year and the **monasteries of Dhafní** and **Kessarianí**, once well outside the city limits, are now approached through more or less continuous cityscape. However, each retains a definite countryside setting and makes for a good respite from the central sights.

The monasteries are easily reached by taxi or by local **city transport**. For Dhafní (9km west of the centre), take bus #A16, #B16 or #A16 from Platía Elefthérias, 300m down Pireós from Omónia; the monastery is to the left of the road, about twenty-minutes' ride (Platía Elefthérias is popularly known as Platía Koumoundoúrou and the return buses are so marked). For Kessarianí, take blue bus #224 from Akadhimías to the last stop, from where the church is a thirty- to forty-minute climb further up the lower slopes of Mount Imittós.

The northern suburb of **Kifissiá** is included in this section as an insight into wealthy Athenian life – it has long been where the rich have their villas – and for natural history students, who may want to check out the Goulandhrís Museum. Kifissiá is the northernmost stop on the metro. Classical enthusiasts may want to continue from Dhafní to the site of **Eleusis** (see p.172), a further twenty-minute ride on the #A16 bus route.

Dhafní

Damaged in the 1999 earthquake, **Dhafní Monastery** was closed at the time of research for restoration work and is due to reopen in 2003. One of the great buildings of Byzantine architecture, the monastery's classic Greek-cross-octagon design is a refinement of a plan first used at Ósios Loukás, on the road to Delphi (see p.315), and its mosaics are considered among the great masterpieces of the Middle Ages.

The monastic church replaced a fortified fifth-century basilica, which in turn had been adapted from the ruins of a sanctuary of Apollo – the name is derived from the *daphnai* (laurels) sacred to the god. Both the church and the fortifications which enclose it incorporate blocks from the ancient sanctuary; a porch featuring Classical columns was present up until two centuries ago, when it was hauled off among Lord Elgin's swag.

The Byzantines only occupied the building for little over a century. When the monastery was established, in 1070, the Greek Church was undergoing an intellectual revival, but the state was in terminal collapse. The following year the Normans took Bari, the last Byzantine possession in southern Italy, and the Seljuk Turks defeated the Byzantine army in Armenia – a prelude to the loss of Asia Minor and, before long, Greece itself. The fortifications and remains of a Gothic cloister show evidence of later building under the Cistercians, who replaced Dhafní's Orthodox monks after the Frankish conquest of Athens in 1204. The monastery today is unoccupied; the Cistercians were banished by the Turks, and Orthodox monks, allowed to return in the sixteenth century, were duly expelled for harbouring rebels during the War of Independence.

Inside the church, the **mosaic cycle** is remarkable for its completeness: there are scenes from the life of Christ and the Virgin, saints (a predominance of Eastern figures from Syria and elsewhere in the Levant), archangels and prophets. The greatest triumph is the *Pandokrátor* (Christ in Majesty) on the dome: lit by the sixteen windows of the drum, and set against a background of gold, this stern image directs a tremendous and piercing gaze, his finger poised on the Book of Judgement. A perfect encapsulation of the strict orthodoxy of Byzantine belief, the scene is rendered poignant by the troubled circumstances in which it was created.

Kessarianí

What it loses in a strict architectural comparison with Dhafní, **Kessarianí monastery** makes up for in its location. Although just 5km from the centre of the city, it is high enough up the slopes of Mount Imittós to escape the *néfos* and the noise. The sources of the river Ilissos provide for extensive gardens hereabouts, as they have since ancient times (Ovid mentions them); Athenians still come to collect water from the local fountains, though it may have become contaminated and should not be drunk.

The monastery buildings date from the eleventh century, though the frescoes in the chapel are much later – executed during the sixteenth and seventeenth centuries. In contrast to Dhafní's clerics, Kessarianí's abbot agreed to submit to Roman authority when the Franks took Athens, so the monastery remained in continuous Greek (if not quite Orthodox) occupation through the Middle Ages. Today the monastery is maintained by a small group of monks, who allow **visits** (Tues–Sun 8.30am–3pm; €2.30). Outside these hours you can while away the time in the well-maintained grounds, full of picnickers in summertime.

On the way up to the monastery, which is fairly obvious from the bus terminal, don't overlook the refugee neighbourhood of Kessarianí. With an attractively ramshackle aspect, its streets were used as a 1920s location for the Greek movie *Rembetiko*. You can also catch a glimpse, to the north, of the uniform blocks of Panepistimioúpoli, the university campus.

Kifissiá

Kifissiá, one of Athens's most desirable suburbs, edges up the leafy slopes of Mount Pendéli, about 10km north of the city centre. A surprising 300m above sea level and a good 5°F cooler than central Athens, it appealed to the nineteenth-century bourgeoisie as a suitable site for summer residence. Their villas – Neoclassical, Swiss, Alsatian and fantasy-melange – still hold their own amid the newer concrete models. Indeed, despite the encroachments of speculators' apartment buildings and trendy boutiques, the suburb's village-like character prevails.

The centre of the old "village" is the crossroads called Plátanos – though the mighty plane tree that gave it its name has long since fallen under the axe of the traffic planners – just at the uphill end of the gardens opposite the Kifissiá metro station. The hub are the two or three streets around Plátanos: *Varsos*, in the middle of the block up Kassavéti from Platía Platánou, an old-fashioned patisserie specializing in home-made yogurts, jams and sticky cakes, acts as a meeting place for the whole neighbourhood. Most other watering holes are trendy and pricey cafés and bars, full of young locals preening themselves and yakking on their mobiles.

If you want some direction to your wanderings around trees and gardens, head for the **Goulandhrís Natural History Museum** (Sat & Sun 9am–2.30pm; €2.30) at Levídhou 13, fifteen-minutes' walk from the metro. The collection has especially good coverage of Greek birds and butterflies and endangered species like the monk seal (*Monachus monachus*; see p.919) and loggerhead sea turtle (*Caretta caretta*; see p.989) and a 250,000-specimen herbarium. The museum has a café and a shop selling superb illustrated books, postcards, posters and prints.

Eating and drinking

As you'd expect in a city that houses almost half the Greek population, Athens has the best and the most varied **restaurants** and **tavernas** in the country – and most places are sources not just of good food but of a good night out.

Starting with **breakfast**, most Athenians survive on a thimbleful of coffee, but if you need a bit more to set you up for the day, you'll easily find a bakery, yogurt shop or fruit stall. Koukáki is particularly good for this, with the *Nestoras Tzatsos* bakery at Veïkoú 45, another at no. 75, and still another on pedestrianized Olymbíou, just off Platía Koukáki, offering excellent wholegrain bread and milk products. Alternatively, you could try one of the places listed under "Tea houses and patisseries" on p.147. For a regular **English breakfast**, there are several options in and around Pláka. For a proper American or Continental breakfast, from croissants and pastries to multi-filling omelettes, head for Neon at Mitropoleos 3.

Later in the day, a host of **snack** stalls and outlets get going. If your budget is low you can fill up at them exclusively, avoiding sit-down restaurants altogether. The standard **snacks** are *souvláki me píta* (kebab in pitta bread), *tyrópites* (cheese pies) and *spanakópites* (spinach pies), along with *bougátses* (cream pies) and a host of other speciality pastries. There is a cluster of good **souvláki** stands around Exárhia square, while those in the immediate vicinity of Omónia are best avoided. At Omónia square 18, however, and at several other points in the city, such as Tsakálof 14, Kolonáki, look out for the *Everest* chain, which does a nice line in pastries, sandwiches and ice cream and stays open past midnight.

Krínos at Eólou 87, an old-fashioned cafeteria operating since 1922 behind the central market, has delectable *loukoumadhes* (pastry puffs soaked in honey-citrus syrup and dusted in cinammon), *tyrópites* and *rizogalo* (rice pudding). There is a *Bagel Café* at Karayeóryi Servías 9b, just below Sýndagma, while the *Aríston* around the corner at Voulís 10 has been famous for years for its good, inexpensive *tyropites*.

For **main meals**, Pláka's hills and lanes provide a pleasant evening setting, despite the aggressive touts and general tourist hype. But for good value and good quality, only a few of the quarter's restaurants and tavernas are these days worth a second glance. For quality Greek cooking, if you're staying any length of time in the city, it's better to strike out into the ring of **neighbourhoods** around: Mets, Pangráti, Exárhia/Neápoli, Koukáki, Áno Petrálona or the more upmarket Kolonáki. None of these is more than a half-hour's walk, or a quick trolleybus or taxi ride, from the centre – effort well repaid by more authentic menus, and often a livelier atmosphere.

Restaurants

The listings below are devoted mainly to **restaurant meals**, grouped according to district and divided into cheap (under €13 per person) and less so (over €13). Note that some of our recommendations are closed in summer (usually Aug), and for five days or so around Easter; this is usually due to hot, un-air-conditioned locales, or the exodus of their regular business trade.

Pláka

Selections here represent just about all of note that **Pláka** has to offer; most are on the periphery of the quarter, rather than on the more travelled squares and stairways. At the latter, don't be bamboozled by the touts, positioned at crucial locations to lure you over to their tavernas' tables – invariably a bad sign. The nearest metro stops for the area are Acropolis or Monastiráki.

Under €13

Damingos (Ta Bakaliarakia) Kydhathinéon 41 ☎ 010/32 25 084. Open since 1865 and tucked away in the basement, this place has dour service, but the old-fashioned operation (hefty barrels in the back room filled with the family's home vintages including a memorable retsina) and excellent *bakaliáro skordhaliá* (cod with garlic sauce) make up for it. Evenings only; closed mid-July to end August.

Iy Klimataria, Klepsýdhras 5 ☎010/32 11 315. Having recently celebrated its centenary and still going strong, this unpretentious and pleasant taverna has decent food, mainly grilled meat and fish. In winter, you're likely to be treated to live, unamplified guitar and accordian music, which inspires sing-alongs by the mostly Greek clientele. In the

summer, the roof opens and the quiet shaded street becomes an oasis.

Skholiarhio To Gerani, Tripódhon 14 ☎010/32 47 605. Attractive split-level taverna, known as *Kouklis* by the Greeks, with a perennially popular summer terrace, sheltered from the street. It has a great selection of mezédhes brought out on long trays so that you can point to the ones you fancy. Especially good are the flaming sausages, *bouréki* (thin pastry filled with ham and cheese) and grilled aubergine. Beware of the house red wine though: it goes down easily but can leave you feeling fragile in the morning.

Over €13

Eden, Lissíou 12, off Mnesikléous ☎010/32 48 858. The city's oldest vegetarian restaurant offers dishes you'll pine for on travels around Greece such as mushroom pie, chilli and soya lasagna. The retro setting, on the ground floor of an old mansion, is pleasant as well. Portions not huge but very tasty. Closed Tues.

Nefeli, cnr Aretoúsas & Pános ☎010/32 12 475. Delightful setting under a secluded grape arbour or in an old mansion with a panoramic view, on a peaceful side street. Does a small but interesting selection of classic Greek dishes such as veal and lamb *stamna* (casserole baked in a clay pot). Subdued live Greek music by a duo and small dance floor. The adjacent synonymous ouzerí overlooking the church of Ayía Anna is a busier local hangout favoured by young Greeks. Dinner only at

taverna, ouzerí open all day.

Palea Taverna Tou Psarra, Erekthéos 16 at Erotokritou ☎010/32 18 733. A restored old mansion in a splendid setting, on a tree-shaded and bougainvillea-draped pedestrian crossroads. You're best making a meal of the mezédhes, which include humble standards as well as seafood and fish concoctions.

O Platanos, Dhioyénous 4 ☎010/32 20 666. One of the oldest tavernas in Pláka, with outdoor summer seating under the namesake tree around the corner from the Roman agora. Specialities include chops and roast lamb with artichokes or spinach and potatoes. The barrelled retsina is the real thing and reasonable. Serves lunch and supper.

Monastiráki, Psyrrí, Gázi and the bazaar

The shift from Pláka to the more genuinely commercial quarter of **Monastiráki** is refreshing, since the area attracts serious eaters. There is a definite character about the streets, too, at its best around the flea market. A few blocks west of Athinás the up-and-coming area of **Psyrrí** is now home to a throng of trendy *mezedhopolía* and bars that line the crossroads of Ayíon Anaryíron and Táki. The newly revitalized district of **Gázi** also has a number of restaurants worth checking out. For a fascinating glimpse of the capital's high and low life at nocturnal play visit one of the trio of places within the **meat market**, open through the night.

Under €13

Bairaktaris/Sigalas, Platía Monastirakioú 2 ☎010/32 13 036. In operation now for more than a century, this gregarious restaurant occupies two buildings, whose walls are lined with wine barrels and photos of schmoozing movie stars and politicians. Some tables are set on the bustling pedestrian walkway at Ermoú, but for a cosier atmosphere, eat inside the second building, closer to Mitropóleos, which is favoured by the Greek regulars and often has some impromptu live Greek music. Straightforward menu of oven dishes such as *tsoutsoukakia* (meatballs in tomato sauce), which can be inspected in pots in front of the kitchen. Daily 7am–3am.

Dirty Ginger, Triptolemou 46, Gazi ☎010/34 23 809. Tasty mixture of Greek and foreign food at moderate prices in a quiet garden. Young crowd and lively recorded music. Open summer only, dinners daily and lunch on Sat & Sun.

Klimataria, Platía Theátrou 2 ☎010/32 16 629. Just west of the central market, the *Klimataria* does good taverna fare in ample portions, including some interesting mezédhes at reasonable prices. Better deal than most establishments in neighbouring Psyrrí. Open courtyard seating in summer and live music on weekends. Open evenings plus Fri & Sat for lunch. Closed Sun.

To Monastiri, central meat market (entrance from Eólou 81). The best of the three restaurants here; the raw ingredients are certainly fresh, and there's *patsás* (tripe and trotter soup) in ever in desperate need of a hangover cure. Daily 24hr.

Iy Stoa Tou Vangeli, Evripídhou 63 ☎010/32 51 513, edge of Psyrrí near the central market. For an authentic Greek atmosphere, pop into this congenial taverna, frequented by workers from the nearby market and offices. The decor includes songbirds in a huge cage and a large butcher block in the corner where your meats are cut to order. Simple taverna appetizers, soups, grills and abundant Greek salads. Open 6am–8pm, liveliest around 3pm. Closed Sun.

Iy Taverna Tou Psyrri, Eskhýlou 12, Psyrrí. One of the most original and cheapest establishments in the area, there is a tasty selection of fare like *thrápsalo* (huge squid), rare fish and chunky *tyrópites*.

O Thanasis, Mitropóleos 69. Reckoned to be the best *souvláki* and *gyros* place in this part of Athens. Always packed with locals at lunchtime. There's no booking so you'll have to fight for a table. Watch for the side dish of peppers, which are really fiery.

Over €13

Café Abysinia, Kynnétou 7, Platía Abysinia, Monastiráki ☎010/32 17 047. Newly remodelled

Should you begin to tire of Greek food, especially during an extended visit, you'll find that, unlike the rest of the country, Athens offers a good selection of foreign cuisine – from highly chichi **French** places, through **Eastern European**, **Armenian** and **Arabic**, to **Japanese** and **Korean**. Listed below are some of the more central places, which don't require a large outlay in taxi fares to reach – others are to be found at the beach suburbs to the south. Eating non-Greek in Athens is comparatively expensive: budget for €17–25 per person.

Unless otherwise indicated, the places listed below are closed in high summer and on Sunday, but otherwise stay open until 1.30am. Reservations are advisable.

ARMENIAN-TURKISH
Tria Asteria, Mélitos 7, Néa Smyrni, at end of #10 trolley line ☎010/93 58 134. Specialities include *tandir kebab* and *kionefe*, a special stuffed-filo dessert. Open in summer.

BRAZILIAN
Yellow Squirrel, Dimitressa 21, Ilisia ☎010/72 11 586. Classic Brazilian meat dishes and mezhédes in a comfortable dining room and garden.

CHINESE
Bee Garden, Kythoníon 30, Néa Smyrni ☎010/93 19 711. Mostly Cantonese dishes with some Mandarin specialities sprinkled on the menu. The Sunday buffet is a good deal at €5.75.
Dragon Palace, Andínoros 3 and Rizari, Pangráti, off map not far from the National Gallery ☎010/72 42 795. Cantonese dishes such as Peking duck. Open in summer and air-conditioned. Lunch and dinner.
Golden Dragon, Olymbíou 27–29/Syngroú 122, Koukáki, off map down Syngroú ☎010/92 32 316. A cut above average: ginger chicken, stuffed chicken wings, beef sate. Open in summer.

CZECH
Bohemia, Dhímou Tséliou, Ambelókipi, a few blocks north of the old Panathinaïkós stadium on Leofóros Alexándras ☎010/64 26 341. Hearty and nicely prepared fare such as *Knedliki*, *svíésová* and Czech beers. Spacious terrace garden in summer. Closed Mon.
Svejk, Roúmbesi 8a, Néos Kósmos, off map east of Syngroú ☎010/90 18 389. Rich stew-like main courses, also duck and carp according to season. Closed Mon.

EGYPTIAN
Alexandra, Metsovou 13 and Rethymnou, National Museum ☎010/82 10 004. Egyptian and Mediterranean specialities in a setting reminiscent of Old Alexandria. Garden. Opens at 2pm, closed Sun.

ETHIOPIAN
Axum, Dhrossopoúlou 183, Platía Koliátsou, close to Patissíon trolley routes #5 and #12 ☎010/20 11 774. Genuine African cuisine, eaten with the fingers and accompanied by traditional music at weekends. Very good value. Closed Tues but open all year.

FRENCH
L'Abreuvoir, Xenokrátous 51, Kolonáki ☎010/72 29 106. Modern ambience with rare specialities like duck steak in cherry vinegar and a wide selection of French wines. Open daily and summer.
Gastra, Platía Dhimáki 2, Lykavitós. Cosy, cavernous bistro with charmingly eccentric decor and taped cabaret music. Open for 25 years and still attracting a loyal fol-

lowing. The menu has a Continental flair but includes chicken Kiev, chili con carne and liver in bacon. Closed Sun and June to mid-Sept.

Prunier, Ipsilándou 63, Kolonáki ☎010/72 27 379. Central and unpretentious bistro. Imported French wines.

GERMAN

Beer Garden Ritterburg Ethnikís Andístasis 214, Kessarianí ☎010/72 22 235. Schnitzels, sausages and Bavarian specialities, best sampled on a variety plate. Closed Mon.

HUNGARIAN

Prasines Tiganites Domates (Fried Green Tomatoes), Aeroporon 10, Amfithea ☎010/94 05 135. Lovely little place with garden, Hungarian dishes in a home-cooked style including goulash. Live Hungarian folk music and songs on Fri and Sat. Menu on Wed is €14.50. Open for lunch and dinner, closed Mon.

INDIAN

Pak Indian, Menandrou 13 ☎010/32 19 412. Handsomely appointed restaurant in the heart of the Indian and Pakistani neighbourhood close to the central market. Dishes such as curries and tandoori are authentic, tasty and nicely presented but make sure extra orders are not brought out without being requested. Air-conditioned. Live concerts with traditional Indian music are occasionally scheduled.

ITALIAN

Al Convento, Anapíron Polémou 4–6, Kolonáki ☎010/72 39 163. Claims to be the oldest Italian restaurant in Athens; the speciality is pasta and scallopine. Open in summer. Closed Sun.

Il Parmigiano, Trivéon 3, Kolonáki ☎010/36 41 414. A trattoria on a pedestrian way that focuses on authentic pastas and crispy pizzas at reasonable prices. Open lunch and dinner. Branches at Yiannitsopoulou 1, Platía Esperidon, Glyfádha and Kifissiá 254, Filothei.

JAPANESE

Furin Kazan, Apollonos 2, Sýndagma ☎010/32 29 170. Strikingly decorated and popular sushi bar in a central location. Open lunch and dinner, closed Sun.

The Sushi Bar, Platía Varnáva, Mets ☎010/75 24 354. Decent range of sushi, tempura and soups in an authentic, bright atmosphere. Takeaway and delivery too. Open daily in summer. Its popularity has spawned two branches at Yeorgiou Vlaxou 38, N. Psyhikó ☎010/67 29 333 and Konstantinoupolis 15, Glyfádha ☎010/89 42 200.

KOREAN

Orient, Lékka 26, Sýndagma ☎010/32 21 192. Also Chinese and Japanese dishes. Open in summer.

Seoul, Evritanías 8, off Panórmou in Ambelókipi ☎010/69 24 669. Speciality Korean barbecue. Garden seating in summer.

LEBANESE

Beyrouth, Saki Karayiórga 13, Glyfádha ☎010/89 43 169. Spicy kebabs, stuffed fowl and taboulé salad served in a classy old house and garden. Special baked dishes on Sundays. Open from midday.

Suzanna, Orféos and Haríton 5, Amfithea ☎010/94 28 129. *Mezodopolío* that serves Anatolian and Lebanese specialities. Open from 1pm.

MEXICAN

Dos Hermanos, Kyriazi 24, Kifissiá ☎010/80 87 906. Well-prepared authentic Mexican classics, as well as memorable margaritas. Open from 1.30pm, closed Mon.
continued overleaf

Foreign-cuisine restaurants continued

POLISH

Diporto, Alexándras 31 and Therianou 12 ☎010/64 35 356. A longtime favourite of expatriate Poles and other residents who like the warm hospitality and find the ample and tasty fare such as *pierogi* to their liking and easy on their wallet. Open from 2.30pm, closed Sun.

RUSSIAN

Tavrida, Aristoyeitonas 12, Kallithéa ☎010/95 98 005. Homey setting and authentic Russian and Pontic specialties, including *pelmeni*, *hatsapouri* and *satsivi*, best accompanied by shots of vodka. Moderate prices. Open from 3pm, closed Mon.
Valentina, Lykoúrgou 235, Kallithéa, not far from metro station ☎010/94 31 871. An array of dishes like borscht and stroganoff at taverna prices. Open in summer.

and expanded, with a handsome dining room, this café has re-emerged as one of the best in Athens, as well as serving some fine dishes. Classics worth trying include the Rembetist's Eggplant, George's Eggs and Cheese Abyssinia.
Dirty Fish, Triptolemou 12, Gazi ☎010/34 74 763. A fish and seafood restaurant, serving a wide selection of dishes from sardines and smelt to thick fillets of sea bass and snapper. Open summer only, dinner daily and lunch on Sat and Sun.
Pro Thermansi, Ayíon. Anaryíron 10, Psyrrí ☎010/33 10 897. *Mezhedopolío* with unusual regional dishes, a bit more expensive than usual, but worth it for a special night out. Outdoor seating on a quiet pedestrian way; avoid the section

devoted to pricey wines by the glass and opt for unusual regional mezédhes. Good live Greek rebétika and laïkó music with no cover for diners.
Zei, Artemisiou 4, Keramikos ☎010/34 60 076. Charming old house serving imaginative Anatolian and Greek mezédhes in an enclosed courtyard. Live rebétika and laïkó music. Closed Mon & Tues.
Zidhoron, Táki 10, Psyrrí ☎010/32 15 368. A typical Psyrrí upscale *mezhedopolío*, painted bright yellow and featuring foods with a Middle Eastern flavour like *pastourmás*, *haloúmi* and hummus, as well as Greek favourites such as baked feta, grilled peppers and baked aubergine. Very popular and situated on a pedestrian street with a good vantage point over the goings-on of Psyrrí. Closed Aug.

Omónia/Exárhia/Platía Viktorías

Exárhia is still surprisingly untrodden by tourists, considering its proximity to the centre. Its eating and drinking establishments are conveniently close to the National Archeological Museum and several recommended hotels, and exploring them gives some insight into how the student/youth/alternative crowd carries on. The nearest metro stop is Omónia.

Under €13

Barba Yannis, Emm. Benáki 94, Exárhia. A neighbourhood treasure with a varied menu of home-style oven food (changes daily and displayed in large pots near entrance) in a relaxed atmosphere, aided and abetted by barrelled wine. Tables outside on pedestrianized street in summer. Very popular with students. Open all day until the small hours.
Oasis, Valtetsíou 44, Exárhia. A wonderful taverna with seating in the garden, and a varied menu of largely meat dishes.
Rozalia, Valtetsíou 58, Exárhia ☎010/33 02 933. The best mezédhes-plus-grill taverna in Exárhia, with renowned chicken and highly palatable white and red barrelled wine. You order from the proffered tray as the waiters thread their way through

the throng. Garden opposite in summer.
Taygetos, Satovriandou 4, Omónia ☎010/52 35 352. No-frills taverna with great *souvláki*, grilled lamb and chicken sold by the kilo. Open from 10am, closed Sun.
The Three Brothers, Elpídhos 7, Platía Viktorías. Wide range of grilled meat and fish plus mezédhes.

Over €13

Ideal, Panepistimíou 46, Omónia ☎010/33 03 000. The 70-year-old original burnt down a decade ago and was replaced with a brighter, more cheerful setting. A staunch favourite with middle-class Greeks who are understandably smitten with its clubby, Art Nouveau atmosphere and the twenty or more fresh, imaginative daily specials. Open from midday, closed Sun.

Neápoli

Neápoli is a long walk or short bus ride up Hariláou Trikoúpi from Exárhia, with a concentration of quieter clubs, bars and cinemas that make it a favourite dining-out area for savvy locals. The food here is good, teetering to either side of the €13 divider. Mavromiháli is parallel to and one street higher up the slopes of **Lykavitós** from Hariláou Trikoúpi.

Alexandra, Zonára 21 Alexandras ☎010/64 20 487. Aubergine croquettes, beetroot salad with walnuts, and meat in various sauces are among the imaginative dishes in this converted old house. Veranda in summer and occasional accordian music. Lunch and dinner; closed Sun.

Ta Bakiria, Mavromiháli 119. Among the less usual dishes are salads with mayonnaise and beef in a mushroom sauce. Atmospheric but smoky interior and a small summer courtyard. Closed Sun.

Iy Lefka, Mavromiháli 121. Beloved old taverna with great *fáva*, black-eyed beans, baked and grilled meat with barrelled retsina. Summer seating in a huge garden enclosed by barrels. Closed Sun.

O Pinaleon, Mavromiháli 152 ☎010/64 40 945. Rich mezédhes (choose from tray brought to table) and meaty entrées, washed down with home-made wine, lovingly brewed by the chef/owner from Híos. Advance booking recommended. Open mid-Oct to late May.

Strefis Taverna tis Xanthis, Irínis Athinéas 5. House specialities include rabbit stew and schnitzel. A delightful old mansion with a roof garden that offers fine views across Lofos Strefi and environs. Mon–Sat 9pm–2am.

Kolonáki

Kolonáki has a ritzy, upmarket reputation that puts off a lot of tourists. Nonetheless, among the boutiques are some surprising finds.

Under €13

Apokentro, end of Dinokratous at Platía Dexameni. This tiny establishment with a few tables inside and a few streetside, serves excellent pizza, a few pasta dishes and the puffiest, tastiest calzone in Athens. Open all day until past midnight.

To Kioupi, Platía Kolonáki 4 ☎010/36 14 033. Subterranean taverna with good-standard Greek fare such as moussaka and stuffed vine leaves. Closed Sun & Aug.

To Kotopoulo, Platía Kolonáki (next to the Citibank). As the name indicates, this tiny hole-in-the-wall is the place for chicken – juicy, crispy rotisseri-stye chicken, the best in Athens. It's strictly no-frills, lit by fluorescent lights and packed with people at all hours. Carry-out orders can be eaten in the nearby National Gardens. Closed Sun.

Over €13

Dhimokritos, Dhimokrítou 23. A bit snooty, but a beautiful building and well-prepared food from a vast menu, much of which is displayed in glass counters near the entrance. Open lunchtime and evenings. Closed late summer & Sun.

Filippou, Xenokratous 19 ☎010/72 16 390. An old-time taverna favourite of office workers and residents. The food is fresher and atmosphere livelier at lunch. Good grills, stews and casseroles. Closed Sat eve & Sun.

47 Maritsa's, Voukourestíou 47. Posh interior and pavement seating. Specializes in seafood like crawfish fritters, lobster spaghetti and grilled mussels.

Rodhia, Aristípou 44, near the base of the funicular. The menu hasn't changed in twenty years but that doesn't bother its many loyal regulars, who like to nestle in the cosy old house. Favourites include beef in lemon sauce, lamb fricassée and octopus in mustard sauce. Tables in the pretty garden are under the namesake pomegranate trees. Closed Sun.

Pangráti and Mets

These two neighbourhoods feature some of the city's best eating places. All the establishments below are a short (if generally uphill) walk across busy Ardhitóu and past the Olympic Stadium, or accessible via a #2, #4 or #12 trolley ride to Platía Plastíra. **Goúva** is an extension of Mets, just south of the First Cemetery.

Under €13

O Ilias, cnr Stasínou/Telesílis, Pangráti. A very good and popular taverna with standard menu. Evenings only. Tables outside in summer.

To Kalyvi, Empedhokléous 26 (off Platía Varnáva), Pangráti. Excellent, traditional mezédhes-type fare. Rustic decor and live music. Closed late May to late Sept.

Karavitis, Arktínou 35, off Leofóros Vas. Konstandínou, Pangráti. Old-style taverna with bulk wine, mezédhes and clay-cooked main courses. Indoor and outdoor seating.

Ta Skalakia, Eyinítou 32, Illisia ☎010/72 29 290. Off some stairs behind the *Holiday Inn*. Although it's not as cheap or unpretentious as it used to be, it still has many classic taverna dishes and a lively crowd.

O Vyrinis, Arhimídhous 11 (off Platía Plastíra), Pangráti. Good-quality taverna, with its own house wine and a wide variety of mezédhes. Tables in garden in summer.

Over €13

Pergoulia, Márkou Moussoúrou 16, Pangráti. Delicious, unusual mezédhes – being English-run there are some set meal options. Air-conditioned in summer.

To Strateri, Platía Plíta 3, Goúva, off map below the cemetery. A good, slightly upmarket *psistariá*. Outdoor seating in the park in summer.

Xanthippi, Arhimidhous 14 & Agras ☎010/75 60 514. Just behind the Olympic Stadium, this converted old house offers interesting mezédhes, crepes and meat combos.

Koukáki

This is one of the most pleasant parts of the city in which to while away the middle of a day or round off an evening. It's very much middle-class, residential Athens – uneventful and a bit early-to-bed, except for the lively pedestrianized streets of Dhrákou, Zínni and Olymbíou, teeming with trendy bars, cafeterias and eateries. The districts straddle the #1, #5 and #15 trolley lines and are also accessible from metro-stop Syngroú-Fix.

Under €13

Ambrosia, Dhrakou and Androutsou. A friendly *psistaría* packed with neighbourhood residents, especially on summer nights when the tables spill out into the pedestrian walkway. Food is simple but delicious; the succulent grilled chicken, pork chops and Greek salads will linger long in the memory. Servers are friendly and attentive.

Iy Gardhinia, Zínni 29. Extremely basic, inexpensive casserole food and barrel wine in a cool, cavernous setting. Lunchtime only in summer.

To Ikositeseroöro, Syngroú 42/44. The name means "open round-the-clock", and that's its main virtue. Fair, if rather overpriced, portions of antihangover food such as lamb tongues and *patsás*. At its liveliest after midnight in summer.

To Meltemi, Zínni 26. A modest-priced ouzerí that shields its customers from street traffic with banks of greenery. Offers a wide range of mezédhes with an emphasis on seafood. Closed Sun.

Ouzeri Evvia, Olymbíou 8, off map further down Veíkou. Hearty food as well as drink served on the pedestrian way, very reasonable and informal.

Iy Rouga, Olymbíou 2, off map further down Veíkou. Lunchtime oven food and evening grill with friendly service.

Over €13

Edodi, Veïkoú 80 ☎010/92 13 013. If you want to be pampered and have only one big splurge evening, have it here, at the finest restaurant in Athens. A more reasonable offshoot of *Bajazzo*, the famed restaurant in Mets, the imaginative fare will dazzle your senses. Waiters show you all of the various creations before you make a choice. A hint: skip the appetizer, as wonderful as they will look (and are) and save your appetite for the main course and dessert: the desserts are a truly splendid finale to a meal to remember. Closed lunch & Sun.

Áno Petrálona

Áno Petrálona, an old refugee neighbourhood on the west flank of Filopáppou Hill, is the least touristy district of central Athens. Just why is a mystery: the range of tavernas is excellent, the #15 trolleybus appears regularly, there's a nearby metro station (Petrálona), and it's a natural choice for eating after an evening at the Dora Stratou folk-dance theatre. There's a trolley stop on the Platía Amalías Merkoúri, from where the main artery of Dhimifóndos is a short stroll northwest. The places listed below are in or just beyond the bottom-left corner of our "Central Athens" map.

Under €13

Ikonomou (sign in Greek), cnr Tróön/Kydhandídhon. Basic home cooking served to packed pavement tables in summer.

To Koutouki, Lakíou 9. Inexpensive traditional taverna with good *fáva* and grilled meat. Like a country house with roof seating overlooking Filopáppou Hill. Closed Sun.

To Monastiri, Dhimifóndos 46. Very popular, moderately priced neighbourhood place with standard fare. Occasional guitar music on an informal basis after 11.30pm.

Ta Sokakia tou Thiakou, Gen. Kolokotroni 58, Platía Filopappou ☎010/92 49 614. Large taverna just down the road from Dora Stratou Theatre. Known for its pasta with lobster, lamb chops and

mixed salads. Outdoor tables. Friendly management and service. Live Greek music on weekends.

To Steki tou Ilia, Eptahálkou 5. This establishment on the pedestrianized road up towards Thissío station is so popular the owners have opened a namesake 200m further down. Fine lamb chops.

Over €13

T'Askimopapo, Iónon 61. A wonderful winter taverna with unusual dishes like meat in creamy sauces. Closed Sun & all summer.

Khryssa, Dhimofóndos 81. This classy restaurant with some pavement seating boasts international cuisine like smoked salmon and duck in various sauces, including curry.

Tea houses and patisseries

With a couple of honourable exceptions, **tea houses** and Continental-style **patisseries** are a recent phenomenon in Athens. Quiet, rather consciously sophisticated places, they're essentially a reaction against the traditional and basic kafenía. Most are concentrated around Pláka and in Kolonáki and the more upmarket suburbs. The pedestrianized streets of Milióni and Valaorítou in Kolonáki, in particular, seem to be one uninterrupted pavement café.

Filion, Skoufá 34, Kolonáki ☎010/36 12 850. One of Athens' intelligentsia's favourite cafés. Besides a variety of coffees, snacks and main dishes, it has exquisite chocolates and pastries. A good place to come for a present if you're invited to a Greek's name-day.

Galaktopolio Iy Amalthea, Tripódhon 16, Pláka. Tasteful if pricey, serving mostly crepes, as well as non-alcoholic drinks.

Gelateria Leonardo da Vinci, Dhimitrakopoúlou 42, cnr Dhrákou, Koukáki. Athens' most extensive range of rich and wonderful Italian *gelati* – not exorbitant for the quality. Also has pasta dishes, beer and wine. Seating indoors and out.

O Glykis, Ag. Geronta 2, Pláka ☎010/32 23 925. A secluded corner under shaded trees just off busy Kydathinéon in Plaká, frequented by a young Greek crowd. It has a mouthwatering array of sweets, as well as cold and hot appetizer plates.

Oasis, west side of National Gardens, opposite cnr of Amalías and Filellínon. An unexpected haven just off the main avenue, offering ice cream, oúzo and mezhédes in the shade.

Strofes, Akarnanías 10, Ambelókipi, off our map near Alexándras/Kifissiá junction. Claims to serve sixty varieties of tea.

La Tasse, Milióni 8, Kolonáki. One of the most popular of the establishments on this pedestrianized lane, just north of Kolonáki square.

To Tristrato, cnr Dedhálou/Angélou Yéronda, Pláka. Coffee, fruit juices, and salads, eggs, desserts, cakes. Exquisitely decorated but expensive. Daily 2pm–midnight.

Zonar's, Roberto Galli 43 ☎010/32 30 336. Traditional upmarket patisserie moved to new quarters in Makriyianni but with an atmosphere much as it was described as a haunt of Harriet and Guy Pringle and Yakimov, in Olivia Manning's *Fortunes of War*.

Ouzerís

Ouzerís – also called *ouzádhika* or *mezedhopolía* – are essentially bars selling oúzo, beer and wine (occasionally just oúzo), along with mezédhes (hors d'oeuvres) to reduce the impact. A special treat is a *pikilía* (usually €4.50–9), a selection of all the mezédhes available; this will probably include fried shrimp, pieces of squid, cheese, olives, tongue, cheese pies, sausage and other delicacies. Ordinarily, you should allow about €20 for two, with drinks, and you never need reservations. As in a Spanish tapas bar, the drink is of equal importance to the food so you don't tend to get as full as in a taverna for the same price. Ouzerís that are more food-oriented are to be found in the restaurant listings.

By far the **best hunting ground** for ouzerís is along the two parallel roads of Themistokléous and Emm. Benáki and their cross streets between Panepistimíou and Exárhia square. Those included below are typical of at least twenty decent establishments in that area.

Athinaikon, Themistokléous 2, cnr Panepistimíou, Omónia ℡010/38 38 485. An old ouzerí in a new location, but retaining its style – marble tables, old posters, etc. Variety of good-sized mezédhes, such as shrimp croquettes and mussels *saganáki* simmered with cheese and peppers. Closed Sun & Aug.

Dhexameni, Platía Dhexamenís, Kolonáki. Caféouzerí that serves drinks and snacks in summer under the trees. The menu is limited, but the setting sublime.

Epistrofi Stin Ithaki, cnr Kolléti and Benáki, Exárhia. Featuring Santoríni wine, this one does a good line in fish and seafood mezédhes. Closed Sun.

Iy Gonia, Arahóvis 59, Exárhia. Mushroom *saganáki*, meatballs, spicy sausages and octopus are among the delights at this place near the square.

O Mitsos, Platía Halandríou, Halándhri (take bus #A6 or #B6 from Har. Trikoúpi or Leofóros Alexándras to the terminal and it's across the square near the big church). Wonderful cheap spot with divine mussels in mustard sauce, fried fish, sausages and various dips. Well worth the trip. Closed Sun.

Iy Oréa Ellás, Mitropóleos 59, Monastiráki. Tucked inside a first-floor cultural centre with outstanding view of the rooftops of Pláka on the slope towards the Acropolis. This atmospheric café has a small but inspired selection of traditional mezédhes at good prices.

Iy Palea Skala, Lepentiotou 25 and Leokoriou ℡010/32 12 677. Seating inside an old house and on a terrace in summer. Excellent mezédhes and wine to accompany the acoustic house band. Generally packed and lots of fun, reasonable prices.

Music and nightlife

Traditional **Greek music** – rebétika and *dhimotiká* – can, at its best, provide the city's most compelling nighttime entertainment. To partake, however, you really need to visit during the winter months; from around May to October most clubs and *boîtes* close their doors, while the musicians head off to tour the countryside and islands. Most of the places that remain open are a tourist travesty of overamplified and overpriced *bouzoúki* noise – at their nadir, not surprisingly, in Pláka.

As for other forms of live music, there are small, indigenous **jazz** and **rock** scenes, perennially strapped for funds and venues, but worth checking out. **Classical** music performances tend to form the core of the summer Hellenic Festival, but with the completion in 1991 of the city's concert hall out on Vasilíssis Sofías there is now a long-running winter season as well. **Discos** and **music bars** are very much in the European mould. The clubs in the city tend to close during the summer, unless they have roof terraces; Athenian youth, meanwhile, move out to a series of huge hangar-like disco-palaces in the coastal suburbs.

Listings information

The **listings** and recommendations in this section are up to date at the time of going to press, but obviously venues change fast and often. Useful additional sources of information include the English-language daily *Athens News*, whose Friday edition has a complete events programme for the weekend, and the Greek-language *Athinorama* (every Fri), the single most reliable source, with screening times for all films and an exhaustive catalogue of nightspots and events. The weekly *Hellenic Times* has good coverage of forthcoming art exhibitions and events, including the summer Hellenic Festival.

For **information** and knowledgeable advice on all kinds of Athenian music – traditional, rock and jazz – look in at the **record shops** 7+7, Iféstou 7, Monastiráki, or Happening, Hariláou Trikoúpi 13. Both of these generally display posters for the more interesting events and have tickets on sale for rock, jazz or festival concerts.

Traditional music

For an introduction to Greek **traditional** and **folk music** see Contexts. In Athens, the various styles can coexist or be heard on alternate evenings at a number of music clubs or *boîtes*. There are purely traditional music venues (such as *To Armenaki*, especially for island music from the Cyclades and Crete), where people go to dance, or to celebrate weddings and other occasions. Most gigs start pretty late – there's little point in arriving much before 10.30pm – and continue until 3 or 4am. After midnight (and a few drinks) people tend to loosen up and start dancing; at around 1am there's generally an interval, when patrons may move to other clubs down the street or across town. Prices tend to be pretty stiff, with expensive drinks (and sometimes food), plus an admission fee or a minimum consumption per set.

Rebétika

For anyone with an interest in folk sounds, **rebétika**, the old drugs-and-outcast music brought over by Asia Minor Greeks, is worth catching live. The form was revived in the late 1970s and, though the fad has waned, there are still good sounds to be heard. If possible, phone to make a reservation and check who's playing. Some of these venues tend more towards **laïkó** (popular) sounds, the descendant of rebétika (see p.1063).

Boemissa, Solomoú 19, Exárhia ☎010/36 43 836. Rebétika and regional folk. Extremely popular with university students, who jam the dance floor and aisles, inevitably ending up writhing on the tabletops as well. Good company of musicians play music from all regions of Greece, but avoid sitting on the second floor where the speakers blast the music. Drinks €5.75 and two drinks minimum. Opens shortly before midnight. Call to make reservations or you may be shut out. Closed Mon and Tues but open all summer.

Deka Entoles, Aharnón 257, Áyios Nikólaos ☎010/83 25 253. Features authentic rebétika by some of the well-known groups such as Athinaiki Compania. Closed Tues.

Diavolos Musiki Spiti, Dhrákou 9 ☎010/92 39 588. Owned by popular singer Yiannis Glezos, who sometimes appears. Music ranges from rebétika to popular, with established singers such as Arletta often on the bill. Cover charge includes one drink. Closed Mon, Tues, May–Sept. Thurs night tango lessons followed by open dancing.

Rebetikí Istoría, Ippokrátous 181, Neápoli ☎010/64 24 967. Fairly genuine sounds from a good company in a large old house. Drinks €5.75 and some tasty cold and hot plates. Closed Wed and July & Aug.

Stoa Athanaton, Sofokléous 19 (in the old meat market) ☎010/32 14 362. Fronted by *bouzoúki* veterans Hondronakos and company. Good taverna food at reasonable prices but expensive drinks. €7.20 minimum. Open 3–6pm and midnight–6am. Closed Sun and May–Aug.

Taxími, Isávron 29, off Hariláou Trikoúpi, Exárhia ☎010/36 39 919. Crowded salon on third floor of a Neoclassical building has been open for twenty years and attracts a crowd of all ages; no cover, but drinks €7. Fruit plates, mixed appetizers. Closed Sun, also July & Aug.

O Yeros Tou Morea, top end of Mniskleous, Pláka. Newly restored club now has a roof and band that plays rebétika and laïkó almost nonstop until three or four in the morning. No cover, reasonable food and drinks.

Dhimotiká (folk) music

There's a real mix of styles at these clubs – everything from Zorba-like Cretan *santoúri* music to wailing clarinet from the mountains of Epirus, from ballroom dancing to lyrical ballads from Asia Minor. Venues are scattered throughout the city and are often pricier than their rebétika equivalents; reservations are advisable.

To Armenaki, Patriárkhou Ioakím 1, short taxi ride from Venizélou/Távros metro station ℡ 010/34 74 716. Island music, with the classic singer Irini Konitopoulou-Legaki often putting in an appearance. Closed Mon & Tues.

Elatos, Trítis Septemvríou 16, nr Omónia square ℡ 010/52 34 262. An eclectic assortment of *dhimotiká*. Closed Wed.

Enallax, Mavromiháli 139, Neápoli ℡ 010/64 37 416. Lively and friendly venue which hosts acts of various folk styles. Live gigs mostly Thurs–Sat. No cover charge but reservation needed. Drinks €5.75.

Kriti, Ayíou Thomá 8, Ambelókipi, off map past Leofóros Alexándras ℡ 010/77 58 258. Specializes in Cretan music. Closed Mon.

Pinakothíki, Ayías Théklas 5, Psyrrí ℡ 010/32 47 741. Small but cosy venue with appearances from revered but less well-known artists like the Cretan Psarandonis and some foreign acts. Closed Sun.

Tsai stin Sahara, Laodhikías 18, Ilíssia. Recently reopened as a folk venue. Admission and first drink typically €10.50.

Jazz and Latin

Jazz has a rather small following in Greece, but the main club, *Half-Note*, has a pleasant environment and usually good musicians. The major events take place as part of the **Jazz and Blues Festival** at the end of June; information and tickets are available from the Hellenic Festival box office (see p.152) and select record stores. Latin and other ethnic music styles are slowly increasing in popularity and the venues where it can be heard are generally very pleasant.

Café Asante, Damaréos 78, Pangráti, off our "Central Athens" map behind the huge Profítis Ilías church ℡ 010/75 60 102. Excellent atmosphere and mainstream to esoteric ethnic music from Afro-Cuban to Indian, Armenian and African. €5.45 entrance.

Half-Note, Trivonianoú 17, Mets ℡ 010/92 13 310. Live jazz most nights, often provided by good musicians brought in from abroad, but closed Tues and for much of the summer.

Hi-Hat Café, Dragoúmi 28 and Krousovou 1, nr *Hilton Hotel* ℡ 010/72 18 171. Crowded, energetic bar that specializes in the blues, but also Latin and jazz. €5.45 minimum.

La Joya, Tsókha 43, nr American Embassy, Ambelókipi, off map along Vas. Konstandínou ℡ 010/64 40 030. Great atmosphere. The live or taped rock, jazz and Latin accounts for some of its considerable success – as does beautiful decor, adventurous food and its popularity as a venue for celebrity parties. Open until 2.30am.

Ninety-five Degrees, Ioánnou Eyísti 18, Gázi. Large bar and dance floor featuring taped jazz, some live performance.

Palenque, Farandaton 41, Platía Ag. Thomas, Ambelókipi ℡ 010/74 87 748. Live Latin music by South American groups, salsa parties, flamenco music and dance lessons.

Parafono, Asklippiou 130a, Exárhia ℡ 010/64 46 512. Features Greek groups in a congenial small club.

Take Five, Patriárkhou Ioakím 37, Kolonáki ℡ 010/72 40 736. Supper club with live jazz bands. Reservations suggested. Closed Mon & Thurs.

Rock: live venues and music bars

The indigenous Greek **rock scene** is small but very solid and its public knowledgeable. Obscure Aussie bands, for example, who would hardly draw a handful of people in London, can be greeted like mini messiahs here. There are occasional appearances by better-known international bands and the annual **Rock Wave Festival**, established in 1997 and held down in Pireás in mid-July, has been attracting the likes of Blur, Garbage, Prodigy and Patti Smith. Local bands still face some difficulties like costly instruments and disfavour from the authorities, but they survive, and groups such as Echo Tattoo, Purple Overdose, Make Believe and Bokomolech are well worth catching if you can. Clubs pop up and disappear like mushrooms, though there is a number of fairly permanent music bars, especially in Exárhia. Many of these host the occasional gig and generally have a dance floor of sorts.

An Club, Solomoú 13–15, Exárhia ☎010/33 05 056. Basement club featuring local and lesser-known foreign rock bands. Entrance from €5.75.

Berlin, Iraklidhón 8, Thissío. Up-to-date indie rock sounds in the air-con interior. Pavement seating but you can't hear the music.

Decadence, Poulherías 2/Voulgaroktónou, Exárhia. Features the savviest indie/alternative sounds. Best in winter, when Dhaskalopoulos, the Greek John Peel, spins the discs on Thurs.

Kittaro Retro Club, Ipírou 48, nr Aharnón. It features live bands, usually playing solid Seventies-style rock. Open Thurs–Sun.

Memphis, Vendíri 5, Ilísia, behind *Hilton Hotel*. Roomy and comfy bar plus garden with good sound system pumping out rock and dance. Eighties parties on Friday.

Mo Better, Kolétti 32, Exárhia. Cramped but fun bar on the first floor of a Neoclassical building. Hip-hop, punk and indie rock. €5.75 entrance includes drink.

Rodhon, Márni 24, Platía Váthis ☎010/52 47 427. The city's most important venue for foreign and Greek rock, soul and reggae groups. Good atmosphere in a converted cinema. Closed in summer.

Discos and clubs

As you would expect of a European capital, Athens has a fair selection of trance, hip-hop and rave showcases. **Rave parties** do happen, with local and foreign DJs, but, as elsewhere, the business operates underground, so look out for posters or ask compulsive clubbers. Expect the unexpected at these clubs: most play recent hits, but don't be surprised if the sound shifts to Greek or belly-dancing music towards the end of the night. Some central Athens air-conditioned clubs remain open through the summer but with the rising temperature the scene really moves out to the coast beyond the airport, where Athens youth congregate at weekends in the beach suburbs of Kalamáki, Glyfádha and Voúla. If you join them, bear in mind that the taxi fare will be the first of several hefty bills, although admission prices usually include a free drink.

Central Athens

Exo, Marko Mousourou 1, Mets ☎010/92 35 818. Foreign rock with a fantastic panoramic view of the Acropolis and Lykavitós. Sushi bar, €11.50 entrance on Fri & Sat.

Q Base, Evripídhou 49, nr Omónia square ☎010/32 18 256. Disco, house and techno grooves.

R-Load, Ermoú 161, Thissío ☎010/34 56 187. This is the best central venue for spacing out to trance and such ambient vibes.

Beach suburbs

Black Hole, Astéria, Glyfádha ☎010/89 46 898. One of the places to be seen and strut your stuff. Drinks €5.75.

Plus Soda, Evryális 2, Glyfádha ☎010/89 40 205. Currently one of the most hip spots for shaking your booty to drum 'n' bass or techno sounds.

Tango, EOT's 2nd Beach, Voúla ☎010/89 56 577. Large veranda and eclectic selection of music, including some Greek, attracts a young crowd.

Gay and lesbian venues

The gay scene is fairly discreet, but Athens has its share of clubs, especially in the Makriyánni district to either side of Syngroú, with an established reputation. For further ideas, check the (brief and not entirely reliable) gay sections in the listings magazines *Athinorama* and *Exodus*.

Alekos Island, Tsakálof 42, Kolonáki. Easy-going atmosphere with small tables and couches and modulated rock/pop music. Owned by Alekos, one of Athens' more colourful bartenders.

Alexander's, Anagnostopoúlou 44, Kolonáki ☎010/36 46 660. Relaxed, slightly middle-of-the-road gay bar in the Kolonáki district. Basement disco with strobe lights rocks.

Granazi, Lembéssi 20, near Syngroú, Makriyánni ☎010/92 44 185. Gay bar close by the transvestite cruising area, Greek music and a crowd said to be "without poses."

The Guys, Lembessi 8, Makriyánni ☎010/92 14 244. Greek and foreign music in a cool lounge.

Koukles, Zan Moreás & Syngroú, Koukáki. The name means "Dolls" and there are humorous live drag acts.

Lambda, Lembéssi 15 & Syngroú 9 ☎010/92 24 202. Popular, with Greek and international music, live shows and gay films, plus "dark room".

Porta, Falirou 10 ☎010/92 43 858. Said to be the only exclusively lesbian bar in Athens, it has a low-key atmosphere and some good recorded music.

Arts and culture

Unless your Greek is fluent, the contemporary **Greek theatre** scene is likely to be inaccessible. As with Greek music, it is essentially a winter pursuit; in summer, the only theatre tends to be satirical and (to outsiders) totally incomprehensible revues. **Dance**, however, is more accessible and includes a fine traditional Greek show, while **cinema** is undubbed – and out of doors in summer.

In addition, in winter months, you might catch **ballet** (and **world music** concerts) at the convenient but acoustically awful Pallas Theatre, at Voukourestíou 1; **opera** from the Greek National Opera Lyrikí Skiní, in the Olympia Theatre at Akadhimías 59; and **classical events** either in the Hall of the Friends of Music (Mégaro Mousikís), out on Leofóros Vasilíssis Sofías next to the US embassy, or at the Filippos Nakas Concert Hall, at Ippokrátous 41. Also worth looking out for are events at the various **foreign cultural institutes**. Among these are: the Hellenic American Union, Massalías 22; the British Council, Platía Kolonáki 17; the French Institute, Sína 29/Massalías 1; and the Goethe Institute, Omírou 14–16.

Hellenic Festival

The summer **Hellenic Festival** has, over the years, come to encompass a broad spectrum of cultural events: most famously **ancient Greek theatre** (performed, in modern Greek, at the Herodes Atticus theatre on the south slope of the Acropolis), but also traditional and contemporary dance, classical music, jazz, traditional Greek music and even a smattering of rock shows. The **Herodes Atticus theatre**, known popularly as the *Iródhio*, is memorable in itself on a warm summer's evening – although you should avoid the cheapest seats, unless you bring along a pair of binoculars and a cushion. Other festival venues include the open-air Lycabettus Theatre on **Lykavitós Hill**, the **mansion of the Duchess of Plaisance** in Pendéli and the great ancient **theatre at Epidaurus** (see p.206), which is best taken in as part of a Peloponnesian tour as excursions from Athens are expensive and exhausting.

Events are scheduled from early June until September, although the exact dates may vary each year. Programmes of performances are best picked up as soon as you arrive in the city, and for theatre, especially, you'll need to move fast to get tickets. The **festival box office** is in the arcade at Stadhíou 4 (☎010/32 21 459, ⓦwww.greekfestival.gr; Mon–Fri 8.30am–8pm, Sat 9am–2.30pm); most events are held in the Herodes Atticus theatre, where the box office is open 6–9pm on the day of performance. Schedules of the main drama and music events are available in advance from OTE offices abroad (though they don't handle tickets). For student discounts, you must buy tickets in advance.

Dance

On the **dance** front, one worthwhile "permanent" performance is that of the **Dora Stratou Ethnic Dance Company** in their own theatre at Arakinthou and Voutie on Filopáppou Hill (☎010/92 14 650). Gathered on a single stage are traditional music, choreography and gorgeous costumes you'd be hard put to encounter in many years' travelling around Greece. Performances are held nightly at 10.15pm (extra show Wed & Sun 8.15pm) from late May to September. To reach the theatre, walk up busy Areopayítou, along the south flank of the Acropolis, until you see the signs. Tickets (€11.50) can almost always be picked up at the door. Somewhat pricey snacks are on offer.

Hat-tricks and hooligans

Greeks are fanatical about football, both their own brand and the big European leagues. They have a particular affinity to the English game and Greek commentaries are sprinkled with English terms like "offside", "foul" and "hat-trick". Sadly, less savoury aspects of the game have also been adopted, and recently there has been an upswing in hooliganism, just as it has been on the wane in Britain, although it is usually of the destructive rather than murderous variety. An example of it was some rather ugly scenes before England's World Cup qualifier in Athens in June 2001.

Most Greeks claim to support one of the big three teams of greater Athens; Panathinaïkós, AEK or Olympiakós. The league title has only occasionally been snatched from the hands of this trio by one of the Thessaloníki outfits and gloriously in 1988 by Lárissa. Of late, the Pireás team Olympiakós has been in the ascendancy again, winning five consecutive championships in 1997–2001 under the expert coaching of Serb Dusan Bajevic, who was at the helm of AEK's similar hat-trick between 1992 and 1994. On either side of that, Panathinaïkós bagged two pairs of titles, completing the Nineties' carve-up.

Most fans stick to their armchairs or kafenío seats throughout the game, and matches are often surprisingly poorly attended apart from local derbies and European games. This makes it easy for the casual visitor to gain admission on the day and even the big matches are not too difficult to obtain tickets for. With Greek sides currently performing well in the Champions League – at the time of writing Panathinaïkós were clear at the top of their group having beaten Arsenal – the chances of catching a famous English, Italian, Spanish or German side in coming seasons remain good. Look out for kiosks in the centre of town selling advance tickets or details in the press.

The thrilling fields
Panathinaïkós (colours green and white) have moved back to their original revamped stadium on Leofóros Alexándhras in central Athens, at least while the Olympic Stadium, where they played for the last decade, is prepared for 2004. Catch the metro to Ambelókipi station, which is right beside the ground.
AEK (colours yellow and black) play at the Níkos Goumás stadium in Néa Filadhélfia; take the metro to Perissós station, from where it's less than ten-minutes' walk under the lines and through residential streets.
Olympiakós (colours red and white) play at Karaïskáki stadium in Néo Fáliro, which is right opposite the metro station of the same name, the last before Pireás itself.

If you've got a liking for the underdog you can always try to see one of the less famous sides like Paniónios in Néa Smýrni, or Ionikós in Níkea, both in the Ethnikí (Premier) division. Otherwise, there are Apóllon in Perissós (near AEK) and Ethnikós (who share Karaïskaki with Olympiakós), both currently in the first division, or the redoubtable Atrómitos (Intrepid) Athinón out in Peristéri, who are now languishing in the second division, but can be likened to Millwall for their small but diehard support.

Cinema

Athens is a great place to catch up on movies. There are literally dozens of indoor cinemas in the city, some relics of the 1930s, but most plushly reno-vated, whilst in summer **outdoor** screens seem to spring up all over the place. Unless they have air conditioning or a roll-back roof, the indoor venues tend to be closed between mid-May and October.

Admission, whether at indoor or outdoor venues, is reasonable: count on €5.20 for outdoor screenings, €6.30 for first-run fare at a midtown theatre. Films are always shown in the original language with Greek **subtitles** (a good way to increase your vocabulary). For **listings**, the weekly magazine *Athinórama* (every Fri; €1.70) is the most reliable source of programme infor-mation if you can decipher Greek script, although foreign film titles are also given in the original language. Films are divided according to category and geographical location of the cinema. English-language cinema listings – less complete – can be found in the weekly *Athens News*.

Among **indoor cinemas**, a cluster showing regular English-language films can be found in three main central areas: Patissíon/Kypséli; downtown, on the three main thoroughfares connecting Omónia and Sýndagma; and Ambelókipi, around the junctions of Leofóros Alexándhras and Kifissías. The posh Village Center in Maroúsi (just off Kifissías, near the Aïdhonákia amuse-ment park) has ten theatres showing current films year round, with the added advantage that you can reserve tickets by phone (☎010/68 05 950). **Oldies** and **art films** tend to be shown at the Asty on Koraï downtown; the Orfeus, Artémonos 57 (a fifteen-minute walk from Pangráti or Koukáki); the Alfaville, Mavromiháli 168; the Aavora, Ippokrátous 180; and the Studio, Stavropoúlou 33, Platía Amerikís (off map up Patissíon). Catch **horror/cult films** at the Petit-Palais (cnr Vasilíou Yeoryíou Víta/Rizári); the Plaza, Kifissías 118, Ambelókipi; the Philip, Platía Amerikís/Thássou 11 (off map up Patissíon); the Amalia, Dhrossopoúlou 197 (off map parallel to Patissíon); the Nirvana, Leofóros Alexándhras 192; the Rialto, Kypsélis 54, Kypséli (off map north of Leofóros Alexándhras); and the Zina, Leofóros Alexándhras 74.

The summer **outdoor screens** show second-run offerings and classics, such as Hitchcock thrillers, as well as festivals featuring prominent European and American directors. To attend simply for the film is to miss much of the point. You may in any case never hear the soundtrack above the din of Greeks crack-ing *passatémpo* (pumpkin seeds), drinking and conversing. Snack bars serve sandwiches, popcorn, pizza and beer and wine; an intermission gives you a chance to stretch your legs and order refreshments. The first screening is at 9pm early in the summer and 8.30pm later in the summer; at late screenings (usu-ally 11pm), the sound is turned right down anyway, so as not to disturb local residents. The most central and reliable outdoor venues are Sine Pari, Kydathinéon 22, Pláka, with a side view of the Acropolis; Thissio, Apostólou Pávlou 7, under the Acropolis; Nea Panathinea, Mavromiháli 165, Neápoli; Zefyros, Tróön 36, Áno Petrálona (good for film noir and 50s oldies); Vox on the platía and Riviera at Valtetsíou 46.

Markets and shops

You can buy just about anything in Athens and even on a purely visual level the city's **markets** and **bazaar** areas are worth an hour or two's wandering. Among the markets, don't miss the Athinás food halls, nor, if you're into bargain-hunting through junk, the Sunday morning **flea markets** in Monastiráki, Thissío and Pireás. The **Athens flea market** spreads over a half-dozen or so blocks around Monastiráki square each Sunday from around 6am until 2pm. In parts it is an extension of the tourist trade – the shops in this area are promoted as a "flea market" every day of the week – but there is authentic Greek (and nowadays Soviet refugee-Greek) junk, too, notably along (and off) Iféstou and Pandhróssou streets. The real McCoy, most noticeable at the Thissío metro station end of Adhrianoú and the platía off Kynéttou near the church of Áyios Fílippos, is just a bag of odds and ends strewn on the ground or on a low table; dive in.

The **Pireás flea market** – at similar times on Sunday mornings – has fewer tourists and more goods. The market is concentrated on Alipédou and Skilítsi parallel to the railroad tracks about 500 metres from the sea. It is a venue for serious antique trading, as well as the sale of more everyday items.

In addition, many Athenian neighbourhoods have a *laïkí agorá* – **street market** – on a set day of the week. Usually running from 7am to 2pm, these are inexpensive and enjoyable, selling household items and dry goods, as well as fresh fruit and vegetables, dried herbs and nuts. The most centrally located ones are: Hánsen in Patissíon on Monday; Lésvou in Kypséli (off map) and Láskou in Pangráti (off map), both on Tuesday; Xenokrátous in Kolonáki, Dragoumi in Ilisia, Tsámi Karatássou in Koukáki and Arhimídhous in Mets, all on Friday; and Plakendías in Ambelókipi (one of the largest; off map) and Kallidhromíou in Exárhia, both on Saturday. Finally, if you're after Greek **plants** or **herbs**, there's a Sunday morning gathering of stalls on Vikéla in Patissíon (off map) and plants and flowers on sale daily at the Platía Ayías Irínis near Ermoú.

For electrical gear, now about as cheap in Greece as elsewhere in Europe, the best place to look is in the streets off Patissíon, just north of Omónia square. The selections below include some of the most enjoyable shops for souvenir-hunting, plus a few more functional places for those in search of books, music and outdoor gear.

Books

Archeological Service Bookstore, Panepistimíou 57, in *stoa* on left. Outlet for the high-quality if dry archeological service publications.

Compendium, Níkis 28 (upstairs), off Sýndagma. The friendliest and best value of the English-language bookshops, with a small secondhand section.

Eleftheroudhakis, Panepistimíou 17. Five floors of English books provide space for an extensive stock; has internet café and excellent cafeteria with a large selection of vegetarian dishes and sweets.

Estia-Kollarou, Sólonos 60. Big Greek-language bookshop, strong on modern history, politics, folk traditions and fiction.

Iy Folia tou Vivliou (The Book Nest), Panepistimíou 25, in the arcade and upstairs. The city's biggest selection of English-language fiction, with a good collection of recent academic work on Greece, and back issues of the *Korfes* hiking magazine. There's also a full-sized travel shop on the ground floor, with the complete line of Rough Guides and Anavasi maps.

Pyrinos Kosmos, Ippokrátous 16. The best shop in town for Greek and English books on philosophy, religion and mysticism.

Reymondos, Voukourestíou 18. Good for foreign periodicals in particular.

Road Editions, Ippokrátous 39. Has a good mix of English and Greek travel guides, plus their own and other companies' maps.

Crafts and antiques

Greek handicrafts are not particularly cheap but the workmanship is usually very high. In addition to the stores listed below, consider those at the **National Archeological Museum**, **Benáki Museum** and **Cycladic Art Museum**, which sell excellent, original designs as well as reproductions, and the cluster of antique shops at the base of **Adhrianoú**, near the corner of Kynéttou, which are good for Ottoman and rural Greek items like backgammon boards, hubble-bubbles, kilims, etc; the best is at Adhrianoú 25.

Amorgos, Kodrou 3, Pláka (across from the *Acropolis House Hotel*). A small shop filled with tasteful woodcarvings, needlework, lamps, lace, shadow puppets and other handicrafts.

Athens Design Centre, Valaorítou 4. A highly original modern potter has her base here. Prices aren't exorbitant considering the quality.

EOMMEX, Mitropóleos 9, Sýndagma, a Greek co-operative for woven rugs.

To Kati yia Sas, Iperídhou 23, Pláka. Eclectic stock of craft items.

Kendro Ellinikis Paradosis, Mitropóleos 59, Monastiráki. As the name suggests, this pleasant upstairs emporium has a wide selection of traditional arts and crafts, especially ceramics and woodcarving, and is mercifully free of the hard sell often encountered in the nearby flea market.

Lalaounis, Panepistimíou 6. Home-base outlet of the world-renowned family of goldsmiths, whose designs are superbly imaginative and very expensive.

Les Amis de Livres, Valaorítou 9, in a cul-de-sac. Prints and engravings.

Manos Faldaïs, Hariláou Trikoúpi 75, Exárhia. Unusual crafts like handmade puppets, wind chimes and scented candles.

Mazarakis, Voulís 31–33. A central outlet for *flokátes*, those hairy-pile wool rugs that are still the best thing to warm up a cold stone floor.

National Welfare Organization, Ipatías 6, cnr Apóllonos, Pláka. Rugs, embroideries, copperware – traditional craft products made in remote country districts.

Stavros Melissinos, Pandhróssou 89, off Monastiráki. The "poet-sandalmaker" of Athens – see p.124. The sandals translate better than the poems but nevertheless an inspiring (and not especially inflated) place to be cobbled.

Health and speciality food

Herbs and herb teas are sold dry and fresh at most street markets and at the Athinás bazaar. Otherwise, the following central outlets are useful.

AB Vassilopoulos The three huge main stores are at Leofóros Kifissías, Psihikó and above Kifissiá on the National Road (all off map), but there are several other outlets throughout the city. Gigantic supermarket stocking esoteric ingredients (their well-known sales pitch is that they stock birds' milk) for just about every cuisine or diet.

Aralus, Sofokléous 17, central bazaar. Fruits, nuts, wholegrain bread, pasta and so on. Also supplements and vitamins.

Bachar, Evripídhou 31, central bazaar. Aromatic bags of teas, herbs and medicinal remedies in large sacks.

Kendro Fyzikis Zois keh Iyias, Panepistimíou 57. Headquarters of the Greek Green Party, but also a tremendously well-stocked store and vegetarian snack bar with a pleasant loft where afternoon snacks are served.

La Tienda, Mihalakopoulou 38, ground floor. Full line of Mexican and Asian staple condiments, from hot sauce to plantains.

Outdoor supplies

Aegean Dive Shop, Pandhóras 42 and Zamanou 53, Glyfádha, off map, on the coast to the southeast ☎010/89 45 409. Diving lessons, equipment rental and good value one-day dive trips to a reef near Vouliagméni, sporadically during the week but regularly on weekends.

Alberto's, Patissíon 37, in the arcade; plus many others on same street heading towards Omónia. This is in effect the "bike bazaar", for repairs, parts and sales. For mountain bikes, try Gatsoúlis at Thessaloníkis 8 in Néa Filadhélfia (off map; #18 trolleybus).

Alpamayo, Panepistimíou 44. Small hiking store which also stocks some *Korfes* back issues (see

also "Books", overleaf).

Mediterranean Dive Shop, Vas. Pávlou 95, Kastélla, nr Pireás (☎010/41 25 376). Efficient and reasonably priced shop for the hire of reliable diving equipment.

No-Name Bike Shop, Trítis Septemvríou 40/cnr Stournári. Bicycles and accessories.

Pindhos, Patissíon 52. Extensive state-of-the-art hiking/climbing gear: Lowe packs, ice axes, stoves, water containers, parkas, foam pads, etc.

Survival, Kynéttou 4, on Ayíou Filíppou square. Good for ponchos, stoves, mess kits, boots, knives and survival gear in general.

Records and CDs

If you hear music you like, or want to explore Greek sounds of bygone days (or today), refer to the discographies in Contexts (p.000) and then try the outlets below. When shopping, beware of records warped by poor stacking in the racks. The big advantage of shopping here is that the **vinyl industry** is still alive and well, having survived the CD onslaught; you may find pressings discontinued elsewhere.

Happening, Hariláou Trikoúpi 13. Good range of heavy metal and indie rock plus tickets, info and magazines.

Jazz Rock, Akadhimías 45. Specializes in just that with forays into rock and ethnic music, also a good source of information and tickets for upcoming concerts.

Metropolis, Panepistimíou 64. Strictly CDs; the branch at #54 sells just vinyl. Often has discounted items; a second branch has opened at the airport and sells CDs only.

7+7, Iféstou 7, Monastiráki. This shop in the flea market has a choice selection of old and new rock and Greek music on vinyl and CD.

Tzina, Panepistimíou 57. Stop in here if Metropolis or Xylouris don't have what you're after; it has its own label of Greek folk.

Virgin Megastore, Stadiou 7–9, Sýndagma. Large selection of Greek rock and folk music and foreign hits at reasonable prices. You can listen to most CDs before you buy.

Xylouris, Panepistimíou 39, in the arcade. Run by the widow of the late, great Cretan singer Nikos Xylouris, this is currently one of the best places for Greek popular, folk and (of course) Cretan music. Stocks items unavailable elsewhere.

Listings

Airlines Most of the following are within 100m or so of Sýndagma: Air Canada, Óthonos 10d ☎010/32 23 206; Air France, Vouliagménis 18, Glyfádha ☎010/96 01 100; Air Greece, Níkis 20 ☎010/32 55 011; Alitalia, Vouliagménis 577, nr airport ☎010/99 88 888; American Airlines, Panepistimíou 15 ☎010/33 11 045; British Airways, Vouliagménis 130, cnr Themistokléous, Glyfádha ☎010/89 06 666; Canadian Airlines (Amfitreon Air Services), 3rd floor, Syngroú 7 ☎010/92 12 470; Cronus, Óthonos 10 ☎010/33 15 502; CSA, Panepistimíou 15 ☎010/32 32 303; Cyprus Airways, F.Fillelínon 10 ☎010/32 47 801; Delta, Óthonos 4 ☎010/33 11 678; easyJet, airport only ☎010/96 70 000; Egyptair, Vouliagménis 26 ☎010/92 12 818; El Al, Voukourestíou 16 ☎010/92 12 818; Kenya Airways, c/o KLM; KLM, Vouliagménis 41, Glyfádha ☎010/96 05 000; Lufthansa, Vas. Sofías 11 ☎010/36 92 11; Malev, Panepistimíou 15 ☎010/32 41 116; Olympic, ticket office at Fillelínon 15 ☎010/92 67 555 for reservations or ☎010/96 66 666, main office at Syngroú 96 ☎010/92 69 111; Qantas (represented by British Airways); Singapore Airlines, Xenofóndos 9 ☎010/32 39 111; South African Airways, Merlin 8, Kolonáki ☎010/36 16 305; Swissair, Óthonos 4 ☎010/32 35 811; Thai, Sekéri 1, Kolonáki ☎010/36 47 610; Turkish Airlines, Fillelínon 19 ☎010/32 46 024;

TWA, Syngroú 7 ☎010/92 13 400.

Airport enquiries ☎010/92 69 111 for Olympic flight enquiries; for all other carriers ☎010/35 30 000.

American Express Poste restante and money changing at the main branch at Ermoú (1st floor), cnr Sýndagma. Mail pick-up desk open in summer Mon–Fri 8am–3pm, Sat 8.30am–1.30pm; shorter weekday hours in winter. Currency exchange only at Ermoú just before Nikis, south side of street. Two Amex offices are open 24hr at the airport.

Banks The normal banking hours are Mon–Thurs 8am–2pm and Fri 8am–1.30pm and just about all banks can do exchange during those hours. The National Bank of Greece at Sýndagma stays open for **exchange** Mon–Thurs 8am–2pm & 3.30–6.30pm, Fri 8am–1.30pm & 3–6.30pm, Sat 9am–3pm & Sun 9am–1pm. The nearby, less crowded Yeniki Trápeza/General Bank cnr Ermoú and Sýndagma, has longer hours: Mon–Thurs 8am–6.30pm, Fri 8am–6pm, Sat 8am–2pm, closed Sun.

Bird-watching The Hellenic Ornithological Society organizes three-day excursions to major nesting and migratory areas such as the Vikos Gorge, Messolónghi wetlands and Préspa lakes. It's located at Emm. Benáki 53, Athens, ☎010/33 01 167.

Buses For information on buses out of Athens (and

the respective terminals), see "Travel Details" at the end of this chapter.

Camera repair Most central at Pikópoulos, Lékka 26, off Ermoú, 3rd floor and Kriton Kremnitsios, Karayeóryi Servías 7, 5th floor.

Car rental A number of companies are to be found on Leofóros Syngroú, including InterRent/EuropCar, at no. 4, ☎010/95 88 990; Holiday Autos (no. 8), Thrifty (no. 24), Eurodollar (no. 29), Just (no. 43), Avanti (no. 50), Antena (no. 52) and Autorent (no. 118); the latter three give student discounts, while Payless is just off Syngroú at Hatzikhrístou 20.

Car repairs, tyres and assistance Mechanics for virtually any make are scattered around Néos Kósmos district, while spares stores congregate along and between Kalliróis and Vouliagménis. If they don't have the part, or the know-how, they'll refer you to someone who does. Tyre stores are grouped between Trítis Septemvríou 60–80 (north of Omónia). **ELPA** – the Greek automobile association – gives free **help and information** to foreign motorists at Leofóros Mesoyíon 2 (northeast of Lykavitós, off map) and at the Athens Tower in Ambelókipi. For **emergency assistance** call ☎104 (free, though you'll pay for any parts).

Dentists Free treatment at the Evangelismos Hospital, Ipsilándou 45, Kolonáki and the Pireás Dentistry School (*Odhondoiatrikó Skholío*), cnr Thívon/Livadhías, well north of the metro and public buses. For private treatment, check the ads in the *Athens News* or ask your embassy for addresses.

Embassies/Consulates include: Albania, Karakhrístou 1 ☎010/72 34 412; Australia, Dhimitríou Soútsou 37 ☎010/64 50 405; Britain, Ploutárhou 1, Kolonáki ☎010/72 36 211; Bulgaria, Stratigoú Kallári 33a, Paleó Psihikó ☎010/67 48 105, Mon–Fri 10am–noon; Canada, Ioánnou Yennadhíou 4 ☎010/72 73 400; Denmark, Vas. Sofías 11 ☎010/36 08 315; Egypt, Vas. Sofías 3 ☎010/36 18 612; France, Vas. Sofías 7 ☎010/33 91 000; Germany, Karaóli Dhimitríou 3 ☎010/72 85 111; Hungary, Kálvou 16, Paleó Psihikó ☎010/67 25 337 (Mon–Fri 9am–noon); India, Kleánthous 3 ☎010/72 16 227; Ireland, Vas. Konstandínou 7 ☎010/72 32 771; Israel, Marathonodhrómou 1, Paleó Psihikó ☎010/67 19 530; Italy, Sekéri 2, Kolonáki ☎010/36 17 227; Japan, Messoghíon 2 ☎010/77 58 101; Netherlands, Vassiléos Konstandínou 5–77 ☎010/72 39 701; New Zealand (consulate), Xenías 24, Ambelókipi ☎010/77 10 112; Norway, Vassiléos Konstandínou ☎010/72 47 605; Romania, Emm. Benáki 7, Paleó Psihikó ☎010/67 28 875 (Mon–Fri 10am–noon); South Africa,

Kifissías 60, Maroússi ☎010/68 06 645; Sweden, Vas. Konstandínou 7 ☎010/72 90 421; Turkey, Vas. Yeorgíou Vita 8 ☎010/72 63 000; US, Vas. Sofías 91 ☎010/72 12 951.

Emergencies Dial the tourist police ☎171 (24hr) for medical or other assistance. In a **medical emergency**, don't wait for an ambulance if you can travel safely – get a taxi straight to the hospital address that the tourist police gives you. If your Greek is up to it, ☎166 summons an ambulance, ☎105 gets you a rota of night-duty doctors, and ☎106 ascertains the best hospital for you to head for. Otherwise, KAT, way out in Kifissiá at Níkis 2, is excellent for trauma and acute complaints if you can hold out that long – it's the designated casualty ward for Greater Athens.

Environment Greenpeace, Zoödhóhou Piyís 52, Exárhia ☎010/38 40 774 (Mon–Sat 9am–4pm). Stop by if you want information, or are staying long-term in Greece and would like to participate in volunteer work and campaigns. WWF Greece, Filellínon 26, 4th floor ☎010/32 47 586 has many excellent field programmes.

Ferries Most central offices for major lines like ANEK, Strintzis, Hellenic Mediterranean, G&A and Ventouris flank Leofóros Amalías between Sýndagma and Hadrian's Arch; a prominent exception is Minoan Lines, on Vasiléos Konstandínou, next to the Olympic Stadium. Phone ☎143 for recorded timetable in Greek or pick up schedule for coming days from the OTE office. Hellas Flying Dolphin tickets are sold an hour before departure at the quay in Marína Zéas (☎010/42 80 001), although it's wise to book tickets in advance during high season at an agent in Athens or Pireás. For Minoan high-speed catamarans to the Cyclades phone ☎010/75 12 356.

Gay groups Akoe Amphi, the Greek National Gay and Lesbian Organization, has an office at Zalóngou 6 ☎010/77 19 221 (Mon–Fri 6–11pm).

Greek-language courses Athens Centre, Arhimídhous 48, Pangráti (☎010/70 12 268, ☎70 18 603) is considered the best for foreigners. The Hellenic American Union, Massalías 22, is more geared to the needs of Greeks learning English.

Hiking Trekking Hellas, Filellínon 7, 3rd floor, arrange hiking tours throughout Greece. The Hellenic Federation of Mountaineering and Climbing, Milioni 5, Kolonáki (☎010/36 45 904) can help with detailed maps for mountain paths and refuges.

Hospital clinics For minor injuries the Hellenic Red Cross, Trítis Septemvríou/Kapodhistríou, is fairly good. For **inoculations**, try the Vaccination Centre, Leofóros Alexándhras 196/cnr Vasilíssis Sofías, Ambelókipi (Mon–Fri 8.30am–12.30pm), where most jabs are free; phone ☎010/64 60 493.

Internet cafés Internet cafés with full email capabilities and access to the Net have been sprouting up all over the city. Some of the more central and reliable places are: *Info Café*, branches at Ippokrátous 31 ☎010/36 15 094 and cnr Botási & Solomoú, Exárhia ☎010/33 04 002; *Museum Internet Café*, Patissíon 46 ☎010/88 33 418; *Café 4U*, Ippokrátous 44 ☎010/36 11 981; *Sofokleous.com Internet Café*, Stadhíou 5 ☎010/32 48 105; and *Tafnet*, Pendélis 3 cnr Mitropóleos, Pláka ☎010/32 49 282. The standard rate is about €5.70 per hour.

Laundry Numerous dry/wet cleaners will do your laundry for you, or there are coin-ops at Dhidhótou 46, Exárhia; cnr Ploutárhou & Karneádhou, Kolonáki; and Ioulianoú 72–78, near the Archeological Museum.

Lost property The transport police have a lost property office (*Grafío Haménon Andikiménon*) at Alexándras 173, 7th floor ☎010/64 21 616. Bring your passport with you.

Luggage storage Best arranged with your hotel; many places will keep the bulk of your luggage for free or a nominal amount while you head off to the islands. Pacific Ltd, Nikis 26, Sýndagma (☎010/32 41 007) has a per piece charge of €1.60 per day, €22.30 per week. It also has a storage area at the airport.

Motorbike rental Available from Motorent, whose head office is at Falírau 5, cnr Makriyánni, Koukáki ☎010/92 34 939, ☎92 34 885.

Mount Áthos permits In Athens, the Ministry of Foreign Affairs, Akadhimías 3, in the arcade, 5th floor, is the first stop in securing a permit; office hours are Mon, Wed & Fri 11am–1pm.

Pharmacies (*farmakía*) The Marinopoulos branches on Patissíon and Panepistimíou are particularly good and also sell homeopathic remedies. Bakakos, on Omónia square is the largest general pharmacy in Athens and stocks just about anything. Call ☎107 for after-hours pharmacies (in Greek) or consult daily listings in *Athens News*. All pharmacies display a daily list of those open after-hours.

Phones You can phone locally from a metered phone at a *períptero* (kiosk), where you pay afterwards or at the airport OTE. Most *períptera* are phasing out their phones, however, since phone boxes that require phonecards are now quite common. The cards cost €2.80 for 100 units and €5.70 for 200 units. These are handy to have and can be used for a quick call home. The Athens OTE no longer has metered phones.

Police Dialling ☎100 gets the flying squad; for thefts, problems with hotel overcharging, etc, contact the **tourist police** at Dimitrakoupoúlou 77, Koukáki ☎171.

Post offices (*Tahydhromía*) For ordinary letters and parcels up to 2kg, the branch on Sýndagma (cnr Mitropóleos) is open Mon–Fri 7.30am–8pm, Sat 7.30am–2pm, Sun 9am–1.30pm. To send home parcels of personal effects, use the post office in the arcade between Voukourestíou and Kriezótou (Mon–Fri 7.30am–2pm) or, closer to Omónia, at Koumoundoúrou 29. Paper and string are supplied – you bring box and twine. "Surface/air lift" will get parcels home to North America or Europe in two weeks. For souvenirs, a branch at Nikis 37 expedites shipments and minimizes duty/declaration problems.

Poste restante The main post office for Athens is at Eólou 100, just off Omónia (Mon–Fri 7.30am–8pm, Sat 7.30am–2pm, Sun 9am–1.30pm).

Scuba diving Greece has gradually been opening up to diving although there are still restrictions because of underwater antiquities. If you want to do an introductory dive or a full PADI course, instruction and certification can be given by bilingual Greek–South African Peter Kastrinoyiannakis ☎010/98 43 851. Or contact the Scuba Diving Center of Vouliagméni, Poseidonos at Vouliagméni Bay ☎010/89 64 609.

Tours Most travel agencies offer a half-day tour of classical Athens including a bus drive around the highlights of the city and guided tour of the Acropolis and Museum for €30. CHAT tours, Zalongou 4, Ayia Paraskevi (tours can be booked at many of the major hotels in central Athens, even if you are not staying there), ☎010/60 72 150, has the best guides and can arrange independent itineraries as well. Tours are also offered to Sounion (€25), Delphi (one day €64, two-day tour with hotel room €87–100) and three days to Delphi and Meteora for €202. Other agencies with tours include GO Tours, Voulis 31–33, ☎010/32 25 591 and Key Tours, Kallirois 4, ☎010/92 33 166.

Train information, reservations and tickets The most central OSE offices are at Filellínon 17 (international trips only) and Sína 6 or you can call ☎010/52 97 002.

Travel agencies Most budget and youth/student agencies are to be found just off Sýndagma, on and around Filellínon and Nikis streets. The cheapest ferry tickets to Italy are usually sold through USIT, Filellínon 1 (☎010/32 41 884). Among other agencies; Periscope, Filellínon 22; Himalaya, Filellínon 7; and Arcturus, Apóllonos 20, are worth scanning for air travel deals, as is

Magic Bus, Filellínon 20 which can also do island packages.

Work/residence permits/visa extensions at the Aliens' Bureau (*Ipiresía Allodhapón*), Leofóros Alexándhras 173; open Mon–Fri 8am–1pm, but go early or you won't get seen. Also, come armed with small notes for revenue stamps, large notes for the extension fee(s), wads of passport photos, pink personalized bank receipts and plenty of patience.

Around Athens: Attica

Attica (Attikí), the region encompassing the capital, is not much explored by tourists. Only the great romantic ruin of the **Temple of Apollo** at Sounion is on the excursion circuit. The rest, if seen at all, tends to be en route to the islands – from the ports of **Pireás**, **Rafína** (a fast and cheap route to many of the Cyclades) or **Lávrio** (which serves Kéa).

The neglect is not surprising. The mountains of **Imittós**, **Pendéli** and **Párnitha**, which surround Athens on three sides, are progressively less successful in confining the urban sprawl, and the routes out of the city to the south and west are unenticing to say the least. But if you're planning on an extended stay in the capital, a day-trip or two or a brief circuit by car can make a rewarding break, with much of Greece in microcosm to be seen within an hour or two's ride: mountainside at **Párnitha**, minor archeological sites in **Brauron** and **Rhamnous** and the odd unspoilt beach, too.

Pireás (Piraeus)

PIREÁS has been the port of Athens since Classical times. Today it is a substantial metropolis in its own right, containing much of Greater Athens' industry, as well as the various commercial activities associated with a port: banking, import–export, freight and so on. For most visitors, though, it is Pireás's interisland ferries that provide the reason for coming (see "The ferries" on p.162 for details).

The port at Pireás was founded at the beginning of the fifth century BC by **Themistocles**, who realized the potential of its three natural harbours. His work was consolidated by Pericles with the building of the **"Long Walls"** to protect the corridor to Athens, and it remained active under Roman and Macedonian rulers. Subsequently, under Turkish rule, the place declined to the extent that there was just one building there, a monastery, by the end of the War of Independence. From the 1830s on, though, Pireás grew by leaps and bounds. The original influx into the port was a group of immigrants from Híos, whose island had been devastated by the Turks; later came populations from Ídhra, Crete and the Peloponnese. By World War I, Pireás had outstripped the island of Sýros as the nation's first port, its strategic position enhanced by the opening of the Suez and Corinth canals in 1862 and 1893 respectively. Like Athens, the city's great period of expansion began in 1923, with the exchange of populations with Turkey. Over 100,000 Asia Minor Greeks decided to settle in Pireás, doubling the population almost overnight – and giving a boost to a pre-existing semi-underworld culture, whose enduring legacy was rebétika, outcasts' music played in hashish dens along the waterside.

The city these days is almost indistinguishable from Athens, with its scruffy web of suburbs merging into those of the capital. Economically, it is at present on a mild upswing, boosted by two successive go-ahead mayors and the prominence of its late MP, former actress and Minister of Culture, Melina Mercouri. An unashamedly functional place, with its port dispatching up to sixty ships a day in season – both to the islands and to a range of international destinations – there are few sights beyond the numbers and diversity of the sailors in the harbour. The ancient walls are long gone – except for small sections on the seafront – and the junta years saw misguided demolition of many buildings of character. On the plus side, there's a nice enough **park** (three blocks back from the main harbour, intersected by Vas. Konstandínou); a scattering of genuine antique/junk shops, plus a big Sunday morning **flea market**, near Platía

CENTRAL PIREÁS

0   200 m

Train Station (Northern Greece)

Train Station (Peloponnese)

Athens

GRAVIAS
AKTI KONDHILI
TH. RESINA
DH. MOUTSOPOULOU
SKILITSI
DHODHEKANISOU
ATHINON

PL. KARAÍSKAKI
K
DH. GOUNARI
New Market
ETHNIKÍS ANDISTÁSIS
FILONOS
KOLOKOTRONI
IROÓN POLYTEKHNIOU

Main Harbour

Customs House
Bus #40 for Athens
AKTI MIAOULI
FILONOS
KOLOKOTRONI
IROÓN POLYTEKHNIOU
Municipal Theatre
PRAXITELOUS
LEOFOROS YEORYÍOU TOU PROTOU
GRIGORI LAMBRAKI
VOULGARI
OMIRIDHOU
Olympiakós Stadium

Archeological Museum
BOUBOULINAS
THEATROU
TSAMADOU
KARAÓLI DHIMITRÍOU
TZAVELLA
Néo Fáliron

Zéa Marina
AKTI MOUTSOPOULOU
ZANNI
IPSILANDHOU
Irinís Ké Filias Stadium

Open-air Theatre
K. SERVIAS
VASILEOS PAVLOU

AKTI THEMISTOKLEOUS
L
Naval Museum
J

Mikrolímano

SAKHTOURI
FILELLINON
G. SOUTZE
HARILAOU TRIKOUPI
KANTHAROU
KENDRIOU

A   Lésvos & Híos Ferries
B   Crete direct
C   Sámos, Ikaría & W. Cyclades
D   Cyclades
E   Sýros, Tínos & Mýkonos;
      Eyína/Methana hydrofoils
F   Argo-Saronic
G   Argo-Saronic
H   Dodecannese & Crete
      via other islands
I   International
J   Argo-Saronic & Peloponnese
      hydrofoils

Ipodhamías, at the top end of Goúnari (behind the train station); and a couple of more than respectable museums.

The Archeological and Maritime museums

The **Archeological Museum** at Hariláou Trikoúpi 31 (Tues–Sun 8.30am–2.30pm; €1.50) is the best time-filler in Pireás, and enthusiasts will certainly want to make a special trip out here. Upper-floor exhibits include a *kouros* (idealized male statue) dedicated to Apollo, which was dragged out of the sea in 1959. Dating from 520 BC, this is the earliest known life-size bronze, and is displayed with two other fifth-century bronzes of Artemis and Athena found in the same manner at about the same time.

On the ground floor are more submarine finds, this time second-century AD stone reliefs of battles between Greeks and Amazons, apparently made for export to Rome. A new room displays Mycenaean chariot figures, musical instruments and pottery. A good selection of funeral stelae and statues includes the twenty-foot Kallithea funeral monument, a miniature temple with statues inside, made in the fourth century BC.

A few blocks away, on Aktí Themistokléous, Freattida square, adjacent to Zéa, the **Maritime Museum** (Tues–Sat 9am–2pm; €1.50) is more specialized, tracing developments with models and actual sections of ancient triremes and ships.

The ferries

If you're staying in Athens prior to heading out to the islands, it's worth going to the tourist office at Amerikís 2 to pick up a **schedule of departures** from Pireás. These can't be relied upon implicitly, but they do give a reasonable indication of what boats are leaving when and for where; note that the Argo-Saronic sailings and ships based on Sýros or Páros are omitted.

The majority of the boats – for the Argo-Saronic, Ikaría or Sámos, and the popular Cyclades – leave between 8 and 9am. There is then another burst of activity between noon and 3pm towards the Cyclades and Dodecanese, and a final battery of sailings from 4 to 10pm (sometimes later), bound for a wide variety of ports, but especially Crete, the northeast Aegean and the western Cyclades. The frequency of sailings is such that, in high season at least, you need never spend the night in Athens or Pireás.

There's no need to **buy tickets** for conventional ferries before you get here, unless you want a cabin berth or are taking a car on board (in which case, consult agents in Athens or Pireás); Flying Dolphin reservations are a good idea during July and August. In general, the best plan is to get to Pireás early, say at 7am, and check with the various **shipping agents** around the metro station and along the quayside Platía Karaïskáki. Keep in mind that many of these act only for particular lines, so for a full picture of the various boats sailing you will need to ask at three or four outlets. This can also be done at the agencies in Sýndagma square a day or two in advance. Prices for all domestic boat journeys are standard, but the quality of the craft and circuitousness of routes vary greatly. If you are heading for Thíra (Santoríni) or Rhodes, for example, try to get a boat that stops at only three or four islands en route; for Crete settle for direct ferries only.

Boats for different destinations leave from a variety of points along the main harbour, usually following the pattern in the box opposite, though it's wise to leave time for wayward ships and look for the signs (indicating name of boat and a clockface with departure time) hung in front of the relevant boats on the waterside railings or on the stern of the boats themselves. The ticket agent should know the whereabouts of the boat on the particular day.

Ferry departure points

Aegean islands (Cyclades/Dodecanese)

These leave from either Aktí Kalimasióti, the quay right in front of the metro station (#3 on the map), from just the other side of Platía Karaïskáki (#4) or from the points listed for specific islands below. The big boats going to the major Dodecanese usually share point #8 with some of the Cretan ferries.

Crete

Those going via the Cyclades or on to the Dodecanese use the dock on Aktí Miaoúli (#8), while direct services leave from #2 on Aktí Kondhíli.

Sýros, Tínos, Mýkonos

The morning departures tend to go from #5, next to the Égina hydrofoils.

Western Cyclades

The ferries for these islands usually depart from Aktí Kalimasióti (#3), right in front of the metro station.

Sámos/Ikaría

Boats ending up at these islands, whether morning or evening services, use the Aktí Kalimasióti (#3) dock as well.

Híos/Lésvos

Most Híos and Mytilíni (Lésvos) boats leave from the newly opened quay (#1) round the harbour past the train station for northern Greece.

Argo-Saronic

Ordinary ferries leave from Aktí Possidhónios (#6) and also just round the corner with Aktí Miaoúli (#7), a ten-minute walk from the metro.

International destinations (Limassol, Haifa, Izmir, etc)

These leave from further around the main harbour (#9), towards the customs house (where you should check passports before boarding).

Hydrofoils

Departures direct to Égina leave from Aktí Tselépi (#5). Aee Hellas flying Dolphin services for Argo-Saronic and Peloponnesian destinations leave from the Zéa marina (#10), a twenty-minute overhill walk from the metro.

Tickets are on sale from the Flying Dolphins office at the quay from about an hour before departure. To be sure of a particular sailing in high season, it is wise to book ahead in Athens. Equally, if your schedule is tight, book your seat back to Pireás when you arrive.

Practicalities

The easiest way to get to Pireás from Athens is on the **metro**. There are central stops in Athens at Platía Viktorías, Omónia, Sýndagma and Monastiráki squares, plus Thissío for those in Veïkou, and Syngroú-Fix or Petrálona for those in Koukáki; the journey takes about 25 minutes from Omónia to the Pireás train-station stop (the end of the line). Metro trains run from 6am, early enough to catch the first ferries, until midnight, long after the arrival of all but the most delayed boats.

Alternatively, you could take a **bus** or a taxi. Bus #40 (about every 20min during the day; hourly 1am–5am) will deposit you on Vasiléos Konstandínou, half a dozen blocks from the docks, but it's very slow – allow nearly an hour from Sýndagma, the most obvious boarding point. The **express buses** (see p.100) are quicker and provide a particularly useful link with the airport. **Taxis** cost about €5.50 at day tariff from the centre of Athens – worth considering, especially if you're taking one of the hydrofoils from the Zéa marina, which is a fair walk from the metro.

Accommodation

Few visitors stay in Pireás, and most of the port's **hotels** are geared to a steady clientele of seamen, resting between ships. For this reason, picking somewhere at random is not always a good idea. There are, however, a few reasonably priced and wholesome places close to the port. One of the nicest, tucked in a side street a block from the metro station is the family-style *Ionion Hotel*, Kapodhistríou 10 (☎010/41 77 537, ℗41 10 613; ❸), a clean place with TV in all the renovated rooms. Opposite each other in the next street along are the functional and very cheap *Hotel Delfini*, Leohárous 7 (☎010/41 23 512, ℗42 27 517; ❷), and *Ikaros*, Leohárous 18 (☎010/41 29 305; ❹), which has TV and a/c in all rooms. Also close by is the *Acropole*, Goúnari 7 (☎010/41 73 313; ❸), a safe but slightly run-down standby with a rooftop bar. A much posher place in a fine setting over the hill in Kastélla is the *Cavo d'Oro*, Vas. Pávlou 19–21 (☎010/41 13 744; ❻), complete with piano music in the lounge bar. *Hotel Mistral*, Vassiléos Pávlou 105, Kastella (☎010/41 17 150; ❺), is a more upscale choice with a nice roof garden, on a hill in Kastella, a picturesque, restored area behind Mikrolímano.

Sleeping rough in Platía Karaïskáki, as some exhausted travellers attempt to do, is unwise. If thieves or the police don't rouse you, street-cleaners armed with hoses certainly will – at 5am.

Eating and drinking

If you're simply looking for food to take on board, or breakfast, you'll find numerous places around the market area, back from the waterside Aktí Miaoúli/Ethnikís Andistáseos, open from 6.30am. Along the waterfront and down its side streets there is also an array of standard *souvláki* and oven-food joints.

For a real blowout, the *Vassilenas* at Etolikoú 72, the street running inland from Aktí Kondhíli, is a fine choice. Housed in an old grocery store, its set menu provides about sixteen different courses of *mezédhes* and main dishes with a fish and seafood emphasis, enough to defy all appetites; at €17 a head, drinks extra, it's not especially cheap but well worth it for the quantity and quality of food you get. Enough Athenians consider it worth the drive that most evenings you need to book a table (☎010/46 12 457). There's a string of ouzerís and seafood tavernas on Aktí Themistokléous, west of the Zéa marina, most of them pretty good and reasonably priced, or try the Indian restaurant *Maharajah* (*Shere-e-Punjab*) at Notará 122 or snack-bar-style *Punjab* at Kolokotróni 136, both genuine and cheap by Greek standards.

Otherwise, a good bet for seafood is *Kefalonitis*, on the corner of Rethýmnis and Tsakálof, up by the open-air theatre. A nearby and equally authentic alternative is *Iy Orea Mykonos*, a simple island-style fish taverna on the corner of Kilkís and Sfakión. A third recommended option is *Margaro*, Hatzikyriakou 126, close to Mikrolímano, a no-frills neighbourhood restaurant, totally low-key and non-touristy, with a small menu of fish and fried crayfish at very reasonable prices (closed Mon).

Entertainment

Culturally, there's not a great deal going on at Pireás, though a **summer festival**, run alongside that of Athens, features events in the open-air theatre set back from the yacht harbour of Mikrolímano (or Tourkolímano, as it has been called for centuries). In winter there's always **football** (see box, p.153): Olympiakós is the port's big team, rival to the capital's AEK and Panathinaïkós, and it plays at Stádhio Karaïskáki beside Néo Fáliro metro station, while **bas-**

ketball and other gymnastic events take place in the indoor arena, Stádhio Irínis & Filías, on the opposite side of the tracks.

The "Apollo Coast", Cape Sounion and Lávrio

The seventy kilometres of coast south of Athens – the tourist-board-dubbed "**Apollo Coast**" – has some good but highly developed beaches. At weekends, when Athenians flee the city, the sands fill fast, as do the innumerable bars, restaurants and discos at night. If this is what you're after, then resorts like **Glyfádha** and **Vouliagméni** are functional enough. But for most foreign visitors, the coast's lure is at the end of the road, in the form of the Temple of Poseidon at **Cape Sounion**.

Access to Sounion (Soúnio in the modern spelling) is straightforward. There are buses on the hour and half-hour from the KTEL terminal on Mavromatéon at the southwest corner of the Pedíou Áreos Park; there's also a more central (but in summer, very full) stop ten minutes later at point "D" on Filellínon, south of Sýndagma (corner of Xenofóndos, in front of the Middle East Airways office). There are both coastal (*paraliakó*) and inland (*mesoyiakó*) services, the latter slightly longer and more expensive. The coast route normally takes around two hours; last departures back to Athens are posted at the Sounion stop.

For Glyfádha/Voúla and Vouliagméni/Várkiza – the main resorts – take the #A3 trunk line from Sýndagma or #E2 express bus from opposite the National Gardens and transfer onto local services #114 and #115. The #A2 trunk-line bus for Glyfádha/Voúla also leaves from Panepistimíou.

The resorts: Glyfádha to Anávissos

Although some Greeks swim at Pireás itself, few would recommend the sea much before **GLYFÁDHA**, half an hour's drive southeast from the city centre. The major resort along the "Apollo Coast", merged almost indistinguishably with its neighbour **VOÚLA**, this is lined with seafood restaurants, ice-cream bars and discos, as well as a couple of marinas and a golf course. Its popularity, though, is hard to fathom, built as it is in the shadow of the airport. The only possible appeal is in the beaches, the best of which is the **Astir**, privately owned and with a stiff admission charge; others are gritty. Hotels are all on the expensive side, and in any case are full of package tours; there is a **campsite** at Voúla (☎010/89 52 712).

VOULIAGMÉNI, which in turn has swallowed up **Kavoúri**, is a little quieter than Glyfádha, and a little ritzier. It is set back from a small natural saltwater and freshwater lake, a pleasant and uncrowded place to swim (admission €4). Vouliagméni itself boasts a water-ski school, some extremely chichi restaurants, and an OTE pay-beach. Again, budget accommodation is hard to come by, though there is a **campsite** – and another OTE pay-beach – just to the south at **Várkiza**. There is also pleasant free swimming to be enjoyed from the popular rocks between Vouliagméni and Várkiza.

South of Várkiza, there are further beaches en route to Sounion, though unless you've a car to pick your spot they're not really worth the effort. The resorts of **Lagoníssi** and **Anávissos** are in the Glyfádha mould, and only slightly less crowded, despite the extra distance from Athens.

Cape Sounion

Cape Sounion – Aktí Souníou – is one of the most imposing spots in Greece, for centuries a landmark for boats sailing between Pireás and the islands, and an equally dramatic vantage-point in itself to look out over the Aegean. On its tip stands the fifth-century BC Temple of Poseidon, built in the time of Pericles as part of a major sanctuary to the sea god.

The Temple of Poseidon

The **Temple of Poseidon** (Tues–Sun 10am–sunset; €2.10) owes its fame above all to **Byron**, who visited in 1810, carved his name on the nearest pillar (an unfortunate precedent) and commemorated the event in the finale of his hymn to Greek independence, the "Isles of Greece" segment of *Don Juan*:

> *Place me on Sunium's marbled steep,*
> *Where nothing, save the waves and I,*
> *May hear our mutual murmurs sweep;*
> *There, swan-like, let me sing and die:*
> *A land of slaves shall ne'er be mine –*
> *Dash down yon cup of Samian wine!*

In summer, at least, there is faint hope of solitude, unless you slip into the site before the tour groups arrive. But the temple is as evocative a ruin as any in Greece. Doric in style, it was probably built by the architect of the Hephaisteion in the Athens Agora. That it is so admired and visited is in part due to its site, but also perhaps to its picturesque state of ruin – preserving, as if by design, sixteen of its 34 columns. On a clear day, the view from the temple takes in the islands of Kéa, Kýthnos and Sérifos to the southeast, Égina and the Peloponnese to the west.

The rest of the site is of more academic interest. There are remains of a fortification wall around the sanctuary; a **Propylaion** (entrance hall) and **Stoa**, and cuttings for two shipsheds. To the north are the foundations of a small **Temple of Athena**.

Beaches – and staying at Sounion

Below the promontory are several **coves** – the most sheltered a five-minute walk east from the car park and site entrance. The main Sounion beach is more crowded, but has a couple of tavernas at the far end – pretty reasonably priced, considering the location. *O Ilias* has the slightly better view and a fair selection of grilled meat and fish. *Akroyiali* is another good choice for fresh fish and octopus.

Places to **stay** include a couple of campsites just around the coast: *Camping Bacchus* (the nearest; ☎02920/39 262) and *Sounion Beach Camping* (5km; ☎02920/39 358). The 1960s-style *Hotel Aegeon* (☎02920/39 262; ❻) is right on the Sounion beach and predictably pricey. A better bargain, with the bonus of a pool, is *Hotel Saron* (☎02920/39 144; ❹), just round the coast by the second campsite.

Lávrio

Ten kilometres north of Sounion, around the cape, is the port of **LÁVRIO**. This has two or three daily ferry connections with Kéa, though extra high-speed services are supposed to be starting up. It can be reached by **bus** from the Mavromatéon terminal in Athens, or from Sounion.

The port's ancient predecessor, Laurion, was famous for its silver mines – a mainstay of the classical Athenian economy – which were worked almost exclusively by slaves. The port today remains an industrial and mining town, though nowadays for less-precious minerals (cadmium and manganese), and also hosts the country's principal transit camp for political refugees: mostly Kurds from Iraq and Turkey at present, with a scattering of eastern Europeans, awaiting resettlement in North America, Australia or Europe. The island off-shore, **Makrónissos**, now uninhabited, has an even more sinister past, for it was here that hundreds of ELAS members and other leftists were imprisoned in "re-education" labour camps during and after the civil war.

As you might imagine, this is not really a place to linger between buses and ferries. If you have time to kill, you'll find the site of **ancient Thoriko** is of some interest. It lies down a zigzag track from the village of Pláka, 5km north of Lávrio. A defensive outpost of the mining area in Classical times, its most prominent ruins are of a theatre, crudely engineered into an irregular slope in the hill.

East of Athens: the Mesóyia and Brauron

The area east of Athens is one of the least visited parts of Attica. The mountain of **Imittós** (Hymettus) forms an initial barrier, with Kessarianí monastery (see p.138) on its cityside flank. Beyond extends the plateau of the **Mesóyia** (Midland), a gentle landscape whose villages have a quiet renown for their retsina and for their churches, many of which date back to Byzantine times. On towards the coast, there is the remote and beautiful site of **ancient Brauron**, and the developing resort of **Pórto Ráfti**.

The Mesóyia

The best-known attraction of the Mesóyia is at the village of **PEANÍA**, on the east slope of Imittós: the **Koutoúki cave** (daily 9.30am–4.30pm; €1.50), endowed with spectacularly illuminated stalactites and stalagmites and multi-coloured curtains of rock. It is fairly easily reached by taking the Athens–Markópoulo bus, stopping at Peanía and then walking up. Close by the village – just to the east on the Spáta road – is the chapel of **Áyios Athanásios**, built with old Roman blocks and fragments.

MARKÓPOULO, the main Mesóyia village, shelters a further clutch of chapels. Within the village, set in a walled garden, stand the twin chapels of **Ayía Paraskeví** and **Ayía Thékla**; ring for admission, and a nun will open them up to show you the seventeenth-century frescoes. Over to the west, on the road to Koropí, is one of the oldest churches in Attica, the tenth-century **Metamórfosi**, the keys to which can be obtained from the Análipsi church in Koropí.

Heading east from Markópoulo, the road runs past the unusual double-naved **Ayía Triádha** (2500m out) and on to the coast at **PÓRTO RÁFTI**, whose bay, protected by islets, forms an almost perfect natural harbour. Buses to Pórto Ráfti from the Mavromatéon terminal sometimes give the final destination as Avláki. The area has been comprehensively developed, with an OTE pay-beach at Avláki and a fair number of tavernas, but remains a good place to **stay** if you can find a room. The *Kiani Akti,* Ayías Marínas 40 (☎02990/86 400, ℱ86 050;

⑤) is a smart modern hotel on the road to Avláki. As for **food**, the most genuine and reasonably priced places are on the old harbour 2km before the bus terminal – try *To Limani*. On the small island in the harbour is a large Roman statue of a woman whose now missing arm held the "first fruits" of crops that were sent each year to the sacred island of Delos. During the sixteenth century the statue was thought to hold scissors, and the port came to be known as the tailor's port, Pórto Ráfti.

Brauron

Over the mountain from Pórto Ráfti lies ancient **Brauron** (site and museum Tues–Sun 8.30am–2.30pm; €1.50), one of the most enjoyable minor Greek sites. It lies just outside the modern village of Vravróna (40km from Athens), in a marshy area at the base of a low, chapel-topped hill. The marsh and surrounding fields are alive with birdsong, only rarely drowned out by traffic noise from the nearby busy road.

The remains are of a **Sanctuary of Artemis**, centred on a vast *stoa*. This was the chief site of the Artemis cult, legendarily founded by Iphigeneia, whose "tomb" has also been identified here. It was she who, with Orestes, stole the image of Artemis from Tauris (as commemorated in Euripides' *Iphigeneia at Tauris*) and introduced worship of the goddess to Greece. The main event of the cult was a quadrennial festival, now shrouded in mystery, in which young girls dressed as bears to enact a ritual connected with the goddess and childbirth.

The **Stoa of the Bears**, where these initiates stayed, has been substantially reconstructed, along with a stone **bridge**; both are fifth century BC and provide a graceful focus to the semi-waterlogged site. Somewhat scantier are the ruins of the temple itself, whose stepped foundations can be made out; immediately adjacent, the sacred spring still wells up, today squirming with tadpoles. Nearby, steps lead up to the chapel, which contains some damaged frescoes. At the site **museum** (Tues–Sun 8.30am–2.30pm; €1.50), left off the main road and over 1km from the ruins, various finds from the sanctuary are displayed, including some marble heads modelled after the little girls and bear masks.

Getting to Brauron from Athens will involve a walk if you're dependent on public transport. Bus #304 from the Záppio passes through **Loútsa** and terminates within 2km of the site. Loútsa itself is also served by buses #316 and #321 and is a lively little spot with a decent sandy beach and row of tavernas and cafés.

Rafína, Marathon and Rhamnous

The port of **RAFÍNA** has **ferries**, a **catamaran** and **hydrofoils** to a wide assortment of the Cyclades, the Dodecanese and the northeast Aegean, as well as to nearby Évvia. It is connected regularly by bus with Athens: a forty-minute trip (from Mavromatéon) through the "gap" in Mount Pendéli.

Boats aside, the appeal of the place is mainly gastronomic. Though much of the town has been spoilt by tacky seaside development, the little fishing harbour with its line of **roof-terrace seafood restaurants** remains one of the most inviting spots on the Attic coast. Of these, *Ta Kavouria tou Asimaki*, the first as you descend to the harbour from the square, is the cheapest and best. A lunchtime outing is an easy operation, given the frequency of the bus service. Evenings, when it's more fun, you need to arrange your own transport back, or make for the beachside **campsite** at nearby Kókkino Limanáki. The town's few **hotels** are often full in summer, so you need to phone ahead to be sure of a room; the best value is the *Corali* (☎02940/22 477; ❷) located in the central Platía Nikifórou Plastíra, while the *Avra* (☎02940/22 780, ℗23 320; ❻), just down from the square and overlooking the sea, is large and rather overpriced.

If you want a **swim**, the pleasant little bay of **Blé Limanáki** is just ten minutes' walk north over the headland above the harbour and avoids the pollution of the longer town beach. There is nothing to eat or drink here, though. Alternatively, you can walk the extra fifteen minutes to **Kókkino Limanáki**, which has a good shady beach and some restaurants and shops.

Marathon

The site of the most famous military victory in Athenian history is not far from the village of **MARATHÓNAS**, 42km from Athens. Buses also leave from the Mavromatéon terminal in Athens, some of them calling first at Rafina. Just over three kilometres after Néa Mákri (4km before the village of Marathónas) there is a turn to the right; the **Týmfos Marathóna** stands to the left of the road 700 metres after this turn. The ancient burial mound was raised over 192 Athenians who died in the city's famous victory over the Persians in 490 BC. Consisting only of overgrown earth piled ten metres high, it is a quietly impressive monument. Another mound, this for the eleven Plataian allies of the Athenians (including a ten-year-old boy) who died in the battle, is about 5km away, near the edge of the mountain. To reach the **Mound of the Plataians** and the **archeological museum**, return to the Rafina–Marathónas road and turn right towards the village of Marathónas. Take a left and follow the small yellow signs for 2.5km to the museum (open, as is the mound precinct, Tues–Sun 8.30am–2.30pm; €1.50), with a sparse collection of artefacts mainly from the local Cave of Pan, a deity felt to have aided the victory.

Marathónas village itself is a dull place, with just a couple of cafés and restaurants for the passing trade. Nearby, though, to the west, and quite an impressive site, is **Límni Marathóna** – Marathon Lake – with its huge marble dam. This provided Athens' entire water supply until the 1950s and is still used as a storage facility for water from the giant Mórnos project in central Greece. You can drive or walk across the top of the dam and there is a scenically situated café/restaurant on the east side.

The coast around ancient Marathon takes in some good stretches of sand, walkable from the tomb if you want to cool off. The best and most popular **beach** is to the north at **SKHINIÁS**, a long, pine-backed strand with shallow water. There is a **campsite**, *Camping Marathon*, midway along the road from Marathónas. Of the tavernas, *Iy Avra* is the best bet and stays open most of the year, at least at weekends.

Rhamnous

Further to the north, the ruins of **RHAMNOUS** (Tues–Sun 8.30am–2.30pm; €1.50) occupy an isolated site above the sea. Among the scattered and overgrown remains is a Doric **Temple of Nemesis**, goddess of retribution. Pausanias records that the Persians who landed nearby before their defeat incurred her wrath by carrying off a marble block – upon which they intended to commemorate their conquest of Athens. There are also the remains of a smaller temple dedicated to Themis, goddess of justice. Rhamnous can be reached just five times daily by bus from the Mavromatéon terminal; the village name to look for is Káto Soúli.

Mount Párnitha and Phyle

Scarcely an hour's bus ride north from Athens' city centre, **Mount Párnitha** is an unexpectedly vast and – where it has escaped fire damage – virgin tract of forest, rock and ravine. If you've no time for expeditions further afield, it will give you a taste of what Greek mountains are all about, including a good selection of mountain flowers. If you're here in March or April, it merits a visit in its own right. Snow lies surprisingly late on the north side and, in its wake, carpets of crocus, alpine squills and mountain windflower spring from the mossy ground, while lower down you'll find aubretia, tulips, dwarf iris and a whole range of orchids.

There are numerous **waymarked paths** on the mountain (look for red discs and multicoloured paint splodges on the trees). The principal and most representative ones are the approach to the Báfi refuge up the **Houni** ravine, and the walk to the Skípiza spring. These, along with a couple of lesser excursions, to the ancient fort at Phyle and one of the many legendary **caves of Pan**, are detailed below.

The hike to the Báfi refuge

On Saturdays and Sundays bus #A12 runs from the corner of Aharnón and Stournári (north side of Platía Váthis) twice a day (6.30am and 2.30pm) up to Párnitha. During the week take the trunk-line bus #A10 or #B10 to the end of the line (Mesiníti) and then the local buses #724 or #737 to the suburb of Thrakomakedhónes, whose topmost houses steal up the flanks of the mountain beside the mouth of the **Houni** ravine. Get off at the highest stop and keep on, bearing left, up Odhós Thrákis to where the road ends at the foot of a cliff beside two new blocks of flats. Keep straight ahead along the foot of the cliff and in a few metres you come to the start of the path, turning down left into a dry streambed, before crossing and continuing on the opposite bank.

The refuge is about two-hours' walk away. The track curves slowly leftwards up the craggy, well-defined ravine, at first through thick scrub, then through more open forest of Greek fir, crossing the stream two or three times. At a junction reached after about 45 minutes, signposted "Katára–Mesanó Neró–Móla", keep straight ahead. At the next fork, some ten minutes later, keep right. After a further five minutes, at the top of a sparsely vegetated slope, you get your first glimpse of the pink-roofed refuge high on a rocky spur in front of you. Another twenty minutes brings you to the confluence of two small streams, where a sign on a tree points left to Ayía Triádha (see below), and a second path branches right to Móla and Koromiliá. Take the third, middle, path, up a scrubby spur. At the top a broad path goes off left to meet the ring road leading to Ayía Triádha. From here, turn right, down into the head of a gully, where the path doubles back and climbs up to the refuge. Normally the refuge warden provides **board and lodging**, particularly on weekends, but it would be wise to check opening times and accommodation policy with the Aharnés EOS (☎010/24 69 777) in advance, or at the Alpine Club of Athens (☎010/32 12 355), which operates the Báfi refuge, as the schedule changes periodically. Water is usually available at the back of the building, except in winter.

To the Skípiza spring

For the walk to the Skípiza spring, you need to get off at the chapel of Ayía Triádha in the heart of the mountains. On the weekends there are two #A12 connections a day: at 6.30am, returning at 8am; and at 2.30pm, returning at 4pm. If you get stuck, you can continue to the *Hotel Mount Parnes* and take the téléférique down if it's operating – otherwise there's a rough trail down a gully near the *Xenia Hotel*, spilling out near the Metóhi picnic grounds.

The **Skípiza spring** is an hour and a half to two-hours' walk away. From the bus stop by the chapel, walk west past the *Hotel-Chalet Kyklamina*, continuing straight on to the ring road. After the first ascent and descent, you come after fifteen minutes to the Paleohóri spring on the right of the road in the middle of a left-hand bend, opposite a piece of flat ground marked with pointed-hat pipes. A beautiful and well-defined path is clearly marked by discs on trees, beginning by the spring and following the course of a small stream up through the fir woods.

From Skípiza you can continue right around the summit to **Móla** (about 90min) and from there, in another hour, back to the Báfi refuge. Alternatively, by setting your back to the Skípiza spring and taking the path that charges up the ridge almost directly behind, you can get to **Báfi** in around forty minutes. Turn left when you hit the paved road after about half an hour; follow it ten minutes more down to the ring road and turn left again. In a few paces you are in the refuge car park. To get back to Ayía Triádha by the road it's about 6km (an hour's walk).

The Cave of Pan

Another highly evocative spot for lovers of classical ghosts is the **Cave of Pan**, which Menander used as the setting for one of his plays. The best approach is by track and trail from the chapel of Ayía Triádha: a map showing local landmarks (labelled in Greek), superimposed on a topographical map, is posted just behind the church.

Phyle

Over to the west of the main Párnitha trails, another route up the mountain will take you to the ruined but still impressive fourth-century BC Athenian fort of **Phyle**, about an hour and three-quarters on foot beyond the village of Filí (known locally as Khasiá). Buses to Filí leave near the Aharnón/Stournára stop on Sourméli. On the way up to the fort you pass the unattractively restored fourteenth-century **monastery of Klistón** in the mouth of the Goúra ravine that splits through the middle of the Párnitha range. The walking, unfortunately, is all on asphalt.

Eleusis and west to the Peloponnese

The main **highway to Kórinthos** (Corinth) is about as unattractive a road as any in Greece. For the first thirty or so kilometres you have little sense of leaving Athens, whose western suburbs merge into the industrial wastelands of first Elefsína and then Mégara. Offshore, almost closing off the bay, is **Salamína** (ancient Salamis), not a dream island in anyone's book but a nicer escape than it looks, and accessible by ferries from the mainland here at Lákki Kalyírou (and at Pérama, near Pireás).

A train or bus direct to Kórinthos or beyond, though, is perhaps the wisest option. Only the site of **ancient Eleusis** is in any way a temptation to stop, and even this is strictly for Classical enthusiasts. **Drivers** should note that the Athens–Kórinthos non-toll road is one of the most dangerous in the country, switching from four-lane highway to a rutted two-laner without warning; it is best driven in daytime, or preserve your sanity and pay the toll for the broad motorway higher up the cliff.

Eleusis

The **Sanctuary of Demeter** at **ELEUSIS**, at the beginning of the Sacred Way to Athens, was one of the most important in the Greek world. For two millennia, the ritual ceremonies known as the Mysteries were perfomed, which had an effect on their ancient initiates the equal of any modern cult. According to Pindar, who experienced the rites in Classical times and, like all others, was bound by pain of death not to reveal their content, anyone who had "seen the holy things [at Eleusis] and goes in death beneath the earth is happy, for he knows life's end and he knows the new divine beginning."

Established in Mycenaean times, perhaps as early as 1500 BC, the cult centred around the figure of Demeter (Ceres to the Romans), the goddess of corn, and the myth of her daughter Persephone's annual descent into and resurrection from the underworld, which came to symbolize the rebirth of the crops (and the gods responsible for them) in the miracle of fertility. By the fifth century BC the cult had developed into a sophisticated annual festival, attracting up to 30,000 people from all over the Greek world. Participants gathered in Athens, outside the Propylaia on the Acropolis, and, after various rituals, including mass bathing and purification in Phaleron Bay, followed the Sacred Way to the sanctuary here at Eleusis. It has been speculated by some, such as the late ethnomycologist R. Gordon Wasson, that one of the rituals entailed the ingestion of a potion containing grain-ergot fungus, the effects of which would be almost identical to those of modern psychedelic drugs. The Mysteries eventually fell foul of Christianity and died out. It is said that Demeter threatened to render the land permanently barren if her worship there ever ceased. Looking at the ecological havoc wreaked by the area's industry, it would seem that the curse has been fulfilled.

The site

The **ruins** (Tues–Sun 8.30am–2.30pm; €1.50) are obscure in the extreme, dating from several different ages of rebuilding and largely reduced to foundations; any imaginings of mystic goings-on are further hampered by the spectacularly unromantic setting. The best plan is to head straight for the **museum**, which features models of the site at various stages in its history. This will at least point you in the direction of the **Telesterion**, the windowless Hall of Initiation, where the priests of Demeter would exhibit the "Holy Things" – presumably sheaves of fungus-infected grain, or vessels containing the magic potion – and speak "the Unutterable Words".

To reach the site from Athens, take **bus** #A16 from Platía Eleftherías, down Pireós from Omónia. Ask to be dropped at the *Heröön* (Sanctuary), to the left of the main road, a short way into Elefsína. The trip can easily be combined with a visit to the monastery at Dhafní (see p.138), on the same road and bus route.

On from Elefsína

Northwest from Elefsína, the **old road to Thebes and Delphi** heads into the hills. This route is described in Chapter Three, and is highly worthwhile, with its detours to **ancient Aegosthena** and the tiny resort of **Pórto Yermenó**. At Mégara another, more minor road heads north to reach the sea at the village of Alepohóri, where it deteriorates to a track to loop around to Pórto Yermenó.

Heading directly west, on towards the Peloponnese, there are shingle beaches – more or less clear of pollution – along the old, parallel coastal road at Kinéta and Áyii Theódhori. This highway, with the Yeránia mountains to the north and those of the Peloponnese across the water, has a small place in pre-Homeric myth, as the route where Theseus slew the bandit Sciron and threw him off the cliffs to be eaten by a giant sea turtle. Thus, Sciron met the same fate as the generations of travellers he had preyed upon.

You leave Attica at Isthmía, a village beside the **Corinth Canal** (see p.187), where most of the buses break the journey for a drink at the café by the bridge. To the north of the canal, Loutráki and Perahóra are technically part of Attica but, as they are more easily reached from Kórinthos, are covered in the Peloponnese chapter.

Travel details

Trains

Trains for Kórinthos and the Peloponnese leave from the Stathmós Peloponníssou, those for northern Greece from Stathmós Laríssis. The stations adjoin each other, just west of Deliyánni, on the #1 trolleybus route. To reach the Peloponnese station, use the metal overpass next to the Laríssis station. The new Inter-City trains are considerably faster and more reliable but there is a hefty extra charge (also levied on rail passes).

Destinations from Stathmós Peloponníssou include: Árgos (6 daily; 3hr 10min); Kalamáta (4 daily; 6hr 30min–8hr); Kórinthos (12 daily; 1hr 30min–2hr); Pátra (8 daily; 3hr 30min–4hr 30min); Pýrgos (7 daily; 5hr 30min–6hr 30min). Destinations from Stathmós Laríssis include: Alexandhroúpoli (2 daily; 16hr); Halkídha (17 daily; 1hr 30min); Thessaloníki (10 daily; 6hr 10min–8hr); Vólos (3 daily; 5–7hr).

Buses

Attica Buses for most destinations in Attica (ie within this chapter) leave from the Mavromatéon terminal (250m north of the National Archeological Museum, at the junction with Leofóros Alexándhras, "B" on the Athens map). Exceptions are specified in the text.
Destinations include: Lávrio (every 30min until 6pm, then hourly until 9pm; 1hr 30min); Marathon Tomb (every 30min until 2pm, hourly thereafter; 1hr 15min); Rafína (every 30min; 1hr); Sounion by the coast (hourly on the half-hour; 1hr 30min); Sounion by the inland route (hourly on the hour; 1hr 45min).
Peloponnese and western/northern Greece Most buses leave from the terminal at Kifissoú 100, a good 4km northeast of the city centre, in the industrial district of Peristéri; the easiest way to get there is on the #051 bus from the corner of Vilára and Menándhrou (near Omónia; "E" on the map).
Destinations include: Árgos (hourly; 2hr 15min); Árta (8 daily; 6hr); Corfu (3 daily; 11hr); Igoumenítsa (3 daily; 9hr 30min); Ioánnina (8 daily; 7hr 30min); Kalamáta (10–11 daily; 4hr 30min); Kefallonía (4–5 daily; 8hr); Kórinthos (every 30min;

1hr 30min); Lefkádha (4 daily; 6hr); Mycenae/Náfplio (hourly; 2hr 30min); Olympia (4 daily; 6hr); Pátra (every 30min; 3hr); Pýlos (2 daily; 6hr); Spárti (11 daily; 4hr); Thessaloníki (10 daily; 7hr 30min); Trípoli (12 daily; 3hr); Zákynthos (4 daily; 7hr).
Central Greece Buses for most other destinations in central Greece leave from the Liossíon 260 terminal, easiest reached by taxi. Alternatively, take either bus #024 at the Amalías entrance of the National Gardens (by Sýndagma), or on Panepistimíou almost to the end of its route (about 25min; the stop is 200m south of the terminal); or the metro from Omónia/ Monastiráki to the Áyios Nikólaos station (800m southeast of the terminal; coming out, go under the rail line, turn left and look out for the buses).
Destinations include: Áyios Konstandínos (hourly at quarter past the hour; 2hr 30min); Delphi (6 daily; 3hr); Halkídha (every 30min; 1hr 15min); Karpeníssi (3 daily; 5hr); Kymi, for Skýros ferries (6 daily; 3hr 30min); Ósios Loukás (2 daily; 4hr); Thíva/Thebes (hourly; 1hr 30min); Tríkala (9 daily; 5hr 30min); Vólos (9–12 daily; 5hr).

Island ferries and hydrofoils

Information For details of ferries from **Rafína** or **Lávrio** call their respective port police offices (Rafína: ☎02940/22 300; Lávrio: ☎02920/25 249). For **hydrofoils** call ☎02940/23 500 or 23 561.

Pireás Ferries and hydrofoils to the Argo-Saronic, Monemvassía, Crete, the Cyclades, Dodecanese and northeast Aegean islands. See p.163 for details of how to get to Pireás.

Lávrio Ferries daily to Kéa. Bus from Mavromatéon.

Rafína Ferries daily to Mármari and Kárystos on Évvia; most days to Ándhros, Tínos, Syros and Mýkonos, plus less frequently to Páros, Náxos and Amorgós; and two or three weekly to Áyios Efstrátios, Lésvos and Límnos. Hydrofoils to Évvia (Stýra, Mármari and Kárystos), Ándhros, Tínos, Mýkonos, Páros, Náxos and beyond. Many ferries from Rafína to the Cyclades leave in the late afternoon – a boon if you've missed the morning Pireás boats. Bus from Mavromatéon.

International ferries

From Pireás Destinations include: Izmir or Çeşme, Turkey (once weekly); Kuşadası, Turkey (once weekly May–Oct); Limassol, Cyprus and Haifa, Israel (at least weekly), via Rhodes or Crete.

Domestic flights

Olympic Airways operates regular flights from the airport to the following destinations: Alexandhroúpoli, Astypálea, Haniá (Crete), Híos, Ikaría, Iráklion (Crete), Ioánnina, Kalamáta, Kárpathos, Kastoriá, Kavála, Kefalloniá, Kérkyra (Corfu), Kós, Kozáni, Kythira, Léros, Límnos, Mílos, Mýkonos, Mytilíni (Lésvos), Náxos, Páros, Préveza, Ródhos (Rhodes), Sámos, Sitía (Crete), Skiáthos, Skýros, Sýros, Thessaloníki, Thíra (Santórini) and Zákynthos. Island services are heavily reduced out of season.

The Peloponnese

CHAPTER 2 # Highlights

* **Acrocorinth** A huge, barren rock arising from and dominating the plains of Kórinthos, crowned by a great medieval fortress. See p.184

* **Mycenae** Agamemnon's legendary palace and possible site of his murder upon his return from the Trojan war. See p.191

* **Náfplio** Genteel and cultured (if slightly faded) nineteenth-century elegance, once the residence of Ioannis Kapodhistrias, first president of Greece. See p.199

* **Monemvasiá** The impregnable rock and stronghold of the Byzantines; once an important port and Mystra's commercial counterpart. See p.215

* **Paleohóra, Kýthira** The ruined medieval island capital; a fortifed town, hidden between ravines. See p.223

* **Máni Towers** Anachronistic medieval architecture; high-rise internecine warfare in the deep south. See p.229

* **Mystra** A visually stunning medieval city that once had a population of 20,000; a superb collection of frescoed Byzantine churches remains. See p.245

* **Loúsios Gorge** Green and luxuriant gorge with extraordinary monasteries clinging to the cliffs. See p.259

* **Olympia** It's worth braving the crowds to see 1400 years of the Olympic Games laid bare along the green valley of the Alfiós. See p.280

* **Vouraïkós Gorge** Greece's most remarkable and scenic railway line, winding through the northern mountains. See p.298

2

The Peloponnese

he appeal of the Peloponnese (Pelopónnisos in Greek) is hard to over-state. This southern peninsula, technically an island since the cutting of the Corinth Canal, seems to have the best of almost everything Greek. Its ancient sites include the Homeric palaces of Agamemnon at **Mycenae** and of Nestor at **Pýlos**, the best preserved of all Greek theatres at **Epidaurus**, and the lush sanctuary of **Olympia**, host for a millennium to the Olympic Games. The medieval remains are scarcely less rich, with the fabulous Venetian, Frankish and Turkish castles of **Náfplio**, **Methóni** and **Kórinthos**; the strange battle towers and frescoed churches of the **Máni**; and the extraor-dinarily well-preserved Byzantine shells of **Mystra** and **Monemvasiá**.

Beyond this incredible profusion of cultural monuments, the Peloponnese is also a superb place to relax and wander. Its **beaches**, especially along the west coast, are among the finest and least developed in the country, and the **landscape** inland is superb – dominated by range after range of forested mountains, and cut by some of the lushest valleys and gorges to be imagined. Not for nothing did its heartland province of **Arcadia** give its name to the concept of a classical rural idyll.

The Peloponnese is at its most enjoyable and intriguing when you venture off the beaten track: to the old hill towns of Arcadia like **Karýtena**, **Stemnítsa** and **Dhimitsána**; the Maniot tower villages such as **Kítta** or **Váthia**; at **Voïdhokiliá** and **Elafónissos** beaches in the south; or the trip along the astonishing **rack-and-pinion railway** leading inland from the north coast at **Dhiakoftó** to **Kalávryta**.

Accommodation price codes

Throughout the book we've categorized accommodation according to the following **price codes**, which denote the cheapest available double room in high season. All prices are for the room only, except where otherwise indicated. Many hotels, especially those in category ❹ and over, include breakfast in the price; you'll need to check this when booking. During low season, rates can drop by more than fifty per-cent, especially if you are staying for three or more nights. Exceptions are during the Christmas and Easter weeks when you'll pay high-season prices. Single rooms, where available, cost around seventy percent of the price of a double.

❶ Up to €24	❹ €43–58
❷ €24–33	❺ €59–72
❸ €34–42	❻ €73 and upwards

Note: Youth hostels and mountain refuges typically charge €7–9 for a dormitory bed. For more accommodation details, see pp.51–54.

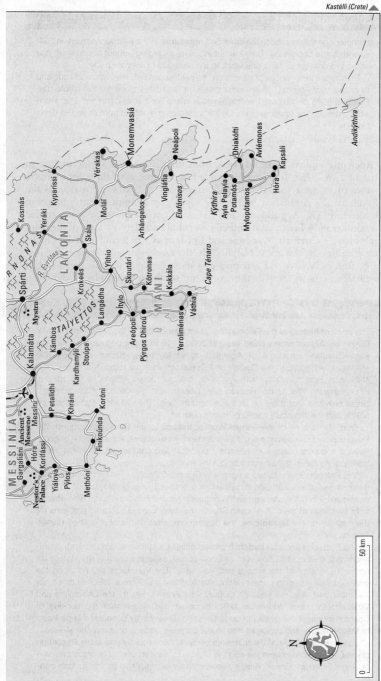

Kastélli (Crete) ▲

Andikýthira

Monemvasiá

Neápoli

Yérakas

Dhiakófti

Avlémonas

Moláï

Kýparissi

Vingláfia

Kapsáli

Arhángelos

Elafónisos

Kýthira

Ayía Pelayía

Hóra

Kosmás

Yeráki

Potamós

Mylopótamos

LAKONÍA

Skála

R. Evrótas

Yíthio

Skoútari

Kótronas

Kokkála

Spárti

Mystra

Krokeés

Itylo

Langádha

Areópoli

MÁNI

Vathia

Cape Ténaro

Kámbos

Kardhamýli

Stoúpa

Pýrgos Dhiroú

Yerolimenás

Kalamáta

Messíni

Petalídhi

Khráni

Koróni

Finikoúnda

MESSINÍA

Gargaliáni Ancient Messene

Hóra Korifássi

Yiálova

Nestor's Palace

Pýlos

Methóni

ÁRNONAS

TAΪYETTOS

50 km

0

N

Anciently known as the **Moreas**, from the resemblance of the outline to that of a mulberry leaf (*morá*), rounded at the top, with three long fingers below (from west to east, Messinía, the Máni and Monemvasiá), plus the thumb of the Argolid, it will amply repay any amount of time that you devote to it. The **Argolid**, the area richest in ancient history, is just a couple of hours from Athens, and if pushed you could complete a circuit of the main sights here – **Corinth**, **Mycenae** and **Epidaurus** – in a couple of days, making your base by the sea in Náfplio. Given a week, you could take in the two large sites of Mystra and Olympia at a more leisurely pace. To get to grips with all this, however, plus the wonderful southern peninsulas of the Máni

Pelopónnissos – Moreas: some history

The **ancient history** of the Peloponnese is very much that of the Greek mainstream. During the **Mycenaean period** (around 2000–1100 BC), the peninsula hosted the semi-legendary kingdoms of Agamemnon at Mycenae, Nestor at Pýlos and Menelaus at Sparta. In the **Dorian** and **Classical** eras, the region's principal city-state was Sparta, which, with its allies, brought down Athens in the ruinous Peloponnesian War. Under **Roman** rule, Corinth was the capital of the southern Greek province. For more on all these periods, see "The historical framework" on p.995, and the individual accounts in this chapter.

From the decline of the Roman Empire, through to the Ottoman conquest, the Peloponnese pursued a more complex and individual course. A succession of occupations and conquests, with attendant outposts and castles, left an extraordinary legacy of medieval remains throughout the region.

The Peloponnese retained a nominally Roman civilization, well after the colonial rule had dissipated, with Corinth at the fore until the city was destroyed by two major earthquakes in the fourth and sixth centuries. Around this time, too, came attacks from barbarian tribes of Avars and Slavs, who were to pose sporadic problems for the new rulers, the **Byzantines**, the eastern emperors of the now divided Roman Empire.

The Byzantines established their courts, castles and towns from the ninth century onward; their control, however, was only partial, as large swaths of the Moreás fell under the control of the Franks and Venetians. The **Venetians** settled along the coast, founding trading ports at Monemvasiá, Pýlos and Koróni, which endured, for the most part, into the fifteenth century. The **Franks**, led by the Champlitte and Villehardouin clans, arrived in 1204, bloodied and eager from the sacking of Constantinople in the piratical Fourth Crusade. They swiftly conquered large tracts of the peninsula, and divided it into feudal baronies under a prince of the Moreas.

Towards the middle of the thirteenth century, there was a remarkable **Byzantine revival**, which spread from the court at Mystra to reassert control over the peninsula. A last flicker of "Greek" rule, it was eventually extinguished by the **Turkish con-**

and Messinía, and the hill towns of Arcadia, you'll need at least a couple of weeks.

If you were planning on a combination of Peloponnese-plus-islands, the Argo-Saronic or Ionian islands are the most convenient, although you would be better off limiting yourself to the mainland on a short trip. The **Argo-Saronic** islands (see p.555) are linked by hydrofoil with the Argolid and Pireás. Of the **Ionian** islands, isolated **Kýthira** is covered in this chapter since closest access is from the southern Peloponnese ports, but **Zákynthos** (see p.984) or **Kefaloniá** (see p.971) can also be reached from the western port of Kyllíni, and Greece's second port city of **Pátra** serves as a gateway to Corfu and to southern Italy.

Travelling about the peninsula by **public transport**, you'll be dependent mostly on the **buses**. These are fast and regular on the main routes between the seven provincial capitals, and from these towns go to most other places at least once a day; travelling between smaller towns in different provinces is considerably more complicated. The Peloponnese **train line**, now over a century old, is in a poor state, especially on its highly scenic southern loop, with trains risking mishaps on defective sleepers if they exceed the leisurely timetable; however they do provide some direct connections and landscape views unavailable on buses. Renting a **car** is worthwhile if you can afford it – even for just a few days – to explore the south from Kalamáta or Spárti, or heartland and coastal Arcadia from Náfplio or Trípoli.

quest between 1458 and 1460, and was to lie dormant, save for sporadic rebellions in the perennially intransigent Máni, until the nineteenth-century **War of Greek Independence**.

In this, the Peloponnese played a major part. The banner of rebellion was raised near Kalávryta on March 25, 1821, by Yermanos, Archbishop of Pátra, and the Greek forces' two most successful leaders – the great, flawed heroes Petros Mavromihalis and Theodhoros Kolokotronis – were natives of, and carried out most of their actions in, the Peloponnese; as you journey around with all the benefits of a present-day transport infrastructure, you will be in the footsteps of Kolokotronis almost everywhere you go. The international naval battle that accidentally decided the war, Navarino Bay, was fought off the west coast at Pýlos; and the first Greek parliament was convened at Náfplio. After independence however, power swiftly drained away from the Peloponnese to Athens, where it was to stay. The peninsula's contribution to the early Greek state became a disaffected one, highlighted by the assassination of Kapodistrias, the first Greek president, by Maniots in Náfplio.

Throughout the **nineteenth** and **early twentieth centuries**, the region developed important ports at Pátra, Kórinthos and Kalamáta, but its interior reverted to backwater status, starting a population decline that continues today. It was little disturbed until **World War II**, during which the area saw some of the worst German atrocities; there was much brave resistance in the mountains, but also some of the most shameful collaboration. The **civil war** which followed left many of the towns polarized and physically in ruins. In its wake there was substantial **emigration** from both towns and countryside, to North America and Australia in particular, as well as to Athens and other Greek cities. Earthquakes still cause considerable disruption, as at Kórinthos in 1981 and Kalamáta in 1986.

Today, the southern Peloponnese has a reputation for being one of the most traditional and politically **conservative** regions of Greece. The people are held in rather poor regard by other Greeks, though to outsiders they seem unfailingly hospitable.

Corinth and the Argolid

The usual approach from Athens to the Peloponnese is along the highway through Elefsína and across the Corinth Canal to modern-day **Kórinthos** (Corinth); buses and trains come this way at least every hour, the former halting at the canal (see p.187). Another, more attractive approach to the peninsula is by ferry or hydrofoil, via the **Argo–Saronic** islands (see p.555); routes run from Pireás through those islands, with brief hops over to the Argolid ports of Ermióni and Pórto Héli, and Náfplio and Paleá Epídhavros in season.

The region that you enter, to the south and southeast of Kórinthos, is known as the **Argolid** (Argolídha in modern Greek), after the city of Árgos, which held sway in Classical times. The greatest concentration of ancient sites in Greece is found in this compact little peninsula, its western boundary delineated by the main road south from Kórinthos. Within an hour or so's journey of each other are Agamemnon's fortress at **Mycenae**, the great theatre of **Epidaurus**, and lesser sites at **Tiryns**, **Árgos** and **Lérna**. Inevitably, these, along with the great Roman site at **Ancient Corinth**, draw the crowds, and in peak season you may want to see the sites early or late in the day to realize their magic.

When ruin-hopping palls, there are the small-town pleasures of elegant **Náfplio**, and a handful of pleasant **coastal resorts**. The best beaches in these parts, however, are to be found along the coast road south from Árgos, at Ástros and Tyrós, where there are some good campsites. Technically outside the Argolid, both of these are easiest reached by bus from Árgos or by hydrofoil from Náfplio (summer only), Pórto Héli or the island of Spétses. The southern continuation of these hydrofoil routes takes you on down the coast to the Byzantine remains of Monemvasiá.

Kórinthos

Like its ancient predecessor, the city of **KÓRINTHOS** (modern Corinth) has been levelled on several occasions by earthquakes – most recently in 1981, when a serious quake left thousands in tented homes for most of the following year. Repaired and reconstructed, with buildings of prudent but characterless concrete, the modern city has little of interest to the outsider; it is largely an industrial and agricultural centre, its economy bolstered by the drying and shipping of currants, for centuries one of Greece's few successful exports (the word "currant" itself derives from Corinth). Perhaps unexpectedly, Kórinthos is the hottest and driest part of the peninsula in summer.

If you wanted to base yourself here for a night or two, you are unlikely to escape from the continuous traffic noise anywhere in the centre of town, so it is worth considering **Arhéa Kórinthos**; 7km to the southwest, it is a quieter, slightly cooler alternative, with magnificent views at night, and close to the remains of ancient and medieval Corinth. Kórinthos itself provides access to Perahóra and a couple of other minor sites (see p.189).

The only specific sight in the modern city is the **Folklore Museum** (daily 8am–1pm; free), located in a tasteful building near the harbour. This contains the usual array of peasant costumes, old engravings and dioramas of traditional crafts.

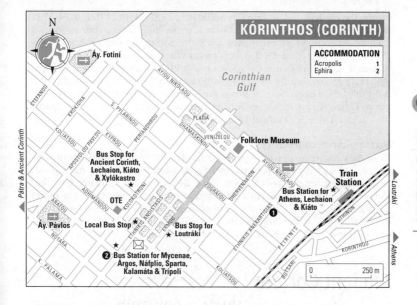

Practicalities

Orientation is straightforward. The centre of Kórinthos is its **park**, bordered on the longer side by Ermoú street and bisected by the parallel Ethnikís Andistásis (formerly Konstandínou). The **bus stop** for some local destinations (including Loutráki and the northeast) is on the Ermoú side of the park, at the corner with Koliátsou. **Buses** to Ancient Corinth (Arhéa Kórinthos), Léheo, Kiáto and Xylókastro go from outside a well-stocked *zaharoplastío* on Koliátsou, west of the park, while buses to other parts of Korinthía province go from Ethnikís Andistásis on the southwest corner of the park. **Long-distance buses** (to Spárti, Kalamáta, Trípoli, Mycenae, Árgos and Náfplio) use a café near the *Ephira* hotel on the other side of the park, at the corner of Ethnikís Andistásis and Arátou. Unlike the others, this station – much used by tourists – has no signboard for destinations and times. Information and tickets are grudgingly provided by the café staff. The **train station** is a few blocks to the east, opposite the KTEL **bus station** for Athens, Lechaion and Kiáto.

You'll find the National and Commercial **banks** along Ethnikís Andistásis, and the main **post office** on Adhimandoú, on the south side of the park. There's a **tourist police** post at Ermoú 5 (☎07410/23 282), and **taxis** wait along the Ethnikís Andistásis side of the park. If you want to rent your own transport, check out Liberopoulos, at Ethnikís Andistásis 27 (☎07410/72 937) for **scooters** and **bikes**, and for **cars**, try Vasilopoulos at Adhimandoú 30 (☎07410/28 437); both are near the southern end of the park.

Accommodation

At most times of year, **hotel rooms** are reasonably easy to find, though almost all suffer from road noise: the *Acropolis*, Ethnikís Anexartisías 25 (☎07410/22 430, ℉22 526; ❹), is on the way into town from the train station; nearer the centre, the modern *Ephira*, Ethnikís Andistásis 52 (☎07410/24 021, ⓕ24 514; ❸), is one block from the park and nearest to the long-distance bus station.

There are a couple of **campsites** along the gulf to the west: *Korinth Beach* (☎07410/27 967; April–Oct) is 3km out at Dhiavakíta – to reach the beach, such as it is, you must cross the coastal road and the railway line. *Blue Dolphin* (☎07410/25 766; April–Oct) is a bit further away at Léheo, but it is on the seaward side of the tracks, and for that alone it's preferable. For both sites, take the bus to Léheo (a part of Ancient Corinth) from alongside the park – or opposite the rail station – in modern Kórinthos.

Eating and drinking

Kórinthos has many fast-food places along the waterfront, mostly reasonably priced, and only a few **tavernas**: *Anexagoras*, Ayíou Nikoláou 31, has a good range of mezédhes and grilled meats, while *24 Ores*, on the same street, on the eastern side of the marina, has a good and tasty selection of snacks and more traditional food. Most other eating places are directly on very busy streets. On the coast road near the campsites, the *Arhontiko* (☎07410/27 968) is very popular with the locals, so phone first before heading off.

Ancient Corinth

Buses to Ancient Corinth, **ARHÉA KÓRINTHOS**, leave modern Kórinthos ten past every hour from 8am to 9pm and return on the half-hour. The ruins of the **ancient city**, which displaced Athens as capital of the Greek province in Roman times, occupy a rambling sequence of sites, the main enclosure of which is given a sense of scale by the majestic ruin of the Temple of Apollo. Most compelling, though, are the ruins of the medieval city, which occupy the stunning acropolis site of **Acrocorinth**, towering 565m above the ancient city.

The ruins of Ancient Corinth spread over a vast area, and include sections of ancient walls (the Roman city had a fifteen-kilometre circuit), outlying stadiums, gymnasiums and necropolises. Only the central area, around the Roman forum and the Classical Temple of Apollo, is preserved in an excavated state; the rest, odd patches of semi-enclosed and often overgrown ruin, you come across unexpectedly while walking about the village and up to Acrocorinth.

The overall effect is impressive, but it only begins to suggest the majesty of this once supremely wealthy city. Ancient Corinth was a key centre of the Greek and Roman worlds, whose possession meant the control of trade between northern Greece and the Peloponnese. In addition, the twin ports of **Lechaion**, on the gulf of Corinth, and **Kenchreai**, on the Saronic Gulf, provided a trade link between the Ionian and Aegean seas – the western and eastern Mediterranean. Not surprisingly, this meant that the city's ancient (and medieval) history was one of invasions and power struggles which, in Classical times, was dominated by Corinth's rivalry with Athens – against whom it sided with Sparta in the Peloponnesian War.

Despite this, Corinth suffered only one major setback, in 146 BC, when the Romans, having defeated the Greek city-states of the Achaean League, razed the site to the ground. For a century the city lay in ruins before being rebuilt, on a majestic scale, by Julius Caesar in 44 BC: initially intended as a colony for veterans, it was later made the provincial capital. Once again

Corinth grew rich on trade – with Rome to the west, and Syria and Egypt to the east.

Roman Corinth's reputation for wealth, fuelled by its trading access to luxury goods, was soon equalled by its appetite for earthly pleasures – including sex. Corinthian women were renowned for their beauty and much sought after as *hetairai* (courtesans); a temple to Aphrodite/Venus, on the acropolis of Acrocorinth, was served by over a thousand sacred prostitutes. **St Paul** stayed in Corinth for eighteen months in 51–52 AD, though his attempts to reform the citizens' ways were met only by rioting – tribulations recorded in his two letters to the Corinthians. The city endured until rocked by two major earthquakes, in 375 and 521, which brought down the Roman buildings, and again depopulated the site until a brief Byzantine revival in the eleventh century.

The excavations

Inevitably, given successive waves of earthquakes and destruction, the **main excavated site** (daily: spring & autumn 8am–7pm; summer 8am–9pm; winter 8am–5pm; €3.50) is dominated by the remains of the Roman city. Entering from the north side, just behind the road where the buses pull in, you'll find yourself in the Roman agora, an enormous marketplace flanked by the substantial foundations of a huge *stoa*, once a structure of several storeys, with 33 shops on the ground floor. Opposite the *stoa* is a *bema*, a marble platform used for public announcements. At the far end are remains of a **basilica**, while the area behind the *bema* is strewn with the remnants of numerous Roman administrative buildings. Back across the agora, almost hidden by a swirl of broken marble and shattered architecture, there's a fascinating trace of the Greek city – a **sacred spring**, covered over by a grille at the base of a narrow flight of steps.

More substantial is the elaborate Roman **Fountain of Peirene**, which stands below the level of the agora, to the side of a wide, excavated stretch of what was the main approach to the city, the marble-paved **Lechaion Way**. Taking the form of a colonnaded and frescoed recess, the fountain occupies the site of one of two natural springs in Corinth – the other is up on the acropolis – and its cool water was channelled into a magnificent fountain and pool in the courtyard. The fountain house was, like many of Athens' Roman public buildings, the gift of the wealthy Athenian and friend of Emperor Hadrian, Herodes Atticus. The waters still flow through the underground cisterns and supply the modern village.

The real focus of the ancient site, though, is a rare survival from the Classical Greek era, the fifth-century BC **Temple of Apollo**, whose seven austere Doric columns stand slightly above the level of the forum and are flanked by foundations of another marketplace and baths. Over to the west is the site **museum** (summer Mon noon–7pm, Tues–Sun 8am–7pm; winter daily 8am–5pm; included in site admission), housing a large collection of domestic pieces, some good Greek and Roman mosaics from nearby and a frieze depicting some of the labours of Heracles (Hercules), several of which were performed nearby at Neméa, Stymfalía and Lérna. The city's other claim to mythic fame, incidentally, is as the home of the infant Oedipus and his step-parents, prior to his travels of discovery to Thebes.

A number of miscellaneous smaller excavations surround the main site. To the west, just across the road from the enclosing wire, there are outlines of two **theatres**: a Roman **odeion** (once again endowed by Herodes Atticus) and a larger Greek theatre, adapted by the Romans for gladiatorial sea battles. To the north are the inaccessible but visible remains of an **Asklepion** (dedicated to the god of healing).

Acrocorinth

Rising almost sheer above the lower town, **Acrocorinth** (summer daily 8am–7pm; winter Tues–Sun 8.30am–3pm; free) is sited on an amazing mass of rock, still largely encircled by two kilometres of wall. The ancient acropolis of Corinth, it became one of Greece's most powerful fortresses during the Middle Ages, besieged by successive waves of invaders, who considered it the key to the Moreás.

Despite the long, four-kilometre climb to the entrance gate (an hour's walk) – or a taxi ride from ancient Corinth, reasonable if shared – a visit to the summit is unreservedly recommended. Looking down over the Saronic and Corinthian gulfs, you really get a sense of the strategic importance of the fortress's position. Amid the extensive remains, you wander through a jumble of chapels, mosques, houses and battlements, erected in turn by Greeks, Romans, Byzantines, Frankish crusaders, Venetians and Turks.

The Turkish remains are unusually substantial. Elsewhere in Greece evidence of the Ottoman occupation has been physically removed or defaced, but here, halfway up the hill, you can see a midway point in the process – the still functioning **fountain of Hatzi Mustafa**, which has been Christianized by the addition of great carved crosses. The outer of the citadel's **triple gates** is also largely Turkish; the middle is a combination of Venetian and Frankish; the inner, Byzantine, incorporating fourth-century BC towers. Within the citadel, the first summit (to the right) is enclosed by a **Frankish keep** – as striking as they come – which last saw action in 1828 during the War of Independence. Keeping along the track to the left, you pass some interesting (if perilous) cisterns, the remains of a Turkish bath house, and crumbling Byzantine chapels.

In the southeast corner of the citadel, hidden away in the lower ground, is the **upper Peirene spring**. This is not easy to find: look out for a narrow, overgrown entrance, from which a flight of iron stairs leads down some five metres to a metal screen. Here, broad stone steps descend into the dark depths, where a fourth-century BC arch stands guard over a pool of water that has never been known to dry up. To the north of the fountain, on the second and higher summit, is the site of the **Temple of Aphrodite**; after its days as a brothel, it saw use as a church, mosque and belvedere.

Practicalities

To explore both ancient and medieval Corinth you need a full day, or better still, to stay here overnight. A modern **village** spreads around the edge of the main ancient site, and there is a scattering of **rooms** to rent in its backstreets – follow the signs or ask at the cafés. A good cheap option, by the Avin garage on the road from Kórinthos, is the hospitable *Hotel Shadow* (☎07410/31 481; ❸), with great views from the rear rooms; a free museum in the lobby includes an extensive and labelled collection of minerals, fossils, petrified wood and local relics. In the centre of the village is *Marinos* rooms (☎07410/31 209; ❸) with an enthusiastically illustrated restaurant. The *Tasos* serves good, traditional Greek taverna **food** at low prices. The solitary modern building up in Acrocorinth is the *Acrocorinthos* café; there is a fully operational restaurant here until early evening during summer months.

Map labels:
- ▲ Loutráki & Perahóra
- Corinthian Gulf
- Diolkos
- N
- AROUND CORINTH
- modern Léheo
- Lechaion
- Sikyon & Xylókastro
- Kórinthos (modern Corinth)
- Corinth Canal
- Isthmós
- Pátra
- Skoutéla
- Ancient Ísthmia
- Kyrás Vrýsi
- Ísthmia
- Athens
- Arhéa Kórinthos
- Ancient Corinth
- Examília
- Acrocorinth
- Kekhriés
- Kenchreai
- Saronic Gulf
- Solomós
- 0   2 km
- Loutrá Elénis
- ▼ Trípoli
- ▼ Neméa, Árgos & Mycenae
- ▼ Epidaurus

Around Corinth

As well as the **Corinth Canal**, which you can't help but cross en route between Kórinthos and Athens, a number of minor sites are accessible by bus (at least most of the way) from Kórinthos, both on the Peloponnese and the western Attic peninsula of Yeránia. Just south of the canal is ancient **Ísthmia**, site of the Panhellenic Isthmian Games. To the northwest are the spa of **Loutráki** and the classical **sanctuary of Hera** at **Perahóra** on Cape Melangávi. If you have a car, there's a grand and rather wild route east from the cape, around the Alkyonidhón Gulf to Pórto Yermenó (see p.331). There are beaches along the way, though little settlement or development, and the final stretch of road beyond Káto Alepohóri is scarcely better than a jeep track.

Back in the Peloponnese proper, **Neméa** – as in the Lion of Hercules' labour – is a brief detour southwest of Kórinthos, off the road to Mycenae and Árgos. **Sikyon** is a bit more remote, 25km up the coast towards Pátra, but again accessible by bus.

The Corinth Canal

The idea for a **Corinth Canal**, providing a short cut and safe passage between the Aegean and Ionian seas, dates back at least to Roman times, when the emperor Nero performed initial excavations with a silver shovel and Jewish slave labour. It was only in the 1890s, however, that the technology became available to cut right across the six-kilometre isthmus. Opened in July 1893, the canal, along with its near-contemporary Suez, helped establish Pireás as a major Mediterranean port and shipping centre, although the projected toll revenues were never realized. Today supertankers have made it something of an anachronism and the canal has fallen into disrepair, but it remains a memorable sight nonetheless.

Approaching on the Athens road, you cross the canal near its southeastern end, often referred to as Isthmós. From Kórinthos you can use the Loutráki buses to get there and back. At both ends of the **bridge** there's a line of **cafés**, where buses from Athens usually stop if they're going beyond Kórinthos – rather than in Kórinthos itself. At the Athens end of the bridge is a KTEL office and bus stop for buses to Athens and the Peloponnese, although getting onto buses here can be a hit-or-miss affair, depending on seat availability. Peering over from the bridge, the canal appears a tiny strip of water until some huge freighter assumes toy-like dimensions as it passes nearly eighty metres below. If you were to take one of the cruise ships from Pireás to the Ionian, you would actually sail through the canal – a trip almost worthwhile for its own sake. At the western end of the canal, by the old Kórinthos–Loutráki ferry dock, there are remains of the **diolkos** (Tues–Sun 8.30am–3pm; free), a paved way along which a wheeled platform used to carry boats across the isthmus. In use from Roman times until the twelfth century, the boats were strapped onto the platform after being relieved temporarily of their cargo.

Ancient Ísthmia

Modern Ísthmia (Isthmía) lies either side of the Saronic Gulf entrance to the canal, and is served by regular buses from Kórinthos. To the west of the modern settlement, on a hillock alongside the present-day village of Kyrás Vrýsi, is the site of ancient **ÍSTHMIA** (summer Tues–Sun 8.30am–3pm; winter daily 8.30am–3pm; free).

There is nothing very notable to see at the site, though the ancient settlement was an important one, due to its **sanctuary of Poseidon** – of which just the foundations remain, much having been incorporated into the seven-kilometre Byzantine Hexamillian Wall – and the Panhellenic Isthmian games. The latter ranked with those of Delphi, Neméa and Olympia, though they have left scant evidence in the form of a **stadium** and **theatre**, together with a few curiosities – including starting blocks used for foot races – in the small adjacent **museum** (same times as site; €1.50), which also houses some of the finds from Kenchreai. There are decent swimming spots and some accommodation at Kekhriés and Loutrá Elénis on the coast heading south towards Paleá Epídhavros. The *Isthmian Beach* campsite (☎07410/37 447, ✉isthmia@otenet.gr) is about 1km north of the Kenchreai site, and provides a free shuttle bus to modern Ísthmia.

Loutráki

Six kilometres north of the canal is the spa resort of **LOUTRÁKI**. The epicentre of the 1981 Corinth earthquake, it has today straight lines of unmemorable concrete buildings. The resort is nonetheless immensely popular, with a larger concentration of hotels than anywhere else in the Peloponnese. The visitors are mostly Greek or Italian, coming here since 1847 for the "cure" at the hot springs, and to sample Loutráki mineral water – the country's leading bottled brand. A sign of the times is the new Pepsi-Cola bottling plant on the outskirts of Loutráki. Others come for the renovated and reopened casino – Greece's oldest – on Posidhónos on the southwest seafront. Near the train station, there is a helpful **tourist kiosk** on E. Venizélou, the main road through town, four blocks south of the bus station, and a second near the thermal baths. The local council has a choice range of well-produced brochures and a town map.

With your own transport, you'd be better off using the town simply as a staging post en route to the site of ancient Perahóra and making Lake Vouliagméni your base (see opposite). Otherwise, Loutráki is connected by bus and special summer trains with Athens, and by bus (every 30min) with Kórinthos. **Car hire** and **exchange** are available from 24 Hours Travel (☎07440/67 666, ℗67 667) on Y. Lékka, near the thermal baths. If you end up staying, *Hotel Brettagne*, at Y. Lékka 28 (☎07440/22 349; ❸), makes a refreshing change from the many expensive spa-resort **hotels**; *Hotel Pappas* (☎07440/23 026; ❺), to the left of the Perahóra road, has better facilities and fine views across the gulf; and the friendly, family-run *Acropole*, P. Tsaldhári 11 (☎07440/22 265, ☞61 171; ❷), has nice, comfortable rooms. To **eat**, the *Harama psistariá* at the corner of Kanári and Ethnikís Andistásis has good grills at decent rates.

Perahóra

mlmlmlmlmlmlThe road to **Cape Melangávi** is enjoyable in itself, running above the sea in the shadow of the Yeránia mountains, whose pine forests are slowly recovering from fire devastation in 1986. En route the road offers a loop through the modern village of **PERAHÓRA** (11km) before heading out to the cape along the shore of **Lake Vouliagméni**, a beautiful two-kilometre-wide lagoon with sheltered swimming, a new hotel, the *Philoxenia* (☎07410/91 294, ☞91 298; ❷), and a small campsite, *Limni Heraiou* (☎07410/91 230), both open all year. Perahóra is connected by hourly bus with Loutráki; one daily bus makes the journey between Loutráki and Lake Vouliagméni, but runs in summer only.

Ancient Perahóra (daily: summer 8am–7pm; winter 8.30am–3pm; free) – also known as Peréa or the Heraion Melangávi – stands just 1km from the western tip of the peninsula, commanding a marvellous, sweeping view of the coastline and mountains along both sides of the gulf. The site's position is its chief attraction, though there are the identifiable ruins of a sanctuary in two parts, the **Hera Akraia** (*akron* is the extremity of the peninsula) and **Hera Limenia** ("of the port"), as well as the **stoa** of the ancient harbour, which provides great snorkelling opportunities.

The initial excavation of Perahóra, between 1930 and 1933, is described by Dilys Powell in *An Affair of the Heart*. Humfry Payne, her husband, directed the work until his death in 1936; he was then buried at Mycenae. The site also features in myth, for it was here that Medea, having been spurned by her husband Jason at Corinth, killed their two children.

Neméa

Ancient **NEMÉA**, the location for Hercules' (Herakles) slaying of its namesake lion (his first labour), lies 6km off the road from Kórinthos to Árgos. To get there by public transport, take the bus to modern Neméa and ask to be dropped en route at Arhéa Neméa, also the name of a village just 300m west of the ruins. Moving on from the site, you can walk back up to the Árgos road and possibly wave down a bus on to Fíkhti for Mycenae.

Like Olympia and Ísthmia, Neméa held athletic games for the Greek world from the sixth century BC, until these were transferred to Árgos in 270 BC. A sanctuary rather than a town, the principal remains at the **site** (daily 8.30am–3pm, closed Mon in summer; €1.50) are of the **Temple of Nemean Zeus**, currently three slender Doric columns surrounded by other fallen and broken drums, but slowly being reassembled by a team of University of California archeologists. Nearby are a **palaestra** with **baths** and a Christian basilica, built with blocks from the temple. Outside the site, half a kilometre east, is a **stadium** whose starting line has been unearthed. There is also a **museum** (same hours), with excellent contextual models, displays relating to the biennial games and items from the area.

The Stymphalian Lake

If you have transport, it's possible to cut across the hills from Neméa towards Arcadia, detouring into another Herculean locale, the **Stymphalian Lake**

at Y. Lékka 28 (☎07440/22 349; ❸), makes a refreshing change from the many expensive spa-resort **hotels**; *Hotel Pappas* (☎07440/23 026; ❺), to the left of the Perahóra road, has better facilities and fine views across the gulf; and the friendly, family-run *Acropole*, P. Tsaldhári 11 (☎07440/22 265, ☞61 171; ❷), has nice, comfortable rooms. To **eat**, the *Harama psistariá* at the corner of Kanári and Ethnikís Andistásis has good grills at decent rates.

at Y. Lékka 28 (☎07440/22 349; ❸), makes a refreshing change from the many expensive spa-resort **hotels**; *Hotel Pappas* (☎07440/23 026; ❺), to the left of the Perahóra road, has better facilities and fine views across the gulf; and the friendly, family-run *Acropole*, P. Tsaldhári 11 (☎07440/22 265, ☞61 171; ❷), has nice, comfortable rooms. To **eat**, the *Harama psistariá* at the corner of Kanári and Ethnikís Andistásis has good grills at decent rates.

(around 35km from ancient Neméa). In myth, this was the nesting-ground of man-eating birds who preyed upon travellers, suffocating them with their wings, and poisoned local crops with their excrement. Hercules roused them from the water with a rattle, then shot them down – one of the more straightforward of his labours.

The lake is known in modern Greek as **Límni Stymfalías**, though it is really more of a swamp: an enormous depression with seasonal waters, ringed by woods and the dark peaks of Mount Olíyirtos on the south. There are no buildings for miles around, save for the ruins of the thirteenth-century Frankish Cistercian **Abbey of Zaráka** (beside the road), one of the few Gothic buildings in Greece.

If you don't have your own transport, the most promising approach to the lake is from Kiáto on the Gulf of Corinth, where there are several hotels and rooms to rent; the road, much better than that from Neméa, has the occasional bus. The nearest places to stay are the pleasant new *Hotel Karteri* (✆07470/31 203; ❸), above the *Taverna Leonidas* in **Kartéri** village, 3km west of the lake, or the *Xenia* (✆07470/61 283; ❹) 3km outside **Kastaniá**, a mountain village famed for its butterflies, 8km further to the west of Kartéri.

Ancient Sikyon

Six kilometres inland from Kiáto (see above), ancient **SIKYON** (Sikyóna) (Tues–Sun 8.30am–3pm; free) is a fairly accessible if little-known site, which deserves more than the few dozen visitors it attracts each year. Six buses a day run from Kiáto (on the bus and train routes from Kórinthos) to the village of Vasilikó, on the edge of a broad escarpment running parallel to the sea, from where it's a kilometre's walk to the site.

In ancient history, Sikyon's principal claim to fame came early in the sixth century BC, when the tyrant Kleisthenes purportedly kept a court of sufficient wealth and influence to entertain suitors for his daughter's hand for a full year. After his death the place was rarely heard of politically, except as a consistent ally of the Spartans, but a mild renaissance ensued at the end of the fourth century when Demetrios Polyorketes moved Sikyon to its present location from the plain below. The town became renowned for sculptors, painters and metallurgic artisans, and flourished well into Roman times; it was the birthplace of Alexander the Great's chief sculptor, Lysippus, and, allegedly, of the art of sculptural relief.

The road from Vasilikó cuts through the site, which is fenced off into a number of enclosures. To the right is the **Roman baths museum** which shelters mosaics of griffins from the second to third centuries AD. To the left are the majority of the public buildings, with a theatre and stadium on the hillside above. As you enter the **main site** (unrestricted access), opposite the Roman baths, the foundations of the **Temple of Artemis** are visible to your left. Beyond it are traces of a **bouleuterion** (senate house) dating from the first half of the third centuries BC. The most important remains in this section are of the **Gymnasium of Kleinias** in the far right-hand corner, at the base of the hill; this is on two levels, the lower dating from around 300 BC, the upper from Roman times.

Although only the first ten rows of seats have been excavated, the outline of the **theatre** – larger than that of Epidaurus – is easy to distinguish and impressive. Pine trees have grown in the upper half, from where there's a marvellous view encompassing the rest of the site, the village of Vasilikó, the lemon and olive groves around Kiáto, plus the Korinthiakós Gulf and distant mountains.

A string of resorts, popular with Greeks although the mountain backdrop was damaged by serious fires in 2000, runs westwards along the Korinthian coast, accessible by bus or train from Kórinthos. There are hotels in Vraháti, Kokkóni, Kiáto, Melíssi and Sykiá, but **XYLÓKASTRO** is of more interest, with both good beaches and accommodation, and a pleasant setting backed by Mount Kyllíni. The main beach, Pefkiás, is lined by a strip of pine woodland. Cheapest of its dozen **hotels** is the hospitable *Hermes* (T07430/22 250; ❸), I. Ioánnou 95, near Pefkiás. Other hotels include the *Kyani Akti*, near the sea at Tsaldhári 68 (T07430/28 930; ❸), and the air-conditioned *Apollon*, housed in a fine old building at I. Ioánnou 119 (T07430/22 239, F25 240; ❺). The long seafront boasts a number of restaurants, of which *Zesti Gonia* is friendly with good fish, while *Palea Exedhra* has more variety. It is only possible to connect westwards with Pátra and Ahaïa by train, not by local buses, since the latter only run to and from Kórinthos.

Mycenae (Mykínes)

Tucked into a fold of the hills just east of the road from Kórinthos to Árgos, Agamemnon's citadel at **MYCENAE** fits the legend better than any other place in Greece. It was uncovered in 1874 by the German archeologist Heinrich Schliemann (who also excavated the site of Troy), impelled by his single-minded belief that there was a factual basis to Homer's epics. Schliemann's finds of brilliantly crafted gold and sophisticated tomb architecture bore out the accuracy of Homer's epithets of "well-built Mycenae, rich in gold".

Mycenaean history and legend

The Mycenae-Árgos region is one of the longest occupied in Greece, with evidence of Neolithic settlements from around 3000 BC. But it is to a period of three centuries at the end of the second millennium BC – from around 1550 to 1200 BC – that the citadel of Mycenae and its associated drama belong. This period is known as **Mycenaean**, a term which covers not just the Mycenae region but a whole Bronze Age civilization that flourished in southern Greece at the time.

According to the **legend** related in Homer's *Iliad* and *Odyssey* and Aeschylus' *Oresteia*, the city of Mycenae was founded by Perseus, the slayer of Medusa the gorgon, before it fell into the bloodied hands of the **House of Atreus**. In an act of vengeance for his brother Thyestes' seduction of his wife, Atreus murdered Thyestes' sons, and fed them to their own father. Not surprisingly, this incurred the wrath of the gods. Thyestes' own daughter, Pelopia, subsequently bore her father a son, Aegisthus, who later murdered Atreus and restored Thyestes to the throne.

The next generation saw the gods' curse fall upon Atreus' son **Agamemnon**. On his return to Mycenae after commanding the Greek forces in the Trojan War – a role in which he had earlier consented to the sacrifice of his own daughter, Iphigeneia – he was killed in his bath by his wife Clytemnestra and her lover, the very same Aegisthus who had killed his father. The tragic cycle was completed by Agamemnon's son, Orestes, who, egged on by his sister Electra, took revenge by murdering his mother,

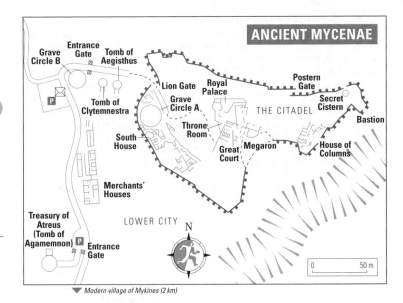

ANCIENT MYCENAE

Grave Circle B — Entrance Gate — Tomb of Aegisthus — Lion Gate — Royal Palace — Postern Gate — Tomb of Clytemnestra — Grave Circle A — THE CITADEL — Secret Cistern — Bastion — Throne Room — Great Court — Megaron — House of Columns — South House — Merchants' Houses — Treasury of Atreus (Tomb of Agamemnon) — LOWER CITY — Entrance Gate — N — 0 — 50 m

▼ *Modern village of Mykines (2 km)*

Clytemnestra, and was pursued by the Furies until Athena finally lifted the curse on the dynasty.

The **archeological remains** of Mycenae fit remarkably easily with the tale, at least if it is taken as a poetic rendering of dynastic struggles, or, as most scholars now believe it to be, a merging of stories from various periods. The buildings unearthed by Schliemann show signs of occupation from around 1950 BC, as well as two periods of intense disruption, around 1200 BC and again in 1100 BC – at which stage the town, though still prosperous, was abandoned.

No coherent explanation has been put forward for these events, since the traditional "Dorian invasions" theory (see p.996) has fallen from favour; but it seems that war among the rival kingdoms was a major factor in the Mycenaean decline. These struggles appear to have escalated as the civilization developed in the thirteenth century BC, and excavations at Troy have revealed the sacking of that city, quite possibly by forces led by a king from Mycenae, in 1240 BC. The citadel of Mycenae seems to have been replanned, and heavily fortified, during this period.

The Citadel

The **Citadel of Mycenae** (daily: summer 8am–7pm (Aug 8am–9pm); winter 8am–5pm; €4.50) is entered through the famous **Lion Gate**, whose huge sloping gateposts bolster walls which were termed "Cyclopean" by later Greeks in bewildered attribution to the only beings deemed capable of their construction. Above them a graceful carved relief stands out in confident assertion: Mycenae at its height led a confederation of Argolid towns (Tiryns, Árgos, Assine, Hermione – present-day Ermióni), dominated the Peloponnese and exerted influence throughout the Aegean. The motif of a pillar supported by two muscular lions was probably the symbol of the Mycenaean royal house, for a seal found on the site bears a similar device. Inside the walls to the right is **Grave Circle A**, the royal cemetery excavated by Schliemann and believed by him to contain the bodies of Agamemnon and his followers, murdered on their triumphant return from Troy. Opening one of the graves, he found a tightly fitting and magnificent gold mask that had somehow preserved the flesh of a Mycenaean noble; "I have gazed upon the face of Agamemnon," he exclaimed in an excited cable to the king of Greece. For a time it seemed that this provided irrefutable evidence of the truth of Homer's tale. In fact, the burials date from about three centuries before the Trojan war, though given Homer's possible accumulation of different and earlier sagas, there's no reason why they should not have been connected with a Mycenaean king Agamemnon. They were certainly royal graves, for the finds (now in the National Archeological Museum in Athens) are among the richest that archeology has yet unearthed.

Schliemann took the extensive **South House**, beyond the grave circle, to be the Palace of Agamemnon. However, a building much grander and more likely to be the **Royal Palace**, was later discovered near the summit of the acropolis. Rebuilt in the thirteenth century BC, this is an impressively elaborate and evocative building complex; although the ruins are only at ground level, the different rooms are easily discernible. Like all Mycenaean palaces, it is centred around a **great court**: on the south side, a staircase would have led via an anteroom to the big rectangular **throne room**; on the east, a double porch gave access to the **megaron**, the grand reception hall with its traditional circular hearth. The small rooms to the north are believed to have been **royal apartments**, and in one of them the remains of a red stuccoed bath have led to its fanciful identification as the scene of Agamemnon's murder.

With the accompaniment of the sound of bells drifting down from goats grazing on the hillsides, a stroll round the ramparts is evocative of earlier times. A more salutary reminder of the nature of life in Mycenaean times is the **secret cistern** at the eastern end of the ramparts, created around 1225 BC. Whether it was designed to enable the citadel's occupants to withstand siege from outsiders, rival Mycenaeans or even an increasingly alienated peasantry is not known. Steps lead down to a deep underground spring; it's still possible to descend the whole way, though you'll need to have a torch and be sure-footed, since there's a drop to the water at the final turn of the twisting passageways. Nearby is the **House of Columns**, a large and stately building with the base of a stairway that once led to an upper storey.

Only the ruling Mycenaean elite could live within the citadel itself. Hence the main part of town lay outside the walls and, in fact, extensive remains of **merchants' houses** have been uncovered near to the road. Their contents included Linear B tablets recording the spices used to scent oils, along with large amounts of pottery, the quantity suggesting that the early Mycenaeans may have dabbled in the perfume trade. The discovery of the tablets has also prompted a reassessment of the sophistication of Mycenaean civilization, for they show that, here at least, writing was not limited to government scribes working in the royal palaces as had previously been thought, and that around the citadel there may have been a commercial city of some size and wealth.

Alongside the merchants' houses are the remains of another **Grave Circle** (B), dating from around 1650 BC and possibly representing an earlier, rival dynasty to the kings buried in Grave Circle A, and two **thólos** (circular chamber-type) tombs, speculatively identified by Schliemann as the **tombs of Aegisthus** and **Clytemnestra**. The former, closer to the Lion Gate, dates from around 1500 BC and has now collapsed, so is roped off; the latter dates from some two centuries later – thus corresponding with the Trojan timescale – and can still be entered.

The Treasury of Atreus

Four hundred metres down the road from the Citadel site is another, infinitely more startling *thólos*, known as the **Treasury of Atreus** or – the currently preferred official name – "Tomb of Agamemnon" (same hours as the Citadel; admission included in Citadel entrance fee). This was certainly a royal burial vault at a late stage in Mycenae's history, contemporary with the "Clytemnestra Tomb", so the attribution to Agamemnon or his father is as good as any – if the king was indeed the historic leader of the Trojan expedition. Whoever it might have belonged to, this beehive-like structure built without the use of mortar, is an impressive monument to Mycenaean building skills. Entering the tomb through a majestic fifteen-metre corridor, you come face to face with the chamber doorway, above which is a great lintel formed by two immense slabs of stone – one of which, a staggering nine metres long, is estimated to weigh 118 tonnes.

Practicalities: Mykínes

The modern village of **MYKÍNES** is 2km from the junction of the main Kórinthos–Árgos highway and the train station, at Fíkhti, but not all trains on the Kórinthos–Árgos line stop here. Buses from Athens to Árgos or Náfplio usually drop passengers at the junction (the café here sells bus tickets), rather than in Mykínes village; crowded local buses from Náfplio via Árgos serve the village and site. The walk in from the main highway is along a beautiful straight road partly lined with eucalyptus trees, through which glimpses of the citadel appear, flanked by the twin peaks of Zára and Ilías. The site is a further two-kilometre uphill walk from Mykínes centre, and in season has a couple of canteens and a **post office** caravan where **currency exchange** is possible.

Accommodation and eating

Unless you have your own transport, you might want to stay at Mykínes, which can be heavily touristy by day, but quiet once the site has closed and the tour buses depart. Along the village's single street, there is quite an array of hotels – most of their names taken from characters in the House of Atreus saga – as well as a number of signs for rooms. Mycenae's two **campsites** are both centrally located, on the way into the village. Both open all year, there's not a great deal to choose between them, though *Camping Mykines* (☎07510/76 121, ℉76 247) is smaller and a little closer to the site than *Camping Atreus* (☎07510/76 221).

All the hotels listed below have **restaurants** catering for the lunchtime tour-group trade, therefore don't raise your expectations too high. Eating places worth trying are the *Electra*, the *King Menelaos* and the *Menelaos*, all along the main street.

Belle Helene ☎07510/76 225, ℉76 179. The village's most characterful hotel, with a good restaurant; converted from the house used by Schliemann during his excavations. Signatures in its visitors' book include Virginia Woolf, Henry Moore, Sartre and Debussy. ❸

Klytemnestra ☎07510/76 451, ℉76 731. Pleasant, modern hotel run by a friendly young Australian. Open all year. ❸

Le Petite Planète ☎07510/76 240, ℉76 610.

A comfortable hotel at the top end of the village, with great views and a swimming pool. Owned by a member of the Dassis clan, this is the nearest hotel to the site. Open April–Oct. ❻

Rooms Dassis ☎07510/76 123, ℉76 124. A pleasant, well-organized set-up, run – along with a useful travel agency below – by Canadian Marion Dassis, who married into the local Dassis dynasty. Good for groups or families. ❸

The Argive Heraion and ancient Midea

The little-visited **Argive Heraion** (daily 8.30am–3pm; free) is an important sanctuary from Mycenaean and Classical times and the site where Agamemnon is said to have been chosen as leader of the Greek expedition to Troy. It lies 7km south of Mycenae, off the minor road which runs east of Árgos through Hónikas, and on to Náfplio. The lonely site is above the village of Hónikas (Néo Iréo); before you reach the village, look out for signs to "Ancient Ireo". There are various Mycenaean tombs near the site, but the principal remains of a temple complex, baths and a *palaestra* (wrestling/athletics gym), built over three interconnnecting terraces, all date from the fifth century BC.

The Heraion makes a pleasant diversion for anyone driving between Mycenae and Náfplio, or an enjoyable afternoon's walk from Mykínes – it takes a little over an hour on foot if you can find the old track southeast from the village, running parallel to the minor road to Ayía Triádha and Náfplio. Hónikas has the occasional bus to Árgos; Ayía Triádha, 5km on, has more frequent connections to Náfplio.

Ancient Midea, in gorgeous countryside between the villages of Midhéa and Dhéndhra, was the third fortified Mycenaean palace of the area, after Mycenae and Tiryns. Excavations have uncovered a fortified area of some six acres, the remains of a young girl – apparently an earthquake victim in the thirteenth century BC – and numerous workshop items, but its most famous find is the remarkable Dendra cuirass, bronze body armour now in the archeological museum in Náfplio.

Árgos

ÁRGOS, 12km south of the Mykínes junction, is said to be the oldest continuously inhabited town in Greece (c. 5000 years), although you wouldn't know it from first impressions. However, this turn-of-the-century trading centre has some pleasant squares and Neoclassical buildings, and a brief stop is worthwhile for the excellent museum and mainly Roman ruins. Try to time your visit to coincide with the regular **Wednesday market**, which draws locals from all the surrounding hill villages; the market square is between the Kapodhístria barracks' three-sided courtyard and the Neoclassical market building, and is unofficially though invariably referred to as the Laïkí Agorá.

The modern **Archeological Museum** (Tues–Sun 8.30am–3pm; €1.50) is just off the pedestrianized Elgas street between the market square and the main church square, Platía Ayíou Pétrou. It makes an interesting detour after Mycenae, with a good collection of Mycenaean tomb objects and armour as well as extensive pottery finds. The region's Roman occupation is well represented here, in sculpture and mosaics, and there are also finds from Lerna on display.

Before you leave Árgos, visit the town's ancient remains which are ten-minutes' walk down the Trípoli road – initially Fidhónos, then Theátrou – from the market square. The **site** (daily 8.30am–3pm; free) is surprisingly extensive; the **theatre**, built by Classical Greeks and adapted by the Romans, looks oddly narrow from the road, but climb up to the top and it feels immense. Estimated to have held 20,000 spectators – six thousand more than Epidaurus – it is matched on the Greek mainland only by the theatres at Megalópolis and Dodóna. Alongside are the remains of an **odeion** and **Roman baths**.

Above the site looms the ancient **acropolis**, on a conical hill capped by the largely Frankish **medieval castle** of Lárissa (Tues–Sun 8.30am–3pm; free), built on sixth-century BC foundations and later augmented by the Venetians and Turks. Massively walled, cisterned and guttered, the sprawling ruins offer wonderful views – the reward for a long, steep haul up, either on indistinct trails beyond the theatre, or a very roundabout road.

Practicalities

You may well need to change **buses** in Árgos since its connections are better than those of Náfplio. There are local bus stops and a ticket kiosk, on Kalléryi, at the southeast corner of the market square near the Dhikastikó Katástima building, for Mykínes and Neméa. Just around the corner, on Kapodhístria, is a KTEL office for buses back towards Athens, and for Trípoli, Spárti and down the coast towards Leonídhi. **Taxis** go from Fidhónos, the central street or market square, as do buses to Kefalári.

For a good meal between buses, try the *Retro Restaurant* on the central square, although there are cheaper in the backstreets. Staying overnight shouldn't be necessary, unless you find Náfplio full – a possibility in high season. **Hotels** on the Ayíou Pétrou main square include the comfortable and reasonable *Telesilla* (T07510/68 317; 3) and *Mycenae* (T07510/68 754, F68 332; 3) – the latter prefers longer-stay guests, groups, families or archeologists.

Tiryns (Tírynthos)

In Mycenaean times **TIRYNS** stood by the sea, commanding the coastal approaches to Árgos and Mycenae. The Aegean shore gradually receded, leaving the fortress stranded on a low hillock in today's plains, surrounded by citrus groves, and alongside the Argolid's principal modern prison. It's not the most enchanting of settings, which in part explains why this accessible, substantial site is undeservedly neglected and relatively empty of visitors. After the crowds at Mycenae, however, the opportunity to wander about Homer's "wall-girt Tiryns" in near-solitude is worth taking. The site lies just to the east of the main Árgos–Náfplio road, and frequent local buses drop off and pick up passengers opposite.

The Citadel

As at Mycenae, Homer's epigrams correspond remarkably well to what you can see on the ground at Tiryns. The fortress, now over three thousand years old, is undeniably impressive, and the site itself had been occupied for four thousand years before that. The walls, 750m long and up to 7m thick, formed of huge Cyclopean stones, dominate the site; the Roman guidebook writer Pausanias, happening on the site in the second century AD, found them "more amazing than the Pyramids" – a claim that seems a little exaggerated, even considering that the walls then stood twice their present height.

The entrance to the site (daily: summer 8am–8pm; winter 8am–2.30pm; €1.50) is on the far side of the fortress from the road, and visitors are restricted to exploring certain passages, staircases and the palace. Despite this, the sophistication and defensive function of the citadel's layout are evident as soon as you climb up the **entrance ramp**. Wide enough to allow access to chariots, the ramp is angled so as to leave the right-hand, unshielded side of any invading force exposed for the entire ascent, before forcing a sharp turn at the top – surveyed by defenders from within. The **gateways**, too, constitute a formidable barrier; the outer one would have been similar in design to Mycenae's Lion Gate, though unfortunately its lintel is missing, so there is no heraldic motif that might confirm a dynastic link between the sites.

Of the **palace** itself only the limestone foundations survive, but the fact that they occupy a level site makes them generally more legible than the ruins of hilly and boulder-strewn Mycenae, and you can gain a clearer idea of its structure. The walls themselves would have been of sun-dried brick, covered in stucco and decorated with frescoes. Fragments of the latter were found on the site: one depicting a boar hunt, the other a life-sized frieze of courtly women, both now in the Náfplio museum. From the forecourt you enter a spacious **colonnaded court** with a round sacrificial altar in the middle. A typically Mycenaean double porch leads directly ahead to the **megaron** (great hall), where the base of a throne was found – it's now in the Archeological Museum in Athens, with miscellaneous finds and frescoes from the site. The massive round clay hearth that is characteristic of these Mycenaean halls – there's a perfect example at Nestor's Palace (see p.275) – is no longer to be seen at Tiryns, because some time in the sixth century BC this part of the palace became the site of a temple to Hera, a structure whose column bases now pepper the ground. **Royal apartments** lead off on either side; the women's quarters are thought to have been to the right, while to the left is the bathroom, its floor – a huge, single flat stone – still intact. The **lower acropolis**, north of the megaron, is currently out of bounds due to the excavation of two underground cisterns discovered at its far end in the late 1980s.

A tower further off to the left of the megaron gives access to a **secret staircase**, as at Mycenae, which winds down to an inconspicuous **postern gate**, although currently both are closed off. The site beyond the megaron is separated by an enormous inner wall and can only be viewed from a distance.

Náfplio

NÁFPLIO (also sometimes known as Nauplia or Navplion) is a rarity amongst Greek towns. A lively, beautifully sited place, it exudes a grand, occasionally slightly faded elegance, inherited from the days when it was the fledgling capital of modern Greece. The seat of government was here from 1829 to 1834 and it was in Náfplio that the first prime minister, Kapodistrias, was assassinated by vengeful Maniot clansmen. It was here also that the Bavarian Prince Otho, put forward by the European powers to be the first King of Greece, had his initial royal residence from 1833 to 1834. Since the 1980s the town has increasingly served as a popular year-round weekend retreat, with the result that hotel rooms and meals have crept up to Athens rates and above, but it remains by far the most attractive base for exploring the Argolid and resting for a while by the sea.

Arrival, information and accommodation

Wedged between the sea and a doubly fortressed headland, the old part of Náfplio is an easy town to find your way around. Arriving by **bus**, you are set down at one of two adjacent terminals just south of the interlocking squares, **Platía Trión Navárhon** and **Platía Kapodhístria**, on Syngroú. The **train** will deposit you near the junction of Polyzoïdhou and Irakléous, where a new station has been built, with two old carriages serving as ticket office and waiting room.

NÁFPLIO

▲ Toló, Neamoní & Epidaurus   ▲ Karathónas beach & Palamídhi

▲ Tiryns & Árgos

▲ Trípoli & Lérna

Kyknos Factory

Wednesday Market

Dia Supermarket

Soccer Stadium

Pool

New Train Station

Old Train Station

Palamídhi Fortress

Karathónas beach

Folk Art Museum

School

Bus Station

OTE

Cathedral

Tourist Police

Bastion

Ay. Spyrídhonos

War Museum

Folk Art Museum

Archeological Museum

National Bank

Clock Tower

Akronafplia Fortress

Nafplia Palace

Arvanitiá beach

Boúrtzi

N

RESTAURANTS
Byzantio Taverna   C
Kakanarakis Taverna   B
Omorfi Taverna   A
Palia Taverna   E
Posidónas taverna   D

ACCOMMODATION
Acronafplia   5   Economou   1
Agamemnon   3   King Othon   4
Byron   7   Leto   8
Dioscouri   6   Park   2

0   300m

▲ Flying Dolphins to the Argo-Saronic & Piréas

The **tourist office** is at 25-Martíou 2 (daily 9am–1pm & 4–8pm ☎07520/24 444), but hours are unpredictable and the information provided is notoriously inaccurate.

Accommodation

Accommodation in Náfplio is generally overpriced for what you get, particularly in the old town, though out of season during the week most **hotels** drop their prices significantly. There are a number of private **rooms** advertised; most cluster on the slope above the main squares. A few other hotels and rooms, generally the last to fill but often more reasonably priced, are located out in the modern town on the road to Árgos. If you come by car, bear in mind that finding a parking place in or near the old town is very difficult in summer. There is nowhere to **camp** in Náfplio itself, but southeast on the stretch of coast from Toló (11km from Náfplio) to Íria (26km away), there are a dozen or so campsites (see p.203).

Acronafplia, Ayíou Spyrídhonos 6 ☎07520/24 481. Good-value pension in five refurbished buildings around town. ❸–❹

Agamemnon, Aktí Miaoúli 3 ☎07520/28 021, ℗28 022. On the waterfront, with an upmarket restaurant and roof garden providing great views. ❺

Byron, Plátonos 2 ☎07520/22 351, ℗26 338, ✆byronhotel@otenet.gr. A beautifully restored old mansion just above Áyios Spyrídhon church. ❺

Dioscouri, Zygomála and Výronos 6 ☎07520/28 550, ℗21 202. A friendly hotel, reached via a steep flight of steps. Rooms at the front overlook the old town and the port. Open all year. ❹

Economou, Argonaftón 22 ☎07520/23 955. To the northeast of town, near the Dia supermarket

on the Árgos road. Recently refurbished, hospitable and excellent value – worth the 15min walk from the centre; some dorm beds available. ❷

King Othon, Farmakopoúlou 2 ☎07520/27 585, ℗27 595. Popular, well-placed hotel, beautifully refurbished with an impressive staircase. Close to the waterfront and Platía Syndágmatos. Open April–Oct. ❺

Leto, Zygomála 28 ☎07520/28 093. Located at the base of the Akronafplía fortress. Open March–Oct; some cheaper rooms (❹) available next door. ❺

Park, Dhervenakíou 1, off Platía Kapodhístria ☎07520/27 428, ℗27 045. Large, well-run 1960s hotel which may well have space when the smaller old-town places are full. ❺

The Town

There's ample pleasure in just wandering about Náfplio: looking around the harbourfront, walking over to the rocky town beach and, when you're feeling energetic, exploring the great twin fortresses of Palamídhi and Akronafplía on the headland. Náfplio also offers some of the best restaurants and shops in the eastern Peloponnese, plus a range of useful facilities including car rental and, in summer, hydrofoils down the coast to Monemvasiá or east to the Argo-Saronic islands.

Palamídhi

The **Palamídhi**, Náfplio's principal fort, was one of the key military flashpoints of the War of Independence. The Greek commander Kolokotronis – of whom there's a majestically bewhiskered statue down in the Platía Kapodhístria – laid siege to the castle for over a year before finally gaining control. After independence, ironically, he was imprisoned in the fortress by the new Greek government; wary of their attempts to curtail his powers, he had kidnapped four members of the parliament.

The most direct approach to the **fortress** (daily: summer 8.30am–3pm; winter 8.30am–5pm; €2.50) is by a stairway from the end of Polyzoïdhou street, beside a Venetian bastion, though there is also a circuitous road up from the town. On foot, it's a pretty killing climb up 890-plus stone-hewn steps and, when you reach the 216-metre summit, you're confronted with a bewilderingly vast complex. Within the outer walls there are three self-contained castles, all of them built by the Venetians between 1711 and 1714, which accounts for the appearance of the city's symbol – the Lion of St Mark – above the various gateways. The middle fort, San Niccolo (Miltiádhes), was the one where Kolokotronis was imprisoned; it later became a notorious prison during the civil war.

The fortress takes its name, incidentally, from Náfplio's most famous and most brilliant legendary son, **Palamedes** – the inventor of dice, lighthouses and measuring scales. He was killed by the Greeks at Troy, on charges of treachery trumped up by Odysseus, who regarded himself as the cleverest of the Greeks.

Akronafplía and Boúrtzi

The **Akronafplía** (*Íts Kalé* – "Three Castles" – in Turkish), to the west of the Palamídhi, occupies the ancient acropolis, whose walls were adapted by three successive medieval restorers – hence the name. The fortifications are today far less complete than those of the Palamídhi, and the most intact section, the lower Torrione castle, has been adapted to house the *Xenia Hotel* (partly closed – the other part a new and very expensive hotel). There's little of interest, but the hotel has meant a road has been carved out over the headland, and this brings you down to a small pay beach, **Arvanitiá** (said to be so named from running red with the blood of Albanian mercenaries slaughtered by Hasan Pasha in 1779), overcrowded in season but nevertheless an enjoyable spot to cool off in the shelter of the forts. In the early evening, it's more pleasant with only a few swimmers, but the refreshment kiosks are shut outside peak hours and out of season. If you walk along the path that continues from the end of the road just past the beach entrance for about ten minutes, you can pick your way down to a couple of small stone beaches below the cliffs; take provisions if you want to stay for a few hours to relax, or you can take the attractive paved route around the western end of Akronafplía, to the main town harbour. A dirt road to the left of Arvanitiá leads to Karathónas beach (see opposite), a 45-minute walk.

The town's third fort, the much photographed **Boúrtzi**, occupies the Ayíou Theodhórou islet offshore from the harbour. Built in 1473 by the Venetians to control the shipping lane to the town and to much of Árgos bay, the castle has seen various uses in modern times – from the nineteenth-century home of the town's public executioner to a luxury hotel in the earlier twentieth century. In her autobiography *I Was Born Greek*, the late actress and politician, Melina Mercouri, claimed to have consummated her first marriage there.

Mosques and museums

In the town itself there are a few minor sights, mainly from the town's Turkish past, and two excellent museums. **Platía Syndágmatos**, the main square of the old town, is the focus of most interest. In the vicinity, three converted **Ottoman mosques** survive: one, in the southeast corner of the square, is an occasional theatre and cinema; another, just off the southwest corner, was the modern Greek state's original **Voulí** (parliament building). A third, fronting nearby Staïkopoúlou, has been reconsecrated as the cathedral of **Áyios Yeóryios**, having actually started life as a Venetian Catholic church. In the same area are a pair of handsome **Turkish fountains** – one abutting the south wall of the theatre-mosque, the other on Kapodhístria, opposite the church of Áyios Spyrídhon. On the steps of the latter, Ioannis Kapodistrias was assassinated by two members of the Mavromihalis clan from the Máni in September 1831; you can still see a scar left in the stone by one of the bullets. The Catholic church, which has also been a mosque, on Fotómara, has a monument to foreigners who died in the War of Independence, including Byron.

The **Archeological Museum** (Tues–Sun 8.30am–3pm; €1.50) occupies a dignified Venetian mansion on the west side of Syndágmatos. It has some good collections, as you'd expect in a town at the heart of the Argolid sites, including a unique and more or less complete suit of Mycenaean armour, the Dendra cuirass from around 1400 BC, and reconstructed frescoes from Tiryns.

The fine **Peloponnesian Folklore Foundation Museum** (Mon & Wed–Sun 9am–3pm, closed Feb; €3) on Vassiléos Alexándrou 1, just off Sofróni, won a European "Museum of the Year" award when it opened in 1981 and features gorgeous embroideries, costumes and traditional household items from all over Greece. At Staïkopoúlou 25 is possibly the world's only **Komboló (Worry-Beads) Museum** (daily 9.30am–9pm; €3), while a little further down at no. 40 you can see shadow puppets being made by Ilias Moros at To Enotion. The **War Museum** (Tues–Sat 9am–2pm, Sun 9.30am–2pm; free) at Amalías 22 has weaponry, uniforms, illustrations and other military memorabilia from the War of Independence to the civil war, including a series of portraits of the heroes of the War of Independence, enabling you to put faces to all those familiar Greek street names.

Ayía Moní

More handicrafts are on sale at the convent of **Ayía Moní**, 4km east of Náfplio on the Epidaurus road, just south of the suburb of Ária. The monastic church, one of the most accomplished Byzantine buildings in the Peloponnese, dates back to the twelfth century. From the outer wall bubbles a nineteenth-century fountain, identified with the ancient spring of Kanthanos, in whose waters the goddess Hera bathed each year to restore her virginity. Modern Greeks similarly esteem the water, though presumably with less specific miracles in mind.

Karathónas beach

The closest proper beach to Náfplio is at **Karathónas**, a fishing hamlet just over the headland beyond the Palamídhi fortress, which can be reached by a short spur off the drive going up to the ramparts. A more direct dirt road, theoretically closed to traffic, around the base of the intervening cliffs can make a pleasant 45-minute walk; however, women alone are occasionally pestered by local moped drivers. There are four morning bus services from Náfplio in season.

The narrow **sandy beach** stretches for a couple of kilometres, with a summer taverna at its far end. There were plans to develop it during the junta years, when the old road here was built, along with the concrete foundations of a hotel, but the project was suspended in the 1970s and has yet to be revived. At present Karathónas attracts quite a few Greek day-trippers in season, along with a handful of foreigners in camper vans; there are cafés in summer, plus windsurf boards for rent.

Eating, drinking and nightlife

Waterside **Bouboulínas**, where the locals take their early evening vólta, is lined with luxurious cafés where the beautiful people meet; tourists not wearing designer clothes and gold jewellery may feel a little out of place here. A cosier place to start restaurant menu-gazing in Náfplio is **Staïkopoúlou**, off which are many enjoyable if touristy **tavernas**. For **breakfast or coffee**, it's hard to beat the *Propylaion* right beside the bus station; assorted bakeries and juice bars around Platía Syndágmatos are also worth investigating. Eating out is oriented towards evening rather than lunchtime meals, but **nightlife** can be low key, with fewer late-night bars than one might expect and the occasional seasonal disco on and around Bouboulínas and Syngroú. A quieter drink can be had at the **cafés** on Platía Syndágmatos, which stay open late. The summer-opening *Mouria* café, next to Áyios Spyrídhon church, has live traditional music. The real night-out haunts around town are the numerous huge discos and nightclubs such as *Perama* on the beach road out towards Néo Kíos, or *Zorba's* outside Toló.

Byzantio, Vassiléos Aléxandrou 15. Excellent and friendly taverna, on a quiet corner of a beautiful street, with a varied menu and large portions. Specialities include home-made sausages.

Kakanarakis, Vassilísis Ólgas 18, ☎07520/25 371. A lively place serving a variety of dependably good mezédhes, plus dishes such as braised cockerel (*kókoras*) with noodles, and *kokkinistó* (meat simmered in tomato sauce). Open evenings only; popular with Greeks so arrive early or book ahead.

Omorfi Tavernaki, Vassilísis Ólgas 16. Local specialities include *kolokotroneïko* (pork in a rich wine and basil sauce), and courgette balls. Very dependable, with prompt service.

Palia, Staïkopoúlou 6. A *mayireftá* taverna since 1810. Friendly, with good food and prices.

Posidonas/Haris, Sidhirás Merarhías. Eating out in the park, with tasty, well-prepared mezédhes, at low prices.

Listings

Banks are concentrated around Platía Syndágmatos and along Amalías. The National Bank branch on Sidhirás Merarhías has an automatic exchange machine.

Bookshops Odyssey, on Platía Syndágmatos (April–Oct 8am–10pm; Nov–March 8am–2pm), has a good stock of English-language books, newspapers, cassettes, CDs and videos.

Car rental Pick from: Safeway, Eyíou 2 ☎07520/22 155; AutoEurope, Bouboulínas 51☎07520/24 160, ⓕ24 164; or the helpful Staïkos Travel, Bouboulínas 50 ☎07520/27 950, ⓕ28 000, who are agents for rail tickets and can also book ferries and flights.

Hydrofoils Náfplio is a stop for Hellas Flying Dolphin hydrofoils from June to September only, although even during this period the service is unreliable so check well in advance. Services connect the town with Spétses and the other Argo-

Saronic islands, plus Pireás and Monemvasiá; some involve a change at Pórto Héli. The ticket office, Yannopoulos, is at Platía Syndágmatos ☎07520/28 054, ⓕ22 393.

Laundries At Papanikoláou 33; Bubbles at Asklipíou 61 (the Toló road).

Post office The main branch (Mon–Fri 7.30am–2pm) is on the northwest corner of Platía Kapodhístria.

Scooter, motorbike and bicycle rental From Nikopoulos, Bouboulínas 49; or MotorTraffic, Sidhirás Merarhías 15 ☎07520/22 702.

Taxis There's a rank on Syngroú, opposite the bus station.

Tourist office 25-Martíou 2 ☎07520/24 444; open daily, officially 9am–1pm & 4–8pm.

Tourist police On the right at top of Syngroú ☎07520/28 131. Helpful and open daily 7.30am–9pm.

Beaches around Náfplio: Toló, Kastráki and beyond

Southeast from Náfplio are the ever-expanding resorts of **Toló** and **Kastráki** – popular and established enough to feature in some British package-holiday brochures. Inevitably, this means that they get packed at the height of the season, although they're still more tranquil than the big island resorts; you can always seek refuge at the low-key places further along the coast.

Toló (Tolon)

TOLÓ, 11km from Náfplio (hourly buses in season; last back at 10pm), is frankly overdeveloped, with a line of thirty or more hotels and campsites swamping its limited sands. Out of season it can still be quite a pleasant resort and the new bypass should, when complete, improve traffic in the central area, but in summer it is about as un-Greek an experience as you'll find in the Peloponnese. Redeeming features include views of the nearby islets of Platía and Romví, and in summer a good range of watersports (windsurfing, waterskiing, paragliding), but the local mosquitoes can be a problem.

Hotels in Toló tend to be block-booked through the summer but you could try some of the smaller places, like the *Hotel Artemis* (☎07520/59 458, ❻59 125; ❹) and *Hotel Tolo* (☎07520/59 248, ⓦwww.hoteltolo.gr; ❺). If they're full or beyond your budget, it's usually possible to find **rooms** by asking around or following the signs, but be prepared for inflated summer prices. The **campsites** charge similar rates to the rooms: first try *Sunset* (☎07520/59 556; March–Oct); failing that, there's the quieter *Lido II* (☎07520/59 369). The seafront taverna, *Chez-Gilles*, at Bouboulínas 14, is highly rated, with well-prepared French and Greek **food**.

In July and August, there are **hydrofoils** to the Argo-Saronic islands of Ídhra (Hydra) and Spétses.

Kastráki and ancient Assine

A pleasant alternative to Toló, especially if you're looking for an inexpensive campsite, is the longer beach at **KASTRÁKI**, 2km to the east; coming from Náfplio by bus, ask to be let off where the road reaches the sea – it forks right to Toló and left (500m) to Kastráki, marked on some maps as Paralía Asínis. Here, too, development is under way, but it's a fair bit behind that of Toló, limited to a scattering of small-scale hotels and campsites. *Camping Kastraki* (☎07520/59 386; April–Oct) is on the beach, and has windsurfing equipment, pedaloes and canoes for hire.

If you get tired of the water, wander along the beach to the scrub-covered rock by the Náfplio road junction. This is, or was, **ancient Assine** (daily 8.30am–3pm; free), an important Mycenaean and Classical city, destroyed by the jealous and more powerful Árgos in retribution for the Assinians having sided with the Spartans against them. There's little to see other than a 200-metre length of ancient wall, but it's an oddly atmospheric spot.

East to Íria

Further around the coast, to the east of Kastráki, the road runs on to **DHRÉPANO**, a sizeable village with four **campsites** and a very expensive hotel. The best campsite is *Triton* (☎07520/92 228; March–Nov); it's 1.2km from the main square of Dhrépano – follow signs to the beach. Beyond Dhrépano, the **Vivári lagoon** has a couple of good **tavernas** on its shore, including the *Mermaid* which is popular with the locals both for its excellent fresh fish and seafood, and for its wonderful view along the bay. If you continue this way for another 13km, you reach a turning and poor track down to the beach and the *Poseidon* campsite (☎07520/913 41; May to mid-Oct) at Paralía Iríon, below Íria village.

For the coast southeast of here towards Pórto Héli, Ermióni, Galatás and Méthana (each a local port for the Argo-Saronic islands) see p.207.

Epidaurus (Epídhavros)

EPIDAURUS is a major Greek site (daily: summer 8.30am–9pm; winter 8am–5pm; €4.50), visited for its stunning **ancient theatre**, built by Polykleitos in the fourth century BC. With its extraordinary acoustics, this has become a very popular venue for the annual Athens Festival productions of **Classical drama** which are staged on Friday and Saturday nights from June through until the last weekend in August. The works are principally those of Sophocles, Euripides and Aeschylus; given the spectacular setting, they are worth arranging your plans around, whether or not you understand the modern Greek in which they're performed. Should you wish to have a better grasp of what you are watching, English translations of the plays are available at the Odyssey bookshop in Náfplio (see p.202). Note that for festival performances the theatre is open after 7pm, but the rest of the site is closed.

The theatre, however, is just one component of what was one of the most important sanctuaries in the ancient world, dedicated to the healing god,

Asclepius, and a site of pilgrimage for half a millennium, from the sixth century BC into Roman times, and now as a World Heritage site.

The ancient theatre and Asklepion

The dedication of the sanctuary at Epidaurus to **Asclepius**, the legendary son of Apollo, probably owes its origin to an early healer from northern Greece who settled in the area. There were Asklepian sanctuaries throughout Greece (Athens has ruins of one on the south slope of its Acropolis) and they were sited, rationally enough, alongside natural springs. Epidaurus, along with the island of Kós, was the most famous and inspirational of them all, and probably the richest. The sanctuary was much endowed by wealthy visitors and hosted a quadrennial festival, including drama in the ancient theatre, which followed the Isthmian games. Its heyday was in the fourth and third centuries BC; after which Rome, when ravaged by an epidemic in 293 BC, sent for the serpent that was kept in the sanctuary.

This aspect of the site, however, along with most of the associated Asklepian ruins, is incidental for most visitors since it is Epidaurus's **ancient theatre** which is simply a wonderful sight. With its backdrop of rolling hills, this 14,000-seat arena merges perfectly into the landscape, so well in fact that it was rediscovered and unearthed only in the nineteenth century. Constructed with mathematical precision, it has an extraordinary equilibrium and, as guides on the stage are forever demonstrating, near-perfect natural acoustics – such that you can hear coins, or even matches, dropped in the circular orchestra from the highest of the 54 tiers of seats. Constructed in white limestone (red for the dignitaries in the front rows), the tiered seats have been repaired, but otherwise restoration has been minimal, with the beaten earth stage being retained, as in ancient times.

The museum

Close by the theatre is a small **museum** (summer Mon noon–7pm, Tues–Sun 8am–7pm; winter closes 5pm; entrance fee included in site ticket price), which is best visited before you explore the sanctuary. The finds displayed here show the progression of medical skills and cures used at the Asklepion; there are tablets recording miraculous and outrageous cures – like the man cured from paralysis after being ordered to heave the biggest boulder he could find into the sea – alongside quite advanced surgical instruments.

In 86 BC, by which time Epidaurus's reputation was in decline, the Roman consul Sulla, leader of the forces invading the Peloponnese, looted the sanctuary and destroyed its buildings. Hence, most of the ruins visible today are just foundations and a visit to the museum helps identify some of the former buildings.

The sanctuary

The **Asklepian sanctuary**, as large a site as Olympia or Delphi, holds considerable fascination, for the ruins here are all of buildings with identifiable functions: hospitals for the sick, dwellings for the priest-physicians, and hotels and amusements for the fashionable visitors to the spa. Their setting, a wooded valley thick with the scent of thyme and pine, is evidently that of a health farm.

The reasonably well-labelled **site** begins just past the museum, where there are remains of **Greek baths** and a huge **gymnasium** with scores of rooms leading off a great colonnaded court; in its centre the Romans built an **odeion**.

To the southwest is the outline of the **stadium** used for the ancient games, while to the northeast, a small **sanctuary of Egyptian gods** reveals a strong presumed influence on the medicine used at the site.

North of the stadium are the foundations of the **Temple of Asclepius** and beside it a rectangular building known as the **Abaton** or **Kimitirion**. Patients would sleep here to await a visitation from the healing god, commonly believed to assume the form of a serpent. He probably appeared in a more physical manifestation than expected; harmless snakes are believed to have been kept in the building and released at night to bestow a curative lick.

The deep significance of the serpent at Epidaurus is elaborated in the circular **Tholos**, one of the best-preserved buildings on the site and designed, like the theatre, by Polykleitos. Its inner foundation walls form a labyrinth which is thought to have been used as a snakepit and, according to one theory, to administer a primitive form of shock therapy to the mentally ill. The afflicted would crawl in darkness through the outer circuit of the maze, guided by a crack of light towards the middle, where they would find themselves surrounded by writhing snakes. Presumably, on occasions, it worked. Another theory is that the labyrinth was used as an initiation chamber for the priests of Asclepius, who underwent a symbolic death and rebirth in it.

Practicalities

Most people take in Epidaurus as a day-trip, though there is a **hotel** at the site – the unattractive and expensive *Xenia* (℡07530/22 005, ℻22 219; April–Oct; prices differ by season). There are better and more modestly priced hotels on the way to and in nearby **LYGOURIÓ** village, 25km from Náfplio and 5km northwest of the site. Possibilities here include the *Hotel Alkion* (℡ & ℻ 07530/22 552; ❸) at the turning off the main road to the village, or *Hotel Koronis* (℡07530/22 267; ❸) in the village itself; both are open all year but fully booked long in advance for the festival period. Alternatively, it's possible to **camp** in the grass car park on days of performances, though you must wait until an hour after the play's end before setting up a tent. Pleasant beachside accommodation is available at Paleá Epídhavros, 15km to the northeast (see opposite). Lygourió itself has a few tavernas and cafés, but little of interest other than the Byzantine church of Áyios Ioánnis Elémonos and a Mycenaean pyramid on the northeast road.

For meals, the nearest **restaurant** is the *Oasis* on the Lygourió road, although there is a café at the *Xenia*. Much better is *Taverna Leonides* (℡07520/22 115),

---

Tickets and transport

Theatre tickets cost €12–25. In recent years there have been chaotic scenes with overselling and ticket-holders being turned away at the gates. Tickets for the plays are available at the site on the day of performance, or in advance in Athens (at the festival box office – see p.152) or possibly in Náfplio at the bus station. Advance information is usually unavailable until just before the festival. In Athens you can buy all-inclusive tickets for performances and return bus travel. There are also special evening buses from the site to Náfplio after the show; check at Náfplio bus station. English translations of the plays are available at the site and at the Odyssey bookshop in Náfplio. Normally there are six buses daily from Náfplio to the site; they are marked "Theatre", "Asklipion" or "Epidhavros" and shouldn't be confused with those to the modern villages of Néa or Arhéa (Paleá) Epídhavros (see opposite).

in the village proper, a friendly spot with a garden out the back; you'd be wise to book ahead if your visit coincides with a performance at the ancient theatre. Actors eat here after shows, and photos on the wall testify to the patronage of Melina Mercouri, the Papandreous, François Mitterrand and Sir Peter Hall.

Paleá Epídhavros

The closest beach resort to Epidaurus is **Paleá Epídhavros** (officially Arhéa Epídhavros), which has expanded since the improvement of the direct coast road from Kórinthos, but remains pleasantly small-scale. The recent discovery of ancient remains at the village means that some road signs for the beach now indicate "Ancient Epidavros", while the main inland site is referred to as "Ancient Theatre of Epidavros". As far as the remains are concerned, excavations are still in progress but they are worth a quick visit. A smaller classical theatre (Tues–Sun 8.30am–3pm; free) on the headland, past the small town beach, is a festival venue for weekend musical shows in July and August, for which advance information is available at the hotel *Christina* or from Athens (☎010/72 82 333). You can find some small, open, Mycenaean *thólos* tombs behind the main street through town; turn inland up Odhós Ippokrátous by the BP petrol station, then left just above it.

Facing the harbour and town beach, there are a number of **hotels** and purpose-built **rooms**, with more, plus campsites, on the road south to Yialási beach. All are full with festival patrons in season. If you want to book ahead, two friendly hotels to try are the *Christina* (☎07530/41 451, ☞41 655; ❹), with excellent home-made breakfasts, on the waterfront square, and the *Paola Beach* (☎07530/41 397 ☞41 697; closed in winter; ❹), the last hotel beyond the church at Vayioniá beach. The *Elena* rooms (☎07530/41 207; ❸) are comfortable apartments, with air conditioning for an extra charge. Three of the four **campsites** are on the beach to the south of the village in the district known as Yialási: they are *Verdelis* (☎07530/41 425; March–Oct), *Bekas* (☎07530/41 714; March–Oct) and *Nicholas II* (☎07530/41 445; April–Oct). **Buses** from Náfplio are scheduled to run late morning and return mid-afternoon, some via Epidaurus, though they can be unreliable – the central bus stop is at the *Platanos* café. Taxis can be summoned on ☎07530/41 723 if you are stuck. A **hydrofoil** route from Pireás via Égina during summer months provides alternative easy access from Athens – the local agents are Syroyiannouli (☎07530/42 010).

The Saronic ports: Méthana to Pórto Héli

The roads across and around the southern tip of the Argolid are sensational scenic rides, but the handful of resorts here are lacking in character, have disappointing beaches and are generally overdeveloped. With a car, you can pick your route and take a leisurely drive back to Náfplio, perhaps exploring the site of **ancient Troezen** and the **Lemonodhássos** lemon groves. Otherwise, you'll probably travel this way only if heading for one of the **Argo–Saronic islands**: **Méthana** has local connections to Égina (Aegina) and Póros; **Galatás** to Póros; **Ermióni** to Ídhra (Hydra) and Spétses; and **Kósta** and **Pórto Héli** to Spétses. Geographically part of the Peloponnese, Galatás, Trizína and

Méthana are, like the Argo-Saronic islands, administratively in the province of Pireás, and sometimes prices are inflated to match those on the islands.

Méthana and ancient Troezen

It's a sixty-kilometre drive from Epidaurus to **MÉTHANA**, the last section along a cliff-hugging corniche road. Set on its own volcanic peninsula, Méthana is a disappointing spa-town, whose devotees are attracted by foul-smelling sulphur springs. Of the half-dozen hotels, the most pleasant is the seafront *Avra* (☎02980/92 382; ❹). The agent for the **hydrofoil** is Palli (☎02980/92 460). The sixty-metre deep **volcanic crater of Hephaistos** at Kaïméni Hóra ("Burnt Village"), on the northwest side of the peninsula is semi-dormant, though Strabo recorded an eruption two thousand years ago. Access paths have been blocked to discourage casual visitors.

Two kilometres west of the village of Trizína, itself just south and inland of the turning to the Méthana peninsula, are the ruins of ancient **TROEZEN**, the legendary birthplace of Theseus and location of his domestic dramas. The root of his problems was Aphrodite, who, having been rejected by Theseus's virgin son Hippolytus, contrived to make Phaedra – Theseus's then wife – fall in love with the boy (her stepson). Phaedra, too, was rejected and responded by accusing Hippolytus of attempted rape. Hippolytus fled, but, when his horses took fright at a sea monster and he was killed, Phaedra confessed her guilt and committed suicide. Originally told by Euripides (later reworked by Racine), a full account of the tragedy, together with a map of the ruins' remains, is on sale for €1 in the modern village. For romantics, Theseus's "autobiography" in Mary Renault's *The King Must Die*, starts, "The Citadel of Troizen, where the palace stands, was built by giants before anyone remembers. But the Palace was built by my great-grandfather. At sunrise . . . the columns glow fire-red and the walls are golden. It shines bright against the dark woods on the mountainside."

Such **remains** as exist of the ancient town are spread over a wide site. Most conspicuous are three ruined Byzantine chapels, constructed of ancient blocks, and a structure known as the Pýrgos Dhiatihísmatos or **Tower of Theseus**, whose lower half is third century BC and top half is medieval. This stands near the lower end of a gorge, the course of an ancient **aqueduct**, which you can follow in fifteen-minutes' walk up a dirt road; a short, signed path leads to the **Dhiavoloyéfyro** ("Devil's Bridge"), natural rock formations spanning the chasm. On the far side, a short path to the right leads down to the lower bridge; a path to the left continues upstream past attractive rockpools – a rare black butterfly is said to be endemic in the valley here.

Galatás and Lemonodhássos

Workaday **GALATÁS** lies only 350m across the water from the touristy island of Póros, with which it is connected by skiffs, sailing more or less continuously in the summer months (5min; €0.30). The town has a cluster of **hotels**, of which the best value are the *Saronis* (☎02980/22 356; ❸) and the friendly *Papasotiriou* (☎02980/22 841; ❺), with a taverna; there are also **rooms** for rent around the waterfront, a **bike rental** place and **taxis**. The town is connected by daily buses with Epidaurus and Náfplio, and has local services to Trizína and Méthana.

On the coast road to the south is the small, unattractive **Pláka** beach (2km); two left turns shortly after bring you to the slightly better **Alykí** beach (4km), backed by a small salt lake. From a church on the main paved road behind Alykí, a route, signposted "Taverna Kardassi", leads into the **Lemonodhássos**

– a vast, irrigated lemon grove. Paths meander through 30,000 lemon trees, heading upwards (20min) to an inspiringly positioned **taverna** serving fresh lemonade on its shady terrace. Henry Miller recounts a visit here in *The Colossus of Maroussi*, hyperbolizing that "in the spring young and old go mad from the fragrance of sap and blossom". There is also a café and a good seafront taverna at Alykí beach, both seasonal. Further along the main road is the longer, cleaner Lemonodhássos beach (5km).

Ermióni, Kósta and Pórto Héli

Continuing clockwise around the coast from Galatás, you follow a narrow, modern road, cut from the mountainside to open up additional resorts close to Athens. **Plépi** (part of Aktí Ídhras – "Hydra Beach") is a villa-urbanization, visited by boats from beachless Ídhra opposite. **ERMIÓNI** (ancient Hermione) is better: a real village, enclosed by a rocky bay, overlooking Dhokós and Ídhra, and perhaps saved from development by lack of a sandy beach. It has several modest **hotels**, including the *Akti* (℡07540/31 241; ❸) and the *Filoxenia* (℡07540/31 218, ℻32 177;❹); as well as the *Ganossis Filoxenia* apartments (❹) along the beach. Aris Skouris, on the seafront south of the harbour, has **bikes** and scooters for rent. The agent for the **hydrofoil** is Koustas (℡07540/31 170, ℻31 600) on the waterfront.

Further round, **KÓSTA**, facing Spétses, and much larger **PÓRTO HÉLI**, squeezed between two enclosed bays, are purpose-built resorts that have swallowed up their original hamlets. Beyond the pretty waterfront views, both feature a rather soulless mix of package-tour hotels and facilities for yachters exploring the Argo-Saronic islands. If you want or have to stay in Kósta, there is a campsite – *Camping Costa* (℡07540/51 571) to the west of Kósta – as well as some fairly upmarket **hotels** like the *Hotel Lido* (℡07540/57 393, ℻57 364; ❺). There are more reasonable options near the harbourfront in Pórto Héli: *Flisvos* (℡07540/51 316, ℻51 011;❹) is on Platía Karaïskáki, where you'll also find the bus stop; *Limani* (aka *Porto* ℡07540/51 410;❸) is on the war-memorial square, as is Hellenic Vision Travel (℡07540/51 453, ℻52 375) which books hydrofoils and can find accommodation. There are numerous restaurants and cafés as well as car and bike rental. Pórto Héli is the only Argolid port which has direct **hydrofoil** connections to Monemvasiá and Kýthira. Kósta connects four times a day by **ferry** to Spétses (tickets available on the boat; €0.50). About 2km east of Kósta is the excellent *Limanaki* taverna, at the attractive small beach at **Áyios Emilianós**. With your own transport, you can go further to the very long, part-sand, part-pebble beach of Kranídhi bay, east across the peninsula from Pórto Héli; there are no facilities.

The circuitous route back to Náfplio from Pórto Héli runs inland, via attractive Kranídhi (7km), then scrambling its way up through the mountains past the 1121-metre viewpoint peak of Mount Dhídhymo. It is covered 3–4 times daily by a bus, which usually dovetails in Pórto Héli and Kósta with ferries and hydrofoils to and from Spétses and elsewhere; in low season, however, you may have to change buses in Kranídhi.

The east coast: Náfplio to Leonídhi

The **coastline** between Náfplio and Leonídhi is mountainous terrain, increasingly so as you move south towards Monemvasiá where the few villages seem carved out of their dramatic backdrop. Considering its proximity to Náfplio –

and Athens – the whole stretch is enjoyably low key and remarkably unexploited, remaining more popular with Greek holiday-makers than with foreign tourists; the accommodation at resorts before Leonídhi may be fully booked well in advance for the mid-June to mid-August Greek school holidays.

Getting to the **beaches** – Parália Ástrous, Áyios Andhréas, Paralía Tyroú and Pláka – is perhaps best done by car, though there are also **buses** twice daily from Árgos to Leonídhi, while **Paralía Tyroú** and **Pláka** (the port/beach of Leonídhi) are served by the Flying Dolphin **hydrofoils** en route from Spétses/Pórto Héli to Monemvasiá. However you travel, change money in advance, as there are few **banks** between Náfplio and Leonídhi.

Right at the beginning of the route, around the coast from Náfplio, the minor site of **ancient Lérna** makes an interesting halt. If you are travelling by train from Árgos to Trípoli, you could stop off at the station of Mýli, only 500m from the site; alternatively, a trip there makes a nice ride around the coast via Néo Kíos beach if you rent a bike in Náfplio.

Ancient Lérna

The site of ancient **LÉRNA** (daily 8.30am–3pm; €1.50) lies 10km south of Árgos and 12km from Náfplio by the minor road around the coast via Néa Kíos. On the way in from Árgos there is an interesting detour possible to the cave-lake **monastery** at Kefalári, where even today some locals still wash their carpets in the nearby freshwater springs. A further 4km inland is the remarkable fourth-century BC "**pyramid**" (Tues–Sun 8.30am–3pm; free) at Ellinikó village, actually a small fortress on the ancient road from Argos to Arcadia, standing nearly at full height.

The nearest village to Ancient Lérna is Mýli, at the foot of Mount Pontínus, on the bus and train routes from Árgos to Trípoli; there is a good **taverna** at the T-junction here. Just beyond the straggle of the village a narrow lane leads to the prehistoric site, which now lies between the main road and the railway; surrounded by an orange grove and close to the sea, it makes a fine picnic spot. The warden, unused to visitors, may volunteer to show you around this, one of Greece's most important Bronze Age sites. American excavations carried out in the 1950s unearthed ruins of an early **Neolithic house** and a well-preserved **fortification wall**, revealing it as one of the most ancient of Greek settlements, inhabited from as early as 5500 BC.

Another large house at the north end of the site is thought to have been an early palace, but was superseded by a much larger and more important structure known as the **House of Tiles**. Measuring approximately 24m by 9m, this dwelling, labelled as another palace, takes its name from the numerous terracotta roof tiles found inside, where they are thought to have fallen when either lightning or enemy raiders set the building ablaze in approximately 2200 BC. The house represents the earliest known instance of the use of terracotta as a building material, and is the most impressive pre-Helladic structure to have been unearthed on the Greek mainland. A symmetrical ground plan of small rooms surrounding larger interior ones is today sheltered by a huge canopy, with stairs mounting to a now-vanished second storey. The substantial walls, made of sun-dried brick on stone foundations, were originally covered with plaster. Even after its destruction, this palace may have retained some ritual significance, since two Mycenaean **shaft graves** were sunk into the ruins in around 1600 BC, and the site was not completely abandoned until around 1250 BC at the end of the Mycenaean period. Further excavations are taking place in Mýli itself, and an archeological park has been proposed, to connect the two sites.

As implied by the chronology, the founders and early inhabitants of Lérna were not Greeks. Certain similarities in sculpture and architecture with contemporary Anatolia suggest an Asiatic origin but this has yet to be proved conclusively. Excavated finds, however, demonstrate that the Lerneans traded across the Aegean and well up into the Balkan peninsula, cultivated all the staple crops still found in the Argolid and raised livestock, as much for wool and hides as for food. Elegant terracotta sauce tureens and "teaspoons", which may be seen in the Árgos archeological museum (see p.195), hint at a sophisticated cuisine.

According to myth, Hercules performed the second of his labours, the slaying of the nine-headed serpent-like monster, Hydra, at Lérna. As if in corroboration of the legend, the nearby swamps are still swarming with eels.

Coastal Arcadia: Ástros and Paralía Tyroú

The initial section of coast from Lérna to Ástros and Áyios Andhréas is low-lying and less spectacular than the sections further south, but pleasant enough, with a scattering of accommodation at Xiropigádho. The first resort of any size is **PARÁLIA ÁSTROUS**, whose older houses are tiered against a headland shared by a medieval **fort** (Tues–Sun 8.30am–3pm; free) and the ruins of a thirteenth-century BC acropolis. Back from the northern end of the sand-and-gravel beach, which extends 6km south of the fishing harbour, there are a few tavernas, more cafés, numerous rooms to let and some **hotels**: the *Golden Beach* (☎07550/51 294; ❸) has a seafront main square setting, while inland nearby the larger *Hotel Crystal* (☎07550/51 313, ☎51 764; ❹) rooms have fridges; both have air conditioning. The newish *Castro* rooms (☎07550/51 885; ❸) are well appointed and very good value, sleeping up to four per apartment. The *Thirea* campsite (☎07550/51 002; May–Oct) is a lively spot.

To the west and south, a trio of surprisingly neat and compact villages – **ÁSTROS** (site of the second National Assembly in 1823), Korakavoúni and Áyios Andhréas – perch at the foothills of **Mount Párnon** as it drops to meet the lush, olive-green plain. The **Kynouria Archeological Museum** (Tues–Sun 8.30am–3pm; €1.50) in a traditional building in Ástros contains local items – including a collection from the Roman villa of Herodes Atticus at Éva Dholianón, 5km inland on the road to Trípoli. A little beyond Áyios Andhréas (10km from Ástros), the road curls down to the coast and the first in a series of fine-pebbled swimming coves, crammed between the spurs of Párnon. There are seasonal **rooms** at several of the coves, plus the *Arcadia* **campsite** (☎07550/31 190; May–Oct) on the main road, 6km beyond Áyios Andhréas; popular with middle-aged Greeks, the site has a friendly atmosphere but is noisy, particularly at weekends. Few concessions are made to tourists along this stretch of coast, apart from the occasional makeshift taverna; out of season, you'll definitely need your own supplies.

PARALÍA TYROÚ is a fair-sized town, with banks and a post office, and is a popular resort, mostly with older Greeks; younger Greeks tend to go further south along the coast, to Pláka. The place feels sedate, with comfortable, mid-range hotels and cafés spread back from its long pebble beach. **Hydrofoils** call in high season with Politis arranging tickets (☎07570/41 692). **Hotel** accommodation options at the southern end of the beach include *Apollon* (☎07570/41 393; ❸) with fridges in the rooms, and which also has apartments; *Kamvyssis* (☎07570/41 424, ☎41 685; ❹) with TV and air conditioning; and *Galazia Thalassa* (aka *Blue Sea*; ☎07570/41 369; ❸). The well-equipped **campsite**, *Zaritsi* (☎07570/41 429; April–Oct), is a few kilometres north at Zarítsi beach. Twelve kilometres south, en route to Leonídhi, there is a good fish taverna, the *Klimataria*, above pretty Sambatiká beach.

Leonídhi, Pláka and south towards Monemvasiá

Gigantic red cliffs that wouldn't look out of place in deserts of the American Southwest or the Canary Islands, confine **LEONÍDHI** (Leonídhion in formal Greek), the terminus of the Árgos bus route. Set inland, with rich agricultural land spreading down to the sea, this prosperous and traditional market town sees little need to pander to tourists, most of whom head for the coast at Leonídhi's diminutive port, Pláka. The **Tsakonic dialect** – a form of ancient Doric – is still used locally, notably for the Easter Sunday Mass. Also unique is the streaky, pale purple, sweet-tasting Tsakoniki aubergine, celebrated in a Pláka festival each August. If you prefer to stay inland, you might find space in the town's one modest **hotel**, the *Alexaki* (aka *Neon*; ☏07570/22 383; €28), or the few advertised **rooms** for rent such as the *Ithaki* (☏07570/23 394; €26) with air-conditioning and open all year. There are some enjoyable, small-town **tavernas**, such as the *Mouria* near the small square.

Pláka to Yérakas

PLÁKA, 4km away, is a delightful place consisting of a harbour, a couple of **hotels** and some **eating places**. It also has a fine pebble beach, which in recent years has become popular with Greek and European tourists, plus a sporadic influx of yachties. In summer, it would be wise to phone ahead to reserve a balconied room with a sea view in the first-choice *Hotel Dionysos* (☏07570/22 379; ❹), owned by the Bekarou family, who have run the *Michael & Margaret* taverna opposite since 1830. Eat here and you may be rewarded with tales of wartime derring-do by the taverna owner's father. There are excellent meals also to be had at picturesquely situated little places like *Tou Psara* taverna near the harbour. The agent for the **hydrofoils** is Kounia (☏07570/22 206).

The small resort of **POÚLITHRA**, 3km south of Pláka around the bay, marks the end of the coast road – which heads inland to small, isolated, mountain villages. There are tavernas close by the narrow strip of beach; a **hotel**, the *Akroyiali* (☏07570/51 262; ❺); and rooms such as *Kekes* (☏07570/51 205; ❷) and *Spanoudakis* (☏07570/51 325; ❸).

South of Leonídhi, in Lakonía province, the coastline is wilder and sparsely inhabited, with just a couple of coastal settlements cut into the cliffs. To reach the two little settlements – **KYPARÍSSI** and **YÉRAKAS** – you're better off taking the Flying Dolphin **hydrofoil**, which stops at both on the way to Monemvasiá. By road, it's a very roundabout route (though in better shape than it looks on the map) from Moláï, on the Spárti–Monemvasiá road.

Inland from Leonídhi

The route inland from **Leonídhi** is worth taking for its own sake, climbing through the huge **Dhafnón gorge**, past the **monastery of Élonas** – although the views are even better if this route is covered in the reverse direction, descending through the gorge to Leonídhi. The road peaks at the high mountain village of **Kosmás**, providing a temperature shock in the height of summer, but a great place to stop and enjoy the fresh mountain air over a drink in the atmospheric square, shaded by a huge plane tree. The whole route is a decent road for cars, and brings you out near the Byzantine site of **Yeráki**; from there, you have a choice of roads – to Spárti or Yíthio (Gythion) via Skála, or to Monemvasiá and Neápoli via Moláï. Without a car, you'll have to plan very carefully: a daily bus runs from Leonídhi to Yeráki, and goes on to Spárti twice a week – but check first.

Moní Élonas

Visible from Leonídhi, the **Panayías tis Élonas** (Elónis) monastery stands out as a white slash in the mountainside – though as you twist around and up the ravine, it drops away from view. The turn-off to the monastery (visitors permitted from sunrise to sunset) comes 13km from Leonídhi, via a short approach road which ends at a gateway. A cliff path takes you on to the main building, where you can wander down to a small chapel (closed during siesta) crammed with icons and lanterns, and to a spring, whose icy-cold water has supposedly curative powers. Most of the monastery, originally founded in medieval times following the appearance of a miraculous and inaccessible icon by St Luke, was rebuilt following the War of Independence, becoming a nunnery in 1972. Today, it is maintained by four nuns, who sell a classic little history (in Greek only) of the monastery's legends and vicissitudes.

Kosmás

Continuing south, 15km past the Élonas turning, you reach **KOSMÁS**, a handsome alpine village set about a grand platía and giant plane tree, with several tavernas. Straddling the most important pass of Párnon, at 1150m, it can be a chilly place during the spring or winter, but very beautiful, too, with its streams, cherries and walnut trees, and would make a pleasant base for mountain walking. The *Xenonas Maleatis Apollo* (☎07570/31 494; ❸) has rooms with kitchens, sleeping two to four, and a small taverna, in an attractively refurbished eighteenth-century building. Just at the edge of the village, on the Leonídhi side, are the *Kosmas* studios (☎07570/31 483; ❷), also with kitchens. Beyond the village the road runs through a pass, then sweeps downvalley through fir forests to the village and the Byzantine ruins of Yeráki (see overleaf).

The southeast: Lakonia

Lakonía, the ancient territories of the Spartans, covers the area between the high ridges of Mount Taïyetos and Mount Párnonas and everywhere to the south. Exclude the lush Evrótas valley, with Spárti itself and Mystra, and you are left with a dramatic and underpopulated landscape of harsh mountains and poor, dry, rocky soil. Landforms apart, the highlights here are the extraordinarily preserved Byzantine town of **Monemvasiá** – an essential visit for any tour of the southern Peloponnese – and the aridly remote **Máni** peninsula, with its bizarre history of violence and piety, of feuds and unique tower-houses and frescoed churches with barrel roofs. Monemvasiá is a regular stop for Flying Dolphin hydrofoils from Pireás and the Argo-Saronic islands, and would make a superb entry point to the peninsula. In summer, the Maniot port of **Yíthio**

(Gythion), and **Neápoli**, south of Monemvasiá, are additional stops on the hydrofoil and provide the easiest links to **Kýthira**, technically an Ionian island under the administration of Pireás, but covered – due to its Peloponnesian access – in this chapter.

South from Leonídhi: Yeráki

If you choose the southeastern route over Mount Párnon from Leonídhi then it is well worth making the effort to visit the **Byzantine antiquities** at Yeráki. With its **Frankish castle** and fifteen **chapels** spread over a spur of the mountain, Yeráki stands a creditable third to the sites of Mystra and Monemvasiá.

Medieval Yeráki

Yeráki (Tues–Sun 8.30am–3pm; free) was one of the original twelve **Frankish baronies** set up in the wake of the Fourth Crusade, and remained an important Byzantine town through the fourteenth century, straddling the road between Mystra and its port at Monemvasiá. The site is spectacular, with sweeping vistas over the olive-covered Evrótas plain and across to Taïyetos. It stands four kilometres outside and overlooking the current village of Yeráki (see below).

All the main churches are kept locked, and to visit them you should, theoretically, enquire at the café on the village square for a caretaker, one of whom may give a tour, clambering around the rocks to the best-preserved **chapels**. However, they usually only open for organized excursions, and some lone women have experienced hostility at the cafés.

The most substantial remains of the medieval town are of its fortress, the **Kástro**, built in 1256 by the local Frankish baron, Jean de Nivelet, who had inherited Yeráki, with six other lordships, from his father. Its heavily fortified design is based on that of the Villehardouin fortress at Mystra, for this was one of the most vulnerable Frankish castles of the Moreas, intended to control the wild and only partially conquered territories of Taïyetos and the Máni. In the event, Jean retained his castle for less than a decade, surrendering to the Byzantines in 1262 and buying an estate near Kórinthos on the proceeds. In the late seventeenth century it became Venetian, then Turkish in 1715 until being abandoned in the late eighteenth century. Within the fortress are huge **cisterns** for withstanding sieges, and the largest of Yeráki's churches: the thirteenth-century **mitrópolis**, also known as **Áyios Yeóryios**, which features blackened Byzantine frescoes, a Frankish iconostasis and the Villehardouin arms.

The churches on the slope below also mix Frankish and Byzantine features, and many incorporate material from Yeráki's ancient predecessor, Geronthrai. The caretaker may be prepared to unlock two or three, including **Áyios Dhimítrios**, **Zoödhóhos Piyí** and **Ayía Paraskeví** (at the base of the hill), each of which has restored frescoes.

Practicalities

The "modern" village of **Yeráki** has no regular accommodation, though rooms may be negotiable through the café or taverna in the square. If you're dependent on public transport, you'll need to take in Yeráki as a day-trip from Spárti: **buses** run several times daily, but only twice a week along the splendid route over Mount Párnon to Leonídhi.

Monemvasiá

MONEMVASIÁ, standing impregnable on a great island-like irruption of rock, was the medieval seaport and commercial centre of the Byzantine Peloponnese, the secular counterpart of Mystra. Nowadays the lower town is a curious mixture of atmospheric heritage combined with tacky souvenir shops and gawping tourists.

The town's name, an elision of *Moni Emvasis*, "single entrance", is a reference to its approach from the mainland, across a kilometre of causeway and a small bridge built in the twentieth century to replace a sequence of wooden bridges. Such a defensible and strategic position gave it control of the sea lanes from Italy and the west, to Constantinople and the Levant. Fortified on all approaches, it was invariably the last outpost of the Peloponnese to fall to invaders, and was only ever taken through siege.

Some history

Founded by the **Byzantines** in the sixth century, Monemvasiá soon became an important port. It remained in Byzantine possession for almost seven hundred years, passing only very briefly to the Franks – who took it in 1249 after a three-year siege but had to ransom it back for the captured Guillaume de Villehardouin. Subsequently, it served as the chief commercial port of the Despotate of Mystra and was for all practical purposes the Greek Byzantine capital. Mystra, despite the presence of the court, was never much more than a large village; Monemvasiá at its peak had a population of almost 60,000.

Like Mystra, Monemvasiá had something of a golden age in the thirteenth century; during this period, it was populated by a number of noble Byzantine families, and reaped considerable wealth from estates inland, from the export of wine (the famed Malmsey – *Malvasia* – mentioned in Shakespeare's *Richard III* and now being replanted locally – available at the *Lazareto* hotel restaurant) and from roving corsairs who preyed on Latin shipping heading for the East. When the rest of the Moreas fell to the Turks in 1460, Monemvasiá was able to seal itself off, placing itself first under the control of the papacy, later under the **Venetians**. Only in 1540 did the **Turks** gain control, the Venetians having abandoned their garrison after the defeat of their navy at Préveza.

Turkish occupation precipitated a steady decline, both in prestige and population, though the town experienced something of a revival during the period of Venetian control of the Peloponnese (1690–1715). Monemvasiá was again thrust to the fore in the **War of Independence**, when, in July 1821, after a terrible siege and wholesale massacre of the Turkish inhabitants, it became the first of the major Turkish fortresses to fall.

After the war, there was no longer the need for such strongholds, and, at the end of the nineteenth century, shipping routes changed too, with the opening of the Corinth Canal. The population plummeted and the town drifted into a village existence, its buildings for the most part allowed to fall into ruin. By the time of World War II – during which 4000 New Zealand troops were dramatically evacuated from the rock – only eighty families remained. Today there are just ten in permanent residence, but much restoration work has been done to the walls and many of the churches.

The rock: medieval Monemvasiá

From the mainland village of **Yéfira** – where the causeway to **Monemvasiá** (or **Kástro**, as locals call it) begins – nothing can be seen of the medieval town,

MONEMVASIÁ

Ritsos' Birthplace

Gateway

Malvasia (Stellaki)

Áyios Pétros (Mosque & Museum)

PLATIA TZAMIOU

Panayía Myrtidhiótissa

Mitrópolis Elkómenos Khristós

Malvasia (Ritsou)

LOWER TOWN

Áyios Nikólaos

Khrysafítissa

Stairs to Upper Town

Place for Swimming

▲ Ayia Sofia   ▲ Spárti

▲ Neápoli

▲ Yéfira

N

100 m
0

ACCOMMODATION
Malvasia (reception)   1
Byzantío (café/ reception)   2
Kellia   3

MONEMVASIÁ HEADLAND

KÁSTRO

UPPER TOWN

Ayia Sofia

Citadel

LOWER TOWN

Platform for Swimming

YÉFIRA

N

which is built purely on the seaward face of the rock. Little more is revealed as you walk across the causeway, past a Mobil garage, but the long entrance road, used for parking, brings you to huge castellated walls. Once through the fortified entrance gate, narrow and tactically Z-shaped, everything looms into view: piled upon one another, amid narrow stone streets and alleyways, are houses with tiled roofs and walled gardens, and distinctively Byzantine churches. High above, the improbably extended castle walls protect the upper town on the summit.

The Lower Town

The **Lower Town** once numbered forty churches and over eight hundred homes, an incredible mass of building, which explains the intricate network of alleys. A single main street – up and slightly to the left from the gateway – shelters most of the restored houses, and is lined with cafés, tavernas and souvenir shops. One of the tavernas is owned by relatives of the late Yannis Ritsos, one of Greece's leading poets and a lifelong communist, who was born on the rock; a plaque on a house above the main gate commemorates his birthplace.

At the end of this street is the lower town's main square, a beautiful public space, with a cannon and a well in its centre, and the setting for the great, vaulted **cathedral** built by the Byzantine emperor Andronikos II Komnenos when he made Monemvasiá a see in 1293. The largest medieval church in southern Greece, it is dedicated to Christ in Chains, and is thus known as *Elkómenos Khristós*. Across the square is the domed church of **Áyios Pétros**, originally a sixteenth-century mosque, which was reconverted by the Turks back into a mosque and now houses a small museum of local finds (open, but keeps unpredictable hours). Unusually for Ottoman Greece, the Christian cathedral was allowed to function during the occupation, and did so beside this mosque, hence the name of this square, Platía Tzamíou – "the square of the mosque".

Down towards the sea is a third notable church, the seventeenth-century **Khrysafítissa**, whose bell hangs from a bent-over old acacia tree in the courtyard. It was restored and adapted by the Venetians in their second, eighteenth-century, occupation. The **Portello** is a small gate in the sea wall, due south of Platía Tzamíou; you can **swim** safely off the rocks here.

In peaceful times, the town was supplied from the tiny harbour, **Kourkoúla**, outside the town and below the road as you approach the entrance gateway. There are two minor churches just off the main street. **Panayía Myrtidhiótissa**, to the north of the cathedral, is a small, single-aisled basilica with a single dome; inside there is a beautifully carved iconostasis – ask around for the priest if the basilica is locked. The big grey church built alongside the main street, above the Khrysafítissa, is **Áyios Nikólaos**; it dates from the early eighteenth century, and was used for many years as a school.

The Upper Town

The climb to the **Upper Town** is highly worthwhile – not least for the solitude, since most day-trippers stay down below. To get the most from the vast site, it's a good idea to bring some food and drink (from Yéfira – Monemvasiá has no supermarket), to enable you to explore at leisure. There are sheer drops from the rockface, and unguarded cisterns, so descend before dusk and if you have young children, keep them close by.

The fortifications, like those of the lower town, are substantially intact with even the **entrance gate** retaining its iron slats. Within, the site is a ruin, unrestored and deserted – the last resident moved out in 1911 – though many structures are still recognizable. The only building that is relatively complete, even though its outbuildings have long since crumbled to foundations, is the beautiful thirteenth-century **Ayía Sofía**, by the gateway. Founded as a monastery by Andronikos II, along a plan similar to that of Dhafní, its chapel candles still flicker perilously in the wind.

Beyond the church extend acres of ruins; in medieval times the population here was much greater than that of the lower town. Among the remains are the stumpy bases of Byzantine houses and public buildings, and, perhaps most striking, a vast **cistern** to ensure a water supply in time of siege. Monemvasiá must have been more or less self-sufficient in this respect, but its weak point was its food supply, which had to be entirely imported from the mainland. In the last siege, by Mavromihalis's Maniot army in the War of Independence, the Turks were reduced to eating rats and, so the propagandists claimed, Greek children.

Practicalities

Monemvasiá can be approached by road or sea. **Ferries** from Pireás are currently suspended, but there are regular **hydrofoils** in season, linking the town to the north with Leonídhi, Pórto Héli, Spétses and Pireás, and to the south with Neápoli and the island of Kýthira; currently there is no hydrofoil link with Yíthio. Direct **buses** connect with Spárti three times daily and twice (in season only) with Yíthio; occasionally a change at Moláï is necessary. Out of season it's better to alight at Skála, 17km from Yíthio, and take a local bus or taxi.

The hydrofoil will drop you at a mooring midway down the causeway; buses arrive in the modern mainland village of Yéfira. This is little more than a straggle of hotels, rooms and restaurants for the rock's tourist trade, with a pebble beach; for a **beach** day-trip, it's best to head 3–4km north along the coast.

Accommodation on the rock is expensive – in season and out – and from June to September, you'll need to book ahead. Within the walls, the choice is between three very upmarket **hotels**, each of which has attractively restored and traditionally furnished rooms. The most renowned is the *Malvasia* (☎07320/61 323, ℱ61 722; ❹–❺), which occupies three separate locations between the main street and the sea; call first at the hotel reception, well signposted from just inside the main gateway. The similarly characterful *Byzantino* (☎07320/61 254, ℱ61 331; ❹–❺) further along the main street is marginally more expensive: ask at the café of the same name. Down near the Khrysafítissa, looking out over the sea, is the EOT's *Xenonas Kellia* (☎07320/61 520, ℱ61 7 67; ❺), a small and rather isolated place, very exposed to the sun; advance booking is recommended. Several other **furnished apartments** on the rock are available for long-term rental. If you ask around at the shops and taverna on the main street, it's just possible that you might get one of these on a more temporary basis, out of season. Or you could seek the help of Malvasia Travel in Yéfira (see below). The *Byzantino* also owns the *Lazareto* hotel (☎07320/61 991, ℱ61 992; ❺), in the old hospital at the island end of the causeway, with luxurious rooms sympathetically converted. Their *Castellano* restaurant has local specialities and a Peloponnesian wine list (likely to include local Malvasia). **Eating out** in the old village is enjoyable, as much for the location as for food. Of the several restaurants, the best all-round place is *Matoula*, going since the 1960s, which has a leafy garden overlooking the sea.

Yéfira

There's more accommodation in **YÉFIRA**, along with various other useful tourist services including a **bank**, **post office** and a **travel agent**, Malvasia

Travel (☎07320/61 432; ✉malvtrvl@otenet.gr), which can help with rooms, ferry (if any) tickets and **scooter** rental; Agelakos (☎07320/61 219) at the Mobil garage just across the bridge towards the rock handles the **hydrofoils**. There are several **hotels** near or just north of the causeway. The cheapest is the refurbished *Akroyiali* (☎07320/61 360; ❷). The *Aktaion* (☎07320/61 234; ❸) and posher *Filoxenia* (☎07320/61 716; ❹) are under the same management. The friendly *Monemvasia* (☎07320/61 381; ❷) is good value, with large balconies overlooking the sea, while inland just over the road the *Flower of Monemvasia* (☎07320/61 395, ℻61 391; ❹) has rooms with a fridge and TV. If these are full, there are others to choose from, plus **rooms** for rent such as the friendly *Petrino* (☎07320/61 136; ❸), advertised along the waterfront. The nearest **campsite** is 3km to the south, along the coast road; *Kapsis Paradise* (☎07320/61 123) is open year-round, and has water-skis and scooters for rent. Back in the village, the best **taverna** is undoubtedly the *Nikolaos*; if you have transport, you could also try the *Pipinelis* (☎07320/61 044; May–Oct), about 2km out on the road south to the campsite, but ring first to be sure it's open and to make a reservation if the weather's cool, as indoor seating is limited. Even closer to the campsite is the pleasant *Kamares* taverna with good grilled and oven food. For nightlife in Yéfira, try the popular *Rock Café* or the *Santé* bar which plays cutting-edge Greek music.

South to Neápoli and Elafónissos

The isolated southeasternmost "finger" of the Peloponnese below Monemvasiá, locally known as Vátika, is little visited by tourists, except for the area around **Neápoli**, the farthest town south in mainland Greece, which offers access to the islet of Elafónissos, just offshore, and to the larger islands of Kýthira and Andikýthira, midway to Crete. From Monemvasiá the southerly route high over the central ridge via Ellinikó village is the slower but more attractive of the two roads to Neápoli – although the other, longer route is being widened and straightened.

Neápoli
NEÁPOLI is a mix of old buildings and modern Greek concrete behind a grey-sand beach – and mainly of interest for its ferry and hydrofoil connections. For such an out-of-the-way place, it is surprisingly developed, catering mostly to Greek holiday-makers. Besides rooms, there are three modest **hotels**: *Aïvali* (☎07340/22 287; ❸) and *Arsenakos* (☎07340/22 991; ❸) on the seafront and, just behind, the newer, friendly *Vergina* (☎07340/23 443; ❷) with fridges in the rooms; all may need to be booked ahead in summer. If you are waiting for the ferry or hydrofoil, you can **eat** extremely well at *To Konaki tou Zaharia*, by the bridge on the seafront, or have a breakfast snack of tasty, freshly cooked octopus at the *Kyma* ouzerí by the jetty. The agency for the Kýthira ferry and hydrofoil is Alexandrakis (☎07340/22 940, ℻22 071), between the jetty and the bridge. Neápoli has three **banks**; **taxis** can be ordered on ☎07340/22 590; and the KTEL **bus** office is on Dhimokratías, opposite the bus park.

Neápoli **beach** extends northwest to the village of Vingláfia and the recently upgraded harbour of Poúnda, which has between five and fifteen daily ferry crossings (☎07340/61 117, ℻22 897; 10min; €2) over the short strait to the islet of Elafónissos. Nearby Lake Strongýli, south of Áyios Yeóryios, is a nature reserve.

Elafónissos island

Like Neápoli, **Elafónissos** is relatively busy in summer, and again is frequented mainly by Greek visitors. The island's lone village is largely modern and functional, but has plenty of rooms and some good fish tavernas. Three **pensions**, the *Asteri* (☎ & ℱ 07340/61 271; ❷) with a fridge in the rooms, *Elafonisos* (☎07340/61 210; June–Oct; ❸) and *Lafotel* (☎07340/61 138; ❹), are worth booking.

Although otherwise scenically unexciting, the island has one of the best **beaches** in this part of Greece at **Símos**, a large double bay of fine white sand heaped into dunes; it's 5km southeast of the village, from where a kaïki leaves every morning in summer. There's one basic sandwich-and-drinks stand at the beach, and usually a small community of people camping here. Another beach, **Káto Nisí**, to the southwest of the village is quieter but almost as beautiful, with views to Kýthira.

Arhángelos

Further up the coast from Neápoli, just off the more northerly route from Monemvasiá, **ARHÁNGELOS** is a pleasant little resort at the southern end of a quiet sandy and deserted bay. By a quaint twist the village's name means "archangel", yet it is the harbour of Dhemonía ("devilry"), several kilometres inland. Rooms are to be had at the smart, apricot-coloured *Hotel Palazzo* (☎07320/44 111, ℱ44 113, ✉palazzo@travelling.gr; ❺), open all year. The *Anokato* bar is a popular hangout for the whole peninsula, especially in winter.

Kýthira island

Isolated at the foot of the Peloponnese, the island of **Kýthira** traditionally belongs to the Ionian islands, and shares their history of Venetian, and later, British rule; under the former it was known as Cerigo. Administratively it is part of Pireás in mainland Attica – like the Argo-Saronic islands. For the most part, similarities end there. The island architecture of whitewashed houses and flat-roofs looks more like that of the Cyclades, albeit with a strong **Venetian** influence. The landscape is different, too: wild scrub- and gorse-covered hills, or moorland sliced by deep valleys and ravines.

Depopulation has left the land underfarmed and the abandoned fields overgrown, for, since World War II, most of the islanders have left for Athens or Australia, giving Kýthira a reputation of being the classic emigrant island; it is known locally as "Australian Colony" or "Kangaroo Island", and Australia is referred to as "Big Kýthira". Many of the villages are deserted, their platías empty and the schools and kafenía closed. Kýthira was never a rich island, but, along with Monemvasiá, it did once have a military and economic significance – which it likewise lost with Greek independence and the opening of the Corinth Canal. These days, tourism has brought prosperity (and a few luxury hotels), but most summer visitors are Greeks and especially Greek Australians. For the few foreigners who reach Kýthira, it remains something of a refuge, with its undeveloped **beaches** a principal attraction. However, Theo Angelopoulos' film *Taxidhi sta Kythira* ("Journey to Kythira"), and, to a much greater extent, a 1998 popular Greek television serial filmed on the island, have attracted a huge amount of domestic attention and, consequent-

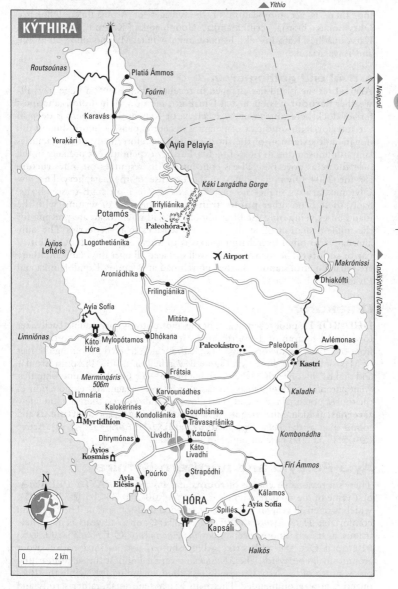

KÝTHIRA

▲ Yíthio

Routsoúnas

Platiá Ámmos

Foúrni

▶ Neápoli

Karavás

Yerakári

Ayía Pelayía

Káki Langádha Gorge

Trifyliánika

Potamós

Paleohóra

 Áyios
Leftéris

Logothetiánika

✈ Airport

▶ Makrónissi

Aroniádhika

Dhiakófti

Frilingiánika

Ayía Sofía

Mitáta

Limniónas

Káto
Hóra

Mylopótamos

Dhókana

Paleokástro

Paleópoli

Avlémonas

▲
Merminqáris
506m

Frátsia

Kastrí

Limnária

Karvounádhes

Kaladhí

Kalokerinés

Goudhiánika

Kombonádha

Myrtidhíon

Kondoliánika

Travasariánika

Dhrymónas

Livádhi

Katoúni

Ayios
Kosmás

Káto
Livadhi

Firí Ámmos

Ayia
Elésis

Poúrko

Strapódhi

Kálamos

HÓRA

Ayía Sofía

Spiliés

N

Kapsáli

Halkós

0   2 km

▶ Andikýthira (Crete)

ly, holiday-makers from the mainland. Much of the accommodation is now
fully booked by Christmas for the entire Greek school-summer-holiday
period; outside of this period some accommodation does not open until June
and closes early in September. The Association of Rental Room Owners (☏
& Ⓕ 07360/31 855) have a list of places to stay: in addition to the follow-

ing, there is accommodation in the villages of Aroniádhika, Dhókana, Dhrymónas, Frátsia, Frilingiánika, Goudhiánika, Kálamos, Kalokerinés, Karvounádhes, Káto Livádhi, Kondoliánika, Mitáta, Mylopótamos, Strapódhi and Travasariánika.

Arrival and getting around

Arrival on the island has changed in recent years. In 1997 a huge new all-weather **harbour** was opened at Dhiakófti, and now all hydrofoils and most ferries dock here instead of Ayía Pelayía or Kapsáli. The airport is deep in the interior, 8km southeast of Potamós; recent expensive refurbishment did not include extension of the short runway, therefore many of the facilities languish unused due to lack of flights. Further expenditure is unlikely in the near future as governing Pireás concentrates its resources on infrastructure for the 2004 Olympic Games at the expense of the periphery. The few Olympic Airways flights are met by taxis, as are most high-season boats. Sadly, there is no other **public transport** at the time of writing, with the island buses being only used for school runs, although locals are pressing for the implementation of, at the least, bus services to meet ferries. The only alternative to often overcharging taxis is to hitch or, more advisedly, hire a **car** or **scooter**. The roads are now well surfaced all over the island and there are reliable petrol stations on the central road at Potamós, Kondoliánika and Livádhi.

Dhiakófti

DHIAKÓFTI, until recently an unsung and relatively inaccessible backwater towards the bottom of the northeast coast, has been catapulted into the forefront of activity by the opening of the harbour, constructed by joining the islet of Makrónisi to the shore by a causeway. Perched on nearby Prasónisi island – and slightly disconcerting when arriving by sea – is a Greek container ship that went aground in 1999. Dhiakófti has a nice sandy beach, and exploitation of the tourist potential is currently fairly low key and seasonal; there are just a few **tavernas**, including the friendly *Notaras* by the causeway, and **apartments** and rooms such as the *Porto Diakofti* (☏07360/33 041; April–Oct; ④–⑤). Active (☏07360/33 207) have an office for **car rental**.

Ayía Pelayía and northern Kýthira

There's a reasonable choice of **rooms** and **tavernas** in **AYÍA PELAYÍA**; best value of the upmarket hotels is *Venardos* (☏07360/34 205, ⓕ33 850; ⑥), which is open all year and can offer very good deals off season. The clean and comfortable *Hotel Kytherea* (☏07360/33 321; ⑤; open all year) is more luxurious, as are the more recent *Filoxenia Apartments* (☏07360/33 100, ⓕ33 610; April–Oct; ⑤), with striking blue shutters and an imaginative layout around small courtyards. The *Moustakias* taverna, amongst the seafront eating places north of the jetty, has good, fresh food, including fish, while the *Paleo* ouzerí is also recommended. The main beaches are small, rather scruffy and disappointing, despite the provision of blue-and-white-striped changing huts; the beach at Kalamítsa, a short dirt track about 2km away to the south, is better.

Potamós and around

From Ayía Pelayía, the main road winds up the mountainside towards **POTAMÓS**, Kýthira's largest village – a pleasant and unspoiled place which, if you have a rented vehicle, makes a good base for exploring the island. It has a few **rooms** with kitchens, such as those at the *Xenonas Porfyra* (☎07360/33 329, ℱ33 924; ④) which have TV, and a pretty terrace and courtyard, and the *Alevizopoulos* (☎07360/33 245; ④) with air conditioning. In addition to **tavernas**, a **bank**, a **post office** and **petrol stations**, facilities include an Olympic Airways office (☎07360/33 688) and the Sirene Travel Club (☎07360/34 371, ℱ34 372), the island's agents for the Neápoli ferry. Most of the shops on the island are here, too, as is the **Sunday market**, Kýthira's liveliest regular event. The *Selana* café can provide **internet** facilities.

From **Logothetiánika**, just south of Potamós, an unpaved road leads down to Áyios Leftéris, where you can **swim** from rocks on the west coast, backed by high cliffs. At Logothetiánika itself, there is a popular taverna, *Karydies* (☎07360/33 664) with live music Thursday to Saturday, when booking is advisable.

Paleohóra

The main reason for visiting Potamós is to get to **PALEOHÓRA**, the ruined **medieval capital** (then called Áyios Dhimítrios) of Kýthira, 3km to the east of the town. Few people seem to know about or visit these remains, though they constitute one of the best Byzantine sites around. The most obvious comparison is with Mystra, and although Paleohóra is much smaller – a fortified village rather than a town – its natural setting is perhaps even more spectacular. Set on a hilltop at the head of the **Káki Langádha gorge**, it is surrounded by a sheer hundred-metre drop on three sides.

The site is lower than the surrounding hills and invisible from the sea and most of the island, something which served to protect it from the pirates that plagued Paleohóra through much of its history. The town was built in the thirteenth century by Byzantine nobles from Monemvasiá, and when Mystra fell to the Turks, many of its noble families also sought refuge here. Despite its seemingly impregnable and perfectly concealed position, the site was discovered and sacked in 1537 by Barbarossa, commander of the Turkish fleet, and the island's seven thousand inhabitants were killed or sold into slavery.

The town was never rebuilt, and tradition maintains that it is a place of ill fortune, which perhaps explains the emptiness of the surrounding countryside, little of which is farmed today. The hills are dotted with Byzantine **chapels**, which suggests that, in its heyday, the area must have been the centre of medieval Kýthira; it is rumoured to have once had eight hundred inhabitants and 72 churches. Now the principal remains are of the surviving churches, some still with traces of frescoes (but kept firmly locked), and the castle. The site is unenclosed and has never been seriously investigated.

If you have your own transport, there's a road to Paleohóra, signposted off the main road from Potamós just north of Aroniádhika: the first 2.4km is asphalt, the remainder driveable gravel. By foot, it's more interesting to take the path from the tiny village of Trifyliánika, just outside Potamós – look out for a rusting sign to the right as you enter the village. The path is overgrown in parts and not easy to follow; the ruins only become visible when you join the road above the gorge.

Karavás

KARAVÁS, 6km north of Potamós, has architecture and a setting – above a deep, partly wooded valley with a stream – which are more reminiscent of the Ionian islands. There is nowhere to stay, but there is a popular **restaurant**, *Amir Ali*, providing a large range of mezédhes (and sometimes live music) in a shady, streamside setting at the northern end of the village, off the road to Platiá Ámmos; food is also available at the German-run *Maina* ("mynah").

Platiá Ámmos, at the end of the valley, and en route to the lighthouse at the island's northern tip, is a sandy beach with a seasonal fish **taverna**. There is also an ouzerí, café, the *Modeas* restaurant, and several **rooms** establishments of which the best is the *Akrotiri* (☎07360/33 216; ❹). Winter storm damage in late 2000 washed away part of the access road, which awaits repair. The little pebble beach at **Foúrni**, 2km south by dirt road, is more attractive.

Kapsáli

KAPSÁLI, in addition to its harbour function, is the one place on Kýthira largely devoted to tourism although much of it closes down from September to June. Most foreign visitors to Kýthira in summer stay here, and it's a popular port of call for yachts heading from the Aegean to the Ionian islands and Italy, particularly since it is sheltered from the strong north winds of summer. Set behind double pebble-and-sand bays, overlooked by Hóra castle, and backed by high grey cliffs on which the tiny white monastery of Áyios Ioánnis Éngremmos perches, it is certainly picturesque. The larger of its two bays has a line of **tavernas**; *Vlastos* is one of the earliest to open in the season, with fish, local dishes, and its speciality, cockerel (*kókoras*) in wine; *Venetsianiko*, halfway along the front, has good food at reasonable prices, but the best is *Hydragogio* at the Hóra end of the beach which serves up good veggie options. For nightlife the liveliest place is *Shaker*, playing the standard mix of Greek and foreign hits.

The best **accommodation** is in high demand and expensive. Top of the tree is the *Porto Delfino* (☎07360/31 940; April–Oct; ❻); a few hundred metres above the bay are *Kalokerines Katikies* (☎ & ❺ 07360/31 265; May–Oct; ❻) and *Hotel Raikos* (☎07360/31 629, ❺31 801; May–Sept; ❻). The *Afroditi Apartments* (☎07360/31 328; ❻) have slightly more reasonable rates, as do *Megaloudi* rooms (☎07360/31 340; ❺). A very basic **campsite** (June–Sept) nestles in the pine trees behind the village.

There's a mobile **post office** in summer, and Panayiotis (☎07360/31 600, ❺31 789, ✉panayoti@otenet.gr) rents **cars**, **motorbikes** and **scooters**, as well as canoes and pedalboats; you can call off-season (☎094/4263757) and get wheels when most places are closed.

Hóra

HÓRA (or Kýthira Town), a steep 2km haul above Kapsáli, has an equally dramatic site, its Cycladic-style houses tiered on the ridge leading to the Venetian **castle**. Access to the fortress is up a modern pathway, but, to the right of this, the original narrow tunnel entrance is still usable. Within the walls, most of the buildings are in ruins, except the paired churches of Panayía Myrtidhiótissa and the smaller Panayía Orfaní (these were Catholic and Orthodox respectively, under the Venetian occupation), and the office of the archives of Kýthira opposite. There are spectacular views down to Kapsáli and out to sea to the striking chunk of inaccessible islet known as Avgó (Egg), legendary birthplace of Aphrodite. On the cliffs grow the yellow-flowered everlasting (*sempreviva*), used locally for making small dried flower arrangements. Below the castle are both the remains of older Byzantine walls and, in Mésa Vouryó, numerous well-signed but securely locked Byzantine churches. A small **museum** (Tues–Sun 8.30am–3pm; free) at the junction of the Hóra–Kapsáli road, houses modest remnants (labelled only in Greek) of the island's numerous occupiers, in particular Minoan finds from excavations at Paleópoli and an Archaic stone lion, as well as a telling selection of gravestones from the English cemetery. The Stavros bookshop, almost opposite, sells a book of walks (mainly in the southern half of the island; a walk book in German has more complete coverage).

Compared with Kapsáli, Hóra stays quiet and many places are closed out of season. Kythira Travel (☎07360/31 390) are agents for the hydrofoils. Other facilities include a couple of **banks**, a **post office** and a branch of Panayiotis vehicle rental (☎07360/31 004). A few **tavernas** open in summer, of which *Zorba* is by far the best, but the climb from Kapsáli discourages the crowds. A popular bar is *Mercato*, which stays open in the winter and also has exhibitions of local art. **Accommodation** is slightly easier to find than in Kapsáli. Options include the *Castello Studios* (☎07360/31 069; ❹), and the *Hotel Margarita* (☎07360/31 711, ⓕ31 325; ❻) in a beautiful 1840s house, with air conditioning and TV in the rooms. The *Xenonas Keiti/Keti/Kaiti* (☎07360/31 318; April–Oct; ❻) has non-smoking rooms in a large 240-year-old characterful house which has seen General Metaxas and George Papandreou as visitors. At **MANITOHÓRI**, 2km further inland, is the more basic *Pension Kythera* (☎07360/31 563; June–Aug; ❸).

The southeast coast

The beach at Kapsáli is decent but not large and gets very crowded in July and August. For quieter, undeveloped beaches, it's better to head out to the east coast, towards Avlémonas.

Firí Ámmos, Kombonádha and Halkós beaches, and Spiliés cave

Firí Ámmos, the nearest good sand beach to Kapsáli, is popular but not overcrowded, even in summer. To get there, you can follow paved roads from Kapsáli or Livádhi as far as the *Filio* taverna (June–Sept; with good traditional food and local specialities) in the scattered settlement of Kálamos; the onward road becomes a four-kilometre dirt track to the beach. Firí Ámmos can also be reached by a second dirt track off the Livádhi–Kálamos road, while another, longer, dirt track, off the Káto Livádhi–Frátsia road leads to **Kombonádha**, the next beach north. There are summer canteens at both beaches. Much smaller, but prettier **Halkós** beach near the southeast corner of the island is signposted from the crossroads at the entrance to Kálamos. Between Kálamos and Kapsáli, a short surfaced road leads south to **Spiliés** village; immediately before the village a signed earth road leads down to a small gorge and a large stalagmite cave with an open-roofed church dedicated to Ayía Sofia (not to be confused with the sea cave near Mylopótamos).

Paleópoli and Avlémonas

PALEÓPOLI, a hamlet of a few scattered houses, is accessible by asphalt roads from Aroniádhika, Frátsia and Kondoliánika. The area is the site of the ancient city of **Skandia**, and excavations on the headland of **Kastrí** have revealed remains of an important Minoan colony. There's little visible evidence, apart from shards of pottery in the low crumbling cliffs, but happily, tourist development in the area has been barred because of its archeological significance. Consequently, there's just one solitary **taverna**, the *Skandia* (June–Oct), on the two-kilometre sand-and-pebble **beach** that stretches to either side of the headland. This place has recently been taken over by seven hippieish Anglo-Greek siblings and has a great atmosphere with home cooking and frequent spontaneous musical evenings.

Paleokástro, the mountain to the west, is the site of ancient Kýthira where there was a sanctuary of Aphrodite, but again, there's little to be seen today. Heading west from Paleópoli, and crossing the river bridge onto the Kondoliánika road, an unpaved road off to the left leads up to a tiny, white-washed church. From there, a rougher track leads down to **Kaladhí**, a beautiful cliff-backed pebble beach with caves, and rocks jutting out to sea.

AVLÉMONAS, on a rocky shoreline 2km east of Paleópoli, is a small fishing port with a bleak end-of-the-world feel as you approach from a distance. It becomes much more attractive once reached, and has a remarkable co-ordination of colour schemes throughout the village. There is a small, unimpressive Venetian fortress, and two **tavernas**, of which *Sotiris* is particularly recommended for a wide selection of fresh, well-prepared and reasonably-priced fish dishes. There are a number of **rooms**, including the swish new apartments of Popi Kastrisiou (☎07360/33 735; ❺), and the older, air-conditioned *Schina* studios (☎07360/33 060; ❹). The Petrohilos family has a number of rooms or studios, including those of Evdokhia (☎07360/34 069; ❹) opposite the *Sotiris*.

North and west of Hóra

LIVÁDHI, 4km north of Hóra, has **rooms** and, on the main road, the *Hotel Aposperides* (☎07360/31 656, ℻31 688; ❺) which, together with the adequate *Toxotis* restaurant opposite, would make a good base if you had transport. Livádhi is also home to the most efficient travel agency on the island, Porfyra Travel, which is the main ANEK/ANEN and Olympic agent (☎07360/31 888, ℻31 889, ✉porfyra@kythira.com), with exchange and car rental; they can also arrange accommodation or transfers.

At **Káto Livádhi**, a kilometre to the east of Livádhi, there is a small museum of Byzantine and post-Byzantine art (Tues–Sun 8.30am–2pm; free) next to the large central church. It contains (labelled in Greek only) frescoes, painstakingly removed from island churches, dating from the twelfth to the eighteenth centuries, a seventh-century mosaic floor and some portable icons. Not far away there is also a co-operative pottery workshop (open all day except 2–4pm) and, on the road to Katoúni, a multiple-arched bridge, said to be the longest stone bridge in Greece and a legacy of the nineteenth century when all the Ionian islands were a British protectorate; like others on the island it was built by a Scottish engineer called McPhail. The best view of it is from beside *Rena's zaharoplastío* in Livádhi. A popular **taverna** nearby is the *Theofilos*.

From Livádhi, a side road heads west to Kalokerinés, and continues 3.6km further to the island's principal monastery, **Myrtidhíon**, set above the wild and windswept west coast, among a dead forest of pines burned in June 2000. The monastery's main icon is said to date from 1160. Beyond the monastery, a track leads down to a small anchorage at **Limnária**; there are few beaches along this rocky, forbidding shore. An early left fork off the Myrtidhíon road out of Livádhi brings you through the hamlet of Poúrko and past the unusual Byzantine church of Áyios Dimítrios. From Poúrko, an increasingly steep road leads up to the **Ayía Elésis**, a nineteenth-century monastery marking the martyrdom of the saint on the hilltop in 375 AD, an event depicted in recent wall-paintings inside the church. For many visitors, however the breathtaking view from the western side of the courtyard is the main reason to visit.

Mylopótamos, Káto Hóra and the Ayía Sofía cave

North of Livádhi, just beyond Dhókana, it is worth making a detour off the main road for **MYLOPÓTAMOS**, a lovely traditional village and an oasis in summer, set in a wooded valley occupied by a small stream. The shady *Platanos* kafenío makes a pleasant stop for a drink above the village's springs and *To Kamari*, in an old restored building, serves snacks and drinks on a lower waterside terrace. Follow the signs for "Katarraktis Neraidha" to find a waterfall, hidden from view by lush vegetation, next to a long-closed café. The valley below the falls is overgrown but contains the remains of the watermill that gave the village its name.

Káto Hóra (Kástro Mylopotamoú), 500m down the road, was Mylopótamos's predecessor, and remains half-enclosed within the walls of a Venetian fortress. The fortress is small, full of locked, well-labelled churches, and has a rather domestic appearance: unlike the castle at Hóra, it was built as a place of refuge for the villagers in case of attack, rather than as a base for a Venetian garrison. All the houses within the walls are abandoned – as are many outside – but are open and accessible. Beyond here, a surfaced but briefly precipitous road continues 5km through spectacular cliffscapes to **Limniónas**, a rocky inlet with a small sand beach, but a fire in June 2000 has left the surrounding countryside unattractive and bereft of vegetation.

The reason most visitors come to Mylopótamos is to see the **cave of Ayía Sofía**, the largest and most impressive of a number of caverns on the island. A half-hour signposted walk from the village, or a short drive by a new dirt road being constructed off the Limniónas road, the cave is open regularly from mid-June to mid-September (Mon–Fri 3–8pm, Sat & Sun 11am–5pm; €2.50). When the cave is closed, you can probably find a guide in Mylopótamos; ask at the village, giving a day's notice if possible. The cave is worth the effort to see: the entrance has been used as a church and has an iconostasis carved from the rock, with important Byzantine frescoes on it. Beyond, the cave system comprises a series of chambers which reach 250m into the mountain, although the thirty-minute guided tour (in Greek and English) only takes in the more interesting outer chambers. These include some startling formations like the "shark's teeth", but you have to ask to be shown "Aphrodite's chambers". A minute new species of disc-shaped insect has been discovered there.

Andikýthira island

Thirteen kilometres to the south of Kýthira, the tiny, wind-blown island of **ANDIKÝTHIRA** has, theoretically, a twice-weekly connection with Crete on the Kýthira–Kastélli–Kýthira run; landings are often impossible due to adverse weather. There are attempts to organize a ferry from Kýthira on August 17 for the festival of Áyios Mýron, returning the following day, but these are frequently thwarted by the wind. Rocky and poor, the island only received electricity in 1984. Attractions include good birdlife and flora, but it's not the place if you want company: with only seventy or so inhabitants divided among a scattering of settlements – mainly in **Potamós**, the harbour, and **Sohória**, the village – people are rather thin on the ground. A resident doctor and a teacher serve the dwindling community (there are three children at the village school, compared with nearly forty in the 1960s). The only official accommodation is the set of **rooms** run by the local community (☎07360/31 390, ℱ33 471) at Potamós, which also has the sole **taverna**, but you'd be recommended to bring plenty of supplies with you. In Sohória the only provisions available are basic foodstuffs at the village shop.

Yíthio (Gythion)

YÍTHIO, Sparta's ancient port, is the gateway to the dramatic Máni peninsula, and one of the south's most attractive seaside towns in its own right. Its somewhat low-key harbour, with occasional ferries to Pireás and Kýthira, gives onto a graceful nineteenth-century waterside of tiled-roof houses – some of them now showing their age. There's a beach within walking distance and rooms are relatively easy to find. In the bay, tethered by a long narrow mole, is the **islet of Marathonísi**, ancient Kranae, where Paris of Troy, having abducted Helen from Menelaus's palace at Sparta, dropped anchor, and where the lovers spent their first night.

The Town

Marathonísi is the town's main sight, a pleasant place to while away an hour or so in the early evening, with swimming off the rocks towards the lighthouse. Amid the island's trees and scrub stands the restored Tzannetákis tower-fortress built around 1810 by the Turkish-appointed Bey of the Máni, to guard the harbour against his lawless countrymen. It now houses a **Museum of the Máni** (officially 9.30am–3pm, though often closed; €1.50), which deals with the exploration of the Máni from Ciriaco de Pizzicoli (1447) to Henri Belle (1861), with captions in Greek and English.

For an aerial view of the islet and town, climb up through Yíthio's stepped streets on to the hill behind – the town's ancient acropolis. The settlement around it, known as **Laryssion**, was quite substantial in Roman times, enjoying wealth from the export of murex, the purple-pigmented mollusc used to dye imperial togas.

Much of the ancient site now lies submerged but there are some impressive remains of a **Roman theatre** to be seen at the northeast end of the town. Follow the road past the post office for about 300m, until you reach the army barracks – the site stands just to the left, inside the outer gate. With most of its stone seats intact, and 50m in diameter, the theatre illustrates perfectly how buildings in Greece take on different guises through the ages: built to one side is a Byzantine church (now ruined) which, in turn, has been pressed into service as the outer wall of the barracks. The archeological museum is currently under restoration, but possesses items from Yíthio and the Lakonian Máni. For some more recent history, visit poet Kostas Vrettos' antiquities shop, Paliatzoures, at Vassiléos Pávlou 25.

Beaches near Yíthio

For swimming, there are a number of places within reach of Yíthio, on both sides of which rise an intermittent sequence of cliffs. To the southeast, the six-kilometre **beach** at Mavrovoúni, by the campsites detailed below, is one of the best but can be very busy, as can the smaller, pebbly Selinítza beach north of the town. Many of the buses serving Yíthio from Spárti routinely continue to Mavrovoúni, but ask on board to be sure. Alternatively, if you've got your own transport, there are the superb beaches in Vathý Bay, further along, off the Areópoli road (see p.233). To the north (7km) the little beach of Trínisa ("three islands") is kept clean by the *Afroditi* café. The coastline eastwards from Trínisa to Kokkiniá has nesting turtles, and the Evrótas delta and Dhivári lagoon are significant migratory bird sites, while the extensive dune areas around the Evrótas are botanically important as refuges for several rare endemic species.

Practicalities

The **bus station** is close to the centre of town, with the main waterfront street, **Vassiléos Pávlou**, right ahead of you, and three **banks** nearby. Moto Makis near the causeway, on the Areópoli road (☎07330/25 111), has **motorbikes and scooters** for rent. You can check **ferry** sailings at the Rozaki Shipping and Travel Agency (☎07330/22 650, ⓕ22 229) on the waterfront; the latter also do **car rental** and will change travellers' cheques and money. An EOT office at Vassiléos Yeoryíou 20 appears to be permanently closed. A trip of at least three days is worth considering for the Máni; the extensive and security-conscious Hasanakos **bookstore** is worth scouring for books on the Máni, and food supplies can be bought from the large supermarket behind the bus station.

Accommodation

Finding **accommodation** shouldn't be hard, with a fair selection of hotels and rooms in town – most along the waterfront, signposted up the steps behind, or facing Marathonísi islet. Despite double-glazing in a number of the waterfront rooms on Vassiléos Pávlou, there is late-night noise from the many music-bars. Out along Mavrovoúni beach, which begins 3km south of the town off the Areópoli road, there are numerous rooms and three **campsites**. The nearest and best of these is the *Meltemi* (☎07330/23 260; April–Oct); a couple of kilometres further on are the *Gythion Bay* (☎07330/22 522) and *Mani Beach* (☎07330/23 450; mid-April to mid-Oct).

Cavo Grosso, ☎07330/22 897, ⓕ23 823. Luxury apartments in Mavrovoúni village. ⑥

Githion, Vassiléos Pávlou 33, ☎07330/23 452, ⓕ23 523. A fine old (1864) hotel on the waterfront, the site of the first poker game played in Greece; good value for money. ④

Kalypso, ☎07330/24 449, ⓕ22 265. Just off the main road, in Mavrovoúni, opposite the *Milton Hotel*. Very good-value rooms with kitchens, air-con and magnificent sea views over Yíthio Bay. ④

Kondogiannis, Vassiléos Pávlou 19 ☎07330/22 518. A small, friendly pension, recently refurbished, up steep steps alongside – and above –

the management's jewellery shop, and next to the police station. ③

Kranai, Vassiléos Pávlou 17, ☎ & ⓕ 07330/24 394. On the waterfront, near *Kondogiannis*; try for a room at the front with a balcony. The restaurant below is very popular. ④

Saga, Tzanetáki ☎07330/23 220, ⓕ24 370. Pension run by a French family, with a restaurant on the ground floor, overlooking the Marathonísi islet. ③

Spanakas rooms, ☎07330/22 490. Homely pension on Vassiléos Yeoryíou – the route into town from Spárti – next to the Panayiotopoulou supermarket. ③

Eating and drinking

For **meals**, the waterside is the obvious location – though choose carefully from among the tavernas since most have inflated prices for fish and seafood. By the small roundabout at the inner end of the harbour, the unpretentious *Korali Ouzeri* has well-prepared food at reasonable prices. Nearby, cheaper still, but with good food and water's-edge tables, is the *Iy Nautilia* ouzerí with excellent seafood and tasty mezédhes, and fine views of the waterfront, sunsets and Mount Profitis Ilías. Both are popular with the locals.

The Máni

The southernmost peninsula of Greece, **the Máni**, stretches from Yíthio in the east to Kardhamýli in the west and terminates at Cape Ténaro, the mythical

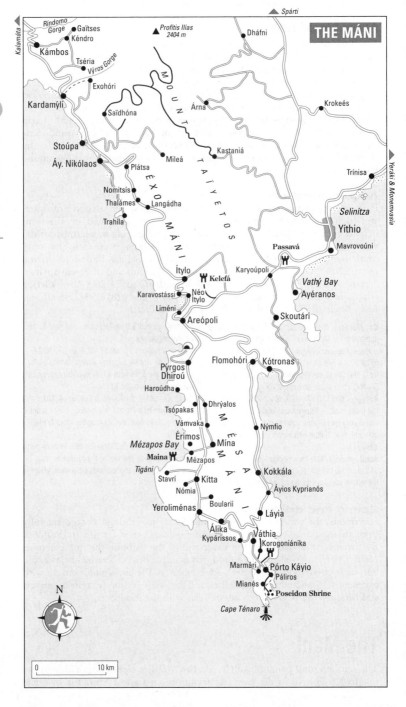

THE MÁNI

Practicalities in the Máni

Getting around can be time-consuming unless you have your own transport, and you may want to consider renting a **scooter** or **motorbike** from Yíthio or Kalamáta, or a **car** from Stoúpa or Kalamáta. Without a vehicle, you will need to walk or hitch to supplement the buses. In Mésa Máni, there are just two services: Areópoli–Yeroliménas–Váthia (daily in summer; three weekly out of season) and Areópoli–Kótronas–Láyia (daily), with the Váthia section being unreliable.

An alternative is to make use of the handful of **taxis**, generally negotiable at Areópoli, Yeroliménas, Kótronas and Yíthio. Currently, for example, a taxi from Areópoli to Váthia would cost €25, and then you could return by bus.

The Mésa Máni has a **bank** at Areópoli (Mon, Wed & Fri 9am–noon). You can sometimes change cash at the **post offices** (Mon–Fri 7.30am–2pm) in Yeroliménas or Areópoli, but it's wiser to bring as much as you think you'll need from either Yíthio or Kalamáta. **Opening hours** of shops, tavernas and almost anything else can be idiosyncratic in the Mésa Máni, so it may also prove wise to bring some general supplies with you – there are well-stocked supermarkets in Yíthio, Stoúpa and Kalamáta.

---

entrance to the underworld. Its spine, negotiated by road at just a few points, is the vast grey mass of Mount Taïyetos and its southern extension, Sangiás. It is a wild landscape, an arid Mediterranean counterpart to Cornwall, or the Scottish highlands, with an idiosyncratic culture and history to match. Nowhere in Greece does a region seem so close to its violent medieval past – which continued largely unaltered until the end of the nineteenth century. Despite, or perhaps because of this, the sense of hospitality is, like nearby Crete, as strong as anywhere in Greece.

The peninsula has two distinct regions: the Éxo (Outer) Máni and the Mésa (Inner or Deep) Máni. The **Mésa Máni** – that part of the peninsula south of a line drawn between Ítylo and Vathý bays – is classic Máni territory, its jagged coast relieved only by the occasional cove, and its land a mass of rocks. It has one major sight, the remarkable caves at **Pýrgos Dhiroú**, which are now very much on the tourist circuit. Beyond this point tourist numbers thin out fast. The attractions include the coastal villages, like **Yeroliménas** on the west coast, or **Kótronas** on the east, but the pleasure is mainly in exploring the **tower-houses** and **churches**, and the solitude. A fair number of the towers survive, their groupings most dramatic at **Kítta**, **Váthia** and **Flomohóri**. The churches are subtler and harder to find, often hidden away from actual villages, but worth the effort. Many were built during the tenth and twelfth centuries, when the Maniots enthusiastically embraced Christianity; almost all retain at least traces of frescoes though many are kept locked, with elusive wardens.

The **Éxo Máni** – the coast up from Areópoli to Kalamáta, much of it in Messinía province – sees the emphasis shift much more to walking and beaches. **Stoúpa** and **Kardhamýli** are both beautiful resorts, developing now but far from spoiled. The road itself is an experience, threading precipitously up into the foothills of Taïyetos before looping down to the sea.

Some Maniot history

The **mountains** offer the key to Maniot history. Formidable natural barriers, they provided a refuge from, and bastion of resistance to, every occupying force of the last two millennia. The Dorians never reached this far south in the wake of the Mycenaeans. Roman occupation was perfunctory and Christianity did not take root in the interior until the ninth century (some five hundred years after the establishment of Byzantium). Throughout the years of Venetian and

Maniot blood feuds

Blood feuds were the result of an intricate **feudal society** that seems to have developed across the peninsula in the fourteenth century. After the arrival of refugee Byzantine families, an aristocracy known as **Nyklians** arose, and the various clans gradually developed strongholds in the tightly clustered villages. The poor, rocky soil was totally inadequate for the population and over the next five centuries the **clans clashed** frequently and bloodily for land, power and prestige.

The feuds became ever more complex and gave rise to the building of strongholds: marble-roofed **battle towers** which, in the elaborate mores of the peninsula, could be raised only by those of Nyklian descent. From these local forts the clans – often based in the same village – conducted vendettas according to strict rules and aims. The object was to annihilate both the tower and the male members of the opposing clan. The favoured method of attack was to smash the prestigious tower roofs; the forts consequently rose to four and five storeys.

Feuds would customarily be signalled by the ringing of church bells and from this moment the adversaries would confine themselves to their towers, firing at each other with all available weaponry. The battles could last for years, even decades, with women (who were safe from attack) shuttling in food, ammunition and supplies. During the really **prolonged feuds**, temporary truces were declared at harvest times; then with business completed the battle would recommence. Ordinary villagers – the non-Nyklian peasantry – would, meanwhile, evacuate for the duration of the worst conflict. The feuds would end in one of two ways: destruction of a family in battle, or total surrender of a whole clan in a gesture of **psyhikó** ("a thing of the soul"), when they would file out to kiss the hands of enemy parents who had lost "guns" (the Maniot term for male children) in the feud; the victors would then dictate strict terms by which the vanquished could remain in the village.

The last full-scale feud took place as late as 1870, in the village of Kítta (see p.236), and required a full detachment of the regular army to put it down.

Turkish control of the Peloponnese there were constant rebellions, climaxing in the Maniot uprising on March 17, 1821, a week before Archbishop Yermanos raised the Greek flag at Kalávryta to officially launch the War of Independence.

Alongside this national assertiveness was an equally intense and violent internal tribalism, seen at its most extreme in the elaborate tradition of **blood feuds** (see box, above), probably prolonged, and certainly exploited, by the **Turks**. The first Maniot uprising against them had taken place in 1571, a year after the Ottoman occupation. There were to be renewed attempts through the succeeding centuries, with plots involving the Venetians, French and Russians. But the Turks, wisely, opted to control the Máni by granting a level of local autonomy, investing power in one or other clan whose leader they designated "Bey" of the region. The position provided a focus for the obsession with arms and war and worked well until the nineteenth-century appointment of **Petrobey Mavromihalis**. With a power base at Liméni he united the clans in revolution, and his Maniot army was to prove vital to the success of the War of Independence.

Unsurprisingly, the end of the war and the formation of an **independent Greece** did not mark the end of Maniot rebellion. Mavromihalis swiftly fell out with the first president of the nation, Kapodistrias and, with other members of the clan, was imprisoned by him at Náfplio – an act which led to the president's assassination at the hands of Petrobey's brothers. The monarchy fared little better until one of the king's German officers was sent to the Máni to enlist soldiers in a special Maniot militia. The idea was adopted with enthusiasm, and was the start of an enduring tradition of Maniot service in the modern Greek military.

Over the last hundred years or so, things have sadly been in decline, with persistent **depopulation** of the villages. In places like Váthia and Kítta, which once held populations in the hundreds, the numbers are now down to single figures, predominantly the old. Socially and politically the region is notorious as the most conservative in Greece. The Maniots reputedly enjoyed an influence during the colonels' junta, when the region first acquired roads, mains electricity and running water. They voted almost unanimously for the monarchy in the 1974 plebiscite, and this is one of the very few parts of Greece where you may still see visible support for the ex-king or the far-right National Party.

Into the Máni: Yíthio to Areópoli

The road from Yíthio into the Máni begins amid a fertile and gentle wooded landscape, running slightly inland of the coast and Mavrovoúni beach, through tracts of citrus and olive groves and between hilltop towers. About 12km beyond Yíthio, the Máni suddenly asserts itself as the road enters a gorge below the Turkish **castle of Passavá**. The castle is one of a pair (with Kelefá to the west) guarding the Máni or perhaps, more accurately, guarding against the Máni. Signed from near the Avin petrol station just to the west, it's quite a scramble up, with no regular path, but the site is ample reward, with views out across two bays and for some miles along the defile from Areópoli. There has been a fortress on Passavá since Mycenaean times; the present version is an eighteenth-century Turkish rebuilding of a Frankish fort (1210) that the Venetians destroyed on their flight from the Peloponnese in 1684. It was abandoned by the Turks in 1780 following the massacre of its garrison and their civilian dependants by the Maniot Grigorakis clan – their vengeance for the arrest and execution by the Turks of the clan chief.

Shortly after Passavá, a turning to the left leads down to an attractive long sandy beach at **Vathý Bay**, which is mostly used by German tourists and local gays. At the southern end of the beach is the grand *Hotel Belle Helene* (☎07330/93 001, ⓕ98 006; April–Oct; ❺), often block-booked by German groups; towards the north end, behind the reasonable *Gorgona* restaurant, the *Kronos* campsite (☎07330/93 320; mid-April to Oct) is well suited to families.

The road beyond the beach deteriorates rapidly, though it is possible to continue through woods to the village of **Ayéranos**, with a tower-house complex, and from there – if you can find your way among the numerous rough tracks – to Skoutári, below which is another reasonable beach with some Roman remains. A better road to Skoutári leaves the main Yíthio-Areópoli road near Karyoúpoli, itself dominated by an imposing tower-house.

Continuing towards Areópoli from Passavá, the landscape remains fertile until the wild, scrubby mass of Mount Kouskoúni signals the final approach to the Mésa Máni. You enter another pass, with **Kelefá castle** (see p.239) above to the north, and beyond it several southerly peaks of the Taïyetos ridge. Areópoli, as you curl down from the hills, radiates a real sense of arrival.

Areópoli and around

An austere-looking town, **AREÓPOLI** sets an immediate mood for the region. Until the nineteenth century it was secondary to Ítylo, 6km north and the gateway to the Mésa Máni, but the modern road has made it, to all intents, the region's centre. Formerly Tsímova, its present name ("Town of Ares" – the god of war) was bestowed for its efforts during the War of Independence. It was here that Mavromihalis (commemorated by a statue in the main platía) declared the uprising.

The town's sights are archetypally Maniot in their anachronisms. The **Áyii Taxiárhes** cathedral, for example, has primitive reliefs above its doors which look twelfth century until you notice their date of 1798. Similarly, the tower-houses could readily be described as medieval, though most of them were built in the early 1800s. On its own, in a little platía, is the church of **Áyios Ioánnis**, the Mavromihalis family church; the interior has strip-cartoon frescoes. Nearby a Byzantine museum is under construction in the Nikolakis tower.

Buses leave Areópoli from the shadeless main square, Platía Athánatos, where the *Europa Grill* is the ticket office; if you are heading north into Messinía, towards Kalamáta, you will probably need to change in Ítylo. On or just off the main platía are a **bank** (Tues & Thurs 9am–noon) with a cash dispenser, a **post office**, several *zaharoplastía*, a useful **supermarket** (especially if heading on south) and the Adhou oti Mani **bookshop**, with an extensive stock of books, mostly in Greek, on the Máni.

There are several **rooms** around the cathedral and two **hotels**: the *Kouris* (℡07330/51 340; ❹) on the main square, and the good-value *Mani* (℡07330/51 190, ℱ51 269; ❹) a few minutes from the square, and between the bank and the EKO petrol station. One of the towers, the *Pyrgos Kapetanakou* (℡07330/51 479; ❹), has been restored by the EOT as a traditional guesthouse; the rooms are austerely beautiful and well priced. Nearby is the upmarket *Londas* (℡07330/51 360, ℱ51 012; ❺), another converted tower-house. The cheaper *Pyrgos Tsimova* (℡07330/51 301; ❹) has more of a lived-in feel. There is a private war museum, covering about two hundred years, in the living room, with a Lewis gun perched on top of the dresser; the owner is a voluble storyteller and staunch royalist – the heroic "George of England" referred to in conversation about World War II (of which the owner is a veteran), is King George VI.

There are a number of **café-restaurants** around the main square; one of the most popular is *Nikola's Corner*, which does good mezédhes. The *inemayirio O Barba Petros* has a little courtyard off a pedestrian street towards *Pyrgos Kapetanakou*.

The Pýrgos Dhiroú caves

Eight kilometres south of Areópoli, at the village of **PÝRGOS DHIROÚ**, the road forks off to the underground caves – the Máni's major tourist attraction. The village itself has an isolated 21-metre tower-house, but is otherwise geared to the cave trade, with numerous tavernas and cafés, and a number of **rooms** for rent. The closest to the caves, and the sea, are at the *Panorama* restaurant (℡07330/52 280; ❹). The rooms have TV, air conditioning, impressive sea views, and the establishment has its own fishing boat. If you want to stay in the village itself, the run-down and overpriced *Hotel Diros* (℡07330/52 306; ❸) is an option.

The **Pýrgos Dhiroú caves** (daily: June–Sept 8am–5.30pm; Oct–May 8am–2.30pm; €12), often referred to as simply "Spílea", are 4km beyond the main village, set beside the sea and a small beach. They are very much a packaged attraction but, unless caves leave you cold, they are worth a visit, especially on weekday afternoons when the wait is shorter. A visit consists of a thirty-minute punt around the underground waterways of the **Glyfádha (Vlyhádha) caves**, well lit and crammed with stalactites, whose reflections are a remarkable sight in the two- to twenty-metre depth of water. You are then permitted a brief tour on foot of the **Alepótrypa caves** – huge chambers (one of them 100m by 60m) in which excavation has unearthed evidence of pre-historic occupation. Unfortunately there is no foreign-language commentary.

You should buy a ticket as soon as you arrive at the caves: this gives you a priority number for the tours. At a mid-season weekend you can wait for an hour or more, so it's best to arrive as early as possible in the day with gear to make the most of the adjacent beach. If time is short, taxis from Areópoli will take you to the caves, then wait and take you back; prices, especially split four ways, are reasonable.

The nearby **museum** (Tues–Sun 8.30am–3pm; €1.50) on a bend of road, contains interesting Neolithic finds from the caves; the few captions are in Greek, although a multilingual leaflet is promised. There is a café down at the end of the road.

South to Yeroliménas

The narrow, raised coastal plain between Pýrgos Dhiroú and Yeroliménas is one of the more fertile parts of the Mésa Máni with a uniform sprinkling of dwarf olive trees. This seventeen-kilometre stretch of the so-called "shadow coast" supported, until the twentieth century, an extraordinary number of small villages. The main road carefully avoids most of them, but many are sited just a kilometre or so to the east or west of it. Very few villages have shops, or facilities such as public phones, so you should carry sufficient water if walking. The area retains a major concentration of **churches**, many of them Byzantine, dating from the ninth to the fourteenth centuries. Though many are now signposted, they can still be hard to find, but are well detailed in Peter Greenhalgh's *Deep Into Mani* (see p.1092). The main feature to look for is a barrel roof. Almost all are kept locked, though a key can sometimes be found by asking around.

Among Greenhalgh's favourites on the seaward side are the eleventh-century **church of the Taxiárhis** at Haroúdha (3km south of Pýrgos Dhiroú), **Trissákia church** by a reservoir near Tsópakas (5km south of Pýrgos Dhiroú) and **Ayía Varvára** at Érimos (8km south of Pýrgos Dhiroú).

Mézapos and the Castle of the Maina

An easier excursion from the main road is to the small village of **MÉZAPOS**, whose deep-water harbour made it one of the chief settlements of Máni, until the road was built in the twentieth century. From the main road, take the side road to Áyios Yeóryios and then to Mézapos, where there are a few rooms. The best of some fine coastal walks leads to the twelfth-century **church of Vlahérna**, which has a few fresco fragments, including a memorable John the Baptist. If you ask at one of the cafés in Mézapos it's sometimes possible to negotiate a boat trip out to Tigáni, or even around the cape to Yeroliménas.

The nearby village of **STAVRÍ** offers traditional **tower-house accommodation** in the converted *Tsitsiris Castle* complex (☎07330/56 297; ❺), much the same price as the tower hotels in Areópoli and Váthia, though much bigger and in a remoter, more exciting setting. The broader plateau here has a confusing network of small, unsigned roads, and even the best maps are hopelessly inadequate. To the north of Stavrí, but within walking distance, is the twelfth-century **church of Episkopí**; the roof has been restored, while inside there are some fine but faded frescoes, and columns crowned by Ionic capitals, with a surprising marble arch at the entry to the iconostasis. Head from Stavrí to the deserted hamlet of **Ayía Kyriakí** for good views, and access to the castle on the bare **Tigáni** ("Frying Pan") **peninsula**. The fortress, by general consensus, seems to have been the **Castle of the Maina**, constructed like those of Mystra and Monemvasiá by the Frankish baron, Guillaume de Villehardouin, and ceded with them to the Byzantines in 1261. Tigáni is as arid a site as any in Greece – a dry Monemvasiá in effect – whose fortress seems scarcely man-made, blending as it does into the terrain. It's a jagged walk out to the castle across rocks fashioned into pans for salt-gathering; within the walls are ruins of a huge Byzantine church and numerous cisterns.

Kítta and Boulariï

Continuing along the main road, **KÍTTA**, once the largest and most powerful village in the region, boasts the crumbling remains of more than twenty tower-houses. It was here in 1870 that the last feudal war took place, only being suppressed by a full battalion of four hundred regular soldiers. Over to the west, visible from the village, is another eruption of tower-houses at Kítta's traditional rival, Nómia.

Two kilometres south of Kítta and east of the main road, **BOULARIÏ** is one of the most interesting and accessible villages in the Mésa Máni. It is clearly divided into "upper" and "lower" quarters, both of which retain well-preserved tower-houses and, in varying states of decay, some twenty churches. The two most impressive are tenth-century **Áyios Pandelímon** (enclosed and locked, with two frescoes that are the earliest in the Máni) and eleventh-century **Áyios Stratigós**, which is just over the brow of the hill at the top of the village. This second church is also kept locked but there are keys with the priest at Eliá village and possibly at the Yeroliménas post office. Entry is well rewarded for the church possesses a spectacular series of frescoes from the twelfth to the eighteenth centuries.

Cape Ténaro (Yeroliménas and south to Mátapan)

After the journey from Areópoli, **YEROLIMÉNAS** (Yerolimín) feels like a village in limbo, of uncertain purpose, but it does make a good base for exploring the southern extremities of the Máni. Despite appearances, the village was only developed in the 1870s – around a jetty and warehouses built by a local (a non-Nyklian migrant) who had made good on the island of Sýros. There are a few shops, a **post office**, a couple of **cafés** and two **hotels**. Of these, the *Akroyiali* (☎07330/54 204, ℻54 272; ❸) is the more comfortable, with some air-conditioned rooms and apartments; a new wing has been added, in traditional style stonework. The *Akrotenaritis* (☎ & ℻ 07330/54 205; ❷), in two buildings, has cheaper rooms with shared facilities in the old part. A couple of other places have rooms with kitchenettes. There are several **eating options** between the two hotels, but the baked fish in lemon juice and olive oil served at the *Akroyiali* takes some beating.

At the dock, occasional boat trips are offered – when the local owners feel like it - around Cape Ténaro, formerly known as Cape Mátapan (see opposite).

Álika to Pórto Káyio and Marmári

South from Yeroliménas, a good road (and the bus) continues to **Álika**, where it divides. One fork leads east through the mountains to Láyia (see opposite), and the other continues to Váthia and across the Marmári isthmus to Páliros. Between Álika and Váthia there are good coves for swimming. One of the best is a place known as **Kypárissos**, reached by following a river bed (dry in summer) about midway to Váthia. On the headland above are scattered Roman remains of ancient Kaenipolis, including (amid the walled fields) the excavated ruins of a sixth-century basilica.

VÁTHIA, a group of tower-houses set uncompromisingly on a scorching mass of high hillside rocks, is one of the most dramatic villages in the Mésa Máni. It features in Colonel Leake's account of his travels, one of the best sources on Greece in the early nineteenth century. He was warned to avoid going through the village in 1805 as a feud had been running between two families for the previous forty years. Today it has the feel of a ghost town. The EOT finally completed its lengthy restoration of a dozen tower-houses to accommodate guests, but the project fell through in 1998.

From Váthia the road south to the cape starts out uphill, edging around the mountain, before slowly descending to a junction. Left brings you down to the beach and laid-back hamlet of **PÓRTO KÁYIO** (7km from Váthia). There are comfortable **rooms** at the *Akroteri* (☎07330/52 013; ❹), and two or three **tavernas**, the best of which is the *Hippocampos*. Across the bay on the north side are the spectacular ruins of a Turkish fortress contemporary with Kelefá and the monastery of Korogoniánika. Above the village, the right branch of the road goes south along the headland, capped by a Maniot tower, to pleasant sandy **beaches** at the double bay of Marmári. Rooms and good food with a sea view are available above the first beach at *To Marmari* (☎07330/52 101; ❸).

On to Cape Ténaro
Starting from the sign to Páliros and the left fork before Marmári, follow the signs on the dirt road – after the second Páliros junction – for the fish taverna, *To Akrotenaro*. After you've wound your way over the Máni's last barren peninsula and down to the taverna, where rooms should be available, the road ends in a knoll crowned with the squat **chapel of Asómati**, constructed largely of materials from an ancient temple of Poseidon.

To the left (east) as you face the chapel is the little pebbly **bay of Asómati**; on the shore is a small **cave**, another addition to the list of sites said to be the mythical entrance to the underworld. Patrick Leigh Fermor, in *Mani*, writes of yet another "Gates of Hades" cave, which he swam into on the western side of the point, just below Marmári. To the right (west) of the Asómati hill, the main path, marked by red dots, continues along the edge of another cove and through the metre-high foundations of a **Roman town** that grew up around the Poseidon shrine; there is even a mosaic in one structure. From here the old trail, which existed before the road was bulldozed, reappears as a walled path, allowing 180-degree views of the sea on its twenty-five-minute course to the lighthouse on **Cape Ténaro**.

The east coast
The east coast of the Mésa Máni is most easily approached from **Areópoli**, where there's a daily **bus** through Kótronas to Láyia. However, if you have transport, or you're prepared to walk and hitch, there's satisfaction in doing a full loop of the peninsula, crossing over to Láyia from Yeroliménas or Pórto Káyio. The east-coast landscape is more barren than the west, little more than scrub and prickly pears. This is the Mésa Máni's "sunward coast", harsher than the "shadow coast" of the west side. There are few beaches, and less coastal plain, with most of the scattered villages hanging on the hillsides.

Láyia to Kokkála
From the fork at Álika (see opposite), it's about a ninety-minute walk by road to **LÁYIA**. Coming from Pórto Káyio it takes around three hours, though

the route, at times on narrow tracks, is more dramatic, passing the virtually deserted hilltop village of **Korogoniánika**. A turning off left, not far above Álika, to Moundanístika, the Máni's highest village, is recommended for spectacular views. Láyia itself is a multi-towered village that perfectly exemplifies the feudal setup of the old Máni. Four Nyklian families lived here, and their four independently sited settlements, each with its own church, survive. One of the taller towers, so the locals claim, was built overnight by the four hundred men of one clan, hoping to gain an advantage at sunrise. During the eighteenth century the village was home to a Maniot doctor – a strategic base from which to attend profitably to the war-wounded all across the peninsula. Today there is a single kafenío, with a few snacks, but the village is showing healthy signs of revival, with ongoing repair and refurbishment of a number of houses.

The first village beyond Láyia, down near the sea, is **ÁYIOS KYPRIANÓS**. It has a few rooms, though the proprietor may prove elusive. Five kilometres on is **KOKKÁLA**, a larger, though visually unexciting, village, enclosed by a rare patch of greenery. It has a small harbour and scruffy beach, a longer beach to the north and walking possibilities. Three kilometres to the northwest, on the mountainside above Nýmfio, is one of the area's few ancient sites, a spot known as Kiónia (columns), with the foundations of two Doric temples. The village boasts several café-restaurants, and rooms for rent above the *Taverna Marathos* (summer only; ☎07330/21 118; ❸) on the beach. Newer is the smart but friendly *Hotel Soloteri* (☎07330/21 126; ❸), which may be the only place open out of high season.

Flomohóri and Kótronas

A further 22km northwards along this comparatively empty coastline, brings you to **FLOMOHÓRI**; the land below is relatively fertile, and the village has maintained a reasonable population as well as a last imposing group of tower-houses. **KÓTRONAS**, a few kilometres downhill, feels like another, softer country. It is still a fishing village, and its pebble beach (there are sandy strips further around the bay) and causeway-islet make it a good last stop in the region. The village is frequented by a fair number of tourists (mainly Germans) each summer, and has a trio of pensions. The most pleasant is the well-priced *Kali Kardia* (aka *4-Asteria*; ☎07330/21 246; ❷) above a seafront café. The coastal dirt road from here to Skoutári, and hence Yíthio, is being widened and paved – when completed there will be no further need to head west across the peninsula back to Areópoli.

The Éxo Máni: Areópoli north to Kalamáta

The forty kilometres of road into Messinía, between Areópoli and Kalamáta, is as dramatic and beautiful as any in Greece, almost a corniche route between the **Taïyetos** ridge and the **Gulf of Messinía**. The first few settlements en route are classic Maniot villages, their towers packed against the hillside. As you move north, with the road dropping to near sea level, there are three or four small resorts, which are becoming increasingly popular but are as yet relatively unspoiled. For walkers, there is a reasonably well-preserved *kalderími* parallelling (or short-cutting) much of the paved route, with a superb **gorge hike** just north of Kardhamýli, and Stoúpa as a good base for local exploration and touring.

North to Liméni

Areópoli stands back a kilometre or so from the sea. **LIMÉNI**, the town's tiny traditional port, lies 3km to the north: a scattering of houses dominated by the restored tower-house of Petrobey Mavromihalis, which resembles nothing so much as an English country parish church. On one of the bends on the road down to Liméni is the newish *Limeni Village* (☎07330/51 111; ⑥), a re-creation of Maniot houses, high above the rocky shore and with its own swimming pool. Further round the bay, on the waterside, there are a few tavernas including *To Limeni*, which has basic rooms (☎07330/51 458; ③).

Ítylo and around

ÍTYLO (Oítylo), 11km from Areópoli, is the transport hub for the region. If you are heading into Messinía province towards Kalamáta, either from Yíthio or Areópoli, you will probably need to change here, at the *Petrini Gonia* café. While waiting for the bus, walk a short distance down to the main church – perched on a balcony overlooking the bay and with a pointed memorial to civil-war dead. The village is currently experiencing a resurgence in fortunes, with many of the old houses, until recently falling into disrepair, now being restored. In earlier days, Ítylo was the capital of the Máni, and from the sixteenth to the eighteenth century it was the region's most notorious base for piracy and slave trading. The Maniots traded amorally and efficiently in slaves, selling Turks to Venetians, Venetians to Turks, and, at times of feud, the women of each others' clans to both. Irritated by the piracy and hoping to control the important pass to the north, the Turks built the sprawling **castle of Kelefá** in 1670. This is just a kilometre's walk from Ítylo across a gorge, and its walls and bastions, built for a garrison of five hundred, are substantially intact. Also worth exploring is the **monastery of Dhekoúlou**, down towards the coast; its setting is beautiful and there are some fine eighteenth-century frescoes in the chapel.

There are a few **rooms** to rent in Ítylo, and a smart guesthouse with a pool just south of town: the *Pyrgos Alevras* (☎07330/59 388; ⑤–⑥), with self-catering studios and views – well positioned if you have your own transport. Another option is to look for accommodation by the beach in **NÉO ÍTYLO**, which is just round the bay from Ítylo's ancient and modern seaport, Karavostássi. Néo Ítylo is a tiny hamlet, but as well as rooms for rent it boasts the luxury *Hotel Itylo* (☎ & ℻ 07330/59 222; ⑤), which also runs the slightly cheaper *Alevras* (④) guesthouse. The *Faros* taverna in Karavostássi makes good fish dishes, and also has en-suite rooms (☎07330/59 204; ③).

Langádha, Nomitsís, Thalámes and Plátsa

If you want to walk for a stretch of the onward route, you can pick up the *kalderími* just below the main road out of Ítylo. As it continues north, the track occasionally crosses the modern road, but it is distinct at least as far as Kotróni or Rínglia. The most interesting of the villages along the way are **LANGÁDHA**, for its setting that bristles with towers, and **NOMITSÍS**, for its trio of frescoed Byzantine churches strung out along the main street. A couple more churches are to be found off the road just to the north; in that of the **Metamórfosis**, there are delightful sculpted animal capitals. Just before Nomitsís, you pass the hamlet of **THALÁMES**, where a local enthusiast has set up a widely advertised **Museum of Maniot Folklore and History** (April–Sept daily 9am–4pm; €2.50). The tag "museum" is perhaps a bit inflated for what is really an unlabelled collection of junkshop items, but it's a nice stop nonetheless and sells local honey and olive oil. **PLÁTSA**, the last village before the road descends has no less than four Byzantine churches: Áyios Dimítrios, Áyios Ioánnis, Áyios Nikólaos and Ayía Paraskeví.

Áyios Nikólaos and Stoúpa

The beaches of the Éxo Máni begin south of **ÁYIOS NIKÓLAOS** (Selenítsa), at the pleasant, tree-shaded Pantazí beach. The village's delightful little harbour is flanked by old stone houses, cafés and tavernas overlooking the fishing boats. The *Limeni* taverna at the southern end of the harbour, with a small shaded extension over the water, does excellent fresh fish. There is a scattering of **rooms** and apartments; one of the best is the *Skafidakia* (☎07210/77 698; ❷) in a stone building near the OTE mast, and near a hidden swimming jetty known as Gnospí; the owner can suggest local walks. The coastal road continues south, through Áyios Dimítrios and then past spectacular cliffs and the Katafíyi cave, one of several, to the end of the road at pretty **Trahíla**. Enquire there at the tower behind the harbour for the spacious and well-priced *Kosta* apartments (☎07210/98 058; ❸).

Just to the north of Áyios Nikólaos, **STOÚPA** is much more developed, and justifiably so. It has possibly the best sands along this coast, with two glorious **beaches** (Stoúpa and the smaller, deeper Kalogriá) separated by a headland, each sloping into the sea and superb for children. Submarine freshwater springs gush into the bay, keeping it unusually clean, if also a bit cold. Ten minutes to the north of Kalogriá beach is the delightful and often deserted cove of Dhelfíni. A further 600m brings you to the pebble beach of Fonéa, wrapped around a rock outcrop and tucked into a corner of the hillside. Stoúpa was home in 1917–18 to the wandering Cretan writer, Nikos Kazantzakis, who is said to have based the title character in *Zorba the Greek* on a worker at the coal mine in nearby Pástrova, though the book itself was written later on Égina island in the Saronic Gulf. Just inland of Stoúpa, in 371 BC, the dominance of the Spartans was finally broken, by the Thebans, at the battle of Leuctra (modern Léfktro).

Out of peak season, Stoúpa is certainly recommended, though in July and August, and any summer weekend, you may find the crowds a bit overwhelming and space at a premium. The area is an excellent base for walkers, with interesting villages and a network of paths that include some magnificently engineered *kalderímia*. A popular walking-guide booklet and largescale map are available: ask at the helpfully efficient Doufexis Travel (☎07210/77 677, ✉douftvl@hellasnet.gr) who can also find accommodation, provide exchange and organize car hire (including car hire and accommodation for the southern Peloponnese during the winter). Accommodation in the resort includes numerous **rooms** and apartments, and several **hotels**. The *Lefktron* (☎07210/77 322; ❸) and the *Stoupa* (☎07210/77 485; ❹) are upmarket but very friendly and reasonably priced. A good rooms option is the *Petros Nikolareas* studios (☎07210/77 063; ❸), seaward of the main church. Over the road from Kalogriá beach is *Kalogria Camping* (☎07210/77 319; June–Oct). Towards Kardhamýli, above Dhelfíni beach, there is another livelier **campsite**, *Ta Delfinia* (☎07210/77 318; April–Sept). There are plenty of **tavernas**, but *Akroyali* at the southern end of the main beach not only has well-prepared food, including fresh fish, but has views after dark of the lights of the mountain village Saïdhóna which look remarkably like an extra constellation of stars. The *Gelateria* home-made ice-cream place at the other end of the beach is justifiably famous. **Bus** services can be unreliable on the Kalamáta–Ítylo route, and **taxis** are in short supply locally; the Stoúpa taxi is on ☎07210/77 477 and the nearest to Áyios Nikólaos is at Plátsa on ☎07210/74 226.

Kardhamýli

KARDHAMÝLI, 8km north of Stoúpa, is also a major resort, by Peloponnese standards at least, with ranks of self-catering apartments and pensions, block-booked by the package trade in season, and suffering from the busy main road that splits it. But once again the **beach** is good, though not sandy – a long pebble strip north of the village and backed by acres of olive trees.

Inland from the platía, it's a nice walk up to "Old Kardhamýli"; here a partly restored citadel of abandoned tower-houses is gathered about the eighteenth-century church of **Áyios Spyrídhon** with its unusual multi-storey bell tower, and the courtyard where the Maniot chieftains Kolokotronis and Mavromihalis played human chess with their troops during the War of Independence. Further back, on the *kalderími* up to Ayía Sofía, is a pair of ancient tombs, said to be of the **Dioskoúri** (the Gemini twins).

On the main road near the platía, you'll find a branch of the Agricultural Bank (Mon–Thurs; summer only) and a **post office** (Mon–Fri). Bookable **hotels** include the *Kardamyli Beach* (☎07210/73 180, ℉73 184; ❻). Also on the way along the beach, near the campsite, is *Lela's* (☎07210/73 541; ❸), a good taverna with fine sea-view **rooms** which should be booked well ahead in summer. The **campsite**, *Melitsina* (☎07210/73 461; May–Sept), is 2km from the village. Among Kardhamýli's **tavernas**, try *Kiki's*, as well as *Lela's* whose eponymous owner was once housekeeper to Patrick Leigh Fermor.

Inland to the Výros gorge

North of Kardhamýli the road leaves the coast, which rises to cliffs around a cape, before finally dropping back to the sea in the bay near Kalamáta. But before moving on, a day or two spent exploring Kardhamýli's immediate environs on foot is time well spent.

The giant **Výros gorge** plunges down from the very summit ridge of Taïyetos to meet the sea just north of the resort, and tracks penetrate the gorge from various directions. From Kardhamýli, the *kalderími* from the citadel continues to the church and village of Ayía Sofía, and then proceeds on a mixture of tracks and lanes either across the plateau up to the hamlet of Exohóri, or down into the gorge, where two **monasteries** nestle deep at the base of dramatic cliffs. An hour or so inland along the canyon, more cobbled ways lead up to either Tséria on the north bank (there's a taverna, but no accommodation) or back towards Exohóri on the south flank. Linking any or all of these points is a reasonable day's hiking at most; forays further upstream require full hiking gear and detailed topographical maps.

Kardhamýli to Kalamáta

Divert west of the road to Kalamáta and you reach the small resorts of Avía and Akroyiáli, and Sándova beach. The *Santova Bungalows* (☎07210/58 496; ❹) are good value, with the apartments sleeping four; there are kitchen facilities, good views and plenty of tavernas nearby.

The heartland: Spárti, Mystra and Taïyetos

The central core of the Peloponnese is the luxuriantly spreading Mount Ménalo, surrounded by some of the most beautiful and verdant landscapes in Greece, though fire damage in summer 2000 has taken its toll. Due south, in the Lakonian Evrótas valley, are **Spárti** and its Byzantine companion, **Mystra**, both overlooked and sheltered from the west by the massive and astonishing wall of the Taïyetos mountain ridge.

Spárti (Sparta)

Thucydides predicted that if the ancient city of **Sparta** were deserted, "distant ages would be very unwilling to believe its power at all equal to its fame". The city had no great temples or public buildings and throughout its period of greatness it remained unfortified: Lycurgus, architect of the Spartan constitution, declared that "it is men not walls that make a city". Consequently, modern **SPÁRTI**, laid out grid-style in 1834, has few ancient ruins, and is today the pleasant organizational centre of a huge agricultural plain. Spárti's appeal is its ordinariness – its pedestrianized side streets, café-lined squares, orange trees and evening vólta. The reason for coming here is basically to see **Mystra**, the Byzantine town, 5km to the west, which once controlled great swaths of the medieval world.

Ancient Sparta

Descending from the mountains that ring Spárti on three sides, you get a sense of how strategic was the location of the ancient city-state of **SPAR-TA**. The ancient "capital" occupied more or less the site of today's town, though it was in fact less a city than a grouping of villages, commanding the Lakonian plain and fertile Evrótas valley from a series of low hills to the west of the river.

The Greek city was at the height of its power from the eighth to the fourth century BC, a period when Sparta structured its society according to the laws of **Lycurgus**, defeated Athens in the Peloponnesian War, established colonies around the Greek world, and eventually lost hegemony through defeat to Thebes. A second period of prosperity came under the Romans – for whom this was an outpost in the south of Greece, with the Máni never properly subdued. However, from the third century AD, Sparta declined as nearby Mystra became the focus of Byzantine interest.

The sites

Traces of ancient Spartan glory are in short supply, but there are some ruins to be seen to the north of the city (daily 8.30am–3pm; free): from the bold **Statue of Leonidas** at the top of Paleológou, follow the track around and behind the football stadium towards the old **Acropolis**, tallest of the Spartan hills. An

SPARTA (SPÁRTI)

N

Trípoli

Altar of
Lycurgus

Heroön

Evrótas River

ODOS TTIN 118

Acropolis

Theatre   Osíos
Níkon

Menelaïon

Sanctuary of
Artemis Orthia

Portico

Stadium

ORTHIAS ARTEMIDHOS

Leonidas' Statue

TON TRIAKOSION

2 **1**

THERMOPYLON

3

Kalamáta

DHIOSKOURON

■ Diethnes Taverna

LISANDHROU
ATRIDOU
AYIDHOS

VRASIDHOU

4 OTE

5

ANANIOU

LYKOURGOU

ARIDHANOU

LYKOURGOU

AYIOS NIKONOS

AVTISIDHOU

Mystra
Bus Stop ★

PALEOLOGOU

Town
Hall

Museum

KONSTANTINOU
KONTOSOLOGOU

LEONIDHOU

PLATIA
KENDRIKI

VYZANTIOU

Mystrás

Lykourgou River

MENELAOU

OTHONOS & AMALIAS

Cathedral

HAMARETOU

KTEL ★
Main Bus
Station

ACCOMMODATION

Apollo	1
Cecil	2
Maniatis	5
Menelaïon	4
Sparta Inn	3

0   250 m

Yíthio

immense **theatre** here, built into the side of the hill, can be quite clearly traced, even though today most of its masonry has gone – hurriedly adapted for fortification when the Spartans' power declined and, later still, used in the building of Byzantine Mystra. Above the theatre a sign marks a fragment of the **Temple of Athina Halkiakou**, while at the top of the acropolis sit the knee-high ruins of the **tenth-century Byzantine church** and **monastery** of Osíos Níkon.

About 500m along the Trípoli road, a path descends to the remains of the **sanctuary of Artemis Orthia**, where Spartan boys underwent endurance tests by flogging. The Roman geographer and travel writer Pausanias records that young men often expired under the lash, adding that the altar had to be splashed with blood before the goddess was satisfied. Perhaps it was the audience potential of such a gory spectacle that led the Romans to revive the custom – the main ruins here are of the spectators' grandstand they built.

They also added shops to supply the audiences at performances. Both of these sites are mostly unenclosed, and you can explore them along pleasant walkways.

Further out is the **Menelaïon** (Tues–Sun 8.30am–3pm; free), a late Mycenaean settlement and a sanctuary of Menelaus and Helen, about 5km to the southeast of town, on the far side of the river. At the modern village of Amýkles, 7km south of Spárti on the road to Yíthio, is the Amyklaïon acropolis and **sanctuary of Apollo Amyklaïos** (same hours), which until the Roman period was the most important Spartan site after the city itself and location for the Hyacinthia festival which celebrated the reconciliation of the Dorians and the Achaians.

The Archeological Museum

All moveable artefacts and mosaics have been transferred to the town's small **Archeological Museum** (Mon–Sat 8.30am–3pm, Sun 9.30am–2.30pm; €1.50) back in town, on Áyios Níkonos. Among its more interesting exhibits are a number of votive offerings found on the sanctuary site – sickles set in stone that were presented as prizes to the Spartan youths and solemnly rededicated to the goddess – and a marble bust of a running Spartan hoplite, found on the acropolis and said to be Leonidas, the hero of Thermopylae (see p.334). There are fragments of Hellenistic and Roman mosaics, and numerous small lead figurines from the Artemis Orthia site.

Practicalities

If it is Mystra that brings you here, and you arrive early in the day, you may well decide to move straight on. Getting out of Spárti is straightforward. The **main bus terminal** (for Trípoli, Athens, Monemvasiá, Kalamáta and the Máni) is on the eastern edge of town at the far end of Lykoúrgou. Buses for **Mystra** leave (hourly on weekdays; less frequently at lunchtime and at weekends) from the main terminal and the corner of Lykoúrgou and Leonídhou; schedules are posted on the window of the café there. Most of the **banks** are on Paleológou. There is a good **map/bookshop** at the corner of Paleológou and Lykoúrgou.

Accommodation

There are usually enough **hotels** to go around, many of them on the main avenue of Paleológou. **Camping** is available at two sites out along the Mystra road; both can be reached via the Mystra bus, which will stop by the sites on request. The nearest, 2.5km from Spárti, is *Camping Mystra* (☎07310/22 724) and is open year-round. Two kilometres closer to Mystra is the *Castle View* (☎07310/93 303), a very clean, well-managed site, with a pool, and a bus stop outside.

Apollo, Thermopýlon 84, cnr Tripoléos ☎07310/22 491, ℗23 936. Open all year; parking area. Facilities include a restaurant and some air-conditioned rooms. ❸

Cecil, Paleológou 125, cnr Thermopýlon ☎07310/24 980, ℗81 318. Small and very friendly, nearest to the sites, recently renovated, most rooms with bathrooms and TV. ❷

Maniatis, Paleológou 72, cnr Lykoúrgou ☎07310/22 665, ℗29 994. Modern, with good

facilities at a reasonable price. The in-house *Dias* restaurant is recommended. ❹

Menelaïon, Paleológou 91 ☎07310/22 161, ℗26 332. A modernized turn-of-the-century hotel, with a swimming pool. Rooms at the front are best avoided as there's an all-night taxi rank outside. ❺

Sparta Inn, Thermopýlon 105, cnr Gortsológlou ☎07310/25 021, ℗24 855. Huge and modern, with a roof garden and two swimming pools. ❹

Eating and drinking

There is a wide choice for meals, with most **restaurants** and **tavernas** concentrated on the main street of Paleológou – including several good *psistariés* towards the south end of Paleológou. One of the most popular music **bars** at present is *Ministry* opposite the *Menelaïon* hotel.

Averof, Paleológou 77. A long-established and reasonably priced taverna with tasty Greek home cooking; outdoor tables in summer.

Diethnes, Paleológou 105. Highly rated by the locals with a wide range of traditional dishes. The interior lacks atmosphere, but a delightful garden behind with orange and lemon trees compensates.

Dionysos. 2km out on the road towards Mystra. Expensive dishes, but served with style outdoors on a summer's evening.

Finikas, Thermopýlon 51. Fine taverna cum *psistariá*.

Semiramis, Paleológou 58. Taverna, tucked away in the basement, with a traditional Greek menu; the house speciality is roast pork with aubergine.

Mystra (Mystrás)

A glorious, airy place, hugging a steep flank of Taïyetos, **Mystra** is one of the most exciting and dramatic sites that the Peloponnese can offer. Winding up the lushly vegetated hillside is an astonishingly complete Byzantine town that once sheltered a population of some 20,000, and through which you can now wander. Winding alleys lead through monumental gates, past medieval houses and palaces and above all into the churches, several of which yield superb and radiant frescoes. The overall effect is of straying into a massive museum of architecture, painting and sculpture – and into a different age.

There are no facilities at the site itself, so you'll need to base yourself at either Spárti (see p.342) or the modern settlement of Néos Mystrás (see p.250).

Some history

Mystra was basically a Frankish creation. In 1249, Guillaume II de Villehardouin, fourth Frankish prince of the Moreas, built a castle here – one of a trio of fortresses (the others were at Monemvasiá and in the Máni) designed to garrison his domain. The Franks, however, were driven out of Mystra by the Byzantines in 1262, and this isolated triangle of land in the southeastern Peloponnese, encompassing the old Spartan territories, became the **Despotate of Mystra** by the mid-fourteenth century. This was the last province of the Greek Byzantine empire and for years, with Constantinople in terminal decay, was its virtual capital.

During the next two centuries, Mystra was the focus of a defiant rebirth of Byzantine power. The despotate's rulers – usually the son or brother of the eastern emperor, often the heir-apparent – recaptured and controlled much of the Peloponnese, which became the largest of the ever-shrinking Byzantine provinces. They and their province were to endure for two centuries before eventual subjugation by the Turks. The end came in 1460, seven years after the fall of Constantinople, when the last despot Demetrius Paleologos, feuding with his brothers, handed the city over to the Sultan Mehmet II.

Mystra's political significance, though, was in any case overshadowed by its **artistic achievements**. Throughout the fourteenth and the first decades of the fifteenth centuries it was the principal cultural and intellectual centre of the Byzantine world, sponsoring, in highly uncertain times, a renaissance in the arts and attracting the finest of Byzantine scholars and theologians – among them a number of members of the imperial families, the Cantacuzenes and Paleologues. Most notable of the court scholars was the humanist philosopher

MYSTRA

KÁSTRO

Kástro

Walls

UPPER

Walls

Pandánassa
Convent

Perivléptos
Monastery

Frangopoulos
House

LOWER TOWN

Laskaris
House

Krevatás
House

Áyios
Khristóforos

Marmara
Fountain

Restaurant

Parking

Néos Mystrás & Spárti

Trýpi & Kalamáta ▲

Parking

Walls

Upper Entrance

2

THE PELOPONNESE | Mystra

Ayía Sofía

TOWN

Palatáki

Náfplio Gate

Áyios Nikólaos

Despots' Palace

Monemvasiá Gate

Mosque

Refectory

Odhiyítria

Vrondohión Monastery

Evangelístria

Ayií Theódorii

Mitrópolis

Walls

Lower Entrance

Canteen

Museum

0   100 m

Gemisthus Plethon, who revived and reinterpreted Plato's ideas, using them to support his own brand of revolutionary teachings, which included the assertions that land should be redistributed among labourers and that reason should be placed on a par with religion. Although his beliefs had limited impact in Mystra itself – whose monks excommunicated him – his followers, who taught in Italy after the fall of Mystra, exercised wide influence in Renaissance Florence and Rome.

More tangibly, Mystra also saw a last flourish of **Byzantine architecture**, with the building of a magnificent palace for the despots and a perfect sequence of churches, multi-domed and brilliantly frescoed. It is these, remarkably preserved and sensitively restored, that provide the focus of this extraordinary site. In the painting, it is not hard to see something of the creativity and spirit of Plethon's court circle, as the stock Byzantine figures turn to more naturalistic forms and settings.

The town's **post-Byzantine history** follows a familiar Peloponnesian pattern. It remained in Turkish hands from the mid-fifteenth to late seventeenth centuries, then was captured briefly by the Venetians under Francesco Morosini in 1687, under whom the town prospered once more, attaining a population of 40,000. Decline set in with a second stage of Turkish control, from 1715 onwards, culminating in the destruction that accompanied the War of Independence, the site being evacuated after fires in 1770 and 1825. Restoration began in the first decades of the twentieth century was interrupted by the civil war – during which it was, for a while, a battle site, with the ruins of the Pandánassa convent sheltering children from the lower town – and renewed in earnest in the 1950s when the last inhabitants were relocated.

The Byzantine city

The site of the Byzantine city (daily: summer 8am–8pm; winter 8am–2pm; €3.50) comprises three main parts: the **Káto Hóra** (lower town), with the city's most important churches; the **Áno Hóra** (upper town), grouped around the vast shell of a royal palace; and the **Kástro** (castle). There are two entrances to the site, at the base of the lower town and up below the *kástro*; once inside, the site is well signposted. A road loops up from the modern village of Néos Mystrás (see p.250) to Trýpi, passing near both upper and lower entrances. Buses from Spárti always stop at the lower entrance, and usually go up to the top as well. It's a good idea to stock up on refreshments before setting out: there's a hygienic mobile snack bar at the lower gate, serving freshly pressed orange or lemon juices, but nothing at the upper one or in the site itself. This lack of commercialism within the site contrasts distinctly with Monemvasiá and contributes to the powerfully historic atmosphere at Mystra.

The Upper Town and Kástro

The **Kástro**, reached by a path direct from the upper gate, maintains the Frankish design of its original thirteenth-century construction, though it was repaired and modified by all successive occupants. There is a walkway around most of the keep, with views allowing an intricate panorama of the town below. The castle itself was the court of Guillaume II de Villehardouin but in later years was used primarily as a citadel.

Following a course downhill from the upper entrance, the first identifiable building you come to is the church of **Ayía Sofía** (1350), which served as the chapel for the Despots' Palace – the enormous structure below. The chapel's finest feature is its floor, made from polychrome marble. Its frescoes, notably a *Pandokrátor* (Christ in Majesty) and *Nativity of the Virgin*, have survived reasonably well, protected until recent years by coatings of whitewash applied by the Turks, who adapted the building as a mosque. Recognizable parts of the refectory and cells of its attached monastery also remain.

Heading down from Ayía Sofía, there is a choice of routes. The right fork winds past ruins of a Byzantine mansion, one of the oldest houses on the site, the **Palatáki** ("Small Palace"; 1250–1300), and **Áyios Nikólaos**, a large seventeenth-century building decorated with unsophisticated paintings. The left fork is more interesting, passing the fortified **Náfplio Gate**, which was the principal entrance to the upper town, and the vast, multi-storeyed, Gothic-looking complex of the **Despots' Palace** (1249–1400) (currently closed for extensive rebuilding and restoration that looks set to continue for a number of years ahead).

Parts of the palace probably date back to the Franks. Most prominent among its numerous rooms is a great vaulted audience hall, built at right angles to the line of the building, with ostentatious windows regally dominating the skyline; this was once heated by eight great chimneys and sported a painted facade. Behind it were various official public buildings, while to the right of the lower wing, flanking one side of a square used by the Turks as a marketplace, are the remains of a **mosque**.

The Lower Town

At the **Monemvasiá Gate**, which links the upper and lower towns, there is a further choice of routes: right to the Pandánassa and Perivléptos monasteries or left to the Vrondohión monastery and cathedral. If time is running out, it is easier to head right first, then double back down to the Vrondohión.

When excavations were resumed in 1952, the last thirty or so families who still lived in the lower town were moved out to Néos Mystrás. Only the nuns of the **Pandánassa** ("Queen of the World") **convent** have remained; currently there are seven in residence and they have a reception room where they sell their own handicrafts and sometimes offer a cooling *vyssinádha* (cherryade) to visitors. The convent's church, built in 1428, is perhaps the finest surviving in Mystra, perfectly proportioned in its blend of Byzantine and Gothic. The **frescoes** date from various centuries, with some superb fifteenth-century work, including one in the gallery (entered by an external staircase but currently closed) which depicts scenes from the life of Christ. David Talbot Rice, in his classic study, *Byzantine Art*, wrote of these frescoes that "Only El Greco in the west, and later Gauguin, would have used their colours in just this way." Other frescoes were painted between 1687 and 1715, when Mystra was held by the Venetians.

Further down on this side of the lower town is a balconied Byzantine mansion, the **House of Frangopoulos**, once the home of the Despotate's chief minister – who was also the founder of the Pandánassa.

Beyond it is the diminutive **Perivléptos monastery** (1310), whose single-domed church, partially carved out of the rock, contains Mystra's most complete cycle of frescoes, almost all of which date from the fourteenth century. They are in some ways finer than those of the Pandánassa, blending an easy humanism with the spirituality of the Byzantine icon traditions, and demonstrating the structured iconography of a Byzantine church. The position of each figure depended upon its sanctity and so here upon the dome, the image of heaven, is the *Pandokrátor* (the all-powerful Christ in glory after the

Ascension); on the apse is the Virgin; and the higher expanses of wall portray scenes from the life of Christ. Prophets and saints could only appear on the lower walls, decreasing in importance according to their distance from the sanctuary.

Along the path leading from Perivléptos to the lower gate are a couple of minor, much-restored churches, and, just above them, the **Laskaris House**, a mansion thought to have belonged to relatives of the emperors. Like the Frangopoulos House, it is balconied; its ground floor probably served as stables. Close by, beside the path, is an old Turkish fountain.

The **Mitrópolis** or cathedral, immediately beyond the gateway, is the oldest of Mystra's churches, built between 1270 and 1292 under the first Paleologue ruler. A marble slab set in its floor is carved with the double-headed eagle of Byzantium, commemorating the spot where Constantine XI Paleologos, the last Eastern emperor, was crowned in 1448; he was soon to perish, with his empire, in the Turkish sacking of Constantinople in 1453. A stone with red stains is said to mark where Bishop Ananias Lambadheris was murdered in 1760. Of the church's frescoes, the earliest, in the northeast aisle, depict the torture and burial of Áyios Dhimítrios, the saint to whom the church is dedicated. The comparative stiffness of their figures contrasts with the later works opposite. These, illustrating the miracles of Christ and the life of the Virgin, are more intimate and lighter of touch; they date from the last great years before Mystra's fall. Adjacent to the cathedral, a small **museum** (included in main admission charge) contains various fragments of sculpture and pottery, though staff may be irritable at having to climb the stairs to keep an eye on you.

Finally, a short way uphill, is the **Vrondohión monastery**. This was the centre of cultural and intellectual life in the fifteenth-century town – the cells of the monastery can still be discerned – and was also the burial place of the despots. Of the two attached churches, the further one, **Odhiyítria** (Afendikó; 1310) has been beautifully restored, revealing early fourteenth-century frescoes similar to those of Perivléptos, with startlingly bold juxtapositions of colour.

Practicalities: Néos Mystrás

Buses run regularly through the day from Spárti to the lower Mystra site entrance, stopping en route at the modern village of **NÉOS MYSTRÁS**. This small roadside community has a half-dozen tavernas, crowded with tour buses by day but reverting to a low-key life at night, except at the end of August when the place buzzes with live music and a gypsy market during the week-long annual *paniyíri* (fête).

In general, staying in Néos Mystrás is worth the bit extra over Spárti, for the setting and easy access to the site, though you will need to book ahead, or arrive early in the day, to find a place. **Accommodation** is limited to a single hotel, the recently refurbished and very pleasant *Byzantion* (✆07310/83 309, ⓕ20 019, ⓔmedotels@otenet.gr; April–Oct; ❹), which is pleasant but over-subscribed for most of the year, and a small number of private rooms – those run by Khristina Vahaviolou (✆07310/20 047; ❸) are especially recommended. There are **campsites** along the Mystrás–Spárti road: see under accommodation details for Spárti on p.244.

The Vahaviolos family also has an excellent **taverna**, while the restaurant opposite the hotel, *To Kastro*, is also good, if a bit on the expensive side.

Mount Taïyetos and the Langádha pass

Moving on from Spárti there is a tough choice of routes: west over the Taïyetos ridge, either on foot or by road through the dramatic **Langádha pass** to Kalamáta; east to the Byzantine towns of Yeráki and **Monemvasiá** (see p.215); or south, skirting the mountain's foothills, to Yíthio and the Máni. For anyone wanting to get to grips with the Greek mountains, there is **Mount Taïyetos** itself. Although the range is one of the most beautiful, dramatic and hazardous in Greece, with vast grey boulders and scree along much of its length, it has one reasonably straightforward path to the highest peak, Profítis Ilías. Three areas, covering different and specialized ecological habitats, in the higher mountains and the gorges of Langádha and Nédhondas, were included for conservation under the EU's NATURA 2000 programme.

Mount Taïyetos

Gazing up at the crags above the castle at Mystra, Mount Taïyetos (Taygettus) looks daunting and inviting in pretty equal measure. If all you want is a different perspective on the mountain, then the simplest course is to take a bus 5km from Spárti to **ÁYIOS IOÁNNIS**, a little way to the south of Mystra and closer to the peaks. From there a spectacular *kalderími* (cobbled way) leads up from the gravel-crushing mill behind the village to **ANAVRYTÍ**, which boasts superb vistas, a single friendly **hotel** – the *Anemodharména Ípsi* ("Wuthering Heights"; ☎07310/21 788; ❸) – and one basic **taverna** aside from the one in the hotel. **Buses** run from Spárti to Anavrytí three times a week, early morning and early afternoon (Mon, Wed & Sat). An alternative, more popular approach involves following the marked E4 overland route, partly on track, partly on trail, up from Néos Mystrás via the **monastery of Faneroméni**. Neither the E4 nor the *kalderími* takes more than two hours uphill, and they can be combined as follows for a wonderful day's outing: bus to Áyios Ioánnis, taxi to rock-crushing mill (2.5km), hike up to Anavrytí for a look around and a meal, then descend via Faneroméni to Néos Mystrás. Note that this route is best tackled from Áyios Ioánnis; the downhill start of the *kalderími* just east of Anavrytí isn't marked, and can be difficult to locate.

Spárti to Kalamáta: the Langádha pass

The **Langádha pass**, the sixty-kilometre route over the Taïyetos from **Spárti to Kalamáta**, was the second ancient crossing after the Kakí Skála (see box overleaf) and is still the only paved road across the mountain. Remote and barren, with long uninhabited sections, it unveils a constant drama of peaks, magnificent at all times but startling at sunrise; sadly the pine forests have suffered extensive damage in the fires of 1998. This route was taken by Telemachus in the *Odyssey* on his way from Nestor's palace at Pýlos to that of Menelaus at Sparta. It took him a day by chariot – good going by any standards, since today's buses take three hours.

Heading from Spárti, the last settlement is **TRÝPI**, 9km out, where there is one of the best **tavernas** in the Spárti area, *Vozola*, and a basic small **hotel**, the *Keadas* (☎07310/98 222; ❷), open Easter to late autumn. Just beyond the village, the road climbs steeply into the mountains and enters the **gorge of**

Most **hikes** beyond Anavrytí need experience and proper equipment, including the relevant Korfes or YIS maps, and should definitely not be undertaken alone – a sprained ankle could be fatal up here. The area is prone to flash floods, so seek advice locally. If you are confident, however, there are various routes to the Profítis Ilías summit and beyond.

The only straightforward route is to follow the **E4 long-distance footpath**, here marked variously by yellow diamonds or red-and-white stripes, for five hours south to the **alpine refuge** at Ayía Varvára (see opposite).

The classic approach to the 2404-metre **Profítis Ilías summit** used to entail a dusty, eleven-kilometre road-walk up from the village of Paleopanayía, a short bus ride south of Spárti off the Yíthio road, to the spring and ex-trailhead at Bóliana (Kryonéri), where there's a single ramshackle hut that serves drinks and sometimes meals in summer. You now have to proceed past Bóliana towards Anavrytí on the E4 track for about thirty minutes, then bear left near a picnic ground and spring (the last reliable water on the mountain). Another half-hour above this, following E4 blazes, what's left of the old trail appears on the right, signposted "EOS Spárti Katafíyio". This short-cuts the new road except for the very last 50m to the Ayía Varvára refuge.

A more challenging option, requiring mountaineering skills and camping equipment, is to adopt the red-dotted trail veering off the E4 early on, and follow it to a point just below the 1700-metre saddle described by Patrick Leigh Fermor in *Mani*, where you must choose between dropping over the pass to the far side of the range or precarious ridge-walking to the Profítis Ilías summit. Crossing the pass would land you at the head of the **Ríndomo gorge**, where you can camp at the deserted chapel-monastery of Panayía Kapsodhematoúsa before descending the next day to either Gaïtsés or Pigádhia, towards the Messinian coast. Keeping to the watershed it is seven tough hours to the peak even in optimum conditions and with a light load, involving exposed rock pinnacles, sheer drops and difficult surfaces. This is not a hike to be lightly undertaken.

Langádha, a wild sequence of hairpins through the pines. To the north of the gorge, at the rock of Keádhas, the Spartans used to leave their sick or puny babies to die from exposure. Beyond the gorge, just before the summit of the pass, 22km from Spárti and 37km from Kalamáta, the *Canadas* **guesthouse** (☏07210/76 281; ❷) is built in the style of an alpine chalet, and is excellent value, with a restaurant that serves good *bakaliáros* (cod), *loukániko* (sausage), smoked pork and bean soup. It's also a good place to sample mountain tea, made from the local herb *sidherítis*. At the **pass**, 3km further on and 125m higher at 1375m, is the (*Touristiko*) *Taïyetou* (☏07210/76236; ❷) hotel and restaurant, also open all year. From here paths and tracks head off north and south along the mountain ridge.

The first actual village on the Kalamáta side is **Artemisía**, where you often have to change buses, before entering the **Nédhondas** gorge for the final zigzagging descent to Kalamáta. There is basic accommodation here, in rooms above one of the cafés, but the *Canadas* and *Touristiko Taïyetou* are far better value for little more cost.

Ayía Varvára to the summit

The **Ayía Varvára refuge** (unstaffed, but open sporadically – more likely at week-ends), above Bóliana, sits on a beautiful grassy knoll shaded by tremendous storm-blasted black pines. The conical peak of Profítis Ilías rises directly above; if you can get your climb to coincide with a full moon you won't regret it. There is plenty of room for camping, and the hut has a porch to provide shelter in bad weather.

The path to the **summit** starts at the rear left corner of the refuge and swings right on a long reach. Level and stony at first, it leaves the treeline and loops up a steep bank to a sloping meadow, where it is ineffectually marked by twisted, rusting signs with their lettering long obliterated. Keep heading right across the slope towards a distinct secondary peak until, once around a steep bend, the path begins to veer left in the direction of the summit. It slants steadily upward following a natural ledge until, at a very clear nick in the ridge above you, it turns right and crosses to the far side, from where you look down on the Gulf of Messinía. Turn left and you climb steeply to the summit in around 25 minutes.

There is a squat stone chapel and outbuildings on the **summit**, used during the celebrations of the feast of the Prophet Elijah (Profítis Ilías) between July 18 and 20. The views, as you would expect, are breathtaking, encompassing the sea to east and west.

Summit to the coast

The ridge terrain **beyond the peak** is probably beyond the ambitions of casual hikers. The easiest and safest way off the mountain towards the Messinian coast is to follow the E4 from Ayía Varvára to the gushing springs at Pendávli, and then over a low saddle to the summer hamlet of **Áyios Dhimítrios**. This takes just a couple of hours and you can camp in the beautiful surroundings. In the morning you're well poised, at the head of the **Výros gorge**, to handle the all-day descent to Kardhamýli through the other great Taïyetan canyon. At one point you negotiate stretches of the **Kakí Skála**, one of the oldest paths in Greece, built to link ancient Sparta and Messene. Dirt roads now also link Áyios Dhimítrios with Saïdhóna (24km), above Stoúpa and Kardhamýli in the west, and via Kastaniá with Yíthio in the southeast.

Arcadia

Arcadia (Arkadhía in modern Greek), the heartland province of the Peloponnese, lives up to its name. It contains some of the most beautiful landscapes in Greece: verdant and dramatic hills crowned by a string of medieval towns, and the occasional Classical antiquity. The best area of all is around **Andhrítsena**, **Stemnítsa** and **Karýtena**, where walkers are rewarded with the luxuriant (and rarely visited) **Loúsios gorge**, and archeology buffs by the remote, though permanently covered, **Temple of Bassae** (Apollo Epikourios). En route, if approaching from **Trípoli**, you may also be tempted by the ancient theatre at **Megalópoli**.

Trípoli

Trípoli is a major crossroads of the Peloponnese, from where most travellers either head **northwest** through Arcadia towards Olympia or Pátra, or **south**

to Spárti and Mystra or Kalamáta (see below). To the **east**, a decent road, looping around Mount Kteniás, connects Trípoli with Árgos and Náfplio, via Lérna. A second road runs southeast across the Tegean plain, then east down to Ástros. To the **southwest**, a winding road over the intervening ridge leads to Megalópoli – and its evocative, scattered ruins – from where a faster road reaches the coast near Kyparissía. To the **northeast**, a fast highway via the Artemisíon Tunnel links Trípoli with Kórinthos and Athens; at the time of writing it extended as far west beyond Trípoli as Mákri, and work continues to connect it with the next section just south of Megalópoli.

The Peloponnese **railway** also passes through Trípoli, continuing its meandering course from Kórinthos and Árgos to Kyparissía or Kalamáta. Those with passes might be tempted to use the train to Trípoli and then take a bus to Spárti, but it's not a good idea, as Árgos–Spárti buses are not scheduled to meet trains in Trípoli and furthermore they often pass through full; it's better to take a direct bus (seven to nine daily from Athens to Spárti, via Árgos

▲ Pýrgos, Pátra & Kalávryta

TRÍPOLI

ACCOMMODATION
Alex	5
Anactoricon	3
Arcadia	4
Artemis	1
Menalon	2

◄ Vytína, Ménalo & Stemnítsa

Árgos ▶

Spárti, Tegéa, Bus Station (Spárti, Yíthio) ▶ & Train Station

Bus Station for Argos & Kórinthos

Local Bus Station

Local Bus Station

Museum

Áy. Dhimítrios

0   100 m

▼ Megalópoli & Kalamáta

and Trípoli), or approach Spárti more enjoyably via the hydrofoil to Monemvasiá.

The Town

Set in a huge upland plain, and surrounded by spectacular mountains, the Arcadian capital doesn't live up to expectations close-up: **TRÍPOLI** is a large, modern town, and home to one of the country's biggest army barracks. It doesn't overwhelm with its charm and has few obvious attractions, although the **Panarcadic Archeological Museum** (Tues–Sun 8.30am–3pm; €1.50), signposted off Vassiléos Yeoryíou and housed in a Neoclassical building with a beautiful rose garden, makes a pleasant diversion; the collection includes finds from much of Arcadia, from Neolithic to Roman. The town's altitude of 650m means an often markedly cooler summer climate and harsh winters. Traffic is chaotic and you may wish to escape to the quiet greenery of Platía Áreos. Medieval Tripolitsa was destroyed by retreating Turkish forces during the War of Independence, when the Greek forces, led by Kolokotronis in one of their worst atrocities, had earlier massacred the town's Turkish population. Tripolitsa's ancient predecessors, the rival towns of Mantinea to the north and Tegea to the south, are the main points of interest to the tourist.

Getting in and out of the town can be fairly complicated. The major **bus terminal**, serving all destinations in Arcadia and the northern Peloponnese, is on Platía Kolokotróni, one of the three main squares. Services to Messinía, Kalamáta, Pýlos, the Máni and Spárti leave from the corner café on Lagopáti, directly opposite the train station, at the southeastern edge of town. If you need to spend a night here, there are a number of reliable **hotels** including the *Arcadia* at Platía Kolokotróni 1 (☎0710/225 551, ℱ222 464; ❹); the *Alex*, Vassiléos Yeoryíou 26 (☎0710/223 465; ❸); the very friendly *Anactoricon* on Ethnikís Andistásis 48 (☎0710/222 545, ℯroinioti@compulink.gr; ❺); the *Menalon* on Platía Áreos (☎0710/222 450; ❸); and the *Artemis*, Dhimitrakopoúlou 1 (☎0710/225 221, ℱ233 629; ❹). Eating establishments are mostly of the functional variety, but for decent food in more pleasant surroundings there are a couple of **tavernas**, *Neos Dionysos* and the more homely *Klimataria*, almost adjacent to one another on Kalavrýton, beyond the Aello cinema and about 100m past the far end of Platía Áreos.

Ancient Mantinea

Ancient **MANTINEA** (Tues–Sun 8.30am–3pm; free), known to Homer as "pleasant Mantinea", was throughout its history a bitter rival of nearby Tegea, invariably forming an alliance with Athens when Tegea stood with Sparta, then switching allegiance to Sparta when Tegea allied with Thebes. Its site stands 15km north of Trípoli, between the road to Pátra and the new Trípoli–Kórinthos highway, and is served by hourly buses from Platía Kolokotróni in Trípoli. The principal remains are a circuit of fourth-century BC **walls**, still more or less intact, though much reduced in height, and a few tiers of its ancient theatre.

Alongside the site, however, is one of the most bizarre sights in Greece: the modern **church of Ayía Fotiní** constructed in an eccentric pastiche of Byzantine and Egyptian styles. Put together in the 1970s by a Greek-American architect, it is dedicated to "The Virgin, the Muses and Beethoven".

Ancient Tegea

Ancient **TEGEA**, 8km south of Trípoli, was the main city of the central Peloponnese in Classical and Roman times, and, refounded in the tenth century, was an important town again under the Byzantines. The diffuse and partially excavated site (Tues–Sun 8.30am–3pm; free) lies just outside the village of Aléa (modern Tegea), on the Spárti road. Local buses from Trípoli stop in the village beside a small **museum** (same hours; €1.50), which is well stocked with sculptures from the site. Take the road to the left as you leave, which leads in 100m to the main remains, the **Temple of Athena Alea**, in whose sanctuary two kings of Sparta once took refuge. Keeping on the road past the site, it's a twenty-minute walk to the village of Paleá Episkopí, whose church – a huge modern pilgrim shrine – incorporates part of ancient Tegea's theatre and a number of Byzantine mosaics.

Megalópoli

Modern **MEGALÓPOLI** (Megalopolis) is an important road and bus junction, and your first thoughts on arrival may be directed towards getting out. It's a rather characterless place, with a military presence and two vast power stations; there's little in the way of hotels or food. The adoption of its ancient name, "Great City", was an altogether empty joke.

However, the impulse to leave should be resisted, at least for an hour or two, because just outside the city to the northwest is one of the most extensive and least touristy sites in the Peloponnese: **ancient Megalopolis**.

Also worth a brief detour is the mountain village of **Vástas**, some 28km southwest of Megalópoli by indirect roads, on the flank of 1389-metre Mount Tetrázio. Below it is the small but remarkable Ayía Theódhora church, which is dwarfed by the seventeen large trees sprouting from the roof.

Practicalities

Megalópoli has regular **bus connections** with Trípoli (and on to Árgos and Athens) and Kalamáta. Moving north or west into Arcadia is slightly more problematic, with just two buses daily to Karýtena/Andhrítsena (currently at noon and 7pm). However, hitching is a viable proposition along this route, as local drivers are aware of the paucity of transport, and it's also possible to negotiate a **taxi** to Karýtena. Facilities such as **banks** and a **post office** are also to be found around the central Platía Gortynías.

There are four or five **hotels** in Megalópoli, catering mostly to local business travellers rather than tourists. Most are in the vicinity of the central platía and include the *Paris*, Ayíou Nikoláou 5 (☎07910/22 410; ❷); and the *Achillion*, Papaioánnou 67 (☎07910/23 276; ❸), which has clean, comfortable rooms with en-suite showers. The *Leontara* **restaurant** on the main square is recommended for baked dishes.

Ancient Megalopolis

Ancient Megalopolis (Tues–Sun 8.30am–3pm; free) was one of the most ambitious building projects of the Classical age, a city intended by the Theban leader Epaminondas, who oversaw construction from 371 to 368 BC, to be the finest of a chain of Arcadian settlements designed to hold back the Spartans. However, although no expense was spared on its construction, nor on its extent – nine kilometres of walls alone – the city never took root. It suffered from sporadic Spartan aggression, and the citizens, transplanted from forty local villages, preferred, and returned to, their old homes. Within two centuries it had been broken up, abandoned and ruined.

As you approach the site, along a tree-lined track off the Andhrítsena road (signposted "Ancient Theatre"), the countryside is beautiful enough; a fertile valley whose steaming cooling towers seem to give it added grandeur; beyond the river-bed is just a low hill, and no sign of any ruins. Suddenly, you round the corner of the rise and its function is revealed: carved into its side is the largest **theatre** built in ancient Greece. Only the first few rows are excavated, but the earthen mounds and ridges of the rest are clearly visible as stepped tiers to the summit where, from the back rows, trees look on like immense spectators. Restoration work is planned.

The theatre was built to a scale similar to those at Argos and Dodona, and could seat 20,000; the **Thersileion** (Assembly Hall) at its base could hold 16,000. Today you're likely to be alone at the site, save perhaps for the custodian (who has plans of the ruins). Out beyond the enclosed part of the site you can wander over a vast area, and with a little imagination make out the foundations of walls and towers, temples, gymnasiums and markets. "The Great City", wrote Kazantzakis in *Journey to the Morea*, "has become a great wasteland". But it's the richest of wastelands, gently and resolutely reclaimed by nature.

Megalópoli to Vytína

North of Megalópoli the best of Arcadia lies before you: minor roads that curl through a series of lush valleys and below the province's most exquisite medieval hill towns. The obvious first stop is **Karýtena**.

Moving on from Karýtena, there is a choice of roads. The "main" route loops west through Andhrítsena to Kréstena, from where irregular buses run to Olympia. An alternative route to the northwest winds around the edge of the Ménalo mountains to the delightful towns of **Stemnítsa** and **Dhimitsána**, meeting the main Trípoli–Langádhia–Olympia–Pýrgos road at Karkaloú. From either of these you can visit the dramatic and remote site of **ancient Gortys** and explore the **Loúsios gorge**, above which, outrageously sited on 300-metre-high cliffs, is the eleventh-century **Ayíou Ioánnou Prodhrómou monastery** (commonly abbreviated to Prodhrómou). North of Dhimitsána is modern **Vytína**, a ski-centre with more extensive tourist facilities. If you have time on your hands, perhaps the most attractive option is to explore the region as far north as Dhimitsána or Vytína, then backtrack through meadows and woodland on Ménalo lanes to Stemnítsa and Karýtena, finally proceeding on to Olympia via Andhrítsena.

Karýtena

Set high above the Megalópoli–Andhrítsena road, **KARÝTENA** may look familiar to Greece aficionados; with its medieval bridge over the River Alfiós (Alpheus), it used to grace the 5000-drachma note. Like many of the Arcadian hill towns hereabouts, its history has Frankish, Byzantine and Turkish contributions, the Venetians having passed over much of the northern interior. It was founded by the Byzantines in the seventh century and had attained a population of some 20,000 when the Franks took it in 1209. Under their century-long rule, Karýtena was the capital of a large barony under Geoffroy de Bruyères, the paragon of chivalry in the medieval ballad *The Chronicle of the Morea*, and probably the only well-liked Frankish overlord.

The village these days has a population of just a couple of hundred, but as recently as the beginning of the nineteenth century there were at least ten times that figure. Approaching, you can stop on the modern bridge over the Alfiós and peer down at the **medieval bridge**, which is immediately adjacent. It is missing the central section, but is an intriguing structure nonetheless, with a small Byzantine chapel built into one of the central pillars.

From the main road, there's a winding three-kilometre road up to the village, in the upper part of which is a small central platía with a kafenío. Off the platía are signposted two Byzantine churches: the fourteenth-century **Zoödhóhos Piyí** (with a Romanesque bell-tower) and the late seventeenth-century **Áyios Nikólaos** (with crumbling frescoes) to the west, down towards the river; ask at the kafenío for the keys. Also off the platía is the **Frourio**, the castle built in 1245 by the Franks, with added Turkish towers. It was repaired by Theodhoros Kolokotronis and it was here that he held out against Ibrahim Pasha in 1826 and turned the tide of the War of Independence – hence the view of Karýtena on the old 5000-drachma note and a portrait of Kolokotronis on the reverse.

There are only two places to rent **rooms**: one signposted opposite the post office, the *Kondopoulos* (℡07910/31 262; ❷); the other, under an isolated house 1km beyond the platía, the *Papadopoulos* (℡07910/31 203; ❷); both are very basic, with shared facilities, and the hotel in Stemnítsa, 15km away (see opposite), is far better value. *To Konaki*, a good **taverna** with typical fare, is on the square.

North through the Loúsios River valley

The site of **ancient Gortys** can be approached either from Karýtena or from Stemnítsa (8km northwest of the site). From Karýtena the most direct route to the valley runs up and through the town to Astíholos (11km), a village 2km southwest of the site; a taxi should cost in the region of €10 return. This route is no more than a jeep track, but is well used. If you don't have your own transport, bus or hitch to Ellinikó, 6km up the Stemnítsa road. From the edge of Ellinikó, a dirt track signposted "Gortys" descends west; a rough six kilometres (ignore right-hand fork to Prodhrómou after 5km) brings you to the bank of the Loúsios River. Here is an old bridge, which you cross to reach the site of ancient Gortys. It is possible to camp overnight at Gortys, or to stay at the nearby monastery of Prodhrómou. The town of Stemnítsa, with its excellent hotel, probably makes the best base for exploring the area, and walkers may want to do so by following the Stemnítsa–Prodhrómou–Gortys–Ellinikó–Stemnítsa circuit (see opposite). There are new dirt roads being made above the Loúsios, which may affect the following routes.

Ancient Gortys

Ancient Gortys is one of the most stirring of all Greek sites, set beside the rushing river known in ancient times as the Gortynios. The remains are widely strewn amongst the vegetation on the west (true right) bank of the stream, but the main attraction, below contemporary ground level and not at all obvious until well to the west of the little chapel of Áyios Andhréas (by the old bridge), is the huge excavation containing the remains of a **temple to Asclepius** (the god of healing) and an adjoining **bath**, both dating from the fourth century BC.

The most curious feature of the site is a circular **portico** enclosing round-backed seats which most certainly would have been part of the therapeutic centre. It's an extraordinary place, especially if you camp with the roar of the Loúsios to lull you to sleep. The only drawbacks are the mosquitoes and the climate: temperatures up here plummet at night, no matter what the season, and heavy mists, wet as a soaking rain, can envelop the mountains from midnight to mid-morning.

The Loúsios gorge and monastery of Prodhrómou

The farmland surrounding ancient Gortys belongs to the monks of the near-by **Prodhrómou monastery**, who have carved a donkey path along the **gorge of the Loúsios** between Áyios Andhréas and the monastery. It's about forty-minutes' walk upstream, with an initially gradual and later steady ascent up a well-graded, switchbacked trail. If you look up through the trees above the path, the monastery, stuck on to the cliff like a swallow's nest, is plainly visible a couple of hundred metres above. A set of park benches by a formal gate indicate the entrance, and the whole area is well stamped about by the monks' mules.

The interior of the monastery does not disappoint; the local villagers accurately describe it as *politisméno* (cultured) as opposed to *ágrio* (wild). Once inside it is surprisingly small; there were never more than about fifteen tenants, and currently there are twelve monks, many of them very young and committed. Visitors are received in the *arhondaríki* (guest lounge and adjoining quarters), and then shown the tiny frescoed *katholikón*, and possibly invited to evening services there. The strictest rules of dress apply, but the monks welcome visitors who wish to stay the night. The only problem, especially at weekends, is that there are only a dozen or so beds, and people from Trípoli and even Athens make pilgrimages and retreats here, arriving by the carload along a circuitous, descending, part-asphalt/part-earth road from Stemnítsa. Be prepared for this possibility, and arrive in time to get back to level ground to camp.

Prodhrómou to Stemnítsa

Beyond Prodhrómou the path continues clearly to the outlying monasteries of **Paleá** and **Néa Filosófou** on the opposite side of the valley. The older dates from the tenth century but, virtually ruined, is easy to miss since it blends into the cliff against which it is flattened. The newer (seventeenth-century) monastery has been restored and recently expanded considerably, but retains frescoes from 1663 inside; there is a permanent caretaker monk. Accommodation is sometimes possible, but mosquitoes can be a hazard.

At Prodhrómou you can pick up the dirt track (described opposite as the fork off the Ellinikó–Gortys track) and head for Stemnítsa. If you are walking it is more pleasant, and quicker, to follow instead the old *kalderími* from Prodhrómou to Stemnítsa – a climb, but not a killing one, of about ninety minutes through scrub oak with fine views over the valley. Usually one of the monks or lay workers will be free to point out the start of the path; follow the road above the modern little chapel at the edge of the canyon, and the path starts near the T-junction above.

If Stemnítsa is your base rather than your destination, you can take this route in reverse by heading out of town on the paved road to Dhimitsána and, 500m after the town-limits sign, bear down and left onto the obvious beginning of the upper end of the *kalderími*. The loop can be completed by following the track all the way back to Ellinikó, where a proper trail leads north back to Stemnítsa.

Stemnítsa

Fifteen kilometres north of Karýtena and at an altitude of 1050m, **STEMNÍTSA** (or Ipsoúnda in its official Hellenicized form – Ipsoús on many maps) was for centuries one of the premier metal-smithing and goldworking centres of the Balkans. Although much depopulated, it remains a fascinating town, with a small folklore museum, an artisan school and a handful of quietly magnificent medieval churches.

The town is divided by ravines into three distinct quarters: the Kástro (the ancient acropolis hill), Ayía Paraskeví (east of the stream) and Áyios Ioánnis (west of the stream). The **Folklore Museum** (Mon & Wed–Fri 6–8pm, Sat 11am–1pm & 6–8pm, Sun 11am–1pm; closed in Feb; free) is just off the main road in the Ayía Paraskeví quarter, and repays the trip out in itself. The ground floor is devoted to mock-ups of the workshops of indigenous crafts such as candle-making, bell-casting, shoe-making and jewellery. The next floor up features re-creations of the salon of a well-to-do family and a humbler cottage. The top storey is taken up by the rather random collections of the Savopoulos family: plates by Avramides (a refugee from Asia Minor and ceramics master), textiles and costumes from all over Greece, weapons, copperware and eighteenth- and nineteenth-century icons. Across the way the **Artisan School** is temporarily closed for refurbishment. Next door to the school is the seventeenth-century **basilica of Tríon Ierarhón**, the most accessible of the town's Byzantine churches; its caretaker lives in the low white house west of the main door.

To visit the other churches, all of which are frescoed and locked, requires more determined enquiries to find a key. The *katholikón* of the seventeenth-century **monastery of Zoödhóhos Piyí** has perhaps the finest setting, on the hillside above Ayía Paraskeví, but the tiny windows do not permit much of an interior view. The little adjoining monastery hosted the first *yeroúsia* (convention) of guerrilla captains in the War of Independence, giving rise to the local claim that Stemnítsa was Greece's first capital.

Near the viewpoint summit of the Kástro hill, overlooking a small gorge, are two adjacent chapels: the tenth-century **Profítis Ilías** (with a convenient window for fresco-viewing) and the twelfth-century **Panayía Vaferón** (with an unusual colonnade). The last of the town's five churches, **Áyios Pandelímon**, is located at the western edge of the town, to the left of the paved road to Dhimitsána.

Accommodation is limited to the very pleasant and hospitable *Hotel Trikolonion* (☎07950/81 297, ☏81 483; ❸), which has rooms and suites in a fine traditional building in the centre of town; the inclusive breakfasts are substantial and the restaurant is cheap and good. The hotel represents the best value in accommodation between Trípoli and Olymbía, and is popular, so advance booking is recommended. You can **eat** here, or in town at the simple *Klinitsa* on the square or pleasant *Kastro* near the hill; vegetarians, however, may find suitable dishes very limited both here and at Dhimitsána. There is one **bus** a day linking Stemnítsa with Trípoli via Dhimitsána.

Dhimitsána

Like Stemnítsa, **DHIMITSÁNA** has an immediately seductive appearance, its cobbled streets and tottering houses straddling a twin hillside overlooking the Loúsios River. Views from the village are stunning: it stands at the head of the gorge, and looking downriver you can just see the cooling towers of the Megalópoli power plant and the bluff that supports Karýtena. To the east are the lower folds of the Ménalo mountains, most visible if you climb up to the local **kástro**, whose stretch of polygonal walls attests to its ancient use.

In the town, a half-dozen churches with tall, squarish belfries recall the extended Frankish, and especially Norman, tenure in this part of the Moreas during the thirteenth century. Yet no one should dispute the deep-dyed Greekness of Dhimitsána. It was the birthplace of Archbishop Yermanos, who first raised the flag of rebellion at Kalávryta in 1821, and of the hapless patriarch, Grigoris V, hanged in Constantinople upon the sultan's receiving news of the insurrection mounted by the patriarch's coreligionist, and of the massacre at Tripolitsa. Grigoris's house is now an **Ecclesiastical Museum** (daily except Wed & Fri, 10am–1.30pm & 5–7pm). During the hostilities the ubiquitous Kolokotronis maintained a lair and a powder mill in the then almost inaccessible town. Before the War of Independence, the nunnery of **Emyalón** (daylight hours except 2–5pm), 3km south towards Stemnítsa, was used by the Kolokotronis clan as a hideout. About 2km south of Dhimitsána, the excellent **Open-Air Water Power Museum** (summer daily 10am–2pm & 5–7pm; winter daily except Tues 10am–4pm; €1.50) has a reconstructed watermill, tannery and powder mill, with restored equipment, and exhibitions on the processes involved. It is possible to follow a marked route down to a bridge over the Loúsios, starting on the low road signed to the Emyalón monastery, then joining a *kalderími* via Paleohóri.

Accommodation is available in an old restored building, the *Xenonas Kazakou*, near the school and church (☎ & ℱ 07950/31 660; ❺), or at rooms such as *Koustenis* (☎07950/31 888; ❷), *Velissaropoulos* (☎07950/31 617; ❷), and *Tsialas* (☎07950/31 583; ❷); the ugly, council-owned hotel *Dimitsana*, 1km out on the road to Stemnítsa, was closed at the time of writing, but the **taverna** *Kali Thea*, just across the road, is reasonably good and not too expensive.

Vytína

Continuing the clockwise circuit around the Ménalo mountains, for a further 19km brings you to the small town of **VYTÍNA**. The local accommodation is intended mainly for winter use during the skiing season, but the town makes a good base for self-drive exploration of the northern mountains; the roads out and facilities are considerably better here than at the other, more traditional villages in this area, and there are up to six buses a day to and from Trípoli. Hotels include the well-equipped *Mainalon* (☎07950/22 217; ❺) in the centre of town, and the older *Aegli* (☎07950/22 216; ❹) towards the bypass. Heading south, deep into Ménalo, on the small road from Vytína to Khrysovítsi, but turning off left to **Limbovísi** (signed in Greek only), brings you to the isolated house, now a small **museum**, in the forest glade where Kolokotronis spent his childhood.

Moving on to Olympia

Keep in mind that through buses from Stemnítsa and Dhimitsána are scarce, and you may well need to hitch (or take a taxi) to Karkaloú junction (or to Vytína), on the main Trípoli–Pýrgos road, where you can pick up buses more easily. Once on the road to Olympia, the most enjoyable halt is **LANGÁDHIA** (18km from Dhimitsána), whose tiers of houses and bubbling sluices tumble downhill to the river far below the road. Often you can stop on a late-morning bus, eat lunch and pick up the next through service with little lost time. If you decide to stay the night, there are a couple of well-priced **hotels** on the main road: the central *Kentrikon* (☎ & ℱ 07950/43 221; ❷) and the even cheaper, council-owned *Langadia Motel* (☎07950/43 202, ℱ43 215; ❷) at the western end.

You may well find that you have fewer changes and stops if you backtrack south to join the **Karýtena–Andhrítsena route** and travel on to Olympia from there. Alternatively, if you're approaching Olympia from the north, through Arcadia from Pátra, then a pleasant staging post is the twin village of

LÁMBIA-DHÍVRI, roughly halfway between Trípoli and Pátra. There is a good *psistariá*, *Iy Divri*, as well as the *Lambia Pension* (☎06240/81 205; ❶), both of which enjoy fine views.

Andhrítsena and the Temple of Bassae

Moving west from Karýtena towards Andhrítsena, the Alfiós River falls away to the north and the hills become mountains – sacred Lýkeo to the south and Mínthi to the west. The route, only slightly less remote than the twists of road around Dhimitsána, is a superb one for its own sake, with the added attractions of **Andhrítsena**, a traditional mountain town, and the **Temple of Apollo Epikourios** at **Bassae** up in the flanks of Mount Lýkeo.

Andhrítsena

ANDHRÍTSENA, 28km west of Karýtena, is a beautiful stop, and the traditional base from which to visit the Temple of Apollo at Bassae up in the mountains to the south. Though very much a roadside settlement today, it too was a major hill town through the years of Turkish occupation and the first century of independent Greece. It remains remarkably untouched, with wooden houses spilling down to a stream, whose clear ice-cold headwaters are channelled into a fountain set within a plane tree in the central platía. There is a small **folk museum**, which opens on demand (€1); contact Vassiliki Tsigouri (☎06260/22 197) at the *Tsigouris* restaurant on a side street near the plane tree.

Hotel accommodation is available only at the *Theoxenia* (☎06260/22 219; March–Oct; ❸) on the Karýtena side of town. For **meals**, try any of the restaurants on the main platía, and especially the one up the steps beside the old (and closed) *Vassae* hotel.

The Temple of Apollo Epikourios at Bassae

Fourteen kilometres into the mountains south from Andhrítsena, the **Temple of Apollo** at **BASSAE** (Vásses) (summer daily 8.30am–3pm; €1.50) is the most remote and arguably the most spectacular site in Greece. In addition, it is, after the Thiseion in Athens, the best-preserved Classical monument in the country, and for many years was considered to have been designed by Iktinos, architect of the Parthenon – though this theory has recently fallen from favour.

There the superlatives must cease. Romantic though the temple was in the past, it is now swathed in a gigantic grey marquee supported on metal girders and set in concrete with wire stays; its entablature and frieze lie dissected in neat rows on the ground to one side. No doubt the **restoration** is badly needed for its preservation – and the marquee is quite a sight in itself – but it has to be said that visitors are likely to be a bit disappointed. If you are not put off, take the Kréstena road out of town and then, almost immediately, turn off to the left and you begin the climb to the temple. The simplest approach is to share a taxi, which should charge around €15 for the round trip, waiting an hour at the site. On foot it's a tiring ascent, with little likelihood of a lift. The site is not enclosed, but has a full-time guardian who lives alongside. It's a lonely place, and must have felt even more isolated in ancient times.

The temple was erected in dedication to **Apollo Epikourios** ("the Succourer") by the Phigalians. It's known that they built it in gratitude for being spared from plague, but beyond this it is something of a puzzle. It is oddly aligned on a north-south axis and, being way up in the mountains, is only visible when you are comparatively near. There are also oddities in the architecture: the columns on its north side are strangely thicker than in the rest of the building, and incorporated into its *cella* was a single Corinthian column, the first known in Greece (though now vanished save for its base). Unusually again, the cult statue, probably a four-metre-high bronze, would have stood in front of this pillar.

Moving on from Bassae or Andhrítsena

Leaving the Bassae/Andhrítsena area, there are a number of choices: from Andhrítsena two daily **buses** head back up towards Karýtena/Megalópoli and two go down to Pýrgos; if you are headed for **Olympia**, take the Pýrgos bus and get off in Kréstena, from where you can hitch or take a taxi 12km along the side road up to the site – you'll certainly save time and maybe some money.

A well-surfaced road winds through the mountains from Bassae down to the coast at **Tholó** (see p.279). It takes quite a while to cover the 46km, but for the unhurried there's an opportunity to stop at Perivólia (10km), which is a surprisingly lively little place with a couple of restaurants, cafés and even a bar full of well-dressed youth. This mountain hamlet has a short dirt road connecting it with the similarly diminutive Figália, close by the ruins of the enormous Classical walls of **ancient Phigalia**.

Messinía: Kalamáta to Kyparissía

The province of **Messinía** stretches from the western flank of the Taïyetos ridge across the plain of **Kalamáta** to the hilly southwesternmost finger of the Peloponnese. Green, fertile and luxuriant for the most part, it is ringed with a series of well-preserved castles overlooking some of the area's most expansive beaches. The pale curve of sand at the bay of **Voïdhokiliá**, sandwiched between sea, rock and lagoon, is one of the most beautiful in Greece. Smaller beaches at **Koróni**, **Methóni** and **Finikoúnda** draw the crowds, but its important archeological sites, such as **Nestor's Palace** near Hóra, rarely see visitors in the quantity of the Argolid sites.

Kalamáta and around

KALAMÁTA is by far the largest city of the southern Peloponnese, spreading for some four kilometres back from the sea, and into the hills. It's quite a metropolitan shock after the small-town life of the rest of the region. The city has a long-established export trade in olives and figs from the Messinian plain,

KALAMÁTA

Spárti

Bus Station

Market

Kástro

DHAMILATIS

KOUTIFARA
LEÍKON

River Nédhon

SPARTIS

AY. YEORYIOU

ALDHANIAS

MITR. MELETIOU

DHOUKAKI

Tís Ipapandís

Museum

BENAKI

Cathedral

SOULIOU

MEROPIS

MESSINIS

IRAS

Áyii
Apóstoli

IPAPANDIS

ANDROUSIS

ARTEMIDHOS

23 MARTIOU

Local Bus Stop

VOLKOU

FILOPIMENOS

KILKIS

KOLIMOUNDHOUROU

ATHINON

SFAKTIRIAS

AYIOU NIKOLAOU

STADHIOU

KALLIPATIRAS

PLATIA
ELEFTHERIAS

PLATIA
MAVROMIHALI

MAVROMIHALI

KOLOKOTRONI

FARON

ANAGNOSTARA

PEROTOU

DHIMAKOPOULOU

PAPATSONI

KAPETANAKI

PALEOLOUGOU

OTE

AVIAS

LAKONIKIS

MEGA ALEXANDHROU

MITROPETROVA

PLATIA
KONSTANDINOU
DHIADHOKHNOU

NIKITARA

ITYLOU

ZOUMBOULI

SARANDAPOROU

YBRONOS

STATHMOU

IATROPOULOU

ARISTOMENOUS

POLYHAROUS

TAXIARHON

KATSARI

FRANTZI

Byzantion

George

VALAORITOU

YEORYOULI

AKRITA

Train
Station

Police

PERIKLEOUS

PALAMA

VAS. YEORYIOU

XENOFONDOS

ARISTODIMOU

VAS. OLGAS

DHIMOSTHENOUS

VAS. SOFIAS

0   200 m

Airport, Tripoli, Messini & Pylos

Areópoli

Waterfront, beach & seafront hotels

KALAMÁTA
WATERFRONT

Railway
Museum

ARISTOMENOUS

KRITIS

LYKOURGOU

IDHRAS

KANARI

FARON

AKRITA

BOUBOULINAS

PSARON

METHONIS

EVANGELISTRIAS

KORONIS

Nevada

SANTAROZA

SALAMINOS

NAVARINOU

0   200 m

Hotels, Beach & Máni

flourishing as a commercial centre during the Turkish period and as one of the first independent Greek towns in 1821, with the first newspaper to be printed on Greek soil five months later. In 1986 however, Kalamáta was near the epicentre of a severe **earthquake** that killed twenty people and left 12,000 families homeless. But for the fact that the quake struck in the early evening, when many people were outside, the death toll would have been much higher. As it was, large numbers of buildings were levelled throughout the town. The intensity of the damage was in part due to the city's position over several subterranean streams, but mostly, it seems, the legacy of poor 1960s construction. The result was an economic depression across the whole area, from which the town is only now recovering properly.

The City

Few visitors plan to linger here; however, if you are travelling for a while, it's a good place to get things done, and there are other simple pleasures such as eating at tavernas among the Neoclassical houses on the waterfront or around the centre, which comprises the wide avenue formed by the long Platía Konstandínou Dhiadhókhnou.

With a little time to fill, a twenty-minute walk north of the centre will bring you to the most pleasing area of the city, around the **Kástro**. Built by the Franks and destroyed and adapted in turn by the Turks and Venetians, the *kástro* survived the quake with little damage; an **amphitheatre** at its base hosts summer concerts. A short way south of the *kástro*, at Polyzóglou 6 is the excellent **Benakion Archeological Museum** (Tues–Sun 8.30am–3pm; €1.50), which houses a modest but well-labelled collection of tomb reliefs, sculptures and smaller artefacts from the surrounding areas, as well as a colourful Roman mosaic from Desylla.

Kalamáta's **beach**, along Navarínou, a ten-minute bus ride (#1) south of the centre, is always crowded along the central section. The gritty sands are functional but improve continuously eastwards until the popular gay area beyond the *Filoxenia Beach Hotel*. If you prefer to walk to the harbour from the centre, it's a thirty-minute walk down Aristoménous, and you can wander in the park alongside the narrow bottom end of the street and admire the old steam engines, rolling stock and mechanical paraphernalia at the open-air Railway Museum.

Practicalities

If you're looking to get transport straight through, arrive early to make connections. The **bus station** (℡07320/23 145) is nearly 1km north of the centre; follow the river, partly covered with carparks, along Nédhondos. The Wednesday and Saturday produce market, one of the region's most colourful, is nearby, across the bridge from the bus station and alongside the road to Spárti. The most regular buses run north to Megalópoli, Trípoli and Athens, and west to Messíni, Koróni or Pýlos; the magnificent route over the Taïyetos ridge to Spárti is covered twice daily, and the one to Kardhamýli, Stoúpa and Ítylo (connection to Areópoli) four times daily.

The **train station** is 200m to the west of Platía Konstandínou Dhiadhókhnou, on Frantzí. Kalamáta is the railhead for trains chugging along the pretty, but slow and at times uncomfortable, route to Kyparissía (and ultimately to Pátra, with a possible detour to Olympia) or inland even more scenically to Trípoli and Árgos. Anyone arriving by slow train from Athens or Trípoli, and heading towards Pýlos or Koróni by bus, could get off at

Aspróhoma station (seven minutes before the main station) and catch the buses nearby, to avoid the long transfer between rail and bus terminals in Kalamáta itself. There are three **flights** a week to and from Athens; tickets are sold at the airport Olympic Airways office. The **airport** (☎07210/69 442) is 9km west of Kalamáta on the highway to Messíni, Pýlos and Koróni, and buses to these destinations pass the entrance. In season there are four charters a week from the UK, all on Sundays. The small terminal has an automatic **exchange** machine.

Taxis usually meet trains; otherwise there is a taxi rank on Aristoménous and another on Navarínou. Three rival agencies offer **car rental**: Maniatis, Iatropoúlou 1 (☎07210/27 694, ✉pelops@emporio.gr); Agni Travel, Kessári 2 (☎07210/20 352); and Stavrianos, Nédhondos 89 (☎07210/23 041). There are two **scooter rental** outlets: Bastakos (also mountain bikes) on Fáron 190 (☎07210/26 638), and Alpha, Výronos 156 (☎07210/93 423).

Most facilities, including the **banks** and **post office**, are in the streets around Platía Konstandínou Dhiadhókhnou, though there is a second **post office** near the customs house at the seaward end of Aristoménous. In the summer, Hobby at Fáron 237 sells English-language newspapers and books.

Accommodation

In the city centre, there are very few mid-range **hotels** left. Two of the best in terms of value for money are the *George*, Frantzí 5 (☎07210/27 225; ❹) and the larger *Byzantion*, Stathmoú 13 (☎07210/86 824; ❸). Both belong to the same management, are very close to the train station, not too far from the buses, and have TV in all rooms. Otherwise you'll do better down by the water-front, where there are many more hotels. Some of these are expensive, though they seem to have spent more on the reception areas than the bedrooms. Even so, they are often full by mid-afternoon and if you have not booked ahead, particularly at weekends, you may have to shop around. Choices include the *Flisvos*, Navarínou 135 (☎07210/82 177; ❺), which has quiet, comfortable rooms, although a little run-down, on the waterfront next to the church of Ayía Anástasi and the nearby *Haïkos*, Navarínou 115 (☎07210/88 902; ❸), a modern hotel with pleasant rooms, TV, air-conditioning and helpful staff. The cosy *Nevada*, Santaróza 9 (☎07210/82 429; ❷), is carefully tended by a Greek matri-arch; there are a number of house rules (in Greek and interpreted by her son). There is no breakfast, but you can eat very cheaply on the waterfront close by.

The nearest **campsites** are to be found along the stretch of beach to the east of the city. The first, about 5km from the waterfront, at Vérga, is the *Elite* (☎07210/80 365; April–Oct), behind the pricey *Hotel Elite* (☎07210/25 015; ❻), where campers can eat, and swim in the pool. If you want to swim off the pebble beach you will have to cross the Areópoli–Kalamáta highway, or stay at the *Maria*, also known as the *Sea and Sun* (☎07210/41 060), a popular and friendly campsite 500m down the road, which fronts onto the sea. However, unless you are stuck, you'd do better heading west towards Petalídhi (see p.268), or southeast to Kardhamýli and Stoúpa (see pp.240–241).

Eating and drinking

The best **restaurants** in the summer months are down by the **harbour**, which has been set up as a yacht marina. From west to east: *Krini* at Evangelistrías 40, is a neighbourhood fish-and-wine taverna open most of the year; *Pyrofani,* at a corner on the waterfront with views of the marina and the lights of the east-ern villages, has a large selection of meat and vegetarian dishes and good local wine; *Katofli* on Salamínos near the marina, has outdoor summer seating and a huge menu – unfortunately all three are accessed through a somewhat insalubrious area of abandoned warehouses and grain silos. Along the main, eastern waterfront are *Meltemi*, near the corner of Navarínou and Fáron, a basic *psistariá* with tasty food; *Tabaki*, Navarínou 91, featuring a wide menu and cheerful service; next door, the *Petrino* has a good selection of mezédhes. There are a couple of well-priced cafés directly opposite the bus station.

Only in winter does the older **centre** of town get into its culinary stride. At this time, pick from *Kannas*, Lakonikís 18, an atmospheric place with occasional live music which featured in Sheelagh Kanelli's novel, *Earth and Water*; or *Kioupi*, Alexíki 52 (off the Areópoli road), idiosyncratically decorated and with clay-pot cooking (as the name implies). For afternoon or evening drinks, the cafés along the central broad Platía Konstandínou Dhiadhókhnou are very pleasant, and less noisy with traffic than waterfront Navarínou. Round the corner, the pace heats up in the **bars** along Frantzí, towards the train station. There are several **cinemas** nearby, some with family entertainment.

If you're not after a full meal, Kalamáta has plenty of *mezedhopolía*, the better among them serving the traditional local snack – roast pork and potatoes. Down at the harbour, the *Karamanos* ouzerí west of the waterfront branch of the post office does nice fish mezédhes.

Ancient Messene

The ruins of ancient **MESSENE** (Ithómi) lie 25km northwest of Kalamáta and 20km northwest of modern Messíni. The ancient city was the fortified capital of the Messenians, and achieved some fame in the ancient world as a showcase of military architecture. The highlights of the widely dispersed site are the outcrops of its giant walls, towers and gates.

The ruins share the lower slopes of Mount Ithómi (800m) with the pretty village of **MAVROMÁTI**. A climb to the summit is rewarded with spectacular views of the region of Messinía and the southern Peloponnese. If you wish to stay and see the sunset from the site of the temple of Zeus which crowns this peak, there are **rooms** at the *Pension Zeus* (☎07240/51 025; ❸), as well as other establishments in the village.

The site is a tricky place to get to, unless you're driving. Buses run only twice a day from Kalamáta (very early morning and early afternoon). With a car it's a fairly easy detour en route to either Kyparissía, Pýlos or Petalídhi/Koróni.

The site

Messene's fortifications were designed as the southernmost link in a defensive chain of **walled cities** (others included Megalópolis and Árgos) masterminded by the Theban leader Epaminondas to keep the Spartans at bay. Having managed to halt them at the battle of Leuctra (near Stoúpa) in 371 BC, he set about building an astonishing nine-kilometre circuit of ten-metre-high walls (which lasted almost undamaged for 750 years) and restoring the Messenians to their native acropolis. The Messenians, who had resisted Spartan oppression from the eighth century BC onwards, wasted no time in re-establishing their capital; the city, so chronicles say, was built in 85 days.

The most interesting of the remains is the **Arcadia gate** at the north end of the site, through which the side road to Meligalás still runs. It consisted of an outer and inner portal separated by a circular courtyard made up of massive chunks of stone precisely cut to fit together without mortar. The outer gate, the foundations of which are fairly evident, was flanked by two square towers from where volleys of javelins and arrows would rain down on attackers. The inner gate, a similarly impregnable barrier, comprised a huge monolithic door-post, half of which still stands. You can still trace the ruts of chariot wheels in paved stretches of ancient road within the gateway.

Further south, and signposted "Ithomi: Archeological site" on the road running northwest from Mavromáti, is a recently excavated **sanctuary of Asclepius**. This site, which was first mistakenly marked out as the agora, consisted of a temple surrounded by a porticoed courtyard. The bases of some of the colonnades have been unearthed along with traces of benches. Next to it you can make out the site of a theatre or meeting place. Excavations continue in the summer with archeologists digging in the shade of semi-permanent canopies.

Other remains are to be seen up Mount Ithómi, an hour's hike along a steep path forking north from the track at the Laconia gate, which is to the southeast of the site. Along the way you pass remains of an Ionic **temple of Artemis**. At the top, on the site of a temple of Zeus, are the ruins of the small **monastery of Voulkanós**, founded in the eighth century but dating in its present form from the sixteenth. Spread below are the lush and fertile valleys of Messinía.

Around the coast to Koróni

Beaches stretch for virtually the entire distance west from Kalamáta then south to Koróni, along what is steadily developing as a major resort coast. At present, however, it is more popular with Greeks than foreigners, and the resorts, tucked away in the pines, consist primarily of campsites at Análypsi and Velíka, interspersed with the odd room for rent. The beach at Boúka, 5km south of modern Messíni, is a fine stretch of sand with views of the Máni. It is popular with the locals, especially as a place to go for Sunday lunch.

The best of the beaches are around **PETALÍDHI**, 25km west around the coast from Kalamáta. The small town itself is not unattractive and there are several **campsites** along this coast: *Petalidi Beach* (☎07220/31 154; April–Sept), 3km north of the village, is well established and reasonably priced. There are ample **tavernas** and cafés around the spacious sea-facing square and some cheap **rooms**. Moving on south, if you have your own transport, there are numerous restaurants, rooms and some hotels along the stretch of coast – and busy road – to Koróni. The *Kalami* and *Sokrates* **tavernas** in **KHRÁNI** are recommended, the latter having very good mezédhes, and the *Sunrise Village* at **KALAMAKÍ** has an unusually good restaurant for a hotel (the rooms themselves are package territory only).

Koróni and Methóni

The twin **fortresses** at Koróni and Methóni were the Venetians' oldest and longest-held possessions in the Peloponnese: strategic outposts on the route to Crete and known through the Middle Ages as "the eyes of the Serene Republic", when it was also noted for the manufacture of siege-engines. Today they shelter two of the more attractive small resorts in the south.

Public **transport** around the Messinian peninsula has improved of late and there are good connections between Kalamáta and Koróni, or Pýlos, with several buses a day from Pýlos to Methóni and Finikoúnda. Direct connections between Methóni and Koróni are still elusive, although a new fast road has been built connecting the two in season (usually early morning and late afternoon), one or two buses a day on the Kalamáta–Koróni route continue to Finikoúnda. If moving on from Koróni to Pýlos, you can change from the Koróni–Kalamáta bus to the Kalamáta–Pýlos bus at the café at Rizómylos junction.

Koróni

KORÓNI has one of the most picturesque sites in Greece, stacked against a fortified bluff and commanding grand views across the Messenian gulf to the Taïyetos peaks. The town is rustically beautiful in itself, with tiled and pastel-washed houses arrayed in a maze of stair-and-ramp streets that can have changed little since the medieval Venetian occupation (1206–1500) when it was a fleet supply base. Buses terminate in the square below the main church, outside a café and excellent *zaharoplastío* and one row back from the waterfront. Koróni's **citadel** is one of the least militaristic-looking in Greece, crowning rather than dwarfing the town. Much of the interior is given over to private houses and garden plots, but the greater part is occupied by the flower-strewn nunnery of **Timíou Prodhrómou**, whose chapels, outbuildings and gardens occupy nearly every bastion.

From the southwest gate of the fortress, stairs descend to the park-like grounds of **Panayía Elestrías**, a church erected at the end of the nineteenth century to house a miraculous icon – unearthed with the assistance of the vision of one Maria Stathaki (buried close by). The whole arrangement, with fountains, shrubbery and benches for watching the sunset seems more like the Adriatic than the Aegean.

Continuing downhill, you reach **Zánga beach** which runs into **Mémi beach**, making a two-kilometre stretch of sand and preternaturally clear water that sets the seal on Koróni's superiority as a place to relax, drink wine and amble about a countryside lush with vineyards, olives and banana trees. The beach is about the only place to go during the afternoon, when Koróni observes the strict siesta. Turtles nest in the Mémi area.

Practicalities

To be sure of a room in summer, it's worth trying to phone ahead. The only large hotel, the *Hotel de la Plage* (℡07250/22 401; ❹), is way out on the road towards Mémi beach. Looking for **private rooms** on arrival, try the places to the right of the fishing port as you face the water, and don't leave it too late in the day; there are also cheaper, quieter rooms in the Panórama district, up behind Zánga beach. Several of the town tavernas rent rooms on a regular basis, including the *Parthenon* (℡07250/22 146; ❷) on a seafront corner below the square, and the *Pension Koroni* (℡07250/22 385; ❷) above the *Symposium/Symposion* restaurant on the main street. An attractive and only slightly more expensive option, with a leafy setting and views of the bay and castle, is *Marinos Bungalows* (℡07250/22 527; April–Oct; ❸) on the road north just out of town. There are two **campsites**: *Memi Beach* (℡07250/22 130; May–Oct), which is 2km south of Koróni as you approach from Methóni, and *Koroni* (℡07250/22 119; May–Sept) on the road into town; both have sandy beaches, though from *Memi Beach* you have to cross the road.

There is a reasonable selection of **restaurants** on the waterfront, and some authentic **tavernas** (barrel-wine and oven-food places) along the main shopping street. The *Parthenon* has good food and efficient service, and the *Symposium* serves moussaka, grills and seafood. The *Flisvos* remains a good restaurant despite its closure as a hotel.

Many people make wine or rakí in their basement and the heady local tipple figures prominently in the **nightlife**. The main venue for nightlife is the sprawling *Astra Club* out towards Mémi beach. There are two or three tavernas on the beach and by night a solitary disco, though all of these close down by mid-September. Otherwise, there are two **banks** (one with a cash dispenser) and a **post office**.

Finikoúnda

FINIKOÚNDA, 18km west of Koróni, is a small fishing village with a superb cove-beach plus another to the east, and a gigantic strand to the west. Over recent years it gained a reputation as a backpackers' – and especially windsurfers' – resort, with half the summer intake at a trio of campsites on either side of the village, the others housed in a variety of rooms including some taken by British package companies. It can be a fun, laid-back place.

To book **rooms** in advance, try the **hotels** *Finikounda* (☎ & ⓕ 07230/71 208; ❹) and *Porto Finissia* (☎07230/71 358, ⓕ71 458; summer only; ❹), or the hospitable *Korakakis Beach* (☎07230/71 221, ⓕ71 232; ❹) which also has self-catering apartments with air conditioning at similar prices. The local **campsites** are the well-equipped *Anemomilos* (☎07230/71 360, ⓕ71 121; open all year), 500m west of town; *Ammos* (☎07230/71 262; May–Oct), 3km west of the village; and the *Loutsa* (☎07230/71 445; June–Sept), 2km to the east. Among the **tavernas**, *Elena* is recommended for good traditional fare and for a drink with a harbour view, while *Psychos* has tasty food, including pasta and pizzas, at good prices; *Theasis* bar features a mixture of old and new rock **music**.

Methóni

In contrast to the almost domestic citadel at Koróni, the fortress at **METHÓNI** is as imposing as they come – massively bastioned, washed on three sides by the sea, and cut off altogether from the land by a great moat. It was maintained by the Venetians in part for its military function, in part as a staging post for pilgrims en route, via Crete and Cyprus, to the Holy Land, and from the thirteenth to the nineteenth centuries it sheltered a substantial town. It was from here, in 1825, that Ibrahim Pasha launched his destructive reinvasion of the Peloponnese that was only finally stopped by the events at Navaríno in 1827 (see box on p.274).

Within the **fortress** (Mon–Sat 8am–8pm, Sun 9am–8pm; closes 3pm in winter; free), entered across the moat along a stone bridge, are the remains of a Venetian cathedral (the Venetians' Lion of St Mark emblem is ubiquitous), along with a Turkish bath, the foundations of dozens of houses and some awesome, but mostly cordoned-off, underground passages. Walking around the walls, a sea gate at the southern end leads out across a causeway to the **Boúrtzi**, a small fortified island that served as a prison and place of execution. The octagonal tower was built by the Turks in the sixteenth century to replace an earlier Venetian fortification. Unusually, and for no obvious reason, photography is forbidden inside the site – probably because of archeological excavations; it seems unlikely that the Greek military regard it as still of strategic significance.

Practicalities

The modern village, on the landward side of the moat, has a **bank** and **post office**, all easily located in the three-street-wide grid. The **bus** stops at the first forked junction in town and there is a timetable in a nearby shop window. The

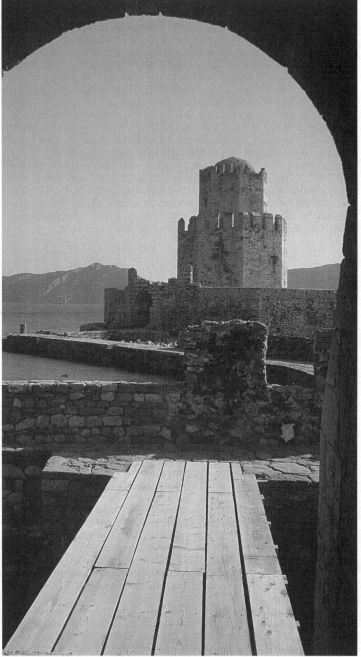

△ The Boúrtzi seen through sea gate of Venetian fort

rather scruffy beach runs eastwards from the castle. In high season, there may be boat trips out to the southern islands of Skhíza and Sapiénza.

Methóni is geared more conspicuously to tourism than Koróni and gets very crowded in season, when accommodation can be expensive and often over-subscribed. Out of season, the **hotels** are cheaper and a number stay open all year. The well-priced *Castello* (☎07230/31 300; ❹) is near the entrance to the fortress, with beautiful gardens, balconies and a stunning view; the friendly *Aris* (☎07230/31 336; ❹) is on a small platía behind *Castello*. The renovated *Anna* (☎07230/31 332; ❹) is also friendly – all rooms have TV and there's a good restaurant. In addition, there is the usual collection of cheaper **rooms** such as the *Mintziras* (☎07230/31 123; ❷) on the hill. At the east end of the beach is a municipal **campsite**, the *Methoni* (☎07230/31 228; May–Oct); it's popular and gets crowded, but the facilities are good and the beach tolerable.

Methóni has several **restaurants**, including the slightly pricey *Klimataria* (☎07230/31 544 reservations suggested; May–Oct, evenings only), which serves a well-prepared selection of dishes (including good veggie choices) in a courtyard garden. At the adequate *Rex*, which is open all day, you can eat in the shade of tamarisk trees. Among the dozen or so other eateries, *Inousses*, 150m along the beach, is also recommended for waterfront dining.

Pýlos and around

PÝLOS is a little like a small-scale, less sophisticated Náfplio – quite a stylish town for rural Messinía. It is guarded by a pair of medieval castles and occupies a superb position on one of the finest natural harbours in Greece, the land-locked **Navarino Bay** (see box on p.274). Given the town's romantic associations with the Battle of Navarino, and, more anciently, with Homer's "sandy Pýlos", the domain of "wise King Nestor" whose palace (see p.275) has been identified 16km to the north, it makes a great base for exploring this part of the Peloponnese, particularly if equipped with a car or scooter – both of which can be rented here. Relying on public transport you'll find the long afternoon gaps in services make complex day-trips impractical.

The Town

The main pleasures of Pýlos are exploring the hillside alleys, waterside streets and fortress. Getting your bearings is easy as it's not a large town, and the buses drop you at the inland end of the central Platía Trión Navárhon which faces the port.

Shaded by a vast plane tree and scented by limes, **Platía Trión Navárhon** is a beautiful public platía, completely encircled by cafés and very much the heart of the town. At its centre is a **war memorial** commemorating admirals Codrington, de Rigny and von Heyden, who commanded the British, French and Russian forces in the Battle of Navarino (see box on p.274). Nearby, just uphill on the Methóni road, the little **Antonopouleion Museum** (Tues–Sun 8.30am–3pm; €1.50) boasts remains from the battle, along with archeological finds from the region.

Further memories of the Navarino battles can be evoked by a visit to the **island of Sfaktiría**, across the bay, where there are various tombs of Philhellenes, a chapel and a memorial to Russian sailors. You can hire a **boat** from the port and also snorkel to see the remains of the Turkish fleet lying on the sea bed; ask at the harbourmaster's office or cafés by the port.

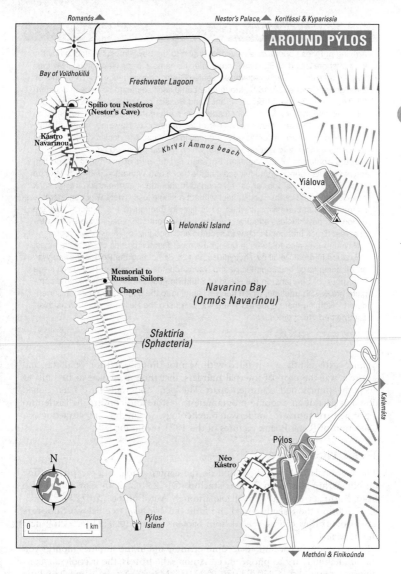

AROUND PÝLOS

Romanós

Nestor's Palace, ▲ Korifássi & Kyparissía

Bay of Voïdhokiliá

Freshwater Lagoon

Spílio tou Nestóros
(Nestor's Cave)

Kástro
Navarínou

Khrysí Ámmos beach

Yiálova

Helonáki Island

Memorial to
Russian Sailors

Chapel

Navarino Bay
(Ormós Navarínou)

Sfaktiría
(Sphacteria)

Kalamáta

N

Pýlos

Néo
Kástro

0   1 km

Pýlos
Island

Methóni & Finikoúnda

The principal sight in town, however, is the **Néo Kástro** (Tues–Sun 8.30am–3pm; €2.50), close by the port on the south side of the bay (further up the Methóni road). The hugely spreading "new castle" was built by the Turks in 1572, and allows a walk around much of the 1500m of arcaded battlements, although unsafe segments are now closed. For much of the eighteenth and nineteenth centuries, it served as a prison and its inner courtyard was divided into a warren of narrow yards separated by high walls, a design completely at odds with most Greek prisons, which were fairly open on the inside. This peculiar feature is explained by the garrison's proximity to the

The battles of Navarino Bay

Arriving at Pýlos your gaze is inevitably drawn to the bay, almost landlocked by the long offshore island of Sfaktiría (Sphacteria). Its name, Órmos Navarínou – Navarino Bay – marks the battle that effectively sealed Greek independence from the Turks on the night of October 20, 1827, though the battle itself seems to have been accidental. The Great Powers of Britain, France and Russia, having established diplomatic relations with the Greek insurgent leaders, were attempting to force an armistice on the Turks. To this end they sent a fleet of 27 warships to Navarino, where Ibrahim Pasha had gathered his forces – 16,000 men in 89 ships. The declared intention was to coerce Ibrahim into leaving Messinía, which he had been raiding.

In the confusion of the night an Egyptian frigate, part of the Turks' supporting force, fired its cannons, and full-scale battle broke out. Without intending to take up arms for the Greeks, the "allies" responded to the attack and, extraordinarily, sank and destroyed 53 of the Turkish fleet without a single loss. There was considerable international embarrassment when news filtered through to the "victors", but the action had nevertheless effectively ended Turkish control of Greek waters and within a year Greek independence was secured and recognized.

Navarino Bay also features in one of the most famous battles of Classical times, described in great detail by Thucydides. In 425 BC, during the Peloponnesian War, an Athenian force encamped in Kástro Navarínou (the old castle of Pýlos) laid siege to a group of Spartans on the island of **Sfaktiría**, just across the straits. In a complete break with tradition, which decreed fighting to the death, the Spartans surrendered. "Nothing that happened in the war surprised the Hellenes as much as this," commented Thucydides.

Máni. So frequently was it filled with Maniots imprisoned for vendettas, and so great was the crop of internal murders, that these pens had to be built to keep the imprisoned clansmen apart. The pens and walls have been pulled down as part of an ongoing programme to restore and convert the castle into a planned **museum** for underwater archeology. So far, the only attraction is a collection of René Puaux pictures of the 1821 revolution.

Practicalities

The National Bank is to be found on the central platía, and the **post office** on Niléos, just west from the **bus station** (℡07230/22 230). **Car rental** (also from Kalamáta airport) is available through AutoEurope (℡07230/22 393, ℗23 400) on the Kalamáta road and from the *Miramare* (see below). **Scooters** and **motorbikes** can be rented from Sapienza Travel (℡07230/23 207) near the *Miramare*.

Pýlos has somewhat limited accommodation and in the summer months you should definitely try to phone ahead. Among the **hotels**, the friendly, air-conditioned *Arvaniti* (℡07230/23 050, ℗22 934; March–Oct; ❸) – up beyond the post office on Niléos – is the best value. The rather faded *Galaxy*, on the platía (℡07230/22 780, ℗22 208; ❹), is a fall-back choice if the *Arvaniti* is closed or full, as is the posher *Karalis*, Kalamátas 26 (℡07230/22 960, ℗22 970; ❺), an attractive seaview hotel with a good restaurant. The *Miramare*, Myrtidhiotíssis 35 (℡07230/22 751, ℗22 226; ❻), has a restaurant and bar and fine views by the port, but is closed between October and March. There are many **rooms** around the winding main road on the hill out towards Kalamáta and Kyparissía. A more relaxed alternative to staying in Pýlos would be the beachfront part of Yiálova (see opposite).

For **drinks**, the Platía Trión Navárhon cafés are the obvious choice. Among **tavernas**, try *Grigori's*, on the road up left of the police station on the platía; the *Lykourgos* opposite is also good. Nightlife revolves around bars on the square, and the larger, summer-only **discos** *Gigi's* and *Zoglo Summer Matter*, both a little out of town. There is also a summer outdoor **cinema**.

The northern rim of Navarino Bay

YIÁLOVA, 6km north out of Pýlos, has tamarisk trees shading its sandy beach and is a delightful base for walkers, naturalists or beach-lovers. The *Navarino Beach* **campsite** (☎07230/22 761; April–Oct) has good facilities including a recommended restaurant, and is popular with windsurfers. Nearer the central jetty there are two **hotels**: the delightful *Zoe* (☎07230/22 025; ❸), with one of the best views in Greece, and *Helonaki House* (☎07230/23 080; ❸) with a variety of rooms and apartments. The *Zoe* also has the *Voula Apartments* (❸) back towards Pýlos. For eating, you can't beat the excellent home cooking at *Oasis* by the corner of the pier, almost next door to the *Zoe*. There is a small shop for picnic supplies between the *Oasis* and the main road; further along the main road is more, though less well-positioned, accommodation.

Pýlos's northern castle, and ancient acropolis, **Kástro Navarínou** (Paleó Kástro), stands on a hill ridge almost touching the island of Sfaktiría, at the end of the bay 5km west of Yiálova. It has substantial walls, and identifiable courtyards and cisterns within fortifications which are a mix of Frankish and Venetian, set upon ancient foundations. The panoramic outlook is tremendous, but the interior is a jungle of shrubs and other vegetation that makes progress through it difficult. It's a ten- to twelve-kilometre trip from Pýlos, for which you'll need some transport. To get there, follow the main road north towards Hóra, but when the road swings right to Korifássi, go left on a side road signed to Romanós and Navarino castle. If you find your way, you will end up at one of the best beaches in the Peloponnese – a lovely crescent of sand curling around the spectacular **Bay of Voïdhokiliá**. A simpler alternative is to go north through Yiálova, turn left at the sign to Voïdhokiliá and Golden Beach (the Pýlos–Hóra bus will bring you this far); at the end of the surfaced road, go left until the dirt road ends below the castle hill. From here head right along the footpath between the lagoon and the hill until you reach the Voïdhokiliá dunes and beach. The lagoon is an important bird conservation area under NATURA 2000, and vehicles are not allowed on the earth road around the eastern rim of the lagoon. Near the end of the asphalt, a signed nature trail has been laid out. Turtles still breed at Voïdhokiliá (and at the beaches of Romanoú and Máti, further north), but a small population – the only one in mainland Europe – of slow-moving chameleons amongst the dune shrubs is endangered by illegal drivers and camper vans.

A path from the Voïdhokiliá dunes ascends to the **Spílio tou Nestóros** (Nestor's Cave), and then more steeply up to the castle. This impressive bat-cave with a hole in the roof is fancifully identified as the grotto in which, according to the *Odyssey*, Nestor and Neleus kept their cows, and in which Hermes hid Apollo's cattle. It is not impossible that the cave sparked Homer's imagination, for this area is reckoned by archeologists to have been the Mycenaean-era harbour of King Nestor (see below), and later of the Classical town of Korifasio.

North to Nestor's Palace

Nestor's Palace (also known as the Palace of Englianós, after the hill on which it stands) was discovered in 1939, but left virtually undisturbed until after World War II; thus its excavation – unlike Mycenae, or most of the other major Greek sites – was conducted in accordance with modern archeological techniques. In consequence, its remains are the best preserved of all the Mycenaean royal palaces, though they shelter rather prosaically beneath a giant metal roof. The site guide by excavators Carl Blegen and Marion Rawson is an excellent buy.

The palace is located some 16km from modern Pýlos, a half-hour drive. Using public transport, take any of the **buses** from Pýlos towards Kyparissía (3–6 daily); these follow the main road inland past Korifássi to the site and its museum at Hóra (4km to the east).

The palace site

Flanked by deep, fertile valleys, the **palace site** (daily 8.30am–3pm; €1.50) looks out towards Navarino Bay – a location perfectly suiting the wise, measured and peaceful king described in Homer's *Odyssey*. The scene from the epic that is set here is the visit of Telemachus, son of Odysseus, who had journeyed from Ithaca to seek news of his father from King Nestor. As Telemachus arrives at the beach, accompanied by the disguised goddess Pallas Athena, he comes upon Nestor with his sons and court sacrificing to Poseidon. The visitors are welcomed and feasted, "sitting on downy fleeces on the sand", and although the king has no news of Odysseus he promises Telemachus a chariot so he can enquire from Menelaus at Sparta. First, however, the guests are taken back to the palace, where Telemachus is given a bath by Nestor's "youngest grown daughter, beautiful Polycaste", and emerges, anointed with oil, "with the body of an immortal".

By some harmonious twist of fate, a bathtub was unearthed on the site, and the palace ruins as a whole are potent ground for Homeric imaginings. The walls stand a metre high, enabling you to make out a very full plan. Originally, they were half-timbered (like Tudor houses), with upper sections of sun-baked brick held together by vertical and horizontal beams, and brilliant frescoes within. Even in their diminished state they suggest a building of considerable prestige. No less should be expected, for Nestor sent the second largest contingent to Troy – a fleet of "ninety black ships". The remains of the massive complex are in three principal groups: the **main palace** in the middle, on the left an earlier and **smaller palace**, and on the right either **guardhouses** or **workshops**.

The basic design will be familiar if you've been to Mycenae or Tiryns: an internal court, guarded by a sentry box, gives access to the main sections of the principal palace. This contained some 45 rooms and halls. The **megaron** (throne room), with its characteristic open hearth, lies directly ahead of the entrance, through a double porch. The finest of the frescoes was discovered here, depicting a griffin (perhaps the royal emblem) standing guard over the throne; this is now in the museum at Hóra. Arranged around are domestic quarters and **storerooms**, which yielded literally thousands of pots and cups during excavations; the rooms may have served as a distribution centre for the produce of the palace workshops. Further back, the famous **bathroom**, with its terracotta tub *in situ*, adjoins a smaller complex of rooms, centred on another, smaller megaron, identified as the **queen's quarters**. Finally, on the other side of the car park there is a *thólos* (beehive) tomb, a smaller version of the famous ones at Mycenae.

Archeologically, the most important find at the site was a group of several hundred tablets inscribed in **Linear B**. These were discovered on the first day of digging, in the two small rooms to the left of the entrance courtyard. They were the first such inscriptions to be discovered on the Greek mainland and proved conclusively a link between the Mycenaean and Minoan civilizations; like those found by Sir Arthur Evans at Knossos on Crete, the language was unmistakably Greek. The tablets were baked hard in the fire which destroyed the palace at the time of the Dorian invasion around 1200 BC, perhaps as little as one generation after the fall of Troy.

The museum at Hóra

At Hóra (Hóra Trifylías), a small town despite the name, the **museum** (officially Tues–Sun 8.30am–3pm, but can be erratic; €1.50) on S. Marinátou, signed above the main square and Friday morning produce market, adds significantly to a visit to the site. If you've no transport, it might be better to take a bus here first, to the central bus station stop, and then walk the 45 minutes to the site after viewing the exhibits. In spring or autumn this is a pleasure; shy golden orioles have been seen in trees alongside the road. In hot weather, or if pressed for time, you can hitch fairly easily or get a taxi.

Pride of place in the display goes to the **palace frescoes**, one of which, bearing out Homer's descriptions, shows a warrior in a boar-tusk helmet. Lesser finds include much pottery, some beautiful gold cups and other objects gathered both from the site and from various Mycenaean tombs in the region.

The coast north of Pýlos

The stretch of **coast** between Pýlos and Pýrgos is defined by its **beaches**, which are on a different scale to those elsewhere in the Peloponnese, or indeed anywhere else in Greece – fine sands, long enough (and undeveloped enough) to satisfy the most jaded Australian or Californian. Their relative anonymity is something of a mystery, though one accounted for in part by poor communications. For those without transport this entails slow and patient progress along the main "coast" road, which for much of the way runs two to five kilometres inland, and a walk from road junction to beach.

Heading north from the Bay of Voïdhokiliá, near the turning inland to Korifási and Nestor's Palace, you can take a paved road, flanked by orange and olive orchards. This keeps close to the sea for most of the way to Kyparissía, allowing access to isolated beaches and villages.

If you're travelling to Olympia by **train** from this coast (once the Pýrgos–Olympia service is reinstated; see p.287), you can save the detour to Pýrgos (not an exhilarating town – see p.288) by getting a connection at Alfiós, a tiny station at the junction of the Olympia line and as bucolic a halt as any on the network (but not to be confused with next stop Alfioúsa station). Alfiós is eleven minutes down the line from Pýrgos, and 25 from Olympia.

Marathópoli and Filiatrá

If you are looking for the rudiments of accommodation and a little more than a village café, then Marathópoli, the harbour of Gargaliáni, holds most promise. **MARATHÓPOLI** has a long beach, rockier than most along this coast and faces the islet of Próti, shaped like a long-tailed turtle and once a pirate refuge. It has two **hotels**: on the beach, the *Artina* (☎07230/61 400, ℱ61 402; ❹) has en-suite facilities, small kitchenettes and should be booked in advance. There are some **rooms** for rent; a **campsite**, *Proti* (☎07230/61 211; May–Oct), with a swimming pool; and two or three summer **tavernas** by the sea. A small taxi boat makes the short crossing to the islet of Próti, with its sandy beach and monastery, for a reasonable fixed rate.

Further on, the road passes through Ayía Kyriakí, a fishing village with a sweet little harbour and a few rooms, before reaching **FILIATRÁ**, which is on the bus route between Pýlos and Kyparissía. By a curious pattern of emigration, just as Kýthira is home to Greek-Australians, the villages along the Kyparissía coast have a concentration of returned Greek-Americans, virtually all of them having done a stint of work in New York or New Jersey. Disgraced American ex-Vice President (1968–73) Spiro Agnew was perhaps the most infamous local boy. However, the Greek-American who has left most mark on his home domain is one Haris Fournakis, also known as **Harry Fournier**, a doctor from Chicago who came back in the 1960s and started building his fantasies. At the northern entrance to Filiatrá, Fournier constructed a garden-furniture version of the **Eiffel Tower** (illuminated at night by fairy lights) and a mini-replica of the globe from the 1964 New York Expo. His most ambitious project, however, was his **Kástro ton Paramythíon** ("Castle of the Fairytales"; daily 9am–2pm & 5–8pm; €1.50), a truly loopy folly with white concrete battlements and outcrops of towers, plus thirty- to forty-foot-high statues of Poseidon's horse (flanked by vases of flowers) and the goddess Athena. The castle is located right on the sea, and can be reached from Filiatrá by following the road for 6km north, through the hamlet of Agríli. Apart from Fournier's castle, the only feature of the town is the pleasant central square with a large, functioning fountain, the bus station and numerous cafés. There is no good beach.

Kyparissía

KYPARISSÍA is a small, congenial agricultural and market town, positioned in the shadow of the eponymous peak, part of the spectacular Egáleo mountain ridge. On a lower outcrop of the range is a Byzantine-Frankish **castle** (free), around which spreads the **old town**. The ochre-hued mansions stand abandoned, having suffered heavy damage during the civil war, though a couple of **tavernas** still function here, lovely old places and very welcoming.

Below the hill, the modern town goes about its business, with a small harbour and real shops. A few tourist boutiques and a nightclub or two have sprung up recently, but it's still a pleasant place to rest up, and possibly preferable to a night in Kalamáta if you're on your way to Olympia by bus or train (Kyparissía is the junction of the Kalamáta and Pýrgos lines). Within walking distance of town are long, near-deserted sands – turtle breeding-grounds – and rocky cliff paths.

Practicalities

The centre of the modern town, just south of the adjacent **bus** (☎07610/22 260) and **train stations** (☎07610/22 283), is Platía Kalantzákou, where you'll find three **banks**, the **post office** and a remarkable number of cafés. Given a choice, Kyparissía is the most convenient place to change between bus and train if you have luggage. Accommodation consists of a half-dozen **hotels**, divided between the town and the beach. The cheapest place to stay in town is the *Trifolia*, 25-Martíou 40 (☎07610/22 066; ❶), a down-to-earth and welcoming pension, just east of the square and round the corner from the bus station. Other hotels are the *Vasilikon*, Alexopoúlou 7 (☎07610/22 655, ℱ24 413; ❹), almost opposite the large church, which is well kept, though without any particular charm, and the nearby comfortable *Ionion* (☎07610/22 511,

Ⓕ22 512; ❹), facing the train station; by the beach is the **campsite**, *Kyparissía* (☎07610/23 491). Beyond this beach, over a small rocky headland there's a better beach used by naturists, though with strong currents at times. There are a handful of no-nonsense **restaurants** and pizzerias in the streets around Platía Kalantzákou; one of the best is *Nynio*, at 25-Martíou 52 on a corner by the bus station. For atmosphere it's better to eat down at the beach, where the taverna *Ta Porákia*, towards the campsite, is a fine choice, or up at the old town, where the liveliest place to dine is the *Psistariá Arcadia*.

Beaches north from Kyparissía

Between Kyparissía and Lake Kaïáfas, the road and rail lines continue, a kilometre or so back from the coast, with the occasional **campsite** advertising its particular stretch of beach. Unofficial camping in the pine forest behind the beach at **Eliá** is possible – on the beach itself there's an ecological kiosk with information about the turtles that nest there, and behind the forest there's a good shady taverna, *O Mythos*. Authorized campsites include the *Apollo Village* (☎06250/61 200; May–Oct) at **Yianitsohóri** (18km along), and, a few kilometres further on, a better site at **Tholó** – the *Tholo Beach* (☎06250/61 345; March–Oct). **Neohóri**, just past Tholó, has a few **rooms** to rent, as does Yianitsohóri.

All of the hamlets on this coast have long stretches of sandy beach, often edged with olive groves, reed-beds or pinewoods – their lack of development seems almost miraculous. One of the more accessible of the beaches (5min from the rail station and 25 from the main highway) is 5km beyond Tholó at **KAKÓVATOS**, which combines breakers with incredibly shallow, slowly shelving waters – though lacking any shade. The area is slightly more commercialized now with the *To Kohyli* (*Grigoris*) taverna and the *Baywatch* café (complete with watchtower) on the beach, while the village has a number of pensions, including *Kallifidhas* (☎06250/31 167; ❶) and *Timoleon* (☎06250/32 253; ❷).

Just north, at **ZAHÁRO**, the largest town between Kyparissía and Pýrgos, and a train stop, there are numerous shops and four **hotels**, though a shortage of tavernas. Near the main crossroads, on the railway station side, is the *Rex* (☎06250/31 221; ❸), with kitchenettes in some of its rooms; the *Nestor* (☎06250/31 206; ❸) has clean rooms and old-fashioned hospitality; while the *Sugar Town* (☎06250/31 985; ❶) opposite is newer and above a café. The *Diethnes* (☎06250/31 208; ❷) is near the church at the top, inland end of the village. The railway station is just under a kilometre from the crossroads, on the road to the sea; midway from the station to the excellent beach is the *Banana Place* (☎06250/34 400; April–Oct; ❷), which offers chalet-type accommodation with cooking facilities – booking is advisable. Afternoon buses through the Zaháro **bus station** – east of the crossroads and right – are few and far between; **taxis** in Zaháro are on ☎06250/31 357.

Another enormous strand, backed by sand dunes and pine groves, is to be found at **Kaïáfas** just before the roads loop inland. At the beach there's just a single, rather uninspired taverna and the train station, both on the main road, opposite the entrance to the spa. On a side road a couple of kilometres inland, however, the village of **LOUTRÁ KAÏÁFAS** assumes the atmosphere of a spa. Strung out alongside the reed-screened lagoon is a scattering of hotels and pensions, frequented mainly by Greeks seeking hydrotherapy cures. Each morning a small shuttle-boat takes the patients from their hotels to the sulphurous and often foul-smelling hot springs across the lagoon. The best deal for accommodation is probably at the friendly *Hotel Jenny* (☎06250/32 234; ❷), which has a decent restaurant, as does the clean and comfortable *Archaea Sami* ☎06250/32 257, ℱ34 639; spring–Oct; ❸) which is the nearest accommodation (1.5km) to the main highway; the latter has cheaper rooms with shared bathrooms, intended for its Greek summer clientele. Two kilometres north of the lake, as the national road loops around a spur in the hills, you can just make out the walls of ancient Samikón on the hillside.

Ilía and Ahaïa: the northwest

Dominated economically by the sprawling city of **Pátra**, the large province of **Ahaïa** combines high mountains and a narrow, densely populated coastal strip; from **Dhiakoftó** in the north, one of Greece's most remarkable railway lines follows the Vouraikós Gorge, up to the memorials of **Kalávryta**. To the southwest of Ahaïa, the flat coastal plains of **Ilía** support a series of undistinguished market towns and are bordered on the west by long, narrow, often underused beaches. The **Olympia** archeological site is the jewel of the fertile Alfiós valley and this area's main tourist attraction.

Olympia (Olymbía)

The historic associations and resonance of **OLYMPIA**, which for over a millennium hosted the most important **Panhellenic games**, are rivalled only by Delphi or Mycenae. It is one of the largest and most beautiful sites in Greece, and the setting is as perfect as could be imagined: a luxuriant valley of wild olive and plane trees, spread beside the twin rivers of Alfiós (Alpheus) – the largest in the Peloponnese – and Kládhios, and overlooked by the pine-covered hill of Krónos. Sadly, the actual ruins of the sanctuary are jumbled and confusing, and seem to cry out for reconstruction, even on a modest scale. The great temple columns lie half-buried amid the trees and undergrowth: picturesque and shaded, perfect ground for picnics, but offering little real impression of their ancient grandeur or function. Their fame, however, prevails over circumstance, and walking through the arch from the sanctuary to the stadium it is hard not to feel in awe of the Olympian history. Despite the crowds, the tour buses, the souvenir shops and other trappings of mass tourism, it demands and deserves a lengthy visit.

The modern village of Olymbía acts as a service centre for the site, and has little in the way of distractions, save for a somewhat dutiful **Museum of the Olympic Games** (Mon–Sat 8am–3.30pm, Sun 9am–4.30pm; €1.50), on the street above the *Hotel Phedias*, with commemorative postage stamps and the odd memento from the modern games, including the box that conveyed the heart of Pierre de Coubertin (reviver of the modern games) from Paris to its burial at Olympia.

The site

From its beginnings the **site** (daily: May to mid–Oct 8am–7pm, Aug until 9pm, Sept until 8pm; mid–Oct to April 8am–5pm, Sat & Sun 8.30am–3pm; €3.50 or €6 for combined site and museum) was a sanctuary, with a permanent population limited to the temple priests. At first the games took place within the sacred precinct, the walled, rectangular **Altis**, but as events became more sophisticated a new **stadium** was built to adjoin it. The whole sanctuary was, throughout its history, a treasure trove of public and religious statuary. Victors were allowed to erect a statue in the Altis (in their likeness if they won three events) and numerous city-states installed treasuries. Pausanias, writing in the second century AD, after the Romans had already looted the sanctuary several times, fills almost a whole book of his *Guide to Greece* with descriptions.

The entrance to the site leads along the west side of the **Altis wall**, past a group of public and official buildings. On the left, beyond some Roman baths, is the **Prytaneion**, the administrators' residence, where athletes were lodged and feasted at official expense. On the right are the ruins of a **gymnasium** and a **palaestra** (wrestling school), used by the competitors during their obligatory month of pre-games training.

Beyond these stood the Priests' House, the **Theokoleion**, a substantial colonnaded building in whose southeast corner is a structure adapted as a Byzantine church. This was originally the **studio of Pheidias**, the fifth-century BC sculptor responsible for the great cult statue in Olympia's Temple of Zeus. It was identified by following a description by Pausanias, and through the discovery of tools, moulds for the statue and a cup engraved with the sculptor's name. The studio's dimensions and orientation are exactly those of the *cella* in which the statue was to be placed, in order that the final effect and lighting matched the sculptor's intentions.

To the south of the studio lie further administrative buildings, including the **Leonidaion**, a large and doubtless luxurious hostel endowed for the most important of the festival guests. It was the first building visitors would reach along the original approach road to the site.

The Altis

In the earlier centuries of the games, admission to the **Altis** was limited to freeborn Greeks – whether spectators or competitors. Throughout its history it was a male-only preserve, save for the sanctuary's priestess. An Olympian anecdote records how a woman from Rhodes disguised herself as her son's trainer to gain admission, but revealed her identity in joy at his victory. She was spared the legislated death penalty, though subsequently all trainers had to appear naked.

The main focus of the precinct, today as in ancient times, is provided by the great Doric **Temple of Zeus**. Built between 470 and 456 BC, it was as large as the almost contemporary Parthenon, a fact quietly substantiated by the vast column drums littering the ground. The temple's decoration, too, rivalled the finest in Athens; partially recovered, its sculptures of Pelops in a chariot race, of Lapiths and Centaurs, and the Labours of Hercules, are now in the museum. In the *cella* was exhibited the (lost) gold-and-ivory cult statue by Pheidias, one of the seven wonders of the ancient world. Here, too, the Olympian flame was kept alight, from the time of the games until the following spring – a tradition continued at an altar for the modern games.

Museum (200 m) ▲

Olympia village (500 m) ◀

Entrance

Roman Baths

Prytaneion

Gymnasium

River Kladhios

Philippeion

Palaestra
(wrestling
school)

Pelopion

Theokoleion
(Priests' House)

Greek
Baths

Studio of
Pheidias

Roman
House

Propylon

N

Bouleuterion
(council
chamber)

Leonidaion
(hostel)

Hill of Kronos

Fountain House

Treasuries

Temple of Hera

Metroön

Altis (Sacred Precinct)

Stadium

Stoa

Temple of Zeus

Altar

Hippodrome

Ceremonial Gate

House of Nero

Altar of Oaths

South Hall

Tripoli

0   50 m

The Olympic games: some history

The origins of the games at Olympia are rooted in **legends** – the most predominant relating to the god **Pelops**, revered in the region before his eclipse by Zeus, and to Hercules (**Herakles**), one of the earliest victors. Historically, the contests probably began around the eleventh century BC, growing over the next two centuries from a local festival to the quadrennial celebration attended by states from throughout the Greek world.

The impetus for this change seems to have come from the **Oracle of Delphi**, which, with the local ruler of Elis, **Iphitos**, and the Spartan ruler **Lykourgos**, helped to codify the Olympic rules in the ninth century BC. Among their most important introductions was a **sacred truce**, the *Ekeheiria*, announced by heralds prior to the celebrations and enforced for their duration. It was virtually unbroken throughout the games' history (Sparta, ironically, was fined at one point) and as host of the games, Elis, a comparatively weak state, was able to keep itself away from political disputes, meanwhile growing rich on the associated trade and kudos.

From the beginning, the main Olympic **events** were athletic. The earliest was a race over the course of the stadium – roughly 200m. Later came the introduction of two-lap (400m) and 24-lap (5000m) races, along with the most revered of the Olympiad events, the **pentathlon**. This encompassed running, jumping, discus and javelin events, the competitors gradually reduced to a final pair for a wrestling-and-boxing combat. It was, like much of these early Olympiads, a fairly brutal contest. More brutal still was the **pancratium**, introduced in 680 BC and one of the most prestigious events. *Pancratium* contestants fought each other, naked and unarmed, using any means except biting or gouging each others' eyes; the olive wreath had on one occasion to be awarded posthumously, the victor having expired at the moment of his opponent's submission. Similarly, the **chariot races**, introduced in the same year, were extreme tests of strength and control, only one team in twenty completing the seven-kilometre course without mishap.

The great gathering of people and nations at the festival extended the games' importance and purpose well beyond the winning of olive wreaths; assembled under the temporary truce, **nobles** and **ambassadors** negotiated treaties, while **mer-**

The smaller **Temple of Hera**, behind, was the first built in the Altis; prior to its completion in the seventh century BC, the sanctuary had only open-air altars, dedicated to Zeus and a variety of other cult gods. The temple, rebuilt in the Doric style in the sixth century BC, is the most complete building on the site, with some thirty of its columns surviving in part, along with a section of the inner wall. The levels above this wall were composed only of sun-baked brick, and the lightness of this building material must have helped to preserve the sculptures – most notably the *Hermes of Praxiteles* – found amid the earthquake ruins.

Between the temples of Hera and Zeus is a grove described by Pausanias, and identified as the **Pelopeion**. In addition to a cult altar to the Olympian hero, this enclosed a small mound formed by sacrificial ashes, among which excavations unearthed many of the terracotta finds in the museum. The sanctuary's principal altar, dedicated to Zeus, probably stood just to the east.

West of the Temple of Hera, and bordering the wall of the Altis, are remains of the circular **Philippeion**, the first monument in the sanctuary to be built to secular glory. It was begun by Philip II after the Battle of Chaironea gave him control over the Greek mainland, and may have been completed by his son, Alexander the Great. To the east of the Hera temple is a small, second-century AD **fountain house**, the gift of the ubiquitous Herodes Atticus. Beyond, lining a terrace at the base of the Hill of Kronos, are the **state treasuries**. All chants chased contacts and foreign markets. **Sculptors** and **poets**, too, would seek commissions for their work. Herodotus read aloud the first books of his history at an Olympian festival to an audience that included Thucydides – who was to date events in his own work by reference to the winners of the *pancratium*.

In the early Olympiads, the **rules of competition** were strict. Only free-born male Greeks could take part, and the rewards of victory were entirely honorary: a palm, given to the victor immediately after the contest, and an olive branch, presented in a ceremony closing the games. As the games developed, however, the rules were loosened to allow participation by athletes from all parts of the Greek and Roman world, and nationalism and professionalism gradually crept in. By the fourth century BC, when the games were at their peak, the athletes were virtually all professionals, heavily sponsored by their home states and, if they won at Olympia, commanding huge appearance money at games elsewhere. Bribery became an all too common feature, despite the solemn religious oaths sworn in front of the sanctuary priests prior to the contests.

Under the **Romans**, predictably, the commercializing process was accelerated. The palms and olive branches were replaced by rich monetary prizes, and a sequence of new events was introduced. The nadir was reached in 67 AD when Emperor Nero advanced the games by two years so that he could compete in (and win) special singing and lyre-playing events – in addition to the chariot race in which he was tactfully declared victor despite falling twice and failing to finish.

Notwithstanding all this abuse, the Olympian tradition was popular enough to be maintained for another three centuries, and the games' eventual **closure** happened as a result of religious dogma rather than lack of support. In 393 AD Emperor Theodosius, recently converted to Christianity, suspended the games as part of a general crackdown on public pagan festivities. This suspension proved final, for Theodosius's successor ordered the destruction of the temples, a process completed by barbarian invasion, earthquakes and, lastly, by the Alfiós River changing its course to cover the sanctuary site. There it remained, covered by seven metres of silt and sand, until the first excavation by German archeologists in the 1870s.

except two of these were constructed by cities outside of Greece proper, as they functioned principally as storage chambers for sacrificial items and sporting equipment used in the games. They are built in the form of temples, as at Delphi; the oldest and grandest, at the east end, belonged to Gela in Sicily. In front of the treasuries are the foundations of the **Metroön**, a fourth-century BC Doric temple dedicated to the mother of the gods.

The ancient ceremonial entrance to the **Altis** was on the south side, below a long **stoa** taking up almost the entire east side of the precinct. At the corner was a house built by the Roman emperor Nero for his stay during the games. He also had the entrance remodelled as a triumphal arch, fit for his anticipated victories. Through the arch, just outside the precinct, stood the **Bouleuterion** or council chamber, where before a great statue of Zeus the competitors took their oaths to observe the Olympian rules. As they approached the stadium, the gravity of this would be impressed upon them: lining the way were bronze statues paid for with the fines exacted for foul play, bearing the name of the disgraced athlete, his father and city.

The stadium

In the final analysis, it is neither foundations nor columns that make sense of Olympia, but the two-hundred-metre track of the **stadium** itself, entered by way of a long arched tunnel. The starting and finishing lines are still there, with the judges' thrones in the middle and seating ridges banked to either side.

Originally unstructured, the stadium developed with the games' popularity, forming a model for others throughout the Greek and Roman world. The tiers here eventually accommodated up to 20,000 spectators, with a smaller number on the southern slope overlooking the **hippodrome** where the chariot races were held. Even so, the seats were reserved for the wealthier strata of society. The ordinary populace – along with slaves and all women spectators – watched the events from the hill of Krónos to the north, then a natural, tree-less grandstand.

The stadium was unearthed only in World War II, during a second phase of German excavations between 1941 and 1944, allegedly on the direct orders of Hitler.

The Archeological Museum

Olympia's site **museum** (May to mid-Oct Mon noon–7pm, Tues–Sun 8am–7pm; mid-Oct to April Mon 10.30am–5pm, Tues–Fri 8am–5pm, Sat & Sun 8.30am–5pm; €3.50 or €6 for combined museum and site) lies a couple of hundred metres north of the sanctuary; some of the signposts still refer to it as the "New Museum". It contains some of the finest Classical and Roman sculptures in the country, all superbly displayed.

The most famous of the individual sculptures are the **head of Hera** and the **Hermes of Praxiteles**, both dating from the fourth century BC and discovered in the Temple of Hera. The Hermes is one of the best preserved of all Classical sculptures, and remarkable in the easy informality of its pose; it retains traces of its original paint. On a grander scale is the **Nike of Paionios**, which was originally ten metres high. Though no longer complete (it's well displayed in a special area), it hints at how the sanctuary must once have appeared, crowded with statuary.

The best of the smaller objects include several fine bronze items, among them a **Persian helmet**, captured by the Athenians at the Battle of Marathon, and (displayed alongside) the **helmet of Miltiades**, the victorious Athenian general; both were found with votive objects dedicated in the stadium. There is also a superb terracotta group of **Zeus abducting Ganymede** and a group of finds from the workshop of **Pheidias**, including the cup with his name inscribed.

In the main hall of the museum is the centrepiece of the Olympia finds: statuary and sculpture reassembled from the **Temple of Zeus**. This includes three groups, all of which were once painted. From the *cella* is a frieze of the **Twelve Labours of Hercules**, delicately moulded and for the most part identifiably preserved. The other groups are from the east and west pediments. The east, reflecting Olympian pursuits, depicts Zeus presiding over a **chariot race** between Pelops and Oinamaos. The story has several versions. King Oinamaos, warned that he would be killed by his son-in-law, challenged each of his daughter Hippomadeia's suitors to a chariot race. After allowing them a start he would catch up and kill them from behind. The king (depicted on the left of the frieze) was eventually defeated by Pelops (on the right with Hippomadeia), after – depending on the version – assistance from Zeus (depicted at the centre), magic steeds from Poseidon or, most un-Olympian, bribing Oinamaos's charioteer to tamper with the wheels.

The west pediment, less controversially mythological, illustrates the **Battle of the Lapiths and Centaurs** at the wedding of the Lapith king, Peirithous. This time, Apollo presides over the scene while Theseus helps the Lapiths defeat the drunken centaurs, depicted, with fairly brutal realism, attacking the women and boy guests. Many of the metope fragments are today in the Louvre in Paris, and some of what you see here are plaster-cast copies.

In the last rooms of the museum are a collection of objects relating to the games – including *halteres* (jumping weights), discuses, weightlifters' stones and other sporting bits and pieces. Also displayed are a number of **funerary inscriptions**, including that of a boxer, Camelos of Alexandria, who died in the stadium after praying to Zeus for victory or death.

Practicalities: Olympía

Modern **OLYMBÍA** is a village that has grown up simply to serve the excavations and tourist trade. It's essentially one long main avenue, **Praxitéles Kondhýli**, lined with gold shops, and with a few short side-streets. Nevertheless, Olympía is quite a pleasant place to stay, and is probably preferable to Pýrgos (see p.288), with the prospect of good countryside walks along the Alfiós River and around the hill of Krónos.

Most people arrive at Olympía **via Pýrgos**, which is on the main Peloponnese rail line and has frequent bus connections with Pátra and four daily with Kyparissía. The **train** link from Pýrgos to Olympía is currently closed for refurbishment; previous timetabling had five daily services. If you have time to kill between buses or trains in Pýrgos, the city square Platía Karayiórga, two blocks north of the bus station, is tolerable in an otherwise unexciting town. **Buses** leave hourly between Pýrgos and Olympía, some signed to "Vasiláki" beyond Olympía; the last service is at 9pm. The only other direct buses to Olympía are **from Trípoli**, via Langádhia. These run twice daily in either direction. If you are approaching **from Andhrítsena**, either take the bus to Pýrgos and change, or stop at Kréstena and hitch or take a taxi the final 12km on from there.

There is a **tourist office** (May–Oct Mon–Sat 9am–3pm; Nov–April Mon–Sat 11am–5pm; ☎06240/23 100), on the right of Praxitéles Kondhýli as you head towards the site. Olympía has three **banks** on the main avenue, and a **post office** just uphill. **English-language books** are to be found in a couple of shops near the tourist office.

Accommodation

Accommodation is fairly easy to come by, with a swift turnaround of clientele and a range of hotels and private rooms whose prices are kept modest by competition. A few **rooms** are signposted on Stefanopoúlou or on the road parallel to and above Praxitéles Kondhýli, though you may well be offered one on arrival. As elsewhere, rates can drop substantially out of season (never precisely defined), though many of the smaller and cheaper places close; it's best to check in advance. There are three **campsites**, closest of which is *Diana* (☎06240/22 314), 1km from the site, with a pool and good facilities. The others are *Alphios* (☎06240/22 950; April–Sept), 1km out on the Kréstena road (from where there are good views of the area), and *Olympía* (☎06240/22 745; April–Oct), 2km out on the Pýrgos road.

Achilles, Stefanopoúlou 4 ☎06240/22 562. A pension on a side street behind the National Bank; large and comfortable if somewhat noisy rooms above a snack bar. ❷

Antonios ☎06240/22 547. A hotel in the woods on the Kréstena road; expensive and not particu-

larly well furnished, but peaceful, with a swimming pool and a stunning view; open April–Oct. ❻

Hercules ☎06240/22 696. A welcoming hotel by the church and school on a side street off Praxitéles Kondhýli; big breakfasts and small balconies. ❷

Hermes ☎06240/22 577. A comfortable hotel near the Shell garage 400m out on the Pýrgos road; rooms have private facilities and there is a good restaurant. ❷

Pelops, Barélas 2 ☎06240/22 543, ℉22 213, ✉hotel-pelops@hotmail.gr. On a square by the church and school; a hotel run by a Greek/Australian couple. Open March–Oct. ❹

Praxiteles, Spiliopoúlou ☎06240/22 592. Quiet hotel next to the police station; there's an acceptable restaurant, and both meals and rooms are competitively priced. Open April–Oct. ❸

Youth Hostel, Praxitéles Kondhýli 18 ☎06240/22 580; €6 per person.

Eating and drinking

Many of the hotels have reasonable **restaurants** where nonresidents can eat. The main avenue is lined with **tavernas**, which offer standard tourist meals at mildly inflated prices in high season – some cafés have positively Athenian prices – but there is a growing number of fast-food kerbside cafés which are often far better value. The *Kladhios* taverna, out of the village on the banks of the Kládhios River, serves good food in a pleasant setting. In **Miráka** village (1km out on the Trípoli road), the family-run *Taverna Drosia* offers a friendly service and fresh, home-made food; the excellent house wine is made by the owner's father. The *Klimataria Taverna* in **Kokkinés** village, a few kilometres northeast, is also recommended. For picnics, bread from the bakery 2km along on the road to Kréstena is very good.

The northwest coast to Pátra

Despite the proximity of Olympia and Pátra, the northwest corner of the Peloponnese is not much explored by foreign visitors. Admittedly, it's not the most glamorous of coasts, although there are some very attractive beaches including the glorious one at **Kalogriá**, but a visit to the old port of **Katákolo** or around **Loutrá Kyllínis/Arkoúdhi** can provide a pleasant enough diversion.

If heading for Delphi, or central or western Greece, car-drivers and pedestrians alike can save backtracking to Athens by using the **ferry links** across the Gulf of Kórinthos between either Río and Andírio (the shortest and most frequent) or Éyio and Áyios Nikólaos. From Kyllíni there are regular crossings to Zákynthos, and in summer to Kefalloniá, while Katákolo has (summer-only) kaïkia to Zákynthos.

Pýrgos

PÝRGOS has a grim recent history. When the Germans withdrew at the end of World War II, it remained under the control of Greek Nazi collaborators. These negotiated surrender with the Resistance, who were met by gunfire as they entered the town. Full-scale battle erupted and for five days the town burned. Today, though friendly enough, it's simply a large, functional, modern Greek town and proudly hosts the Currant Institute of the Autonomous Currant Organization; if you can avoid an enforced overnight stay, do so. Diversions are nonexistent for the tourist, except for the avid clothes shopper (clothes shops here are abundant and well stocked and priced), although there are plans to convert the Neoclassical Central Market building into an archeological museum. If you have to stay the night, the cheapest hotels are the *Marily*, Deliyiánni 48 (☎06210/28 133, ℉27 066; ❸), and the *Pantheon*, Themistokléous 7 (☎06210/29 748, ℉36 791; ❺).

The main escape routes are by **train** or **bus** to Pátra, Olympia or Kyparissía – though services to the last are not well timed for onward connections; the bus station is at the top of the hill, on Manolopoúlou, and the train station 400m away at the bottom on Ipsilándou, so allow a little time for interchange. There is a daily, but often crowded bus to Itéa, usually in the morning and this should put you within striking distance of Delphi on the same day. Closer to hand, there are frequent buses to Katákolo by local bus #4; these go from opposite the Dhikastikón Mégaron building on 28-Oktovríou, which is parallel to and next above Manolopoúlou (but buy tickets first from the Manolopoúlou bus station).

Katákolo

Thirteen kilometres west of Pýrgos, **KATÁKOLO** is somewhat more enticing: a decayed, ramshackle old port with good beaches close by. Until the last few decades, when new roads improved connections with Pátra, it controlled the trade for Ilía province. Today only a few tramp steamers rust at anchor, though the navy calls occasionally and, oddly, the port remains a stop for Italian summer-cruise ships. Consequently, the town has become aware of a potentially lucrative tourist trade, and most of the old warehouses have been converted into boutiques and trinket shops. The main drag can be noisy at night, belying the town's torpid daytime appearance, but arriving from Pýrgos it feels an easy place to settle into, and to the south there's a pleasant twenty-minute walk out to the **lighthouse**, set on a plateau among arbutus and pine.

There are several **room** establishments, with cabins fronted by peach and apricot trees, and the small hotel *Zefyros* (☎06210/41 170; ❸). For **meals**, there is a handful of good tavernas on the quay.

Beaches

Katákolo's beach, the **Spiándza**, stretches away for miles to the southeast, a popular spot with Greeks, many of whom own shuttered little cottages set just back from the sea. Though it is sandy, it is hard-packed and more of a spot for football or jogging, with the sea too shallow for real swimming. However, a thirty-minute walk north, past the overgrown Byzantine-Frankish **castle of Pondikón** (Pondikókastro, Beauvoir), will take you to much better swimming at **Áyios Andhréas** beach, the port of Ancient Pheia: two hundred metres of sloping, outcrop-studded sand, with views over a few attendant islets and out to Zákynthos. There are summer **tavernas** here, the comfortable **hotel** *Brynioti* (☎06210/41 294; ❺), plus a few rooms to let. An even better beach is to be found at **Skafidhiá**, 3km north of Katákolo and accessible by road via Korakohóri. There is hotel **accommodation** at **MYRTIÁ**, 2km inland, at *Zorbas* (☎06210/54 238; ❹). Further northwest is the beach at **Kouroúta**, with several campsites.

The cape north of Pýrgos

North from Pýrgos, road and rail meander through a series of uneventful market towns, but there are two forks west to a sandy cape and the coast. The first is at Gastoúni and heads for the spa of **Loutrá Kyllínis** (occasional buses from Pýrgos and Pátra); the second is at Kavásilas, where a side road (buses from Pátra) heads down to **Kyllíni** (port) proper. Take care not to confuse the two.

LOUTRÁ KYLLÍNIS has a long beach, and at its north end you'll find a crop of upmarket **hotels** catering for the resort's spa trade, including the overpriced and under-resourced *Kyllini Spa Xenia Tourist Complex*. It's better to walk south where the development soon gives way to sand dunes. There are two **campsites** – the *Anginara Beach* (☎06230/96 411) and the *Ionian Beach* (☎06230/96 395), both bordered by trees and beaches of fine shingle and sand – further to the southeast and best approached via Lygiá on the road from Gastoúni.

Only a few kilometres south of the EOT complex, at the point where this most westerly coast of the Peloponnese bends back east into the long bay that curves towards Katákolo, is **ARKOÚDHI**, a far better place to stay. This compact village resort has something of an island feel to it and a fine sandy bay enclosed by a rocky promontory. As well as a **campsite**, there is a surprising number of **hotels and rooms**. On the edge of the village is the posh but good-value hotel *Arkoudi* (☎06230/96 480; April–Oct; ❹), which has a pool. In the village centre more spacious apartments with kitchen and fridge are available at *Soulis* (☎06230/96 379; ❹). For meals try the central *Spyros psistariá*, or the *Akrogiali*, which offers a sea view and a wide selection of dishes.

Cheerless little **KYLLÍNI** (accessible by taxi from Loutrá Kyllínis) has little more to offer than its **ferry connections**. It is the principal port for **Zákynthos** (7–9 daily in summer, 5 in winter; ☎06230/92 385; car €6.50, passengers €3.50) and **Kefalloniá** (to Argostoli 2–3 daily in summer, 1–2 in winter; and to Póros 3 daily in summer, 1–2 in winter; ☎06230/92 351). If you're stuck overnight in Kyllíni, **places to stay** are limited: the choice is between the *Hotel Ionian* (☎06230/92 318; ❹) on the main street where some rooms have private facilities, rooms (also on the main street) – or sleeping on the beach. The *Taverna Anna*, beyond the harbour, serves a wide range of traditional dishes and is particularly popular with locals at Sunday lunchtimes.

Using Loutrá Kyllínis, Arkoúdhi or Kyllíni as a base, it's worth taking time to hitch or walk to the village of **KÁSTRO**, at the centre of the cape. Looming above the village and visible from miles around is the Frankish **castle of Khlemoútsi** (Castel Tornese; summer 8.30am–8pm, winter 8.30am–3pm; free), a vast hexagonal structure built in 1220 by Geoffrey de Villehardouin. Its function was principally to control the province of Ahaïa, though it served also as a strategic fortress on the Adriatic. Haze permitting, there are sweeping views across the straits to Zákynthos, and even to Kefalloniá and Itháki, from the well-preserved and restored ramparts. Kástro has the welcoming *Chryssi Avgi* rooms, at Loutrópoleos 9 (☎06230/95 224; May to mid-Oct; ❹), with rooms with kitchen facilities. You can **dine** well at the nearby *Apollon* taverna.

Kalogriá and Niforéïka Patrón

Midway between Kyllíni and Pátra, **KALOGRIÁ** is an eight-kilometre strand of beach, partly naturist, bordered by a swathe of **pine forests**. A fair proportion of Pátra, including the gay community, descends here at the weekend as it's the nearest good **beach** to the city, but it's also a protected place (the beach for its sands and the forest for its birdlife) and permanent development remains low key. It is not actually a village – the nearest bona fide town is Metóhi – but rather a cluster of tavernas and stores. At the far north end of the beach there's the *Kalogria Beach* (☎06930/31 276; ❹), a large **hotel complex** with many facilities including a pool, nightclub and tennis courts. There's not much official accommodation apart from that, but free camping is tolerated among the pines behind the beach. A novelty for wildlife aficionados are the estuaries nearby in which you may find yourself swimming alongside harmless metre-long watersnakes – the whole area is part of the Strofyliá Forest-Kotykhí Wetland National Park.

Around the northwest coast towards Pátra, 3km west of Káto Ahaïa, another busy little resort is that of **NIFORÉÏKA PATRÓN**, where accommodation options include the pricey *Hotel Acheos* complex (☎06930/22 561, ⓔhotelach@otenet.gr; ⑥), with cheaper bungalows attached (⑤), and *Alikes* camping (☎06930/22 730). There is a choice of several restaurants.

Pátra

PÁTRA (Patras) is the largest town in the Peloponnese and, after Pireás, the major port of Greece; from here you can go to Italy as well as to certain Ionian islands. The city is also a hub of the Greek-mainland transport network, with connections throughout the Peloponnese and, via the ferry at Río, across the straits to Delphi or western Greece.

Unless you arrive late in the day from Italy, you shouldn't need to spend more than a few hours in the city. A conurbation of close to a quarter of a million souls, it's not the ideal holiday retreat: there are no beaches and no particular sights. Traffic noise goes on well into the night and starts earlier than you'd want to get up. Nor has there been much effort to make the place attractive to visitors, save for a **summer festival** which sponsors events from late June to mid-September. These include Classical plays and the occasional rock concert in the Roman **odeion** and art and photographic exhibitions that bring a bit of life to the warehouses by the harbour (details from the EOT, the tourist police or the theatre on Platía Yeoryíou). The three-week **carnival** (ending on the Sun before Lent Mon – *Kathará Dheftéra*) is one of the biggest in the country, with a grand parade through the city centre on the final day.

Arrival, information and accommodation

If you are driving in or through Pátra, you will find the traffic and one-way system no less frustrating than Athens; an EOT map showing the direction of traffic, if not vital, will at least save time and probably maintain sanity. For **tourist information**, on weekdays try the **EOT** office, at the entrance to the Italy ferry terminal (Mon–Fri 7am–9pm; ☎0610/620 353); otherwise the helpful **tourist police** (daily 7am–11pm; ☎0610/451 893) are inside the same building.

Accommodation

Most of Pátra's **hotels** are on Ayíou Andhréou, one block back from Óthonos & Amalías, or on Ayíou Nikoláou, which runs back from the sea, near the train station and Platía Trión Symáhon. Don't expect too much in the way of standards or value for money; most of the places cater for a very passing trade and don't make great efforts. Most of the older hotels nearer the waterfront have closed, or indeed collapsed. Of those still standing, choices include the following.

Adonis, Kapsáli ☎0610/224 213, ⓕ226 971. On the junction with Kapsáli opposite the bus station. It's well furnished and maintained and includes a buffet-style breakfast; good value. ④

Astir, Ayíou Andhréou 16 ☎0610/277 502. Modern hotel with a swimming pool, sauna, roof garden and car parking, which still don't justify the price. ⑥

Atlanta, Záïmi 10 ☎0610/220 098, ⓕ220 019.

Central hotel, but still good value; out of season you should get a competitive price. ③

El Greco, Ayíou Andhréou 145 ☎0610/272 931, ⓕ226 179. A good bargain hotel and top of its class with refurbished rooms; the manager is attentive and speaks English. ③

Galaxy, Ayíou Nikoláou 9 ☎0610/275 981. A well-placed hotel, if a touch pretentious; serves a good breakfast. ⑤

Río & Athens

PÁTRA

ACCOMMODATION
Adonis	1
Astir	3
Atlanta	2
El Greco	8
Galaxy	5
Méditerranée	7
Rannia	4
St George	6

Glyfádha Jetty

Italy Ferry Terminal, EOT & Tourist Police

Gate 6

Triándi Jetty

Ionian Ferry Terminal

★ Bus Station to Mesolóngi & Lefkádha

Main Bus Station ★

Train Station

Áy. Nikólaou (Rousvelt) Jetty

Museum

Banks

Buses to Delphi & Arta ★

★ Local Bus 5 & 6

Buses to Zákynthos, Kefalloniá & Lamia ★

Kástro

Hamam

Krini

Gounári Jetty
Gate 1

Tourist Police

Odeion

Fishing Harbour

OTE

Áyios Andhréas

Achaïa Clauss Factory (7 km) & Kalávryta

0   500 m

Pýrgos & southwest

Méditerranée , Ayíou Nikólaou 18 ☎0610/279 602. Modern and adequate hotel, if undistinguished, with helpful staff. ❹

Rannia , Platía Ólgas & Ríga Feréou ☎0610/220 114, ℻220 537. Very friendly, clean and well placed on the square, with a café and snack bar. ❹

Saint George Hotel , Ayíou Andhréou 73 ☎0610/225 092. A good, new, clean and central hotel. ❹

Youth Hostel , Iróön Polytekhníou 62 ☎0610/427 278. Cheap, but a long (1.5km) walk from the centre. €6 per person.

The Town

For relaxation, the best places to make for are the café-table-studded **Platía Psilá Alónia** with its monument to Bishop Yermanos, or the **Kástro** (daily

8am–7pm; free), a mainly Frankish-Byzantine citadel a fifteen-minute walk up from the water. This partly restored fortress is not particularly exciting, but it is away from the city bustle, surrounded by a park and with woodland beyond. Nearby, at Boukaoúri 29, is the **Hamam** (Turkish bath), still functioning after 600 years, while the Roman **odeion** (Tues–Sun 8.30am–3pm; free) is on Sotiriádhou, near the castle. Like many a Greek metropolis in summer, Pátra is perhaps at its best after dark, when the heat is not so oppressive, the concrete structures less overpowering, and the city life and lights rather brighter; a stroll down to the huge jetty at the foot of Ayíou Nikoláou can bring you to cool sea breezes – and some of the cheapest coffee around, at the port kiosk just over the railway lines. Join the evening *vólta* here, or watch the sunset and departing ferries, with the spectacular mountains of Étolo-Akarnanía to the northwest and the 1924-metre backdrop of Mount Panahaïkó to the east. The recently pedestrianized bottom end of Ayíou Nikoláou is now a lively area at night, with cafés spread across the street and a couple of popular cinemas. At the southwest end of the waterfront itself is the huge neo-Byzantine **church of Áyios Andhréas**, which opened in 1979 and houses relics of St Andrew, said to have been martyred on this spot. The church is a massive confection of yellow-and-cream walls, blue-tiled domes and marmoreal excess that takes in the pillars and arches. A small **archeological museum** (Tues–Sun 8.30am–3pm; free) on the corner of Mézonos and Arátou contains a number of exquisite objects from the province of Ahaïa dating from the Mycenaean to the Roman eras.

Swimming near Pátra isn't really advisable with the sea polluted for some kilometres to the southwest. Locals go to the **beaches** around Río (7km northeast; bus #6 goes frequently from the stop on Yerokostópoulou, near Zákynthos bus station) or to Kalogriá (40km southwest, see p.290; 3 daily buses in season from the KTEL station).

The Achaïa Clauss factory

The **Achaïa Clauss** factory (daily tours 9am–5pm), founded 1854, is an out-of-town time-filler, 8km southeast of Pátra; take the #7 bus from stop 5 or 6. Tours show you around the wine-making process, and feature some treasured, century-old barrels of Mavrodhafni – a dark dessert wine named after the woman Clauss wanted to marry. You're given a glass of white wine to sample on reaching the factory's rather Teutonic bar, an echo of its founder's nationality. Along the walls are signed letters from celebrity recipients of Mavrodhafni. A shop sells all the factory's products, if you want a bottle for yourself.

Eating and drinking

Pátra's **restaurants** are fairly uninspiring, with countless fast-food places around Platía Trión Symáhon, and along Ayíou Andhréou and Ayíou Nikoláou. But even here there are some reliable restaurants with character, and some mouth-watering patisserie-bakeries. For fish, the best places are a couple of tavernas down by the fishing harbour, home to a somewhat half-hearted fleet, while for spit-roast specialities, several *psistariés* are grouped around Platía Omonías and Platía Konstandínou. **Nightlife** in town is largely concentrated around a noisy selection of bars at the steps of Ayíou Nikoláou.

If you're stuck for the night and feel the urge to escape to a quieter stretch of sea, hop on any #5 blue bus labelled "Tsoukaleíka" and alight at either **Monodhéndhri** or **Vrahnéïka**, 10km southwest of the city. There is now a practically unbroken chain of tavernas stretching 2km between these resorts, of

Ferry routes and companies

Innumerable ticket agents along or near the waterfront each sell different permutations of **ferry crossings** to Italy on one or more of the lines detailed below. It is worth spending an hour or so researching these, especially if you're taking a car, since costs, journey times and routes all differ from one company to another. Glossy ferry company **brochures** quoting times and prices are freely available from the agents. En route to Italy, it is possible to make stopovers on Kefaloniá and Itháki or, more commonly, Igoumenítsa and Corfu (Kérkyra). Domestic tickets to Kefaloniá and Itháki are also available from Pátra.

Routes

Pátra–Ancona has become the standard route. Until recently this entailed two nights on board, but high-speed ferries operated by ANEK, Minoan Lines, Strintzis and Superfast Ferries can now complete the crossing in 18–24hr. Other routes include Pátra–Brindisi, Pátra–Bari, Pátra–Trieste and Pátra–Venice.

High season

All frequencies of ferry crossings detailed opposite are for the high season, the definition of which varies slightly from company to company. Broadly, for crossings from Italy to Greece, high season is between early July and mid-August; from Greece to Italy, it is between early August and early September. Check with company agents for exact dates. Out of season, all services are reduced.

Fares

All companies offer a variety of fares for cabin, airline-type seats and deck passage, with reductions according to age and student or rail card status. High-speed ferries cost only fractionally more than the normal ones. All ferry companies offer a substantial discount (normally thirty percent) on return trips if booked together with the outward journey. Travellers with camper vans are often allowed to sleep in them, thus saving the cost of a cabin.

Embarkation tax

All international departures carry a levy of €6.50 per person and per car.

Checking in

If you have bought tickets in advance, or from a travel agent other than the official agent listed opposite, you must check in (to the appropriate agent's office, or at their booth in the departure hall) at least two hours before departure.

Stopovers

Free if you specify them when booking, though you may have to pay re-embarkation taxes.

---

which *Thalassa Ouzeri* has the best selection of food. The others vary in price, range and quality but all share the seaside and sunset view. Real gourmets will want to check out the terrific cuisine at *Mesogeios/Mouragios*, in the suburb of **Boznítika**, 6km east of Pátra. Specialities include artichoke soufflé and seafood pasta served in a conch shell; the prices are reasonable. Choices in Pátra include the following:

Faros , cnr Óthonos & Amalías and Sahtoúri. One of the best fish tavernas for quality and prices.

Krini , Pandokrátoros 57. An endearing place at the top of the old town, by the *kástro*. It has a limited but exemplary menu, and is a favourite with locals; it's possible to eat in the little garden at the back.

Majestic , Ayíou Nikoláou 2/4. Old-style *estiatório*, where you can choose from the day's hot dishes,

Companies, agents and destinations

Adriatica
Cacouris, Óthonos & Amalías 8 ☎0610/421 995, ⓦwww.adriatica.it.
Shuttle coach runs Pátra–Athens in summer.
Brindisi: via Igoumenítsa and Corfu alternate days (19hr); direct daily in summer (14hr).

ANEK
United Ferries, Óthonos & Amalías 25 ☎0610/226 053, ⑤620 462, ⓦwww.anek.gr.
Ancona: Tues, Fri direct (23hr); Wed, Sat & Sun via Igoumenítsa (32–33hr).
Trieste: Mon via Igoumenítsa (33hr); Wed & Thurs via Igoumenítsa and Corfu (32–34hr).

Blue Star Ferries/Strintzis
Tsimaras Shipping, Óthonos & Amalías 14 ☎0610/622 602, ⑤623 110, ⓦwww.strintzis.gr.
Ancona: Mon, Tues & Sun direct (22hr); Fri & Sat via Igoumenítsa and Corfu (30hr); otherwise direct.
Itháki: daily via Sámi on Kefalloniá (3hr 45min).
Venice: Mon–Thurs via Igoumenítsa and Corfu (32–36hr).

HML-Hellenic Mediterranean Lines
Elmes Travel Services, Pénde Pigadhíon 2 and Iróön Polytekhníou ☎0610/452 521, ⑤452 775, ⓦwww.hml.it.
Brindisi: daily via Kefalloniá, Igoumenítsa and Corfu (19hr 30min).

Marlines
Marlines, Athinón 16 ☎0610/454 933, ⓦwww.marlines.it.
Ancona: Mon, Tues & Thurs via Igoumenítsa (36hr).

MedLink Lines
Giannatos Travel, Óthonos & Amalías 15 ☎0610/623 011, ⑤623 320, ⓦwww.mll.gr.
Brindisi: daily (13–14hr), in summer some via Kefalloniá and/or Igoumenítsa (14–16hr).

Minoan Lines
Fotopoulos-Sotiropoulos, Athinón 2 ☎0610/421 500, ⑤420 800, ⓦwww.minoan.gr.
Ancona: via Igoumenítsa Tues–Sun (20hr).
Venice: daily via Corfu and Igoumenítsa (33–37hr).

Superfast Ferries
Filopoulos-Parthenopoulos, Óthonos & Amalías 12 ☎0610/622 500, ⑤623 574, ⓦwww.superfast.com.
Ancona: daily direct (19hr).
Bari: daily via Igoumenítsa (15hr).

Ventouris
Express United Shipping, Iróön Polytekhníou 44–46 ☎0610/454 873, ⑤454 875, ⓦwww.ventouris.gr.
Bari: direct alternate days (17hr 30min); via Kefalloniá alternate days (18hr).

which are tasty but expensive.
Nikolaras, Ayíou Nikoláou 50. Another old-style *estiatório*, serving good, traditional food on a cheap self-serve basis.

Listings

Airlines Olympic, Arátou 8 ☎0610/222 901.
Banks and money exchange National Bank of Greece, Platía Trión Symáhon (normal banking hours plus 6–8pm); Kapa foreign exchange bureau, southeast cnr Platía Trión Symáhon (☎0610/437 261).
Books and newspapers Book's Corner, Ayíou Nikoláou 32, stocks useful maps and English-language newspapers. Lexis, Mézonos 38 and Patréos 90, stocks maps and a selection of

Penguins. English-language papers are available from kiosks on the waterfront. The Ermis bookshop at Záïmi stocks ROAD's map of Ahaïa.

Car rental Major operators include: Alamo/National, Ayíou Andhréou 1 ℡ 0610/273 667, ℻ 277 864, ✉ m.konstantinou@nationalcar.gr; AutoUnion/Thrifty, Ayíou Dhionysíou 2 ℡ 0610/623 200, ℻ 622 201, ✉ mmiglia@hellasnet.gr; Avis, Kapsáli 13 ℡ 0610/275 898; Budget, Óthonos & Amalías 14, ℡ 0610/623 200; Delta, Óthonos & Amalías 44, ℡ 0610/272 764; Eurodollar, Albatros Travel, Óthonos & Amalías 48, ℡ 0610/220 993; Hertz, 28-Oktovríou 2 ℡ 0610/220 990; InterRent-EuropCar, Ayíou Andhréou 6 ℡ 0610/621 360; Sixt, Ayíou Andhréou 10 ℡ 0610/275 677.

Consulates Britain, Vótsi 2 ℡ 0610/277 079, ℻ 225 334; Germany, Mézonos 98 ℡ 0610/221 943; Sweden, Óthonos & Amalías 62 ℡ 0610/271 702.

Ferry agents Óthonos & Amalías (see box overleaf).

KTEL bus terminal Óthonos & Amalías ℡ 0610/273 936 for other towns in the Peloponnese, Athens, Ioánnina, Thessaloníki and Vólos; services to Mesolóngi and Agrínio leave from the terminal on Faviérou; buses to Crete, Kefalloniá, Lefkádha and Zákynthos, also Árta, Lamía, Tríkala and Itéa (for Delphi), leave from Snakbar Sami, Óthonos & Amalías 58 ℡ 0610/272 246.

OTE cnr Goúnari and Kanakári (daily 7am–midnight).

Post office cnr Mézonos and Záïmi (Mon–Fri 7.30am–8pm); also near cnr Gounári and Ayíou Andhréou.

Train station Óthonos & Amalías. Trains travel west (changes at Alfiós or Pýrgos) to Olympia – when the line is reinstated (see p.287) and Kaló Neró (Kyparissía); inland and east to Dhiakoftó, Kalamáta, Trípoli, Kórinthos, Athens and Pireás.

Travel agents These can help with information and reservations, and line Óthonos & Amalías: Albatros Travel ℡ 0610/220 993; Marine Tours ℡ 0610/621 166; Olympias Shipping and Travel Enterprises ℡ 0610/275 495.

The north coast and the Kalávryta railway

From Pátra you can reach Kórinthos in two hours by **train** or **bus** along the national highway; the onward journey to Athens takes another ninety minutes. The resorts and villages lining the Gulf of Kórinthos are nothing very special, though none of them is overdeveloped. At most of them you find little more than a narrow strip of beach, a campsite, a few rooms for rent and a couple of seasonal tavernas. At both **Río** and **Éyio**, you can cross the gulf to the mainland by ferry. Beyond **Dhiakoftó**, if you're unhurried, it's worth taking the old **coast road** along the Gulf of Kórinthos; this runs below the national highway, often right by the sea.

However, to travel from Pátra to Kórinthos without taking the time to detour along the **Kalávryta railway** from Dhiakoftó would be to miss one of the best treats the Peloponnese has to offer – and certainly the finest train journey in Greece. Even if you have a car, this trip should still be part of your plans.

Río and Éyio

RÍO (Ríon), connected by local bus #6 to Pátra in thirty minutes (or by train in ten, though with a long walk from the station to the harbour), signals the beginning of swimmable water, though most travellers stop here only to make use of the **ferry** across the gulf to Andírio – which will be replaced in a few years by a suspension bridge. This ferry (℡ 09320/74 717) runs every fifteen minutes through the day and evening (every 30min thereafter), shuttling cars (€5 including driver) and passengers (€0.50) across to the central mainland. It is a long-established crossing, testimony to which are the squat Turkish **forts** paired on either side of the gulf; the opening times of the Rio fortress, with its marine moat, are unreliable (officially Tues–Fri 8am–7pm, Sat & Sun 8.30am–3pm).

If you are crossing into the Peloponnese via Andírio, you might be tempted to stop by the sea here, rather than at Pátra. There are several **hotels**, including the inland *Georgios* (☎0610/991 134; ❹), in town towards the train station, or, both on the seafront south of the jetty, the *Rion Beach* (☎0610/991 422, ⓕ991 390; ❹) and the ultraswish *Hotel Porto Rio* and casino (☎0610/992 102, ⓕ992 115; ❻). There are two **campsites**: the *Rio Mare* (☎0610/990 762; May–Oct), just east of the jetty and fortress, and the *Rion* (☎0610/991 585, ⓕ993 388; open all year), south of the jetty but closer to the beach, which is poor just here but improves a little as you go south. The best of the **restaurants** is the *Tésseres Epohes* ("Four Seasons") with bargain prices in a romantic setting by the train station. Río seafront also boasts some of the most tub-thumping disco bars in the Pátra area – *Mojo* is particularly popular.

Moving east, there are better beaches, and a further **campsite**, the *Tsolis* (☎06910/31 469), at **ÉYIO**. Although not a place many people would choose to stay, there are a few hotels and rooms in Éyio. It's more likely you might want to **eat** there, though, and the main town, inland and uphill, has several decent *psistariés*, while just east of the harbour around Dhódheka Vrýsses square are more eating establishments; the *Plessas Inomayirio* taverna is authentic and cheap – nearby stands an ancient plane tree supposedly from 200 AD and dedicated to the theoretically near-contemporaneous historian Pausanias. Local cliffs cut sharply into the hillside near the impressive Panayía Trypití church, marking the spot where resident hero Miralis escaped from the Turks in 1821 by jumping over with his horse. A **ferry** crosses the gulf five to nine times daily (5.15am–8.30pm; car and driver €10, passengers €1.60; ☎010/42 20 175) to Áyios Nikólaos, well placed for Delphi. Buses from Pátra stop at the bus station on the inland side of town, a considerable and inconvenient distance from the harbour or the railway station.

The best sands are at the village of **RHODHODHÁFNI**, 2km northwest of Éyio; the *Corali Beach* (☎06910/71 546; May–Sept) and the *Aeoli Beach* (☎06910/71 317; April–Oct) **campsites** are close to the beach.

Dhiakoftó and beyond

It is at **DHIAKOFTÓ** (officially Dhiakoptó) that the rack-and-pinion railway heads south up into the Vouraïkós gorge for Kalávryta (see p.299). If you arrive late in the day, it's worth spending the night here and making the train journey in daylight; the town can, in any case, be an attractive alternative to staying overnight in Pátra. The climate is very pleasant, less humid than Pátra and less furnace-like than Korinthía province to the east. There are four **hotels**: the pleasant, upmarket *Chris-Paul* (☎06910/41 715, ⓕ42 128; ❹), which has a pool; the basic *Helmos* (☎06910/41 236; closed in winter, occasionally at other times; ❷); the very friendly *Lemonies* (☎06910/41 229; ❸), opposite the school on the road to the beach, with its own retsina; and the *Panorama* (☎06910/41 614; ❹), 800m along the beach with a reasonable restaurant. The seafront *Kohyli* **taverna** on the corner of the beach road has excellent seafood. A few minutes inland of the station, on the road out to the main highways, there is a good map/bookshop.

Travelling east beyond Dhiakoftó there is a pleasant beach at **Plátanos**. **AKRÁTA**, the final minor resort in Ahaïa, before the coastal strip of Korinthía province, is a small town with a beach annexe, but is a little crowded, with three hotels and three campsites set along a drab, exposed stretch of beach.

Dhiakoftó to Kalávryta: the rack-and-pinion railway

Even if you have no interest in trains, the **rack-and-pinion railway** from Dhiakoftó to Kalávryta is a must. It can be hot, crowded and uncomfortable, but the track is a crazy feat of Italian engineering, rising at gradients of up to one in seven as it cuts inland through the **Vouraïkós gorge**. En route is a toy-train fantasy of tunnels, bridges and precipitous overhangs.

The railway was built between 1889 and 1896 to bring minerals from the mountains to the sea. Its 1896 steam locomotives were replaced some years ago – one (*O Moutzouris*) remains by the line at Dhiakoftó Station (☎06910/43 206) with other relics, and another at Kalávryta – but the track itself retains all the charm of its period. The tunnels, for example, have delicately carved window openings, and the narrow bridges zigzagging across the Vouraïkós seem engineered for sheer virtuosity.

It takes up to an hour to get from Dhiakoftó to Zakhloroú (confusingly listed on timetables as Méga Spiléou), and about another twenty minutes from there to Kalávryta. The best part of the trip is the stretch to **Zakhloroú** (see below), along which the gorge narrows to a few feet at points, only to open out into brilliant, open shafts of light beside the Vouraïkós, clear and fast-running even in midsummer. In peak season the ride is very popular (there are just four trains a day), so you'll probably need to buy tickets some hours before your preferred departure (including the return journey). Despite only covering some 22km, trains on this line can be subject to the same lengthy delays (or cancellations) as their grown-up counterparts on the main line below.

Zakhloroú and Méga Spiléou

ZAKHLOROÚ is as perfect a train stop as could be imagined: a tiny hamlet echoing with the sound of the Vouraïkós River, which splits it into two neighbourhoods. It's a lovely, peaceful place with an old, en-suite wooden hotel, the very friendly and very reasonably priced *Romantzo* (☎06920/22 758; ❷), which has a fine restaurant below. The only other hotel-restaurant is the adjacent and basic *Messina* (☎06920/22 789; ❷), sometimes closed during summer.

The eight-storey **Monastery of Méga Spiléou** ("Great Cave"; closed 1–3pm), built at a sixty-metre cave entrance under a 120-metre cliff, is a 45-minute walk from the village, up a rough donkey track along the hillside; this joins a road, then an access drive along the final stretch, which is often chock-a-block with tour buses. The monastery is reputedly the oldest in Greece, but it has been burned down and then rebuilt so many times that you'd hardly guess at its antiquity – from a distance it looks like a misplaced hotel. The last major fire took place in 1934, after a keg of gunpowder left behind from the War of Independence exploded. In 1943, the Nazis killed many of the residents and looted seventy lorryloads of furniture and relics, much of it later recovered. Dress conduct for visitors is strict: skirts for women, and long sleeves and trousers for men. Only men are allowed to stay overnight, at the precipitous *xenónas*, and the monks like visitors to arrive before 8pm, serving up a rough repast before closing the gates.

The view of the gorge valley from the monastery is for many the principal attraction. However, the cloister once had 450 monks and was among the richest in the Greek world, owning properties throughout the Peloponnese, in Macedonia, Constantinople and Asia Minor. In consequence, its treasury, arranged as a small **museum** (€1), is outstanding. In the main church, among its icons is a charred black wax and mastic image of the Virgin, one of three in

Greece said to be by the hand of St Luke (but more probably from the tenth century); a smaller chapel houses a remarkable collection of body parts from various saints. The monastery was founded by Saints Theodhoros and Simeon, after a vision by the shepherdess Euphrosyne in 362 AD led to the discovery of the icon in the cave (Ayiásma) behind the site of the later church; cardboard cut-outs now model the story, including flames leaping from the icon to destroy a serpent.

If returning to Dhiakoftó from Zakhloroú, it is possible to walk alongside the 12km of railway line down through the gorge – part of the E4 walk route – in about two hours. You should of course be aware of the times that trains are due on that section of line – the most photogenic points are around the 5.8km mark above Dhiakoftó. The walk may not be easy for vertigo sufferers, since it involves crossing some rather precipitous bridges.

Kalávryta and around

From Méga Spiléou a scenic road has been constructed 28km down to coastal Trápeza, and another has been hacked 10km through to **KALÁVRYTA**. The train line is more in harmony with the surroundings, but coming from Zakhloroú the drama of the route is diminished as the gorge opens out. Kalávryta itself is beautifully positioned, with Mount Helmós as a backdrop, though it has a sad atmosphere. During World War II, on December 13, 1943, the German occupiers carried out one of their most brutal reprisal massacres, killing the entire male population – 1436 men and boys – and leaving the town in flames, because of partisan activity in the area. Rebuilt, it is both depressing and poignant. The first and last sight is a mural, opposite the station, that reads: "Kalavryta, founder member of the Union of Martyred Towns, appeals to all to fight for world peace." The left clocktower on the central church stands fixed at 2.34pm – the hour of the massacre. In the old primary school is the **Museum of the Sacrifice of the People of Kalavryta**, while out in the countryside behind the town is a shrine to those massacred, with the single word "Peace" (*Iríni*).

The Nazis also burned the tenth-century **monastery of Ayías Lávras**, 6km out of Kalávryta. As the site where Yermanos, Archbishop of Pátra, raised the flag to signal the War of Independence, the monastery is one of the great Greek national shrines. It, too, has been rebuilt, along with a small historical museum.

Staying at Kalávryta has a sense of pilgrimage about it for Greeks, and it's crowded with school parties during the week and with families at weekends. The general attitude to foreigners – perhaps understandably – is business-like rather than overtly friendly, and the town will probably not have the same appeal for the casual visitor. If you miss the last train back to Zakhloroú (currently at 7.30pm, but check upon arrival) there are several pleasant **hotels** whose rates drop outside of winter weekends. Among them are the hospitable *Polyxeni*, Lohagón Vassiléos Kapóta 13 (☎06920/22 141; ❸); the friendly, good-value (in summer) and luxurious *Filoxenia*, Ethnikís Andistásis 20 (☎06920/22 422, Ⓕ23 009, ⒺFiloxenia@otenet.gr; ❹); and the *Villa Kalavrita* (☎06920/22 712; ❺) across the rail track from the station, which has comfortable, modern rooms with a fridge and TV. There are several adequate **restaurants** around the square – *To Tzaki* has a nice atmosphere and good, mostly grilled food. Kalávryta is also the main base for the **Helmos Ski Centre** (☎06920/22 174), which is rapidly growing in popularity. There are a number of shops which can hire out equipment, give information about the state of the slopes and maybe help with transport up to the centre.

A thirty-minute drive southeast of Kalávryta, and 1.5km north of Kastriá is the **Spílio tón Límnon** or Cave of the Lakes (summer daily 9am–6pm; winter Mon–Fri 9.30am–4.30pm, Sat & Sun 9.30am–6.30pm; €6; ☎06920/31 633). Mineral-saturated water trickling through a two-kilometre cavern system from the Apanókambos plateau has precipitated natural dams, trapping a series of small underground lakes. Only the first 300m or so are as yet open to the public, but the chambers are still well worth the trip.

The cave is on the same **bus** line from Kalávryta as the villages of Káto Loussí, Kastriá and Planitéro, and is 2km north of Kastriá. Buses also run from Kalávryta to Pátra four times daily.

Mount Helmós

The highest peaks of the imposing Helmós (Aroánia) range rear up a dozen or so kilometres to the southeast of Kalávryta. **Mount Helmós** itself, at 2355m, is only 50m short of the summit of Taïyetos to the south. However, the walk from Kalávryta is not an interesting approach, the trail having vanished under a paved road and the new ski centre (1900m) approached by it. To get the most from hiking on the mountain you need to climb up from the village of **Sólos**, on the west side – a five-hour-plus walk which takes you to the **Mavronéri waterfall**, source of the legendary Styx (Stýga, Stygós), the river which souls of the dead had to cross in order to enter Hades.

The hike from Sólos

To reach the path opening at Sólos, start at **Akráta** on the Pátra-Kórinthos road. From here it's a slow but beautiful 35-kilometre haul up a winding paved road. Buses run only three times a week, but hitching isn't too difficult in high summer.

SÓLOS is a tiny place, a cluster of stone cottages on a steep hillside just below the fir trees, and inhabited only in summer. Facing it across the valley is the larger but more scattered village of Peristéra, past which runs the easiest of the routes to Mavronéri.

Follow the **track** through Sólos, past the combined inn (all of ten beds) and *magazí* (café-store), where you can get a simple meal. Beyond the last houses the track curves around the head of a gully. On the right, going down its wooded flank, is a good path which leads to a bridge over the river at the bottom. Just beyond (15min; this and all subsequent times are from Sólos), you reach another track. There is a **chapel** on the left, and, on the wall of a house on the right, a sign saying "Pros Gounariánika" that points up a path to the left. Follow it past a **church** on a prominent knoll and on to the jeep track again, where, after 75 minutes, you turn left to the half-ruined hamlet of **Gounariánika**. From there continue steadily upwards along the west (right) flank of the valley through abandoned fields until you come to a stream–gully running down off the ridge above you on your right. On the far side of the stream the fir forest begins. It's an ideal camping place (2hr 30min; 1hr 30min going back down).

Once into the **woods**, the path is very clear. After about an hour (3hr 30min) you descend to a boulder-strewn **stream bed** with a rocky ravine to the right leading up to the foot of a huge bare crag, the east side of the Neraïdhórahi peak (2238m) visible from Kalávryta. Cross the stream and continue leftwards up the opposite bank. In June there are the most incredible wild flowers, including at least half a dozen different orchids, all the way up from here, plus rare blue butterflies.

After fifteen-minutes' climb above the bank, you come out on top of a **grassy knoll** (3hr 30min), then dip back into the trees again. At the four-hour mark, you turn a corner into the mouth of the **Styx ravine**. Another five-minutes' walk brings you to a **deep gully** where enormous banks of snow lie late into the spring. A few paces across a dividing rib of rock there is a second gully, where the path has been eroded and you have to cross some slippery scree.

Here you come to a wooded spur running down from the crag on the right. The trail winds up to a shoulder (4hr 20min), descends into another gully, and then winds up to a second shoulder of level rocky ground by some large black pines (4hr 30min), known as *Tò Dhiáselo toú Kynigoú* (the Hunter's Saddle). From there you can look into the Styx ravine. Continue down the path towards the right until it dwindles at the foot of a vast crag (4hr 45min). You can now see the **Mavronéri waterfall**, a 200-metre-long, wavering plume of water pouring off the red cliffs up ahead.

To get to it, angle across the scree bank without losing altitude – the track is obliterated soon after the saddle – until you reach the base of the falls (5hr). There's a small **cave** under the fall, where a rare columbine grows. It is possible to continue up the valley, past some turf next to a seasonal pond where people camp, but the summit area proper is a bit of a let-down after the majesty of the Styx valley. Fairly clear and easy trails lead down from the south side of the watershed to join the E4 trail between the villages of Káto Loussí (12km above Kalávryta) or Planitéro (8km from Klitoría); the appropriate Korfes or YIS maps have more details on these routes.

Travel details

Trains

There are two types of train: ordinary and express (Intercity or IC); the latter only stop at the larger stations and incur variable, often large, supplementary fares. Some small stations are unmanned and trains only stop on request. There are two main Peloponnesian lines:

Athens–Kórinthos–Dhiakoftó–Pátra–Pýrgos–Kyparissía–Kalamáta; one train daily makes the full run in each direction. Another 8 daily run between Athens and Pátra, 7 continuing to Pýrgos, 5 as far as Kyparissía. Another train daily covers the route between Pátra and Kalamáta, with a change at Kaló Neró or Kyparissía. In summer extra services may run from Pátra to Éyio (3 daily Mon–Sat; 45min) and to Dhiakoftó (3 daily Mon–Sat; 45min–1hr).
Approximate journey times are:
Athens–Kórinthos (1hr 30min–2hr)
Kórinthos–Dhiakoftó (1hr–1hr 30min)
Dhiakoftó–Pátra (45min–1hr 25min)
Pátra–Pýrgos (1hr 30min–2hr 15min)

Pýrgos–Kyparissía (1hr–1hr 35min)
Kyparissía–Kalamáta (1hr 40min–2hr).
Athens (starts in Pireás)–Kórinthos–Mykínes (Mycenae)–Árgos–Trípoli–Kalamáta; three trains daily cover the full route, four returning.
Approximate journey times are:
Athens–Kórinthos (1hr 30min–2hr)
Kórinthos–Mykínes (50min)
Mykínes–Árgos (10min)
Árgos–Trípoli (1hr 20min–1hr 35min)
Trípoli–Kalamáta (2hr 5min–2hr 20min).

In addition, there are the following branch lines:
Árgos–Náfplio 2 daily (20min) – this section has a large supplementary fare.
Pýrgos–Olympía 5 trains daily (36min) – but service suspended for refurbishment of the line.
Pýrgos–Katákolo 1–2 daily (25min) – but service suspended for refurbishment of the line.
Dhiakoftó–Zakhloroú–Kalávryta 4 daily (Dhiakoftó–Zakhloroú 46min; Zakhloroú–Kalávryta 21min).

Buses

Buses detailed usually have similar frequency in each direction, so entries are given just once; for reference check under both starting-point and destination. Bus station timetables rarely indicate when there is a change of bus en route – this can involve a long wait. Long-distance buses from Athens often have a break at Isthmós, by the Corinth Canal.

Connections with Athens: Árgos (hourly; 2hr 15min); Hóra (4 daily; 5hr 30min); Kalamáta (12–13 daily; 4hr 30min); Kalávryta (1–2 daily; 3hr 30min); Kórinthos (hourly; 1hr–1hr 30min); Koróni (1 daily; 7hr); Kyparissía (4 daily; 5hr 30min); Loutráki (9 daily; 1hr 30min); Monemvasiá (2 daily; 6hr); Mykínes-Fíkhti (for Mycenae; hourly; 2hr); Náfplio (hourly; 3hr); Olympía (4 daily; 5hr 30min); Pátra (28 daily from 2.30am to 9.30pm; 3hr); Pýlos (2 daily; 5hr 30min–7hr); Pýrgos (8 daily; 5hr); Spárti (9 daily; 4hr); Tíryns (hourly; 2hr 45min); Trípoli (14 daily; 2hr 30min–3hr); Yeroliménas (2 daily in season only; 7hr); Yíthio (4–5 daily; 5hr).

Areópoli to: Ítylo (4 daily, 20min); Kalamáta (4 daily changing at Ítylo; 1hr 30min–2hr 30min); Láyia (daily; 1hr); Váthia (daily in season; 1hr 30min); Yeroliménas (2 daily in season; 1hr).

Árgos to: Andhrítsena (1 daily; 3hr); Ástros (3 daily Mon–Fri; 1hr); Ayía Triádha (8 daily; 20min); Kórinthos (15 daily; 1hr); Leonídhi (3 daily Mon–Fri; 3hr); Midhéa (3 daily; 40min); Mykínes (Mycenae; 5 daily; 30min); Mýli (for Lerna; 5–10 daily; 25min); Náfplio (15–17 daily; every 30min; 30min); Neméa (2 daily; 1hr); Néo Kíos (11 daily; 20min); Olympía (3 daily on weekdays; 4hr 30min); Spárti (8 daily; 3hr); Tíryns (every 30min; 15min); Trípoli (4 daily Mon–Fri, 3 daily Sat–Sun; 1hr 20min).

Galatás to: Méthana (2–4 daily; 45min); Trizína (4 daily; 15min).

Kalamáta to: Exohóri (2 daily; 1hr 30min); Finikoúnda (4 daily, changing at Pýlos; 2hr 15min); Hóra (5 daily, changing at Pýlos, plus 3 direct; 2hr); Kardhamýli (4 daily; 50min); Kórinthos (7 daily; 4hr); Koróni (8 daily; 1hr 20min–2hr); Kyparissía (5 daily; 2hr); Megalópoli (8 daily; 1hr 15min); Messíni (frequent except Sun; 25min); Methóni (6 daily, via Pýlos; 2hr); Pátra (2 daily, via Pýrgos); 4hr–4hr 30min); Pýlos (9 daily; 1hr 30min); Saïdhóna (2 daily); Stoúpa (4 daily; 1hr); Trípoli (8 daily; 1hr 45min–2hr).

Kórinthos to: Loutráki (every 30min; 20min); Mykínes (Mycenae; hourly; 30min); Náfplio (hourly; 1hr 30min); Neméa (5 daily; 45min); Spárti (8 daily; 4hr); Tíryns (hourly; 1hr 15min); Trípoli (9 daily; 1hr 30min).

Kyparissía to: Filiatrá (7 daily; 20min); Pýlos (3 daily changing at Hóra; 2hr); Pýrgos (2–4 daily;

1hr); Trípoli (2 daily; 2hr); Zaháro (4 daily; 25min).

Megalópoli to: Andhrítsena (2 daily; 1hr 15min); Pýrgos (2 daily; 4hr).

Náfplio to: Dhrépano (6–9 daily, except Sun; 20min); Epidaurus (5 daily; 45min); Ermióni (3–4 daily; 2hr 15min); Galatás for Póros (2–3 daily; 2hr); Íria (2 daily; 1hr); Karathónas beach (4 daily; 20min); Kósta (3–4 daily; 2hr 15min); Kranídhi (3–4 daily; 1hr 50min); Lygourió (7 daily; 40min); Midhéa (3 daily; 40min); Mykínes (Mycenae; 3 daily; 1hr); Néo Kíos (11 daily; 20min); Paleá Epídhavros (3 daily; 1hr); Pórto Héli (3–4 daily; 2hr); Tíryns (15–17 daily, every 30min; 15min); Toló (hourly; 25min); Trípoli (3–4 daily; 2hr).

Pátra to: Aháïa (26 daily; 40min); Éyio (12–18 daily; 1hr); Itéa (for Delphi; 2 daily, Mon–Sat; 3–4hr); Ioánnina (4 daily; 5hr); Kalamáta (2 daily; 4hr); Kalávryta (4 daily; 2hr 15min); Kalogriá (1 daily in season; 1hr 15min); Pýrgos (6–10 daily; 2hr); Thessaloníki (3 daily; 9–10hr); Trípoli (2 daily, via Lámbia; 4hr); Vólos (1 daily; 6hr); Zákynthos (4 daily; 2hr 30min including ferry from Kyllíni).

Pýlos to: Finikoúnda (4 daily; 45min); Hóra (6 daily; 40min); Kyparissía (3–6 daily, sometimes changing in Hóra; 2hr); Methóni (6 daily; 20min).

Pýrgos to: Andhrítsena (2 daily; 2hr); Kalamáta (2 daily; 2hr); Katákolo (9 daily; 30min); Kyllíni (3 daily; 1hr); Kyparissía (2 daily; 1hr); Olympía (hourly, but none 12.30–3.30pm; 45–60min); Pátra (10–11 daily; 2hr).

Spárti to: Areópoli (2–3 daily; 2hr); Kalamáta (2 daily; 2hr–2hr 30min); Moláï (6 daily; 2hr); Monemvasiá (3 daily; 2hr 30min–3hr); Mystra (12 daily, 6 on Sun; 15min); Neápoli (3–4 daily; 4hr); Pýrgos Dhiroú (1 daily; 2hr 30min); Trípoli (9–10 daily; 1hr 30min–1hr 20min); Yeroliménas (2 daily; 3hr); Yíthio (5 daily; 1hr).

Trípoli to: Andhrítsena (2 daily; 1hr 30min); Ástros (2 daily Mon–Sat; 1hr 30min); Dhimitsána (1 daily; 1hr 30min); Kalávryta (1 daily; 2hr 30min); Karýtena (2 daily; 1hr); Kyparissía (2 daily; 1hr 30min); Klitoría (1–2 daily; 2hr); Leonídhi (1–2 daily; 3hr 30min); Megalópoli (9 daily Mon–Fri, 6 daily; Sat–Sun; 40min); Neápoli (2 daily; 5hr 30min); Olympía (2 daily Mon–Fri, 1–3 Sat–Sun; 5hr); Pýlos (3 daily; 3hr); Pýrgos (3 daily; 3hr); Stemnítsa (1 daily; 1hr 15min); Tegéa (hourly; 20min); Vytína (6 daily; Mon–Fri, 4 Sat–Sun; 1hr 15min); Yíthio (3 daily; 2hr 30min).

Yíthio to: Areópoli (4 daily; 35–50min); Láyia (daily; 1hr); Monemvasiá (2 daily; 2hr 30min); Pýrgos Dhiroú ("Spílea"; 1 daily; 1hr 10min); Váthia (1 daily, Mon, Wed, Fri; 2hr); Yeroliménas (3 daily 2hr).

Ferries

Across the Gulf of Kórinthos: Andírio–Río (every 15min, every 30min between 11pm and 7am; 10–20min); Éyio–Áyios Nikólaos (5.15am–8.30pm; 9 daily June–Oct, 7 daily Nov–May; 35–50min).

Galatás to: Póros (every 15min from dawn till past midnight; 5min).

Kalamáta to: Kýthira (1–2 weekly in season; 5hr).

Kósta to: Spétses (4 daily; 20min).

Kyllíni to: Zákynthos (daily 7–9 summer, 5 winter; 1hr 30min); Kefalloniá (daily 3–6 summer, 2–4 winter; 1hr 15min–2hr 15min).

Kýthira to: Andikýthira (2 weekly in season); Kastélli, Crete (4–6 weekly in season; 2hr 15min; 5hr via Andikýthira); Pireás (2 weekly in season).

Neápoli to: Elafónissos (5–15 daily; 10 min); Kýthira (1 daily in low season, 2–3 daily mid-season, 3–4 daily late July–Aug; 1hr).

Pátra to: Igoumenítsa and Corfu (2–3 daily; 6–11hr/8–11hr); Kefalloniá and Itháki (1–2 daily; 2hr 30min/3hr 45min); also to Brindisi, Ancona, Bari, Trieste and Venice (Italy).

Yíthio to: Kýthira (1–3 weekly in season; 2hr 30min); contact Rozaki (☎07330/22 207) for current information.

Hydrofoils

For details and frequencies of services, which vary drastically with season, contact local agents or the Minoan Flying Dolphins' main office in Pireás (Aktí Themistokléous 8 ☎010/41 28 001).

Flying Dolphin hydrofoils run between the following ports:

Yérakas/Kyparíssi/Monemvasiá/Leonídhi/Tyroú to Pórto Héli, Spétses, Ídhra and Pireás.

Neápoli (summer only) to Kýthira, Monemvasiá, Kyparíssi, Leonídhi and Pireás.

Kýthira to Monemvasiá, Kyparíssi, Leonídhi, Pórto Héli, Spétses, Ídhra and Pireás.

Méthana to Póros, Ídhra, Ermióni, Égina and Pireás.

Ermióni to Spétses, Pórto Héli, Ídhra, Póros, Méthana and Pireás.

Náfplio (midsummer only) to Monemvasiá, Toló, Spétses, Póros and Pireás.

Paleá Epídhavros (summer only) to Égina and Pireás.

Summer-only excursion boats

Kósta and Pórto Héli: Water-taxis to Spétses according to demand (10–20min).

Flights

To/from **Athens–Kalamáta** (3 weekly; 50min); **Athens–Kýthira** (1–2 daily; 50min).

Thessaly and
central Greece

N

0   100 km

CHAPTER 3 **Highlights**

＊ **Ósios Loukás** A fine
Byzantine monastery deco-
rated with vivid mosaics
from the eleventh century.
See p.315

＊ **Delphi** Site of the famous
oracle and believed by the
ancient Greeks to be the
centre of the earth.
See p.317

＊ **Galaxídhi** The most perfectly
preserved settlement on the
Gulf of Corinth, this was one
of Greece's major ports in
the nineteenth century.
See p.328

＊ **Náfpaktos** A lively market
town with a stage-set old
harbour and swooping castle
walls. See p.331

＊ **Karpenisiótis valley** This
green but alpine valley,
known as the "Greek
Switzerland", is an all-year
recreation paradise.
See p.336

＊ **Mount Pílio** Hiking trails link
mansion-filled villages clinging to wooded hillsides; the
mythical home of the cen-
taurs. See p.346

＊ **The northeast Pílio coast**
Superb, pale-sand beaches
provide respite after arduous
hiking. See p.250

＊ **The Metéora** Meaning
"rocks in the air"; bizarre and
stunning scenery and exquisite Byzantine monasteries.
See p.370

3

Thessaly and central Greece

C entral Greece is a region of scattered highlights, above all the site of the ancient oracle at **Delphi** (modern Dhelfí), and, further north, the other-worldly rock monasteries of the **Metéora**. The area as a whole, dominated by the vast agricultural plain of Thessaly, is less exciting, with rather drab market and industrial towns. The southern part of this region, below Thessaly proper, is known as **Stereá Elládha** – literally "Greek Continent", a name that reflects its mid-nineteenth-century past as the only independent Greek mainland territory, along with Attica and the quasi-island of the Peloponnese. It corresponds to the ancient divisions of Boeotia and Phocis, the domains respectively of Thebes (modern Thíva) and Delphi. Most visitors head straight through these territories to Delphi, but if you have time there are some rewarding detours to the monastery of **Ósios Loukás** – containing the finest Byzantine mosaics in the country – and **Glas**, the largest and most obscure of the Mycenaean sites. For hikers there is also the opportunity of climbing **Mount Parnassós**, the Muses' mountain.

The basin of **Thessaly** (Thessalía) formed the bed of an ancient inland sea – rich agricultural land that was ceded reluctantly to the modern nation by the

---

Accommodation price codes

Throughout the book we've categorized accommodation according to the following **price codes**, which denote the cheapest available double room in high season. All prices are for the room only, except where otherwise indicated. Many hotels, especially those in category ❹ and over, include breakfast in the price; you'll need to check this when booking. During low season, rates can drop by more than fifty percent, especially if you are staying for three or more nights. Exceptions are during the Christmas and Easter weeks when you'll pay high-season prices. Single rooms, where available, cost around seventy percent of the price of a double.

❶ Up to €24	❹ €43–58
❷ €24–33	❺ €59–72
❸ €34–42	❻ €73 and upwards

Note: Youth hostels and mountain refuges typically charge €7–9 for a dormitory bed. For more accommodation details, see pp.51–54.

▲ Árta & Lefkádha

Turks in 1878. This region's attractions lie at its periphery, hemmed in by the mountain ranges of Ólymbos (Olympus), Píndhos (Pindus), Óssa and Pílio (Pelion). East from the major port city of Vólos extends the hilly peninsula of **Mount Pílio**, whose luxuriant woods and idyllic beaches are easily combined with island-hopping to the Sporades. To the west, **Kalambáka** gives access to the Metéora (not to be missed) and across the dramatic **Katára pass** over the Píndhos to Epirus. To the north, the horizon is dominated by **Mount Olympus** (covered in Chapter Five), home of the ancient gods.

Looming across a narrow gulf from Stereá Elládha, and joined by a bridge at Halkídha, is the island of **Évvia** (Euboea). Though this feels – especially in summer – like an extension of the mainland (from where there are many ferry crossings), it is nonetheless a bona-fide island and its attractions are detailed in Chapter Eleven.

Stereá Elládha: routes to Delphi and beyond

The inevitable focus of a visit to Stereá Elládha is **Delphi**, 150km northwest of Athens. Buses cover the route from the capital several times a day, or they can be picked up at **Livadhiá**, the nearest rail terminus. However, if you're in no hurry and/or have your own transport, there are ample rewards in slowing your progress: take the "old road" to Thebes (Thíva), or detour from Livadhiá to the Byzantine monastery of **Ósios Loukás** or to Mycenaean **Glas**.

To the northeast of the Athens–Delphi road, traffic roars along **National Road 1** towards Lárissa and Thessaloníki, skirting the coast for much of the way, with the long island of Évvia only a few kilometres across the gulf. Along this route there are ferries over to Évvia at **Arkítsa**, **Áyios Konstandínos** (where you can also pick up ferries or hydrofoils to the Sporades) and **Glýfa**.

Moving on from Delphi and Lamía, the town immediately north, two routes cross Thessaly: northwest to the Metéora, or northeast to Pílio. Another road leads southwest to the Gulf of Corinth, offering an approach to – or from – the **Peloponnese**, via the ferry services Andírio–Río or Áyios Nikólaos–Éyio, or the thinly populated province of Étolo-Akarnanía. A fourth, more remote route leads due west from Lamía to **Karpeníssi** and then across the southern-most extensions of the Píndhos mountains.

The Old Road to Thebes (Thíva)

The ancient road from Athens to Delphi began at the Parthenon as the **Sacred Way to Eleusis**, and from there climbed northwest into the hills towards Thebes. It is possible to follow this route, almost unchanged since Oedipus supposedly trod it, by taking the minor road, signposted for "Mándhra", north off the motorway at modern Elefsína. Leaving the polluted and industrial port, matters improve quickly, as the road winds up and out into a landscape of pines and grey stony hills. There are two buses daily along this road to Thíva and connections from there on to Livadhiá and Delphi.

Pórto Yermenó, Aegosthena and Eleutherai

The first thing to tempt you off the Thebes road is a look at the best-preserved stretch of ancient walls in Greece – the fourth-century BC fort of **Aegosthena** – 23km from the Elefsína–Thíva road (no bus), above the mouth of a valley running between mounts Kytherónas and Patéras, overlooking a secluded arm of the Gulf of Kórinthos. Historically it is insignificant, being merely an outpost of Sparta's ally Megara, but the ruins themselves are impressive, the two end towers rising up more than 12m above the walls. The seaward ramparts have mostly vanished; up on the acropolis, a church with frescoes survives from a medieval monastery which took root here.

A kilometre below on the shore at this extreme northeast corner of the Gulf sprawls **PÓRTO YERMENÓ**, a little resort popular with the working-class districts of western Athens. Three gravel-sand beaches here are divided by tiny, low headlands, with pine- and olive-draped hills as a backdrop, and are certainly the cleanest near Athens. If you avoid high summer and shoulder-season weekends, when the place gets packed out, Pórto Yermenó makes an excellent first-night halt by the sea, especially if you've started late out of Athens. Give the overpriced, inland *Hotel Egosthenion* a miss in favour of the 1980s-vintage **rooms and apartments** just above the northerly beach: *Vassiliki Mastroyianni* (☎02630/41 394; ❸) is representative. At peak season, up to a dozen **tavernas**, pizzerias, and fast-food takeaways operate, but for year-round reliability *Psarotaverna O Dhimos* (weekends only winter), out behind the southerly beach of Ayios Nikólaos, is hard to better for its meat/fish grills, salads and own-made retsina; their fresh-fish meals shouldn't exceed €15 each. In town, the *Avra* is the most accomplished and northernmost of several seafood tavernas in a row on the pedestrianized lane behind the north beach.

Back on the Thebes road, a kilometre north of the Pórto Yermenó turning, you pass another fortress – fourth-century BC **Eleutherai**. Signposted from the road, 400m to the east, the fort is again well preserved, with its northeast side almost intact and six of its circuit of towers surviving to varying degrees. The scant ruins of Eleutherai town itself lie down by the Aegosthena junction, while the fort defends a critical pass above; both sites have unlimited access.

Thíva (Thebes)

The modern town of **THÍVA** lies 20km north of Eleutherai, built right on the site of its mighty predecessor. For this very reason, there are almost no traces of the past: archeologists have had little success in excavating the crucial central areas, and the most interesting visit is to the excellent **archeological museum** (summer Mon noon–7pm, Tues–Sun 8am–7pm; winter may close earlier; €1.50). This is to be found at the north (downhill) end of Pindhárou, the main street; look out for the enormous Frankish tower in its forecourt, where archeologists can often be seen at work in their labs. The collection is strongest on Bronze Age to Classical Boeotia, in particular votive offerings from religious centres, though as so often labelling is spotty and tends to be by group rather than by item. Room A features funerary stelae, in particular one from the sixth-century BC depicting a youth holding a cockerel and sniffing a lotus; from the same era are two *kouroi* (idealized Archaic male figures) from an Apollo shrine at Ptóön, reminiscent of the larger one found on Sámos (see p.834). Room D is devoted to a unique collection of painted *larnakes* (sarcophagi) from Mycenean Tanagra, dating to 1350–1250 BC. Bold expressionistic strokes display heavy Cretan influence; along with floral and abstract patterns there are well-observed hunting scenes, and women lamenting their dead.

There are no direct **buses** from Thíva to Delphi, but services run frequently to Livadhiá (where there are better connections) and a couple of times a day to Halkídha, gateway to Évvia. If you get stranded between buses, there are two central if rather overpriced **hotels** opposite each other on Epaminónda; the *Niobe* at no. 63 (☎02620/27 949; ❹) is preferable.

Livadhiá and around

Livadhiá lies at the edge of a great **agricultural plain**, much of it reclaimed lakebed, scattered with a few minor but enjoyable sites. It's a part of Greece that sees few tourists, most of whom are in a hurry to reach the glories of the Parnassós country just to the west.

Livadhiá

LIVADHIÁ is a pleasant town on the banks of the Érkyna, a river of ancient fame which emerges from a dark gorge at the base of a fortress. It's an attractive place for a brief stop, with paired ancient and medieval sights, but bear in mind the last bus or train connection out, since overnighting here will prove costly.

The older curiosity is the site of the **Oracle of Trophonios**, a ten-minute walk from the main square, beside an Ottoman-era bridge. Here the waters of the Érkyna rise from a series of springs, now channelled beside the (signposted) *Xenia* café. Above the springs, cut into the rock, are niches for votive offerings – in one of which, in a large chamber with a bench, the Turkish governor would sit for a quiet smoke. In antiquity, all who sought to consult the Oracle of Trophonios first had to bathe in the Springs of Memory and Forgetfulness. The oracle, a circular structure which gave entrance to caves deep in the gorge, has been tentatively identified at the top of the hill, near the remains of an unfinished temple of Zeus. It was visited by the Greek traveller-scholar Pausanias, who wrote that it left him "possessed with terror and hardly knowing himself or anything around him".

The **kástro**, or castle, which overlooks the springs, provides the medieval interest; its entrance lies just around the corner up the hill to the west. An impressive and well-bastioned square structure, it was built in the fourteenth century and was a key early conquest in the War of Independence. But its early history is more compelling. The castle was the stronghold of a small group of Catalan mercenaries, the Grand Company, who took control of central Greece in 1311 and – appointing a Sicilian prince as their ruler – held it for sixty years. They were a tiny, brutal band who had arrived in Greece from Spain in the wake of the Fourth Crusade. They wrested control from the Franks, who were then established in Athens and Thebes, in a cunning deviation from traditional rules of engagement. As the Frankish nobility approached Livadhiá, the vastly outnumbered Catalans diverted the river to flood the surrounding fields. The Frankish cavalry advanced into the unexpected marsh and were cut down to a man.

Practicalities

The town today is a minor provincial capital with a trade in milling cotton from the area. Though completely off the tourist route, landscaping and gentrification in the vicinity of the river springs make it an enjoyable daytime pause before, or after, Delphi. Be warned that in season buses on towards Delphi often arrive and leave full, though two local ones start from Livadhiá around noon. Arriving by **bus**, you'll be dropped near the central square, **Platía Dhiákou**; the **train station** is a few kilometres out, but arrivals may be met by a shuttle bus (or more likely taxis) into town.

Staying overnight is highly problematic since virtually all of Livadhiá's budget hotels closed their doors in the early 1990s. The exception, included only for the record, is the *Erkyna*, a depressing, overpriced dosshouse, just downriver from the park area at Ioánni Lápa 6 (℡02610/28 227; ❸). If your budget doesn't run to the pricey *Livadhia* on Platía Kotsóni at the main junction (℡02610/23 611; ❻), or if you don't fancy the noisy *Philippos*, a modern pile at the east outskirts (℡02610/24 931; ❺) and closed for renovations at the time of writing, you'd be well advised to press on towards Aráhova and Delphi. **Eating out** here is a better proposition; in the pedestrianized zones surrounding the riverside park are a number of grills, *mezedhopolía* and cafés, some only active by night and two housed in converted water mills. *Neromylos*, one of the after-dark mill restorations on the pedestrianized riverbank, is OK as a suppertime ouzerí, and not too expensive; for lunch, *Iy Krya*, officially at Trofoníou 2 (the first establishment on the right, facing upriver), is acceptable as a simple grill.

Orchomenos

Just 10km northeast of Livadhiá (hourly buses) is the site of **ancient ORCHOMENOS**, inhabited from Neolithic to Classical times. As the capital of the Minyans, a native Thessalian dynasty, it was one of the wealthiest Mycenaean cities.

Near the middle of the rather drab modern village of Orhomenós, along the road signposted for Dhiónysos village, is the **"Treasury" of Minyas** (Tues–Sat 9am–3pm, Sun 10am–2pm), a stone *thólos*-type tomb similar to the tomb of Atreus at Mycenae, and also excavated by Heinrich Schliemann in 1880. The roof has collapsed but it is otherwise complete, and its inner chamber, hewn from the rock, has an intricately carved marble ceiling. Closer to the road are the remains of a fourth-century BC **theatre**, and behind, on the rocky hilltop, a tiny fortified acropolis from the same period.

Across the road from the theatre is the ninth-century Byzantine **church of Panayía tís Skripoús**, built entirely of blocks from the theatre and column drums from a classical temple – as is the minute Byzantine church in the main village square. The larger triple-apsed church has some fine reliefs, including a sundial, with the remains of a monastery just to the south.

The citadel of Glas

Continuing east, in a highly worthwhile diversion, it's a further 16km (2 buses daily, 2.30pm & 7.15pm) to the village of Kástro, right next to the motorway towards Lárissa. If you cross the highway and then walk south (towards Athens) for about 100m you come to the signposted side road which leads, within about 300m, to the Mycenaean citadel of Glas.

An enormous and extraordinary site, **GLAS** (unrestricted entrance) stands within a three-kilometre circuit of Cyclopean walls – a far larger citadel than either Tiryns or Mycenae. Almost nothing, however, is known about the site, save that it was once an island in Lake Kopaïs (which was drained late in the nineteenth century) and that it may have been an outpost of the Minyans. The **walls** and **city gates** still stand to five metres in places, and are almost three kilometres in length, despite having been damaged when the city fell. Inside, on the higher ground, what is thought to have been a huge Mycenaean **palace** has been revealed; it appears to include a *megaron* (throne room) and various storerooms, though archeologists are puzzled by differences from the standard Mycenaean palace form. Further down, and currently being excavated, is a vast walled area believed to have been the **marketplace**.

Chaironeia

Directly north of Livadhiá, on the main road to Lamía, is **Chaironeia**, once the home of the writer Plutarch, but more famous as the site of one of the most **decisive battles** of ancient Greece. Here, in 338 BC, Philip of Macedon won a resounding victory over an alliance of Athenians, Thebans and Peloponnesians put together by Demosthenes. This defeat marked the death of the old city-states, from whom control passed forever into foreign hands: first Macedonian, later Roman.

Set beside the road, at modern **Herónia**, is a remarkable six-metre-high **stone lion**, originally part of the funerary monument to the Thebans (or, some say, to the Macedonians) killed in the battle. Adjacent is a small museum of local finds, and there are remains of ancient **acropolis** fortifications, with a theatre at their base, above the village.

The Oedipus crossroads, Ósios Loukás and Aráhova

West from Livadhiá, the landscape becomes ever more striking as Mount Parnassós and its attendant peaks loom high above the road. After 22km, about halfway to Delphi, you reach the so-called **Schist** (Split) or **Triodos** (Triple Way) **crossroads** – also known as the **Oedipus crossroads** – which was the intersection of the ancient roads from Delphi, Daulis (today Dávlia), Thebes (Thíva) and Ambrossos (Dhístomo). The old road actually lay in the gorge, below the modern one.

Pausanias identified this crossroads as the site of Oedipus's murder of his father, King Laius of Thebes, and all but one of his retainers (who later, unwilling-ly, identifies Oedipus). According to the **myth**, Oedipus was returning on foot from Delphi while Laius and his entourage was speeding towards him from the opposite direction on a chariot. Neither would give way, and in the altercation that followed Oedipus killed them, ignorant of who they were. It was to be, in the supreme understatement of Pausanias, "the beginning of his troubles". Continuing to Thebes, Oedipus solved the riddle of the Sphinx, which had been ravaging the area, and was given the hand of widowed Queen Iocaste (Jocasta) in marriage – unaware that he was marrying his own mother.

Getting to Ósios Loukás: Dhístomo

If you have transport, you can turn left at the crossroads and follow the minor road to Dhístomo, and thence 8km east to the **monastery of Ósios Loukás**. Travelling by bus, you may need to take a more roundabout route: first from

Livadhiá to Dhístomo, then another bus on from there towards Stíri and Kyriáki – getting off at the fork to Ósios Loukás, leaving just a 2.5km walk. Alternatively, it's possible to hire a taxi in **DHÍSTOMO**, which also has a couple of small **hotels** on the town square facing the church: the *America* (☎02670/22 079; ❸) and *Koutriaris* (☎02670/22 268; ❸).

Despite valiant attempts at beautification in its centre, Dhístomo remains a drab place, distinguished historically by one of the worst World War II **atrocities** in Greece: German occupying forces shot 232 of the inhabitants on June 10, 1944, looting and burning part of the village for good measure. The event is immortalized in a bleak grey-and-white memorial, erected in 1996 on a nearby hilltop – follow the signs to the marble-clad "mausoleum". On one plaque are the names of the victims; on two others apologetic sentiments from a German citizens' group and then-President, Roman Herzog.

Ósios Loukás monastery

The **monastery of Ósios Loukás** (daily: May to mid-Sept 8am–2pm & 4–7pm; winter 8am–5pm; €2.40) was a precursor of that last defiant flourish of **Byzantine art** that produced the great churches at Mystra in the Peloponnese. It is modest in scale, but from an architectural or decorative point of view ranks as one of the great buildings of medieval Greece. The setting, too, is exquisite – as beautiful as it is remote, especially in February when the many local almond trees are in bloom. As one approaches from Dhístomo, the monastery suddenly appears on its shady terrace, overlooking a spectacular sweep of the Elikónas mountain range and an intervening valley.

The main structure comprises two domed churches, the larger **katholikón** of Ósios Loukás and the adjacent chapel of the **Theotókos**. They are joined by a common foundation wall but otherwise share few architectural features. Ten monks still live in the monastic buildings around the courtyard, but the monastery is essentially maintained as a museum, with snack and souvenir stalls in the grounds.

The katholikón

The **katholikón** (main church), built in the early eleventh century, is dedicated to a local beatified hermit, Luke of Stiri (not the Evangelist). Its design formed the basis of Byzantine octagonal-plan churches, and was later copied at Dhafní and at Mystra. Externally it is modest, with rough brick-and-stone walls surmounted by a well-proportioned dome. The interior, however, is startling. Built to a conventional cross-in-square plan, its atmosphere switches from austere to exultant as the eye moves along walls lined in red, grey and green marble to the gold-backed mosaics on the high ceiling. Light filtering through marble-encrusted windows reflects across the curved surfaces of the mosaics in the nave and bounces onto the marble walls, bringing out the subtlety of their shades.

The original **mosaics** were damaged by an earthquake in 1659, and in the dome and elsewhere have been replaced by unremarkable frescoes, but surviving examples testify to their glory. On the right as you enter the narthex are a majestic *Resurrection*, rivalled only by the version at Néa Moní on Híos (see p.860), and *Thomas Probing Christ's Wound*. The mosaic of the *Niptir* (*Washing of the Apostles' Feet*) on the far left (north side) of the narthex is one of the finest here; its theme is an especially human one, the expressions of the apostles ranging between diffidence and surprise. This dynamic and richly humanized approach is again illustrated by the *Baptism*, high up in the naos, on the northwest squinch. Here the naked Jesus reaches for the cross amidst a swirling mass of water, an illusion of depth created by the angle and curvature of the wall. On other squinches (the curved surfaces supporting the dome), the Christ Child reaches out to the High Priest Simeon in *The Presentation*, while in *The Nativity*, angels predominate rather than the usual shepherds. The church's original **frescoes** are confined to the vaulted chambers at the corners of the cross plan and, though less imposing than the mosaics, employ subtle colours and shades, notably in *Christ Walking towards the Baptism*.

The Theotókos chapel and crypt

The chapel of the **Theotókos** (literally "God-Bearing", meaning the Virgin Mary) is a century older than the *katholikón*. From the outside it overshadows the main church with its elaborate brick decoration culminating in a highly Eastern-influenced, marble-panelled drum. The interior (currently shut for restoration) seems gloomy and cramped by comparison, highlighted only by a couple of fine Corinthian capitals and an original floor mosaic, now dimmed by the passage of time.

Finally, do not miss the vivid frescoes in the **crypt** of the *katholikón*, entered on the lower right-hand (south) side of the building. It's a good idea to bring a torch, since illumination is limited to three spotlights to preserve the colours of the post-Byzantine frescoes.

Aráhova

Arriving at **ARÁHOVA**, the last town east of Delphi (just 11km further on), you are well and truly in Parnassós country. The peaks stand tiered above, sullied somewhat by the wide asphalt road cut to a ski-resort – the winter-weekend haunt of well-heeled Athenians. If you want to **ski**, it's possible to hire equipment on a daily basis at the resort, or even to get an all-in day-package from Athens through the Klaoudatos department store. The resort's main problem – besides ever-dryer and -warmer winters which mean it operates twelve weeks a year at best – is high winds, which often lead to lift closure, so check the forecast before you set off.

Skiing aside, the town is appealing (if fairly desolate in summer), despite being split in two by the Livadhiá–Delphi road, and fairly comprehensive après-ski commercialization. If you're not making for any other mountain areas, Aráhova is worth an afternoon's pause before continuing to Delphi; those with their own transport may prefer staying here, as opposed to modern Dhelfí village. A dwindling number of houses in Aráhova retain their vernacular architecture, flanking narrow lanes twisting north up the slope or poised to the south on the edge of the olive-tree-choked Plistós gorge. The area is renowned for its strong purplish wines, honey, candied fruits and nuts, cheese, the novelty noodles called *hilopíttes*, *tsípouro* and woollen weavings; all are much in evidence in the roadside shops, though most of the woven goods are nowadays imported from northern Greece and/or machine-loomed. Also of note is the local **festival of Áyios Yeóryios** (April 23, or the Tues after Easter if this date falls within Lent), centred on the church at the top of the hill, and one of the best opportunities to catch genuine folk-dancing during almost two days of continuous partying.

Practicalities

In the summer most people just stop for a meal and to souvenir-shop, so finding **accommodation** is easy, even though several establishments close down. In winter, particularly at weekends, rooms are at a premium in all senses, with prices bumped up at least one category from the summer. At the cheaper end of the scale, there are two pleasant if modest **hotels**, with shared bathrooms, side by side at the Livadhiá end of town: the *Apollon* (☎02670/31 427; ➊) and the *Parnassos* (☎02670/31 307; ➊), both with good views. Near the centre of the village, away from the busy through road, is Aráhova's one restoration **inn**, *Paradhosiakos Xenonas Maria* (☎02670/31 803, ➋32 091; ➌ summer B&B, ➌–➎ winter), a lovely old building with an array of rustic-decor doubles, triples and quads. At the Delphi end of town, choose from among the plain but spacious *Apollon Inn* (☎02670/31 057, ✉Arachova-Inn@United-Hellas.com; ➊–➋), an annexe of the *Apollon Hotel* with some en-suite rooms; the *Pension Nostos* (☎02670/31 385, ➋31 765, ✉nostos@otenet.gr; ➌ summer, ➏ winter B&B), with balconies in most of the smallish rooms; or the 1997-refurbished *Xenia Hotel* (☎02670/31 230; ➌ summer, ➍–➏ winter), with its own parking, gorgeous views from all rooms and buffet breakfast included in the price. Certainly the best value in this neighbourhood, though, is the 1999-built *Xenonas Petrino* (☎02670/31 384, ➋32 663; ➋ summer, ➎ winter), whose plain but attractive galleried rooms function as doubles or quads; there's also a basement breakfast bar.

During summer, a good fifty percent of Aráhova's eateries close down, but an amazing number of state-of-the-art bars and sweet shops continues to serve the trendy local youth. As testimony to the village's dual personality, the kafenío tables on the main fountain square remain packed out with their loudly discussing elders until late. Among the more durable and consistently open **tavernas** is the excellent *Karathanasi*, also on the square, with soups in the cooler months, bulk wine and assorted meat dishes; it has roof-terrace seating on summer nights. For milk-based sweets, there's *Galaktopolio En Arahovi*, up the steps from the main fountain-plátia, with indoor and outdoor seating.

Six **buses** daily go to Athens and seven to Delphi and Itéa, one or two of which go on to Pátra; bus timetables are displayed at the *Celena Cafeteria Bar*, open all day, right opposite the smaller square which doubles as a bus stop and taxi rank. Two **banks** with cash dispensers round off the list of essential amenities.

Delphi (Dhelfí)

With its site raised on the slopes of a high mountain terrace and dwarfed to either side by the massive, ominous crags of Parnassós, it's easy to see why the ancients believed **DELPHI** to be the centre of the earth. But more than the natural setting or even the occasional earthquake and avalanche were needed to confirm a divine presence. This, according to Plutarch, was achieved through the discovery of a rock chasm that exuded strange vapours and reduced all comers to frenzied, incoherent and undoubtedly **prophetic** mutterings.

The oracle: some history

The first **oracle** established on this spot was dedicated to **Gea** ("Mother Earth") and to **Poseidon** ("the Earth Shaker"). The serpent **Python**, son of Gea, was installed in a nearby cave, and communication made through the Pythian priestess. Python was subsequently slain by **Apollo**, whose cult had been imported from Crete (legend has it that he arrived in the form of a dolphin – hence the name *Delphoi*). The **Pythian Games** were established on an eight-year cycle to commemorate the feat, and perhaps also to placate the ancient deities.

The place was known to the **Mycenaeans**, whose votive offerings (tiny striped statues of goddesses and worshipping women) have been discovered near the site of Apollo's temple. Following the arrival of the **Dorians** in Greece at the beginning of the twelfth century BC, the sanctuary became the centre of the loose-knit association of Greek city-states known as the **Amphyctionic League**. The territory still belonged however, to the nearby city of Krissa, which, as the oracle gained in popularity, began to extort heavy dues from the pilgrims arriving at the port of Kirrha. In the sixth century BC the League was called on to intervene, and the first of a series of **Sacred Wars** broke out. The League wrested Delphi from the Krissaeans and made it an autonomous state. From then on Delphi experienced a rapid ascent to fame and respect, becoming within a few decades one of the major sanctuaries of Greece, with its tried and tested oracle generally thought to be the arbiter of truth.

For over a thousand years thereafter, a steady stream of **pilgrims** made its way up the dangerous mountain paths to seek divine direction in matters of war, worship, love or business. On arrival they would sacrifice a sheep or a goat and, depending on the omens, wait to submit questions inscribed on lead tablets. The Pythian priestess, a simple and devout village woman of fifty or more years in age, would chant her prophecies from a tripod positioned over the oracular chasm. Crucially, an attendant priest would then "interpret" her utterings and relay them to the enquirer in hexameter verse.

Many of the **oracular answers** were equivocal: Croesus, for example, was told that if he embarked on war against neighbouring Persia he would destroy a mighty empire; he did – his own. But it's hard to imagine that the oracle would have retained its popularity and influence for so long without offering predominantly sound advice. Indeed, Strabo wrote that "of all oracles in the world, it had the reputation of being the most truthful." One explanation is that the Delphic priests were simply better informed than any other corporate body around at the time. Positioned at the centre of the Amphyctionic League, which became a kind of "United Nations" of the Greek city-states, they were in a position to amass a wealth of political, economic and social information, and, from the seventh century BC onwards, Delphi had its own network of informants throughout the Greek world.

The **influence** of the oracle spread abroad with the Classical age of colonization and its patronage grew, reaching a peak in the sixth century BC, with powerful benefactors such as Amasis, King of Egypt, and the unfortunate King Croesus of Lydia; many of the Greek city-states also dedicated treasuries at this time. Privileged position and enormous wealth, however, made Delphi vulnerable to Greek rivalries; the first Sacred Wars left it autonomous, but in the fifth century BC the oracle began to be too closely identified with individual states. Worse, it maintained a defeatist, almost treacherous attitude towards the Persian invasions – only partially mitigated when a Persian force, sent by Xerxes to raid Delphi, was crushed at the entrance to the sanctuary by a well-timed earthquake.

It never quite regained the same level of trust – and consequently of power – after these instances of bias and corruption. However, real **decline** did not set in until the fourth century BC, with the resumption of the Sacred Wars and the emergence of Macedonian control. Following prolonged squabbling among the Greek city-states, the sanctuary was seized by the Phocians in 356 BC, leading to Philip of Macedon's intervention to restore the Amphyctionic League to power. Seven years later, when the League again invited Philip to settle a dispute, this time provoked by the Amphissans, he responded by invading southern Greece. The independence of the city-states was brought to an end at the Battle of Chaironeia, and Delphi's political intriguing was effectively over.

Under **Macedonian** and later **Roman** control, the oracle's role became increasingly domestic and insignificant, dispensing advice on marriages, loans, voyages and the like. The Romans thought little of its utterances, rather more of its treasure: Sulla plundered the sanctuary in 86 BC and Nero, outraged when the oracle pronounced judgement on the murder of his mother, carted away some five hundred bronze statues. Finally, with the demise of paganism under Theodosius late in the fourth century AD, the oracle became defunct.

In modern times, the sanctuary site was rediscovered towards the end of the seventeenth century and explored haphazardly from the 1840s onwards. Real **excavation** of the site came only in 1892 when the French School of Archeology leased the land, in exchange for a French government agreement to buy the Greek currant crop. There was little to be seen other than the outline of a stadium and theatre, but the villagers who lived there were persuaded (with the help of an army detachment) to move to a new town 1km west, and digging commenced. Over the next decade or so most of the excavations and reconstruction visible today were completed.

The most interesting development in Delphi's recent history came through the efforts of the poet Angelos Sikelianos and his American wife Eva Palmer to set up a "University of the World" in the 1920s. The project eventually failed, though it inspired an annual **Delphic Festival**, held now in June of each year, with performances of Classical drama in the ancient theatre.

The sites

Split by the road from Aráhova, the ancient site divides essentially into three parts: the **Sacred Precinct**, the **Marmaria** and the **Castalian spring**. In addition there is a worthwhile **museum**, still poorly presented despite a recent rejigging and face-lift. All in all Delphi is a large and complex ruin, best taken in two stages, with the sanctuary ideally at the beginning or end of the day, or (in winter) at lunchtime, to escape the coached-in crowds. Make sure you have sturdy footwear as there's a lot of clambering up rough stone steps and paths, and take food and drink if you're planning a full day's visit; good picnicking spots are the theatre with its panorama of the sanctuary (its seats, alas, off-limits), or try the stadium for fewer interruptions.

DELPHI: THE SITES

The Sacred Precinct

The **Sacred Precinct** (daily: summer 7.30am–7pm; winter 8am–5pm; €3.50, or €5.90 joint ticket with museum), or Temenos (Sanctuary) of Apollo, is entered, as in ancient times, by way of a small **agora** enclosed by ruins of Roman porticoes and shops for the sale of votive offerings. The paved **Sacred Way** begins after a few stairs, and zigzags uphill between the foundations of memorials and treasuries to the Temple of Apollo. Along each edge is a jumble of statue bases where gold, bronze and painted-marble figures once stood; Pliny counted more than three thousand on his visit, and that was after Nero's infamous raid.

The choice and position of these **memorials** were dictated by more than religious zeal; many were used as a deliberate show of strength or as a direct insult against a rival Greek state. For instance, the **Offering of the Arcadians** on the right of the entrance (a line of bases that supported nine bronzes) was erected to commemorate their invasion of Laconia in 369 BC, and pointedly placed in front of the Lacedaemonians' own monument. Beside this, and following the same logic, the Spartans celebrated their victory over Athens by erecting their **Monument of the Admirals** – a large recessed structure, which once held 37 bronze statues of gods and generals – directly opposite the Athenians' **Offering of Marathon**.

Further up the path, past the Doric remains of the **Sikyonian Treasury** on the left, stretch the expansive foundations of the **Siphnian Treasury**, a grandiose Ionic temple erected in 525 BC. Ancient Siphnos had rich gold mines and intended the building to be an unrivalled show of opulence. Fragments of the caryatids that supported its west entrance, and the fine Parian marble frieze that adorned all four sides, are now in the museum. Above this is the **Treasury of the Athenians**, built, like the city's "Offering", after Marathon (490 BC). It was reconstructed in 1904–06 by matching the inscriptions that completely cover its blocks. These include honorific decrees in favour of Athens, lists of Athenian ambassadors to the Pythian Festival and a hymn to Apollo with its musical notation in Greek letters above the text.

Next to it are the foundations of the **Bouleuterion**, or council house, a reminder that Delphi needed administrators, and above sprawls the remarkable **Polygonal Wall** whose irregular interlocking blocks have withstood, intact, all earthquakes. It, too, is covered with inscriptions, but these almost universally refer to the emancipation of slaves; Delphi was one of the few places where such freedom could be made official and public by an inscribed register. An incongruous outcrop of rock between the wall and the treasuries marks the original **Sanctuary of Gea**. It was here, or more precisely on the recently built-up rock, that the Sibyl, an early itinerant priestess, was reputed to have uttered her prophecies.

Finally, the Sacred Way leads to the temple terrace where you are confronted with a large altar, erected by the island of Chios (Híos). Of the main body of the **Temple of Apollo**, only the foundations stood when it was uncovered by the French. Six Doric columns have since been re-erected, giving a vertical line to the ruins and providing some idea of the temple's former dominance over the whole of the sanctuary. In the innermost part of the temple was the *adyton*, a dark cell at the mouth of the oracular chasm where the Pythian priestess would officiate. No sign of cave or chasm has been found, nor any vapours that might have induced a trance, but it is likely that such a chasm did exist and was simply opened and closed by successive earthquakes. On the architrave of the temple – probably on the interior – were inscribed the maxims "Know Thyself" and "Moderation in All Things".

DELPHI: THE SACRED PRECINCT

Theatre

Temenos of Dionysos

Stage

Temenos of Poseidon

Stadium

Sacred Way

Altar of Apollo

Temple of Apollo

Sacred Way

Terrace

Polygonal Wall

Sanctuary of Gea

Bouleuterion

Sacred Way

Treasury of the Athenians

Monument of the Admirals

Theban Treasury

Siphnian Treasury

Sikyonian Treasury

Sacred Way

Main Entrance

Offering of the Arcadians

Athenians' offering of Marathon

N

0   20 m

The theatre and stadium used for the main events of the Pythian Festival lie on terraces above the temple. The **theatre**, built in the fourth century BC with a capacity of five thousand, was closely connected with Dionysos, the god of ecstasy, the arts and wine, who reigned in Delphi over the winter months when the oracle was silent. A path leads up through cool pine groves to the **stadium**, a steep and longish walk which discourages many of the tour groups. Its site was artificially levelled in the fifth century BC, though it was banked with stone seats (giving a capacity of seven thousand) only in Roman times – the gift, like so many other public buildings in Greece, of Herodes Atticus. For even greater solitude, climb up above to the pine trees that have engulfed the remains of the fourth-century BC walls.

The museum

Delphi's **museum** (summer Mon–Fri 7.30am–6.45pm, Sat & Sun 8.30am–2.45pm; winter earlier weekday closure; €3.50, or €5.90 joint ticket with site) contains a rare and exquisite collection of sculpture spanning the Archaic to the Roman eras, matched only by finds on Athens' Acropolis. It features pottery, bronze articles and friezes from the various treasuries and temple pediments, which, grouped together, give a good picture of the sanctuary's riches. Labelling, however, is poor, often only in Greek or French; serious students will want to buy a catalogue.

The most famous exhibit, placed alone at the far south end of the central corridor, is the **Charioteer**, one of the few surviving bronzes of the fifth century BC. It was unearthed in 1896 along with other scant remains of the "Offering of Polyzalos", which probably toppled during the earthquake of 373 BC. The charioteer's eyes, made of onyx and set slightly askew, lend it a startling realism, while the demure expression sets the scene as a lap of honour. It is thought that the odd proportions of the body – the torso seems far too abbreviated when seen straight on – were designed by the sculptor (possibly Pythagoras of Samos) with perspective in mind; they would be "corrected" when the figure was viewed, as intended, from below.

Other major pieces include two huge **kouroi** from the sixth century BC, in the room straight ahead of you from the top of the entry stairs. Like so many of this genre, they betray clear Asiatic/Egyptian stylistic traits. Immediately to their right (north) is a room dedicated to objects in ivory and precious metals; the star exhibit here is a life-size, sixth-century BC votive **bull** fashioned from hammered silver sheeting.

To the right of the main entrance are large chunks of the beautiful and meticulously carved **Syphnian frieze**; they depict Zeus and other gods looking on as the Homeric heroes fight over the body of Patroclus, as well as Herakles and Apollo engaged in a tug-of-war over an oracular tripod. Another portion of this frieze shows a battle between gods and giants, including a lion graphically mauling a warrior. In the same room is an elegant Ionic sculpture of the winged **Sphinx of the Naxians**, dating from 565 BC.

Just left (south) of the main entrance is the **Athenian Treasury** (490 BC), represented by fragments of the metopes which depict the labours of Herakles, the adventures of Theseus and a battle with Amazons. Further on, the room just outside the Charioteer's home is dominated by a group of three colossal **dancing women**, carved from Pentelic marble around an acanthus-topped column. The badly damaged figures, celebrating Dionysos, probably formed the stand for a tripod. Opposite, in the same room, is an exquisite second-century AD figure of **Antinoös**, favourite of Roman emperor Hadrian. In the rear central hall are two lion-spouted marble rain gutters (sixth century BC) from the Apollo temple, while scattered across several rooms are bronze *protomes* or **griffin heads**, used extensively during Archaic times on the edge of cauldrons.

The Castalian spring

Following the road east of the sanctuary, towards Aráhova, you reach a sharp bend. To the left, marked by niches for votive offerings and by the remains of an archaic fountain house, the celebrated **Castalian spring** still flows from a cleft in the Phaedriades cliffs.

Visitors to Delphi (only men were allowed in the early centuries) were obliged to purify themselves in its waters, usually by washing their hair, though murderers had to take the full plunge. **Byron**, impressed by the legend that it succoured poetic inspiration, also jumped in. This is no longer possible, since the spring is fenced off owing to sporadic rock-falls from the Phaedriades cliffs.

The Marmaria

Across and below the road from the spring is the **Marmaria** (daily: summer 8am–7pm; winter 8am–5pm; free), or Sanctuary of Athena, whom the Delphians worshipped as Athena Pronoia ("Guardian of the Temple"). *Marmariá* means "marble quarry" and derives from the medieval practice of filching the ancient blocks for private use.

The most conspicuous building in the precinct, and the first visible from the road, is the **Tholos**, a fourth-century BC rotunda. Three of its dome-columns and their entablature have been set up, but while these amply demonstrate the original beauty of the building (which is *the* postcard image of Delphi), its purpose remains a mystery.

At the entrance to the sanctuary stood the **Old Temple of Athena**, destroyed by the Persians and rebuilt in the Doric order during the fourth century BC; foundations of both can be traced. Outside the precinct on the northwest side (above the Marmaria) is a **gymnasium**, again built in the fourth century BC, but later enlarged by the Romans who added a running track on the now collapsed terrace; prominent among the ruins is a circular plunge bath which, filled with cold water, served to refresh the athletes after their exertions.

Practicalities: Modern Dhelfí

Modern Dhelfí is as inconsequential as its ancient namesake, 1500m to the east, is impressive. Entirely geared to tourism (including Greek skiers), its attraction lies in its mountain setting, proximity to the ruins and access to Mount Parnassós (see p.325).

There is a single **bus terminal**, located at the Itéa (west) end of town, where the upper and lower commercial streets link up. Westbound buses go to Ámfissa (whence you can pick up connections north), Itéa and (usually with a change) Náfpaktos, while eastbound services go only to Aráhova, Livadhiá or Athens. The main difficulty, since all coaches originate elsewhere, is that seats allocated for the Dhelfí ticket booth are limited and they sell out some hours in advance. If you're going to be stuck standing all the way to Athens, it's better to get off at Livadhiá and continue by train. Bus timetables are available from the helpful **tourist office** (Mon–Fri 7.30am–2.30pm; ☎02650/82 900) in the town hall on the lower main thoroughfare. Other amenities include several **banks** (with cash dispensers) and a **post office**, again along the lower main street.

Accommodation

Accommodation is plentiful if not especially good value; like most Greek site villages, Dhelfí has a quick turnaround of visitors and, with over twenty hotels and pensions, finding an actual vacancy should present few problems. However, there is no set peak season – indeed winter weekends can see top rates charged, courtesy of the ski-trade spillover from Aráhova (see p.316) – so scope for bargaining depends on current traffic. As a somewhat arcane alternative to Dhelfí

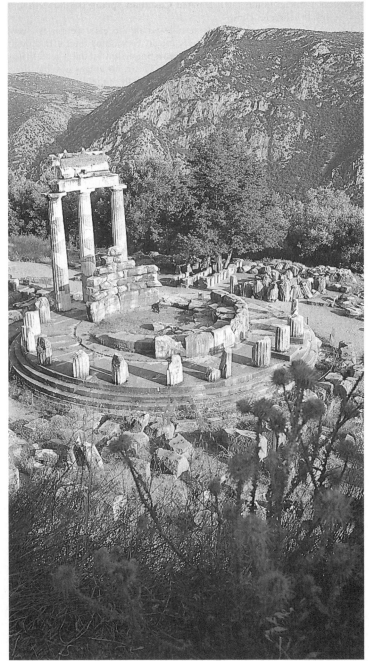

△ The Tholos, Delphi

or Aráhova, you might consider **KHRISSÓ** village, 13km downhill towards the gulf; it's thus far untouristed, with considerable character in its centre where there are a few *psistariés* and **tavernas** under the plane trees and a *xenónas* (**inn**) attached to one of them.

There are two **campsites** in the immediate area. Closest is *Camping Apollon* (℡02650/82 762, 🌐www.campingclub.gr; open all year), alongside the road to Ámfissa/Itéa and less than 1km west of Dhelfí, with a pool and restaurant but more caravan than tent space. *Camping Delphi* (℡02650/82 475, 🌐www.delphi.camping.com; March to mid-Nov) lies 3km further along the same road, just above Khrissó, is slightly roomier, and has a few more amenities.

Athena, Vas. Pávlou ké Fredheríkis 55 ℡02650/82 430 or 094/4698866, ℗02650/82 239. Near the bus station at the Itéa (west) end of town, this hotel has wood-decor, well-kept if smallish rooms, mostly en suite, and views of the gulf from rear units. Variety of breakfasts extra. Shut Nov–Christmas and weekdays Christmas–end March. ❸

Hermes, Pávlou ké Frederíkis 27 ℡02650/82 318. Quiet and clean, if overpriced, with wonderful views. ❺

Odysseus Pension, Iséa 1, cnr Filellínon, the street below and parallel to Pávlou ké Fredheríkis ℡02650/82 235. Non-en-suite and spartan 1970s rooms, but quiet, with a flowered terrace for unobstructed views. ❸

Orfeas, Ifiyenías Syngroú 35 ℡02650/82 077, ℗82 079. Rooms are 1970s vintage but spacious and well maintained; superb views and air conditioning; may shut in Nov; fifteen percent discount to Rough Guide readers. ❹

Pan, Pávlou ké Fredheríkis 53 ℡02650/82 294, ℗82 320. Adequate and comfortable with fine views of the gulf; the best, newest rooms, with small bathtubs, are in the attic. ❹

Pythia, Pávlou ké Fredheríkis 68 ℡02650/82 328. Close to the site and museum; run as an annexe of the *Pan*, where you usually have to enquire first. ❹

Sun View Pension, Apóllonos 84, far west end of upper commercial street, near *Amalia Hotel* ℡02650/82 349, ℗82 815. Fair-sized, inexpensive if rather neutral white-and-pine rooms, with new bathrooms; rear-facing ones are a bit dark. Run by the shop below; easy parking adjacent. ❸

Varonos, Pávlou ké Fredheríkis 25 ℡ & ℗ 02650/82 345. Large, slightly kitsch en-suite rooms (pink and pastel-pattern decor), but well kept and equipped with hair dryers and air conditioning. Copious breakfasts extra. ❹

Eating and drinking

Meals out are not a Dhelfí strong point, despite the winter Athenian-skier custom; too many coach parties have had a predictable effect. The two "quality" tavernas, adjacent each other on Apóllonos, the upper through road, are *Taverna Vakchos* (no. 31) and *Lekaria* (no. 33); each generate praise and disparagement in equal measure, so it's best not to count on anything other than the views both establishments enjoy from their terraces. A newer and pricier (€15 each) entrant on the scene is *Epikouros*, down at Pávlou ké Fredheríkis 33. The cheap-and-cheerful backpackers' grills, where you can fill up for a fraction of that, are *Omfalos* on Apóllonos, and *Gargandouas* at the west end of Pávlou ké Fredheríkis.

Mount Parnassós

For a taste of the Greek alpine scene, **Parnassós** is probably the most convenient peak in the land, though its heights no longer rank as wilderness, having been disfigured by the ski-station above Aráhova and its accompanying paraphernalia of lifts, snack bars and access roads. The best routes for walkers are those up from Dhelfí to the **Corycian cave** (practicable from April to Nov, but not in midsummer without a dawn start), or the **Liákoura summit ascent** (May to Oct only). Those with their own transport can take advantage of a ride along sealed **roads** up the mountain from Aráhova on the south, or

Lílea, Polýdhrosos or Amfilia on the north slope, any of which could easily be combined with a walk. For extended explorations, Road Editions' 1:50,000 **map** no. 42, *Parnassos*, is a wise investment, though as ever it's by no means infallible; an attached booklet summarizes a slightly alternative route to the Corycian cave.

Dhelfí to the Corycian cave

To reach the **trailhead** for this walk – and the initial path up the mountain – take the right-hand (approaching from Athens), uphill street through Dhelfí village, officially Apóllonos. At the top of the slope, by the church, turn right onto a road that doubles back to the **museum-house** (daily except Tues 9am–3pm; €1.50) where the poet **Angelos Sikelianos** – he of the revived ancient festival – once lived. There is a bust of him outside.

Continue climbing from here, with more zigzags along a gravel surface, until you reach the highest point of the fence enclosing the sanctuary ruins. Where the track ends at a gate, don't go into the site, but adopt a trail on your left, initially marked by a black-and-yellow rectangle on a white background. From the top of the hill the trail continues, well marked by more black-on-yellow metal diamonds: it's part of the **E4 European long-distance trail**. Initially steep, the way soon flattens out on a grassy knoll overlooking the stadium, and continues along a ridge next to a line of burned cypresses.

Soon after, you join up with an ancient cobbled trail coming from inside the fenced precinct, the **Kakí Skála**, which zigzags up the slope above you in broad arcs. The view from here is fantastic, stretching back over the Gulf of Kórinthos to the mountains of the Peloponnese. The cobbles end near two concrete inspection covers in Dhelfí's water supply, an hour-plus above the village, at the top of the Phaedriades cliffs. Nearby stand some rock pinnacles, from one of which those guilty of sacrilege in ancient times were thrown to their deaths – a custom perhaps giving rise to the name *Kakí Skála* or "Evil Stairway".

E4 markers remain visible in the valley which opens out ahead of you. You can get simultaneous views south, and northeast towards the Parnassan summits, by detouring a little to the left to a wooden hut and a barn, then to a slight rise perhaps 150m further. The principal route becomes a gravel track bearing northeast; forsake the E4 diamonds and follow instead a metal sign pointing toward the cave, by taking the right fork near a spring and watering troughs, with some shepherds' huts scattered under the trees. This track passes a picnic ground and a chapel of Ayía Paraskeví within the next fifteen minutes, and acquires intermittent paved surface. Continue along this track for some forty minutes beyond the chapel, heading gently downhill and passing another sign for the cave, until you emerge from the fir woods (a bit over 2hr 30min from Dhelfí) with a view east and ahead to the rounded mass of the Yerondóvrahos peak (2367m) of the Parnassós massif.

Another fifteen minutes bring you to a spring, followed by another chapel (of Ayía Triádha) on the left, with a spring and picnic ground. To the left rises a steep ridge, on whose flank lies the ancient **Corycian cave**, in Greek the *Korýkio Ándro*. Ignore the Greek-only sign just behind the chapel, which indicates a dangerous and disused old trail, and persevere along the road about five more minutes to where a white bilingual sign points to a newer path, marked by orange paint splodges. After a forty-minute scramble up the slope, you meet another dirt road; turn left and follow it five minutes more to the end, about 10m below the conspicuous cave mouth at an altitude of 1370m.

The cave was sacred to Pan and the nymphs in ancient times, the presiding deities of Delphi during the winter months when Apollo was said to desert the oracle. Orgiastic rites were celebrated in November at the cave by women acting as the nymphs, who made the long hike up from Delphi on the Kakí Skála by torchlight. The cavern itself is chilly and forbidding, but if you look carefully with a torch you can find ancient inscriptions near the entrance; without artificial light you can't see more than a hundred metres inside. By the entrance you'll notice a rock with a man-made circular indentation – possibly an ancient altar to hold libations.

Descending to Dhelfi takes slightly less than the four-hour ascent – you'll need to allow a full day for the outing, and take ample food. The marked E4 route, on the other hand, continues almost due north – more on track than on path, it must be said – to the large village of **EPTÁLOFOS**, on the Arákhova–Lílea–Graviá paved road. This, just below the forest with sweeping views north, is a popular Greek "hill station" and a prominent staging point on the E4; accordingly, there are a half-dozen places to **stay**, including the "*Hotel*" *Panorama* (☏02340/61 302; ③) or the *Mavrodhimos* rooms (☏02340/61 309; ③), plus lots of **psistariés** around the plane-shaded platía.

The Liákoura summit

Liákoura is Parnassós's highest and finest peak (2457m) and can be approached either from the Dhelfi side or from the northeastern foothills of the mountain. The latter is the best walk, starting **from Áno Tithoréa**, but it involves taking a bus or train and then local taxi to the trailhead – plus camping out on the mountain. If you want a more casual look at Parnassós, it's probably better to walk up **from the Dhelfi side**, as a continuation of the Corycian cave outing, staying overnight at the hamlet of **Kalývia** on the Livádhi plateau, some 45-minutes' walk beyond the cave. Here there are numerous chalet-hotels for skiers and a number of tavernas, some of them shut during summer.

For the energetic, it's possible to traverse the whole massif in around two long days' walking time, starting from Dhelfi and descending at Áno Tithoréa, or vice versa. You will, however, need full camping equipment, as springs are poorly spaced, and the alpine shelters near the summit are either locked or very primitive.

Áno Tithoréa to Liákoura via the Velítsa ravine

The principal surviving wilderness route up Parnassós to Liákoura involves starting with a trip by train or bus as far as Káto Tithoréa, which is on the Livadhià–Amfíklia road and the Athens–Thessaloníki railway. You then need to get to the higher, twin village of **Áno Tithoréa**, a four-kilometre haul easiest accomplished by taxi (usually available, but bargain for the price beforehand). You should allow at least six hours for the ascent, and around four and a half hours for the descent, so it's best to arrive early in the day; come equipped for camping out on the mountain as lodging can be difficult to find.

From the platía in Áno Tithoréa, head southwest out of town until you reach some park benches overlooking the giant **Velítsa ravine**. Adjacent is a "waterfall" (in reality a leak in an aqueduct) which crosses the path beginning here a few minutes above the benches. A hundred metres further, bear left away from what seems to be the main track and descend towards the bed of the canyon. Once you're on the far side you can see the aqueduct again, now uncovered. Follow it until you reach the isolated chapel of Áyios Ioánnis (1hr from Áno Tithoréa).

Past the chapel, a fine alpine path heads off through the firs in front of you. The way is obvious for the next ninety minutes, with tremendous views of the crags filing up to the Liákoura summit on your right across the valley. You emerge on a narrow neck of land, with a brief glimpse over the Ayía Marína valley and a monastery of Kímisis Theotókou to the east (left) – as well as a dirt track which nearly meets your route. The path, faint for an interval, heads slightly downhill and to the right to meet the floor of the Velítsa at the Tsáres spring (3hr 30min) – it's the last reliable water supply, so best fill up.

On the far bank of the river, head up a steep, scree-laden slope through the last of the trees to some sheep pens (4hr), then climb up to another pastoral hut (4hr 30min) at the base of the defile leading down from the main summit ridge. Beyond this point the going is gentler for much of the final ascent to the northwest (top right-hand) corner of this valley. A brief scramble up a rockfall to a gap in the ridge and you are at the base of Liákoura (5hr 30min). Orange paint-splashes – primarily oriented for those descending – stake out most of the approach from the Tsáres spring.

The **final ascent** is an easy twenty-minute scramble more or less up to the ridge line. On a clear morning, especially after rain, you're supposed to be able to see Mount Olympus in the north, the Aegean to the east, the Ionian to the west and way down into the Peloponnese to the south. The best viewing is said to be in midsummer, but all too often you can see only cloud.

Along the gulf: Delphi to Náfpaktos

The train-less, almost beach-less north shore of the **Gulf of Kórinthos** is far less frequented than the south coast. The arid landscape, with harsh mountains inland, can be initially off-putting, but there are bits of cultivated valley and coastal plain, and attractive, low-key resorts in **Galaxídhi** and **Náfpaktos**, both reasonably well connected by bus. This coast also offers convenient access south to the Peloponnese, via the ferries at Áyios Nikólaos–Éyio or Andírio–Río. From both Éyio and Río, you can reach Pátra by rail or road. Alternatively, heading in the opposite direction, it is easy to reach Dhiakoftó and the Kalávryta rack-and-pinion railway.

All buses heading southwest of Delphi towards the Gulf of Kórinthos stop first at Itéa, a gritty little industrial town (literally, owing to the bauxite tailings piled at the outskirts) and unlikely resort-for-Greeks where you may have to change buses for the next leg of the journey.

Galaxídhi

GALAXÍDHI, a quiet port rearing mirage-like out of an otherwise lifeless shore 17km southwest of Itéa, is the first place you'd want to break a journey voluntarily. The old town stands on a raised headland, crowned by the eighteenth-century church of Áyios Nikólaos (the old, basilica-like one, not the more obvious belfryed structure), patron saint of sailors. With its protected double harbour, the place would have been irresistible to early settlers, and sure enough you see stretches of Pelasgian walls – all that's left of **ancient Oianthe** – between the two churches and the water on the headland dividing the two anchorages. Amazingly, Galaxídhi was once one of Greece's major harbours, with a fleet of over four hundred two- and three-masted kaïkia and schooners, built alongside Hirólakkas anchorage, north of the headland. But shipowners failed to convert to steampower after 1890, and the town's prosperity vanished. Clusters of nineteenth-century shipowners' mansions, reminders of those heady days, don't match the rest of Fokídha province architecturally, but reflect borrowings from Venice, testament to the sea-captains' far-flung travels. Lately they've become the haunt of Athenian second-homers, but despite their restorations and a bit of a marina ethos down at the main southern harbour, the town still remains just the right side of tweeness, with an animated commercial high street and a good range of places to eat and drink.

Just uphill from the south harbour, a small **maritime museum** (Tues–Fri 9.30am–1pm, Sat & Sun 9.30am–2pm; €1.50) contains paintings and models of ships as well as old figureheads, while a modest **folk art museum** (daily except Tues 9.30am–1.30pm; €1.50), in an imposing tower-mansion just inland from Hirólakkas, has three rooms of turn-of-the-century embroideries and fashions. Both are set to move into a combined museum, under construction, close to the existing maritime display.

If you stroll around the pine-covered headland flanking the south harbour, you'll find tiny pebbly **coves** where most people swim, with chapel-crowned islets offshore. The closest "real" beach is **Kalafátis** just north of town, though this isn't brilliant – harsh shingle underfoot and occasionally turbid water. The only other local diversion is the four-kilometre drive up to the **monastery of Metamórfosis Sotíros**, well signposted under the flyover just west of town; the magnificent view is the attraction, as the thirteenth-century *katholikón* is visibly unsound structurally and bare of frescoes – a single nun lives in the modern cloister alongside.

Practicalities

Accommodation is on the pricey side and hard to find in summer, or at weekends year-round, though all of it is en suite and usually with air conditioning. The three least expensive places are the modern *Hotel Koukonas* (☏02650/41 179;③ –④), inland from the end of the new harbour, with clean if plain air-conditioned rooms; the *Pension Votsalo* (☏02650/41 788; ③ –④) above Hirólakkas, just three en-suite rooms with air-con and old-fashioned decor, but again no views; or the better-placed *Rooms Hirolakkas* (☏02650/41 170 or 41 230;③), in a modernized old building beside the folk museum, where the sea breeze from Hirólakkas bay does duty for air conditioning. Among several top-flight outfits, the clear winners are the delightful Italian-run *Ganimede Hotel* (☏02650/41 328 or 097/2295719, ℱ02650/42 160, ⓦwww.gsp.gr/ganimede.gr;④ ; closed Nov), just six rooms in an old sea captain's house off the market street, with courtyard fountain garden and good-value breakfasts featuring proprietor Bruno's own patés and jams, plus advantageous half-board rates though *Il Posto* (see overleaf); the *Hotel Galaxa* (☏02650/41 620, ℱ42 053;④), occupying an old house on the hillside beyond Hirólakkas, somewhat casually run and maintained but with a garden bar for views plus private parking; or the 2000-built *Arhondiko* (co-managed with *Pension Votsalo;⑤), in a secluded spot beyond Hirólakkas with easy parking, partial sea-views and themed, mock-traditional rooms (including a mirrored-ceiling one) with self-catering breakfast facilities.

Tavernas, mostly on the southerly quay, are generally of a fairly high standard, though a few, like *Steki* and *Tò Porto*, are overpriced and worth avoiding. The only real budget choice is *Albatross*, inland on the street near Áyios Nikólaos, which has limited quantities of well-executed dishes from a similarly restricted menu. *Tassos* is best for fish, while *Barko Maritsa* near the far east end of the esplanade features savoury, non-greasy *píttes* and seafood risotto –

allow €15 a head with bulk wine. But for a real treat (evenings only), look no further than *Il Posto*, opposite (and co-managed with) the *Ganimede Hotel*. By law there's an à la carte menu, but fast all day and plump instead for chef Bruno's four-course table d'hôte (€20 with house wine) – salad, pasta, meat dish and home-made sweet in sufficient quantity to defeat most appetites. As for **nightlife**, a half-dozen bars on the quay cater to sophisticated Athenian forty- and fifty-somethings. Beyond the traces of ancient Oianthe, *Di Bar* incorporates a sand-strewn lido, while there's another beach bar at Kalafátis, the main youth hangout. The only establishment at Hirólakkas, and worth special mention, is *Liovtrivi*, ideal for a home-made dessert or a nightcap on the water. Proprietor George Minas is a painter of some note, and the building has been in his family since 1925 (working as a bar since 1977). Galaxídhi is large enough to support a **post office** and a **bank** with a cash dispenser; **buses** call at the landscaped central plaza-roundabout.

West of Galaxídhi

West of Galaxídhi lies some of the sparsest scenery along the Greek shoreline; there are a few villages with scrappy beaches, few of them warranting a stop. At **Áyios Nikólaos**, however, there's a year-round **ferry** across the gulf to the Peloponnese – an alternative to the crossing at Andírio–Río, 60km further west (see p.332). These ro-ro boats require forty minutes for the journey (7 times daily in summer, 6.30am–10pm, around €2 per passenger, €10 per small car; ☎02660/31 854 or 06910/22 792 for current info). Westbound bus timings are perversely (some say deliberately) designed to just miss coinciding with ferry departures; if you miss the last sailing, **accommodation** possibilities include Theodore Katharakis's rooms (☎02660/31 177; ❸), just east of the pebble beach. On a bluff, high above the coast road, sits a well-maintained campsite, the *Doric* (☎02660/31 195; May–Sept), which also offers six bungalows to rent (❹).

Trizónia and Monastiráki

The Gulf of Kórinthos has about a dozen islets, but **TRIZÓNIA** – roughly halfway between Áyios Nikólaos and Náfpaktos, just across a narrow strait – is the largest and only inhabited one (permanent population around 55). Green with vegetation and blissfully vehicle-free (except for a handful of service trucks), it has long been a favourite stopover for yachters, and makes an idyllic retreat for conventional travellers despite a lack of good beaches. To reach the island, follow signs from the main highway down to the settlement of Hánia (only its neighbour Glyfádha is shown on most maps), where a little boat shuttles across eleven times daily until about 9pm (€0.70 per person; more frequent service in midsummer). This calls at the appealing fishing harbour with its three fish **tavernas**, among which *Ta Dhyo Limania* and *Porto Trizonia* both prove reasonable and friendly. The sole **accommodation** is the modern but well-designed *Hotel Drymna* (☎02660/71 204, ℱ71 304; ❹), most of whose peaceful rooms overlook the yacht anchorage – and *Lizzie's Yacht Club* on the hillside opposite, a revered institution amongst the boating fraternity but open to all, constitutes the island's main **nightlife**. The access track to it continues towards Trizónia's southeast tip, where the small, red-sand beach at **Poúnda**, a half-hour in total from the village, is the best of several swimming coves on the far side of the island.

Beyond Trizónia, the most pleasant spot along the approach to Náfpaktos is **MONASTIRÁKI**, some 11km shy of the former. Monastiráki retains plenty of old stone houses, along a serpentining, tree-studded quay; there are no short-term places to stay but there is a handful of **seafood tavernas**, much the best being *Iliopoulos* (closed Mon in winter) around the easterly headland. This has a superb selection of wild-caught fish, plus a few seafood appetizers and home-made *píttes*; reckon on €16–17 for fish, two appetizers and a beer. For a pre- or post-prandial swim, there's a pebble **beach** just below the *Iliopoulos* terrace, or another much larger, less windy but shadeless one west of the main port, backed by a lagoon.

Náfpaktos

The other place that stands out west of Galaxídhi, and indeed the largest settlement on the gulf's north shore, is **NÁFPAKTOS**, a lively market town and resort which straggles for some distance along a plane-tree-shaded seafront, below its rambling Venetian castle. The planes are nurtured by numerous running springs, which attest to deceptively water-rich mountains just inland. Some two-hours' drive from Dhelfí, or an hour by buses and ferry from Pátra, it makes a convenient and attractive stopover, though diversion of the relentlessly heavy traffic through town would enhance its charm.

The pine-tufted **kástro** provides a picturesque backdrop, plus an enjoyable stroll through old houses to the top of its fortifications. The curtain walls plunge down to the sea, enclosing the oval-shaped old harbour and the westerly beach, with one of the original gates giving access to one end of the latter. The castle was long a formidable part of the Venetian Greek defences, and the **Battle of Lepanto** (Náfpaktos's medieval name) was fought just offshore from here in 1571. An allied Christian armada commanded by John of Austria devastated an Ottoman fleet – the first European naval victory over the Turks since the death of the dreaded pirate-admiral Barbarossa; Cervantes, author of *Don Quixote*, lost his left arm to a cannonball during the conflict, and now has a Spanish-erected statue honouring him at the old harbour. But Western supremacy on the high seas proved fleeting, since the Ottomans quickly replaced their navy and wrested Cyprus from the Venetians the following year.

Practicalities

Buses run northwest to Agrínio (where you can pick up services to Ioánnina or Lefkádha), and east to Itéa and Ámfissa (for connections north into Thessaly). Local blue-and-white city buses go frequently to the ferry at Andírio, or you can sometimes get a seat on a long-distance bus heading to Pátra.

Despite ten hotels and a similar number of rooms or apartments, **accommodation** can be in short supply or overpriced in summer, and noisy at midtown locales. The cleaner, more popular westerly beach of **Psáni**, with Navmahías as its frontage road, is both central and relatively quiet; if your finances will stretch that far, go for the spotless *Plaza House* (☎06340/22 226, ⓕ23 174; ❺) at no. 37, or the apartments *Regina*, at the east end of the esplanade near the old port (☎06340/21 555 or 094/4875384, ⓕ06340/21 556; ❹). Budget options are restricted to the non-en-suite, noisy *Hotel Aegli* (☎06340/27 271; ❷), at main east–west thoroughfare Ilárhou Kósta Tzavéla 75, or the more central but equally basic *Hotel Amaryllis* (☎06340/27 237; ❶), a 1960s relic on Platía Liménos; its ground-floor restaurant has to be seen to be believed, and it's a long hike to the showers from clean if spartan rooms with wash basins. For a return to more tranquillity and comfort, head for the easterly beach of **Grímbovo** (Paralía Grimbóvou), just 1km east of the old port. Here, one block inland, you've the *Afroditi*, Filikís Eterías corner Filíppou

Plastirá (☎06340/29 922, ℮29 924; ❹), with bland but medium-sized bal-conied rooms plus an enormous, slightly kitsch lounge/breakfast salon, or the somewhat higher-standard, better-value *Akti* (☎06340/28 464, ℮24 171; ❹) right beside the creek flowing to the sea, with partial gulf views from about half the rooms, en suites with baths and an airy, cheerful breakfast salon. There's a good **campsite**, *Platanitis Beach* (☎06340/31 555; mid-May to Sept), 5km west of the town towards Andírio; to get there, catch a blue city bus from the main square – the last one leaves at 10pm.

Most of Náfpaktos' full-service **tavernas** and ouzerís line the esplanade at Grímbovo, some half-dozen strong and all fairly comparable in quality. The only eateries near the old port are *To Steki tou Dhyti* (dinner only) and *Papoulis Ouzeri*, near the mosque missing its minaret, and the more traditional *Tsaras* (Thurs–Sun dinner only), dedicated to *mayireftá*. But otherwise the medieval harbour is ringed by cafés and bars which provide a fair proportion of Náfpaktos's **nightlife** and daytime dalliance as well. In general, a local sweet tooth is attested to by an improbable number of **sweet shops** offering crepes, waffles and ice cream – for example the hygienic and friendly, if not so allur-ingly set, *Kreperi* at Mesolongíou 9.

The Andírio–Río ferry

The ferry at **Andírio** runs across the Gulf of Kórinthos to Río every fifteen minutes from 6.45am until 10.45pm, and less frequently during the night. The trip takes barely fifteen minutes, and fares are around €0.50 per passenger, €5 per car and driver. However, all this will be a thing of the past after 2004, when an enormous, anti-seismic **suspension bridge**, one of the largest in the world, is completed by a French consortium; the pier-bases have already been anchored to the bottom, and giant tower-cranes swivel in the straits.

Once across to Río, you can generally pick up a city bus immediately for Pátra, but as through bus services between the Dhelfí area and Pátra exist fair-ly reliably, it might be worth getting one of these in Náfpaktos or even soon-er. In summer, drivers should count on waiting for around thirty minutes to be loaded onto the ferry. There are a few snack bars and – in the unlikely event you get stuck – the *Hotel Andirrion* (☎06340/31 450; ❸), or the *Dounis Beach* campsite (☎06340/31 565; May–Nov) on the Náfpaktos–Andírio road, 1km east of the ferry quay.

North to Lamía

Lamía is a half-day's journey north from Dhelfí by bus (much less with your own car), with a connection at Ámfissa: a pleasant route skirting mounts Parnassós, Gióna and (to the northwest) Íti. At the historic pass of **Thermopylae**, 12km shy of Lamía, the road joins the **coastal highway** from Athens.

Inland via Ámfissa

The inland road west from Dhelfí climbs slowly through a sea of groves, source of the acclaimed local green olives, to **ÁMFISSA**, a small town in the foothills of Mount Gióna. Its medieval name of Sálona is still used conversationally; like Livadhiá, this strategic military location was a base for the Catalan Grand Company, who left their mark on the **castle**. If you have time to kill between buses (the **KTEL** is on the main square), its ruins, which incorporate remnants of an ancient acropolis, make for a pleasant walk, if only to enjoy the shade of the pine trees and examine a few stretches of Classical polygonal masonry. The **market** quarter of the town also repays a stroll: Ámfissa was once one of the major bell-making centres in the Balkans, and copper-alloy sheep bells are still produced and sold here. You would be unlucky to get stranded here, but if so, the *Apollon* at Gidhoyánnou 14, one block east of the platía (℡02650/72 261; ❹) is the best and least overpriced of two modest **hotels**. More likely you'll only patronize one of several café-bars on the partly pedestrianized square.

Serious **walkers** may want to use Ámfissa as a jumping-off point for the mountains west and north towards Karpeníssi: **Gióna**, **Vardhoússia** and **Íti**. There are bus routes, some only running once or twice weekly, to various trailhead villages in the foothills of these peaks, as well as to Lidhoríki, due west of Ámfissa, with better access to Vardhoússia and Gióna. Most travellers, however, continue north along the scenic **Lamía road**, dividing mounts Parnassós and Gióna, or along the **rail line** from Livadhiá to Lamía. This is one of the most dramatic stretches of railway in Europe, and has a history to match: it runs through the foothills of Gióna and Íti, and over the precipitous defile of the **Gorgopótamos River**, where in late November 1942 the Greek Resistance – all factions united for the first and last time, under the command of British intelligence officer Brigadier Eddie Meyers – blew up a critical railway viaduct, cutting one of the Germans' vital supply lines to their army in North Africa for three months.

The coastal highway

The first 60km of the **Athens–Lamía** coastal motorway are fast, efficient and generally dull, its massive improvement completed with EU funds during the late 1990s. Generally flat, it initially runs a fair distance inland, skirting various pockets of seasonal lakebed, like Límni Ilíki, north of Thíva, before reaching the coast just before Atalándi, home to many of Greece's beer breweries. The most interesting stop, along with Thíva (see p.311), is the Mycenaean citadel of Glas (see p.313), just behind the Ilíki lake near the village of Kástro.

There are also various links with the island of **Évvia** (see p.926): first at Halkídha (where there's a causeway); then by ferry at **Arkítsa** to Loutrá Edhipsoú (every hour in season, every 2hr (hourly at weekends) out of season, last ferry at 9.30pm, 11pm July–Aug; 45min; passengers around €1.60, cars €10). Arkítsa itself is a rather upmarket resort, popular mainly with Greeks, as are all the coastal settlements hereabouts.

Áyios Konstandínos and Kaména Voúrla

ÁYIOS KONSTANDÍNOS is the closest port to Athens if you're heading for the islands of the Sporades. There are at least three daily car **ferries** or **catamarans**, usually at 8.30am, noon or 1pm and 6.45 or 7.30pm, to Skiáthos, with all midday departures continuing on to Skópelos, and all evening schedules calling at Alónissos too. Since the advent of the "Flying Cat" craft, the old-fashioned **hydrofoil** service has been cut back to just once daily, typically 10am to all three islands cited. For current ferry information contact Alkyon Travel (℡02350/31 920); for catamaran or hydrofoil information call the Bilalis agency (℡02350/31 614), adjacent on the main square.

There should be no reason to stay in Áyios Konstandínos, but if you're stranded you can choose from among eight **hotels** – try the D-class *Hotel Poulia* (℡02350/31 663; ❷ –❸) with some en-suite rooms, or the more pleasant *Amfitryon* (℡02350/31 702; ❸) on the waterfront – and a **campsite**,

Camping Blue Bay (☎02350/314 25). *O Faros Taverna* by the sea serves up a variety of **seafood** delights.

KAMÉNA VOÚRLA, 9km west, has a better beach; this is, however, very much a resort, used mainly by Greeks attracted by the spas here and at nearby Loutrá Thermopylíon (see below). Seafood aficionados are well looked after at the long line of decent fish **tavernas** along the promenade here, particularly at *Falaraïka* in Áyios Pandelímon district, and there are scores of acceptable **hotels** and rooms on the main street and shady backstreets.

Thermopylae, its spa and Bodonítsa castle

Just before joining the road descending north from the mountains, the motorway enters the **Pass of Thermopylae** (modern Thermopýles), where Leonidas and three hundred Spartans made a last stand against Xerxes' thirty-thousand-strong Persian army in 480 BC. The pass was much more defined in ancient times: a narrow defile with Mount Kallídhromo to the south and the sea – which has silted and retreated nearly 4km – to the north.

The tale of Spartan bravery is described at length by **Herodotus**. Leonidas, King of Sparta, stood guard over the pass with a mixed force of seven thousand Greeks, confident that it was the only approach an army could take to enter Greece from Thessaly. By night, however, Xerxes sent an advance party of his forces along a mountain trail and broke through the pass to attack the Greeks from the rear. Leonidas ordered a retreat of the main army, but remained in the pass himself, with his Spartan guard, to delay the Persians' progress. He and all but two of the guard fought to their deaths.

Loutrá Thermopylíon, midway through the pass, is named for the hot springs present here since antiquity. The grave mound of the fallen Spartans lies 500m away, opposite a gloriously heroic statue of Leonidas. The **spa** and restaurant facilities are intimidatingly built up and the surroundings generally tatty, but there are a few cascades and drainage sluices where you can bathe undisturbed in the open air, the latter rather permeated with a sulphurous stench.

From just east of the spa, a paved road leads southeast 14km to the village of Mendhenítsa on the flank of Mount Kallídhrómo, overlooked by the fine **castle of Bodonítsa**. This is reached by a short, sharp climb, rewarded by the sweeping view north and substantial remains of the citadel. Built in 1205 by a clan from Parma, it soon passed to the Venetians, who held it until a successful Ottoman siege in 1410.

Lamía and onward routes

LAMÍA is a busy provincial capital and an important transport junction for travellers. It sees few overnight visitors, but has a worthwhile sight in its Catalan castle, and abounds in excellent ouzerís and kafenía.

Heading **north from Lamía** there's a choice of three routes: to Tríkala and Kalambáka, to Lárissa, or around the coast to Vólos, but none is especially memorable. Fársala and Kardhítsa, on the routes to Lárissa and Tríkala respectively, are small, rather nondescript country towns. The **Vólos road**, however, leading east along the coast, has a little more to delay your progress.

Lamía

The town centre is arranged around three main squares: Platía Párkou, Platía Eleftherías and Platía Laoú, the latter two good venues for sipping a drink and watching Greek life go by. **Platía Eleftherías** is the town's social hub and scene of the evening *vólta*, with outdoor café tables and a little bandstand-gazebo. The cathedral and Neoclassical provincial government building flank the square on the north, with the Galaxias two-plex winter **cinema** tucked into the southwest corner. Just east and downhill from Eleftherías is the atmospheric **Platía Laoú**, shaded by plane trees crowded in autumn with migratory birds. The third square, **Platía Párkou**, lies amidst the main shopping area, with several **banks** (with cash dispensers) grouped around it, and blue city buses flocking here to spawn, as it were. On Saturdays, the streets below Párkou turn into a lively **market**, with everything from rheumatism cures to plastic combs on sale.

Looking down on the city from the north is the fourteenth-century Catalan castle, which boasts superb views and also houses an **archeological museum** (Tues–Sun 8.30am–2.30pm; €1.50) exhibiting a variety of finds – Neolithic, Mycenaean, Classical, Hellenistic and Roman – in a Neoclassical building dating from the 1850s; the displays are well arranged, but many items labelled in Greek only. Other diversions in Lamía include a state **theatre** on Ipsilándou (which leads northwest from Laoú), used for art exhibitions and in winter as an art-film cinema.

Practicalities

Buses, including a local service from the train station (6km out), arrive at terminals scattered throughout the town, though none is much further than ten-minutes' walk away from Platía Párkou. Karpeníssi services use a terminal on Márkou Bótsari, near the disused, in-town train station on the now-closed Stylídha spur line; those for Ámfissa and Lárissa use a terminal (the remotest) out on Thermopýlon, southeast of the centre just past the train tracks; those for Tríkala, from a terminal a block southeast of the Ámfissa stop; those for Vólos, the more central stop at the corner of Levadhítou and Rozáki-Ángeli; while buses for Athens and Thessaloníki go from the corner of Papakyriazí and Satovriándou, near the Karpeníssi station. The most convenient **taxi** rank is at the top end of Andhroútsou, behind the cathedral.

Accommodation prospects are vastly overpriced and poorly sited in Lamía. There are a couple of drab hotels on Ódhos Rozáki-Ángeli, convenient for the nearby meat-and-fish market; the dire *Thermopylae* (☎02310/21 366; ❹) at no. 36, and the preferable, better-value *Athina* (☎02310/20 700; ❺) across the way at no. 41, which does have the bonus of an underground car park (parking is a major hassle in Lamía). The *Samaras* (☎02310/42 701; ❻) opposite the **post office** on pretty Platía Dhiákou, south of Eleftherías, is a more attractive alternative, but disinclined to bargain much; the *Apollonio* at one corner of Párkou (entrance on Vasakári ☎02310/22 668; ❹) makes a reasonable compromise.

By contrast, you're spoilt for choice in the matter of **food and drink**, making Lamía a good lunch halt. On or just off Platía Laoú you'll find three decent *mayireftá* tavernas: *Megalexandhros* on the square; around the corner at Aristotélous 3, *Gogos* (closed July–Sept, evenings only except Sun); and the *Ilysia* – the last of those in particular offers a wide variety of reasonably priced casserole specialities. Leading off from one corner of the platía is Karaïskáki, a vegetarian's nightmare of a street, with whole sheep roasting on spits and the smell of *patsás* (tripe soup) wafting though the air. Andhroútsou, a mostly pedestrianized lane threading between platías Laoú and Eleftherías, is crammed full of attractive ouzerís, of which *Aman Aman* and *Allo Skedhio* are reckoned the best; the former (evenings only) is beyond the cathedral, the latter is one of three clustered in a nameless tiny plaza just down some steps from Eleftherías. The most durable cafés on Platía Eleftherías are the *Viva*, *Remezzo* and *Contratto*; just north of the platía, at Ipsilándi 6, is Lamía's most central **internet café**.

Lamía to Vólos

The first temptation on the coast road to Vólos is **AYIA MARÍNA**, 12km east of Lamía, where the seafood tavernas – a popular weekend jaunt for Lamian families – are much better than the rather pathetic beach.

A couple of kilometres further, **STYLÍDHA** was once one of the major ports of the Aegean; it was at the opera house here that Maria Callas's grandfather outsang a visiting Italian star. Today the unsightly town is chiefly concerned with olive-oil bottling and cement – not an inspiring prospect – and there is no longer any hydrofoil service from here to the Sporades to prompt a stop. At Karavómylos and Akhládhi, 8km and 19km east of Stylídha respectively, the fish tavernas are again more inviting than the beaches, though you'll need your own transport.

The best beaches along this route are near **GLÝFA** 30km further north, actually 11km off the motorway and served only by one afternoon bus from Lamía. It has the mainland's northernmost ferry crossing to **Évvia**: eight times daily in July and August to Áyiokambos (last ferry at 8.30–9.30pm summer, 5.30pm winter; 30min; passengers €1.20, cars €9). **Rooms** are on offer, plus there are several **hotels**, the cheapest of which is the *Oasis* (☎02380/61 353;❷).

Finally, rounding the Pagasitic Gulf towards Vólos – you'll exit the motorway for access to Vólos – car drivers might want to stop at **Néa Anhíalos**, where five **early Christian basilicas** have been uncovered right next to the road. Their mosaics and the small site museum are interesting, though perhaps not enough to make it worth risking a three-hour wait between buses; moreover, excavations are ongoing, with photography prohibited.

West to Karpeníssi – and beyond

The road west from Lamía climbs out of the Sperhiós valley, with glimpses on the way of mounts Íti, Gióna and Vardhoússia, 10km to the south. If you want to do some **hiking**, there are satisfying routes on Mount Íti (the classical Oeta), easiest approached from the village of Ipáti. The **Karpeníssi valley** also lends itself to treks amid a countryside of dark fir forest – conspicuously ravaged of late by either acid rain or some mysterious disease – and snow-fringed mountains, which the EOT promotes (with some justice) as "the Greek Switzerland". Besides walking, skiing on Mount Tymfristós and summertime rafting on the local rivers are the main outdoor activities.

Since the mid-1990s, both summer and winter tourism, mostly domestic, has really taken off here, such that accommodation prices in the Karpeníssi area are also authentically Swiss. They've been ratcheted up by an habitual clientele of conspicuously consuming Athenians and Thessalonians, likely as not to arrive in convoys of late-model sports cars; backpackers and budget travellers don't really get a look-in unless they've paid to be on an organized activity group.

Ipáti and Mount Íti

Mount Íti is one of the most beautiful of Greek mountains – its green northeast slopes constituting a national park – and also unusually accessible by Greek standards. There are buses almost hourly from Lamía to Ipáti, the usual trail-head; if you arrive by train, these can be picked up en route at Lamía's "local" station, Lianokládhi, 6km from the town. Be sure not to get off the bus at the sulphurous spa of Loutrá Ipátis, 5km north of and below Ipáti proper.

IPÁTI is a medium-sized village, clustered below a much-ruined Byzantine/Catalan castle. Two modest **hotels** cater mainly for Greek families: the courteous *Panorama* (℡02310/98 222; ❶), just above the square and open most of the year, or the more basic and noisy *Panhellinion* (℡02310/98 340; ❶) right on the platía, open in high summer only. There are also a couple of reasonable **tavernas**, such as *To Hani* on the road into town.

Route-finding on Mount Íti has been eased recently by the availability of two decent, rival topographic maps, published respectively by Road Editions (no. 43, 1:50,000, with route summaries in English) and Anavasi (no. 10, 1:50,000), also with a useful booklet in bilingual text. The classic full traverse of the range from Ipáti to Pávliani, taking in the 2150m summit of Pýrgos, is an ambitious undertaking of between ten and eleven hours, best spread over two days; a limited day-outing, however, should be feasible if you've reasonable orientation skills. The way out of Ipáti, starting from the square, is marked with red paint splodges or square placards; the actual path starting at the top of the village leads in around four hours to an EOS refuge known as **Trápeza** (usually locked, but with a spring and camping space nearby). This is a steep but rewarding walk, giving a good idea of Íti's sheer rock ramparts and lush meadows. From there you could return on a different path via Zapandólakka to Ipáti for a full-day loop hike, overnighting twice in the village. Otherwise, continue more or less due south to the flat-topped peak of Pyrá ("the pyre"), where in legend Herakles (Hercules) immolated himself to escape the agony of the poisoned tunic which his wife Deinaneira had given him. From there, proceed southwest via the Piyés and Katavóthra plateaus, on a mixture of track, path and cross-country surface, to the villages of **Áno/Káto Pávliani** where there are uncertain bus connections back to Lamía, as well as **accommodation** in the lower village at the *Xenonas Petrino* (℡02310/83 111; ❹).

Karpeníssi

The main road west from Lamía and Ipáti, after scaling a spur of Mount Tymfristós, drops down to the town of **KARPENÍSSI**. An all-year tunnel below the snowline opened in 2000, but few people use it during summer as it means spending three claustrophobic kilometres underground. Karpeníssi's site is spectacular – huddled at the base of the peak and head of the Karpenisiótis valley, which extends south all the way to wall-like Mount Panetolikó – but the town itself is entirely nondescript, having been destroyed in World War II by the Germans and again during the civil war. During the latter, it was captured and held for a week by Communist guerrillas in January 1949. During the fighting, an American pilot was shot down – thereby gaining, as C.M. Woodhouse observes in *Modern Greece* (see "Books" p.1077), "probably the unenviable distinction of being the first American serviceman to be killed in action by Communist arms".

Practicalities

Except on summer weekends or during the skiing season, **accommodation** is easily found, if not that appealing; most of the seven hotels are noisy or over-priced, though bargaining at midweek year-round is always productive. **Parking** in the town centre is difficult and/or heavily controlled, so we've indicated lodging where this is less of a problem. Best value and quietest are **rooms** kept by Kostas Koutsikos, up some steps behind the KTEL and opposite the *dhimarhío* (℡02370/21 400; ❷), or the *Hotel Galini* (℡02370/22 914; ❹) on Ríga Feréou 3, a lane (parking feasible) in the bazaar downhill from the main thoroughfare, 250m southeast of the *Panorama* restaurant (see below). For more comfort, try the well-kept *Hotel Elvetia* at Zinopoúlou 27 (℡02370/22 465, ℱ80 112; ❺), recently converted to all en suite. Zinopoúlou leads into town from the east, arriving at the leafy, café-table-staked-out central square and the adjacent **KTEL terminal**. The main street continues out of town as Ethnikís Andístasis, just off of which stands one more hotel – the *Lefkon Oros/Mont Blanc* (℡02370/80 330, ℱ80 332, ✉hmb@otenet.gr; ❹), now under new management, fairly quiet with en-suite rooms and easy parking nearby, but overpriced and still in need of maintenance.

   Eating options are somewhat limited; central exceptions to the plethora of fast-food outlets and après-ski *barákia* are the *Psistaria Spitiko Poniras*, opposite the bus station, or (for *mayireftá*) *Iy Klimataria*, around the corner from and just below *Hotel Galini*. For a bit more, locals prefer *Esy Oti Pis*, past the police station, at the start of the road to Agrínio, or (going a bit further, then left) the garden-seating *Panorama*, which offers both *mayireftá* and grills; it's at Ríga Feréou 18, just below an unmissable unfinished hotel.

Around Karpeníssi

Your first conceivable halt in the Karpenissiótis valley, 5km by road south of town, is the rather embalmed village of **KORYSKHÁDES**, whose stone houses are famous for their ornate wooden balconies with views across the valley to Mount Kaliakoúdha. All but three of the permanent population have decamped, selling up to an enterprise which has meticulously restored several mansions as premier **accommodation** – rooms, suites, family apartments – priced in Swiss fashion (℡02370/25 102, ℱ23 456; ❻ B&B). The only place to **eat or drink** is the combination kafenío-restaurant-breakfast salon, also the scheme's contact office, on the repaved platía.

Megálo Horió, Gávros and Mikró Horió

For villages with more of a lived-in feel to them, deeper into the stunning countryside, head 16km downriver, again on the main valley-floor, to **MEGÁLO HORIÓ** and **MIKRÓ HORIÓ** ("Big Village" and "Little Village"); buses make the trip from Karpeníssi twice daily. Megálo, on the east side of the valley, has several places to stay and eat, but again no lodging bargains. The friendliest, best sited and least expensive **accommodation** is the *Agnandi* (℡02370/41 303; ❸ summer, ❻ winter), to your left on the approach road, which has modern but tasteful rooms with knockout views across the village to the mountains, and a communal ground-floor kitchen providing self-service breakfast; the proprietor is helpful and knowledgeable about the area. Otherwise try, right in the heart of things, the "high-rise" *Antigone Hotel* (℡02370/41 395, ℱ41 450; ❹ summer, ❺ winter) which doubles as the main bar/restaurant; rooms were thoroughly overhauled in 2000, with carpeting for winter and pastel-coloured bedding and drapery. There are a few other tentative eateries in the village centre, but for the best meals you're advised to head down to **GÁVROS**, a little suburb of Megálo Horió on the valley floor (in this case the name means "hornbeam", which once abounded here, not "anchovy"). Several **tavernas** lining the through road are all better than anything up the hill, but *To Spiti tou Psara* gets top marks; a superb meal here of grilled trout, *hortópitta*, *kafterí* or spicy cheese dip, and a half-litre of own-made wine will barely top the €11 mark, with seating on the rear terrace overlooking the riverside trees. There's also **accommodation** here worth considering, by the bridge: the 2000-built *Pension Agrambeli* (℡02370/41 148; ❸ summer, ❺ winter), which has cool, cave-like rooms in a variety of formats, but all with balconies or verandas, and an indoor bar/breakfast area and medium-size swimming pool sharing space on a riverside lawn.

Mikró Horió, visible opposite Megálo at the foot of Mount Helidhóna, has a turbulent history; it was a major centre for local resistance during World War II, with a clandestine printing press. On Sunday, January 13, 1963, after two weeks of uninterrupted rain, an avalanche wiped out the western two-thirds of the village, killing thirteen (the death toll would have been far higher except that many locals were in church). The place was already in bad official odour because of its wartime stance, and every goverment since the disaster has exerted pressure in various ways to move the survivors 4km downhill to the replacement community of **Néo** (New) **Mikró Horió**. Here "Swiss" silliness reaches its apotheosis in the pretentious *Country Club Hellas Hotel* (℡02370/41 570, ℻41 577; ❻), which hosts Athenian society weddings and where you can drop €147–335 a night on a room or a luxury suite if you're so inclined – you're paying for the vast common areas and service, not for the rooms themselves. There are a few other, considerably more reasonable, **rooms** options scattered along the grid of streets in the purpose-built village, its stone-built houses not so wretched as many such disaster responses are. Two of the best are *Iy Gonia* near the top of the hill (℡02370/41 393; ❸ summer, ❹ winter), modern rooms with mountain views from their verandas, or (200m downhill on the same street) *Fotini Zara*'s (℡02370/41 236 or 094/5449172; ❸ summer, ❹ winter) units, with fireplaces. Both are well-signposted from the bottom of the village, and the serviceable, inexpensive *psistariá* attached to *Iy Gonia* has been operating since the 1963 resettlement.

You might prefer to continue to road's end at **Paleó** (Old) **Mikró Horió**, where the municipally run, en-suite *Helidhona Hotel* (℡02370/41 221, or 097/2555637; ❸ summer, ❹ winter) by the fountain and plane tree is about the most reasonable lodging in the valley, with rare single rates and knockout views out back towards Mount Tymfristós – not surprisingly, booking is mandatory, especially since a comprehensive refurbishment in 2000. Cooking at the ground-floor restaurant, *Iy Kyra Maria*, has also improved a bit from its former profile of cheap and merely sustaining. There are no shops in the moribund village, so come equipped for the three-hour hike west up Mount Helidhóna (1973m), indicated by blue or yellow waymarks. The first half of this is along forestry track, rather than path, with a potential detour early on to visit a small natural lake near the village entrance.

Up Mount Kaliakoúdha

The full-day **hike** up and down **Mount Kaliakoúdha** (2098m), the peak which dominates Megálo Hório, is one of the most popular outings in the Karpenisiótis valley. There's a good, waymarked path much of the way, but a certain amount of shadeless track-tramping near the top, and the final ascent conquers one of the sharpest grades in the Greek mountains – advanced peak-bagging skills are essential. The route, and geographical features, are shown more or less correctly on Anavasi Editions 1:50,000 map no. 13, *Karpenisi Prousos*. You'll want an early start, to polish off most of the 1250-metre altitude difference before the sun catches you.

From the village square near the *Hotel Antigoni*, leave Megálo Horió heading southeast, following painted red or yellow waymarks. Adopt a corniche path for just under half an hour, which briefly becomes an old and not too onerous bulldozer track which ends by a cement cistern with an overflow valve – fill up, this is the last water for some time. The proper trail resumes, climbing steadily through fir forest; you'll notice that about one in twenty trees are dead or dying, but the survivors provide welcome shade. There's also substantial deadfall and litter obscuring parts of the path, making you dependent on the frequent waymarks, especially at the half-dozen crossings of the modern dirt track heading up the mountain.

About two hours from the village, the path ends for now just below treeline, at a sharp bend in the track with a culvert; just to the left, in a clump of firs, is **Malakássa**, the only other reliable spring this side of the mountain. After topping up again, you're forced to adopt the track for about 45 minutes, with shortcuts only possible once beyond a fenced-in "base camp" for a trekking company. Between the spring and the "base camp", you'll pass a small chapel with an unreliable fountain, two crude *stánes* or pastoral huts, and a memorial to an 1823 battle here during the War of Independence. With or without shortcuts through a couloir, three-hours' hike from Megálo Horió should see you up on the saddle at the northeast flank of the peak.

The track over the saddle continues down and south into the signposted territory of Dhomnísta municipality; for Kaliakoúdha, however, head west and relentlessly up, following red-paint waymarks. The trail is poor-to-nonexistent, well strewn with scree midway along, but there's little danger of getting lost and on a fine summer's day you'll have plenty of company. Just under an hour (roughly 4hr from the village) is required to reach the **summit** and trig point (missing its "2098" disc); the staggering **views** over much of central Greece are your reward. The Vardhoússia and Íti ranges loom to the east; the Ágrafa region unfolds beyond Mount Tymfristós to the north-northeast; while Mount Panetolikó approximates the provincial border south-southwest. Due south, you see Stournára village in the Krikellopótamos valley, poised just above **Pandavréhi**, a popular beauty spot and trekkers' destination where waterfalls pour year-round from a rock wall. Many hikers elect to continue there rather than return to Megálo Horió; there's no confirmed lodging in Stournári, so you should plan to camp out. Return to the saddle takes about an hour owing to the scree and the sharp grade, and from there the descent back to Megálo Horió requires three-and-a-half hours, for a nearly eight-hour walking day.

Proussós: monastery and village

Beyond Gávros, the valley narrows to a spectacular **gorge** with two narrows at Klidhí and Patímata tís Panayías before emerging at Dhípotama, the mingling of the Karpenisiótis and Krikellopótamos rivers to form the Trikeriótis, a favourite put-in point of rafting outfitters. A paved if steep road through the canyon has made a visit to the monastery and village of **PROUSSÓS** (33km out of Karpeníssi) easier than before, though only three afternoon buses a week do the trip. The **monastery**, amazingly set on a cliff in a bend of a tributary to the Krikellopótamos, opposite two rock pinnacles, is flanked by two eighteenth-century defensive towers associated with Yiorgos Karaïskakis, the revolutionary war figure who used the place as a stronghold. Massive and much rebuilt after a succession of fires (started by candles), "Proussoú" (the official nomenclature) is presently inhabited by just two monks plus some layworkers. Coachloads of pilgrims revere the icon of the Panayía Proussiótissa in the ninth-century *katholikón*. Here, or in the treasury (*skevofylakíon*), you can see curiosities such as paper made from the skin of a goat embryo and an icon of the Panayía with its eyes gouged out. (According to the locals, the Communist rebels of the 1940s were responsible for this, though Muslim Turks were wont to perform the same sacrilege, and credulous villagers attributed magical powers to the dust thus obtained.)

Houses of the **village**, a kilometre further on, are dispersed across incredibly steep slopes, duly plagued by the sort of earth movements that did for Mikró Horió. The central neighbourhood has a drab community **hotel**, the *Agathidis* (☎02370/80 813 or 91 248; ❸) and several meat-oriented, evening-only tavernas around the central square; more reliably open, and with good, cheap *mayireftá*, is the *Proussiotissa Taverna*, just off the side-drive to the monastery.

Routes beyond Karpeníssi

Roads west or north from Karpeníssi climb high into the mountains of **Ágrafa**, the southernmost extension of the Píndhos. The road south of Proussós, only paved in 2000, creeps over the **Panetolikó** range separating Evrytanía province (which encompasses the Karpenisiótis valley and most of the Ágrafa region) from Étolo-Akarnanía. In winter critical passes are generally closed, but through the summer they're open. With your own transport, any of these routes is enjoyable, and much the quickest way out in the directions indicated.

West to Agrínio

The road west, then southwest to Agrínio is well paved and fairly broad, but extremely sinuous, so it still takes the one morning bus from Karpeníssi a good three and a half hours to cover the 114km (cars will easily make it in 3hr). The beauty of the first three-quarters of the journey up to Áyios Vlásios cannot be overemphasized; it's largely empty country, with the only place of any size being the double village of **FRANGÍSTA**, which straddles a compact valley – Anatolikí Frangísta, 39km from Karpeníssi, with three simple *xenónes*, and Dhytikí Frangísta, 3km further, offering another **inn**, a filling station and four **psistariés**, of which the most reliable two are *To Steki* and *Trikorfo* (meat platter, chips, salad and a beer for under €9). Beyond Frangísta, the road uses a causeway to cross the giant, surprisingly scenic **Kremastón reservoir** on the Tavropós, Trikeriótis and Ahelóös rivers, with a clutch of fish tavernas (exactly halfway to Agrínio) on the far side. Next the route climbs again, skirting Panetolikó, until the fir trees stop at Áyios Vlásios and the still-narrow road winds down through tobacco-planted hills to Agrínio.

If you wish to explore the Ágrafa wilderness northwest of Karpeníssi, take an afternoon bus to Kréndis; with your own vehicle, the junction for this village (along with Vinianí and Kerasohóri) is well signposted 30km out of Karpeníssi, on the west bank of the Tavropós. **KRÉNDIS** is rapidly becoming one of the gateways for exploring the Ágrafa region and can offer a high-quality **inn** with attached **restaurant**: the *Xenonas Makkas* (☎02370/31 350; ❹).

South to Náfpaktos

Another exceedingly scenic route, again with no bus service, is the one **south** from Proussós **to Náfpaktos**, a three-hour drive. The route is entirely paved, but for most of the first 35km of the journey extremely narrow, slow going. Landslides are already nibbling away at the pavement up to the pass in Panetolikó giving a last, vast panorama of Evrytanía, before it drops down to Lambíri, the first village in Étolo-Akarnanía. This and succeeding communities up to Kallithéa have a wild, God-forsaken aspect; there's little evidence on this side of the watershed of the prosperity introduced by alpine tourism to the Karpenisiótis valley. At livelier Kallithéa you have your first, sweeping views of

THESSALY AND CENTRAL GREECE | Routes beyond Karpeníssi

341

Lake Trihonídha, the largest body of fresh water in Greece; it's of irrigational rather than recreational use, the shore by turns sheer or reedy, but apparently in pretty good ecological shape, with three native fish species caught for food.

About ninety minutes out of Proussós you reach **THÉRMO**, a surpisingly large place – almost a small town – dominating a fertile upland just invisible from the lake; it has a pleasant, plane-shaded square, petrol, shops, **tavernas**, regular **buses** to Agrínio if needed, **banks** (with cash dispensers), and a D-class **hotel** on the right as you approach the square, the *Aetolia* (T06440/22 394; ❷), with some rooms en suite. Of potentially more interest is the town's pred-ecessor, **ancient Thermon** (Tues–Sun 8.30am–3pm; €1.50), well signposted 1.5km southeast of the centre. This, excavated between 1994 and 1999, was not a city per se but the main religious shrine of the Aetolians; a shelter covers many of the digs, and a small site museum highlights the local finds.

Beyond Thérmo the way drops to the lush, intensely cultivated southeast shore of the lake before climbing again over surprisingly green hills into the valley of the **Évinos River**, the last undammed one in this part of Greece. Accordingly there are a handful of **rafting outfitters** at or near **Háni Baniás** at the river bridge, as well as a restaurant and *xenónas*, but these all tend to work only at high-water season (March–May), with most clients coming for the day from Náfpaktos, just 15km further. Incidentally, if you are reversing these direc-tions, take the road out from Platía Liménos labelled "Kástro", but keep going straight rather than up and right.

North to Kardhítsa

Again with your own transport, one of the best options – giving direct access to the Metéora (see p.370) – is the **route north to Kardhítsa**, which takes off from the top of the pass in the old road east of Karpeníssi, directly above the tunnel. Except for a few short dirt patches – being repaired – the way is paved and wide, a beautiful drive where sweeping vistas over central Greece alternate with fir forest. It's 28km around Mount Tymfristós to the turning for **FOURNÁ** village, with a hotel there (*Wild Beauty* T02370/51 223; ❸) if needed; then 64km more to Kardhítsa, with little in between other than **Loutropiyí**, where you may pause to munch on *souvláki*; **Loutrá Smokóvou**, where you can drown any sorrows in the little spa; and Kédhros, with the first fuel since Karpeníssi, and where the road straightens out for the final flat, straight approach to Kardhítsa. Allow just over two hours from Karpeníssi – a considerable saving in time and mileage versus going all the way back to Lamía, and then northwest across the dull Thessalian plains.

Thessaly

The highlights of travelling through **Thessaly** are easily summarized. Over to the east, curling down from the industrial port-city of Vólos, is the mountain-ous **Pílio** (Pelion) peninsula. The villages on its lush, orchard-covered slopes are among the most beautiful in the country – a long-established resort area for Greeks and numerous foreign car-equipped tourists, though still with many unspoiled corners. To the west is a sight not to be missed on any mainland exploration: the extraordinary "monasteries in the air" of the **Metéora**.

The **central plains** are something to be passed through, rather than visited. That said, **Tríkala**, capital of the eponymous province, is making itself into a relatively pleasant city, besides providing efficient connections by bus to nearby **Kalambáka**, gateway to the Metéora, and to Vólos (via dreary **Lárissa**).

Heading north or west from Lárissa, you'll find yourself in one mountain range or another. The dramatic route over the Píndhos, from Kalambáka to Ioánnina, is covered in the following chapter. North from Kalambáka there are reasonable roads, though few buses, into western Macedonia, with the lakeside town of Kastoriá an obvious focus. Most travellers, however, head north from Lárissa towards Thessaloníki, an attractive (though currently much dug-up) route in the shadow of Mount Olympus (see Chapter Five).

Vólos

Arriving at the city of **VÓLOS** gives little hint of Pílio's promise. It's hard to imagine the mythological past of this busy modern port, but this is the site of ancient Iolkos, from where Jason and the Argonauts set off on their quest for the Golden Fleece. One of Greece's fastest-growing industrial centres and a major depot for long-distance truck drivers, Vólos was rebuilt in utilitarian style after a series of devastating earthquakes between 1947 and 1957, and is now edging to its natural limits against the Pílio foothills behind. This admitted, it's a lively place with a large university-student population, beginning to revel in recently acquired prosperity, and you could do worse than spend a few hours or even a night here while waiting for a bus up the mountain or a boat to Skiáthos (see p.908), Skópelos (see p.913) or Alónissos (see p.917), for which Vólos is the **main port**.

The most attractive place to linger is along the eastern waterfront esplanade, between the landscaped **Platía Yeoryíou** and the archeological museum, which is itself a highly recommended diversion. Imaginatively laid out and clearly labelled in English, the **Archeological Museum** (Tues–Sun 8.30am–2.30pm; €1.50) features a unique collection of painted Hellenistic grave *stelae* depicting, in now-faded colours, the everyday scenarios of fifth-century BC life, as well as a variety of graves complete with skeletons. It also has one of the best European collections of Neolithic pottery, tools and figurines, from the local sites of Sesklo and Dimini (both of which – respectively 15km and 3km west of Vólos – can be visited). Sesklo remains of essentially specialist interest, but since the 1990s **ancient Dimini** (open Tues–Sun, no fixed hours; €1.50) has emerged as something of a local attraction, with the circuit of Neolithic walls clean and labelled, plus two fairly intact Mycenaean *thólos*-type tombs. Adjacent to the site, and still closed for excavations, is a large Mycenaean palace complex which some think may actually be ancient Iolkos.

Along with Lárissa, Halkídha and Ioánnina, Vólos was historically home to one of the larger **Jewish communities** of central Greece. Local Jews were well integrated into the social and political life of the town, such that during World War II only 155 out of the thousand-strong community were caught and murdered by the Nazis; the rest joined the Resistance or were otherwise hidden on Mount Pílio. The victims have a prominent, sculpted memorial in one corner of Platía Ríga Feréou, donated by one of the survivors.

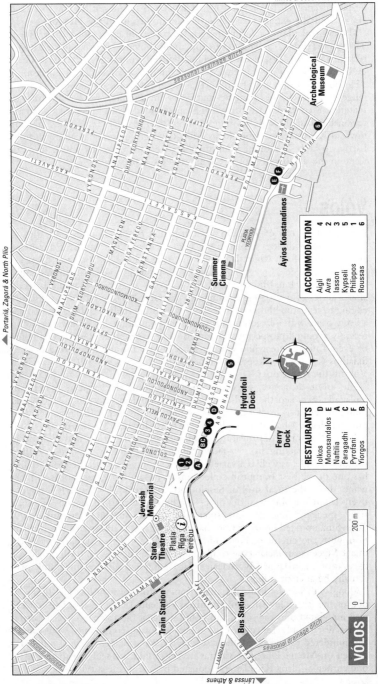

Miliés & South Pílio ▲

▲ Portariá, Zagorá & North Pílio

Lárissa & Athens ▲

Ágios Konstandínos

ACCOMMODATION

Aigli	4
Avra	2
Iasson	3
Kypseli	5
Philippos	1
Roussas	6

RESTAURANTS

Ioikos	D
Monosandalos	E
Naftilia	A
Paragadhi	C
Pyrofani	F
Yiorgos	B

Archeological Museum

Summer Cinema

Hydrofoil Dock

Ferry Dock

Jewish Memorial

State Theatre

Platía Ríga Feréou

Train Station

Bus Station

N

0   200 m

VÓLOS

seasonal drainage ditch

Practicalities

The nearest **airport**, opened to civilian charter flights in 1998 (but not yet domestic flights), is at Néa Anhíalos, 26km southwest. Ferries and hydrofoils call at the port's **main quay**, and most other services are found within a couple of blocks. An exception is the **bus station** on Grigoríou Lambráki, ten minutes' walk southwest of the main square, **Platía Ríga Feréou**. Arrayed around the latter are the **train station** and the fairly useless **EOT** office (Mon–Fri 7.30am–2pm; July & Aug may also open 6–8pm; ☎04210/23 500 or 37 417), which mostly confines itself to stocking leaflets and maps, but may be able to provide information on bus and ferry services. Better maps, and a selection of foreign-language books and periodicals, can be found at Papasotiriou, on Dhimitriádhos on the corner of Koumoundhoúrou, or at Tsekouras, Venizélou 1, just by the quay.

Like Áyios Konstandínos, Vólos has regular ferries and, in summer, frequent and quicker hydrofoils to the Sporades. **Ferries** leave three to five times daily in July and August for Skiáthos, Skópelos and Alónissos; the last departure is generally around 5.30pm. For current information ring ☎04210/20 336, or go straight to Vis Travel's dedicated Sporádhes booth on the quay. **Hydrofoils** (Hellas Flying Dolphins, book through Falcon Tours, Argonaftón 34, ☎04210/21 626) run three to five times daily to Skiáthos, Skópelos and Alónissos; as of writing, any link with remoter Skýros has been suspended. In midsummer there are also daily hydrofoils to the islands from **Tríkeri** at the foot of Mount Pílio (see overleaf); the more frequent service from Platanía has been discontinued. For the regular sailings to the Cyclades and Crete (occasional summer service to Lésvos is unreliable), contact Vis Travel's main office just a few steps back from the waterfront at Andonopoúlou 3 (☎04210/25 666 or 31 059). For information after-hours try the port police in their dockside booth (☎04210/38 888).

If you want to **rent a car** to explore Mount Pílio, try one of the following agencies: European at 79–83 Iássonos (☎04210/36 238); Budget, Iássonos 5, corner Sólonos (☎04210/21 535); or Hertz, Iássonos 97 and at the airport (☎04210/22 544).

Accommodation

Hotels are fairly plentiful if not for the most part great value, with a concentration of acceptable ones in the grid of streets behind the port. Budget options (relatively speaking) include the double-glazed *Iasson* (☎04210/26 075; ❸), partly facing the port at Pávlou Melá 1; the seaside *Kypseli* at Ayíou Nikoláou 1 (☎04210/24 420; ❷–❸), with some en-suite rooms; or, further out at Iatrou Tzánou 1, the basic but well-equipped en-suite *Roussas* (☎04210/21 732, ℉22 987; ❷), easily the best value and best reserved in advance, with relatively easy parking, convenience to the museum and ouzerís, and helpful staff offsetting occasional nocturnal motorcycle noise outside. Mid-range places include the air-conditioned *Avra* at Sólonos 3 (☎04210/25 370, ℉28 980; ❹), thoroughly refurbished in 2000; the comfortable *Philippos* (☎04210/37 607, ⓦwww.philippos.gr; ❹), inland at Sólonos 9; or the recently expanded *Aigli* (☎04210/24 471; ℉33 006; ❺) at Argonaftón 24–26, a restored Art Deco complex on the quayside.

Restaurants and entertainment

Vólos specializes in one of Greece's most endearing and enduring institutions – the authentic **ouzerí**, serving a huge variety of mezédhes washed down, not necessarily with oúzo but with *tsípouro*, the favoured spirit of the northern mainland. Among the ouzerís strung out along the waterfront street of Argonaftón, *O Yiorgos* at no. 15 has good seafood if slack service (Greek-only menu); *Naftilia* at no. 1, *Paragadhi* at no. 19 or *Iolkos* at no. 32 also get good marks. About a half-dozen more pricey seafood-strong ouzerís are found at the start of Nikifórou Plastíra, near the enormous Áyios Konstandínos church, interspersed with cafés and *barákia*. Of these, the best two are widely reckoned to be the adjacent *Pyrofani* and *Monosandalos*, most reliably open evenings and all day weekends, with waterside seating. At *Monosandalos* the bill for two starters, a beer and a portion of house-special *garidhokrokétes* (shrimp patties) will run to about €13, or €50 for a group of four passing plates around.

As for **entertainment**, concerts and plays are frequently performed in the open-air **theatre** or the closed one on Platía Ríga Feréou (tickets can be bought at Kehaïdis music store at the corner of Iásonos and Kartáli streets, one block in from the waterfront), while the summer **cinema** Exoraïstiki occupies one corner of Platía Yeoryíou. There are dozens of **discos** at the west edge of town past the train station, particularly on Lahaná, though in summer many of these transfer operations to the easterly beach suburbs or even to the Sporádhes.

Mount Pílio (Pelion)

The **Mount Pílio peninsula**, with its lush orchards of apple, pear and nut trees and dense forests of beech and oak, seems designed to confound stereotypical images of Greece. Scarcely a rock is visible along the slopes, and the sound of water comes gurgling up from fountains or aqueducts beside every track; summer temperatures here can be a good 10°F cooler than on the baking Thessalian plains. Pílio is reputed to be the land of the mythical centaurs – thus the name *Kentavros* (Centaur) for various hotels and bars – and the site of revelries by ancient gods.

Pílio **villages** are equally idiosyncratic, often spread out over wide areas due to easy availability of water, their various quarters linked by winding cobbled paths. They formed a semi-autonomous district throughout the Ottoman occupation, and during the eighteenth century became something of a nursery for Greek Orthodox culture, fostered by semi-underground education and a revival of **folk art** and **traditional architecture**. There is also a strong regional **cuisine**, with specialities such as *spedzofaí* (sausage and pepper casserole), *kounéli kokkinistó* (rabbit stew) and *gída lemonáti* (goat stew with lemon sauce). To wash it down there's widely available, surprisingly palatable wine bottled by the Dhimitra Co-op at Nea Anhíalos. In the far south, the gastronomic pattern changes a bit: obvious touristic tavernas are confined to the coast, while unassuming-looking kafenía on most village squares function, after dark, as *tsipourádhika* producing *tís óres* titbits plus a few ready dishes. Herbs, a wide range of fruit, home-made preserves and honey are important local products and souvenirs, pitched at the roadside.

Many of the communities have changed little in appearance over the centuries, and reward visits with their ornate mansions, churches and sprawling platías – invariably shaded by several vast plane trees, sheltering the local cafés. The slate-roofed **churches** are highly distinctive, built in a low, wide style, often with a detached bell-tower, marble reliefs on the apse and always ornamented inside with carved wood. Two villages, **Makrinítsa** and **Vyzítsa**, have been designated by the EOT as protected showpieces of the region, but almost every place offers its own unique attractions.

Add to the above the delights of a dozen-plus excellent **beaches**, plus a growing number of maintained **hiking** routes (see box overleaf), and you have a recipe for an instant holiday idyll – or disaster, if your timing is wrong. Lying conveniently between Athens and Thessaloníki, Pílio is a long-established favourite with Greek holiday-makers, who inundate the place at Eastertime or Christmas week, from mid-July to mid-August and during any three-day weekend year-round. At such times you'd really be pushing your luck to show up without a reservation, when, in any case, prices are the highest on the mainland. Additionally, many of the mansions restored as accommodation are typically unattended, their owners absent in Vólos unless they know they'll have customers; thus it's essential to reserve such lodging in advance year-round.

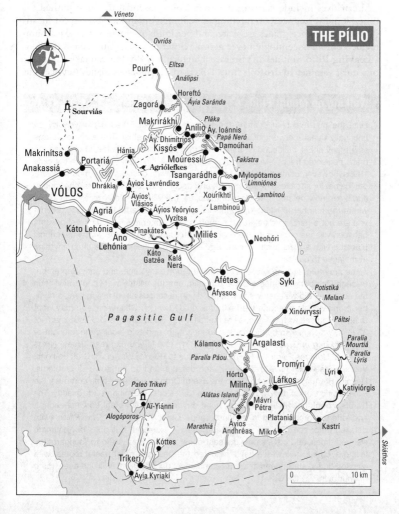

THE PÍLIO

0   10 km

Getting around Pílio

The peninsula is divided into three regions, the best concentration of distinctive communities lying just **north and east** of Vólos and along the **northeast coast**. The **southwest coast** is less scenically interesting, with concentrated development along the Pagasitic Gulf, despite its lack of decent beaches. The far **south**, relatively low-lying and sparsely populated, has just two major resorts – Plataniá and Milína – plus a few scattered inland villages.

Travelling between the villages can be tricky without your own transport. **Buses** to the east cover two main routes: Vólos–Hánia–Zagorá (2–5 daily) and Vólos–Tsangarádha–Áyios Ioánnis via Miliés (2 daily), with just one daily service linking Zagorá and Tsangarádha to complete the loop. The far south is equally sparsely served, with just two or three departures a day to Tríkeri, Plataniá and Katiyórgis, though the respective northern and western highlights of Makrinítsa and Vyzítza both have more frequent connections.

Alternatives include **renting a car** in Vólos (essential if you're pushed for time), some very uncertain hitching or walking. Any mode of transport means slow progress, since grades are sharp, and perilously narrow roads snake around ravine contours, seemingly never getting closer to villages just across the way.

Leaving Pílio, you needn't necessarily return to Vólos but can take advantage of regular summer **hydrofoils** from Tríkeri to the Sporades islands (services out

---

Walking on Mount Pílio

Until the mid-twentieth century, the Pílio villages were linked exclusively by an unusually dense network of **kalderímia** (old cobbled paths). The automobile age saw many either bulldozed or consigned to disuse, and in the local hothouse climate, neglected trails were blocked by vegetation within a few years. Since the early 1990s, however, committed local residents and village councils have mounted various campaigns to clean, restore, mark and document these superb walking routes, and it can now be said that, along with Epirus, the Pílio is the only region of Greece where the number of hiking opportunities is growing rather than dwindling. Even if you are not a hard-core trekker, the refurbished paths provide essential short-cuts between villages or down to the beaches. You'll see lots of metal yellow directional placards with a black walking-man logo – sometimes helpful, more often anything from vague to useless.

The preferred walking seasons are May through early June, and early September through October; summer is hot and humid, and the winter mist- and snowline in the north can dip well below the villages. If you're serious about hiking here, a number of individuals (noted in the text) offer guided walks. Otherwise, you may want to equip yourself with some or all of the following: Road Editions' 1:50,000 map no. 33 *Pílio*, which is also by far the best touring map, and sold locally; the now out-of-print *Trekking in Greece* (see "Books" p.1091); and (if you can read Greek) Nikos Haratsis' *Odhigos Piliou Yia Peripatites* ("Guide to Pílio for Walkers"), Grafi Editions, Vólos. These each have their virtues and defects, and do not solve all problems. Despite Haratsis' participation, and the use of Ordnance Survey-type contours, the Road Editions map does not trace walking routes or some minor roads exactly. The Haratsis book itself has non-scale, hand-drawn maps with crabbed Greek script, and often imprecise text directions. Lance Chilton's *Walks in The Pilion* (with detailed map; see "Books" p.1091) is generally excellent, but does not estimate elapsed times, and covers only the east-coast villages from Anílio to Tsangarádha. In the accounts below, we have indicated the best and most useful routes, with elapsed times, start points and brief summaries; doubtless you will find a few more of your own.

of Plataniá and Áyios Ioánnis are suspended at present). **Arriving** fairly directly in Pílio **from overseas** is now possible, using summer-only charter flights to either Skiáthos (frequent) or Anhiálos, near Vólos (once weekly only), followed by a short transfer. UK package companies Sunsail, Sunvil and Tapestry have the lion's share of such airplanes, though seats for flight-only or fly-drive packages are usually in short supply.

The north

Before crossing over to the popular east coast on the main Vólos–Zagorá route, consider pausing at either **Portariá** or **Makrinítsa**. Both villages have intrinsic attractions and make good first or last stops on any touring circuit.

Anakassiá and Portariá

The first encountered Pílio village, **ANAKASSIÁ** is just 4km out of town, and few casual visitors give more than a passing glance to what is essentially a suburb of Vólos. What they miss is a small but very beautiful museum (signposted) dedicated to the "naive" painter **Theophilos** (1873–1934). A great eccentric, originally from Lésvos, Theophilos lived for long periods in both Athens and Vólos, where he wandered around, often dressed in traditional costumes, painting frescoes for anyone prepared either to pay or feed him. In Pílio you find his work in the most unlikely places, mostly unheralded, including a number of village tavernas and kafenía. Here, the **museum** (Mon–Fri 8am–2.30pm; free) occupies the **Arhondikó Kóndos**, an eighteenth-century mansion whose first floor Theophilos frescoed entirely with scenes from the Greek War of Independence – one of his favourite themes.

  PORTARIÁ, 14km east of Vólos, has a more mountainous feel with a soundtrack of running streams. Regrettably, the areas closest to the busy road have become tacky and commercialized (right down to a convenient Commercial Bank cash dispenser), but the backstreets are still rewarding. The chief glory, as so often in Pílio, is the main square, shaded by tremendous plane trees, one planted in 1220. If you decide to stay, you can pick from among more than a dozen traditional inns and **hotels**; the obvious, modern (and noisy) *Filoxenia* and *Pelias* just off the main square are worth shunning in favour of restored pensions such as the *Arhondiko Athanasaki* (☎04280/99 235, Ⓕ90 091; ❹ B&B summer, ❻ winter) just above the road but quiet, with private parking and plain but large rooms, or the smaller, more secluded *Arhondiko Klitsa* (☎04280/99 418, Ⓕ27 551; ❹). For those on a budget, the less characterful *Viky's* (☎04280/99 520; ❸) just outside Portariá on the road to Makrinítsa, is the main choice.

Makrinítsa

From Portariá many buses detour 2km northwest to **MAKRINÍTSA**, 17km from Vólos, where stone houses straggle picturesquely down the mountainside. Founded in 1204 by refugees from the first sacking of Constantinople, it offers six outstanding churches plus a monastery, and a group of **traditional mansions** – many restored as accommodation. If your time in Pílio is limited, Makrinítsa is perhaps the best single target, since the village ranks as one of Greece's prettiest. Inevitably, there is blight on the main lane into the centre from tatty souvenir shops, and plenty of (Greek) day-trippers, but both are easy to escape, and the views over the Pagasitic Gulf are splendid.

  There's a two hundred-metre altitude difference between the upper and lower quarters of Makrinítsa, so to get a full sense of the village takes a half-day's rambling. Most impressive of the churches are **Áyios Ioánnis**, next to the fountain on the shady main platía, and the beautiful eighteenth-century **monastery of Panayía Makrinítissa**, right under the clocktower. Many of the sanctuaries and frescoes here are only a few centuries old, but the marble relief work on some of the apses (the curvature behind the altar) is the best of its type in Greece. A few metres on from the Áyios Ioánnis square there are **Theóphilos frescoes** (see overleaf) in a café.

If you are looking for a **challenging walk** in Pílio, the village is also the starting point for the five-hour-long trek to the deserted, frescoed **monastery of Sourviás**. This begins at the little plaza known as Bránis, and sticks largely to *kalderími* and path surface. There is another route via the chapel of Panayía Leskhianí which takes only three-and-a-half hours one way, and which also starts at Platía Bránis, but in this case you begin on a steep cement track west past the monastery of Ayíou Yerasímou, though trail resumes for most of the way once Makrinítsa is out of sight.

Accommodation in Makrinítsa is abundant but, as everywhere on Pílio, not cheap. Three of the "traditional inns" (*Xiradhaki* to the east of the main square, and the more remote *Mouslí* and *Sissilianou*) are beginning to show their age – early 1980s-vintage restoration – and are not necessarily the best choices here. They are co-managed (☎04280/99 250 or 99 256, ⓕ90 151; ❹–❺), and almost uniquely offer singles, some en suite, but are often noisy and very spartanly furnished. Better, privately run options include the atmospheric, slightly funky *Arkhondiko Diomidi* (☎04280/99 430, ⓕ99 114; ❸–❹), which has some en-suite rooms, directly overhead if gazing from the platía church; the *Theophilos* (☎04280/99 435; ❹), with contemporary furnishings; and the cosy *Rooms Routsou* (☎04280/99 090; ❹), in an older building on the way to the platía. There are a few rather commercialized **tavernas** right on the platía, but the series of three tucked behind the church are the most atmospheric and most locally patronized.

Hánia

Travelling on over the mountain, beyond Portariá, the road hairpins up to the **Hánia pass**, and the eponymous "village", a string of modern houses and a smattering of hotels which you shouldn't need to use. Its **tavernas**, however, may come in handy as a lunch stop for hikers **trekking** between Portariá or Dhrákia and Zagorá, five- to six-hour undertakings, mostly on path. A minor road leads 4km southeast to the small Agriólefkes **ski resort** (all of four lifts and four runs; open Jan–March at most, global warming permitting). Once past Hánia, the view suddenly opens to take in the whole northeast coast of the peninsula as you spiral down to a fork: the left turning leads to Zagorá, the right towards Tsangarádha. The old *kalderími* between Hánia and Zagorá has been cleaned and repaired, but the main problem with this three-hour walk is that you're never far out of sight or sound of the busy road, and the final approach to Zagorá is entirely on asphalt.

The northeast coast

Pílio's best (and most popular) beaches, plus its lushest scenery, are found on the Aegean-facing **northeast coast**, which bears the brunt of winter storms. A relatively humid climate and shady dells nurture exotic flowers such as gardenias and camelias, locally bred and sold at the roadside. The "county town" of the region and major producer and packer of fruit is **Zagorá**, the apple capital of Greece.

Zagorá and Pourí

The largest Pílio village, **ZAGORÁ** has a life more independent of tourism than its neighbours, though government studies give the fruit orchards only until the year 2020 to survive, owing to depleted soil and overuse of pesticides. Raspberries are being proposed as a potential breakaway from apple monoculture; most of the residents are opposed to tourism, and wish to continue somehow as farmers.

Visitors often jump to unfavourable conclusions from the workaday, concrete main street where the bus calls; in fact there are four well-preserved and architecturally more varied areas, based around the squares of **Ayía Paraskeví**, **Ayía Kyriakí**, **Áyios Yeóryios** and **Metamórfosis (Sotíra)**, strung out over five kilometres. Coming from Vólos, turn left at the first filling station to find Ayía Paraskeví (Perahóra) up the hillside, with its pleasant, unvisited platía. Ayía Kyriakí is effectively the centre of Zagorá. Bearing left away from the turning for Horeftó will bring you to the broad platía of Áyios Yeóryios, in the shadow of its lovely plane tree and beautiful eighteenth-century church, while Sotíra lies beyond this, above the road to Pourí. At the second bend of the road down to Horeftó beach stands the **Ríga Feréou "secret" school**, now a gallery/folk museum, kept open in July and August.

The prime **accommodation** choice in Zagorá is Wolf Keil and Ingrid Brink's *Villa Horizonte* (☎04260/23 342, ℻23 176, @www.villa-horizonte.com; ❹), 400m down a signposted, narrow dirt track heading east from the "secret" school. Though still functioning on demand as a cultural centre which organizes and hosts concerts, seminars and craft exhibitions, emphasis has shifted recently to walking holidays (led by Wolf) and accommodation in designer-decor, themed rooms, with generous, healthy buffet breakfast included. Other, more conventional lodging in Zagorá is often more reasonably priced than elsewhere in the region. There are a few rooms places, such as *Marika Vlahou* (☎04260/22 153; ❷), above a metal shop in Ayía Kyriakí, or the simple but warmly welcoming *Yiannis Halkias* (☎04260/22 159; ❸), near the turn for Horeftó, as well as an impeccably restored mansion, the *Arhontiko Gayanni* (☎04260/23 391, ℻22 671; ❻ B&B), with a beautiful garden and breakfasts of *Villa Horizonte* standard. All four parish squares host grill-**tavernas**: *O Takis* in Ayía Kyriakí is reasonable, *Kyriazis* in Sotíra is best for mezédhes, while *O Petros* (aka *Fani's*) and *Venizelos* at Áyios Yeóryios are good allrounders. There's also a **post office**, **internet** facilities (at Alma Computers) and a **bank** in Ayía Kyriakí, the latter with an all-important cash dispenser – the only one in the remote Pelion.

The road from Zagorá to **POURÍ**, one of the northernmost communities on Pílio, is a spectacular approach to a regally situated village. Theoharis Hiotis rents **rooms** (☎04260/23 168; ❸) here in his modern pension 250m beyond the square, though eating options are limited to a kafenío doing simple mezédhes below the platía. Also worth a stop are a carpet-weaving shop with hand-knotted carpets, and a sculpture/pottery gallery. The two dazzling, usually deserted beaches of **Elítsa** and **Ovriós** below the village give you an idea of what Horeftó and Áyios Ioánnis looked like until 1980. Pourí is also a major trailhead for **ambitious treks** such as the five-and-a-half-hour hike to Sourviás monastery, initially track but then trail, or the eight-hour expedition to Véneto, the northernmost village in Pílio, via the abandoned hamlet of Paleá Mintzéla. Either requires more stamina and orientation skills than the usual Pílio outing; if you're not confident, Wolf of *Villa Horizonte* leads group treks at appropriate times of year (April–May & Sept–Oct).

Horeftó

Eight twisting kilometres down the mountain, **HOREFTÓ** (4 buses daily from Tsangarádha in summer, 2 off-season) makes an excellent coastal base. There is a choice of beaches here: the long, decent one in front of the former fishing village; secluded **Ayía Saránda** 2km south; and two coves at Análipsi, to the north. A brief hike from the end of the frontage road brings you to the first cove, a little paradise popular with nudists and freelance campers taking advantage of a spring behind the sand. Determined explorers can follow a coastal path for twenty minutes more to the northerly cove, road-accessible and rockier. There are also two hour-plus *kalderímia* up to Zagorá, one of them passing by the Ríga Feréou school, which can be combined to make an enjoyable loop.

Horeftó supports half a dozen hotels and an equal number of studio apartments for rent. The best-value and best-located **hotels** are – near the quieter south end of the coast road – the high-standard *Hayiati* (☎04260/23 540, ℉22 405; ❹; open all year), with off-street parking, spacious garden bar, wheelchair access and fridges in the mostly sea-view rooms, which are heated in winter; the simpler *Erato* (☎04260/22 445; ❸), more of a "*dhomátia*" in that breakfast isn't available, a 1970s block with partial sea views and fridges; and, above the final curve on the road in, the simple, homey *Aegeus* (☎04260/22 778, ℉22 784; ❸), often full and making an attempt to soften the communal areas with textiles. Attractive studio possibilities include Kosta Kapaniri's simple but spotless units (☎04260/63 779;❹), among the trees. If you show up without booking during midsummer you're likely to end up at the unlicensed **campsite** (no phone), at the extreme south end of the main beach. You can continue past the campsite to the unmarked but paved and very useful shortcut up to Makriráhi, saving the long way around back through Zagóra.

Eating options in Horeftó are decent, with *O Petros* (a branch of the one in Zagorá) being an excellent all-rounder, while *Ta Dhelfínia* proves a competent ouzerí, where fried fish and two starters (including stuffed olives) with a beer should be around €10. *To Milo tis Eridhos*, run by the Apple Growers Cooperative, has always received highly mixed reviews – patronize at your own risk. Two or three **bars** provide evening distraction.

Kissós

The easterly turning at the junction below Hánia leads through or past resolutely untouristy Makriráhi, a perennial traffic bottleneck; north-facing Anílio (meaning "without sun"); and the upper edge of Áyios Dhimítrios before reaching the side road for **KISSÓS**. This unspoilt corner of Pílio lies 1km off the main road, virtually buried in foliage, with sleepy residential quarters ascending in terraces either side of eighteenth-century **Ayía Marína**, one of the finest churches on the peninsula. It's protected (and kept locked) by the archeological service, but you can still admire fine frescoes above the south door.

Accommodation here tends to be simple but good-value, for example the modern, bland *Rooms Sofia Gloumi-Hanou* (☎04260/31 267 or 097/2821841; ❸), uphill from the multilevel platía – the largest on the mountain – with an evening-only *psistariá* on the ground floor. The smallish rooms at *Xenonas Kissos* (☎04260/31 214; ❸, also triples and quads) opposite the church, have wood trim, bright curtains and fridges; its more versatile, all-day **taverna** (*Iy Klimataria*) on the ground floor, under new management in 2001, has a fine terrace. The more prosaically set *Makis* across the street is also excellent. If you're based here, the hike up to Hánia is a good two-hour jaunt, mostly on path.

Áyios Ioánnis to Damoúhari

Heading for the coast via Áyios Dhimítrios, you tackle 6km of twisting paved road down to **ÁYIOS IOÁNNIS**, once the port and boat-building yards for Áyios Dhimítrios but now eastern Pílio's major resort. A score of densely packed hotels and private rooms were thrown up during the mid-1980s in a manner now decidedly illegal, but despite these numbers finding a bed here in peak season is as problematic as anywhere on the peninsula with a significant package presence. Budget **accommodation** options include the *Hotel Evripidis* (℡04260/31 338; ❸) on the seafront or the *Hotel Marina* (℡04260/31 239 or 31 097; ❷) in a peaceful cul-de-sac at the south end of the strip, an annexe of the adjacent *Hotel Eleana* which fills first with packages. With a bit more to spend, try the civilized, good-taste *Anesis* (℡04260/31 123, ⓦwww.geocities.com/anesis; ❹), which welcomes walk-ins to its pastel-decor rooms; the kitschly furnished *Zephyros* (℡04260/31 335; ❸) at the quieter, south end of the strip; the superbly sited but somewhat unwelcoming *Manthos Beach* (℡04260/31 137, ⓦwww.hotelmanthos.gr; ❹), at the northern, pedestrianized end of the front; and the somewhat impersonal but good-value *Aloe* (℡04260/31 240; ❺), sprawling behind its lawn-garden. **Restaurants** along the front are all much of a touristy muchness, though *Akroyiali* and *Poseidon* have their virtues. For something more unusual, the *Ostria* inland (well-signed) acquits itself well as a *kultúra* taverna, with rich, generic-Mediterranean recipes making good use of herbs and other strong flavourings; proprietress Hariklia spent years in Florence, so pasta dishes are emphasized. It's worth the splurge of about €18 a head, plus wine (either very good bulk or Rapsani bottled), but seating is limited so reserve on ℡04260/32 132.

The **beach** at Áyios Ioánnis is popular and commercialized, with windsurfing boards and waterskis for rent. For more ambitious activities, such as sea-kayaking, mountain-biking and horse-riding, contact local **travel agency** Les Hirondelles (℡04260/31 181, ⓦwww.les-hirondelles.gr), which also changes money and arranges accommodation if necessary. For a quieter time and finer sand, walk either ten minutes north to **Pláka** beach, with its mostly young, Greek clientele and popular beach bar/taverna, or fifteen minutes south (past the **campsite** ℡04260/49 238; June–Sept) to **Papa Neró** beach, the best tanning spot in the vicinity, and accordingly cluttered with sunbeds. At present it's fronted by just a few rooms for rent – *Iy Orea Ammoudhia* (℡04260/31 219, ⒡31 965; ❸) being one of the best, and the only one not controlled by Les Hirondelles – and two good tavernas, though a mass of building sites on the slope above suggest its peaceful days are numbered.

South from the campsite, a narrow paved road leads to **DAMOÚHARI**, a hamlet set amid olive trees and bordering a secluded port. The construction of another road down from Moúressi has put an end to its seclusion, and villas are springing up fast amongst the olive trees. However, cars are excluded from the shoreline area, which offers a large pebble beach, the overgrown ruins of a Venetian castle, and three **tavernas**, best of which by some way is *Kafezythestiatorio Barba Stergios*, where you can dine on excellent wild fish, two starters and bulk wine for under €18, or assorted meat grills and *mayireftá* for far less. Top **accommodation** choice here is the attractive, unobtrusive *Hotel Damouhari* (℡04260/49 840, ⒡49 841; ❺), a mock-trad "village" of stone-built studio cottages and rooms, with antiques and wood trim in the units and fine decor in the bar which is better known as *Kleopatra Miramare*. A small pool, more of a gathering place, was added in 2001. Unfortunately for on-spec travellers, they're block-booked much of the year by British companies Simply and

Tapestry; local alternatives are the comparatively modest *Rooms Kastro* (☎04260/49 475; ❸) and *Rooms Thomas Olkas* (☎04260/49 872; ❸).

From Damoúhari, it's possible to walk to **Tsangarádha** in 75 minutes, a popular and rewarding trip (though most folk do it downhill in something under an hour). At the mouth of the ravine leading down to the larger bay, a spectacular *kalderími* begins its steep ascent, allowing glimpses of up to six villages simultaneously, and even the Sporades on a clear day, from points along the way. Subsequently there is deep shade, and springwater approaching Ayía Kyriakí; the path emerges in the Ayía Paraskeví quarter of Tsangarádha, just downhill from the post office.

Tsangarádha and Moúressi

TSANGARÁDHA is the largest northeastern village after Zagorá, though it may not seem so at first since it's divided into four distinct quarters – **Taxiárhes**, **Ayía Paraskeví**, **Ayía Kyriakí** and **Áyios Stéfanos** – strung along several kilometres of road. Each of these is scattered around a namesake church and platía, the finest of which is **Ayía Paraskeví**, shaded by reputedly the heftiest plane tree in Greece – pushing a thousand years in age, and requiring eighteen men to encircle.

Most **accommodation** in this area is pricey, and on the noisy main road. Exceptions in one respect or another include the friendly, en-suite *Villa ton Rodhon* (☎04260/49 340; ❹), right by the top of the cobbled path to Damoúhari, a 1970s construction where most plain rooms have sea views and balconies; the *Arhondiko Hatzakou* (☎04260/49 911; ❹), a somewhat over-modernized mansion well below the highway in Taxiárhes quarter; or the slightly pricier but good-value *Konaki Hotel* (☎04260/49 481 or 53 842; ❹), just south of the Ayía Paraskeví square but set back from the road. All rooms here have fridges and views, some equipped with iron beds and balconies, and there's a pleasant basement breakfast area. If money's no object, push the boat out at the antiques-furnished, British/American-run *Lost Unicorn* (☎04260/49 930, ℉49 931; ❻, effectively less through Houses of Pelion or Sunvil – see "Basics"), just behind Ayía Paraskeví square and its giant tree. The common areas are set up like a British club, with high tea on offer and game forming part of half-board menus. Tsangarádha's independent **eating** options are less than brilliant; the oft-cited exception, *Aleka's* on the main road at Ayía Paraskeví, has gotten stodgy and overpriced of late, with shambolic service to boot.

In general, better meals are to be had at any of the four **tavernas** in **MOÚRESSI**, 3km northwest on the road. Both *To Tavernaki* or the nearby *Iy Dhrosia* up on the main highway are famously dour, but you can get specialities like *fasólies hándres* (delicately flavoured pinto beans) and assorted offal on a spit. Good food at the taverna by Moúressi's atmospheric platía offsets service worthy of *Fawlty Towers*, while *O Vangelis*, 300m down the road to Áyios Ioánnis, is an inexpensive and friendly grill with good bulk wine (though it gets null points for prefried chips). Down in the village centre, there's also a prime en-suite **accommodation** choice: *The Old Silk Store* (☎04260/49 086 or 093/7156780, ℉04260/49 565, ⓦwww.hotels-in-greece.com/magnisia/metaxourgio-e.htm, also bookable through Houses of Pelion or Sunvil; ❹; closed Feb), a lightly restored nineteenth-century mansion with a garden, barbecue area and high-ceilinged, wood-floored rooms (including one self-catering studio). Breakfasts change daily but always include excellent bread and own-made preserves; Cornish proprietress Jill Sleeman can help with travel arrangements and also leads walking tours in the area. An excellent short stroll, very useful for reaching the beach or completing a loop via Áyios Ioánnis, is the 45-minute descent to Damoúhari; look out for the start of the trail on the bend in the road about 100m past *O Vangelis*.

The coast: Mylopótamos to Lambinoú

From Tsangarádha, ninety-minute paths from both Taxiárhes and Ayía Paraskeví, or a seven-kilometre hairpin road snake down to **MYLOPÓTAMOS**, a collection of attractive pebble coves. The two largest are separated by a naturally tunnelled rock wall, with a pair of musical beach bars just above. They attract mostly Greek summer crowds, who pack into **accommodation** lining the approach road; one of the nearest is *Diakoumis* (℡04260/49 203; ❸), with popular, mock-traditional rooms spread over two rambling buildings, and spectacular views from wooden terraces. Another bend uphill stands the blindingly white rooms of *Dhimitris Angelikas* (℡04260/49 588 or 097/4044364; ❸) – the same family manages the fish **taverna**, widely praised for consistent quality, just above the Mylopótamos parking area. Finally, about halfway back towards the Ayía Paraskeví quarter of Tsangarádha, there's the *Hotel Tsangarada* (℡04260/49 014, ℻49 763; mid-June to mid-Sept; ❹), which has large if anodyne white-tile rooms with views and (mostly) balconies.

If you want more solitude, try **Fakístra beach**, the next swimmable cove to the north. It's most satisfyingly reached on foot from Damoúhari, via a coastal corniche trail which takes off between two prominent stakes, fifteen minutes uphill from the latter beach. Just beyond, there's been some disruption from an illegal road threatening the *kalderími*, but persevere – the way goes through. Green-dot waymarks lead you down towards sea level through olive groves. After about half an hour, you cross Makrolítharo bay with its rocky shore and striking promontory; the path, unmarked now, continues from the far side, climbing gradually through more olives to a spectacular viewpoint taking in a cliff-cave which was purportedly another "secret school" in bygone times. Some thirty minutes past Makrolítharo, you pass the marked side-trail accessing the school, and then almost immediately the end of the road-for-the-lazy down from Ayía Kyriakí; it's unpaved the last 3km, with a tiny parking area, from which it's a few minutes more (total 80min from Damoúhari) to the cliff-girt, pea-gravel-and-sand bay with a shattered castle atop the southerly palisade.

Southeast of Mylopótamos lie two more attractive **beaches**: Limniónas and Lambinoú. Both can be reached along the coast by rough dirt track, but most people arrive via the inland village of Lambinoú, from where a paved road leads 3km down past the abandoned monastery of Lambidhónas. **Lambinoú** cove, with a snack bar, is a narrow, deep square of sand where three parties would constitute a crowd. **Limniónas** is reached via a separate track system from the monastery.

Just above the main road en route from Tsangarádha to Lambinoú, the non-descript village of Xouríkhti is the eastern trailhead for an enjoyable three-hour **hike to Miliés**. The path proper, which wends its way through a mix of open hillside and shady dell, starts about fifteen minutes southwest of the platía (follow signs to Áyios Dhimítrios), branching left off the track system; from here on the route is obvious and well-marked, with stretches of restored *kalderími*. Before the road around the hill via Lambinoú and Kalamáki was opened in 1938, this was the principal thoroughfare between the railhead at Miliés and the Tsangarádha area. It is quite feasible to do this walk one-way and then, with an eye to bus schedules, take an afternoon KTEL back to your starting point.

The west

Lying in the "rain shadow" of the mountain, the western Pílio villages and coast have a drier, more Mediterranean climate, with olives and arbutus shrubs predominating, except in shady, well-watered ravines. The beaches, at least until you get past Kalá Nerá, are far more developed than their natural endowments merit and lack the character of those on the east side. Inland it is a different story, with pleasant foothill villages and – for a change – decent bus services. **Vyzítsa** and **Pinakátes** in particular both make good bases for car-touring or hiking.

Miliés

Like Tsangarádha, the sizeable village of **MILIÉS** (sometimes Miléës or Mileaí) was an important centre of culture during the eighteenth century. It retains a number of imposing mansions and an interesting church, the **Taxiárhis** (unpredictable hours; most likely open at 6pm), decorated throughout with brilliant frescoes. There is also a small **folk museum** (Tues–Sun 10am–2pm; free), which displays local artefacts and sponsors a crafts festival in early July.

Accommodation is somewhat limited, since most people stay nearby at Vyzítsa; the choice boils down to either a couple of pricey EOT-run mansions – the *Filippidi* and *Evangelinaki* (T04230/86 714, F90 151, ❺) – or *O Paleos Stathmos* (T04230/86 425, F86 736; ❹), accessible by *kalderími* from the main square, whose very plain rooms are only worth it if you get a balconied front unit. Quality **eating and drinking** options are limited; the simple grill, *Panorama*, occupying a wedge-shaped building just above the platía, is about the most consistent. The famous restaurant attached to *O Paleos Stathmos* has, alas, taken a sharp dive in quality since the mid-1990s and can no longer be whole-

The Pílio trenáki

A prime attraction in the western Pílio is the old *trenáki* or **narrow-gauge railway** which originally ran between Vólos and Miliés. The sixty-kilometre line, in service until 1971, was laid out between 1894 and 1903 by an Italian consortium under the supervision of engineer Evaristo de Chirico, father of the famous artist Giorgio de Chirico. The boy, born in Vólos in 1888, spent his formative years with his father on the job-site, which accounts for the little trains which chug across several of his paintings (such as *The Hour of Silence* and *The Seer's Reward*, both 1913). To conquer the maximum 2.8 percent grade and numerous ravines between Lehónia and Miliés, the elder de Chirico designed six multiple-span stone viaducts, buttressing with blind arches, tunnels and a riveted iron trestle bridge, all justly considered masterpieces of form and function. The bridge, some 700m west of the terminus in Miliés, spans a particularly deep gorge and can be crossed on a **pedestrian catwalk**; indeed, following the entire route down to Áno Lehónia is a popular three-hour walk, with occasional springs and picnic spots en route.

In 1997, after years of rumours, an excursion service, using one of the original **Belgian steam locomotives**, was resumed as a tourist attraction during weekends and holidays year-round, and several of the Belle Epoque stations restored. The train leaves Áno Lehónia on the coast at 11am, taking 90 minutes to reach Miliés, from where it returns at 5pm. Tickets are currently a hefty €13, whether you travel one-way or round trip, and go on sale at 9–9.30am. However, groups often book out the handful of carriages, so you're well advised to make enquiries at Vólos station a few days in advance. There is talk of extending the run from Lehónia to Vólos, but this would involve expensive rerouting of the track or at least prising it free from the asphalt road in which it's embedded from Káto Lehónia to Vólos.

heartedly recommended. The most distinctive food in town comes from the excellent *Korbas* bakery down by the Vólos road junction by the bus stop, which cranks out every kind of Pílio bread, pie, turnover and cake imaginable.

Vyzítsa

VYZÍTSA, 3km further up the mountain from Miliés and alive with water in streams and aqueducts, has been designated a "traditional settlement" by the EOT. It has a more open and less lived-in feel than either Makrinítsa or Miliés, though it draws surprisingly large crowds of day-trippers in summer. Nonetheless it's an excellent base, with several privatized, ex-EOT lodges in converted mansions. Pick of this **accommodation**, from the standpoint of decor and quiet, would be the *Arhondiko Vafiadi* (☎04230/86 765, ⓕ86 045; ❹ room only, ❺ B&B), two floors of very plush rooms and original art in the common areas; or the slightly plainer but airy *Arhondiko Kondou* (☎04230/86 793, ⓔvikonto@otenrt.gr; ❺), both a five-minute walk up-slope from the car-park platía. About the best value here, with the feel of staying in an *arhondikó* without the expense, is the *Thetis* (☎04230/86 111 or 04210/53 122; ❷ summer, ❸ winter), conveniently just west of the car park but calm enough, with good breakfasts included at the adjacent stone-built café. The approach road to the village is lined with more prosaically located inns; best of these are the non-en-suite *Xenonas Dimou* (☎04230/86 718, ⓕ04210/21 222; ❸), small and set back a bit from the road, with a breakfast salon; or the *Hotel Stoïkos* (☎04230/86 406, ⓕ86 061; ❹), most of whose well-executed modern rooms appointed in mock-trad style have views. Another fairly inexpensive option, and probably the last to fill at busy times, is the relentlessly modern *Rooms Afroditi* (☎04230/86 484; ❷ summer, ❹ winter), some 200m past the tiered upper platía. This, with its fountains and three plane trees, each larger than the last, offers three **tavernas**, acceptable though nothing extraordinary; probably the best eating is available at *O Yiorgaras*, out on the main road next to *Hotel Stoïkos*.

Vyzítsa sits at the nexus of a number of trails down to the coast at Kalá Nerá, which can be combined into **loop-hikes** of a half-day's duration. From the chapel of Zoödhóhou Piyís in Vyzítsa, a sporadically marked route takes you around a vast landslip zone, and then across two ravines (bridges provided) and a brief stretch of farm track until dropping to Kalá Nerá, via Aryireïka hamlet, just under two hours later (if you're going uphill, the opening to this path is conspicuously signposted). Once down on the main highway, you can bear left (east) and adopt the oblique cemetery track (actually signposted for two monasteries and Aryireïka) which begins the ninety-minute hike up to Miliés. Alternatively, and preferably perhaps, turn right (west) and complete a circuit by turning onto the well-indicated *kalderími* taking off just before the filling station, opposite the OTE circuit building. This climbs, in just over ninety minutes, to Pinakátes, almost entirely along a cleaned and meticulously restored *kalderími*, with superb views over the ravine separating Olgá hamlet from Aryireïka, and de Chirico's five-arched rail bridge there. Once in Miliés or Pinakátes, the final link back to Vyzítsa may be tricky; there is a signposted *kalderími* from Miliés, but the nominally half-hour path from the edge of Pinakátes to Vyzítsa's upper square has been damaged by a landslide halfway along, so it will probably take you closer to an hour.

Pinakátes

PINAKÁTES, tucked at the top of a densely forested ravine, was once among the least visited and most desolate of the west Pílio villages, despite being the terminus of a bus line from Vólos. No longer: the sealing of the road in from

Vyzítsa, and trendy Greeks buying up crumbling mansions for restoration, have seen to that. For the moment it remains a superbly atmospheric spot, with just enough food and lodging to make it a practical base. In the village centre there are two mansion-**inns**: the *Alatinou*, a few steps below the square (☎04230/86 995 or 097/2838282; ❹), has simple en-suite rooms with dark-wood decor and a basement breakfast salon; and the much grander *Xiradhakis* (☎04230/86 375, ✉info@dasco-hotels.gr; ❺ summer, ❻ winter), a bit further down the same lane. The shaded platía offers a single **taverna** and a little kafenío by the metal church belfry where you can sample twenty flavours of *glyká koutalioú* or "spoon sweets", but the best eating for some distance around – and where the villagers themselves prefer to hang out – is at *Iy Dhrosia* (alias *Taverna tou Papa*), at the far western edge of Pinakátes. The food – including leafy *dolmádhes* and *gídha lemonáti* – uses local, free-range meat and poultry; there are also excellent *mezédhes* available (off-menu) to accompany a *karafáki* of *tsípouro* – or a jug of their deceptively potent red bulk wine. The same friendly family also keeps small but sweet en-suite **rooms** upstairs, with wood floors and ceilings (☎04230/86 772, ◍www.filoxenia.gr; ❷ Aug, ❸ winter, ❶ otherwise; discount to Rough Guide readers).

Áyios Yeóryios to Dhrákia – and walks

The next village on the road (and bus route) west to Vólos, **ÁYIOS YEÓRYIOS NILÍAS**, should be a major walkers' mecca – except that amenities are limited to a lone platía-**taverna** and two traditional mansion-**inns**: the eighteenth-century *Arhondiko Dereli* (☎ & ⓕ 04280/93 163; ❹), a courtyarded house just below the through road; and the nineteenth-century, pricier-than-usual *Arhondiko Tzortzis* (☎04280/94 923, ⓕ94 252; ❺ summer, ❻ winter), at the start of the path up the mountain, both of them likely to be unattended without prior notice.

The **two long hikes** from here, however, are superb; both initially use the same path, but 25 minutes above the village square, at a cement aqueduct, there's a division, with a left run taking you up to the **Agriólefkes ski centre** within three-and-a-half hours, mostly through beech woods with long stretches of path underfoot. Continuing straight, following profuse red or blue paint dots/arrows (as well as the occasional sign), brings you to **Taxiárhes of Tsangarádha** within five hours. This scenic, trans-Pelion traverse goes at a much higher contour than the Xouríkhti Miliés one, attaining an elevation of 1057m at Kourvéndelis ridge, just over two hours along. The changes in landscape – from apple orchards to dense beech forest – are marvellous, drinking water abundant, and the views southeast from the heights magnificent; the main drawback is that just under half the distance is along track rather than trail, with a dreary final-hour descent from the Mylopótamos springs to the main highway.

Another, much briefer *kalderími* links Áyios Yeóryios with Áyios Vlásios, the next village downhill – no accommodation, just a taverna-café for a halt before continuing ninety minutes north on foot over a *kalderími* to **ÁYIOS LAVRÉNDIOS**, a quietly homogenous village with **accommodation**: the *Hotel Kentavros* (☎04210/96 224, ⓕ96 100; ❸ summer; ❺ winter), and the spacious, wood-floored *Rooms Thalpori* (☎04280/96 310; ❸). This has no public transport from Vólos; nor does **DHRÁKIA**, just across the top of the valley here and an hour away on foot (mostly by dirt track). At Dhrákia there are two **rooms** establishments – *Haralambos Koumoutsis* (☎04280/92 610; ❸) and *Spyridhon Mantzanis*, (☎04280/96 152; ❸), both open all year – plus you're poised for hikes onward to Hánia (90min) or Portariá (2hr 30min).

The coast

Most of the coast between Vólos and Korópi (below Miliés) is unenticing, and for much of its course the road runs well inland. At Agriá, for example, a giant Hercules Cement factory casts its shadow over rashes of hotels and neon-garish tavernas, while spilling a horrid brown sludge into the Pagasitic Gulf. The little settlements beyond are very much suburbs of Vólos, with city bus #5 plying as far as Áno Lehónia, handy for catching the weekend *trenáki* (see box on p.356). Heading southeast, things improve slightly at the little resort and narrow beach of Maláki, the first place anyone gets in the water. Olive groves line the road at Káto Gatzéa, where there are three **campsites**, of which *Hellas* (☎04230/22 267) and *Sykia* (also with bungalows, and its own beach; ☎04230/22 279; March–Oct), almost in Kalá Nerá, are the best two. The next place, Kalá Nerá is, as noted above, an important trailhead for some of the best Pílio walks, but otherwise of little intrinsic interest.

The south

Once **south** of the road linking Kalá Nerá, Miliés and Tsangarádha, Pílio becomes drier, lower and more stereotypically Mediterranean. The region was hit hard by wildfires during the mid-1990s, such that the only undamaged pine forests are found around Neohóri, southeast of Miliés; the terrain overall is less dramatic, the villages more scattered. There are, however, some interesting pockets, and considerably less tourism inland, though a number of busy coastal resorts attract a mixed clientele of foreigners and locals.

The area can be reached a little tortuously by bus or car, but much more comfortably by sea. In summer, **hydrofoils** from Vólos call at least daily at the port of Ayía Kyriakí (Tríkeri) after first pausing at the little island of Paleó Tríkeri; they used to continue to the resort of Platanía and may resume doing so in the future.

Argalastí and around

AFÉTES is the first village encountered on the land approach, and worth the brief detour for its vast platía with five plane trees, ornate church, dinner-only taverna and single-arch bridge below the car park. A few kilometres downhill lies Áfyssos, a busy resort bulging with weekend apartments for Greeks.

ARGALASTÍ, 12km southeast, is much the biggest place in the south, with a post office and shops (including two bakeries). You can **stay** a bit west of the main through road at the high-standard *Agamemnon* (☎ & ℱ 04230/54 557, Ⓔhotagam@otenet.gr; ❹ high, ❸ low season), a restored nineteenth-century mansion hotel with a swiming pool and English breakfast; it's available only through Tapestry (UK) from May to October, but open to all comers in winter. On the platía, admittedly not as attractive as some others on the mountain, *Sfindio* is the most reliable of three **tavernas**, quick-serving and reasonable, with *tsipouromezédhes* at night.

Argalastí is close to the Pagasitic Gulf, just a brief walk or drive west; a half-day loop taking in Kálamos resort (1hr west by path), Paralía Páou (fine coastal trail south) and the walled monastery of Páou (locked), just uphill. The beach at **Kálamos** is long and one of the sandiest on the Pagasitic side, but the fairly busy road runs just behind it; there are literally dozens of rooms (mostly ❹) and several tavernas, plus a discernible package presence. Secluded **Paralía Paoú**, reached by a different, dead-end road if you don't walk over from Kálamos, is by contrast fine gravel, one of the best on the Pagasitic, but devoid of amenities other than a few private villas.

Potistiká to Páltsi: the east coast

Better, less developed beaches are found on the east coast, with fine views across to the islands of Skiáthos, Skópelos and (on clear days) Alónissos, though late-1990s fire damage has made their hinterlands decidedly unscenic. Closest to Argalastí, reached along a paved road (10km) via the dozy village of Xinóvryssi, is **POTISTIKÁ**. This is stunning, and just out of the burn zone, if a little windy; huge rock formations at the south end separate it from more private **Melaní**, also reachable by a rough track system from Xinóvryssi but without facilities. Potistiká has enough places to stay and eat to make it a potential base. Top two **accommodation** picks are *Bungalows The Garden* (☎04230/55 360 or 094/5516787;❸), well-kept if small studios set well inland in an orchard with ample parking, and the welcoming *Hotel Elytis* (☎ & ℱ 04230/54 482 or 097/7735775; ❸), all of whose bland, white-tiled rooms face the sea, with heating for year-round operation and one of the only full-service **tavernas** here (*Aïdhonofolies*, next to *The Garden*, is the other).

The beach at **Páltsi** lies 12km from Argalastí via a partly paved turning from the Xinóvryssi road (it's officially signposted at points as "Áyios Konstandínos"). The sandy beach is marred somewhat by a reef in the middle, but the edges are fine, with islets and outcrops to dive off or swim towards. Melaní beach can also be reached by a marked dirt track (3km) from the inland side of Páltsi hamlet.

Páltsi facilities comprise three independent **tavernas**, two of them inland (of these *Levendis* by the chapel has cheap, sustaining *mayireftá*), and a single, somewhat overpriced **hotel**, *Erovios* (☎04230/54 210; ❹), a ziggurat-like 1970s structure whose main selling point is its large seaview balconies; at the time of writing it's in the throes of a management change and faces an uncertain future, so ring first. Otherwise there are a few **rooms**, for example *Olga* (☎04230/55 300;❷) right behind the beach.

Hórto to Marathiá via Láfkos: the west coast

Continuing due south from Argalastí, you reach the sea again after 7km at **HÓRTO**, a quiet little resort largely protected from exploitation by its mediocre beaches. **Accommodation** is mostly self-catering, and handled by tour companies; three **tavernas** intersperse themselves among a like number of coves here.

Just 3km further, **MILÍNA** is far more commercialized, attended mostly by folk from Vólos, with a half-dozen **accommodation** establishments on the water (such as *Xenon Athina* ☎04230/65 473; ❸), many more in the backstreets and four or five bona fide **tavernas**, none really standing out. There's also a hillside olive-grove **campsite**, the *Olizon* (☎04230/65 236), though this tends to be monopolized by caravans all summer. The beach, moreover, is the scanty Pagasitic norm; Milína is mostly a place to watch magnificent sunsets over the offshore islets and distant mainland ridges. Of potentially more interest is the local travel agency To Pilioritiko (☎04230/65 471), which organizes walking tours locally and is also the trading office of the recommended Houses of Pelion agency (see "Basics").

Milína is also one terminus of a pair of hour-long *kalderímia* linking the coast with the inland village of Láfkos, which can be combined for an enjoyable circuit. Beginning from the church on the shore road in Milína, head ten minutes inland along the side road until you see the recently restored *kalderími* erupting in an olive grove; from Láfkos, the return route starts at the far end of its platía, exiting the village from its lowest houses.

LÁFKOS itself is a handsome, ridgetop village graced by another respectable, car-free platía with a record number of plane trees in residence and a few cafés; more interesting perhaps, on the lane in from the south edge of the village, is one of the last wood-fired bakeries in the region. Just off the start of the path down to Milína are two high-standard restoration **inns**, both monopolized by Tapestry (UK) from May to October: the *Xenon Lafkos* (☎04230/65 017; ❺) and the even more sumptuous Arhondiko Parissi (☎04230/65 856, ℉66 098; ❺), the latter open year-round.

Beyond Milína, there are no more real villages on the coast and the landscape becomes increasingly bleak, with only the occasional weekend villa or moored boat to vary the horizon. Some 4km along, at landlocked **Valtoúdhi Bay**, yachts anchored in the lee of Alátas islet (Sunsail has an office here) are beginning to outnumber fishing boats, but the roadside *Favios* taverna at **Mávri Pétra** hamlet, 3km out of Milína, is still a reliable venue for retsina and fresh fish. About 1km past this, a side road on the right leads to the little anchorage of **Áyios Andhréas**, where the fishermen sit about talking shop and *O Pingouïnos* is another good bet for somewhat pricey fish (allow over €20 for a meal), in particular the bass-like, much-esteemed *sykiós*. All along this stretch, people tend to play on the water rather than in it, as the gulf here is apt to be warm, with plenty of flotsam and garbage washed down from Vólos. About the best swimming beach hereabouts is at **Marathiá(s)**, 7km further, where each of two rival tavernas maintains its own access drive and parking area.

The far southeast coast: Paralía Mourtiá to Kastrí

Heading east from Láfkos, you'll again find better beaches on the east-facing coast. About halfway to the Aegean you pass through **Promýri**, spilling down the slope where it's been hidden, out of sight from the sea and prying pirate eyes. After climbing northeast out of the ravine, you dip to the sea again at **Paralía Mourtiá**, a tiny but fairly attractive beach with a single rooms outfit. Most will continue one bay south to **Paralía Lýris**, bigger and sandier than its neighbour although less secluded, with a reliably open taverna and some rooms. Like most of the little coves on the coast south of Potistiká, these spots are hugely popular with German caravanners.

The main road passes through inland Lýri (no facilities) before arriving at the little port of **KATIYIÓRGIS**, the only sizeable coastal settlement in these parts, and the terminus of a twice-daily bus line from Vólos. The miniscule sandy bay here isn't great for swimming owing to the numbers of fishing boats and yachts at anchor, but Katiyiórgis makes a good lunch stop, with terrace seating opposite Skiáthos, just three nautical miles distant. The more venerable of two **tavernas** is *Flisvos* (April–Oct), with both *mayireftá* and famously fresh fish, at only slightly bumped up prices considering the number of excursion boats which call here from Skiáthos; budget €15 for a quarter-kilo of fish, two starters and a beer, served at tables on the sand. They also have cheap self-catering **rooms** upstairs (☎04230/71 071, ℉71 072; ❷ Aug, ❶ otherwise).

From 500m north of the quay, a good dirt road leaves the asphalt, heading southwest through as-yet-unburnt olives and pines, with big eyefuls of Skiáthos and Évvia across the straits. After 7km it emerges on the paved road linking Promýri and Láfkos with Plataniá and **KASTRÍ**. Bearing left leads to the latter, a protected, medium-sized sandy bay with a small **campsite** (☎04230/54 248) and a few self-catering studios, for example *Kastri* (☎04230/71 201; ❹) or *Ktena* (☎04230/71 345; ❸).

Plataniá and Mikró

Turning down and right from the above-cited junction brings you shortly to **PLATANIÁ** (sometimes spelled "Plataniás"), on the south coast of Pílio, 10km in total from Láfkos. Taking its name from the robust plane trees in the stream valley which meets the sea here, this is the biggest resort in the south after Milína, with a regular bus service (but currently no hydrofoils) from Vólos. The small beach is OK, but always oversubscribed by a mix of local and foreign holiday-makers; from the olive grove just inland an obvious path, threading spectacularly above the coast with some patches of cobbles, leads ten minutes west to the much bigger and better strand of **Mikró**. Plataniá is also a good base for longer walks, such as the six-hour loop via Láfkos and Promýri, which – while blighted by the usual proportion of useless bulldozer tracks – includes a particularly appealing stretch of *kalderími* south of Promýri.

One of the first Pílio beaches to be developed, Plataniá is essentially a collection of junta-era low-rises, but innocuous enough outside of high season. Among six licensed **hotels**, much the best and quietest is the *Platania*, east of the river mouth, on the waterfront (☎04230/71 266; ❸; open all year). At this rambling complex, all rooms have a fridge and balcony, though most with mountain rather than sea views; there are also family units suitable for four, and a respectable **taverna** (*To Steki*) on the ground floor. None of the handful of other waterside restaurants really stands out, having grown used to a not-very-discriminating clientele. Accommodation alternatives include the forbidding *Drossero Akroyiali* (☎04230/71 210, ☎71 211; ❷), whose only advantage is a car park, or the old-fashioned, secluded *Helena Apartments* in the olive grove behind the beach (☎04230/71 012; ❷), accessible by path or roundabout road, with all units en suite and some with kitchen. On the road into Plataniá there's also a large **campsite**, the *Louisa* (☎04230/71 260).

MIKRÓ is arguably more attractive as a base, and served by an 8.5-kilometre dirt road from the Láfkos–Promýri asphalt. There are some pleasant cafés on the sand, a **taverna** up the slope and a single **rooms** outfit, the *Mikro* (☎04230/71 212; ❸).

Tríkeri

Forming a "crab claw" at the extreme southeast end of Pílio, the semi-peninsula of **Tríkeri** still feels very remote. During the Greek War of Independence, the Trikeriots put their considerable fleets at the disposal of the insurrection. More recently, the area was used after the 1946–49 civil war as a place of exile for political prisoners (along with the island of Paleó Tríkeri), and until a few years ago there was no real road connecting it with the rest of Pílio. It now boasts the best highway in Pílio, connecting it with Milína in less than thirty minutes. There are a couple of daily buses from Vólos, but the area can also be reached by hydrofoil from Vólos or the Sporades (daily June to mid-Sept; perhaps a few weekly May & autumn); for current information ring the local agent, Yeroyiannis (☎04230/91 251).

The hilltop village of **TRÍKERI** (called simply "Horió" in local parlance) has few amenities for outsiders other than some simple, evening-only kafenía and grills on the little square, shaded in this arid climate by pea-family trees rather than the usual planes. The new road has prompted a spate of cement construction and re-roofing, and donkeys as a mode of transport are on the wane, but the half-hour *kalderími* down to the port of **AYÍA KYRIAKÍ** is still well used (drivers face a winding, 6km road). This is principally a working fishing village, something of a rarity in modern Greece, and much the most attractive spot on this coast. In the local boatyard, large kaïkia, and occasionally yachts, are built in much the same way they have been for the last hundred years, continuing the seafaring tradition put to use during the War of Independence. There are a few **rooms** to rent in the backstreets and at Mýlos cove, 1km west (*O Lambis* ☎04230/91 587; ❷), but otherwise minimal concessions to tourism, perhaps because there's no good beach close by. However, multicoloured fishing boats, views across the straits to Évvia, cheap petrol for the trip out and excellent seafood combine to make it a captivating, unspoilt little spot. Facing east from the car park and bus turnaround area, you can see three **tavernas**, the best being the easternmost, *Mouragio*; their fish is reliably fresh and unfarmed, though as everywhere in Pílio within reach of Vólos, not as cheap as you might think.

Paleó Tríkeri islet

"Horió" is something of a walkers' focus, with intact if shadeless paths 45 minutes northeast to Kóttes ("Chickens"), the winter port, and two hours north to Alogóporos ("Ford of the Horse"), a pebble cove and informal crossing point for **Paleó Tríkeri** (also called Nisí Tríkeri – Tríkeri island – and Nisí Panayías, after the main monastery dedicated to the Virgin). This island was the original site of Tríkeri, inhabited from prehistoric times until sixteenth-century piracy compelled its abandonment and the move to "Horió". Today there's a population of under a hundred, two places to stay, a couple of tavernas and clean sea – which perhaps makes Paleó Tríkeri the smallest Greek island with everything you really need. Little more than 2.5km from end to end, it consists of a few olive-covered hills and a fringe of small, rocky beaches.

The port and lone village of **Aï-Yiánni**, is tiny, with a single shop and a good independent **taverna** by the harbour. Following a track up from the village for around ten minutes, you reach the nineteenth-century **Evangelistrías monastery** (daily nominal hours 8am–3pm & 6–8pm), home to just an elderly lady caretaker who may let you stay the night, at the centre of the island. Past here, you reach a large bay and the lone **hotel**, the *Palio Tríkeri* (☎04230/91 432; ❸; April–Sept), with a restaurant overlooking the water. The *Galatia Apartments* (☎04230/55 233 or 55 505; April–Oct) are high-standard studios suitable for two (❷) to five (❺) persons.

Besides the hydrofoil services detailed above, you can reach Paleó Tríkeri by getting to Alogóporos via the newish dirt track from just north of "Horió" – which cuts across the path – and hailing a **small boat** to come fetch you from the far side of the narrow strait here. You might also phone one of the two lodgings or the *Skala* taverna (☎04230/55 240), who will provide a free **shuttle** if you eat there.

Lárissa

LÁRISSA stands at the heart of the Thessalian plain: a large market centre approached across a prosperous but dull landscape of wheat and corn fields. It is also a major garrison town: army camps surround it, the airport remains reserved for use by the Greek Air Force, and the Thessalonian writer Yorgos Ioannou, rusticated here in 1958 as a teacher, slammed Lárissa as an "arrogant, nouveau-riche provincial town full of horrific army officers and their majestic wives". The southwestern part of the city – for such it is now, with nearly half a million inhabitants – is dominated by ranks of military housing, and a particularly nasty piece of graffiti by the north–south through road ("A bullet in the head for every Turk") would seem to suggest that international peace and friendship is not uppermost on everyone's minds here.

Despite such unpromising impressions, undeniably modern and unremarkable Lárissa retains a few old streets that hint at its less recent past as ancient/Byzantine Larissa, and later an Ottoman provincial capital called Yenişehir. The highest point of the town – the ancient acropolis of Áyios Ahíllios – is dominated by the remains of a medieval **kástro** (closed to the public) and the foundations of an ancient **Athena temple**. Just south and below are the excavated and fairly impressive remains of the **ancient theatre**. Further south in the flatlands, the city centre consists of a pair of landscaped squares (Sapká and Makaríou), connected by pedestrianized streets lined with the usual upmarket boutiques.

Save an hour for the **archeological museum** at 31-Avgoústou 2 (Tues–Sun 8.30am–3pm; free), with its fascinating collection of Neolithic finds and grave *stelae*. The modern Greek paintings in the **Pinakothíki** (Tues–Sun 10.30am–2.30pm & 5.30–8.30pm, Sat & Sun am only; €0.40), at Roosevelt 59, are considered second only to those in the National Gallery in Athens. Otherwise, the **Alkazar** park beside the Piniós, Thessaly's major river, remains relatively cool throughout the summer, when Lárissa as a whole bakes.

As a major **road and rail junction**, the town has efficient connections with most places you'd want to reach: Vólos to the east; Tríkala and Kalambáka to the west; Lamía to the south; the Vale of Témbi (see below), Mount Olympus and Thessaloníki along the national highway to the northeast. The main **KTEL** is on Yeoryiádhou, about 200m east of the acropolis, but all buses towards Tríkala leave from a substation on Iróön Polytekhníou southwest of the centre, near the military housing, and a few other random services use a third stop on Ptoleméou, opposite the **train station**, 1km southeast of the central plazas.

You probably won't need or choose to stay in Lárissa, but if you do there are numerous, often pricey **hotels**. Among a trio of D-class places in the square by the train station, the *Pantheon* (☎0410/236 726; ❷) is probably the most appealing. More central, savoury options, also handy for the main KTEL station, include the *Lido* at Iféstou 2 (☎0410/255 097; ❸), more or less opposite the ancient theatre, or the *Acropole* nearby, towards the river at Venizélou 142 (☎0410/536 315; ❷–❹). For a bit more comfort, the *Adonis* on Alékou Papagoúli 8A (☎0410/534 648; ❹) is fine, its underground garage a blessing in a town with difficult parking.

As so often in untouristed parts of the mainland, **eating** is more apt to be rewarding than staying. By far the best lunch stop is *Tsipouradhiko To Spitaki*, 3km northeast in the suburb refugee village of Yiannoúli (#17 or #9 city bus). At no. 45 (west side) of the through road, it's the sort of place where local business- and tradesmen drink the afternoon away, but everyone's welcome and the fare – strong on seafood – is some of the best on the mainland: *toúrsi* (pickled vegetables) and salt herring included with your *karafáki*, *tyrokafterí*, fried vegetable slivers, butterflied fresh sardines in herbs, lemon and oil, plus a house sweet for about €11. Back in town, the *kultúra* taverna niche is occupied by *Rodhi* (daily except Sun/Mon lunch), on a little alley just off Filellínon on the acropolis hill, where carefully presented *mayireftá* will run €15 and up. It's the only real eatery along pedestrianized Filellínon, home to much of Lárissa's after-dark bar and café life. Trendy daytime cafés are on Platía Makaríou, which features several fountains, flowerbeds and statues, plus tables shaded by smart white umbrellas.

North towards Mount Olympus: the Vale of Témbi and the coast

Travelling north from Lárissa, the motorway heads towards Thessaloníki, a highly scenic route through the **Vale of Témbi**, between mounts Olympus and Óssa, before emerging on the coast. Accounts of the valley and the best of the **beaches** east of Mount Óssa follow; for details on Mount Olympus, see p.476. If you are driving, be aware that the upgrading programme for the motorway has now reached the Vale of Témbi – and more or less stalled there while some gargantuan tunnels are bored. This means highly dangerous, two-lane conditions, best avoided at night, between Lárissa and Kateríni until at least 2004.

Ambelákia

If you have time, or a vehicle, a worthwhile first stop in the Témbi region is **AMBELÁKIA**, a large village in the foothills of Mount Óssa. During the eighteenth century, this community supported the world's first **industrial co-operative**, producing, dyeing and exporting textiles, and maintaining its own branch offices as far afield as London. With the co-operative came a rare and enlightened prosperity. At a time when most of Greece lay stagnant under Ottoman rule, Ambelákia was largely autonomous; it held democratic assemblies, offered free education and medical care and even subsidized weekly performances of ancient drama. The brave experiment lasted over a century, eventually succumbing to the triple ravages of war, economics and the industrial revolution. In 1811 Ali Pasha raided the town, and a decade later any chance of recovery was lost with the collapse of the Viennese bank in which the town's wealth was deposited.

Until World War II, however, over six hundred mansions survived in the town. Today there are just 36, many in poor condition but some finally benefiting from renovation. You can still get some idea of the former prosperity by visiting the **Mansion of George Schwarz**. The home of the co-operative's last president, this *arhondikó* (Tues–Sat 8.45am–3pm, Sun 9.30am–2.30pm; €1.80) is built in grand, old-Constantinople style. The exterior has been admirably restored, and the charming Ottoman-Rococo interior is also currently undergoing conservation work. Schwarz, incidentally, was a Greek, despite the German-sounding name, which was merely the Austrian bank's translation of his real surname, Mavros (Black).

Without being twee, Ambelákia is an attractive, un-self-conscious place, with a cobbled high street, a couple of old fashioned bakeries and three *psistariés* on the plane-and-mulberry-shaded square. The middle one, *O Platanos*, also offers simple **rooms** in a quiet house (☎04950/93 130; ❶); there are more available through the Women's Agrotourism Co-operative (☎04950/93 401; ❶), visitable in person at their café, *To Rodi*. There's also a mock-traditional **hotel**, the *Ennea Mousses* (☎04950/93 405; ❹), on the left entering town just before the square, but like so many mansion-lodges on Pílio, this operates on demand only and if you're intent on staying there, ring the owner first in Lárissa (☎0410/550 744).

The town is connected by bus with Lárissa (3 daily); or you can walk up a cobbled way in about an hour from the Témbi train station, part of the recently designated **O2 long-distance trail**. This continues within three hours to Spília village, high up on Mount Óssa, and from there over the top to Stómio or Karítsa.

The Vale of Témbi

Two kilometres beyond the Ambelákia turn-off, you enter the **Vale of Témbi**, a valley cut over the eons by the Piniós, which runs for nearly ten kilometres between the steep cliffs of the Olympus (Ólymbos) and Óssa ranges. In antiquity it was sacred to Apollo and constituted one of the few possible approaches into Greece – being the path taken by both Xerxes and

Alexander the Great – and it remained an important passage during the Middle Ages. Walkers might consider a hike along the valley, which can also be traversed by canoe on the Piniós. However, both motorway and railway forge through Témbi, impinging considerably on its beauties. Halfway through the vale (on the right, coming from Lárissa) are the ruins of the **Kástro tís Oreás** (Castle of the Beautiful Maiden), one of four Frankish guardposts here, while marking the northern end of the pass is a second **medieval fortress** at Platamónas (summer Tues–Fri 8am–7pm; winter Tues–Fri 8.30am–5pm; all year Sat & Sun 8.30am–3pm), also Crusader-built. An impressive citadel, it's been restored for use in the Olympos Festival (July–Aug), while a new rail tunnel has been bored right under it. A steep dirt track leads to it from the busy main highway, for the expected views.

Platamónas marks the beginning of **Macedonia** and heralds a rather grim succession of dull resorts fronting the narrow, pebbly beaches of the Thermaïkós Gulf. The coast south of the castles is a better bet. Inland, the mountain spectacle continues, with **Mount Olympus** (Óros Ólymbos) casting ever-longer shadows; the trailhead for climbing it is Litóhoro (see p.476).

Stómio and the Óssa coast

A side road, close by the Kástro tís Oreás, takes you the 12km to **STÓMIO**, an unexceptional seaside village near the mouth of the river Piniós. The beach here is a relatively new phenomenon – a 1950s flood changed the river's course, creating a vast sandspit behind the abandoned riverbed. The dense beech trees of Óssa march down almost to the shore, masking some of Stómio's more uninspired recent construction; the place is cheerfully downmarket and resolutely Greek working-class, though an influx of EU money has resulted in cosmetic "improvements". The marshes flanking the old river-branch make the beach a fine spot for bird-watchers, and swimmers can bathe in clear waters, while gazing at Mount Olympus.

Outside July and August – when Stómio draws big crowds from the hinterland – you shouldn't have any trouble finding **accommodation**, though rooms closest to the waterfront are apt to be noisy. Much the best choice is the ebulliently welcoming *Hotel Panorama* (T04950/91 345 or 094/4288581; ❷), in a calm uphill setting; all rooms have orthopedic beds, veranda access and ceiling fans, while some allow for self-catering. The municipal beachside **campsite** divides into two zones: one fenced with showers and power hook-ups for caravans, the other free, with cold taps and toilets only, squalid and used mostly by impecunious tenters and the occasional gypsy party. Of the four **tavernas** on the seafront road leading to the fishing port, the furthest – *To Tsayezi* ("River-mouth" in Turkish) – has squirmingly fresh fare, *krítamo* (samphire) garnish and normal prices; *Iy Gorgona* is a likely alternative. A few bars, like *O Faros* just below the *Panorama*, offer a semblance of nightlife.

Down the coast towards Pílio, towards which the road is entirely paved, Koutsoupiá and Kókkino Neró have smaller beaches and serve as rather scruffy resorts for Larissans and Trikalans. **Ayiókambos** and **Velíka**, east and southeast of the attractive Óssa hill villages of **Ayiá** and **Melívia**, have long sandy beaches and get a more international crowd. All four villages are served by bus from Lárissa; for **accommodation** try the *Golden Beach* (T04940/51 222; ❺) at Ayiókambos, which has a pool and tennis courts, or the modest eight-room *Melivia Beach* (T04940/51 128; ❷) on the shore at Velíka. There are also three licensed campsites in the area.

West from Lárissa: Tríkala, the Pýli region and the route to Árta

West from Lárissa, the road trails the river Piniós to **Tríkala**, an enjoyable provincial town with a scattering of Byzantine monuments nearby. For most travellers, it's simply a staging post en route to Kalambáka and the Metéora; frequent buses join it with Lárissa, and there are connections north and west as well. The rail line linking Lárissa, Tríkala and Kalambáka was refitted with standard-gauge track in the year 2000, but it seems unlikely that a projected high-speed train link from Vólos to Igoumenítsa through the Píndhos mountains will ever materialize.

Tríkala

TRÍKALA is quite an attractive and manageable (pop. 60,000) metropolis compared to most of Thessaly; it's evenly divided by the Lethéos, a tributary of the Piniós, and backed by the mountains of the Kóziakas range rising abruptly to the west. Tríkala was the capital of the nineteenth-century Ottoman province and retains quite a few houses from that era, in the Varoúsi district below the fortress clocktower at the north end of town. Downriver from the bus station on the same bank, the **Koursoun Tzami**, a minaret-less yet very stately and recently restored sixteenth-century mosque, also survives, a graceful accompaniment to the town's numerous stone churches; by 2002 it should be open to the public.

The town's inner **fortress**, a Turkish and Byzantine adaptation of a claimed fourth-century BC foundation, is closed to the public except for special events, but the outer walls host attractive gardens and a pleasantly shaded terrace café. Down in the flatlands, on busy Saráfi, lie the meagre, half-excavated remains of a **sanctuary of Asclepius**; according to some accounts, the cult of the healing god originated here in ancient Trikke. The liveliest part of town, encompassing what's left of the old **bazaar**, are the streets around the central Platía Iróön Polytekhníou on the riverside, with a statue of local hero Stefanos Sarafis, commander of ELAS during the civil war. Rebétika great Vassilis Tsitsanis (see p.1063 in Contexts) also hailed from here, and he too is honoured by the street bearing his name, heading east from the platía.

Practicalities

The **post office** is situated off Platía Iróön Polytekhníou, as are several **banks** with cash dispensers. The **bus station** is on the west bank of the river, 300m southeast of the square; the main **taxi** ranks are on Iróön Polytekhníou and its continuation across the river, Platía Ríga Feréou. As ever, drivers should be mindful of the pay-and-display **parking** scheme, easily enough avoided by parking slightly out of the centre.

Accommodation, as usual for untouristed mainland towns, is problematic; the cheapest, non-en-suite hotel, the *Palladion* (☎04310/28 091; ❸), still vastly overpriced, lies within sight of the two squares at Výronos 4. Three "mid-range" alternatives are pretty comparable in price, so you may as well plump for the most distinctive and historic of them: the 2000-refurbished, Neoclassic *Panellinion* at one corner of Platía Ríga Feréou (☎04310/73 545, ℉27 350; ❺), away from traffic noise. Dating from 1914, it hosted leading Greek politicians and artists of the era, and served as the Italian and German HQ during World War II. En-suite rooms are parquet-floored and air-conditioned, some with balconies and small tubs; there's a mezzanine bar and a decent ground-floor restaurant, the *Aigli*.

Other **eateries** are scattered throughout the town, on either bank of the river. A good, cheap *mayireftá* lunch can be had between bus connections at *Katarahias*, Óthonos 10, by the KTEL; another west-bank possibility is *Pliatsikas* on Iouliéttas Adhám 8, which runs perpendicular to Karnasíou and roughly parallel to Asklipíou. Pedestrianized Asklipíou itself, forging southwest from Ríga Feréou towards the train station, is the town's daytime social hub, with plenty of fancy cafés and *zaharoplastía* to choose from. Near the train station, at Pýlis 2, *Hani* (supper only) occupies an old inn, specializing in casserole and fried dishes more than grilled items. Around the east-bank Platía Ethnikís Andístasis, opposite Ríga Feréou, are a few tavernas with riverside seating, such as *Psatha* and the carnivorous *Psitopolio Kostaras*.

Pýli

It takes some exercise of will to delay immediate progress to Kalambáka and the Metéora. Byzantine aficionados, however, may be tempted by a detour to **PÝLI**, 19km southwest of Tríkala, for the thirteenth-century church of **Pórta Panayía**, one of the unsung beauties of Thessaly, in a superb setting at the mouth of a gorge. Nearby, there is an outstanding cycle of frescoes at the monastery of **Ayíou Vissaríonos Dousíkou** (men only admitted), which would be a major tourist attraction were it not overshadowed by its spectacular neighbour, Metéora.

Regular **buses** run to Pýli from Tríkala, almost hourly during the day. Near Pórta Panayía and beside a fountain-fed oasis on the north bank there are two simple **psistariés** – a nicer lunch stop than Tríkala; one of these, the *Porta Panayia*, has a single room for rent (❶). Pýli village across the river can offer only a rather drab, overpriced **hotel**, the *Babanara* (☎04310/22 325; ❹). Just upstream from the village on the south bank, near the old bridge, *Taverna Kamara* has excellent trout and salads, but check bills (which shouldn't much exceed €9 per person) carefully – as foreigners have been overcharged here.

Pórta Panayía

The church of **Pórta Panayía** (daily: summer 8am–noon & 4–8pm; winter 9am–noon & 3–5pm; €1.20) is a ten-minute walk uphill from the bus stop in Pýli village. Cross the Portaïkós River on the footbridge, then bear left on the far bank until you see its dome in a clump of trees below the north-bank frontage road; cars must use a slightly longer route via a one-lane vehicle bridge. The caretaker lives in a white house below the nearby tavernas.

Much of the church was completed in 1283 by one Ioannis Doukas, a prince of the Despotate of Epirus. Its architecture is somewhat bizarre, in that the current narthex is probably a fourteenth-century Serbian remodelling of the original dome and transept. The original nave on its west side collapsed in an earthquake, and its replacement to the east gives the whole a "backwards" orientation. In the Doukas section, perpendicular barrel vaults over a narrow transept and more generous nave lend antiseismic properties, with further support from six columns. The highlights of the interior are a pair of **mosaic icons** depicting the adult Christ plus Mary and the Child, and a marble iconostasis. The **frescoes** have fared less well, with many of the figures blackened by fire and barely discernible. The most interesting image is next to the tiny font, over Ioannis Doukas's tomb, where a lunette shows the Archangel Michael leading a realistically portrayed Doukas by the hand to the enthroned Virgin with Child; there's also an interesting, late Holy Trinity over the apse, showing the influence of the Renaissance.

A kilometre upstream, easiest reached along the Pýli bank of the river, a graceful **medieval bridge** (currently scaffolded) spans the Portaïkós at the point where it exits a narrow mountain gorge. A couple of cafés and snack bars take advantage of the setting; the whole area being a very popular weekend outing venue for the locals, so that its tranquil beauty is best appreciated on a weekday. You can cross the bridge to follow paths some distance along the gorge on the opposite side; the EU Leader II programme is currently cleaning and marking more to make long traverses possible on Mount Kóziakas.

Ayíou Vissaríonos Dhousíkou

The monastery of **Ayíou Vissaríonos Dhousíkou** – known locally as Aï-Vissáris – has a stunning setting, 500m up a flank of Mount Kóziakas, looking out over most of Thessaly. The small community of monks seems keen to maintain its isolation, excluding women from visits and admitting foreign men with occasional reluctance. In theory, visits are allowed from 8am to noon and 3.30pm to 7pm (3–6.30pm in winter), with preference given to Orthodox visitors and/or Greek speakers. To reach the monastery, cross the single-lane road bridge over the Portaïkós as if heading for Pórta Panayía, but turn right instead, then left almost instantly onto a signed dirt track which leads up for 4.5km. This is slowly being paved from the top down; in theory walkers will soon be able to reach the place directly from the old Pýli bridge on one of the Leader paths.

The monastery was founded in 1530 by Vissarionos (Bessarion), a native of Pýli, and contains a perfect **cycle of frescoes** by Tzortzis – one of the major painters of Mount Athos – executed between 1550 and 1558 and restored to brilliance during the early 1990s. These, and the institution as a whole, miraculously escaped damage in 1940, when two Italian bombs fell in the courtyard but failed to explode.

Originally, the monastery perched on a cliff as steep as any at Metéora, but in 1962 the abyss was largely filled in with kitchen gardens, and a new road and gate opened. This rendered ornamental the pulleys and ladder on the east wall, which like much of the place had survived intact since its foundation. In its heyday, nearly three hundred monks lived at the monastery; currently there are around ten.

The route to Árta: alpine resorts

West of Tríkala and Pýli lies a wild, impressively scenic alpine region that has long been known to Greek holiday-makers, but is beginning to pitch itself to foreigners. Villages and attractions line a surprisingly good road network, which (with just a few unmade patches) can be followed all the way to Árta, via Voulgarélli (see p.420).

Eláti, Pertoúli and Neraïdhohóri

Just 4km west of Pýli, signs indicate the turning left for the most direct, though not the best surfaced, way to Árta, via Stournareïka. Most will continue another 10km on the widest road to **ELÁTI**, a "hill station" for Trikalans and nestled in fir trees as the place-name implies. There are numerous places to stay and eat, though **accommodation** is apt to be noisy – on the upper, through highway from traffic noise, on the lower *agorá* from late-night revelling. The *Lingeri* on the upper road (T04340/71 196, F71 454; ❺ summer, ❻ winter B&B), a modern but stone-clad structure with fireplaces in some rooms, represents the highest standard here; the nearby, utilitarian *Rooms Stefania Plakia* (T04340/71 213; ❸) are more affordable, as is the *Koziakas* down on the commercial street (T04340/71 270, F71 106; ❺), whose ground-floor restaurant runs to such exotica as ostrich steak in plum sauce and an eighty-label-strong wine cellar.

Another 10km takes you past the **Pertoúli ski resort** at 1200m – all of one downhill run, plus some nordic pistes – to a junction with the side road north marked "Kalambáka 38km". The sign's grossly underestimated – it's more like 51km – but it's still a quicker way back to the Metéora region than retracing your tyre treads, and allows a satisfying circuit of mounts Kóziakas and Kerkétio via Khryssomiliá. The uplands here – the so-called Pertouliótika Livádhia – form part of the Píndhos watershed; behind you all rivers drain eventually into the Aegean, while from all points west streams find their way into the Ahelóös and eventually the Adriatic near Pátras.

PERTOÚLI village itself lies 4km west of this intersection in some of the densest stands of local fir, even more attractive and upmarket than Eláti, and with facilities priced accordingly. Among several places to **stay** and **eat**, nothing could be classed as budget; the stone-built *Arhondiko Dhivani* (☎04340/91 252, ℉91 111; ●), with a respected restaurant, is typical of offerings here. The cost-conscious might continue another 3km to **NERAÏDHOHÓRI**, the last place of any size and the end of the bus line; it's frankly more of a collection of roadside businesses, but does offer the more affordable *Hotel Niavis* (☎04340/91 201; ●). In summer both Pertoúli and Neraïdhohóri are start-points for day-long walks up the peaks immediately north.

Beyond to Tría Potámia

Just 2km west of Neraïdhohóri, the medieval roadside church of **Ayía Paraskeví** (partly open) – with its high hexagonal cupola, fine masonry and slate roof – is the last outpost of civilization. Beyond, the valley opens up dramatically to easily twice the breadth of the Karpenisiótis, with bony ridges rising everywhere above the fir forest. Most villages are tucked away up side valleys, though not remotely enough to have saved them from the pyromaniac vengeance of the German army in 1943; it's lonely country, with only the occasional goatherd and his flock for human scale.

At **Tría Potámia**, the Aspropótamos descending from Timíou Stavroú and the Komnaïtikos you've been following unite to form the Ahelóös – thus the "Three Rivers" of the name. It's a popular **kayaking venue**, as numerous "put-in" signs indicate, but for how much longer is a moot point. Bearing south along 15km of dirt road to Mesahóra village takes you both back to the main Árta route and the site of Greece's **most controversial dam**. It was approved by ex-prime minister Constantine Mitsotakis back in 1993, during the dying months of his administration, in the face of strenuous opposition. If completed, it would not only flood a half-dozen upstream settlements, but a concomitant scheme would divert vast quantities of water to the Thessalian plains for agricultural use. Together these plans would doom the wetlands at the mouth of the Ahelóös, together with the birdlife and rich fisheries which depend on a reasonable flow. As of writing the European Union has pulled the financial plug on the project, and the Greek Council of State has sided with conservationist litigants, but construction does not seem to have completely ceased. Expect drastic road re-routing here in the event of rising waters.

The monasteries of Metéora

The **monasteries of Metéora** are indisputably one of the great sights of mainland Greece. These extraordinary buildings, perched on seemingly inaccessible pinnacles of rock, occupy a valley just to the north of **Kalambáka**; the name *metéora* means literally "rocks in the air", and *kalabak* is an Ottoman Turkish word meaning roughly the same thing. Arriving at the town, your eye is drawn inexorably towards the outermost of these weird grey cylinders. Overhead to the right you can make out the closest of the monasteries, Ayíou Stefánou, firmly ensconced on a massive pedestal; beyond stretches a chaos of pinnacles, cones and stubbier, rounded cliffs. These are remnants of river sediment which flowed into a prehistoric sea that covered the plain of Thessaly around twenty-five million years ago, subsequently moulded into bizarre shapes by the combined action of fissuring from tectonic-plate pressures and erosion by the infant Piniós River.

Some history

The Meteoran monasteries are as enigmatic as they are spectacular. Legend has it that **St Athanasios**, who founded Megálou Meteórou (the Great Meteoron) – the earliest of the buildings – flew up to the rocks on the back of an eagle. A more prosaic version suggests that the villagers of Stáyi, the medieval precursor of Kalambáka, may have become adept at climbing, and helped the original monks up. The difficulties of access and building are hard to overstate; a German guide published for rock climbers grades almost all the Metéora routes as "advanced", even with modern high-tech climbing gear.

The earliest religious communities here appeared in the late tenth century, when groups of **hermits** made their homes in the caves that score many of the rocks. In 1336 they were joined by two monks from Mount Athos: **Gregorios**, Abbot of Magoula, and his companion, **Athanasios**. Gregorios returned shortly to Athos but he left Athanasios behind, ordering him to establish a monastery. This Athanasios did shortly after 1344, whether supernaturally assisted or not, imposing a particularly austere and ascetic rule. He was quickly joined by many brothers, including, in 1381, **John Paleologos**, who refused the throne of Serbia to become the monk Ioasaph.

The royal presence was an important aid to the **endowment** of the monasteries, which followed swiftly on all the accessible, and many of the all-but-inaccessible, rocks. They reached their zenith during the reign of the Ottoman sultan Süleyman the Magnificent (1520–66), by which time 24 of the rocks had been surmounted by monasteries and hermitages. The major establishments accumulated great wealth, flourishing on revenues of estates granted them in distant Wallachia and Moldavia, as well as in Thessaly itself. They retained these estates, more or less intact, until the eighteenth century, at which time monasticism here, as elsewhere in Greece, began to decline.

During the intervening centuries, numerous disputes arose over power and precedence among the monasteries. However, the principal factors in the Metéora's fall from glory were physical and economic. Many of the buildings, especially the smaller hermitages, were simply not built to withstand centuries of use and, perhaps neglected or unoccupied, gradually disintegrated. The grander monasteries suffered **depopulation**, conspicuously so in the nineteenth century as a modern Greek state was established to the south – with Thessaly itself initially excluded – and monasticism lost its exclusive identification with Greek nationalism and resistance to Turkish rule.

During the twentieth century the crisis accelerated after the monastic lands and revenues, already much reduced from their heyday, were taken over by the state for use by Greek refugees from Asia Minor, after the Greco-Turkish war of 1919–22. By the 1950s, there were just five active monasteries, struggling along with little more than a dozen monks between them – an era superbly chronicled in Patrick Leigh Fermor's *Roumeli*. Ironically, before their expropriation for **tourism** in the 1970s, the monasteries had begun to revive a little, attracting a number of young and intellectually rigorous brothers. Today, put firmly on the map by appearances in such films as James Bond's *For Your Eyes Only*, the four most accessible monasteries and convents are essentially showcase monuments. Only the two easterly foundations, **Ayías Triádhos** (the Holy Trinity) and **Ayíou Stefánou**, continue to function with a primarily religious purpose.

Practicalities: Kalambáka and Kastráki

Visiting the Metéora demands a full day, which means staying at least one night in **Kalambáka** or, preferably, at the village of **Kastráki**, 2km to the northwest, which wins hands down on atmosphere and situation, set as it is right in the shadow of the rocks. The older, upper quarters of the village make for pleasant strolls, and had some of their lanes repaved in 1998 with EU funding. Kastráki also offers much better value for money lodging-wise, and has two of the best local campsites.

Kalambáka

KALAMBÁKA has no particular allure, save for its position near the rocks. The town was burned by the Germans during World War II and very few pre-war buildings remain, among them the **Mitrópolis** or old cathedral. This, dedicated to the *Kímisis tís Theotókou* ("Dormition of the Virgin"; daily 8am–1pm & 4–8pm; €1.20), stands a couple of streets above its modern successor, at the top end of the town. It was founded in the sixth century on the site of a temple to Apollo and incorporates various classical drums and fragments in its erratically designed walls. The interior is overarched by a unique, coffered-wood ceiling and dominated, equally unusually for a Greek church, by a great double marble pulpit in the central aisle, itself staked out by marble columns. The thirteenth- and fourteenth-century Byzantine frescoes are best preserved in the narthex, stressing the miracles of Christ's ministry (*Healing the Paralytic, The Storm on Galilee, Raising Lazarus, The Wedding at Cana*), though there's also a vivid portrayal of Hell on the south wall.

Arriving by bus or train in season, you're likely to be offered a **room** by waiting proprietors. Unfortunately, not all of them are reputable – the *Totis Rooms* in particular have generated reader complaints – so preferably hunt for accommodation independently, to avoid being cheated. This should not be difficult, as there are numerous signs on the road into town from the bus station and plenty of rather undistinguished **hotels**, most of them prone to road noise, with minimal views or character and above-average rates, reflecting the commercialization of the Metéora. The best budget choice is the welcoming *Hotel Meteora* (℡04320/22 367, ℻75 550; ❷) at Ploutárhou 13, a quiet side-street up to the right as you leave Kalambáka for Kastráki, at the foot of the extraordinary rocks. This has a wide variety of room formats, air-con/heating, and adequate parking; breakfasts are enhanced with home-made cakes and cheese, while proprietors Nikos and Kostas Gekas are a fount of information on the area, and have mountain bikes for rent. Also in the upper, most "villagey" part of town, some 700m up from the main square, near the Mitrópolis and start/end of the trail to Ayías Triádhos at Kanári 21, are the *Koka Roka Rooms* (℡04320/24 554, ✉kokaroka@yahoo.com; ❷), with rooms both en suite and not, and internet facilities. It's a classic backpackers' hangout, if a fairly salubrious one, though service at the ground-floor grill (cheap and cheerful meals from €6.50) is decidedly leisurely. If they're full – they've only a few rooms – the closest comparable option is *Alsos House* just a few steps downhill at Kanári 5 (℡04320/24 097 or 097/2544825; ❶–❷); the cheaper ground-floor rooms are gloomy but en suite, with a shared fridge – top-floor units are definitely preferable.

Mid-range options include the en-suite *Odyssion* (℡04320/22 320, ℻75 307; ❸) on the main through road at the Kastráki end of things; it's a bit of a 1960s barracks, though it has adequate parking, and the balconied rooms are fair-sized. The *Helvetia* more or less opposite (℡04320/23 041, ℻25 241; ❹) also has parking facilities, but it's a bit closer to the road and the somewhat smaller rooms are of the same grim vintage.

As with hotels, so with **restaurants**: lots of mediocre ones, used to a quick turnover of a captive audience. The *Panellinion*, with fountainside seating on the upper of two platías, is tolerable, and as a break from the carnivorous tastes of the deep mainland, the *Kreperi Lotos* at Dhimoulá 1, does both savoury and sweet crepes.

Kastráki

KASTRÁKI is twenty-minutes' walk out of Kalambáka along the busy and somewhat dangerous road; with EU funds, a proper pedestrian route is being prepared from the vicinity of the Mitrópolis. In season (May 15–Sept 15) there are regular buses throughout the day to Kastráki.

Entering the downhill end of the village, you pass the first of two **campsites** here, *Camping Vrachos* (☎04320/22 293, ℱ23 134), which offers **rock-climbing** and **hang-gliding** lessons in English: sign up on the premises. The other, *Camping Boufidhis/The Cave* (☎ & ℱ 04320/24 802; May–Oct) at the top end of the through road, is a bit more cramped but wonderfully grassy (except in a dry year) and shady for tents, incomparably set on the far side of the village with the monasteries of Ayíou Nikoláou and Roussánou rearing above. Both have swimming pools, as do the other more distant sites out on the Tríkala and Ioánnina roads – the best placed of which is probably the *Meteora Garden*, 1km southwest of Kastráki (☎04320/22 727).

The village has scores of **rooms** for rent, mostly of a very high standard, as well as five bona fide hotels. It's vital, however, to get off the main through road up to the monasteries, which has coaches rumbling through much of the day. Meeting this criterion is *Doupiani House* (☎04320/77 555, ℱ75 326, ℮doupiani-house@kmp.forthnet.gr; ❸–❹), well signposted left of the road near *The Cave*, with superb views from the pricier, front-facing air-conditioned rooms; proprietors Thanassis and Toula serve breakfast in the finest hotel garden of Kastráki, and can point walkers to the start of various hikes. *Ziogas Rooms* (☎04320/24 037; ❸), further downhill and again set well back from the road, offers large, balconied units, most with superb views and heating for winter; there's also a huge breakfast salon on the ground floor. Closer to the road, but still peaceful if you get one of the predominantly rear-facing units, is the friendly, spotless *Hotel Tsikelli* (☎04320/22 438, ℱ77 872; ❸). *The Cave* campsite also offers the remote *Villa San Giorgio* (❸), in a calm lane at the top of the village, plus noisier rooms (❷) by the campsite, with swimming-pool privileges for both.

Among about a dozen **places to eat** (overwhelmingly *psistariés*), the favourite among locals is *Yiorgos Ziogas* (dinner only), on the through road near the eponymous rooms; the interior's tiny but after dark the traffic lessens and all sit outside in the courtyard, downing excellent lamb chops, salads and dips which with drink won't cost over €10.50 per head. Runners-up, open at lunch also, include the *Plakia Gardhenia*, just below the church in the village centre, or *Iy Triandafyllia* on the road near *Camping Vrachos*, with cool seating under the trees, the food a tad cheaper than at *Ziogas* but also not quite as good. One pub-gelateria, *Alpha Beta Gamma* on the through road, provides formal **nightlife** and sweets.

Visiting the monasteries

There are six Metéora monasteries, each open to visits at slightly different hours and days (see below). To see them all in a day, start early to take in Ayíou Nikoláou, Varlaám and Megálou Meteórou before 1pm, leaving the afternoon for Roussánou, Ayías Triádhos and Ayíou Stefánou.

The road from **Kastráki to Ayíou Stefánou** is just under 10km long, often narrow and dangerous with speeding cars; if you're on foot, we recommend you follow the hiking directions given below to spare you the tarmac as much as possible – by using the trails and dirt tracks available you can avoid most of the asphalt. Ayíou Stefánou is in a cul-de-sac for both drivers and hikers; the through road signposted Kalambáka just before Ayías Triádhos is a highly indirect 5km. In season there are a number of daily buses (most reliably at about 9am and 1pm) from Kalambáka up the road as far as Megálou Meteórou/Varlaám; even taken just part of the way they will give you the necessary head start to make a hiking day manageable. Hitching is also pretty straightforward.

You may want a local **map** in addition to that provided on p.371, especially if you intend to leave the beaten track. A lot of dross is sold in Kalambáka, but the only two products worth having are sold at the newsagent on the upper platía. The *Panoramic Map with Geology* (co-produced by Karto Atelier, Switzerland and Trekking Hellas; €4.50) is aerial-view art format, but fairly accurate and good enough to follow the main routes. Andonis Kaloyirou's Greek-only text booklet, with topographic map in back (Road Editions, €11.80) is superior, and many will find the map alone worth the investment.

Before setting out it is worth buying **food and drink** to last the day; there are only a couple of drinks/fruit stands on the circuit, by Varlaám and Megálou Meteórou. And finally, don't forget to carry money with you: each monastery levies an admission charge – currently €1.50, with students half price except at Ayías Triádhos.

For visits to all the monasteries, **dress code** is strict. For women this means wearing a skirt – not trousers; for men, long trousers. Both sexes must cover their shoulders. Skirts or simple wraps are often lent to female visitors, but it's best not to count on this. Finally, it's worth noting that **photography** and **videoing** are strictly **forbidden** in all of the monasteries.

Ayíou Nikoláou Anápavsa

North of Kastráki the road threads between the huge rock outcrops of Áyion Pnévma and Doupianí, the latter named for a long-vanished chapel-hermitage, among the first monastic settlements. To avoid covering the paved road on foot, use instead the street, then track which takes off from the northwest corner of Kastráki's village square.

This deposits you, after twenty minutes, at the base of the stair-path up to **Ayíou Nikoláou Anápavsa** (April–Oct daily except Fri 9am–3.30pm; winter hours vary). A small monastery restored during the 1980s, this has some superb early sixteenth-century frescoes in its *katholikón* (main chapel) by the Cretan painter Theophanes. Oddly, the tiny *katholikón* faces almost due north rather than east because of the rock's shape. On the east wall of the naos, a shocked disciple topples over in a back somersault at the *Transfiguration*, an ingenious use of the cramped space; in the *Denial of Peter* on the door arch, the protagonists warm their hands over a fire in the pre-dawn. On the west wall of the narthex, a stylite (column-dwelling hermit) perches in a wilderness populated by wild beasts, while an acolyte prepares a basket of supplies to be hoisted up – as would have been done in real life just outside when the fresco was new. Other Desert Fathers rush to attend the event: some riding beasts, others – crippled or infirm – on litters or piggyback on the strong. As well as the Theophanes paintings there are later, naive images that show Adam naming the animals, including a basilisk – the legendary lizard-like beast that could kill by a breath or glance.

Next to Ayíou Nikoláou, on a needle-thin shaft, sit the shattered wall fragments of **Ayía Moní**, abandoned after an earthquake in 1858. Beyond this, some 250m past the parking area and steps for Ayíou Nikólaou, a cobbled and partly shaded path leads northwest from the road; fifteen minutes up this path bear right at an unsigned T-junction to reach Varlaám monastery in ten minutes, or turn left for Megálou Meteórou within ten slightly steeper minutes. There is no other direct route between the two (other than the unpleasantly cluttered access roads serving both); if you visit Megálou Meteórou first, re-descend the path to pick up the Varlaám turning.

Megálou Meteórou (Great Meteora)

The **Megálou Meteórou** (daily except Tues 9am–1pm & 3.20–6pm) is the grandest and highest of the monasteries, built on the Platýs Líthos ("Broad Rock") 615m above sea level. It had extensive privileges and held sway over the area for several centuries: in an eighteenth-century engraving (displayed in the museum) it is depicted literally towering above the others. How Athanasios got onto this rock is a mystery.

The monastery's **katholikón**, dedicated to the *Metamórfosis* (Transfiguration), is the most magnificent in Metéora, a beautiful cross-in-square church, its columns and beams supporting a lofty dome with a *Pandokrátor*. It was enlarged in the fifteenth and sixteenth centuries, with the original chapel, constructed by the royal Serbian Ioasaph in 1383, forming just the *ierón*, the sanctuary behind the intricately carved *témblon*, or altar screen. Frescoes, however, are much later (mid-sixteenth century) than those of the preceding monasteries and not as significant artistically; those in the narthex concentrate almost exclusively on grisly martyrdoms.

The other monastery rooms comprise a vast, arcaded cluster of buildings. The *kellari*, or storage cellar, holds an exhibit of rural impedimenta; in the domed and vaulted refectory, still set with the traditional silver/pewter table service for monastic meals, is a **museum**, featuring a number of exquisite carved-wood crosses and rare icons (though other precious exhibits seem to be in storage as of writing). You can also visit the ancient domed and smoke-blackened kitchen adjacent, with its bread oven and soup-hearth.

Varlaám (Barlaam)

Varlaám (daily except Thurs 9am–2pm & 3.20–5pm) is one of the earliest established monasteries, standing on the site of a hermitage established by St Varlaam – a key figure in Meteorite history – shortly after Athanasios' arrival. The present building was founded by two brothers from Ioánnina in 1517 and is one of the most beautiful in the valley.

The monastery's *katholikón*, dedicated to Ayíon Pándon (All Saints), is small but glorious, supported by painted beams and with walls and pillars totally covered by frescoes. A dominant theme, well suited to the Metéora, are the desert ascetics, and there are many scenes of martyrdom. The highly vivid *Last Judgement* (1566), has a gaping leviathan swallowing the damned, and, dominating the hierarchy of paintings, a great *Pandokrátor* (Christ in Majesty) in the inner of two domes (1544) – the outer dome has an equally fine *Ascension*. In the refectory is a small museum of icons, inlaid furniture and textiles; elsewhere the monks' original water barrel is displayed.

Varlaám also retains intact its old **ascent tower**, with a precipitous reception platform and dubious, now inactive windlass mechanism (replaced by an electric winch), though the original rope and "basket" are still used. Until the 1920s the only way of reaching most of the Meteorite monasteries was by being hauled up in a net drawn by rope and windlass, or by the equally perilous retractable ladders. Patrick Leigh Fermor, who stayed at Varlaám in the 1950s, reported a macabre anecdote about a former abbot: asked how often the rope was changed, he replied, "When it breaks."

Steps were eventually cut to all of the monasteries on the orders of the Bishop of Tríkala, doubtless unnerved by the vulnerability of his authority on visits. Today rope-baskets are used only for carrying up supplies and building materials, often supplemented by aerial cable cars bridging chasms from the nearest car park.

THESSALY AND CENTRAL GREECE | Visiting the monasteries

Roussánou

To hike from Varlaám to Roussánou, the most efficient path, with the least unneccesary altitude change and amount of road-tramping, is as follows. Proceed down the access road for Varlaám to a point about 100m past where the access drive for Megálou Metéorou joins up. Leave the road, keeping an eye out for blue-paint waymarks, and adopt paths with (except initially) decent surface underfoot; you thread around (and briefly over) some minor, rounded monoliths, the Plákes Kelaraká, until you reach the bed of a ravine, with a few puddles even in July, just above a sharp bend in the road. Cross the streambed and head briefly up the canyon on the far bank, then bear right into the trees on another path after about 50m. You'll emerge on the ascending road, right below Roussánou, some 35 minutes after leaving Varlaám, with only a final twenty-metre scramble where the path has been ruined by rubble-dumping.

More or less opposite, a well-signed and cobbled path ascends to the tiny and compact convent of **Roussánou** (daily: summer 9am–6pm; winter 9am–1pm & 3.20–6pm), also known as Ayías Varváras; there's another descending trail off a still higher loop of road, but in either case the final approach is across a dizzying bridge from an adjacent rock. Roussánou has perhaps the most extraordinary site of all the monasteries, its walls edging right up to sheer drops all around. Inside, the narthex of its main chapel has particularly gruesome seventeenth-century frescoes of martyrdom and judgement, the only respite from sundry beheadings, spearings and mutilations being the lions licking Daniel's feet in his imprisonment (near the window); diagonally across the room, two not-so-friendly lions are engaged in devouring the saint Ignatios Theoforos.

If you need to return to Kastráki directly from Roussánou, there's an excellent trail shortcut. From the lower access path, walk downhill some thirteen minutes, through the first hairpin bend, to the point by the roadside with another sharp-bend warning sign and a transformer pole. Take the path which drops from here south to the course of the Paleokraniés stream, and then follow this until you emerge at a small pumping station on the Kastráki–Ayíou Nikoláou farm track noted above. This takes about twenty minutes on foot, and saves nearly as much compared to using the road.

Ipapandí, Ayías Triádhos and Ayíou Stefánou

If you are visiting the valley in midsummer, you may by this point be impressed by the buildings but depressed by the commercialization and crowds (and the shocking amount of roadside litter), which together detract from the wild, spiritual romance of the valley. The remaining monasteries on the "east loop" are less visited, and for a real escape, you can take a short walk north from near Megálou Metéorou to the tiny hermitage of **Ipapandí**.

From the car park for Megálou Metéorou, head northeast along multiple traces visible beside a downed metal fence; after about five minutes, you'll reach a prominent pass in the ridge where several trails cross and the main, wide path begins descending, still northeast, through oak woods. This arcs twice around the tops of ravines, until some thirty minutes along you hit the rough service track going ten more minutes west towards Ipapandí, now visible wedged into its cliff-face. Its lengthy restoration was completed in late 2000, but there are not yet any resident monks to receive visitors come to admire the fine frescoes in the fourteenth-century chapel here. Until and unless this happens, the best view is from the next round-topped monolith along, with a statue of a heroic monk, a crucifix and a circular area with a flagpole. It's possible (and a popular option) to follow the dirt track southwest, then southeast as it loops around the rock formations to emerge on the main paved road between Ayíou Nikoláou and Doupianí.

From the base of Roussánou's lower access path, descend the main road for seven minutes until the first curve and then adopt the path signposted for Ayías Triádhos. After about ten-minutes' climb you reach a ridge, beyond which lies the rugged canyon called Houní Ayías Triádhos. There is no way straight across this; instead bear left, following red dots, to climb more gently to a point on the circuit road about 600m shy of your goal – this won't save a huge amount of time compared to the half-hour road walk from Roussánou, but as ever is far more pleasurable. The final approach from the parking area of **Ayías Triádhos** (daily except Thurs: summer 9am–5pm; winter 9am–12.30pm & 3–5pm) consists of 130 steps carved into a tunnel in the rock. You emerge into a light and airy compound, renovated during the 1980s. There are small displays of weavings and kitchen/farm implements, but in lieu of labelling there are maxims from Corinthians 1:13 emblazoned everywhere: "Love is Patient", "Love Does not Criticize", etc.

The frescoes in the *katholikón* have finally been completely cleaned and restored to their former glory, and fully justify a visit. On the southwest wall, the *Dormition* is flanked by the *Judgment of Pilate* and the *Transaction of Judas*, complete with the thirty pieces of silver and subsequent self-hanging. Like others in the Metéora, this church was clearly built in two phases, as evidenced by two domes, each with a *Pandokrátor* (the one by the *témblon* very fine), and two complete sets of Evangelists on the squinches. In the south arch is a rare portrait of a beardless Christ Emmanuel, borne aloft by four cherubs. Relatively few tour buses stop here, and the life of the place remains essentially monastic, even if there are only four brothers to maintain it – including the voluble senior monk Ioannis, who has been here since 1975 and who, he will proudly tell you, was cured of blindness in one eye by the Virgin (though he lost the other).

Ayíou Stefánou (Tues–Sun 9am–1pm and 3.20–6pm), the last and easternmost of the monasteries, is fifteen-minutes' walk beyond here (no path shortcut possible), appearing suddenly at a bend in the road. Again it is active, occupied this time by nuns (who are keen to peddle trinkets), but the buildings are a little disappointing, having been bombed during World War II and then occupied by the Communists during the civil war, and it's the obvious one to miss if you're short of time. That said, the fifteenth-century refectory contains an apsidal fresco of the Virgin, beyond the museum graced by a fine Epitáfios covering embroidered in gold thread.

Although Ayías Triádhos teeters above a deep ravine and the little garden ends in a precipitous drop, there is an obvious, well-signposted **path** from the bottom of the monastery's access steps which leads back to **Kalambáka**. This is about a 45-minute descent, saving a long trudge back around the circuit; it's a partly cobbled, all-weather surface in decent shape. By contrast, the old trail towards Kalambáka from Ayíou Stefánou is said to be disused and dangerous – you would have to find a safe way to the chapel of Análipsi, from where a track descends to town.

Other local walks

Once they've toured the monasteries, many visitors – especially during low season – are seduced into staying an extra day by the otherworldly scenery. There are a number of other hikes to hidden attractions on and around some of the lesser monoliths, where you're virtually assured of solitude.

One of the easier walks is to the **cave-chapel of Áyion Pnévma**. From the Kastráki platía, get onto the fieldstoned lane just above and north, heading northeast towards the last house on this side of the ravine dividing the village. Behind it a clear but unmarked path heads off into the wilds. Once through the last abandoned fruit and nut groves, this route enters scrub and boulder falls, with the wall-like Áyion Pnévma monolith to your left. Roussánou pops into sight as the path excecutes a hairpin and begins scaling a ravine, essentially a fissure in the side of the rock. Some 35 minutes out of town you'll reach a level spot overhung by the monolith on two sides; to the right (west) the cave-chapel of Áyion Pnévma has been dug out of the rock strata. This was once a hermit's quarters, and inside – otherwise all whitewash and modern icons – you'll see a sarcophagus for his (vanished) bones, again carved from the rock. To the left of the chapel door is the rain cistern which supplied the hermit; the adept can scramble a few minutes further, onto the rock surface with the metal belfry, for superb views.

A slightly more advanced stroll – though still not quite up to abseiling standard – is the steep scramble from the edge of Kastráki up to the partly frescoed **cave-church of Áyii Apóstoli**, the highest sacred monument of the Metéora atop its 630-metre namesake monololith. From beside the prominent village cemetery, a good path leads steeply up for fifteen minutes to the obvious "finger" of Adrakhtí; the easy going is over now, and you must find the hard-to-spot continuation of the route up the steep gully to the right, keeping to the left side. After five minutes on all fours, you reach the proper onward path. There's a ladder and a fixed chain at the trickiest point near the top, but overall this isn't an outing for the acrophobic.

Those really intent on solitude should head for the area around the **cave-chapel of Áyios Andónios**. On the southeastern outskirts of Kastráki, opposite *Taverna To Harama*, turn onto the narrow road signposted towards "Old Habitation of Kastráki" in English. Drive or walk a short distance up this, then bear right onto a one-lane cement drive which soon becomes dirt, then stops at a new but attractive chapel built in traditional style. (With a good map, you can also find your way here by track from the Kastráki cemetery.) Overhead to the east, wedged into the cliff-face, is the restored monastery of **Ayíou Nikoláou Bandóvas**, a dependency of Ayías Triádhos, now used as a hermitage; visits are not allowed, and if you approach, a huge monk with a snowy, Old Testament beard may emerge to shoo you away. But the real reason you've come here, ideally at sunset, is bang in front of you, on the side of the Pixári monolith: the cave-chapel of Áyios Andónios (alas, locked in 2001) and a series of rickety wooden platforms jammed into natural cavities in the cliff face, with half-rotten ladders dangling from them. These **askitíria** or extreme hermitages are now home only to rock-doves, but they were inhabited well into the twentieth century, and on their patron saint's day a monk used to be levered up to conduct a liturgy until the 1960s. Here then in the raw, without souvenirs, multilingual guides and tour buses, are the origins and impulse of Metéora contemplative life.

On from Kalambáka

One of the most dramatic roads in Greece forges **west** from Kalambáka, negotiating the **Katára pass** across the Píndhos mountains to Métsovo and Ioánnina. This route, taking you into northern Epirus, is covered at the beginning of the next chapter.

Another road leads **north** from Kalambáka through Grevená into Macedonia, and then forks: northwest to Kastoriá, or northeast to Siátista, Kozáni, Véria and Thessaloníki (see Chapter Five). The **Grevená-bound road** is scenic, well graded and little travelled; its only drawback is that there is just one daily bus to ghastly Grevená itself, and not a lot of other transport. Finally, there's a possible side-trip into the mountains west of Metéora to visit one of Greece's most peculiar churches.

The church of Timíou Stavroú

If you have your own transport, the flamboyant medieval **church of Timíou Stavroú**, 42km west of Kalambáka, between the villages of Kranía (Kranéa on some maps) and Dholianá, is well worth a visit. The church itself, originally eighteenth century but seeming far older, is a masterpiece of whimsy, matched in concept only by two specimens in Romania and Russia. It sports no fewer than twelve turret-like cupolas, higher than they are wide: three are over the nave, one over each of the three apses, and six over the ends of the triple transept. The church is in perfect repair, despite some hasty postwar restoration (it was badly damaged in 1943) and bulldozing, and a terrace below with a wooden table (and a water tap nearby) makes an ideal picnic spot.

To reach the church, head 10km north of Kalambáka and instead of taking the Métsovo/Ioánnina-bound highway, bear left into a narrower road at Mourgáni, the junction festooned with multiple signposts for high villages. Climb steadily over a pass on the shoulder of Mount Tringía and then drop sharply into the densely forested valley of the Aspropótamos River, one of the loveliest in the Píndhos. From the *Aspropótamos* taverna, continue 1.5km further south to a tiny bridge and a track on the left, signposted in Greek as "Prós Ierán Monín Timíou Stavroú Dholianón". This leads after 700m to the church, at a height of 1150m. There's a bus from Tríkala to nearby Kranía most days in the summer; on the village platía there's a small **hotel-taverna**, the *Aspropotamos* (☎04320/87 235; ❸), is open from June to September only.

From the church or Kraniá it's an easy matter to continue 17km further down-valley to Tría Potámia, where you can either press on southwest to Árta or carry on east through Pertoúli and Eláti to loop back to Tríkala.

Travel details

Trains

Athens–Thíva–Livadhiá–Lianokládhi (Lamía)–Lárissa
Eleven trains daily in each direction: six of these are expresses (marked IC on schedules) which may skip Thíva or Livadhiá (sometimes Lamía too), and take only four hours to reach Lárissa. Approximate non-express journey times:
Athens–Thíva (1hr 15min)
Thíva–Livadhiá (25min)
Livadhiá–Lianokládhi (1hr 10min–1hr 40min)
Lianokládhi–Lárissa (1hr 45min–2hrmin)

Lárissa–Platamónas–Kateríni–Thessaloníki
Nine daily in each direction, four of these express. Approximate journey times:
Lárissa–Platamónas (45min)
Lárissa–Kateríni (1hr 10min)
Kateríni–Thessaloníki (1hr 10min).
Lárissa–Thessaloníki (express 'IC'; 2hr)

Vólos–Athens
Two daily IC in each direction via Lárissa (5hr); through service without changing.

Vólos–Lárissa
Eleven daily slow trains in each direction (1hr 5min).

Vólos–Kalambáka
Two slow through trains daily each direction (2hr 45min).

Kalambaka–Athens
Two express trains daily each direction (5hr); through service without changing.

Kalambáka–Thessaloníki
Two express trains daily each direction (4hr); may change at Lárissa.

Buses

Buses detailed have similar frequency in each direction, so entries are given just once; for

reference check under both starting-point and destination.

Connections with Athens Dhelfí (6–7 daily; 3hr); Karpeníssi (2 daily; 6hr); Lamía (hourly; 3hr 15min); Lárissa (6 daily; 4hr 30min); Livadhiá (hourly; 2hr 10min); Thíva (hourly; 1hr 30min); Tríkala (9 daily; 5hr 30min); Vólos (10 daily; 5hr 30min).

Ámfissa to: Lamía (3 daily; 2hr 30min); Náfpaktos (4–5 daily; 2hr).

Andírio to:Agrínio (12 daily; 80min); Mesolóngi (12 daily; 40min).

Dhelfí to: Ámfissa (7 daily; 40min); Itéa (5–6 daily; 30min); Pátra (3 daily, 1 direct; 3hr).

Elefsína to: Thíva (Thebes; 2 daily; 1hr 30min).

Galaxídhi to: Itéa (5 daily Mon–Fri, 4 Sat–Sun; 30min); Náfpaktos (5 daily Mon–Fri, 3 Sat,1 Sun to Áyios Nikólaos ferry only; 1hr 15min).

Kalambáka to: Grevená (1 daily; 1hr 30min); Ioánnina (2 daily; 3hr 30min); Métsovo (2 daily; 1hr 30min); Vólos (4 daily; 2hr 30min).

Karpeníssi to: Agrínio (1 at 9am most days, extra at 1.30pm Fri; 3hr 30min); Megálo/Mikró Horió (2 daily; 15min); Proussós (Mon, Wed & Fri at 1pm; 1hr).

Lamía to: Karpeníssi (4 daily; 2hr); Lárissa (4 daily; 3hr 30min); Thessaloníki (2 daily; 4hr 30min); Tríkala, via Kardhítsa (4 daily; 3hr); Vólos (2 daily; 3hr).

Lárissa to: Kalambáka (hourly; 2hr); Litóhoro junction (almost hourly; 1hr 45min); Stómio (4 daily Mon–Fri, 5 daily weekends/hols; 1hr 25min); Tríkala (20 daily; 1hr); Vólos (hourly; 1hr).

Livadhiá to: Aráhova (6 daily; 40min); Dhelfí (6 daily; 1hr); Dhístomo, for Ósios Loukás (10 daily; 45min); Ósios Loukás, direct (daily at 12.45pm; 1hr).

Náfpaktos: frequent blue city bus to Andírio for most connections.

Thíva to: Halkídha (2 daily; 1hr 20min); Livadhiá (hourly; 1hr).

Tríkala to: Grevená (1 daily; 2hr); Ioánnina (2 daily; 4hr); Kalambáka (roughly hourly; 30min); Métsovo (2 daily; 2hr); Pertoúli, via Eláti (3 daily Mon–Fri, 2 Sat–Sun; 1hr 15min); Pýli (13 daily Mon–Fri, 11 Sat–Sun; 20min).

Vólos to: Áyios Ioánnis (2 daily; 2hr 30min); Makrinítsa (10 daily; 50min); Miliés (6 daily Mon–Fri, 5 Sat–Sun; 1hr); Milína via Hórto (5 daily; 1hr 40min); Plataniá (3 daily; 2hr); Portariá (10 daily; 40min); Thessaloníki (5 daily; 3hr 20min); Tríkala (4 daily; 2hr 30min); Tríkeri (2 daily; 2hr 30min); Tsangarádha (2 daily; 2hr); Vyzítsa (6 daily Mon–Fri, 5 Sat–Sun; 1hr 10min); Zagorá (4 daily; 2hr).

Zagorá to: Horeftó (4 daily; 15min).

Ferries

Áyios Konstandínos to: Alónissos (1daily; 4hr 40min); Skiáthos (1–2 daily; 2hr 30min); Skópelos (1–2 daily; 3hr 30min). ☎02350/31 759 for port police, ☎31 614 for current agent.

Vólos to: Alónissos (1–2 daily; 5–6hr); Skiáthos (2–4 daily; 2hr 30min–3hr); Skópelos (2–4 daily; 4–5hr). Also one weekly service to select Cyclades and Crete (Iráklio). ☎04210/20 336 for Sporádhes service, ☎04210/31 059 for long-haul services, ☎04210/38 888 for port police.

To Évvia Arkítsa–Loutrá Edhípsou (at least hourly July–Sept 15, every 1–2hr otherwise, last at 10–11pm/8–9pm; 45min); Glýfa–Ayiókambos (8–11 daily summer, 4 in winter; last sailing at 8.30pm/5pm; 30min).

Hánia–Trizónia (11 daily spring/autumn 7am–9pm, more in summer; 5min journey; no cars taken).

Across the Gulf of Kórinthos Andírio–Río (every 15min, much less often after midnight; 15min journey); Áyios Nikólaos–Éyio (7 times daily in summer, well-spaced 6.30am–10pm; 35–40min journey).

Catamarans

Áyios Konstandínos 1daily (evening) June to mid-Sept to Skiáthos, Skópelos, Alónissos and Thessaloníki.

Hydrofoils

Hellas Flying Dolphins run from the following ports. "In season" means June to mid-September.

Áyios Konstandínos 1 daily (mid-morning) in season to Skiáthos, Skópelos and Alónissos.

Plataniá Service currently suspended, but historically 5–6 weekly in season to Skiáthos, Skópelos and Alónissos, 4–5 weekly to Vólos.

Tríkeri/Paleó Tríkeri 1 daily in season to Skiáthos, Skópelos, Alónissos and Vólos.

Vólos 3–5 daily in season to Skiáthos, Skópelos and Alónissos last reliable departure 7pm; 1 daily (midday) calls at Tríkeri/Paleó Tríkeri.

For details of services, which vary drastically with the seasons, you are advised to contact local agents (in Áyios Konstandínos ☎02350/31 614; in Vólos ☎04210/21 626; in Tríkeri ☎04230/91 251); or call ☎010/41 99 000 for information on any route.

Epirus and the west

0   100 km

CHAPTER 4

Highlights

✳ **Ioánnina** The Ottoman citadel, lake front and island associated with locally infamous hero/villain, Ali Pasha. See p.397

✳ **Dodona** Remote and ancient theatre and ruins of the Oracle of Zeus. See p.401

✳ **The Víkos Gorge** One of the longest in Europe and a rival to its Cretan counterpart. See p.404

✳ **Zagóri** Old stone *arhondiká* (mansions) and villages set in rugged mountain scenery. See p.403

✳ **Karavostási** Perhaps the best of many good beaches on the Thesprotían coast from Igoumenítsa to Préveza. See p.426

✳ **The Ahérondas river** From the gorge at its wild upper reaches to the sea at the pleasant beach resort of Ammoudhiá. See p.430

✳ **Ancient Kassopi** Underrated but atmospheric remains of a former city-state, abandoned in 31 BC. See p.432

✳ **Byzantine monuments** These abound in and around Árta, a former autonomous Byzantine despotate; the monastic church of Panayía Vlahernón particularly stands out. See p.435

4

Epirus and the west

pirus (*Ípiros* in modern Greek) has the strongest regional identity in mainland Greece. It owes this character to an unrelentingly mountainous terrain: the rugged peaks and passes, forested ravines and turbulent rivers of the **Píndhos** (Pindus) **range**. They have always protected and isolated Epirus from outside interference, securing it a large measure of autonomy even under Ottoman rule.

Because of this remoteness, the region's role in Greek affairs was peripheral in ancient times. There are just four archeological sites of importance, two of them chosen by oracles for their isolation. At **Dodona**, the sanctuary includes a spectacular Classical theatre; at **Ephyra**, the weird remains of a Necromanteion (Oracle of the Dead) was touted by the ancients as the gateway to Hades. **Kassopi** and **Nikopolis**, both near Préveza, are more conventional ancient cities.

In more recent times, **Lord Byron** has been the region's greatest publicist. He passed through in 1809 when tyrannical local ruler Ali Pasha was at the height of his power, and the poet's tales of passionate intrigue, fierce-eyed brigandage and braggadocio sent a shiver down romantic Western spines. Byron went on to distinguish himself in the southern province of **Étolo-Akarnanía** by supplying and training troops for the Greek War of Independence, and of course by dying during it at **Mesolóngi**.

Despite eventual Greek victory in the War of Independence, the Ottomans remained in Epirus, and were not finally ousted until March 1913. A disputed

Accommodation price codes

Throughout the book we've categorized accommodation according to the following **price codes**, which denote the cheapest available double room in high season. All prices are for the room only, except where otherwise indicated. Many hotels, especially those in category ❹ and over, include breakfast in the price; you'll need to check this when booking. During low season, rates can drop by more than fifty percent, especially if you are staying for three or more nights. Exceptions are during the Christmas and Easter weeks when you'll pay high-season prices. Single rooms, where available, cost around seventy percent of the price of a double.

❶	Up to €24	❹	€43–58
❷	€24–33	❺	€59–72
❸	€34–42	❻	€73 and upwards

Note: Youth hostels and mountain refuges typically charge €7–9 for a dormitory bed. For more accommodation details, see pp.51–54.

ALBANIA

Mt. Grámmos
2520m

Plikáti

Siátista

Mt.
Smólikas

Samarína

MAKEDHONÍA

Kerásovo

Paleosélli

Grevená

Molyvdhosképastos

Kónitsa

Pádhes

Dhístrato

Pápingo

Mt.
Gamíla
2497m

Vovoússa

P
I
N
D
H
O
S

Kakaviá

Vikos
Gorge

Tsepélovo

Monodhéndhri

Katára
Pass

Kípi

ZAGÓRI

Zítsa

Mt. Mitsikéli

Métsovo

Metéora

Pérama

Lykiádhes

Kalambáka

Ioánnina

Pamvótidha

Filiátes

Sýráko

Kallarítes

Prámanda

Melissourgí

VIA EGNATIA EXPRESSWAY (UNDER CONSTRUCTION)

Dodona

E P I R U S

Mt.
Tzoumérka
2393m

Corfu
(Kérkyra)

Igoumenítsa

Paramythiá

Pláka

Lefkími

Platariá

Sývota

Karavostási

S O Ú L I

Aráknthos River

Ahelóös River

Sarakíniko

Anthoússa

Glykí

Tríkastro

Theodhóriana

Paxí

Párga

Ahérondas
River

Necromanteion of Ephyra

Voulgarélli

Ammoudhiá

Mesopótamo

Kanalláki

Paxí

Loútsa

Filipiádha

Panayía Vlahernón

Paralía Vráhou

Lygiá

Kassopi

Arta

Káto Panayía

Italy

Kremastón
Dam

Nikopolis

Koronissía

Menídhi

Préveza

Áktio

Vónitsa

Amvrakikós
Gulf

I O N I A N   S E A

Lefkádha

Páleros

Amfilohía

É T O L O -

Lefkádha

Nydhrí

Mýtikas

A K A R N A N Í A

Vassilikí

Kálamos

Lake
Ozerós

Agrínio

Hóra

Lake
Trihonídha

Átokos

Astakós

Ahelóös River

 Itháki

Fiskárdho

Fríkes

Oeniadae

Etolikó

Pleuron

Ássos

Itháki

Mesolóngi

Kefalloniá

Tourlídha

N

0   25 km

Sámi

Argostóli

frontier territory throughout the nineteenth century, the region never recovered its medieval prosperity. When the Italians invaded in 1940, followed by the Germans in 1941, the Pindus mountains became first a stronghold of the Resistance, then a battleground for rival political factions and finally, after 1946, the chief bastion of the Communist Democratic Army in the **civil war**. The events of this period (see the box below) are among the saddest of modern Greek history, and still reverberate today, not least in Epirus's consistent ranking in European Union studies as one of the poorest parts of Western Europe.

However, for visitors the **mountains** remain the best place to head for in Epirus. The people – especially away from the most visited spots – are friendly and hospitable, and certain aspects of their traditional way of life are still in

World War II and the civil war in Epirus

In **November 1940**, the **Italians** invaded Epirus, pushing down from Albania as far as Kalpáki, just south of Kónitsa. United as a nation for the first time in decades, the Greeks repulsed the attack and humiliated Mussolini. However, the euphoria was short-lived as the following April the Germans attacked and rapidly overran Greece. When parcelling out various portions of the country to their allies for administration, the Germans initially assigned Epirus to the Italians, who trod lightly in the province where they had recently been so soundly beaten. After Mussolini's capitulation in September 1943 the Germans assumed direct responsibility for Epirus, and conditions worsened. Together with the mountains of central Greece to the south, the Epirot Píndhos was the main staging point for various **partisan bands**, foremost among them the Communist-dominated **ELAS**. Resistance, harassment and ambush of the occupying forces incurred harsh reprisals, including the burning in early 1944 of essentially every village along the Aóös River.

The wartime flight to the cities from the mountains dates more or less from these atrocities, and the vicissitudes of the subsequent **civil war** (1946–49) dashed any lingering hope of a reasonable existence in the mountains. Victims of reprisals by either the Communists or the Royalist/Nationalist central government, villagers fled to safety in the cities, and many never returned. In the backcountry, off the tourist-trodden byways, you'll still hear older people talk of these times. Some blame the Communists, some blame the Nationalists and all blame the British: "They set us at each other's throats," many will say, and with some justice.

Since 1975, many men (and a few women) who fought in ELAS, either as volunteers or conscripts, have returned to their villages – some of them after over thirty years of exile in what was the USSR and other East Bloc countries. Numerous others had been carried off as children to Albania, and made to work in labour camps before being distributed to various East European states. The political Right claims that this *pedhomázema* – the roundup of children – was a cynical and merciless ploy to indoctrinate an army of dedicated revolutionaries for the future. The Left retorts that it was a prudent evacuation of noncombatants from a war zone.

One thing, however, is certain. The Right won, with the backing of the British and, more significantly, the Americans, and they used that victory to maintain an undemocratic and vengeful regime for the best part of the following quarter-century. Many Epirot villagers, regardless of political conviction, believe that the poverty and backwardness in which their communities long remained was a deliberate punishment for being part of Communist-held territory during the civil war. For decades they were constantly harassed by the police, who controlled the issue of all sorts of licences and certificates needed to find public-sector work, to travel, to put children in better schools, to run one's own business and so forth. Only since 1981 have things really changed, and the past finally treated as another, and separate, age.

force. Latinate-speaking Vlach and Doric-speaking Sarakatsan shepherds (see "Greek Minorities" in Contexts, p.1023) continue to bring their flocks to the high mountain pastures in summer. Bears leave footprints on riverbanks or raid beehives, risking an (illegal) bullet in the head, while increasing numbers of wolves keep a hungry eye out for stray ewes and goats.

The best single area to visit is around **mounts Gamíla** and **Smólikas**, with the **Aóös** and **Víkos gorges** to walk through and the splendid **villages of Zagóri** to stay in. You have to explore on foot to get a full flavour of the place, and not surprisingly the Píndhos has become a popular hiking and trekking venue, with increasing international caché.

Some of the road itineraries offer less strenuous travelling highlights – above all the Kalambáka–Ioánnina highway as it negotiates the **Katára pass**, though this trunk route will soon be diverted via a tunnel, one of nearly sixty on the showcase **Via Egnatia motorway**, ostensibly due for completion before the 2004 Olympics but unlikely to be inaugurated before 2007. Roughly halfway between Ioánnina and the Metéora (see p.370) stands **Métsovo**, perhaps the easiest location for a taste of mountain life, though baldly commercialized of late. **Ioánnina**, Ali Pasha's capital, remains a town of some character, with its island and lake, and the main transport hub for trips into Zagóri. Other than **Árta**, prettily set and with some fine Byzantine churches, there are few urban attractions.

The coast, in both Epirus and Étolo-Akarnanía, is in general disappointing. **Igoumenítsa** is a useful ferry terminal for Corfu and Italy, but otherwise will win few admirers. **Párga**, *the* major Epirot resort, has been developed beyond its capacity, though **Préveza** has retained some character against the odds and is now a major gateway and nightspot for package-holiday patrons. Between these two towns is a series of attractive, sandy and not unduly developed **beaches**, while just inland beckons a scenic highlight – the **gorge of the Aheróndas River**.

South of Préveza, you enter a low, marshy landscape of lakes and landlocked gulfs hemmed in by bare hills – of interest mainly to the bird-watcher and fish-dinner enthusiast. For better beach escapes in this part of the world you need islands, fortunately close at hand in the Ionian group – **Lefkádha** (see p.964) is actually connected to the mainland by a moveable bridge.

The Píndhos mountains

Even if you have no plans to go hiking, the **Píndhos range** deserves a few days' detour. The remoteness and traditional architecture, the air, the peaks, all constitute a very different Greece to the popular tourist image and, despite increasing popularity as a trekking destination, the area remains relatively unspoilt – attempts to establish a package industry, for example, have largely foundered.

If you are coming from central Greece, the best of the main routes is **Kalambáka–Métsovo–Ioánnina**, which divides the **north Píndhos** from the **south Píndhos**. If you are arriving by ferry at Igoumenítsa, getting up to

Ioánnina enables you to reverse this itinerary, which is quite the most attractive route into the central mainland. **Walkers** will want to make directly for the **Zagóri**, north of Ioánnina, where trekking opportunities abound.

A number of **hiking routes** are detailed in the text; others can be found in specialist guides (see "Books" in Contexts, p.1077). Most of the routes are arduous and lonesome, rather than dangerous. But all the same, this is high-mountain country, with unpredictable microclimates, and it's inadvisable to set off on the longer, more ambitious itineraries without any previous trekking experience.

Kalambáka to Ioánnina

West of Kalambáka (see p.373), the 1694-metre Katára pass cuts across the central chain of the Píndhos to link Thessaly and Epirus. This route, the only motor road across these mountains kept open in winter (except during blizzards), is one of the most spectacular in the country and worth taking for the journey alone. Though nominally the shortest east–west crossing in Greece, distances here are deceptive. The road switchbacks and zigzags through folds in the enormous peaks, which rise to more than 2300m around Métsovo, and from November to April the snowline must be crossed. All this, however, will soon be optional, as several enormous tunnels have been bored through the ridges here as part of the pharaonically ambitious **Via Egnatia** expressway, designed to spare drivers (especially of lorries) the dangerously curvy existing highway. However, the actual road works – 129km in total from Katára to Igoumenítsa – have been delayed by the necessity of routing 28km of the route through nearly sixty expensive tunnels, often linked by viaducts.

Just two buses daily cover the entire existing route across the mountains, running between Tríkala and Ioánnina, with stops at Kalambáka and Métsovo. If you're driving, allow half a day for the journey from Kalambáka to Ioánnina (114km), and in winter check on conditions before setting out. Anyone planning on hitching from Kalambáka should take a lift only if it's going through to Ioánnina or Métsovo, for there's nothing but forest in between, except for a few small villages without significant facilities.

Métsovo

MÉTSOVO spreads just west of the Katára pass, right below the Kalambáka–Ioánnina highway (and just above the new Via Egnatia expressway). It is a small, often rainy alpine town, built on two sides of a ravine and guarded by a forbidding range of peaks to the south and east. This startling site is matched by a persistently traditional way of life and architecture. Immediately below the highway begin tiers of eighteenth- and nineteenth-century stone houses with wooden balconies. These dwellings spill down the slope to and past the main platía, where a dwindling number of old men still loiter, especially after Sunday Mass, magnificent in their full traditional dress, from flat black caps to pompommed shoes; you're more likely to see them strolling in groups in "civilian" dress, chatting loudly in Vlach (or Arouman, to give the language its proper name). The women, enveloped in rich blue weave and a headscarf over a pair of braids, have a more subdued appearance but are more regularly seen in such garb.

If you arrive outside of the two high seasons (midsummer and Christmas week), stay overnight and take the time to walk in the valley below, the place can seem magical. Otherwise your experience may not be so positive as Métsovo has become a favourite target for tour-buses full of Greeks, and its beauty veers perilously close to the artificially quaint. Souvenir shops selling kitsch wooden artefacts and "traditional" weavings (too often mass-produced these days) have proliferated – the Zouvias and Tsiroyiannis storefronts at the very top of town more reliably stock hand-loomed items. Also, the former stone roofs of the mansions have been completely replaced by ugly pantiles – it's claimed the slates cracked too readily under the weight of the yearly snow-fall.

Nonetheless, it would be a shame to pass through Métsovo too speedily, for its history and status as the Vlach "capital" (see "Greek Minorities" in Contexts, p.1023) are unique. Positioned astride the only commercially and militarily viable route across the Píndhos, it won a measure of independence, both political and economic, in the earliest days of Ottoman rule. These privileges were greatly extended in 1659 by a grateful Turkish vizier who, restored to the sultan's favour, wanted to say a proper "thank you" to the Metsovite shepherd who had protected him during his disgrace and exile.

Métsovo's continued prosperity, and the preservation of some of its traditions, are largely due to Baron Mihaïl Tositsas (1888–1950), banker offspring of a Metsovot family living in Switzerland, who left his colossal fortune to an endowment that benefits industries and crafts in and around the town.

The town and around

The Métsovo **museum** occupies the eighteenth-century **Arhondikó Tosítsa** (daily except Thurs: summer 8.30am–1pm & 4–6pm; winter 3–5pm; group tours only every 30min; €1.50), the old Tosítsa mansion just off the main thoroughfare. This has been restored to its full glory, and with its panelled rooms, rugs and fine collection of Epirot crafts and costumes, gives a real sense of the town's wealth and grandeur in that era.

The other major Métsovo attraction is the relatively remote monastery of **Áyios Nikólaos**, signposted from the main platía but in fact fifteen-minutes' walk below town, just off the half-cemented-over *kalderími* bound for **Anílio**, the village across the ravine. The *katholikón*, topped by a simple barrel vault, was built in the fourteenth century to an unconventional plan. What might once have been the narthex became over time a *yinaikonítis* or women's gallery, something seen rarely elsewhere in Greece, except Kastoriá (see p.496). The brilliant **frescoes** exhibit an unconventional style dating from 1702, and were cleaned and illuminated during the 1960s, courtesy of the Tositsa Foundation. Since there is no dome, the Four Evangelists are painted on four partly recessed columns rather than on pendentives, as is usual; between them are scenes from the life of Christ, and assorted martyrdoms. The barrel vault features four medallions – the Virgin and Child, the Holy Trinity, an Archangel and a *Pandokrátor* (Christ in Majesty) – forming an unusual sequence. Otherwise the iconography is the norm for post-Byzantine churches: a *Crucifixion* on the west wall, and a *Virgin Enthroned* in the conch of the apse, flanked by the *Communion of the Apostles* (six to each side). A warden family live on the premises and receive visitors until 7.30pm. You'll be shown the monks' former cells, with insulating walls of mud and straw, and the abbot's more sumptuous quarters; a purchase of postcards or souvenirs is expected.

The village of **ANÍLIO** ("Sunless", because of its north-facing position) is a further half-hour down, then up, and you'll have to make the gruelling trek back the same way – assuming, of course, that the Via Egnatia does not bull-doze through the *kalderími* in the near future. Like Métsovo, its population is

4

Vlach-speaking, and its life is more genuinely traditional. There are no pretensions to tourist appeal, with its architecture executed in dull cement. You can, however, get a sustaining, reasonably priced lunch at the platía before starting back.

For more advanced **hikes** over tracks or trails, ranging in length from a few hours to a few days, consult the folding map which the Development Enterprise of Métsovo Municipality has prepared (available free locally, but labelled and described in Greek only).

In winter, global warming permitting, a small **ski centre** operates between Anílio and the Katára pass; it's considered a joke among serious skiers, merely providing an extra excuse for Athenians to show up at weekends. For the record, there are presently three drag lifts serving just six runs, mostly green- and blue-rated; a hopefully more reliable piste on a north-facing slope is being prepared across the valley.

Practicalities

The **bus stop** is on the main platía, the **post office** is on the main street some 200m uphill, while five **banks** with cash dispensers are scattered between the two.

Métsovo has a wide range of **accommodation**, with thirteen hotels plus quite a few rooms for rent, virtually all of it en suite. Outside Christmas week, the town's festival (July 26) or late August, you should have little trouble in getting a bed or bargaining posted rates down a category. However, **budget** options are somewhat limited since the indefinite occupation of the very central *Hotel Athinai/Athens* by Via Egnatia engineers; its rival the *Acropolis*, at the top of town, is erratically managed and overpriced (☎06560/41 672; ❸) for rooms with mostly shared facilities. Better to head for the *Athinai's* still-running, en-suite annexe, *Rooms Filoxenia* (☎06560/41 021, ☞42 009; ❸), just behind the grassy hillock of the central park; never mind the gruff proprietor, it's excellent value, with valley views out of the rear rooms. The rather stark *Rooms Elli Tsanaka* nearby (☎06560/41 806; ❷) is another, less exalted possibility, though strangely they can fill with Greek tours. **Mid-range hotels** include the rustic-style *Flokas* (☎06560/41 309, ☞41 547; ❹ winter, ❷ summer), on the street leading south from the square, with views from the top-floor rooms; all rooms at the much larger *Kassaros* a few steps away (☎06560/41 800, ☞41 262, ⓦwww.hotels-in-greece.com/ioannina/kassaros-e.html; ❺ Christmas, ❹ rest of year) have views over to Anílio. Perhaps the most welcoming choice in this category is the *Bitounis* (☎06560/41 217 or 093/2584069, ☞06560/41 545, ⓔbitounis@met.forthnet.gr; ❹), at the top of the main street, whose affable proprietor Tolis lived in London for eight years. All rooms got a thorough overhaul in 2001, and over two-thirds of them have balconies with valley views; there are attic suites suitable for four, plus a sauna for skiers. The *Andonis*, quietly sited just above the main square (☎06560/42 300, ☞42 298, ⓦwww.metsovo.com/Apollon; ❺ B&B peak, rest of year ❹ room only), has the largest, most plushly appointed rooms in town; if they're full, you'll be sent to their affiliate, the *Hotel Apollon* (❺), below the main square.

Meals are overwhelmingly meat-oriented, as befits a pastoral centre. Four of the simpler grills are *Kryfi Folia* on the main platía, *To Tzaki* next door, *To Koutouki tou Nikola* (also with some non-meat dishes), directly below and behind the post office, and *To Arhondiko* opposite; all function principally in the evening. The main vegetarian and lunchtime option, with the fullest menu, is the ground-floor restaurant under the *Hotel Athinai Athens*, which does no-nonsense casserole food, accompanied by decent house wine. The restaurant attached to the nearby *Hotel Galaxias* offers a similar menu, and the chance to sit out on the lawn under giant trees, but isn't as good value. **Wine** buffs may want to try the fabled Katóyi, available in some of these restaurants, in local shops and fairly widely across Greece. It's a moderately expensive limited bottling from tiny vineyards down on the Árakhthos River, though the quality of the main label – Averoff – is variable (the Ktima line is best). This, and other **local specialities** such as *trahanádhes* (a porridge base of milled wheat and soured sheep's milk, either sweet or savoury), the smoked *metsovóne* cheese and *hilópites* (like tagliatelli with added egg, long or chopped into cubes) can be obtained at local shops such as Iy Piyi or O Vlahos, just downhill from the *Hotel Bitoúnis*.

Nightlife takes the form of a few conspicuously noisy pubs, cafés and discos uphill from the post office on the main street; their identity, though not their location, tends to change yearly.

Villages of eastern Zagóri

For a taste of wilder, remoter scenery, and a truer, grittier picture of contemporary mountain life, follow the paved road north into the **eastern Zagóri** district from just west of the Baldhoúma bridge on the Métsovo–Ioánnina highway. This precipitous route snakes its way north along the valley of the Várdhas River, through a lush landscape of broad-leafed trees and scrub. At **GREVENÍTI**, 21km along and the first of a series of predominantly Vlach villages, a black pine forest takes over and cloaks the Píndhos virtually all the way to Albania; you can stay here at **rooms** run by Anastasia Panayiotopoulou (☎06560/31 212; ❸).

The neighbouring villages of **Flambourári** and **Elatohóri** also have basic *xenónes* (inns) and places to **eat**, plus bus services from Ioánnina three days weekly in common with Vovoússa (see below), though the villages are badly depopulated, having failed to recover from wartime destruction inflicted by the Germans in pursuit of Resistance fighters. What remains, however, is very attractive: stone-roofed churches, vine-shaded terraces and courtyards full of flowers and logs stacked for winter. Best of all is the beautiful village of **Makrinó** and its fine monastery, an hour's glorious walk across the ravine from Elatohóri (or a more circuitous twenty-minute drive by car).

The main road continues, winding northeast to the asphalt's end at **VOVOÚSSA**, which lies right on the Aóös River 51km from the main highway, its milky-green waters spanned here by a high-arched, eighteenth-century **bridge**. On either side, wooded ridges rise steeply to the skyline, culminating in the 2177-metre Avgó peak just east, which presides over the **Vália Kálda**, heart of a small national park, threaded by the E6 long-distance trail and home to numbers of bears. The village itself, the last one before the border with Grevená province in Macedonia, has a handful of **psistariés**; the most characterful of these is *Angelos*, which triples as a kafenío and basic shop, with limited terrace seating overlooking the river. There are several licensed **rooms** establishments in Vovoússa, such as those of Khrysoula Avdhikou (☎06560/31 050; ❷); Kaloyerou and Kouskou (☎06560/31 303; ❷); or Athanasios Stangoyiannis (☎06560/31 365; ❸). If you prefer to camp, walk about fifteen minutes downstream to where a stretch of riverbank meadow makes an idyllic site. Fresh paw-prints are often seen in the riverside mud here, but the locals swear bears are timid creatures who avoid contact with humans.

There is an infrequent **bus service** to Vovoússa from Ioánnina at 2pm on Monday and Friday, returning to Ioánnina the next morning at 6am; Sundays they leave from Ioánnina at 7.30am, returning at 2.30pm. Alternatively, you could hike along a marked long-distance route down the Aóös River valley to Dhístrato on Mount Smólikas, where there are several inns and an early morning bus service (Tues, Thurs & Sat am, plus Sun pm) to Kónitsa (see p.414). The trek, partly along trail and partly on abandoned forestry track, keeps to the east bank of the Aóös, is shown more or less correctly on the Métsovo municipality's map, and takes a full day to accomplish.

Ioánnina and around

Moving west from Métsovo, you drop first into the Árakhthos river valley, then climb again over a shoulder of Mount Mitsikéli before the final descent to the north margin of the great, reed-fringed **lake of Pamvótidha** (Pamvótis). On its south shore, the old town of **IOÁNNINA** (often Yiánnena) covers a rocky promontory jutting out into the water, its fortifications punctuated by bastions and minarets. From this base, Ali Pasha carved out – at the expense of the sultan's authority – a fiefdom that encompassed much of western Greece and present-day Albania: an act of contemptuous rebellion that portended wider defiance in the Greeks' own War of Independence.

Disappointingly, most of the city is **modern** and undistinguished, a testimony not so much to Ali (although he did raze much of it to the ground while under siege in 1820), as to developers in the 1960s – and the fact that Ioánnina is one of Greece's fastest-growing provincial capitals, with the city and suburbs' **population** recently reaching about 130,000. Much of this has been sucked inward from moribund villages in the remoter reaches of the province, but it also includes some 25,000 students at the major university here, who keep things lively, plus military personnel and their dependants – Ioánnina has served as a strategic garrison town since its incorporation into Greece.

However, there are still a pair of stone-built **mosques** (and a synagogue) to evoke the Ottoman era, two worthwhile **museums**, and the fortifications of Ali Pasha's citadel, the **Kástro**, the latter surviving more or less intact. Ioánnina is also the jump-off point for visits to the **caves of Pérama**, some of Greece's largest, on the western shore of the lake, and the longer excursion to the mysterious and remote Oracle of Zeus at **Dodona**, as well as to Epirus's most rewarding corner, **Zagóri** (see p.403).

Arrival, orientation and information

Ioánnina **airport** is on the road out to the Pérama caves, 5km from the centre; so far only domestic flights with Olympic and Aegean/Cronus land here (☎06510/23 120 and ☎65 200 respectively), but given the town's exponential growth it may not be long before seasonal charters and no-frills airlines from northern Europe begin calling. The airport is connected to the town by city bus #7 (the most frequent); #1 and #13 also pass by. All such blue-and-white buses leave Ioánnina from a series of stops below the central **Platía Pýrrou**; buy tickets from adjacent booths beforehand, and cancel them when boarding.

KTEL buses arrive at one of two terminals. One station is at **Zozimádhon 4**, north of Platía Pýrrou; this serves most points north and west, including Métsovo, Kalambáka, Igoumenítsa, Kónitsa and the Zagóri villages. Another terminal at **Bizaníou 19** connects Árta, Préveza, Dodona and all villages in the south or east parts of Epirus. It is advisable, especially on summer weekends, to buy tickets for both coast and mountains the day before. For more efficient explorations of the poorly served Zagóri area, consider **car rental**, all on the same street, Dhodhónis, from the likes of Avis at no. 96 (☎06510/46 333), Budget at no. 109 (☎06510/43 901), European at no. 48 (☎06510/67 715), Hertz at no. 105 (☎06510/77 796), Reliable at no. 42 (☎06510/46 450) or Tomaso, also at no. 42 (☎06510/66 900). Despite the number of outlets, don't expect any bargains for short hire periods. **Taxis** are dark green; the most central ranks are marked on the map.

The airport, campsite, Pérama Caves, Lykiádhes, Igoumenítsa & Zagóri ◀

IOÁNNINA

Lake Pamvótidha

Boats to the Island

0   200 m

N

Grotto of Skylosofos

MÓLOS

PLATIA MAVILI

Aslan Pasha Tzami (Municipal or Popular Art Museum)

KÁSTRO

Jewish Deportation Memorial

Silverwork Hall

Fethiye Tzami

INNER CITADEL

Byzantine Museum

Bus Station

Taxi Rank

OLD BAZAAR

Town Hall

PLATIA DHIMOKRATIAS

Cathedral

Archeological Museum

PLATIA AKADHIMIAS

METSOVOU

Blue City Buses

Provincial Government Hall

PLATIA PYRROU

Market

Taxi Rank

Olympic Airways

Bus Station (Préveza/Árta)

PLATIA TZAVELA

RESTAURANTS, CAFÉS & BARS	
Filippos	D
Gallery	E
Hackers	I
Ivi	J
Kyknos	A
Paleopanos	K
Select	L
Stin Ithaki	C
Syn 2	B
To Kourmanio	G
To Manteio	H
Vrettania	M
Yperokeanio	F

ACCOMMODATION	
Egnatia	3
Esperia	6
Galaxy	7
Kastro	1
Metropolis	5
Politeia	2
Tourist	4

▼ Dodona, Préveza, Árta & Athens

Ali Pasha, a highly ambivalent "heroic rebel", is the major figure in recent Ioanninan and Epirot history. The so-called "Lion of Yiannena", on balance a highly talented sociopath, pursued a policy that was consistent only in its ambition and self-interest. His attacks on the Ottoman imperial government were matched by acts of appalling and vindictive **savagery** against his largely Orthodox Christian subjects. Despite all this, he is still held in some regard by locals, the justifications apparently being "a son of a bitch, but at least *our* son of a bitch", and his perceived role as a defier of Istanbul, the common enemy – a platía in the citadel is even named after him.

Ali was born in 1741 in Tepelene, now in modern Albania, and rose to power under imperial patronage, being made pasha of Tríkala in 1787 as reward for his efforts in the sultan's war against Austria. His ambitions, however, were of a grander order, and the following year he **seized Ioánnina**, an important town since the thirteenth century, with a population of 30,000 – probably the largest in Greece at the time. Paying sporadic tribute to the sultan, he operated from this power base for the next 33 years, allying himself in turn, and as the moment suited him, with the Ottomans, the French or the British.

In 1809, when his dependence upon the sultan was nominal, Ali was visited by the young **Lord Byron**, whom he overwhelmed with hospitality and attention. (The tyrant's sexual tastes were famously omnivorous, and it is recorded that he was particularly taken with the poet's "small ears", a purported mark of good breeding.) Byron, impressed for his part with Ali's daring and stature, and the lively **revival of Greek culture** in Ioánnina (which, he wrote, was "superior in wealth, refinement and learning" to any town in Greece), commemorated the meeting in *Childe Harold*. The portrait that he drew, however, was an ambiguous one, since he was well aware that beneath Ali's splendid court and deceptively mild countenance there were "deeds that lurk" and "stain him with disgrace". In fact, when writing to his mother he was more explicit, concluding that "His highness is a remorseless tyrant, guilty of the most horrible cruelties, very brave, so good a general that they call him the Mahometan Buonaparte . . . but as barbarous as he is successful, roasting rebels, etc, etc".

Of those who rebelled against Ali, the most illustrious was Lambros Katsandonis who, wracked by smallpox, was captured by Ali in a cave in the Ágrafa mountains. He imprisoned the unfortunate wretch in a waterlogged lakeside dungeon and finally executed him in public by smashing his bones with a sledgehammer. Ali himself met nearly as grisly an end: in 1821, resolved to eliminate the Epirot threat to his authority before tackling the Greek revolutionary insurgents, the Ottoman sultan sent an army of 50,000 to Ioánninna to besiege and capture Ali. He was lured from the security of his citadel to a monastery on the lake island with false promises of lenient surrender terms, but was shot and decapitated instead in an ambush there. His severed head was displayed in all the provinces he had terrorized, to assure folk that the monster was dead – and that the sultan's writ ran once again – before being sent off to Istanbul. The rest of Ali still purportedly lies in a corner of the citadel.

4

The axis of the town centre is the confusing, oddly angled jumble of streets between Platía Pýrrou and the **Kástro**, Ali Pasha's old citadel. Near the latter is the old bazaar area – still in part an artesans' marketplace. Within sight of Platía Pýrrou are all the essential services: most of the **banks** (all with cash dispensers) and the central **post office** (Mon–Fri 7.30am–8pm), the latter on 28-Oktovríou. There's a second post office closer to the lake on Yeoryíou Papandhréou (same hours) that's more handy for the campsite. **Information** on current bus timetables is most easily obtained from the friendly OTE (Sept–June Mon–Fri 7.30am–2.30pm; additional hours, staff permitting, July–Aug Mon–Fri 5.30–8.30pm & Sat 9am–1pm) at Dhodhónis 39, past the *Xenia Hotel*, though they seem to keep very little printed literature in English. For quality maps and a respectable stock of books in English (including a few Rough Guides), head for Papasotiriou **bookstore** at Mihaíl Angélou 6, just off Platía Pýrrou.

Accommodation

Most Ioánnina **hotels** are noisy, badly placed and expensive for what's on offer, though at slow times they may cut prices by a category. High season tends to be Christmas and Easter more than summer, and weekends year-round can see the better places packed out. The town's pay-and-display **parking** scheme is pretty comprehensive, with punch-out cards permitting only two hours at a time; thus hotels with their own parking or garages are indicated.

If you arrive early enough in the day, and value tranquillity above luxury, it's worth heading straight out to Nissí island (see p.398), where the inn run by the Dellas family offers about the most attractive budget accommodation. You will also find more than twenty licensed **rooms** outfits in Pérama village (see p.401), between the main highway and the caves. If you can afford the better mid-range Ioánnina hotels, you could pay about the same at quality lodgings in the stunningly set nearby village of Lykiádhes, halfway up the slopes of Mount Mitsikéli, which closes off the lake to the north.

Camping, unusually for a town, is an attractive option and *Camping Limnopoula*, 2km out of town on the Pérama road (city bus #2 or 20min walk from Platía Mavíli), is a pleasant, well-equipped, mosquito-free site, though a bit cramped and more geared towards camper vans than tents.

Egnatia, Danglí 2, cnr Aravandinoú ☎06510/25 667, ℱ75 064. A decent hotel near the Zozimádhon bus station, especially if you get a side room. Favoured by trekking outfitters and sometimes block-booked; has a garage. ❹

Esperia, Kaplání 3 ☎06510/24 111, ℱ77 498. One of the few savoury, quiet cheapies in town, with large, balconied, en-suite rooms (though furnishings are distressed 1970s vintage) and private parking out back. ❸

Galaxy, Platía Pýrrou, south corner ☎06510/25 056, ℱ30 724. Comfortable and quiet rooms with spectacular mountain/lake views from the balconies, air-con and small tubs in the bathrooms. You don't get much more central; limited street parking. ❹

Kastro, Andhroníkou Paleológou 57, inside the Kástro ☎06510/82 866, ℱ22 780, ⓦwww.epirus.com/hotel-kastro. A tastefully restored inn on the way to the Fethiye Tzami, whose seven unique rooms are mostly equippped with double beds. Cooler downstairs units (fans but no air-con) are cheaper. Rates include breakfast. Limited street parking. ❺

Metropolis/Metropole, Krystálli 2, cnr Avéroff ☎06510/26 207. Pretty basic and noisy rooms with shared facilities, but a clean enough budget hotel. ❷

Orizon/Horizon, Lykiádhes village, 12km from Ioánnina ☎06510/86 180 or 094/4836473, ℱ06510/81 530, ⓦwww.epirus.com/horizon. The name says it all – knockout views over the entire lake basin from this well-designed, newish hotel. The en-suite, double-glazed rooms are huge, all with balconies and some with tubs in the bathrooms; an ample breakfast is served out on the terrace or in the large lounge. Adequate parking, but a steep drive to reach it. ❹–❺

Politeia, Anexartisías 109 ☎06510/30 090 or 097/2001570, ⓦwww.etip.gr. Built on the site of an old tradesmen's hall, this apart-hotel retains some period details (stone walls) and its arrangement around a courtyard. Handy for the bus station, but fairly quiet; standard self-catering units have baths and air-con, though ground-floor ones are a bit dark. No breakfast provided, but there's a bar-café in the courtyard. ❺

Sotiris & Evangelos Dellas ☎06510/81 494, ℱ79 380. A good if simple pension on Nissí with six non-en-suite rooms; you'll find the proprietors at the house right next to the school, or on the ground floor of the inn-building in their newly inaugurated, as-yet-unnamed snack bar. ❶

Tourist, Kolétti 18, cnr Krystálli (☎ 06510/26 443, ℱ20 002. Around the corner from the *Metropolis*, but quieter and more comfortable. En-suite rooms and shared bathrooms available. ❸–❹

The town

The **Kástro** is an obvious point to begin your explorations. In its heyday the walls dropped abruptly to the lake, and were moated on their landward (southwest) side. The moat has been filled in, and a quay-esplanade now extends below the lakeside ramparts, but there is still the feel of a citadel; inside nestles a quiet residential zone with narrow alleys and its own shops.

Signs inside direct you to the **Municipal (Popular Art) Museum** (summer Mon–Fri 8am–8pm, Sat–Sun 9am–8pm; winter Mon–Fri 8am–3pm, Sat–Sun 9am–3pm; €2), an elegantly arranged collection of Epirot costumes, guns and jewellery. More poignant is a section devoted to synagogue rugs and tapestries donated in the early 1990s by the dwindling Jewish community of about thirty; their *hávra* or **synagogue** at Ioustinianoú 16 can be visited on application to the community office at Iosíf Eliyía 18B (the unmarked, ground-floor storefront – only Greek or Hebrew spoken). Some 150m west of the clocktower over the *kástro* gate, a municipally erected, trilingual **memorial** honours the 1850 local Jews deported on March 25, 1944 to their deaths at Auschwitz.

The museum's so-called Muslim wing features a walnut and mother-of-pearl suite, complete with the pipe of Esat Pasha, last Ottoman governor here. The museum is housed in the well-preserved, floodlit **Aslan Pasha Tzami**, allowing a rare glimpse of the interior of a Greek mosque; it retains painted decoration in its dome and *mihrab* (niche indicating direction of Mecca), as well as the recesses in the vestibule for worshippers' shoes. The mosque dates from 1618, built on the site of an Orthodox cathedral pulled down in reprisal for a failed local revolt of 1611. Its instigator, Skylosofos (The Dog-Sage), was a charismatic religious hermit who lived in a dank cave directly underneath the cathedral and its replacement; the grotto is now signposted from the lake esplanade.

In the adjacent, arcaded *medresse* or Muslim seminary, tradition places Ali's attempted rape in 1801 of Kyra Phrosyne, the mistress of his eldest son. In return for refusing the 62-year-old tyrant's sexual advances, she was bound, weighted and thrown alive into Lake Pamvótidha, together with seventeen of her companions. The incident gave rise to several folk songs (and not a few kitsch postcards); her ghost is still said to hover over the water on moonlit nights. The *medresse* is currently home to the **Fotis Rapakousis Museum** (same hours as museum; free, but items labelled only in Greek), a huge collection of medieval weaponry and jewellery.

To the east of the Aslan Pasha Tzami lies the "Its Kale" or **inner citadel** of the fortress (daily 7am–10pm; free); the grounds are often used for concerts after-hours, and there's a pleasant, reasonably priced café near the entrance. The citadel was used for some years by the Greek military and most of its buildings – including Ali's palace where Byron was entertained – have unfortunately been adapted or restored in a way that they can no longer be recognized as eighteenth-century structures. One of two Ottoman graves in front of the old **Fethiye Tzami** (Victory Mosque), surmounted by an elegant wrought-iron cage, may be that of Ali Pasha, though neither is identified as such. The tyrant's former palace has been pressed into service as the **Byzantine Museum** (summer Mon 12.30–7pm, Tues–Sun 8am–7pm; winter Tues–Sun 8.30am–5pm; €1.50), a remarkably thin and emphatically post-Byzantine collection which can be skipped if time is short of if you're heading towards Kastoriá (see p.496). Its six rooms contain masonry from assorted collapsed Epirot basilicas, troves of coins, medieval pottery and a few post-Byzantine icons, mostly sixteenth- and seventeenth-century, but far too many Cibachrome prints of frescoes *in situ* elsewhere. The only genuinely Byzantine painting is a fresco fragment of *The Betrayal*, from a damaged church in Voulgaréli. A few paces away, in the purported treasury of Ali Pasha's seraglio, is a marginally better auxiliary exhibit, labelled as the **"Silverwork Hall"**, devoted to Ioánnina's long-running silver industry, featuring both secular and ecclesiastical work from the nineteenth century, and an explanatory mock-up of a smith's work-bench.

Apart from the Kástro, the town's most enjoyable quarter is that of the **old bazaar**, a roughly semicircular area focused on the citadel's main gate. This retains a cluster of Ottoman-era buildings (including some imposing houses with ornate window grilles), as well as a scattering of copper- and tinsmiths, plus the silversmiths that were for centuries a mainstay of the town's economy.

Just off the central Platía Dhimokratías (recently renamed Andhréa Papandhréou), set beside a small park behind the National Bank, is the decently presented **archeological museum** (Tues–Sun 8.30am–3pm; €1.50). It's certainly a must if you're planning a visit to the theatre and oracle of Dodona, for on display here – along with some exceptionally well-crafted bronze seals – is a fascinating collection of lead tablets inscribed with questions to the oracle. In the same room are numerous bronze statuettes, including two Hellenistic children – one throwing a ball and one holding a dove. In adjacent galleries, Roman artefacts include ornate relief-carved sarcophagi from Paramythiá and Igoumenítsa, while there are earlier funerary and votive bronze or ceramic items from Ambrakia (Árta), Aheron (the Necromanteion of Ephyra) and Vítsa.

The oldest item, part of a small exhibit on prehistoric Epirus, is a crudely hewn hand-axe, dated to 200,000 BC, the earliest such tool known in Greece. There is also a wealth of finds from a Molossian cemetery at Liatovoúni near Kónitsa, almost all of it from Corinth; the ancient Corinthians colonized both the entire Epirot coast and the tastes of the Molossian tribe, for the latter used the proceeds from trading excess livestock and crops to buy Corinthian luxury goods. Corinthian excess is most evident in the eye-catching "Treasures of Amvrakia" display, which includes oak-leaf wreaths, cupid-shaped earrings, and rings with inset gems, all executed in gold.

Nissí island

The island of **Nissí** in Lake Pamvotídha is connected by water-buses (half-hourly in summer, hourly otherwise, 8am–11pm; €0.80) from the Mólos quay northwest of the Kástro on Platía Mavíli. The beautiful island village, founded in the sixteenth century by refugees from the Máni in the Peloponnese, is flanked by several **monasteries**, providing a perfect focus for an afternoon's visit. By day the main lane leading up from the boat dock is crammed with stalls selling jewellery and kitsch souvenirs. Except at three overpriced restaurants on the waterfront and another cluster by Pandelímonos, quiet descends with the sun as it sets superbly over the reedbeds that fringe the island. Only cars belonging to islanders are allowed, which are hauled across on a chain-barge to the mainland opposite.

The **monastery of Pandelímonos**, just to the east of the village, is perhaps the most dramatic of Ioánnina's Ali Pasha sites, though it is in fact a complete reconstruction, as the original building was smashed some years ago by a falling tree. In January 1822 Ali was assassinated here, his hiding place having been revealed to soldiers of the Ottoman sultan, who had finally lost patience with his intrigues. Trapped in his rooms on the upper storey, he was shot from the floor below, then decapitated (supposedly on the second step from the top), with his head sent to Istanbul as a trophy. The fateful bullet holes in the floorboards form the centrepiece of a small **museum** (daily: summer reasonable daylight hours;

winter hours vary; €0.50) devoted to Ali, along with numerous wonderful peri-od prints and knick-knacks like his splendid hubble-bubble on the fireplace.

Three other **monasteries** – **Filanthropinón**, **Ayíou Nikoláou Stratigopoúlou** or **Dilíou**, and **Eleoússas** (closed indefinitely for extensive restoration) – lie south of the village in the order cited. They are quite clearly signposted and stand within a few hundred yards of one another along a lovely tree-lined lane; the first two are maintained by resident families, who allow brief visits except during siesta hours (knock for admission if the doors are shut). Both monasteries are attractively situated, with pleasant courtyards, though visits essentially consist of being shown their main chapel, or *katholikón*. These feature late and post-Byzantine **frescoes**, in various states of preservation.

The finest are those of Filanthropinón, a simple barrel-vaulted structure with a blind narthex and two *pareklísia* (side chapels). A complete cycle of Christ's life in the inner nave dates from just after the monastery's foundation in 1292; there are plenty of episodes on boats in the Sea of Galilee, as befits a lake-island church. Lower down, throughout the building, are the saints, including (just east of the door to the south *pareklísion*) the apocryphal Khristóforos (Christopher). Higher up, in the outer nave and north *pareklísion*, graphic mar-tyrdoms predominate and include sundry beheadings, draggings, impalings and boilings. At the east end of the north chapel, Adam names the beasts in the Garden of Eden, while the ceiling of the narthex holds a fine *Transfiguration*. In the south chapel, just west of the door, ancient Greek sages (Solon, Aristotle, Plutarch) make a rare appearance, indicating that this may have been a school for Hellenic culture during the Turkish period.

Lake Pamvótidha and its ecology

Murkily green and visibly polluted, **Lake Pamvótidha** is in desperate straits. The springs which historically fed it along its north shore suddenly dried up in the early 1980s, leaving runoff as its main replenishment. This – from Ioánnina and surround-ing farmland – is heavily **contaminated** with lead from auto fuel, rubber tyre parti-cles, pesticides and fertilizers. The lake only drains toward the Ionian Sea in winter, via a ditch near Pérama linking it to the Kalamás River; in dry years Pamvótidha may fail to drain at all, with water levels falling up to 2m in a lake that's at best 15m deep. Swimming is forbidden, though few would want to under present circumstances.

In the face of all this, the inhabitants of the island struggle to continue **fishing**. The lake was stocked with three species from Hungary in 1986, though all but one of these, the hardy, carp-like *kyprínos*, have been fished out as they failed to repro-duce. Another Hungarian bass-like fish was later introduced, and did thrive – it attains two kilos in weight within two years, and a monstrous fifteen kilos by four years of age. But Ioánnina inhabitants generally refuse to eat anything caught in the lake, so the islanders are forced to sell their catch at a pittance for shipment to Thessaloníki, where it retails for ten times the price. Given such dire economics, fish-ing continues mainly to pass the time and supplement local diets. The only lake items on Nissí restaurant menus are the legs of frogs caught in the surrounding reedbeds, some of the eels, the *kyprínos*, and those leviathans at two kilos and up.

Lake Pamvótidha also boasts a 2000-metre **rowing course** – the longest in Greece. Rather churlishly, the Greek Olympic committee hasn't seen fit to share some of the Olympiad bonanza with Ioánnina, and instead has mandated the construction from scratch of rowing facilities on pristine wetlands in Attica – thus generating another environmental disaster. This decision is currently being challenged in the courts, but even if the environmentalists win it seems likely that a course will be built near the old Athens airport, rather than Ioánnina's facilities being used.

The frescoes in Dilíou are being slowly cleaned, and should eventually equal Filanthropinón's in interest. Currently the narthex offers, from the Life of the Virgin, a fine *Adoration of the Magi* and a *Flight into Egypt* on the west wall, plus a typically surreal *Apocalypse* over the door to the naos. There's a fine touch to the *Nativity*, where an angel sternly awakens Joseph with a wagging finger.

Beyond these three monasteries the track loops anticlockwise around the island until you emerge by a fourth monastery, **Ioánnou Prodhrómou**, right behind Pandelímonos, which holds the keys. However the interior is of less interest than the exterior's three-windowed gables and brickwork.

Eating, nightlife and entertainment

For eating, **the island** is admittedly an atmospheric location with its expensive tavernas by the boat dock featuring freshwater specialities like eel (*héli*), crayfish (*karavídhes*) and frogs' legs, as well as lake carp (*kyprínos*). But only foreign and Greek tourists eat there; if Ioanninots want a lake view, they go elsewhere nearby, especially to **Lykiádhes village**, directly above the island on Mount Mitsikéli, always several degrees cooler year-round. Here, both *Exostis* and *Mitsikeli* tavernas provide good-value grills of local meat, and *orektiká* (*Exostis* has an airier terrace, as the name implies). For a seafood blowout, look no further than *Kastellorizo* (open all year for lunch and dinner; reserve on ☎06510/81 915 at weekends/holidays), well signed in Drambátova shore district of **Amfithéa village** and a recent franchise of a successful Athens chain, it's not cheap at about €76 for two, but this gets you a four-course meal (plus their own wine from Sitía, Crete) and far and away the most professional service and presentation in the Ioánnina area. Back up on the main road, in Amfithéa proper, *Iy Veranda* gets high marks for less expensive, well-executed mezédhes and grills.

For lakeside dining **in Ioánnina itself**, head northwest along Odhós Pamvótidhas from the Mólos quay, where a half-dozen *psistariés* and mezedhopolía beckon, the two functions often combined. Of these, *Filippos* is competent and reasonable at about €10–11 for a three-course meal (meat or fish) with beer, while the remoter *Syn 2* (pronounced "Sýn Dhýo"), rates highly for an imaginative and lengthy menu, reasonable prices and a loyal clientele. Between these two, *Stin Ithaki* has an even more ambitious menu, including *hortópitta* with nettles and stuffed corn-flour crepes, with huge portions making it excellent value – two courses should be enough for most appetites – but overall, the promised "traditional Mediterranean cuisine" tends towards the stodgy. Inland, cheaper, more standard fare can be found around the *kástro* gate; try the *Ivi* restaurant for basic, inexpensive *mayireftá*, or, for grills, the worthy rivals *To Kourmanio* and *To Manteio*, both exactly opposite the gate.

For **snacks**, note that Ioánnina is the original home of the *bougátsa* (custard-tart), fresh at breakfast time with sweet or savoury fillings from *Select* at Platía Dhimokratías (aka Andhréa Papandhréou) 2, whose decor has seemingly remained unchanged for thirty years. An alternative, with the same retro design sense, is *Paleopanos* at Avéroff 3. For a more contemporary environment, the patisserie *Vrettania*, under the (not recommended) eponymous hotel at Platía Dhimokratías 11/A, also has excellent own-made ice cream.

Nightlife and coffee society oscillates between the calmer **cafés** around Platía Pýrrou and along nearby Leofóros Dhodhónis, and the café-bars on Platía Mavíli, heart of the Mólos or lakefront. The most durable of these are *Yperokeanio* and *Gallery*, active by day as well; at night, a gas-lantern-lit carnival atmosphere prevails at Mólos, enlivened by sellers of Fársala *halvás* (sweetmeat) and roast corn. About 100m beyond *Syn 2* is *Kyknos*, a music bar aimed at the student crowd, which only really gets going after 11pm. There are more wine bars, creperies and kafenía scattered across the approaches to the castle, along completely gentrified Karamanlí, and at the far end of Ethnikís Andístasis, at the southern corner of the citadel, and in the little platía behind a former craftsmen's bazaar. The most central **internet café** is *Hackers*, on Averoff immediately opposite the *Ivi* taverna.

Back up around Platía Pýrrou, there are also three **cinemas**, which – thanks to the university students – usually host quite a decent programme of first-run films. From mid-July to mid-August, there are formal music/theatre events of various sorts, usually kicking off with a folk festival featuring various international groups. Most performances take place in the hillside EHM **theatre** (also known as the Fróntzos), just outside the town, with fine views down to the town and lake. Some years there are a few performances of Classical drama and contemporary music at the ancient **theatre of Dodona** (see overleaf). Information and tickets for all these events are available from the OTE office.

North to the Pérama caves

Five kilometres north of Ioánnina, the village of **PÉRAMA** claims to have Greece's largest system of **caves** (daily: summer 8am–7pm; winter 8am–sunset; €4.50, students €2), which extend and echo for kilometres beneath a low hill. They were discovered during World War II by a Resistance fighter hiding from the Germans. The 45-minute mandatory tours of the complex are Greek-only, save a brief printed summary in English, and are a little perfunctory (consisting in the main of a student reeling off the names of various suggestively shaped formations), but not enough to spoil the experience. The same might not be said for the ugly concrete path which has been threaded through nearly a kilometre of the caverns.

To reach the caves on public transport, take a #8 blue city bus from the terminal below Platía Pýrrou to Pérama village; the caves are a ten-minute walk inland from the bus stop, past tacky souvenir shops. If you are driving, you can make a circuit of it. The road splits shortly after Pérama: one fork leads up towards Métsovo, with superb views down over Ioánnina and Pamvótidha, while the other runs around the lake, veering off at Amfithéa and passing, just shy of halfway, the **monastery of Dhouraháni**, now run as a vocational school for disadvantaged children.

Dodona: the Oracle of Zeus

At **DODONA**, 22km southwest of Ioánnina, in a mountainous and once-isolated region, lie the ruins of the ancient **Oracle of Zeus** (daily: summer 8.30am–7pm; winter 8.30am–5pm; €1.50), dominated by a vast and elegant theatre. "Wintry Dodona" is mentioned in Homer, and the worship here of Zeus and of a sacred oak tree seems to have been connected with the first Hellenic tribes who arrived in Epirus around 1900 BC.

The origins of the oracle – the oldest in Greece – are shadowy. Herodotus relates an enigmatic story about the arrival of a *peleiae* or dove from Egyptian Thebes which settled in an oak tree and ordered a place of divination to be made. In ancient Greek, *peleiae* could mean both dove and old woman, so it's possible that the legend refers to an original priestess – perhaps captured from the Middle East and having some knowledge of Asiatic cults and divination. The **oak tree**, stamped on the ancient coins of the area, was central to the cult. Herodotus also recorded that the oracle spoke through the rustling of the oak's leaves in sounds amplified by copper vessels suspended from its branches. These would then be interpreted by frenzied priestesses and strange priests who slept on the ground and never washed their feet. Legend also asserts that the Argonauts used timber from this oak to build their ship, with the presumably charmed properties of the wood enabling them to get out of numerous tight spots.

The site

Entering the site past a few seat-tiers of a third-century BC **stadium**, you are immediately confronted by the massive western retaining wall of the **theatre**. Built during the time of King Pyrrhus (297–272 BC), this was one of the largest on the Greek mainland, rivalled only by those at Argos and Megalopolis. Later, the Romans made adaptations necessary for their blood sports, adding a protective wall over the lower seating and also a drainage channel, cut in a horseshoe shape around the orchestra. What you see today is a meticulous late nineteenth-century reconstruction, since until then the theatre had been an almost incomprehensible jumble of stones.

The theatre is used occasionally, to marvellous effect, for weekend ancient drama and music performances during the summer (see p.401). This is one of the most glorious settings in Greece, facing out across a green, silent valley to the slopes of Mount Tómaros. At the top of the *cavea*, or seating curve, a grand entrance gate leads into the **acropolis**, an overgrown and largely unexcavated area. The foundations of its walls, mostly Hellenistic, are a remarkable four to five metres wide.

Beside the theatre, and tiered uncharacteristically against the same slope, are the foundations of a *bouleuterion*, beyond which lie the complex ruins of the **Sanctuary of Zeus**, site of the oracle itself. There was no temple as such until the end of the fifth century BC; until then, worship had centred upon the sacred oak, which stood alone within a circle of votive tripods and cauldrons. Building began modestly with a small stone temple-precinct, and in the time of Pyrrhus the precinct was enclosed with Ionic colonnades. In 219 BC the sacred house was sacked by the Aetolians and a larger temple was built with a monumental *propylaion*. This survived until the fourth century AD, when the oak tree was hacked down by Christian zealots. It is the remains of the later precinct that can be seen today, distinguishable by a modern oak planted at the centre by a helpfully reverent archeologist. Ruins of an early Christian **basilica**, constructed on a sanctuary of Hercules (Herakles), are also prominent nearby – distinguished by rounded column stumps. Excavations on the site have resumed, which should result in greater comprehensibility when completed.

Many **oracular inscriptions** were found scattered around the site when it was first systematically excavated in 1952. Now displayed in Ioánnina's archeological museum, they give you a good idea of the oracle's lingering influence in the years after it had been eclipsed by Delphi. More interestingly, they also afford a glimpse of the fears and inadequacies that motivated the pilgrims of the age to journey here, asking such domestic questions as: "Am I her children's father?" and, memorably, "Has Peistos stolen the wool from the mattress?"

Practicalities

Relatively few people make the detour to Dodona, so the site and **DHODHÓNI** – the little village to the west of it – are completely unspoilt. **Transport** is accordingly sparse, with buses direct from Ioánnina only three days a week (Mon, Wed, & Fri 6.30am & 3.30pm) to Melingí village, via the site. Alternatively, buses for the village of Zotikó (Mon, Wed & Fri at 2pm) pass within 2km of the site; the bus conductor will point out the kafenío where you should alight for the final, downhill walk, and the "real" return bus calls at the site car park at about 4.40pm, giving you over two hours to look around. Hitching to the site from the junction 7km south of Ioánnina should be feasible in summer, or a round trip by taxi from Ioánnina with an hour at the site can be negotiated for a reasonable amount – about €18 per carload.

Alternatively, you could always stay the night here. There are some lovely spots to **camp**, a friendly if basic **taverna** in the village, which has a couple of **rooms** run by Stefanos Nastos (☎06510/71 106, ❷) and a small **hotel** close to the site, the *Andromachi* (☎06510/91 196; ❹), which fills (and charges full rates) only at festival time – it also has its own restaurant.

Zagóri

Few parts of Greece are more surprising or more beguiling than **Zagóri**. A wild, thinly populated region, it lies to the north of Ioánnina, bounded by the roads to Kónitsa and Métsovo on the west and south, and the Aóös River valley to the northeast. The beauty of its landscape is unquestionable: miles of forest, barren limestone wastes, rugged mountains deeply furrowed by foaming rivers and partly subterranean streams. But there is hardly an arable inch anywhere, and scarcely a job for any of its few remaining inhabitants other than herding sheep or cutting timber. The last place, in fact, that one would expect to find some of the most imposing architecture in Greece.

Yet the **Zagorohória**, as the 46 villages of Zagóri are called, are full of grand stone *arhondiká* (mansions) enclosed by semi-fortified walls, with deep-eaved gateways opening onto immaculately cobbled streets. Though they look older, the *arhondiká* date mostly from the late eighteenth or early nineteenth century. By the 1960s, many had fallen into disrepair or been insensitively restored, but the government now ensures (in several listed villages, anyway) that repairs are carried out in the proper materials, rather than cheap brick and sheet metal; new structures are required to have local stone cladding. Inside, the living quarters are upstairs, arranged on an **Ottoman** model. Instead of moveable furniture, low platforms line the rooms on either side of an often elaborately hooded fireplace; strewn with rugs and cushions, they serve as couches for sitting during the day and sleeping at night. The wall facing the fire is usually lined with panelled and sometimes painted storage cupboards called *misándres*. In the grander houses the intricately fretted wooden ceilings are often painted as well. Additionally, most houses have a *bímsa* (secret, fireproof bunker) for hiding the family gold and perhaps a wife and child or two whenever Albanian or other Muslim marauders threatened; even if the house was torched, the survivors could dig out their wealth and start over again.

As for the countryside, much the best way of savouring it is on foot, **hiking** the dozens of paths which, gliding through forest and sheepfold or slipping over passes and hogbacks, connect the outlying villages. The most popular outing – now very much part of holiday trekking-company programmes – is along the awesome **Víkos gorge** and then up over the Astráka pass to an alpine lake. It's not to be missed, though for more of a feel of the backcountry, you may want to continue northeast, over **Mount Gamíla** towards the remoter Vlach villages at the base of **Mount Smólikas** (see p.416).

If you would rather have things organized for you, Robinson Expeditions, Ogdhóïs Merarkhías 10, Ioánnina (☎06510/29 402 or 74 989, best to fax or email them from abroad: ℗25 071, ⓦwww.robinson.gr), near the campsite by a BP filling station, runs **group treks** for a number of overseas hiking companies but welcomes walk-in custom. If you arrange things in advance, or are prepared to wait a few days, they will do their best to fit you in.

The Víkos gorge and western Zagóri

The walls of the **Víkos gorge** are nearly 1000m high in places, cutting right through the limestone tablelands of Mount Gamíla, and separating the villages of the western and central Zagóri. It is quite the equal of the famous Samarian gorge in Crete, and a **hike** through or around it – depending on your abilities and time – is likely to be the highlight of a visit to the Zagóri. Since 1975 a national park has encompassed both Víkos and the equally gorgeous Aóös River canyon to the north and, to date at least, various plans for ski centres, téléfériques and dams have been fought off.

Touristic development, however, has come on apace since the early 1980s, when British and French trekking companies first began coming here, and today almost every hamlet within spitting distance of the canyon (and indeed any sizeable village elsewhere in Zagóri) has some form of accommodation,

Hiking warnings

Despite the Víkos Gorge's popularity and periodic attempts at trail maintenance, mapping and waymarking, it is worth emphasizing that it is not a Sunday stroll and that there is still plenty of scope for getting lost or worse. During April or early May, snowmelt often makes the Monodhéndhri end impassable due to high run-off, and during a rainstorm the sides of the gorge can become an oozing mass of mud, tree-trunks and scree.

At the best of times it's not really a hike to be undertaken in trainers and with PVC water bottles, as so many do. It is also strongly recommended that walkers go in parties of four or more, since isolated hikers are more vulnerable to attack by desperate, possibly armed **Albanians** who sometimes live rough in the bushes while transiting illegally between Albania and Greece. A stout stick for warding off snakes and belligerent livestock, and for stability when traversing bald or scree-laden slopes, would not go amiss either. Finally, owing partly to the decrease in grazing and the gradual reforestation of the area, the local **bear population** is on the increase; sightings of tracks and actual individuals are becoming commonplace, especially around Kípi and Pápingo, though they are shy and (except for females with cubs) flee humans who stumble on them.

In 1995, the EU-funded **"Life" programme** signposted some thirty "Z"-prefixed trails in western and central Zagóri, but the walking-times given are often unreliable, waymarking en route – often vandalized by hunters and other interested parties – can be haphazard and trail maintenance since then has been spotty to nonexistent. A folding map-booklet, *Orivatikos Odhoiporikos Hartis Zagoriou* (1:100,000; €3), may still be sold locally, but the text is in Greek only, and the actual map, with its blurry ink and faint contour lines, is virtually useless. You really do need access to a specialist guide – for example, photocopies of pp.167–85 of the out-of-print *Trekking in Greece* (see "Books" in Contexts, p.1077) – and some trekking nous if you plan to venture off the most trodden routes. Currently the **best topographical map** is Anavasi Editions' 1:50,000 folding sheet *Zagori*, available in Athens, Ioánnina or map specialists abroad (€3 in Greece). This is waterproof and fairly easy to read, with 100-metre contour intervals and useful text on the back, but again far from flawless – it unaccountably omits many of the better Z-trails (while rating some tracks as paths), and like most sources shows a nonexistent route through the Vikákis ravine from Tsepélovo to Kípi.

usually open all year, and tavernas. Be warned, though, that the area's popularity is such that you won't get a room to save your life from mid-July through late August, when a tent provides an essential fallback. During the rest of the year, weekends and bank holidays are also unwise times to show up without advance reservations. Moreover, you may have to settle for staying in some of the outlying villages, away from the immediate environs of the gorge – though this can work out slightly less expensive, and the "second choice" village may have a more genuine community feel.

Monodhéndhri is the most popular starting point for a traverse of the gorge, but is by no means the only one; explorations in the area generally lend themselves to linear or loop trips of some days' length, rather than basing yourself somewhere for a week.

Monodhéndhri

Near the south end of the gorge, perched right on the rim, stands the handsome village of **MONODHÉNDHRI**. It is one of the best preserved of the western Zagóri communities, all of which escaped the wartime devastation suffered by their eastern cousins. The wide, rather artless modern *kalderími* leading off from the far end of the lower platía reaches, after 900m (not "500m" as signed) the eagle's-nest monastery of **Áyia Paraskeví**, teetering on the very brink of the gorge and now uninhabited, though left open. If you have a good head for heights, continue on around the adjacent cliff-face and the path eventually comes to a dead end near **Megáli Spiliá**, a well-hidden cave where the villagers used to barricade themselves in times of danger. In all, count on just under an hour for visiting these sites. For an even more spectacular view of the gorge, follow signs towards **Oxiá** (7km by car, slightly shorter by the Z8 path), where a short *kalderími* leads out from the road's end onto a natural balcony where all of Víkos is spread vertiginously at your feet.

There are **buses** here from Ioánnina (Mon, Wed & Fri, 6.15am & 4.15pm); those with their own transport should leave vehicles at the car park by the lower, cobbled platía. If you take the later bus, be advised that the handful of **inns** by the upper, asphalt platía where the bus calls are relatively pricey. Among these, *Arhondiko Kalderimi* (☎06530/71 510 or 094/5211241; ❹ July–Aug, ❺ winter room only, ❸ B&B low season) is, with its wood-floored, occasionally balconied rooms and snug breakfast bar, better value than *Arhondiko Zarkadas* (☎06530/71 305; ❸). The only real budget option is the *Monodendri*, aka *Katerina's* (☎06530/71 300; ❷), with plain but adequate rooms both en suite and not. For **meals**, best options, both on or near the upper plaza, are either *O Dhionysos* (which can get coach tours), featuring local recipes such as *alevrópitta* (a surprisingly pricey egg, flour and milk fry-up), or the less inspired *Iy Haradhra tou Víkou*; the eatery at the more appealing lower plaza, with seating under the plane tree, was shut at the time of writing for a management change. There is no shop, so bring supplies for trekking in the gorge.

Alternative bases and walks

During busy times of the year, you may choose – or be forced – to stay in other villages near this end of the gorge. At nearby **VÍTSA**, 2km below Monodhéndhri, additional en-suite accommodation is available at *Arhondiko Dhanou* (☎06530/71 371; ❸), in the upper quarter, though it's often unstaffed so ring ahead. The *Hotel Selini* (☎06530/71 471, ℻71 350; ❹), in the lower of the two ridgeline neighbourhoods, has its own, 300-metre access drive well marked, and private parking, though the rooms are modern-anodyne, rather sterile and overpriced. To some tastes Vítsa is a less claustrophobic, more attractive village than Monodhéndhri, with a few **tavernas**, a fine platía and alternative access to the gorge. This is via the signposted Skála Vítsas, a half-hour's gentle descent along the **Z9** path, partly on engineered stair-path, to the handsome single-arched Misíou bridge; from there it's possible to continue upstream to Kípi village via the O3 path (see opposite), or veer downstream along the heart of the gorge.

From either Vítsa or the bridge, the **Z15** trail leads south to Dhílofo; the start of the path in Vítsa is trickier to find than the branch leading from the bridge, but once accomplished it's a twenty-minute descent to a streambed (ford, no bridge), where the Misíou branch joins it, then there's a climb along a crumbled *kalderími* which peters out in schist badlands. After another stream crossing with no waymarks to help, the path resumes before becoming a track system leaving you at the outskirts of **DHÍLOFO**, just over an hour along. One of the most handsome of the Zagorian villages, formerly called **Sopetséli**, it also has road access (though cars must be left at the outskirts) and has been "discovered" since the mid-1990s. You may **stay** at the *Aithrio Inn*, on the plane-tree platía, which has five rooms (three with fireplace, but none en suite) run by the *Lithos Bar Restaurant* at the village entrance (☎06530/61 362, 22 600 or 094/4153644; ❸ , ❹ holidays). The *Lithos* hosts special events on summer weekends, though the *Tzimoyiannis* **taverna**, actually nearer the inn, is more traditional and has excellent food, when they can be bothered to cook.

From Dhílofo walkers can continue down to the chapel of Áyios Minás on the main valley-floor road. From this point, the **Z24** path gives access to Eláti village, but nearly half of the one-hour course is along asphalt or bulldozer track, with path only near the end, so you may as well visit **ELÁTI** by car. You're rather distant here from the gorge country, but there are fine views north to the peaks of Gamíla, plus a good but seldom full **hotel-restaurant**, the *Elati* (☎06530/71 180, ℻71 181; ❹), run by Alex Yiannakopoulos, an engaging Canadian Greek.

If you still have no luck with vacancies in any of the foregoing spots, **ÁNO PEDHINÁ**, 4km west of Vítsa and Monodhéndhri and sharing the same bus service, offers two rooms establishments and two superior **hotels**. Longest-running of the latter is Dutch co-managed *Spiti tou Oresti* (☎06530/71 202 or 06510/32 686; open all year; ❹ B&B, ❻ major holidays) at the very top of the village, its double-glazed rooms warmly furnished, and with an adequate attached restaurant. A comparable alternative is the *Ameliko* (☎06530/71 501 or 094/4772638, ⓦwww.epirus.com/ameliko; ❹–❺ B&B), recently done out in traditional style, with an alarmingly bright colour scheme in the comfortable double and quad en-suite rooms. At the base of the village, to your right as you approach, stands the old **convent of Evangelístria**, which after seventy years of neglect was restored in 1997 and is now inhabited by four young nuns who welcome visitors – especially Sister Ephrosyne, originally from Wood Green, in North London. The *katholikón* has a magnificent carved *témblon* and vivid, cleaned frescoes from 1793, though the structure is much older.

From Áno Pedhiná, the **Z5** and **Z4** routes, via Elafótopos, take you around most of the Víkos Gorge at problematic times of the year, ending up at Víkos village (see opposite) after three-plus hours; this trail is still intact – no bulldozing allowed within the national park limits – but overgrown or scree-strewn in spots. **ELAFÓTOPOS** itself, on a hillside, has just a single **grill** (*T'Alonia*) and an unreliably open if attractive stone-built **hotel**, the *Elafotopos* (☎ & ℻ 06530/71 001; ❸) – ring first before showing up.

Monodhéndhri to Pápingo: through the gorge

All of the above notwithstanding, the most-used **path down to the gorge**
begins beside the arcaded church of Áyios Athanásios in Monodhéndhri's
lower platía. Having first passed the village's municipal amphitheatre, the path
is paved for most of the way down to the riverbed, whose stony course you
can quite easily parallel for the first hour or so of the walk. The walk along the
gorge is not difficult to follow, since the entire route is waymarked, in parts a
bit faintly, by red-paint dots and white-on-red stencilled metal diamonds with
the legend O3. This refers to a long-distance path, which begins south of Kípi
at Lykiádhes on Mount Mitsikéli and as of writing can be followed across
Mount Gamíla all the way to Mount Smólikas. In the future, trail maintenance
works are planned to prepare a route well up on the wooded, true left bank;
until then expect a certain amount of boulder-hopping in the gorge bed, and
slippery, land-slid patches on the sides.

About two and a half hours out of Monodhéndhri you draw even with the
mouth of the **Mégas Lákkos ravine**, the only major breach in the eastern
wall of the gorge; a spring here has been improved with piping to make it more
reliable later in the year. Another forty-minutes' level tramping brings you past
the small, white shrine of **Ayía Triádha** with a recessed well opposite. A further hour yet (around 4hr 30min from Monodhéndhri) sees the gorge begin
to open out and the sheer walls recede.

As the gorge widens you are faced with a choice. Continuing straight, on the
best-defined path, takes you close to a beautifully set eighteenth-century
chapel of the Panayía, past which the route becomes a well-paved *kalderími*,
climbing up and left to the village of **VÍKOS** (alias Vitsikó, also accessible by
5km paved road from Arísti). This section has been kept in good repair by the
locals and takes half an hour to ascend. This underrated village has two **inns**,
of which the one kept by Ioannis and Olga Dinoulis (☎06530/42 112; ➍),
right where the gorge trail arrives, is preferable with modern but comfortable
rooms and an on-site restaurant which will do vegetarian food on request. Up
on the square, with its handsome church, there's an independent **restaurant**
and the other, larger inn run by Kostas Karpouzis (☎06530/41 176; ➌), a bit
impersonally run and with rooms not quite up to their rival's standard.

Most walkers, however, prefer to follow the marked O3 route to the two
Pápingo villages, crossing the gorge bed at the **Voïdhomátis springs**, some
five hours from Monodhéndhri. This trail was regraded and rerouted in 1985
and is fairly straightforward to follow. It's about two-hours' walk to Mikró
Pápingo, slightly less to Megálo, with the divide in the trail nearly ninety minutes above the riverbed crossing. Midway, after an initial steep climb, there's a
fine view down into the north end of the gorge in the vicinity of some weathered, tooth-like pinnacles, before the trail traverses a stable rock slide to the
fork. Should you be taking the same route, but in reverse, the start of the path
in each Pápingo village is currently signposted in Greek only.

The Pápingo villages and around

MEGÁLO PÁPINGO is, as its name suggests, the larger of these paired villages (ⓦwww.epirus.com/papigo): two distinct quarters comprising fifty or so
houses along a tributary of the Voïdhomátis River, which served as the location for the filming of *Signs and Wonders*, starring Charlotte Rampling, in 1999.
Even before this, it had long been a haunt of wealthy, trendy Greeks, making
it a poor choice of base in peak season, though it is still delightful at other
times, when most **accommodation** proprietors will knock a category off
room rates. Behind the central café is the refurbished eighteen-bed *Pension*

Koulis (☎06530/41 138 or 093/2847752;❸) with en-suite rooms, the historic original inn run by the Khristodhoulou family, who are also the local EOS representatives. As such, they can advise on space in the Astráka hut and walks towards Mount Gamíla (see opposite), and the managers, Nikos and Vangelis, speak English. Mr Koulis also has a tiny shop with basic tinned/dried trekking staples and camera film. On the south side of the village, a second inn, *Xenonas Kalliopi* (☎ & ☞ 06530/41 081;❸ ,❹ winter), offers en-suite rooms with views and good home-style meals at the only year-round-reliable taverna (reservations suggested); there are cheaper *dhomátia* at no. 5 of the lane leading there. If money is no object, Nikos and Poli's *Ta Spitia tou Saxoni* (☎06530/41 615, ☞41 891;❸), an immaculate, eighteen-bed pension on the lane leading to the Klidhoniá path (see below), is one place to part with it; another, better-value venue, way at the far north end of the village, is the *Xenonas Papaevangelou* (☎06530/41 135 or 094/6044260, ☞06530/41 988;❺), with large, variable rooms, a self-catering studio amidst well-tended gardens, inviting common areas and genial, multilingual manager, Yiorgos. On the way there you'll pass the *Xenonas Astraka* (☎06530/41 693 or 06510/35 801, ☞06530/41 693;❺ , credit cards by arrangement), fairly well run with large rooms.

By far the best of several stand-alone **tavernas** in the village is the *Ouzerí Nikos Tsoumanis*, with huge salads, tasty lamb and regional dishes, including *amilétita* (livestock testicles) for the bold, plus an unimproveable view of the Pýrgi from the terrace; by contrast *Yiorgos Ioannidhes*, opposite the hexagonal belfry, is overpriced, so best avoided, except perhaps for a drink.

MIKRÓ PÁPINGO, around half the size of its neighbour, crouches below an outcrop of grey-limestone rocks known as the *Pýrgi* (Towers). The village has one main **inn**, *Xenon O Dhias* (☎06530/41 257, ☞41 892; ❸), up to Megálo Pápingo standards, whose proprietor, Kostas Tsoumanis, often gives discounts to trekkers. There is also a resident mountain guide, Panos Sotiropoulos. Slightly less pricey are various rented **rooms** around the inn, for example those of Kostas and Evangelia Pantazi (☎06530/41 110;❸).

Bus journeys from Pápingo back to Ioánnina can be rather haphazard affairs since the service is erratic. Departures from Ioánnina (Mon, Wed & Fri 5.15am & 2.30pm) turn around for the return trip immediately upon arrival at Megálo Pápingo, an hour or so later; in midsummer there may also be a service on Sunday, leaving Ioánnina at 9.30am and getting back to town in the late afternoon. If you miss the bus, the best course is to walk to the village of Kalývi Klidhoniás on the Kónitsa–Ioánnina highway, which has regular services. It's around a two-and-a-half-hour walk west from Megálo Pápingo, via the nearly abandoned hamlet of **Áno Klidhoniá**, on a better-than-average marked path, most of it unbulldozed, and certainly quicker than the dreary 23-kilometre haul to the highway along the paved road which passes through Arísti.

The lower Voïdhomátis River valley

There are almost always **accommodation** vacancies in **ARÍSTI**, southwest of the Voïdhomátis River; best value of three inns here is the *Zissis* (☎06530/41 147, ☞42 148;❹), with small but appealing rooms in mock-traditional style, and a good attached restaurant; it's near the bottom of the village en route to the Pápingos.

Roughly halfway between the Kónitsa–Ioánnina highway and Megálo Pápingo, the paved side-road descends sharply from Arísti to cross the Voïdhomátis as it flows out of the Víkos gorge. The immediate environs of the bridge (built 1923) are a popular picnic area in summer (no camping allowed), but riverbank trails allow you to hike to more peaceful, tree-shaded spots upstream before the gorge blocks further progress. **Kayaking** and **rafting** are the only ways to visit these narrows; swimming in the Voïdhomátis is a privilege enjoyed only by the (not-to-be-fished) trout, though anyone ignoring the ban would probably perish anyway in the icy waters. Downstream lies the restored, cliff-clinging **monastery of Spiliótissas** (always locked); a signposted track (closed to cars) leads to it through a plane grove, west of the road, about 400m before the bridge. The best views of the monastery, however, are from the road as it begins ascending to Pápingo.

If you're up for a more substantial **walk through the river gorge**, start from Víkos village, where a good trail brings you down to the road bridge, and then on past Spiliótissas, finishing out at the historic, single-arch bridge – the national park boundary – near Kalývi Klidhoniás. The last bit on the true right bank is along a fake "*kalderími*" laid in garishly inappropriate white fieldstone, but it's still a worthwhile outing that gives you a close look at the river environment. It's a three-hour one-way hike downhill from Víkos; return by retracing your steps, or stay at one of the clutch of rather expensive hotels and *dhomátia* near the old bridge, catering mostly to the rafters and kayakers who emerge here.

Hikes across the Gamíla range

For walkers keen on further, fairly arduous hiking, there are a number of routes beyond the Pápingo villages, over and across the **Gamíla** range into the central Zagóri. These are served by the aforementioned O3 long-distance trail, and several of the more ambitious 'Z' paths.

Packhorse bridges

A perennial pleasure as you stumble down boulder-strewn ravine beds that are bone-dry an hour after a thunderstorm, is coming upon one of the many fine stone **"packhorse"** bridges that abound in the Zagóri. One-, two- or even three-arched, these bridges, and the old cobbled paths serving them, were the only link with the outside world for these remote communities until motor roads were opened up in the 1950s. They were erected mainly in the nineteenth century by gangs of itinerant craftsmen and financed by local worthies.

Like the semi-nomadic Vlach and Sarakatsan shepherds of Epirus, these wandering construction gangs or *bouloúkia* were away from home between the feasts of Áyios Yeóryios (Saint George's Day) in April and Áyios Dhimítrios (Saint Demetrius) in October. As in other mountainous regions of Europe they came from remote and poor communities: Pyrsóyianni and Voúrbiani in the Kónitsa area in particular, and Ágnanda, Prámanda and Houliarádhes southeast of Ioánnina. Closely guarding the secrets of their trade with their own invented argot, they travelled the length and breadth of Greece and the Balkans, right up to World War II.

While you're in the Zagóri region, a good side-trip, easiest done from Vítsa, Dhílofo, Kípi or Koukoúli, would be to take a look at the half-dozen fantastic bridges in the vicinity. One, the Misíou, lies below Vítsa; the Kokorós stands right beside the main valley road; the Kondodhímou nestles between Kípi and Koukoúli; and the remainder are scattered to either side of Kípi – one spectacular triple span (the Plakídha) downstream, three more upstream from the village. These bridges span the upper reaches of the Víkos gorge and its tributaries, and constitute the most representative and accessible examples of the vanished craft of packhorse-bridge building.

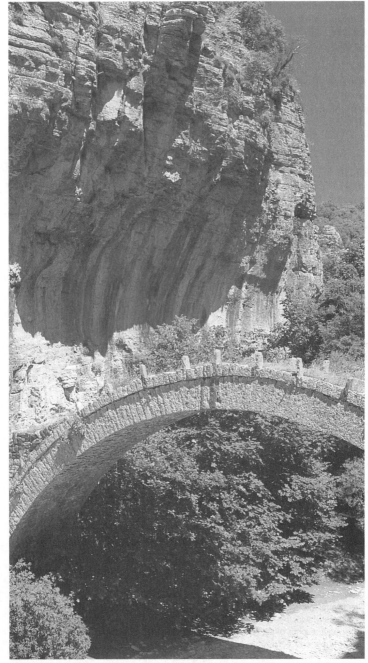

△ Bridge over Voidhomátis River

Pápingo to the Astráka refuge

All onward hikes east into Gamíla begin with the steep but straightforward ascent to the **refuge** on **Astráka col**. Though the refuge is clearly visible from Megálo Pápingo, the trail essentially starts at Mikró Pápingo. The two villages are linked by a three-kilometre asphalt road, which takes 45 minutes to walk; it's better to take the marked, short-cutting, restored *kalderími* off the road, via a historic bridge, which reduces the journey time to half an hour. If you do take the road, just before the bend – at an obvious spot adorned by low masoned walls – you can detour to the **kolymvitíria** or natural swimming pools, a few paces up the streambed.

At the top of Mikró Pápingo, the well-signposted, maintained O3 trail resumes. Ten minutes out, you pass a chapel of Áyios Pandelímon, then head through forest to the Antálki spring (about 40min from Mikró Pápingo). From here the forest thins as you climb towards the Tráfos spring (1hr 40min from Mikró). Twenty minutes beyond Tráfos, a signposted trail branches right towards the **Astráka summit** (2436m), which is a three-hour round-trip from this point. If you ignore this trail, and keep straight with the O3 markers, in around 35 minutes you will reach the **EOS refuge**, perched on the saddle joining Astráka with Mount Lápatos (2hr 45min from Mikró Pápingo).

The hut is open and permanently staffed from mid-May to mid-October, but until a (currently stalled) expansion to sixty bunks is completed, space is at a premium; fees are the refuge standard of €9 (twenty percent discount for affiliated European alpine club members), and meals are also relatively expensive. If you want to squeeze in amongst the Greek and foreign trekking/climbing groups, phone direct on mobiles ☎094/5794748 or 097/4556526 or have either the *Pension Koulis* or *Xenon O Dhias* (who are in radio contact with the hut) make the necessary arrangements.

East of Astráka

Northeast of the refuge, on the far side of the boggy Lákka Tsoumáni valley below, the gleaming **lake of Dhrakólimni**, alive with newts, is tucked away on the very edge of the Gamíla range. This lies about an hour from the refuge, along a well-grooved and waymarked path.

East of the refuge, the O3 route takes you on a strenuous nine-hour hike to the village of Vryssohóri via the **Karterós pass**. Despite waymarking, the casual walker may find this an intimidating trip; it's best attempted only if you're an experienced trekker and equipped with the appropriate maps. At first, the path heads towards **Mount Gamíla** (2497m), itself a good two-and-a-half-hour climb from the refuge, but then veers off south from the final summit approach to negotiate the pass between the Karterós and Gamíla peaks, with a nasty scree slide on the far side. Near the usually empty sheepfold of Kátsanos, this route eventually joins an easier, unmarked trail coming over from the village of Skamnélli in the south, plus another path arriving from Stomíou in the northwest, before the final descent to Vryssohóri (see p.413 for details).

South to central Zagóri

A more obvious, less demanding onward trek from Astráka col is the six-hour route, on an often faint trail – designated as the Z1 – south across the Gamíla uplands, via the Mirioúli sheepfold and the head of the Mégas Lákkos gorge, to the villages of central Zagóri. Besides water at Mirioúli, there is only one other tiny spring en route, and for the most part the scenery consists of forbidding limestone-dell-scape, but **TSEPÉLOVO**, the main destination, is among the finest of the Zagorohória. The major local attraction is the

monastery of Rangovoú, about 1km southwest of the village, just off (and below) the main road. Dedicated to Áyios Ioánnis Pródhromos (Saint John the Baptist), it was founded in the eleventh century; its partly cleaned frescoes are much later but still well worth a look. The *katholikón* is most likely to be open on summer Sundays, when it's a popular venue for weddings and baptisms. From the perimeter wall of the grounds, a new cobble trail leads to a dead-end overlook of the Vikákis ravine and a miniscule bridge; allow one hour return.

New **pensions and hotels** seem to open here all the time, making it the biggest tourist centre in Zagóri after the Pápingo villages. The oldest, least expensive and one of the friendliest is the 1996-renovated *Hotel Gouris* (☎06530/81 214, 81 288 or 094/4789909; ❷ B&B, ❸ HB), founded by the late and much lamented Alexis Gouris, tourism pioneer hereabouts, its management now assumed by his widow Anthoula and English-speaking daughter Nikoletta. Rooms are en suite, with parquet floors and restrained decor. A good second choice is *Tò Palió Arhondikó* (☎06530/81 216 or 094/6844385; ❸), an unmissable gaily painted restored mansion just below the platía, with en-suite, slightly kitsch rooms and half-board available. Right on the platía in another older building are the well-appointed *Deligiannis Rooms* (☎06530/81 232; ❸), with a small self-catering area for making breakfast; also on the square, and the lane leading up to it from the main road, are most of Tsepélovo's **tavernas**. Three pairs of weekly **buses** (Mon, Wed & Fri) connect the village with Ioánnina; they leave Ioánnina at 7am (6.15am in summer) and at 3.15pm, ending their run in Skamnélli and then returning via Tsepélovo an hour or so later.

The adjacent village of **SKAMNÉLLI**, 3.5km along, isn't the most prepossessing place with its tin-and-tile roofs, but it's a useful base in its own right, as the start of a schematically marked hiking route to Stomíou monastery in the Aóös valley, via the Goúra plateau and the Tsoúka Roússa pass (see opposite). The *Hotel Pindhos* down by the road (☎06530/81 280; ❸) is institutional and on the modern side, with the biggest restaurant for miles around; *Paradhisos* rooms, at the very top of the village (☎06530/81 378; ❸), are quieter and more traditionally built.

Descending 12km by road from Tsepélovo towards Ioánnina brings you to the celebrated cluster of **old bridges** (see box on p.415) around Kípi, passing en route the amazing coiled-spring *kalderími* linking Kapésovo and Vradhéto. The bridges span the very upper reaches of the Víkos gorge, which can be reached nearly as easily from here as it can from Monodhéndhri or Vítsa. If you haven't a vehicle, by far the best way of heading down-valley is via a path due west out of Tsepélovo, across the ravine, which links up with the Z23 descending to Vradhéto. From Vradhéto, use the marvellous "skála" (see opposite) to reach the edge of Kapésovo, from where the old track can be used to shortcut the asphalt road to Koukoúli. From Koukoúli, proceed on the Z31 path (see opposite) to Kípi. Be warned that the Z13–Z12 combination from Tsepélovo to Kípi is strictly dreary track-walking and that no real path exists through the Vikákis ravine between the two villages – the crossing of this gorge is a late-summer canyoning exercise for those willing to swim or (preferably) don neoprene suits.

Kapésovo, Koukoúli and Kípi

Of the three villages closest to the bridges, **KAPÉSOVO** is the highest; an attractive place, mostly invisible from the road and offering yet another possible access to the Víkos gorge. The gigantic former schoolhouse, dating from 1861, is now home to an informal ethnographic collection, including wolf-traps, and also hosts special events. The local **inn**, *Tò Kapesovo* (☎06530/71 723; ❸), though well appointed and featuring historic wall paintings, is neurotically managed, with more rules than a Victorian orphanage; the **café-taverna** on the platía does evening meals. Besides the famous *kalderími* up to Vradhéto, signposted at the village edge as "Skála Vradhétou", there's a brief corniche route (the "Katafí") to an overlook of the Mezariá ravine. The conventional trail down to Víkos, though a bit weedy, is well marked through oak forest.

Some 4km downhill from Kapésovo, **KOUKOÚLI** is another scarcely commercialized, atmospheric village, with cars banned from the village proper and nightingales audible by day until June. There are two **accommodation** options here: the *Xenon Koukouli* (☎06530/71 070, ⓦwww.epirus.com/koukouli; ❹) occupies three separate buildings – the best units are in the old monastery, and breakfast is served in the old school; it's co-managed with the *Hotel Ameliko* in Áno Pedhiná, and rooms share the same striking colour scheme. English residents Roy and Effi Hounsell offer *The Hamlet* (☎06530/71 743; ❸): four large pine-and-white rooms, and an apartment, overlooking a spacious garden – a rarity in Zagória. There's a breakfast bar on the ground floor; for other meals, patronize the central **kafenío-snack bar** by the church. Koukoúli, too, has relatively direct access to the gorge: an unmarked but still useable path leads from the southwest entrance of the village down to the O3 threading between Kípi and the Misíou bridge. Alternatively, the well-marked **Z31** path heads southeast, with a *kalderími* descent to the Kondodhímou bridge, reaching Kípi within 45 minutes.

KÍPI, by road 2km up a side turning 6km below Kapésovo, is another handsome village, which until the 1920s was known as Báya, and served as the administrative centre for the whole area. There's **accommodation** at Mina Vlahopoulou's en-suite *Pension stou Artemi* (☎06530/71 644 or 06510/75 678; ❸); the rooms of Evangelia Dherva (☎06530/71 658; ❸) are the alternative. Down on the main road stands what's considered the best **taverna** in the area, *Stou Mihali*, emphasizing local ingredients (beans, greens) and recipes (various *píttes*) at fair prices, washed down by a lovely purple wine. Also on the through road is an **activity centre** run by Robinson Expeditions (ring first as it's not always open – ☎06530/71 041 or 094/4525324), which in addition to offering regular guided walks will also organize canyoning, mountain-biking, rock-climbing and paragliding outings. On the same road, at the east edge of town, is the **Tolis Agapios Folklore Museum** (daily, any reasonable hour – knock next door). These days every Zagorian village claims to have such a display, but this one, with some 50,000 articles crammed in, really is the business. The regular **bus** (Mon, Wed & Fri), the same one serving Tsepélovo and Skamnélli, leaves for Ioánnina at 7am and 5pm on the days indicated.

North to the Aóös valley and north Píndhos

Beyond Skamnélli, forest appears, extending north to the **Aóös valley**. Fourteen kilometres or so out of the village, the road branches north towards Vryssohóri, which has two buses a week from Ioánnina. Rather than follow this relatively dull road on foot, you can get there in seven hours from Skamnélli by walking over a pass between the peaks of **Megála Lithária** (2467m) and **Tsoúka Roússa** (2377m). This is a rather easier hike than that through the Karterós pass previously described, and covered by many of the organized trekking groups. An added bonus is the unrivalled display of mountain wild flowers in the **Goúra valley**, directly below Tsoúka Roússa.

After the approach, **VRYSSOHÓRI** is a little anticlimactic, being almost swallowed by the dense woods at the base of Tsoúka Roússa peak. Tiny and ramshackle (this was one of the settlements burned by the Germans in the war), the village has just one, three-room **inn** run by Stamatia Tsoumani (☎06530/81 497 or 06510/20 974; ❸), but no proper taverna or even a store.

If necessary, you can camp at the edge of town by one of two springs on either side of the O3 coming down from Karterós.

The O3 used to continue as a trail across the Aóös from Vryssohóri to **Paleosélli** in the north Píndhos, but the path was bulldozed into a dirt track in 1989. If you want to avoid road-tramping, you will have to follow a slightly longer, pretty, but as yet unmarked trail from Vryssohóri via Áyios Minás chapel down to the Aóös. Ford the river (possible at low water only), and bushwhack a bit on the other side up to Paleosélli. You would need to allow about three and a half hours for this stretch, which permits direct access to the villages of Paleosélli and Pádhes on the southern slopes of Mount Smólikas (see p.416). Alternatively, the O3 resumes after a fashion on the far side of the bridge, cutting across the curves of the new road en route to Pádhes.

The north Píndhos

The region **north of the Aóös River** is far less visited than Zagóri. Its landscape is just as scenic but its villages are very poor relatives – almost all those within sight of the river were burned by the Germans during early 1944, accounting for their present thrown-together appearance. The villagers claim that before this disaster their houses exceeded in splendour those of Zagóri, since they had ample timber to span huge widths and for carved interiors.

The region is dominated by mounts **Smólikas** and **Grámmos**, two of the highest peaks in Greece. The former can be approached on foot from **Mount Gamíla** (see p.411) or by vehicle from **Kónitsa**, the largest settlement in these parts, just off the Ioánnina–Kastoriá highway.

Kónitsa and around

KÓNITSA is a sleepy little town whose most memorable features are a famous bridge and a view. The **bridge**, over the Aóös, is a giant, built around 1870 but looking far older. The **view** comes from the town's amphitheatre-like setting on the slopes of Mount Trapezítsa, above a broad flood plain where the Aóös and Voïdhomátis rivers mingle with the Sarandáporos before flowing through Albania to the sea.

The town was besieged by the Communist Democratic Army over New Year 1948, in their last, unsuccessful bid to establish a provisional capital. Much was destroyed in the fighting, though parts of the old bazaar and a tiny Ottoman neighbourhood near the river survive, as well as (near the top of town) a very dilapidated mansion which was apparently the birthplace of Hamko Hanim, mother of Ali Pasha (see p.395). However, in July 1996 a severe earthquake damaged numerous buildings in the lower quarters; a few families are still living in "temporary" pre-fab emergency structures.

The **bus terminal** (4–7 buses daily to Ioánnina and connections to most villages in this section) is on the central platía; the **bank** (with cash dispenser) and **post office** are just to the south. Kónitsa is now a recognized kayakers' and walkers' centre: outfits include No Limits (℡06550/23 777), down at the main-highway river-bridge (not the old one) who organize river trips, and Alpiki Zoni (℡06550/24 822 or 094/4909590). Accordingly, *dhomátia* have sprung up like mushrooms on the serpentine approach road up from the main highway, and along the minor lane to the historic bridge. Longest established, and one of the best, is en-suite *Tò Dhendro* (℡06550/23 982, ℻22 055,

@ www.epirus.com/todendro; **②**), whose English-speaking proprietor Yiannis Mourehidhes, one of the characters of Epirus, is a mine of local information, also arranges kayaking outings, and is fixing up a luxury hotel (opening 2003). Cooking at the attached restaurant is good too, featuring baked goat (*gástra*) and Yiannis' (in)famous *fétta psití*, baked feta cheese spiked with hot green chillies. Amongst other rooms, the best choice from the standpoint of calm is *Yerakofolia* (**①**06550/22 168; **②**), 300m along the road to Pádhes. The *Kouyias* (**①**06550/23 830; **③**), up on the main street near the post office and bank, is the one bona fide hotel in the town centre, with a ground-floor café and cheerful rooms. The only really fancy spot is the *Gefyri*, down by the old bridge (**①**06550/23 780, **②**gefyri@yahoo.com; **⑤**), and while the rooms (one or two with river view) are decent enough, noise from the adjacent nightclub may mean you don't get your money's worth. Apart from *To Dhendro*, *O Sourloukas* on the central platía is a good, inexpensive taverna.

The Aóös gorge

Kónitsa can serve as a base for a fine afternoon's walking, or even longer treks. Beginning at the old bridge over the Aóös, either of two interweaving paths on the south bank leads within ninety minutes to the eighteenth-century **monastery of Stomíou**, perched on a bluff overlooking the narrowest part of the Aóös gorge. The *katholikón* here is of minimal interest, and the premises have been rather brutally restored, but the setting is sublime. There are two springs to drink from, and many visitors camp in the surroundings, after bathing in the river below.

Beyond Stomíou the slopes are shaggy with vegetation constituting one of the last pristine habitats for lynx, roe deer and birds of prey. A minimally way-marked path climbs from the monastery gate up to the **Astráka area** (see p.411). This is a five-hour uphill walk, rather less in reverse, and a very useful trekkers' link between the Gamíla and the Smólikas regions, provided you have a good map. It is less arduous than the Astráka–Vryssohóri route and allows all sorts of loops through both Gamíla and the north Píndhos.

Molyvdhosképastos: village and monastery

The tiny hillside village of **MOLYVDHOSKÉPASTOS** hugs the Albanian border 23km west of Kónitsa. The place was once a haunt of the seventh-century emperor Constantine IV Pogonatos, though only a few of his monuments survive intact. One of these is the tiny chapel of **Ayía Triádha**, on a crag below; another is the present parish church of **Áyii Apóstoli**, right on the frontier. If you can get in, the church has fine frescoes, and the view from its terrace – into Albania, over the Aóös valley, and east to Smólikas and Gamíla – is among the finest in Epirus. Unfortunately, photography is forbidden hereabouts, and near the sporadically manned military checkpoint back at the Aóös bridge.

A weekday **bus** comes out to Molyvdhosképastos at 8am and 2.45pm from Kónitsa, but departs mornings only at weekends, in which case the only **place to stay** is at the overpriced *Hotel Bourazani* (T06550/61 283, F61 321, Wwww.burazani.gr; 6), set in its own safari/game park by the river bridge 10km before Molyvdhosképastos (the menu principally features beasts shot on request). On June 29, the village itself comes to life for the **festival** of its patron saints, Peter and Paul, with music and feasting until dawn.

Five kilometres below the village is the **monastery of Molyvdhoskepástou**, the most important of the emperor's surviving monuments. Repopulated early in the 1990s and attractively restored by its half-dozen monks, it enjoys a bucolic setting on the bank of the Aóös. The curiously long and narrow church, with a precariously high Serbian-type dome, is thirteenth century. The nave ceiling is supported by arches and vaults; the airier exonarthex was a later addition, and the frescoes throughout are in a poor state. This is a working monastery, so don't visit between 3pm and 5pm; the monks are also quite fanatical, not uncommon in cases of monastic revival, with lots of ecclesiastical literature (in Greek) on sale. Prominent, too, is the **exomoloyitírio** or confessional chapel, where (unlike in the Catholic tradition) the penitent sits at right angles to the priest at his desk, facing the altar where an icon of Christ presumably gazes into their very soul.

East of Kónitsa: Mount Smólikas

Mount Smólikas (2637m) is the second highest peak in Greece. It dominates a beautiful and very extensive range, covering a hundred square kilometres of mountain territory above 1700m in elevation, and including a lovely mountain lake, **Dhrakólimni** (not to be confused with its namesake on Mount Gamíla). The region is also one of the last heartlands of traditional shepherd life, which is best witnessed in summer at the Vlach village of **Samarína**.

Kónitsa–Dhístrato **buses** (Mon, Wed & Fri 2.30pm, Sun 7.45pm) roll through the mountains, stopping en route at Paleosélli and Pádhes, the two best trailheads on the mountain's southern flank. **PALEOSÉLLI** is much more of a going concern, with two simple stores, a pair of kafenía and an **inn-taverna** on the post-office plaza run by Yiorgos Tzimas **PÁDHES**, 3km further along, has rather less to offer: a single, stone-built building in the centre, the former school, which triples as the shop, **taverna** and **inn** (seventeen dorm-style beds) – the catch being that it operates only in the early morning and after 6pm, when someone motorbikes in from the nearby village of Ármata to unlock the premises.

Asphalt road surfacing has been extended the 20km from Pádhes to **DHÍSTRATO** at the end of the bus line; this large, relatively thriving village has no fewer than four licensed conventional **rooms** establishments, thanks to the ski centre nearby just over the provincial border on Mount Vassilítsa. From just before Dhístrato it's possible to drive north to Samarína (see below), but it's nineteen pretty-rutted kilometres, passable only from May until the first snows, and needing a jeep or high-clearance vehicle even then.

Hiking from Paleosélli

There is a fine trail from Paleosélli up to **Dhrakólimni** (a little over 4hr), and from there you can make an ascent of **Mount Smólikas** (another 90min). There is also a marked path to the lake from Pádhes, though a dirt road cuts across it at several points.

The Paleosélli–Dhrakólimni route has been waymarked as part of the O3 and a **refuge** established midway, at a spring and sheepfold known as Náneh, an idyllic little spot 1600m up with camping space, an external water supply and a toilet. Keys for this shelter are available from the Paleosélli inn. Beyond the refuge, the trail becomes less distinct but waymarks lead you up onto a ridge aiming for the summit of Mount Smólikas, though the path markings disappear at the treeline. Just over two walking hours from the refuge you should emerge into the little depression containing the **lake**. You can camp here, but level space is at a premium, the lake itself isn't drinkable (use sheep-free springs nearby) and you'll need a tent to protect against the cold and damp. Moving along the ridge above the lake, you can reach the **summit of Smólikas**, by tackling a rather steep, pathless slope with grass and stone underfoot. It is not unusual to see chamoix near the top.

The easiest way down from Smólikas is a scenic and well-trodden two-and-a-half-hour path to the hamlet of **AYÍA PARASKEVÍ** (also known as Kerásovo). The path leads off at a sheepfold in the vale between the lake and the summit. There are a couple of basic **tavernas** in the village, including one on the ground floor of the central *Kerassovo* hotel (☎06550/41 215 or 41 435; ❸), open all year; if it's full, camping near the village is tolerated. There's also a **bus** service to Kónitsa (currently Mon, Tues, Thurs & Fri around 7.30am, returning the same day at 2.30 or 3pm).

Hiking from Dhrakólimni to Samarína

If you have a good head for heights, and you're not carrying too heavy a pack, the best hiking route from **Dhrakólimni to Samarína** involves tracing the ridge east from the summit, the start of a seven-hour walking day. After an hour-plus of cross-country progress, you'll reach a small, bleak pass in the watershed, where you link up with a real path coming up from the village of Pádhes, hereabouts marked by faint yellow paint splodges on the rocks. Once through this gap, you descend into the rather lunar, northwest-facing cirque which eventually drains down to the hamlet of Ayía Paraskeví.

Next you traverse the base of one of Smólikas's secondary peaks as a prelude to creeping up a scree-laden rock "stair". From the top of this waymarks change from yellow to red, and a line of cairns guides you across a broad, flat-topped ridge. The path soon levels out on another neck of land. To the left yawns a dry gully (to be avoided) and way off to the right (south) can be glimpsed the other of Smólikas's lakes, as large as Dhrakólimni but difficult to reach. Try not to stray in either direction in poor visibility, as there are steep drops to either side.

Beyond, you encounter the leading edge of the black-pine forest, at the foot of a peak, which is capped by a wooden altimeter. The trail threads between this knoll and another, at the foot of which lies Samarína. Twenty minutes or so beyond this pass, a spring oozes from serpentine strata, some six hours from the Smólikas summit. There follows a sharper descent through thick forest, with a second spring gurgling into a log trough set in a beautiful mountain clearing, to which there is now a direct road. Below this, the woods end abruptly and you'll emerge on a bare slope directly above Samarína.

Samarína

At 1450m, just over the border in Grevená province, **SAMARÍNA** is claimed to be the highest village in Greece. It's principally inhabited in the summer when it fills up with Vlachs from the plains of Thessaly, and their sheep – some 50,000 of them, their odour alive or cooked permeating the air (and everything else). The village was burned during both World War II and the civil war, and was rebuilt in brutalist, cheap-and-easy style, with no concessions to "olde worlde" town planning. Thus, while Samarína may seem like the Bright Lights after several days' trekking, it's emphatically not somewhere you'd go out of your way to visit. This acknowledged, it's a thriving and friendly place, very proud of its Vlach traditions. The high point of the year is the **Feast of the Assumption** on August 15, when there is much music and merry-making and the place is swamped by nostalgic Vlachs from Athens and all over the country.

The interior of the main church, the **Panayía**, is superb, with frescoes and painted ceilings and an intricately carved *témblon*, where the angels, soldiers and biblical figures are dressed in mustachios and *fustanélles* (the Greek kilt). Though it looks a lot older, like many other churches in the region it dates from around 1800. Its special hallmark is an adult black pine growing out of the roof of the apse, and no one can remember a time without it. The keys are with the priest, who lives opposite the main gate.

The improbably large stone building that confronts you at the top of the village is a **hotel** (℡04620/95 216; ❸), now open all year, with winter sports to hand and for whose sake an improved, all-weather road is being graded in from Grévena. There are less pricey en-suite **rooms** on or just off the stone-paved platía: those of Ioannis Parlitis (℡04620/95 279; ❷), some with cooking facilities, or noisier ones above *O Yeros Smolikas*, one of six **grills** here. Yet more basic are the breeze-block rooms in the "*Hotel*" *Kyparissi* (℡04620/95 253; ❶), out on the east edge of the village, though these tend to operate only in July and August. Failing all of these, no one will mind if you camp in the pastures beyond the village itself.

Leaving Samarína, you have two choices. There is a bus to **Grevená**, 40km away on the Kalambáka–Kastoriá road, from June to September, but not every day, though a lift is not too hard to get if you ask around. If you are committed to staying in Epirus, follow the E6 trail via the monastery of Ayía Paraskeví and Goúrna ridge to **Dhístrato** (p.417), which has lodging and where you might coincide with an early-morning bus back to Kónitsa, or keep going to Vovoússa on the east bank of the Aóös, with its less frequent buses to Ioánnina.

North of Kónitsa: Mount Grámmos

It was on **Mount Grámmos** that the Communist "Democratic Army" made its last stand in the civil war. Its eventual retreat into Albania followed a bitter campaign which saw tens of thousands of deaths and the world's first use of napalm (supplied by the United States). The upper slopes of the mountain remain totally bare, and as you walk the high ridges you still see collapsed trenches and rusty cartridges from the fighting.

If you want to visit the range, and peer down into the wilds of Albania, the most useful base is the village of Plikáti. The simplest way here is from Kónitsa by **bus** (Mon, Wed & Fri 2pm). Coming here from the Smólikas area, you're best off walking out to **Ayía Paraskeví**, where there are **buses** to Kónitsa (see p.414); if you're too impatient to wait for the afternoon bus to Plikáti, the turn-off to it is just 10km north of the Ayía Paraskeví side-road, and you could always try your luck hitching.

Plikáti and a hike up Mount Grámmos

There's a singularly end-of-the-world feel to **PLIKÁTI** – it's the closest Greek village to the Albanian frontier, and trailhead for Greece's remotest, least fre-quented trekking area. Some eighteen paved kilometres off the main highway, the village is a traditional-looking place, with stone houses, the usual tiny per-manent population, a couple of exceedingly basic **inns** (those of Prokopis Natsis ☎06550/31 423; ❶, or two rooms rented by Angeliki Theologou) and a combination taverna/general store. Brace yourself to be stared at, as relative-ly few foreigners make it up here nowadays.

Mount Grámmos (2520m) is the fourth loftiest Greek peak, and in mak-ing the ascent you should plan on a round trip of eight hours from Plikáti. The easiest strategy is to angle northeast up the gentler slopes leading to Perífano (2442m), second highest point in the range, rather than tackling head-on the badly eroded and steep incline immediately below the main peak. The route in the indicated direction is clear for the first two hours out of the village, cross-ing the river and switchbacking up through bushes and then beech trees before it peters out at a sheepfold. Just above this are the last water sources on this side of the ridge: various trickles feeding a pond. Bearing west along a plain trail, you can thread along the crest for roughly an hour up to the **summit**, its cairn covered in a babel of initials and multilingual graffiti. Below, to the west, a cul-tivated Albanian valley stretches to the barns of Erseke, 5km away.

In the opposite direction from the summit, you can follow the watershed to the lower **Aréna massif**, which is garnished with a trio of small lakes and clumps of beech trees. The summer-only village of Grámmos is visible from the summit ridge, and though a clear trail leads to the place (which is in Kastoriá province), there is no onward means of transport.

The south Píndhos

Most hikers arriving at Ioánnina have their sights firmly set northwards, espe-cially on the Víkos gorge and the Zagóri villages. If you're feeling adventurous, however, and are not too particular about where you sleep or what you eat, the **remote villages** of the south Píndhos provide an interesting, and far less touristy, alternative. They perch on the beetling flanks of **mounts Tzoumérka** and **Kakardhítsa**, two overlapping ridges of bare mountains linked by a high plateau, plainly visible from Ioánnina. There are few special sights, but you'll get a solid, undiluted experience of Epirot life.

On weekdays **buses** leave from Ioánnina's southern station at 5am and 3.30pm for Ágnanda and Prámanda, with an additional Saturday service at

3.30pm and on Sundays at 2.30pm; there is also a service from Árta to Prámanda and beyond. Buses run a couple of times daily in either direction along the secondary road between Árta and Ioánnina, stopping at **Pláka**, which has an eighteenth-century bridge over the Arahthós amid stunning scenery; here you can flag down one of the twice-daily Árta-based buses continuing along the sideroad east as far as Melissourgí.

Ágnanda to Melissourgí

The first village of any size is 12km above Pláka at **ÁGNANDA**, heavily damaged in World War II and not particularly attractive, though it does have one **inn** (☎06850/31 332; ❸). It's better to continue on to **PRÁMANDA**, which is no more distinguished architecturally than Ágnanda, but enjoys a wonderful setting strewn across several ridges. The village is dominated by Mount Kakardhítsa behind and commands fine views of the Kallaritikós valley. Nearby there is a huge cave, inhabited in Neolithic times, to which any villager will give you directions if you ask for the *spília*. The enormous church of **Ayía Paraskeví** almost uniquely escaped wartime devastation, and as an example of nineteenth-century kitsch it is hard to beat. The village has a **post office**, a rather primitive central **inn**, plus a handful of **tavernas** and *psistariés*, though there is a more comfortable **hotel**, the *Tzoumerka* (☎06590/61 590, ☏61 336; ❹) in the tiny hamlet of **TSÓPELAS**, 2km out on the road to Melissourgí.

MELISSOURGÍ, 5km to the southeast of Prámanda, is more rewarding. The village escaped destruction during the war, though most buildings – including the historic church – have lost their slate roofs in favour of ugly pantiles. There is a **taverna** and one large **inn** (☎06590/61 357; ❸), run by a Mr Karadhimas, though it is not to be counted on in midsummer, when all accommodation is likely to be booked by holidaying relatives from the cities. There are two daily weekday **buses** to Árta from Melissourgí, at 6am and 5pm.

Hikes from Melissourgí

Melissourgí is a good base for rambles on the **Kostelláta plateau** to the south. This upland separates Mount Kakardhítsa (2429m), which looms sheer above the village, from the more pyramidal Mount Tzoumérka (2399m). Heading south, you can cross these high pastures in a day and a half. The initial stretch of path from Melissourgí is very faintly waymarked with red-paint arrows, and there are intermittent *stánes* (summer sheepfolds) if you need water or directions. You can descend to the villages of **THEODHÓRIANA** or **VOULGARÉLLI** (officially Dhrossopiyí), at the edge of the Ahelóös river basin; both have daily early-morning buses to Árta, as well as modest **inns** and **tavernas**. In Voulgarélli, the not-so-modest *Arhondiko Villa Sofia* beckons (☎06850/22 713; ❹); however, it's car-inaccessible at the top of a slope and overpriced, so luckily two more-reasonable, less-publicized outfits, including the *Galini* (☎06850/22 135; ❸) are available lower down the hill.

Prámanda to Syráko

On weekdays the afternoon **bus** from Ioánnina continues to **Matsoúki**, the last village on the provincial route, beautifully set near the head of a partly forested valley and offering easy access to Mount Kakardhítsa, as well as a few beds. Most days the bus also calls at the hamlet of **Kipína**. A famous namesake **monastery**, founded in 1381 but uninhabited today, hangs like a martin's nest from the cliff-face a half-hour's walk beyond the hamlet.

Kallarítes

Beyond Kipína monastery, you can follow the road upstream for around half an hour through a tunnel and past a road bridge to join the remnant of a wonderful *kalderími* climbing up to the village of **KALLARÍTES**, perched superbly above the upper reaches of the Kallaritikós River. This depleted village, one of the southernmost Vlach settlements in the Píndhos, was a veritable El Dorado until the close of the nineteenth century. Fame and fortune were based on its specialization in gold- and silversmithing, and even today the craftsmen of Ioánnina are mostly of Kallaritiot descent – as is Bulgari, one of the world's most exclusive contemporary jewellers. Though the village is all but deserted except during summer holidays, the grand houses of the departed rich are kept in excellent repair by their descendants. The flagstoned platía has probably remained unchanged for a century, with its old-fashioned stores and *stele* commemorating local emigré Kallaritiots, who helped finance the Greek War of Independence. There are two **café-grills** on the platía, and a like number of small **inns**: those of Pavlos and Evripidha Patounis (℡06510/79 917; ❷) and Napoleon Zanglis (℡06590/61 518; ❷).

Khroússias gorge and Syráko

Just beyond Kallarítes, the awesome **Khroússias gorge** separates the village from its neighbour Syráko, visible high up on the west bank but a good hour's walk away. The trail is spectacular, including a near-vertical "ladder" hewn out of the rockface. Down on the bridge over the river you can peer upstream at a pair of abandoned water mills. The canyon walls are steep and the sun shines down here for only a few hours a day, even in summer.

SYRÁKO, hugging a steep-sloped ravine, is even more strikingly set than Kallarítes, with well-preserved *arhondiká*, archways and churches more reminiscent of those in the Zagóri. Not to be upstaged by Kallarítes, the village has also erected a number of monuments to various national figures (including the poet Krystallis) who hailed from here. There is a **taverna** (summer only), a kafenío and a very few unofficial **rooms**; if these are unavailable, you can beg a mattress on the floor in the school during the summer. Bus service is nonexistent except July 1 to August 15 (Fri dawn and Sun evening), so if you've hiked here at other times you should plan on hitching or walking out.

The Epirot coast and Étolo-Akarnanía

The **Epirot coast** has some attractive beaches between Igoumenítsa and Préveza, though they can't compare to Zagória or the Píndhos overall for uniqueness or scenic distinction. **Igoumenítsa** itself is a purely functional ferry port, while the first beaches you'd detour for are at **Sývota**, a few kilometres south. **Párga**, the most attractive resort on the way to Préveza, has become overdeveloped and is best left for out-of-season visiting. Head a little inland, however, and things start looking up. Close by Párga, the **Nekromanteion of Ephyra** (the legendary gate of Hades) is an intriguing detour; the **gorge of the Aheróndas River** offers fine hiking; and the imposing ruins of **Kassopi** and **Nikopolis** break the journey to **Préveza**, a fairly low-key provincial capital at the mouth of the Amvrákikos gulf. **Árta** is another interesting town surrounded by Byzantine churches, approached either around the gulf from Préveza, or more impressively along the plane-shaded Loúros river gorge from Ioánnina.

Moving south into **Étolo-Akarnanía**, the landscape becomes increasingly desolate with little to delay your progress to the island of Lefkádha (see p.964) or to Andírio, for the ferry to the Peloponnese. Committed hermits might hole up on **Kálamos** island, south of Vónitsa and reached from the enjoyable little coastal settlement of **Mýtikas**. Lord Byron's heart is buried at wall-girt **Mesolóngi**; it's otherwise an unglamorous town, though tolerable enough for a few hours.

Igoumenítsa and around

IGOUMENÍTSA is Greece's third passenger port, after Pireás and Pátra, with almost hourly ferries to Corfu and several daily to Italy. As land travel through most of ex-Yugoslavia remains a dodgy option, sea traffic between Greece and Italy has increased significantly. With the impending completion of the Via Egnatia expressway segment from Thessaly to here, it will soon become the country's leading cargo port; a megaterminal is being built at the harbour to service lorries exiting the motorway.

These seagoing functions and its waterfront apart, the town is pretty unappealing; Igoumenítsa was levelled during World War II and rebuilt in a sprawling, utilitarian style. If you can arrange it, try to get a ferry out on the day you arrive; virtually every day in season there are sailings to Italy almost around the clock. To take a vehicle, or get a cabin berth on afternoon or evening sailings (see box on pp.424–425), it's best to make reservations in advance. If you find yourself stuck for the day, you are better off taking one of the limited range of **excursions** from Igoumenítsa than hanging around the town.

Practicalities

At present, **boats depart** from various locations along the quay, though once the new south terminal is completed you can expect most international services to be shifted there. When buying tickets, ascertain exactly where your boat is berthed to avoid last-minute dashes. Local ferries to Corfu or Paxí are unlikely to move from their current home just north of the new port. Close to the central part of the quay, you'll still find the OTE **office** (daily 7am–2.30pm; ☎06650/22 227), next to the customs house. The **bus station** is five minutes away at Kýprou 47. Driving your own car, beware of Igoumenítsa's **fee-parking** scheme, nominally in effect 8am–10pm (though enforcement on two recent visits was lax): you buy tickets at kiosks, not at pay-and-display machines.

The town is not large but **hotels** are plentiful, if rather lugubrious and overpriced; most are to be found either along or just back from the waterfront. The nearest budget hotel to the port, at Ethnikís Andístasis 58A, is the *Acropolis* (☎06650/22 342; ❷), non-en-suite but with sea views. More comfortable and closer to the dock is the C-class *Oscar* at Ayíon Apostólon 149, also on the seafront (☎06650/23 338; ❹). Inland, at the southeast corner of the main platía, stands the more comfortable, air-conditioned *Egnatia*, at Eleftherías 1 (☎06650/23 648; ❸); ask for a rear room facing the pine grove. Perhaps the best budget choice is the non-en-suite *Stavrodhromi*, Soulíou 14, the street leading diagonally uphill and northeast from the square (☎06650/22 343; ❶), with a pleasant atmosphere and a restaurant that makes its own wine. The closest **campsite** is the *Kalami Beach* (☎06650/71 211; April–Oct), just before Platariá, a nine-kilometre bus ride away.

Not surprisingly, **restaurants** and **cafés** are generally pretty uninspiring and thin on the ground; for lunch, try *Martinis Sotiriou* inland at pedestrianized Grigoríou Lambráki 32, or *Ouzeri To Kohyli* at the south end of Lambráki, near Venizélou, for seafood. After dark several fish tavernas and ouzerís at the very north end of the front, near the Dhrépano turning, come to life, as does the *Psarotaverna O Timios*, just south of the new port. Several **banks** with cash dispensers are scattered along the south end of the front; at the north end, just inland on Evangelistrías, is the **post office**.

Around Igoumenítsa

The best brief escapes are probably to the **beach**. The closest strand lies 5km west at **Dhrépano**, a crescent-shaped sand spit (the name means "sickle") shaded by myrtle and closing off a lagoon. Local city buses serve it, and there are a few simple snack bars along its two-kilometre length.

Inland, few destinations reward the effort expended to get to them, despite earnest promotion in OTE brochures. There is a regular bus to the "traditional village" of **Filiátes**, 19km north of Igoumenítsa, but it proves to be a drab place, with a paltry number of old Epirot houses and little else, not even a taverna, to redeem it. The old hill town of **Paramythiá**, 38km to the southeast (2 buses daily), is another disappointment. A castle is scarcely in evidence, the Byzantine cemetery church of Kímisis Theotókou on the outskirts has little of note inside or out, and despite being touted as a centre for copper-working, just two mediocre metal shops remain in a tiny bazaar much encroached on by 1960s architecture – nothing comparable to what you'd more easily and conveniently see in Ioánnina. For an inland excursion, your time would be much better spent at the remarkable **Nekromanteion of Ephyra** or the **Aheróndas gorge** (see opposite).

South along the coast, other beaches flank the campsites at Kalámi (9km) and Platariá (12km), but the beaches at Sývota (23km), and Karavostási and Sarakíniko further south, are by far the most attractive options in this direction.

Sývota

The sleepy resort of **SÝVOTA**, surrounded by olive groves, drapes itself over some evocative coastal topography while gazing out to Corfu and Paxí. Greeks favour the place for their holidays, so summer apartments predominate, though foreign package companies have discovered Sývota since the early 1990s. The north bay and its small port has been developed and prettified with pedestrianization; it's a popular berthing for yachts, despite fierce afternoon winds, and renting a small boat is a good way of exploring the convoluted coast. The village centre – such as it is – lies a kilometre inland, with smaller, sandier bays found just off the road south to Pérdhika (and eventually, Párga, a link not shown on older maps). In order of occurrence going south, there's small, shady **Závia**, bigger, sunnier **Méga Ámmos**, **Mikrí Ámmos** (now rechristened "BB Beach"), **Méga Tráfos** with its two secluded coves, and **Ayía Paraskeví**, with an islet to swim to. There are also sandy patches on the island of **Mávro Óros**, joined to the mainland by the sandspit of **Bélla Vráka**; you can reach

Igoumenítsa ferry companies

In recent years there has been a winnowing out of the flakier ferry companies, and a healthy spreading of **departure times** across the day. Thus it's risky to generalize, but you can expect ferries to leave for different Italian destinations between 5am and 3pm, fairly evenly spaced, with another cluster of evening departures between 7pm and 2am (most commonly 10pm–midnight). Ticket agencies tend to stay open until the last boat which they handle has departed.

Except where noted, frequencies of ferry crossings detailed opposite are for the **high season**, the definition of which varies slightly between companies. Broadly, for crossings from Italy to Greece, high season is between early July and mid-August, especially at weekends; from Greece to Italy, it is between early August and early September. Out of season, services are reduced to two or three weekly on many lines.

Most **ticket agencies** for international ferries are found along waterfront Ethnikís Andístasis and its continuation, Ayíon Apostólon, south towards the new harbour. Tickets for domestic services are purchased at little booths on the domestic ferry quay, a bit north of the new port. All companies offer a variety of **fares** for cabin, "airplane" seats and deck passage, as well as reductions for student-cardholders and hefty discounts on return tickets. High-season fares to Bari, for example, range from €50–63.50 for the cheapest seats to €115–140.50 for two-berth cabins with baths. Cars are carried on all ferries; as a guideline count on €50–58.50 for a small sedan to Bari. Bicycles go free, motorcycles usually do so too, or cost next to nothing. Ventouris, Superfast and Med Link allow you to sleep in your camper or van on deck, sparing you the cost of a cabin. It pays to shop around, as fares and conditions vary significantly from company to company, according to boat quality and speed; the new generation of high-speed craft, basically huge catamarans, have cut optimum travel times by a third and pushed many slower boats out of business. Whether by high-speed or conventional ferry, Brindisi tends to be marginally less expensive as a destination than Bari, Ancona rather more; Venice and Trieste are vastly more costly destinations, but many drivers reckon it worth the extra money in terms of savings on expensive Italian fuel and skipping hazardous motorway travel.

All international departures carry an **embarkation tax** of €4.50–6 per person *and* per car; this figure is usually, but not always, included in a company's quoted prices. If you have bought tickets in advance, or from a travel agent other than the local authorized agent – and most waterfront agencies sell cheerfully and promiscuously for several companies – you must **check in** (to the appropriate *official* agent as listed opposite, or at their booth in the port) at least two hours before departure. Unlike sailings from Pátra, ferries from Igoumenítsa to Italy are not allowed to sell tickets

this overland using the track, then path, from a side spur of the access road for the exclusively German Club Robinson, though it has mostly novelty value – the shore here is gritty and dominated by the Club Robinson clients. Another potential problem at Sývota is reaching the southerly beaches; they're spread out along more than 6km, there's limited local transport hire, and only a rudimentary **bus** service through here (3 Mon–Fri, 2 Sat) to Pérdhika and Párga.

Among **hotels** taking walk-in trade, there's the tree-shrouded *Hellas* (☎06650/93 227; ❸) in the village centre, with a decent restaurant, or the studio apartments *Long Summer* (☎06650/93 260; ❹), further towards the beach but still inland. There are also numerous places around and behind the round platía at the north harbour, best of these the well-maintained *Villa Anneta* gallery apartments (☎06650/93 457 or 27 386; ❹) for up to four people, in a lovely garden setting 150m inland – the friendly managing family has some tours but keeps a few units for walk-ins. Right on the same roundabout, overlooking the harbour with a **stopover** on Corfu. You can, however, take the regular Corfu ferry over and then pick up most ferry routes on from there, though the fare will be the same as from Igoumenítsa (and, in many cases, as from Pátra).

International ferry companies, destinations and agents

Agoudimos Brindisi (9hr), July to mid-Aug daily at 10am, mid-Aug to mid-Sept 10pm, much less often till Christmas and April–June. Nikos Zois, Ethnikís Andístasis 32 ☎06650/21 175.

ANEK Ancona (13hr), mid-May to Oct 6 weekly at 11pm or 1am, Jan–April 4 weekly; Trieste (20hr), mid-May to Oct 6 weekly at 10am, Jan–April 4 weekly. Eleftherios Revis, Ethnikís Andístasis 34 ☎06650/22 104.

Blue Star Ancona (15hr 30min), Oct–March only daily 7.30pm; Venice (25hr 30min), year-round Mon, Tues, Fri & Sat at 7.30am; Brindisi (9hr) April–Oct daily at 11.30pm; Ayíon Apostólon 145 ☎06650/29 260.

Fragline Brindisi (8hr 15min) via Corfu, mid-June to early Oct daily at 7.45 or 11am; April to mid-June mix of morning and 10pm sailings, almost daily. Eleftherios Revis, Ethnikís Andístasis 34 ☎06650/27 906.

Marlines Bari (12hr–12hr 30min), July to mid-Oct only 4 varying days weekly (always Sun & Fri), 2 via Corfu. Marlines, Ethnikís Andístasis 42 ☎06650/23 911.

Med Link Lines, Brindisi direct (9hr 30min), Aug to mid-Sept sporadic days at 2am. Eleni Pantazi, Ethnikís Andístasis 70 ☎06550/26 833.

Minoan Lines Brindisi via Corfu (8hr 30min), mid-May to late Sept daily at 11.30pm. Oscar Travel, Ayíon Apostólon 147 ☎06650/26 410.

Superfast, Bari (9hr 30min), Jan–Feb daily at midnight except certain days; Ancona (15hr), year round daily at 11.30pm except "rest" day every two weeks. Pitoulis, Ayíon Apostólon 61 ☎06550/28 150.

Ventouris Bari via Corfu (11hr 30min), June to mid-Sept daily at 10pm, mid-Sept to Dec 3–4 weekly, April–May roughly 5 weekly; Brindisi via Corfu (4hr high speed), late April to late June 1 daily 11am, late June to Aug 3 daily at 8.30am–7/8pm, Aug 1 daily Fri–Sun via Paxí; Brindisi via Corfu (9hr conventional boat), late June to mid-Aug daily 11pm, mid-Aug to mid-Sept daily 11am. Milano Travel, Ayíon Apostólon 11B ☎06650/24 237.

Domestic ferries and hydrofoils

Corfu (Town) (1hr–1hr 15min) Almost hourly ferries in season from 4.30am to 10pm.
Corfu (Lefkími) (30min) 6 daily ferries, 7.30am–9.30pm (1hr); 1–2 daily hydrofoils.
Paxí (Gaïos) (1hr 20min) 1 daily ferry Mon–Fri (4pm), 2 daily Sat–Sun (10.30am & 4pm); 1–2 daily hydrofoils (40min).

next to the police station, there's also the comfortable *Hotel Fylakas* (☎06650/93 345; ❺). You'll get more facilities for your money out at the beaches: at Méga Ámmos by far the better of two hotels is the *Mikros Paradisos* (☎06650/93 281, ⓕ93 501; ❹), also with pricier air-con bungalows (❺) and family units scattered across lovely grounds with a tennis court. There are some packages here; advantageous half-board rates include home-made wine. There's also a **campsite** (☎06650/93 275; May–Sept) just north of the harbour.

The beaches all have grills or simple snack bars, but for relatively haute cuisine the harbour is the place, where about ten **tavernas** vie for your custom. *O Faros* (*Tzimas*) at mid-quay is a reliable all-rounder, with fish, appetizers and *mayireftá*, though other eateries excel at their specialities: *Trehandiri* (the first in line) for seafood, remoter *Ostria* for *mezédhes*. At the port you can also catch the seasonal **ferry** to Paxí, less reliable and pricier (€14.70–22 one-way depending on type of craft) than Parga's or Igoumenítsa's; contact Isabella Travel (☎06650/93 317 or

93 050, @Isabella@otenet.gr) for current details. This agency also **rents cars and bikes**, arranges accommodation and can **change money**, though there's now a freestanding cash dispenser in the village.

Karavostási and Sarakíniko

About 11km south of Sývota "town" centre, you reach the edge of Pérdhika village and the poorly marked but well-paved side road (6km) down to **Karavostási** beach – its hotels are better signposted. The 450-metre beach itself – generally conceded the best on the Thesprotian coast – usually has a light surf, but the water is clean and brisk, with just a few rental sunbeds and camper vans at the far end. At the river mouth (a protected environment) there's a snack/drink bar but no other facilities independent of the three **hotels** here. Of these, the Intourist-style *Regina Mare* has a funicular to plonk its patrons at the north end of the strand, the *Elina* is perennially booked by Italian groups, leaving the B-class *Karavostasi Beach* as your best-value option (☎06650/91 104, ⓕ91 568, ⓦwww.karavostasi.com; ❹, ❶ low). Some of the marble-clad rooms have sea views, while the well-designed pool-bar area makes an attractive breakfast venue. **Aríllas**, the next bay north and reached from a split in the road 1500m above Karavostási, doesn't have nearly as good a beach, but does offer two or three proper **restaurants** and a yachting/fishing anchorage.

Beyond Karavostási, you cross the provincial border into Préveza and just before Ayiá meet the paved, five-kilometre road down to scenic **Sarakíniko**, a short (about 150m) if broad cove of sand and pebbles, with currents making for a cool sea year-round, and a certain amount of day-trip patronage from Párga (see below). Just inland sits one of the region's best **tavernas**, *Christos*, where it's advisable to book and preorder during peak season (☎06840/35 207 or 097/7982207). Only a few select dishes per day are cooked, but the quality is high, prices fair and seafood (excepting squid or octopus) is served fresh or not at all. Among a handful of places to **stay**, try for the peaceful, friendly rooms of Periklis and Simela Nanos, 300m south (☎06840/35 292; ❸), run as a sideline to their vast farm; it too must be prebooked from July through mid-August.

Párga and around

PÁRGA is a photogenic and popular coastal town, approximately 50km south of Igoumenítsa on the Epirot shoreline. An arc of tiered houses, set below a Norman-Venetian **kástro**, and superb local **beaches**, with a string of rocky islets offshore, constitute as enticing a resort as any in western Greece. However, since the late 1980s this has been swamped by concrete apartments at the outskirts, and package tourism has even engulfed the next village, Anthoússa, 3km west, where numerous tavernas and accommodation places nestle under a tiny, hatbox castle between Ayiá and Tríkorfo, nocturnally illuminated for tourists' benefit. In peak season, it's hard to recommend more than a brief stopover in Párga (if you can find a room) before taking the twice-daily local **ferry to Paxí**, which in July and August must also be reserved in advance. The Corfu model, presumably, was just too close to ignore, though plans to enlarge the harbour to accommodate cruise liners have fortunately been suspended.

Párga's fate is all the more poignant given its idiosyncratic **history**. From the fourteenth to the eighteenth centuries Párga was a lone Venetian toehold in Epirus, complementing the Serene Republic's offshore possessions in the

Ionian islands. The Lion of St Mark – symbol of Venice – is still visible on the *kástro* keep. Under Venetian rule, a small community of Jews prospered here from the export of citrons to western Europe for liturgical use; they, and the citrons, are long gone but lemon groves remain at Anthoússa. Later, the Napoleonic French took Párga for a brief period, leaving additional fortifications on the largest **islet**, a 200-metre swim from the harbour beach.

At the start of the nineteenth century, the town enjoyed a stint of independence, being self-sufficient through the export of olives, still a mainstay of the region's agriculture. After that, the British acquired Párga and subsequently sold it to Ali Pasha, who rebuilt all the local castles. The townspeople, knowing his reputation, decamped to the Ionian islands, the area being resettled by Muslims who remained until the exchange of populations in 1923, when they were replaced in part by Orthodox Greeks from the area around Constantinople.

The town and its beaches

The town is dominated by the blufftop **Kástro** (open all day; free at present), a haven from Párga's bustle. A long stair-street leads up to the ruined, cypress-tufted ramparts, which offer excellent views of the town, its waterfront and a mountainous backdrop. A visitor centre inside the castle is approaching completion, after which you can expect some sort of perfunctory museum and an admission charge.

Párga's fine **beaches** line three consecutive bays, split by the fortress headland, and get very crowded in midsummer. The small bay of **Kryonéri** lies opposite the church-studded islet, an easy swim away (or reachable by self-drive motorboat, a popular option). Immediately beyond the *kástro* (and on foot easiest reached by the long ramp from the *kástro* gate; also frequent water-taxis in season from the town dock) lies **Váltos beach**, more than a kilometre in length as it arcs around to the hamlet of the same name. **Lýkhnos**, 3km in the opposite (southeast) direction, is a similarly huge beach; a shaded path through the olive groves, starting beyond the supermarket and bakery behind Kyronéri, shortcuts the winding road in, or again taxi-boats spare you the walk.

Practicalities

Buses link Párga with Ioánnina, Igoumenítsa and Préveza four or five times daily on weekdays, less at weekends; the stop is up on the bypass road, near the start of Spýrou Livadhá (the way to Váltos) and Avis (☏06840/26 632) **car rental**. The **post office** is on Alexándhrou Bánga, start of the main market street, which also has two **banks** with cash dispensers. A half-dozen travel agencies, concentrated on the waterfront, cater mostly to package tourists, but they also rent motorbikes or cars, and run boat tours up the Aheróndas River to the Nekromanteion of Ephyra, allowing good views of the delta birdlife en route (though this is more easily and cheaply arranged in Ammoudhiá, see p.432). ITS (☏06840/31 833) is one of the more useful agencies, acting as ticket-sales point for the regular morning and evening ferry to Paxí (about €4 one way), much the cheapest and quickest means of getting there.

Accommodation

From late June to early September package tourists monopolize most of the hotels and quality apartments; in the UK, Direct Greece and Sunvil offer some of the better-sited and -appointed properties. This leaves the balance, often reserved by Italians for weeks in advance; only during May, early June and October will you more or less have the run of the place. Just a bare handful of

hotels remain which are not block-booked by companies. The potentially noisy *Ayios Nektarios* (☎06840/31 150, ℻32 150, ⓦwww.epirus.com/hotel-nectarios; ❹), on the edge of town at the corner of Livadhá and the road in, has a small self-catering kitchen and fair-sized rooms, with those facing the sea the best. The *Galini* (☎06840/31 581, ℻32 221; ❸), set nearby in an orchard, is as quiet as the name ("Serenity") implies, with enormous rooms; the almost adjacent *Alkyon* (☎06840/31 022; ❸) is also worth considering. The *Torini*, far enough up Spýrou Livadhá to avoid most (though not all) traffic noise (☎06840/31 219; ❹ high, ❷ low season), offers anodyne, medium-sized rooms with fridge and balconies. Better than any of these, however, are the *Magda Apartments* (☎06840/31 332, ℻31 690, ⓔmagdas@otenet.gr; ❺), also on the road to Váltos before the *kástro* turning. Two- to four-person units are superbly appointed and enjoy a fine hillside garden environment with mountain and partial sea views – though as with anything of this standard in Párga, there's a heavy package presence.

Rooms are theoretically plentiful, but the plushest are again contracted out. The best hunting strategy for the rest is to take the stair-street up to the castle entrance, where the lane leading perpendicularly away along the ridge (officially Patatoúka, popularly called Tourkopázaro) is one solid line of rooms, many with unbeatable views over Váltos beach – outside peak season you'll be approached with offers of accommodation. Representative of ones left for on-spec tourists are the incredibly friendly and resolutely basic ones of Kostas and Katerina Pappas at no. 36 (☎06840/31 301), with a roof terrace, small kitchen and mixed bathless (❷) and en-suite (❸) rooms.

There are **campsites** just behind Kryonéri beach at *Parga Camping* (☎06840/31 161), and a newer, unobtrusive site, *Valtos* (☎06840/31 287; May–Sept), at the far end of Váltos beach by the new yacht harbour, but the enormous *Enjoy Lyhnos Camping* (☎06840/31 171) straddles the road access to Lýkhnos beach, making you feel compelled to use their facilities.

Eating and drinking

For **meals**, there are easily two dozen full-service tavernas around the town, though most have had their menus predictably warped by the mass-tourist trade. Exceptions include long-running *To Kantouni*, at the rear of the market on Platía Ayíou Dhimitríou, which maintains high standards, and *Psarotaverna Zorbas* (aka *Triadha's* after the proprietress) on the west waterfront of Kamíni, which is a good venue for fish. On the busier east quay, where you'll see quite a few Greek holiday-makers eating, *To Souli* ranks as far and away the best of several here, offering reasonably priced, non-greasy if standard *mayireftá*; people dine on fish at *Dionysos*, at the far end overlooking Kryonéri from an elevated position. Párga's one and only ouzerí is *Apangio*, up a stair-lane from the east quay, next to the *Kamares* disco; it's savoury but a bit pricey (reckon on €12–14 for three dishes including seafood, and a *karafáki*), with a mixed local and foreign clientele. Up on Patatoúka leading off the castle gate, few of several establishments are worth considering; *Sakis*, while cheapish, is greasily mediocre, however, *Filomila* some 100m beyond makes a decent fist of Italian pasta dishes, and is the only spot in Párga to secure fresh mussels. Lastly, *Creperie Eden/Edem* on Platía Ayíou Dhimitríou can be confidently recommended for full breakfasts and desserts, with consistent quality since the early 1990s. Incidentally, most Párga tavernas offer local wine from the barrel; the red is generally excellent. For more extended drinking, **nightlife** centres around a half-dozen well-behaved bars on the main quay, pumping out 1960s and 1970s sounds to match the largely forty- and fifty-something crowd; Párga isn't primarily a youth mecca.

Southeast: the Necromanteion of Ephyra

The **Necromanteion of Ephyra** (or Sanctuary of Persephone and Hades, **Nekromandío** in modern Greek) stands just above the village of Mesopótamo, 22km southeast of Párga. Compared with Greece's other ancient remains, the site has few visitors, and this, coupled with its evocative location, makes it a worthwhile and slightly unusual excursion. The sanctuary is sited on a low, rocky hill, above where, in ancient times, the Acheron (Ahérondas in modern Greek), associated with the mythical Styx, river of the underworld, the Kokytos, "River of Lamentation", and the Pyriphlegethon, "River of Flaming Fire", all flowed into the marshy lake of Acherousia. According to mythology, this was the spot from where Charon rowed departed souls across the lake to the gates of Hades, and from Mycenaean to Roman times it maintained an elaborate oracle of the dead. Ephyra never achieved the stature of Delphi or Dodona, but its fame was sufficient for Homer, writing (one assumes) in the ninth century BC, to use it as the setting for Odysseus's visit to Hades. Circe describes it explicitly, when advising Odysseus: "You will come to a wild coast and to Persephone's grove, where the hill poplars grow and the willows that so quickly lose their seeds. Beach your boat there by Ocean's swirling stream and march on into Hades' Kingdom of Decay. There the River of Flaming Fire and the River of Lamentation, which is a branch of the Waters of the Styx, unite around a pinnacle of rock to pour their thundering streams into Acheron. This is the spot, my lord, that I bid you seek out . . . then the souls of the dead and departed will come up in their multitudes."

The sanctuary

Trees still mark the sanctuary's site (daily: summer 8am–7pm; winter 8am–3pm; €1.50; site booklet €4.50 extra), though today they are primarily cypresses, emblems of the dead throughout the Mediterranean. The ancient Lake Acherousia, which once enclosed the island-oracle, has receded to the vague line of the Ahérondas skirting the modern, marshy plain of Fanári, which still floods in winter; from the sanctuary you can pick out its course from a fringe of Homer's willows. All the mythological rivers still exist, though the Pyriphlegethon has taken the modern name Vovós.

As for the sanctuary itself, its **ruins**, flanked by an early **Christian basilica**, offer a fascinating exposé of the confidence tricks pulled by its priestly initiates. According to contemporary accounts, **pilgrims** arriving on the oracle-island were accommodated for a night in windowless rooms. Impressed by the atmosphere, and by their mission to consult with the souls of the dead, they would then be relieved of their votive offerings while awaiting their "day-trip" to the underworld. When their turn came, they would be sent groping along labyrinthine corridors into the heart of the sanctuary, where, further disorientated by having ingested psychoactive lupin seeds, they would be lowered into the antechamber of "Hades" itself to witness whatever spectral visitation the priests might have devised.

The remains of the sanctuary – walls of polygonal masonry standing up to head height – allowed excavators to identify the function of each room, and there is a rudimentary plan at the entrance. At the very top, visible from a considerable distance, sits a **medieval chapel** of Ayíou Ioánnou Prodhrómou, retaining eighteenth-century fresco fragments; just below, *pithária* or giant storage urns have been left *in situ*. At the centre of the site is a long room with high walls, flanked by chambers used for votive offerings. From here metal steps lead to the damp, vaulted underground chamber where the necromantic audiences took place. Originally this descent was by means of a precarious windlass mechanism, which was found on the site.

Practicalities

The Necromanteion is most easily reached by boat **tour** from Párga or Ammoudhiá (see p.432), or by motorbike. Puny scooters will not cope well with the grades and speeds of the improved main highway between the two points – you'll need at least a 90cc bike. **Buses** from Párga stop at Kastrí (2km before Kanalláki), 5km from the site, but they do not call at Mesopótamo or Ammoudhiá, which are on the direct coast road to Préveza, and a different bus line. Buses from Párga and Préveza also pass through the county town of **KANALLÁKI**, where scooters (a more feasible mode of transport from here) can be rented in summer. There are two basic **hotels** in Kanalláki, the *Ephyra* (☎06840/22 128; ❷) and *Aheron* (☎06840/22 241; ❷), beside each other near the main platía, plus a few *psistariés*. In theory, the village could make a useful base for leisurely exploration of both the Necromanteion and the Soúli area (see below), but in fact it's an ugly, dusty place bearing all the hallmarks of massive wartime destruction and/or hasty refugee settlement. Ammoudhiá (see p.432) is a far more amenable base, and slightly closer to the Necromanteion in any case.

East into Souliot country

The highland region four valleys east of Párga was the traditional heartland of the **Souliots**, an independent-spirited tribe of Albanian Orthodox Christians, who inhabited eleven separate villages here. From 1787 until their initial defeat and dispersal in 1803, these 12,000 doughty mountain warriors conducted a perennial rebellion against Ali Pasha and his Muslim Albanians from their strongholds above the **Ahérondas gorge** and in the mountains to the south. In 1820 they allied themselves with Ali Pasha and were allowed to return to their homes, but following the sultan's final victory over Ali, the Souliots were exiled permanently as punishment. Today the region remains impoverished and deserted, though celebrated as a linchpin of resistance against Ottoman rule.

Although it seems hard to think now of the placid Ahérondas near the Necromanteion of Ephyra as the way to Hell, just a few kilometres inland its waters cut deep into rock strata and swirl in unnavigable eddies as the river saws a course through its gorge, which begins its downstream course at the remote village of Tríkastro. While not in quite the same league as the Víkos (see p.404), it is certainly a respectable wilderness, and if you're looking for a solitary adventure inland from Párga you won't find better (except at weekends, when locals will be out in force).

Local walks

Hikes up the gorge start at **GLYKÍ**, 12km from Kanalláki on the inland road between Préveza and Paramythiá (one daily bus from the former). The river, still relatively calm here, is flanked on one bank by several mediocre, overpriced *exóhika kéndra* eateries and on the other (the south or true left bank) by a sign reading "Skála Tzavélainas", pointing up a paved road. Following this, you can bear left after 800m towards the signposted *Piyes Aheronda* **taverna** (1400m in total from the main road), much better and cheaper than its rivals, with abundant, hygienic grilled fare. There's also shaded seating in the river sand, plus good wading for kids and adults alike to the nearby *piyés* (**springs**) themselves upstream on the far bank, which augment the Ahérondas' flow.

Continue along the main road parallel to the river, and bear left towards a modern chapel, about 1km from the bridge; some 400m further on, EU money has funded a flagstoned car park and picnic benches. Here the way deteriorates to a track which ends 1.8km from Glykí at a laboriously wrought tunnel which often has cars parked inside, as well as beside it. The **Skála Tzavélainas** begins just to its left; in Souliot days it was a vertiginous corniche path several hundred metres long, named in honour of a local woman who managed to traverse it on a donkey when her menfolk declined to do so. This too has been tamed for tourists with a retaining wall, and the formerly washed-out course of the *skála* down and to the left rehabilitated. Below, the canyon walls squeeze together, and upstream a carpet of greenery covers a wilderness, rolling up to the plainly visible castle of Kiáfa.

Beyond the *skála*, the main trail into Soúli, waymarked sporadically with blue arrows, yellow rectangles and newer red squares, descends towards the Ahérondas. About 25 minutes along, there's a junction right for the path to Tríkastro village, via the **Piyés Ádhi** (Gates of Hell) **narrows** and Póros Pyrás spring, five-hours' hike one-way upstream, waymarked with red diamonds. Since there's no bus to Tríkastro, probably the best way to do this traverse is to take a taxi or hire car there, walk downstream, have lunch at *Piyes Aheronda*, and return the same way if necessary or take another taxi home.

Most visitors, however, will continue on the main path, crossing a modern bridge over the Ahérondas and reaching (half an hour from the tunnel) the much older Dála bridge over the tributary Tsangariótiko stream, known locally as the **Piyés Soulíou** (Souliot Springs). Beyond here the marked route climbs up through the oaks out of the Ahérondas valley, arriving at another path junction (1hr) below a circular, roofed gazebo. This, waymarked with green triangles, leads steadily up within another 35 minutes to a pass (*kiáfa* in Albanian) just below the castle, with goat pens, robust plane trees and a few wells on the col. The south gate of **Kiáfa castle**, more of a fortified manor built by Ali Pasha to overawe the Souliots, lies another quarter-hour's scramble up a scree slope with a poor path. The interior is ruinous, patrolled by cows, but the climb's justified by fine views west to Paxí and north to the conical hill where the **fortified monastery of Koúngi** used to sit until Souliot rebels under the monk Samuel blew themselves up rather than surrender – a newer chapel marks the spot.

At the base of the Koúngi hill, reached by a rough descending track from the col (another 35min), is impoverished **Samoníva** (Samonídha on some official maps), the only one of the eleven Souliot villages still inhabited after a fashion – though there are no reliable facilities, so bring any snacks and water along. At a little church below Samoníva's scattered houses, you can pick up the red-rectangle path for the return journey to the tunnel and car park; allow just over an hour for this, for a generous half-day outing.

South to Préveza

Approaches to Préveza (see opposite) from the Necromanteion and Aheróndas area feature a few more minor sites and resorts before edging out onto the landlocked **Amvrakikós (Ambracian) Gulf**, where in 31 BC Octavian defeated Antony and Cleopatra at the Battle of Actium. Suitably enough, the most substantial of the ruins is Octavian's "Victory City" of **Nikopolis,** just south of the point where the Igoumenítsa–Préveza and the Árta–Préveza highways meet.

Ammoudhiá and the coast road

Two daily local **buses** cover the coastal route to Préveza from **AMMOUD-HIÁ**, a surprisingly unspoilt little beach-resort 5km due west of the Necromanteion at the mouth of the Ahérondas. By the roundabout at the entrance to the village is a worthwhile **visitor information centre** (daily except Sun according to staff whim; free), whose intelligent, non-jingoistic exhibits highlight the unique ecology of the river and its marshes, as well as the history and ethnology of Soúli. There are various booklets, some of the best presented available in Greece, both free and for sale, though these only partially offset bouts of Greek-only labelling of the displays.

As with most of the spots along this coast, tourists equipped with camper vans occupy the eucalyptus grove separating the rather scrappy village, only founded after the 1950s draining of the Fanári marsh, from the 700-metre sandy **beach**. There's usually washed-up flotsam, and the water can be chilly, but it's clear and scenic enough, with the mountains visible beyond the headland closing off the funnel-shaped bay. If the main beach fails to suit for any reason, there are two more sandy coves a short distance south, across the river: **Keréntza** and **Alonáki**.

The Ahérondas meets (and cools) the sea here, bounding the village on the south; the quay is packed with fishing boats and excursion boats for the jaunt upriver to the Necromanteion, and lined with most of Ammoudhiá's **tavernas** and cafés. One of the best for fish, easternmost in the series, is *Iy Roxani* (aka *Thanasis Babos*). If you want to stay, there are various rooms and apartments, as well as several bona-fide **hotels**, among which the simple but adequate and en-suite *Glaros* (☎06840/41 300, ℉41 118; ❶), one block behind the river esplanade, is the most convenient and quiet enough.

Other places to break your journey, south of Ammoudhiá, especially if you take this route with your own vehicle, are at **LYGIÁ**, unmarked on some maps, or **LOÚTSA** and **PARALÍA VRÁHOU** immediately north (shared exit from the newish main highway). At Lygiá there are **rooms** to rent (rather than the mega-hotels found further south at Kanáli), an impromptu campsite, several **tavernas** and an enormous, boulder-strewn beach, all overlooked by a crumbling castle in the distance; the run-together beach of Loútsa and Paralía Vráhou is longer and sandier, with a similar range of amenities behind. The long-distance buses to and from Párga or Igoumenítsa don't pass this way, but head inland at Mórfi junction, before rejoining the coast road near Nikopolis.

Inland: Zálongo and ancient Kassopi

Some 28km from Mesopótamo on the inland route, you pass a turning east to the village of **Kamarína** (3km), overlooked by the monastery and monument of Zálongo and the ruins of ancient Kassopi. These are a steep, shadeless six-kilometre climb from the main highway, though a daily **bus** from Préveza goes direct to the site each morning at 6am and at 2pm. An early start does have its rewards, since both places are glorious vantage points from which to watch the sunrise. Otherwise a taxi or your own transport is a good idea; there's also an approach (unsignposted) through the village of Kryopiyí, also 3km off the main road, somewhat quicker if you're approaching from the north.

The **monastery of Zálongo** is a staple of Greek schoolbook history, immortalized by the defiant mass suicide of a group of Souliot women. In 1803, Ali Pasha's troops, commanded by his son Veli, cornered in the monastery a large band of Souliots who were fleeing the destruction of Koúngi. As this refuge was overrun, about sixty Souliot women and children fled to the top of the cliff above and, to the amazement of the approaching Albanian Muslims, the mothers danced one by one, with their children in their arms, over the edge of the precipice. This act is commemorated by a truly hideous modern cement-and-stone **sculpture**, approached by several hundred steps. Along with the monastery just below (closed 2–4pm & Thurs) which is of no intrinsic interest, the monument attracts regular coach tours of Greek schoolchildren and (at weekends) adults.

Slightly to the west of the monastery, on a natural balcony just below the summit of a similar bluff, are the remains of **ancient Kassopi** (Tues–Sun 8.30am–3pm; €1.50), a minor Thesprotian city-state today approached via a long path through a pine grove. The ruins date mainly from the fourth century BC, with extensive second-century rebuilding after the city was sacked by the Romans; the place was definitively abandoned in 31 BC when its citizens were commanded to inhabit Nikopolis (see below). An excellent site plan affixed to the warden's hut helps to locate highlights, including the central agora, a tiny, eroded odeion and (most impressive) a *katagoyeion* or hostelry for representatives of the Kassopian federation. Principally, though, Kassopi is memorable for its superb location – some 600m above sea level, with the Ionian Sea coastline and Lefkádha laid at your feet.

Nikopolis

The "Victory City" of **NIKOPOLIS** was founded by Octavian on the site where his army had camped prior to the Battle of Actium. An arrogant and ill-considered gesture, it made little geographical sense. The settlement was on unstable ground, water had to be transported by aqueduct from the distant springs of the Loúros, and a population had to be forcibly imported from towns as far afield as the Gulf of Corinth. However, such a *folie de grandeur* was perhaps understandable. At **Actium**, Octavian had first blockaded and then largely annihilated the combined fleets of Antony and Cleopatra, gathered there for the invasion of Italy. The rewards were sweet, subsequently transforming Octavian from military commander to emperor of Rome, under the title of Augustus.

The subsequent history of Nikopolis is undistinguished, with much of its original population drifting back to their homes. As the Roman Empire declined, the city suffered sacking by Vandals and Goths. Later, in the sixth century AD, it was restored by Justininan and flourished for a while as a Byzantine city, but within four centuries it had sunk again into the earth, devastated by the combined effect of earthquakes and Bulgar raids.

The site and museum
The far-flung and overgrown monuments begin 7km north of Préveza, on either side of the main road. Travelling by **bus**, you could just ask to be set down here, though it's a long walk back to town. It would be better to hire a taxi in Préveza for a couple of hours, or visit with a rental car, as the site is really too scattered to tour on foot.

The ruins (access generally unrestricted, certain items fenced) look impressive from the road. A great **theatre** stands to the east and as you approach the site museum, past remnants of the **baths**, there is a formidable stretch of sixth-century Byzantine **fortified walls**. But as you walk around, the promise of this enormous site is unfulfilled; few other remains reward close inspection, though they're home to snakes, butterflies, the odd tortoise and, in spring, numerous wild flowers.

From the scant foundations of the sixth-century **basilica of Alkysonos**, it's a two-kilometre walk to the main **theatre**, whose arches stand amidst dangerously crumbling masonry. To the left of this you can just make out the sunken outline of the **stadium**, below the modern village of Smyrtoúna. Octavian's own tent was pitched upon the hill above the village, and a massive **podium** remains from the commemorative monument that he erected. On a terrace alongside, excavations have revealed the remains of "beaks" (ramming protuberances) of some of the captured warships, which he dedicated to the gods.

The dull **museum** (Tues–Sun 8.30am–2.30pm; €1.50) consists of two rooms containing a rather uninspiring collection of Roman sarcophagi and coins. Its caretaker's main function used to be wardenship of the Roman and Byzantine mosaics unearthed amidst the foundations of the sixth-century **basilica of Doumetios** nearby, but these are now covered by a protective layer of sand and polythene. The caretaker may escort you to the Roman **odeion**, for which he has the keys. This dates from the original construction of the city and has been well restored for use in the local summer festival (see "Préveza", below).

Préveza

Modern **PRÉVEZA**, at the mouth of the Amvrakikós Gulf, is a relatively insignificant successor to Nikopolis, but not without its charm. Numerous **cafés** line the east waterfront, facing Actium (modern Áktio) where the forces of Antony and Cleopatra were defeated. Since the advent of international flights to nearby Áktio airport from the 1980s, this provincial capital has had a facelift of sorts, and more character remains in the pedestrianized old quarter than at Párga. Préveza merits a brief stopover, not only for Nikopolis, but also for its enjoyable evenings and the **tavernas** in its commercial quarter, offering the most reasonably priced and varied fare for some way around.

Charter flights arriving at nearby Áktio **airport** generally have transport laid on to Lefkádha or Párga; otherwise there are taxis for the seven-kilometre trip to town. The **bus station** in Préveza is on Leofóros Irínis, 1km southwest of the new ferry dock at the north end of the quay, with the massive castle of Ayíou Andhréou interposed between the two. Ro-ro **ferries** ply constantly across the gulf to Áktio jetty, where you can pick up buses (four or five daily) to Vónitsa and Lefkádha (times are displayed on the quayside ticket office). However within in the lifetime of this edition, this is set to be replaced by a new, high-tech tunnel – a less impressive project than the Río–Andírio bridge, but equally vital.

The **post office** is on Spiliádhou, near the castle; there is no longer a tourist office. Several **banks** with cash dispensers are found at the north end of the waterfront, on the way to the new ferry dock. Olympic Airways, for **flights to Athens**, is out at Irínis 37; a potential source of one-way charter seats back to Britain is Karyatis Travel, just in from the waterfront at Navarínou 10 (☎06820/60 745).

Accommodation

The four in-town **hotels** are neither especially inviting nor geared to budget travellers; it's assumed that any clued-up tourist will be staying at beachfront resort hotels to the north, and only coming to town after dark for the lively nightlife. Most obvious, and most expensive, is the noisy *Preveza City* at Irínis 61, 200m south of the KTEL (☎06820/27 365, ℱ23 872; ❹), which seems to specialize in hosting Greek conventions; much better is the *Dioni* on Platía Papayeoryíou, a quiet pedestrian zone more or less just behind (☎06820/27

381, Ⓕ27 384; Ⓞ). The *Minos*, a bit south on 21-Oktovríou (Ⓣ06820/28 424; Ⓞ), is bargainable from the rack rates, but it's not the friendliest place in town; the only seafront establishment is the 1998-renovated and marginally more affordable *Avra* at Venizélou 19 (Ⓣ06820/21 230, Ⓕ26 454; Ⓞ). Failing these, there are a few rooms on the shore road towards the far side of the peninsula; follow this road south out of town about 2km, curling around the Venetian **Pandokrátoras** castle (a shell) at the peninsula tip, and you'll pass them.

The nearest **campsite** is *Kalamitsi* (Ⓣ06820/22 368; open all year), around 4km north of town on the broad highway which skims along a few hundred metres back from the coast. Any bus running towards Kanáli (15km out, and not to be confused with Kanalláki) will pass the summer-only sites of *Monolithi* (Ⓣ06820/51 755) and *Kanali* (Ⓣ06820/22 741), on either side of the road at **Monolíthi** beach, a fine stretch of sand beginning 11km from Préveza.

Eating, drinking and nightlife

There are at least a dozen **tavernas** scattered around the inland market lanes in central Préveza, with cafés and bars on the pedestrianized portion of waterfront boulevard Venizélou. Good inland choices include *Psatha*, Dhardhanellíon 4–6 (one block south of the Venetian clocktower along the main shopping thoroughfare, then west), for standard oven fare, and the long-running *Amvrosios*, specializing in grilled sardines and barrel wine at budget prices, on the lane – officially Grigoríou toú Pémptou – leading seaward (east) from the clocktower. If this is shut for any reason, try its adjacent competitors *Tou Stavraka* or *Iy Trata*, or the *Ouzeri Kaixis* at Parthenogoyíou 7, three lanes south. By night, these bazaar alleys, particularly within a 100-metre radius of the fishmarket building and the clocktower, come alive with an assortment of **bars**, **cafés** (including *Netcafe Ascot* at Vasilíou Bálkou 6–8) and shops, patronized by a mixture of locals and guests from the surrounding resorts. In terms of organized culture, July and August see a range of musical and theatrical events as part of the **Nikopolia festival**, held at Nikopolis, plus there's a summer outdoor **cinema** south of town on the road to Pandokrátoras.

Árta and around

Fifty kilometres northeast of Préveza lies **ÁRTA**, finely situated in a loop of the broad Árakhthos River as it meanders towards the **Amvrakikós Gulf**, 20km to the south. It is one of the more pleasant Greek-mainland towns: a quiet place, very much the provincial capital, with an old centre that retains much of its Ottoman-bazaar aspect (including a covered market on Pýrrou), and some celebrated medieval monuments.

From the west, you enter town within sight of the 1993-restored packhorse **bridge**, subject of song and poetry throughout the mainland. A grisly legend – found elsewhere in the Balkans as well – maintains that the bridge builder, continually thwarted by the current washing his foundations away, took the advice of a bird and sealed up his wife in the central pier; the bridge finally held but the woman's voice haunted the place thereafter.

The town

Árta was known anciently as Ambracia and had a brief period of fame as the capital of Pyrrhus, king of Epirus; it was the base for the king's hard-won campaigns ("Another such victory and I am lost") in Italy – the original Pyrrhic

ÁRTA

Árakhthos River

0   200 m

N

RING ROAD

ORFEAS
Summer
Cinema

Modern
Cathedral

FROÚRIO

Théatro
Kástrou

Ayios
Vassilíos

Ayía Theodhóra

Amvrakia

Skalinon

Papadhákos

PLATIA
ETHNIKIS
ANDISTASIS

Odeion

Temple of Apollo

Cronos

PLATIA
KILKIS

PLATIA
SKOUFA

En Artí

Panayía
Parigorítissa

KOMMENOU

Káto Panayía (2km)

Old Bridge (400m), Ioánnina, Préveza Koronissía, Vlahérna, ●Club Mylos, ■O Protomástoras & ■Yéfira (400m)

▲ Bus Station (200m), Menídhi & Amfilohía

victories. The foundations of a **temple of Apollo** and an **odeion** lie to either side of Odhós Pýrrou, but otherwise there are very few remains from this period. At the northeast end of the street is the **Froúrio**, the ancient acropolis and the citadel in every subsequent era; regrettably, it is now locked, except for performances at its open-air theatre.

More substantial monuments date from Árta's second burst of glory, following the 1204 fall of Constantinople, when the town was the centre of the **Despotate of Epirus**, an autonomous Byzantine state. The despotate, which stretched from Corfu to Thessaloníki, was governed by the Angelos dynasty (the imperial family expelled from Constantinople) and survived until 1449, when the garrison surrendered to the Turks.

Most striking and certainly the most bizarre of the Byzantine monuments is the **Panayía Parigorítissa** (sometimes rendered Parigorítria; Tues–Sun

8.30am–3pm; €1.50), a grandiose, five-domed cube that rears above Platía Skoufá, at the southwest end of that street. The interior is almost Gothic in appearance, the main dome being supported by an extraordinary cantilevered-pilaster system that looks unwieldy and unsafe. Up top, this insecurity is accentuated by a looming *Pandokrátor* (Christ in Majesty) mosaic in excellent condition, overshadowing the sixteenth- and seventeenth-century frescoes in the sanctuary and nave. The church, flanked by two side chapels, was built between 1283–96 by Despot Nikiforos I as part of a monastic complex; of this, sixteen cells and the refectory remain east and south of the church, along with the excavated foundations of an early shrine, and there are tentative plans to restore them as an archeological museum.

Two smaller Byzantine churches from the same period also survive in the town. Both have a more conventional structure but are enlivened by highly elaborate brick and tile decorations on the outside walls. They're usually locked, but this is no tragedy since the exteriors are the main interest. **Ayía Theódhora**, containing the fine marble tomb of the wife of Epirot ruler Michael II, stands in its own courtyard halfway down Pýrrou. A little further north, opposite the produce market, is thirteenth-century **Áyios Vassilíos**, ornamented with glazed polychrome tiles and bas-reliefs.

Nearby monasteries and churches

Amid the orange groves surrounding Árta, a number of **monasteries and churches** were built during the despotate, many of them by members of the imperial Angelos dynasty; all are well signposted with yellow-on-brown placards.

Within easy walking distance (2km along Odhós Komménou, past the hospital turning) stands the **monastery of Káto Panayía** (daily: May–Sept 7am–1pm & 4.30–7.30pm; Oct–April 8am–1pm & 3–6pm; ring for admission), erected by Michael II between 1231 and 1271. This is now a working convent occupied by a dozen nuns and, in one corner of the garden, several caged peacocks. The *katholikón* in a shaded courtyard has extravagant exterior decoration, and frescoes inside showing Christ in three guises. The gabled roof of the triple-aisled nave is supported by six columns; one of the two cross-vaults serves as a narthex. Many of the frescoes are badly smudged, but the highlight is an undamaged version of Christ as Emmanuel in the front vault. The west outer wall sports a graphic *Last Judgement*, but this is definitely a case where the interior is more compelling than the exterior.

Further out of Árta, 6km north by a circuitous route (11–12 buses daily from the ring-road stop), the monastic church of **Panayía Vlahernón** in Vlahérna village is engaging both inside and out. To the basic three-aisled twelfth-century plan, Michael II added the trio of domes in the following century, as well as the narthex; one of the two tombs inside is thought to be his. Having found the key custodian at the nearby kafenío, you enter the south narthex door under a fine **relief** of the Archangel Michael. Dissimilar columns support the added cupolas, but the church is more remarkable for what is normally hidden from view. The warden will lift a section of carpet to reveal a magnificent **mosaic**, just one portion of a vast marble floor punctuated with such tessellations. Only a few of numerous **frescoes** thought to be under plaster are exposed. This is the most beautiful of Árta's churches, worth contemplating at length from the kafenío.

If you get hooked, there are three more churches within easy reach of Árta, all signposted after a fashion; these have apparently never been associated with a monastery, and today serve as the graveyard chapels for the nearest village.

Panayía tís Bryónis lies 800m up the side road towards Megárhi, the turning 6km out of Árta en route to Amfilohía; dating from 1232, with some fine brickwork, it unhappily got hideous new roof tiles in 1998. By taking the road for Kostáki and Anéza from the historic bridge, and then turning west towards Plisí, you should reach **Áyios Dhimítrios Katsoúris** after 5km, partly eleventh-century in vintage, with a freestanding belfry. If the priest is in at the neighbouring cottage, you'll get to see a frescoed interior. Some 2km further north, at the edge of Kirkizátes village, stands **Áyios Nikólaos tís Rodhiás**, a thirteenth-century, single-apsed chapel with contemporary frescoes in fair condition.

Practicalities

Arriving by **bus**, you'll be dropped at a terminus on the riverbank, on the northern outskirts of town, though there is a discretional stop on the ring road east of both the modern and the Byzantine bridges. From the main station it's a ten-minute walk southwest along **Odhós Skoufá**, the main thoroughfare, to the central **Platía Ethnikís Andístasis**. Skoufá, Árta's main commercial street and pedestrianized for much of its length (as are most of its narrower perpendiculars), and its parallel streets, Pýrrou and Konstandínou, wind through the oldest part of town. If you come by car, beware of the city-centre **fee-parking scheme** in effect during business hours: a red strip on the sign means parking of one to two hours – get a pay-and-display ticket from kerbside machines – while a green strip denotes long-term parking for residents only.

There are just two **hotels**, normally enough for the trickle of tourists and business visitors, though as at Préveza neither constitutes great value. The *Amvrakia*, Priovólou 13 (☎06810/28 311, ⓕ78 544; ❷–❸), is the best choice, with comfortable rooms – some en-suite – and a good position on a pedestrian way, just off Platía Ethnikís Andístasis. The *Cronos* (☎06810/22 211; ❹) on Platía Kilkís is noisier – despite recent pedestrianization of the square – and vastly overpriced.

Árta **restaurants**, what few there are, can be excellent value, catering for locals rather than tourists. Best in the centre is the *Skalinon*, just next to the *Amvrakia* hotel, open lunch only Monday to Saturday; with more than usual attention to decor, it provides ample choice for vegetarians. A more ordinary option for *mayireftá* is the *Papadhakos* at Skoufá 31. Most visitors, however, will gravitate towards the old bridge, where you can admire the structure at leisure over a coffee or a meal. *O Protomastoras* offers adequate, inexpensive fare to a young crowd under a shady plane, as does adjacent *Yefira*; the *Club Mylos* at the far end of the pedestrianized span is an after-hours *baráki*. In the evenings, people tend to perform their *vólta* around Platía Ethnikís Andístasis or congregate in its cafés; a slightly less central, pleasant one, within sight of Panayía Paregorítissa, is *En Arti*, with seating by a fountain and plane tree.

The Amvrakikós Gulf

Árta is the exceptional bright spot close to the **Amvrakikós Gulf**. Further around, and in fact all the way south to the open sea, there is little to prompt a stop. Locals from Árta head at weekends for seafood meals at nearby coastal villages, and you might imitate them if passing through.

MENÍDHI (21km southeast) is a far better place to get stuck between buses than Amfilohía (see opposite); it's slightly off the main road, with three **hotels**, including the *Sorokos* at mid-quay (☎06810/88 213; ❸), and plenty of fish **tavernas**. Of these, *Vouliagmeni* (*Pandioras*), the first on the left as you drop down from the highway, is famous for its fresh shrimps from the gulf, but has seen prices climb lately with fame – budget €18 per person. The final approach to **KORONÍSSIA** (25km southwest of Árta), more or less in the middle of the gulf, lies along a wave-lashed causeway flanked by a scrappy beach popular with windsurfers. Today the village, once an island, offers a few fish **tavernas** (the most celebrated of these is *Myrtaria*, again no cheaper than those at Menídhi), some rooms and, up on the hill, yet another Byzantine church, the rather lopsided, tenth-century **Yénnisis tis Theotókou**, surveying the gulf and lagoons below.

AMFILOHÍA is promisingly situated at the head of the gulf, but in reality proves an exceedingly dull, small town. The chance for a swim would also seem from the map to be a redeeming feature, but the water here is at its most stagnant, with only a miniature municipal beach as a way in (another is being prepared across the bay). If you're marooned here, the best emergency fallback **hotel** is the *Helena* (☎06420/22 509; ②), near the "old" beach on the road north out of town.

If you need to stay the night on this coastline, **VÓNITSA**, 35km west of Amfilohía, would be a more convenient and pleasant choice. Again it's not a wildly exciting place, and frustratingly distant from real sea, but represents a definite improvement on Amfilohía with its lively waterside, tree-lined squares and a substantial Byzantine **castle** above. Among three surviving **hotels**, pick of the litter is the comfortable enough *Bel Mare* (☎06430/22 394, ℉22 564; ④) on the castle end of the *paralía*. As at Préveza across the gulf, sardines figure prominently on the menus of a half-dozen waterfront **tavernas**; bars and cafés are found on the front, or the little platía just inland. Infrequent local **buses** cover the 14km to the south ferry terminal across the gulf from Préveza (and possibly through the new tunnel when it's ready), passing Áktio airport.

The Etolo-Akarnanian coast

Heading south for Mesolóngi and the Gulf of Kórinthos, there is not much of interest, at least on the more direct **inland route**. Beyond Amfilohía, you pass a few swampy lakes like Amvráki and Ozerós, pumped for irrigating the local tobacco. Halfway along the Amfilohía–Mesolóngi road, in-your-face ugly **AGRÍNIO** – also the hottest town in Greece during summer – is of scant note except as the public transport link for this area, with buses northwest to Árta/Ioánnina, northeast to Karpeníssi and south to Andírio, from where there are local buses to Náfpaktos, as well as the ferry across the Gulf of Kórinthos to the Peloponnese.

Mýtikas and Kálamos island

The **coast south from Vónitsa** is bleakly impressive, with a quiet stretch of road that skirts the shoreline, with nothing but parched wilderness inland. However, if you have transport there are great opportunities for finding tiny deserted pebble beaches along the 10km south from Páleros. The next settlement is sleepy but pleasant **MÝTIKAS**, whose rows of old-fashioned houses strung along a pebbly shore look out onto the island of Kálamos, with a backdrop inland of sheer, amphitheatric mountainside. Coming northwest from Andírio, it's the first place that would prompt thoughts of an overnight stay, and there's nothing as inviting going south until you reach Náfpaktos (see p.331).

You'll probably need to stay here to catch the boat across to the island of Kálamos (see overleaf); among three **hotels**, best is the *Kymata* (☎06460/81

258 or 81 311; ❷), above a well-attended sweet shop. Among **rooms**, most atmospheric are those above *O Glaros* **taverna** (☎06460/81 240; ❶) – utterly spartan, with baths down the hall but unbeatable views on the gulf side. Fish meals downstairs are inexpensive and well-grilled; the only other alternative, *Ouzeri Stou Thoma* at the far end of the village, is more elaborate but still very reasonable. Beyond it, *O Barba Panos* is another *zaharoplastío* with tables in the shore pebbles (or even in the sea if you wish).

Kálamos

The island of **Kálamos**, the largest of a mini-archipelago west of Astakós, is essentially a partly wooded mountain rising abruptly from the sea. Though officially part of Lefkádha in the Ionian group, all utility and transport links are to the mainland opposite. In summer there are usually a few yachts moored in the small harbour below the main village, Hóra, but otherwise the island, with a permanent population of about three hundred, sees few visitors and is ill equipped to host them. The only regular connection is a daily kaïki from Mýtikas, which leaves the mainland at about noon and returns from the island at 7.30am the next day; in summer the same craft may do group day-trips, but otherwise you must charter the entire boat for €21 (one way). There is just one **place to stay** in Hóra – rooms kept by the Lezentínos family (☎06460/91 238; ❶) – but it only operates during July and August, when it will probably be full anyway, so come with camping gear if you intend to stay the night (though even this is difficult, given the lack of flat ground).

HÓRA, spread out among gardens and olive groves on the south coast, largely survived the 1953 earthquake which devastated so many of the Ionian islands, though there's been no lack of insensitive building since. There are two basic kafenía/tavernas and a "supermarket" by the harbour, plus a bakery and sweetshop higher up, next to a **post office**. The gravelly village **beach**, fifteen minutes southwest (follow the seaward lane from the quay, bearing left at every option) has no reliable facilities; the much better beach of **Merithiá** lies twenty minutes northeast of the port, via a rough scramble along the shore. Your reward will be 500m of sand and fine gravel which could easily fit in all the tourists Kálamos is ever likely to get, and this could be one of the better places to camp, though there's no shade or fresh water.

Kástro, an old fortified settlement at the north tip of the island facing Mýtikas, is linked to the port by a seven-kilometre asphalt road; the ninety-minute walk is drudgery, despite pine-shade and views, so try and hitch the sparse traffic. The small, five-bastioned castle here may possibly be Byzantine, and surveyed the straits between here and Mýtikas, as suggested by the name of the road's-end hamlet 2km beyond, Episkopí ("Overlook"). Its walls are surrounded by a dozen or so houses, mostly roofless and abandoned, and the overgrown bailey is now used by villagers to keep their hens and sheep. A spring just above the road provides water, and a damp church of Áyios Nikólaos huddles beside the fortifications. Down towards Kástro's harbour, a few more houses are still inhabited, though there's no shop or café. Small, exquisite beaches dot the coast between Hóra and Kástro, though they can only be seen and reached by sea, not from the road.

Southwest of Hóra, a broad mule-and-tractor track leads to **Kefáli (Pórto Leóne)**, near the island's southern tip, which shelters a deep bay protected in all weathers and thus beloved of Ionian yacht flotillas. The lower village has been deserted since the 1953 earthquake; a higher, pirate-proof settlement, nearly invisible now in its dereliction, was abandoned a few centuries ago. It's a shadeless, two-hour walk across scrub-covered mountainside from Hóra, with only views across to the neighbouring island of Kastós to compensate; as ever in this region, you're best off going by boat.

Astakós, Oeniadae and Etolikó

South of Mýtikas, the coast road offers stunning views west over Kálamos, Kastós, Itháki and Kefalloniá – one of the most dramatic seascapes in Greece. After 31km you reach **ASTAKÓS**, a place whose name means "lobster". Patrick Leigh Fermor, in *Roumeli*, fantasizes about arriving at this gastronomic-sounding place and ordering its namesake for supper; it turned out to be a crashing non-event, and you'd still be very lucky to get lobster at any of the half-dozen tavernas which line its quay on the north flank of the all-but-beachless gulf here. Like Amfilohía, the location of the village is its most attractive attribute, though yacht flotillas call to take on water, and many of the older buildings have been preserved.

Arriving by land, the KTEL (two through connections with Athens daily, five via Agrínio) is at one end of the quay, while the single, vastly overpriced hotel, *Stratos* (☎06460/41 911, ⓕ41 227; ⑥), sprawls at the other, overlooking the tiny, gravelly town beach; in peak season numbers of cheaper studio-type rooms are on offer elsewhere. The **ferries** which used to cross over to **Itháki and Kefalloniá** are currently suspended; if they are reinstated, expect once-daily service in midsummer only.

Beyond here the scenery becomes greener as the road winds 26km over oak-covered hills and then down onto the floodplain of the Ahelöós River. At Katohí, by the river, there's a turning for the eight-kilometre detour west to **ancient Oeniadae** (unenclosed; free), also known by its medieval name Trikardhókastro. In ancient times, when the river delta was not so far advanced as today, Oeniadae was the most prominent port of western Greece, and irresistible to any conqueror; accordingly a section of the 7km of still-extant Hellenistic **walls and gates** loops around to defend it. The American School first excavated it in 1901, after which the city became overgrown again; recently the undergrowth has been cleared to reveal a small **theatre**, backed into an oak-shaded hill and used in a local summer festival.

East of the Ahelöós delta stands **ETOLIKÓ**, built on an island in the eponymous, rather sumpy lagoon and reached by two causeways. The town is visibly less prosperous than Mesolóngi (see below), of which it seems a miniature version – there's an obvious shanty-town west of the centre – but it could make a good emergency halt, with a perfectly acceptable en-suite **hotel** on the west-facing quay: the *Alexandra* (☎06320/23 019; ②). Next door is the town's fanciest **restaurant**, *To Stafnokari*, specializing in local seafood, and there's the usual complement of bars and kafenía in the centre, plus a bank and post office. Occasional buses ply to Mesolóngi, just 10km southeast, past the salt factories that are today the area's mainstay.

Mesolóngi

Mesolóngi (Missolongi), for most visitors, is irrevocably associated with the name of **Lord Byron**, who died in the town, to dramatic effect, while organizer of the local Greek forces during the War of Independence (see box overleaf). Mesolóngi can claim some attention for this literary past but, as in Byron's time, it's a fairly shabby and rather unromantic place: wet during autumn and spring, and comprised mostly of drab, modern buildings. Amazingly, it, rather than larger Agrínio, is the capital of Étolo-Akarnanía, a decision surely taken more on sentimental than practical grounds. To be fair, the town has been spruced up of late, especially around the centre, but if you come here on a pilgrimage, it's still best to plan on moving on within the day.

The town

You enter the town from the northeast by the **Gate of the Exodus**, whose name recalls an attempt by nine thousand men, women and children to break out during the Ottomans' year-long siege in 1826. In one wild dash they managed to get free of Mesolóngi, leaving a group of defenders to destroy it in their wake. But those fleeing were betrayed, ambushed in the supposed safety of nearby Mount Zygós and massacred by a large Albanian mercenary force.

O Iórdhos Výronos: Byron in Mesolóngi

Lord Byron arrived at Mesolóngi, a squalid and inhospitable place surrounded by marshland, in January 1824. The town, with its small port allowing access to the Ionian islands, was the western centre of **resistance** against the Turks. The poet, who had contributed much of his personal fortune to the war effort, as well as his own fame, was enthusiastically greeted with a 21-gun salute.

On landing, he was made **commander-in-chief** of the five thousand soldiers gathered at the garrison, a role that was as much political as military. The Greek forces, led by klephtic brigand-generals, were divided among themselves and each faction separately and persistently petitioned him for money. He had already wasted months on the island of Kefalloniá, trying to assess their claims and quarrels before finalizing his own military plan – to march full force on Náfpaktos and from there take control of the Gulf of Corinth – but in Mesolóngi he was again forced to delay.

Occasionally Byron despaired: "Here we sit in this realm of mud and discord", he wrote in his journal. But while other Philhellenes were returning home, disillusioned by the squabbles and larceny of the Greeks, or appalled by the conditions in this damp, stagnant town, he stayed, campaigning eloquently and profitably for the cause. Outside his house, he drilled soldiers; in the lagoon he rowed, and shot, and caught a fever. On April 19, 1824, Byron died, pronouncing a few days earlier, in a moment of resignation, "My wealth, my abilities, I devoted to the cause of Greece – well, here is my life to her!" It was, in fact, the most important contribution he could have made to the struggle.

The news of the poet's death reverberated across northern Europe, swelled to heroic proportions by his admirers. Arguably it changed the course of the war in Greece. When Mesolóngi fell again to the Ottomans, in 1826, there was outcry in the European press, and the French and English forces were finally galvanized into action, sending a joint naval force for protection. It was this force that accidentally engaged an Egyptian fleet at Navarino Bay (see p.274), striking a fatal blow against the Ottoman navy.

Byron, ever since independence, has been a Greek national hero. Almost every town in the country has a street – Výronos – named after him; not a few men still answer to "Vyron" as a first name; and there was once an eponymous brand of cigarettes (perhaps the ultimate Greek tribute). Most importantly, the respect he inspired was for many years generalized to his fellow countrymen – before being dissipated after 1943 by British interference in the civil war and bungling in Cyprus.

Just inside this gate, on the right, partly bounded by the remains of the fortifications, is the **Kípos Iróön**, or **Garden of Heroes** (daily: summer 9am–1.30pm & 5–7pm; winter 9am–1.30pm & 4–7pm; free) – though it is signposted in English as "Heroes' Tombs" – where a tumulus covers the bodies of the town's unnamed defenders. Beside the tomb of the Greek Souliot commander, Markos Botsaris, is a **statue of Byron**, erected in 1881, under which is buried the poet's heart (some sources claim it's his lungs). The rest of Byron's remains were taken back to his family home, Newstead Abbey, despite his dying request: "Here let my bones moulder; lay me in the first corner without pomp or nonsense." Perhaps he knew this would be disregarded. There is certainly a touch of pomp in the carving of Byron's coat of arms with a royal crown above; there had been speculation that Byron would be offered the crown of an independent Greece. Among the palm trees and rusty cannons there are other monuments – busts, obelisks, cenotaphs – to an astonishing range of American, German and French Philhellenes.

Elsewhere in the town, traces of Byron are sparse. The **house** in which he lived and died was destroyed during World War II and its site is marked by a clumsy memorial garden. It's on Odhós Levídhou, reached from the central platía by walking down to the end of Hariláou Trikoúpi and turning left.

Back in the central Platía Bótsari, the mock-Neoclassical town hall houses a small **museum** devoted to the revolution (Mon–Fri 9am–1.30pm & 4–7pm, Sat & Sun 9am–1pm & 4–7pm, closes 6pm winter; free), with some emotive paintings of the independence struggle on the upper floor (including a copy of Delacroix's *Gate of the Sortie*), reproductions of period lithographs and a rather desperate collection of Byronia on the ground floor, padded out with a brass souvenir plaque of Newstead Abbey. The credibility of the museum is further overstretched by a central display of ephemera from the Nottinghamshire town of Gedling, which is twinned with Mesolóngi. Pride of place, by the entrance, goes to an original edition of Solomos's poem "Hymn to Liberty", now the words to the national anthem. Perhaps in realization of the evident thinness of the current exhibits, plans for a new "Lord Byron Museum" west of town have now been cancelled.

Perhaps more interesting and enjoyable than any of this is a walk across the **lagoon**, past two **forts** which were vital defences against the Turkish navy. The lagoon, with its saltpans and fish farms, attracts coastal birds: migrant waders pass through and, in spring, avocets and black-winged stilts nest here. A causeway extends for about 5km and reaches the open sea at **TOURLÍDHA**, a hamlet of pre-fab summer cottages on stilts, and a pair of tavernas which may only function in summer.

Some 4km north of town, on the road to Etolikó, lies **ancient Pleuron** (unenclosed, free), which reached its zenith in Hellenistic times. The most obvious remains – reachable by signposted dirt track – are stretches of massive wall and a small theatre.

Practicalities

Long-distance **buses** arrive at the KTEL on Mavrokordhátou 5, next to the central Platía Bótsari, while the local blue-and-white ones park just a few paces away. You can **rent bicycles** from the *Theoxenia* hotel should you wish to explore the lagoon; they are a popular option among locals, given the town's unrelenting flatness. The **post office** stands just a block east of the square; the big telecoms antenna marks the spot.

Hotels in Mesolóngi are a bit cheerless, expensive and often block-booked by Greek tour groups. Etolikó (see p.441), 10km to the west, could be a cheaper, less crowded alternative for the night. If you need or want to stay in the town, a good option is the *Avra,* Hariláou Trikoúpi 5 (☎06310/22 284; ❸); it's adjacent to the central platía and close to the best of Mesolóngi's eating and drinking venues. More upmarket and impersonal choices include the massive *Liberty,* Iróön Polytekhníou 41 (☎06310/28 050; ❺), overpriced though with park views from most rooms, one block from the Garden of Heroes, or the *Theoxenia* (☎06310/22 493; ❻), a small, more pleasant complex amidst landscaping just south of town on the lagoon shore.

Since the mid-1990s, the prevailing Greek craze for cutting-edge ouzerís and *barákia* has swept through Mesolóngi, resulting in a vastly improved **eating and drinking** scene, making a lunch stop here something to plan rather than dread. The place is especially famous for its eels, hunted with tridents in the lagoon and then smoked. The main concentration of establishments is along Athanasíou Razikotsíka, a pedestrianized street one block south of Hariláou Trikoúpi. *O Nikos* at no. 7 has been tried and passed muster, but there is also *Stin Agora* next door, *Poseidhon* opposite at no.4 and *Marokia* at no. 8, interspersed with bars. In the narrow alleys linking these two broader streets are more bars, kafenía and ouzerís, including the *Rodhon* which has an impressive range of imported beers.

Travel details

Buses

Buses detailed have similar frequency in each direction, so entries are given just once; for reference check under both starting-point and destination.

Agrínio to: Corfu (bus/ferry, 2 daily in season; 4hr); Ioánnina (6 daily; 2hr 20min); Karpeníssi (1 daily, 2 Fri; 3hr 30min); Lefkádha (5 daily; 2hr); Mesolóngi–Andírio (12 daily; 1hr–1hr 30min).

Áktio to: Lefkádha (5 daily; 20min).

Árta to: Ioánnina (10 Mon–Fri, 6 Sat/Sun; 2hr 30min); Prámanda and Melissourgí (2 daily 5am/2pm; 1hr 30min); Préveza (5 Mon–Fri, 2 Sat/Sun; 1hr); Theodhóriana (daily Mon–Fri at 2pm; 1hr 15min).

Igoumenítsa to: Athens (4 daily; 8hr); Párga (4 daily, 3 Sat, 1 Sun; 1hr 30min); Préveza (2 daily; 3hr); Sývota (bus marked Pérdhika; 3 daily, 2 Saturday; 30min); Thessaloníki (1 daily; 8hr 30min).

Ioánnina to: Athens (9 daily; 7hr 30min); Dodona (Mon, Wed & Fri 6.30am & 3.30pm; 40min); Igoumenítsa (9 daily, 7 Sat/Sun; 2hr); Kastoriá, via Kónitsa (2 daily, change at Neápoli; 6hr); Kónitsa (7 daily, 4 Sat/Sun; 1hr 30min); Métsovo (3 daily, 2

Sun; 1hr 30min); Monodhéndhri (Mon, Wed & Fri 6.15am/4.15pm; 45min); Pápingo (Mon, Wed & Fri 5.15am/2.30pm; 1hr); Párga (1 daily; 2hr 30min); Pátra via Agrínio (4 daily; 4hr 30min); Prámanda (2 daily Mon–Fri 5am/3.15pm, Sat–Sun 3.15pm only; 2hr); Préveza (10 daily, 8 Sun; 2hr 30min); Thessaloníki (6 daily; 8hr); Tríkala, via Métsovo and Kalambáka (2 daily, 3 Fri & Sun; 3hr); Tsepélovo (2 daily Mon, Wed & Fri 6.15am & 3.15pm; 1hr); Vólos (1 daily; 5hr 30min); Vovoússa (Mon & Fri 2pm, Sun 7.30am; 1hr 30min).

Kónitsa to: Dhístrato (Mon, Wed & Fri 2.30pm, Sun 7.45pm; 1hr 15min); Molydhosképastos (2 daily Mon–Fri, 1 daily Sat/Sun am; 30min); Plikáti (Mon, Wed & Fri 2pm; 1hr).

Mesolóngi to: Astakós (2 daily; 1hr 15min); Athens (8 daily; 4hr); Ioánnina (6 daily, 2hr 30min); Pátra (8 daily; 1hr 30min).

Préveza to: Glykí (1 daily; 1hr); Lefkádha (4 daily; 35min including ferry trip); Párga (4 daily Mon–Fri, 3 Sat/Sun; 1hr 30min).

Vónitsa to: Áktio (3 daily; 20min); Lefkádha (5 daily; 20min).

Ferries/hydrofoils

Igoumenítsa to: Corfu Town (almost hourly, 4.30am–10pm; 1hr–1hr 15min); Lefkími in southern Corfu (6 daily, 7.30am–9.30pm; 1hr); Paxí (Gaïos; 1 daily ferry Mon–Fri, 2 Sat–Sun; 1hr

20min; 1–2 daily hydrofoils, via Corfu; 40min). Also to Bari, Brindisi, Ancona, Trieste and Venice (Italy). See box on pp.424–425 for details.

Párga to: Paxí (daily 9.30am & 5.30pm

June–Sept, 3–4 weekly May/Oct; 1hr 20min).
Préveza to: Áktio (every 20min 9am–9pm, every
30min 6am–9am & 9pm–midnight, every hour

midnight–6am; 10min).
Sývota to: Paxí (1–2 weekly in season; 2hr).

Flights

All on Olympic unless otherwise specified.
Ioánnina to: Athens (2–3 daily; 1hr 20min; plus 2
daily on Aegean-Cronus; 1hr 10min); Thessaloníki
(6 weekly; 50min).

Préveza to: Athens (5 weekly; 1hr 10min).
Also regular **international charters** between
Préveza (Áktio) and Britain.

5

Macedonia and Thrace

CHAPTER 5 Highlights

* **Thessaloníki** Balkan in atmosphere, Greece's second city offers monuments from its rich Roman, Byzantine, Ottoman, and Jewish past – plus a vibrant nightlife. See p.452

* **Mount Olympus** The rewards of the three-day hike to the summit – Greece's highest – and mythical home to the gods include pristine scenery and riots of wild flowers. See p.476

* **Vergina** Beguiling treasures unearthed in the poignant burial chambers of Macedonia's royal dynasty. See p.484

* **Édhessa** Cliff-top wooden houses from Ottoman times and impeccably restored water-mills make this environment-conscious town one of Greece's most inviting. See p.488

* **Kastoriá** On the shores of Lake Orestiádha, this unusual resort is still the country's fur capital. See p.496

* **The Préspa Lakes** Forming the leading ornithological reserve in the region, the reed-fringed shores are a haven for nature lovers. See p.492

* **Mount Áthos** Timeless Orthodox monasteries set among unspoiled landscapes in a semi-independent republic run by monks – controversially for men only. See p.512

* **Dhadhiá** Oak and pine forests draped over volcanic ridges are home to black vultures and other rare raptors. See p.543

5

Macedonia and Thrace

T he two northern regions of **Macedonia** and **Thrace** have been part of the Greek state for just less than three generations. Macedonia (*Makedhonía*) was surrendered by the Turks after the Balkan wars in 1913; Greek sovereignty over western Thrace (*Thráki*) was not confirmed until 1923. As such, they stand slightly apart from the rest of Greece, an impression reinforced for visitors by architecture and scenery, customs and climate that seem more Balkan than typically Mediterranean. The two regions even have their own government ministry, in recognition of their specific nature and needs. In physical terms, Macedonia is characterized by dense forests and a brood of lakes to the west, and in the east by heavily cultivated flood plains and deltas of rivers with sources in former Yugoslavia or Bulgaria. Essentially continental in nature, the climate is harsher than in the rest of the country, with steamy summers and bitterly cold winters, especially up in the Rodhópi mountains on the border with Bulgaria.

These factors, along with a dearth of good beaches and thus fewer direct charter flights from abroad, plus often overpriced accommodation, may explain why northern Greece is relatively little known to outsiders. Only Halkidhikí

Accommodation price codes

Throughout the book we've categorized accommodation according to the following **price codes**, which denote the cheapest available double room in high season. All prices are for the room only, except where otherwise indicated. Many hotels, especially those in category ❹ and over, include breakfast in the price; you'll need to check this when booking. During low season, rates can drop by more than fifty percent, especially if you are staying for three or more nights. Exceptions are during the Christmas and Easter weeks when you'll pay high-season prices. Single rooms, where available, cost around seventy percent of the price of a double.

❶ Up to €24	❹ €43–58
❷ €24–33	❺ €59–72
❸ €34–42	❻ €73 and upwards

Note: Youth hostels and mountain refuges typically charge €7–9 for a dormitory bed. For more accommodation details, see pp.51–54.

and Mount Olympus draw more than a scattering of visitors, even at the height of summer. **Halkidhikí**'s three mountainous peninsulas trailing below Thessaloníki serve as a beach-playground for the inhabitants of Greece's second city. More hard-won pleasures – including stunning views – are available on the slopes of **Mount Olympus**, the mythical abode of the gods.

Although the north is less obviously appealing than the Peloponnese, say, visitors who spend some time getting to know the area find that it has much to offer. Part of its charm lies in its vigorous day-to-day life, independent of tourism, at its most evident in the sybaritic Macedonian capital of **Thessaloníki** (Salonica) and the north's second port-city, **Kavála**. The north also has some outstandingly beautiful spots, especially the **Préspa national park** in rugged western Macedonia. The nearby lakeside city of **Kastoriá** and the clifftop town of **Édhessa** are among Greece's most beguiling urban centres, thanks to a belated but determined attempt to restore some fine old buildings. Admittedly, the region's monuments are on the whole modest, though there is one notable exception: the ancient, awe-inspiring Macedonian tombs discovered at **Veryína** in the 1970s. Not so well known are the Macedonian and Roman sites at **Pella**, with its fabulous mosaics, and at **Philippi**, St Paul's first stop in Greece, as well as an up-and-coming trio of archeological digs along the Thracian seaboard: **Abdera**, **Maroneia** and **Mesembria**. Few travellers on their way to Bulgaria or Turkey stray from the dull trunk road through eastern Thrace, but the well-preserved town of **Xánthi**, the waterfowl reserves of the **Évros delta** and the **Dhadhiá Forest**, with its black vultures, deserve more than just a meal stop. Other attractions are two sharply antithetical islands just off the coast – popular **Thássos** and introverted **Samothráki**, covered in Chapter 10.

If you are male, over 18 and interested enough in monasticism – or Byzantine art, music and architecture – to obtain a pilgrimage permit, **Mount Athos** may prove to be a highlight of a visit to Greece. This "Monks' Republic" occupies the spectacular easternmost prong of Halkidhikí, and maintains control over twenty monasteries and numerous dependencies and hermitages. **Women** (and most female animals) have been **excluded** from the peninsula since a decree of 1060, although it is possible for both sexes to view the monasteries from the sea by taking a boat tour from the resorts of Ierissós and Ouranoúpoli in the "secular" part of Athos.

Public **transport** in the north is somewhat limited. Unreliable and infrequent trains link some of the urban centres, but the railway line east from Thessaloníki curls unhelpfully inland, bypassing Kavála altogether and leaving buses or your own transport as the only alternatives. The road system has improved beyond recognition in recent years, and the partly-EU-funded "Via Egnatia" highway – sections of which are already operational – will provide an uninterrupted link between the west coast and the Bulgarian and Turkish borders within a few years. The Athens–Thessaloníki motorway is also nearing completion.

Thessaloníki and western Macedonia

Thessaloníki is the fulcrum, and focus, to travel in northern Greece. The train ride west from here to Flórina via the appealing town of **Édhessa** and Lake Vegorítidha, is one of the most scenic in the country. **Kastoriá**, for those who like their towns remote and speckled with Byzantine monuments, is also highly rewarding. Way up in the northwestern corner, the secluded **Préspa lakes**, straddling the frontiers of three countries, constitute one of the finest wildlife refuges in the Balkans, but are virtually inaccessible unless you have your own transport. The biggest natural attraction in this part of Macedonia, however, has to be **Mount Olympus** (Óros Ólymbos); the fabled home of the gods soars high above the town of **Litóhoro**, easily approached from the highway or rail line between Thessaloníki and Lárissa. Near the town of **Véria**, another transport hub, lie the region's most fascinating ancient finds, the tombs of Philip II of Macedonia and other members of his dynasty at **Veryína**. Macedonia's southwestern reaches, around **Kozáni**, are less interesting, despite some fine views towards the natural barrier of the Píndhos mountains.

Thessaloníki (Salonica)

Greece's pleasant second city and the administrative centre for the two northern regions, **THESSALONÍKI** – or Salonica, as the city was known in western Europe until well into the twentieth century – has a very different feel to Athens: more Balkan-European and modern, less Middle Eastern and villagey. Situated at the head of an eponymous gulf, a horseshoe-shaped inner recess of the Thermaïkós bight, it also seems more open.

The "modern" quality of Thessaloníki is due largely to a disastrous **1917 fire** which levelled most of the old plaster houses along a labyrinth of Ottoman lanes, including the entire Jewish quarter with its 32 synagogues, rendering 70,000 – nearly half the population – homeless. The city was rebuilt over the following eight years on a grid plan prepared under the supervision of French architect and archeologist Ernest Hébrard, with long central avenues running parallel to the seafront, and cross-streets densely planted with shade trees. Hébrard's prohibition of high-rises was blithely disregarded within two decades, but Thessaloníki is still a more liveable, though arguably less interesting, city than Athens. It has a wider ethnic mix and more wealth, stimulated by its major university, international trade fair and famously avant-garde live music and entertainment scene. The food is generally superior, too: there are some very sophisticated restaurants, but also flavoursome traditional fare on offer in ouzerís and undeniably Turkish-influenced tavernas. The city's opulence is epitomized by the locals' sartorial elegance, but the recent upsurge in prosperity, owing to a stable economy and, undoubtedly in part, EU subsidies, has resulted in a new class of "yuppies", in contrast to a permanent floating underclass living in shantytowns near the port: Pontic (Black Sea) Greeks flog substandard goods at the street markets, while unemployed Albanians and eastern European refugees eke out a meagre living by selling contraband cigarettes or cleaning car windscreens.

Athenians have always delighted in disparaging their rival city as "Bulgaria", especially at football matches, but it might be more accurately nicknamed "Anatolia", for Thessaloníki is the 1923 refugees' metropolis *par excellence*, their presence most obvious in the preponderance of Turkish surnames (such as Dereli, Mumtzi and Aslanoglu) and the spicy Anatolian food seen nowhere else in Greece.

Before 1923, the population was as varied as any in the Balkans, with Greek Orthodox Christians in a distinct minority. Besides Ottoman Muslims, who had called the city "Selanık" since their arrival in 1430, a generation before the conquest of Constantinople, there were Slavs (who knew it as "Solun"), Albanians, Armenians and, after the Iberian expulsions at the end of the fifteenth century, the largest European **Jewish community** of the age: 80,000, or nearly half the inhabitants, for whom "Salonik or Salonicco" ranked as a "Mother of Israel" – until, that is, the first waves of emigration to Palestine, western Europe and the United States began after World War I. Numbers had dropped to fewer than 60,000 at the onset of World War II, when all but a tiny fraction were deported from Platía Eleftherías to the concentration camps and immediate gassing, in one of the worst atrocities ever committed in the Balkans. The vast Jewish cemeteries east of the city centre, among the world's largest, were desecrated in 1942; to add insult to injury, the area was later covered over by the new university and expanded trade-fair grounds in 1948. At last, however, the role of the Jewish community in making the city what it is has received some recognition in the form of a new **museum**, inaugurated in 2001, and a **memorial** to the victims of the 1943 deportations.

You can catch glimpses of "Old Salonica" today in the walled **Kástra** quarter, often known as the **Áno Pólis**, on the hillside beyond the modern grid of streets. Even amidst the post-1917 flatlands below, there are pockets of Ottoman buildings which miraculously survived the fire. The same goes for Greek Art Deco piles dating from the city's heyday and put up in time for the first International Trade Fair in 1926. In addition, the city's many **churches** constitute a showcase of Orthodox architecture through the ages. A smaller number of **Islamic monuments** – virtually all of them from the fifteenth century – attests to Thessaloníki's status as the premier Ottoman Balkan city, when Athens was still a backwater. For most visitors, however, the sight that

▼ The Sporades, Crete, Lésvos, Límnos & Cyclades

ACCOMMODATION								RESTAURANTS	
ABC	14	Averof	13	Emborikon	9	Nea Mitropolis	6	Ta Adhelfia tis Pixarias	U
Amalia	15	Bill	5	Esperia	3	Orestias Castorias	2	Aristotelous	S
Argo	7	Capsis Bristol	19	Ilisia	11	Park	1	Doré Zythos	b
Atlantis	10	City	17	Kinissi Palace	8	Pella	4	Iy Gonia tou Merakli	N
Atlas	12	Electra Palace	19	Macedonia Palace	20	Palace	16	Hiotis	B
						Tourist	18		

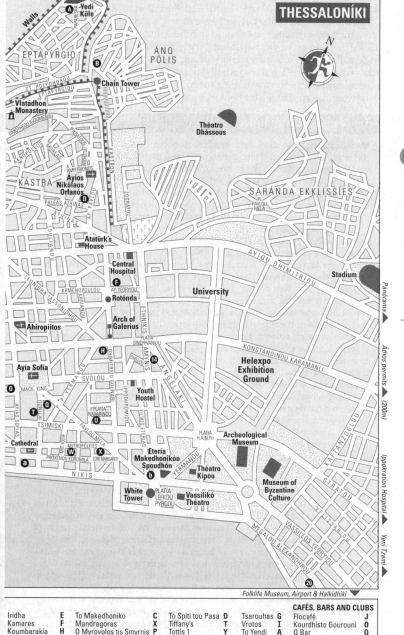

THESSALONÍKI

Panórama ▶

Áthos permits ▶ (200m)

Ippokration Hospital ▶

Yeni Tzami ▶

Folklife Museum, Airport & Halkidhikí ▼

Iridha	E	To Makedhoniko	C	To Spiti tou Pasa	D	Tsarouhas	G	CAFÉS, BARS AND CLUBS	
Kamares	F	Mandragoras	X	Tiffany's	T	Vrotos	I	Flocafé	J
Koumbarakia	H	O Myrovolos tis Smyrnis	P	Tottis 1	Y	To Yendi	A	Kourdhisto Gourouni	O
Louloudhadhika	R	Nea Ilyssia	L	Tottis 2	a	Zythos	V	Q Bar	Q
Loutros	M	Platia Athonos	K					Santé	W
								Tribeca	Z

stands out is Thessaloníki's excellent **Archeological Museum**, albeit depleted since the transfer of most Philip II-related exhibits back to Veryína.

The downside, for visitors as well as residents, is a complex of **problems** all
too reminiscent of those experienced in Athens. Industries and residences alike
discharge their waste, untreated, into the gulf (with slight improvements of
late), and traffic on the main avenues, despite a comprehensive one-way system
and a ring-road, is often at a standstill. After years of planning and sporadic discussion, bids for a contract to dig a metro system have finally been tendered,
with work due to start as this book goes to press.

The Macedonian controversy

Macedonia has been the subject of much controversy since the early 1990s and,
although the brouhaha has dropped from the fever pitch that it reached back then,
the Macedonian question remains the subject of fiery arguments in Greece. Although
inter-ethnic strife is nothing new in the Balkans, what sets this specific disagreement
apart is the **ancient historical dimension**, exploited by modern states in their quest
for a communal identity. The name Macedonia is a geographical term of long standing, applied to an area that has always been populated by a variety of races and cultures. It is today divided unequally between Greece (the lion's share), Bulgaria and the
Former Yugoslav Republic of Macedonia (FYROM) with a tiny fraction in Albania.

The original Kingdom of Macedonia, which gained pre-eminence under **Philip II**
and his son **Alexander the Great**, was part of the Greek cosmos; **Aristotle**, born at
Stageira, Halkidhikí, tutored Alexander. It is thought that the Macedons may have
originally migrated from central Europe. Almost nothing is known of their "native"
tongue, but Greek was used as the lingua franca, especially for cultural activities. The
capital, first established at **Veryína**, was transferred around 400 BC to **Pella**, which
shortly afterwards became the capital of Greece. The **empire** lasted for little more
than two centuries, exhausted by its galloping expansion: under Alexander's dynamic and despotic leadership Macedonia spread as far as Egypt and India. The lands
were then controlled successively by the Romans, Saracens and Bulgars, while
pockets were settled by Albanians and Serbs; it was part of the cosmopolitan
Byzantine empire before eventual subjugation under Ottoman Turkish rule.

In the late nineteenth century, when the disintegration of the **Ottoman empire**
began to raise the issue of future national territories, the name Macedonia denoted
simply the geographical region. Its highly heterogeneous population included
Greeks, Jews, Vlachs, Albanians and Turks and various Slavs. While no one ethnic
group predominated overall (the Greek Orthodox community was in a minority), the
Greek language remained the lingua franca. The first nationalist struggles for the territory began in the 1890s, when small armies of Greek *andartes*, Serbian *chetniks*
and Bulgarian *comitadjis* took root in the mountains, battling each other ferociously
before uniting briefly against the Ottomans in the first Balkan War (1912).

Following Turkish defeat, the **Bulgarians**, traditionally Greece's second foe, laid
sole claim to Macedonia in the second Balkan War (1912–13), but were defeated by
a Greco–Serb alliance; a 1913 agreement between the victors divided much of
Macedonian territory between them, roughly along linguistic/ethnic lines. The Greek
government was even prepared to let Bulgaria have most of Macedonia, as "recovering" the Asia Minor coast had become a nobler goal; at all events, during World
War I the Bulgarians occupied much of Greek Macedonia, before capitulating in
1917. After Versailles, a small part of Slav-speaking Macedonia remained in
Bulgaria, and Greek-speakers living in Bulgaria were "exchanged" for Bulgarian-
speakers in Greece, under the 1919 Treaty of Neuilly. Then, under the terms of the
Treaty of Lausanne in 1923, hundreds of thousands of ethnic Greek refugees from
Asia Minor were settled throughout Greece (what would now be called ethnic
cleansing). In the north they swamped the remaining Slavophones.

Arrival, orientation and information

Arriving in Thessaloníki is fairly straightforward. The **train station** on the west side of town, with convenient bus links and a reliable taxi rank, is just a short walk from both the central grid of streets and the harbour. **Buses** arrive at a variety of points, mostly within sight of each other, near the train station; the most useful are detailed in "Listings", p.472. The efficient international **airport** is located 15km south of the city centre. Facilities include a tourist booth, operating restricted hours, and cash dispensers, located near the first-floor café,

The position of Yugoslavia, however, under Tito, was more ambiguous. Yugoslavia had established the **Socialist Republic of Macedonia** in its share of the historical territory, and from time to time Belgrade issued thinly veiled irredentist threats. The Serb-dominated federation also "reinvented" the Macedonian language in an attempt to bring it closer to Serbo–Croat than Bulgarian; the republic, a neglected backwater, was encouraged to have a separate but pro-Serb identity. When the Yugoslav federation fell apart chaotically and violently in mid-1991, and the population of Yugoslav Macedonia voted overwhelmingly for an independent state, many Greeks predicted that the tiny resourceless country would not survive, especially given its "ethnic heterogeneity". But under wily autocrat President Gligorov the population rallied together. Both officially and at grassroots level, Greek reaction was vitriolic, especially when the fledgling nation provocatively adopted the sixteen-pointed star of Veryína (the symbol of the ancient Macedonian dynasty) on its flag and coinage (later abandoned). Foreign ministers did the rounds of EU capitals, imploring their allies not to recognize the new state; increasingly rebuffed by the international community, the PASOK government instigated a unilateral **economic boycott** of the new republic, eventually lifted.

After negotiations, the country was recognized by the international community (officially) as the Former Yugoslav Republic of Macedonia (**FYROM**). Greeks grudgingly accepted this *fait accompli*, but virtually all still refuse to use the name. The media refer to it as *Ta Skópia* and its people as *Skopianí*; Greek tabloids tend to use the phrase "pseudo-statelet of Skopje" and the press is not allowed to refer in print to Yugoslav "Macedonia" – the Greek rendition of the official acronym is "pYDM" (próin Yougoslavikí Dhimokratía tis Makedhonías). Icons of ancient Macedonian culture, such as the sixteen-pointed star of Veryína (albeit sometimes missing four rays) and images of the heroic figure of Alexander the Great, are ubiquitous in northern Greece. At the height of the crisis, official posters and stickers throughout Greece proclaimed that Macedonia had always been part of Greece, for "three thousand years" no less, and further exhorted visitors to "read history".

All this has been bad news for the estimated 40,000 **Slav-speakers**, most of them elderly, living in Greek Macedonia (and Thrace). Nation states have often maltreated linguistic minorities and Greece seems to be no exception; activists leafleting for recognition of the Slav-speaking minority in the 1990s were arrested, and in 1994, a respected Greek professor working in the US, Anastasia Karakasidou, received death threats in her native city of Thessaloníki after presenting highly publicized research establishing that the region had only become "Greek" politically and ethnically since the early twentieth century, by means of a deliberate process of Hellenization. Her manuscript, *Fields of Wheat, Hills of Blood,* was declined for publication by Cambridge University Press, despite a ringing endorsement from its editorial review board, for fears about the safety of CUP personnel in Greece and of endangering CUP's lucrative sale of TEFL materials in Greece. Karakasidou, who teaches at SUNY Stony Brook, had her work published by the University of Chicago (see "Books" in *Contexts*), but the episode highlights the sensitivity of this issue in Greece.

on departures level. City bus #78 (€0.40) shuttles back and forth hourly between 6am and 11pm; it leaves from the base of the kerbside luggage-cart ramp going up to arrivals/departures. The most convenient city stops are Platía Aristotélous and the train station. That said, a **taxi** into town won't set you back more than €7.30, or a bit more at night. All **ferries and hydrofoils** call at the passenger port, within walking distance of the train station, at the western end of the seafront. For all ferry agencies, see "Listings" on p.472; Aegean routes and frequencies are given in the "Travel details" at the end of the chapter.

Once you're within the central grid of streets, **orientation** is made relatively straightforward by frequent sightings of the bay and a series of main avenues: Ayíou Dhimitríou, Egnatía, Tsimiskí and Mitropóleos. All run parallel to the quay, but confusingly change their names repeatedly as they head east into the city's post-medieval annexe. The divide between the older and newer parts of town is marked by the exhibition grounds and the start of the seaside park strip, known locally as Zoo Park and dominated by the **Lefkós Pýrgos** or White Tower, the city's enduring symbol.

City transport

There are two types of **local buses**: the orange articulated "caterpillar" models which operate within the city, and the deep-red or blue buses which travel further afield. The fare within the city is €0.30, to the suburbs €0.40 and out to nearby villages €0.50. In most cases there's an automatic ticket machine on the bus (correct money only), but there are still a few where you pay the conductor at the rear entrance. Useful lines include #10 and #11, both of which ply the length of Egnatía/Karamanlí. From Platía Eleftherías (just behind the seafront), buses initially run east along Mitropóleos; line #5 takes you to the archeological and folklore museums, and #22/28 heads north through Kástra to the highest quarter, known as Eptapýrgio. **Taxis** (dark-blue and white) are plentiful and reliable.

If you bring your own **car**, it's best to use the attended fee-parking area that occupies all of Platía Eleftherías, where you pay on exit. Otherwise, finding a kerbside space is a fairly hopeless task, even in the suburbs; if you do manage to find a space you then usually have to go to a *períptero* to buy blue-and-red strip cards which you cancel yourself for an hour at a time (€0.90 per hour) – buy as many as you need in advance for display in the windscreen. Fees are payable 8am to 8pm Monday to Friday, 8am to 3pm on Saturday. If you intend to drive around the city, you're advised to arm yourself with a map that shows the one-way system (such as the one published by EOT).

Information

The overstretched and poorly equipped main **EOT** office is at Platía Aristotélous 8 (Mon–Fri 7.30am–3pm, Sat 8.30am–3pm, Sun 10am–5pm; ☎0310/271 888). When this is closed, try the **tourist police** post (daily 8am–2pm; Tues, Thurs & Fri also 5–9pm; ☎0310/554 870/871) at Dhodhekaníssou 4, off Platía Dhimokratías.

Quite good free **maps** are available from the tourist office. For something more detailed, we recommend the map published by Emvelia, which also includes Halkidhikí and the immediate surroundings of the city; they also do a folding map of Thessaloníki if you don't want the indexed atlas. A useful **book**, with a large-scale folding map, is *Monuments of Thessaloníki* by Apostolos Papayiannopoulos (€4.50), technically out of print but still possibly available at Áyios Dhimítrios church (and in German at many bookshops). Other recommended regional archeological guides, *Wandering in Byzantine Thessaloniki* and

Monuments of Thessaloniki (see box, p.465), are easier to find locally but have rudimentary street plans.

Accommodation

From after Easter until August, reasonably priced **hotel** rooms are fairly easy to find, albeit not always attractively situated. You will, however, find accommodation relatively expensive – over ten percent more than in Athens or the Peloponnese for equivalent facilities. During the **International Trade Fair** (Sept) and the autumn festival season (Oct and Nov) hotels are allowed to add a **twenty-percent surcharge** to the standard rate. From September to Easter high-season rates apply in any case, this being a business-oriented city rather than a tourist resort.

At the lower end of the price range, none of the city hotels officially charging less than €20 can be recommended, while most of the modest to comfortable hotels cluster around the southwestern end of Egnatía, or "Lower Egnatía" – although many of the establishments here are plagued by street noise. Others are concentrated on or around quieter Syngroú and in the more agreeable zone between Eleftherías and Aristotélous squares.

The unofficial **youth hostel** at Svólou 44 (☎0310/225 946; €7.50 per person) is well located if nothing else; take bus #10 from the train station to the Kamára stop. However, it continues to generate complaints about filth (especially in the basement showers), lack of security and generally poor management; if you're not put off, you should know that the office is closed from 11am to 7pm, so only turn up in the morning or evening.

The closest **campsites** are at the small resorts of Ayía Triádha and Órmos Epanomís, 24km and 33km away respectively; see pp.474–475 for more information. Both are EOT sites and, of the two, the further is the better – as is the beach there. Take bus #73 from Platía Dhikastiríon for Ayía Triádha, bus #69 for Órmos Epanomís.

Lower Egnatía

Argo, Egnatía 11 ☎0310/519 770. An old affair with basic but acceptable rooms, some of which have private facilities. ❶

Atlantis, Egnatía 14 ☎0310/540 131. Mostly non-en suite, with the better rooms facing a side street. ❸

Atlas, Egnatía 40 ☎0310/537 046. A very friendly hotel, centrally located and the furthest of the Egnatía hotels from the train station. Some rooms are en suite. Those at the front are noisy. ❷

Averof, Sófou 24, south of Egnatía ☎0310/538 840, ℻543 194. A good, friendly if musty cheapie, not too noisy and used to foreigners' needs. Some rooms were converted to ensuite in 1998. ❶

Ilisia, Egnatía 24 ☎0310/528 492. A good deal, this hotel has purpose-built en-suite facilities and extends a courteous welcome. ❷

Syngróu and around

Bill, Syngroú 29, cnr Amvrossíou ☎0310/537 666. In a quiet, tree-lined side street, this is a good find, if getting a bit well worn; balconies, and origi-

nal bathrooms in en-suite units (avoid the bathless rooms, in dire need of refurbishment). ❸

Emborikon, Syngroú 14, cnr Egnatía ☎0310/514 431. Good value, despite the shared bathrooms, and with helpful staff. ❷

Esperia, Olýmbou 58 ☎0310/269 321, ℻269 457. Refurbished in 1995, though slightly overpriced, with views north to the hills. ❹

Kinissi Palace, Egnatía 41 and Syngroú ☎0310/508 081, ℻523 904, ✉info@kinissi.gr. This impressive newcomer is by far the smartest in the area and is unbeatable value. Comfortable rooms with all mod cons; sauna, hammam and massage; an appealing bar and a decent restaurant, the *Averof*. ❻

Nea Mitropolis, Syngroú 22 ☎0310/525 540, ℻539 910. Clean, good value and well maintained, not too noisy despite its proximity to Egnatía. ❸

Park, Íonos Dhragoúmi 81 ☎0310/524 121, ℻524 193, 🖳www.psark.net.gr/business/parkhotel. Modern and sterile, but comfortable, spotless, double-glazed rooms with limited sea views. ❺

Pella, Íonos Dhragoúmi 63 ℡ 0310/524 221 or 555 550, ℻ 524 223. A tall, narrow, modern hotel on a moderately quiet street; pleasant, impeccably clean rooms and newly installed bathrooms. ❹

Rest of the city

ABC, Angeláki 41 ℡ 0310/265 421, ℻ 276 542, ⓦ www.hotelabc.gr. Popular with trade-fair and other business visitors, but its well-maintained, neutral rooms, copious buffet breakfast and convenient location make it good value for all. ❻

Amalia, Ermoú 33 ℡ 0310/268 321, ℻ 233 356. A decent, if slightly overpriced hotel, quiet enough at night, and well placed near the market. ❺

Capsis Bristol, Oplopíou 2 and Katoúni ℡ 0310/506 500, ℻ 515 777, ⓦ www.capsisbristol.gr. Thessaloníki's only boutique hotel to date, with twenty period-furnished rooms in an impeccably restored 1870 building; the *Dhipnosofistis* restaurant and *Medusa* bistro are further attractions. ❻

City, Komninón 11 ℡ 0310/269 421–9, ℻ 274 358, ⓦ www.cityhotel.gr. One of the newest establishments in the city, its smart spacious rooms with state-of-the-art bathrooms are obviously aimed at business travellers. Some have balconies offering views of the Upper Town. Beautiful breakfast bar where a bountiful American-style buffet can be sampled. ❻

Electra Palace, Platía Aristotélous 9/A ℡ 0310/232 221, ℻ 235 947. In one of the town's most prestigious positions – but it can get noise from events in the square. That said, it is as palatial inside as out, with large rooms and a good dining room, albeit with a slightly dated air. ❻

Hyatt Regency, near airport, on Halkidhikí road ℡ 0310/401 234, ℻ 401 100, ⓦ www.hyatt.com. The nearest you'll find to world-class service and comfort in the whole of northern Greece, it lives up to the chain's high standards. Excellent restaurant, spacious rooms and a casino. ❻

Macedonia Palace, Meghálou Aléxandhrou 2 ℡ 0310/897 197, ℻ 897 211, ⓔ mpalace@mkp.grecotel.gr. Smart, elegant and spacious rooms and suites in this city establishment hotel, with the best seafront views and an excellent restaurant, the *Porphyra*, famous for its brunch. ❻

Orestias Castorias, Agnóstou Stratiótou 14, cnr Olýmbou ℡ 0310/276 517, ℻ 276 572. With most rooms in this 1920s building recently converted to en suite, this is a prime, friendly choice and one of the quieter hotels in the city; reservations suggested. ❷

Palace, Tsimiskí 12 ℡ 0310/257 400, ℻ 256 589, ⓔ qcas@otenet.gr. Completely refurbished in 1998, this Art Deco hotel is extremely good value: spacious rooms with modern baths and double glazing (but it's still best to ask for a room away from the street). Characterful common areas comprise mezzanine lounge, a ground-floor café and a restaurant. An outstanding buffet breakfast is included. ❻

Tourist, Mitropóleos 21 ℡ 0310/270 501, ℻ 226 865. A friendly, rambling Belle Epoque palace with parquet-floored lounges and breakfast salon and a 1920s Swiss lift; 1990s-refurbished rooms all en suite; just two singles. You'll need to book in advance. ❺

Central Thessaloníki

Most of central Thessaloníki's principal sights are within easy walking distance of each other, many located on either side of the city's busiest main street, **Odhós Egnatía**. One of the city's most outstanding churches, **Ayía Sofía**, houses some superb mosaics, as does the converted Roman mausoleum still known by its Latin name, the **Rotónda**. Further highlights include the emblematic **White Tower**, the Turkish **bazaars** and what remains of the **Jewish city**, now represented by a charming museum. The city's best museum, however, is the remarkable **Archeological Museum** where some of the splendid Veryína treasures are on display. Venture into the city's eastern districts and you'll find some fine early-twentieth-century mansions, as well as **Yeni Camii**, a beautiful Art Nouveau mosque, used at the beginning of the last century by a crypto-Jewish sect outwardly practising Islam.

Odhós Egnatía and around

The social and commercial heart of downtown Thessaloníki is **Odhós Aristotélous**, a partly pedestrianized street with Italianate porticos on either side and lined with freshly painted, pale ochre buildings. It opens out at the seaside end into completely pedestrianized Platía Aristotélous, with views across to Mount

Olympus on clear days, and slopes up to the city's main artery, traffic-infested **Odhós Egnatía**. Although scholarly opinion now holds that Via Egnatia skirted the ancient city walls, there is no doubt that the modern Egnatía follows the course of an important Roman street or processional way. At some point during your time in town you are certain to ride or walk down it, catching glimpses of various monuments – some Roman, some Byzantine, some Ottoman – that lie on or just off it. Remains of Salonica's formative years in the eastern Roman empire are thin on the ground, however. For example, the ruins of the **Roman agora** unearthed in the 1970s in the vast Platía Dhikastiríon have yielded little in the way of structures, give or take a column or two, though they're still being excavated. Rather more prominent is a reconstructed **odeion** at the north corner of the square.

Byzantine monuments surpass the Roman ones; on Egnatía, at the southwestern corner of Platía Dhikastiríon, amid luxuriant palms, cypress and pines, nestles the eleventh-century **Panayía Halkéon** church, a classic though rather unimaginative example of the cross-in-square form (see box on Roman and Byzantine Salonica, p.464). It has been restored, reopening only in 2000, and is worth popping inside to see the fragmentary frescoes in the cupola and some fine icons. As the name indicates, it served during the Ottoman occupation as the copperworkers' guild mosque; the only remnant of this tradition is the handful of kitsch-copper-souvenir shops just across the street. For real antiques – mostly old lamps, bedsteads and wooden furniture, and not particularly cheap – you're best off heading uphill two blocks to Tossítsa, home (along with a courtyard just west) to the city's **flea market**.

Several blocks east and tucked away just out of sight north of the boulevard, the recently-restored, fifth-century, three-aisled basilica of **Panayía Ahiropíitos** is the oldest in the city, featuring arcades, monolithic columns and often highly elaborate capitals – a popular development begun under Theodosius. Only the mosaics inside the arches survive, depicting birds, fruits and vegetation in a rich Alexandrian style.

Ottoman architecture is also easy to spot; near the eastern corner of Platía Dhikastiríon stands the disused **Bey Hamam** or Parádhisos Baths (Mon–Fri 8am–2.30pm; free), the oldest Turkish bathhouse in the city (1444) and in use until 1968. The doorway is surmounted by elaborate ornamentation, while inside is more fine stalactite vaulting. Other nearby Ottoman monuments include the six-domed **Bezesténi** or covered valuables market at the corner of Venizélou and Egnatía, given a face-lift as part of the 1997 works and now housing jewellery and other shops. Directly opposite, on the north side of Egnatía, more modest stores occupy a prominent mosque, the fifteenth-century purpose-built **Hamza Bey Camii** (most mosques in Ottoman Thessaloníki were converted churches), now looking rather ramshackle.

South of Platía Dhikastiríon lies the **main bazaar** area, bounded roughly by Egnatía, Dhragoúmi, Ayías Sofías and Tsimiskí. Much the most interesting bit, and a quiet midtown oasis, is a grid of lanes between Ayías Sofías and Aristotélous, devoted to selling live animals, wood and cane furniture, chair-seat-reweavers and crafts shops.

The Rotónda and the Arch of Galerius

Some way off Egnatía, at the far northeastern end of Filippoú, the **Rotónda**, later converted into the church of **Áyios Yeóryios**, is the most striking single Roman monument in the city – designed, but never used, as an imperial mausoleum (possibly for Galerius) and consecrated for Christian use in the late fourth century by the addition of a sanctuary, an apse, a narthex and rich mosaics. Later it became one of the city's major mosques, from which period the minaret remains. Following lengthy repairs in the wake of the 1978 earth-quake, Áyios Yeóryios is once again open to the public (Tues–Sun 8.30am–3pm; free), though restoration work is ongoing. It ranks as a must-see for the sake of its superb mosaics, the finest of their era outside Constantinople or Ravenna. Ones already visible include a miscellaneous aviary of birds in the south vault; ducks, partridge and woodcock in the southeast vault; while up in the damaged dome the head of a mythical phoenix is visible with angels just outside a circular rainbow. Unfortunately hidden by scaffolding, just down from the dome, are fifteen naturalistically portrayed saints, many Roman sol-dier-martyrs, all sheltering under a fantastic structure where peacocks and birds of paradise perch, meant to symbolize the City of Heaven.

The Rotónda originally formed part of a larger complex which included the **Arch of Galerius**, just off the eastern end of Egnatía, Roman palaces and a hippodrome. Recently rid of scaffolding, the arch is the surviving span of a dome-surmounted arcade that once led towards the palaces. Built to com-memorate the emperor's victories over the Persians in 297 AD, its piers contain rather weathered reliefs of the battle scenes interspersed with glorified poses of Galerius himself. The well displayed remains of **Galerius's palace** can be viewed, below the modern street level, along pedestrianized Dhimitríou Goúnari and into its extension, Platía Navarínou.

Ayía Sofía

Between Egnatía and Navarínou, and not to be confused with the city's undistin-guished modern cathedral on Mitropóleos, the heavily restored eighth-century church of **Ayía Sofía** was consciously modelled on its more illustrious namesake in Constantinople. It replaced an older basilica, the only trace of which remains a few paces south, a below-street-level *ayíasma* or holy well of John the Baptist, itself originally a Roman nymphaeum (sacred fountain). Ayía Sofía's dome, ten metres in diameter, bears a splendid **mosaic** of the *Ascension*, for which you'll need opera glasses or binoculars. Christ, borne up to the heavens by two angels, sits resplen-dent on a rainbow throne, right hand extended in blessing; below, a wry inscrip-tion quotes Acts 1:11: "Ye men of Galilee, why stand ye gazing up into heaven?" The whole is ringed by fifteen figures: the Virgin, attended by two angels, and the twelve apostles shown reacting variously to the miracle above. The dome was restored late in the 1980s; the rest of the interior decoration was plastered over after the 1917 fire. Another fine mosaic of the *Virgin Enthroned* in the apse appar-ently replaced a cross, of which traces are visible, dating from the Iconoclast peri-od. Outside, on the north flank of the building, is a curious Ottoman tower, not the minaret pulled down from the south flank after 1912; the tower lost its dome at the same time as a Byzantine portico on the west side was demolished.

Jewish Salonica

Thessaloníki's only surviving pre-Holocaust **synagogue** is the Monastiriótou at Syngroú 35, with an imposing, if austere, facade; it's usually open for Friday evening and Saturday morning worship. At the very heart of the former Jewish district to the southeast (until 1942 Thessaloníki had no ghetto) sprawls the **Modhiáno**, the central meat, fish and produce market, named after the wealthy Jewish **Modiano family** which long owned it. Unfortunately it has suffered steady decline, with many stalls vacant, but still makes an atmospheric and authentic destination for a meal (see "Eating", p.469).

Just to the south, an early twentieth-century Jewish-owned building has been beautifully renovated to accommodate the impressive **Jewish Museum**, or Museo Djudio de Salonik to give it its Judeo-Spanish name (Tues–Fri & Sun

11am–2pm, Wed & Thurs 5–8pm; free), at Ayíou Miná 13. On the ground floor are a few precious remains (and some moving photographic documentation) of the city's Jewish cemetery which contained half a million graves until it was vandalized by the Nazis in 1942. Outstanding is a marble Roman stele from the third century recycled as a Jewish tombstone for a member of the post-1492 Sephardic community from Iberia. In the middle of the courtyard is a finely sculpted fountain that once stood in a city synagogue. Upstairs, a well-presented exhibition, clearly labelled in Greek and English, traces the history of the Jewish presence from around 140 BC to the present day, and displays some of the few religious and secular items that miraculously survived the 1917 fire and the Holocaust.

The White Tower
The most prominent central post-Byzantine monument is at the far northeastern end of seafront promenade Leofóros Níkis: the **White Tower (Lefkós Pýrgos)**, which formed the southeast corner of the city's Byzantine and Turkish defences before most of the walls were demolished late in the nineteenth century. Prior to this, it was the "Bloody Tower", a place of imprisonment and (in 1826) execution of the janissaries, until the Greeks whitewashed both the building and its image after World War I, removing at the same time a polygonal outer enclosure built by the Ottomans in 1875. Today, stripped of white pigment, it looks a little stagey in its isolation, but is a graceful symbol nonetheless, which for years appeared as the background logo on the evening TV news. It was restored in 1985 for Salonica's 2300th birthday celebrations to house a small but well-presented **museum** of Byzantine secular and sacred art, though at the time of research it had closed for further repairs.

The Archeological Museum
Although some of its star exhibits have been returned to the original site at Veryína (see p.484), it's still worth finding time for the **Archeological Museum** (summer Mon 12.30–7pm, Tues–Sun 8am–7pm; winter Mon 10.30am–5pm, Tues–Sun 8.30am–3pm; €4.50, €6 joint ticket with Museum of Byzantine Culture; see p.465) on Platía H.A.N.T.H., just a few minutes' walk inland from the White Tower. The central gallery, opposite as you enter, is devoted to rich grave finds from ancient Sindos, a few kilometres north of the modern city, while the left-hand wing is taken up by Hellenistic and Roman art, in particular some exquisite blown-glass birds, found in the tumuli or *toúmbes* which stud the plain around Thessaloníki. Downstairs is an exhibition of prehistoric finds from the city and region, of limited interest.

But these are all just appetizers for – or anticlimaxes after – the marvellous **Gold of Macedon exhibition** in the south hall (reached via the right-hand doorway), which displays – and clearly labels in both English and Greek – many of the finds from the royal tombs of Philip II of Macedon (father of Alexander the Great) and others at the ancient Macedonian capital of Aegae, at modern Veryína. They include startling amounts of gold and silver – masks, crowns, necklaces, earrings and bracelets – all of extraordinarily imaginative craftsmanship, both beautiful and practical, as well as pieces in ivory and bronze. Examples include a silver wine strainer with goose-head handles, a perforated bronze lampshade and an enormous bronze *krater* (wine-mixing bowl), which, in its richly ornate rendition of the life of the god Dionysos, prefigures Baroque art. However, the long-running star attractions – the *larnax* or gold ossuary casket of Philip II, plus that of a consort of his, and assorted gold wreaths – have been transferred back to Veryína itself. Philip II's bones are also no longer on view: they have been given a symbolic reburial at Veryína.

Through these finds the museum traces the history of the Macedonian dynasty and empire, and quite overtly uses the discoveries to emphasize the fundamental "Greekness" of the modern province of Macedonia. Although to an outsider it now seems like an accepted and inviolable part of Greece, Macedonia's occupation by Turks until the early twentieth century and the Bulgarian invasion during the two world wars are still very much part of Greek political memory. Archeology in northern Greece has always been a nationalist as well as an academic issue, and the museum itself is a brilliantly executed "educational" endeavour.

Roman and Byzantine Salonica and its churches

Macedonia became a **Roman province** in 146 BC, and **Salonica**, with its strategic position allowing both land and sea access, was the natural and immediate choice of capital. Its fortunes and significance were boosted by the building of the Via Egnatia, the great road linking Rome (via Brindisi) with Byzantium and the East, along whose course Amphipolis, Philippi and Neapolis (now Kavála) were also to develop.

Christianity had slow beginnings in the city. Saint Paul visited twice, being driven out on the first occasion after provoking the Jewish community. On the second, in the year 56AD, he stayed long enough to found a church, later writing the two Epistles to the Thessalonians, his congregation there. It was another three centuries, however, before the new religion took full root. Galerius, who acceded as eastern emperor upon Byzantium's break with Rome, provided the city with virtually all its surviving late Roman monuments – and its patron saint, Demetrius (Dhimítrios), whom he martyred. The first resident Christian emperor was **Theodosius** (reigned 379–95), who after his conversion issued the Edict of Salonica, officially ending paganism.

Under Justinian's rule (527–65) Salonica became the second city of Byzantium after Constantinople, which it remained – under constant pressure from Goths and Slavs – until its sacking by Saracens in 904. The storming and sacking continued under the Normans of Sicily (1185) and with the Fourth Crusade (1204), when the city became for a time capital of the Latin Kingdom of Salonica. It was, however, restored to the Byzantine Empire of Nicea in 1246, reaching a cultural "**golden age**" amidst the theological conflict and political rebellion of the next two centuries, until Turkish conquest and occupation in 1430.

The most prominent of Roman public buildings had been the **basilica**: a large wooden-roofed hall, with aisles split by rows of columns. It was ideally suited for conversion to Christian congregational worship, a process achieved simply by placing a canopied altar at what became the apse, and dividing it from the main body of the church (the nave) by a screen (a forerunner to the *témblon* or iconostasis). The baptistry, a smaller, distinct building, was then added to one side. The upper reaches of wall were adorned with mosaics illustrating Christ's incarnation and man's redemption, while at eye level stood a blank lining of marble. (Frescoes, a far more economical medium, did not become fashionable until much later – during the thirteenth and fourteenth centuries – when their scope for expression and movement was fully realized.)

By the sixth century, architects had succumbed to eastern influence and set

The Byzantine museums

Besides the gallery in the White Tower, there are two other recently inaugurated museums which, with varying degrees of success, attempt to do justice to Byzantine civilization. The state-run **Museum of Byzantine Culture**, in a handsome brick structure at Stratoú 2, just east of the Archeological Museum (summer Mon 12.30–7pm, Tues–Sun 8am–7pm; winter Mon 10.30am–5pm, Tues–Sun 8.30am–3pm; €3, €6 joint ticket with Archeological Museum; see p.463), does a fine job of displaying the early Christian tombs and graves excavated in the city, featuring rescued wall paintings depicting *Susannah and the Elders*, and a naked rower surrounded by sea creatures. The lighting and display techniques are faultless but most of the displays will appeal more to specialists than to lay visitors.

The other museum, in Ladhádhika district at Katoúni 12–14, is the heavily promoted, privately run **Museum of Ancient, Byzantine and Post-Byzantine Musical Instruments** (Mon 9am–3pm, Tues–Sun 9am–3pm &

about improving their basilicas with the addition of a dome. For inspiration they turned to the highly effective Ayía Sofía in Constantinople – the most striking of all Justinian's churches. Aesthetic effect, however, was not the only accomplishment, for the structure lent itself perfectly to the prevailing representational art. The mosaics and frescoes adorning its surfaces became physically interrelated or counterposed, creating a powerful spiritual aid. The eye would be uplifted at once to meet the gaze of the *Pandokrátor* (Christ in Majesty) in the dome, illuminated by the windows of the drum. Between these windows the prophets and apostles would be depicted, and as the lower levels were scanned the liturgy would unfold amid a hierarchy of saints.

The most successful shape to emerge during later experiments with the dome was the "Greek cross-in-square" – four equal arms that efficiently absorb the weight of the dome, passing it from high barrel vaults to lower vaulted chambers fitted inside its angles. Architecturally it was a perfect solution; a square ground plan was produced inside the church with an aesthetically pleasing cruciform shape evident in the superstructure. Best of all, it was entirely self-supporting.

By the mid-tenth century it had become the conventional form. Architects, no longer interested in new designs, exploited the old, which proved remarkably flexible; subsidiary drums were introduced above corners of the square, proportions were stretched ever taller, and the outer walls became masoned with elaborate brick and stone patterning.

Almost all the main Byzantine churches in Thessaloníki are located in the central districts. Under the Turks most of the buildings were converted for use as mosques, a process that obscured many of their original features and destroyed (by whitewashing) the majority of their frescoes and mosaics. Further damage came with the 1917 fire and more recently with the earthquake of 1978. Restoration seems a glacially slow process, guaranteeing that many of the sanctuaries are locked, or shrouded in scaffolding, or both, at any given moment. But, these disappointments acknowledged, the churches of Thessaloníki remain an impressive and illuminating group.

If you're keen to find out more about the subject it's worth trying to get hold of two locally available stone-by-stone **guides**: the succinct *Monuments of Thessaloniki* (Molho Editions), with coverage only of Roman and Christian sites but better site plans, or the more comprehensive but pricier and rather densely written *Wandering in Byzantine Thessaloniki* (Kapon Editions), which includes Ottoman monuments and has better reproductions. One last thing you might consider is arming yourself with a pair of opera glasses, as many of the mosaics are high up and difficult to see.

5–10pm; €4.50) occupying three floors of a purpose-built block. Put charitably, this is a triumph of style over substance – you're paying to see reproductions of artistic presentations of ancient instruments on walls, vases, drinking cups and so forth. Though each type (such as bagpipes or harps) is given a wing to itself, there's nothing in the way of interpretation or context. On the ground floor worthwhile photography exhibitions are regularly staged.

Folklife (Ethnological) Museum of Macedonia

The **Folklife Museum** at Vasilíssis Ólgas 68 (closed at the time of writing but supposedly reopening sometime in 2002), some way to the east of the city centre, is the best of its kind in Greece, with well-written commentaries (English and Greek) accompanying displays on housing, costumes, day-to-day work and crafts. The exhibits, on weaving and spinning especially, are beautiful. And there is a sharp, highly unfolkloric emphasis on context: on the role of women in the community, the clash between tradition and progress, and the yearly cycle of agricultural and religious festivals. Even the traditional costumes are presented in a manner that goes beyond the mere picturesque.

The collection is housed in the elegant early twentieth-century mansion of the **Modiano** family, they of the meat market, and one of several Jewish-built villas hereabouts. The museum is just a twenty-minute walk (or short bus ride) from the Archeological Museum; catch the #5 bus as it runs east along Mitropóleos and Meghálou Aléxandhrou.

The Dönme and the Yeni Camii

The **Dönme** or **Ma'min** were followers of Sabbatai Zvi, the seventeenth-century "False Messiah"; outwardly they embraced Islam after his forced conversion, and were counted as part of the Ottoman Muslim population, but secretly continued certain aspects of Jewish worship and married only among themselves. Numbering about 15,000 of the city's wealthier citizens, they were disproportionately important in the commerce of pre-fire Salonica, and later – following their voluntary emigration or 1923 expulsion – that of republican Turkey.

Concentrated in the wealthy eastern annexe, they were also responsible for numerous sumptuous villas in the same area as the Modiano, many still standing, but their enduring civic contribution is the orientalized Art Nouveau **Yeni Camii**, dating from 1904, the last mosque built in the city. Designed by an Italian architect, it is an engaging folly, often open for special exhibitions; in fact it long served as Thessaloníki's archeological museum after 1923. The interior is nothing other than an Iberian synagogue in disguise, its decor likely to overshadow any displays. It's easy to find, well signposted about 1km northwest up Vasilíssis Ólgas from the Folklife Museum, then 100m up a side street.

Áno Pólis (Kástra and Eptapýrgio)

Above Odhós Kassándhrou rises the Upper Town or **Áno Pólis**, part of which is sometimes referred to as **Kástra**, the main surviving quarter of Ottoman Thessaloníki. Although the streets here are gradually becoming swamped by new apartment buildings, they remain ramshackle and atmospheric, a labyrinth of timber-framed houses and winding steps. In the past few years the stigma of the district's "Turkishness" has been overcome as the older houses have been bought up and restored – indeed it has become one of its draws, and it is justifiably one of the city's favourite after-dark destinations. The best place to start for the walk up is the intersection of Ayíou Nikoláou and Ayíou Dhimitríou. Spare a glance en route for seventeenth-century **Yeni Hamam**, now a summer cinema and music venue, the Aigli (see p.471), and the fifteenth-century **Altaza Imaret mosque**, tucked away in a quiet square diagonally opposite, with a handsome portico and multiple domes.

Áyios Dhimítrios and around

At the very foot of the slope is a massive yet simple church, **Áyios Dhimítrios** (Mon 12.30–7.30pm, Tues–Sun 8am–8pm; free), conceived in the fifth century, though heavily restored since. The de facto cathedral of the city, with pride of place in Thessalonian hearts, it was almost entirely rebuilt after the 1917 fire, which destroyed all but the apse and colonnades. The church is dedicated to the city's patron saint and stands on the site of his martyrdom, and even if you know beforehand that it is the largest basilica in Greece, its immense interior comes as a surprise.

Amid the multicoloured marble columns and vast extents of off-white plaster, six small surviving **mosaics**, mostly on the columns flanking the altar, make an easy focal point; of these, four date back to the church's second reconstruction after the fire of 620. The astonishing seventh-century mosaic of *Áyios Dhimítrios Flanked by the Church's Two Founders*, on the inside of the south (right-hand) pier beside the steps to the crypt, was described by Osbert Lancaster as "the greatest remaining masterpiece of pictorial art of the pre-Iconoclastic era in Greece". This, and the adjacent mosaics of *Áyios Sérgios* and *Áyios Dhimítrios with a Deacon*, contrast well with their contemporary on the north column, a warm and humane mosaic of the saint with two young children. The other two mosaics date back to the fifth century. The one on the north pier is a *Deisis* with the Virgin and Áyios Theódhoros, while the other, high on the west wall of the inner south aisle, depicts a child being presented or dedicated to the saint.

The **crypt** (Mon 12.30–7pm, Tues–Sat 8am–8pm, Sun 10.30am–8pm; free), unearthed after the great fire, contains the *martyrion* of the saint – probably an adaptation of the Roman baths in which he was imprisoned – and a whole exhibit of beautifully carved column-capitals, labelled in Greek only and arrayed around a seven-columned fountain and collecting basin.

Around Áyios Dhimítrios are several more churches, utterly different in feel. West along Ayíou Dhimitríou is the somewhat remote church of **Dhódheka Apóstoli**, built with seven more centuries of experience and the bold Renaissance influence of Mystra. Its five domes rise in perfect symmetry above walls of fine brickwork, while inside are glorious fourteenth-century mosaics, among the last executed in the Byzantine empire. High up in the arches to the south, west and north of the dome respectively are a *Nativity*, an *Entry into Jerusalem*, a *Resurrection* and a *Transfiguration*.

To the west, **Ayía Ekateríni**, built just before Dhódheka Apóstoli, has fine brickwork, exploiting all the natural colours of the stones, though its interior frescoes are now fragmentary. **Profítis Ilías**, between Ayía Ekateríni and Áyiou Dhimítriou, is in the same vein as Dhódheka Apóstoli, though less imposing, and with negligible surviving interior frescoes.

Óssios Dhavídh

A short, stiff but direct climb up from Áyiou Dhimitríou along Ayía Sofía takes you to **Óssios Dhavídh** (Mon–Sat 8am–noon & 5–6pm, Sun 8–10.30am), a tiny fifth-century church on Odhós Timothéou. It doesn't really fit into any architectural progression, since the Ottomans demolished much of the building when converting it to a mosque. However, it has arguably the finest mosaic in the city, depicting a clean-shaven Christ Emmanuel appearing in a vision, surrounded by the Tetramorphs or symbols of the four Gospels. The four Rivers of Paradise, replete with fish, flow from beneath Christ, lapping the feet of the prophets Ezekiel and Habakkuk, who respectively cringe in terror and ponder at the revelation. Ask the curator to switch on the floodlights for a better view; a small donation for a candle will be appreciated. Nearby, up on Eptapyrgíou, the still-functioning **monastery of Vlatádhon** is most noteworthy for its tree-shaded courtyard, with its peacocks, a perfect place to pause during a tour; sometimes you can gain access to the much-restored *katholikón*, which has just a very few fourteenth-century frescoes and a collection of precious icons inside.

The ramparts and Eptapýrgio

Sections of the fourteenth-century **Byzantine ramparts**, constructed with brick and rubble on top of old Roman foundations, crop up all around the northern part of town. The best-preserved portion begins at a large circular keep, the Trigónion or Chain Tower (so called for its encircling ornamental moulding), in the northeast angle where the easterly city walls change direction. A much smaller circuit of walls rambles around the district of **Eptapýrgio** ("seven towers"), enclosing the old eponymous acropolis at the top end. For centuries it served as the city's **prison** (Tues–Sun 8.30am–3pm) – described as a sort of Greek Devil's Island in a number of plaintive old songs entitled "Yedi Küle", the Turkish word for Eptapýrgio – until abandoned as too inhumane in 1989; it is now being restored with European funds, eventually to include a **museum** commemorating its inmates, among whom were many political prisoners. On its south side, the wall is followed by Odhós Eptapyrgíou and edged by a small strip of park – a good place to sit and scan Thessaloníki.

Atatürk's house

If you approach or leave Kástra on its east side, it's worth passing by the Turkish consulate at the corner of Ayíou Dhimitríou and Apostólou Pávlou. In the pink, nineteenth-century building immediately behind it at Apostólou Pávlou 17, **Kemal Atatürk**, creator and first president of the modern secular state of Turkey, was born. The consulate maintains the house as a small **museum** (daily 10am–5pm; free), with its original fixtures and some Atatürk memorabilia. To visit you must apply for admission at the consulate itself, with your passport (☎0310/248 452; chancellery hours Mon–Fri 9.30am–12.30pm; ring the bell). Security is tight and for good reason – Atatürk is not universally popular in Greece. In 1981, a Turkish celebration of the centenary of his birth had to be called off after a Greek stunt pilot threatened a kamikaze dive at the house.

Áyios Nikólaos Orfanós

Fourteenth-century **Áyios Nikólaos Orfanós** (Tues–Sun 8.30am–3pm; entrance from Irodhótou, warden at no. 17) is a diminutive, much-altered basilica to the north of Atatürk's house; the imaginative and well-preserved frescoes inside are the most accessible and expressive in the city. In the south aisle, Áyios Yerásimos of Jordan is seen with anthropomorphic lions, with Christ's miracles set forth in a row above. The naos is devoted to episodes from the Passion, in particular the rarely depicted *Christ Mounting the Cross* and *Pilate Seated in Judgment* at a wooden desk, just like a Byzantine scribe of the era. Above the Virgin Platytera in the apse conch looms the equally unusual *Áyion Mandílion*, an image of Christ's head superimposed on a legendary Turin-style veil sent to an ancient king of Anatolian Edessa. Around the apse is a wonderful *Niptir* (Christ Washing the Disciple's Feet), in which it is thought the painter inserted (in lieu of a signature) an image of himself at the top right above the conch, riding a horse and wearing a white turban. Frescoes in the north aisle, illustrating the Akathistos hymn glorifying the Virgin, are less intact, but do feature a wonderful *Dream of Joseph* on one column capital.

Eating

First impressions are that the city centre is dominated by fast-food outlets, but since the early 1990s there has been an explosion of interesting places to eat and drink in Thessaloníki, parallelling the increasing prosperity of the city. All restaurants listed below have been categorized by price per person. The downtown area listings are all within walking distance of Platía Aristotélous; for the others we've given the appropriate transport connections. The notation "closed in midsummer" means closed from mid-July to mid-August – the time when Thessalonians typically take their summer holidays, a bit earlier than the Athenians. Traditionally, the city's ouzerís will provide some sort of sweet on the house, often semolina *halvás* or watermelon.

There are several recommended places scattered across town where you can get a **breakfast** or **quick snack**. Perhaps the best all-rounder is *Hotpot* at Komninón 15, open 24 hours, with full omelette-based breakfasts, pizzas, salads and pasta dishes. *Family* at Mitrópoleos 67, on the corner of Ayías Sofías, offers pastries, turnovers, sandwiches and good coffee or juice for breakfast, plus pizzas and pasta after midday. There's cheaper self-service at the window stools, or pay extra to be waited on at the sidewalk tables. *Vavel/Babel*, at Komninón 20, uniquely offers crepes, plus a salad bar, fresh juices and coffee in a pleasant indoor/outdoor environment. Lovers of quality biscuits will be in heaven at either *Armenaki*, Venizélou 10, or *Cookie Man*, Mackenzie King 8 (by Ayía Sofía church), both purveying myriad varieties of fresh-baked cookies by weight.

Downtown: between the sea and Odhós Ayíou Dhimitríou

Under €14

Ta Adhelfia tis Pixarias, Platía Navarínou 7. The best of several similar places on this archeological site/square, with delicacies such as *tzigerosarmás* (lamb's liver in cabbage) and *mýdhia saganáki* (mussels with cheese), plus real tablecloths – though the service tends to be haphazard and the portions are on the small side. It's often packed, so you should go early.

Iy Gonia tou Merakli, Avyerinoú, alley off Platía Áthonos. Inexpensive seafood and bulk wine make this about the best of several ouzerís in these atmospheric lanes between Platía Áthonos and Aristotélous.

Iridha, Olýmbou 83. A normal-priced taverna under the hotel *Orestias Kastorias*, offering a wide-ranging menu of *mayireftá*, *mezédhes* and grills. The speciality *soutzoukákia* bear little relation to the usual Greek version, being more like Turkish *inegöl köfte*. Attentive service and real table napery. Seating indoors or outdoors under some of the city's famous acacias; open all year.

Kamares, Ayíou Yeoryíou 11, Platía Rotóndas. Excellent seafood, salads and grilled meat at this year-round place, washed down by bulk wine from Límnos. Summer outdoor seating beside the park.

Koumbarakia, Egnatía 140. Tucked behind the little Byzantine chapel of the Transfiguration, the outdoor tables of this durable ouzerí groan with Macedonian-style grills, seafood and salads, including *túrsi* (pickled vegetables). Closed Sun and midsummer.

Loutros, M. Koundoúra 5. Good fried seafood, simple *orektiká* and excellent retsina next to the Bezesténi. Closed in midsummer.

O Myrovolos tis Smyrnis, in arcade in the Modiano off Komninón 32 ☎0310/274 170. Friendly, crowded ouzerí, also known as *Tou Thanassi* and reckoned the best of several clustered here. Typical fare includes cheese-stuffed squid, Smyrna-style meatballs, stuffed potatoes and grilled baby fish. Attracts a crowd of locals happy to empty several pitchers of *tsípouro* or Límnos bulk wine of an afternoon in the company of buskers. Open all year, air-conditioned in summer; despite ample seating, reservations recommended.

Nea Ilyssia, Sófou 17. Opposite the *Averof* hotel, this popular travellers' restaurant is open long hours (8.30am–2am) and serves highly regarded *mayireftá*.

Platia Athonos, Dhragoúmi, alley off said platía. Another good choice in this popular area, and one that's open for lunch.

Over €14

Aristotelous, Aristotélous 8. Tucked discreetly into a courtyard off Odhós Aristotélous (enter next to Blow Up Records), this stylish ouzerí with its fine arcaded interior and courtyard gets crowded for the sake of standard but well-executed mezédhes. Excellent *tsípouro* is available. Closed midsummer & Sun pm.

Doré Zythos, Tsiroyiánni 7, opposite the White Tower ☎0310/279 010. Younger branch of the original *Zythos* (see below), with food regarded as good as or even better than its parent's, served in stylishly retro decor and accompanied by mellow music. Reservations recommended at weekends.

Louloudhadhika, Komninón 20. An upmarket eatery, with yellow walls and smart tablecloths, serving extremely good food, especially the fresh fish, and the barrel retsina is wonderfully refreshing. Try and get an outside table in front of the old Jewish baths.

Mandragoras, Mitropóleos 98. Run by a man who twice won the state lottery, this is a large and elegant upstairs wine bar with theatrical decor, offering sophisticated if pricey food: the Beluga caviar

weighs in at €73 a serving. Open evenings only; closed in midsummer.

Tiffany's, Iktínou 3. A well-established favourite with locals, specializing in meat dishes, such as veal with okra, and offering delicious appetizers such as aubergine *bourekákia*.

Tottis, Platía Aristotélous 2–3 (plus a seaview branch at Níkis 29). A café, gelateria and (pricey) adjacent restaurant (*Ouzerí To Tavernáki*) all rolled into one – as much a meeting place as a dining spot.

Tsarouhas, Olýmbou 78, near Platía Dhikastiríon. Reputedly the best, and certainly the most famous, of the city's *patsatzídhika* – kitchens devoted to tripe-and-trotter soup. Lots of other *mayireftá*, and Anatolian puddings such as *kazandibí*. Closed midsummer; otherwise open all hours.

Vrotos, Mitropolítou Yennadhíou 6, Platía Áthonos ☎0310/223958. The most imaginative and currently one of the most popular of the half-dozen ouzerís in this area, with something for all tastes: elaborate vegetable dishes with or without cheese, meats, seafood recipes (though not whole fresh fish). Seating from long, narrow premises spills out onto the sidewalk, but space is still limited and so it's wise to book ahead. Open daily for lunch and supper except perhaps late July.

Zythos, Platía Katoúni 5 ☎0310/540 284. One of the best places in the Ladhádhika district. Very decent food is served at midday and in the evening, along with an excellent section of wine and several brews of draught and bottled Greek and foreign beers. Reservations recommended at weekends.

Áno Pólis (Kástra and Eptapýrgio)

The below represent a cross-section of typical Upper Town eateries, mostly reasonably priced and full of atmosphere; buses #22 or #28 from Platía Eleftherías spare you the climb. Incidentally, the garish, neon-lit joints on either side of the Chain Tower are perfectly alright for a terrace-with-a-view drink, but are not noted for their cuisine.

Hiotis, Graviás 2. Just inside the second (eastern) castle gate, near the Chain Tower. Mussels, kebabs and *kokorétsi* served on the terrace under the ramparts, weather permitting. Dinner only in summer, lunch and dinner rest of the year.

To Makedhoniko, Sykiés district. To get here, from the main Portára gate, head west, keeping to the walls as much as practicable, passing a second gate, until you reach the west end of the walls, near a third minor gate. You can also get a bus: #28 goes right through this gateway. A limited menu of *tís óras*, dips, salad and retsina is on offer, but it's cheap and popular with the trendy set as well as locals.

To Spiti tou Pasa, Apostólou Pávlou 35. As the name ("the Pasha's house") suggests, this elegant, two-storeyed house, stylishly but discreetly decorated, lays emphasis on creature comforts – they include tip-top Límnos wine from the barrel and fresh grilled fish and meats, plus impeccable service.

To Yendi, Paparéska 13, at the very top of Kástra, opposite the Yedi Küle citadel. An ouzerí-type menu that changes daily, dished up in largish portions, and accompanied by *tsípouro*, oúzo or house wine. Ample indoor or terrace seating under trees opposite the gate of Yedi Küle, but service can get overstretched owing to popularity. Supper only.

The eastern suburbs

The eastern suburbs are one of the city's more affluent areas and the restaurants tend to be correspondingly more expensive than elsewhere – routinely more than €14 per person; you may need to factor in taxi fares too.

Archipelagos Kanári 1, cnr Platía Eleftherías, Néa Kríni. A fancy seafood place and one of the best in the area. Take bus #5 or a taxi. Open daily 1pm–midnight.

Batis Platía Eleftherías 2, Néa Kríni, opposite the preceding. Much homier and almost normal-priced compared to *Archipelagos*. Grilled octopus and other fish dishes served on the open-air seaview terrace.

Ellinisti Filelínon 11 and Alexandhrias. Oúzo and *tsípouro* accompany excellent mezédhes, followed by some of the best fish in the city, all served in quaintly attractive surroundings.

Krikelas Ethnikís Andistásis 32, in the Vyzándio district, on the way to the airport. A somewhat touristy venue marooned in a desert of private medical clinics and car showrooms, but the chef here is one of the best in Greece, drawing on half a century of experience. Indoor seating only; closed July–Sept.

Vosporos Krítis 60, just east of 25-Martíou and 600m beyond the ethnological museum. Delicious Constantinopolitan–Greek food served in a pleasant three-level designer building; you select from preferred trays of hot and cold mezédhes. Open all year; closed Sun eve and all day Mon.

Drinking, nightlife and entertainment

The city's most fashionable nightlife district is **Ladhádhika**, near the harbour. It used to be rather seedy and run-down, but since the early 1990s has gone considerably more upmarket. Pedestrianized Katoúni, Eyíptou and Platía Morihóvou and surrounding streets are lined with a bewildering mix of cafés, windowless techno-*barákia* (complete with bouncers and sunglass-clad patrons), gelaterie, numerous ouzerís and even a few full-on tavernas. Most establishments have a high turnover rate, so singling them out is fairly pointless: just stroll by and choose according to crowd and noise level. Another profitable hunting ground is **Leofóros Níkis**, the seafront promenade that is a perennial *vólta* favourite, while a cluster of trendy designer bars on the square opposite the **White Tower** is worth checking out. During the warmer months, action shifts to various glitzy, barn-like establishments lining the coast road out to **Kalamariá**, and to pedestrianized Dhimitríou Goúnari, between the Arch of Galerius and the seafront, including bustling **Platía Navarínou** halfway down.

Bars, cafés and music clubs

Aigli cnr Ayíou Nikoláou and Kassándhrou, behind Áyios Dhimítrios church. Predating the 1997 wave of renovations, this classy bar-ouzerí, with Anatolian decor, occupies part of this dependency of the nearby Alatza Imaret mosque. A small events hall takes up the double-domed main chamber of the baths, with bar seating outside in summer, when the garden becomes an outdoor cinema.

Café Amareion ☎0310/248 812. Apostólou Pávlou. This relative newcomer puts on acoustically high-quality music gigs at weekends. It's wise to call ahead.

Flocafé Aristotélous 27. Serves some of the best coffee in the city, and has a strategically-placed terrace by the flowerbeds at the top of this lively, attractive street.

Kourdhisto Gourouni Ayías Sofías 31. Several foreign brews on tap, and a bewildering range of

bottled varieties, at this stylish bar with indoor and outdoor seating; expensive food menu also.

Q Zefxídhos 6, a pedestrian lane between Iktínou and Pávlou Melá. A former ouzerí, now a trendy little café-bar serving fruit juices, espresso and delicious hot chocolate in a contemporary decor of pale wood and cream leatherette with lots of leopardskin.

Santé Mitropóleos 70. Perhaps the most original café in Thessaloníki, with a kitsch decor apparently inspired by the collectors' item packets of the ironically named Santé cigarettes. Good place to find out about music gigs; the tiny dance floor sometimes comes to life later on.

Tribeca Níkis 19. An "in" waterfront hangout, with pricey coffees and alcohol at indoor or sidewalk seating. Purports to be on the exact spot occupied by a pre-1917-fire kafenío.

Events

In **winter**, **dance**, **opera**, **concert** and **theatre** events, often of high quality, mostly take place in one of the State Theatre of Northern Greece (Kratikó Théatro Voríou Elládhos) venues. Downtown this means either the 1997-redone Etería Makedhonikón Spoudhón or the ultramodern Vassilikó Théatro, within sight of each other behind the White Tower. In **summer**, things move to one of a number of outdoor venues: the Théatro Kípou, near the Archeological Museum; well up the hill at the Théatro Dhássous, in the pines east of the upper town, with events from late June to mid-September; or the Théatro Damari, above the Kaftantzoglio Stadium in Triandhría district (just off our map), which hosts big Greek or international stars like Marinella, James Brown or Tito Puente. In the absence of a reliable listings magazine, watch for posters in the windows of the usual ticket vendors: the record stores Blow Up (Aristotélous 8), Albandis (Mitropóleos 14–16), Patsis (Tsimiskí 41) and Virgin (shopping mall at Tsimiskí 43), as well as at Zythos or Doré Zythos (see p.470).

More **cutting-edge events** are held at Mylos, at Andhréou Yeoryíou 56, a multifunctional cultural complex housed in an old flour mill 2km southeast of the centre, founded in 1991. Here you'll find a couple of bars, a live jazz café, a popular *tsipourádhiko* (open for lunch), a summer cinema, concert halls and exhibition galleries of various sizes, plus a theatre. It has spawned various smaller imitators near and far in Greece, including (in Thessaloníki) Moní Lazaristón in Stavroúpoli at Kolokotróni 25 (☎0310/652 020), a deconsecrated Catholic monastery 2km out from the centre along Langadhá. Now officially part of the State Theatre of Northern Greece project, its main and smaller theatres host regular concerts and plays, by top Greek performers and visiting foreign troupes, as well as exhibitions. Buses #34 and #38 go there from Platía Dhikastiríon.

Cinema

Indoor cinemas, closed in summer unless otherwise indicated, tend to cluster between the White Tower and the Arch of Galerius; those known to concentrate on quality first-run material include Alexandhros, Ethnikís Amýnis 1 (open in summer); Egnatia, Patriárhou Ioakím 1, corner Keramopoúlou, by Ayía Sofia; Esperos, Svólou 22 (open in summer); Makedhonikon, Filikís Eterías, corner Dhimitríou Margaríti; Navarinon, on the namesake plaza; and Vakoura, Ioánnou Mihaïl 10. **Open-air cinemas** have all but vanished from downtown Thessaloníki, owing to spiralling property values; the only ones left are the Alex, at Olýmbou 106; the nearby Aigli outside the Yeni Hamam; Ellinis, the summer branch of the Egnatia, on Platía H.A.N.TH.; and the comparatively remote Natali, at the start of Megálou Alexándhrou by the *Macedonia Palace* hotel. Listings are given in the daily Greek papers and in *Parallaxi*, the monthly Greek-language cinema newspaper (🌐www.magnet.gr/parallaxi).

Listings

Airlines Aegean, Venizélou 2 ☎0310/280 050; Alitalia ☎0310/257 707; Cronus, Vas. Yeoryíou 18 ☎0310/870 555; Olympic, Koundourióti 3 ☎0310/230 240. Most other airlines have offices at the airport.

Airport ☎0310/411 977 for flight information.

Books and papers Molho, Tsimiskí 10, is far and away the best shop in the city, with an excellent stock of English-language books (in particular related to Thessaloníki), magazines and newspapers. Promitheus, at Ermoú 75 and Isávron 1, near Platía Navarlnou, and Konstandinidhis, at Egnatía 125, are good alternatives.

Bus terminals Most KTELs are opposite the train station, but specific locations should be checked with EOT. Currently, the most useful ones include: Alexandhroúpoli, at Koloniári 31; Édhessa/Véria, Monastiríou 75; Flórina, Anayenníseos 42; Halkidhikí, Karakássi 68, in the east of town (#10 bus to Bótsari stop); Ioánnina, Khrístou Pípsou 19;

Kastoriá, Anayenníseos 4; Kavála, Langadhá 59; Komotiní, cnr Olympíou Yeorgáki and Irínis; Litóhoro, Sapfoús 10; Pélla, Anayenníseos 22; Tríkala, Monastiríou 65; Vólos, Anayenníseos 22; and Xánthi, Ayíou Nestóros 22.

Camping gear Petridhis, Vas. Iraklíou 43; or World Jamboree, at Íonos Dhelíou 6, off Ethnikís Amýnis.

Car rental Many agencies are clustered near the fairgrounds and Archeological Museum on Angeláki, which is a good place to comparison-shop. The leading agencies have kiosks at the airport, too. Specific outfits include Avis, Níkis 3 ☎0310/227 126; Budget, Angeláki 15 ☎0310/274 272; Eurodollar, Ethnikís Andistásis 157 ☎0310/456 630; Europcar/Inter Rent, Papandhréou 5 ☎0310/826 333; European, Angeláki 15 ☎0310/281 603; Eurorent, Angeláki 3 ☎0310/286 327; Hertz, Venizélou 5 ☎0310/224 906; Thrifty, Angeláki 5 ☎0310/241 241.

Consulates Important for onward travel in the Balkans, but no longer needed for introductory letters to Athos (see below). Bulgaria, Mánou 2 ☎0310/854 004; Canada, Tsimiskí 17 ☎0310/256 350; Denmark, Komminón 26 ☎0310/284 065; Netherlands, Komninón 26 ☎0310/227 477; Romania, Níkis 13, 4th Floor ☎0310/225 481; South Africa, Tsimiskí 51 ☎0310/274 393; Turkey, Ayíou Dhimitríou 151 ☎0310/248 452; UK/Commonwealth: honorary consul is at Venizélou 8, 8th floor (Mon–Fri 8am–1pm; ☎0310/278 006); US, Níkis 59 (Mon–Fri 9am–noon; ☎0310/242 905). Note that there is still no full-blown consulate for the FYROM in Thessaloníki; visas to visit that country, if required, should be obtained in Athens rather than chancing the frontier.

Cultural institutes British Council, Ethnikís Amýnis 9, cnr Tsimiskí; free library and reading room, plus various events in the winter months.

Exchange For changing notes, use the 24hr automatic exchange machine at the National Bank on Platía Aristotélous 6. Thessaloníki has plenty of reliable cash dispensers accepting a variety of foreign plastic.

Ferry ticket agents The main agent for the DANE ferry to Sámos and the Dodecanese, plus G&A sailings to the Dodecanese, is Omikron Travel, Salamínos 4 ☎0310/555 995. Minoan Line or G&A sailings to the Sporádhes, Cyclades and Crete, as well as all hydrofoils to the Sporádhes, are best obtained from Kriti/Crete Air Travel, Íonos Dhragoúmi 1, cnr Koundouriótou ☎0310/534 376. Karacharisis at Koundouriótou 8 ☎0310/524 544 is the main NEL agent, and also deals in all G&A sailings and Minoan Lines.

Football Thessaloníki's main team is PAOK, whose stadium is in the east of the city at Toúmba – off

our map, though visible in square A5 of the EOT *Thessaloniki/Halkidhiki* handout.

Hospitals For minor trauma, use the Yeniko Kendriko at Ethnikís Amýnis 41; otherwise, head for the Ippokration at Konstandinopóleos 49, in the eastern part of town.

Internet café There are dozens, but two of the least noisy are *Link* at Goúnari 50 and *Planet* at Svólou 55.

Laundries Several coin-ops let you leave your clothes to be washed and collect them later, including Bianca, Antoniádhou 3, near the Arch of Galerius (quick service and long hours), and Freskadha, Filíppou 105, beside the Rotónda.

Mount Athos permits Regardless of what you may read in other sources, even official ones, prospective foreign pilgrims no longer need recommendation letters. Proceed directly to the Grafío Proskynitón Ayíou Órous (Pilgrims' Office for Mt Athos), Konstandínou Karamanlí 14, 1st Floor, ☎0310/546 38, some way east of the University. Walk-in hours – bring your passport – are Mon–Fri 9am–2pm, Sat 10am–noon, closed on Sun and major holy days. Telephone bookings (English spoken) are accepted, but you will still have to post a copy of your passport (relevant pages) or EU ID, and reconfirm the reservation closer to the intended date, up to the day before. Ten permits per day are issued to non-Orthodox, one hundred daily to baptized Greek Orthodox of whatever nationality. Non-Orthodox should ring ☎0310/861 611; Greek Orthodox ☎0310/833 733. For more details of the procedure see p.517.

Music Best of Thessaloníki's various record stores for Greek music are Studio 52, Dhimitríou Goúnari 46, basement, with lots of out-of-print vinyl and cassettes plus well-sorted CDs, and En Chordais, Ippodhromíou 3–4, a traditional music school and instrument shop which also has a well-selected stock of folk and innovative CDs.

OTE Ermoú 40, at junction with Karólou Díehl. Open daily 24hr, but only cardphones available.

Post office Main branch (for poste restante and complicated parcel services) is at Aristotélous 26 (Mon–Fri 7.30am–8pm, Sat 7.30am–2.15pm, Sun 9am–1.30pm). There are other post offices around the city: the most useful ones are at Koundouriótou (by the port), Ethnikís Amýnis 9a and Ayíou Dhimitríou 98.

Train tickets All services depart from the antiquated station down on Monastiríou, the southwestern continuation of Egnatía, well served by buses. If you want to buy tickets or make reservations in advance, the OSE office at Aristotélous 18 (Tues–Fri 8am–9pm, Mon & Sat 8am–3pm) is far more central and helpful than the station ticket-windows.

Travel agents Flights out of Thessaloníki have become much cheaper over the last couple of years; most general sales agents and consolidators cluster around Platía Eleftherías, especially on Kalapotháki, Komninón, Níkis and Mitropóleos. Students and youth travellers should try Nouvelles Frontières at Kalopotháki 8 ☏0310/237 700, Etos at Svólou 44, under the youth hostel ☏0310/263 814, or Sunflight – not just for under-30s – at Tsimiskí 114 ☏0310/280 500. For cheap buses to Turkey, try

Bus and Atlantic Tours, Aristotélous 10, 4th Floor ☏0310/226 036. Mountain trekking and other outdoor expeditions are offered by Trekking Hellas, Mitropóleos 60 ☏0310/264 082.

Wine Northern Greece nurtures some fine vineyards, and accordingly Thessaloníki has some excellent bottle-shops affordably selling vintages superior to your average taverna plonk: Iy Tsaritsani, Avyerinoú 9, off Platía Áthonos; Aneroto, Dhimitríou Goúnari 42; and Reklos, Ayíou Dhimitríou 118, cnr Ayías Sofías.

Out from the city

The main weekend escape from Thessaloníki is to the three-pronged Halkidhikí peninsula, but to get to its better beaches requires more than a day-trip. If you just want a respite from the city, or a walk in the hills, consider instead Thessaloníki's own local villages and suburbs. Further out, drivers en route to Néa Moudhaniá can take in the extraordinary cave near Petrálona – though half-day trips with a local tour operator make this a possibility for those without their own transport, too.

Panórama and Hortiátis

On the hillside 11km southeast of town, **PANÓRAMA**, the closest escape from the city, is exactly what its name suggests: a hillside viewpoint looking down over Thessaloníki and the gulf. The original village was razed to the ground by the Germans in retaliation for partisan sabotage during World War II – there's a monument to those burnt alive in the action – and Panórama has been rebuilt with smart villas, coffee shops and a large, modern shopping mall. Of more appeal are a number of cafés, tavernas and *zaharoplastía*, these last selling the premier local speciality, *trígona* (very sweet custard-filled triangular confections), wonderful *dondurma* (Turkish-style ice cream) and, more rarely these days, *salépi*, a beverage made from the ground-up root of *Orchis mascula*. The village can be reached by #58 bus from Platía Dhikastiríon, or by taxi (around €4 one way).

Still more of a retreat is **HORTIÁTIS**, 11km away due east (or 16km direct from Thessaloníki), set in a mountainous area known as *Hília Dhéndhra* (Thousand Trees), which since ancient times has supplied Thessaloníki with water – you can still see the ruined aqueduct to one side of the road. To get there from Thessaloníki, take the #61 bus which meets passengers alighting the #58 at the crossroads where those buses head up to Panórama. Attractions include sweeping views over the city, good walking among the pines and some popular places to eat; the *Tsakis* taverna has a well-deserved reputation, so in summer you should reserve tables in advance (☏0310/349 874) to avoid disappointment.

Seaside resorts

To swim near Thessaloníki you need to get well clear of the gulf, where the pollution is all too visible – and odorous. This means heading southwest towards Kateríni and the "Olympic Riviera" beaches below Mount Olympus (along the fast, four-lane National Road), or southeast towards Halkidhikí.

If all you want is a meal by the sea, then you can take local buses around the gulf. Bus #75 runs to **PERÉA**, 20km from Thessaloníki, a medium-sized weekender resort with good seafront tavernas but brutalist architecture and a rather unpleasant beach. Bus #73 serves **AYÍA TRIÁDHA**, 2.5km further

Anastenária: the fire walkers of Langadhás

On May 21, the feast day of Saints Constantine and Helen, villagers at **LAN-GADHÁS**, 20km north of Thessaloníki, perform a ritual barefoot **dance across a bed of burning coals**. The festival rites are of unknown and strongly disputed origin. It has been suggested that they are remnants of a Dionysiac cult, though devotees assert a purely Christian tradition. This seems to relate to a fire, around 1250, in the Thracian village of Kostí (now in Bulgaria), from where many of the inhabitants of Langadhás originate. Holy icons were heard groaning from the flames and were rescued by villagers, who emerged miraculously unburnt from the blazing church. The icons, passed down by their families, are believed to ensure protection during the fire-walking. Equally important is piety and purity of heart: it is said that no one with any harboured grudges or unconfessed sins can pass through the coals unscathed. The Greek Church authorities, however, refuse to sanction any service on the day of the ritual; it has even been accused of planting glass among the coals to try and discredit this "devil's gift".

Whatever the origin, the rite is still performed most years – lately as something of a tourist attraction, with an admission charge and repeat performances over the next two days. It is nevertheless eerie and impressive, beginning around 7pm with the lighting of a cone of hardwood logs. A couple of hours later their embers are raked into a circle and, just before complete darkness, a traditional Macedonian *daoúli* **drummer** and two **lyra players** precede about sixteen women and men into the arena. These *anastenárídhes* (literally "groaners"), in partial trance, then shuffle across the coals for about a quarter of an hour.

During the 1980s participants in the ritual were subjected to various **scientific tests**. The only established clues were that the dancers' brain waves indicated some altered state – when brain activity returned to normal they instinctively left the embers – and that their rhythmical steps maintained minimum skin contact with the fires. There was no suggestion of fraud, however. In 1981 an Englishman jumped into the arena, was badly burnt and had to be rescued by the police from irate devotees and dancers. Between 1991 and 1994, however, the rites failed to take place, owing to continued pressure from the Church and the *anastenárídhes'* own ire at being viewed merely as freak-show attractions. But by 1998, the event had resumed in public. If you decide to go, arrive early at Langadhás – by 5.30pm at the latest – in order to get a good seat. Frequent buses leave from a dedicated terminal on Odhós Langadhá in Thessaloníki. Be prepared, too, for the circus-like commercialism, though this in itself can be quite fun.

Other *anastenárídhes* used to "perform" at **Melíki**, near Véria, and at the villages of **Ayía Eléni** and **Áyios Pétros** near Sérres. Crowds, though, were reputed to be just as large and fire-walkers fewer. If you're in Greece, anywhere, and moderately interested, you can catch the show on the ET TV news at 9pm.

---

west and marginally more pleasant, where there is an EOT **campsite**, the *Akti Thermaïkou* (☎03920/51 360; open all year), rooms to rent and a few **hotels**, most economical of these the shoreline *Aegean* (☎03920/51 236; ❸), with a good taverna and decent en-suite rooms. The *Galaxias* (☎03920/22 291, Ⓦwww.galaxias-hotels.com; ❻), 1km from the centre, is smart, but frankly overpriced despite its swimming pool.

Bus #69 veers south, via inland Epanomís, to the better strand of **ÓRMOS EPANOMÍS**, 33km from Thessaloníki, although some people prefer to travel on to Néa Kalikrátia before taking to the water. There is a second EOT **campsite** at Órmos Epanomís (☎03920/41 378; April–Oct), more attractive and with more shade than the one at Ayía Triádha.

Petrálona

Fifty kilometres southeast of Thessaloníki and set among handsome mountain scenery, is the **cave of Kókkines Pétres** (Red Stones), discovered in 1959 by villagers from nearby **PETRÁLONA** looking for water. Besides an impressive display of stalagmites and stalactites, the villagers – and, later, academics – found the fossilized remains of prehistoric animals and, most dramatic of all, a Neanderthal skull, all of which are displayed in a decent museum near the cave entrance.

The cave, kitted out with dioramas of prehistoric activities and well worth a visit makes an interesting diversion on the way to or from the Kassándhra peninsula; you'll find the village of Petrálona itself roughly 4km north of Eleohória, on the old road running from Thessaloníki to Néa Moudhaniá at the neck of the peninsula. The cave and museum are open daily (9am to sunset; €4.50; guided tours only, photography forbidden) and there's a small café on site. Doucas Tours in Thessaloníki (Venizélou 8, near the UK consulate), and other outfits, operate a half-day trip.

Mount Olympus (Óros Ólymbos)

The highest, most magical and most dramatic of all Greek mountains, **Mount Olympus** – Ólymbos in Greek – rears straight up to 2917m from the shores of the Thermaïkos Gulf and, when pollution allows, is visible from downtown Thessaloníki, some 100km away, to the northeast. Its summit was believed by the ancient Greeks to be the home of the gods and it seems that quite a few locals still follow the old religion – whether as the result of incredible continuity or a recent revival it's difficult to ascertain. Dense forests cover its lower slopes, and its **wild flowers** are without parallel even by Greek standards. To make the most of it, you need to allow two- to three-days' hiking.

You should go equipped with decent boots and warm clothing, but no special expertise is necessary to get to the top in summer (mid-June to Oct). It's a long hard pull, though, requiring a good deal of stamina; winter climbs, of course, are another matter, with heavy snowfall quite low down adding to the challenge. At any time of year Olympus is a mountain to be treated with respect: its weather is notoriously fickle, with sudden fogs or storms, and it regularly claims lives.

Olympus practicalities and Litóhoro

By far the best base for a walk up the mountain is the small town of **LITÓHORO** on the eastern side. An intrinsically dull, rough-and-ready garrison town with two huge army camps on the approach road, its setting in good weather affords intoxicating dawn-of-climb views into the heart of the range. Reaching Litóhoro is fairly easy: it has its own motorway turn-off, and buses to the central platía **KTEL** from Thessaloníki or the market town of Kateríni are frequent. A train station is due to open soon.

At the budget end of **accommodation** you're best off looking for **rooms** (❶), by asking in the cafés and tavernas around the main square. The best, those in the hospitable *Xenonas Papanikolaou* (☎03520/81 236; ❷), are particularly good value, albeit slightly more expensive than the others, and hidden away in a quiet part of town (signposted). Low-price **hotels** include the very basic *Markesia* at Dhionýsou 5 (☎03520/81 831; ❶), off 28-Oktovríou some way from the central platía – if it's unattended, enquire at the novelty shop nearby. You could also try the exceedingly plain but en-suite *Park* on the main drag,

MOUNT OLYMPUS (ÓLYMBOS)

Litóhoro

Takis Boundolos ('D') Refuge

Enípeas (Mavrólongos) Canyon

Dhiakládhosi (Gortsiá)

Old Ayíou Dhionysíou Monastery

Petróstrounga

Strángo

Mandhres 2241m

Skoúrta 2485m

Lemós

Pápa Alóni Ravine

Profítis Ilías 2803m

Diosapítho Mousón

Refuge C (Khristos Kakalos)

Zonária

Yíosos Apostolídhis (SEO) Refuge

Stefáni 2909m

Mýtikas 2917m

Loúki

Skála 2866m

Kazánia

Skolió 2911m

Áyios Andónios 2817m

Spílios Agápitos ('A') Refuge

Pritónia (Taverna)

Gólna 926m

Déli

Káto Tsouknídha

Ano Tsouknídha 1498m

Palaio Vouthiá

Livadháki

Simeóforos 2381m

Págos 2676m

Kalóyeros 2701m

Frángou Alóni 2677m

Metamórfosi 2699m

MACEDONIA

THESSALY

Kokinoplós

Enípeas (Mavrólongos) Canyon

	Contour
	Cross-country route
	Refuge
	Spring

0   2 km

N

Ayíou Nikoláou at no. 23 (☎03520/81 252; ❶), towards the lower part of town. At the newish, spotless *Enipefs/Enipeas* (☎03520/81 328 or 84 328; ❸), beyond the main square near the National Bank, upper rear rooms have the best views in town; attic rooms with skylight only are cheaper. Immediately opposite stands the *Aphrodite* (☎03520/81 415; ❸) with only averagely clean rooms, few of which have any view. For much of the year, there's little price difference between Litóhoro hotels, so you may as well go up a notch at the comfortable *Myrto* on Ayíou Nikoláou, just before the main square (☎03520/81 398, ⓕ82 298; ❹; open all year). Finest of all, if not the best located, tucked away two or three streets back from Ayíou Nikoláou, is *Villa Drossos*, at Arheláou 18 (☎03520/84 561, ⓕ84 563; ❹), which boasts smart rooms, an attractive swimming-pool, and an open fire in winter, plus parking space and Litóhoro's top breakfasts; meals can also be laid on.

When it comes to **eating**, you'll find a rash of fast-food places in the square and on Ayíou Nikoláou but, on the uphill side streets near the central platía, there are more attractive possibilities, such as the *Ouzeri Manos* at 28-Oktovríou 3, just down from the **post office** at no. 11, with a limited menu of seafood tit-bits; or the *Dhamaskinia*, higher up on Vasiléos Konstandínou. Even better is the *Ouzeri Pazari* nearby on Platía 3-Martíou, serving locally caught octopus and squid. If you're keen to stock up on carbohydrates before a climb, try the pasta at the *Fournos*, on the roundabout at the bottom of Ayíou Nikoláou. At the start of the road towards the mountain (signposted "Olymbos"), just above the SEO office, is a couple of cheap-and-cheerful, sit-down *psistariés* – the *Zeus* in particular passes muster. For sustenance while walking, you'll need to buy food at the well-stocked stores in Litóhoro, though water can wait until you're in the vicinity of either of two trailheads (see opposite).

Accommodation on **Olympus** itself is better organized than on any other mountain in Greece. There are two staffed **refuges**: the EOS-run *Spilios Agapitos* at 2100m (open May 15 to Oct 15; ☎03520/81 800, reservations recommended in summer), commonly known as Refuge "A", and the SEO-managed *Yiosos Apostolidhis* hut at 2700m (open July–Sept only, though its glassed-in porch is always available for climbers in need). There is no set phone number for this refuge, since the wardenship is often in a state of flux; contact the SEO information office in Litóhoro on ☎03520/82 300 (evenings only). Both currently charge around €9 for a bunk (you can camp at Refuge "A" for €2.60, using their bathroom), with lights out and outer door locked at 10pm, so bring a torch. Meals at either shelter are relatively expensive, and mandatory since no cooking is allowed inside; bring more money than you think you'll require, as bad weather can ground you a day or two longer than planned. A couple of **banks** in Litóhoro have cash dispensers.

This guide contains all you need to know to head up the mountain immediately on arrival if you so desire, since **information** sources in Litóhoro can be patchy. EOS (summer only Mon–Fri 9.30am–12.30pm & 6.30–8.30pm, Sat 9am–noon) maintains a well-signposted office 200m west of the *Hotel Myrto*, but they've no set hours off-season, and their free leaflet is quite useless. Rival club SEO is tucked away along the road to the national park, just 50m along, behind and below the *psistariés* cited above, and opens only in the evenings. The best, most easily available commercial **trekking map** is Road Editions' no. 31 *Olymbos* at 1:50,000, available from specialist map shops abroad (see p.37 for some recommended outlets) or in Athens or Thessaloníki; a good alternative is one of the same scale that is co-produced by *Korfes* magazine and EOS. One or other is usually available at a shop on Ayíou Nikoláou opposite the start of the Ólymbos road, but they often run out. Trekking Hellas at Ayíou Nikoláou

64 (☎ & ⑤ 03520/814 131, ⓦ www.olympus.gr/trekking) can organize **treks** and other activities for those not wanting to go it alone.

The mountain

To reach alpine Olympus, you've a choice of road or foot routes. With your own vehicle, you can **drive** deep into the mountain along a fairly decent road, the first 11km of which is now paved – with the same treatment controversially planned soon for the remainder. There is an information booth at Km3, where (in high season anyway) your nationality is recorded and you're given some literature advising you of the park rules, but so far there's no admission charge. It is much better, however, to **walk** in from Litóhoro, as far as the monastery of Ayíou Dhionysíou, and beyond to the two trailheads following.

As for the final **ascent routes**, there are two main paths: one beginning at Priónia, just under 18km up the mountain at the road's end, where there's a spring, toilets and a primitive taverna (May–Oct); the other at a spot called Dhiakládhosi or Gortsiá (13km along), marked by a signboard displaying a map of the range. The Priónia path is more frequented and more convenient, the Dhiakládhosi trail longer but more beautiful. A 1800-metre driveway, appearing on the main road at 15.5km (about halfway between the two trailheads), leads down to Ayíou Dhionysíou. At the spot called Stavrós, 9km above Litóhoro along the road, there's a third **refuge** (really a roadhouse, officially called *Takis Boundolos*; ☎ 03520/84 519), but it's not conspicuously welcoming and usually booked up, though it does have the highest cardphone on the mountain.

The Enipéas (Mavrólongos) canyon and Ayíou Dhionysíou monastery

Some time ago the Greek overland-trail committee rehabilitated old paths in the superlatively beautiful Enipéas (Mavrólongos) river canyon to make a fine section of the **E4 overland trail**, thus sparing hikers the drudgery of walking up the road or the expense of a taxi. Black-on-yellow diamond markers begin near Litóhoro's central platía; follow road signs for Mýli and bear down and right at the cemetery. Once out of town, waymarks lead you along a roller-coaster course by the river for four hours to Ayíou Dhionysíou. It's a delightful route, but you'll need basic hiking skills, as there are some scrambles over steep terrain, and a few water crossings.

The **monastery** itself was burned by the Germans in 1943 for allegedly harbouring anti-occupation guerrillas, and the surviving monks, rather than rebuilding, relocated to new premises nearer Litóhoro. After years of dereliction and vandalism, Ayíou Dhionysíou is undergoing a snail's-pace restoration; so far only the *katholikón* has been re-erected. If you ask the resident warden, Father Anthimios, nicely and contribute your mite to the restoration, you may stay in any vacant ground-floor cells (iron bedsteads). There's potable water just outside, much used by people camping along the riverbanks below the perimeter wall (tolerated despite falling within national park territory), though you may have to contend with wild boar, reintroduced locally by Greek ecologists.

From Ayíou Dhionysíou it's just under an hour more upstream along the riverside E4 to Priónia, or slightly less up the driveway and then east to the Dhiakládhosi trailhead.

The ascent from Priónia

The E4 carries on just uphill from the taverna, by an EOS signpost giving the time to the refuge as two hours thirty minutes, though it actually takes more like three hours, even at a brisk pace. You cross a stream (last water before the

Spilios Agapitos refuge, purification advisable) and start to climb steeply up through woods of beech and black pine. This path, the continuation of the E4, is well trodden and marked, so there is no danger of getting lost. As you gain height there are majestic views across the Enipéas (Mavrólongos) ravine to your left and to the peaks towering above you.

The *Spilios Agapitos* **refuge** perches on the edge of an abrupt spur, surrounded by huge storm-beaten trees. The resident warden runs a tight ship, and you need to let him know in good time if you want a meal and a bed. It's best to stay overnight here, as you should make an early start (certainly pre-8am) for the three-hour ascent to Mýtikas, the highest peak at 2917m. The peaks frequently cloud up by midday and you lose the view, to say nothing of the danger of catching one of Zeus's thunderbolts, for this was the mythical seat of the gods. Besides, nights at the refuge are fantastic: a log fire blazes, you watch the sun set on the peaks and dawn break over the Aegean, and there are billions of stars.

The summit area

The E4 path continues behind the refuge (your last **water source** on the ascent), climbing to the left up a steep spur among the last of the trees. Having ignored an initial right fork towards the usually unstaffed *Khristos Kakalos* hut (Refuge "C"), within about an hour you reach a signposted **fork** above the treeline. Straight on takes you across the range to Kokkinopylós village with the E4 waymarks, or with a slight deviation right to Mýtikas, via the ridge known as Kakí Skála (1hr 30min–2hr). An immediate right turn leads to the *Yiosos Apostolidhis* hut in one hour along the so-called Zonária trail, with the option after forty–fifty minutes of taking the very steep Loúki couloir left up to Mýtikas; if you do this, be wary of rockfalls.

For the safer **Kakí Skála route**, continue up the right flank of the stony, featureless valley in front of you, with the Áyios Andónios peak up to your left. An hour's dull climb brings you to the summit ridge between the peaks of Skolió on the left and Skála on the right. You know you're there when one more step would tip you over a 500-metre sheer drop into the Kazánia chasm; take great care. The Kakí Skála ("Evil Stairway") begins in a narrow cleft on the right just short of the ridge; paint splashes mark the way. The route keeps just below the ridge, so you are protected from the drop into Kazánia. Even so, those who don't like heights are likely to be reduced to a whimpering crouch.

You start with a slightly descending rightward traverse to a narrow nick in the ridge revealing the drop to Kazánia – easily negotiated. Continue traversing right, skirting the base of the Skála peak, then climb leftwards up a steepish gully made a little awkward by loose rock on sloping footholds. Bear right at the top over steep but reassuringly solid rock, and across a narrow neck. Step left around an awkward corner and there in front of you, scarcely a hundred metres away, is **Mýtikas summit**, an airy, boulder-strewn platform with a trigonometric point, tin Greek flag and visitors' book. In reasonable conditions it's about forty minutes to the summit from the start of Káki Skála; three hours from the refuge; five and a half hours from Priónia.

A stone's throw to the north of Mýtikas is the **Stefáni peak**, also known as the Throne of Zeus, a bristling hog's back of rock with a couple of nastily exposed moves to scale the last few feet.

Descending from Mýtikas, you can either go back the way you came, with the option of turning left at the signpost (see above) for the *Yiosos Apostolidhis* hut (2hr 30min from Mýtikas by this route), or you can step out, apparently into space, in the direction of Stefáni and turn immediately down to the right into the mouth of the Loúki couloir. It takes about forty minutes of downward scrambling to reach the main path where you turn left for the hut, skirting the impressive northeast face of Stefáni (1hr), or go right, back to the familiar signpost and down the E4 to *Spílios Agapitos* (2hr altogether).

The ascent from Dhiakládhosi (Gortsiá)

Starting from the small parking area beyond the information placard, take the narrow path going up and left via faint steps – with a wood railing and wooden awning – not the forest track heading down and right. An hour along, you reach the meadow of **Bárba**, and two hours out you'll arrive at a messy junction with a modern water tank and various placards – take left forks en route when given the choice. The signs point hard left to the spring at **Strángo**; right for the direct path to Petróstrounga; and straight on for the old, more scenic way to **Petróstrounga**, passed some two and a half hours along.

Beyond this summer pastoral colony, there's an indicated right, then the trail wanders up to the base of **Skoúrta** knoll (4hr 15min), above the treeline. After crossing the Lemós (Neck) ridge dividing the Papá Alóni and Enipéas (Mavrólongos) ravines, with spectacular views into both, five and a quarter hours should see you up on the Oropédhio Musón (Plateau of the Muses), five and a half hours to the *Apostolídhis* refuge, visible the last fifteen minutes. But you should count on seven hours, including rests, for this route; going down takes about four and a half hours, a highly recommended descent if you've come up from Priónia.

It takes about an hour, losing altitude, to traverse the onward Zonária path linking *Apostolídhis* and the E4, skimming the base of the peaks – about the same time as coming the other way as described above.

The southern ridge route

To experience complete solitude on Olympus, continue past Áyios Andónios, the peak just south of Skála and the E4 trail, and begin to ridge-walk the line of peaks that bounds the Enipéas (Mavrólongos), to the south. Much of this trek past Metamórfosi, Kalóyeros and Págos summits is cross-country, but with the recommended map, route-finding is easy on a clear day. It's six and a half walking hours from the *Apostolídhis* hut to the dilapidated but serviceable, unstaffed shelter at **Livadháki**, with unreliable cistern water only – you'll need to carry at least a couple of litres in with you. From Livadháki a good trail descends via the ridges of Pelekoudhiá and Tsouknídha, coming out over three hours on at the meadow of **Déli**, where you're just above a forest road which leads 7km down to Litóhoro.

Alternatively, a faint but followable trail at Déli (on our map, but not on the Road Editions or EOS products) dips down into a ravine and up onto **Gólna** knoll, intersecting another, sporadically marked path up from Litóhoro that leads over into the Enipéas (Mavrólongos) watershed to join up with the E4. Just above the junction, woodcutters have rather messed up the path, but persevere, and you'll suddenly drop down on to the E4 about halfway along its course, some ninety minutes out of Déli. This last section makes a beautiful, if challenging walk.

Dion

Ancient **DION**, in the foothills of Mount Olympus, was the Macedonians' sacred city. At this site – a harbour before the river mouth silted up – the kingdom maintained its principal sanctuaries: to Zeus (from which the name *Dion*, or *Dios*, is derived) above all, but also to Demeter, Artemis, Asclepius and, later, to foreign gods such as the Egyptians Isis and Serapis. Philip II and Alexander both came to sacrifice to Zeus here before their expeditions and battles. Inscriptions found at the sanctuaries referring to boundary disputes, treaties and other affairs of state suggest that the political and social importance of the city's festivals exceeded a purely Macedonian domain.

Most exciting for visitors, however, are the finds of mosaics, temples and baths that have been excavated since 1990 – work that remains in progress whenever funds allow. These are not quite on a par with the Veryína tombs (see below), but still rank among the major discoveries of ancient Macedonian history and culture. If you're near Mount Olympus, they are certainly worth a detour, and the abundance of water and vegetation make it cooler and more pleasing on the eye than many sites. The frog-ponds and grazing geese in a lush landscape littered with voluptuous statuary lend the place the air of a decadent Roman villa and its gardens.

At the village of **DHÍON** (Malathiriá until the archeological discovery), 7km inland from Litóhoro beach or reached by #14 bus from Kateríni, take a side road 400m east from the *Hotel Dion*, past the remains of a **theatre**, put to good use during the summer Olympus Festival. The main **site** or "park" lies ahead (daily: summer 8am–7pm; winter closes 5pm; €2.40). A direct, signposted, paved road links Dion to Litóhoro (see above), crossing a formerly out-of-bounds army firing range; coming from Litóhoro take the Olympus road and keep going ahead instead of turning left up the mountain. Recommended for an **overnight** stay is the decent *Hotel Dion*, which stands at the crossroads by the bus stop (☎03510/53 682; ❹), 100m below the museum; on the pedestrian street linking the two are a few tavernas firmly pitched at the tourist trade. The nearest campsites are on the beach at Varikó, 11km away: *Stani* (☎03520/61 277) and *Niteas* (☎03520/61 290), both open all year round.

The integrity of the site and its finds is due to the nature of the city's demise. At some point in the fifth century AD, a series of earthquakes prompted an evacuation of Dion, which was then swallowed up by a mudslide from the mountain. The place is still quite waterlogged, and constant pumping against the local aquifer is necessary. The main visible excavations are of the vast **public baths** complex and, outside the city **walls**, the **sanctuaries** of Demeter and Aphrodite-Isis. In the latter, a small temple has been unearthed, along with its cult statue – a copy of which remains *in situ*. Two Christian **basilicas** attest to the town's later years as a Byzantine bishopric in the fourth and fifth centuries AD. An observation platform allows you to view the layout of the site more clearly.

In the village, a large but poorly labelled **museum** (Mon 12.30–7pm, Tues–Sun; winter Mon–Fri closes at 5pm; €2.40) houses most of the finds. The sculpture, perfectly preserved by the mud, is impressive, and accompanied by various tombstones and altars. In the basement sprawls a mosaic of Medusa, along with the finest **mosaics** so far discovered at the site: they would have paved the banquet room and depict the god Dionysos on a chariot. Upstairs, along with extensive displays of pottery and coinage, is a collection of everyday items, including surgical and dental tools perhaps connected with the sanctuary of Asclepius, the healing god. Pride of place, however, goes to the remains of a first-century BC **pipe organ**, discovered in 1992 and exhibited on the upper storey.

Véria and Veryína

The broad agricultural plain extending due west from Thessaloníki eventually collides with an abrupt, wooded escarpment, at the panoramic edge of which several towns have grown up, including Édhessa (see p.488) and Náoussa (see p.489). The largest of these, **Véria** (Karaferiye to the Turks), has few outstanding sites or monuments, but it is one of the more interesting northern Greek communities, thanks to its mixed Jewish, Muslim and Christian heritage, and lies within twenty-minutes' drive of the history-changing excavations of ancient Aegae at **Veryína**.

Véria

If you don't have your own transport the best way to get to **VÉRIA** (ancient Berrhoea or Berea) is by bus, as the train station is hopelessly inconvenient, a good 3km east of the centre. The bus drops you at the main **KTEL** and from here there are regular onward services to Veryína and all regional destinations, except Kozáni and Thessaloníki (for connections to these see below). Heading south from the KTEL along Odhós Venizélou you come to a fork in the road. Fashionable Odhós Eliás, to the left, takes you to Platía Eliás, known locally as the Belvedere. From here Leofóros Aníxeos snakes east and north along the cliff edge, past Véria's most prestigious district, to rejoin Venizélou. En route, Aníxeos passes the **archeological museum** (daily except Mon 8.30am–3pm; €1.50), which contains mostly Roman oddments from the immediate area. Meanwhile, the right fork, partly pedestrianized, one-way **Mitropóleos**, heads west towards the central Platía Konstandínou Raktiván – universally called **Platía Oroloyíou**, after a long-vanished clock tower – passing on its way the **post office** on side-street Dhionysíou Solomoú, various banks (with cash dispensers) and the nondescript new cathedral. On the far western side of Platía Oroloyíou is the **KTEL** terminal for Kozáni and Thessaloníki services.

The ramshackle twelfth-century **old cathedral**, opposite a gnarled plane tree from which the conquering Turks hanged the town's archbishop in 1430, is just off Odhós Vassiléos Konstandínou (also known as **Kendrikís**), which links Venizélou and Platía Raktiván; with its chimney-like truncated minaret, added when it was converted to a mosque, it looks like some disused factory. Near the tree, what remains of the old **bazaar** straddles Kendrikís; downhill and to the northwest tumbles the riverside Ottoman quarter of **Barboúta**, sometimes known as the Barboúti. Largely **Jewish** before the 1943 deportations annihilated the 1000-strong community, it is today more or less abandoned, though EU-funded restoration of the crumbling houses – many bearing Hebrew inscriptions and ornate frescoes – is now proceeding apace. The disused **synagogue** can be reached either along pedestrianized Odhós Sófou, or via Odhós Dhekátis Merarhías, another stepped lane taking off from behind the yellow officers' club up on Platía Oroloyíou. When you reach a plaza with a small amphitheatre, look for a long stone building, partly ochre-painted with an awning over the door, sometimes left ajar, allowing you to look at the rambling, arcaded interior. Survivals of the **Muslim** presence in Véria are more numerous and more conspicuous: a wonderful *hamam* complex on Loutroú, west of Mitropóleos; a small mosque on Kendrikís; and a larger one on Márkou Bótsari, just south of Platía Oroloyíou.

Christianity has a venerable and long history here: Saint Paul preached in Véria (Acts 17:10–14) on two occasions, between 50 and 60 AD, and a gaudy alcove shrine at the base of Mavromiháli marks the supposed spot of his sermons. The town is famed for sixty or so small medieval **churches**, mostly dating from the sixteenth to eighteenth century and earning it the moniker of "Little Jerusalem". In order to avoid offending Muslim sensibilities, they were once disguised as barns or warehouses, with little dormer windows rather than domes to admit light; but today, often surrounded by cleared spaces and well labelled, they're not hard to find. They are, however, generally locked, only viewable (with a good scholarly reason) by application to the 11th Ephorate of Byzantine Antiquities. The only church regularly open is the well-signposted **Resurrection of Christ, or Anastásseos Christoú** (daily except Mon 8.30am–3pm; free), with cleaned fourteenth-century frescoes, near the fork end of Mitropóleos. The most striking images here are a *Dormition/Assumption* over the west door; a *Transfiguration* on the south wall, with one disciple somersaulting backwards in fear; and on the north wall a rare image of Christ mounting the Cross on a ladder. The key-keeper may offer to show you the nearby tenth-century chapel of **Kýrikos and Ioulíta**, down a lane to the southwest, but its frescoes are alas uncleaned and likely to remain so, since churches in Kastoriá and Kozáni provinces seem to have priority in this respect.

Practicalities

The bare handful of **hotels** scattered across Véria is generally overpriced and/or noisy in typical mainland fashion. The least expensive is the adequate and clean en-suite *Veroi* at Kendrikís 4, just off Platía Oroloyíou (✆03310/22 866; ❸). A slightly smarter, better-value choice is the *Villa Elia*, Elías 16 (✆03310/26 800, 🄵21 880; ❹), but prone to street noise. Best of all is the *Makedhonia*, Kondoyeorgáki 50 (✆ & 🄵 03310/66 902; ❹), with a roof garden and substantial breakfasts, and far enough past the bars (see below) for nocturnal peace.

The town does rather better when it comes to **restaurants**. A pair of tavernas, *To Steki tou Goulara* and *Nikos*, sit opposite each other on pedestrianized Patriárhou Ioakeím, 100m southwest from the new cathedral. The former in particular is friendly and appetizing, and serves up grilled quail and vegetarian mezédhes. This lane is also lined with old Ottoman houses, many of them housing café-bars. Elsewhere, an enduring favourite for supper is *Kostalar* (closed Mon) in Papákia district at Afrodhítis 2/D, reached by following Mavromiháli uphill from the Saint Paul shrine to a plane-tree-shaded square with rivulets; this place has been going since 1939, offering clay-pot oven dishes and grills. Another popular spot is the *Ouzeri Yiaze stin Petra*, on the corner of Aníxeos and Koundourióti; although not in the most inspired location, it serves up consistently good grills and appetizers.

In the daytime, by far the most pleasant place for a coffee or a beer is the city-run **tourist pavilion** at the edge of the Belvedere, with its shady terrace overlooking the plain (though meals here are not recommended). Just further along Aníxeos, *Kamelot*, opposite the large church near the junction with Odhós Pastér, is a relatively quiet café-bar, with a shady courtyard and upstairs rooms for playing *távli*, popular with a broad spectrum of Veriots. For the best ice cream in town head for *Prapas* at Mitropóleos 51.

If you crave more action after dark, the pedestrianized area southwest of Mitropóleos, crammed full with noisy *barákia* installed in restored Ottoman houses, comes into its own. Most of these **clubs** are on Kondoyeorgáki, heading downhill from the Resurrection church, and its perpendicular Ellis.

Veryína: ancient Aegae

The site of **VERYÍNA**, 16km southeast of Véria, undoubtedly qualifies as one of the most memorable experiences, and not just archeological, that Greece has to offer. The main finds consist of a series of **chamber tombs** unearthed by Professor Manolis Andronikos in November 1977 – the culmination of decades of work on the site – and unequivocally accepted as those of Philip II, the father of Alexander the Great, and other members of the Macedonian royal family. This means that the site itself must be that of **Aegae**, the original Macedonian royal capital before the shift to Pella, and later the sanctuary and royal burial place of the Macedonian kings. It was here that Philip II was assassinated, cremated and buried – and tradition maintained that the dynasty would be destroyed if any king were buried elsewhere, as indeed happened after the death of Alexander the Great in Asia. Until Andronikos's finds, Aegae had long been assumed to be lost beneath modern Édhessa. Its discovery at Verýina has been exploited by Greek nationalists to support their argument that Macedonia has always been Greek and always will be (for more on the Macedonian question see p.456).

Finds from the site and tombs, the richest Greek trove since the discovery of Mycenae, are exhibited in the complex. Some are also on display at Thessaloníki's Archeological Museum (see p.463), though recently many have been returned to Verýina. The main tombs remain *in situ*, while the magnificent treasures found inside are shown off in remarkably well-lit cases, along with erudite texts in Greek and English. Visitors walk down narrow underground passages into a climate-controlled bunker which allows them to see the ornamental facades and the empty chambers beyond; overhead, the earth of the tumulus has been replaced. It's best to try and get here very early or visit at siesta time (it's refreshingly cool inside during the fierce summer heat) in order to avoid crowds and the increasing number of Greek school parties.

The modern village of Verýina right next door has limited facilities, with a slew of tourist-trap **tavernas**, a **cash dispenser** and foreign-note changer. For somewhere to **stay** try decent *Pension Vergina* (☎03310/92 510 or 25 703; ❸), conveniently located near the stop for Véria-bound buses; it offers en-suite rooms with fans and balconies and a copious breakfast is included in the price.

The Royal Tombs

Under a tumulus just outside modern Verýina, Andronikos discovered several large and indisputably Macedonian chamber tombs, known simply as the **Royal Tombs** (Mon 12.30–7pm, Tues–Sun 8am–7pm; close 5pm winter; €3.60. Photography forbidden). From outside, all that's visible is a low hillock with skylights and long ramps leading inside, but once underground you can admire the facades and doorways of the tombs, which are well illuminated and behind glass.

A clockwise tour takes you round the tombs in the order IV-I-II-III. Tomb IV, the so-called "Doric", was looted in antiquity; so too was **Tomb I**, or the "**Persephone tomb**", but it retained a delicate and exquisitely crafted **mural** of the rape of Persephone by Hades, the only complete example of an ancient Greek painting that has yet been found. **Tomb II**, confidently identified as that of **Philip II**, is a much grander vaulted tomb with a Doric facade adorned by a sumptuous painted **frieze** of Philip, Alexander and their retinue on a lion hunt. This – incredibly – was intact, having been deliberately disguised with rubble from later tomb pillagings. Among the treasures to emerge – now displayed in the dimly lit but well-labelled hall here – were a marble sarcophagus containing a **gold ossuary** (*larnax*), its cover embossed with the exploding, sixteen-pointed star symbol of the royal line. Still more significantly, five small **ivory heads** were found, among them representations of both Philip II and Alexander. It was this clue, as well as the fact that the skull bore marks of a disfiguring facial wound Philip was known to have sustained, that led to the identification of the tomb as his. Also on view are a fabulous **gold oak-leaf**

wreath – so delicate it quivers – and a more modest companion *larnax* found in the antechamber, presumed to contain the carefully wrapped bones and ashes of a legitimate queen or concubine, quite probably a Thracian aristocrat, married for political reasons, and who, according to some sources, stepped into the dead king's pyre of her own accord.

Tomb III is thought to be that of Alexander IV, "the Great's" son, murdered in adolescence – thus the moniker "**Prince's Tomb**". His bones were discovered in a silver vase. From the tomb frieze, a superb **miniature of Dionysos and his consort** is highlighted. You should also spare a moment or two to view the excellent **video**, subtitled in English, which brings the archeological finds to life.

⑤ Macedonian Tomb

The so-called "**Macedonian Tomb**", actually five adjacent tombs, can also be visited after a fashion (same times as above; same admission ticket). They are about 500m uphill and south of the village and, like the Royal Tombs, lie well below ground level, protected by a vast tin roof. When he's around, the guard will let you into the dig, though not into the tombs themselves. Excavated by the French in 1861, the most prominent one, thought to be that of Philip's mother Eurydike, is in the form of a temple, with an Ionic facade of half-columns breached by two successive marble portals opening onto ante- and main chambers. Inside you can just make out an imposing marble throne with sphinxes carved on the sides, armrests and footstool. The neighbouring two pairs of tombs, still undergoing snail-paced excavation, are said to be similar in design.

Palace of Palatítsia

On a slope southeast of the village, across a ravine and 1km by road beyond the main village crossroads and a vast new car park, the ruins of the **Palace of Palatítsia** (daily summer 8am–7pm; €1.50) occupy a low hill. This complex was probably built during the third century BC as a summer residence for the last great Macedonian king, Antigonus Gonatas. Little more than the foundations remain, but amidst the confusing litter of column drums and capitals you can make out a triple *propylaion* (entrance gate) opening onto a central courtyard. This is framed by broad porticoes and colonnades which, on the south side, preserve a well-executed mosaic now, alas, invisible under protective sand and gravel following frost damage. Despite its lack of substance, Palatítsa is an attractive site, dominated by a grand old oak tree looking out across the plains, scattered with Iron Age (tenth- to seventh-century BC) tumuli and who knows what else. The only substantial items dug up to date are the first two tiers of the **theatre** just below, where Philip II was assassinated in 336 BC, some say at the wedding of his daughter.

Pella

PELLA was the capital of Macedonia throughout its greatest period, and the first "real capital" of Greece after Philip II forcibly unified the country around 338 BC. It was founded some sixty years earlier by King Archelaos, who transferred the royal Macedonian court here from Aegae (see p.484), and from its beginnings it was a major centre of culture. The royal palace was decorated by the painter Zeuxis and said to be the greatest artistic showplace since the time of Classical Athens. Euripides wrote and produced his last plays at the court, and here, too, Aristotle was to tutor the young Alexander the Great – born, like his father Philip II, in the city.

The site today is a worthwhile stopover to Édhessa and western Macedonia. Its main treasures are a series of pebble mosaics, some in the museum, others *in situ*. For an understanding of the context, it is best to visit after looking around the Archeological Museum at Thessaloníki, from where the site can also be visited comfortably on a rewarding day-trip.

The site

When Archelaos founded Pella, it lay at the head of a broad lake, connected to the Thermaïkós Gulf by a navigable river. By the second century BC the river had begun to silt up and the city fell into decline. It was sacked by the Romans in 146 BC and never rebuilt; an earthquake caused further damage around two centuries later. Today its **ruins** (April–Oct Mon noon–7pm, Tues–Sun 8am–7pm; closes 3pm rest of year; €1.50, €2.40 combined ticket with museum) stand in the middle of a broad expanse of plain, 40km from Thessaloníki and the sea.

Pella was located by chance finds in 1957; preliminary excavations have revealed a vast site covering over 485 hectares. As yet, only a few blocks of the city have been fully excavated but they have proved exciting, and investigations are continuing. The **acropolis** at Pella is a low hill to the west of the modern village of Pélla. Excavation is in progress on a sizeable building, probably a palace, but at present it's illuminating mainly for the idea it gives you of the size and scope of the site. To the north of the road, at the main site, stand the low remains of a grand official building, probably a government office; it is divided into three large open courts, each enclosed by a *peristyle*, or portico (the columns of the central one have been re-erected), and bordered by wide streets with a sophisticated drainage system.

The three main rooms of the first court have patterned geometric floors, in the centre of which were found intricate **pebble mosaics** depicting scenes of a lion hunt, a griffin attacking a deer and Dionysos riding a panther. These are now in the excellent **museum** across the road (April–Oct Mon noon–7pm, Tues–Sun 8am–7pm; Nov–March 8am–3pm, closed Mon; same price as site), next to the car park. But in the third court three late fourth-century BC mosaics have been left *in situ* under sheltering canopies; one, a stag hunt, is complete, and astounding in its dynamism and use of perspective. The others represent, respectively, the rape of Helen by Paris and his friends Phorbas and Theseus, and a fight between a Greek and an Amazon.

It is the graceful and fluid quality of these compositions that sets them apart from later Roman and Byzantine mosaics, and which more than justifies a visit. The uncut pebbles, carefully chosen for their soft shades, blend so naturally that the shapes and movements of the subjects seem gradated rather than fixed, especially in the action of the hunting scenes and the rippling movement of the leopard with Dionysos. Strips of lead or clay are used to outline special features; the eyes, now missing, were probably semi-precious stones.

The mosaics are inevitably a hard act to follow, but the museum merits another half-hour of perusal for the sake of its other well-presented exhibits. Highlights include rich grave finds from the two local necropolises, delicately worked terracotta figurines from a sanctuary of Aphrodite and Cybele, a large horde of late Classical/early Hellenistic coins, and – on the rarely seen domestic level – metal door fittings: pivots, knocker plates and crude keys.

The nearest **hotels** to the site are at Néa Halkidhóna, a major junction 8km east. Opposite each other on the Véria road, 1km from the junction with the Thessaloníki road, are the decent enough *Kornelios* (☎03910/23 888, Ⓦwww.hotelkornelios.gr; ❷) or the slightly more appealing *Filippos* (☎03910/22 125, Ⓕ22 198; ❷). **Buses** from Véria and Veryína to Thessaloníki stop right in front of the *Hotel Kornelios*. The site of Pella lies on the main Thessaloníki–Édhessa road and is served by half-hourly buses, stopping in **Néa Halkidhóna**, in either direction.

Édhessa and around

The main gateway to the intriguing northwest corner of Macedonia, a land of lofty peaks and mirror-like lakes, **Édhessa**, teetering atop the same escarpment as Véria, has been resolutely turning itself into a regional centre for tourism since the late 1990s. With considerable style it has recently started renovating its old buildings, including some handsome water mills, and now offers a wide range of activities both within the town and in the nearby mountains. The town makes a good base from which to visit the unspoilt archeological site of **Lefkádhia** and the viticultural centre of **Náoussa**.

Édhessa

ÉDHESSA, like Véria, is a delightful place for a stopover but with rather better accommodation; its modest fame is attributed to the waters that flow through the town. Descending from the mountains to the north, these waters flow swiftly through the middle of town in several courses and then, just to the east, cascade down a dramatic ravine, luxuriant with vegetation, to the plain below. Most of the town's architecture is humdrum, but the various streamside parks and wide pedestrian pavements are a rare pleasure in a country where the car is tyrant – indeed, Édhessa was the pioneering town in Greece for pedestrianization.

The most interesting neighbourhood in the town is the **Varóssi**, tottering atop the cliffs just west of the waterfalls. Its mills and old Balkan-style houses, some decorously decaying, some recently restored with considerable style, reward aimless wanderings. Many of the **water mills** have been renovated as part of a scheme to create an "open-air water museum", due for completion in 2002. Several churches and chapels, new and restored, are proudly signposted but the only real monument as such is a delightful little **folklore museum** (Tues–Sun 10am–6pm; €1.50), on Megálou Aléxandhrou, near Áyia Paraskeví church; it displays various household objects and other traditional items of the kind that would have graced every home in the district in days gone by.

Practicalities

Édhessa's **train and bus stations** are both well placed for breaking a journey. The main KTEL is on the corner of Filíppou (the main road into the town centre) and Pávlou Melá; there's a second, smaller terminal for Flórina/Kastoriá services only, nearby at the corner of Egnatía and Pávlou Melá. The train station is in the north of town. The town's excellent new **tourist information office** is in the park at Garéfi and Pérdhika (daily 10am–8pm; ☎03810/20 300 or 23 101, Ⓦwww.edessacity.gr) and is far and away the best in the region. English-speaking staff can provide information about activities, such as trekking, rafting, kayaking and skiing in the surrounding region. You'll find the **post office** on Dhimokratías, while several **banks** sport cash dispensers.

Accommodation at the lower end of the scale is available at the slightly shabby but friendly *Pella*, Egnatia 26–30 (℡03810/23 541; ❷), or the more comfortable *Alfa*, virtually next door at no. 36 (℡03810/22 221; ❷). Quieter but less friendly is the *Elena* at Dhimitríou Rízou 4, on the corner of Platía Timenídhon (℡03810/23 218; ❷), whose management (unlike the others) may refuse to bargain at slack times. Far more upmarket, the A-class *Xenia* (℡03810/21 898; ❺), signposted off Filíppou, is the town's most expensive hotel, yet its comfortable rooms and deluxe facilities make it good value. All four are a ten-minute walk or less from either bus terminal. For some real old-fashioned hospitality, however, try the popular *Varossi*, in the eponymous district at Arh. Meletíou 45–47 (℡03810/21 865, ℻28 872; ❹), run by a charming local lady and her daughters and an absolute delight, with open fire, cosy en-suite rooms decorated in a vernacular style, and delicious breakfasts.

The range of **restaurants** is more limited. *Paeti* at 18-Oktovríou 20 is the undisputed top choice, offering a small but flavoursome range of *mayireftá* and *tis óras*, and specializing in roast suckling pig and delicious barrelled wine. Apart from the municipal restaurant in the *Katarraktes* complex by the tourist office, you'll also find a couple of decent tavernas and a pizzeria at the eastern or park end of Tsimiskí, plus various standard eateries, including a rash of fast-food outlets, around town.

Café and **bar** life mostly happens in the pedestrian zones flanking the rivulets, especially on Angelí Gátsou. Away from here, the municipal café-bar *Psilos Vrahos*, perched atop its namesake vantage point from where it commands fabulous views of the valley, is worth a visit for a beer or fruit juice. However, Édhessa's – and possibly the whole country's – most unusual entertainment venue is dramatically-sited *To Kanavouryio*, a recently converted hemp factory, complete with intact machinery, that doubles up as a café-bar-cum-restaurant and **live music** locale (jazz, rock and folk). Located at the foot of the cliffs, it can be reached by two giddying glass-lifts accessible from a platform near Áyios Vassílis chapel at the edge of the Varóssi district (signposted). Anyone whose nerves aren't up to it or who doesn't quite trust the engineering can get there the long way (3km), via a signposted road off the main route towards Pélla, down in the valley.

Lefkádhia and Náoussa

Thirty kilometres south of Édhessa on the road to Véria, **LEFKÁDHIA** has not been positively identified with any Macedonian city, but it is possible that it was Mieza, where Aristotle taught. The modern village lies just west of the main road, but for the ancient site you should turn off east at a sign reading "To the Macedonian Tombs". There are, in fact, four subterranean tombs in all – though only one has a guard, who keeps the keys to the other three.

The staffed one, the so-called **Great Tomb** or **Tomb of Judgement** (currently closed for restoration), east of the main road just past the train tracks, is the largest Macedonian temple-tomb yet discovered. Despite extensive cement protection, it has been badly damaged by creeping damp from the very high local water table; extensive consolidation work is currently underway, probably involving its complete dismantling and reconstruction. It dates from the third century BC, and was probably built for a general, who is depicted in one of the barely surviving frescoes, on the left, being led by Hermes in his role of conductor of souls. Other faded frescoes on the right represent the judges of Hades – hence the tomb's alias. A once-elaborate double-storeyed facade, half-Doric and half-Ionic, has almost completely crumbled away; on the entablature frieze you can barely make out a battle between Persians and Macedonians.

The **Anthimíon Tomb**, 150m further along the same country road, is more impressive, with its four Ionic facade columns, two marble interior sarcophagi with inscribed lids, and well-preserved frescoes. The tympanum bears portraits of a couple, presumably the tomb occupants, though the man's face has been rubbed out. Ornamental designs and three giant *akrokerámata* (cornice ornaments) complete the pediment decoration. Between the double set of portals, the ceiling frescoes are perhaps stylized representations of octopuses and other water creatures.

The other two local tombs are of essentially specialist interest. The one signposted "**Kinch's Macedonian Tomb**", after the Dane who discovered it, is on the east side of the main road, on the way back towards the village. The tomb of **Lyson-Kallikles** is signposted west of the main road, before the turning to the village, at the end of a one-kilometre dirt track through peach orchards; to visit, you have to lower yourself through a usually locked grating in the ceiling, the original entrance having been long since buried.

Four kilometres south of the tombs is a turning west, off the main road, to the small country town of **NÁOUSSA**. Although pleasant enough, Náoussa is less distinguished than the other escarpment towns of Édhessa and Véria. Its vintners, however, the **Boutari** company, produce some of Greece's best wines, and, along with Véria, the town is at the heart of the country's main peach-growing region – excuse enough for at least a stop in July. Besides wine and peaches, the town also turns out vast numbers of brightly-coloured acrylic blankets for the nation's hotels. It also hosts one of Macedonia's most elaborate pre-Lenten carnivals. In winter, it becomes a busy ski resort: nearby Mount Vérmion has two excellent **ski centres**.

Náoussa's main visitor attraction is the parkland of **Áyios Nikólaos**, 4km beyond town (itself 6km west of the main road), an oasis of giant plane trees nourished by the streams that bubble from the earth here. Most of the space is filled by a fun-fair and go-kart track. The riverbanks are additionally lined with several similarly priced tavernas featuring farm-raised trout (the *Nissaki* is the most pleasantly set). Just upstream, the *Hotel Vermion* (☎03320/29 311; ➍) is open year-round and has a decent restaurant.

South of the large belfried church, which you pass as you wind up from the main road, there's a small park strip, lined with the bulk of Náoussa's **restaurants** and bars; one of the town's most reputed eateries is taverna *Spíleo* at Spíleo 34. The only **accommodation** in town is the well-priced, en-suite *Hellas* at Megálou Alexándhrou 16 (☎03320/22 006; ➌). The **KTEL** is at the lower end of town, while the **train station** is a good 7km distant.

West from Édhessa: Nymféo, Flórina and the lakes

Visiting this northwestern nook of the region entails a complicated detour from the direct Édhessa–Kastoriá route and so is really best tackled only if you have your own transport. Its highlights are a set of lakes, especially the bird-rich **Préspa** pair, nestling in a strategic spot where Greece, Albania and FYROM meet; and a handsome mountain village, **Nymféo**. The area's main urban centre is **Flórina**, a rather charmless place, whose one attraction is its Archeological Museum.

Lake Vegorítidha

West of Édhessa lies **Lake Vegorítidha**, the first but not the most beautiful of a series of lakes that punctuates the landscape on the way to Kastoriá and beyond. The rail line between Édhessa and Flórina traces the lake's northwest shore: a fine journey which could be broken at the village of Árnissa. A scenic road skirts the northern side of the lake, passing through one or two picturesque villages and rocky sheep pasture, and offering panoramic glimpses of the lake; fairly frequent buses from Flórina to Áyios Athanássios ply this route.

Of the two lakeside settlements, **ÁRNISSA** has perhaps the better setting, opposite an islet and amidst apple orchards; for a swim, head for the water, then walk right for a quarter of an hour until you find a break in the shoreline reedbeds. The one-street village itself is a little drab, with no commendable accommodation, but it does come alive on Tuesdays when the weekly market attracts families from miles around, using their tractors as taxis.

To the north of the village rises **Mount Kaïmaktsalán**, scene of one of the bloodiest and most important battles of World War I, which raged intermittently from 1916 to 1918 until a Serbian–Greek force managed to break through the German–Bulgarian lines. The 2524-metre summit, marks the Greek–"Yugoslav" frontier, currently out of bounds, and bears a small memorial chapel to the fallen. The area has recently been developed as the **Vórras ski resort** (℡03810/82 169 or 20 300), one of the highest and best in northern Greece.

The more attractive of the lakeside villages architecturally is **ÁYIOS PANDELEÍMONAS**, with its red-roofed houses, crowned by a ruined windmill. It also has a small beach, though the waters are slightly algae-ridden. The lakeside *Epiheirisi* **restaurant** keeps watch over a basic, informal **campsite**, the village's only form of accommodation. Rail and road go on from here to the junction town of Amýndeo (no reputable accommodation, and a dire place to get stuck), from where paved roads lead north, west and south to Flórina (see overleaf), Kastoriá (see p.496) and Kozáni respectively. Some 2km west of Amýndeo, a short diversion to the right brings you to the smaller lake of **Petrón** and the hillside ruins of Hellenistic Petres on the west shore, excavated during the early 1990s and the subject of a moderately interesting display on the first floor of Flórina's Archeological Museum (see p.492).

Nymféo

Perched at 1300m on the eastern flank of Mount Vítsi, some 25km west of Amýndeo and 60km northeast of Kastoriá, lies the well-groomed mountain village of **NYMFÉO**, popular of late with prosperous young Greek professionals looking for "alternative" recreational activities in retreats far from the city. To get there take the poorly marked turn-off at the village of Aetós; you then climb up an incredibly steep side road with hairpin bends.

Facilities are priced accordingly, and the least expensive **accommodation** is also the least attractive: central *Xenonas Neveska* (℡03860/31 442; ❸). You might also find **rooms** at the *Ederne* which has self-catering facilities (℡03860/31 230 or 31 351; ❹) or at *La Galba* (℡03860/22 818 or 097/2210955; ❹), for a little more atmosphere. The professionally run **inn** at the entrance to the village, *Ta Linouria* (℡03860/31 030 or 0310/300 050, ℻03860/31 133; ❻), offers attractively decorated suites and is also a reliable source of decent, if pricey, **food**; otherwise try one of the cheaper tavernas in the village centre. If money is no object, consider a night at one of Greece's most exclusive hotels, *La Moará*

(☎0310/287 626, ⓕ287 401; closed July; ❻), a short way uphill and run by nationally renowned wine-makers, the Boutari family.

Flórina

Surrounded by steep hills carpeted with beech woods, **FLÓRINA** is the last Greek town before the FYROM border, 13km to the north. The frontier is open to road traffic, but at present there are no trains, just an infrequent service to Thessaloníki from the semi-derelict station. Though it has a lively market, Flórina is a rather charmless place, with ugly Communist-style concrete buildings. Its only attraction to speak of is the **Archeological Museum** (Tues–Fri 8.30am–3pm; €1.50), which is just up from the train station and houses among other things some fine icons rescued from the shores of the Préspa lakes (see below).

The local economy relies on agriculture, but has been hard hit by the various post-Yugoslavia crises, mainly because locals from over the border no longer come here to shop. This has not had a salutory effect on **hotel** prices, which remain exorbitant; you're better off staying in Édhessa, Kastoriá or by the lakes. If you do end up staying, you'll find the cheapest place to stay is the *Ellinis* at Pávlou Melá 31 (☎03850/22 671; ❹), beyond the museum.

Although it has numerous cafés, bars and fast-food places – mostly on Pávlou Melá – Flórina doesn't score highly on **restaurants**. The best, notwithstanding its location on the grim Soviet-style square beneath the KTEL, is the *Tò Koutouki*, open daily for lunch and dinner and serving decent barrelled wine with the usual array of dishes. Another option is *Iy Prespa* (closed Tues) on Tyrnóvou, a side street off Pávlou Melá, but its half-dozen indoor tables soon fill up.

There's no longer any direct bus to **Kastoriá**, and it's easy to see why, as there's little in between other than dense forest and a few crumbling villages, half-deserted since the civil war. There are, however, two daily buses (currently 6.45am & 5pm) to **Áyios Yermanós** in the **Préspa** basin, and if Kastoriá-bound you could conceivably take these to the Préspa turn-off and hitch the remaining 35km to Kastoriá, rather than going all the way around via ghastly Amýndeo.

The road out of Flórina snakes up the alpine-looking valley to the 1600-metre Pisodhéri saddle, site of one of the livelier villages en route and the **Vígla** ski lift. **PISODHÉRI** village offers the *Xenonas Modestios* (☎03850/45 928, ⓕ45 801; ❸), a restored traditional **inn** that's far better value than anything in Flórina; you can eat nearby at *Kyra Panayiota's* simple streamside **diner**. From here the road follows the headwaters of the Aliákmonas River, the longest and one of the most beautiful in Greece, most of the way to Kastoriá.

The Préspa lakes

Climbing west out of the Aliákmonas valley on the serpentine paved side road towards Préspa, you have little hint of what's ahead until suddenly you top a pass, and a shimmering expanse of water riven by islets and ridges appears. It is not, at first glance, postcard-pretty, but the basin has an eerie beauty and a back-of-beyond quality that grows on you with further acquaintance. It also has a turbulent recent history that belies its current role as one of the Balkans' most important wildlife sanctuaries.

During the Byzantine era, Préspa became a prominent place of exile for troublesome noblemen, so accounting for the surprising number of **ecclesiastical monuments** in this backwater. In the tenth century it briefly hosted the court of the Bulgarian Tsar Samuel before his defeat by Byzantine Emperor Basil II. Under the Ottomans the area again lapsed into obscurity, only to regain the dubious benefits of strategic importance in just about every European war of the last century, culminating in vicious local battles during the 1947–49 Greek civil war. In 1988, a forest fire on the eastern ridge treated observers to a dangerous fireworks display, as dozens of unexploded artillery shells were touched off by the heat. After World War II Préspa lay desolate and largely depopulated, as the locals fled abroad to either Eastern Europe or North America and Australia, depending on which side they fought on. Their emigration was partly in response to a punitive government policy of forced assimilation operating against Slavophones or Macedonian-speakers – as all the lake-dwellers are. It is only since the late 1970s that the villages, still comparatively primitive and neglected, have begun to refill during the summer, when beans and hay are grown as close to the two lakes as the national park authorities allow – ecologists, self-styled or bona fide, are not popular here, as farmers resent proposed restrictions on land use, pesticides and chemical fertilizers. A common sight everywhere are lake-reeds, cut and stacked for use as bean-poles.

Mikrí Préspa, the southerly lake, is mostly shallow (9m maximum depth) and reedy, with a narrow fjord curling west and just penetrating Albanian territory. The borders of Greece, Albania and FYROM meet in the middle of deeper **Megáli Préspa**, dividing its waters unequally, making the area doomed to play some role in whatever Balkan unrest may lie in the future. During the past few years a steady stream of Albanian refugees has used the basin as an exit corridor into Greece. Though they used to be routinely caught and returned to Albania by the army, their presence as illegal agricultural workers is now tolerated, as farms in the area are perennially short-handed. Considering that for years you needed an official permit to visit Préspa, and given the uncertain future, the Greek military presence is surprisingly unobtrusive and sovereignty lightly **exercised**. As indicated above, the border here is extremely porous – though freelance forays into Albania are emphatically not recommended – and a considerable amount of smuggling in duty-free goods goes on.

The core of the **national park**, established in 1971, barely encompasses Mikrí Préspa and its shores, but the peripheral zone extends well into the surrounding mountains, affording protection of sorts to a variety of land mammals. You'll almost certainly see foxes crossing the road, though the wolves and bears up on the ridges are considerably shyer. The lakes have a dozen resident fish species, including *tsiróni* – a sort of freshwater sardine – and *grivádhi*, a kind of carp. But it's **birdlife** for which the Préspa basin, particularly the smaller lake, is most famous. There are few birds of prey, but you should see a fair number of egrets, cormorants, crested grebes and pelicans, which nest in the spring, with the chicks out and about by summer. They feed partly on the large numbers of snakes, which include vipers, whip snakes and harmless water snakes which you may encounter while swimming. Observation towers are available at Vromolímni and near Áyios Ahíllios, but dawn spent anywhere at the edge of the reedbeds with a pair of binoculars will be immensely rewarding (though bear in mind that you are not allowed to boat or wade into the reeds). There are **park information centres** in the villages of Áyios Yermanós and Psarádhes (see below).

While you may arrive from Flórina by bus, you really can't hope to tour the area without some **means of transport** – either a mountain bike or a car. Similarly, in view of the area's past underdevelopment, don't expect much in the way of **facilities**: food is adequate and inexpensive, but exceedingly simple; the same might be said of local accommodation, though this has improved since the early 1990s. Indeed, Préspa is becoming increasingly popular, and you'd be wise to reserve the few accommodations listed during midsummer, especially at weekends.

The way in: Mikrolímni

MIKROLÍMNI, 5km up a side road off the main route into the valley, would be your first conceivable stop. The small shop and fish taverna owned by Yiorgos Hassou, on the shoreside square, has a few **rooms** to let (☎03850/61 221 or 45 931; ❶). In the evening, you can look towards sunsets over reedbeds and the snake-infested Vidhronísi (or Vitrinítsi) islet, though swimming isn't good here, or anywhere else on Mikrí Préspa for that matter. At the far end of the hamlet is a sporadically used biological observation station, literally the last house in Greece, and beyond that the lake narrows between sheer hillsides on its way to Albania. A prominent trail, much used by fleeing Albanians, leads there, paralleling the long inlet, but it would be unwise to walk its full length.

Regain the main road, which reaches a T-junction 16km from the main Flórina–Kastoriá highway, on the spit which separates the larger and smaller lakes. It's probable that at one time there was just one lake here, but now there's a four-metre elevation difference. Bearing right at the junction leads within 4km to Áyios Yermanós; the left option splits again at the west end of the spit, bearing south towards the islet of Áyios Ahillíos or northwest towards the hamlet of Psarádhes.

Áyios Yermanós

The district "capital", **ÁYIOS YERMANÓS** proves a surprisingly large village of tile-roofed houses, overlooking a patch of Megáli Préspa in the distance. It's worth making the trip up just to see two tiny late Byzantine churches, whose frescoes, dating from the time when the place belonged to the bishopric of Ohrid, display a marked Macedonian influence. The lower church, **Áyios Athanásios**, was renovated in 1995, but if it's open (a rare event) you can glimpse a dog-faced *St Christopher* among a line of saints opposite the door.

Far more impressive, however, is the tiny, eleventh-century parish church of **Áyios Yermanós** up on the square, hidden behind a new monster awkwardly tacked onto it in 1882. The Byzantine structure has its own entrance, and the frescoes, skilfully retouched in 1743, can be lit; the switch is hidden in the narthex. There are more hagiographies and martyrdoms than possible to list here, but there's a complete catalogue of them (in Greek and English) by the door. Among the best are the dome's *Pandokrátor*; a *Nativity* and *Baptism* right of the dome; a *Crucifixion* and *Resurrection* to the left; plus the saints *Peter and Paul, Kosmas and Damian, Tryphon and Pandelimon* by the door. Less conventional scenes include the *Entry into Jerusalem* and *Simon Helping Christ with the Cross*, opposite the door, and the *Apocalypse*, with the *Succouring of Mary the Beatified by Zosimas*, in the narthex. Mary was an Alexandrine courtesan who, repenting of her ways, retired to the desert for forty years. She was found, a withered crone on the point of death, by Zosimas, abbot of a desert monastery, and is traditionally shown being spoon-fed like an infant.

In the village is the excellent **Préspa information centre** (daily 9.30am–2.30pm), focusing on the wildlife of the national park; given sufficient warning, the centre can arrange guides for trips into the park. It also sells locally farmed organic products. The village has a **post office** – the only one in the Préspa basin – and just one place to **stay**: a set of pleasant, renovated old houses at the very top of the village, run by the local Women's Cooperative and heated by wood stoves in winter. Reservations (☎03850/51 320 or 51 355; ❷) are strongly advised, especially in August when a folk-dance seminar takes place in the village. These premises – plus a larger, centrally heated building at the bottom of the village – are open year-round. The best **taverna** is *Lefteris*, nearby.

Across the spit: Koúla beach and Psarádhes

At the far end of the wide causeway dividing the two lakes, 4km from the T-junction, is **Koúla beach**, and a cluster of what passes for tourist development hereabouts: a patch of reed-free sand from where you can swim in Megáli Préspa, a free but basic camping area, now bereft of its water tap, plus an army post. Tents are also pitched near the run-of-the-mill taverna *Plaz Prespon*; *Iy Koula*, up by the army post, is the only (not very good, and overpriced) alternative. Just below it, you can see where the waters of Mikrí Préspa trickle into Megáli Préspa.

If you don't intend to camp, it's best to bear right just above the army post, reaching after 6km of panoramic corniche the rickety village of **PSARÁDHES** (*Nivitsa* in Slav dialect), whose lanes make for a pleasant stroll. Unfortunately, the wonderful old houses lining them are increasingly derelict, with nothing being done either to preserve them, or check the spread of unsightly modern construction. There are some **rooms** for rent in the village such as the spartanly furnished ones above the *Taverna Syndrofia* (☎03850/ 46 107; ❶), a good spot to sample lake fish and the proprietor Lazaros Khristianopoulos' wine. You won't find the fish fried here anywhere else in Greece; similarly, the cows ambling through Psarádhes are a locally adapted dwarf variety. Of the other **tavernas**, *Paradhosi* seems the best of the bunch and the most reliably open. The village elders who used to gabble away in mixed Macedonian and Greek at the inland-platía kafenío have been turfed out and the place refurbished as a *baráki*, *Mythos*, which does creditable coffees; similarly, the waterfront has been paved and landscaped, with parking provided for tour coaches.

The only activity on offer in Psarádhes is a **boat excursion** to (and past) various medieval shrines and *askitíria* (hermitages) tucked into the shore leading around the promontory to Albania. The going rate per boat is €20, so you'll probably want to assemble a small party. The ride alone is well worth it, as cormorants, gulls and pelicans skim the limpid waters of Megáli Préspa, in which the mountains of Albania are reflected. Your guide will point out a fifteenth-century icon of the Virgin painted onto the rock opposite the village, and (on the far side of the peninsula) the thirteenth-century hermitage of Metamórfosis, whose icons have either been stolen or taken to the safety of the Flórina museum (see p.492). Usually, your only landfall is the spectacular fifteenth-century rock-church of **Panayía Eleoússas**, concealed at the top of a deep chasm some 500m before the frontier. From the top of the long stairway up, you've a fantastic framed view of the lake and the Albanian shore; the deceptively simple vaulted chapel contains a plethora of expressive, naive frescoes. They commemorate critical episodes from the life of Christ: to the right of the door, Mary Magdalene washes Christ's feet, with the *Transfiguration* just above, while opposite are a moving *Lamentation*, the two Marys at the sepulchre and an unusual *Resurrection* showing only Adam.

Áyios Ahíllios

If you keep straight at the end of the causeway, instead of turning right, the road soon brings you to a floating footbridge, 1500m in length, and recently constructed with EU funding, which leads across to the islet of **Áyios Ahíllios** and its impoverished hamlet. Five families totalling under thirty members still live on the islet, outnumbered by their cattle. A five-minute walk from the footbridge is the ruined Byzantine basilica of **Áyios Ahíllios**, while another ruin, a sixteenth-century monastery, Panayía Porfýras, lies at the southern end of the islet. For unrivalled views of Mikrí Préspa climb up to the summit of the islet's hill. Should you want to **stay** the night or get some refreshment, you'll find rooms, a café and decent **taverna** at *Xenónas* (☎03850/46 601, ℉46 931; ❸), outwardly rather unprepossessing, but pleasant inside.

Kastoriá and around

Set on a hilly, wooded peninsula extending deep into a slate-coloured lake, **KASTORIÁ** is one of the most interesting and attractive towns of mainland Greece. It's also wealthy by Greek standards and has been so for centuries as the centre of southeast Europe's fur trade; although the local beavers (*kastóri* in Greek) of the name had been trapped to extinction by the nineteenth century, Kastoriá still supports a considerable industry of furriers who make up coats, gloves and other items from fur scraps imported from Canada and Scandinavia and, increasingly, from the pelts of locally farmed beavers. Animal-rights activists will find the place heavy going as the industry is well-nigh ubiquitous: you'll see scraps drying on racks, and megastores line all the approach highways, pitched at Russian mafiosi buying mink coats for their womenfolk, to judge from the profuse Cyrillic signposting.

For most visitors, however, Kastoriá's main appeal lies in traces of its former prosperity: dozens of splendid *arhondiká* – **mansions** of the old fur families – dating from the seventeenth to nineteenth centuries, plus some fifty Byzantine and medieval **churches**, though only a handful is visitable and of compelling interest. About the only reminder of Muslim settlement is the minaretless Kursun Tzami marooned in a ridgetop car park; there's also a patch of an originally Byzantine-fortification wall down on the neck of the peninsula.

Kastoriá suffered heavy damage during both **World War II** and the **civil war** which followed it. Platía Van Fleet, by the lakeside at the neck of the promontory, commemorates the US general who supervised the Greek Nationalist Army's operations against the Communist Democratic Army in the final campaigns of 1948–49. The town was nearly captured by the Communists in 1948, and Mount Vítsi (2128m), the mountain dominating the northeastern shore of the lake, was, together with Mount Grámmos (2520m) to the west, the scene of their last stand in August 1949. However, most of the destruction of Kastoriá's architectural heritage is not due so much to 1940s munitions as to 1950s neglect, 1960s development and 1970s "renovation". It is miraculous that so many isolated specimens of Balkan vernacular and Neoclassical townhouses survive, mostly higher up on the peninsula where the steep grades have frustrated cement mixers.

The town has a strong tradition of **rowing**, and rowers can be seen out daily on the lake opposite Odhós Megálou Alexándhrou. Even the Oxford and Cambridge Blues have been known to practise their strokes here. The less energetic might prefer to take one of the regular **boat trips** on the lake during the spring and summer months; they leave from the jetty near the fish market on the northern side of town (☎04670/61 758 or 74 289; noon and 6pm; €3).

Town museums

For a sense of what Kastoriá must once have been during its heyday, head for the former lakeside quarter officially called **Karýdhis** but better known as **Dóltso** around and below recently renovated Platía Emmanouíl. On the platía itself, a Museum of Macedonian Struggle is being installed in a particularly fine mansion and is due to open in 2002. Nearby, at Kapetán Lázou 10, the splendidly opulent seventeenth-century Aïvazís family mansion has been turned into a **Folklore Museum** (daily 10am–noon & 3–6pm; €0.60). The house was inhabited until 1972 and its furnishings and most of its ceilings are in excellent repair, having miraculously survived German shelling; the Ottoman-style kiosk sports a set of stained-glass windows, three of them original, the others (blown out during bombardments) replaced by a local craftsman. Other features are an oriental fireplace in the master bedroom and the kitchen with all the original pots and pans.

▲ Flórina 70km

KASTORIÁ

Byzantine Wall

Tourist Boats

★ KTEL

Olympic Airways

Mosque Kursun Tzámi

Byzantine Museum

Áyii Anáryiri

Panayía Koumbelídhiki

Áyios Nikólaos Kasnítsi

Áyios Stéfanos

Taxiárhes tis Mitropóleos

Áyios Athanássios

Cathedral

Museum of Macedonian Struggle

KARYDHIS (DOLTSO)

Traditional Costume Musuem

Arhondikó Bassáras

Arhondikó Natzís

Folklore Museum

Lake Orestiádha

Lake Orestiádha

Lake Orestiádha

0   200 m

ACCOMMODATION

Anessis	1
Arhondiko tis Venetoulas	12
Arhondiko tou Vergoula	11
Castor Palace	4
Eolis	6
Evropa	5
Filoxenia	10
Idhiston	9
Kastoria	7
Keletron	2
Orestion	3
Xenia	8

RESTAURANTS

Arhondariki	F
Katergo	A
Krasostamo	D
Krondiri	E
Mantziaris	C
Omonoia	B

◄ Airport 10km & Kozáni 90km

◄ 700m

► 100m & Mavriótissa monastery 3km

► 400m

Mavriótissa monastery 1300m ▼

The caretaker, on request, will show you some of the other nearby *arhondiká*. The most notable are **Bassáras** and **Natzís**, close together on Vyzandíon; the latter was admirably restored in the 1990s. A third, also close by, on Platía Dóltso, now houses the **Traditional Costume Museum** (☎04670/22 697; open by appointment; free), a magical display of traditional clothing from western Macedonia and a chance to see another magnificent interior.

The **Byzantine museum** (Tues–Sun 8.30am–3pm; free) up on Platía Dhexamenís, opposite the *Xenia Limnis* hotel, is rather more rewarding than Ioánnina's (see p.397), wisely going for quality over quantity in this well-lit collection spanning the twelfth to the sixteenth centuries. Highlights include an unusually expressive thirteenth-century icon of Áyios Nikólaos and a fourteenth-century *Ayii Anaryiri*, plus a later one depicting the life of St George. There are also a few double-sided icons, including a rare *Deposition*, intended for use in religious processions.

Byzantine churches

Note that Kastoriá's noteworthy Byzantine **churches** can only be visited by application to the curator of the Byzantine museum (see above), or her friendly and knowledgeable assistant, the key-keeper, who alas speaks only Greek. The churches are small structures which almost certainly began life as private chapels founded by wealthy donors from amongst the mansion owners. **Áyii Anáryiri** dates from the eleventh century, with three layers of frescoes spanning the following two hundred years. Some of the frescoes, especially the soldier-saints, have been cleared of all the grime. Nearby **Áyios Stéfanos** dates from the tenth century and has been little changed over the years. Its frescoes are insignificant but it does have an unusual women's gallery or *yinaikonítis*.

The excellent frescoes of twelfth-century **Áyios Nikólaos Kasnítsi** were returned to their former glory during the late 1980s. The unusual epithet stems from the donor, who is shown with his wife on the narthex wall presenting a model of the church to Christ. Lower down are ranks of exclusively female saints, to console the women congregated in the narthex which long served as a women's gallery. High up on the west wall of the nave, the *Dormition* and the *Transfiguration* are in good condition, the former inexplicably backwards (the Virgin's head is usually to the left). **Taxiárhes tis Mitropóleos**, the oldest (ninth-century) church, was built on the foundations of an earlier pagan temple, of which recycled columns and capitals are visible. Its more prominent frescoes, such as that of the *Virgin Platytera and Adoring Archangels* in the conch of the apse, and a conventional *Dormition* on the west wall, are fourteenth century. In the north aisle is the tomb of Greek nationalist Pavlos Melas, assassinated by Bulgarians at a nearby village in 1906, and commemorated by streetnames across northern Greece; his widow, who survived to the age of 101 (she died in 1974), is interred with him. Lastly, the **Panayía Koumbelidhikí**, so named because of its unusual dome (*kübe* in Turkish), is undergoing much-needed repairs, but it still retains one startling and well-illuminated fresco: a portrayal – almost unique in Greece – of God the Father in a ceiling mural of the *Holy Trinity*. The building was constructed in stages, with the apse completed in the tenth century and the narthex in the fifteenth. The dome was meticulously restored after being destroyed by Italian bombing in 1940.

If tracking down churches seems too much like hard work, one of the most pleasant things to do in Kastoriá is to follow the narrow road along the tree-lined water's edge all around the **peninsula** to the east of town; at the tip vehicles must circulate anticlockwise, but the route is mainly used by joggers and the odd walker. Although the lake itself is visibly polluted, wildlife still abounds – frogs, tortoises and water snakes especially, and on a spring day numerous fish break water. Near the southeastern tip of the peninsula, some 3km along from the *Hotel Kastoria*, stands the **Mavriótissa monastery**, flanked by peacocks and a fair-value restaurant. Two much-restored churches are all that remains of the monastery: a smaller fourteenth-century chapel, with fine frescoes of scenes from Christ's life, abutting the larger, wood-roofed eleventh-century *katholikón* on whose outer wall looms a well-preserved *Tree of Jesse*, showing the genealogy of the Saviour. The warden-priest runs a very basic **campsite** a few paces away, if none of the town hotels (see below) is for you.

Practicalities

The **airport** is 10km south of town and Olympic Airways' in-town air terminal is at Megálou Alexándhrou 15. Arriving at the **bus station**, you'll find yourself at the western edge of the peninsula. Coming by **car**, beware of the fee-parking scheme in effect across much of the city centre, operated by ticket-machines; only a couple of central hotels have free or off-street parking, and they are the more expensive ones. Kastoriá has a locally-based **car-rental** outfit, Tomazo at Gramou 147 (☎04670/84 000).

The **tourist office** (Mon–Fri 8am–2.30pm & 3–7pm, Sat, Sun & hols 8am–1.30pm; ☎04670/26 777), for what it is worth, dispenses leaflets, brochures and limited information from a room in the town hall on Platía Van Fleet.

For lower-priced, traditional **restaurants** head for Platía Omonías, where the *Omonoia*, on the square proper, and the *Mantziaris*, opposite at Valallá 8, are both excellent for *mayireftá*, with outdoor tables in good weather. Lakeside dining has taken off in recent years: *Katergo* at Orestíon 19 is a trendy ouzerí featuring specialities such as aubergines stuffed with bacon and cheese. A couple of stylish tavernas are located on Orestiádhos: the *Krondiri* at no. 13, which some say serves the town's best food, specializes in fancy *mezédhes*, gratins and "soufflés" in attractive clay pots, and has tables on the lake bank. Further along at no. 87, *Arhondariki* is somewhat less sophisticated, but the barrelled wine accompanying fish and other delicacies is very good indeed. Round the bend at Megálou Aléxandhrou 45 is another reliable taverna, *Krasostamo*, where you can feast on particularly flavoursome *mayireftá*. **Cafés, bars and nightlife** are mostly to be found at the water's edge: there are some near the fish market and more stylish ones on the western side of the promontory.

Accommodation

Many of Kastoriá's **hotels**, especially those within easy walking distance of the bus station, are rather noisy with prices above average; moreover, despite this, they tend to be full pretty much year-round with people on fur-buying sprees, so it's worth phoning ahead to book. All addresses given below are en suite, unless specified, and fairly central; along the lakeside road towards the airport and Kozáni you'll find more, mostly sizeable establishments, which could be useful overflows if no central accommodation is going; these all lie on the bus route.

Anessis, Grámou 10 ☎04670/83 908 or 83 909, 🖷83 768. After sorely needed renovation, this hotel is now modern, clean and eminently appealing, with charmingly decorated rooms and all mod cons, spoiled only by a noisy location. ④
Arhondiko tis Venetoulas, Ayíon Theológon 6 ☎ & 🖷 04670/22 446. A mansion conversion oozing charm. Great location and friendly, attentive serv-

ice; breakfast included in the price. ⑤
Arhondiko tou Vergoula, Aïdhítras 14 ☎04670/23 415 or 23 416, 🖷23 676, 📧sfinas@otenet.gr. Kastoriá's leading boutique hotel, housed in a handsome mid-nineteenth-century mansion, is in a particularly quiet part of the Dóltso. Rooms with a view are heftily surcharged, but all are faultlessly done out in traditional yet

comfortable style. The ground-floor wine bar, serving Greek vintages, is open for patrons and outsiders every Friday and Saturday evening. ❺

Castor Palace, Grámou 237 ☎04670/82 160, ℱ82 161. The nearest palace hotel to the town centre, bizarrely located near the lakefront overlooking a military camp. Impeccable rooms and extremely comfortable throughout; good breakfast included. ❺

Eolis, Ayíou Athanassíou 30 ☎04670/21 070 or 21 080, ℱ21 086, ⓦwww.topnet.com.gr/greekhotels/hotels/aiolis.htm. Designer-magazine interiors, tip-top service and every comfort – minibar, hairdryer, hydro-massage – make this 1930s villa one of the town's leading hotels. A full breakfast served in your room or the smart dining-room included. ❻

Evropa, Ayíou Athanassíou 12 ☎04670/23 826, ℱ25 154. With the town's fur-inflated hotel rates, this is the least expensive hotel that can be unreservedly recommended. Clean, decent rooms and relatively quiet location. ❸

Filoxenia, no address, nr Profítis Elías church ☎04670/22 162. Kastoriá's nearest thing to budget accommodation, this hostel is well located. Some of its modest rooms enjoy lake views and cost more accordingly. Clean but simple. ❷–❸

Idhiston, Megálou Aléxandhrou 75 ☎04670/22 250. Self-catering apartments in a prime location over one of the town's trendy bars, with lake views. Run by a returnee from Canada whose passion for his native town is contagious. Book well ahead. ❺

Kastoria, Leofóros Níkis 122 ☎04670/29 453, ℱ29 608. At the far end of the northern waterfront, this smart, traditional establishment, renovated and upgraded in 1998, offers lake views from its balconied, air-conditioned front rooms, plus free parking. ❻

Keletron, 11-Noemvríou 52 ☎04670/22 676. Rather shabby but passable hotel with entrance on a side street and some rooms overlooking leafy Platía Van Fleet. ❸

Orestion, Platía Dhaváki 1 ☎04670/22 257 or 22 258. Clean, well-run, modern hotel with small but decent rooms, all en suite. Helpful reception but fairly noisy location. Breakfast included. ❹

Xenia, Platía Dhexamenís ☎04670/22 565, ℱ26 391. Peacefully set near the top of town, it has private parking, and its wood-floored rooms are comfortable enough, if 1970s vintage. Breakfast extra. ❹

Around Kastoriá

If you have your own transport, you might make a trip 14km southwest to **OMORFOKLISSIÁ**, an eerie village of mudbrick houses inherited post-1923 from Muslim peasants. It has a fourteenth-century Byzantine church with a lofty cupola, belfry and, inside, a huge, primitive carved-relief wooden **icon of St George** thought to date from the eleventh century.

SIÁTISTA, draped along a single ridge in a forbiddingly bare landscape 70km south of Kastoriá, is also a worthy destination and possible stopover. Located just above the point where the road splits for Kozáni or Grevená (and the Metéora beyond), it too was an important fur centre, and also boasts a handful of eighteenth-century mansions or *arhondiká*, which you can visit. The eighteenth-century house of **Hatzimihaïl Kanatsoúli** at Mitropóleos 1, near the police station, is still lived in but you can ring to be shown around. The first two floors are occupied; upstairs, a corner room has naive murals of mythological scenes (including Kronos's castration of Ouranos). The warden of the dilapidated **Nerantzópoulos mansion** (Mon–Sat 8.30am–3pm, Sun 9.30am–2.30pm), on the upper square, has the keys for several other houses, of which the largest and most elaborate is the **Manoússi mansion**, dating from 1763, in a vale below the Kanatsoúli, along with various other surviving *arhondiká*. The church of **Áyia Paraskeví**, on the lowest platía, behind a tall belfry, has soot-blackened seventeenth-century frescoes inside. You can view them by calling the warden on ☎04650/21 359 or 097/4816566, but until the scheduled cleaning takes place you're probably better off just looking at the exterior frescoes.

Most of what you'll need in Siátista – **banks** with cash dispensers and the **post office** – can be found on the single, long main street, Meghálou Aléxandhrou. This is also the location of the large and comfortable *Archontikon*

hotel (☎04650/21 298, ℱ22 835; ❹), which has a reasonable restaurant and café on the ground floor, despite the TV; rooms often fill with tours, so check for space in advance. Other options for **eating** out tend to have rather boozy male-dominated environments, such as the *Psistaria Ouzeri O Platanos*, just below Áyia Paraskeví or the slightly more appealing *To Xani*, nearby. The most frequent **bus** connections are with Kozáni, 28km to the southeast, which has good onward connections to Thessaloníki.

Halkidhikí and eastern Macedonia

Halkidhikí, easily reached by bus from Thessaloníki, is the clear highlight of Macedonia's eastern half. Its first two peninsulas, Kassándhra and Sithonía, shelter the north's main concentration of beaches; the third, **Athos**, the country's finest, though most secretive, monasteries.

Further east, there are a few more good beaches en route to **Kavála**, but little of interest inland, with a scattering of small market towns serving a population that – as in neighbouring Thrace – produces the main Greek tobacco crop.

Kassándhra, Sithonía and secular Athos

The squid-shaped peninsula of **Halkidhikí** begins at a perforated edge of shallow lakes east of Thessaloníki, then extends into three prongs of land – Kassándhra, Sithonía and Athos – trailing like tentacles into the Aegean Sea. **Mount Athos**, the easternmost peninsula, is in all ways separate, a "Holy Mountain", whose monastic population, semi-autonomous within the Greek state, excludes all women – even as visitors. For men who wish to experience Athonite life, a visit involves recently simplified procedures which are detailed, with the monastic sights, in the section beginning on p.512. The most that women can do is to glimpse the buildings from offshore cruise kaïkia sailing from the two small resorts on the periphery of the peninsula – Ierissós and Ouranoúpoli – on the "secular" part of the Athos peninsula.

Kassándhra and **Sithonía**, by contrast, host some of the most overblown holiday resorts in Greece. Up until the late 1980s these were popular mainly with Greeks, but they've since been fairly comprehensively developed, with most European package-tour companies maintaining a presence at often monstrously huge complexes. On Kassándhra especially, almost any reasonable beach is accompanied by a crop of villas or several hotel developments, while huge billboards advertise campsite complexes miles in advance. Still larger signs at the entrance to each peninsula of Halkidhikí remind you that camping outside authorized sites is strictly prohibited, although in theory it's possible, as

HALKIDHIKÍ: KASSANDHRA, SITHONIA AND SECULAR ATHOS

Alistráti

1103m

Thessaloníki

Mt Kerdhýlio
1092m

Amphipolis

Kaválla

Kaválla

Mt Vólvis
659m

Lake
Korónia

Lake Vólvi

Asproválta

Orfanós Gulf

Stavrós

Olymbiádha   Stageira

N

Stáyira

Cape
Eléfthera

Paleohóra   Arnéa

Stratóni

Áyios Pródhromos

Paleohóri

Ierissós Gulf

Gomáti   Ierissós

Petrálona

Políyiros

Néa Ródha

Trypití

Metangítsi   Pyrgadhíkia

Amouliani   Ouranoúpoli

Néa Tríglia

Paralía Salonikioú

Ólynthos

Metamórfosi   Áyios Nikólaos

Mt Athos

Yerakiní

Órmos Panayiás

Sigitikos Gulf
(Áyion Óros Gulf)

Néa
Moudhaniá

Nikíti   Sithínia

Néa Potídhea   Potidaia

Vourvouroú

Kassándhra Gulf

Parthenónas   Mt Sithonía
817m

Néa Fókea

Áfytos (Áthytos)

Néos Marmarás

Sárti

Sáni   Kallithéa

Ljkithos

Sykiá

Kassándhria   Kryopiyí

Paralía Sykiás

Síviri   Polýkhrono

Cape Papadhiá

Haniótis   Pefkohóri

Tristiníka

Possídhi   Mála   Mt Kassándhra
307m

Ayía Paraskeví

Toróni   Kalamítsi

Cape Kassándhras

Kalándra

Pórto Koufó

Néa Skióni   Palioúri   Kánistro

Cape
Lemós

Loutrá   Cape Ayíou
Nikoláou

0   10km

Sporádhes

most beaches here are equipped with free freshwater showers. You should have no trouble getting accommodation outside the busy midsummer period (mid-July to mid-August). The beaches themselves consist of white sand, ranging in consistency from powder to coarse-grained; less appealing are the fortunately stingless jellyfish which drift about nearly everywhere.

Both Kassándhra and Sithonía are connected to Thessaloníki by a four-lane expressway which ends at Néa Moudhaniá, from where a network of fast two-lane roads extend around their coastlines. Buses run frequently to all the larger resorts. In spite of this, neither peninsula is that easy to travel around if you are dependent on **public transport**. You really have to pick a place and stay there, perhaps **renting a motorbike** or **car** for excursions.

Kassándhra

Vaguely boot-shaped **Kassándhra**, the nearest of Halkidhikí's three peninsulas to Thessaloníki, is also by far the most developed, though beyond the grain fields around Kallithéa, extensive forest survives unscathed along the hilly spine of the peninsula. Its population took part in the independence uprising of 1821, but was defeated and massacred; the handful of attractive villages, mostly inland and lower down, essentially date from just after, though often built atop ancient or medieval foundations. On the coast, there were only a few small fishing hamlets here until after 1923, when the peninsula was resettled by refugees from around the Sea of Marmara – these have since burgeoned into holiday venues. Unless very pushed for time, most travellers choose to keep going to Sithonía or the top end of Athos.

Néa Moudhaniá

The first resort you come to, **NÉA MOUDHANIÁ**, is not on the peninsula proper but lies on the coast, just to the north. A sizeable town, complete with several **banks** (with cash dispensers) and a **post office**, it's also a minor passenger port. Catamarans sail from here to Skiáthos, Skópelos, Alónissos and beyond, at least twice a week from June to mid-September only: check and book with Moudania Tours at Platía Omónia 7 (☎03730/22 888 or 21 450, ⓔmoutours@otenet.gr). The best of an unattractive half-dozen **hotels** are the *Filippos* (☎03730/21 461, ⓔhotel-sokrates@hol.gr; ❹), located inland opposite the school, and the soulless *Thalia* (☎03730/23 106; ❹). There are also plenty of **rooms** for rent and a campsite on a sandy beach 3km southeast – the *Ouzouni Beach* (☎03730/42 100; May–Sept). Waterfront **eating** is on offer at a number of decent fish tavernas, but far and away the best food is served at the charmingly decorated *Kapilio*, set one street back from the harbour, and where a range of dishes is accompanied by golden wine from the barrel.

Néa Potídhea and Néa Fókea

NÉA POTÍDHEA, some 6km beyond Néa Moudhaniá and across the ancient canal which severs the narrow neck of Kassándhra, is a bit of an eyesore like all of the coastal refugee settlements. The seafront promenade resembles a mini-Coney Island/Blackpool with its mechanical animals, and fast-food joints alternating with bars. This accepted, the front is in fact pedestrianized and well landscaped, and the beach itself broad, sandy and reef-free. Greek families rent summer apartments here long-term, making it a poor bet for a quick overnight, while an otherwise fairly young crowd lends a laid-back feel. The way to the fishing port at the west end of the canal is flanked by the ruined fortifications of ancient Potidaia; at the end you'll find two worthy **fish tavernas**, *Kastro* (perched amidst bits of wall) and *Marina*, overlooking the sea and another, half-submerged, bit of antiquity.

The next resort, **NÉA FÓKEA**, is by comparison a modest place rendered picturesque by a Byzantine watchtower on a grassy headland. There are several fish **tavernas** in the delightful little harbour, right by the main road, from where a long beach heads north under cliffs, improving as you distance yourself from the tower. As at Néa Potídhea, apartments predominate.

Áfytos

Some 5km south of Néa Fókea, you reach the turning east for **ÁFYTOS** (or Áthytos), by far the most attractive spot on Kassándhra, if a bit self-consciously so. This large village of tiled-roofed, traditional houses spreads over a series of ravines furrowing the bluff here, which ends in a sharp drop to the sea. Near the cliff bottom a series of springs oozes from a rock overhang, nurturing a little oasis – and doubtless a spur in the founding of Aphytis, the village's ancient predecessor. Be warned that the beach here is poor by Halkidhikí standards, marred by rock sills with lots of sea urchins, a fact which (along with a local preservation order) has probably kept Áfytos from going the sorry way of most coastal resorts here. On the square, focus of a mesh of slightly twee cobbled lanes closed to traffic for the nightly *vólta* (promenade), stands a handsome church in post-Byzantine style, dating only from 1850 but seeming much older.

There is inevitably a strong package presence, but independent travellers have a choice of **rooms**, best sited for sea views at the cliff-edge (though you'll get mosquitos from the oasis) and priced at ❸–❹, often with some sort of self-catering facility. For a bona-fide **hotel**, try the charming *Stamos* (☎03740/91 520, ℉91 234;❺) on the minor road leading to the cliff-edge; it has a flowery courtyard and pool, and its studios for three or four make it good for families. Down on the shore, the medium-sized *Blue Bay* (☎03740/91 644, ℉91 646; ❻) dominates one of the most usable patches of beach, but tends to fill in peak season with tour groups.

Eating out is best at no-nonsense *To Perasma*, with reliable *tis óras* fare and excellent wines or, in season, the upmarket *Soussouradha*, next to the bakery. By the church is the anonymous ouzerí, the old boys' hangout, serving copious drink, salads and one dish of the day only. For full **buffet breakfast** at a fair price, look no further than *Gastronomia*, near the *Stamos* (no relation to the namesake in the centre) – it's worth trying their Italian fare by night as well. **Nightlife** is fairly lively and not entirely tourist-pitched, with Greek musicians often playing the bars at summer weekends, sometimes under the aegis of the **Kassándhra Festival** which Áfytos shares with Síviri (see opposite): performances include Shakespearean and ancient Greek plays, blues, soul, classical and Greek music.

From Kallithéa to Palioúri

Another 4km to the south, you reach the horrible roadside strip-development of **KALLITHÉA**, a complete contrast to Áfytos and with only **banks** (cash dispensers) and **car/motorbike/windsurfer rental** to its credit. There are half-a-dozen mammoth hotels (❻ plus) on the beach, plus a like number of apartments in the ❹ category that may have vacancies on spec.

More of the same is to be found at **KRYOPIYÍ**, just under 6km further; most of the development is concentrated along the steep roads that cascade down to the water, where there's a steeply shelving beach, but Kryopiyí has preserved its old village core up the hill, on the land side of the main road. By the somewhat gentrified "platía" is a couple of **tavernas**: the *Platia* has a slight edge over the *Anoyi*. A regular **shuttle bus** from the beach area stops by the church in the summer.

Beyond Kryopiyí, you head towards the "toe" of the Kassandhrian boot via three consecutive coastal resorts – Polýkhrono, Haniótis and Pefkohóri. Each vies to exceed its neighbour in tackiness and excess capacity (signs with offers of vacant rooms abound); at **HANIÓTIS** in particular, you have to wend your way through some fairly downmarket if low-rise development – three dozen hotels and apartment units of it – to reach the long but narrow beach (standing room only from the day school breaks up). Just southeast of

PEFKOHÓRI, which has an official **campsite**, a lagoon enclosed by a pine-tufted spit is just about the only spot on the peninsula where rough camping seems to be winked at. At the bay of **Khroussoú**, there are two more recognized **campsites** and rather more low-key development than at the preceding. From here, rather than continuing to the disappointing "toe"-cape, you're better off heading west and inland along the main road to the rambling ridge-top village of **PALIOÚRI**, also full of lodging.

The southern shore

The southern shore of Kassándhra is in general developed more for Greek weekenders rather than foreigners, with plenty of *ikismí* (garden-villa or apartment clusters) pitched at Thessalonians. Some 6km beyond hilltop Palioúri you emerge at **AYÍA PARASKEVÍ**, a delightful village with sea views, mostly untouched save for a pair of simple **tavernas** and a fancy-paved central roundabout. However, a 1998 fire did for most of the pine forest from here down to **LOUTRÁ** on the coast – an altogether missable place with its outdated thermal spa and handful of hotels. **NÉA SKIÓNI**, 6km northwest, makes a far better conventional base, with its unburnt backdrop, good clean beach and appealing seafront. Here a string of tavernas is supplied by a tiny fleet in the fishing port, and the best, open for lunch and all year, is *Yiorgos*, opposite the jetty entrance. Amongst the apartments are some **rooms** (❸–❹). **Mala**, nominally 8km northwest, is not really a village but a string of weekend real estate which blocks access to most of the coast from just outside Néa Skióni. Hidden away up on the cape is the picturesque village of **KALÁNDHRA**, just off the route to **Posídhi beach**, which itself isn't wonderful, though beyond the lively beach bar, at the lighthouse cape, the rock reef abates and you can skinny-dip. The campsite in the nearby pine grove is for University of Thessaloníki students only, and the access road dead-ends rather than continuing along the coast.

The west coast

Some 9km north of Kálandra, **SÍVIRI** is a larger, busier version of Néa Skióni. It has a lovely **beach**, good **tavernas** (*Dhiamandis* has the prime position) and lively summer nightlife. It's also one of the best spots on the peninsula for sunset views across the gulf to Mount Olympus. There's just the one **hotel**, the 1999-vintage *Samel* (☎03740/23 400, ✉samel@otenet.gr; late April to Sept; ❸), with very smart rooms, a pool and a stylish bar.

From Síviri there's no direct coastal access to **SÁNI**; you'll need to take the trans-peninsular road to Kallithéa. Just north of Néa Fókea, an eight-kilometre paved side road takes you westwards through bucolic countryside to the municipally-run *Blue Dream* **campsite** (☎03740/31 435; May–Sept). Otherwise there are only several luxury megacomplexes. The town is noted for its summer **festival**, with a cosmopolitan billing of world music, salsa, jazz and cutting-edge Greek stars.

Sithonía

As you move east across Halkidhikí and away from the frontline of tourism, the landscape becomes increasingly green and hilly, culminating in the isolated and spectacular scenery of the Holy Mountain, looming across the gulf lapping Sithonía's east coast. The **Sithonía** peninsula is more rugged but better cultivated than Kassándhra, though here there are even fewer true villages, and those that do exist mostly date from the 1920s resettlement era. Pine forests cover many of the slopes, particularly in the south, giving way to olive groves on the coast. Small sandy inlets with relatively discreet pockets of campsites and tavernas make a welcome change from sprawling megaresorts.

If you're travelling under your own steam, some 6km past the last motorway exit at Néa Moudhaniá en route to Sithonía it's worth making the slight detour to splendidly located **ancient Olynthos** (Tues–Sun 8am–2.30pm; €1.50), atop a hill offering mountain and sea views. This is a rare example of an unmodified Classical town laid out to the grid plan of Hippodamus. There's an initially off-putting walk of 700m, partly up a slope, from the ticket booth, but well-excavated streets, houses and even some mosaics to see once you arrive. Like the new, informative museum near the entrance, it is clearly labelled in Greek and English. The modern village of **ÓLYNTHOS**, 1km west across the riverbed here, has **food** and a **hotel**, the central *Olynthos* (☎03790/91 666; ❸).

Metamórfosi

Suitably enough, **METAMÓRFOSI** ("Transfiguration"), at the western base of Sithonía, signals the transformation. Its beach is only adequate, but there's good swimming, and the village, while relentlessly modern, has an easy-going air. In addition to the friendly *Hotel Golden Beach* (☎03750/22 063; ❻; May–Sept), with its cool courtyard and café backing onto the village square, there are two **campsites**: *Sithon*, 5km west (☎03750/22 414; May–Sept), and the preferable *Mylos*, 3km east, on the beach side of the road. In high season, both campsites and village can be a little crowded, but there's a fair number of **tavernas** clustered in and around the village square which seem to soak up business.

Moving on to Sithonía proper, it's best to follow the loop road clockwise around the east coast, so that the peak of Athos is always before you. **Bus services** are sparse, however: there are up to five buses daily around the west coast to Sárti, and up to three a day direct to Vourvouroú, but there's no KTEL connection between these two endpoints. A complete circuit is only really possible with your own transport.

Órmos Panayiás and Vourvouroú

ÓRMOS PANAYIÁS, first of the east-coast resorts, is nowadays well developed; ranks of villas dwarf the picturesque hamlet and tiny harbour, and the nearest decent beaches lie 4km north en route to Pyrgadhíkia, below the inland village of Áyios Nikólaos. The only conceivable reason to stop at Órmos would be to catch the excursion boats that sail around Athos from here, but these are expensive and often prereserved for tourists bused in from the big Halkidhikí resorts (for better alternatives see Ouranoúpoli, p.511).

VOURVOUROÚ, 8km down the coast from Órmos, is not a typical resort, since it's essentially a vacation-villa project for Thessaloníki professors, established in the late 1950s on land expropriated from Vatopedhíou monastery on Athos. There is a fair amount of short-term **accommodation**: as well as numbers of **rooms**, there's the seafront **hotel** *Dhiaporos* (☎03750/91 313; ❹; half-board may be obligatory), with its cool rooftop restaurant, and the plain but en-suite *Vourvourou* (☎03750/91 261; ❸; June–Sept), plus the rather sterile *Rema* just inland (☎03750/91 071 or 91 142, ☏91 198; ❺; half-board sometimes obligatory), which often has low-season specials. The strange feel of the place is accentuated by those plot owners who haven't bothered to build villas (so far very scattered) and merely tent down, making it hard to tell which are the real campsites. Islets astride the mouth of the bay make for a fine setting, but the beach, while sandy, is extremely narrow, and Vourvouroú is really more of a yachters' haven. **Tavernas** are relatively inexpensive because they're banking on a return clientele; the *Itamos*, inland from the road, is the best; the *Gorgona/Pullman*, while the nicest positioned – on the waterfront – gets coach tours as the alias implies. There are two **campsites**: *Dionysos* (☎03750/91 214; April–Oct), simple but adequate, part of which faces the beach, and *Glaros* (no phone; mostly caravans), facing Karýdhi beach at the eastern end of things.

Some of Sithonía's best **beaches** lie off the thirty kilometres of corniche road between Vourvouroú and Sárti: five signposted sandy coves, each with a **campsite** and little else. The names of the bays, such as Koutloumousíou or Zográfou, reflect the fact that most of the land here belonged to various Athonite monasteries until confiscated by the Greek government to resettle Anatolian refugees.

Sárti

Concrete-grid **SÁRTI**, rising to a ridge on the north, is set slightly back from its broad, two-kilometre-long beach, with only the scale of the bay protecting it from being utterly overrun in summer by tourists. There are hundreds of **rooms** (though often not enough to go around), the choicest being in the southerly part of town, and not all of these block-booked by foreign companies. At the far south end of the beach is another cluster of development, including some **hotels**, among them the *Sarti Beach* (☎03750/94 250; ❹), and the shady *Camping Sarti Beach* (☎03750/94 629; May–Sept), the campsite laid out between the road and the hotel grounds. *Iy Neraïda* and *O Stavros* are two of the less expensive **tavernas** lining the landscaped shore esplanade, but the perennial (if pricey) favourite amongst Greeks, *Ta Vrahakia*, stands at the far north end of the beach, overlooking the "little rocks" of the name, and dishing up rich *mayireftá*. Inland you'll find a short-hours **bank** and a rather tattily commercialized square ringed by forgettable fast-food joints – plus the big local travel agency, Sithon Travel (☎03750/94 066, ✉sithon@otenet.gr), which does **car rental**.

Paralía Sykiás and Kalamítsi

PARALÍA SYKIÁS, 8km further along, has a beach somewhat inferior to Sárti's and thus less developed so far. What there is, however, seems not very user-friendly despite a fine setting: just a few tavernas well back from the sea along 2km of coastal highway, with much of the intervening space fenced off for some unaesthetic incipient development. At the north end of the beach a **campsite**, *Melissi* (☎03750/41 631), shelters in some trees. The best strategy here is to follow the side road at the south end of the beach towards the more scenic coves at **Linaráki**, where *Pende Vimata stin Ammo* is the most noteworthy of several **tavernas** along here, or beyond to Pigadháki. For a **post office** and shops head for **SYKIÁ**, 2km inland, hemmed in by a bowl of rocky hills.

KALAMÍTSI, another 8km south of Paralía Sykiás, consists of a beautiful double bay, with relatively little commercialization to date. At the sheltered north bay of Pórto, there's a basic **campsite** (☎03750/41 346). There's a **taverna**, *O Yiorgakis*, next door, with varied, reasonably priced food, and good **rooms** behind (☎03750/41 338; ❸). The small beach just out front can get cramped in summer, at which time you can easily swim out to the main islet for less company. The equally sandy south bay is rather monopolized by the fancier *Camping Kalamitsi* (☎03750/41 411; May–Sept).

Pórto Koufó, Toróni and Tristiníka

The forest cover gets progressively thinner the further south you go from Sárti, and as you round the tip of the peninsula it vanishes completely, with bare hills spilling into the sea to create a handful of deep bays. **PÓRTO KOUFÓ**, just northwest of the cape, is the most dramatic of these, almost completely cut off from the open sea by high cliffs. The name Koufó ("deaf" in Greek) is said to come from one's inability to hear the sea within the confines of this inlet, which served as an Axis submarine shelter during World War II. There's a decent beach near where the road drops down from the east, as well as a small, stark, pricey **hotel** and a few **rooms**. The north end of the inlet, 1km from the beach area, is a yacht and fishing harbour with a string of somewhat expensive seafood **tavernas**.

    TORÓNI, 3km north, is the antithesis of this, an exposed, two-kilometre-long crescent of sand with wooded hills behind. It's probably your best Sithonian bet as a base if you just want to flop on a beach for a few days; for more stimulation there is a minimal **archeological site** (currently off-limits) on the southern cape, sporting the remains of an ancient fortress, while near-by is an early Christian basilica. After being overlooked until the late 1990s, it has "arrived" touristically in a modest way. Open spaces are slowly filling, too, with apartments for Greek weekenders, though the Sykiá municipality has banned beachfront building. Half a dozen combination **taverna-studio rooms** are scattered the length of the beach, among them *Haus Sakis* (☎03750/51 261; ❸), at the northernmost end, with comfortable rooms upstairs and good food plus German beer on tap at street level.

    Just 2km north is the turning for less-developed **TRISTINÍKA**, with anoth-er outstanding two-kilometre beach, reached by a bumpy, 1800-metre sand-and-dirt track. On the way you pass a taverna-and-rooms outfit, with a tiny hamlet 1km off the main road. At the south end of the sand, served by its own access drive, is *Camping Isa* (☎03750/51 235; May–Sept).

    Some 5km further north along the main road, there's a turning for the rec-ommended, friendly *Camping Areti* (☎03750/71 430, ☏71 573) nestled between Cape Papadhiá and Lýkithos hamlet, with views of three islets over its private beach. Besides tent space in well-landscaped olive groves, there are also wood chalets with all amenities at ❸ rates.

Pórto Carrás to Parthenónas

Beyond Tristiníka, you edge back into high-tech-resort territory, epitomized by Greece's largest planned holiday complex, **PÓRTO CARRÁS**. Established by the Carras wine and shipping dynasty, it features an in-house shopping cen-tre, golf course and vineyards, while from the ten-kilometre private beach in front, you can indulge in every imaginable watersport. Since the death of founder John Carras, the complex has been sold off and split into three futur-istic luxury hotels: *Meliton Beach*, *Village Inn* and *Sithonia Beach*. However, both more affordable and desirable is the *Kelyfos* **hotel** (☎03750/72 833, ☏72 247; ❻), 1km north of the Pórto Carrás turn-off and impressively located on a hill-top; the smart, new rooms have sea views and all mod cons.

    The nearest proper town to all this, with **banks** (cash dispensers), **tavernas** and a **post office**, is **NÉOS MARMARÁS**, a once-attractive fishing port with a small beach. Nowadays, it's popular with Greeks who stay in a score of modest hotels and a like number of apartment developments. Some 3km to the north lies a decent **campsite**, the *Castello* (☎03750/71 095; May–Sept) – at which point the beach is sandy, and there's tennis, volleyball and a restaurant. Exceptionally good *yíros* is carved at *Fast Food O Dhimitris*, between the church and the bus stop.

    A visit to **PARTHENÓNAS**, the lone "traditional" village on Sithonía, will give you some idea of what Sithonía must have looked like before the developers moved in. Crouched at the base of 808-metre Mount Ítamos, it's 5km up from Néos Marmarás and reached via a good road lined with pine- and olive-groves. Parthenónas was abandoned in the 1960s in favour of the shore, and never even provided with mains electricity; its dilapidated but appealing houses are now slowly being sold off to wealthy Greeks and Germans. The *Pension Parthenon* (☎094/438 2384; ❹) in a fine stone house on high ground offers some of the peninsula's most charming accommodation. *To Steki tou Meniou* serves very basic fare in a pleasant hut, but don't go out of your way.

East to secular Athos

From Órmos Panayiás a road winds around the coast and up over a ridge to the head of the Athos peninsula. The principal place you'd think to stop is **PYRGADHÍKIA**, a ravine-set fishing village jutting out into the Sigitikós gulf. However, it can offer no more than a few basic, unenticingly placed **hotels**, such as the *Possidon* (☎03750/93 357; ❶), but you still might lunch here at one of the waterfront tavernas. There's little beach to speak of, although there are some good ones dotted along the stretch between here and **PARALÍA SALONIKIOÚ**, located 6km to the southwest and offering studio rooms and more tavernas.

Inland Halkidhikí

From Pyrgadhíkia the road heads inland towards Paleohóri and Arnéa, while a turn-off via dull Gomáti takes you to Ierissós through unspoilt moors. No buses cover these routes, however, and if you're dependent on public transport you'll have to backtrack as far as Yerakiní and then inland to Halkidhikí's capital, **POLÝIROS**, a drab market town with an unexciting archeological museum. At Áyios Pródhromos, 20km north, you can pick up one of the frequent buses heading for Athos via **ARNÉA**. This small, quaint town has some fine old quarters with attractive Balkan-style houses, one of which has been turned into a moderately interesting **folk museum** (erratic opening; free), and a reputation for carpets and other colourful handwoven goods, along with delicious honey. Although it has a dearth of good places to eat – you'll be forced to fall back on pizzerias – Arnéa does have some high-quality accommodation in the form of a restored old mansion just off the central platía: *Archontiko Mitsiou* (☎03720/22 744, ℱ22 988; ❹), with large, wood-decor rooms. More accommodation can be found in town and also at **PALEOHÓRI**, 5km further east towards Stáyira (and not to be confused with Paleohóra, 16km to the west of Arnéa), where the genial *Park Hotel Tasos* (☎03720/41 722, ℱ41 858; ❹), on the westerly outskirts, has exceptionally quiet, if 1970s-vintage, rooms. The ground-floor lounge is a veritable museum of "Macedoniana", or good-natured kitsch; none of the several tavernas on the road through town is up to much, so if the hotel restaurant is open, take advantage. From the high, partly forested plateau here, the road drops down to the sea again at Stratóni, then veers south to Ierissós, taking you through some fine scenery reminiscent of Mount Athos itself.

Ierissós and Néa Ródha

With its good, long beach and a vast, promontory-flanked gulf, **IERISSÓS** is the most Greek-patronized of the "secular Athos" resorts, although the sizeable town itself, built well back from the shore and with room to expand, is a sterile concrete grid dating from after a devastating 1932 earthquake. The only hint of pre-touristic life is the vast kaïki-building dry dock to the south.

There's an inexpensive **hotel** – the en-suite, friendly if sometimes noisy *Marcos* (☎03770/22 518; ❷), overlooking its own garden and car park at the south end of town, as well as numerous **rooms for rent**, such as pleasant *Aliki* (☎03770/22 363; ❶), on the water's edge to the far north of the town. One of the two basic **campsites** is situated at the northern edge of town, while the other, *Delfini* (☎03770/22 208), lies en route to Néa Ródha. The beach is surprisingly uncluttered – if rather straight-arrow dull – with just a handful of **bars** behind the landscaped promenade. Currently, the best of several mediocre **tavernas** is *O Iosif*, just inland on the main drag, with decent *mezédhes*, but establish prices before ordering. Rounding off the list of amenities, there's a **post office**, two **banks** and a summer **cinema** by the campsite. Ierissós is also the main **port** for the northeast shore of Athos; see p.517 for details.

The road beyond Ierissós passes through the resort of **NÉA RÓDHA**, with a small beach and no more claim to architectural distinction than its neighbour, but worth knowing about as an alternative point for picking up the morning boat from Ierissós. Just beyond here your route veers inland to follow a boggy depression that's the remaining stretch of **Xerxes' canal**, cut by the Persian invader in 480 BC to spare his fleet the shipwreck at the tip of Athos that had befallen the previous expedition eleven years before.

Amoulianí

You emerge on the southwest-facing coast at **Trypití** ("Perforated"), not a settlement but merely the western exit of Xerxes' canal and now also the ferry jetty for the small island of **AMOULIANÍ** (15min; up to 7 daily crossings in summer; €0.50, €6.20 for a car). This is Macedonia's only inhabited Aegean island apart from Thássos, and after decades of eking out an existence from fishing, the island's population, refugees from the Sea of Marmara, has in recent years had to adjust to an influx of holiday-makers. Like anywhere else in Halkidhikí, it's impossibly oversubscribed in July and August, but in spring or autumn this low-lying, scrub- and olive-covered islet can make an idyllic hideaway.

The only town, where the ferries dock, is another unprepossessing grid of concrete slung over a ridge, with few pre-1960s buildings remaining; it is, however, chock-a-block with **rooms**, many self-catering, and there are two **hotels** plainly visible on the left as you sail in. The better of these is the *Sunrise* (☎03770/51 273, ℉51 174; ❸), with its own swimming jetty and reliable hot water. Of the village's half-dozen **tavernas**, *Alekos* (on the front), *Iy Klimataria* (on the road out) and *Yannis* (facing the rear Limanáki port) get high marks for hygiene and good value. There are a few shops for self-caterers, but **no bank or post office**. As for **nightlife**, you've two bars (one, *Barka*, does breakfasts) and two discos a few hundred metres out of town on the main island road.

Two kilometres southwest of the town lies **Alykés**, the islet's most famous beach, with a namesake salt-marsh inland, a taverna and separate café behind the sand, and a rather parched campsite. Amoulianí's best beaches however, lie in the far southeast, facing the straits with the Athos peninsula. To reach them, bear left off the pavement 1500m out of town where the *Agionissi* luxury resort is signposted, onto a smooth, sand-dirt track. Some 2km along this, you pass the tiny chapel and cistern of **Áyios Yeóryios** overlooking the excellent eponymous beach. Just beyond stands the popular lunchtime-only *Sarandis*, but it's pricier than the exceedingly simple fare warrants, and you might prefer to continue to the far end of the beach to the better-value *Gripos Ouzeri*. This also offers a half-dozen upstairs rooms of considerable charm (☎03770/51 049; ❷), with copper antiques, beam ceilings, terracotta floor tiles and large balconies.

Nikos, the affable owner, keeps pheasants and other exotic fowl, whose squawkings vie with those of the gulls nesting on the rock islets of the Dhrénia archipelago just offshore. You can continue a final 500m to even more idyllically set **Megáli Ámmos** beach, where there's a café with seats in the sand, a seasonal taverna and a pleasant, olive-shaded campsite. Still other, less accessible beaches beckon in the northwest of the island, served in season by excursion boats from the town; a popular map-postcard on sale will give necessary hints on how to reach them on foot or rented bicycle.

Ouranoúpoli

Fifteen kilometres beyond Ierissós, **OURANOÚPOLI** is the last community before the restricted monastic domains, with a centre that's downright tatty, showing the effects of too much tourism. Somewhat mysteriously, it has become a major resort aside from its function as the main gateway to Mount Athos; local beaches, stretching intermittently for several kilometres to the north, are sandy enough but narrow and cramped – certainly not the best Halkidhikí has to offer. If you're compelled to stay the night while waiting for passage to Athos, the best temporary escape would be either to take a cruise, or to **rent a motor boat**, to the mini-archipelago of **Dhrénia** just opposite, with almost tropical sandy bays and tavernas on the larger islets.

The only other diversion in Ouranoúpoli is the Byzantine **Phosphori tower** by the bus stop, visible from some distance. Here for nearly thirty years lived Sydney Loch, author of *Athos: the Holy Mountain*, published posthumously in 1957 and still an excellent, if now rather nostalgic, guide to the monasteries. Loch and his wife Joyce, who died in the tower in 1982, were a Scots-Australian missionary couple who devoted most of their lives to the refugees of Halkidhikí. The cottage industry of carpet-weaving, which they taught the local villagers, is increasingly less in evidence.

Two **ferries** – the *Ayios Nikolaos* and the *Axion Esti* – take turns calling along the southwest shore of Athos, and they're probably the main reason you're here. Throughout the year there's just one daily departure, at around 9.45am; tickets, the price of which depends on destination, should be purchased before boarding from the Athoniki agency, near the Phosphori tower. One of these, or perhaps another craft, also offers coed half-day **cruises** in season (€12 a head; departs 10.30am), which skim along the Athonite coast, keeping their contaminating female presence 500m offshore as required by the monastic authorities.

If you need to **stay** – and fortunately proprietors are fairly used to one-night stays, en route to or from Athos – there are a fair number of rooms and a similar quantity of hotels, virtually all of them en suite. Less expensive ones include the *Diana* (☎03770/71 052; ❷) and the adjacent *Rooms Lazaros Antonakis* (☎03770/71 366; ❷), both on the road leading down from the pilgrims' office. On the southerly seafront there's the *Akroyali* (☎03770/71 201, ℱ71 395; ❸), which shares management with the *Makedonia*, slightly uphill and inland (☎03770/71 085, ℱ71 395; ❸), a pleasantly quiet spot with a small package presence. About 300m out of town towards the monastic border, the *Avra* (☎03770/71 189, ℱ71 095; ❹) isn't wildly friendly, but the sea-view rooms are clean and spacious. If money's no object, the closest high-grade hotel to town that isn't utterly dominated by packages is the *Xenia*, on the beach (☎03770/71 412, ℱ71 362, ℮xenia@papcorp.gr; ❺ half-board), with substantial bargains outside peak season. A **campsite**, better appointed than those in Ierissós, lies 2km north of the village, amidst a crop of luxury hotel complexes. The half-dozen waterfront **tavernas** all tout identical rip-off menus, though you're unlikely to care much about value for money before (or especially after) several lean days on Athos. On the south waterfront, respectively just before and after the town limits sign, are two more appealing alternatives: *Mantho*, a traditional-format *estiatório* with plenty of *mayireftá*, and the fancier *Athos*, next to the hotel *Avra*, with a huge menu featuring grilled vegetables, soups and sweets. Ouranoúpoli has a **post office**, but no bank.

Mount Athos: the monks' republic

The population of the **Mount Athos** peninsula has been exclusively male – farm animals included – since the *ávaton* edict, banning females permanent or transient, was promulgated by the Byzantine emperor Constantine Monomachos in 1060. Known in Greek as the **Áyion Óros** (Holy Mountain), it is an administratively autonomous province of the country – a "monks' republic" – on whose slopes are gathered twenty monasteries, plus a number of smaller dependencies and hermitages.

Most of the **monasteries** were founded in the tenth and eleventh centuries; today, all survive in a state of comparative decline but they remain unsurpassed in their general and architectural interest, and for the art treasures they contain. If you are male, over 18 years old and have a genuine interest in monasticism or Greek Orthodoxy, sacred music or simply in Byzantine and medieval architecture, a visit is strongly recommended. It takes less than an hour to arrange in Thessaloníki (see p.473 for details), though for much of the year you'll need to plan your visit well in advance, and the rewards more than justify any efforts. In addition to the religious and architectural aspects of Athos, it should be added that the peninsula, despite some horrific fires and heavy logging in recent years, remains one of the most beautiful parts of Greece. With only the occasional service vehicle, two buses and sporadic coastal boats, a visit necessarily involves walking between settlements – on paths through dense woods, up the main peak or above what is perhaps the Mediterranean's last undeveloped coastline. For many visitors, this – as much as the experience of monasticism – is the highlight of time spent on the Holy Mountain.

The Theocratic Republic: some history

By a legislative decree of 1926, Athos has the status of **Theocratic Republic**. It is governed from the small town and capital of Karyés by the *Ayía Epistasía* (Holy Superintendency), a council of twenty representatives elected for one-year terms by each of the monasteries. At the same time Athos remains a part of Greece. All foreign monks must adopt Greek citizenship and the Greek civil government is represented by an appointed governor and a small police force.

Each monastery has a distinct place in the **Athonite hierarchy**: Meyístis Lávras holds the prestigious first place, Konstamonítou ranks twentieth. All other settlements are attached to one or other of the twenty "ruling" monasteries; the dependencies range from a *skíti* (either a group of houses, or a cloister-like compound scarcely distinguishable from a monastery) through a *kellí* (a sort of farmhouse) to an *isihastírio* (a solitary hermitage, often a cave). Numerous laymen – including many Muslim Albanians of late – also live on Athos, mostly employed as agricultural or manual labourers by the monasteries.

The **development of monasticism** on Athos is a matter of some controversy, and foundation legends abound. The most popular asserts that the Virgin

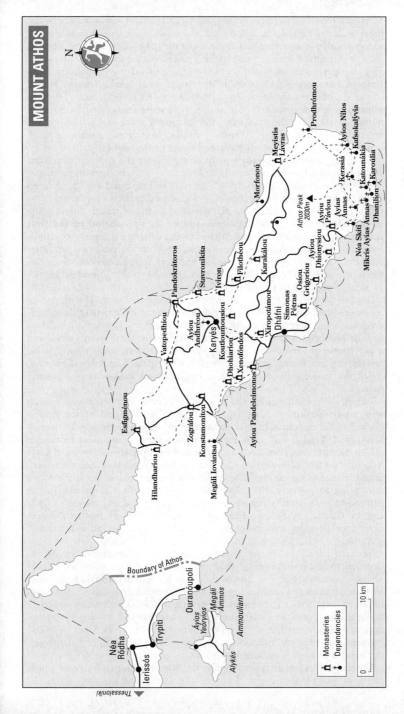

MOUNT ATHOS

N

Thessaloníki

Ierissós
Néa Ródha
Trypití
Ouranóupoli
Boundary of Athos
Áyios Yeóryios
Megáli Ámmos
Ammoulianí
Alykés

Esfigménou
Hilandharíou
Zográfou
Konstamonítou
Megáli Ioνántsa
Áyiou Pandeleímonos
Xenofóndos
Dhohiaríou
Vatopedhíou
Áyiou Andhréou
Karyés
Koutloumousíou
Pandokrátoros
Stavronikíta
Íviron
Filothéou
Karakálou
Xiropotámou
Dháfni
Símonas Pétras
Osíou Grigoríou
Áyiou Dhionysíou
Athos Peak 2030m
Áyiou Pávlou
Áyias Ánnas
Néa Skíti
Mikrís Áyias Ánnas
Dhanílíou
Karoúlia
Katounákia
Kafsokalývia
Áyios Nílos
Kerasiá
Morfonoú
Meyístis Lávras
Prodhrómou

Monasteries
Dependencies

0   10 km

Mary was blown ashore here on her way to Cyprus; she was overcome by the great beauty of the mountain and a celestial voice consecrated the place in her name. Another tradition relates that Constantine the Great founded the first monastery in the fourth century, but this is certainly far too early. The earliest historical reference to Athonite monks is to their attendance at a council of the Empress Theodora in 843; probably there were some monks here by the end of the seventh century. Athos was particularly appropriate for early Christian monasticism, its deserted and isolated slopes providing a natural refuge from the outside world – especially from the Arab conquests in the east, and during the Iconoclastic phase of the Byzantine empire (eighth to ninth centuries). Moreover, its awesome beauty facilitated communion with God.

The most famous of the **early monks** were Peter the Athonite and Saint Euthymios of Salonica, both of whom lived in cave-hermitages on the slopes during the mid-ninth century. In 885 an edict of Emperor Basil I recognized Athos as the sole preserve of monks, and gradually hermits came together to form communities known in church Greek as *koinobia* (literally "life in common"). The year 963 is the traditional date for the **foundation of the first monastery**, Meyístis Lávras, by Athanasios the Athonite; Emperor Nikiforos Fokas provided considerable financial assistance. Over the next two centuries, with the protection of other Byzantine emperors, foundations were frequent, the monasteries reaching forty in number (reputedly with a thousand monks in each), alongside many smaller communities.

Troubles for Athos began at the end of the eleventh century. The monasteries suffered sporadically from pirate raids and from the settlement of three hundred Vlach shepherd families on the mountain. After a reputedly scandalous episode between the monks and the shepherdesses, the Vlachs were ejected and a new imperial *chryssobull* ("golden" edict) was issued, confirming that no female mammal, human or animal, be allowed to set foot on Athos. This edict, called the *ávaton*, remains in force today, excepting various cats to control rodents.

During the twelfth century, the monasteries gained an international – or at least, a **pan-Orthodox** – aspect, as Romanian, Russian and Serbian monks flocked to the mountain in retreat from the turbulence of the age. Athos itself was subjected to Frankish raids during the Latin occupation of Constantinople (1204–61) and, even after this, faced great pressure from the Unionists of Latin Salonica to unite with western Catholics; in the courtyard of Zográfou there is still a monument to the monks who were martyred at this time while attempting to preserve the independence of Orthodox Christianity. In the early fourteenth century the monasteries suffered two disastrous years of pillage by Catalan mercenaries but they recovered, primarily through Serbian benefactors, to enjoy a period of great prosperity in the fifteenth and sixteenth centuries.

After the fall of the Byzantine empire to the Ottomans, the fathers wisely declined to resist, maintaining good relations with the early sultans, one of whom paid a state visit. The later Middle Ages brought **economic problems**, with heavy taxes and confiscations, and as a defence many of the monasteries dissolved their common holdings and reverted to an idiorrhythmic system, a self-regulating form of monasticism where monks live and worship in a loosely bound community but work and eat individually. However, Athos remained the spiritual centre of Orthodoxy, and during the seventeenth and eighteenth centuries even built and maintained its own schools.

The mountain's real decline came after the **War of Independence**, in which many of the monks fought alongside the Greek revolutionary forces. In

Macedonia the insurrectionists were easily subdued, the region remaining under Ottoman control, and the monks paid the price. A permanent Turkish garrison was established on the mountain and monastery populations fell sharply as, in the wake of independence for southern Greece, monasticism became less of a focus for Greek Orthodox Christianity.

At the end of the nineteenth century and beginning of the twentieth, **foreign Orthodox** monks, particularly Russian ones, tried to step in and fill the vacuum. But the Athonite fathers have always resisted any move that might dilute the Greek character of the Holy Mountain, even – until recently – at the expense of its material prosperity. During the early 1960s, numbers were at their lowest ever, barely a thousand, compared to 20,000 in Athos's heyday. Today, however, the monastic population has climbed to about two thousand, its average age has dropped significantly, and the number of well-educated monks has increased markedly.

This revival is due in part to the increasing appeal of the contemplative life in a blatantly materialistic and morally relativistic age; some would also put it down to a wave of militant sectarian sentiment, which has swept world Orthodoxy at large. Successful recruitment has produced a number of novices from around the world, particularly visible in such monasteries as Símonos Pétras, Filothéou and Vatopedhíou. There have, however, been complaints that efforts to recruit brothers from abroad have been hampered by the authorities, and unlike Greek clerics and novices, those from Serbia, Russia, Romania and Bulgaria must be approved for entry by the Ecumenical Patriarchate in Istanbul.

While welcoming the revival, some monks and observers feel there are too many outward signs of unwordliness on the Mountain, such as faxes and mobile phones, and parts of the peninsula resemble a building site, with extensive, ongoing restoration or new building works underway at several monasteries.

Athonite terms

Arhondáris Guestmaster of a monastery or *skíti*, responsible for all visitors; similarly, *arhondaríki*, the guest quarters themselves.

Arsanás Harbour annexe of each monastery or *skíti*, where ro-ro ferries or kaïkia anchor; they can be a considerable distance from the institution in question.

Cenobitic/Idiorrythmic Historically, this is (increasingly, was) the major distinction between religious foundations on the Mountain. At cenobite establishments the monks eat all meals together, hold all property in common and have rigidly scheduled days. Those remaining foundations that are idiorrhythmic are more individualistic: the monks eat in their own quarters and study or worship when and as they wish. Beginning in the mid-1980s, all of the remaining idiorrhythmic monasteries reverted to cenobitic status, with Pandokrátoros the last hold-out until 1992. Currently monks wishing to follow a more independent path must take up residence in an idiorrhythmic *skíti* (most of them are) or a *kellí*.

Dhíkeos The "righteous one" – head of an idiorrhythmic foundation.

Dhókimos A novice monk.

Fiáli The covered font for holy water in some monastery courtyards; often very ornate.

Igoúmenos Abbot, the head of a monastery.

Katholikón Main church of a monastery.

Kyriakón Central chapel of a *skíti*, where the residents worship together once weekly.

Trápeza Refectory, or dining room.

Yérondas A novice's spiritual elder and supervisor, not necessarily the abbot; akin to the *staretz* of the Russian Orthodox tradition.

△ Mount Athos frescoes

Permits and entry

Until a few decades ago foreigners could visit Athos quite easily, but during the early 1970s the influx of tourists grew so great that the monasteries could no longer cope. Since then a permit system has been instituted, limiting the numbers of visitors, though Greek Orthodox have a larger quota. It has been argued, incidentally, by some in the foreign press, that Athos, as a subprovince of Greece, may be obliged to cease controlling its own borders and stop barring women, but the Mountain and its sympathizers promise to fight any such changes, and the permit system seems likely to remain in place.

The first step in acquiring the necessary **dhiamonitírion** (permit) to visit and stay on Athos is to telephone or call in at the **Pilgrims' Office** (*Grafío Proskynitón Ayíou Órous*) in Thessaloníki (see "Listings" on p.473); staff there are helpful and speak English. You will then be issued a reservation confirmation valid for residence on Athos for up to three nights/four days, specifying a date for initial entry to the monastic republic; you will need a slip which you can either have posted or faxed to you if you can't drop by the office in person. This may not be the date of your choice, especially from May to September; to go at Orthodox Easter time, you'll need to apply for permission several weeks in advance. Reservations can be made up to a maximum of six months ahead.

To reach Athos from Thessaloníki, first take a Halkidhikí KTEL bus from its terminal at Karakássi 68 to Ouranoúpoli or Ierissós (see "East to secular Athos", p.509). From Ouranoúpoli just one **boat** daily throughout the year sails at 9.45am as far as **Dháfni**, the main port on the southwestern coast of Athos, stopping at each *arsanás* or coastal monastery, en route; from Dháfni, there's a connecting service onward to the *skíti* of Ayías Ánnas. If you're setting out on the day your permit starts, you'll have to take the earliest (6am) KTEL departure to connect with the boat. From Ierissós, the boat leaves at 8.30am (daily in summer; Sept 13–June Thurs–Mon), but will usually wait for the first bus to arrive; an overnight stop here reduces the risk of missing the boat. This latter service, along the northeast shore, goes as far as the monastery of **Ivíron**, but it may not stop at every *arsanás* on the way, and there's no longer any boat service up to Meyístis Lávras. Ouranoúpoli–Dháfni takes about ninety minutes, Ierissós–Ivíron more than two hours; the boats turn around for the return trip more or less immediately upon arrival. Fares are inexpensive, for example about €3 from Ouranoúpoli to Dháfni, or €0.50–1 from one of the southwest coastal monasteries back to Dháfni.

In Ouranoúpoli, you must call at the **Grafío Proskynitón** (or Pilgrims' Office; daily 8.10am–2pm), at the entry to the town, behind the Jet Oil filling station. If you've stayed overnight, it's suggested that you arrive well before opening time, as the little office is mobbed once the 6am bus from Thessaloníki arrives. This is where you exchange your reservation confirmation slip for your permit proper (€24, or €12 for card-carrying students under 27), which entitles you to stay at any of the main monasteries or *skítes*. Armed with this, you may get off the boat at the *arsanás* of any of the southwest coastal monasteries. Starting from Ierissós or Néa Ródha, passengers will be granted this permit from a police post at the *arsanás* of Hilandharíou, the first monastery on the northeast coast; they are then free to disembark or continue with the boat to a dock of another monastery of their choice.

As of writing, eleven of the twenty monasteries and two *skítes* require **advance reservations** by phone or fax throughout the year; those showing up on spec will, in theory, be turned away, though experience suggests that most of the *arhondáridhes* are not consistently strict on this point. All thirteen institutions are identified in the text, and **telephone numbers** given for all of them. If the phone isn't answered at once, be persistent, and only call during the specified time slot, Monday to Saturday, and don't expect an answer on major holy days.

Many visitors wish to arrange for an **extension** of the basic four-day period. This can theoretically be done at the *Ayía Epistasía* (Holy Superintendancy) in Karyés, though you should have a good reason; two or three extra days are normally granted, and your chances are much better out of season. If you and a particular monastery are particularly taken with each other, and you intend to become a novice, an *idhikó dhiamonitírio* (special sojourning permit) can be arranged. In the past nobody was terribly bothered if you stayed five days or even a week on the mountain, except in summer when monastic accommodation gets quite crowded; the four-day limit was originally enforced to discourage gawkers and others with frivolous motives for visiting. Nowadays, however, most guestmasters ask to see your *dhiamonitírion*, and if you strike the monks as behaving presumptuously or inappropriately, no amount of time remaining on your permit will persuade them to host you. As signs on walls repeatedly remind you, "Hospitality is not obligatory."

The way of life

With *dhiamonitírion* in hand, you will be admitted to stay and eat in the main monasteries – and certain *skítes* – free of charge. If you offer money it will be refused, though all pilgrims are encouraged to buy candles, incense, CDs of liturgical music and icon reproductions of varying quality at those *skítes* which specialize in their production, or at monastery shops supplied by them. **Accommodation** is typically in dormitories, and fairly spartan, but there's usually a shower down the hall (sometimes hot) and you're always given sheets and blankets, so you don't need to lug a sleeping bag around if you don't want to. Athos grows much of its own **food**, and the monastic diet is based on tomatoes, beans, olives, green vegetables, coarse bread, cheese and pasta, with occasional treats like *halvás* and fruit included. After Sunday morning service, wine often accompanies fish (fresh or tinned) in the heartiest meal of the week. Normally only two meals a day are served, the first at mid-morning, the latter about an hour and a half to two hours before sunset. You will need to be partly self-sufficient in provisions – especially dried fruits, nuts and other energy-rich food – both for the times when you fail to coincide with meals and for the long walks between monasteries. (If you arrive after the morning or evening meal you will generally be served leftovers set aside for latecomers.) There are a few shops in Karyés, but for better selection and to save valuable time you should stock up before coming to Athos.

If you're planning to **walk between monasteries**, you should get hold of one of two **maps**: the first simply entitled *Athos*, produced in Austria at a scale of 1:50,000 by Reinhold Zwerger (Wohlmutstr 8, A 1020 Wien; ☎43/222/262205 or 43/2641/67212), is no longer available in Greece but may still be stocked by specialist map shops like Stanford's in London (see p.37). The other, a simple sketch map of all the roads and trails on Mount Athos, was prepared by Theodhoros Tsiropoulos of Thessaloníki (☎0310/430 196), who has marked most of the surviving Athonite trails with white-lettering-on-red-field wooden signposts. The map provided by *Korfes* magazine is now obsolete and contains potentially dangerous errors, but it's still more useful than any of the fanciful tourist productions sold in Ouranoúpoli. Even equipped with the better maps, you'll still need to be pointed to the start of trails at each monastery, and confirm walking times and path conditions. New roads are constantly being built, and trails accordingly abandoned, and in the humid local climate they become completely overgrown within two years if not used, though moves are afoot to clear and restore these.

If need be, you can supplement walking with the regular **kaïki** service provided by the little *Ayia Anna* on the southwest coast only. This departs from the *skíti* of Kavsokalývia, near the southern tip of the peninsula, via all intervening *arsanádhes*, to Dháfni at about 9.15am in summer, with onward connections towards the "border" just after noon. There is no longer any regular linking service between Kavsokalývia and Meyístis Lávras, nor between the latter and Ivíron. Sleek Landrover minibuses are scheduled (in theory) to coincide with the arrival times of the larger ferries; they can be expensive and, if they're driven by lay-workers, you should establish a price beforehand.

However you move around, you must reach your destination **before dark**, since all monasteries and many *skítes* lock their front gates at sunset – which would leave you outside with the wild boars. Upon arrival you should ask for the *arhondáris* (**guestmaster**), who will proffer the traditional welcome of a *tsípouro* (distilled spirits) and *loukoúmi* (Turkish delight) before showing you to your bed. These days many guestmasters speak good English, a reflection of the increasing numbers of Cypriot, Australian or educated Greek novices on Athos.

You will find the monastic **daily schedule** somewhat disorienting, and adapted according to the seasonal time of sunrise and sunset. On the northeast side of the peninsula 12 o'clock is reckoned from the hour of sunrise, and on the opposite side clock towers show both hands up at sunset, in the traditional Byzantine manner. Yet Vatopedhíou keeps "worldly" time, as do most monks' wristwatches, and in most monasteries two wall-clocks are mounted side-by-side: one showing secular time, including daylight savings, the other "Byzantine" time. However, the **Julian calendar**, a fortnight behind the outside world, is universally observed, in particular for the frequent holy days. Most monasteries have electric power from generators – though this may be switched on for just a few hours at dusk, powering feeble bulbs – and all now have phones, sometimes faxes as well. But these have affected the round of life very little; both you and the monks will go to bed early, shortly after sunset. Sometimes in the small hours your hosts will awake for solitary meditation and study, followed by *órthros*, or matins. Around sunrise there is another quiet period, just before the *akolouthía*, or main liturgy. Next comes the morning meal, anywhere from 9.30am to 11.30am depending on the time of year and day of week. The afternoon is devoted to manual labour until the *esperinós*, or vespers, often announced by a carillon "concert" of some musicality, and actually almost three hours before sunset in summer (much less in winter). This is followed immediately by the evening meal and the short *apódhipno*, or compline service.

A few words about **attitudes and behaviour** towards your hosts (and vice versa) are in order, as many misunderstandings arise from mutual perceptions of disrespect, real or imagined. For your part, you should be fully clad at all times, even when going from dormitory to bathroom; this in effect means no shorts, no hats inside monasteries and sleeves that cover all or nearly all the arm. If you swim, do so where nobody can see you, and certainly don't do it naked. Smoking in most foundations is forbidden, though a few allow you to indulge out on the balconies. It would be criminal to do so on the trail, given the chronic fire danger; you could give it up as a penance for the duration of your stay. Singing, whistling and raised voices are taboo; so is standing with your hands behind your back or in your pockets or crossing your legs when seated, both considered overbearing stances. If you want to photograph monks you should always ask permission, though photography is forbidden altogether in many monasteries, and video cameras are completely banned from the mountain. It's best not to go poking around corners of the buildings where you're not specifically invited, even if they seem open to the public.

Monasteries, and their tenants, tend to vary a good deal in their handling of visitors, and their reputations, deserved or otherwise, tend to precede them as a favourite subject of trail gossip among foreigners. You will find that as a non-Orthodox you may be politely ignored; signs at some institutions specifically forbid you from attending services or sharing meals with the monks. Other monasteries put themselves at the disposal of visitors of whatever creed; it is possible to be treated to ferocious bigotry and disarming gentility at the same place within the space of ten minutes, making it tricky to draw conclusions about Athos in general and given monasteries in particular. If you are non-Orthodox, and seem to understand enough Greek to get the message, you'll probably be told at some point, subtly or less so, that you ought to convert to the True Faith. It's worth remembering that even if they don't receive them the monks expect religious pilgrims, and their role is to be committed, rather than tolerant. Generally speaking, you can expect those monks with some level of education or smattering of foreign languages to be benignly interested in you, and to pursue a very soft-sell in the form of a reading library of pamphlets and books put at your disposal. Incidentally, idiorrhythmic *skítes* (see box on p.515) tend to provide exceedingly basic accommodation and food, even by austere monastic standards, and *kelliá* are not bound by the monastic rule of hospitality, so you really need to know someone at a *kellí* in order to stay the night in one.

The monasteries

Obviously you can't hope to visit all twenty monasteries during a short stay, though if you're able to extend the basic four-day period for a few days you can fairly easily see the peninsula's most prominent foundations. The dirt road linking the southwestern port of Dháfni with the northeastern coastal monastery of Ivíron by way of Karyés, the capital, not only cuts the peninsula roughly in two but also separates the monasteries into equal southeastern and northwestern groups; the division is not so arbitrary as it seems, since the remaining path system seems to reflect it and the feel of the two halves is very different.

The southeastern group

Ivíron

The vast **IVÍRON** monastery (☏03770/23 643; booking required noon–2pm) is not a bad introduction to Áthos, and is well poised for walks or rides in various directions. Although founded late in the tenth century by Iberian (Georgian) monks, the last Georgian died in the 1950s and today it is a cenobitic house of forty monks. Many of them moved here from nearby Stavronikíta, under the tutelage of the abbot Vasilios, one of the luminaries of the monastic revival, who to his credit has also spoken out on occasion against the unseemly modernization of life on the Mountain. The focus of pilgrimage is the miraculous **icon** of the *Portaítissa*, the Virgin Guarding the Gate, housed in a special chapel to the left of the entrance. It is believed that if this protecting image ever leaves Áthos, then great misfortune will befall the monks. The **katholikón** is among the largest on the mountain, with an elaborate mosaic floor dating from 1030. There are various pagan touches such as the Persian-influenced gold crown around the chandelier, and two Hellenistic columns with rams-head capitals from a temple of Poseidon which once stood here. Because of the Georgian connection, Russians were lavish donors to this monastery and one of their most notable gifts is a silver-leaf lemon tree crafted in Moscow. The bare-white refectory is, unusually, unadorned except for a pulpit on the south wall, formerly used to deliver the mealtime homily. The monastery is also endowed with an immensely rich library and treasury-museum, presided over by the kindly Father Iakovos, who speaks excellent French and English, and sells copies of the abbot's monographs.

Karyés and around: minor monasteries

Though you no longer have to call in here except for extensions of the *dhiamontírion*, a look around **KARYÉS** is rewarding: the main church of the Protáton, dating from 965, contains exceptional fourteenth-century **frescoes** of the Macedonian school. Karyés also has a few **restaurants**, where you may be able to get heartier fare than is typical in the monasteries, and a simple inn. At the northern edge of "town" sprawls the enormous cloister-like *skíti* of **Ayíou Andhréou**, a former Russian dependency of the great Vatopedhíou monastery, erected hurriedly in the nineteenth century but today virtually deserted.

A signposted trail leads up and west within an hour to small but tidy **KOUTLOUMOUSÍOU** (☎03770/23 226; booking required noon–2.30pm), at the very edge of Karyés. Much the most interesting thing about it is its name, which appears to be that of a Seljuk chieftain converted to Christianity.

From Ivíron another path stumbles south uphill, tangling with roads, to reach **FILOTHÉOU** (☎03770/23 256, ☎23 674), which was at the forefront of the monastic revival in the early 1980s, courtesy of its abbot Ephraim, and hence one of the more vital monasteries. It is not, however, one of the more impressive foundations from an architectural or artistic point of view – though the lawn surfacing the entire courtyard is an interesting touch – and it's one of those houses where the non-Orthodox are forbidden from attending church or eating with the monks.

The same is true at **KARAKÁLOU** (☎03770/23 225; booking required noon–2pm), 45-minutes' walk (mostly on paths) below Filothéou, also accessible via a short trail up from its *arsanás*. The lofty keep is typical of the fortress-monasteries built close enough to the shore to be victimized by pirates. Between here and Meyístis Lávras the trail system has been destroyed and replaced by a road that makes for six hours of dreary tramping, so it's advisable to arrange a lift with a service vehicle. Fairly regular transfers are provided by Landrover minibus from the boat jetty at Ivíron; such vehicles tend to show up between 12.30 and 1pm, and you should pay no more than €6 to get to Meyístis Lávras or the *skíti* or Prodhrómou just beyond. If a monk is driving, you may just get a lift for free; the drive takes just over an hour to Meyístis Lávras, nearly ninety minutes to Prodhrómou.

Meyístis Lávras and the Athonite wilderness

MEYÍSTIS LÁVRAS (the "Great Lavra"; ☎03770/23 758) is the oldest and foremost of the ruling monasteries, and physically the most imposing establishment on Athos, with no fewer than fifteen chapels within its walls. Although there is a fair number of additions from the nineteenth century, it has (uniquely among the twenty) never suffered from fire. The treasury and library are both predictably rich, the latter containing over two thousand precious manuscripts, though the ordinary traveller is unlikely to view them; as is usual, several monks (out of the 25 here) have complementary keys which must be operated together to gain entrance. At mealtimes you can enjoy the superior **frescoes** in the **trápeza**, executed by Theophanes the Cretan in 1535.

Hagiographies and grisly martyrdoms line the apse, while there's a *Tree of Jesse* (the genealogy of Jesus) in the south transept, the *Death of Athanasios* (the founder) opposite and an *Apocalypse* to the left of the main entry. In the western apse is a *Last Supper*, not surprisingly a popular theme in refectories. Just outside the door stands a huge **fiáli**, largest on the mountain, with recycled columns from a pagan temple supporting the canopy. The **katholikón**, near the rear of the large but cluttered courtyard, contains more frescoes by Theophanes.

Beyond Meyístis Lávras lies some of the most beautiful and deserted wilderness on the peninsula – the so-called Athonite "desert", beloved of ascetics – now partly compromised by a track bulldozed over the most direct path south to one of Meyístis Lávras's many dependencies, **Skíti Prodhrómou**. Under the aegis of the saintly elder Petronios, it is now full of young Romanian monks who keep the place immaculate. Just ten minutes away by marked path there's the **hermitage-cave of St Athanassios**, watched over by five skulls.

Most first-time visitors will, however, proceed without delay from Meyístis Lávras on a traverse of up to six hours across the tip of Athos, through incomparably rugged territory along paths unlikely to be destroyed in the future – the local monks intend to keep it this way, and this is currently one of the few places on Athos where trails are at all maintained. A few minutes past the point where the ascending paths from Meyístis Lávras and Prodhrómou link up, there's a turning down and left towards the *kellí* of **Áyios Nílos**, reached by crossing an intimidating but stabilized rockfall. There's a welcome **spring** here – many on Athos are neglected and dried up – and you can visit the cave of the medieval hermit Nilos on the far side of the prominent crag here. Otherwise, it's plainly visible after you descend through a fearsome ravine and climb up the far side; Nilos's tomb, towards the base of the same cliff, is difficult to reach.

About an hour past Áyios Nílos, or nearly three from Meyístis Lávras, you come to the sizeable *skíti* of **Kavsokalývia (Ayías Triádhas)**, where donkeys are much in evidence toiling up between the tiered cottages. The community took root around the tombs of the saints Maximios and Akakios, and there's a surprisingly large and comprehensively frescoed *kyriakón* beside the small and rather plain guest quarters.

To rejoin the main trail from here involves a punishing climb over a 500-metre altitude difference, which can be avoided by taking the daily morning kaïki from Kavsokalývia's *arsanás*, a half-hour below. Disembark at the next port for the hermitages of Karoúlia and Katounákia, where you face a much more manageable climb of 200m (45min) up to the **Dhanilíon** academy, where monks and laymen perfect their technique of Byzantine chanting. From here it's an hour-plus walking on a gentle contour path to the *skíti* of Ayías Ánnas, via incongruously modernized Mikrís Ayías Ánnas, whose helipad and solar-powered villas would not disgrace a trendy Greek island.

However, the commonest strategy involves heading directly west from Prodhrómou, via the only water at the Krýa Nerá stream, to **Skíti Ayías Ánnas** (☎03770/23 320; booking required – no specific booking times), whose buildings tumble downslope to a perennial-summer patch of coast capable of ripening lemons. This, with its renovated *arhondaríki*, is the usual "base camp" for the climb of **Athos peak** itself (2030m) – best left for the next morning, and the months May–June and September.

With a (pre-)dawn start, you gain the necessary mercy of a little shade and can expect to be up top in just over four walking hours from Ayías Ánnas, with the combination refuge-church of **Panayía** passed a little over an hour before reaching the summit. Some hikers plan an overnight stop at this shelter, to watch the sunrise from the peak, but for this you must be self-sufficient in **food**. There's no spring **water** en route – you drink from cisterns at Panayía or at **Metamórfosis**, the tiny chapel atop the peak.

Returning from the peak before noon, you'll still have time to reach one of the monasteries north of Ayías Ánnas; the scenic path continues past **Néa Skíti** (☎03770/23 629; booking required 8am–1.30pm) and affords a sudden, breathtaking view of **AYÍOU PÁVLOU** (☎03770/23 250) as you round a bend. Except for the ugly scar of the new access road off to the left, which continues down to its *arsanás*, little can have changed in the perspective since Edward Lear painted it in the 1850s. Up close, the monastery, about ninety minutes from Ayías Ánnas, does not fulfil the promise of first sight; the courtyard lacks charm, as does the echoing, hospital-like guest area. Traditionally home to monks from the island of Kefaloniá, Ayíou Pávlou now has far more Cypriot brothers.

The "hanging" monasteries

From Ayíou Pávlou it's another hour to **DHIONYSÍOU** (☎03770/23 687, ⓕ23 686), a fortified structure perched spectacularly on a coastal cliff, and among the most richly endowed monasteries. It is one of those houses where the non-Orthodox must eat separately from the monks, though there's a neat and airy *arkhondaríki* that comes as a relief after so many claustrophobic facilities. Sadly, it is difficult to make out the sixteenth-century **frescoes** by the Cretan Tzortzis in the hopelessly dim *katholikón*, likewise an icon attributed to the Evangelist Luke; however, those of Theophanes on the inside and out of the **trápeza** are another story. The interior features *The Entry of the Saints into Paradise* and *The Ladder to Heaven*; the exterior wall bears a version of the *Apocalypse*, complete with what looks suspiciously like a nuclear mushroom cloud. Unusually, the Cypriot warden may offer a tour of the **library** with its illuminated gospels on silk-fortified paper, wooden carved miniature of the Passion week and ivory crucifixes. You've little chance, however, of seeing Dhionysíou's great treasure, the three-metre-long **chryssobull** of the Trapezuntine emperor Alexios III Komnenos. Extensive modernization has been carried out here, with mixed results: clean electric power is supplied by a water turbine up-canyon, but the old half-timbered facade has been replaced with a rather brutal concrete-stucco one.

The onward path to **OSSÍOU GRIGORÍOU** (☎03770/23 668, booking required 11am–1pm) is a bit neglected but spectacular and still usable, depositing you at the front door within an hour and a quarter of leaving Dhionysíou. Of all the monasteries and *skítes* it has the most intimate relation with the sea, though every building dates from after a devastating fire in 1761. Owing to yet another charismatic abbot, some forty monks live here, usually vastly outnumbered by Greek pilgrims attracted by the place's reputation and quality of chanting. In the old guest quarters there's an attractive "common room"-library with literature on Orthodoxy; the guest overflow stays in a wood-trimmed hostel outside the gate, by the boat dock.

The southwest coastal trail system ends ninety minutes later at **SÍMONOS PÉTRAS** (abbreviated **Simópetra**; ☎03770/23 254, ⓕ23 707, reservations required 1–3pm) or "The Rock of Simon", after the foundation legend asserting that the hermit Simon was directed to build a monastery here by a mysterious light hovering over the sheer pinnacle. Though entirely rebuilt in the wake of a fire a century ago, Simópetra is perhaps the most visually striking monastery on Athos. With its multiple storeys, ringed by wooden balconies overhanging sheer 300-metre drops, it resembles nothing so much as a Tibetan lamasery. As at Dhionysíou, of which it seems an exaggerated rendition, the courtyard is quite narrow. Thanks to the fire there are no material treasures worth mentioning, though the monastery rivals Filothéou in vigour, with sixty monks from a dozen countries around the world, and the choir is generally acknowledged to be the best on Athos. Unfortunately, because of the spectacle it presents, and its feasibility as an easy first stop out of Dháfni, Simópetra is always crowded with foreigners and Orthodox alike, and might be better admired from a distance, especially during summer.

Further walking is inadvisable and it's best to arrange a lift northwest up the peninsula, or catch the morning boat in the same direction.

The northwestern group

Dháfni port and the Russian monastery

Though you may not ever pass through Karyés, at some point you'll make the acquaintance of **DHÁFNI**, if only to change boats, since the service on this coast is not continuous. There's a **post office**, some rather tacky souvenir shops and a **customs** post – much more vigilant when you leave than upon entry; all passengers' baggage is inspected to check traffic in smuggled-out treasures. A number of eagle-brooch-capped Athonite police skulk about as well, ever ready to pounce on real or imagined violations of the Athonite dress and behaviour codes. There's a **taverna** where you can get a beer and the dish of the day (usually frugal), but no shops adequate for restocking on food and drink.

The kaïki usually has an hour's layover here before heading back towards Ayías Ánnas, during which time the captain can often be persuaded (for a reasonable fee) to take groups as far as the Russian monastery of **AYÍOU PAN-DELEÍMONOS** (alias **Roussikó**; ☎03770/23 252; booking required 10am–noon), sparing you a dull forty-minute walk from the port. Many of the monks are Russian, an ethnic predominance strongly reflected in onion-shaped **domes** and the softer faces of the frescoes. The majority of the buildings were erected at speed just after the mid-1800s, as part of Tsarist Russia's campaign for eminence on the Mountain, and have a utilitarian, barracks-like quality. The sole unique features are the corrosion-green lead roofs and the enormous **bell** over the refectory, the second largest in the world, which always prompts speculation as to how it got there. Otherwise, the small population fairly rattles around the echoing halls, the effect of desolation increased by ranks of outer dormitories gutted by a fire in 1968. If you're an architecture buff, Roussikó can probably be omitted without a twinge of conscience; students of early twentieth-century kitsch will be delighted, however, with mass-produced saints' calendars, gaudy reliquaries and a torrent of gold (or at least gilt) fixtures in the seldom-used *katholikón*. It's worth trying to get into a service in the top-storey chapel north of the belfry for the sake of the Slavonic chanting, though it must be said that the residents don't exactly put themselves out for non-Slavs.

Actually closer to Dháfni, a bit inland on what remains of the old path towards Karyés, stands the square compound of **XIROPOTÁMOU** (☎03770/23 251; booking required 11.30am–1.30pm), with most of its construction and church frescoes dating from the eighteenth century, except for two wings that were fire-damaged in 1952. Like Filothéou, this monastery was at the forefront of the 1980s "renaissance"; here again non-Orthodox are kept segregated from the faithful at meal times.

Greek coastal monasteries

From the vicinity of Dháfni or Roussikó, most pilgrims continue along the coast, reaching **XENOFÓNDOS** (℡03770/23 633; booking required noon–2pm) along a mix of trail and tractor track an hour after quitting the Russian monastery. Approached from this direction, Xenofóndos's busy sawmill gives it a vaguely industrial air. The enormous, sloping, irregularly shaped court, expanded upwards in the nineteenth century, is unique in possessing two *katholiká*. The small, older one, decorated with exterior frescoes of the Cretan school, was outgrown and replaced during the 1830s by the huge upper one. Among its many icons are two fine **mosaics** of saints George and Demetrios. The guest quarters occupy a modern wing overlooking the sea at the extreme south end of the perimeter.

A half-hour's walk separates Xenofóndos from **DHOHIARÍOU** (℡03770/23 245), one of the more picturesque monasteries on this coast but not conspicuously friendly to the non-Orthodox. Early 1990s renovations left untouched the spare but clean *arhondaríki*, which sees few foreigners. An exceptionally lofty, large **katholikón** nearly fills the court, though its Cretan-school frescoes, possibly by Tzortzis, were clumsily retouched in 1855. Much better are the late seventeenth-century ones in the long, narrow **refectory**, with its sea views some of the nicest on Athos. Even Orthodox pilgrims have trouble getting to see the wonder-working icon of *Gorgoipikóou* ("She who is quick to hear"), housed in a chapel between church and *trapezaría*.

The far northern monasteries

The direct trail inland and up to **KONSTAMONÍTOU** (also known as Kastamonítou) has been reclaimed by the forest, so to get there you have to go in a roundabout fashion 45 minutes along the coast to its *arsanás*, and then as much time again sharply up on a track which has regrettably buried the old cobbled way. Hidden up in a thickly wooded valley, Konstamonítou (℡03770/23 228), seems as humble, bare and poor as you'd expect from the last-ranking monastery; the *katholikón* nearly fills the quadrangular court where the grass is literally growing up through the cracks. Non-Orthodox and believers are segregated, not that many foreigners make it this far.

From here you can continue on foot for ninety minutes to Zográfou, more usually reached directly from its *arsanás* (second stop on the boat route from Ouranoúpoli) within an hour by a track which has obliterated eighty percent of the old path. **ZOGRÁFOU** (℡03770/23 247), the furthest inland of the monasteries, is populated by a handful of elderly Bulgarian monks whose numbers are not being replenished, owing to long-standing indifference by both the Greek and Bulgarian governments. A stroll down the empty, rambling corridors past the scarcely maintained seventeenth- and eighteenth-century cells lends an appreciation of the enormous workload that falls on so few shoulders, yet even here building materials are piled high for the imminent makeover. "Zográfou" means "of the Painter", in reference to a tenth-century legend: the Slavs who founded the monastery couldn't decide on a patron saint, so they put a wooden panel by the altar, and after lengthy prayer a painting of Saint George – henceforth the institution's protector – appeared.

From Zográfou the direct trails to Esfigménou and Vatopedhíou have been bulldozed, so the best option if you're crossing the peninsula is to follow the one surviving path which begins as a shaded *kalderími* and is only sullied by tracks for about twenty minutes near the high point. After some three hours on this high-quality route, you suddenly drop down to **HILANDHARÍOU** (**Hilandar** in Serbian; ℡03770/23 797), hidden in a shady glen and fringed by vast, mechanically tilled gardens and orchards. This enormous, irregularly shaped monastery has been hard hit by the Balkan conflict which has pretty much cut off the flow of Serbian pilgrims, and, all things considered, the twenty, mostly young, monks who come in rota from Serbia are amazingly civil and hospitable to all visitors, whatever their nationality. Hilandharíou has been Serbian since its thirteenth-century patronization by Serbian kings, and as you'd expect for a beacon of medieval Serbian culture, the library and treasury are well endowed. The **katholikón**, at the bottom end of the sloping, triangular courtyard, dates from the fourteenth century, but its frescoes, similar in style to those in the Protáton at Karyés, have been retouched. On the south side of the church, an allegedly 800-year-old grapevine sprouted miraculously of its own accord from a holy tomb; the monks make raisins of its grapes, to which are ascribed various miraculous properties. Opposite the door of the **refectory**, there's a fresco of the *Ouranóskala* or Stairway to Heaven, in which righteous monks are being assisted upwards by angels, while a few wicked ones are being yanked down by demons to the mouth of Hell. Last but perhaps not least, the reception area is the most sumptuous and tasteful on the Mountain, more like the lobby of a Spanish parador, and the *arhondaríki* is also among the most salubrious.

Northeast coast monasteries

From Hilandharíou purists can follow a path east, then north, with considerable elevation change, to **ESFIGMÉNOU** monastery (℡03770/23 796), though most will opt for the easier, though duller hour-long track walk north, then east. Built directly at sea level in fortress style, it is the strictest foundation on Athos, such that it does not recognize the authority of current Patriarch Vartholomeos and in its schismatic state has little to do with the other nineteen monasteries. Some of its ninety monks have erected a sign facing the sea, reading "Orthodoxy or Death", which does not encourage a casual visit; the premises, lit by oil lamp, have an accordingly harsh feel despite a courtyard full of citrus and banana trees.

Nonetheless, Esfigménou marks the start of one of the more wonderful surviving Athos treks, the three-and-a-half hour coastal trek to Vatopedhíou (which, incidentally, tends to close an hour *before* sunset). There's track for the initial twenty minutes, then a path heads off left (seawards); shortly after the high point of the route, an hour along the path, a well-preserved *kalderími* kicks in for the long descent through the thick Dhafnára laurel groves to emerge briefly on the coast, two-and-a-half hours along, before heading slightly inland again as a *kalderími* on the final approach.

VATOPEDHÍOU (℡03770/23 219; booking required 10am–4pm) exceeds Meyístis Lávras in size, nearly matches it in importance and wealth, and makes a good beginning or farewell to Athos. The cobbled, slanting court with its freestanding belfry seems more like a town plaza, ringed by stairways and stacks of cells for more than three hundred monks. The **katholikón**, one of the oldest on the mountain, contains a set of exceptional fourteenth-century **frescoes** of the Macedonian school and three **mosaics** flanking the door of the inner narthex: Gabriel (left) and the Virgin (right) comprising an *Annunciation*, with the *Deisis* (the Virgin, Christ and John the Baptist) above, and some more wonderful mosaics in the nave. The growing international population of eighty-plus welcoming monks, mostly young and some Cypriot or Australian in background, makes this a good place to get to grips with Orthodoxy, with plenty of English-speakers to talk to and reading material provided in the *arhondaríki*. Even if you're not staying, it's possible to have a small snack here and retire from the heat of midday before resuming progress to other monasteries.

Continuing southeast, you can initially short-cut dust-tracks on the *kalderími* for the first hour-plus up to the ridge, but the ninety-minute trail from there to Pandokrátoros was chewed up by bulldozers in 1998 and is now all but impossible to find going in this direction. Allow nearly three hours to reach **PANDOKRÁTOROS** (☎03770/23 253; booking required 11.30am–2pm & 7.30–9pm). Other than a hilltop setting overlooking its own picturesque fishing harbour, and the courtyard with its eight Valencia orange trees, there is little of artistic note – perhaps still less given ambitious renovations – though the thirty-odd young monks are welcoming, and the guest wing overlooks the sea. In a valley above looms its dependent *skíti* of **Profítis Ilías**, a relic of the Russian expansion drive and today home to a handful of monks from several different countries.

Continuing on the now-shady, roller-coastering shoreline trail, it's under an hour door-to-door to tiny **STAVRONIKÍTA** (☎03770/23 255; booking required 1–3pm). With some of the best views of Athos peak available, it's also the best example of an Athonite coastal fortress-monastery and distinctly vertical in orientation on its surf-lashed promontory. Long one of the poorest houses, Stavronikíta was completely revitalized under the abbot Vasilios before his move to Ivíron, and, surrounded by aqueduct-fed kitchen gardens, remains pin-neat. The narrow **katholikón** occupies virtually all of the gloomy courtyard, and the **refectory**, normally opposite, had to be shifted upstairs to the south wing; it's a spartan room with a single window on the water, and fresco fragments by Theophanes of the *Death of Áyios Nikólaos* (the patron) and the *Last Supper*. Many Australians, including the most recent abbot, number among the two dozen monks, who really are strict about bookings for the small, oil-lamp-lit guest quarters and who will roust all, Orthodox and infidel alike, for 3.30am matins. All non-Orthodox guests will be sent on their way an hour or so after sunrise, after coffee and biscuits. Despite (or because of) the foregoing, this is a popular monastery with young, educated city Greeks. From here an hour's walk, mostly on path, separates you from Ivíron.

The coastal road to Kavála

Heading towards Kavála from Sithonía or Athos by public transport is surprisingly tricky, since buses from the two peninsulas run only to Thessaloníki. However, the gap between the Thessaloníki–Halkidhikí and Thessaloníki–Kavála services is only 17km wide at one point, with a couple of places you wouldn't mind getting stuck at along the way, so if you don't have your own transport but plenty of energy, you could always walk.

To begin, you should get off the Ouranoúpoli–Thessaloníki bus at the drab coastal village of **STRATÓNI**. The bay here is dominated by the local mine workings, and there is little incentive to stay, though there are several tavernas on the grey–black beach and even one basic hotel, the *Angelika* (☎03760/22 075; ❷). From Stratóni, the scenic road glides over the forested ridge north 17km to the beach resort of Olymbiádha, from where regular buses run to the Thessaloníki–Kavála highway – ending up, incidentally, in Thessaloníki at a special terminal at Irínis 17, behind Langadhás 16; they ply the route four times daily Monday to Friday, three times on Saturday and twice on Sunday all year round.

OLYMBIÁDHA (aka Olymbiás) itself is very low-key. In the late 1990s an Athens-based mining company, TVX, pushed to establish a highly polluting gold-processing plant here, and the locals were understandably up in arms at the prospect of losing their pristine environment; demonstrations and criminal prosecutions for sabotage of company equipment gave the village nationwide media attention, and all-round pressure forced TVX to abandon their scheme.

You can stay in **rooms**, a pair of shaded, streamside campsites – *Olympias* and *Corali* (☎03760/51 304) – 1km north and 500km inland respectively, or a pair of co-managed hotels: the quieter *Liotopi* at the south edge of town, with breakfast served in a lush garden, and the central *Germany* with an atmospheric ground-floor taverna (both ☎03760/51 362, ℱ51 255; ❹ half-board). There are more **tavernas** on the southern bay, the cheapest and most characterful being the *Kapetan Manolis/Platanos* by the concrete jetty. All along this shore the local speciality is **mussels** (*mýdhia*), farmed in floating nursery beds and typically served in a spicy cheese sauce, or sold raw for home use at roadside stalls.

The small town **beaches** are fine, but there are other ones – such as Próti Ammoudhiá, where the water can be murky – 2km back towards Stratóni, behind the promontory containing **ancient Stageira**, birthplace of Aristotle. This covers two hilltops joined by a saddle, and is under continuous summer excavation; it's completely fenced off, but when the gates are open you're free to have a wander around, though there's not much on view yet apart from the western wall and towers guarding the landward approach, a few paved streets and house foundations. It is, however, perhaps unique in ancient Greece for having been a city built of granite rather than marble or limestone.

STAVRÓS, 12km north of Olymbiádha – the interval dotted with semi-accessible coves – is a much bigger, busier place than Olymbiádha: a neon-lit, fun-faired vulgarity. It does, though, have a beautiful seafront of plane trees, and up to ten daily orange buses to Thessaloníki's Irínis 17 terminal. Among five modest **hotels**, the *Athos* (☎03970/61 353; ❷) is the best placed and represents best value; **tavernas** such as *Iy Amalthia* or *Iy Platania*, at the far south end of town, are the most authentic.

From here you're only 4km from the main E90 highway, where just east of the junction the first coastal place of any size – **ASPROVÁLTA** – will come as a jolt after the relative calm of Halkidhikí. Minimally attractive, it's essentially a summer suburb of Sérres or Thessaloníki, with a frequent bus service to and from the latter.

Fourteen kilometres east of Asproválta, the road to Kavála crosses the **River Strymónas**, recorded as one of the most polluted in Europe owing to dumping of toxic substances near its sources in Bulgaria. If you bear onto a minor road signposted for Nigríta, rather than continuing over the river bridge, after less than 1km you'll find on your left the colossal marble **Lion of Amphipolis**. This was reconstructed in 1937 from fragments found when excavating the nearby ancient city of Amphipolis, and is thought to date from the end of the fourth century BC. **Ancient Amphipolis** itself (Tues–Sun 9am–3pm), some 3km further on, beyond the old iron bridge across the Strymónas, figured largely in Thucydides' *Peloponnesian Wars*. It's worth the slight detour, preserving considerable chunks of fortification wall, foundations of a fifth-century BC river bridge and an early Christian basilica with mosaic floors.

Beyond the Strymónas, there's a choice of routes east: the shorter, but slower inland road via the villages at the base of Mount Pangéo, or the slightly longer but quicker coast highway, which is the one long-distance buses to Kavála tend to use. This is being upgraded to motorway status as part of the "Via Egnatia" project, though there's not a great deal along the way other than some vineyards, an occasional crumbled medieval watchtower and duney, white-sand **beaches**, the best in eastern Macedonia, scarcely developed and relatively free from riverborne pollution. The first place of any size, **NÉA PÉRAMOS**, 14km before Kavála and connected by regular buses, sports an unheralded **castle** at one corner of its sandy, sheltered bay. This isn't a bad place to spend a couple of hours, especially before taking one of the several daily **ro-ro ferries** (but only once a day off season) to Skála Prínou on the island of Thássos (see p.894). *Camping Anatoli* (☎05940/21 027; May–Sept) at the west end of things, with a saltwater swimming pool, can be recommended if you want to spend the night. The only other **campsites** between here and Kavála are the *Estella*, 5km east, or the pricier *Batis*, 10km along and already hedged by Kavála's sprawl.

Inland to Kavála via the Alistráti caves

An alternative way of reaching Kavála and/or Xánthi is the busy but scenic route that climbs northeast out of Thessaloníki, first taking you via the prosperous but not terribly interesting town of Sérres before heading towards Dhráma and Philippi along a quieter road that offers majestic panoramas of Mount Meníkio (1963m), Mount Pangéo (1956m) and Mount Falakró (2230m). Regular buses from Thessaloníki and between Sérres and Dhráma ply the road.

Just over 20km before you reach Sérres you come to the village of **ALISTRÁTI**, a pleasant cluster of houses blessed with one or two decent **tavernas**. The only **hotel** is a delightfully restored mansion, *Arhondiko Voziki* (☎03240/20 400, ⊜20 408, ⓦwww.hotelboziki.gr; ❺), with beautifully furnished rooms and a swimming pool. The village is well placed for exploring the nearby mountains. The main reason for coming here, though, is to visit the impressive **caves** (9am–7pm Easter to Sept 30; 9am–5pm rest of year; guided tours only, 1hr; €6 with reductions; ⓦwww.alistraticave.gr), reached down a scenic side road 6km southeast of the village. First explored in the mid-1970s, these impressive caves, which easily rival those at Pérama (see p.401), are claimed to be the most extensive of their kind in Europe not requiring special speleogical equipment or training to visit. Dating from the Quaternary Period, these gigantic limestone cavities are over two million years old, and bristle with a variety of wonderful formations, including the relatively rare "eccentrites" and "helictites", respectively stalactites sticking out at angles, rather than hanging vertically, and twisted forms resembling branches. The impressive entrance, a long tunnel bored into the hillside, takes you right into the caverns, and a winding path weaves its way through masses of stalagmites, many of them outstandingly beautiful, and some exceeding 15m in length.

Kavála

Backing onto the easterly foothills of Mount Sýmvolo, **KAVÁLA** is the second-largest city of Macedonia and the second port for northern Greece. Although its attempt to style itself as the Azure City, on account of its position at the head of a wide bay, is going a little overboard, it does have a characterful centre, focused on the nineteenth-century harbour and old tobacco warehouses. A picturesque citadel looks down from a rocky promontory to the east, and an elegant Turkish aqueduct leaps over modern buildings into the old quarter on the bluff.

KAVÁLA

Folk & Modern
Art Museum

Alexandhroúpoli
★ Bus Stop

Archeological
Museum

Olympic
Airways

KTEL

OTE

Tourist Police

City
Bus Stop ★

Thássos
Ferry &
Hydrofoil
Dock

Miliadhes
Ferry Agent

Aegean
Ferry Dock

Arsinoi Agent

Citadel

Imaret

PANAYÍA

Mehmet Ali's House

Statue

RESTAURANTS

Antonia	D
O Kanadhos	C
To Koutoukaki	E
Panos Zafira	A
To Tavernaki tis Pares	B

ACCOMMODATION

Akropolis	4
Esperia	2
Nefeli	1
Panorama	3
Rooms Yiorgos Alvanos	5

N

0   200 m

Known in ancient times as Neapolis, the town was for two centuries or more a staging post on the Via Egnatía and the first European port of call for merchants and travellers from the Middle East. It was here that Saint Paul landed en route to Philippi (see p.532), on his initial mission to Europe. In later years, the port and citadel were occupied in turn by the Byzantines, Normans, Franks, Venetians, Ottomans and (during both world wars) Bulgarians. Kavála is also one of the main departure points for Thássos (see p.894) and, to a lesser extent, Samothráki (see p.889).

The town

Although the remnants of Kavála's Turkish past are mostly neglected, the wedge-shaped **Panayía** quarter to the east of the port preserves a scattering of eighteenth- and nineteenth-century buildings with atmospheric lanes wandering up towards the citadel. The most conspicuous and interesting of its buildings is the **Imaret**, overlooking the harbour on Poulídhou. An elongated, yellowish multidomed structure with plaques inscribed with Arabic script over many doorways, it was originally a combination soup kitchen-cum-hostel, housing three hundred *softas*, or theological students. After many decades of dereliction it was partly refurbished during the early 1990s appropriately enough as a bar–restaurant (see "Eating and drinking", p.532). Claimed to be the largest Islamic public building in Europe, it was endowed by **Mehmet (or Mohammed) Ali**, pasha of Egypt and founder of the dynasty which ended with King Farouk. The splendid **house** where Mehmet Ali was born to an Albanian family in 1769, near the corner of Pavlídhou and Mohámet Alí, is maintained as a monument. It provides an opportunity to look over a prestigious Islamic house, with its wood-panelled reception rooms, ground-floor stables and first-floor harem (daily except Mon 10am–2pm; officially free but easiest in a group; tip the non-English-speaking guide). Nearby rears an equestrian bronze statue of the great man, one of the finest of its kind in Greece.

Wonderful views can be had from the Byzantine **citadel** (daily 10am–7pm, sometimes closed for siesta; free), signed "castle". You can explore the ramparts, towers, dungeon and cistern, and in season it co-hosts the Philippi–Thássos Festival of drama and music in its main court. From here, down towards the middle of town, the **aqueduct**, built on a Roman model during the reign of Süleyman the Magnificent (1520–66), spans the traffic in Platía Nikotsára.

Finally, on the other side of the harbour from the old town, there are two museums of moderate interest. The **Archeological Museum** (Tues–Sun 8.30am–3pm; €1.50) on Erythroú Stavroú contains a fine dolphin and lily mosaic upstairs in the Abdera room, plus painted sarcophagi in the adjacent section devoted to Thasian colonies. Downstairs in the ground-floor rear left gallery is a reconstructed Macedonian funeral chamber, with many terracotta figurines still decorated in their original paint and gold ornaments from tombs at Amphipolis. Just inland, wedged between former tobacco warehouses at Filíppou 4, is the **Folk and Modern Art Museum** (Mon–Fri 8am–2pm, Sat 9am–1pm; free). Along with various collections of traditional costumes and household utensils, this has some interesting rooms devoted to the Thássos-born sculptor Polygnotos Vayis (see p.899).

Practicalities

The main **bus station** is on the corner of Mitropolítou Khryssostómou and Filikís Eterías, near the Thássos ferry and hydrofoil dock; buses for Alexandhroúpoli stop some blocks away on Erythroú Stavroú, in front of the *Hotel Oceanis*, while buses from Komotiní tend to drop passengers off on the same street. **Taxis** are deep orange; if you're **driving** in, you can usually (just) find a space on the quay car park near the Thássos dock. In the main square, Platía Eleftherías, you'll find an **EOT** office, which can provide details (and sell tickets) for the summer Philippi–Thássos Festival. Right next door is a long-hours money **exchange** booth, Midas, and the Ionian Bank has erected an automatic note-changer on the fishing wharf, though the square is ringed by several banks with cash dispensers. Kavála's **airport**, used by package holiday-makers en route to Thássos and providing domestic flights to and from Athens, lies 29km southeast.

Accommodation

Abundant, good-value **hotel** rooms are not the order of the day in Kavála, though proprietors can often be bargained down a category or two in the off-season. If you're arriving on an afternoon charter in summer, you might well prefer to transfer from the airport to Keramotí for a ferry to Thássos with its wide choice of accommodation (see p.894), reserving Kavála for a day-trip. While there are some dosshouses on the pedestrian streets just off Platía Eleftherías, for most travellers the cheapest acceptable outfits will be the *Panorama* (☎0510/224 205; ❸), at Venizélou 26–32/C, west of Platía Eleftherías and in dire need of refurbishment, or the *Akropolis* (☎0510/223 543, ☎830 752; ❸), opposite at Venizélou 29, with English-speaking management and large, eccentric but not unpleasant rooms. Infinitely better value are two nearly adjacent hotels on Erythroú Stavroú: although it's been recently refurbished, the C-class *Nefeli* at no. 50 (☎0510/227 441, ☎227 440; ❹) doesn't have all the advantages of the smart B-class *Esperia* (☎0510/229 621, ☎220 621; ❹), with its air conditioning, good breakfasts on a terrace and availability of quieter side or back rooms. The only accommodation in the old town is *Yiorgos Alvanos* at Anthemíou 35 (☎0510/228 412;❶), with comfortable rented rooms in a beautifully restored old house just below the castle – you need to arrive early in the day, however, to be sure of a room. The closest **campsite** is *Irini* (☎0510/229 785; open all year), on the shore 3km east of the port and served by city bus #2.

Eating and drinking

Eating out in Kavála is a more cheerful prospect than staying the night; most places on the waterfront, however, are tourist-traps, though *Panos Zafira* fish taverna on Platía Karaolí Dhimitríou deserves its good reputation. You're far better off walking up into the Panayía district, where a cluster of tavernas with outdoor seating on Poulídhou, interspersed with café-bars, tempts you with good and reasonably priced grills and seafood. Starting opposite the lower end of the Imaret as you proceed uphill, on your left are *To Tavernaki tis Pareas*, *O Kanadhos*, *Antonia* and *To Koutoukaki*, all with their own loyal clientele and perfectly adequate. For coffee or a drink with *mezédhes* you might try the **Imaret** itself, certainly the most atmospheric premises in the province. The courtyard floor is a café-bar; somewhat limited-menu meals are served on the upper gallery overlooking whitewashed arcades and the harbour, with stunning views at sunset.

Ferry services

Car ferries sail from Kavála to **Thássos** almost hourly from 6am to 9pm in season; virtually all run to the port of Skála Prínou (1hr 15min). At the time of research the regular seasonal **hydrofoil** service to and from the island (30min each way) seemed to be in jeopardy, so you'll need to check locally for details. From September to April, when services drop to just a handful of boats daily, you may be better off taking the bus or driving to Keramotí, 46km southeast, and then using the car ferry from there to Thássos. **KERAMOTÍ** itself provides an alternative, though unexciting, stopover. It's a small, rather drab village amidst corn fields in the Néstos delta, 9km beyond the airport turn-off, with a decent beach backed by pines, a few rooms and a half-dozen hotels which you shouldn't have to patronize, as the last ferry leaves for Thássos at 9.30pm. If you do miss it (or get a late boat from Thássos) try the *Golden Sands* (☎05910/51 509;❷), tucked away in a quieter part of town.

Other ferry services from Kavála are fairly predictable as to basic weekly pattern, though specific days vary. From late July until late August, there are in theory five weekly departures to **Samothráki** (typically Mon–Wed, Fri & Sat; 4hr), though these don't run every year; on the other hand, in some years they've started as early as Easter, so you'll need to check. Far more certain are the four boats a week to **Límnos** (Tues, Thurs, Sat & Sun; 5hr), dwindling to two off-season. For much of the year two or three of these continue to various islands and mainland ports, among them Áyios Efstrátios, Lésvos, Híos and Rafina/Pireás. Details for Límnos and beyond are available from Nikos Miliadhes, behind Platía Karaolí Dhimitríou (☎0510/226 147 or 223 421), while the Samothráki services can be checked at the agency Arsinoi-Saos (☎0510/835 671), a little further along the harbour front.

Philippi

As you might expect, **PHILIPPI** (*Filippoi* on some maps and signs) was named after Philip II of Macedon, who wrested the town from the Thracians in 356 BC for the sake of nearby gold mines on Mount Pangéo. However, it owed its later importance and prosperity to the Roman construction of the Via Egnatia, which ran from the Adriatic to Byzantium. With Kavála/Neápolis as its port, Philippi was essentially the easternmost town of Roman-occupied Europe.

Here also, as at Actium, the fate of the Roman empire was decided on Greek soil, at the **Battle of Philippi** in 42 BC. After assassinating Julius Caesar, Brutus and Cassius had fled east of the Adriatic and, against their better judgement, were forced into confrontation on the Philippi plains with the pursuing armies of Antony and Octavian. The "honourable conspirators", who could have successfully exhausted the enemy by avoiding action, were decimated by Octavian in two successive battles, and, as defeat became imminent, first Cassius, then Brutus killed himself – the latter running on his comrade's sword with the purported Shakespearian sentiment, "Caesar now be still, I killed thee not with half so good a will."

Saint Paul landed at Kavála and visited Philippi in 49 AD and so began his mission in Europe. Despite being cast into prison he retained a special affection for the Philippians, his first converts, and the congregation that he established was one of the earliest to flourish in Greece. It has furnished the principal remains of the site: several impressive, although ruined, basilican churches.

Philippi is easily reached from Kavála, just 14km distant; buses (which continue to the dull market town of Dhráma) leave every half-hour, and drop you by the road that now splits the site.

The site

Of the churches at the site (Tues–Sun 8.30am–6pm; €2.40) the most conspicuous is the **Direkler** (Turkish for "columns" or "piers"), to the south of the modern road which here follows the line of the Via Egnatia. Also known as Basilica B, this was an unsuccessful attempt by its sixth-century architect to improve the basilica design by adding a dome. In this instance the entire east wall collapsed under the weight, leaving only the narthex convertible for worship during the tenth century. The central arch of its west wall and a few pillars of reused antique drums stand amid remains of the Roman **forum**. A line of second-century porticoes spreads outwards in front of the church, and on their east side are the foundations of a colonnaded octagonal church which was approached from the Via Egnatia by a great gate. Behind the Direkler and, perversely, the most interesting and best-preserved building of the site, is a huge monumental **public latrine** with nearly fifty of its original marble seats still intact.

Across the road on the northern side, stone steps climb up to a terrace, passing on the right a Roman crypt, reputed to have been the **prison of Saint Paul** and appropriately frescoed. The terrace flattens out onto a huge paved atrium that extends to the foundations of another extremely large basilica, the so-called Basilica A. Continuing in the same direction around the base of a hill you emerge above a **theatre** cut into its side. Though dating from the original town it was heavily remodelled as an amphitheatre by the Romans – the bas-reliefs of Nemesis, Mars and Victory (on the left of the stage) all belong to this period. It is now used for performances during the annual summer Philippi–Thássos Festival (see p.531). The **museum**, above the road at the far end of the site, is rather dreary.

The best general impression of the site – which is extensive despite a lack of obviously notable buildings – and of the battlefield behind it can be gained from the **acropolis**, a steep climb along a path from the museum. Its own remains are predominantly medieval.

Thrace (Thráki)

Separated from Macedonia to the west by the Néstos River and from (Turkish) Eastern Thrace by the Évros River and its delta, **Western Thrace** is the Greek state's most recent acquisition. The area was under effective Greek control from 1920. The Treaty of Lausanne (1923) confirmed Greek sovereignty and also sanctioned the forced evacuation of 390,000 Muslims, principally from Macedonia and Epirus, in exchange for more than a million ethnic Greeks from Eastern Thrace and Asia Minor (both now part of the modern Turkish state). But the Muslims of Western Thrace, in return for a continued Greek presence in and around Constantinople, were exempt from the exchanges and continue to live in the region.

Thrace was originally inhabited by a people with their own, non-Hellenic, language and religion. From the seventh century BC onwards it was colonized by Greeks, and after Alexander's time the area took on a strategic significance as the land route between Greece and Byzantium. It was later controlled by the Roman and Byzantine empires, and after 1361 by the Ottoman Turks.

Nowadays, out of a total population of 360,000, there are around 120,000 Muslims, made up (approximately) of 60,000 **Turkish-speakers**, 40,000 **Pomaks** and 20,000 **gypsies**. These figures are disputed by Turkish Muslims who put their numbers alone at something between 100,000 and 120,000. The Greek government lumps all three groups together as "a Muslim minority" principally of Turkish descent, and provides all of them with Turkish-language education (despite the fact that the Pomaks speak a language very similar to Bulgarian). Greek authorities also point to the hundreds of functioning mosques, the Turkish-language newspapers and a Turkish-language radio station in Komotiní as evidence of their goodwill. However, since 1968 only graduates from a special Academy in Thessaloníki have been allowed to teach in the Turkish-language schools here – thus (deliberately) isolating Thracian Turks from mainstream Turkish culture – and on various occasions the Greek authorities have interfered with Muslim religious appointments. In 1991, the Greeks appointed a new Muslim leader in Xánthi, without consulting the Muslim community.

There is no doubt in the minds of local Turks and Pomaks that in secular matters, too, they are the victims of **discrimination**. Muslim villages, they say, receive less help from the state than Greek villages; until the late 1990s a few were still without electricity, and many lacked proper roads. Muslim schools are underfunded; Muslims are unable to join the police force; and it is extremely difficult for them to buy property or get bank loans – although most ethnic Turks do also acknowledge that they are still materially better off than their counterparts in Turkey.

There have been occasional explosions of intercommunal violence, and matters have only worsened since the reincorporation, in neighbouring Bulgaria, of the Turkish minority into the commercial and political life of that country, with the Greeks becoming increasingly aware of the potential for unrest. In 1991 the Greek government put forward a plan to demilitarize the whole of Thrace, including Bulgarian and Turkish sectors. The plan received a positive reply from the Bulgarian government, but, ominously, Turkey reserved its position, and Greece remains fearful of Turkish agitation in Western Thrace that might lead to a Cyprus-type military operation where Turkish forces "come to the assistance" of an "oppressed" minority. The Turkish consulate at Komotiní has long been considered a conduit for fifth-column activities, with incumbent consuls regularly expelled by Greece for "activities incompatible with diplomatic status". These activities constitute not espionage, but alleged attempts to foment local disturbances. Occasionally the Greek secret service has been accused of playing rougher, as in the case of the outspoken former MP for Thrace, Ahmet Sadiq, who was killed in an allegedly "manufactured" road accident in 1995.

As an outsider you will probably not notice the intercommunal tensions, but you will not be able to avoid the many military installations in the border zones of the province. However, there are mixed villages where Muslims and Greeks appear to coexist quite amicably, and Thracians, both Muslim and Orthodox, have a deserved reputation for hospitality.

Compared to the rest of the mainland, there is little tangible to see, and most travellers take a bus straight through to **Alexandhroúpoli**, for the ferry to Samothráki, or head straight on to **Istanbul**. But Thrace's many rulers left some mark on the area, and there are a few well-preserved monuments, most significantly the remains of the coastal cities of Abdera, south of **Xánthi**, Maroneia, southeast of **Komotiní**, the regional capital, and Mesembria, west of Alexandhroúpoli – Greek colonies in the seventh century BC that were abandoned in Byzantine times when the inhabitants moved inland to escape pirate raids. Otherwise, it is the landscape itself that holds most appeal, with the train line forging a circuitous but scenic route below the foothills of the Rodhópi mountains: the best stretch is the **Néstos valley** between Paranésti and Xánthi. Unfortunately, many of the towns and villages have lost their charm, owing to unattractive twentieth-century architecture, but if you make time to explore the backstreets or venture up to tiny, isolated villages in the Rodhópi mountains, you'll find an atmosphere quite unlike any other part of Greece.

Xánthi and around

Coming from Kavála, after the turning to the airport and shortly after the turning to Keramotí you cross the Néstos River, which with the **Rodhópi mountains** forms the border of Greek Thrace. The Greek/Turkish, Christian/Muslim demographics are almost immediately apparent in the villages: the Turkish settlements, long established, with their tiled, whitewashed houses and pencil-thin minarets; the Greek ones, often adjacent, built in drab modern style for the refugees of the 1920s.

Xánthi

XÁNTHI (*Iskeçe* to the Turks), the first town of any size, is perhaps the most interesting point to break a journey. There is a busy market area, good food, and – up the hill to the north of the main café-lined square – a very attractive old quarter. The town is also home to the University of Thrace, which lends a lively air to the place, particularly in the area between the bazaar and the campus, where bars, cinemas and bistros are busy in term time. Try if you can to visit on Saturday, the day of Xánthi's **street fair** – a huge affair, attended equally by Greeks, Pomaks and Turks, held in an open space near the fire station on the eastern side of the town.

The narrow, cobbled streets of the **old town** are home to a number of very fine mansions – some restored, some derelict – with highly coloured exteriors, bay windows and wrought-iron balconies; most date from the mid-nineteenth century when Xánthi's tobacco merchants made their fortunes. One of them has been turned into a **folk museum** (closed for repairs at the time of research), at Odhós Antíka 7, at the bottom of the grade up into the right-bank quarter of the old town. Originally built for two tobacco magnate brothers, its home is a beautiful semi-detached pair of mansions worth seeing for their exterior alone; some years back the interior was lovingly restored with painted wooden panels and decorated plaster and floral designs on the walls and ceilings. The displays include Thracian clothes and jewellery, a postcard collection and cakes of tobacco.

Further up, the roads become increasingly narrow and steep, and the Turkish presence (about fifteen percent of the total urban population) is more noticeable: most of the women have their heads covered, and the more religious ones wear full-length cloaks. Churches and mosques hide behind whitewashed houses with tiled roofs, and orange-brown tobacco leaves are strung along drying frames. Numerous houses, no matter how modest, sport a dish for tuning into Turkish satellite television.

To the north, overlooking the town from on high, is the **Panayía convent**, while beyond stands the **Áyios Nikólaos monastery**, from where there are fine views north into the forested Rodhópi mountains. To reach them by car from the river bridge, follow road signs for "Monasteries"; on foot, walk fifteen minutes up through the left-bank neighbourhood of Samakóv.

Practicalities

The **train station** lies just off the Kavála road, 2km south of the centre (taxis await arrivals and are green with white tops; approximately €2), while buses draw in at the new **KTEL**, over 1km north of the centre. The main south–north thoroughfare is 28-Oktovríou, lined with fast-food outlets and sundry shops. One end is marked by the Kendrikí Platía, recognizable by its prominent, if unsightly clocktower. Xánthi's pay-and-display **parking** scheme is pretty comprehensive, with fees payable in the centre from 8.30am to 9pm, Monday to Saturday. The **post office**, signposted, and Olympic Airways are both very close to the platía, on its uphill side. Several **banks** with cash dispensers line the square.

Downtown **hotel** choices are limited and rather overpriced, and disappointingly there's no official accommodation in the atmospheric old town. Nearest the centre is the recently refurbished *Democritus*, 28-Oktovríou 41 (T05410/25 111, F25 537; ❹), where you should insist on a room away from the street. More or less around the corner at Mihaïl Karaolí 40, the 1996-vintage *Orfeas* (T05410/20 121, F20 998; ❹) has spacious, bright, en-suite rooms. Smartest and quietest, however, is the business-oriented but good-value *Xanthippion*, 28-Oktovríou 212 (T05410/77 061, F77 076; ❹), a short walk from the centre and not far from the KTEL.

Choices in **restaurants** are somewhat better. Tucked away just to the north of the Kendrikí Platía, at Yeoryíou Stavroú 18, is the eminently reasonable *Taverna Midhos* (more of an ouzerí), with a delightful summer garden out the back, efficient service and a mix of mezédhes and *mayireftá*. At the lower reaches of cobbled Paleológou and Odhós P. Christídhi, you'll find a gaggle of taverna-cum-ouzerís, of which the best is arguably *Myrovolos* – all with identical prices and similarly predictable menus, but featuring wonderful barrel retsina. For a good-value summertime grilled supper from a limited menu but in a superb setting, look no further than the *Nissaki* on the banks of the Podhonífi River dividing the town. To find it, follow Odhós Pindhárou upstream from behind the abandoned *Xenia* hotel, to this street's end at the base of the old town.

Xánthi's buzzing **nightlife** is focused on Odhós Vasilíssis Sofías, which forks off Paleológou at the little park sporting a bust of war hero Antíkas, and on the platía itself. Doyen of the various bars on the former is the enormous *Kyverneio*, boasting a huge terrace, while a whole cluster of see-and-be-seen **café-bars** on the platía vie for your custom. For a coffee and cake the "traditional" *zaharoplastío Vyzándio*, also on the platía, may look fake, but the pastries, chocolates and ice cream are divine and the coffee's the best in town. There's a quality **cinema**, Olympia, at the bottom of the old town behind the municipal library, or in summer premises next to the town hall.

North of Xánthi

Much of the countryside north of Xánthi, towards the Bulgarian border, is a military "controlled area", dotted with signs denoting the fact. Greeks will tell you that access is restricted because of the sensitivity of the frontier with Bulgaria; ethnic Pomaks claim the army uses the border as an excuse to keep tabs on them, and until the 1990s foreigners needed a special pass to visit the area.

If you do venture up into the western Rodhópi range here, the main reward is some magnificent scenery; there's not much arable land amidst the wild, pine-forested hills, and what there is – down in the river valleys – is devoted entirely to tobacco, hand-tilled by the blonde, fair-haired Pomaks, who, claims of Greek nationalists to the contrary, are about as close as you'll find to the original ancestral Thracians. They were Bogomil-Christian Slavs, who were forcibly converted to Islam in the sixteenth century and still speak a dialect of Bulgarian with generous admixtures of Greek and Turkish.

There is a number of Muslim villages though, with a modest increase in material prosperity since the 1980s, they have mostly lost their traditional architecture to concrete multistorey apartments. **SMÍNTHI**, a large and dispersed Pomak settlement with a mosque and tall minaret, has two *psistariés* on the through road, the only thing remotely resembling tourist facilities in the region. **EHÍNOS**, encroached on by oak and beech woods, no longer has much appeal, but remains the main market town for the region. **ORÉO**, 6km up a side road northwest of Smínthi, is dramatically set on a steep hillside with cloud-covered peaks behind and terraces falling away to the riverbed. The ground floors of the houses are used for corralling animals or storing farm produce, but it has no coffeehouse, at least not for visitors. Because of the hard time they've had, Pomaks tend to keep themselves to themselves.

South of Xánthi

South of Xánthi, the coastal plain, bright with cotton, tobacco and cereals, stretches to the sea. Heading towards modern Ávdhira, you'll pass through **YENISSÉA** (Yeniçe), an unspectacular farming village with one of the oldest **mosques** in Thrace, dating from the sixteenth century. Now derelict, it's a low whitewashed building with a tiled roof, crumbled wooden portico and truncated minaret.

Regular buses serve the village of **ÁVDHIRA**, 10km further on, and, in summer, run on to the **beach** of Paralía Avdhíron, 7km beyond, passing through the site of **ancient Abdera** (daily 8am–2pm; free), founded in the seventh century BC by Clazomenians from Asia Minor. The walls of the ancient acropolis are visible on a low headland above the sea, and there are fragmentary traces of Roman baths, a theatre and an ancient acropolis. The remains are unspectacular, and the setting not particularly attractive, but the **archeological museum** (daily 11am–2pm; free), located in the village and inaugurated in 2000, puts it all into context with a stunning and beautifully presented exhibition, accompanied by extensive English texts. A rich collection of ceramics, coins, oil-lamps, mosaics and jewellery is dominated by a moving section devoted to burial customs, including some spectacular reconstructions of graves dating from the seventh to fifth centuries BC.

For the most part, the coast east from here is flat and dull. At the southern end of brackish Lake Vistonídha stands **PÓRTO LÁGOS**, a semi-derelict harbour partly redeemed by the nearby monastery of **Áyios Nikólaos** (open reasonable hours except 1–5pm) built on two islets in the lagoon, though the structure itself is modern and, on closer inspection, undistinguished. The surrounding marshland, a major site for birdlife, is more accessible, though less important, than the Évros delta (see p.542); a few observation towers have been provided along the reedy shoreline.

Nearby, 7km southeast and 32km from Xánthi, the small resort of **FANÁRI** has a long, sandy beach – one of the better ones in Thrace – backed by two co-managed **places to stay**: the all-white, modern *Fanari Hotel* (☎05350/31 300, ℉31 388, ✉fanarih@otenet.gr; ❸), set well back from the beach at the eastern edge of the village, and the smaller, potentially noisier *Villa Theodora* (☎ & ℉ 05350/31 242; ❸), out on the village promontory by the fishing port. Given the cost and unattractiveness of accommodation in both Xánthi and Komotiní, this could be an option worth considering, and you could visit each town on daytrips. The *Fanari* has a restaurant and there are other fish **tavernas**. An EOT campsite, the *Fanari* (☎05350/31 270; May–Oct), lies 500m east of the *Fanari Hotel*, just before the public beach. Fanári village is a popular gathering point in the evenings and at weekends, and its beach gets busy in the high summer, but there are less crowded spots on the coast a few kilometres east.

Komotiní and around

The fertile central plains of Thrace, with their large ethnic Turkish population, are one of the least visited areas of the country, but not without some appeal. Though outwardly unattractive, the market town of **Komotiní** rewards a closer look, with its two well-presented museums, one devoted to folk life and history, the other to archeological finds fom the region. The contents of the latter are complemented by the delightful ancient site of **Maroneia**, on the coast, and newly excavated **Mesembria**, further east.

Komotiní

Lying 48km east of Xánthi along the direct road skirting the Rodhópi foothills, **KOMOTINÍ** is larger and markedly more Turkish than Xánthi. On first impression, it's a rather charmless place, with ranks of apartment buildings and gridded suburbs to the south and west, their noisy streets clogged with traffic. It does, however, have a couple of worthwhile museums, a lively bazaar and some of the region's best food. It also has more than a dozen functioning mosques. Social mixing between the different ethnic groups, however – roughly at parity population-wise – is almost nonexistent, although Orthodox and Muslims live in the same neighbourhoods. Recently, the town has become even more polyglot, with an influx of Greek, Armenian and Georgian

Christians from the Caucasus, and the authorities have bent over backwards to integrate them.

During the thirteenth century, the city gained importance owing to its position on the Via Egnatia. When the Ottomans took the city in 1361, they changed its name to Gümülçine, and it's still known as this to its ethnic Turks. In 1912, at the outbreak of the First Balkan War, Komotiní fell to the Bulgarians; it was liberated by Greek forces in the following year, only to be taken once more by the Bulgarians during World War I. It was finally and definitively joined to Greece on May 14, 1920.

The old **bazaar**, to the north of Platía Irínis, is a little bit of Istanbul, lodged between fine mosques and an elegant Ottoman-era **clocktower**. Alongside shady cafés tiny shops sell everything from dried apricots to iron buckets, and it's especially busy on Tuesdays when the villagers from the surrounding area come into town to sell their wares. Behind this old quarter, you can see the remains of Komotiní's **Byzantine walls**, in one corner of which once stood a fine synagogue, demolished after its dome collapsed in the late 1980s.

Traditionally a city with both Greek and Turkish inhabitants, Komotiní began to be dominated by Greek influence in the waning years of the Ottoman empire, when rich Greeks funded schools in the city to develop Greek culture and ideals. Some of these educational foundations still survive: one, a handsome half-timbered building at AyíouYeoryíou 13, has become the **Museum of Folk Life and History** (daily except Sun 10am–1pm; free), displaying examples of Thracian embroidery, traditional Thracian dress, silverware, copperware and a collection of religious seals, but avoiding any mention of the ethnic Turkish community. The **Archeological Museum** at Simeonídhi 4 (daily 9am–6pm; free) is also worth a visit, giving a lucid overview of Thracian history, by means of plans and finds from local sites, from its beginnings up to the Byzantine era.

Practicalities

The **train station** is over 1km to the southwest of the centre, but **taxis** (red or maroon, mostly with white tops) await arrivals. The **KTEL** (also with a taxi rank) is some way to the south of central Platía Irínis, via Énou. Should you need to stay, be aware that the **hotel** situation is nearly as unpromising as Xánthi's. Basic in a quaint way, and very friendly, is the *Hellas* at Dhimokrítou 31 (T05310/22 055; ❷), with shared showers and toilets, at a noisy intersection in the west of town. The more central, air-conditioned, all en-suite *Olympos*, at Orféos 37 (T05310/37 690; ❹), tends to fill with business types. Marginally quieter, but overpriced, is the *Astoria*, a Neoclassical inn restoration at Platía Irínis 28 (T05310/35 054; ❻); calmer still, but a long way out, beyond the war memorial, at the east end of Platía Irínis, is the *Anatolia*, Anhiálou 53 (T05310/36 242; ❺).

The best **eating** is to be found at *Inopion* at Platía Irínis 67, in the form of conventional, impeccably prepared dishes served with considerable style. Tucked away in the narrowest lanes of the bazaar just north of Orféos, two decent ouzerís, *Apolafsis* and *Yiaxis* (the better of the two) put out tables under arbours; there's also a good *psistariá* opposite the clocktower, behind the main mosque, run by ethnic Turk Mumin Mehmet Muhsin.

Marónia and Mesimvría

Just off the E90 motorway, southeast of Komotiní, lie two archeological sites that make a good break in the journey to Alexandhroúpoli, if nothing else. Clearly indicated from the Sápes turn-off is **ancient Maroneia**, a set of ancient and Byzantine ruins scattered among seaside olive-groves. It's just below the modern village of **MARÓNIA**, served by six daily buses from Komotiní via the old road. Maróina has held onto a few surviving old Thracian mansions with balconies, and you can find some **rooms** (☎05330/41 158; ●) offered through a women's co-operative; they will also supply daily meals during July and August, but only at weekends, if at all otherwise.

To get to the ruins, attractively situated at the foot of Mount Ísmaros, follow the signs to Maróina's harbour of **Áyios Harálambos**, taking care not to enter the airforce camp nearby. The founder of the city is reckoned to be Maron, the son of the god of wine, Dionysos (Ísmaros is known locally as the Mountain of Dionysos), and the city became one of the most powerful in all of ancient Thrace. Mostly unexcavated, the remains can be explored at will but are badly signposted. Even so, you should be able to track down traces of a theatre, a sanctuary of Dionysos and various buildings including a house with a well-preserved mosaic floor. The land walls of the city are preserved to a height of two metres, together with a Roman tower above the harbour. Over time, the sea has done its own excavation, eroding the crumbling cliffs, revealing shards of pottery and ancient walls.

The port area, below the edge of the archeological site and 4km south of the modern village, was (along with the road down) "improved" during the 1990s in anticipation of a tourism boom that never happened; it's not a very enticing place, baking in the heat of the surrounding red cliffs, with no usable beach and two overpriced, overstretched tavernas. By contrast, **Platanítis**, 4km west of Maróina by another paved but unsigned road (just look for signs to various hotels), has a small but adequate gravel-and-sand beach – essentially a gap in the red cliffs – and a good, reasonably priced fish taverna, *O Yerasimos*.

A more worthwhile site, **ancient Mesembria**, or **MESIMVRÍA** in modern Greek (Mon 7am–2.30pm, Tues–Fri 7am–4pm, Sat & Sun 9.30am–4pm; free) is clearly signposted from the motorway and is reached via the nondescript village of Dhíkela. Thanks to its unspoiled seaside location, fruitful recent excavations and a well-thought-out display, it easily qualifies as the most appealing of the three ancient sites on the Thracian coastline. You can stay nearby at the smart, seaview **hotel** *Klio* (☎05510/71 311, ☎71 411; ●), with a decent restaurant at Ayía Paraskeví, near Mákri, a fishing village 11km west of Alexandhroúpoli along the old road.

Alexandhroúpoli

Some 120km southeast of Xánthi, the modern city of **ALEXANDHROÚPOLI** (Dedeağaç to the Turks), designed by Russian military architects during the Russo-Turkish war of 1878, does not, on first acquaintance, have much to recommend it: a border town and military garrison, with overland travellers in transit and Greek holiday-makers competing in summer for limited space in the few hotels and the campsite.

The town became Greek in 1920, when it was renamed Alexandhroúpoli after a visit from Greece's King Alexander. There are no obvious sights and the heavy military presence can be oppressive. The Turkish quarter, literally on the wrong side of the tracks, may or may not whet the appetite for the unadulterated article across the border. Otherwise it's the lively seafront that best characterizes the town; dominated by a seventeen-metre-tall **lighthouse** built in 1880 (and adopted as the town's symbol), it comes alive at dusk when the locals begin their evening *vólta*. In summer, café tables spill out onto the road and

ACCOMMODATION
Erika	3
Lido	2
Majestic	5
Metropolis	4
Okeanis	1

RESTAURANTS
Psarotaverna Anesti	B
Café del Mar	E
Daily	D
To Diethnés	F
Naftikos Omilos	C
To Nissiotiko	A

ALEXANDHROÚPOLI

Áyios Nikólaos

Ecclesiastical Museum

Bus Station

Kykon Travel

Town Hall

Theatre

Main Post Office

Samothráki Ferries

Train Station

Port Police

Ferry Terminal

Hydrofoil Berth

Olympic Airways (250m)

Airport (7km), Dhidhymóthio & Kipi

Samothráki

0   300 m

around the lighthouse; makeshift stalls on the pavements sell pirate cassettes, pumpkin seeds and grilled sweetcorn.

Practicalities

Arriving by **train**, you'll be deposited conveniently next to the port; the **KTEL** is at Venizélou 36, several blocks inland. **Drivers** will find it prudent to enter town from the west along coastal Megálou Alexándhrou, signposted for the ferries and restaurants, since the prevailing craze for pedestrianization, one-way systems and fee parking effectively block movement between Dhimokratías – local name for the Via Egnatia – and the sea. There is a rudimentary, seasonal **tourist office** in the town hall building at the corner of Dhimokratías and Mitropolítou Kavíri.

For the island of **Samothráki** (see p.889), whose dramatic silhouette looms 50km off the coast, there are at least four **ferries** weekly year-round and, in July and August, at least two a day. Tickets can be bought from the Vatissis agency at Kýprou 5 (☎05510/26 721 or 23 512). Drivers should be aware that this is a somewhat expensive monopoly sailing: €33 for a small car on the one-way, two-hour thirty-minute journey, a price that would normally get you several hours of travel. **Hydrofoil** departures to Samothráki (Easter to late autumn) and occasionally to destinations beyond (high summer only) are handled by Arsinoi. Occasional NEL sailings for north Aegean islands, as well as the once-weekly G&A ferry to Rhodes and several intervening islands (seasonal departures only), are represented by Kykon Tours at Venizélou 68 (☎05510/25 455).

The closest **hotel** to the train station is the *Majestic*, Platía Eleftherías 7 (☎05510/26 444; ●), a decent, old-fashioned, non-en-suite cheapie; second nearest is the reliable, no-frills *Erika* at Karaóli Dhimitríou 110 (☎05510/34 115; ●), with impeccably clean en-suite rooms; a bit farther away is the somewhat overpriced *Metropolis*, Athanasíou Dhiákou 11 (☎05510/26 443; ❹), where rooms are spotless if basic. Better value than all three is the bright and cheerful *Lido* at Paleológou 15 (☎05510/28 808; ❷), with its large en-suite rooms. More luxury means either the slick *Okeanis* at Paleológou 20 (☎05510/28 830; ❹), behind the KTEL, or best of all the tastefully renovated *Ira/Hera* at Dhimokratías 179 (☎05510/23 941–3; ✉herahtl@hotmail.com; ❺), where ultrasmart rooms are extremely good value.

For **restaurants**, check out the row of good tavernas with terraces, near the train station – at a pinch the best is *To Diethnés* (or *Kyras Dimitras*), where a wide range of vegetable dishes accompany fried fish. Two commendable addresses are *To Nissiotiko* at Bouboulínas 2 and *Psarotaverna Anesti* at Athanassíou Dhiákou 5; the former, with its picturesque decor, serves a delicious dill-flavoured seafood risotto (*piláfi thalássino*). Good fish cuisine and an attractive location make the *Naftikos Omilos*, or *Marine Club*, next to the ferry terminal, also worth heading for.

The Évros Valley and northeastern Thrace

The **Évros Valley**, extending northeast of Alexandhroúpoli, is a prosperous but dull agricultural area. Most towns are ugly, modern concrete affairs full of bored soldiers, with little to delay you; others, such as **Souflí** and **Dhidhymótiho**, retain some character and medieval monuments, and the main route through the valley as far as **Orestiádha** is well served by public transport, while the main road is being upgraded and bypasses are being built. The standout here by some way is the **Dhadhiá Forest** and wildlife reserve, also reachable by bus; you'll need your own transport to head east from Alexandhroúpoli to the **Évros delta**, one of Europe's most important wetland areas for birds – and one of Greece's most sensitive military areas.

The Évros delta

To the southeast, the **Évros delta** is home to more than 250 different species of birds, including sea eagles, pygmy cormorants and the lesser white-fronted goose. The way to get there (if you have a car) is to leave Alexandhroúpoli on the main road (E90/E85) towards Turkey and Bulgaria. Some 10km after the airport, you'll reach the turn-off to **Loutrá Traianópolis**, the site of an ancient Roman spa and its modern continuation Loutrós. Either of the two following hotels in the vicinity would make a good base for exploring the delta: the *Athina* (☎05510/61 208; ❷) and the *Plotini* (☎05510/61 106; ❷). The delta is best approached by turning right off the main road, opposite the side road to the hotels; the lane is tarmacked only as far as the level-crossing but remains good thereafter. The delta is crisscrossed with tracks along the dykes used by farmers taking advantage of the plentiful water supply for growing sweetcorn and cotton. The south is the most inspiring part, well away from the army installations to the north; as you go further into the wetlands, the landscape becomes utterly desolate, with decrepit clusters of fishing huts among the sandbars and inlets. At the mouth of the delta sprawls a huge saltwater lake called **Límni Dhrakónda**. Obviously what you see depends on the time of year, but even if birdlife is a bit thin on the ground, the atmosphere of the place is worth experiencing.

Féres: Panayía Kosmosótira

Northeast into the valley proper, 28km from Alexandhroúpoli, the otherwise unremarkable town of **FÉRES**, draped over several hills and ravines, offers the imposing twelfth-century Byzantine church of **Panayía Kosmosótira**. Though rather vaguely signposted, it's recognizable from afar by its broad, lead-sheathed dome and commanding hilltop position. Founded by a member of the Komnenos dynasty, it was originally part of a fortified monastery, of which only two ruined towers on the south remain. The church's exterior seems a bit unpromising, with the original masonry covered by many layers of rendering, and the frescoes inside have been obliterated except for some saints at the transept ends. Mostly what impresses are the huge capitals of the paired pier-columns, and the lofty airiness of the twelve-windowed cupola, surrounded by four subsidiary domes – a design rare in Greece outside of Thessaloníki. If you have to change buses en route to the border post at Kípi, as sometimes happens, and have some time to wait, the church is well worth seeking out; it's just a few paces east of the main commercial street.

The Dhadhiá Forest

To the north, the next attraction is the **Dhadhiá Forest Reserve**, consisting of 35,200 hectares of protected oak and pine forest and covering a succession of volcanic ridges. The diversity of landscape and vegetation and the proximity of important migration routes make for an extremely diverse flora and fauna, but raptors are the star attraction, and main impetus for this WWF project. The reserve is reached by a clearly marked road off to the left 1km after passing the second right-hand turn-off to Likófi (Likófos). After a drive of 7km through the rolling, forested hills, you reach the reserve complex (March–Nov daily 9am–7pm; Dec–Feb Mon–Thurs 10am–4pm, Fri–Sun 9am–6pm), with its information centre and exhibition about the region's wildlife.

All cars – except for a special tour van which makes sorties several times daily (€2.20) – are banned from core areas totalling 7200 hectares, and foot access is restricted to two marked trails: a two-hour route up to the reserve's highest point, 520-metre **Gíbrena** with its ruined Byzantine castle, and another ninety-minute loop-route to an observation hide overlooking **Mavrórema** canyon. The region is one of two remaining European homes of the majestic **black vulture** (*Aegypius monachus*), the other being the Extremadura region of Spain. Their numbers have increased from near extinction when protection began in 1980 to some one hundred individuals, and they and griffon vultures (*Gyps fulvus*) make up the bulk of sightings from this post. In all, 36 of Europe's 38 species of diurnal birds of prey, including eagles, falcons, hawks and buzzards, can be sighted at least part of the year.

It's a good idea to stay the night, as the best raptor viewing is in the early morning or evening in summer (but virtually all day Oct–March). Next to the visitors' centre is the best accommodation for miles around, a comfortable "**ecotourism hostel**" run by Dhadhiá village (☎05540/32 263; ❸), where the en-suite rooms have been given bird names instead of numbers (keys from the café across the car park, until 11pm). The café supplies breakfast, drinks and cold meals, but for hot **meals** you'll have to retire to the village where you can try the inexpensive *Psistaria Pelargos* on the platía, plus there's an active nightlife at a handful of **bars**.

Souflí

The nearest town to Dhadhiá, 7km north of the side-turning and set among lush mulberry-groves, is **SOUFLÍ**, renowned for a now all-but-vanished silk industry. The town's history as Greece's silk centre in Byzantine and Ottoman times and a fascinating explanation of the whole silk-making process are documented (with English text) in a **folk/silk museum** (daily except Tues: Easter to mid-Oct 10am–2pm & 5–7pm; rest of year 10am–4pm; €1.20), a little way uphill and west of the main through road. It's lodged in a fine old yellow mansion, one of a number of surviving vernacular houses, including semi-ruined *bitziklíkia* (cocoon-houses), which lend Souflí some distinction. Accommodation is limited to just two **hotels**, both on the noisy main highway: the basic, non-en-suite *Egnatia* (⊕05540/24 124; ❷) at no. 225, or the overpriced *Orfeas/Orpheus* (⊕05540/22 922; ❹), at no. 172. **Eating** and **drinking** options aren't great either, consisting mostly of pizzerias, *souvladzídhika* and *barákia*.

North of Souflí

A pleasant scenic alternative to the trunk-road, especially if Bulgaria is your destination, is the labyrinthine, but well-signposted, network of smaller roads that heads inland through isolated villages and beautiful countryside of rolling hills and deciduous woods. It has been a state priority to establish a Greek population in this extremely sensitive and strategic corner of Thrace, hemmed in on three sides by Bulgaria and Turkey, and the many signs forbidding photography of bridges, rivers and dams should be heeded. Military barracks and traffic police are conspicuous throughout the hinterland and along the eastern border with Turkey.

METAXÁDHES, reached from the village of Mándhra, 5km north of Souflí, is one of the most handsome villages in the area, sited on a steep hill. Once fought over by Bulgars and Turks, Metaxádhes used to support a Turkish community, but now its population is exclusively Greek. Beyond Metaxádhes, you descend north into the vast, fertile **Árdhas river plain**. Rich farmland supports a large number of modern villages. One of the most picturesque is hilltop **PENDÁLOFOS**. The nearby **hotel**, *To Thirama* (⊕05560/61 242; ❻ half-board; summer only), is the sole accommodation for miles around and is unusual in that it doubles up as a game reserve. The restaurant, open at weekends only outside high season, specializes in delicious venison, wild boar and hare dishes. Accommodation consists of comfortable rooms with mod cons, and the hotel's lonely but attractive setting is definitely part of the appeal.

Dhidhymótiho and Orestiádha

DHIDHYMÓTIHO, 30km northeast of Souflí, is the last place on the trunk route into Turkey of any interest. The old part of town is still partially enclosed by the remains of double Byzantine fortifications, and some old houses and churches survive, but the area has a feeling of decay despite continuing efforts at restoration. Like Komotiní, the town once had a fine synagogue for its thousand-strong Jewish community, but this was sold and demolished in 1985, after having been ransacked during World War II at the instigation of the Nazis, who had spread about the (false) rumour that treasure was secreted in its walls. Below the fortified hill, on the central platía, stands the most important surviving monument, a fourteenth-century **mosque**, the oldest and second-largest in the Balkans. A great square box of a building with a pyramidal metal roof, its design harks back to Seljuk and other pre-Ottoman prototypes in central Anatolia, and you'll see nothing else like it between here and Divriği or Erzurum in Turkey. Unfortunately, the interior is closed indefinitely for restoration, though you can still admire the ornate west portal.

Staying presents a problem, as neither of the town's two **hotels** is wonderful; you're much better off waiting till you reach Orestiádha. If you do stay, you'll find the cheaper and more central one is the none-too-welcoming *Anessis* (☎05530/24 850; ❸), 250m northwest of the mosque at Vassiléos Alexándhrou 51. Your other choice is the *Plotini* (☎05530/23 400; ❹), a rather gaudy building, 1km south of town across the river, on the west side of the road. For a **meal**, try the *Zythestiatorio Kypselaki* in the central market hall just above the mosque.

The main town beyond Dhidhymótiho and the last before the border post is **ORESTIÁDHA**, a lively but far from attractive post-1923 market centre with restaurants, bars and lots of cake shops around its main square. Its several banks, with cash dispensers, could be specially useful when entering Greece from Bulgaria or Turkey, though you'll get a poor rate exchanging your remaining lev or lira. **Accommodation** is better here than at Dhidhymótiho or Souflí, though fairly expensive. All within walking distance of the main platía are the smart *Alexandros* (☎05520/27 000; ❹) at Vassiléos Constantínou 10, the appealing and popular *Selini* (☎05520/22 636; ❹), at Skra 44, and the comfortable *Elektra* (☎05520/23 540; ❹) at Pandazídhou 50. Pandazídhou also hosts a string of decent **tavernas** and ouzerís, though the best reputation is enjoyed by nearby *O Petinos*, at Lohagoú Dhiamándi 7. The **cafés** (some with internet) in this neighbourhood are surprisingly chic and trendy.

On to Turkey or Bulgaria

Getting to Turkey from Alexandhroúpoli is still somewhat complicated and currently there's only one daily rail link to Bulgaria via **PÝTHIO**. Current times for rail departures should be confirmed locally, as they are in a constant flux. There are two road crossing-points into Turkey along a heavily guarded frontier: **KÍPI,** where the motorway now passes (open 24hr) and **KASTANIÉS** (9am–4pm daily). Some nationalities require a **Turkish visa**; for British passport holders it costs £10 at the border, for US citizens it's $45. Border guards can be very exigent about linking currencies to nationalities – Brits for example, can only pay with sterling – and will often only accept other denominations (even Turkish money) with ruinous surcharges, so come prepared. **Bulgarian visas** are required for all nationals and are expensive; prices fluctuate around the $70 mark (have US currency ready) for a transit pass at the border, somewhat less if you obtain it at a consulate, such as the one in Thessaloníki, beforehand.

By bus to Turkey

The simplest way to travel from northern Greece to Turkey, if you can get a ticket, is to go by **bus** direct to Istanbul. There is currently just one departure daily, run by OSE (tickets from the main train stations), but the problem is that it starts in Thessaloníki and, by the time it reaches the border area, will probably be full. There used to be a few private coaches, but service is currently suspended; ask for current details at travel agents in Xánthi, Komotiní or Alexandhroúpoli, some of which also run excursions to Istanbul (Constantinople).

An alternative is to take a bus from Alexandhroúpoli to the border at Kípi (6 daily). You are not allowed to cross the frontier here on foot, but it is generally no problem to find a driver who'll shuttle you the extra 500m across to the

Turkish post, and perhaps even give you a lift beyond. The nearest town is Ipsala (5km further on), but if possible get as far as Keşan, (another 25km), from where buses to Istanbul are much more frequent.

By train to Turkey

Travelling by **train** to Istanbul should in theory be simpler. However, the only through connection leaves Alexandhroúpoli just after noon, crossing the border at Pýthio two hours later and taking (in theory) nine more hours (including a long halt at the frontier) to reach Istanbul. On the Greek side this service has official express status, but don't be surprised if the train – which originates in Thessaloníki – shows up late.

You could also take a more frequent local train to Pýthio and on to Kastaniés, opposite Turkish **Edirne** (Adhrianoúpoli to the Greeks). You must use a morning departure from Alexandhroúpoli (check times) to reach Kastaniés while the **border post** (see above) is still open. There's no accommodation in Kastaniés, but in theory you are allowed to walk across the border (under army escort). Once on the Turkish side, there's an infrequent bus service to the first Turkish village, Karaağaç, 2km beyond the frontier; it's then only another 4km to the centre of Edirne – an attractive and historic city with some important Ottoman monuments; frequent buses make the three-hour onward trip to Istanbul. An easier, quicker but more expensive alternative is to get a **taxi** from Kastaniés all the way to Edirne (€30 one way, including customs fee). For more information, see the *Rough Guide to Turkey*.

Into Bulgaria

To Bulgaria from Alexandhroúpoli there is just one connecting **train** daily, leaving at about 5am and reaching the Greek border hamlet of Orménio (also a road crossing) some three hours later, where you may have to change trains for the fifteen-minute journey to Svilengrad inside Bulgaria. This turns around less than an hour later for a service back to Alexandhroúpoli. From Svilengrad (which has only expensive accommodation) it's best to plan on moving on the same day towards Plovdiv. For further details, see the *Rough Guide to Bulgaria*.

Travel details

Note: onward services in the states of former Yugoslavia are currently sharply reduced and, with the exception of trains into the FYROM from Thessaloníki, it is impossible to obtain reliable information on schedules, so check locally; in the wake of the recent various conflicts and in the light of continuing instability, these routes are, in any case, inadvisable for independent travellers.

International trains

Alexandhroúpoli–Istanbul (Turkey) Semi-direct "express", arriving Istanbul after at least 9hr, including an hour or longer wait at the border; change at Pýthio (Greece) or Uzunköprü (Turkey).

Alexandhroúpoli–Dhidhymótiho–Orestiádha–Kastaniés (for Edirne) 6 daily, but only earlier departures reach the frontier post before 4pm when it closes; scheduled as 2hr 45min to Kastaniés.

Alexandhroúpoli–Svilengrad (Bulgaria) 1 daily; 3hr.

Thessaloníki–Gevgelija (FYROM) 1 daily; 1hr 30min–2hr.

Thessaloníki–Promahónas/Kulata, Bulgarian frontier 1 daily; 2hr 30min.

Domestic trains

Thessaloníki–Kateríni/Lárissa/Athens 4 express, 5 slower trains daily in each direction (6–7hr 30min for entire journey).
Thessaloníki–Lárissa 3 daily in each direction (2hr 45min), 1 continuing to Vólos (4hr total).
Thessaloníki–Véria/Édhessa/Amýndeo/Flórina 3–4 daily to Flórina (3hr 30min), changing as necessary at Amýndeo; connections between Amýndeo and Kozáni (3hr 30min) 6 times daily; 1 daily only up to Édhessa (2hr).
Thessaloníki–Sérres/Dhráma/Xánthi/Komotiní/Alexandhroúpoli 2 daily expresses, well spaced, plus 3 slower trains (Thessaloníki–Xánthi 4–5hr; Xánthi–Alexandhroúpoli 1hr 30min–2hr).

Buses

Alexandhroúpoli to: Dhadhiá (2 daily; 1hr 20min); Dhidhymótiho (17 daily Mon–Fri, 14 daily Sat–Sun; 2hr); Istanbul (daily OSE bus; 8hr); Kípi (5 daily; 45min); Komotiní (14 daily; 1hr).
Édhessa to: Flórina (4 daily; 2hr); Kastoriá (4 daily; 2hr 30min, change at Amýndeo); Véria (6 Mon–Sat, 2 Sun; 50min).
Flórina to: Préspa basin (2 daily; 1hr).
Kastoriá to: Flórina (4 daily indirect services via Amýndeo; 3hr including layover).
Kateríni to: Dhión (12 daily; 20min); Litóhoro, for Mt Olympus (18 Mon–Sat, 12 Sun; 30min).
Kavála to: Keramotí (12 daily; 1hr); Komotiní (half-hourly 6am–9pm; 2hr); Philippi (half-hourly 6am–8.30pm; 20min); Xánthi (half-hourly 6am–9pm; 1hr); Alexandhroúpoli (5 daily; 3hr).
Komotiní to: Fanári (7 daily Mon–Fri, 6 Sat, 5 Sun; 45min).
Kozáni to: Grevená (8 daily; 1hr); Siátista (4 daily; 30min).
Thessaloníki to: Alexandhroúpoli (5 daily; 6hr); Arnéa (5–7 daily; 2hr); Athens (16 daily; 7hr); Édhessa (hourly; 1hr 30min); Flórina (6 daily; 3hr 30min); Ierissós (5–7 aily; 3hr 30min); Ioánnina (5 daily; 7hr); Istanbul (almost daily with OSE, occasional privately operated; 14hr); Kalambáka (7 daily; 4hr 30min); Kastoriá (5 daily; 4hr); Kavála (hourly 6am–10pm; 2hr 15min–3hr); Litóhoro, for Mt Olympus (7 daily; 1hr 30min); Ouranoúpoli (5–7 daily; 3hr 30min); Pélla (hourly; 1hr); Sárti, via Políyiros (3 daily; 4hr 30min); Sofia (daily with OSE; 7hr 30min); Véria (half-hourly; 1hr 15min); Vólos (4 daily; 4hr); Vourvouroú, via Políyiros (3 daily; 3hr).
Véria to: Édhessa, via Náoussa (6 daily; 1hr 15min); Kozáni (8 daily; 1hr).
Xánthi to: Kavála (half-hourly, 6am–9pm; 1hr); Komotiní (17–18 daily, via coast or inland; 50min); Thessaloníki (6–7 daily; 4hr).

Ferries

Alexandhroúpoli to: Límnos, Lésvos, Híos, Sámos, Kós or Kálymnos, Rhodes (1 weekly); Samothráki (2–3 daily in season, 4 weekly out of season; 2hr 30min).
Kavála to: Lésvos and Híos (2–3 weekly; 12 hr); Límnos (5hr) and Áyios Efstrátios (2–4 weekly; 8hr); Samothráki (2–5 weekly late April to Sept; 5hr); Thássos (Skála Prínou) (4–15 daily, average 8, depending on season; 1hr 15min).
Keramotí to: Thássos (Liménas) (10 daily, year round; 40min).
Thessaloníki to: Iráklion (Crete) via Skiáthos, Tínos, Sýros, Mýkonos, Páros, Náxos and Thíra (2–5 weekly March–Oct); Límnos, Lésvos and Híos (1–2 weekly June–Sept); Sámos, Léros or Kálymnos, Kós, Rhodes (1 weekly May–Oct).

Hydrofoils

Alexandhroúpoli to: Samothráki (1–2 daily April–Nov; 1hr 10min).
Kavála to: Thássos (Liménas) (8–15 daily; 40min); Thássos (west-coast resorts) (1–3 daily).
Thessaloníki to: Skiáthos, Skópelos and Alónissos (June to mid-Sept, at least daily); Skýros and Áyios Ioánnis (Pílio) (2–4 weekly early July to mid-Sept).

Flights

Aegean, Cronus and Olympic all compete on most of these routes, though some destinations listed from Thessaloníki may be via Athens, direct only in high season.
Alexandhroúpoli to: Athens (2 daily; 1hr).
Kastoriá to: Athens (3–4 weekly; 1hr 15min).
Kavála to: Athens (2–3 daily; 1hr).
Kozáni to: Athens (3–4 weekly; 1hr 10min).
Thessaloníki to: Athens (8–10 daily; 50min); Corfu (2–5 weekly; 1hr); Haniá, Crete (1–2 daily; 2hr); Híos (2 weekly; 1hr 50min); Ioánnina (1 daily; 50min); Iráklion, Crete (1–2 daily; 2hr); Lésvos (1 daily; 1–2hr); Límnos (4–7 weekly; 50min); Sámos (4 weekly; 1hr 40min); Thíra (3 weekly summer only; 1hr 30min).

the islands

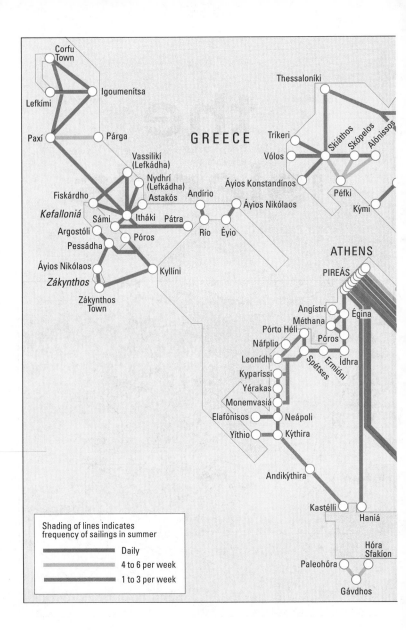

GREECE

Corfu Town
Igoumenítsa
Lefkími
Paxí
Párga

Thessaloníki
Tríkeri
Skíathos
Skópelos
Alónissos
Vólos
 Áyios Konstandínos
Péfki
Kými

Vassilikí (Lefkádha)
Nydhrí (Lefkádha)
Fiskárdho
Andírio
Astakós
Áyios Nikólaos
Kefalloniá
Sámi
Itháki
Pátra
Argostóli
Póros
Río
Éyio
Pessádha
Áyios Nikólaos
Kyllíni
Zákynthos
Zákynthos Town

ATHENS
PIREÁS

Angístri
Égina
Méthana
Pórto Héli
Póros
Náfplio
Ídhra
Leonídhi
Ermióni
Spétses
Kyparíssi
Yérakas
Monemvasiá
Elafónisos
Neápoli
Yíthio
Kýthira

Andikýthira

Kastélli
Haniá

Hóra Sfakíon
Paleohóra
Gávdhos

Shading of lines indicates
frequency of sailings in summer

——— Daily
——— 4 to 6 per week
——— 1 to 3 per week

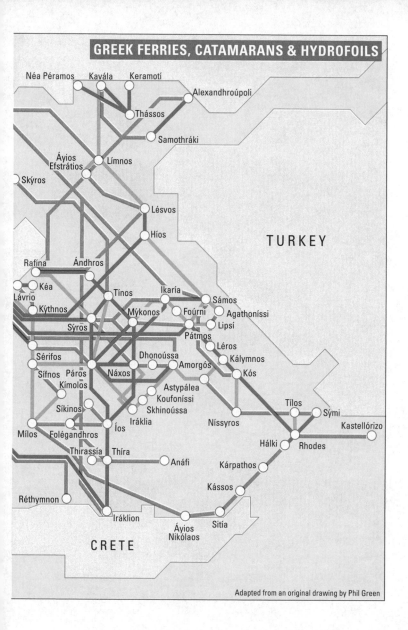

GREEK FERRIES, CATAMARANS & HYDROFOILS

Néa Péramos Kavála Keramotí

Alexandhroúpoli

Thássos

Samothráki

 Áyios Efstrátios Límnos

Skýros

Lésvos

Híos

TURKEY

Rafína Ándhros

Kéa

Lávrio

Kýthnos

Tínos

Ikaría

Sámos

Mýkonos Foúrni Agathoníssi

Sýros Lipsí

Pátmos

Léros

Dhonoússa Kálymnos

Sérifos

Amorgós Kós

Sífnos Páros

Náxos

Kímolos

Astypálea

Koufoníssi

Síkinos Skhinoússa Tílos

Íos Iráklia

Níssyros Sými

Mílos Folégandhros Kastellórizo

Thirassía Thíra Hálki Rhodes

Anáfi Kárpathos

Kássos

Réthymnon

Iráklion Sitía

Áyios Nikólaos

CRETE

Adapted from an original drawing by Phil Green

6

The Argo-Saronic

CHAPTER 6

Highlights

* **Temple of Aphaia, Égina**
  The best preserved Archaic
  temple on any island, set on
  a pretty pine-wooded hill.
  See p.560

* **Paleohóra, Égina** Explore
  some of the now deserted
  town's 365 tiny churches.
  See p.558

* **Póros Town** Climb up the
  clocktower for a view over
  the Argo-Saronic gulf and
  the Peloponnese. See p.564

* **Ídhra Town** A perfect
  horseshoe-shaped harbour
  surrounded by grand eighteenth-century mansions.
  See p.567

* **Spétses** Admire the house
  and beautiful surroundings
  used as the setting for John
  Fowles' *The Magus*. See p.570

6

The Argo-Saronic

T

he rocky, volcanic chain of **Argo-Saronic** islands, most of them barely an
olive's throw from the Argolid, differs to a surprising extent not just from
the mainland but from one another. Less surprising – given their proximity to the mainland – is their massive popularity, with Égina (Aegina) almost
becoming an Athenian suburb at weekends. Ídhra (Hydra), Póros and Spétses
(Spetsai) are not far behind in summer, though their visitors tend to be predominantly cruise- and package-tourists. More than any other group, these islands are
at their best out of season, when populations fall dramatically and the port towns
return to a quieter, more provincial life.

Égina, important in antiquity and more or less continually inhabited since then,
is the most fertile of the group, famous for its pistachio nuts, as well as for one of the
finest ancient temples in Greece. Its main problem – the crowds – can be escaped
by avoiding weekends, or taking the time to explore its satellite isle, **Angístri**.

The three southerly islands, **Spétses**, **Ídhra** and **Póros**, are pine-cloaked and comparatively infertile. They were not extensively settled until medieval times, when
refugees from the mainland – principally Albanian Christians – established themselves
here. In response to the barrenness of their new homes the islanders adopted piracy
as a livelihood. The seamanship and huge fleets thus acquired were placed at the disposal of the Greek nation during the War of Independence. Today, foreigners and
Athenians have replaced locals in the rapidly depopulating harbour towns; windsurfers
and sailboats are faint echoes of the massed warships and kaïkia once at anchor.

The closest island of the Argo-Saronic group, **Salamína**, is virtually a suburb of
Pireás, just over a kilometre offshore to its east, and almost touches the industrial

Accommodation price codes

Throughout the book we've categorized accommodation according to the following
price codes, which denote the cheapest available double room in high season. All
prices are for the room only, except where otherwise indicated. Many hotels, especially those in category ❹ and over, include breakfast in the price; you'll need to
check this when booking. During low season, rates can drop by more than fifty percent, especially if you are staying for three or more nights. Exceptions are during the
Christmas and Easter weeks when you'll pay high-season prices. Single rooms,
where available, cost around seventy percent of the price of a double.

❶ Up to €24	❹ €43–58
❷ €24–33	❺ €59–72
❸ €34–42	❻ €73 and upwards

Note: Youth hostels and mountain refuges typically charge €7–9 for a dormitory bed.
For more accommodation details, see pp.51–54.

▼ *Monemvasiá & Kýthira*

city of Mégara to the west. It is frequented by Athenian weekenders or is a base for commuting to the capital, but sees very few foreign visitors. Despite its proximity to the metropolis, it is noted for its distinct folk dances and costumes.

Salamína (Salamis)

Salamína is the quickest possible island hop from Athens. Take the Kifissiá–Pireás train to the end of the line in Pireás and then one of the green buses marked Pérama to the shipyard port of Pérama, just west of Pireás, and a ferry (daily 5am–midnight; €0.40) will whisk you across to the little port of Paloukía in a matter of minutes. The ferry crosses the narrow strait where, in 480 BC, the Greek navy trounced the Persian fleet, despite being outnumbered three to one; this battle is said by some to be more significant than the battle of Marathon, ten years earlier. Alternatively, ferries run from Pireás, next to the

Details of ferry routes, together with approximate journey times and frequencies, are to be found at the end of each chapter in the "Travel details" section. Please note that these are for general guidance only. Ferry schedules change with alarming regularity and the only information to be relied upon is that provided by the port police in each island harbour. Ferry agents in Pireás and on the islands are helpful, of course, but keep in mind that they often represent just one ferry line and won't necessarily inform you of the competition. Be aware, too, that ferry services to the smaller islands tend to be pretty skeletal from mid-September through to April.

In many island groups, ferries are supplemented by catamarans and hydrofoils, which tend to take half the time and be twice the price. Most of the major hydrofoil routes are operated from May to early September, with lesser ones sometimes running in July and August only.

Argo-Saronic Flying Dolphins berth (every 30min, 8am–5pm; 45min; €1.05), calling en route at Ambelákia. On arrival in Paloukía, you won't be rewarded by desirable or isolated beaches – the pollution of Pireás and Athens is a little too close for comfort, although the water has much improved in recent years – but you may escape the capital's smog and city pace.

Paloukía, Salamína Town and Selínia

By the ferry dock in **PALOUKÍA** is a bus station, with services to the contiguous capital Salamína Town (3km) and beyond, though the large selection of signed destinations can be confusing.

SALAMÍNA TOWN (also known as Kouloúri) is home to 18,000 of the island's 23,000 population. It's a depressing place, with a couple of banks, a fish market and motorway-like traffic. Pretty much uniquely for an island town – and emphasizing the absence of tourists – there is no bike or moped rental outlet, and also no hotel (not that you'd want to stay). Bus services link most points on the island, though information about them is scanty. **Iliaktí beach** is pleasant enough, some 5km to the west.

Buses marked **Faneroméni** run to the port at the northwest tip of the island, the **Voudóro peninsula**, where there are ferries across to Lákki Kalomírou, near Mégara on the Athens–Kórinthos road. En route it passes close by the frescoed seventeenth-century **monastery of Faneroméni** (6km from Salamína), rather majestically sited above the gulf.

Around 6km to the south of Paloukía is a third island port, **SELÍNIA**, which has connections direct to the Pireás ferry dock (winter 9.30am, summer five crossings daily between 8am and 2.30pm; 30min; €1.10). It can also be reached direct by bus from Paloukía. This is the main summer resort, with a pleasant waterfront, a bank, several tavernas and two inexpensive hotels, the *Akroyali* (☎010/46 73 263; ❷) and *Votsalakia* (☎010/46 71 334; ❷).

Eándio and the south

South from Salamína Town, the road edges the coast towards Eándio (6km; regular buses). There are a few tavernas along the way, but the sea vistas are not inspiring. **EÁNDIO**, however, is quite a pleasant village, with a little pebble beach and the island's best **hotel**, the *Gabriel* (☎010/46 62 275; ❸), which overlooks the bay, whose waters are said to be returning to health, although the Salamína waterfront opposite can be less than sweet-smelling.

Two roads continue from Eándio. The one to the southeast runs to the unassuming village resorts of Peráni and Paralía (both around 4km from Eándio). The more interesting route is southeast towards Kanákia (8km from Eándio; two buses daily), over the island's pine-covered mountain, and passing (at around 5km) a monastery – dedicated, like most Salamína churches, to Áyios Nikólaos. At the monastery, turn off left to the harbour and small-scale resort of Peristéria (5km). This is a much more attractive settlement than the littered beach and scruffy huts of Kanákia itself.

Égina (Aegina)

Égina was a major power in Classical times, rivalling Athens. It carried trade to the limits of the known world, maintained a sophisticated silver coinage system (the first in Greece) and had prominent athletes and craftsmen. During the fifth century BC, however, the islanders made the political mistake of siding with their fellow Dorians, the Spartans. Athens seized on this as an excuse to act on a long-standing jealousy; her fleets defeated those of the islanders in two separate sea battles and, after the second, the population was expelled and replaced by more tractable colonists.

Subsequent history was less distinguished, with the pattern of occupation familiar to central Greece – by Romans, Franks, Venetians, Catalans and Turks – before the War of Independence brought a brief period as seat of government for the fledgling Greek nation. For a time it was a prison island and only comparatively recently has it shaken off the consequent unfavourable reputation. The grim Égina prison still stands behind the stadium, but is currently used as a stray-dog shelter. These days, the island is most famous for its **pistachio orchards**, whose thirsty trees lower the water table several feet annually – hence the notices warning you of the perennial water crisis.

Athenians regard Égina as a beach annexe for their city, being the closest place to the capital most of them would swim at, though for tourists it has a monument as fine as any in the Aegean in its beautiful fifth-century BC **Temple of Afaia**. This is located on the east coast, close to the port of **Ayía Marína**, and if it is your primary goal, you'd do best to take one of the ferries or hydrofoils which run directly there in season. Hydrofoils are more frequent than ferries, run from the same quay in Pireás as the conventional boats, and cost hardly any more. If you plan to stay, then make sure your boat docks at **Égina Town**, the island capital. Ferries and hydrofoils also stop at **Souvála**, a Greek weekend retreat between the two ports devoid of interest to outsiders.

Égina Town

A solitary column of the Temple of Apollo beckons as your ferry or hydrofoil steams around the point into the harbour at **ÉGINA TOWN**. The island's capital, it makes an attractive base, with some grand old buildings from the time (1826–28) when it served as the first capital of Greece during the War of Independence. And for somewhere so close to Athens, it isn't especially overrun by foreign tourists, although accommodation prices are high, particularly at weekends.

The **long harbour** waterfront combines the workaday with the picturesque, but is nonetheless appealing: fishermen talk and tend their nets, and kaïkia selling produce from the mainland bob at anchor. North of the port, behind the small town beach, a lone column on a low hill, known, logically enough, as **Kolóna** (Column) marks the remains of the temple of Apollo and the ancient acropolis. Near the entrance to the ruins (Tues–Sun 8.30am–3pm; €1.50), a small but worthwhile **archeology museum** has finds from the extensive excavations that have revealed five thousand years and ten layers of settlement; a free pamphlet gives a history and explains the objects on display. On the north flank of Kolóna hill there's an attractive bay with a very small, sandy **beach** – the best spot for swimming in the immediate vicinity of the town.

The town's other sights include the restored **Markélos Tower**, seat of the first Greek government, uphill from the middle of the harbour, near the large **Church of Áyios Nikólaos**. The frescoed thirteenth-century church of **Ómorfi Ekklisía** is a fifteen-minute walk east of the port. In the suburb of Livádhi, just to the north, a plaque marks the residence of **Nikos Kazantzakis**, when he was writing his most celebrated book, *Zorba the Greek*.

Arrival and accommodation

The **bus station** is on the spacious Platía Ethneyersías, just north of the ferry arrival point, with excellent services to most villages; buy your tickets before you get on the bus. Horse buggies and taxis are found nearby. The **post office** is across the square, and the **tourist police** post (☎02970/23 333) is immediately behind it in the same building as the regular police. Several offices on and behind the main waterfront rent cars, mopeds, motorbikes and mountain bikes – Égina is large and hilly enough to make a motor worthwhile for anything other than a pedal to the beaches towards Pérdhika. Four **banks** line the main waterfront. Aegina Island Holidays (☎02970/26 430) on the waterfront near the church, offers excursions to the Epidaurus theatre festival (see p.206), handles tickets for the hydrofoils to Souvála and Ayía Marína, and books accommodation.

Good inexpensive **accommodation** can be found in the *Electra* rooms (☎02970/23 360, ℗26 715; ❷) on Leonárdhou Ladhá, above the square. On the seafront between the square and the Kolóna are the *Avra* (☎02970/22 303, ℗23 917; ❸) and the friendly *Plaza Hotel* (☎02970/25 600; ❷), where seaview rooms may be a bit noisy. The pleasantly situated *House of Peace* on the corner of Kanari and Aphroditi is under new management and has rooms and apartments (☎02970/23 790, ℗28 818, ✉the_house_of_peace@yahoo.com). Up above the Markélos Tower is the attractively restored *Traditional Pension* (*Eyinitiko Arhondiko*; ☎02970/24 968, ℗24 156; ❹) and on the other side of the church the *Stone House* (*To Petrino Spiti*, ☎ 02970/23 827) has pleasant studios for three (❹). Aegina Island Holidays can book air-conditioned doubles with private facilities (❷).

Eating and entertainment

There are enough reasonable **tavernas** in the town: directly behind the fish market on P. Irióti is *Psarotaverna Agora*, particularly good for inexpensive seafood and with outdoor seating on the cobbles in summer; near the *Avra* hotel, the small *Lekkas* is excellent for no-nonsense meat grills by the waterside; and nearby *Flisvos* offers charcoal-grilled food by the sea. Further south along the main quay, near the Ionian Bank, the *Estiatorinon Economou* serves good traditional food, while a couple of kilometres south, in the suburbs, the *Stratigos* serves straightforward but well-prepared food overlooking the little harbour at Fáros. Self-caterers will find good prices and a large selection at the Kritikou supermarket on the Ayía Marína road, just beyond the stadium and prison.

In terms of **nightlife**, Égina Town boasts two summer **cinemas**: the Olympia near the football grounds before the *Miranda* hotel, and the new Akroyiali at the south end of the harbour on the Pérdhika road, which shows quality foreign films; the winter cinema, the Titina, is by the park of the medieval tower-house, a block below the OTE. The young and lively might try the *Apocalypse* or *Perdiotika* **bars**, or Petros' *Tropic* all-night café. The well-heeled can sample genuine live *bouzoúki* at Athenian prices at *Kanellas*, also on the waterfront. Most **discos** are across the island in Ayía Marína, but the vast *Vareladiko* disco is in Fáros, just beyond the *Stratigos* taverna.

The free *Essential Aegina* is a useful **listings** booklet, updated regularly during the summer season and available from tourist offices, and some hotels and restaurants.

The Temple of Afaia

The Doric **Temple of Afaia** (Mon–Fri 8am–7pm, Sat & Sun 8am–3pm; €2.40) lies 12km east of Égina Town, among pines that are tapped to flavour the local retsina, and beside a less aesthetic radio mast. It is one of the most complete and visually complex ancient buildings in Greece, its superimposed arrays of columns and lintels evocative of an Escher drawing. Built in the fifth century BC to replace a destroyed sixth-century original, it slightly predates the Parthenon. The dedication is unusual: Afaia was a Cretan nymph who had fled from the lust of King Minos, and seems to have been worshipped almost exclusively on Égina. As recently as two centuries ago the temple's pediments were intact and virtually perfect, depicting two battles at Troy. However, like the Elgin marbles they were "purchased" from the Turks – this time by Ludwig I of Bavaria, which explains their current residence in Munich's Glyptothek museum.

Buses from Égina Town to Ayía Marína stop at the temple, or you could walk from Ayía Marína along the path that takes up where Kolokotróni leaves off, but rented transport allows you to stop at the monastery of Áyios Nektários and at the island's former capital of Paleohóra.

Áyios Nektários and Paleohóra

Áyios Nektários, a whitewashed modern convent situated around halfway to the Temple of Afaia, was named in honour of the Greek Orthodox Church's most recent and controversial saint, Anastasios Kefalas, a rather high-living monk who died in 1920 and was canonized in 1962. An oversized church – the largest in Greece – was recently completed on the main road below. Opposite the convent car park a partly paved road leads up into the hills towards the seventeenth-century convent of Khryssoleóndissa – primarily worth seeing for its views.

Paleohóra, a kilometre or so further east, was built in the ninth century as protection against piracy, but failed singularly in this capacity during Barbarossa's 1537 raid. Abandoned in 1827 following Greek independence, Paleohóra is now utterly deserted, but possesses the romantic appeal of a ghost village. You can drive right up to the site: take the turning left after passing the new large church and keep going about 400m. Some twenty of Paleohóra's reputed 365 churches and monasteries – one for every saint's day – remain in a recognizable state, and can be visited, but only those of Episkopí (locked), Áyios Yeóryios and Metamórfosis (on the lower of the two trails) retain frescoes of any merit or are in any state of preservation. Little remains of the town itself; when the islanders left, they simply abandoned their houses and moved to Égina Town.

The east: Ayía Marína and Pórtes

The island's major package resort of **AYÍA MARÍNA**, 15km from Égina Town, lies on the east coast of the island, south of the Afaia temple ridge. The concentrated tackiness of its jam-packed high street rivals anything found on Corfu: signs abound for Guinness and cider, burger bars and salaciously named cocktails. The beach is packed and overlooked by constantly sprouting, half-built hotels, and the water is not clean. It's really only worth coming here for connections to Pireás. There are around five ferries a day in season, with departures in the morning and late in the afternoon.

Beyond the resort, the paved road continues south 8km to **PÓRTES**, a low-key shore hamlet. Among the uneasy mix of new summer villas-in-progress (no short-term accommodation) and old basalt cottages are scattered a few tiny fish **tavernas** and snack bars, with a functional beach between the two fishing anchorages. The road climbs to the village of Anitséou, just below a major saddle on the flank of Mount Óros, and then forges west towards the scenic village of **Pahiá Ráhi**, almost entirely rebuilt in traditional style by foreign owners. From here, a sharp, winding descent leads to the main west-coast road at Marathónas (see below), or a longer, paved and tree-lined route heads back to Égina Town.

Mount Óros

Just south of the saddle between Pahiá Ráhi and Anitséou, mentioned above, are the foundations of the shrine of **Ellaníou Dhiós**, with the monastery of Taxiárhis squatting amid the massive masonry. The 532-metre summit cone of **Mount Óros**, an hour's walk from the highest point of the road, is capped by the modern chapel of Análipsi (the Ascension) and has views across the entire island and much of the Argo-Saronic Gulf.

Gerald Thompson's *A Walking Guide to Aegina*, available locally, describes in detail a series of walks across the range of mountains and wooded valleys between Mount Óros and the Afaia temple and down to the port of Souvála, all avoiding main roads.

The west: Marathónas, Pérdhika and Moní islet

The road due south of Égina Town running along the west coast of the island is served by regular buses (8–10 daily). Small but sprawling **MARATHÓNAS**,

5km from Égina, has the biggest of the west coast's small and rather scruffy sand beaches, and is tolerable enough, with a scattering of rooms, tavernas and cafés along the shore.

PÉRDHIKA, 9km along at the end of the coastal road, scenically set on its little bay, is the most pleasant and picturesque village on the island and certainly has the best range of nonpackaged **accommodation** outside Égina Town. There are rooms on the main road, and just off it, immediately before the waterfront, is the well-priced *Hotel Hippocampus* (☎02970/61 363; ❸). On first sight the elongated village can appear characterless; however, further exploration reveals a relaxed, seaside-holiday atmosphere, very different from the rest of the island. On the attractive, pedestrianized waterfront esplanade, overlooking a panorama of Moní islet and the Peloponnese, are a dozen **tavernas** and cafés; probably the best food is at *O Nondas*.

The only other diversion at Pérdhika is a trip to the pale-limestone offshore islet of **Moní** (10min; several departures daily; €1.50 one way). There are no facilities on the island and most of it is fenced off as a nature conservation area. It's really only worth the trip for a swim in wonderfully clear water, as Pérdhika bay itself is of questionable cleanliness and has very small beach areas.

Angístri

Angístri, fifteen minutes by catamaran from Égina, is small enough to be over-looked by most island-hoppers, though it is now in many foreign holiday brochures. The island fosters an uneasy coexistence between Athenian and German old-timers, who bought property here years ago, and British new-comers on package trips. Beaches, however, remain better and less crowded than on Égina, and out of season the pine-covered island succumbs to a leisurely village pace, with many islanders still making a living from fishing and farming. Headscarves worn by the old women indicate the islanders' Albanian ancestry, and until recently they still spoke Arvanítika – a dialect of medieval Albanian with Greek accretions – amongst themselves.

The Angístri dock in Égina Town is immediately south of the main harbour. **Boats and catamarans** from Égina and Pireás call at Skála, and possibly at Mýlos. **From Pireás**, a direct ferry runs at least twice daily in season, once a day out of season, taking two hours; the fast catamaran three times a day, via Égina, takes one hour. A water taxi is based in Angístri, but will be more expensive.

Skála and Mýlos

The essentially modern resort of **SKÁLA** is dominated by many new apartment buildings and hotels with little to distinguish them, spreading west halfway along the north shore of the island. The popular town beach, Angístri's only sandy one, nestles against the protected south shore of this headland, below the big white church. Just inland of the ferry dock is the attractive hotel *Yana* (☎02970/91 228; ❷), sharing a pool with the *Alter Ego* self-catering apartments; both are run by the helpful Nektarios (Nick) Panou of Skala Travel (☎02970/91 356, ⓕ91 342, ⓔnik.panou@otenet.gr), who can also arrange reservations for other **accommodation**. On summer weekends you would be well advised to reserve ahead. For **food**, there's the *Neptune* taverna in Skála and *Alter Ego* serves excellent crepes; in Mýlos the *Sailor* and *Konaki* are recommended.

Both **mopeds** and **mountain bikes** are available for rent; Limenária, near the end of the trans-island road, is less than 8km distant, so in cooler weather

ANGÍSTRI

Epidaurus

MÝLOS

SKÁLA

Metóhi

Dhragonéra

Halikádha

Apónissos

Lake

Dhoroússa

Limenária

Máriza

N

0   1 km

you can comfortably cross Angístri on foot or by bike. A road to the left of the harbour leads within fifteen minutes to the *Angistri Club*, with a disco-bar on the rocks above the sea, and the nearby *Alkyoni* taverna. From there, it's another ten-minutes' walk to the secluded **Halikádha** pebble beach backed by crumbling cliffs and pine-covered hills; along with Dhragonéra (see below), this is the best that the island has to offer, and is clothing-optional.

Metóhi, the hillside hamlet just above Skála, was once the main village, and in recent years has been completely bought up and restored by foreigners and Athenians; there are no facilities.

Ever-spreading Skála threatens in the future to merge with **MÝLOS** (Megalohóri), just 1.5km west along the north coast. Once you penetrate a husk of new construction, you find an attractive, traditional Argo-Saronic-style village centre. Although there's no decent beach nearby, it makes an alternative base to Skála, with plenty of rented **rooms** and some **hotels**. The *Milos Hotel* (☎02970/91 241; ❷) is a good, well-positioned choice.

The rest of the island

A regular bus service, designed to dovetail with the ferry schedule, connects Skála and Mýlos with Limenária on the far side of the island – or you could hike from Metóhi along a winding dirt road through the pine forest, with views across to Égina and the Peloponnese. The paved west-coast road takes you past the turning for **Dhragonéra**, a broad pebble beach with a dramatic panorama across to the mainland.

LIMENÁRIA is a small farming community set at the edge of a fertile plateau in the southeast corner of the island, and still largely unaffected by tourism. There are two tavernas – *Tasos* is very good – and a few rooms. A sign points to a misleadingly named "beach", really just a spot, often monopolized by male naturists, where you can swim off the rocks. A half-hour walk west of Limenária, on the old path which parallels the road, will bring you past a shallow salt lake, to a seasonal taverna overlooking the tiny islet of Apónissos and larger Dhoroússa beyond.

Póros

Separated from the mainland by a 450-metre strait, **Póros** ("the ford") barely qualifies as an island, and far more than any other Argo-Saronic island it is package-tour territory. Its proximity to Pireás also means a weekend Athenian invasion. The island town has character though, and the topography is interesting: Póros is in fact two islands, **Sferiá** (Póros Town) and the much more extensive **Kalávria**, separated from each other by a shallow engineered canal, which is now silting up.

In addition to its regular ferry and hydrofoil connections with Pireás and the other Argo-Saronics, Póros has frequent boats shuttling across from the workaday mainland port of **Galatás** in the Peloponnese, and there's a car ferry every twenty minutes from near the Naval Academy. These allow for some interesting excursions – locally to the lemon groves of Lemonodhássos, ancient Troezen near Trizína, and the nearby Devil's Bridge (see p.208). Further afield, day-trips to Náfplio or to performances of ancient drama at the great theatre of Epidaurus are possible by car, or by taking an excursion, available through travel agents in Póros Town (see below).

Póros Town

Ferries from the Argo-Saronics or from Galatás drop you at **PÓROS**, the main town on the island, which rises steeply on three sides of the tiny volcanic Sferiá. The harbour and town are picturesque, and the cafés and waterfront lively. Fishermen sell their catches direct from the boat and it is possible to arrange fishing trips. Particular sights are the hilltop clocktower and a small, well-labelled **archeological museum** (Mon–Sat 9am–3pm; free), with items from the mainland site of Troezen and elsewhere.

Near the main ferry dock is the helpful Family Tours (☎02980/23 743, 🖷24 480) which has a variety of rooms available. Also on the waterfront are three other **travel agents**: Marinos Tours (☎02980/23 423), sole agents for the Hellas Flying Dolphin hydrofoils and with well-priced local maps, Hellenic

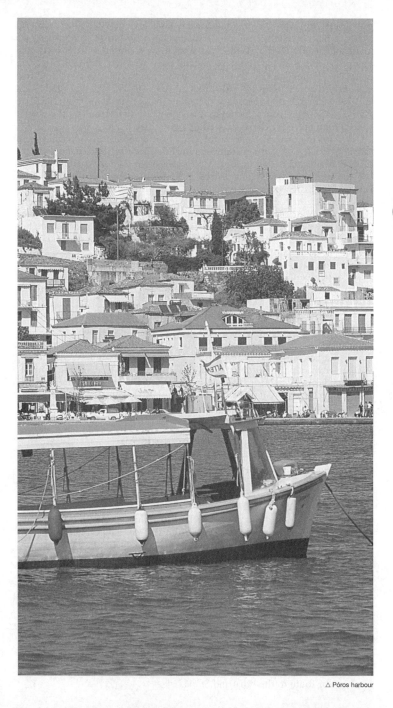

△ Póros harbour

Sun Travel (☎02980/25 901) and Saronic Gulf Travel (☎02980/24 555). All these agencies **exchange** money, arrange **accommodation** in rented rooms and handle **tours** off the island. If you want to look around on your own, quieter places to stay are up on the hill behind the clocktower, although prices are generally on the high side. To the right of the road to Kalávria you'll find two reasonable hotels: *Dimitra* (☎02980/22 697, ℱ25 653; ❷) and *Latsi* (☎02980/22 392; ❷). Most of the other hotels are across the canal on Kalávria. Camping is not encouraged anywhere on the island and the nearest official campsite, *Kyrayelo*, is just west of Galatás (see p.208).

Down on the quayside, among the cafés, bars, creperies and souvenir shops facing Galatás, good-value **restaurants** include *Grill Oasis* and *Mouragio*, at the far end away from the ferry dock. *Moskhoyiannis* has traditional Greek food in the souvenir lane which runs between the Alpha Bank and the post office square. A well-signed lane, between the *Latsi* and the school, leads gently up, past the police station and the Ergani weaving shop, to the upper square. Here, by the ÁyiosYeóryios cathedral are a cluster of good tavernas: *Platanos, Perasma, Dimitris* – the last run by a local butcher, so offers excellent meat – and, just beyond, the *Kipos* (*Garden*). The *Lithos* bar is nearby and the *Korali* and *Sirocco* **discos** provide nightlife, with both Greek and foreign music.

Additional facilities around the waterfront include **moped** and **bicycle** rental outlets (you can take either across on boats to the mainland), four **banks**, a **post office**, the summer-only Diana **cinema** and the helpful **tourist police** (☎02980/22 462; mid-May to Sept).

Kalávria

Most of Póros's **hotels** are to be found on Kalávria, the main body of the island, just across the canal beyond the Naval Cadets' Training School. They stretch for a couple of kilometres on either side of the bridge, with some of those to the west in Neório ideally situated to catch the dawn chorus – the Navy's marching band. If you'd rather sleep in, head beyond the first bay where the fishing boats tie up. Two kilometres from the bridge, in **Megálo Neório**, is the pleasant *Pavlou* hotel (☎02980/22 734, ℱ22 735; ❺–❺), a larger beach and a watersports centre.

Alternatively, turn right through **Askéli**, where posh hotels and villas face good clear water. Two **bus** routes run half-hourly from Poros Town waterfront to Askéli and Zoödhóhou Piyís, and to Neório.

The monastery of Zoödhóhou Piyís and Temple of Poseidon

At the end of the four-kilometre stretch of road through Askéli lies the eighteenth-century **monastery of Zoödhóhou Piyís** ("Life-giving Spring") whose monks have fled the tourists and have been replaced by a caretaker. It's a pretty spot, with a couple of summer tavernas at the beach below.

From here you can either walk up across to the northern side of the island through the pines, or bike along the road. Initially, Kalávria appears to be mostly pine forest, but the far side has fertile plateaus, olive terraces, small deserted beaches in narrow inlets and magnificent panoramic views. Foot or bike routes lead you to a saddle in the hills and the few columns and ruins that make up the sixth-century BC **Temple of Poseidon**. Keep your eyes open or you may miss them; look for a small blue caretaker's hut. It was here that Demosthenes, fleeing from the Macedonians after taking part in the last-ditch resistance of the Athenians, took poison rather than surrender. The road leads on, back down in a circular route to the canal and Sferiá.

Ídhra (Hydra)

The port and town of **Ídhra**, with tiers of substantial greystone mansions and white-walled, red-tiled houses climbing up from a perfect horseshoe harbour, are a beautiful spectacle. The whole island is treated as a national monument, blessedly free of traffic – except for an occasional garbage lorry – making it one of the most peaceful and refreshing destinations in Greece. Unfortunately, thousands of others think so too, so the town's busy from Easter until September. In summer, especially with the midday crush of cruise-ship day-trippers and the weekend invasion of Athenians, it's packed to the gills; the front becomes one long outdoor café and souvenir stall, the hotels are full and the discos flourish. Once a fashionable artists' colony, established in the 1960s as people restored the grand old houses, it has experienced a predictable metamorphosis into one of the more popular (and expensive) resorts in Greece. Good beaches are also notably scarce. But this acknowledged, a visit is still recommended, especially out of peak season and during the week.

Ídhra Town

The waterfront of **ÍDHRA TOWN** is lined with mansions, most of them built during the eighteenth century, on the accumulated wealth of a remarkable merchant fleet of 160 ships which traded as far afield as America and, during the Napoleonic Wars, broke the British blockade to sell grain to France. Fortunes were made and the island also enjoyed a special relationship with the Turkish Porte, governing itself and paying no tax, but providing sailors for the sultan's navy. These conditions naturally attracted Greek immigrants from the less-privileged mainland, and by the 1820s the town's population was nearly 20,000 – an incredible figure when you reflect that today it is under 3000. During the War of Independence, Hydriot merchants provided many of the ships for the Greek forces and consequently many of the commanders.

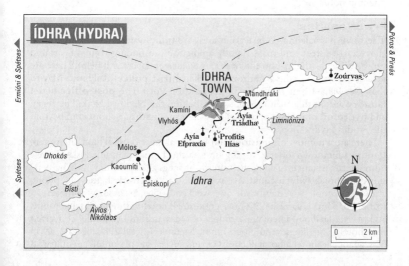

On the second or third weekend in June, Ídhra Town celebrates the **Miaoulia**, in honour of Admiral Andreas Miaoulis whose **fire boats**, packed with explosives, were set adrift upwind of the Turkish fleet during the War of Independence. The highlight of the celebrations is the burning of a boat at sea as a tribute to the sailors who risked their lives in this dangerous enterprise.

On an altogether more peaceful note, the **International Puppet Theatre Festival** takes place here at the end of July and appeals to children of all ages.

Easter is a particularly colourful and moving experience here. Ídhra's prosperity allows for grand celebrations, with a special emphasis on performances of choral music. Reservations must be made well ahead of time for all of these festivals.

The **mansions** (*arhóndika*) of these merchant families, designed by Venetian and Genoese architects, are still the great monuments of the town. A town map is available locally, if you are interested in seeking them out – some are labelled at the entrance with "*Oikía*" (home) and the family name. On the western waterfront, and the hill behind, are the **Voulgaris** mansion, with its interesting interior, and the **Tombazis** mansion, used as a holiday hostel for arts students. Set among pines above the restored windmill on the western point, the **Koundouriotis** mansion was the home of George Koundouriotis, a wealthy shipowner who fought in the War of Independence and whose great grandson, Pavlos Koundouriotis, was president of republican Greece in the 1920s. It is being refurbished as a museum with EU funding. On the eastern waterfront are the **Kriezis** mansion, the **Spiliopoulos** mansion and the **Tsamados** mansion – now the national merchant navy college which you can sometimes visit between lectures. The **historical archives museum** is also on the eastern waterfront (Tues–Sun 9am–2.30pm; €3).

Ídhra is also reputedly hallowed by no fewer than 365 churches – a total claimed by many a Greek island, but here with some justice. The most important is the church of **Panayía Mitropóleos**, set in a monastic courtyard by the port, with a distinctive clocktower and a **Byzantine museum** of uncertain opening hours.

Practicalities

The town is small and compact, but away from the waterfront the streets and alleyways are steep and maps slightly ambiguous, so finding your way around can be difficult (the map in the free *This Summer in Hydra* will help). There are several **banks** along the waterfront, and the **tourist police** (daily mid-May to mid-Oct 9am–10pm; ☎02980/52 205) are on Vótsi. The **post office** and a **laundry** are on the small market square, behind the National bank. The **ferry** and **hydrofoil** offices are upstairs on the eastern waterfront, about 10m beyond the Studio Hydra shop.

There are a number of **pensions** and **hotels** along, or just behind, the waterfront in Ídhra town, often charging up to a third more than usual island rates. Some of the restaurants along the waterfront act as agents for the outlying pensions and hotels, which could save you time and footwork; better still, phone ahead and book – certainly for any weekend. The *Amarillis* at Tombázi 15 (☎02980/53 611, ☏52 249; ●) is a good small hotel with comfortable rooms and private facilities. There are a couple of old mansions beautifully converted into hotels: *Angelica*, several blocks up at Miaoúli 42 (☎02980/53 202, ☏53 698, ✉angelicahotel@hotmail.com; ●), and *Hydra*, steeply uphill at Voulgari 8

(☎ & ☎ 02980/52 102, ✉hydrahotel@aig.forthnet.gr;④). Of the pensions, try the *Erofili* (☎02980/54 049;②).

There's no shortage of **restaurants** and cafés around the waterfront, but for good tavernas you would do better to head a little inland. The *Garden* taverna, known for tasty meat dishes, is on the road heading up from the hydrofoil dock, with the equally good *Xeri Elia* down the narrow street outside the *Garden*'s wall. Above the *Amarillis Hotel* is the small *Barba Dimas* taverna, which has wonderful mezédhes, snails and fish. Further up on the same road, *To Kryfo Limani* is a pleasant taverna in a small garden, while further yet will bring you excellent home cooking at the *Yeitoniko* (also known as *Manolis & Christina's*), which has tables on its roof and a small veranda. For light snacks and refreshments, try the small and friendly *Pigadi* café, below the *Amarillis*.

For **nightlife** you might start at a portside bar: try the *Pirate* or *To Roloi*. Or hike up the hill west of town to *Heaven*, a disco favoured by the younger set. A few minutes further west on the way to Kamíni you'll have no trouble locating the *Scirocco* disco, if it's open.

Beaches around Ídhra Town

The town's only sandy beach is at **MANDHRÁKI**, 1.5km east of the harbour along a concrete road; it's the private domain of the *Miramare Hotel* (☎02980/52 300;⑥), although the windsurfing centre is open to all.

On the opposite side of the harbour, to the southwest, a broad coastal path leads around to **KAMÍNI**, about a twenty-minute walk. Just as you reach Kamíni on the right is a small pension, *Antonia* (☎02980/52 481;③) On the left, across the street, Eléni Petrolékka has a popular rival pension and apartments (☎02980/52 701;③). Also on the left is the *Kondylenia* restaurant, with fresh fish and wonderful views of the sunset. About 50m up the dry, paved streambed to the left is *Christina's*, a fine traditional Greek fish taverna.

Thirty-minutes' walk beyond Kamíni (or a boat ride from the port) will bring you to **VLYHÓS**, a small hamlet with three tavernas, rooms, a small beach and a restored nineteenth-century bridge. The *Iliovasilema* taverna enjoys sunset views from the water's edge, near the small jetty, while just beyond are the attractive *Antigone* rooms (☎02980/53 228, ☎53 042;④) and café. Any of these establishments can call a water taxi to whisk you back to town. **Camping** is tolerated here (though nowhere else closer to town) and the swimming in the lee of an offshore islet is good. Further out is the steep-sided island of **Dhokós**, large but only seasonally inhabited by goatherds and people tending their olives.

The rest of the island

There are no motor vehicles on Ídhra, except for a few lorries to cart away rubble and rubbish, and no surfaced roads away from the port; the island is mountainous and its interior accessible only by foot or hoof. The net result is that most tourists don't venture beyond the town, so by a little walking you can find yourself in a dramatically different kind of island. The pines devastated by forest fires in 1985 are fortunately now growing back.

Following the streets of the town upwards and inland behind the *Angelica* you reach a path which winds up the mountain for about an hour's walk to the **monastery of Profítis Ilías** and the **convent of Ayía Efpraxía**. Both are beautifully situated; the nuns at the convent (the lower of the two) offer hand-woven fabrics for sale. A path continues behind Profítis Ilías to a saddle overlooking the south coast and a steeply descending *kalderími* onwards to scattered houses and chapels near the sea. From the saddle, a faint path climbs to the right for twenty minutes to the 588-metre summit of Mount Éros, the Argo-Saronic islands' highest viewpoint. To the east of Profítis Ilías are four more monasteries, the nearest to town being **Ayía Triádha**, occupied by a few monks (no women admitted). From here a path continues east for two more hours to the cloister of **Zourvás** in the extreme east of the island.

A dirt road continues west of Vlyhós, past a busy boat-repair yard, to **Episkopí**, a high plateau planted with olives and vineyards and dotted by a scattering of homes (no facilities), and then climbs above Mólos Bay, the property of an Athenian hospital owner, and closed to the public. From Episkopí itself, vague tracks lead to the southwestern extreme of the island, on either side of which the bays of **Bísti** and **Áyios Nikólaos** offer solitude and good swimming. Bísti has a pebble beach with rocks for swimming off at one side; Áyios Nikólaos has a small sand beach.

The best cove of the many on the south coast is **Limnióniza** (beyond Ayía Triádha), with a pebble beach and pine trees; the overland access path is long (1 hr 15 min from town) and rough, though well-marked and obvious.

Points on the coast can be reached much more easily by **water taxis**, which will drop you off and then pick you up again at any time you arrange.

Spétses (Spetsai)

Spétses was the island where the author John Fowles once lived and which he used, thinly disguised as Phraxos, as the setting for *The Magus*. It is today very popular with well-to-do Athenians and with foreigners, and seems to have risen above the bad 1980s reputation earned by an unhealthy proportion of cheap package tours and lager louts. The architecture of Spétses Town is distinct and distinguished, though less photogenic than that of Ídhra. Lacking any dramatic topography, and despite a bout of forest-fire devastation in 1990, hints of the landscape described by Fowles are still to be seen: "away from its inhabited corner [it is] truly haunted . . . its pine forests uncanny". Remarkably, at Áyii Anáryiri, Spétses' best beach, development has been restrained to a scattering of holiday villas.

Spétses Town

SPÉTSES TOWN is the island's port – and its only settlement. It shares with Ídhra the same history of late eighteenth-century mercantile adventure and prosperity, and the same leading role in the War of Independence, which made its foremost citizens the aristocrats of the newly independent Greek state. Pebble-mosaic courtyards and streets sprawl between 200-year-old mansions, whose architecture is quite distinct from the Peloponnesian styles across the water. Though homeowners may bring private cars onto the island, their movement inside the town limits is prohibited. A few taxis supplement the horse-drawn buggies, whose bells ring cheerfully night and day along the long waterfront, though animal welfare activists are justifiably worried by the condition of some of the horses by summer's end. Motorbikes, mopeds and noisy three-wheel mini-trucks are the preferred mode of transport, and career continuously through the town streets, making life almost as difficult for pedestrians as if cars had been allowed.

The sights are principally the majestic old houses and gardens, the grandest of which is the magnificent Mexis family mansion, built in 1795 and now used as the **local museum** (Tues–Sun 8.30am–2.15pm; €1.50), housing displays of relics from the War of Independence that include the bones of the Spetsiot admiral-heroine Laskarina Bouboulina. One of Bouboulina's homes, to the rear of the cannon-studded main harbour known as the **Dápia**, has been made into a **museum** (daily morning and late afternoon; €3) by her descendants and is well worth visiting. Guided tours (30min) are given in English several times a day.

Just outside the town, Fowles aficionados will notice **Anáryiros Koryalénos College**, a curious Greek re-creation of an English public school where the author was employed and set part of his tale; it is now vacant, save for the occasional conference or kids' holiday programme. Like the massive waterfront **Hotel Posidonion,** where kings and presidents once slept, the college was endowed by Sotirios Anaryiros, the island's great nineteenth-century benefactor. An enormously rich self-made man, he was also responsible for replanting the pine forest that now covers the island. His former residence, behind the *Hotel Roumani*, is a Pharaonic monument to bad taste.

Walking east from the Dápia, you pass the **Old Harbour** inlet, still a well-protected mooring, and the church of **Áyios Nikólaos** with its graceful belfry, "Freedom or Death" memorial and some giant pebble mosaics. At the end of the road you reach the **Baltíza** inlet where, among the sardine-packed yachts, half a dozen boatyards continue to build kaïkia in the traditional manner; it was one of these that re-created the *Argo* for Tim Severin's re-enactment of the "Jason Voyage". An extensive new housing development behind Baltíza will probably edge local prices even higher.

Practicalities

A good way to get around the island is by bike, and, despite the hills, you can reach most points or make the 25km circuit without too much exertion. Several reliable **bike** and **moped** rental outlets are scattered through town.

All kinds of **accommodation** are available in Spétses Town, but be warned that prices are inflated in high season, although the town is smaller and less steep than Ídhra, so hunting around for a good deal is not such hard work. If you don't fancy pounding the streets yourself, try Alasia Travel (☎02980/74 098), Melédon Tourist and Travel Agency (☎02980/74 497) or Pine Island Tours (☎02980/72 464), all by the Dápia. Simple but comfortable hotels include *Faros* (☎02980/72 613, ℗72 614; ❸) on Platía Oroloyíou ("Clocktower Square"), *Stelios* (☎02980/72 971; ❸) on the waterfront, and *Star* (☎02980/72 214, ℗27 872; ❺), which is quieter because its pebble-mosaic pavement makes it off-limits to vehicles. A few hotels – the *Faros* (see above), the *Alexandris* (☎02980/72 211; ❸), above the petrol station, and the waterfront *Klimis* (☎02980/72 334; ❹) – stay open all winter. Inland a few blocks from the ferry landing the *Villa Christina* (☎02980/72 218; ❹), an old villa in its own quiet garden, has doubles and studios with a fridge, some with views of the harbour. You might even want to spring for the recently renovated *Posidonion* (☎02980/72 308, ℗72 209; ❻).

In Spétses Town, **food** and **drink** tend to be overpriced. Among the better options are *Roussos*, 300m east of the Dápia, just beyond the *Klimis*; or the *Lazaros* taverna, about 400m up from the Dápia, which are better-priced and have good food. For fish, go to the *Bouboulina* ouzerí opposite the fish market, which is before *Klimis*, or the long-established *Patralis* near the water in Kounoupítsa, west towards the *Spetses* hotel. The *Bakery Restaurant*, above the popular bakery just up from the ferry landing, offers more updated fare, including a fine artichoke moussaka. The ouzerí *Byzantino* is popular, characterful, but expensive, as are many other places around the Old Harbour.

By day, *Tó Kafenío*, near the Flying Dolphin office at the Dápia, remains steadfastly traditional, with drinks and lunchtime mezédhes – a good place to watch and wait for your ferry. By night, clubbers head for *Figaro*, in the Old Harbour, and the places at the other end of town around Kounoupítsa. Few of these places shut until the fishermen are setting out.

The **post office** is near the *Roussos* taverna, while a couple of **banks** are behind the Dápia, near the *Roumani* hotel. There's also a **laundry** behind Platía Oroloyíou.

Around the island

For **swimming** you need to get clear of the town. Beaches within walking distance are at **Ayía Marína** (twenty minutes east, with the very pleasant *Paradise* restaurant), at various spots beyond the Old Harbour, and several other spots half an hour away in either direction. The tempting smaller isle of **Spetsopoúla**, just offshore from Ayía Marína, is off-limits: it's the private property of the heirs of shipping magnate Stavros Niarchos.

For heading further afield, you'll need to hire a **bike** or **moped**, or use the **kaḯkia** rides from the Dápia, which run to beaches around the island in summer. A very expensive alternative are **water taxis**, though they can take up to ten people. **Walkers** might want to go over the top of the island to Áyii Anáryiri; forest fire has ravaged much of the southern side's pines between Ayía Marína and Áyii Anáryiri, though happily they are growing back. There is a **bus** service to Áyii Anáryiri from near the *Roussos* taverna, running several times a day in season. Routes out of town start from beyond the *Lazaros* taverna, and pass the forest service firewatch tower. Brave the precariously attached steps and you're rewarded with the island's highest and best viewpoint.

West from Spétses Town

Heading west from the Dápia around the coast, the road is paved or in good condition almost all around the island. The forest that survived the fires stretches from the central hills right down to the western shores and makes for a beautiful coastline with little coves and rocky promontories, all shaded by trees. *Panas Taverna* at Ligonéri, run by a Greek-American woman, provides wonderful respite from the bustle of town. You can swim below and then have lunch or dinner under the pines. A regular bus service runs to Ligonéri in season from in front of the *Hotel Posidonion*. A (not always reliable) timetable is posted at the stop.

Vréllos is the next place you come to, at the mouth of a wooded valley known locally as "Paradise", which would be a fairly apt description, except that, like so many of the beaches, it becomes littered every year with windblown rubbish. However, the entire shore is dotted with coves and in a few places there are small, seasonal tavernas – there's a good one at **Zogeriá**, for instance, where the scenery and rocks more than make up for the small beach.

Working your way anticlockwise around the coast towards Áyii Anáryiri you reach **Áyia Paraskeví** with its small church and beach – one of the most beautiful coves on Spétses and an alternate stop on some of the kaïki runs. There's a basic beach café and watersports here in summer. On the hill behind is the house John Fowles used as the setting for *The Magus*, the **Villa Yasemiá**, available for rent to Fowles aficionados; contact Pine Island Tours (℡02980/72 464, ℱ73 255).

Áyii Anáryiri

Áyii Anáryiri, on the south side of the island, is the best, if also the most popular, beach: a beautiful, long, sheltered bay of fine sand. Gorgeous first thing in the morning, it fills up later in the day with bathers, windsurfers and, at one corner, speedboats driving waterskiers. On the right-hand side of the bay, looking out to sea, there's a sea cave, which you can walk or swim to and explore, if you're not discouraged by the ominous rockfall on the access steps. There's a good seafront taverna and another, *Tassos*, just behind, run by one of the island's great eccentrics.

Travel details

Ferries

From the central harbour at Pireás at least 4 boats daily run to Ayía Marína (1hr) and 11 to Égina (1hr 30min); 1–2 daily to Skála and Mýlos (2hr); 4 daily to Póros (3hr 30min); 1–2 daily to Ídhra (4hr 30min) and Spétses (5hr 30min). About 4 connections daily between Égina and Póros; 4–5 daily between Égina and Angístri; from Angístri about 4 weekly to Paleá Epídhavros, far less frequently to Póros and Méthana.

Most of the ferries stop on the Peloponnesian mainland at Méthana (between Égina and Póros) and Ermióni (between Ídhra and Spétses); it is possible to board them here. Some continue from Spétses to Pórto Héli. There are also constant boats between Póros and Galatás (10min) from dawn until late at night, boat-taxis between Spétses and Pórto Héli, and 4 daily ferries between Spétses and Kósta.

NB there are more ferries at weekends and fewer out of season (although the service remains good); for Égina and Póros they leave Pireás most frequently between 7.30am and 9am, and 2pm and 4pm. Do not buy a return ticket as it saves no money and limits you to one specific boat. The larger landing-craft ferries are generally less expensive, but the smaller regular boats are somewhat faster. A schedule is posted at the small Port Police kiosk on the quay, and tickets can be purchased at nearby stalls. The general information number for the Argo-Saronic ferries is ℡010/41 75 382.

Flying Dolphin hydrofoils

Approximately hourly services from Aktí Tselépi at Pireás to Égina 6am–8pm in season, 7am–7pm out of season (40min); Saronic Dolphins craft for Póros, Ídhra and Spétses leave from further south-east on the same quay (4–6 daily, 2hr 30min to Spétses).

All other hydrofoils going beyond Égina leave from the Zéa Marina: 4–15 times daily to Póros (1hr), Ídhra (1hr 40min) and Spétses (2hr–2hr 30min). All these times depend upon the stops en route, and frequencies vary with the season.

Égina is connected with Méthana and Póros 1–3 times a day; Póros, Ídhra and Spétses with each other 5–7 times daily. Some hydrofoils also stop at Méthana and Ermióni and most of those to Spétses continue to Porto Héli (15min more). This is a junction of the hydrofoil route – in season there is usu-ally one a day onwards to Toló and Náfplio (and vice versa; 30 and 45min) and another to Monemvasía (2hr). The Monemvasía hydrofoil continues 2–4 days a week (Fri–Sun) to the island of Kýthira.

NB Services are heavily reduced out of season, though all the routes between Pórto Héli and Pireás still run. Hydrofoils are usually twice as fast and twice as expensive as ordinary boats, though to Égina the price is little different. You can now buy round-trip tickets to destinations in the Argo-Saronic Gulf. In season, it's not unusual for departures to be fully booked for a day or so at a time.

Details and tickets available from the Hellas Flying Dolphins office in Athens at 2 Vas. Konstandinou (☎010/75 20 540) or in Pireás at Ákti Themistokléous 8 (☎010/41 99 000). Tickets can be bought at the departure quays on Aktí Tselépi in Pireás and at Zéa Marina.

The Cyclades

CHAPTER 7

Highlights

* **Delos** The Cyclades' sacred centre and holiest ancient site, birthplace of Apollo and Artemis. See p.616

* **Caldera of Thíra** A spectacular geographical wonder, this crater left by a colossal volcanic explosion averages five miles in diameter. See p.654

* **Akrotíri, Thíra** The best preserved of all Minoan cities, and possibly part of legendary Atlantis. See p.660

* **Mýkonos Town** Charming labyrinthine lanes filled with restaurants, boutiques and nightlife but is overpriced and overrun by tourists in season. See p.610

* **Ermoúpolis, Sýros** Once Greece's busiest port, the elegant capital of the Cyclades, with arcaded central platía and an opera house, is now a UNESCO heritage site. See p.618

* **Boat tour around Mílos** Take in the geological diversity of this volcanic island, with swimming and a late lunch on nearby Kímolos. See p.595

* **Tragéa, Náxos** This fertile inland plain, covered with orchards, shelters most of the villages on the Cyclades' largest island. See p.637

* **Church of Ekatondapylianí, Paríkia, Páros** A picturesque and interesting sixth-century Byzantine church. See p.624

* **Hóra, Folégandhros** The least spoiled capital in the Cyclades, atop a spectacular cliff and free of traffic, with a handsome old *kástro* and white churches. See p.653

* **Hóra, Íos** The party capital of Greece, yet surprisingly pretty and charming. See p.648

7

The Cyclades

amed after the circle they form around the sacred island of Delos, the **Cyclades** (Kykládhes) is the most satisfying Greek archipelago for island-hopping. On no other group do you get quite such a strong feeling of each island as a microcosm, each with its own distinct traditions, customs and path of modern development. Most of these self-contained realms are compact enough to walk around in a few days, giving you a sense of completeness and identity impossible on, say, Crete or most of the Ionian islands.

The islands do share some features, with the majority of them (Ándhros, Náxos, Sérifos and Kéa excepted) being arid and rocky; most also share the "Cycladic" style of brilliant-white, Cubist architecture. The extent and impact of tourism, though, is markedly haphazard, so that although some English is spoken on most islands, a slight detour from the beaten track – from Íos to Síkinos, for example – can have you groping for your Greek phrasebook.

But whatever the level of tourist development, there are only two islands where it has come completely to dominate their character: **Íos**, the original hippie-island and still a paradise for hard-drinking backpackers, and **Mýkonos**, by far the most popular of the group, with its teeming old town, selection of nude beaches and sophisticated clubs and gay bars. After these two, **Páros**, **Sífnos**, **Náxos** and **Thíra** (Santoríni) are currently the most popular, with their beaches and main towns drastically overcrowded at the height of the season. To avoid the hordes altogether – except in August, when nearly everywhere is overrun and escape is impossible – the most promising islands are

Accommodation price codes

Throughout the book we've categorized accommodation according to the following **price codes**, which denote the cheapest available double room in high season. All prices are for the room only, except where otherwise indicated. Many hotels, especially those in category ❹ and over, include breakfast in the price; you'll need to check this when booking. During low season, rates can drop by more than fifty percent, especially if you are staying for three or more nights. Exceptions are during the Christmas and Easter weeks when you'll pay high-season prices. Single rooms, where available, cost around seventy percent of the price of a double.

❶ Up to €24	❹ €43–58
❷ €24–33	❺ €59–72
❸ €34–42	❻ €73 and upwards

Note: Youth hostels and mountain refuges typically charge €7–9 for a dormitory bed. For more accommodation details, see pp.51–54.

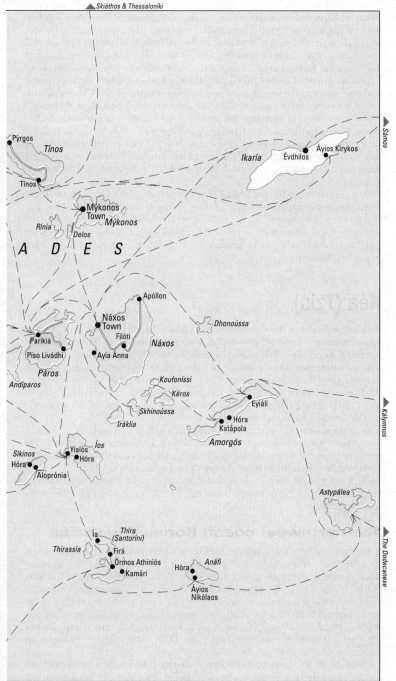

Skiáthos & Thessaloníki

▶ Sámos

▶ Kálymnos

▶ The Dodecanese

Pýrgos

Tínos

Tínos

Ikaría   Évdhilos   Áyios Kírykos

Mýkonos Town   Mýkonos

Rínia

Delos

A   D   E   S

Apóllon

Náxos Town

Filóti   Náxos

Parikiá

Píso Livádhi   Ayía Ánna

Dhonoússa

Páros

Andíparos

Koufoníssi

Kéros

Skhinoússa

Iráklia

Eyiáli

Hóra

Katápola

Amorgós

Astypálea

Síkinos   Íos

Hóra   Yialós   Hóra

Aloprónia

Ía   Thíra (Santoríni)

Thirassía

Firá

Órmos Athiniós

Kamári

Hóra   Anáfi

Áyios Nikólaos

(Crete)

Síkinos, Kímolos or Anáfi, or the minor islets around Náxos. For a different view of the Cyclades, visit **Tínos** and its imposing pilgrimage church, a major spiritual centre of Greek Orthodoxy, or **Sýros** with its elegant townscape and (like Tínos) large Catholic minority. Due to their closeness to Athens, adjacent **Kýthnos** and **Kéa** are predictably popular – and relatively expensive – weekend havens for Greeks. The one major ancient site is **Delos** (Dhílos), certainly worth making time for: the commercial and religious centre of the Classical Greek world, it's visited most easily on a day-trip, by kaïki or jet boat from Mýkonos.

When it comes to **moving on**, many of the islands – in particular Mílos, Páros, Náxos and Thíra – are handily connected with Crete (easier in season), while from Tínos, Mýkonos, Sýros, Páros, Náxos, Thíra or Amorgós you can reach many of the Dodecanese by direct boat. Similarly, you can regularly get from Mýkonos, Náxos, Sýros and Páros to Ikaría and Sámos (in the eastern Aegean).

One consideration for the timing of your visit is that the Cyclades often get frustratingly **stormy**, particularly in early spring or late autumn, and it's also the group worst affected by the *meltémi*, which blows sand and tables about with ease throughout much of July and August. Delayed or cancelled ferries are not uncommon, so if you're heading back to Athens to catch a flight leave yourself a day or two's leeway.

Kéa (Tziá)

Kéa is the closest of the Cyclades to the mainland and is extremely popular in summer, and at weekends year-round, with Athenians. Their impact is mostly confined to certain small coastal resorts, leaving most of the interior quiet, although there is a preponderance of expensive apartments and villas and not as many good tavernas as you might expect because so many visitors self-cater. Midweek or outside peak season, Kéa is a more enticing destination, with its rocky, forbidding perimeter and inland oak and almond groves. It's an excellent destination for those who enjoy a rural ramble.

As ancient Keos, the island and its strategic, well-placed harbour supported four cities – a pre-eminence that continued until the nineteenth century when Sýros became the main Greek port. Today, tourists account for the sea traffic with regular (in season) **ferry connections** with Lávrio on the mainland (only a ninety-minute bus ride from Athens), plus useful hydrofoils and ferries to and from Pireás, Sýros and Kýthnos; there may also be Mega Dolphin services to and from Zéa (near Pireás).

The northwest coast: Korissía to Otziás

The small northern ferry and hydrofoil port of **KORISSÍA** has fallen victim to uneven expansion and has little beauty to lose; if you don't like its looks upon disembarking, try to get a bus to Písses (16km), Otziás (6km) or Ioulídha (6km). Buses usually meet the boats; during July and August there's a regular fixed schedule around the island, but at other times public transport can be very elusive. There are a few **taxis** on Kéa, and two motorbike rental outfits: Adonis (✆02880/21 097), close to the *Karthea* hotel, and Moto Center (✆02880/21 844), a little inland near the **OTE**, both of them being more expensive than on most islands.

There's a list of rooms in the seafront **tourist information** office, and the kindly agents for the Flying Dolphin hydrofoils (To Stegadhi bookshop), sell maps and guides, and can phone around in search of **accommodation**. The best choices are the *Nikitas* pension (☎02880/21 193; ❷), open all year and very friendly; *Hotel Korissia* (☎02880/21 484; ❸–❹), well inland along the stream bed; *Hotel Tzia Mas* (☎02880/21 305; ❷–❹), right behind the east end of the otherwise uninspiring port beach; and the somewhat noisy *Karthea* (☎02880/21 204; ❹), which does, however, boast single rooms and year-round operation, a cameo appearance in recent Greek history: when the junta fell in July 1974, the colonels were initially imprisoned for some weeks in the then-new hotel, while the recently restored civilian government pondered what to do with them; Kéa was then so remote and unvisited that the erstwhile tyrants were safely out of reach of a vengeful populace. For **eating**, *Iy Akri* and *Angyrovoli* near the *Karthea* hotel have standard fare, while near the jetty *Apothiki* seems more popular than its smarter neighbour, *Lagoudera*. There's good swimming at **Yialiskári**, a small, eucalyptus-fringed beach between Korissía and Vourkári; the *Yialiskari* rooms (☎02880/21 197; ❷) enjoy a good view.

VOURKÁRI, a couple of kilometres to the north, is more compact and arguably more attractive than Korissía, serving as the favourite hangout of the yachting set; there's no real beach or accommodation here. Three fairly expensive and indistinguishable **tavernas** serve up good seafood dishes, and there's a very good ouzerí – *Strofi tou Mimi* – located where the road cuts inland towards Otziás. The few **bars** include *Vourkariani*, popular with an older crowd, and the slightly more happening *Kokko Cafe* and *Emage*.

Another 4km to the east, **OTZIÁS** has a small beach that's a bit better than that at Korissía, though more exposed to prevailing winds; facilities are limited to a couple of tavernas and a fair number of apartments for rent. Kéa's only functioning monastery, the eighteenth-century **Panayía Kastrianí**, is an hour's walk along a dirt road from Otziás. Although more remarkable for its fine setting on a high bluff than for any intrinsic interest, the hostel at the monastery (☎02880/21 348) is the cheapest accommodation deal on the island, albeit rather basic, isolated and not dependably open. From here you can take the pleasant walk on to the island capital, Ioulídha, in another two hours.

Ioulídha

IOULÍDHA (ancient Ioulis), aka Hóra, was the birthplace of the renowned early fifth-century BC poets Simonides and Bacchylides. With its numerous red-tiled roofs, Neoclassical buildings and winding flagstoned paths, it is by no means a typical Cycladic village, but, beautifully situated in an amphitheatric fold in the hills, it is architecturally the most interesting settlement on the island, and the best base for exploring it. Accordingly Ioulídha has "arrived" in recent years, with numerous trendy bars and bistros much patronized at weekends, but during the week it's quiet, its narrow lanes excluding vehicles. The **archeological museum** (Tues–Sun 8.30am–3pm; free) displays finds from the four ancient city-states of Kéa, although the best items were long ago spirited away to Athens. The lower reaches of the town stretch across a spur to the **Kástro**, a tumbledown Venetian fortress incorporating stones from an ancient temple of Apollo. Fifteen-minutes' walk northeast, on the path toward Panayía Kastrianí, you pass the **Lion of Kea**, a sixth-century BC sculpture carved out of an outcrop of rock, six metres long and three metres high. There are steps right down to the lion, but the effect is most striking from a distance.

There are a couple of **pensions** in Ioulídha: the somewhat pokey *Filoxenia* (☎02880/22 057; ❷), perched above a shoeshop in the middle of town, with no en-suite plumbing and saggy beds; and the more comfortable *Ioulis* (☎02880/22 177; ❸), which has its own terrace restaurant, up in the *kástro*.

You're spoiled for choice when it comes to **eating** and **drinking** though, with quality generally higher here than in Korissía. *Iy Piatsa*, just as you enter the lower town from the car park, has a variety of tasty dishes, while *Iy Dafni*, reached by a path from the bus stop, and *To Kalofagadhon*, up on the platía, both enjoy great views, the latter being the best place for a full-blown meat feast. Further up there is good standard fare on the terrace of *To Steki tis Tzias*. The aptly named *Panorama* serves up pastries and coffee and is a good place to watch the sun set, while after-dark action seems to oscillate between such bars as *Kamini*, *Leon* and, best of all, *Mylos*. *Ta Pedhia Pezi* (which means "the guys are playing"), is a lively hangout a few kilometres out of town off the road towards Písses and is terrific for a full-on *bouzoúki* night. A **post office** and **bank agent** round up the list of amenities.

The south

About 8km southwest of Ioulídha, reached via a mix of tracks and paths, or by mostly paved road, the crumbling Hellenistic watchtower of **Ayía Marína** sprouts dramatically from the grounds of a small nineteenth-century monastery.

Beyond, the paved main road twists around the startling scenic head of the lovely agricultural valley at **PÍSSES**, emerging at a large and little-developed beach. There are two tavernas, plus a pleasant **campsite**, *Camping Kea*, which has good turfy ground and also runs the studios (☎02880/31 302) further inland. Of the tavernas, the best is *Tó Akroyiali*, with a good range of dishes and excellent rosé wine, as well as rooms to rent upstairs (☎02880/31 301 or 31 327; ❷).

Beyond Písses, the asphalt – and the bus service – peters out along the 5km road south to **KOÚNDOUROS**, a sheltered, convoluted bay popular with yachters; there's a taverna behind the largest of several sandy coves, none cleaner or bigger than the beach at Písses. The luxury *Kea Beach* hotel (☎02880/31 230; ❹–❺) sits out on its own promontory with tennis courts, pool, and a hamlet of dummy windmills built as holiday homes. At the south end of the bay, *St George Bungalows* (☎02880 31 277; ❸) has smart rooms at very reasonable prices, as well as its own taverna which is recommended. A further 2km south at **Kambí**, there's a nice little beach and a good taverna, *Tó Kambí*.

Besides the very scant ruins of ancient Poiessa near Písses, the only remains of any real significance from Kéa's past are fragments of a temple of Apollo at **ancient Karthaia**, tucked away on the southeastern edge of the island above Póles Bay, with an excellent deserted twin beach that's easiest reached by boat. Otherwise, it's a good three-hour round-trip walk from the hamlet of Stavroudháki, some way off the lower road linking Koúndouros, Hávouna and Káto Meriá. Travelling by motorbike, the upper road, which plies more directly between Písses and Káto Meriá, is worth following as an alternative return along the island's summit to Ioulídha; it's paved between Ioulídha and Káto Meriá, and the entire way affords fine views over the thousands of magnificent oaks which are Kéa's most distinctive feature.

Kýthnos (Thermiá)

Though perhaps the dullest and certainly the most barren of the Cyclades, a short stay on **Kýthnos** is a good antidote to the exploitation likely to be encountered elsewhere. Few foreigners bother to visit and the island is much quieter than Kéa. It's a place where Athenians come to buy land for villas, go spear-fishing and sprawl on generally mediocre beaches without having to jostle for space. You could use it as a first or, better, last island stop; in season there are several **ferry connections** a week with Kéa and Lávrio, a frequent ferry and hydrofoil service to and from Sérifos, Sífnos and Pireás, plus further direct ferry and hydrofoil connections with Mílos and Kímolos.

Mérihas and around

In good weather boats dock on the west coast at **MÉRIHAS**, a rather functional ferry and fishing port with most of the island's facilities. This fact almost obliges you to stay here, and makes Mérihas something of a relative tourist ghetto, but it's redeemed by proximity to the island's best beaches. The closest beach of any repute is **Episkopí**, a 500-metre stretch of averagely clean grey sand with a single taverna, thirty-minutes' walk north of the town; you can shorten this considerably by sticking to coast-hugging trails and tracks below the road. Far better are the adjacent beaches of **Apókroussi**, which has a canteen, and **Kolóna**, the latter essentially a sandspit joining the islet of Áyios Loukás to Kýthnos. These lie about an hour's walk northwest of Episkopí, and are easiest reached by boat-trip from the harbour. Camping is generally toler-

ated, even on Martinákia beach, the nearest to Mérihas, which has an eponymous taverna.

Owners of **accommodation** often meet the ferries in high season. There are
numerous rooms to let, but they tend to be large and equipped for visiting
families, so they can be on the expensive side – although with some opportunity for bargaining during the week. Out of season, owners are often not on
the premises, but a contact phone number is usually posted up. Few places have
sea views, one exception being the *Kythnos Hotel* (☎02810/32 247; ❷), near
the ferry dock, which has the added bonus of being open all year round. A little inland, behind the small bridge on the seafront, *Panayiota* (☎02810/32 268;
❸) is a decent choice; and there are plenty of other rooms and studios of similar price and quality along the same road. The Milos Express agency may be
able to help you find a room (☎02810/32 104, ☏32 291).

The best **restaurants** are *To Kandouni*, furthest from the ferry, a tasty grill
with tables right by the water and specialities like *sfougáto*; and *Kissos*, a little
inland from the middle of the harbour, where you pay for the food rather than
the setting. There's also a bakery on the road to Dhryopída. Among purveyors
of a modest nightlife, by far the friendliest and liveliest place is *To Vyzantio*.
Remezzo behind the beach plays good popular music, while eclectic Greek folk

can be heard at the modern *New Corner*, 100m along the road to Dhryopídha. The latest addition of any significance is *Akrotiri Club*, perched up on the headland above the south end of the harbour, playing that popular island blend of summer hits and Greek music.

The **bus service**, principally to Loutrá, Hóra, Dhryopídha and Kanála, is reasonably reliable, in season at least; the only motorbike rental is through the main Milos Express agency and is noticeably more expensive than on many islands. The Cava Kythnos shop doubles as the official **National Bank** outlet (exchange all day, credit cards accepted for a €3 fee), and is the agent for hydrofoil tickets and the boat to Kéa.

Hóra and Loutrá

HÓRA lies 6km northeast of Mérihas, set in the middle of the island. Tilting south off an east–west ridge, and laid out to an approximate grid plan, it's an awkward blend of Kéa-style gabled roofs, Cycladic churches with dunce-cap cupolas, and concrete monsters. Hóra supports a **post office** (open only until noon); the closest accommodation at present is at Loutrá. You can **eat** at *To Kentro* taverna run by Maria Tzoyiou near the small square, or at *To Steki* grill; *Paradisos*, on the approach road from Mérihas is another reasonable option. As well as a rather sophisticated kafenío on the square, there is a very pleasant bar, *Apokalypsi*, a little further up, with outdoor seating.

The much-vaunted resort of **LOUTRÁ** (3km north of Hóra and named after its thermal baths) is scruffy, its nineteenth-century spa long since replaced by a sterile modern construction. The best **taverna**, *Katerini*, is a little out on a limb in the neighbouring bay to the west. Otherwise there are a few seafront bars and tavernas offering basic services, such as showers, to yachting crews. There is no shortage of places to sleep: **pensions** such as *Delfini* (☎02810/31 430; ➋), the *Meltemi* (☎02810/31 271; ➋, furnished apartments ➍–➎) and *Porto Klaras* (☎02810/31 276; ➌) are acceptable choices. You can also stay in the state-run *Xenia* baths complex (☎02810/31 217; ➌), where a twenty-minute bath plus basic check-up – blood pressure, heart rate and weight – costs about €3. The small bay of Ayía Iríni, just a kilometre east of Loutrá, is a more pleasant place to swim and boasts the decent *Trehandiri* taverna on the hill above the bay.

Dhryopídha and the south

You're handily placed in Hóra to tackle the most interesting thing to do on Kýthnos: the beautiful **walk** south to Dhryopídha. It takes about ninety minutes, initially following the old cobbled way that leaves Hóra heading due south; critical junctions in the first few minutes are marked by red paint dots. The only reliable water is a well in the valley bottom, reached after thirty minutes, just before a side trail to the triple-naved **chapel of Áyios Spyrídhon** which has recycled Byzantine columns. Just beyond this, you collide with a bulldozed track between Dhryopídha and Áyios Stéfanos, but purists can avoid it by bearing west towards some ruined ridgetop windmills and picking up secondary paths for the final forty minutes of the hike.

More appealing than Hóra by virtue of spanning a ravine, **DHRYOPÍDHA**, with its pleasing tiled roofs, is reminiscent of Spain or Tuscany. A surprisingly large place, it was once the island's capital, built around a famous cave, the Katafíki, at the head of a well-watered valley. Tucked away behind the cathedral is a tiny **folklore museum** that opens erratically in high season. Beside the cathedral is a cheap *psistariá*, *To Steki*, and a good local ouzerí called O

Apithanos ("the unbelievable guy"). Some people let rooms in their houses, but the nearest official accommodation is 6km south at Kanála.

KANÁLA is a good alternative to Loutrá. There are some rooms in the older settlement up on the promontory and a good taverna, *Louloudhas*, with a huge terrace overlooking the larger western beach, **Megáli Ámmos**, which also has rooms and a combination snack bar and taverna. Two adjacent **pensions** on the beach are *Anna* (☎02810/32 035;❷) and the B&B *Margarita* (☎02810/32 265; ❷–❹), with the latter warmly recommended for its home-like atmosphere.

From Kanála, a succession of small coves extends up the east coast as far as **ÁYIOS STÉFANOS**, a small coastal hamlet with two high-season tavernas opposite a chapel-crowned islet linked by a causeway to the body of the island. Southwest of Dhryopídha, reached by a turning off the road to Kanála, **Flamboúri** is the most presentable beach on the west coast. The extension of the asphalted road southwards makes the double bay of **Ayíou Dhimitríou** more accessible than before; although not too exciting, there are a couple of tavernas and rooms to rent in high season.

Sérifos

Sérifos has long languished outside the mainstream of history and modern tourism. Little has happened here since the legendary Perseus returned with Medusa's head, in time to save his mother, Danaë, from being ravished by the local king Polydectes – turning him, his court and the green island into stone. Many would-be visitors are deterred by the apparently barren, hilly interior which, with the stark, rocky coastline, makes Sérifos appear uninhabited until the ferry turns into Livádhi bay. The island is recommended for serious **walkers**, who can head for several small villages in the little-explored interior, plus some isolated coves. Modern Serifots love seclusion, and here, more than anywhere else in the Cyclades, you will find farmsteads miles from anywhere, with only a donkey path to their door. Many people still keep livestock and produce their own wines, and many also cultivate the wild narcissus for export.

Few islanders speak much English; even a few select words of amateur Greek will come in handy and will be warmly received. American yachties drop anchor here in some numbers as well, to take on fresh water which, despite appearances, Sérifos has in abundance.

Livádhi and the main beaches

Most visitors stay in the port, **LIVÁDHI**, set in a wide greenery-fringed bay and handy for most of the island's beaches. The usually calm bay here is a magnet for island-hopping yachts, whose crews chug to and fro in dinghies all day and night. It's not the most attractive place on Sérifos and mosquitoes abound, but Livádhi and the neighbouring cove of Livadhákia are certainly the easiest places to find rooms and any amenities you might need, all of which are very scarce elsewhere.

Unfortunately, the long **beach** at Livádhi is nothing to write home about: the sand is hard-packed and muddy, and the water weedy and prone to intermittent jellyfish flotillas – only the far northeastern end is at all usable. Turn left up the main business street, or climb over the southerly headland from the cemetery, to reach the neighbouring, far superior **Livadhákia**. This golden-sand beach, shaded by tamarisk trees, offers snorkelling and other watersports, as well as an acceptable taverna. If you prefer more seclusion, five-minutes' stroll across the headland to the south brings you to the smaller **Karávi** beach, which is cleaner and almost totally naturist, but has no shade or facilities.

A slightly longer 45-minute walk north of the port along a bumpy track leads to **Psilí Ámmos**, a sheltered, white-sand beach considered the best on the island. Accordingly it's popular, with two rival tavernas which tend to be full in high season. Naturists are pointed – via a ten-minute walk across the headland – towards the larger and often deserted **Áyios Ioánnis** beach, but this is rather exposed with no facilities at all, and only the far south end is inviting. Both beaches are theoretically visited by kaïkia from Livádhi, as are two nearby sea caves, but don't count on it. Additionally, and plainly visible from arriving ferries, two more sandy coves hide at the far southeastern flank of the island opposite an islet; they are accessible on foot only, by a variation of the track to Psilí Ámmos. The more northerly of the two, **Áyios Sóstis**, has a well with fresh water and is the most commonly used beach for secluded camping.

Practicalities

The helpful Krinas Travel (☎02810/51 448, ⨏51 073, ⓔsertrav@otenet.gr), near the jetty, sells **hydrofoil** and **boat** tickets. The public **bus stop** and posted schedule are at the base of the yacht and fishing-boat jetty. You can rent a **bike** or **car** from Blue Bird next to the filling station on the main street or from Krinas Travel.

Accommodation proprietors don't always meet ferries, with the exception of the *Coralli Camping Bungalows*, which regularly sends a minibus, but in high season you'll have to step lively off the boat to get a decent bed. The most rewarding hunting grounds are on the headland above the ferry dock, or Livadhákia beach (see opposite); anything without a sea view will be a notch cheaper. Up on the headland, the *Pension Cristi* (☎02810/51 775; ❷) has an excellent, quiet position overlooking the bay; the nearby *Areti* (☎02810/51 479; ❷–❹) is a little smarter but less friendly. Alternatively, down in the flatlands, the inexpensive seafront rooms of *Anna* (☎02810/51 263; ❷) and *Fani* (☎02810/51 746; ❷) are friendly and spotlessly clean, though the rooms at the front get some traffic noise. The *Hotel Anna* (☎02810/51 666; ❸–❹), above the pizzeria by the yacht harbour, is another fall-back, while the cheapest rooms in Livádhi are next to each other at the far end of the bay: *Margarita* (☏02810/51 321; ❶) and *Adonios Peloponnisos* (☏02810/51 113; ❶).

Livadhákia, ten- to fifteen-minutes' walk south, offers more nocturnal peace, choice and quality, though it has a more touristy feel and the mosquitoes are positively ferocious – bring insecticide coils or make sure your room is furnished with electric vapour pads. One of the oldest and largest complexes of rooms and apartments, close to the beach and with verdant views, is run by Vaso Stamataki (☏02810/51 346; ❷). Newer and higher-standard choices include the *Helios Pension* (☏02810/51 066; ❸), just above the road as you arrive at Livadhákia, and, further along, the *Medusa* (☏02810/51 127; ❸). Cheaper are the rooms in adjacent buildings just after *Helios*, run by two sisters, Yioryia (☏02810/51 336; ❷) and Mina (☏02810/51 545; ❷–❸) – the latter place has sea views. Further along are *Dhorkas* (☏02810/51 422; ❹) and, right by the beach above a restaurant, *O Alexandros* (☏02810/51 119; ❸). Near the built-up area, beside one of only two public access tracks to the beach and behind the best patch of sand, *Coralli Camping Bungalows* (☏02810/51 500, ⓦwww.coralli.gr; ❸–❹) has a restaurant, bar, shop and landscaped camping area.

A makeshift road runs the length of the Livádhi seafront, crammed with restaurants, clubs, shops, supermarkets, and a **cashpoint** at the Alpha Bank. Turn up the road across from the yacht jetty to reach the main street; the *Mylos* bakery – look for the windmill painted on its corner – has exceptionally good cheese pies and wholegrain bread, and there's a **pharmacy** up on the right.

Like most islands, **tavernas** near the quay tend to be slightly pricier, but *Mokkas* fish taverna is recommended nonetheless. Walk up the beach and meals get less expensive; the two best traditional tavernas are the busy *Perseus* and *Cyclades*. Another 500m brings you to *Stamatis*, a favourite with locals for inexpensive home-style food. At the extreme far northeast end of the beach, *Sklavenis* (aka *Margarita's*) has a homely feel and courtyard seating, but the food can be overly deep-fried and quite pricey. Closer to the yacht harbour, *Meltemi* is a good, if slightly expensive, ouzerí – something out of the ordinary for the island. For crepes and ice cream, try *Meli*, in the commercial centre by the port police.

Nightlife is surprisingly lively, and most of it's clustered in or near a mini-mall on the seafront just up from the yacht jetty, so you should be able to quickly find something to suit your taste. The *Roman Cafe Bar*, inside the mall, has a pool table and plays a sophisticated mix of jazz, blues, Latin and adventurous modern. *Alter Ego*, at the back, offers more typically Greek music while *Captain Hook*, upstairs, is louder and more rocking. *Vitamin C* and *Karnayio* are two popular bars next door, and further up the beach is the *Sérifos Yacht Club*, which is actually just a dolled-up kafenío.

Buses connect Livádhi with Hóra, 2km away, some ten times daily, but only manage one or two daily trips to Megálo Livádhya, Galaní and Kállitsos. You may well want to walk, if you're travelling light; it's a pleasant if steep forty minutes up a cobbled way to Hóra, with the *kalderími* leading off from a bend in the road about 300m out of Livádhia. By the beginning of October, you'll have no choice, since the bus – like nearly everything else – ceases operation for the winter.

Hóra

Quiet and atmospheric **HÓRA**, teetering precariously above the harbour, is one of the most spectacular villages of the Cyclades. The best sights are to be found on the town's borders: tiny churches cling to the cliff-edge, and there are breathtaking views across the valleys below. At odd intervals along its alleyways you'll find part of the old castle making up the wall of a house, or a marble statue leaning incongruously in one corner. A pleasant diversion is the hour-long **walk** down to **Psilí Ámmos**: start from beside Hóra's cemetery and aim for the lower of two visible pigeon towers, and then keep close to the phone wires, which will guide you towards the continuation of the double-walled path descending to a bend in the road just above the beach.

Among two or three **tavernas**, the nicest place is *Zorbas*, near the church on the upper square, serving local dishes such as wild fennel fritters; *Stavros*, just east of the bus-stop platía, is friendly and dependable and can arrange **rooms** too (☎02810/51 303; ❶). The island's **post office** is found in the lowest quarter, and a few more expensive rooms for rent lie about 200m north of town, on the street above the track to the cemetery.

The north

North of Hóra, the island's high water-table sometimes breaks the surface to run in delightful rivulets swarming with turtles and frogs, though in recent years many of the open streams seem to have dried up. Reeds, orchards and even the occasional palm tree still take advantage of the unexpected moisture, even if it's no longer visible. This is especially true at **KÁLLITSOS** (Kéndarhos), reached by a ninety-minute path from Hóra, marked by fading red paint splodges along a donkey track above the cemetery. Once at Kállitsos (no facilities), a paved road leads west for 3km to the fifteenth- to seventeenth-century **monastery of Taxiarhón**, designed for sixty monks but presently home only to one of the island's two parish priests – part of a dying breed of farmer-fisherman monks. If he's about, the priest will show you treasures in the monastic church, such as an ivory-inlaid bishop's throne, silver lamps from Egypt (to where many Serifots emigrated during the nineteenth century) and the finely carved *témblon*.

As you loop back towards Hóra from Kállitsos on the asphalt, the fine villages of Galaní and Panayía (named after its tenth-century church) make convenient stops. In **GALANÍ** you can sometimes get simple **meals** at the central store, which also sells excellent, tawny-pink, sherry-like wine; its small-scale production in the west of the island is highly uneconomic, so you'll find it at few other places on Sérifos. Below the village, trails lead to the remote and often windswept beach of **Sykaminiá**, with no facilities and no camping allowed; a better bet for a local swim is the more sheltered cove of **Platýs Yialós** at the extreme northern tip of the island, reached by a partly paved track (negotiable by moped) that branches off just east of Taxiarhón. The neighbouring beach has a taverna, *Nikoulias*, with a couple of very basic rooms (☎02810/52 174; ❷), which nonetheless have great views. The church at **Panayiá** is usually locked, but comes alive on its feast day of Xilopanayía (August 16). Traditionally the first couple to dance around the adjacent olive tree would be the first to marry that year, but this led to unseemly brawls so the priest always goes first these days.

The southwest

A little way south of Panayía, you reach a junction in the road. Turn left to return to Hóra, or continue straight towards **Megálo Horió** – the site of ancient Sérifos, but with little else to recommend it. **Megálo Livádhi**, further on, is a remote and quiet beach resort 8km west of Hóra, with two lovely tavernas whose tables are practically on the beach. *Iy Mardhitsa* taverna has some simple rooms behind the beach (☎02810/51 003; ❶). Iron and copper ore were once exported from here, but cheaper African deposits sent the mines into decline and today most of the idle machinery rusts away, though some gravel-crushing still goes on. At the north end of the beach there's a monument to four workers killed during a protest against unfair conditions in 1916. An alternate turning just below Megálo Horió leads to the small mining and fishing port of **Koutalás**, a pretty sweep of bay with a church-tipped rock, and a long if narrow beach. It has become rather a ghost settlement and the workers' restaurants have all closed down, but there is one snack bar/taverna, catering mainly for yachting crews. The winding track above the village leads to Livádhi, and apart from the pleasant **Gánema** beach, which has a taverna of the same name, there are no places to rest or buy refreshments on the long journey back.

Sífnos

Sífnos is a more immediately appealing island than its northern neighbours since it's prettier, more cultivated and has some fine architecture. This means that it's also much more popular, and extremely crowded in July or August, when rooms are very difficult to find. Take any offered as you land, come armed with a reservation or, best of all, time your visit for spring or autumn, though bear in mind that most of the bars and the souvenir shops aren't likely to be open. In keeping with the island's somewhat upmarket clientele, freelance camping is forbidden, while nudism is tolerated only in isolated coves. The locals tend to be more cosmopolitan and aloof than on neighbouring islands, but in the more out-of-the-way places they're usually hospitable.

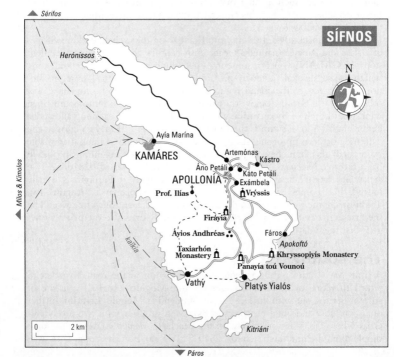

The island's modest size – no bigger than Kýthnos or Sérifos – makes it eminently explorable. The **bus service** is excellent, most of the roads quite decent, and there's a network of paths that are fairly easy to follow. Sífnos has a strong tradition of pottery and was long esteemed for its distinctive cuisine, although most tourist-oriented cooking is only a little above average. However, the island's shops and greengrocers are well stocked in season.

Ferry connections have improved in recent years, keeping pace with the island's increasing popularity. The *Express Milos* and *Express Dionysos* ply a regular shuttle via Kýthnos and Sérifos, then on to Mílos and Kímolos before heading east to Folégandros, Síkinos, Íos and Thíra, from where the course is reversed back to Pireás. Links with the central Cyclades are provided by the infrequent visits of the *Georgios Express* to Páros or Sýros and backed up by an almost daily hydrofoil service which also goes to Náxos and Mýkonos several times a week.

Kamáres

KAMÁRES, the island's port, is tucked away at the foot of high, bare cliffs in the west, which enclose a beach. A busy, fairly downmarket resort with concrete blocks of villas edging up to the base of the cliffs, Kamáres' seafront road is crammed with bars, travel agencies, ice-cream shops and fast-food places. You can store luggage at the Aegean Thesaurus **travel agency** while hunting for a room (proprietors tend not to meet boats); they also change money and can book accommodation throughout the island.

Accommodation is relatively expensive, though bargaining can be productive outside peak season. Try the reasonable *Hotel Stavros* (☎02840/31 641; ❷) or, further along above the town beach, the good but pricier *Boulis Hotel* (☎02840/32 122; ❸–❹), which has very friendly management. Above the *Boulis*, the welcoming *Makis* **campsite** (☎ & ℗02840/32 366) has good facilities and good-value air-conditioned rooms (❸). Continue past the *Makis* and turn right up from the end of the beach to find newer, quieter accommodation in Ayía Marína, including the *Mosha Pension* (☎02840/31 719; ❷), and the newly remodelled *Delphini Hotel* (☎02840/33 740; ❻), which has its own pool.

The best **restaurants** are the *Meropi*, ideal for a pre-ferry lunch, the *Boulis* (under the same management as the *Boulis Hotel*) with its collection of huge retsina barrels, the *Kamares* ouzerí and *Kira Margena* at the far end of the beach in Ayía Marína. Kamáres also has a little **nightlife**: the *Collage Bar*, good for a sunset cocktail, and *Folie-Folie*. The best place to **hire a moped** is at Dionysos.

Apollonía and Artemónas

A steep twenty-minute bus ride (hourly service until late at night) takes you up to **APOLLONÍA**, the centre of Hóra, an amalgam of three hilltop villages which have merged over the years into one continuous community. With white buildings, flower-draped balconies, belfries and pretty squares, it is eminently scenic, though not self-consciously so. On the central platía itself, the **folk museum** (daily 9.30am–2pm & 6–10pm; €1) is worth a visit. As well as an interesting collection of textiles, lace, costumes and weaponry, there are paintings by Nikolaos Tselemendi, a celebrated cookery teacher.

Radiating out from the platía is a network of stepped marble footways and the main pedestrian street, flagstoned Odhós Styliánou Prókou, which leads off to the south, lined with shops, restaurants, bars and churches, including the cakebox cathedral, **Áyios Spyrídhon**, and the eighteenth-century church of **Panayía Ouranoforía**, which stands in the highest quarter of town, incorporating fragments of a seventh-century BC temple of Apollo and a relief of Áyios Yeóryios over the door. **Áyios Athanásios**, next to Platía Kleánthi Triandafýlou, has frescoes and a wooden *témblon*. Some 3km southeast, a short distance from the village of Exámbela, you'll find the active monastery of **Vrýssis** which dates from 1612 and is home to a good collection of religious artefacts and manuscripts.

ARTEMÓNAS, fifteen minutes south of Apollonía on foot, is worth a morning's exploration for its churches and elegant Venetian and Neoclassical houses alone. **Panayía Gourniá** (the key is kept next door) has vivid frescoes; the clustered-dome church of **Kohí** was built over an ancient temple of Artemis (also the basis of the village's name); and seventeenth-century **Áyios Yeóryios** contains fine icons. Artemónas is also the point of departure for **Herónissos**, an isolated hamlet with two tavernas and a few potteries behind a deeply indented, rather bleak bay at the northwestern tip of the island. There's a motorable dirt track there and occasional boat trips from Kamáres, though these are only worth the effort on calm days.

Practicalities

The **post office** and **bus stop** edge onto Apollonía's central platía. The **bank** and **police station** are located on the main road leading north out of town. There are rooms scattered all over the village, making them hard to find; however, there are some obvious choices along the road towards Fáros (thus a bit noisy), the *Margarita* (℡02840/31 032; ❷) being fairly representative. The *Hotel Sifnos* (℡02840/31 624, ℻33 067; ❸), on the main pedestrian street, is the most traditional in its architecture and furnishing, and is operated by the friendly Diareme family. All the central hotels are sure to be noisy when the nearby clubs are open during the summer, and if you want quieter premises with a better view, be prepared to pay more: *Margarita Kouki* (℡02840/33 152; ❷), above the luxurious *Hotel Petali* (℡02840/33 024; ❺–❻), north of the square on the pedestrian lane, is a welcome exception. Probably your best bet is to look on the square for the main branch of the excellent travel agency, Aegean Thesaurus (℡02840/31 151, ℻32 190, ✉aegean@thesaurus.gr), which can book you into rooms of all categories. They also sell a worthwhile package consisting of an accurate topographical map, bus/boat schedules and a short text on Sífnos for about €1.50.

There are a number of **restaurants** in Apollonía, including *Iy Orea Sifnos*, with good food despite its kitchy decor, on the central square; for excellent pizza and pasta find *Mama Mia* up the pedestrian lane to the north; and *Cafe Sifnos*, next to the *Hotel Sifnos* on the main pedestrian street, serves something for nearly every taste and is open all day. There are several tavernas up in the backstreets: *To Apostoli to Koutouki* is quite good for standard Greek fare and very reasonable; probably the best and most famous place to eat on the island, owing to its highly-rated chef, is *Liotrivi* (*Manganas*) on the square up in Artemónas, where there's also an excellent bakery.

Most of the **nightlife** can be found on the main pedestrian street south of the square, where you'll find *Isidora*, *Cafe Folie* and *Argo* – the biggest and loudest. The *Camel Club*, on the road to Fáros, is another popular place for late-night action. For *bouzoúki* there's the *Aloni*, just above the crossroad to *kástro*.

The east coast

Most of Sífnos's coastal settlements are along the less precipitous eastern shore, within a modest distance of Hóra and its surrounding cultivated plateau. These all have good bus services, and a certain amount of food and accommodation,

Kástro being far more appealing than the resorts of Platýs Yialós and Fáros which can get very overcrowded in July and August.

Kástro

An alternative east-coast base which seems the last place on Sífnos to fill up in season, **KÁSTRO** can be reached on foot from Apollonía in 35 minutes, all but the last ten on a clear path beginning at the fork in the road to Kástro, threading its way via Káto Petáli hamlet. Built on a rocky outcrop with an almost sheer drop to the sea on three sides, the ancient capital of the island retains much of its medieval character. Parts of its boundary walls survive, along with a full complement of sinuous, narrow streets graced by balconied, two-storey houses and some fine sixteenth- and seventeenth-century churches with ornamental floors. Venetian coats of arms and ancient wall-fragments can still be seen on some of the older dwellings; there are the remains of the ancient acropolis (including a ram's head sarcophagus by one of the medieval gates), as well as a small **archeological museum** (Tues–Sun 8am–2.30pm; free), which does not always stick closely to the official opening hours, installed in a former Catholic church in the higher part of the village.

Among the several **rooms**, the modernized *Aris* apartments (☎02840/31 161; ②–④) have something for most budgets and are open all year. More rooms are available at the lower end of the village, of which the friendly *Marianna* (☎02840/33 681; ②) is a good basic option. The *Star* and *Leonidas* are the obvious **tavernas** to try out, while the *Cavos Sunrise* café-bar is laid-back and has a fantastic view. On the edge of town, the *Castello* disco-bar is a livelier hangout.

There's nothing approximating a beach in Kástro; for a swim you have to walk to the nearby rocky coves of **Serália** (to the southeast, and with more rooms) and **Paláti**. You can also hike – from the windmills on the approach road near Káto Petáli – to either the sixteenth-century monastery of **Khryssostómou**, or along a track opposite the cliff-face that overlooks the church of the **Eptá Martíres** (Seven Martyrs); nudists sun themselves and snorkel on and around the flat rocks below.

Platýs Yialós

From Apollonía there are almost hourly buses to the resort of **PLATÝS YIALÓS**, some 12km distant, near the southern tip of the island. Despite claims to be the longest beach in the Cyclades, the sand can get very crowded. Diversions include a pottery workshop, but many are put off by the continuous row of snack bars and rooms to rent, which line the entire stretch of beach, and the strong winds which plague it. **Rooms** are expensive, although the comfortable *Pension Angelaki* (☎02840/71 288; ③), near the bus stop, is more reasonably priced, while the *Hotel Efrossyni* (☎02840/71 353; ④) next door is comfortable, and breakfast is included in the price. The local **campsite** is rather uninspiring – a stiff hike inland, shadeless and on sloping, stony ground. Among several fairly pricey **tavernas** are the straightforward *To Steki* and *Bus Stop*, and there is *Mama Mía* for pizza and pasta.

A more rewarding walk uphill from Platýs Yialós brings you to the convent of **Panayía toú Vounoú** (though it's easy to get lost on the way without the locally sold map); the caretaker should let you in if she's about.

Fáros and around

Less crowded beaches are to be found just to the northeast of Platýs Yialós (though unfortunately not directly accessible along the coast). **FÁROS**, again with regular bus links to Apollonía, makes an excellent fall-back base if you don't strike it lucky elsewhere. A small and friendly resort, it has some of the cheapest **accommodation** on the island, as well as a couple of smarter places, including the recommended *Apéranto* guesthouse (☎02840/71 473;❸) at the far end of the bay. *To Kyma* is a pleasant seafront **taverna**, and the smart *On the Rocks*, perched on the headland at the far end of the beach, serves a tasty selection of snacks as well as full meals. The closest beaches are not up to much: the town strand itself is muddy, shadeless and crowded, and the one to the northeast past the headland is not much better. Head off in the opposite direction, however, through the older part of the village, and things improve at **Glyfó**, a longer, wider family beach about twenty minutes away.

Continuing from Glyfó, a fifteen-minute cliffside path leads to the beach of **Apokoftó**, with a couple of good tavernas, and, up an access road, to the *Hotel Flora* (☎02840/71 278; ❷ -❸), which has superb views. The shore itself tends to collect seaweed, however, and a rock reef must be negotiated to get into the water. Flanking Apokoftó to the south, marooned on a sea-washed spit and featuring on every OTE poster of the island, is the disestablished, seventeenth-century **Khryssopiyís monastery**, where until recently cells were rented out as tourist accommodation. According to legend, the cleft in the rock appeared when two village girls, fleeing to the spit to escape the attentions of menacing pirates, prayed to the Virgin to defend their virtue.

The interior and Vathý

Apollonía is a good base from which to start your explorations of remoter Sífnos. You can rent **bikes** at Moto Apollo, beside the petrol station on the road to Fáros, but the island is best explored on foot.

Taking the path out from Katavatí (the district south of Apollonía) you'll pass, after a few minutes, the beautiful empty **monastery of Firáyia** and – fifteen minutes along the ugly new road – the path climbing up to **Áyios Andhréas**, where you'll be rewarded with tremendous views over the islands of Sýros, Páros, Íos, Folégandhros and Síkinos. Just below the church is an enormous Bronze Age archeological site.

Even better is the all-trail walk to Vathý, around three hours from Katavatí and reached by bearing right at a signed junction in Katavatí. Part way along you can detour on a conspicuous side-trail to the **monastery of Profítis Ilías**, on the very summit of the island, with a vaulted refectory and extensive views.

Vathý

A fishing village on the shore of a stunning funnel-shaped bay, **VATHÝ** is the most attractive and remote base on the island. However, the highway there has been recently improved, so it's poised for development, with a new luxury hotel with a huge pool. There are an increasing number of **rooms**, the best deals probably being at *Manolis* taverna (☎02840/71 111;❷), or those attached to the tiny **monastery of the Archangel Gabriel**. Unusually, camping rough meets with little objection from the locals, a reflection of their friendly attitude towards outsiders. For **food**, *Manolis* does excellent grills and has a fascinating gyrating clay oven in the courtyard; *Iy Okeanidha* has good mezédhes such as chickpea balls and cheesy aubergine patties; while *To Tsikali* behind the monastery is cheaper but less varied.

Now that there are regular **buses** (8 daily in high season, 2 daily at other times) the kaïkia no longer run from Kamáres. It is possible to walk to Platýs Yíalos in ninety minutes, but the path is not well marked. At the far end of the bay a traditional pottery still functions.

Mílos

Volcanic **Mílos** boasts amazing geological diversity, weird rock formations, hot springs, good beaches and sensational views. Minoan settlers were attracted by obsidian, and other products of its volcanic soil made the island one of the most important of the Cyclades in the ancient world. Today the quarrying of barite, perlite and porcelain has left deep scars on the landscape but given the island a relative prosperity and independence. It hasn't had to tart itself up to court tourism – the main reason it's worth a stay of several days.

You get a good preview of the island's geological wonders as your ferry enters Mílos Bay, one of the world's most striking natural harbours, shaped by an ancient explosion. Off the north coast, accessible only by excursion boat, the Glaroníssia (Seagull Isles) are shaped like massed organ pipes, and there are more weird formations on the southwest coast at Kléftiko. Inland, too, you frequently come across strange, volcanic outcrops, and thermal springs burst forth.

Like most volcanic islands, Mílos is quite fertile: away from the summits of **Profítis Ilías** in the southwest and lower hills in the east, a gently undulating countryside is intensively cultivated to produce grain, hay and orchard fruits. The island's domestic architecture, with its lava-built, two-up-two-down houses, isn't as immediately impressive as its more pristine neighbours, but is charming nonetheless. There's an excellent free guide booklet, *Welcome to Mílos*, which can be picked up from tourist offices, hotels and restaurants.

Adhámas

The main port of **ADHÁMAS**, known as Adhámandas to locals, was founded by Cretan refugees fleeing a failed rebellion in 1841. With a handsome new marble-paved esplanade around its natural headland it's now among the most attractive ports in the Cyclades, lively enough, with all the requisite facilities.

Most **accommodation** is concentrated on the hill above the harbour and on or just off the main road to Pláka, and ranges from real cheapies with shared facilities, like that of Anna Gozadhinou (☏02870/22 364; ❶), to smart rooms with TV and all mod cons, like *Thalassitra* (☏02870/23 570; ❹). Best choices include the *Delfini* (☏02870/22 001; ❷ -❸), one block behind the town beach to the left from the ferry landing, the smart, central, double-glazed *Portiani Hotel* (☏02870/22 940; ❸ -❺) and the luxury *Santa Maria Village* (☏02870/21 949; ❹ -❻), 300m behind the beach. During high season the highly organized **tourist office** opposite the ferry dock has a daily updated list of available rooms around the island, and a handy brochure with all the numbers at any given time. Until recently freelance **camping** went undisturbed at the small **Frangomnímata** beach, ten-minutes' walk northwest by the French war memorial, but with the arrival of the first official campsite at Hivadolímni beach (☏02870/31 410) things seem set to change. As is the case with many campsites in Greece, bungalows are also available ❹); a campsite minibus meets ferries.

Flisvos, near the jetty, is a good place to **eat**. Of the three adjacent tavernas along the seafront towards the long tamarisk-lined beach south of town, *Navagio* is the best value, although the service is slow. Just off the main street inland, *Ta Pitsounakia* is a good cheap *psistariá* with a pleasant courtyard. The local internet café (☏02870/28 011, ✉pmayros@yahoo.com) is up near the Ayía Triáda church. Apart from the obvious string of cafés along the main seafront drag, *Akri*, above the jetty, is a more hip **bar**, with a pleasant veranda. *Micro Cafe*, on the way to the first beach east of town, has an English-speaking owner who plays varied music and plays requests, and *Fuego*, above the far end of the beach, goes on until sunrise playing a mixture of summer hits and Greek pop.

On the quayside, several **travel agencies** sell ferry tickets and maps, have information about coastal boat-trips and rent motorbikes and cars. Dolfin Tours (☏02870/23 183, ℉23 409), near the Emboriko Bank, is particularly friendly and helpful, and sells tickets to Crete and the Dodecanese. There are also several **banks** and a **post office**. Adhámas is the hub of the island's **bus services**, which run hourly to Pláka, nine times daily in high season to Pollónia, seven times daily to Paleohóri via Zefiria and to Provatás. The taxi rank is nearby – call ☏02870/22 219 to book. Some visitors arrive by plane from Athens; most seats, however, are reserved by the local mining industry. The new, but already inadequate **airport** is 5km southeast of the port, close to Zefiria.

The **Mining Museum of Mílos** (daily 9.30am–1pm & 5–8pm; free), housed in a new building towards the south beach, charts the mining history of Mílos. Take a **boat tour** round the island on one of three boats; weather permitting, these normally leave at 9am and make several stops at inaccessible swimming spots like the magnificent Kléftiko, with a late lunch on Kímolos (see p.599 and p.600).

The northwestern villages and ancient Melos

The main appeal of Mílos is in an area that has been the island's focus of habitation since Classical times, where a cluster of villages huddle in the lee of a crag, four kilometres northwest of the harbour.

PLÁKA (**MÍLOS**) is the largest of these communities and the official capital of the island, with a hospital and **post office**. There is also a **motorbike rental** outfit near the archeological museum (see below). There are **rooms** available scattered around the village, with those on the west side offering spectacular views (there's a map and listing in *Welcome to Mílos*). Among the nicest of these are the pretty studios of Sotiria & Stavros Karamitsou (☎02870/23 820; ❹) and those of Stratis Vourakis (☎02870/21 702; ❹). Kaliopi Moraitou (☎02870/41 353; ❹) has newly refurbished rooms in the house where the Venus de Milo was allegedly hidden following its discovery (see below), and Maria Kentrota (☎02870/21 572; ❸) has a couple of charming, if basic, studios close to the archeological museum. There are also three or four blocks of modern accommodation overlooking the busy approach road. A number of ouzerís have opened up in recent years, making Pláka a real **eating** paradise: highly recommended are *Arhondoula*, *Dhiporto* and *To Kastro* up in the centre of the village, as well as *Plakiani Gonia* on the approach road. The *Utopia Cafe* is a fine place to stop for a coffee or a drink and take in the sensational view, especially at sunset.

Pláka boasts **two museums**. Behind the lower car park, at the top of the approach boulevard through the newer district, the **archeological museum** (Tues–Sun 8.30am–3pm; €1.50) contains numerous obsidian implements, plus a whole wing of finds from ancient Phylakopi (see p.599) whose highlights include a votive lamp in the form of a bull and a rather Minoan-looking terracotta goddess. Labelling is scant, but isn't really needed for a plaster cast of the most famous statue in the world, the Venus de Milo, the original of which was found on the island in 1820 and appropriated by the French; her arms were knocked off in the melée surrounding her abduction. Up in a mansion of the old quarter, the **folk museum** (Tues–Sat 10am–2pm & 6–9pm; €1.50) offers room re-creations, but is otherwise a Greek-labelled jumble of impedimenta pertaining to milling, brewing, cheese-making, baking and weaving, rounded off by old engravings, photos and mineral samples.

A stairway beginning near the police station leads up to the old Venetian **Kástro**, its slopes clad in stone and cement to channel precious rainwater into cisterns. The enormous chapel of **Panayía Thalassítra** looms near the summit, where the ancient Melians made their last stand against the Athenians before the massacre of 416 BC. Today it offers one of the best views in the Aegean, particularly at sunset in clear conditions.

The attractive village of **TRYPITÍ** (meaning "perforated"), which takes its name from the cliffside tombs nearby and covers a long ridge a kilometre south of Pláka, is another good base if you're after a village environment. There are a few modest **rooms**, two of which are just down the steep street from the tiny platía below the main church. The best place to **eat** is *Ta Glaronisia*, on the main street and there's a nice little bar, *Konaki*, near the main square. From Trypití, it's a pleasant 45-minute walk down to Adhámas via Skinópi on the winding old *kaldeŕími*, which begins on the saddle linking Trypití with the hamlet of Klimatovoúni.

TRIOVÁSSALOS and its twin **PÉRAN TRIOVÁSSALOS** are more workaday, less polished than Pláka or Trypití. There are "rooms to rent" signs out here as well, but they'll inevitably be noisier. Péran also offers the idiosyncratic taverna *O Hamos* (which means "a mess") and a naive pebble mosaic in the courtyard of **Áyios Yeóryios church** – created in 1880, it features assorted animal and plant motifs.

Local sites and the coast

From Pláka's archeological museum, signs point you towards the **early Christian catacombs** (Tues–Sun 8.30am–3pm; free), 1km south of Pláka and

just 400m from Trypití village; steps lead down from the road to the inconspicuous entrance. Some 5000 bodies were buried in tomb-lined corridors
stretching some 200m into the soft volcanic rock, but only the first 50m is illuminated and accessible by boardwalk. Don't miss the adjacent ruins of **ancient
Melos**, extending down from Pláka almost to the sea. There are huge Dorian
walls, the usual column fragments lying around and, best of all, a well-preserved
Roman **amphitheatre** (unrestricted access) some 200m west of the catacombs
by track, then trail. Only seven rows of seats remain intact, but these evocatively
look out over Klíma to the bay. Between the catacombs and the theatre is the
signposted spot where the Venus de Milo was found; promptly delivered to the
French consul for "safekeeping" from the Turks, this was the last the Greeks saw
of the statue until a copy was belatedly forwarded from the Louvre in Paris.

At the very bottom of the vale, **KLÍMA** is the most photogenic of several
fishing hamlets on the island, with its picturesque boathouses tucked underneath the principal living areas. There's no beach to speak of, and only one
place to stay – the impeccably sited, if a little basic *Panorama* (℡02870/21 623;
❷–❹), with an acceptable balcony taverna.

Pláthiena, 45-minutes' walk northwest of Pláka, is the closest proper beach, and
thus is extremely popular in summer. There are no facilities, but the beach is fairly well protected and partly shaded by tamarisks. Head initially west from near the
police station on the marked footpath towards **ARETÍ** and **FOURKOVOÚNI**,
two more cliff-dug, boathouse-hamlets very much in the Klíma mould. Although
the direct route to Pláthiena is signposted, it no longer goes via Fourkovoúni; both
hamlets are reached by side-turnings off the main route, which becomes a jeep
track as you approach Fourkovoúni. By moped, access to Pláthiena is only from
Plakés, the northernmost and smallest of the five northwestern villages.

The south

The main road to the south of the island splits at **Kánava junction**, a dreary
place at first glance owing to the large power plant here. But opposite this,
indicated by a rusty sign pointing seaward, is the first of Mílos's **hot springs**,
which bubble up in the shallows and are much enjoyed by the locals.

Taking the left or easterly fork leads to **ZEFYRÍA**, hidden among olive
groves below the bare hills; it was briefly the medieval capital until an eighteenth-century epidemic drove out the population. Much of the old town is
still deserted, though some life has returned, and there's a magnificent seventeenth-century church.

South of here it's a further 8km down a winding road to the coarse-sand
beach of **Paleohóri**. Actually a triple strand totalling 800m in length, it's indisputably the island's best; clothing's optional at the westerly cove, where steam
vents heat both the shallow water and the rock overhangs onshore. There are a
number of **places to stay**, such as the inland *Broutsos* (℡010/34 78 425;❹),
the purpose-built rooms at the *Artemis* restaurant (℡02870/31 221;❹) nearer
the beach, and Panayiota Vikelli's rooms (℡02870/31 228; ❹). The place to eat
is *Pelagos*, which has a large raised patio.

The westerly road from Kánava junction leads past the airport gate to
Hivadholímni, considered to be the best beach on Mílos bay itself. Not that
this is saying much: Hivadholímni is north-facing and thus garbage-prone, with
shallow sumpy water offshore, although there is a taverna, a disco-bar and a
sizeable community of campers during the summer. It's better to veer south to
Provatás, a short but tidy beach, closed off by colourful cliffs on the east. Being
so easy to get to, it hasn't escaped some development: there are two **rooms**

establishments plus, closer to the shore, a newer, luxury complex, *Golden Milos Beach* (T02870/31 307; ❹–❻). The best value for food and accommodation is the *Maistrali* (T02870/31 206; ❸).

Some 2km west of Provatás, you'll see a highway sign for **Kípos**. Below and to the left of the road, a small **medieval chapel** dedicated to the *Kímisis* (Assumption) sits atop foundations far older – as evidenced by the early Christian reliefs stacked along the west wall and a carved, cruciform baptismal font in the *ieron* behind the altar screen. At one time a spring gushed from the low-tunnel cave beside the font – sufficiently miraculous in itself on arid Mílos. Several kilometres before Provatás, a road forks east through a dusty white quarry to the trendy and popular beach of **Firipláka**. Further east, **Tsigrádho** beach is accessible by boat, or by the novel means of a rope hanging down a crevice in the cliff-face.

For the most part **Hálakas**, the southwestern peninsula centred on the wilderness of 748-metre Profítis Ilías, is uninhabited and little built upon, with the exception of the **monastery of Sidherianós**. The roads are memorable, if a little tiring, and several spots are worth making the effort to see. **Emboriós** on the east side of the peninsula has a fine little beach and a great local taverna with a few cheap rooms (T02870/21 389; ❸). On the mostly rugged west coast, **Triádhes** is one of the finest and least spoilt beaches in the Cyclades, but you'll have to bring your own provisions. **Kléftiko** in the southwest corner is only reachable by boat, but repays the effort to get there with its stunning rock formations, semi-submerged rock tunnels and colourful coral.

The north coast

From either Adhámas or the Pláka area, good roads run roughly parallel to the **north coast** which, despite being windswept and largely uninhabited, is not devoid of interest. **Mandhrákia**, reached from Péran Triovássalos, is another boathouse settlement, and **Sarakíniko**, to the east, is a sculpted inlet with a sandy seabed and a summer beach café. About 8km from Adhámas, the little hamlet of **Páhena**, not shown on many maps, has a small beach and cluster of rooms – try *Terry's* (T02870/22 640; ❸). About a kilometre beyond this, the remains of three superimposed Neolithic settlements crown a small knoll at **Fylakopí** (ancient Phylakope); the site was important archeologically, but hasn't been maintained and is difficult to interpret. Just before the site is another one of Milos's coastal wonders: the deep-sea inlet of **Papáfranga**, set in a ravine and accessible through a gap in the cliffs.

Pollónia

POLLÓNIA, 12km northeast of Adhámas, must be the windiest spot on the island, hence the name of its longest-lived and best **bar**, *Okto Bofor* (meaning "Force 8 gales"), near the church. The second resort on Mílos after Adhámas, it is, not surprisingly, immensely popular with windsurfers, and a diving centre has further increased its popularity among watersports enthusiasts. Pollónia is essentially a small harbour protected by a storm-lashed spit of land on the northeast, where self-catering units are multiplying rapidly, fringed by a long but narrow, tamarisk-fringed beach to the rear, and closed off on the south by a smaller promontory on which the tiny original settlement huddles. Besides the town beach, the only other convenient, half-decent beach is at **Voúdhia**, 3km east, where you will find more of the island's hot springs, although it is effectively spoiled by its proximity to huge mining works, which lend it the desolate air of a *Mad Max* location.

On the quay are several **tavernas** and a couple of very mediocre café/snack bars. Inland and south of here you'll find a concentration of **accommodation**, more simple rooms and fewer apartments, most with the slight drawback of occasional noise and dust from quarry trucks. Among the highest-quality units here are the *Kapetan Tasos Studios* (☎02870/41 287; ❹), with good views of the straits between Mílos and Kímolos; *Flora* (☎02870/41 249; ❹), on the road towards the spit, is a more reasonable option, as are *Efi* rooms (☎02870/41 396; ❹), above the far end of the beach; *Andreas* (☎02870/41 262; ❹) has triple studios with stunning views and easy access to the quiet neighbouring bay. Pollónia has no bank or post office, but the friendly Axios Rent A Car office (☎02870/41 442) can change money and advise you on accommodation matters. A **motorbike rental** place and a well-stocked **supermarket** complete the list of amenities. There is a huge map fixed on a metal frame near the bus stop, which shows all the facilities and gives telephone numbers.

Getting to Kímolos may be the main reason you're here. The *Tria Adhelfia* makes the trip daily year-round at 6.45am and 2pm, returning from Kímolos an hour later. During high season, there is also an open ferry boat, so that there are at least five crossings a day.

Kímolos

Of the three islets off the coast of Mílos, Andímilos is home to a rare species of chamois, Políegos has more ordinary goats, but only **Kímolos** has any human habitation. Volcanic like Mílos, with the same little lava-built rural cottages, it profits from its geology and used to export chalk (*kimolía* in Greek) until the supply was exhausted. Fuller's earth is still extracted locally, and the fine dust of this clay is a familiar sight on the island, where mining still outstrips fishing and farming as an occupation. Rugged and barren in the interior, it has some fertile land on the southeast coast where wells provide water, and this is where the population of about eight hundred is concentrated.

Kímolos is sleepy indeed from September to June, and even in August sees few visitors. This is probably just as well, since there are fewer than a hundred beds on the whole island, and little in the way of other amenities.

Psathí and Hóra

Whether you arrive by ferry, or by kaïki from Pollónia, you'll dock at the hamlet of **PSATHÍ**, pretty much a non-event except for the excellent *To Kyma* **taverna** midway along the beach. The laissez-faire attitude towards tourism is demonstrated by the fact that there are no rooms here. **Ferry tickets** are sold only outside the expensive café at the end of the jetty, an hour or so before the anticipated arrival of the boat; the *Tria Adhelfia* and another open ferry come and go from Pollónia on Mílos from the base of the jetty five times a day in summer. There is no bus on the island, but a licence has been obtained for a taxi, so now only a driver is required. The friendly locals will sometimes offer you a lift.

Around the bay there are a few old windmills and the dazzlingly white **HÓRA** perched on the ridge above them. Unsung – and neglected, although there are plans to reconstruct it and build government rooms – is the magnificent, two-gated sixteenth-century *kástro*, the best preserved of such fortresses built against marauding pirates in the Cyclades; the perimeter houses are intact and inhabited but its heart is a jumble of ruins. Just outside the *kástro* to the north stands the conspicuously unwhitewashed, late-sixteenth-century church of **Khryssóstomos**, the oldest and most beautiful on the island. It takes fifteen minutes to walk up to the surprisingly large town, passing the adequate *Villa Maria* (☎02870/51 392; ❷), about five minutes along the way and nearer to Psathí. Further accommodation is available in Hóra itself, where Margaro Petraki (☎02870/51 314; ❶), has rooms tucked away in the rather unglamorous maze of backstreets, as does Nikos Ventouris (☎02870/51 329; ❶) above his kafenío nearby. Sofia Ventouris (☎02870/51 219; ❸) has a few new studios with sea views, close to the church. The aptly named *Panorama*, near the east gate of the *kástro*, is the most elaborate and consistently open **taverna**. *Meltémi*, to the west of the village, is a good, new taverna which also has some rooms (☎02870/51 360; ❷). There are a couple of basic *psistariés*, as well as *1860*, a surprisingly sophisticated **café-bar**. Self-catering is an easy proposition – and may be a necessity before June or after August – with a well-stocked supermarket, produce stalls and a butcher. Finally, there are a couple of boat agencies, and a **post office** in the west of the village. The small **archeological museum** (Tues & Fri 8am–2pm, Wed, Thurs, Sat, Sun 8am–1pm), currently on the road into Hóra, is due to move to more spacious premises near the church; its collection comprises pottery from the Geometric to the Roman period.

Around the island

During summer at least, the hamlet of **ALYKÍ** on the south coast is a better bet for staying than Psathí and Hóra; it only takes about thirty minutes to walk there on the paved road that forks left just before the *Villa Maria*. Alykí is named after the salt pan which sprawls between a rather mediocre beach with no shade or shelter, and has a pair of **rooms** – *Sardis* (☎02870/51 458; ❸) and *Passamihalis* (☎02870/51 340; ❷) – and simple **tavernas**. You can stroll west one cove to **Bonátsa** for better sand and shallow water, though you won't escape the winds. Passing another cove you come to the even more attractive beach of Kalamítsi, with better shade and the good little taverna and rooms of *Ventouris* (❸). To the east, between Alykí and Psathí, the smaller, more secluded beach of **Skála** is better for camping.

The 700m coarse-sand beach of **Elliniká** is 45-minutes' walk west of Alykí: starting on the road, bear left – just before two chapels on a slope – onto a narrower track which runs through the fields at the bottom of the valley. Divided by a low bluff, the beach is bracketed by two capes and looks out over Dhaskalió islet; it tends to catch heavy weather in the afternoon, and there are no facilities here.

Another road leads northeast from Hóra to a beach and radioactive springs at **Prássa**, 7km away. The route takes in impressive views across the straits to Políegos, and there are several shady peaceful coves where it's possible to camp out. Innumerable goat tracks invite exploration of the rest of the island; in the far northwest, on Kímolos's summit, are the ruins of an imposing Venetian fortress known as **Paleókastro**. The local community has plans to open an official campsite at Klíma Bay 2km northeast of Hóra, once it has relocated the rubbish dump that currently befouls the place.

Ándhros

Ándhros, the second largest and northernmost of the Cyclades, has a number of fine features to offer the visitor and is a great place for serious walkers. Thinly populated but prosperous, its fertile, well-watered valleys have attracted

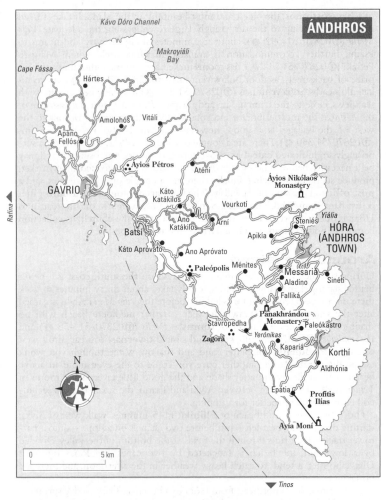

scores of Athenian holiday villas whose red-tiled roofs and white walls stand out among the greenery. Some of the more recent of these have robbed many of the villages of life and atmosphere, turning them into scattered settlements with no nucleus, and creating a weekender mentality manifest in noisy Friday and Sunday evening traffic jams at the ferry dock. The island doesn't cater to independent travellers, and it can be difficult to find a bed during high season, especially at weekends. On the positive side, the permanent population is distinctly hospitable; traditionally working on ships, they are only too happy to try out their English on you. Together with some of the more idiosyncratic reminders of the Venetian period, such as the *peristereónes* (pigeon towers) and the *frákhtes* (dry-stone walls, here raised to the status of an art form), it is this friendliness that lends Ándhros its charm.

Ferries connect the island with Rafina on the mainland, only an hour from Athens on the bus, and you can loop back onto the central Cycladic routes via

Mýkonos, Tínos or Sýros. A bus usually meets arriving ferries and runs to Batsí and on to Hóra at least six times a day in the high season.

Northern and western Ándhros

All ferries and catamarans arrive at the main port, **GÁVRIO**, a moderately attractive holiday resort. Few venture onto the adjacent windswept beach; however, there are plenty more attractive alternatives just to the south, where you'll find some of the area's better accommodation. A converted dovecote houses a sporadically functioning **tourist office**, and there are half a dozen ferry **ticket agents**, a **bank**, and a **post office** on the waterfront.

The cheapest **accommodation** is in the basic *Galaxias* (☎02820/71 228; ❷), which serves as a late-arrival fall-back. There are more room and studio outfits along and above the main coastal road to Batsí: *Aktion* (☎02820/71 607; ❸) is fairly representative, while *Andros Holiday Hotel* (☎02820/71 384; ❻) is a good upmarket choice. **Restaurants** worth trying include the good if basic *estiatório, Tria Asteria*; the *Veggera* taverna 100m inland with its pleasant leafy courtyard; and the smart *Trehandiri* ouzerí opposite the catamaran dock. **Nightlife** revolves around a string of cafés and bars along the harbourfront, of which *Marlin* is a popular choice. Alternatively, there are one or two lively venues on Áyios Pétros beach several kilometres south, including *Marabou* taverna which frequently features live guitar music. Along the same stretch the excellent *Yiannouli* taverna is worth checking out for lunch.

The road north begins behind the *Hotel Gavrion Beach*. Around 3km northwest are two beaches named **Fellós**: one with holiday villas and a taverna, the other hidden beyond the headland and popular with freelance campers. Beyond Ápano Fellós, the countryside is empty except for a few hamlets inhabited by the descendants of Albanians who settled here and in southern Évvia several hundred years ago.

Most visitors head 8km south down the coast, past the lively Khryssí Ammos beach, and the *Perakkis Hotel* above it (☎02820/71 456; ❸), to **BATSÍ**, the island's main resort, with large hotels and bars around its fine natural harbour. The beautiful though often crowded beach curves round the port, and the sea is cold, calm and clean (except near the taxi park). **Hotels** range from the central, comfortable *Chryssi Akti* (☎02820/41 236; ❸) to the upmarket *Aneroussa Beach Hotel* (☎02820/41 045; ❸–❺), south of town past the Stivári area towards Áyia Marína beach – a picturesque cove with *Yiannoulis* fish taverna and studios (☎02820/41 963; ❸). Besides these there are plenty of other rooms, and good **food** can be had, especially at *To Akroyiali* and *Pizza Ritsa*. Other choices include *Stamatis*, an established taverna with a nice atmosphere, and *Ta Delfinia,* which has a pleasant, sheltered balcony. For something a little different have a shrimp feast at *Restaurant Sirocco*, on the inland path above the village. There are several café-bars, such as *Capriccio* and *Select*, a half a dozen or so loud indoor bars featuring the standard foreign/Greek musical mix, and even an outdoor cinema with a different movie every night in the summer. There are two banks, with cash dispensers. For information on walking tours, a free copy of the informative *Island of Andro*, or other travel needs go to Greek Sun Travel (☎02820/41 198, ℻41 239, ✉greeksun@traveling.gr), upstairs near the taxi park.

From Batsí you're within easy walking distance of some beautiful inland villages. At **KÁTO KATÁKILOS**, one hour inland, there are a couple of seasonal **tavernas** including *O Gregos*; a rough track leads to **ATÉNI**, a hamlet in a lush, remote valley. **ÁNO KATÁKILOS** has a couple of undervisited tavernas with fine views across the village. A right-hand turning out of Katákilos heads up the mountain to **ARNÍ**, whose lone taverna is often shrouded in mist. Another rewarding trip is to a well-preserved, twenty-metre-high tower at **Áyios Pétros**, a mystery even to locals, 5km from Gávrio or 9km coming from Batsí.

South of Batsí along the main road are **Káto** and **Áno Apróvato**. Káto has rooms, including *Galíni* (℡02820/41 472; **②**), a taverna and a path to a quiet beach, while nearby is the largely unexplored archeological site of **Paleópolis**. Áno has the excellent taverna *To Balkóni tou Egeou*, which can be most easily visited on one of the "Mezédhes Nights" organized from Batsí by Greek Sun Travel and various hotels, though for a more authentic evening you may be better off making your own way there.

Hóra and around

A bus service links the west coast with **HÓRA**, aka **ÁNDHROS TOWN**, 35km from Gávrio. With its setting on a rocky spur cutting across a huge bay, the capital is the most attractive place on the island. Paved in marble and schist from the still-active local quarries, the buildings around the bus station are grand nineteenth-century affairs, and the squares with their ornate wall fountains and gateways are equally elegant. The hill quarters are modern and rather exclusive, while the small port on the west side of the headland has a yacht supply station and ferry landing. There are beaches on both sides of the headland, the better of which is Parapórti, to the east, though it's somewhat exposed to the *meltémi* winds in summer.

The few **hotels** in town are on the expensive side and tend to be busy with holidaying Greeks, although you could try the traditional *Aigli* (℡02820/22 303; **②**), opposite the big church on the main walkway. Most rooms are clustered behind the long **Nimbório** northwest of town, and range from cheap family guesthouses like *Firíou* (℡02820/22 921; **①**) and good clean rooms like those of *Villa Stella* (℡02820/22 471; **③**) to modern apartments such as the *Alkíoni Inn* (℡02820/24 522; **④**). The *Paradise Hotel* (℡02820/22 187, ⓔmarlos@mail.otenet.gr; **⑤–⑥**), with its swimming pool and tennis court, is the most upmarket choice. For **eating**, most cafés are up in Hóra: *Plátanos* has a generous mezédhes selection which can be enjoyed with an oúzo under the plane trees; the appropriately named *O Stathmos* right by the bus station is good; and there's a decent *psistariá* on the main drag. The nicest taverna is *O Nonas*, tucked away at the town end of the beach behind the ugly *Xenia* hotel; *Nostos*, a smart new pizzeria nearby on the seafront, is another popular choice. Up in Hóra there's the *Rock Café* for a **drink**, but Nimboúrio beach is the epicentre of **nightlife** with the two-storey *Veggera*, a thumping disco halfway along, and the huge *Kavo* right at the end, which plays Greek music till after 4am. There's a post office and bank around town, a couple of travel agents and three motorbike rentals behind the beach.

From the square right at the end of town you pass through an archway and down to windswept **Platía Ríva**, with its statue of the unknown sailor scanning the sea. (This stolid bronze, a gift from the Soviet Union, was recently toppled and broken by a high wind, but locals plan to restore it.) Beyond lies the thirteenth-century Venetian *kástro*, precariously joined to the mainland by a narrow-arched bridge, which was damaged by German munitions in World War II. Don't be discouraged by the stark modern architecture of the **archeological museum** (Tues–Sun 8.30am–2.30pm; €1.50), on the main street; it proves to be well laid out and labelled, with instructive models. Its prize item is the fourth-century "Hermes of Ándros", reclaimed from a prominent position in the Athens archeological museum. Behind it, the **Modern Art Museum** (Wed–Mon 10am–2pm, also 6–8pm in summer; €3) has a sculpture garden and a permanent collection with works by Picasso, Matisse, Kandinsky, Chagall and others, as well as temporary shows.

Hiking is particularly inviting south and west from Ándros, where there are lush little river valleys. One obvious destination is **MÉNITES**, a hill village just up a green valley choked with trees and straddled by stone walls. The church of the **Panayía** may have been the location of a temple of Dionysos, where water was turned into wine; water still flows continuously from the local rocks. Nearby is the medieval village of **MESSARIÁ**, with the deserted twelfth-century Byzantine church of **Taxiárhis** below and the pleasantly shady *Platanos* taverna. The finest monastery on the island, **Panakhrándou**, is only an hour's (steep) walk away, via the village of Falliká: reputedly tenth-century, it's still defended by massive walls but occupied these days by just three monks. It clings to an iron-stained cliff southwest of Hóra, to which you can return directly with a healthy two- to three-hour walk down the creek valley, guided by red dots.

Hidden by the ridge directly north of Hóra, the prosperous nineteenth-century village of **STENIÉS** was built by the vanguard of today's shipping magnates; just below, at Yiália, there's a small pebble beach with a taverna. Nearby on the road to Strapouriés is a wonderful taverna, *Bozakis*, which boasts a view all the way down to the coast and excellent food. Beyond Steniés is **APIKÍA**, a tidy little village which bottles Sariza-brand mineral water for a living; there are a few **tavernas**, including *O Tassos* which has a lovely garden setting and specialities such as goat and rabbit. There are a very limited number of **rooms** here, as well as the "luxury" hotel *Pigi Sariza* (℡02820/23 799 or 23 899; ❸-❺), which is getting a bit tatty around the edges. The road is now asphalted up to Vourkotí and even past this point is quite negotiable via Arní to the west coast. There are some stunning views all along this road but bike riders need to take care when the *meltémi* is blowing – it can get dangerously windy.

Southern Ándros

On your way south, you might stop at **Zagorá**, a fortified Geometric town – unique in having never been built over – that was excavated in the early 1970s. Located on a desolate, flat-topped promontory with cliffs falling away on three sides, it's worth a visit for the view alone. With your own transport, the sheltered cove of Sinéti south of Hóra is also worth a detour.

The village of **KORTHÍ**, the end of the line, is a friendly place which is slowly waking up to its tourist potential. Set on a large sandy bay, cut off from the rest of the island by a high ridge and so relatively unspoiled, it is pleasant enough to merit spending the night at *Villa Aristidou* (℡02820/62 122;❷) or at the austere-looking *Hotel Korthion* (℡02820/61 218;❷ -❸). There are also several good seafood **restaurants**, and a number of pleasant café-bars including *Erolo Cafe* on the seafront. You could also take in the nearby convent of **Zoödhóhou Piyís** (open to visitors before noon), with illuminated manuscripts and a disused weaving factory.

To the north is **PALEÓKASTRO**, a tumbledown village with a ruined Venetian castle and a legend about an old woman who betrayed the stronghold to the Turks, then jumped off the walls in remorse, landing on a rock now known as "Old Lady's Leap". In the opposite direction out of Korthí are **AÏDHÓNIA** and **KAPARIÁ**, dotted with pigeon towers (*peristereónes*) left by the Venetians.

Tínos

Tínos still feels one of the most Greek of the larger islands. A few foreigners have discovered its beaches and unspoiled villages, but most visitors are Greek, here to see the church of **Panayía Evangelístria**, a grandiose shrine erected on the spot where a miraculous icon with healing powers was found in 1822. A local nun, now canonized as Ayía Pelayía, was directed in a vision to unearth the relic just as the War of Independence was getting underway, a timely coincidence which served to underscore the links between the Orthodox Church and Greek nationalism. Today, there are two major annual pilgrimages, on March 25 and August 15, when, at 11am, the icon bearing the Virgin's image is carried in state down to the harbour over the heads of the faithful.

The Ottoman tenure here was the most fleeting in the Aegean. **Exóbourgo**, the craggy mount dominating southern Tínos and surrounded by most of the island's sixty-odd villages, is studded with the ruins of a Venetian citadel which defied the Turks until 1715, long after the rest of Greece had fallen. An enduring legacy of the long Venetian rule is a persistent **Catholic minority**, which accounts for almost half the population, and a sectarian rivalry said to be responsible for the numerous graceful belfries scattered throughout the island – Orthodox and Catholic parishes vying to build the tallest. The sky is pierced, too, by distinctive and ornate dovecotes, even more in evidence here than on Ándhros. Aside from all this, the inland village architecture is striking and there's a flourishing folk-art tradition which finds expression in the abundant local marble. The islanders have remained open and hospitable to the relatively few foreigners and the steady stream of Greek visitors who touch down here, and any mercenary inclinations seem to be satisfied by booming sales in religious paraphernalia to the faithful.

Tínos Town and the southern beaches

At **TÍNOS TOWN**, trafficking in devotional articles certainly dominates the streets leading up from the busy waterfront to the Neoclassical **church** (daily 8am–8pm) which towers above. Approached via a massive marble staircase, the famous **icon** inside is all but buried under a dazzling array of jewels; below is the crypt (where the icon was discovered) and a mausoleum for the sailors drowned when the Greek warship *Elli*, at anchor off Tínos during a pilgrimage, was torpedoed by an Italian submarine on August 15, 1940. Museums around the courtyard display more objects donated by the faithful (who inundate the island for the two big yearly festivals), as well as icons, paintings and work by local marble sculptors.

The shrine aside – and all the attendant stalls, shops and bustle – the port is none too exciting, with just scattered inland patches of nineteenth-century buildings. You might make time for the **Archeological Museum** (Tues–Sun 8.30am–3pm; €1.50) on the way up to the church, whose collection includes a fascinating sundial from the local Roman sanctuary of Poseidon and Amphitrite (see p.608).

Practicalities

Ferries dock at any of three different **jetties**; which one depends on weather conditions. There are at least two boats a day from Pireás and Sýros, and four from Rafina and Ándhros going on to Mýkonos, as well as a useful hydrofoil, and less-frequent ferry connections to Páros, Náxos and Thíra. When you're leaving, ask your ticket agent which jetty to head for. **Buses** leave from a small

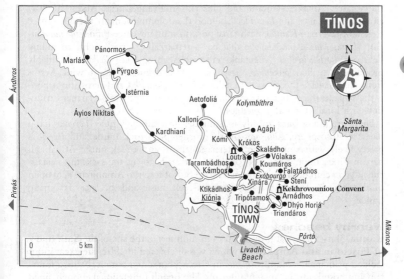

parking area in front of a cubbyhole-office on the quay, to Pánormos, Kallóni, Stení, Pórto and Kiónia (timetables available here; no buses after 7.30pm). A **motorbike** is perhaps a more reliable means of exploring – Vidalis at Zanáki Alavánou 16 is a good rental agency.

Windmills Travel (☎ & ℗ 02830/23 398, ℮ tinos@windmills-travel.com), on the front towards the new jetty, can help with information as well as hotel and **tour bookings**; they even have a book exchange. In season an excursion boat does day-trips taking in Delos (see p.616) and Mýkonos (Tues–Sun; €15 round trip); this makes it possible to see Delos without the expense of staying overnight in Mýkonos, but only allows you two and a half hours at the site. The **tourist police** are located on the road to the west of the new jetty.

To have any chance of securing a reasonably priced **room** around the pilgrimage day of March 25 (August 15 is hopeless), you must arrive several days in advance. At other times there's plenty of choice, though you'll still be competing with out-of-season pilgrims, Athenian tourists and the ill and disabled seeking a miracle cure. Of the hotels, the *Eleana* (☎02830/22 561;❷), east of the quay about 200m inland from the Commercial Bank and taxi stand, is a good budget option. Slightly pricier options include the *Avra* (☎02830/22 242;❸), a Neoclassical relic on the waterfront, and the *Vyzantio* (☎02830/22 421; ❹), three blocks inland on the road to Pórto. The *Favie Suzanne* (☎02830/22 693, ℗25 993;❹), across the small square is probably a bit quieter, while the newly-renovated *Hotel Tinion* (☎02830/22 261, ℗24 754;❹), behind the post office, is a stylish 1920s hotel. The *Vyzantio* (above) and the *Meltémi* (☎02830/22 881;❸) at Filipóti 7, near Megaloháris, are the only places open out of season. Finally, there is a smart hotel, the *Aeolos Bay* (☎02830/23 410;❹) with a swimming pool, near the beginning of the beach road east of the promontory. Otherwise, beat the crowds by staying at *Tinos Camping*, which also has a few nice rooms to let (☎02830/22 344;❶); follow the signs and it's a ten-minute walk from the port.

As usual, most seafront **restaurants** are rather overpriced and indifferent, with the exception of a friendly *psitopolió* right opposite the bus station, and the smarter *Xinari* restaurant and pizzeria on Evangelístrias. About midway along the port near the *Leto Hotel*, behind the dolphin fountain, there are three excellent tavernas: *Kanilio*, with tasty pork in mustard sauce (*hirinó mé moustárda*); *Metaxi Mas*, a *mezedopolio* that has a remarkably varied menu, including delicious *hortokeftédhes* (vegetable croquettes); and *Palea Pallada*, justifiably proud of its grilled *loukániko*, sharp local feta and smooth house wine. Across from *Palea Pallada* there's a small bakery, *Psomi Horiatiko*, and across from both is the Palláda, the public square where every morning there's a farmer's **market** with local fruit and vegetables.

There are a few **bars**, mostly in a huddle near the new quay. *Fevgatos* has a pleasant atmosphere, *Koutsaros* on the corner plays rock music, and *Pyrsos* is pretty lively with a mixture of international hits and Greek music. At 3am all bars in Tínos Town close, but for those not ready to hit the sack, the *Paradise* and *Veggera* club duplex on the main road out of town to Amphitrite stay open until dawn, the former playing mainly Greek music and the latter favouring trance.

Nearby beaches

Kiónia, 3km northwest (hourly buses in summer), is the site of the **Sanctuary of Poseidon and Amphitrite** which was discovered in 1902; the excavations yielded principally columns (*kiónia* in Greek), but also a temple, baths, a fountain and hostels for the ancient pilgrims. The **beach** is functional enough, lined with rooms to rent and snack bars, but it's better to walk past the large *Tinos Beach Hotel* (☎02830/22 626; ❻), the last stop for the bus, and follow an unpaved road to a series of sandy coves beyond.

The beach beyond the headland east of town starts off rocky but improves if you walk 500m further along. Further east, **Pórto** (six buses daily) boasts two good beaches, with a couple of good tavernas as well as **rooms** at the reasonably priced restaurant belonging to *Akti Aegeou* (☎02830/24 248; ❹), on the first beach of Áyios Pandelímon, as well as the smart studios of *Porto Raphael* (☎02830/22 403; ❸), above Áyios Ioánnis. *Porto Tango* (☎02830/24 410; ❻) is an excellent upmarket hotel here, with a lovely pool setting.

Northern Tínos

A good beginning to a foray into the interior is to take the stone stairway – the continuation of Odhós Ayíou Nikoláou – that passes behind and to the left of the Evangelístria. This climbs for ninety minutes through appealing countryside to **KTIKÁDHOS**, a fine village with a good seaview taverna, *Iy Dhrosia*. You can either flag down a bus on the main road or stay with the trail until Xinára (see opposite).

Heading northwest from the junction flanked by Ktikádhos, Tripótamos and Xinára, there's little to stop for – except the fine dovecotes around Tarambádhos – until you reach **KARDHIANÍ**, one of the most strikingly set and beautiful villages on the island, with its views across to Sýros from amid a dense oasis. Nestled in the small sandy bay below is a fine little restaurant by the name of *Anemos*, which serves octopus stew and other dishes at good prices. Kardhianí has been discovered by wealthy Athenians and expatriates, and now offers the exotic *To Perivoli* taverna. **ISTÉRNIA**, just a little beyond, is not nearly so appealing but there is some accommodation on offer, including the *Lameras Hotel* (☎02830/31 215; ❷). The *Tavsternia* taverna commands stunning panoramic views and there are a few cafés, perched above the turning for **Órmos Isterníon**, a comparatively small but overdeveloped beach.

Five daily buses along this route finish up at **PÝRGOS**, a few kilometres further north and smack in the middle of the island's marble-quarrying district. A beautiful village, its local artisans are renowned throughout Greece for their skill in producing marble ornamentation; ornate fanlights and bas-relief plaques crafted here adorn houses throughout Tínos. Pýrgos is also home to the School of Arts, and the **Museum of Tinian Artists** (daily 11am–2pm & 5.30–6.30pm; €1) contains numerous representative works from some of the island's finest artists. There are two **kafenía** and a **snack bar** on the attractive shady platía, and one acceptable **taverna** opposite the bus station. Pýrgos is popular in summer, and if you want to stay there are some new **studios** for rent on the main road coming into the village; alternatively ask the locals on the platía.

The marble products were once exported from **PÁNORMOS** (Órmos) harbour, 4km northeast, with its tiny but commercialized beach; there's little reason to linger, but if you get stuck there are rooms and some tavernas.

Around Exóbourgo

The ring of villages around **Exóbourgo** mountain is the other focus of interest on Tínos. The fortified pinnacle itself (570m), with ancient foundations as well as the ruins of three Venetian churches and a fountain, is reached by steep steps from **XINÁRA** (near the island's major road junction), the seat of the island's Roman Catholic bishop. Most villages in north central Tínos have mixed populations, but Xinára and its immediate neighbours are purely Catholic; the inland villages also tend to have a more sheltered position, with better farmland nearby – the Venetians' way of rewarding converts and their descendants. Yet **TRIPÓTAMOS**, just south of Xinára, is a completely Orthodox village with possibly the finest architecture in this region – and has accordingly been pounced on by foreigners keen to restore its historic properties.

At **LOUTRÁ**, the next community north of Xinára, there's an Ursuline convent and a good **folk art museum** (summer only 10.30am–3.30pm; free) in the old Jesuit monastery; to visit, leave the bus at the turning for Skaládho. From Krókos, 1km northwest of Loutra, which has a scenically situated restaurant, *O Krokos*, it's a forty-minute walk to **VÓLAKAS** (Vólax), one of the most remote villages on the island, a windswept oasis surrounded by bony rocks. Here, half a dozen elderly Catholic basketweavers fashion some of the best examples in Greece. There is a small **folklore museum** (free) which you have to ask the lady living in the house opposite the entrance to open, and the charming outdoor **Fontaine Theatre** which in August hosts visiting theatre groups from all over Greece. Accommodation is hard to come by, but there are a couple of places to eat, including the recommended *O Rokos* taverna.

At Kómi, 5km beyond Krókos, you can take a detour for **KOLYMBÍTHRA**, a magnificent double beach: one part wild, huge and windswept (temporary residence to pink flamingos migrating to Africa during May), the other sheltered and with a couple of tavernas including *Kolibithra Beach* (☎02830/51 213), which also has rooms (④). The bus to Kallóni goes on to Kolymbíthra twice a day in season; out of season you'll have to get off at Kómi and walk 4km.

From either Skaládho or Vólakas you go on to Koúmaros, where another long stairway leads up to Exóbourgo, or skirt the pinnacle towards Stení and Falatádhos which appear as white speckles against the fertile Livádha valley. From Stení you can catch the bus back to the harbour (seven daily). On the way down, try and stop off at one of the beautiful settlements just below the important twelfth-century **convent of Kekhrovouníou**, where Ayía Pelayía had her vision. Particularly worth visiting are **DHÝO HORIÁ**, which has a fine main square where cave-fountains burble, and **TRIANDÁROS**, which has two reasonable **eating** places: *Iy Lefka* and *Eleni's* (a tiny place at the back of the village). If you have your own transport, there are quite wide and fairly negotiable tracks down to some lovely secluded bays on the east of the island from the area of Stení. One such is **Sánta Margaríta**; given the lack of tourist development here, it's a good idea to take something to drink.

This is hardly an exhaustive list of Tiniot villages; armed with a map and good walking shoes for tackling the many old trails that still exist, you could spend days within sight of Exóbourgo and never pass through the same hamlets twice. Take warm clothing out of season, especially if you're on a scooter, since the forbidding mountains behind Vólakas and the Livadhéri plain keep things noticeably cool.

Mýkonos

Originally visited only as a stop on the way to ancient Delos, **Mýkonos** has become easily the most popular (and the most expensive) of the Cyclades. Boosted by direct air links with Britain and domestic flights from Athens, it sees an incredible 800,000 tourists pass through in a good year, producing some spectacular overcrowding in high summer on Mýkonos's 75 square kilometres. But if you don't mind the crowds, or – and this is a much more attractive proposition – you come out of season, the prosperous capital is still one of the most beautiful of all island towns, its immaculately whitewashed houses concealing hundreds of little churches, shrines and chapels.

The sophisticated nightlife is pretty hectic, amply stimulated by Mýkonos's former reputation as *the* gay resort of the Mediterranean – a title shared in recent years with places like Ibiza and Sitges in Spain; whatever, the locals take this comparatively exotic clientele in their stride. Unspoiled it isn't, but the island does offer excellent (if crowded) beaches, picturesque windmills and a rolling arid interior. An unheralded Mykonian quirk is the legality of scuba diving, a rarity in Greece, and dive centres have sprung up on virtually every beach.

Mýkonos Town

Don't let the crowds put you off exploring **MÝKONOS TOWN**, the archetypal postcard image of the Cyclades. Its sugar-cube buildings are stacked around a cluster of seafront fishermen's dwellings, with every nook and cranny scrubbed and shown off. Most people head out to the beaches during the day, so early morning or late afternoon are the best times to wander the maze of narrow streets. The labyrinthine design was intended to confuse the pirates who plagued Mýkonos in the eighteenth and early nineteenth centuries, and it still has the desired effect.

You don't need any maps or hints to explore the convoluted streets and alleys of town – getting lost is half the fun. There are, however, a few places worth seeking out. Coming from the ferry quay you'll pass the **Archeological Museum** (Tues–Sat 9am–3.30pm, Sun 10am–3pm; €1.50) on your way into town, which displays some good Delos pottery; the town also boasts a **Maritime Museum** displaying various nautical artefacts, including a lighthouse re-erected in the back garden (Tues–Sun 8.30am–3pm; €1).

MÝKONOS TOWN

RESTAURANTS & BARS

Café Express	B
La Cathedral	H
Edem	I
Gatsby's	N
El Greco	J
Kostas	K
Kounelas	E
Nikos' Taverna	C
Pelican	F
Pierros Bar	D
Remezzo Bar	A
The Sesame Kitchen	M
Spiro's	G
Yiavroutas Estiatorio	L

Accommodation Office
Tourist Police
Island Ferries

Archeological
Museum
Buses to Áno Méra
★ & Ay. Stéfanos

OTE

A

N

Boats to Délos

Folklore Museum

Kástro

Paraportianí

KAMBANI

PLATIA
M. MAVROYENOUS

C

E

KAMBANI

National Bank
& Port Police

B

D

3

4

KALOYERA

5

Maritime
Museum

F

Mitrópolis

H

K

L

J

M

Mýkonos
Accommodation Center

N

I

Alefkándhra
('Venice Quarter')

Tría Pigádhia

Windmills

LITTLE VENICE

Laundry

Buses to
Platýs Yialós,
Paránga &
Paradise Beach

Olympic
Airways

Scooter
Rental

Scooter Rental

8

9

Scooter
Rental

Scooter
Rental

6

7

10

Áno Méra

ACCOMMODATION

Apollon	2
Belvedere	7
Delfine's	3
Elysium	10
Pension Marina	8
Philippi	5
Semeli	6
Terra Maria	4
La Veranda	1
Villa Giovani	9

0   100 m

▼ Órnós

Alternatively, behind the two banks there's the **library**, with Hellenistic coins and late medieval seals, or, at the base of the Delos jetty, the **Folklore Museum** (Mon–Sat 4–8pm, Sun 5–8pm; free), housed in an eighteenth-century mansion and cramming in a larger-than-usual collection of bric-a-brac, including a vast four-poster bed. The museum shares the same promontory as the old Venetian *kástro*, the entrance to which is marked by Mýkonos's oldest and best-known church, **Paraportianí**, which is a fascinating asymmetrical hodgepodge of four chapels amalgamated into one.

The shore leads to the area known as "Little Venice" because of its high, arcaded Venetian houses built right up to the water's edge. Its real name is **Alefkándhra**, a trendy district packed with art galleries, chic bars and discos. Away from the seafront, behind Platía Alefkándhra, are Mýkonos's two **cathedrals**: Roman Catholic and Greek Orthodox. Beyond, the famous **windmills** look over the area, a little shabby but ripe for photo opportunities. Instead of retracing your steps along the water's edge, follow Énoplon Dhinaméon (left off Mitropóleos) to **Tría Pigádhia** fountain. The name means "Three Wells", and legend has it that should a maiden drink from all three she is bound to find a husband.

Arrival and information

There is some accommodation information at the **airport**, but unless you know where you're going it's easier to take a taxi for the 3km into town, and sort things out there. The vast majority of visitors arrive by boat at the new northern **jetty**, which is 1km north of town in Toúrlos, where a veritable horde of room-owners pounces on the newly arrived. The scene is actually quite intimidating, and so, if you can avoid the grasping talons, it is far better to go a hundred metres further where a row of offices deal with official hotels, rented rooms and camping information, or get the bus into town to the extremely helpful Mykonos Accommodation Centre on Énoplon Dhinaméon near Tría Pigádia (☎02890/23 160, ℻24 137, ⓔmac@mac.myk.forthnet.gr).

The **tourist police** and local **accommodation centre** (open high season only) can be found up from the ferry stalls near the old ferry landing. The harbour curves around past the dull, central Polikandhrióti beach, off the north end of which you'll find the **north bus station**, for Toúrlos, Áyios Stéfanos, Elía and Áno Méra. The **south bus station**, for beaches to the south, is across town, in the Lákka area where the **post office**, Olympic Airways office and several **motorbike** agencies can be found. Buses to all the most popular beaches and resorts run frequently until the early hours. **Taxis** run from Platía Mavroyénous on the seafront and from the south bus station, and their rates are fixed and quite reasonable; try Mykonos Radio Taxi (☎02890/22 400). Find a copy of the free *Mykonos Summertime* magazine or, better yet, the Athinorama *Mykonos Guide* (€1.50) which can be purchased from tourist offices or bookshops.

Hydrofoil and ferry tickets are sold at several separate and uncooperative **travel agencies** on the harbour front. Check out the various possibilities, and if your boat leaves from the new harbour, catch the bus up from the old ferry landing across from the Eurobank.

Accommodation

Accommodation prices in Mýkonos rocket in the high season to a greater degree than almost anywhere else in Greece. In town, try the friendly *Apollon* on the harbour (☎02890/22 223; ❸), *Delfine's* on Mavroyénous (☎02890/22 292; ❻), *Terra Maria* at Kaloyéra 18 (☎02890/24 212; ❹–❻) or the *Philippi* at Kaloyéra 25 (☎02890/22 294, ⓔchrico@otenet.gr; ❹). There are plenty of very expensive hotels like *Semeli Hotel* (☎02890/27 466, ℻27 467; ❻) above town on Ayíou Ioánnou, which has a pool, whirlpool and very tastefully decorated rooms, or the *Belvedere Hotel* (☎02890/25 122, ✉belvedere@myk.forthnet.gr; ❻) next door. *La Veranda* (☎02890/23 670; ❻) is a hidden gem, located on the hillside above town, with rooms set around a small pool. Unsurprisingly, most accommodation is extremely gay-friendly: *Elysium* (☎02890/23 952; ❻) is almost exclusively gay. Two recommended **pensions** are on the south side of town above the bus station: *Villa Giovanni* (☎02890/22 485; ❺) and *Pension Marina* (☎02890/24 960; ❺) on Ayiou Ioánnou and Láka. There are two **campsites**: *Mykonos Camping* (☎02890/24 578) above Paránga beach is smaller and has a more pleasant setting than nearby *Paradise Camping* on Paradise beach (☎02890/22 852, ✉PARADISE@paradise.myk.forthnet.gr); however, the latter also has bungalows (❹). Both are packed in season, and dance music from the 24-hour bars on Paradise Beach makes sleep difficult. The overpriced campsite restaurants serving poor food are best avoided. Hourly bus services to Paránga and Paradise Beach continue into the early hours but can get very overcrowded.

Eating and nightlife

Even **light meals** and **snacks** are expensive in Mýkonos, but there are several bakeries, supermarkets and fruit stalls, some concentrated near the south bus station. For good *tyrópites* and *milópites* try Anemomilos (Karapis), on the right about fifty metres up Mavroyénous.

The area around Alefkándhra is a promising place to head for a full **meal**: *La Cathedral*, by the two cathedrals on the platía, has standard fare; *Pelican*, behind the cathedrals, is pricey but well sited; and *Kostas*, also nearby, has competitive prices, a good wine list including barrelled wine (not easily found on Mýkonos) and friendly service. Less than fifty metres further along Mitropóleos, the small *Yiavroutas Estiatorio* is probably the least expensive and most authentically Greek place on the island, again with good barrelled wine. *Kounelas* is a good fish taverna with more reasonable prices than *Spiro's* on the seafront. *Edem*, close to Panakhrándou, offers poolside dining. *El Greco* at Tría Pigádhia is expensive but romantic, and *Gatsby's* on Tourlianís is a gay-friendly restaurant with an adventurous menu. *The Sesame Kitchen* on Énoplon Dhinaméon is an acceptable vegetarian restaurant; however, most of the smarter restaurants in Mýkonos do cater well for vegetarians anyway. Just behind the town hall is *Nikos' Taverna* – crowded, reasonable and recommended. For **late-night** snacks, most of the cafés on Kambani stay open until the small hours, and *Cafe Express* is open all night.

Nightlife in town is every bit as good as it's cracked up to be – and every bit as pricey. *Remezzo* (near the OTE) is one of the oldest bars, now a bit over the hill but a lively spot nonetheless, and a good place to have a drink before moving onto *Mercedes Club* next door; both are popular with young Athenians. *Skandinavian Bar-Disco* is a cheap-and-cheerful party spot, as is the nearby *Irish Bar*, and there are more sophisticated bars on Andhroníkou Matoyiánni and Énoplon Dhinaméon. *Katerina's*, *Caprice* and *Kastro*, in Little Venice, are ideal for sunset cocktails; the first serves delicious fresh fruit juices, and the latter plays classical music and is popular with an older gay crowd. Back (northeast) towards the harbour, *La Mer* is a popular disco/bar playing a lively mix of Greek and dance music, while *Porta* is a popular gay haunt near *Kounelas* restaurant. *Pierro's* and *Icarus* (upstairs), just off Platía Mavroyénous, become the focal point of gay activity later on, the latter having great drag shows and welcoming proprietors. *Cavo Paradiso*, near *Paradise Camping*, is the after-hours club where die-hard party animals of all persuasions come together.

The beaches

The closest **beaches** to town are those to the north, at **Toúrlos** (only 2km away but horrid) and **Áyios Stéfanos** (4km, much better), both developed resorts and connected by a very regular bus service to Mýkonos Town. There are tavernas and rooms to let (as well as package hotels) at Áyios Stéfanos, away from the beach; *Mocambo Lido* taverna at the far end of the bay has a pleasant setting and good food.

Other nearby destinations include southwest peninsula resorts, with undistinguished beaches tucked into pretty bays. The nearest to town, 1km away, is **Megáli Ámmos**, a good beach backed by flat rocks and pricey rooms, but nearby Kórfos bay is disgusting, thanks to the town dump and machine noise. Buses serve **Ornós**, an average beach, and **Áyios Ioánnis**, a dramatic bay with a tiny, stony beach, which achieved its moment of fame as a location for the film *Shirley Valentine*. The taverna *To Iliovasilema* has an excellent selection of fish and is highly recommended, if a little pricey.

The south coast is the busiest part of the island. Kaïkia ply from town to all of its beaches, which are among the straightest on the island, and still regarded to some extent as family strands by the Greeks. You might begin with **Platýs Yialós**, 4km south of town, though you won't be alone: one of the longest-established resorts on the island, it's not remotely Greek any more, the sand is monopolized by hotels, and you won't get a room to save your life between June and September. **Psaroú**, next door to the west, is very pretty – 150m of white sand backed by foliage and calamus reeds, crowded with sunbathers. Facilities here include a diving club (☎02890/23 579), waterskiing and windsurfer rental, but again you'll need to reserve well in advance to secure a room between mid-June and mid-September.

Just over the headland to the east of Platýs Yialós is **Paránga beach**, which is actually two beaches separated by a smaller headland. The highly recommended *Nicolas* taverna and rooms (☎02890/23 566; ❹) on the first beach is worlds apart from its noisy neighbour which is home to a loud beach bar and *Mýkonos Camping*. A dusty footpath beyond Platýs Yialós crosses the fields and caves of the headland across the clifftops past Paranga, and drops down to **Paradise Beach**, a crescent of golden sand that is packed in season. Behind are the shops, self-service restaurants and noisy 24-hour beach bars of *Paradise Camping*. The next bay east contains **Super Paradise** (officially "Plindhrí") beach, accessible by footpath or by kaïki. One of the most fun beaches on the island, it has a decent taverna and two bars at opposite ends of the beach pumping out cheesy summer hits. One half of the beach is very mixed, getting progressively more gay as you walk away from where the kaïkia dock towards the beach bar perched in the hills, below which the beach is almost exclusively gay and nudist.

Probably the **best beach** on Mýkonos is **Eliá**, the last port of call for the kaïkia. A broad, sandy stretch with a verdant backdrop, it's the longest beach on the island, though split in two by a rocky area. It's gay-friendly, but also increasingly popular with families because of the proximity of Watermania (10am–midnight; adults €12, under 12s €6, under 5s free; there's a free daily bus from Mýkonos Town; ☎02890/71 685) the island's biggest **waterslide park**, and several restaurants, including the excellent *Matheos*. If the crowds have followed you this far, one last escape route is to follow the bare rock footpath over the spur (look for the white house) at the end of Eliá beach. This cuts upwards for grand views east and west and then winds down to **Kaló Livádhi** (seasonal bus service), a stunning beach adjoining an agricultural valley scattered with little farmhouses; even here there's a restaurant (a good one at that) at the far end of the beach. **Liá**, further on, is smaller but delightful, with bamboo windbreaks and clear water, plus another taverna.

East of Eliá, roughly 12km by road from the town, **Ayía Ánna** boasts a shingle beach and taverna, with the cliffs above granting some fine vistas. **Tarsaná**, on the other side of the isthmus, has a long, coarse-sand beach, with watersports, a taverna and smart bungalows on offer. **Kalafáti**, almost adjacent, is more of a tourist community, its white-sand beach supporting a few hotels, restaurants and a disco. There's a local bus service from here to Áno Méra (see below), or you can jump on an excursion boat to **Tragoníssi**, the islet just offshore, for spectacular coastal scenery, seals and wild birds. The rest of the east coast is difficult – often impossible – to reach: there are some small beaches, really only worth the effort if you crave solitude, and the region is dominated by the peak of Profítis Ilías, sadly spoiled by a huge radar dome and military establishment. The **north coast** suffers persistent battering from the *meltémi*, plus tar and litter pollution, and for the most part is bare, brown and exposed. **Pánormos Bay** is the exception to this – a lovely, relatively sheltered beach. Despite a good restaurant, a relaxed beach bar and the rather conspicuous *Albatros Club Hotel* (☎02890/25 130; ❺), Pánormos remains one of the least crowded beaches on the island.

Áno Méra

From Pánormos Bay, it's an easy walk to the only other settlement of any size on the island, **ÁNO MÉRA**, where you should be able to find a **room**. The village prides itself on striving to maintain a traditional way of life, although the result is rather pseudo and wishy-washy: the so-called traditional kafenío has long since ditched Greek coffee for cappuccino and traditional sweets for "ice-cream special". There are, however, several acceptable **tavernas** on the platía, of which *Tou Apostoli to Koutouki* is most popular with locals, and a large **hotel** – *Hotel Ano Mera* (☎02890/71 276; ❸–❻). The red-roofed church near the square is the sixteenth-century **monastery of Panayía Tourlianí**, where a collection of Cretan icons and the unusual eighteenth-century marble baptismal font are worth seeing. It's not far, either, to the late twelfth-century **Paleokástro monastery** (also known as Dárga), just north of the village, in a magnificent green setting on an otherwise barren slope. To the northwest are more of the same dry and wind-buffeted landscapes, though they do provide some enjoyable, rocky walking with expansive views across to neighbouring islands – head to Áyios Stéfanos for buses back to the harbour.

Delos (Dhílos)

The remains of **ancient Delos**, Pindar's "unmoved marvel of the wide world", though skeletal and swarming now with lizards and tourists, give some idea of the past grandeur of this sacred isle a few sea-miles west of Mýkonos. The ancient town (Tues–Sun 8.30am–3pm; €4.40) lies on the west coast on flat, sometimes marshy ground which rises in the south to **Mount Kýnthos**. From the summit – an easy walk – there's a magnificent view across the Cyclades: the name of the archipelago means "those [islands] around [Delos]".

The first excursion boats to Delos leave Mýkonos daily at 8.30am (€5.80 round trip), except Mondays when the site is closed. You have to return on the same boat, but in season each does the trip several times and you can choose what time you leave. The last return is usually about 3pm, and you'll need to arrive early if you want to make a thorough tour of the site. In season a daily kaïki makes return trips from the beaches (€9) with pick-up points at Platýs Yialós and Órnos, but only allows you three hours on the island. It's a good idea to bring your own food and drink as the tourist pavilion's snack bar is a rip-off.

Some history

Delos's ancient fame was due to the fact that Leto gave birth to the divine twins Artemis and Apollo on the island, although its fine harbour and central position did nothing to hamper development. When the Ionians colonized the island around 1000 BC it was already a cult centre, and by the seventh century BC it had become the commercial and religious centre of the **Amphictionic League**. Unfortunately Delos also attracted the attention of Athens, which sought dominion over this prestigious island; the wealth of the Delian Confederacy, founded after the Persian Wars to protect the Aegean cities, was harnessed to Athenian ends, and for a while Athens controlled the Sanctuary of Apollo. Athenian attempts to "purify" the island began with a decree that no one could die or give birth on Delos – the sick and the pregnant were taken to the islet of Rheneia – and culminated in the simple expedient of banishing the native population.

Delos reached its peak in the third and second centuries BC, after being declared a free port by its Roman overlords. In the end, though, its undefended wealth brought ruin: first Mithridates (88 BC), then Athenodorus (69 BC) plundered the treasures and the island never recovered. By the third century AD, Athens could not even sell it, and for centuries, every passing seafarer stopped to collect a few prizes.

The site

As you land, the Sacred Harbour is on your left, the Commercial Harbour on your right and straight ahead is the **Agora of the Competialists**. Competialists were Roman merchants or freed slaves who worshipped the Lares Competales, the guardian spirits of crossroads; offerings to Hermes would once have been placed in the middle of the agora, their position now marked by a round and a square base. The **Sacred Way** leads north from the far left corner; it used to be lined with statues and the grandiose monuments of rival kings. Along it you reach three marble steps which lead into the **Sanctuary of Apollo**; much was lavished on the god, but the forest of offerings has been plundered over the years. On your left is the Stoa of the Naxians, while against the north wall of the House of the Naxians, to the right, a huge statue of Apollo stood in ancient times. In 417 BC the Athenian general Nikias led a procession of priests across a bridge of boats from Rheneia to dedicate a bronze palm tree; when it was later blown over in a gale it took the statue with it. Three **Temples of Apollo** stand in a row to the right along the Sacred Way: the Delian Temple, that of the Athenians and the Porinos Naos, the earliest of them, dating from the sixth century BC. To the east towards the museum you pass the **Sanctuary of Dionysos**, with its marble phalluses on tall pillars.

The best finds from the site are in Athens, but the **museum** still justifies a visit, if only to see the famous **lions**, their lean bodies masterfully executed by Naxians in the seventh century BC (of the original nine, three have disappeared and one adorns the Arsenale in Venice). To the north stands a wall that marks the site of the **Sacred Lake** where Leto gave birth, clinging to a palm tree, guarded by excellent reproductions of the lions. On the other side of the lake is the City Wall, built in 69 BC – too late to protect the treasures.

Set out in the other direction from the Agora of the Competialists and you enter the residential area, known as the **Theatre Quarter**. Many of the walls and roads remain, but there is none of the domestic detail that brings such sites to life. Some colour is added by the mosaics: one in the **House of the Trident**, and better ones in the **House of the Masks**, most notably a vigorous portrayal of Dionysos riding on a panther's back. The **theatre** itself seated 5500 spectators, and, though much ravaged, offers some fine views. Behind the theatre, a path leads past the **Sanctuaries of the Foreign Gods** and up **Mount Kýnthos** for more panoramic sightseeing.

Sýros

Don't be put off by first impressions of **Sýros**. From the ferry it looks grimly industrial, but away from the Neórion shipyard things improve quickly. Very much a working island with only a relatively recent history of tourism, it is among the most Greek of the Cyclades. You probably won't find, as Herman Melville did when he visited in 1856, shops full of "fez-caps, swords, tobacco, shawls, pistols, and orient finery", but you're still likely to appreciate Sýros as a refreshing change from its more touristic neighbours. Of course, outsiders do come to the island; in fact there's a thriving permanent foreign community, and the beaches are hardly undeveloped, but everywhere there's the underlying assumption that you're a guest of an inherently private people.

Ermoúpoli

The main town and port of **ERMOÚPOLI** was founded during the War of Independence by refugees from Psará and Híos, becoming Greece's chief port in the nineteenth century. Although Pireás outstripped it long ago, Ermoúpoli is still the largest town in the Cyclades, and the archipelago's capital. Medieval Sýros was largely a Catholic island, but an influx of Orthodox refugees during the War of Independence created two distinct communities; now almost equal in numbers, the two groups today still live in their respective quarters, occupying two hills that rise up from the sea.

Ermoúpoli itself, the **lower town**, is worth at least a night's stay, with grandiose buildings a relic of its days as a major port. The long, central **Platía Miaoúli** is named after an admiral of the revolution whose statue stands there, and in the evenings the population parades in front of its arcades, while the children ride the mechanical animals. Up the stairs to the left of the town hall is the small **Archeological Museum** (Tues–Sun 8.30am–3pm; free), with three rooms of finds from Sýros, Páros and Amorgós. To the left of the clocktower more stairs climb up to **Vrondádho**, the hill that hosts the Orthodox quarter. The wonderful church of the **Anástassi** stands atop the hill, with its domed roof and great views over Tínos and Mýkonos – if it's locked, ask for the key at the priest's house.

Up from the right of the square you'll find the **Apollon Theatre**, a copy of Milan's La Scala, which has recently undergone a major renovation and occasionally hosts performances. Up from it is the handsome Orthodox church of **Áyious Nikólaos**, and beyond it to the right is **Vapória**, where the island's wealthiest shipowners, merchants and bankers built their mansions.

On the taller hill to the left is the intricate medieval quarter of **Áno Sýros**, with a clutch of Catholic churches below the cathedral of St George. There are fine views of the town below, and, close by, the **Cappuchin monastery of St Jean**, founded in 1535 to do duty as a poorhouse. It takes about 45 minutes of tough walking up Omírou to reach this quarter, passing the Orthodox and Catholic cemeteries on the way – the former full of grand shipowners' mausoleums, the

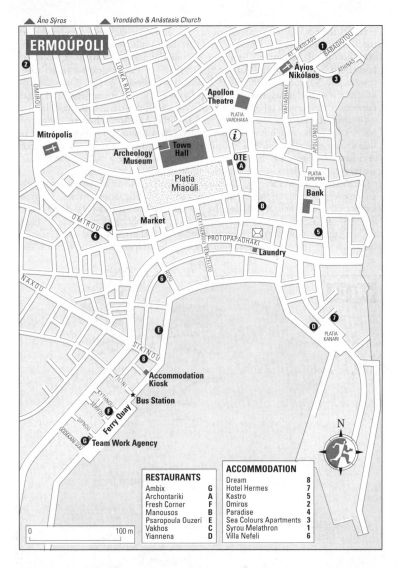

ERMOÚPOLI

Áno Sýros   Vrondádho & Anástasis Church

Áyios
Nikólaos

Apollon
Theatre

PLATIA
VARDHAKA

Mitrópolis

Archeology
Museum

Town
Hall

OTE

Platía
Miaoúli

PLATIA
TSIROPINA

Bank

Market

PROTOPAPADHAKI

Laundry

PLATIA
KANARI

N

Accommodation
Kiosk

Bus Station

Ferry Quay

Team Work Agency

RESTAURANTS	
Ambix	**G**
Archontariki	**A**
Fresh Corner	**F**
Manousos	**B**
Psaropoula Ouzerí	**E**
Vakhos	**C**
Yiannena	**D**

ACCOMMODATION	
Dream	**8**
Hotel Hermes	**7**
Kastro	**5**
Omiros	**2**
Paradise	**4**
Sea Colours Apartments	**3**
Syrou Melathron	**1**
Villa Nefeli	**6**

0   100 m

latter with more modest monuments and French and Italian inscriptions (you can halve the walking time by taking a shortcut onto the stair-street named Andhréa Kárga, part of the way along). Once up here it's worth visiting the local art and church exhibitions at the Vamvákeris **museum** (daily 10.30am–1pm & 7–10pm; €1.50), and the Byzantine museum attached to the monastery.

Arrival, facilities and accommodation

The harbour is still busy, though nowadays it deals with more tourists than industrial shipping; Sýros is a major crossover point on the ferry-boat routes. There are several **travel agencies** for various ferries and hydrofoils, the most helpful of which is TeamWork (📞02810/83 400, 📠83 508, 📧teamwork@otenet.gr). Also on the harbourfront is the **bus station**, along with the **tourist police** and several **motorbike** rental places, of which Apollon on Andíparou, one block behind the seafront, is recommended. **Odhós Híou**, the market street, is especially lively on Saturday when people come in from the surrounding countryside to sell fresh produce.

Keeping step with a growing level of tourism, **rooms** have improved in quality and number in recent years; many are in garishly decorated, if crumbling, Neoclassical mansions. Good choices include *Kastro* rooms, Kalomenopóulou 12 (📞02810/88 064; ❷), *Dream*, on the seafront near the bus station (📞02810/84 356; ❸), and *Paradise*, Omírou 3 (📞02810/83 204; ❸). Particularly recommended are the traditionally decorated rooms of *Villa Nefeli*, Parou 21 (📞02810/87 076; ❸), and *Sea Colours Apartments* (📞02810/88 716; ❹), located at Áyios Nikólaos beach, a quieter corner of town. A notch up in price and quality is the well-sited *Hotel Hermes* (📞02810/83 011; ❺–❻) on Platía Kanári, overlooking the port. A more stylish traditional hotel is the *Omiros* (📞02810/84 910, 📠86 266; ❹–❺) or, for luxury, try the *Syrou Melathron* (📞02810/86 495, 📠87 806; ❻), beyond Áyios Nikólaos in Vapória. TeamWork agency (see above), on the waterfront, is a useful source of information and able to help with your accommodation needs. In the summer you might try the kiosk belonging to the Rooms and Apartments Association of Sýros (📞02810/87 360), also on the waterfront.

Eating, drinking and nightlife

Numerous shops sell *loukoúmia* (Turkish delight), *madoláta* (nougats) and *halvadhópita* (sweetmeat pie) for which the island is famed.

The most authentic and reasonably priced of the harbour **eateries** are the *Yiannena Estiatorio* on Platía Kanári and the popular *Psaropoula Ouzeri*. East of Platía Miaoúli, the *Manousos* taverna is a good traditional place, as is *Archontariki*, which serves delicious *patátes me keséri* (fries with cheese). The most respected traditional taverna is *Vakhos*, near the market, with specialities like rabbit casserole and haddock in garlic sauce. *Ambix*, near where the ferries dock, is a good Italian restaurant; for snacks resist the glitzy *Goody's* hamburger-joint and have a *yíros* at the more authentic *Fresh Corner* nearby. In Áno Sýros, the *Thea* taverna, signposted in Greek from the car park, is fine and affords the views its name would suggest; *Iy Piatsa* ouzerí is also worth a try.

Sýros still honours its contribution to the development of **rebétika**; *bouzoúki*-great Markos Vamvakaris hailed from here, and a platía in Áno Sýros has been named after him. **Taverna-clubs** such as *Xanthomalis* (up in Áno Sýros) with music at weekends, now take their place beside a batch of more conventional disco-clubs down near the Apollon Theatre. There are several other (often expensive) *bouzoúki* bars scattered around the island, mostly strung along routes to beach resorts. The seafront has a rash of lively **bars**: the *Cotton Club* café seems to be the focal point of activity in this area. There's a more interesting cluster around the Platía Miaoúli: *Clearchos* piano bar is rather smooth, *Agora* has imaginative decor, good DJs and a lovely garden, and *Piramatiko* is heaving, playing a loud and varied mix from indie to house. The big venue for night-owls is *Rodo*, a huge club in a converted warehouse out past the Neórión shipyard opposite the turning to Vári. The *Aegean Casino* on the seafront features live music at the restaurant, and is open till 6am for those who have money to burn (and are sufficiently well-dressed). Above it, *Muses* has live music on Friday and Saturday nights; the €7.35 entrance includes your first drink.

Around the island

The main loop road (to Gallissás, Fínikas, Mégas Yialós, Vári and back), and the road west to Kíni, are good: **buses** ply the routes hourly in season, and run until late. Elsewhere, expect potholes – especially to the **north** where the land is barren and high, with few villages. The main route north from Áno Sýros has improved and is quite easily negotiable by bike; en route, the village of **Mýtikas** has a decent taverna just off the road. A few kilometres further on the road forks, with the left turn leading, after another left, to the small settlement of **Syríngas**, where there's an interesting cave to explore. Straight on leads to **Kámbos**, from where a path leads down to Liá Beach; the right fork eventually descends to the northeast coast after passing an excellent kafenío, *Sgouros*, with views across to Tínos.

The well-trodden route **south** offers more tangible and accessible rewards. Closest to the capital, fifteen minutes away by bus, is the twin-beach coastal settlement of **KÍNI**. Good accommodation includes the *Sunset Hotel* (☏02810/71 211; ❸–❹), with the excellent *Zalounis* taverna just below and, just away from the seafront, the *Hotel Elpida* (☏02810/71 224; ❷–❹). **Dhelfíni**, just to the north, is also a fine beach.

GALISSÁS, a few kilometres south, but reached by different buses, has developed along different lines. Fundamentally an agricultural village, it's been taken over since the mid-1980s by backpackers attracted by the island's only **campsites** – both have good facilities and send minibuses to all boats, but *Camping Yianna* (☏02810/42 418) has the advantage over the newer *Two Hearts* (☏02810/42 052) of being closer to the sea – and a very pretty beach, more protected than Kíni's. This new-found popularity has created a surplus of unaesthetic **rooms**, which at least makes bargaining possible, and six bona fide hotels, of which the cheapest are *O Petros* and *Semiramis* (☏02810/42 067; both ❸–❹), though the *Benois* (☏02810/42 833; ❸–❺) is decent value, with buffet breakfast included. Among the many **eating** choices, *To Iliovasilema*, next to *Benois*, is an acceptable fish taverna, and *Cavos*, part of a luxury complex, the *Dolphin Beach Hotel* (☏02810/42 924; ❻), has great views overlooking the bay. Galissás's identity crisis is exemplified by the proximity of bemused, grazing dairy cattle, a heavy-metal music pub and upmarket handicrafts shops. Still, the people are welcoming, and if you feel the urge to escape, you can rent a scooter, or walk ten minutes past the headland to the nudist beach of **Arméos**, where there's fresh spring water. Note that buses out are erratically routed; to be sure of making your connection you must wait at the high-road stop, not down by the beach.

A pleasant forty-minute walk or a ten-minute bus ride south from Galissás brings you to the more mainstream resort of **FÍNIKAS**, purported to have been settled originally by the Phoenicians (although an alternative derivation could be from *fínikas*, meaning "palm tree" in Greek). The beach is narrow and gritty, right next to the road but protected to some extent by a row of tamarisk trees; the pick of the hotels is the *Cyclades* (☏02810/42 255; ❹–❺), and there is an acceptable restaurant just in front, while the *Amaryllis* rooms (☏02810/42 894; ❸) are slightly cheaper. The fish taverna *O Barpalias* on the seafront is recommended.

Fínikas is separated by a tiny headland from its neighbour **POSSIDHONÍA** (or Delagrazzia), a nicer spot with some idiosyncratically ornate mansions and a bright blue church right on the edge of the village. It's worth walking ten minutes further south, past the naval yacht club and its patrol boat to **Agathopés**, with a sandy beach and a little islet just offshore. Komitó, at the end of the unpaved track leading south from Agathopés, is nothing more than a stony beach fronting an olive grove. **Accommodation** around Possidhonía ranges from the smart *Possidonion* hotel (☏02810/42 100; ❹–❺) on the seafront to basic rooms inland, while *Meltémi* is a good seafood taverna.

The road swings east to **MÉGAS YIALÓS**, a small resort below a hillside festooned with brightly painted houses. The long, narrow beach is lined with shady trees and there are pedal boats for hire. Of the **room** set-ups, *Mike and Bill's* (☎02810/43 531; ❷) is a reasonable deal, and the pricier *Alexandra Hotel* (☎02810/42 540; ❹–❺), on the bay, enjoys lovely views. **VÁRI** is more – though not much more – of a town, with its own small fishing fleet. Beach-goers are in a goldfish bowl, as it were, with tavernas and **rooms** looming right overhead, but it is the most sheltered of the island's bays, something to remember when the *meltémi* is up. The *Kamelo* hotel (☎02810/61 217; ❹) provides the best value and has TV in all the rooms. The adjacent cove of **AKHLÁDHI** is far more pleasant and boasts two small good-value hotels, including the *Emily* (☎02810/61 400; ❸–❹), on the seafront, and has one taverna.

Páros and Andíparos

Gently and undramatically furled around the single peak of Profitis Ilías, **Páros** has a little of everything one expects from a Greek island: old villages, monasteries, fishing harbours, a labyrinthine capital, and some of the best nightlife and beaches in the Aegean. Parikía, the hóra, is the major hub of interisland ferry services, so that if you wait long enough you can get to just about any island in the Aegean. However, the island is almost as touristy and expensive as Mýkonos – in peak season, it's touch-and-go when it comes to finding rooms and beach space. At such times, the attractive inland settlements or the satellite island of **Andíparos** handle the overflow. Incidentally, the August 15 festival here is one of the best such observances in Greece, with a parade of flare-lit fishing boats and fireworks delighting as many Greeks as foreigners, but it's a real feat to secure accommodation around this time.

Parikía and around

PARIKÍA sets the tone architecturally for the rest of Páros, with its ranks of typically Cycladic white houses punctuated by the occasional Venetian-style building and church domes. The busy waterfront is jam-packed with bars, restaurants, hotels and ticket agencies. Continue inland from the **windmill** past the tourist information office and taxi station to reach **Mavroyénous Square**, around which you'll find a maze of houses designed to thwart both the wind and pirates, and the telephone office, police station (and tourist police), banks and Olympic Airlines office.

Just beyond the central clutter, though, to the left (southeast) of the windmill, the town has one of the most architecturally interesting churches in the Aegean – the **Ekatondapyliani**, or "The One-Hundred-Gated". What's visible today was designed and supervised by Isidore of Miletus in the sixth century, but construction was actually carried out by his pupil Ignatius. It's said that it was so beautiful on completion that the master, consumed with jealousy, grappled with his apprentice on the rooftop and both of them fell to their deaths. They are portrayed kneeling at the column bases across the courtyard, the old master tugging at his beard in repentance and his rueful pupil clutching a broken head. The church was substantially altered after a severe earthquake in the eighth century, but its essentially Byzantine aspect remains, its shape an imperfect Greek cross. Enclosed by a great wall to protect its icons from pirates, it is in fact three interlocking churches; the oldest, the chapel of Áyios Nikólaos to the left of the apse, is an adaptation of a pagan building dating from the early fourth century BC. To the right of the courtyard, the **Byzantine Museum** (daily 9am–1pm & 5.30–9.30pm; €1.50, free on Tues) displays a collection of icons. Behind Ekatondapiliani, the **Archeological Museum** (Tues–Sun 8am–3pm; €1.50) has a fair collection of antique bits and pieces, its prize exhibits being a fifth-century winged Nike and a piece of the *Parian Chronicle*, a social and cultural history of Greece up to 264 BC engraved in marble.

These sights apart, the real attraction of Parikía is simply to wander the town itself, especially along the meandering **old market street**. Arcaded lanes lead past Venetian-influenced villas, traditional island dwellings and ornate wall-fountains. The town culminates in a seaward Venetian *kástro*, whose surviving east wall incorporates a fifth-century BC round tower and is constructed using masonry pillaged from a temple of Athena. Part of the base of the temple is still visible next to the beautiful, arcaded church of Áyios Konstandínos and Ayía Eléni which crowns the highest point, from where the fortified hill drops sharply to the quay in a series of hanging gardens.

If you're staying in town, you'll want to get out into the surroundings at some stage, if only to the beach. The most rewarding **excursion** is the hour's walk along the road starting just past the museum up to the **Áyii Anáryiri** monastery. Perched on the bluff above town, this makes a great picnic spot, with cypress groves, a gushing fountain and some splendid views.

There are **beaches** immediately north and south of the harbour, though none are particularly attractive when compared with Páros's best. In fact, you might prefer to avoid the northern stretch altogether and head **south** along the asphalt road instead. The first unsurfaced side-track you come to leads to a small, sheltered beach; fifteen minutes further on is **PARASPÓROS**, with an attractively landscaped and relatively quiet **campsite** (☎02840/21 100) and beach near the remains of an ancient temple to Asklepios (see p.795), the god of medicine and son of Apollo. Continuing for 45 minutes (or a short hop by bus) brings you to arguably the best of the bunch, **AYÍA IRÍNI**, with good sand and a taverna next to a farm and shady olive grove.

Off in the same direction, but a much longer two-hour haul each way, is **PETALOÚDHES**, the so-called "Valley of the Butterflies", a walled-in oasis where millions of Jersey tiger moths perch on the foliage during early summer (June–Sept 9am–8pm; €1.20). The trip pays more dividends when combined with a visit to the eighteenth-century nunnery of **Khristoú stoú Dhássous**, at the crest of a ridge twenty minutes to the north. Only women are allowed in the sanctuary, although men can get as far as the courtyard. The succession of narrow drives and donkey paths linking both places begins just south of Parikía. Petaloúdhes can be reached from Parikía by bus (in summer), by scooter or on an overpriced excursion by mule.

Arrival, information and accommodation

Ferries **dock** in Parikía by the windmill; the **bus stop** is 100m or so to the left. Bus routes extend to Náoussa in the north, Poúnda (for Andíparos) in the west, Alikí in the south and Dhrýos on the island's east coast (with another very useful service between Dhrýos and Náoussa). Buses to Náoussa carry on running hourly through the night, while other services stop around midnight. The **airport** is around 12km south of town, close to Alykí – from where ten daily buses run to Parikía.

Most of the island is flat enough for bicycle rides, but motorbikes are more common and are available for rent at several places in town; Forget-Me-Not, along the seafront west of the bus stop, offers a professional and friendly service. Polos Tours, left of the windmill, is one of the more together and friendly **travel agencies**, issuing air tickets when Olympic is shut, and acting as agents for virtually all the boats. Luggage can be left at Santorineos Travel, 50m beyond Polos Tours.

As for **accommodation**, Parikía is a pleasant and central base, but absolutely mobbed in summer. You'll be met off the ferry by locals offering rooms, even at the most unlikely hours; most rooms and hotels are to the left of the windmill, and some can be a long walk. One of the best deals to be had is at the *Pension Festos* on the backstreets inland, managed by young Brits (☎02840/21 635; €11.75 per person); it has beds in shared rooms, making it a good choice for single travellers. Of the hotels, the smart, family-run *Argonauta* (☎02840/21 440, ℱ23 442, ℮hotel@argonauta.gr; ❹), at the back of Mavroyénous Square near the National Bank, is highly recommended. Other acceptable hotels include the *Dina* (☎02840/21 325; ❸), further inland, in the market; the *Oasis* (☎02840/21 227; ❹), near the windmill; the small, family-run *Kypreou* (☎02840/21 383; ❹) across from Ekatondapilianí church; and the *Pension Antoine* (☎02840/24 435 ❶), also near the church. Irini Triandafilou (☎02840/23 022; ❸) has a few basic rooms within the *kástro*, some with good sea views. *Argonauta Appartments* (☎02840/23 888; ❹) have some smart accommodation in the Livádhia area in the north of town. *Koula Camping* (☎02840/22 081), along the seafront east of the bus stop, has good facilities but can get noisy. *Krios Camping* (☎02840/22 081), across the bay to the north has a nice beach.

Eating, drinking and nightlife

Most of the eating establishments in Parikía are along the waterfront to the right (south) of the windmill. Many are run by outsiders operating under municipal concession, so there is year-to-year variation in proprietors and quality. *Magic*, near the *kástro*, is a good place for breakfast, and *Hibiscus*, next to the Town Hall, offers generous-sized wood-oven-baked pizzas. Head inland for more substantial meals: *Koutouki Thanasis*, on a backstreet to the left of the Town Hall, serves oven food for locals and bold tourists; *Argonauta Restaurant*, near the hotel of the same name, across from the National Bank, is dependably good; and further back in the market is the popular taverna, *Garden of Dionysos*. *May Tey* serves average Chinese food at moderate mark-up, while Italian dishes can be found at *Cavo D'Oro* in the Livádhia area. *Trata*, behind the ancient cemetery left of the windmill, is recommended for fish; *Le Coq Fou*, in the Market near *Dionysos*, is a good breakfasting spot, serving excellent crepes; *Ragousis Bakery*, behind the National Bank, is a good place for sandwiches and pastries; and beyond it you'll find the *Happy Green Cow*, a nice vegetarian café. *Cookies Cyber Cafe* (ⓦwww.paroslink.com), about midway along the old market, is a friendly place that offers free internet access with the purchase of its snacks.

Parikía has a wealth of **pubs**, **bars** and low-key **discos**, not as pretentious as those on Mýkonos or as raucous as the scene on Íos, but certainly everything in between. The most popular cocktail bars extend along the seafront, mostly to the south of the windmill, tucked into a series of open squares and offering competing but staggered (no pun intended) "happy hours", so that you can drink cheaply for much of the evening. Beware of anything too cheap as some places still sell *bómba*, a local hooch that can get you really drunk fast and really sick afterwards. A rowdy crowd favours the conspicuous *Saloon D'Or*, while the *Pirate Bar*, behind the Town Hall, features jazz and blues. *Evinos* and *Pebbles* are more genteel, the latter pricey but with good sunset views and classical music. The "theme" pubs are a bit rough and ready for some – most outrageous is the *Dubliner/Paros Rock Complex*, comprising four bars, a snack section, disco and seating area.

Finally, a thriving cultural centre, Arhilohos (near Ekatondapilianí) caters mostly to locals, with occasional **film** screenings – there are also two open-air cinemas, Neo Rex and Paros, where foreign films are shown in season.

Náoussa and around

The second port of Páros, **NÁOUSSA** is a major resort town grown up around a charming little port. Modern concrete hotels and attendant trappings have all but swamped its original character, though down at the small harbour, fishermen still tenderize octopuses by thrashing them against the walls, and with a little patience you can still find some of its winding, narrow alleys and simple Cycladic houses. The local festivals – an annual Fish and Wine Festival on July 2, and an August 23 shindig celebrating an old naval victory over the Turks – are also still celebrated with enthusiasm; the latter tends to be brought forward to coincide with the August 15 festival of the Panayía. Most people are here for the local beaches (see opposite) and the relaxed nightlife; there's really only one sight, a **museum** (daily 9am–1.30pm & 7–9pm; free) in the monastery of Áyios Athanásios, with an interesting collection of Byzantine and post-Byzantine icons from the churches and monasteries around Náoussa.

Despite encroaching development, the town is noted for its nearby beaches and is a good place to head for as soon as you reach Páros. Because it's newer and more fashionable than Parikía, accommodation is more expensive. There is a helpful local council **information centre** just over the bridge, west from the harbour, and Nissiotissa Tours (☎02840/51 480, ⓕ51 189), off the left side of the main square, which can help you find a room, though it specializes in transport. The *Sea House* (☎02840/52 198; ❹) on the rocks above Pipéri beach was the first place in Náoussa to let rooms and has one of the best locations. Out of season you should haggle for reduced prices at the *Madaki* (☎02840/51 475; ❹), just over the bridge west of the harbour, and at the basic, but well-located *Stella* (☎02840/52 198; ❸), several blocks inland from the old harbour. If you don't mind a five-minute climb, the friendly *Papadakis* (☎02840/52 504; ❺) has excellent views. There are two **campsites** in the vicinity: the relaxed and friendly *Naoussa* (☎02840/51 565), out of town towards Kolymbíthres (see below), and the newer *Surfing Beach* (☎02840/51 013) at Sánta Mariá, northeast of Náoussa; both run courtesy minibuses to and from Parikía.

Most of the harbour **tavernas** are surprisingly good, specializing in fresh fish and seafood; *O Barbarossas* ouzerí is the best of these. There are more places to eat along the main road leading inland from just beside the little bridge over the canal. *Glaros*, with good barrelled unresinated wine, and the *Vengera* opposite stay open until the early morning hours. **Bars** cluster around the old harbour: *Linardo* and *Agosta* play dance music, *Camaron* plays mainly Greek music, and *Café Sante*, inland, off the main drag, is a cool spot playing easy-listening, and mellower dance grooves. There are several big clubs up from the bus station, including *Nostos* and *Privilege,* popular with a younger late-night crowd.

Local beaches

Pipéri beach is a couple of minutes' walk west of Náoussa's harbour; there are other good-to-excellent beaches within walking distance, and a summer kaïki service to connect them. To the west, an hour's tramp brings you to **Kolymbíthres** ("Basins"), where there are three tavernas and the wind- and sea-sculpted rock formations from which the place draws its name. A few minutes beyond, **Monastíri** beach, below the abandoned Pródhromos monastery, is similarly attractive, and partly nudist. If you go up the hill after Monastíri onto the rocky promontory, the island gradually shelves into the sea via a series of flattish rock ledges, making a fine secluded spot for diving and snorkelling, as long as the sea is calm. Go northeast and the sands are better still, the barren headland spangled with good surfing beaches. **Langéri** is backed by dunes; the best surfing is at **Sánta María**, a trendy beach connected with Náoussa by road, which also has a couple of tavernas, including the pleasant *Aristofanes*; and **Platiá Ámmos** perches on the northeastern tip of the island.

The northeast coast and inland

AMBELÁS hamlet marks the start of a longer trek down the **east coast**. Ambelás itself has a good beach, a small taverna and some rooms and hotels, of which the *Hotel Christiana* (☎02840/51 573; ❸) is good value, with great fresh fish, local wine in the restaurant and extremely friendly proprietors. From here a rough track leads south, passing several undeveloped stretches on the way; after about an hour you reach **Mólos beach**, impressive and not particularly crowded. **MÁRMARA**, twenty minutes further on, has rooms to let and makes an attractive place to stay, though the marble that the village is built from and named after has largely been whitewashed over.

If Mármara doesn't appeal, then serene **MÁRPISSA**, just to the south, might – a maze of winding alleys and ageing archways overhung by floral balconies, all clinging precariously to the hillside. There are rooms here too: *Afendakis* (☎02840/41 141; ❷) has clean and modern rooms and furnished apartments (❻), and you can while away a spare hour climbing up the conical Kéfalos hill, on whose fortified summit the last Venetian lords of Páros were overpowered by the Ottomans in 1537. Today the monastery of **Áyios Andónios** occupies the site, but the grounds are locked; to enjoy the views over eastern Páros and the straits of Náxos fully, pick up the key from the priest in Márpissa before setting out (ask in the minimarket of his whereabouts). On the shore nearby, **PÍSO LIVÁDHI** was once a quiet fishing village, but has been ruined by rampant construction in the name of package tourism. The main reason to visit is to catch a (seasonal) kaïki to Ayía Ánna on Náxos; if you need to **stay** overnight here, *Hotel Andromache* (☎02840/41 387 or 42 565; ❷–❹) is a good place behind the beach, as is the *Akteon Hotel* (☎02840/41 873; ❷–❺) at **Logarás beach** next door. The *Captain Kafkis Camping* (☎02840/41 479) – a small quiet **campsite** – is out of town on the road up to Márpissa.

Inland

The road runs west from Píso Livádhi back to the capital. A medieval flag-stoned path once linked both sides of the island, and parts of it survive in the east between Mármara and the villages around Léfkes. **PRÓDHROMOS**, encountered first, is an old fortified farming settlement with defensive walls girding its nearby monastery, while **LÉFKES** itself, an hour up the track, is perhaps the most beautiful and unspoiled settlement on Páros. The town flourished from the seventeenth century on, its population swollen by refugees fleeing from coastal piracy; indeed it was the island's hóra during most of the Ottoman period. Léfkes's marbled alleyways and amphitheatrical setting are unparalleled and, despite the few rooms, a disco (*Akrovatis*), a taverna on the outskirts and the presence of two oversized hotels – the *Hotel Pantheon* (☎02840/41 646; ❷–❹), a large 1970s hotel at the top of the village, and *Lefkes Village* (☎02840/41 827 or 42 398; ❹–❻), a beautiful hotel on the outskirts, with stunning views – the area around the main square has steadfastly resisted change; the central kafenío and bakery observe their siestas religiously.

Thirty minutes further on, through olive groves, is **KÓSTOS**, a simple village and a good place for lunch in a taverna. Any traces of path disappear at **MARÁTHI**, on the site of the ancient marble quarries which once supplied much of Europe. Considered second only to Carrara marble, the last slabs were mined here by the French in the nineteenth century for Napoleon's tomb. From Maráthi, it's easy enough to pick up the bus on to Parikía, but if you want to continue hiking, strike south for the monastery of **Áyios Minás**, twenty minutes away. Various Classical and Byzantine masonry fragments are worked into the walls of this sixteenth-century foundation, and the friendly custodians can put you on the right path up to the convent of **Thapsaná**. From here, other paths lead either back to Parikía (two hours altogether from Áyios Minás), or on up to the island's summit for the last word in views over the Cyclades.

The south of the island

There's little to stop for south of Parikía until **POÚNDA**, 6km away, and then only to catch the ferry to Andíparos (see opposite). What used to be a sleepy hamlet is now a concrete jungle, and neighbouring **ALYKÍ** appears to be permanently under construction. The **airport** is close by, making for lots of unwelcome noise; the sole redeeming feature is an excellent beachside restaurant, by the large tamarisk tree. The end of the southern bus route is at Angeriá, about 3km inland of which is the **convent of Áyii Theodhóri**. Its nuns specialize in weaving locally commissioned articles and are further distinguished as *paleomeroloyítes*, or old-calendarites, meaning that they follow the medieval Orthodox (Julian) calendar, rather than the Gregorian one.

Working your way around the **south coast**, there are two routes east to Dhryós. Either retrace your steps to Angeriá and follow the (slightly inland) coastal road, which skirts a succession of isolated coves and small beaches, or keep on across the foothills from Áyii Theodhóri – a shorter walk. Aside from an abundant water supply (including a duck pond) and surrounding orchards, **DHRYÓS** village is mostly modern and characterless, lacking even a well-defined platía. Follow the lane signed "Dhryós Beach", however, and things improve a bit.

Between here and Píso Livádhi to the north are several sandy coves – Khryssí Aktí ("Golden Beach"), Tzirdhákia, Mezádha, Poúnda and Logarás – prone to pummelling by the *meltémi*, yet all favoured to varying degrees by campers and by windsurfers making a virtue out of necessity. **KHRYSSÍ AKTÍ** is now thoroughly overrun with tavernas, room complexes and the whole range of watersports; there are also tavernas at Logarás, but other facilities are concentrated in Dhryós, which is still the focal point of this part of the island.

Andíparos

Andíparos was once quiet and unspoiled, but now the secret is definitely out. The waterfront is lined with new hotels and apartments, and in high season it can be full, though in recent years families seem to be displacing the young, international crowd. It has managed to hold on to much of its friendly small island atmosphere and still has a lot going for it, including good sandy beaches and an impressive cave, and the rooms and hotels are less expensive than on Páros.

Most of the population of eight hundred live in the large low-lying northern **village**, across the narrow straits from Páros, the new development on the outskirts concealing an attractive traditional settlement around the *kástro*. A long, flagstoned pedestrian street forms its backbone, leading from the jetty to the Cycladic houses around the outer wall of the *kástro*, which was built by Leonardo Loredano in the 1440s as a fortified settlement safe from pirate raids – the Loredano coat of arms can still be seen on a house in the courtyard. The only way into the courtyard is through a pointed archway from the platía, where several cafés are shaded by a giant eucalyptus. Inside, more whitewashed houses surround two churches and a cistern built into the surviving base of the central tower.

Andíparos's **beaches** begin right outside town: **Psaralíki**, just to the south with golden sand and tamarisks for shade, is much better than Sifnéïko (aka "Sunset") on the opposite side of the island. Villa development is starting to follow the newly paved road down the east coast, but has yet to get out of hand. **Glyfa**, 4km down, is another good beach and, further south, **Sorós** has rooms and tavernas. On the west coast there are some fine small sandy coves at **Áyios Yeóryios**, the end of the road, and another long stretch of sand at **Kalóyeros**. Kaïki make daily trips round the island and, less frequently, to the uninhabited islet of Dhespotikó, opposite Áyios Yeóryios.

The great **cave** (summer daily 10.45am–3.45pm; €3) in the south of the island is the chief attraction for day-trippers. In these eerie chambers the Marquis de Nointel, Louis XIV's ambassador to Constantinople, celebrated Christmas Mass in 1673 while a retinue of five hundred, including painters, pirates, Jesuits and Turks, looked on; at the exact moment of midnight explosives were detonated to emphasize the enormity of the event. Although electric light and cement steps have diminished its mystery and grandeur, the cave remains impressive. Tour buses (€2.35 one-way) – buy a one-way fare so you can return on the first available bus – and public buses (€1.10 one-way) run from the port every hour in season; bus services and opening hours are reduced and in winter you'll have to fetch the key for the cave from the mayor or village council (℡02840/61 218).

Practicalities

To get here, you have a choice of **boats** from Parikía (hourly; 40min), arriving at the jetty opposite the main street, or the car ferry from Poúnda (every 30min; 10min), arriving 150m to the south. In season there's no need to use the car ferry unless you take a scooter over or miss the last boat back to Parikía; the car ferry keeps running until midnight. The service to Parikía is reduced out of season and runs only once a day in winter.

There are plenty of **hotels** along the waterfront, including *Anargyros* (℡02840/61 204; ❷), which has good, basic rooms. More upmarket places to the north of the jetty include *Mantalena* (℡02840/61 206; ❸–❺) and *Artemis* (℡02840/61 460; ❹–❻), while inland there are some cheaper rooms as well as the *Hotel Galini* (℡02840/61 420; ❷–❺) to the left of the main street. The popular **campsite** (℡02840/61 221) is a ten-minute walk northeast along a track, next to its own nudist beach; the water here is shallow enough for campers to wade across to the neighbouring islet of Dhipló. For peace and quiet with a degree of comfort try *Studios Delfini* (℡093/275 911; ❹) at Áyios Yeóryios, a long stretch of beach with several tavernas, of which *Captain Pipinos* is recommended.

The best of the waterfront **tavernas** is *Anargyros*, below the hotel of the same name. The main street leads up beside it, and *Klimataria*, 100m inland off to the left, has tables in a pleasant, shady garden. *The Corner Cafe*, also on the main street, has excellent coffee. *To Kastro* is one of the better restaurants outside the *kástro*, where you'll also find the excellent *To Kendro* sweetshop. There are plenty of **bars** around this eucalyptus-filled platía, where a festive atmosphere prevails at night. *Café Margarita* is a pleasant street-side hangout on the way up to this platía. For quiet music and views of the mountains try *Café Yam*, an outdoor café-bar near the *Klimataria*. A short-schedule **bank**, a **post office**, a cinema and several **travel agents** round up the list of amenities.

Náxos

Náxos is the largest and most fertile of the Cyclades, and, with its green and mountainous highland scenery, seems immediately distinct from many of its neighbours. The difference is accentuated by the **unique architecture** of many of the interior villages: the Venetian Duchy of the Aegean, which ruled from the thirteenth to the sixteenth century, left towers and fortified mansions scattered throughout the island, while medieval Cretan refugees bestowed a singular character upon Náxos's eastern settlements.

Today Náxos could easily support itself without tourists by relying on its production of potatoes, olives, grapes and lemons, but it has thrown in its lot with mass tourism, so that parts of the island are now almost as busy and commercialized as Páros in season. But the island certainly has plenty to see if you know where to look: the highest mountains in the Cyclades, intriguing central valleys, a spectacular north coast and marvellously sandy beaches in the southwest.

Náxos Town

A long causeway, built to protect the harbour to the north, connects **NÁXOS TOWN** (or Hóra) with the islet of Palátia – the place where, according to legend, Theseus abandoned Ariadne on his way home from Crete. The famous stone **Portára** that has greeted visitors for 2500 years is the portal of a temple of Apollo, built on the orders of the tyrant Lygdamis in the sixth century BC, but never completed. Most of the town's life goes on down by the crowded port esplanade or just behind it; back streets and alleys behind the harbour lead up through low arches of the old town, Boúrgos, to the fortified *kástro*, from where Marco Sanudo and his successors ruled over the Cyclades. Only two of the *kástro*'s original seven towers remain, though the north gate (approached from Apóllonos) survives as a splendid example of a medieval fort entrance. The Venetians' Catholic descendants, now much declined in numbers, still live in the old mansions which encircle the site, many with ancient coats of arms above

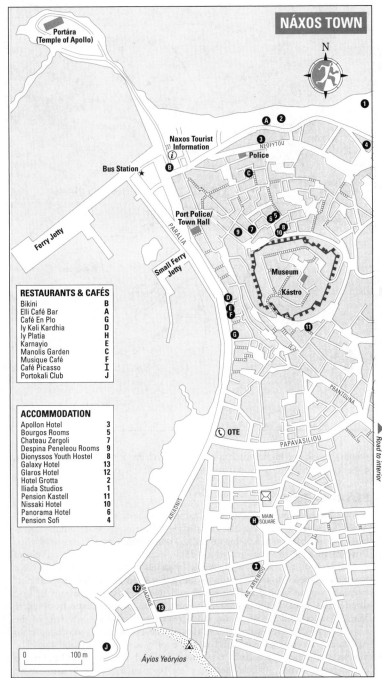

NÁXOS TOWN

N

Portára
(Temple of Apollo)

Naxos Tourist
Information
(i)

Police

Bus Station ★

Port Police/
Town Hall

Ferry Jetty

Small Ferry
Jetty

Museum

Kástro

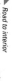
Road to interior

PRANTOUNA

OTE

PAPAVASILIOU

ARIADNIS

MAIN
SQUARE

AG. ARSENIOU

ABIADNIS

Áyios Yeóryios

0   100 m

RESTAURANTS & CAFÉS

Bikini	B
Elli Café Bar	A
Café En Plo	G
Iy Keli Kardhia	D
Iy Platia	H
Karnayio	E
Manolis Garden	C
Musique Café	F
Café Picasso	I
Portokali Club	J

ACCOMMODATION

Apollon Hotel	3
Bourgos Rooms	5
Chateau Zergoli	7
Despina Peneleou Rooms	9
Dionyssos Youth Hostel	8
Galaxy Hotel	13
Glaros Hotel	12
Hotel Grotta	2
Iliada Studios	1
Pension Kastell	11
Nissaki Hotel	10
Panorama Hotel	6
Pension Sofi	4

crumbling doorways. One of these, the **Domus Della-Rocca-Barozzi** (opening hours vary; €1.50), is open to the public; the tour even includes a tasting from the family's wine cellar. Other brooding relics survive in the same area: a seventeenth-century Ursuline convent and the Roman Catholic cathedral, restored in questionable taste in the 1950s, though still displaying a thirteenth-century crest inside. Nearby was one of Ottoman Greece's first schools, the French School; opened in 1627 for Catholic and Orthodox students alike, its pupils included, briefly, Nikos Kazantzakis. The school building now houses an excellent **archeological museum** (Tues–Sun 8.30am–2.30pm; €3), with finds from Náxos, Koufoníssi, Keros and Dhonoússa, including an important collection of Early Cycladic figurines. Archaic and Classical sculpture and pottery dating from Neolithic through to Roman times are also on display. On the roof terrace a Hellenistic mosaic floor shows a nereid surrounded by deer and peacocks.

As well as archeological treasures, Náxos has some very good sandal-makers – try the Markos store on Papavassilíou. The island is also renowned for its cheese – sharp *kefalotíri* and milder *graviéra* – wines and *kítron*, a sweet citron liqueur.

Arrival, transport and information

Large **ferries** dock along the northerly harbour causeway; all small boats and the very useful *Skopelitis* ferry use the jetty in the fishing harbour, not the main car-ferry dock. The **bus station** is at its landward end: buses run five times a day to Apóllon (€3.40), and one of the morning services to Apóllon takes the newly paved coastal road via Engarés and Abrámi, and is much quicker though not any cheaper. There are six buses a day to Apíranthos via Filóti, two of these going on to Moutsoúna on the east coast. Buses run (every 30min 8am–midnight) to Áyios Prokópios, Ayía Ánna and as far as the *Maragas* campsite on Pláka beach, and four times a day to Pirgáki. Printed timetables are available from the bus station. **Naxos Tourist Information** (☎02850/25 201, ℻30 285), on the seafront near the jetty, is a wealth of information and also has details of rooms.

Accommodation

There's plenty of accommodation in Náxos and you should have no problem finding somewhere to stay. Once you've run the gauntlet of touts on the jetty, there are three basic areas to look for **rooms** in Náxos Town: in the old quarter near the *kástro*, where they are hard to find and relatively expensive; up to the left (north) of town in Grótta; and south of town near Áyios Yeóryios beach, where they are most abundant and less expensive, but with significant nighttime noise from clubs and discos. *Despina Panteleou* (☎02850/22 356; ❸), the newer *Bourgos Rooms* (☎02850/25 979; ❸) and *Pension Kastell* (☎02850/23 082, ✉pension.kastell@gmx.net; ❸) are good choices near the *kástro*, where you'll also find the *Dionyssos Youth Hostel* (☎02850/22 331; €14.70 dorm bed). In Grotta, try *Pension Sofi* (☎02850/25 582; ❸) or *Iliada Studios* (☎02850/23 303 or 24 277, ✉ILIADA@naxos-island.com; ❹) on the cliff beyond, with good views over the town and out to sea.

Hotel choices near the *kástro* include the charming traditional *Chateau Zevgoli* (☎02850/22 993; ❻), with antique-furnished, air-conditioned rooms, and *Panorama* (☎02850/24 404; ❹). Across from the cathedral near the ancient agora you'll find one of the newest and best, the *Apollon* (☎02850/22 468, ℻25 200, ✉apollon-hotel@naxos-island.com; ❹). Up in Grótta there's the friendly *Hotel Grótta* (☎02850/22 215; ❸–❹), while near Áyios Yeóryios beach there's the *Nissaki* (☎02850/25 710; ❹), with a pool; the *Glaros* (☎02850/23 101; ❸); and the more upscale *Galaxy* (☎02850/22 422; ❺–❻) further along, and plenty more to choose from.

Eating, drinking and nightlife

One of the best quayside breakfast bars is the *Bikini* creperie. Further along to the south are a string of relatively expensive but simple oven-food **tavernas** – *Iy Kali Kardhia* is typical, serving acceptable casserole dishes washed down with barrelled wine. *Iy Platia* on the main square, near Áyios Yeóryios beach, serves traditional fare and is popular with Greeks, while the nearby *Cafe Picasso* serves Mexican food (evenings only) to a mixed crowd. On the front *Karnayio* is a good, if a little pricey, fish taverna; *Cafe En Plo* and *Musique Café* are two reasonable places in the middle of the quay, both popular with locals. *Manolis Garden Taverna*, nearby the ancient agora, is one of the most pleasant of the Boúrgos tourist eateries. *Elli Cafe Bar Restaurant* behind Grótta beach is a little more expensive but serves imaginative food, and *Portokali Club* on the headland to the south of town is a club, café and restaurant with good views over Áyios Yeóryios bay. There's a good **bakery** about midway along the harbour front. For local cheese, wine, *kítron*, spices and other dried comestibles head for Tirokomika Proionia Naxou, a delightful old store on Papavassilíou.

Much of the evening action goes on at the south end of the waterfront, where you'll find *Day & Night*, *Cream*, *Veggera* and *Med*. The *Ocean Club Disco*, further south, above the near end of Áyios Yeóryios beach, is probably the hottest place for dancing to loud and lively pop. *Sugar Island*, also popular with the younger set, is near Grótta while *Lakridi*, behind the town hall, plays jazz and blues for those wanting something more sedate. There's also an open-air **cinema**, the Ciné Astra, on the road to the airport at the southern end of town; it's a fair walk out, but the Ayía Ánna bus stops here.

The southwestern beaches

The **beaches** around Náxos Town are worth sampling. For some unusual swimming just to the **north** of the port, beyond the causeway, **Grótta** is easiest to reach. Besides the caves after which the place is named, the remains of submerged Cycladic buildings are visible, including some stones said to be the entrance to a tunnel leading to the unfinished temple of Apollo. The finest spots, though, are all **south** of town, the entire southwestern coastline boasting a series of excellent **beaches** accessible by regular bus. **ÁYIOS YEÓRYIOS**, a long sandy bay fringed by the southern extension of the hotel "colony", is within walking distance. There's a line of cafés and tavernas at the northern end of the beach, and a windsurfing school, plus the first of four **campsites**, whose touts you will no doubt have become acquainted with at the ferry jetty. This first campsite, *Camping Naxos* (☎02850/23 500), isn't recommended; *Maragas* and *Plaka* have far more attractive locations on Pláka beach (see p.636). A word of warning for campers: although this entire coast is relatively sheltered from the *meltémi*, the plains behind are boggy and you should bring along mosquito repellent.

Buses take you to **ÁYIOS PROKÓPIOS** beach, with plenty of reasonably priced hotels, rooms and basic tavernas, plus the relaxed *Apollon* campsite (☎02850/24 117) nearby. *Hotel Lianos Village* (☎02850/23 366, ✉lianos-village@nax.forthnet.gr; ❹–❻) is an upmarket choice with a pleasant pool setting; of the restaurants *Pizzeria Promponas* has a varied menu and nice setting. Rapid development along this stretch means that this resort has blended into the next resort of **AYÍA ÁNNA** (habitually referred to as "Ayi'Ánna"), further along the busy road; here you will find accommodation of similar price and quality. The seaview *Hotel Ayia Anna* (☎02850/42 576; ❸) and adjacent *Gorgona* taverna are recommended, as is *Bar Bagianni* on the road from Áyia Ánna to Áyios

△ Temple of Apollo, Náxos

Prokópios, a colourful and popular bar which serves vegetarian food. Moving along the coast, away from the built-up area, the beach here is nudist.

Beyond the headland stretch the five kilometres of **PLÁKA** beach, a vegetation-fringed expanse of white sand. Things are not so built up here, and parts of the beach are nudist (past *Plaka* campsite). There are two suitably laid-back and friendly **campsites** here: *Maragas* (☎02850/24 552) which also has double rooms (❶), and the newer *Plaka* campsite (☎02850/42 700), a little further along, which is small and quiet with a few inexpensive bungalows (❶); be aware, however, that it's 6km into town, and the camp's bus will not run at your convenience (they usually run in concurrence with the ferry service). The *Hotel Orkos Village* (☎02850/75 321, ✉orkos@nax.forthnet.gr; ❺) has apartments in an attractive location, on a hillside above the coast between Pláka beach and Mikrí Vígla.

For real isolation, go to the other side of Mikrí Vígla headland, along a narrow footpath across the cliff-edge, to **KASTRÁKI** beach; towards the middle of the beach *Areti* (☎02850/75 292; ❺) has apartments and a restaurant. A few people camp around the taverna on the small headland a little further down. In summer this stretch, all the way from Mikrí Vígla down to Pyrgáki, attracts camper vans and windsurfers from all over Europe. On the Alíko promontory to the south of Kastráki there is a small nudist beach.

From Kastráki, it's a couple of hours' walk up to the Byzantine castle of **Apalírou** which held out for two months against the besieging Marco Sanudo. The fortifications are relatively intact and the views magnificent. **Pyrgáki** beach has a couple of tavernas and a few rooms; four kilometres further on is **Ayiássos** beach.

The rest of the **southern coast** – indeed, virtually the whole of the southeast of the island – is remote and mountain-studded; you'd have to be a dedicated and well-equipped camper/hiker to get much out of the region.

Central Náxos and the Tragéa

Although buses bound for Apóllon (in the north) link up the central Naxian villages, the core of the island – between Náxos Town and Apíranthos – is best explored by motorbike or on foot. Much of the region is well off the beaten track, and can be a rewarding excursion if you've had your fill of beaches; Christian Ucke's *Walking Tours on Naxos*, available from bookshops in Náxos town, is a useful guide for hikers.

Once out of Hóra, you quickly arrive at the neighbouring villages of **GLINÁDHO** and **GALANÁDHO**, forking respectively right and left. Both are scruffy market centres: Glinádho is built on a rocky outcrop above the Livádhi plain, while Galánadho displays the first of Náxos's fortified mansions and an unusual "double church". A combined Orthodox chapel and Catholic sanctuary separated by a double arch, the church reflects the tolerance both by the Venetians during their rule and by the locals to established Catholics afterwards. Continue beyond Glinádho to **TRÍPODHES** (ancient Biblos), 9km from Náxos Town. Noted by Homer for its wines, this old-fashioned agricultural village has nothing much to do, but you can enjoy a coffee at the shaded kafenío. The start of a long but rewarding walk is a rough road (past the parish church) which leads down the colourful Pláka valley, past an old watchtower and the Byzantine church of **Áyios Matthéos** ("mosaic pavement"), and ends at the glorious Pláka beach (see above).

To the east, the twin villages of **SANGRÍ**, on a vast plateau at the head of a long valley, can be reached by continuing to follow the left-hand fork past

Galanádho, a route which allows a look at the domed eighth-century church of **Áyios Mámas** (on the left), once the Byzantine cathedral of the island but neglected during the Venetian period and now a sorry sight. Either way, **Káto Sangrí** boasts the remains of a Venetian castle, while **Áno Sangrí** is a comely little place, all cobbled streets and fragrant courtyards. Thirty-minutes' stroll away, on a path leading south out of the village, are the partially reconstructed remains of a Classical temple of Demeter.

The Tragéa

From Sangrí the road twists northeast into the **Tragéa** region, scattered with olive trees and occupying a vast highland valley. It's a good jumping-off point for all sorts of exploratory rambling, and **HALKÍ** is a fine introduction to what is to come. Set high up, 16km from the port, it's a noble and silent town with some lovely churches. The **Panayía Protóthronis** church, with its eleventh- to thirteenth-century frescoes, and the romantic **Grazia (Frangopoulos) Pýrgos**, are open to visitors, but only in the morning. Tourists wanting to stay here are still something of a rarity, although you can usually get a room in someone's house by asking at the store. *Yiannis* taverna is the focal point of village activity and has a good selection of fresh *mezédhes* to enjoy with a glass of oúzo. Nearby is the distillery and shop of Vallindras Naxos Citron, whose charming proprietors explain the process of producing this speciality citrus liqueur (*kítron*), followed by a little tasting session. The olive and citrus plantations surrounding Halkí are crisscrossed by paths and tracks, the groves dotted with numerous Byzantine chapels and the ruins of fortified *pyrgi* or Venetian mansions. Between Halkí and Akadhimí, but closer to the latter, sits the peculiar twelfth-century "piggyback" church of **Áyii Apóstoli**, with a tiny chapel (where the ennobled donors worshipped in private) perched above the narthex; there are brilliant thirteenth-century frescoes as well.

The road from Halkí heads north to **MONÍ**. Just before the village, you pass the sixth-century monastery of **Panayía Dhrossianí**, a group of stark, grey-stone buildings with some excellent frescoes; the monks allow visits at any time, though you may have to contend with coach tours from Náxos Town. Moní itself enjoys an outstanding view of the Tragéa and surrounding mountains, and has four tavernas, plus some rooms. The main road leads on to Kinídharos, with an old marble quarry above the village; a few kilometres beyond, a signpost points you down a rough track to the left, to **FLÉRIO** (commonly called Melanés). The most interesting of the ancient marble quarries on Náxos, this is home to two famous **koúri**, dating from the sixth century BC, that were left recumbent and unfinished because of flaws in the material. Even so, they're finely detailed figures, over five metres in length. One of the statues lies in a private, irrigated orchard; the other is up a hillside some distance above, and you will need to seek local guidance to find it.

From Flério you could retrace your steps to the road and head back to Hóra via Mýli and the ruined Venetian castle at Kouronohóri, both pretty hamlets connected by footpaths. If you're feeling more adventurous, ask to be directed south to the footpath which leads over the hill to the Potamiá villages. The first of these, **ÁNO POTAMIÁ**, has a fine taverna and a rocky track back towards the Tragéa. Once past the valley the landscape becomes craggy and barren, the forbidding Venetian fortress of **Apáno Kástro** perched on a peak just south of the path. This is believed to have been Sanudo's summer home, but the fortified site goes back further, if the Mycenaean tombs found nearby are any indication. From the fort, paths lead back to Halkí in around an hour. Alternatively, you can continue further southwest down the Potamiá valley towards Hóra, passing first the ruined **Cocco Pýrgos** – said to be haunted by one Constantine Cocco, the victim of a seventeenth-century clan feud – on the way to **MÉSO POTAMIÁ**, joined by some isolated dwellings with its twin village **KÁTO POTAMIÁ**, nestling almost invisibly among the greenery flanking the creek.

At the far end of the gorgeous Tragéa valley, **FILÓTI**, the largest village in the region, lies on the slopes of Mount Zás (or Zeus) which, at 1000m, is the highest point in the Cyclades. Under the shade of the plane trees on the main platía are several pleasant kafenía, as well as *Babulas Grill-Restaurant* (☎02850/31 426; ❶), which has the best rooms in the village. To get an idea of the old village, climb the steps up the hill starting at the platía. A turning at the southern end of the village is signposted to the **Pýrgos Hímárou**, a remote twenty-metre Hellenistic watchtower, and **Kalándou** beach on the south coast; beyond the turning the road is unpaved. There are no villages in this part of the island, so bring supplies if you're planning to camp. From the village, it's a round-trip walk of three to four hours to the summit of Zás, a climb which rewards you with an astounding panorama of virtually the whole of Náxos and its Cycladic neighbours. From the main Filóti–Apóllon road, take the side road towards Dhánakos until you reach a small chapel on the right, just beside the start of the waymarked final approach trail. (Save yourself the rather tedious walk along the tarmac road by taking the bus towards Apóllon and asking the driver to let you off at the Dhánakos turning. There is a sign before the turnoff to the Zas Cave, a pleasant place for a picnic, but not a good point from which to tackle the steep ascent to the summit.)

APÍRANTHOS, a hilly, winding 10km beyond, shows the most Cretan influence of all the interior villages. There are four small **museums** and two Venetian fortified mansions, while the square contains a miniature church with a three-tiered bell tower. Ask to be pointed to the start of the spectacular path up over the ridge behind; this ends either in Moní or Kalóxilos, depending on whether you fork right or left respectively at the top. Cafés and tavernas on the main street look out over a terraced valley below. Rooms are available but are not advertised – ask in the cafés or in the embroidery shop. Apíranthos is a good quiet place to stay for a few days, and being high in the mountains is noticeably cooler and greener than the coast.

Apíranthos has a beach annexe of sorts at **Moutsoúna**, 12km east. Emery mined near Apíranthos used to be transported here by means of an aerial funicular and then shipped out of the port. The industry collapsed in the 1980s, and the sandy cove beyond the dock now features a growing colony of holiday villas. An unpaved road heads south along the coast to a remote sandy beach at **Psilí Ámmos** – ideal for self-sufficient campers, but you must take enough water. From here a track carries on to **Pánormos** beach in the southeastern corner of the island.

Northern Náxos

The route through the mountains from Apíranthos to Apóllon is very scenic, and the road surface is in good condition all the way. Jagged ranges and hairpin bends confront you before reaching Kóronos, the halfway point, where a road off to the right threads through a wooded valley to **Liónas**, a tiny and very Greek port with a pebble beach. You'd do better to continue, past Skadhó, to the remote, emery-miners' village of **KOMIAKÍ** which is a pleasing, vine-covered settlement – the highest village in the island and the original home of *kítron* liqueur.

Back on the main road, a series of slightly less hairy bends leads down a long valley to **APÓLLON** (Apóllonas), a small resort with two beaches: a tiny and crowded stretch of sand backed by cafés and restaurants, and a longer and quieter stretch of shingle, popular mainly with Greek families. If you are staying, try the friendly rooms of *Maria* (T02850/67 106; ❷) behind the harbour. The only major attraction is a **koúros**, approached by a path from the main road just above the village. Lying *in situ* at a former marble quarry, this largest of Náxos's abandoned stone figures is just over ten metres long, but, compared with those at Flério, disappointingly lacking in detail. Here since 600 BC, it serves as a singular reminder of the Naxians' traditional skill; the famous Delian lions (see p.618) are also made of Apollonian marble. Not surprisingly, bus tours descend upon the village during the day, and Apóllon is now quite a popular little place. The local festival, celebrated on August 28–29, is one of Náxos's best.

From Náxos town there is now a daily bus service direct to Apóllon (taking about an hour). It's easy to make a round trip of the north coast and inland villages by bus in either direction. The coastal road is spectacularly beautiful, going high above the sea for most of the way – it's more like parts of Crete or the mainland than other islands. Ten kilometres past the northern cape sprouts the beautiful **Ayiá** *pýrgos*, or tower, another foundation (in 1717) of the Cocco family. There's a tiny hamlet nearby, and, 7km further along, a track leads off to **Abrámi** beach, an idyllic spot with a highly recommended family-run taverna and **rooms** to let, *Pension and Restaurant Efthimios* (T02850/63 244; ❷). Just beyond the hamlet of Hília Výssi is the abandoned **monastery of Faneroménis**, built in 1606. Carrying on along the coastal road you will reach Engarés valley, at the foot of which is another quiet beach, **Amití**, which can be reached via one of two dirt tracks, the most obvious being the one leading down from Galíni, only 6km from Hóra. On the final stretch back to the port you pass a unique eighteenth-century Turkish fountain-house and the fortified monastery of **Ayíou Ioánnou Khryssostómou**, where a couple of aged nuns are still in residence. A footpath from the monastery and the road below lead straight back to town.

Koufoníssi, Skhinoússa, Iráklia and Dhonoússa

In the patch of the Aegean between Náxos and Amorgós there is a chain of six small islands relatively neglected by tourists and by the majority of Greeks, few of whom have heard of them. **Kéros** – ancient Karos – is an important archeological site but has no permanent population, and **Káto Koufoníssi** is inhabited only by goatherds. However, the other four islands – **Áno Koufoníssi**, **Skhinoússa**, **Iráklia** and **Dhonoússa** – are all inhabited, served by ferry and can be visited. Now increasingly discovered by Greeks and foreigners alike, the islets' popularity has hastened the development of better facilities, but they're still a welcome break from the mass tourism of the rest of the Cyclades, especially during high season. If you want real peace and quiet – what the Greeks call *isykhiá* – get there soon.

A few times weekly in summer a Pireás-based **ferry** – usually the *Express Adonis*, *Express Hermes* or the *Georgios Express* – calls at each of the islands, linking them with Náxos and Amorgós and (usually) Páros and Sýros. A small local ferry, the *Express Skopelitis*, is a reliable daily fixture, leaving the little ferry quay in Náxos in mid-afternoon for relatively civilized arrival times at all the islets.

Koufoníssi and Kéros

Áno Koufoníssi is the most populous island of the group; there is a reasonable living to be made from fishing and, with some of the best beaches in the Cyclades, it is attracting increasing numbers of Greek and foreign holidaymakers. Small enough to walk round in a morning, the island can actually feel overcrowded in July and August.

The old single-street village of **HÓRA**, on a low hill behind the harbour, is being engulfed by new room and hotel development, but still has a friendly, small-island atmosphere. A map by the jetty shows where to find all the island's **rooms**: *To Limani* (☎02850/71 851 or 71 450; **②**) is a café with rooms near the harbour; the popular restaurant and pension *Melissa* (☎02850/71 454; **②**) is another good choice. The most upmarket options include *Hotel Aegeon* (☎02850/74 050 or 74 051; **⑤**), by the village beach, or *Ostria Village* (☎02850/71 671; **④**), on the hillside to the east of the village. *Akroyiali* (☎02850/71 685; **③**) is on the front just beyond the beach; Yeoryia Kouveou has beautifully situated rooms at *Hondros Kavos* (☎02850/71 707; **②**), outside the village to the east; and the *Petros Club* (☎02850/71 728; **④**) is in a quiet position inland, with excellent views.

Koufoníssi is noted for its fish **tavernas**; *To Nikitouri*, up in Hóra, has very personable Greek-American management, and the *Karnayio* ouzerí on the bay to the west of the harbour is cheaper than most and has a fine array of seafood. The nearby *To Steki Tis Marias* is a good breakfast place with a few rooms (**②**), and has views over the narrow channel to Káto Koufoníssi. The most popular nightspot is *Soroccos*, a lively café-bar on the front, while good alternatives include *Ta Kalamia*, with a quieter choice of music; *Nikitas*; and *Skholeio*, a creperie and bar. *To Palio Fanari*, to the west of the village, is the club favoured by locals, playing a mix of dance and Greek music. The OTE office and ticket agency are on the main street, and money, unusually, of late, can be changed at the somewhat improvised "post office" (limited hours), north of the town hall.

All the good beaches are in the southeast of the island, getting better as you go east along a dirt path that skirts the coastline along the edge of low cliffs. **Fínikas**, a ten-minute walk from the village, is the first of four wide coves with gently shelving golden sand, where there are rooms and an acceptable taverna. Further east is **Harakópou**, which has a windswept **campsite** (☎02850/71 683) with cane shade and rather poor facilities on the headland before the next beach, **Thános**. Next is **Platiá Púnda**, where caves have been hollowed out of the cliffs. Further east, the path rounds a rocky headland to **Porí**, a much longer and wilder beach, backed by dunes and set in a deep bay. It can be reached more easily from the village by following a track heading inland through the low scrub-covered hills.

KÁTO KOUFONÍSSI, the uninhabited island to the southwest, has a seasonal taverna and some more secluded beaches; a kaïki shuttles people across until late in the evening. A festival is held here on August 15, at the church of the Panayía. The island of **Kéros** is harder to reach, but if there is a willing group of people keen to visit the ancient site, a boat and boatmen can be hired at around €45 for the day.

Skhinoússa

A little to the southwest, the island of **Skhinoússa** is just beginning to awaken to its tourist potential. Boats dock at the small port of Mersíni, which has one pension (☎02850/71 157; **④**) and a couple of cafés; a road leads up to **HÓRA**, aka Panayía, the walk taking just over ten minutes. As you enter the village, the well-stocked "**Tourist Centre**" is one of the first buildings. Yiorgos

Grispos is a mine of information and is personally responsible for the island's map and postcards, as well as being the boat/hydrofoil agent, having a metred phone and selling Greek and foreign press.

Accommodation is mostly in fairly simple rooms, such as *Pension Meltemi* (☎02850/71 195; ❹), *Anesis* (☎02850/71180; ❷) and the pleasant *Provaloma* (☎02850/71 936; ❷), which also has a taverna. The rooms belonging to Anna (☎02850/71 161; ❷) are particularly recommended, as is the modern *Hotel Sunset* (☎02850/71 948; ❷–❹) which enjoys stunning views of the harbour. The main concentration of **restaurants**, cafés and bars is along the main thoroughfare, including the popular *Bar Ostria* and a lively ouzerí.

There are no fewer than sixteen **beaches** dotted around the island, accessible by a lacework of trails. **Tsigoúri** is a ten-minute walk southwest from Hóra; largely undeveloped except for the new *Tsigouri Beach Villas* (☎02850/71 175; ❸), which has a good taverna with great views. The only other beach with any refreshments is **Almyrós**, a half-hour southeast of Hóra, which has a simple canteen.

Iráklia

In an attempt to accommodate increasing visitor numbers, **Iráklia** (pronounced Irakliá by locals), the westernmost of the minor Cyclades, is losing its charm as the number of purpose-built rooms increases.

Ferries and hydrofoils call at **ÁYIOS YEÓRYIOS**, a small but sprawling settlement behind a sandy tamarisk-backed beach. Irini Koveou (☎02850/71 488; ❷) has a café-restaurant and rooms opposite the harbour, and more rooms and places to eat can be found along the old road to Livádhi beach. *Anna's Place* (☎02850/71 145; ❷) has rooms with shared cooking facilities, and *Mestrali* (☎02850/71 807; ❷) has newer rooms as well as its own café-cum-taverna. Theofanis Gavalas (☎02850/71 565; ❷), Dhimítrios Stefanídhis (☎02850/71 484; ❷), Alexandra Tournaki (☎02850/71 482; ❷) and Angelos Koveos (☎02850/71 486; ❷) all have rooms nearby. *O Pefkos* is a pleasant **taverna**, with tables shaded by a large pine tree, while the café/shop *Melissa* acts as the main ticket agency for ferries. The recommended *Perigiali* taverna also has a small shop selling maps showing the mule path to a fine **cave** of Ayíos Ioánnis on the west side of the island.

Livádhi, the best beach on the island, is a fifteen-minute walk southeast of town. There is shade, but bring refreshments, as the taverna might not be open. The village of Livádhi, deserted since 1940, stands on the hillside above, its houses ruined and overgrown; among the remains are Hellenistic walls incorporated into a later building, and fortifications from the time of Marco Sanudo. Marietta Markoyianni (☎02850/71 252; ❷) has the only rooms on the beach; *Zografos Rooms* (☎02850/71 946; ❹), above the road to Panayía, has fine views but is rather remote.

PANAYÍA or **HÓRA**, an unspoiled one-street village at the foot of Mount Papás, is another hour's walk inland along the paved road. It has a bakery/minimarket, two café/shops and the excellent and cheap *O Kritikos* ouzerí, but no rooms. A track to the east heads down to Pigádhi, a rocky beach with sea urchins, at the head of a narrow inlet. To the west a track from the near-deserted hamlet of **Áyios Athanásios** leads back to the port.

The **cave of Áyios Ioánnis** lies behind the mountain, at the head of a valley leading to Vourkária bay. From Panayía, follow a signposted track west before zigzagging up to a saddle well to the north of the summit, with views over Skhinoússa, Koufoníssi, Kéros, Náxos and Amorgós; the path drops down to the south around the back of the mountain. A painted red arrow on the left indicates the turning to the cave, just over an hour's walk from Panayía. A church bell hangs from a cypress tree above the whitewashed entrance; inside there's a shrine, and the cave opens up into a large chamber with stalactites and stalagmites. It can be explored to a depth of 120m and is thought to be part of a much larger cave system, yet to be opened up; a festival is held here every year on August 18.

The main trail continues beyond the cave to a small sandy beach at **Alimiá** but this can be reached more easily with the beach boat from Áyios Yeóryios. In season the boat sails daily to either Skhinoússa, Alimiá or the nearby pebble beach of Karvounólakos.

Dhonoússa

Dhonoússa is a little out on a limb compared with the other minor Cylclades, and ferries and hydrofoils call less frequently. Island life centres on the pleasant port settlement of **STAVRÓS**, spread out behind the harbour and the village beach.

Rooms, most without signs, tend to be booked up by Greek holiday-makers in August; try Mihalis Prasinos (☎02850/51 578; ❹ based on four people sharing), with rooms along a lane behind the church; Dhimitris Prasinos (☎02850/51 579; ❷), with rooms open year-round near the *Iliovasilema* restaurant; or Nikos Prasinos (☎02850/51 551; ❹), who has good new studios above the rocks west of the harbour. *Ta Kymata* is the most popular of the four **tavernas** but *Meltemi* is also good, as is the friendly *Aposperitis*, right on the village beach. Nikitas Roussos (☎02850/51 648) has a **ticket agency** above the harbour and can book rooms and change money – at high rates so you would be wise to bring enough with you.

The hills around Stavrós are low and barren and scarred by bulldozed tracks, but a little walking is repaid with dramatic scenery and a couple of fine beaches. Campers and nudists head for **Kéndros**, a long and attractive stretch of sand fifteen minutes to the east, although shade is limited and there are no facilities. A road has been built on the hillside above, replacing the donkey track to the farming hamlets of Haravyí and Mersíni; these have more hens and goats in the streets than people, and there are no cafés, shops or rooms. **Mersíni** is an hour's walk from Stavrós and has a welcome spring beneath a plane tree, the island's only running water. A nearby path leads down to Livádhi, an idyllic white sand beach with tamarisks for shade. In July and August there's a daily beach boat from the port.

The road to **KALOTARÍTISSA**, on the northeast coast is now paved and no longer an especially attractive walk. You might want to head inland from Stavrós toward Papás, the island's highest point, from where a valley drops down rapidly to the tiny village with a simple **taverna** and one room to rent (☎02850/51 562; ❶). There are two small pebble beaches and a path that continues above the coast to Mersíni. It takes four to five hours to walk round the island.

Amorgós

Amorgós, with its dramatic mountain scenery and laid-back atmosphere, is attracting visitors in increasing numbers; most ferries and hydrofoils call at both Katápola in the southwest and Eyiáli in the northeast – with these destinations, rather than Amorgós, on schedules – and there is a regular bus service between both ports. The island can get extremely crowded in midsummer, the numbers swollen by French paying their respects to the film location of Luc Besson's *The Big Blue*, although few actually venture out to the wreck of the *Olympia*, at the island's west end, which figured so prominently in the movie. In general it's a low-key, escapist clientele, happy to have found a relatively large, interesting and uncommercialized island with excellent walking.

The southwest

KATÁPOLA, set at the head of a deep bay, is actually three separate hamlets: **Katápola** proper on the south flank, **Rahídhi** on the ridge at the head of the gulf and **Xilokeratídhi** along the north shore. There is a beach in front of Rahídhi, but the beach to the west of Katápola is better, though not up to the standards of Eyiáli in the northeast. In season there is also a regular kaïki to nearby beaches at **Maltézi** and **Plákes** (€1.20 return) and a daily kaïki to the islet of **Gramvoússa** off the western end of Amorgós (€6 return).

There are plenty of small **hotels** and **pensions** and, except in high summer when rooms are almost impossible to find, proprietors tend to meet those boats arriving around sunset – though not necessarily those that show up in the small hours. A good clean place next to the beach at the western end of Katápola is *Eleni Rooms* (℡02850/71 543 or 71 628; ④); *Dhimitri's Place* in Rahídhi (℡02850/71 309; ①) is a compound of interconnecting buildings in an orchard with shared cooking facilities; on the same road, *Angeliki Rooms* (℡02850/71 280; ②) is well run, friendly and good value; the smart traditional *Hotel Minoa* (℡02850/71 480; ③–⑤) on the waterfront may be a bit too noisy for some, who might try the *Valsamitis* (℡02850/71 148; ②–⑤), off the northeast corner of the port. *Panayiotis Rooms* (℡02850/71 890; ②) in Xilokeratídhi is also good value and inland, south of the port you'll find the *Hotel Anna* (℡02850/71 218; ②), with a lovely setting and basic cooking facilities. There are several similarly priced pensions further east, including *Big Blue* and *Sofia*. The **campsite** (℡02850/71 802) is well signed between Rahídhi and Xilokeratídhi.

In Katápola proper, *Mourayio* is the most popular **taverna** in town; alternatively try the *Akrogiali*. There are four tavernas near the campsite near Xilokeratídhi, of which the first is a friendly fish taverna, and of the others around the corner *Vitzentzos* is by far the best. What **nightlife** there is focuses on a handful of cafés and pubs. A bar called *Le Grand Bleu* in Xilokeratídhi regularly shows *The Big Blue* on video but there are other less obvious and less expensive places to drink, such as *The Moon Bar* next door or *45 Strofes*, a café and bar on the front at Rahídhi.

Prekas is the one-stop **boat ticket agency**, and there are several **motorbike rental** outlets including the friendly Corner Rentabike, though the local bus service is more than adequate and the walking trails are delightful.

Steps, and then a jeep track, lead south out of Katápola to the remains of **ancient Minoa**, which are apt to disappoint close up: some polygonal wall four or five courses high, the foundations of an Apollo temple, a crumbled Roman structure and bushels of unsorted pottery shards. The setting, however, with views encompassing Hóra and ancient Arkessíni, is memorable. Beyond Minoa the track dwindles to a trail, continuing within a few hours to Arkessíni (see overleaf) via several hamlets – a wonderful **excursion** with the possibility of catching the bus back.

The **bus** shuttles almost hourly until 11pm between Katápola and Hóra, the island capital; several times daily it continues to Ayía Ánna via Hozoviotíssas monastery, and once a day (9.45am) out to the "Káto Meriá", made up of the hamlets of Kamári, Arkessíni and Kolofána. **HÓRA**, also accessible by an hour-long path beginning from behind the Rahídhi campsite, is one of the best-preserved settlements in the Cyclades, with a scattering of tourist shops, cafés, tavernas and rooms. Dominated by a rock plug wrapped with a chapel or two, the thirteenth-century Venetian fortifications look down on countless other bulbous churches – including Greece's smallest, **Áyios Fanoúrios**, which holds just three worshippers – and a line of decapitated windmills beyond. Of the half-dozen or so **places to stay**, *Pension O Ilias* (℡02850/71 277; ❷) is recommended. *Liotrivi* restaurant, down the steps from the bus stop, is probably the best place to **eat** in town. In addition to a pair of traditional tavernas, *Kastanis* and *Klimataria*, there are several noisy bistro/café/pubs, with *To Plateaki* in the upper plaza perennially popular in the late afternoon, and *Giulia Kafeneon*, near the bus stop, livelier later on. Also in the upper square is the island's main **post office**.

From the top of Hóra, near the upper satellite-dish tower, a wide cobbled *kalderími* drops down to two major attractions, effectively short-cutting the road and taking little longer than the bus to reach them. Bearing left at an inconspicuous fork after fifteen minutes, you'll come to the spectacular **monastery of Hozoviotíssas** (daily 8am–1pm; donation expected, modest dress required), which appears suddenly as you round a bend, its vast wall gleaming white at the base of a towering orange cliff. Only four monks occupy the fifty rooms now, but they are quite welcoming considering the number of visitors who file through; you can see the eleventh-century icon around which the monastery was founded, along with a stack of other treasures. Legend has it that during the Iconoclastic period a precious icon of the Virgin was committed to the sea by beleaguered monks at Hózova, in the Middle East, and it washed up safely at the base of the palisade here. The view from the *katholikón's* terrace overshadows all for most visitors, and to round off the experience, you are ushered into a comfy reception room and treated to a sugary lump of *loukoúmi*, a fiery shot of *kítron* and a cool glass of water.

The right-hand trail leads down, within forty minutes, to the pebble **beaches** at **Ayía Ánna**. Skip the first batch of tiny coves in favour of the path to the westernmost bay, where naturists cavort, almost in scandalous sight of the monastery far above. As yet there are no tavernas here, nor a spring, so bring food and water for the day.

For alternatives to Ayía Ánna, take the morning bus out toward modern Arkessíni, alighting at **Kamári** hamlet (where there's a single taverna) for the twenty-minute path down to the adjacent beaches of **Notiná**, **Moúros** and **Poulopódhi**. Like most of Amorgós's south-facing beaches, they're clean, with calm water, and here, too, a freshwater spring dribbles most of the year. The road is paved as far as **Kolofána**, where there is one place with **rooms**. From here unpaved roads lead to the western tip of the island, and remote beaches at Káto Kámbos and at Paradhísa, facing the islet of Gramvoússa.

Archeology buffs will want to head north from Kamári to Vroútsi, start of the overgrown hour-long route to **ancient Arkessini**, a collection of tombs, six-metre-high walls and houses out on the cape of Kastrí. The main path from Minoa also passes through Vroútsi, ending next to the well-preserved Hellenistic fort known locally as the "Pýrgos", just outside modern **ARKESSÍNI**. The village has a single taverna with rooms, and, more importantly, an afternoon bus back to Hóra and Katápola.

The northeast

The energetically inclined can walk the four to five hours from Hóra to Eyiáli, either continuing on the faint trail just beyond Hozoviótissas, or taking the scenic and sheltered valley track through Terláki and Rikhtí. The two routes, and the modern jeep road, more or less meet an hour out of Hóra. Along most of the way, you're treated to amazing views of **Nikouriá islet**, nearly joined to the main island, and in former times a leper colony. The only habitations en route are the summer hamlet of **Asfodhilítis**, with well water but little else for the traveller, and **Potamós**, a double village you encounter on the stroll down towards Eyiáli bay.

EYIÁLI (Órmos) is smaller than Katápola but more picturesque, so it's gaining in popularity. The road inland, behind the harbour, leads to a group of **hotels** of similar price and quality. *Nikitas* (☎02850/73 237; ❷) is the most pleasant, in that it stands on its own in a field, commanding unobstructed sea views. Above is a row of hotels including *Pension Christine* (☎02850/73 236; ❷), *Akrogiali* (☎02850/73 249; ❸) and *Hotel Pelagos* (☎02850/73 206; ❷). Above on the main road is *Poseidon Studios* (☎02850/73 453; ❹), which have fully equipped kitchens. Along the beach is the *Lakki* (☎02850/73 244; ❹) and behind this the pleasant *Pension Askas* (☎02850/73 333; ❹) – both of which have their own shaded tavernas. Next to *Pension Askas* there is a very friendly official **campsite**, *Amorgos Camping* (☎02850/73 500), usually less crowded than that in Katápola. Overlooking the bay on the road up to Tholária is a luxury hotel with a swimming pool, the *Egialis* (☎02850/73 393; ❹–❻). For **eating out**, try *To Limani* (aka *Katerina's*) on the single inland lane, packed until midnight by virtue of its excellent food and barrel wine. Other good options are the *Amorgialos* kafenío right by the harbour, which serves up octopus, and *Delear*, a smart beach bar with live music some evenings and rather pricey drinks. A few seasonal music **bars**, such as *Blé Café*, attempt to compete with *Katerina's*. The *Corte Club* at the *Egialis* hotel is a typical holiday resort disco playing northern European dance music and Greek pop. For a more active adventure you can take advantage of the new **diving** centre, Dive Ventures (☎02850/73 611), which organizes daily boat and shore dives.

The main Eyiáli **beach** is more than serviceable, getting less weedy and reefy as you stroll further north, the sand interrupted by the remains of a Roman building jutting into the sea. A trail here leads over various headlands to an array of clothing-optional bays: the first sandy, the second mixed sand and gravel, the last shingle. There are no facilities anywhere so bring along what you need.

There is a **bus service** up to each of the two villages visible above and east of Eyiáli, with eight departures daily up and down (a timetable is posted by the harbour bus stop), but it would be a shame to miss out on the beautiful **loop walk** linking them with the port. A path starting at the far end of the beach heads inland and crosses the road before climbing steeply to **THOLÁRIA**, named after vaulted Roman tombs found around Vígla, the site of ancient Eyiáli. Vígla is on a hill opposite the village but there is little to see beyond the bases of statues and traces of city walls incorporated into later terracing. Another path winds down behind the hill to a tiny pebble beach at Mikrí Vlihádha far below. There are a few **taverna-cafés**, including a handsome wooden-floored establishment near the church, and several places to stay, including some comfortable **rooms** (reserve through *Pension Lakki* in Eyiáli), the large and upmarket *Vigla* (☎02850/73 288; ❸–❺) and the *Thalassino Oneiro* (☎02850/73 345; ❷), which has a fine restaurant and an extremely friendly owner.

LANGÁDHA is another hour's walk along a path starting below Tholária; to the left of the trail is the chapel of Astrátios with an altar supported by the capital of a Corinthian column. Past here there are views down to the inlet of Megáli Vlihádha and, on a clear day, across to Ikaría in the north. The path descends through the village of Stroúmbos, abandoned apart from a few houses restored as holiday homes, and into a small gorge before climbing the steps up to Langádha. The place is home to a sizeable colony of expatriates – reflected in the German-Greek cooking at the beautifully located *Nikos'* **taverna** at the lower end of the village, which also runs the attached *Pagali* hotel (☎02850/73 310; ❹). The *Loza* taverna, at the top of the village also owns a more straightforward pension with rooms (☎02850/73 315; ❷).

Beyond Langádha, another rocky path leads around the base of the island's highest peak, the 821-metre-high **Kríkellos**, passing on the way the fascinating church of **Theológos**, with lower walls and ground plan dating to the fifth century. Somewhat easier to reach, by a slight detour off the main Tholária-Langádha trail, are the church and festival grounds of **Panayía Panohoriáni** – not so architecturally distinguished but a fine spot nonetheless.

Íos

No other island is quite like **Íos**, nor attracts the same vast crowds of young people, although attempts are being made to move the island's tourism upmarket. Buildings are now painted white with blue trim, instead of garish psychedelic hues; camping rough is discouraged; and Greece's early closing laws (3am except Fri & Sat) are enforced, and bars no longer stay open all night. (There is still, however, a lingering problem with *bómba*, a cheap local drink that gets you drunk fast and then makes you sick. It might be worth resisting drinks that are suspiciously cheap.)

The only real villages – **Yialós**, **Hóra** and **Mylopótamos** – are in one small corner of the island, and until recently development elsewhere was restricted by poor roads. As a result there are still some very quiet beaches with just a few rooms to rent. Yialós has one of the best and safest natural harbours in the Cyclades, with a newly paved esplanade, and there is talk of building a new yacht marina.

Most visitors stay along the arc delineated by the port – at Yialós, where you'll arrive (there's no airport), in Hóra above it or at the beach at Mylopótamos; it's a small area, and you soon get to know your way around. **Buses** constantly shuttle between Koumbára, Yialós, Hóra and Mylopótamos, with a daily service running roughly from 8am to midnight; you should never have to wait more than fifteen minutes during high season, but at least once try the short walk up (or down) the stepped path between Yialós and Hóra. Various travel offices run their own buses to the beaches at Manganári and Ayía Theodhóti; they sell return tickets only and are a bit expensive. To rent your own transport, try Jacob's Car and Bike Rental (☎02860/91 047) in Yialós or Vangelis Bike Rental (☎02860/91 919) in Hóra; unlike most of the other islands, here you'll need a valid motorcycle license.

Despite its past popularity, **sleeping on the beach** on Íos is discouraged these days. Crime and police raids are becoming more frequent as the island strains under the sheer impact of increasing youth tourism, and the police have been known to turn nasty. They prefer you to sleep in the official campsites and, given the problem of theft, you should probably take their advice.

Yialós and Hóra

From **YIALÓS** quayside, **buses** turn around just to the left, while Yialós **beach** – surprisingly peaceful and uncrowded – is another five-minutes' walk in the same direction. You might be tempted to grab a room in Yialós as you arrive: owners meet the ferries, hustling the town's **accommodation**, and there are also a couple of kiosks by the jetty that will book rooms for you. In shoulder season you can bargain for prices considerably lower than those listed below, but the town won't be in full swing. *Hotel Mare Monte* (☎02860/91 585; ❹), about halfway down the beach, has clean modern rooms and a small pool; *Galini Rooms* (☎02860/91 115; ❹), down a lane behind the beach, is a good quiet choice, if a little out of the way. One of the best choices is the quiet family-owned *Golden Sun* (☎02860/91 110; ❹), about 300m up the road to Hóra, which has a large pool. There are more rooms on the stepped path from Yialós to Hóra although they can be noisy at night: the *Hotel-Bar Helios* (☎02860/91 500; ❹) has a few simple, older rooms, and smarter options nearby include *Armadoras* (☎02860/91 201; ④), with a pleasant pool and bar, and *Hotel Poseidon* (☎02860/91 091; ④). *Ios Camping* (☎02860/91 329) is friendly and clean and has a rather luxurious swimming pool and café area. Yialós has other essentials, including a reasonable supermarket and a few **tavernas**. The *Octopus Tree*, a small kafenío by the fishing boats, serves cheap fresh seafood caught by the owner, while on the front heading towards the beach the *Waves Restaurant* does good Indian food. A twenty-minute stroll over the headland at **KOUMBÁRA**, there's a smaller and less-crowded beach, with a rocky islet to explore, and the *Polydoros* taverna, one of the better places to eat on Iós – well worth the walk or bus ride.

HÓRA (aka Íos Town), a twenty-minute walk up behind the port, is one of the most picturesque towns in the Cyclades, filled with meandering arcaded lanes and whitewashed chapels, though it's overwhelmed by crowds of young revellers in the high season. It divides naturally into two parts: the old town climbing the hillside to the left as you arrive, and the newer development to the right.

There are plenty of basic **rooms** in the old part, although the bars can make sleep difficult. Your best strategy for a modicum of quiet is to wend your way up to the left where you find several establishments, including *Francesco's* (☎02860/91 223; ③). Lower down there's the *Hotel Filippou* (☎02860/91 290; ③), above the National Bank and next to the cathedral, and Yannis Stratis (☎02860/91 494; ②) has a few very simple rooms next door. Your best chances for affordable rest will be found in the newer quarter: *Markos Pension* (☎02860/91 059; ④; ask for the ten percent discount for *Rough Guide* readers), with a poolside bar; *Lofos (The Hill) Pension* (☎02860/91 481: ④), to the right up from the Rollan supermarket; *Katerina Rooms* (☎02860/91 997; ④), just out of town down a path past the *Iós Club*; the new *Village Twins* (☎02860/92 211; ④), up to the left before the *Scorpion Club*; and the friendly *Four Seasons Pension* (☎02860/91 308 or winter ☎02860/92 081; ④), up from Vangelis Bike Rental.

Every evening in summer Hóra is the centre of the island's **nightlife**, its streets throbbing with music from ranks of competing discos and clubs – mostly free, or with a nominal entrance charge, though drinks tend to be expensive. Most of the smaller **bars** and pubs are tucked into the thronging narrow streets of the old village on the hill, offering something for everyone – unless you just want a quiet drink – and you'll have no trouble finding them. A welcome exception to the techno-pop dancing fodder can be found at the *Ios Club*, perched right up on the hill, which plays quieter music, has reasonable food and is a good place to watch the sunset. The larger **dancing clubs**, include the *Mojo*, which plays techno and trance music, *Scorpion* and *Cavos*, on the main road to Mylopótamos.

Eating is a secondary consideration but there are plenty of cheap and cheerful *psistariés* and takeaway joints: sound choices include the Italian restaurant *Pinocchio*, and the *Lord Byron* mezedhopolíon in an alley up to the left in the old quarter – it's open year round and tries hard to re-create a traditional atmosphere, with old rembétika music and some good, unusual Greek food.

Culturally things are improving with the recent opening of the **Archeological Museum of Ios** (Tues–Sun 8am–2pm; €1.50), on the second floor of the yellow town hall, which hopes to attract a more diverse range of visitors to the island. The outdoor theatre of Odysseus Elytis, behind the windmills, provides a beautiful setting in which to enjoy concerts and plays, details of which can be found at the travel agent/information booth next to the archeological museum.

Around the island

The most popular stop on the island's bus routes is **MYLOPÓTAMOS** (universally abbreviated to Mylópotas), the site of a magnificent beach and a mini-resort. Due to the large number of young travellers in Íos, **camping** is a popular option. *Far Out* (☎02860/91 468), the better of the campsites also has bungalows (●); it has an attractive setting and excellent facilities, including an air-conditioned cafeteria, but it's very popular and can get noisy and crowded. *The Purple Pig* (☎02860/91 302, ☻purplpig@otenet.gr), a friendly Australian-run backpackers' complex, by the road up to Hóra, has clean bungalows ●–●, good camping facilities and plenty of other pleasurable distractions, including its own club and a poolside bar. Up the road at the far end of the beach, *Gorgona* (☎02860/91 307; ●) and *Dracos* (☎02860/91 281 or 91 010; ●) have reasonable rooms, and *Dracos* also has a good taverna on its own little quay, serving freshly caught fish. The *Far Out Hotel* (☎02860/91 446 or 91 702; ●), on the road down from Hóra, and the luxurious *Ios Palace Hotel* (☎02860/91 269; ●), above the near end of the beach, are the most upmarket choices. On the rocks, beyond the *Ios Palace*, the *Harmony Restaurant* is one of the better places to eat, serving pizzas and Mexican food. The restaurants and self-service cafés behind the beach are uninspiring, and only the *Faros Café* rates a mention for staying open through the night to cater for the crowds returning from Hóra in the early hours. Mylopótamos itself has surprisingly little in the way of nightlife.

From Yialós, daily boats depart at around 10am (returning in the late afternoon) to **Manganári** on the south coast, where there's a beach and a swanky hotel; you can also get there by scooter. There's an expensive speedboat (€12) from Yialós to Manganári, but most people go by private buses run by travel agencies (€5 return), which leave Yialós about 11am, calling at Hóra and Mylopótamos and return later in the afternoon. Predominantly nudist, Manganári is the beach to come to for serious tans, although there's more to see, and a better atmosphere at **Ayía Theodhóti** up on the east coast. There's a paved road across the island to Ayía Theodhóti – the daily excursion bus costs €3 return. A couple of kilometres south of Ayía Theodhóti is a ruined Venetian castle which encompasses the ruins of a marble-finished town and a Byzantine church. In the unlikely event that the beach – a good one and mainly nudist – is too crowded, try the one at **Psathí**, 14km to the southeast. Frequented by wealthy Athenians, this small resort has a couple of pricey tavernas, making it better for a day-trip than an extended stay. The road is very poor and not really safe for scooters, although there are plans to improve it. Another island beach is at **Kálamos**: get off the Manganári bus at the turning for Kálamos, which leaves you with a four-kilometre walk.

"**Homer's**" **tomb** can be reached by motorbike along a safe unpaved road (turning left from the paved road to Ayía Theódhoti 4.5km from Hóra). The town itself has long since slipped down the side of the cliff, but the rocky ruins of the entrance to a tomb remain, as well as some graves – one of which is claimed to be Homer's, but which in reality probably dates only to the Byzantine era.

Síkinos

Síkinos has so small a population that the mule ride or walk up from the port to the village was only replaced by a bus late in the 1980s and, until the new jetty was completed at roughly the same time, it was the last major Greek island

▼ Thíra, Crete & Dodecanese

where ferry passengers were still taken ashore in launches. With no dramatic characteristics, nor any nightlife to speak of, few foreigners make the short trip over here from neighbouring Íos and Folégandhros or from sporadically connected Páros, Náxos or Thíra. There is no bank on the island, but there is a **post office** up in Kástro-Hóra, and you can sometimes change cash at the store in Aloprónia.

Aloprónia and Kástro-Hóra

Such tourist facilities as exist are concentrated in the little harbour of **ALOPRÓNIA**, with its long sandy beach and extended breakwater and jetty. More and more formal **accommodation** is being built here, but it's still possible to camp or just sleep out under the tamarisks behind the beach. For rooms, try *Flora* (☎02860/51 214; ❶), near the main road leading to Hóra, *Loukas* (☎02860/51 076; ❶–❹), which has rooms and studios around town to suit most budgets, or the recommended *The Rock* (☎02860/51 135; ❷), above the *Vrachos Pizzaria/Rock Cafe*; alternatively, the comfortable and traditional *Hotel Kamares* (☎02860/51 234; ❷) has a nicer setting than the conspicuous *Porto Sikinos* luxury complex (☎02860/51 247; ❹). *To Meltemi* **taverna** on the quay is the locals' hangout, while the fancier *Ostria* is affiliated with the *Hotel Kamares* and the *Loukas* provides standard fare. The *Rock Cafe* above the quay plays a more varied music selection than its name would suggest and attracts a good mix of people, while *Vengera* music bar on the opposite side of the bay is a smoother joint.

The double village of **KÁSTRO-HÓRA** is served by the single island bus, which shuttles regularly from early morning till quite late in the evening between the harbour and here, though the route should soon be extended to Episkopí with the completion of the new road. On the ride up, the scenery turns out to be less desolate than initial impressions suggest. Draped across a ridge overlooking the sea, Kástro-Hóra makes for a charming day-trip, and the lovely oil-press **museum** (July to mid-Sept 6.30–8.30pm; free), run privately by a Greek-American, is highly recommended. A partly ruined monastery,

Zoödhóhou Piyís ("Life-giving Spring", a frequent name in the Cyclades), crowns the rock above. The architectural highlight of the place, though, is the central quadrangle of **Kástro**, a series of ornate eighteenth-century houses arrayed defensively around a chapel square, their backs to the exterior of the village. The quality of **rooms** has improved, and both Markos Zagoreos (☎02860/51 263; ❶) and Haroula (☎02860/51 212; ❶) have competitive prices – the former has great views. A good selection of **food** is available, along with fine local wine, at both *Klimataria* and *To Steki tou Garbi* next door. The kafenía up here are very traditional affairs and you might feel more welcome at the café-bars *Kastro* or *Platía*.

Around the island

West of Kástro-Hóra, an hour-plus walk (or mule ride) takes you through a landscape lush with olive trees to **Episkopí**, where elements of an ancient temple-tomb have been ingeniously incorporated into a seventh-century church – the structure is known formally as the Iróön, though it's now thought to have been a Roman mausoleum rather than a temple of Hera. Ninety minutes from Kástro-Hóra, in the opposite direction, lies **Paleokástro**, the patchy remains of an ancient fortress. The beaches of **Áyios Yeóryios** and **Áyios Nikólaos** are reachable by a regular kaïki from Aloprónia; the former is a better option because it has the daytime *Almira* restaurant. It is possible to walk to them, but there is no real path at the later stages. A more feasible journey by foot is to the pebble beach at **Áyios Pandelímonas**: just under an hour's trail walk southwest of Aloprónia, it is the most scenic and sheltered on the island, and is also served by a kaïki in season.

Folégandhros

The cliffs of **Folégandhros** rise sheer in places over 300m from the sea – until the early 1980s as effective a deterrent to tourists as they always were to pirates. It was used as an island of political exile right up until 1974, but life in the high, barren interior has been eased since the junta years by the arrival of electricity and the construction of a lengthways road from the harbour to Hóra and beyond. Development has been given further impetus by the recent exponential increase in tourism and the mild commercialization this has brought.

A veritable explosion in accommodation for most budgets, and improvement in ferry arrival times, means there is no longer much need for – or local tolerance of – sleeping rough on the beaches. The increased wealth and trendiness of the heterogeneous clientele is reflected in fancy jewellery shops, an arty postcard gallery and a helipad. Yet away from the showcase Hóra and the beaches, the countryside remains mostly pristine, and is largely devoted to the spring and summer cultivation of barley, the mainstay of many of the Cyclades before the advent of tourism. Donkeys and donkey paths are also still very much in evidence, since the terrain on much of the island is too steep for vehicle roads.

Karavostássi and around

KARAVOSTÁSSI, the rather unprepossessing port whose name simply means "ferry stop", serves as a last-resort base; it has several **hotels** but little atmosphere. Best value if you do decide to stay is *Hotel Aeolos* (☎02860/41

205; ❷), while the *Poseidon* (☎02860/41 272; ❹) throws in breakfast at its decent restaurant *To Kati Allo*, which means "Something Else" and the new *Vrahos Hotel* (☎02860/41 304; ❹) has some nice rooms on the far side of the bay. *Iy Kali Kardhia* **taverna** above the harbour is recommended, and there are a couple of pleasant beach **bars** including the *Smyrna Ouzeri*, housed in a converted boathouse. There are many buses a day in summer to Hóra, three continuing to Áno Meriá; if you're feeling adventurous try Jimmy's motorbike rental (☎02860/41 448), which is cheaper than its counterparts in Hóra.

The closest **beach** is the smallish, but attractive enough, sand-and-pebble **Vardhiá**, signposted just north over the headland. Some twenty-minutes' walk south lies **Loustriá**, a rather average beach with tamarisk trees and the island's official **campsite**, *Livadi Camping* (☎02860 41 304), which is good and friendly, although the hot water supply can be erratic.

Easily the most scenic beach on Folégandhros, a 300-metre stretch of pea-gravel with an offshore islet, is at **Katergó**, on the southeastern tip of the island. Most people visit on a boat excursion from Karavostássi or Angáli, but you can also get there on foot from the hamlet of Livádhi, a short walk inland from Loustriá. Be warned, though, that it's a rather arduous trek, with some nasty trail-less slithering in the final moments.

Hóra

The island's real character and appeal are to be found in the spectacular **HÓRA**, perched on a clifftop plateau some 45 minutes' walk from the dock; an hourly high-season **bus** service (6 daily spring/autumn) runs from morning until late at night. Locals and foreigners – hundreds of them in high season – mingle at the cafés and tavernas under the almond, flowering Judas and pepper trees of the two main platías, passing the time unmolested by traffic, which is banned from the village centre. Towards the cliff-edge, and entered through two arcades, the defensive core of the medieval *kástro* is marked by ranks of two-storey houses, whose repetitive, almost identical stairways and slightly recessed doors are very appealing.

From the square where the bus stops, a zigzag path with views down to both coastlines climbs to the cragtop, wedding-cake church of **Kímisis Theotókou**, nocturnally illuminated to grand effect. Beyond and below it hides the **Khryssospiliá**, a large cave with stalactites, accessible only to proficient climbers; the necessary steps and railings have crumbled away into the sea, although a minor, lower grotto can still be visited by kaïki from the port.

Practicalities

Hóra's **accommodation** seems slightly weighted to favour hotels over rooms, with concentrations around the bus plaza at the eastern entrance to the village and at the western edge. Many of the tavernas and shops advertise rooms in their windows; otherwise try the purpose-built complex run by Irini Dekavalla (☎02860/41 235; ❸), east of the bus stop. The nearby *Hotel Polikandia* (☎02860/41 322; ❹) has an engaging proprietress and lower rates off-season. The most luxurious facilities are at the cliff-edge *Anemomilos Apartments* (☎02860/41 309; ❺), immaculately appointed and with stunning views; the new *Meltemi* (☎02860/41 328; ❸), just opposite, has clean, comfortable rooms. The only hotel within Hóra is the traditional *Castro* (☎02860/41 230; ❸–❹), built in 1212 and fully renovated in 1992, with three rather dramatic rooms looking directly out on an alarming drop to the sea. At the western edge of Hóra near the police station, a dense cluster of rooms tend to block each other's views; the least claustrophobic is the recently renovated *Odysseas* (☎02860/41 276; ❸), which also manages some attractive apartments near the *Anemomilos*, the *Folgeandros Apartments* (☎02860/41 239; ❹). By the roadside on the way to Áno Meriá, the *Fani-Vevis* (☎02860/41 237; ❷–❹), in a Neoclassical mansion overlooking the sea, seems to function only in high season; 100m beyond are some smart new studios (☎02860/41 274; ❺) managed by *Iy Kali Kardhia* (see p.653).

Hóra's dozen or so **restaurants** are surprisingly varied. The *Folegandros* ouzerí in water-cistern plaza, is fun, if a bit eccentrically run. Breakfast can be enjoyed on the adjacent Platía Kondaríni at *Iy Melissa*, which does good fruit and yogurt, omelettes and juices. *Iy Piatsa* has a nightly changing menu of well-executed Greek dishes, while their neighbour and local hangout *O Kritikos* is notable only for its grills. *Iy Pounda* near the bus stop is the most traditional place and has a small garden, while *Apanemo* at the far end of town has good food and a quieter setting, despite its proximity to the main bar area. Self-catering is an attractive option, with two well-stocked fruit shops and two supermarkets. Hóra is inevitably beginning to sprawl unattractively at the edges, but this at least means that the burgeoning **nightlife** – two dance bars and a number of music pubs and ouzerís – can be exiled to the north, away from most accommodation. *Avli* and *Greco* are two lively bars and both play up-to-date sounds, while *Kellari* is a rustic and charming wine bar where the atmosphere is more relaxed. A **post office** (no bank or OTE) completes the list of amenities, though the single **ferry agent** also does money exchange, as does the friendly and competent Italian-run Sottavento agency, which offers a wide range of services.

The rest of the island

Northwest of Hóra a narrow, paved road threads its way towards **ÁNO MERIÁ**, the other village of the island; after 4km you pass its first houses, clustered around the three churches of Áyios Pandelímonas, Áyios Yeóryios and Áyios Andhréas. Four **tavernas** operate in high season only: *Barba Kostas* is at the beginning of the village, *O Mimis* is about halfway along, *Iy Sinandisi* is at the turning for Áyios Yeóryios beach, while *Iliovasilema*, at the far end of the sprawling village, completes the list. Several **rooms** are also available, including *Stella's* (☎02860/41 329; ❶) and *Irini's* (☎02860/41 344; ❶).

Up to six times a day in high season a **bus** trundles out here to drop people off at the footpaths down to the various sheltered beaches on the southwest shore of the island. Busiest of these is **Angáli** (aka Vathý), with four rather basic rooms outfits including *Vangelis* (☎02860/41 105; ❶) and *Panagiotis* (☎02860/41 116; ❷) and two equally simple summer-only tavernas, reached by a fifteen-minute walk along a dirt road from the bus stop.

Nudists should take the paths which lead twenty minutes east or west to **Firá** or **Áyios Nikólaos** beaches respectively; the latter in particular, with its many tamarisks, coarse sand and view back over the island, is Katergó's only serious rival in the best-beach sweepstakes. At Áyios Nikólaos, a lone taverna operates up by the namesake chapel; Firá has no facilities at all. From the *Iliovasilema* taverna, a motorable track continues north to a point from where a 500-metre path takes you down to the pleasant little bay of **Ambéli**.

Thíra (Santoríni)

As the ferry manoeuvres into the great caldera of **Thíra**, the land seems to rise up and clamp around it. Gaunt, sheer cliffs loom hundreds of feet above, nothing grows or grazes to soften the awesome view, and the only colours are the reddish-brown, black and grey pumice striations layering the cliff-face. The landscape tells of a history so dramatic and turbulent that legend hangs as fact upon it.

From as early as 3000 BC the island developed as a sophisticated outpost of Minoan civilization, until sometime between 1647 and 1628 BC (according to latest estimates) when catastrophe struck: the volcano-island erupted, its heart sank below the sea leaving a crater (caldera) 10km in diameter, and earthquakes reverberated across the Aegean. Thíra was destroyed and the great Minoan civilization on Crete was dealt a severe blow. At this point the island's history became linked with legends of Atlantis, the "Happy Isles Submerged by Sea". Plato insisted that the legend was true, and Solon dated the cataclysm to 9000 years before his time – if you're willing to accept a mistake and knock off the final zero, a highly plausible date.

These apocalyptic events, though, scarcely concern modern tourists, who come here to take in the spectacular views, stretch out on the island's dark-sand beaches and absorb the peculiar, infernal atmosphere; as recently as a century ago, Thíra was still reckoned to be infested with vampires. Though not nearly so predatory as the undead, current visitors have in fact succeeded in pretty much killing off most genuine island life, creating in its place a rather expensive and stagey playground.

Arrival and departure

Ferries dock at the somewhat grim port of **Órmos Athiniós**; **Skála Firás** and **Ía** in the north are reserved for local ferries, excursion kaïkia and cruise ships. **Buses**, astonishingly crammed, connect Athiniós with the island capital Firá, and, less frequently, with Ía and the main beaches at Kamári and Périssa. Disembark quickly and take whatever bus is going, if you want to avoid a long wait or a tedious hike up. You'll be accosted at Athiniós by people offering rooms all over the island; in the summer it might be a good idea to pay attention to them, given the scramble for beds, in Firá especially. From Skála Firás, you have the traditional route of 580 steps (about 45 minutes) up to Firá – not too difficult a walk, if you don't mind mule manure – or you can go by mule (€3, negotiable in off-season) or cable car (summer only 6.40am–10pm, every 20min; €3), so exhilarating a ride that you may want to take it for fun. The **airport** is on the east side of the island, near Monólithos; there is a regular shuttle-bus service to the Firá bus station, which runs until 10pm.

When it comes to **leaving** – especially for summer/evening ferry departures – it's best to buy your ticket in advance. Note, too, that although the bus service stops around midnight, a shared taxi isn't outrageously expensive (about €6 from Firá to Athiniós). Incidentally, **ferry information** from any source is notoriously unreliable on Thíra and rival agencies don't inform you of alternatives – Nomikos Travel (☎02860/23 660), with seven branches, is the largest and most reliable – so you should enquire about the possibilities at several agencies and triple-check departure times. If you do get stranded in Athiniós, there's no place to stay, and the tavernas are pretty awful. With time on your hands, it's probably worth calling for a taxi (☎02860/22 555) or zigzagging the 3.5km up to the closest village, **MEGALOHÓRI**. Between Megalohóri and Pýrgos village, near the junction of the main and Athiniós road, is *Hotel Zorbas* (☎02860/31 433; ⊙), and at the centre of Megalohóri, the *Yeromanolis* is a surprisingly reasonable and tasty grill which offers the increasingly rare home-made Santoríni wine.

Firá

Half-rebuilt after a devastating earthquake in 1956, **FIRÁ** (also known as Thíra or Hóra) still clings precariously to the edge of the enormous caldera, affording astonishing views. You will, of course, have to pay for such a beautiful setting. It's so thoroughly commercialized and, in summer, so inundated with cruise-ship passengers and day-trippers that it can get overwhelming; it is definitely worth phoning for accommodation in advance.

However, the view is still thrilling, and Firá also has several excellent museums. The **Archeological Museum** (Tues–Sun 8am–2.30pm; €3), near the cable car to the north of town, has a collection which includes a curious set of erotic Dionysiac figures. The handsome **Museum Megaro Ghyzi** (Mon–Sat 10.30am–1.30pm & 5–8pm, Sun 10.30am–4.30pm; €1.50) above the Archeological Museum in an old mansion owned by the Catholic diocese of Santoríni, has been restored as a cultural centre, and has a good collection of old prints and maps as well as photographs of the town before and after the 1956 earthquake. Further north along the caldera the **Thira Foundation**, housed in galleries carved into the cliffside, contains superb life-size 3D colour photo reproductions of the frescos of Akrotíri (Tues–Sun 8.30am–3pm; €3). At the other end of town, between the cathedral and bus station, the **Museum of Prehistoric Thira** (Tues–Sun 8.30am–3pm; free), a newly opened museum housed in a handsome building, has interesting displays of fossils, Cycladic art, and astonishing finds from Akrotíri.

Practicalities

For a caldera-view **hotel** in Firá consider the excellent *Loucas* (☎02860/22 480, ℉24 882, Ⓔloucasason@ath.fortnet.gr; ❺–❻), a traditional hotel with barrel-ceilinged caves – to prevent collapse during an earthquake – carved into the cliffside, and a beautiful new pool; or the nearby *Kavalari* (☎02860/22 455, ℉22 603; ❻). There are plenty of rooms without caldera views at the back of town. *Villa Haroula* (☎02860/24 226; ❺) is a good smart option on the road down to *Santorini Camping* (☎02860/22 944), the nearest **campsite**. (The newest and best campsite on the island is *Caldera View Camping* (☎02860/82 010) near Akrotíri village.) Along the same road *Pension Petros* (☎02860/22 573; ❹) and *Pension Soula* (☎02860/23 473; ❺) are two reasonable, if not very exciting, alternatives. There are two **youth hostels** north of the main square on the road to Ía, not far from each other: *Thira Youth Hostel* (☎02860/22 387) and *International Youth Hostel Kamares* (☎02860/24 472), both budget-priced (€6 per person) but noisy at night.

FIROSTEFÁNI, between Firá and Imerovígli, is the best bet for reasonably priced rooms with views over the caldera. Rooms in Firostefáni of varying prices and standards include *Apartments Gaby* (☎02860/22 057; ❺), *Hotel Mylos* (☎02860/23 884; ❹), *Kafieris Hotel* (☎02860/22 189; ❸–❹) and the rooms of Ioannis Roussos (☎02860/22 611 or 22 862; ❹). For something smarter, *Manos Apartments* (☎02860/23 202; ❺–❻) is highly recommended.

Another good location, where you don't have to pay for the (caldera) view, is **KARTERÁDHOS**, a small village about twenty-minutes' walk southeast of Firá, where you'll find pleasant *Hotel Albatross* (☎02860/23 435, ℉23 431; ❺), the charming *Cyclades* (☎02860/24 543; ❺) and the welcoming *Pension George* (☎02860/22 351; ❸). Nomikos Travel can help you find a room (see below).

Firá's **restaurants** are primarily aimed at the tourist market, but for dependably good food with a sensational view find *Aris*, below the *Loucas Hotel*, or *Flame of the Volcano*, the last of the caldera-side restaurants north past the cable-car station (towards Firostefáni). On Erythroú Stavroú, the first street up from the main square, *Nikolas* is an old and defiantly traditional taverna, but it can be hard to get a table; the best budget choice is *Naoussa*, further north on the same street, upstairs on the right. Otherwise try *Koutouki* on 25-Martíou, the road to Ía, the welcoming *Mama's Cyclades*, a little further up on the same road, or *Aktaion* in Firostefáni. Most of the **nightlife** can be found northwest of the central square on Erythroú Stavroú: *Town Club*, *Amnesia*, *Murphy's* and, just above, *Enigma* and *Koo*. The best bars from which to admire the caldera are *Franco's*, a rather exclusive and pricey cocktail bar, and the more relaxed *Renaissance*, below the *Loucas Hotel*.

Nomikos Travel (☎02860/23 660) on 25-Martíou, opposite the OTE, is friendly and organizes excursions and trips to ancient Thíra and Thirassía in conjunction with Kamari Tours (☎02860/31 390). **Buses** leave Firá from just south of Platía Theotokopoúlou to Périssa, Perívolos, Kamári, Monólithos, Akrotíri Órmos, Athiniós and the airport. **Taxis** (☎02860/22 555) go from near the bus station. If you want to see the whole island in a couple of days a rented **motorbike** might do, though you must be very careful – especially since local drivers seem to enjoy antagonizing tourists on difficult and precipitous roads; try Moto Chris at the top of the road that leads down to *Santorini Camping*.

The north

Once outside Firá, the rest of Thíra comes as a nice surprise, although development is beginning to encroach. The volcanic soil is highly fertile, with every available space terraced and cultivated: wheat, tomatoes (most made into paste), pistachios and grapes are the main crops, all still harvested and planted by hand. The island's *vysándo* and *nikhtéri* wines are a little sweet for many tastes but are among the finest produced in the Cyclades.

A satisfying – if demanding – approach to Ía, 12km from Firá in the northwest of the island, is to walk the stretch from **IMEROVÍGLI**, 3km out of Firá, using a spectacular footpath along the lip of the caldera; the walk takes around two hours. Imerovígli is crowded with luxury, caldera-side **apartments** such as *Chromata* (☎02860/24 850; ❻) and *Astra* (☎02860/23 641; ❻), requiring reservations well in advance; *Katerina* (☎02860/22 708; ❹–❺) is a more moderately priced hotel, with caldera views from the large balcony/bar area only. Between the *Katerina* and *Chromata*, *Altana* is a small caldera-side **café** whose position and relaxed atmosphere make for a pleasing breakfast spot. Continuing to Ía, you'll pass Toúrlos, an old Venetian citadel on Cape Skáros.

ÍA, the most delightful village on the island, was once a major fishing port of the Aegean, but it has declined in the wake of economic depression, wars, earthquakes and depleted fish stocks. Partly destroyed in the 1956 earthquake, the town has been sympathetically reconstructed, its pristine white houses clinging to the cliff-face. Apart from the caldera and the village itself there are a couple of things to see, including the **Naval Museum** (daily except Tues 9am–1pm & 5–8pm) and the very modest remains of a Venetian castle. With a **post office**, a couple of travel agencies – Karvounis (☎02860/71 290, ☏71 291, ✉mkarvounis@otenet.gr), on the pedestrian street, is the older and more reliable – and several **bike-rental** offices (of which Motor Fun is particularly good), Ía is a fine, and quieter, alternative to Firá.

Much of the town's **accommodation** is in its restored old houses, including the traditional *Hotel Lauda* (☎02860/71 204; ❸–❻), the *Hotel Anemones* (☎02860/71 342; ❸–❹) and the *Hotel Fregata* (☎02860/71 221; ❺). Near the bus terminal, also reachable by the main road that continues round to the back end of the village, is an excellent hostel – the *Oia Youth Hostel* (☎02860/71 465), with a terrace and shady courtyard, a good bar, clean dormitories and breakfast included. Generally, the further you go along the central ridge towards the new end of Ía, the better value the **restaurants**: the *Anemomilos* and *Laokastri* are two such examples. The *Neptune*, near the church square, with good Greek dishes and vegetable specials, has a pleasant rooftop garden. **Nightlife** revolves around sunset-gazing, for which people are coached in from all over the island, creating traffic chaos; when this pales, there's *Petra* and *Alitana*, two bars on the road leading down to the youth hostel, both playing easy listening in pleasant garden surroundings.

Below the town, 200-odd steps switchback hundreds of metres down to two small harbours: **Ammoúdhi**, for the fishermen, and **Arméni**, where the excursion boats dock. Both have excellent fish tavernas. *Sunset* taverna at Ammoúdhi is recommended, and at Arméni there is a taverna which specializes in grilled octopus lunches. **FINIKIÁ**, 1km east of Ía, is a very quiet and traditional little village. *Lotza Rooms* (☎02860/71 051; ❷) are located in an old house in the middle of the village, while *Hotel Finikia* (☎02860/71 373; ❸), above the village near the main road, is a smarter option. Just north of Ía is **Baxédhes** beach, a quiet alternative to Kamári and Périssa (see opposite), with a few tavernas including the *Paradhisos*, which has good food and reasonable prices.

The east and south

Beaches on Thíra, to the east and south, are bizarre – long black stretches of volcanic sand which get blisteringly hot in the afternoon sun. They're no secret, and in the summer the crowds can be a bit overpowering. Closest to Firá, **MONÓLITHOS** has a couple of tavernas but is nothing special. Further south, **KAMÁRI** has surrendered lock, stock and barrel to the package-tour operators and there's not a piece of sand that isn't fronted by concrete villas. Nonetheless it's quieter and cleaner than most, with some beachfront **accommodation**, including *Hotel Nikolina* (☎02860/31 702; ❷), with basic but cheap rooms towards the southern end of the beach, as well as the *White House* (☎02860/31 441; ❹) and the friendly *Sea Side Rooms* (☎02860/33 403; ❷) further along the beach. *Rose Bay Hotel* (☎02860/33 650; ❻) is a far pricier option, with a pleasant pool setting, set back away from the noisy beach thoroughfare. *Kamari Camping* (☎02860/31 453), a fifteen-minute walk on the road out of Kamári, is a small municipal-run site with limited facilities and no points for a warm welcome.

Psistaria O Kritikos, a taverna-grill frequented by locals rather than tourists, is one of the best places to **eat** on the island. It's a long way out of Kamári on the road up to Messariá, and too far to walk, but the bus stops outside. There are plenty of cafés and restaurants behind the beach, though many are expensive or uninspired. *Saliveros*, in front of the *Hotel Nikolina*, has taverna food at reasonable prices, and *Almira*, next to *Sea Side Rooms*, is a smarter restaurant and only a little more expensive. Kamári is a family resort with little in the way of clubs and nightlife, but there is a good open-air **cinema** near the campsite, and in summer buses run until 1am, so there's no problem getting back to Firá after seeing a film.

Things are scruffier at **PÉRISSA**, around the cape. Because of its attractive situation and abundance of cheap rooms, it's noisy and crowded with backpackers. *Camping Perissa Beach* (☎02860/81 343) is right behind the beach and has plenty of shade but is also next to a couple of noisy late-night bars. There is also a youth hostel on the road into Périssa: *Anna* (☎02860/82 182; €10 per person) has dorm beds as well as a few simple studios closer to the beach. There are plenty of cheap rooms in the same area and some upmarket hotels behind the beach; the modern *Meltemi Hotel* (☎02860/81 325; ❷–❺) is a sensible choice. The beach itself extends almost 7km to the west, sheltered by the occasional tamarisk tree, with beach bars dotted along at intervals; *Wet Stories*, about ten-minutes' walk from Périssa village, has a fun atmosphere and a varied snack selection.

Kamári and Périssa are separated by the Mésa Vounó headland, on which stood **ancient Thíra** (Tues–Sun 9am–3pm), the post-eruption settlement dating from the ninth century BC. Excursion buses go up from Kamári (€15), staying two hours at the site (ask at Kamári Tours behind the beach) but you can walk the **cobbled path** starting from the square in Kamári by the Argo General Store. The path zigzags up to a whitewashed church by a **cave**, containing one of Thíra's few freshwater springs, before crossing over to meet the road and ending at a saddle between Mésa Vounó and Profítis Ilías, where a refreshments van sells expensive drinks. From here, the path to the site passes a chapel dating back to the fourth century AD before skirting round to the Temenos of Artemidoros with bas-relief carvings of a dolphin, eagle and lion representing Poseidon, Zeus and Apollo. Next, the trail follows the sacred way of the ancient city through the remains of the agora and past the theatre. Most of the ruins (dating mainly from Hellenistic and Roman times) are difficult to place, but the site is impressively large and the views are awesome. The site can also be reached by a path from Périssa, and either way it's less than an hour's walk.

Inland along the same mountain spine is the monastery of **Profítis Ilías**, now sharing its refuge with Greek radio and TV pylons and the antennae of a NATO station. With just one monk remaining to look after the church, the place only really comes to life for the annual Profítis Ilías festival, when the whole island troops up here to celebrate. The views are still rewarding, though, and from near the entrance to the monastery an old footpath heads across the ridge in about an hour to ancient Thíra. The easiest ascent is the thirty-minute walk from the village of Pýrgos.

PÝRGOS itself is one of the oldest settlements on the island, a jumble of old houses and alleys that still bear the scars of the 1956 earthquake. It climbs to another Venetian fortress crowned by several churches and you can clamber around the battlements for sweeping views over the entire island and its Aegean neighbours. By way of contrast **MESSARIÁ**, a thirty-minute stroll north, has a skyline consisting solely of massive church domes that lord it over the houses huddled in a ravine.

Akrotíri

Evidence of the Minoan colony that once thrived here has been uncovered at the other ancient site of **Akrotíri** (Tues–Sat 8.30am–3pm; €15), at the southwestern tip of the island. Tunnels through the volcanic ash uncovered structures, two and three storeys high, first damaged by earthquake then buried by eruption; Professor Marinatos, the excavator and now an island hero, was killed by a collapsing wall and is also buried on the site. Only a small part of what was the largest Minoan city outside of Crete has been excavated thus far. Lavish frescoes adorned the walls, and Cretan pottery was found stored in a chamber; most of the frescoes are currently exhibited in Athens, though you can see excellent reproductions at the Thira Foundation in Firá (see p.656). Visit early to avoid crowds and heat.

Akrotíri itself can be reached by bus from Firá or Périssa; the excellent *Glaros* taverna, on the way to Kókkini Ámmos beach, has fine food and barrelled wine. Kókkini Ámmos is about 500m from the site and is quite spectacular with high reddish-brown cliffs above sand the same colour (the name means "red sand"). There's a drinks stall in a cave hollowed into the base of the cliff. It's a better beach than the one below the site, but gets crowded in season.

The Kaméni islets and Thirassía

From either Firá or Ía, boat excursions and local ferries run to the charred volcanic islets of **Paleá Kaméni** and **Néa Kaméni**, and on to the relatively unspoiled islet of Thirassía, which was once part of Thíra until shorn off by an eruption in the third century BC. At Paleá Kaméni you can swim from the boat to hot springs with sulphurous mud, and Néa Kaméni, with its own mud-clouded hot springs, features a demanding hike to a volcanically active crater.

The real attraction though, is **Thirassía**, the quietest island in the Cyclades. The views are as dramatic as any on Thíra, and tourism has little effect on island life. The downside is that there is no sandy beach, no nightlife and nowhere to change money.

Most tour boats head for **Kórfos**, a stretch of shingle backed by fishermen's houses and high cliffs. It has a few tavernas, including *Tonio* which stays open when the day-trippers have gone, but no rooms. From Kórfos a stepped path climbs up to **MANOLÁS**, nearly 200m above. Donkeys are still used for transport, and stables can be seen in both villages. Manolás straggles along the edge of the caldera, an untidy but attractive small island village that gives an idea of what Thíra was like before tourism arrived there. It has a bakery, a couple of shops and a few tavernas, including the friendly *Panorama*, that opens only for the midday rush; the **restaurant** at the *Hotel Cavo Mare* (T02860/29 176; ❹) wins out by giving diners the use of the swimming pool. Dhimítrios Nomikós has **rooms** (T02860/29 102; ❷) overlooking the village from the south.

The best **excursion** from Manolás is to follow the unmade road heading south; about halfway along you pass the church of Profítis Ilías on a hilltop to the left. From here an old and overgrown trail descends through the deserted caldera-side village of **Kerá**, before running parallel with the road to the **monastery of the Kímisis** above the southern tip of the island. Minoan remains were excavated in a pumice quarry to the west of here in 1867, several years before the first discoveries at Akrotíri, but there is nothing to be seen today.

Ferries run to Thirassía four times a week in season and three times a week through the winter. There is no problem taking a car or rental bike over, but fill up with petrol first. Day-trips take in Néa Kaméni and Paleá Kaméni but are quite expensive (€18) and only stay two or three hours on Thirassía.

Anáfi

A ninety-minute boat ride to the east of Thíra, **Anáfi** is the last stop for ferries and hydrofoils and something of a travellers' dead end, with no longer any high season ferries on to Crete or the Dodecanese. Not that this is likely to bother most of the visitors, who intentionally come here for weeks in midsummer, and take over the island's beaches with a vengeance.

At most other times the place seems idyllic, and indeed may prove too sleepy for some: there are no bona fide hotels, scooters, discos or organized excursions, and donkeys are still the main method of transport in the interior. Anáfi, though initially enchanting, is a harsh place, its mixed granite/limestone core overlaid by volcanic rock spewed out by Thíra's eruptions. Apart from the few olive trees and vines grown in the valleys, the only plants that seem to thrive are prickly pears.

The harbour and Hóra

The tiny harbour hamlet of **ÁYIOS NIKÓLAOS** has a single taverna, *To Akroyiali*, with a few rooms (T02860/61 218; ❶), while *Dave's Cafe*, with straw umbrellas above the beach, is a colourful English-run drinking spot. Jeyzed Travel (T02860/61 253, F61 352) can provide information as well as issue ferry tickets, change money and book rooms. In August there are enough Greek visitors to fill all the rooms on the island, so it's a good idea to book ahead. Most places to stay are in Hóra. In season a bus runs from the harbour every two hours or so, 9am to 11pm, to stops at both ends of the village.

HÓRA itself, adorning a conical hill overhead, is a stiff, 25-minute climb up the obvious old mule path which shortcuts the modern road. Exposed and blustery when the *meltémi* is blowing, Hóra can initially seem a rather forbidding ghost town. This impression is slowly dispelled as you discover the hospitable islanders taking their coffee in sheltered, south-facing terraces, or under the anti-earthquake barrel vaulting that features in domestic architecture here.

The modern, purpose-built **rooms** run by Kalliopi Halari (T02860/61 271; ❶) and Voula Loudharou (T02860/61 279; ❶), and those run by Margarita

Kollidha (☎02860/61 292; ❷) at the east edge of the village, are about the most comfortable – and boast stunning views south to the islets of Ftená, Pahiá and Makriá, and the distinctive monolith at the southeastern corner of Anáfi. Evening **diners** seem to divide their custom between the simple, welcoming *To Steki*, with reasonable food and barrel wine served on its terrace, and the more upmarket *Alexandhra's* on the central walkway. *Armenaki* is a lively taverna/ouzerí which hosts regular *bouzoúki* nights. Otherwise nightlife revolves around the two bars: *Mylos*, in a converted windmill in the village, and *Mantres* on the main road between the port and Hóra. Several shops, a bakery and a **post office** round up the list of amenities.

East along the coast: beaches and monasteries

The glory of Anáfi is a string of south-facing beaches starting under the cliffs at Áyios Nikólaos. Freelance campers head for **KLISÍDHI**, a short walk to the east of the harbour, which has 200m of tan, gently shelving sand. Above the calamus-and-tamarisk oasis backing the beach there are two cafés and a taverna, including the *Kafestiatorion tis Margaritas*, with popular rooms (☎02860/61 237; ❷). The *Villa Apollon* on the hillside above has the island's most upmarket accommodation (☎02860/61 348; ❷). Klisídhi can be reached by road but it's quicker to take the clifftop path starting behind the power station at the harbour. East of here the beaches can only be reached by foot or boat.

From a point on the paved road just east of Hóra, the **main path** skirting the south flank of the island is signposted "Kastélli – Paleá Hóra – Roúkouna – Monastíri". The primary branch of this trail roller-coasters in and out of several agricultural valleys that provide most of Anáfi's produce and fresh water. Just under an hour along, beside a well, you veer down a side trail to **Roúkounas**, easily the island's best beach, with some 500m of broad sand rising to tamarisk-stabilized dunes, which provide welcome shade. A single taverna, *Tou Papa*, operates up by the main trail in season; the suggestively craggy hill of **Kastélli**, an hour's scramble above the taverna, is the site both of ancient Anáfi and a ruined Venetian castle.

Beyond Roúkounas, it's another half-hour on foot to the first of the exquisite half-dozen **Katelímatsa** coves, of all shapes and sizes, and 45 minutes to **Monastíri** beach – all without facilities, so come prepared. Nudism is banned on Monastíri, because of its proximity to the monasteries.

The monasteries

Between Katelímatsa and Kálamos, the main route keeps inland, past a rare spring, to arrive at the **monastery of Zoödhóhou Piyís**, some two hours out of Hóra. A ruined temple of Apollo is incorporated into the monastery buildings to the side of the main gate; according to legend, Apollo caused Anáfi to rise from the waves, pulling off a dramatic rescue of the storm-lashed Argonauts. The courtyard, with a welcome cistern, is the venue for the island's major festival, celebrated eleven days after Easter. A family of cheesemakers lives next door and can point you up the start of the spectacular onward path to **Kalamiótissa**, a little monastery perched atop the abrupt pinnacle at the extreme southeast of the island. It takes another hour to reach, but is eminently worthwhile for the stunning scenery and views over the entire south coast. Kalamiótissa comes alive only during its September 7–8 festival; at other times, you could haul a sleeping bag up here to witness the amazing sunsets and sunrises, with your vantage point often floating in a sea of cloud. There is no water up here, so bring enough with you. It's a full day's outing from Hóra to Kalamiótissa, so you might wish to take advantage, in at least one direction, of the excursion **kaïki** that runs from Áyios Nikólaos to Monastíri (6 times daily in high season). There is also a slightly larger mail and supplies boat (currently Mon & Thurs 11am) which takes passengers to and from Thíra (Órmos Athiniós), supplementing the main-line ferries to Pireás.

Travel details

Ferries

Most of the Cyclades are served by main-line ferries from Pireás. Boats for Kéa depart from Lávrio, which will become increasingly important as work proceeds on the new highway to the new international airport at Spáta. There are daily services from Rafína to Ándhros, Tínos and Mýkonos, with less frequent sailings to Sýros, Páros, Náxos and Amorgós, and the north and east Aegean. All three ports are easily reached by bus from Athens. From June to September there are also a few weekly sailings from Thessaloníki to the most popular islands.

The frequency of sailings given below is intended to give an idea of services from April to October, when most visitors tour the islands. During the winter expect departures to be at or below the minimum level listed, with some routes cancelled entirely. Conversely, routes tend to be more comprehensive in spring and autumn, when the government obliges shipping companies to make extra stops to compensate for numbers of boats still in dry dock.

All agents are required to issue computerized tickets, using a computerized booking system. This was designed to conform to EU regulations and prevent the overcrowding of ferries so common in the past. It means that, in high season, certain popular routes may be booked up days in advance, so if you're visiting a few islands it is important to check availability on arrival in Greece, and book your outward and final pre-flight tickets well ahead. There is not usually so much problem with space between islands as there is to and from Pireás.

Amorgós 6–8 ferries weekly to Náxos and Páros, one of these continuing to Rafína rather than Pireás; 3–4 weekly to Sýros; 2–3 weekly to Tínos and Mýkonos; 2–3 weekly to Ándhros, Koufoníssi, Skhinoússa, Iráklia and Dhonoússa; 2–3 weekly to Astypálea.

Anáfi 6–8 weekly to Pireás (12hr 30min), mostly via Thíra (1hr 30min), Íos, Náxos, Páros; 1 weekly to Astypálea; 1 weekly to Sýros, Síkinos and Folégandhros; 2 weekly mail boats to Thíra (2hr).

Ándhros At least 3 daily to Rafína (2hr), Tínos (2hr) and Mýkonos; 4 weekly to Sýros; 2 weekly to

Amorgós and Náxos; 1–4 weekly to Paros.

Dhonoússa 3–4 weekly to Amorgós; 2–3 weekly to Náxos, Koufoníssi, Skhinoússa, Iráklia and Páros; 1 weekly to Pireás, Mýkonos, Tínos and Sýros; 2 weekly to Astypálea.

Íos At least 3 daily to Pireás (10hr), Páros (5hr), Náxos (3hr) and Thíra (several of which continue to Anáfi); 4–5 weekly to Síkinos and Folégandhros; 1 weekly to Crete; 1 weekly to Mílos, Kímolos, Sérifos and Sífnos; 2–3 weekly to Sýros and Kássos; daily to Mýkonos.

Kéa 1–3 daily to Lávrio (1hr 30min); 4 weekly to Kýthnos; 2 weekly to Sýros.

Kímolos 2 daily kaïkia to Mílos (Pollónia) year-round, 5 in summer; 2–5 weekly to Mílos (Adhámas), Sífnos, Sérifos, Kýthnos and Pireás (7hr); 2 weekly to Folégandhros, Síkinos and Thíra.

Koufoníssi, Skhinoússa, Iráklia 2–3 weekly to Náxos; 1–2 weekly to Páros, Sýros and Tínos and Mýkonos; 1 weekly to Dhonoússa, Amorgós and Pireás.

Kýthnos 4–12 weekly to Pireás (3hr 15min); 4–10 weekly to Sérifos, Sífnos, Kímolos and Mílos; 3–4 weekly to Thíra and Folégandhros; 1–2 weekly to Síkinos, Sýros, Íos and Kéa.

Mílos At least daily to Pireás (8hr); Thurs–Sat to Sífnos (2hr), Sérifos and Kýthnos; 2–5 daily kaïkia or 4–6 weekly ferries to Kímolos; 2–3 weekly to Folégandhros, Síkinos, Íos and Thíra; 2 weekly to Sýros; 2 weekly to Crete (Iráklion or Sitía); 2 weekly to Kássos and Kárpathos; 1 weekly to Hálki and Rhodes.

Mýkonos At least 2 daily to Pireás (5hr), Rafína (3hr 30min), Tínos (1hr), Ándhros (2hr 30min) and Sýros (2hr); 2–3 weekly to Amorgós; 2 weekly to Crete (Iráklion), Skiáthos and Thessaloníki; 1–2 weekly to Dhonoússa, Koufoníssi, Skhinoússa and Iráklia; 1 weekly to Pátmos and Foúrni; 3–4 weekly to Ikaría and Sámos; daily to Íos, Náxos and Páros; daily (except Mon) excursion boats to Delos.

Náxos At least 3 daily to Pireás (8hr), Páros (1hr), Íos and Thíra; 6–8 weekly to Sýros; 5–7 weekly to Amorgós; 3 weekly to Crete (Iráklion); 5–6 weekly to Amorgós; 4–5 weekly to Tínos; 5 weekly to Síkinos and Folégandhros; 2 weekly to Ándhros and Rafína; 3 weekly to Anáfi; 3–4 weekly to Rhodes; 2–4 weekly to Ikaría and Sámos; 4 weekly to Astypálea; 1–2 weekly to Kássos and Kárpathos; 1 weekly to Kós and Foúrni; 2–3 weekly to Skiáthos and Thessaloníki; 3–6 weekly to Iráklia, Skhinoússa, Koufoníssi and Dhonoússa.

Páros At least 3 daily to Pireás (7hr), Andíparos, Náxos, Íos, Thíra; 6–8 weekly to Sýros and Tínos; 4

weekly to Iráklion (Crete); 3–6 weekly to Ikaría and Sámos; 4–6 weekly to Síkinos, Folégandhros and Amorgós; 4 weekly to Rafína and Ándhros; 2–3 weekly to Skiáthos and Thessaloníki; daily to Rhodes; 4–6 weekly to Anáfi; 1–2 weekly to Foúrni, Kós, Kássos and Kárpathos; 4 weekly to Astypálea; 2–4 weekly to Koufoníssi, Skhinoússa, Iráklia and Dhonoússa; 1 weekly to Vólos; 1 weekly to Pátmos and Kálymnos; 3–6 weekly to Ikaría and Sámos; at least 1 daily to Mýkonos; at least hourly (from Parikía) to Andíparos in summer, dropping to 3 weekly in winter. There is also a car ferry from Poúnda to Andíparos at least hourly throughout the year.

Sérifos and Sífnos 5–12 weekly to Pireás (4hr 30min), Kýthnos and each other; 5–10 weekly to Mílos; 2–5 weekly to Kímolos; 2–3 weekly to Folégandhros, Síkinos and Thíra; once weekly to Íos; 2 weekly to Sýros; 1–2 weekly to Crete from Sífnos only; twice weekly from Sífnos to Páros.

Síkinos and Folégandhros 6 weekly between each other, and to Pireás (10hr); 2 weekly to Sýros, Kýthnos, Sérifos, Sífnos, Mílos and Kímolos; 3–6 weekly to Íos, Thíra, Páros and Náxos.

Sýros At least 2 daily to Pireás (4hr), Tínos (1hr), Mýkonos (2hr), Náxos and Páros; at least 2 weekly to Rafína (3hr 30min) and Ándhros; 3 weekly to Amorgós and the islets behind Náxos; 2–4 weekly to Íos and Thíra; 1 weekly to Síkinos and Folégandhros; 3 weekly to Ikaría, Sámos and Astypálea; 2 weekly to Kéa, Kýthnos, Sérifos, Sífnos, Mílos and Kímolos; 1 weekly to Pátmos, Léros and Lipsí; 2–4 weekly to Skiáthos and Thessaloníki.

Thíra At least 3 daily to Pireás (10–12hr), Páros, Íos and Náxos; 5–6 weekly to Iráklion, Crete (5hr) and Thessaloníki; 6–8 weekly to Síkinos and Folégandhros; 4–6 weekly to Anáfi and Sífnos; daily to Mýkonos; 6–8 weekly to Sýros; 3–5 weekly to Tínos and Skiáthos; 2–4 weekly to Mílos and Kímolos; 1–2 weekly to Kárpathos, Kássos and Sérifos; 2 weekly to Rhodes; 1 weekly to Vólos; 4–6 weekly to Thirassía (plus lots of expensive daily excursion boats in season); 2 weekly mail boats to Anáfi.

Tínos At least 2 daily to Pireás (5hr), Rafína (4hr), Ándhros, Sýros and Mýkonos; 3–4 weekly to Páros and Náxos; 3 weekly to Thíra and Iráklion (Crete); 2–4 weekly to Skiáthos and Thessaloníki; 3 weekly to Amorgós; 1 weekly to Íos, Koufoníssi, Skhinoússa, Iráklia and Dhonoússa; also excursion boats calling at Delos and Mýkonos, 1 daily except Mon.

Other services

To simplify the lists above, certain strategic hydrofoil and small-boat services have been omitted. Of these, the *Express Skopelitis* plies daily in season between Mýkonos and Amorgós, spending each night at the latter and threading through all of the minor isles between it and Náxos, as well as Náxos and Páros (Píso Livádhi), in the course of a week; however, it's unreliable and often overcrowded. The *Seajet* catamaran – a small-capacity (and expensive) jet-boat (☎010 41 41 250 for details) – operates daily during summer out of Rafína and connects Sýros, Ándhros, Tínos, Mýkonos, Páros, Náxos and Thíra. Cycladic routes are pretty well mapped out by the three hydrofoil companies – Minoan Flying Dolphins, Speed Lines and Cruises (Santorini Dolphin) and Dolphin Sea Line, with regular services from Zéa (Pireás), Thíra and Rafína respectively. Hydrofoil travel is expensive; however, when time is an issue, or for more regular connections to some of the less commonly serviced routes such as the minor islets around Náxos, these handy flying machines are a welcome addition to the conventional fleet.

Flights

There are airports on Páros, Mýkonos, Thíra, Sýros, Mílos and Náxos. In season, or during storms when ferries are idle, you have little chance of getting a seat with Olympic Airways at less than three-days' notice. Olympic's Athens–Mílos route is probably the best value for money, but it's usually booked by the island's mining executives; the other destinations seem deliberately overpriced, in a usually unsuccessful attempt to keep passenger volume manageable. Axon and Aegean Cronus have summer flights to Thíra and Mýkonos. Expect off-season (Oct–April) frequencies to drop by at least eighty percent. Flights are on Olympic unless otherwise stated.

Athens–Mílos (1–2 daily; 45min)
Athens–Mýkonos (5–6 daily on Olympic; 2–3 daily on Axon; 45min)
Athens–Náxos (6 weekly; 45min)
Athens–Páros (3–4 daily; 45min)
Athens–Sýros (6 weekly on Olympic; 3 daily on Axon & Aegean-Cronus; 35min)
Athens–Thíra (5–6 daily on Olympic)
Mýkonos–Rhodes (2 weekly; 1hr)
Mýkonos–Thessaloníki (3 weekly; 1hr 15min)
Mýkonos–Thíra (3–7 weekly; 30min)
Thíra–Iráklion (Crete) (2 weekly; 40min)
Thíra–Rhodes (3–6 weekly; 1hr)
Thíra–Thessaloníki (3 weekly; 1hr 30min)

8

Crete

CHAPTER 8 # Highlights

✳ **Archeological Museum, Iráklion** The world's foremost Minoan museum. **See p.677**

✳ **Minoan Sites** Knossós is the most exciting, but Mália, Festós, Zákros and other archeological ruins across the island are also worth a visit. **See p.683**

✳ **Beach resorts** Although those on the Iráklion coast are overcrowded, Mátala, Paleohóra, Plakiás and Sitía still have bags of charm and excellent strands. **See p.690**

✳ **Lasíthi Plateau** This green and fertile high mountain plateau has picturesque agricultural villages and unique white cloth-sailed windmills. **See p.700**

✳ **The Dhiktean cave** Stunningly situated on the Lasíthi Plateau, and, like many Cretan caves, has ancient historical connections. **See p.701**

✳ **Haniá and Réthymnon old towns** These atmospheric centres display haunting vestiges of their Venetian and Turkish pasts and are a joy to wander around. **See p.721 and p.712**

✳ **Gorge of Samariá** A magnificent gorge, but often gets too crowded in summer, so try and seek out the lesser-known Ayía Iríni and Zákros gorges. **See p.732**

8

Crete

Crete (Kríti) is a great deal more than just another Greek island. In many places, especially in the cities or along the developed north coast, it doesn't feel like an island at all, but rather a substantial land in its own right – a mountainous, wealthy and surprisingly cosmopolitan one. But when you lose yourself among the mountains, or on the lesser-known coastal reaches of the south, it has everything you could want of a Greek island and more: great beaches, remote hinterlands and hospitable people.

In **history**, Crete is distinguished above all as the home of Europe's earliest civilization. It was only at the beginning of the twentieth century that the legends of King Minos and of a Cretan society that ruled the Greek world in prehistory were confirmed by excavations at **Knossós** and **Festós**. Yet the **Minoans** had a remarkably advanced society, the centre of a maritime trading empire as early as 2000 BC. The artworks produced on Crete at this time are unsurpassed anywhere in the ancient world, and it seems clear that life on Crete in those days was good. This apparently peaceful culture survived at least three major natural disasters. Each time the palaces were destroyed, and each time they were rebuilt on a grander scale. Only after the last destruction, probably the result of an eruption of Thíra (Santoríni) and subsequent tidal waves and earthquakes, do significant numbers of weapons begin to appear in the ruins. This, together with the appearance of the Greek language, has been interpreted to mean that Mycenaean Greeks had taken control of the island. Nevertheless, for nearly 500 years, by far the longest period of peace the island has seen, Crete was home to a culture well ahead of its time.

Accommodation price codes

Throughout the book we've categorized accommodation according to the following **price codes**, which denote the cheapest available double room in high season. All prices are for the room only, except where otherwise indicated. Many hotels, especially those in category ❹ and over, include breakfast in the price; you'll need to check this when booking. During low season, rates can drop by more than fifty percent, especially if you are staying for three or more nights. Exceptions are during the Christmas and Easter weeks when you'll pay high-season prices. Single rooms, where available, cost around seventy percent of the price of a double.

❶ Up to €24	❹ €43–58
❷ €24–33	❺ €59–72
❸ €34–42	❻ €73 and upwards

Note: Youth hostels and mountain refuges typically charge €7–9 for a dormitory bed. For more accommodation details, see pp.51–54.

The Minoans of Crete probably came originally from Anatolia; at their height they maintained strong links with Egypt and with the people of Asia Minor, and this position as meeting point and strategic fulcrum between east and west has played a major role in Crete's subsequent history. Control of the island passed from Greeks to Romans to Saracens, through the Byzantine empire to Venice, and finally to Turkey for more than two centuries. During World War II, the island was **occupied** by the Germans and attained the dubious distinction of being the first place to be successfully invaded by paratroops.

Today, with a flourishing **agricultural economy**, Crete is one of the few islands which could probably support itself without tourists. Nevertheless, **tourism** is heavily promoted. The northeast coast in particular is overdeveloped, and though there are parts of the south and west coasts that have not been spoiled, they are getting harder to find. By contrast, the high mountains of the interior are still barely touched, and one of the best things to do on Crete is to **rent a vehicle** and explore the remoter villages.

Where to go

Every part of Crete has its loyal devotees and it's hard to pick out highlights, but generally if you want to get away from it all you should head west, towards **Haniá** and the smaller, less well-connected places along the south and west coasts. It is in this part of the island that the White Mountains rise, while below them yawns the famous **Samarian Gorge**. The **far east**, around **Sitía**, is also relatively unscathed with a string of isolated beaches worth seeking out to the south of the over-popular **Váï beach**, which lures crowds attracted by its famous palm grove. However, Sitía's new international airport, currently under construction, could change things significantly here in the next few years.

Whatever you do, your first main priority will probably be to leave **Iráklion** (Heraklion) as quickly as possible, having paid the obligatory, and rewarding, visit to the **Archeological Museum** and nearby **Knossós**. The other great Minoan sites cluster around the middle of the island: **Festós** and **Ayía Triádha** to the south (with Roman **Górtys** to provide contrast), and **Mália** on the north coast. Almost wherever you go you'll find a reminder of the island's history, whether it's the town of **Gourniá** near the cosmopolitan resort of **Áyios Nikólaos**, the exquisitely sited palace of **Zákros** in the far east, or the lesser sites scattered around the west. Unexpected highlights include Crete's Venetian forts at **Réthymnon** and **Frangokástello**; its hundreds of frescoed Byzantine churches, most famously at **Kritsá**; and, at Réthymnon and Haniá, the cluttered old Venetian and Turkish quarters.

Climate

Crete has by far the longest summers in Greece, and you can get a decent tan here right into October and swim at least from May until November. The one seasonal blight is the *meltémi*, a northerly wind which regularly blows harder here and more continuously than anywhere else in Greece – the best of several reasons for avoiding an **August** visit if you can. It's far from an ill wind, however, as it also lowers humidity and makes the island's higher summer temperatures more bearable.

Iráklion, Knossós and central Crete

Many visitors to Crete arrive in the island's capital, **Iráklion** (Heraklion), but it's not an outstandingly beautiful city, nor one where you'll want to stay much longer than it takes to visit the **Archeological Museum** and nearby **Knossós**. Iráklion itself, though it has its good points – superb fortifications, a fine market, atmospheric old alleys and some interesting lesser museums – is for the most part an experience in survival: despite a recent makeover of central areas by the city hall it remains modern, raucous, traffic-laden and overcrowded.

The area immediately around the city is less touristy than you might expect, mainly because there are few decent beaches of any size on this central part of the coast. To the west, mountains drop straight into the sea virtually all the way to Réthymnon, with just two significant coastal settlements: **Ayía Pelayía**, a sizeable resort, and **Balí**, which is gradually becoming one. Eastwards, the main resorts are at least 30km away, at **Hersónissos** and beyond, although there is a string of rather unattractive developments all the way there. Inland, there's agricultural country, some of the richest on the island, a cluster of Crete's better vineyards, and a series of wealthy but rather dull villages. Directly behind the capital rises **Mount Ioúktas** with its characteristic profile of Zeus; to the west the Psilorítis massif spreads around the peak of **Mount Psilorítis** (Ídha) the island's highest mountain. On the south coast there are few roads and little development of any kind, except at **Ayía Galíni** in the southwest, a nominal fishing village long since swamped with tourists, and **Mátala**, which has thrown out the hippies that made it famous and is now crowded with package-trippers. **Léndas** has to some extent occupied Mátala's old niche.

Despite the lack of resorts, there seem constantly to be thousands of people trekking back and forth across the centre of the island. This is largely because of the superb archeological sites in the south: **Festós**, second of the Minoan palaces, with its attendant villa at **Ayía Triádha**, and **Górtys**, capital of Roman Crete.

Iráklion

The best way to approach **IRÁKLION** is by sea: that way you see the city as it should be seen, with Mount Ioúktas rising behind and the Psilorítis range to the west. As you get closer, it's the city walls that first stand out, still dominating and fully encircling the oldest part of town; finally you sail in past the great Venetian **fort** defending the harbour entrance. Unfortunately, big ships no longer dock in the old port but at great modern concrete wharves alongside, which neatly sums up Iráklion itself. Many of the old parts have been restored from the bottom up, but they're of no relevance to the bustle and noise that characterizes much of the city today. In recent times, however, Iráklion's administrators have been giving belated attention to dealing with some of the image problems, and large tracts of the centre – particularly the focal Platía Eleftherías – have been landscaped and refurbished with the aim of presenting a less daunting prospect to the visitor.

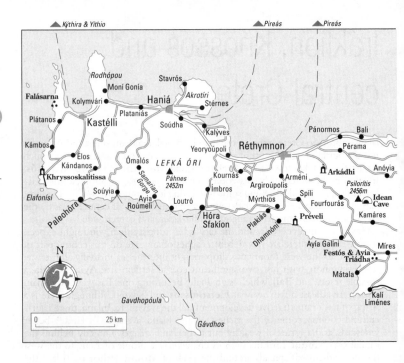

Orientation, arrival and information

Virtually everything you're likely to want to see in Iráklion lies within the walled city, and even here the majority falls into a relatively small sector – the northeastern corner. The most vital thoroughfare, **25-Avgoústou**, links the harbour with the commercial city centre. At the bottom it is lined with shipping and travel agencies and rental outlets, but further up these give way to banks, restaurants and stores. **Platía Venizélou** (or Fountain Square), off to the right, is crowded with cafés and restaurants; behind Venizélou lies **El Greco Park** (actually a rather cramped garden), with more bars, while on the opposite side of 25-Avgoústou are some of the more interesting of Iráklion's older buildings. Further up 25-Avgoústou, **Kalokerinoú** leads down to Haniá Gate and westwards out of the city; straight ahead, **Odhós–1821** is a major shopping street, and adjacent 1866 is given over to the animated **market**. To the left, Dhikeosínis heads for the city's main square, **Platía Eleftherías**, paralleled by the touristy pedestrian alley, Dedhálou, the direct link between the two squares. The newly revamped Eleftherías is very much the traditional centre of the city, both for traffic – which swirls around it constantly – and for life in general; it is ringed by more expensive tourist cafés and restaurants and comes alive in the evening with crowds of strolling locals.

Points of arrival

Iráklion **airport** is right on the coast, 4km east of the city. **Bus** #1 leaves for Platía Eleftherías every few minutes from the car park in front of the terminal; buy your ticket (€0.55) at the booth before boarding. There are also plenty of **taxis** outside (which you'll be forced to use when the buses stop at 11pm), and prices to major destinations are posted here and in the domestic departures hall

MEDITERRANEAN SEA

– it's about €4 to the centre of town. Get an agreement on the fare before taking a cab and beware if the driver extols the virtues of a particular place to stay and offers to drop you there – he'll usually be getting a kickback from the proprietors. To avoid such hassles ask to be dropped at the central Platía Eleftherías, from where everything is in easy walking distance.

There are three main **bus stations** and a small terminus. Services along the coastal highway to or from the **east** (Mália, Áyios Nikólaos, Ierápetra, Sitía and so on) use the terminal just off the main road between the ferry dock and the Venetian harbour; the #2 local bus to Knossós runs from the city bus stop, adjacent to the east bus station. Main road services **west** (Réthymnon and Haniá) leave from a terminal close to the east bus station on the other side of the road. Buses for the **southwest** (Festós, Mátala or Ayía Galíni) and along the inland roads west (Týlissos, Anóyia) operate out of a terminal just outside Haniá Gate, a very long walk from the centre along Kalokerinoú (or jump on any bus heading down this street). From the wharves where the **ferries** dock, the city rises directly ahead in steep tiers. If you're heading for the centre, for the archeological museum or the tourist office, cut straight up the stepped alleys behind the bus station onto Dhoúkos Bofór and to Platía Eleftherías; this will take about fifteen minutes. For accommodation though, and to get a better idea of the layout of Iráklion's main attractions, it's simplest to follow the main roads by a rather more roundabout route. Head west along the coast, past the major eastbound bus station and on by the Venetian harbour before cutting up towards the centre on 25-Avgoústou.

Information

Iráklion's **tourist office** has had its hours cut to weekdays only (Mon–Fri 8.30am–5pm; ☎0810/228 225, ⓕ226 020) and is located just below Platía

IRÁKLION

ACCOMMODATION

Hellas	10
Kris	5
Kronos	1
Lato	2
Marin	8
Mirabello	6
Olympic	11
Rea	7
Rodos	9
Vergina	3
Youth Hostel	4

S. VENIZELOU

SKORDHILON

ODHOS 1878

Priouli Fountain

St Andrew's Bastion

MAKARIOU

SAVATHIANON

SEAKION

AYIOU DHEONOS

DEDHIDHAKI

KALOKERINOU

PLATIA EKATERINIS

Áyios Minas

Cathedral

Pantokratóros Bastion

Pórta H.

South/West Bus Station

62 MARTYRON

PLASTIRA

KARDIOTISSIS

◀ Haniá & Festós

THERISSOU

THENON

TOMBAZI

YIANIKOU

ROMANDU

PLASTIRA

N

KONDILAKI

Kazantzakis' Tomb

Martinengo Bastion

0   250 m

Castle

Venetian Harbour

S. VENIZELOU
Áyios Petros 1 A
B
C
Historical Museum
GAZI
3
7
HORTATSON
HANDHAKOS
THEOTOKOPOULOU
MINOTAVROU
VYRONOS
6
D
4
Arsenali
EPIMENIDHOU
25-AVGOUSTOU

West-bound Bus Station
Ferry Dock
East Bus Station

2
5
DHOUKOS BOFOR
8

National Bank
F 9
Áyios Títos
G
El Greco Park
OTE
PSAROMILIGON
10
PLATIA VENIZELOU
Loggia
MIRABELOU
Sabbionera Bastion
Archeological Museum

MIHELIDHAKI
Morosini Fountain
J
San Marco
ANDHROYEO
DEDHALOU
H
K
I
MILATOU
KORAI
i
SAPOUTIE
ANTHOUDHIDHOU
DHOUKOS BOFOR
IKAROU

Ayía Ekaterini
1821
OD. FOTIOU THEODHOSAKI
DHIKEOSINIS
M. YIANARI
SMYRNIS
Tourist Police
PLATIA ELEFTHERIAS
PLATIA DHASKALOYIANNI

▶ Airport & the east

Market
1866
Olympic Airways
AVEROF
PEDHIADHOS

Bembo & Turkish Fountain
PLATIA ARKADHIOU
VIKELA
11
PLATIA KORNAROU
EVANS
PEDHIADHOS

Public Gardens
Vitouri Bastion

Pórta Kenoúria
★ **Southeast Bus Terminal**
PLATIA KYPROU
Jesus Bastion

KNOSSOU
KHRISSOSTOMOU
TOMBAZI
DHIMOKRATIAS

RESTAURANTS
Bougatsa Kirkor   J
Chilis   E
Geroplatanos   G
Ippokampos   A
Kapetanios   D
Katsina   B
Loukoulos   I
New China   H
Pagopoleion   F
Taverna Giovanni   K
Vareladika   C

8

CRETE | Iráklion

675

▼ Knossós & Natural History Museum

Eleftherías, opposite the Archeological Museum at Zanthoudhídhou 1. A sub-office at the **airport** (April–Sept daily 9am–9pm) is good for basic information and maps. The **tourist police** – more helpful than most – are at Dhikeosínis 10 (☎0810/283 190), halfway between Platía Eleftherías and the market.

Accommodation

Finding a **room** can be difficult in season. The best place to look for inexpensive rooms is in the area around Platía Venizélou, along Hándhakos and towards the harbour to the west of 25-Avgoústou. Other concentrations of affordable places are around El Greco park and in the streets above the Venetian harbour. Better hotels mostly lie closer to Platía Eleftherías, to the south of Platía Venizélou and near the east- and westbound bus stations. The dusty park between the main bus station and the harbour is often crowded with the sleeping bags of those who failed to find, or couldn't afford, a room; however, the police are far less tolerant to rough sleepers these days, and while crashing here is a possibility, a pleasant environment it certainly is not.

There are no **campsites** near Iráklion. The nearest sites both lie to the east of the city: *Creta Camping* at Káto Goúves (☎08970/41 400), 16km east, and *Caravan Camping* (☎08970/22 025) at Hersónissos, 28km east.

Hellas, Hándhakos 24 ☎0810/288 851, ℱ284 442. Hostel-type place with simple doubles, and dormitory rooms (€6 per bed) favoured by younger travellers. Also has a roof garden and snack bar. ❶

Kris, Dhoúkos Bofór 2, near the Venetian harbour ☎0810/223 944. Apartment-style rooms with kitchenette, fridge, great balcony views and friendly female proprietor. ❸

Kronos, Agaráthou 2, west of 25-Avgoústou ☎0810/282 240, ℱ285 853. Pleasant, friendly and modern hotel with sea view and baths in all rooms. ❷

Lato, Epomenídhou 15 ☎0810/228 103, ℱ240 350. Stylish and luxurious hotel where the air-con rooms have minibar, TV and sea view balcony with breakfast included. ❺

Marin, Dhoúkos Bofór 10 ☎0810/224 736, ℱ224 730. Comfortable and good-value rooms with bath, overlooking the Venetian harbour; get a balcony room at the front for a great view. Very convenient for the bus stations and the Archeological Museum. ❸

Mirabello, Theotokopoúlou 20 ☎0810/285 052, ℱ225 852, ℮mirabhot@otenet.gr. Good-value, family-run place with some rooms en-suite in a quiet street close to El Greco Park. ❷–❸

Olympic, Platía Kornárou ☎0810/288 861, ℱ222 512. Overlooking the busy platía and the famous Bembo and Turkish fountains. One of the many hotels built in the 1960s, but one of the few that has been refurbished; rates include breakfast. ❹

Rea, Kalimeráki 1 ☎0810/223 638, ℱ242 189. A friendly, comfortable and clean pension in a quiet street. Some rooms with washbasin, others with own shower. ❶

Pension Rodos, Platía Áyios Títos ☎0810/228 519. Homely and clean no-frills doubles and triples on a picturesque square with a great breakfast bar next door. ❶

Vergina, Hortátson 32 ☎0810/242 739. Basic but pleasant rooms with washbasins in a quiet street and set around a courtyard with a giant banana tree. ❶

Youth Hostel, Víronos 5 ☎0810/286 281, ℱ222 947. Formerly Iráklion's official youth hostel, it has been stripped of its HI status. It is in fact a good place to stay, family run and very friendly and helpful. There's plenty of space and some beds (albeit illegal) on the roof if you fancy sleeping out under the stars. Private rooms (€13.50) as well as dormitories (€5.90 per bed); hot showers, breakfast and other meals available.

The Town

From the port, the town rises overhead, and you can cut up the stepped alleys for a direct approach to Platía Eleftherías (Liberty Square) and the Archeological Museum. The easiest way to the middle of things, though, is to head west along the coast road, past the main bus stations and the *arsenáli*, and then up 25-Avgoústou, which leads into Platía Venizélou. This is crowded with

Iraklian youth patronizing outdoor cafés (marginally cheaper than those on Eleftherías), and with travellers who've arranged to meet in "Fountain Square". The recently restored **Morosini Fountain** itself is not particularly spectacular at first glance, but on closer inspection is really a very beautiful work; it was built by Venetian governor Francesco Morosini in the seventeenth century, incorporating four lions which were some three hundred years old even then. From the platía you can strike up Dhedhálou, a pedestrianized street full of tourist shops and restaurants, or continue on 25-Avgoústou to a major traffic junction. To the right, Kalokerinoú leads west out of the city, the market lies straight ahead, and Platía Eleftherías is a short walk to the left up Dhikeosínis.

Platía Eleftherías and the Archeological Museum

The recently revamped **Platía Eleftherías**, with seats shaded by palms and eucalyptuses is very much the traditional heart of the city: traffic swirls around it constantly, and on summer evenings strolling hordes jam its expensive cafés and restaurants. Most of Iráklion's more expensive shops are in the streets leading off the platía.

The **Archeological Museum** (Mon noon–7pm, Tues–Sun 8am–7pm; €4.40) is nearby, directly opposite the OTE office. Almost every important prehistoric and Minoan find on Crete is included in this fabulous, if bewilderingly large, collection. The museum tends to be crowded, especially when a guided tour stampedes through, but it's worth taking time over. You can't hope to see everything, nor can we attempt to describe it all (several good museum guides are sold here; the best probably being the glossy one by J.A. Sakellarakis), but highlights include the **mosaics** in Room 2 (the galleries are arranged basically in chronological order), the famous **inscribed disc** from Festós in Room 3 (itself the subject of several books), most of Room 4, especially the magnificent bull's head **rhyton** (drinking vessel), the **jewellery** in Room 6 (and elsewhere) and the engraved **black vases** in Room 7. Save some of your time and energy for upstairs, where the **Hall of the Frescoes**, with intricately reconstructed fragments of the wall paintings from Knossós and other sites, is especially wonderful.

The Archeological Museum's renovation

A long-overdue **renovation** of the archeological museum is planned to begin in the near future which, once completed, should place it in the forefront of museum design in Greece. New buildings are planned to house the administration offices, freeing up more space for exhibits, and a new subterranean floor is to be excavated beneath the museum to stage special exhibitions.

Preliminary soundings for the latter section have – perhaps predictably – uncovered the remains of a **Roman villa**, a **Venetian aqueduct** as well as the remnants of a **Franciscan monastery**, all of which previously occupied the site at different times. These will need to be properly investigated before any work can begin, thus making any starting or completion dates difficult to forecast. A further brake on the timetable at the time of writing is a government freeze applied to all public expenditure not directly connected with the staging of the Olympics in 2004. When work does get under way and while it is in progress, there will inevitably be some frustration for visitors as rooms are closed and items moved around. All this means that our account may not be entirely accurate, but it should still be possible to identify the major exhibits in the collection without too much difficulty.

△ Archeological Museum interior, Irálklion, Crete

Walls and fortifications

The massive **Venetian walls**, in places up to fifteen metres thick, are the most obvious evidence of Iráklion's later history. Though their fabric is incredibly well preserved, access is virtually nonexistent. It is possible, just, to walk along them from St Andrew's Bastion over the sea in the west, as far as the Martinengo Bastion where lies the **tomb of Nikos Kazantzakis**, Cretan author of *Zorba the Greek*, whose epitaph reads: "I believe in nothing, I hope for nothing, I am free." At weekends, Iraklians gather here to pay their respects and enjoy a free view of the soccer matches played by one of the city's two team's in the stadium below. If the walls seem altogether too much effort, the **port fortifications** are very much easier to see. Stroll out along the jetty (crowded with courting couples after dark) and you can get inside the sixteenth-century **castle** (Tues–Sat 8.30am–3pm, Sun 10am–3pm; €1.45, students €0.60) at the harbour entrance, emblazoned with the Venetian Lion of St Mark. Standing atop this, you can begin to understand how Iráklion (or Candia as it was known until the seventeenth century) withstood a 22-year siege before finally falling to the Ottomans. On the landward side of the port, the Venetian **arsenáli** (arsenals) can also be seen, their arches rather lost amid the concrete road system all around.

Churches and other museums

From the harbour, 25-Avgoústou will take you up past most of the rest of what's interesting. The **church of Áyios Títos**, on the left as you approach Platía Venizélou, borders a pleasant little platía. Byzantine in origin but substantially rebuilt by the Venetians, it looks magnificent principally because, like most of the churches here, it was adapted by the Turks as a mosque and only reconsecrated in 1925; consequently it has been renovated on numerous occasions. On the top side of this platía, abutting 25-Avgoústou, is the Venetian **city hall** with its famous loggia, again almost entirely rebuilt. Just above this, facing Platía Venizélou, is the **church of San Marco**, its steps usually crowded with the overflow of people milling around in the platía. Neither of these last two buildings has found a permanent role in its refurbished state, but both are generally open to house some kind of exhibition or craft show.

Slightly away from the obvious city-centre circuit, but still within the bounds of the walls, there are a couple of lesser museums worth seeing if you have the time. First of these is the excellent collection of **icons** in the **church of Ayía Ekateríni** (Mon–Fri 9.30am–2.30pm; €1.45), an ancient building just below the undistinguished cathedral, off Kalokerinoú. The finest here are six large scenes by Mihaïl Damaskinos (a near-contemporary of El Greco) who fused Byzantine and Renaissance influences. Supposedly both Damaskinos and El Greco studied at Ayía Ekateríni in the sixteenth century, when it functioned as a sort of monastic art school.

The **Historical Museum** (Mon–Fri 9am–5pm, Sat 9am–2pm; €3) is some way from here, down near the waterfront opposite the stark *Xenia* hotel. Its display of folk costumes and jumble of local memorabilia includes the reconstructed studies of both Nikos Kazantzakis and Emanuel Tsouderos (the latter both Cretan statesman and former Greek prime minister). There's enough variety to satisfy just about anyone, including the only El Greco painting on Crete, *View of Mount Sinai and the Monastery of St Catherine*.

A new **Natural History Museum** (June–Sept daily 9am–7pm; Oct–May Mon–Fri 9am–3pm, Sun 10am–6pm; €4.40, concessions €1.50; Ⓦ www.nhmc.uoc.gr) is definitely worth the trek out to visit it. Covering three floors, as well as the usual flora and fauna displays, it has exhibits detailing the island's geological evolution, the arrival of man and the environment as it would have appeared to the Minoans. The museum lies 2km south of the Pórta Kenoúria (a gate in the walls) along the road to Knossós. Bus #2 from Platía Eleftherías will drop you there (ask for the "Pagritio School" stop) or take a taxi (about €2.50).

The beaches

Iráklion's **beaches** are some way out, whether east or west of town. In either direction they're easily accessible by bus: #6 heads west from the stop outside the *Astoria* hotel in Platía Eleftherías; #7 east from the stop opposite this, under the trees in the centre of the platía.

Almyrós (or Ammoudhári) to the west has been subjected to a degree of development, comprising a campsite, several medium-size hotels and one giant one (the *Zeus Beach*, in the shadow of the power station at the far end), which makes the beach hard to get to without walking through or past something built up.

Amnissós, to the east, is the better choice, with several tavernas and the added amusement of planes swooping in immediately overhead to land. This is where most locals go on their afternoons off; the furthest of the beaches is the best, although new hotels are encroaching here, too. Little remains here to indicate the once-flourishing port of Knossós aside from a rather dull, fenced-in dig. If you're seriously into antiquities, however, you'll find a more rewarding site in the small Minoan villa, known as **Nírou Háni** (Tues–Sun 8.30am–3pm; free) at Háni Kokkíni, the first of the full-blown resort developments east of Iráklion.

Eating

Big city as it is, Iráklion disappoints when it comes to eating. The cafés and tavernas of platías **Venizélou** and **Eleftherías** are essential places to sit and watch the world pass, but their food is expensive and mediocre. One striking exception is *Bougatsa Kirkor*, by the Morosini fountain in Venizélou, where you can sample authentic Cretan *bougátsa* – a creamy cheese pie sprinkled with sugar and cinnamon; alternatively, try a plate of *loukoumádhes* (dough fritters), available from a number of cafés (*Aktarika* is good) near the junction of Dhikeosínis and 25-Avgoústou. The cafés and tavernas on **Dhedhálou**, the pedestrian alley linking the two main platías, are very run of the mill, with persistent waiters enticing you in with faded photographs of what appears to be food.

A more atmospheric option is to head for the little alley, **Fotíou Theodhosáki**, which runs through from the market to Odhós Evans. It is entirely lined with the tables of rival taverna owners, certainly authentic and catering for market traders and their customers as well as tourists. Compared with some, they often look a little grimy, but they are by no means cheap, which can come as a surprise.

A relaxed lunchtime venue in the **centre** of town is *Geroplatanos* with tables on the leafy Platía Ayíou Títou beside the church of the same name. Across from here is one of Iráklion's most stylish bars, *Pagopoleion* ("Ice Factory"), also good for lazy terrace breakfasts and snacks; the same place has now added an excellent restaurant and although medium priced, the food is consistently good – their recommended *mezedhákia* buffet (Sat & Sun 1–4pm) allows you to fill a plate for €4.50. *Pagopoleion* is the creation of photographic artist Chrissy Karelli, who has preserved a strident inscription on one wall, left by the Nazi occupiers who used local labour to run what was then Iráklion's only ice factory. Still near the centre, just off Eleftherías at **Platía Dhaskaloyiánni** (where the post office is), are some inexpensive and unexceptional tavernas; by day the platía is however a pleasant and relaxing venue, if not for a meal then to sit at one of its cafés, which transform themselves into more raucous and crowded music bars after dark. Nearer Venizélou, try exploring some of the backstreets to the east, off Dhedhálou and behind the loggia. The *Taverna Giovanni*, on the alley Koráï parallel to Dhedhálou, is one of the better tavernas in Iráklion, although the pricey food and an expensive wine list seem aimed more at Iráklion's smart set than the casual visitor. Should you have a craving for non-Greek food, there is Italian at the equally expensive *Loukoulos* and Chinese at the *New China Restaurant*, both with leafy courtyards and in the same street as the *Taverna Giovanni*. More reasonable prices are on offer at the very good new taverna-ouzerí *Vareladika*, Monís Agaráthou 13, close to the Venetian harbour which offers a wide range of Cretan specialities in a stylish setting. Mexican tacos and beers are on offer at *Chilis*, Hándhakos 71 on the west side of the central zone – an area with many lively bars and cafés.

The **waterfront** is dotted with fish tavernas with little to recommend them. Instead, turn left at the bottom of 25-Avgoústou and cross the road to *Ippokampos*, which specializes in excellent-value fish dishes and mezédhes at moderate prices. It is deservedly popular with locals and is often crowded late into the evening: you may have to wait in line or turn up earlier than the Greeks eat. Even if you see no space it is worth asking as the owner may suddenly disappear inside the taverna and emerge with yet another table to carry further down the pavement. For simple and cheap seafood mezédhes, slightly south from here, *Katsina* at Marineli 12 is a simple and friendly ouzerí with outdoor tables; this alley has a whole bunch of similar places popular with locals, ending with *Kapetanios*, opposite the pint-sized chapel of Áyios Dimítrios.

For **snacks** and **takeaways**, there's a whole group of *souvláki* stalls clustering around the top of 25-Avgoústou at the entrance to El Greco Park, which is handy if you need somewhere to sit and eat. For *tyrópita* and *spanakópita* (cheese or spinach pies) and other pastries, sweet or savoury, there are no shortage of *zaharoplastía* and places such as *Everest* – just north of the Morosini fountain – which does takeaways of these as well as a whole bunch of other savouries. If you want to buy your own food, the **market** on Odhós 1866 is the place to go; it's an attraction in itself, and does a great line in modestly priced Cretan herbs (including saffron) to take home.

Drinking, nightlife and entertainment

Iráklion is a bit of a damp squib as far as **nightlife** goes, certainly when compared with many other towns on the island. If you're determined, however, there are a few city-centre possibilities, and plenty of options if all you want to do is sit and **drink**. In addition, there are a number of **cinemas** scattered about: check the posters on the boards by the tourist police office.

Bars

The city's most animated **bars** are located around **Platía Koráï** behind Dhedhálou (up from the *Giovanni* restaurant listed above) and along the alley of the same name to the west. On summer nights these places are packed with Iráklion's younger set and you don't really need a guidebook to direct you. *Flash* and *To Avgo* are the most popular venues on the platía itself while along the alley are places such as *Rebels* and the glitzy new *Korais*, with plant-festooned terrace, movie-screens and music – currently *the* place to be seen. A little to the north, *Pagopoleion* (see opposite) beside the church of Áyios Títos is a less frenetic after-dark alternative with a DJ and laid-back Latin and modern Greek sounds. After ten at night a lively bar scene also fans out into the streets around Hándhakos;

among a number of new-style places *Jasmin*, Ayiostefanitón 6, is tucked in an alley on the left, midway down Hándhakos, and serves a variety of teas (including the Cretan *dhíktamo* – a panacea used by the ancients) with easy jazz and rock as background music. Nearby, *Orianas* at Psaromíligon 15 is a new music and drinks bar on two floors which has a varied programme of live music at weekends including jazz, blues, reggae and rock acts.

In and around **Platía Venizélou** (Fountain Square), there are many bars, again some are very fashionable, with *Andromeda* and *Aktarika* being a couple of the most popular. These represent a new breed of kafenío emerging in Iráklion, attracting a younger crowd: the drinks are **cocktails** rather than *rakí*, the music is Western or modern Greek, and there are prices to match. There are similar bars along Kandanoléon, off El Greco Park, and on the east side of the park itself.

Clubs and discos

For **discos** and **clubs** proper, there is a large selection, even if they all play techno at the moment, interspersed with Greek music (not the type played for tourists). *Privilege* is the most popular, down towards the harbour at the bottom of Dhoúkos Bofór, below the Archeological Museum. The nearby *Yacht Club* provides it with competition, and along Ikarou, downhill from Platía Eleftherías, another group of clubs is gathered including *Minoica*, *Korus Club* and *Athina*, all playing similar music and popular with young Iraklians. *Aman*, at the junction of Odhós Ay. Títos and Idomeneos and just east of the Áyios Títos church, with cine screens around its dance floor and three bars, is another more central alternative.

Listings

Airlines Aegean, Dhimokratias 11 ☎0810/344 394; Axon, Ethnikís Andístasis 134, ☎0810 331 310; Cronus Air, Odhós-1821 10, near El Greco Park ☎0810/397 368; Olympic, Platía Eleftherías ☎0810/229 191. Charter airlines flying in to Iráklion mostly use local travel agents as their representatives.

Airport For airport information call ☎0810/245 644. Bus #1 runs from Platía Eleftherías to the airport every few minutes; buy a ticket (€0.45) from the booth outside the *Astoria Hotel* first.

Banks There are now 24hr cash dispensers all over town, but the main bank branches are on 25-Avgoústou.

Car and bike rental 25-Avgoústou is lined with rental companies, but you'll often find cheaper rates on the backstreets; it's always worth asking for discounts. Good places to start include: Blue Sea, Kosmá Zótou 7, near the bottom of 25-Avgoústou ☎0810/241 097, for cars and bikes, which gives a twenty percent discount to Rough Guide readers; Sun Rise, 25-Avgoústou 46 ☎0810/221 609, also does both cars and bikes. For cars: Reliable, Epimenidou 8 off the east side of the same street ☎0810/344 212; Motor Club, Platía Ánglon 1 at the bottom of 25-Avgoústou facing the port ☎0810/222 408; and Ritz in the *Hotel*

Rea, Kalimeráki 1 ☎0810/223 638, are other possibilities. All offer free delivery to hotels and airport.

Ferry tickets Available from Minoan Lines, 25-Avgoústou 78 ☎0810/229 646 (handles the islands and Athens), ANEK Lines, 25-Avgoústou 33 ☎0810/222 481 (Athens only), or any of the travel agents listed opposite. Another source for tickets and ferry information is the long-established Paleologus Travel, 25-Avgoústou 5 ☎0810/346 185; their comprehensive website, ⓦwww.ferries.gr, is excellent.

Hospital Most central is the hospital on Apollónion, southwest of Platía Kornárou, between Albér and Moussoúrou.

Internet Iráklion now has a number of internet cafés located in and around the city centre. *Netcafé*, Odhós-1878 4 (daily 10am–midnight, near the sea to the west of the Historical Museum; €3.50 for 1hr; ⓦwww.the-netcafe.net) is good; other central places with similar charges and hours are *Istos*, Malakoúti 2 near the Arsenali; *Gallery Games*, Korai 6; and *Konsova*, Dhikeosínis 25.

Laundry Washsalon, Hándhakos 18 (Mon–Sat 8am–8pm) is reliable and also does service washes (€5.90 for 6kg). Laundry Perfect at Malikoúti 32, north of the Archeological Museum, will do the same for €5.30 (Mon–Sat 9am–9pm).

Left luggage Offices in the eastbound and south-west bus stations (daily 6.30am–8pm; €0.90 per bag per day), as well as a commercial agency at Hándhakos 18 (daily 24hr; large locker €1.50 per day). You can also leave bags at the youth hostel (even if you don't stay there) for €1.50 per bag per day. If you want to leave your bag while you go off on a bike for a day or two, the rental company should be prepared to store it.

Newspapers and books For English-language newspapers and novels, as well as local guides and maps, Dhedhálou is the best bet, where Bibliopoleío (no. 6) stocks a wide selection of books in English. The excellent Planet International Bookstore, on four floors behind Platía Venizélou at the corner of Hándhakos and Kydhonías (☎0810/281 558), has the island's biggest stock of English-language titles and is a great place to browse; they also buy, sell and exchange second-hand books in English.

Pharmacies Plentiful on the main shopping streets – at least one is open 24hr on a rota basis; the others will have a sign on the door indicating which it is. There are traditional herbalists in the market.

Post office Main office in Platía Dhaskaloyiánnis,

off Eleftherías (Mon–Fri 7.30am–8pm). There's also a temporary office (a van) at the entrance to El Greco Park (daily 7.30am–7pm).

Taxis Major taxi ranks in Platía Eleftherías and by the Morosini Fountain (Platía Venizélou), or call ☎0810/210 102 or 210 168. Prices displayed on boards at the taxi stands.

Telephones The OTE head office is on the west side of El Greco Park; it's open 8am–11pm, but most overseas destinations can now be phoned from street booths using a phonecard (*telekárta*) obtainable from a *períptero* (street kiosk).

Toilets In El Greco Park and the public gardens near the cathedral, or at the bus stations and the Archeological Museum (no entrance charge).

Travel agencies Budget operators and student specialists include the extremely helpful Blavakis Travel, Platía Kallergón 8, just off 25-Avgoústou by the entrance to El Greco Park ☎0810/282 541, and Prince Travel, 25-Avgoústou 30 ☎0810/282 706. For excursions around the island, villa rentals and so on, the bigger operators are probably easier: Irman Travel, Dhedhálou 26 ☎0810/242 527, or Creta Travel Bureau, Epimenídhou 20–22 ☎0810/227 002. The latter is also the local American Express agent.

Knossós

KNOSSÓS, the largest of the **Minoan palaces**, reached its cultural peak more than three thousand years ago, though a town of some importance persisted here well into the Roman era. It lies on a low, largely man-made hill some 5km southeast of Iráklion; the surrounding hillsides are rich in lesser remains spanning 25 centuries, starting at the beginning of the second millennium BC.

Barely a hundred years ago the palace existed only in mythology. Knossós was the court of the legendary King Minos, whose wife Pasiphae bore the Minotaur, half-bull, half-man. Here the labyrinth was constructed by Daedalus to contain the monster, and youths were brought from Athens as human sacrifice until Theseus arrived to slay the beast and, with Ariadne's help, escape its lair. The discovery of the palace, and the interplay of these legends with fact, is among the most amazing tales of modern archeology. Heinrich Schliemann, the German excavator of Troy, suspected that a major Minoan palace lay under the various tumuli here, but was denied the necessary permission to dig by the local Ottoman authorities at the end of the nineteenth century. It was left for Sir Arthur Evans, whose name is indelibly associated with Knossós, to excavate the site, from 1900 onwards.

The #2 and #4 local **buses** set off every ten minutes from Iráklion's city bus stands (adjacent to the eastbound bus station), proceed up 25-Avgoústou (with a stop just south of Platía Venizélou) and out of town on Odhós-1821 and Evans. This is also the route you should also take if **driving** (follow the signs from Platía Eleftherías); a **taxi** from the centre will cost around €2.50. At Knossós, outside the fenced site, stands the *caravanserai* where ancient wayfarers

PALACE OF KNOSSÓS

Royal Road   Theatral Area

North Entrance

Lustral Basin   Bull Relief

West Court

Storage Pits

Site Entrance

Statue
West Entrance

Storerooms   Piano Nobile   Throne Room   Workshops

Giant "Pithoí"

Central Court

Grand Stairway

Priest-King Fresco

Royal Apartments

South House

South-east House

0   25 m

would rest and water their animals. Head out onto the road and you'll find no lack of watering holes for modern travellers either – a string of rather pricey tavernas and tacky souvenir stands. There are several **rooms** for rent here, and if you're really into Minoan culture, there's a lot to be said for staying out this way to get an early start. Be warned, though, that this zone is expensive and unashamedly commercial.

The site

As soon as you enter the **Palace of Knossós** (daily: April–Sept 8am–7pm; Oct–March 8.30am–3pm; €4.40) through the West Court, the ancient cere-monial entrance, it is clear how the legends of the labyrinth grew up around it. Even with a detailed plan, it's almost impossible to find your way around the site with any success. The best advice is not to try; wander around for long enough and you'll eventually stumble upon everything. If you're worried about missing the highlights, you can always tag along with one of the constant guid-ed tours for a while, catching the patter and then backtracking to absorb the detail when the crowd has moved on. Outside the period December to February you won't get the place to yourself, whenever you come, but explor-ing on your own does give you the opportunity to appreciate individual parts of the palace in the brief lulls between groups.

Knossós was liberally "restored" by Evans, and these restorations have been the source of furious controversy among archeologists ever since. It has become clear that much of Evans's upper level – the so-called *piano nobile* – is pure con-jecture. Even so, his guess as to what the palace might have looked like is certainly as good as anyone else's, and it makes the other sites infinitely more meaningful if you have seen Knossós first. Without the restorations, it would be almost impossible to imagine the grandeur of the multistorey palace or to see the ceremonial stairways, strange, top-heavy pillars and gaily painted walls that distinguish the site. For some idea of the size and complexity of the palace in its original state, take a look at the cutaway drawings (wholly imaginary but probably not too far off) on sale outside.

Royal Apartments

The superb **Royal Apartments** around the central staircase are not guess-work, and they are plainly the finest of the rooms at Knossós. The **Grand Stairway** itself is a masterpiece of design: not only a fitting approach to these sumptuously appointed chambers, but also an integral part of the whole plan, its large well bringing light into the lower storeys. Light wells such as these, usually with a courtyard at the bottom, are a constant feature of Knossós and a reminder just how important creature comforts were to the Minoans, and how skilled they were at providing them.

For evidence of this luxurious lifestyle you need look no further than the **Queen's Suite**, off the grand **Hall of the Colonnades** at the bottom of the staircase. Here, the main living room is decorated with the celebrated **dolphin fresco** (a reproduction; the original is now in the Iráklion archeological museum) and with running friezes of flowers and abstract spirals. On two sides it opens out onto courtyards that let in light and air; the smaller one would prob-ably have been planted with flowers. The room may have been scattered with cushions and hung with plush drapes, while doors and further curtains between the pillars would have allowed for privacy, and provided cool shade in the heat of the day. Remember, though, that all this is speculation and some of it is pure hype; the dolphin fresco, for example, was found on the courtyard floor, not in the room itself, and would have been viewed from an upper balcony as a sort of trompe l'oeil, like looking through a glass-bottomed boat. Whatever the truth, this is an impressive example of Minoan architecture, the more so when you follow the dark passage around to the queen's **bathroom**. Here is a clay tub, protected behind a low wall (and again probably screened by curtains when in use), and the famous "flushing" toilet (a hole in the ground with drains to take the waste away – it was flushed by throwing a bucket of water down).

The much perused **drainage system** was a series of interconnecting terra-cotta pipes running underneath most of the palace. Guides to the site never fail to point these out as evidence of the advanced state of Minoan civilization, and they are indeed quite an achievement, in particular the system of baffles and overflows to slow down the runoff and avoid any danger of flooding. Just how much running water there would have been, however, is another matter; the water supply was, and is, at the bottom of the hill, and even the combined efforts of rainwater catchment and hauling water up to the palace can hardly have been sufficient to supply the needs of more than a small elite.

Going up the Grand Stairway to the floor above the queen's domain, you come to a set of rooms generally regarded as the **King's Quarters**. These are chambers in a considerably sterner vein; the staircase opens into a grandiose reception chamber known as the **Hall of the Royal Guard**, its walls deco-rated in repeated shield patterns. Immediately off here is the **Hall of the Double Axes**, believed to be have been the ruler's personal chamber, a dou-ble room that would allow for privacy in one portion while audiences were held in the more public section. Its name comes from the double-axe symbol carved into every block of masonry.

The Throne Room and the rest of the palace

Continuing to the top of the Grand Stairway, you emerge onto the broad **Central Court**, a feature of all the Minoan palaces. Open now, this would once have been enclosed by the walls of the buildings all around. On the far side, in the northwestern corner of the courtyard, is the entrance to another of Knossós's most atmospheric survivals, the **Throne Room**. Here, a worn stone throne – with its hollowed shaping for the posterior – sits against the wall of a surprisingly small chamber; along the walls around it are ranged stone benches, suggesting a king ruling in council, and behind there's a reconstructed fresco of two griffins. In all probability in Minoan times this was the seat of a priestess rather than a ruler (there's nothing like it in any other Minoan palace), and its conversion into a throne room seems to have been a late innovation wrought by the invading Mycenaeans, during their short-lived domination prior to the palace's final destruction in the fourteenth century BC. The Throne Room is now closed off with a wooden gate, but you can lean over this for a good view, and in the antechamber there's a wooden copy of the throne on which everyone perches to have their picture taken.

The rest you'll see as you wander, contemplating the legends of the place which blur with reality. Try not to miss the giant *pithoi* in the northeast quadrant of the site, an area known as the palace workshops; the storage chambers which you see from behind the Throne Room, and the reproduced frescoes in the reconstructed room above it; the fresco of the Priest-King looking down on the south side of the central court, and the relief of a charging bull on its north side. This last would have greeted you if you entered the palace through its north door; you can see evidence here of some kind of gatehouse and a lustral bath, a sunken area perhaps used for ceremonial bathing and purification. Just outside this gate is the **theatral area**, an open space a little like a stepped amphitheatre, which may have been used for ritual performances or dances. From here the **Royal Road**, claimed as the oldest road in Europe, sets out. At one time, this probably ran right across the island; nowadays it ends after about a hundred yards in a brick wall beneath the modern road. Circling back around the outside of the palace, you get more idea of its scale by looking up at it; on the south side are a couple of small reconstructed Minoan houses which are worth exploring.

Beyond Knossós

If you have transport, the drive beyond Knossós can be an attractive and enjoyable one, taking minor roads through much greener country, with vineyards draped across low hills and flourishing agricultural communities. If you want specific things to seek out, head first for **MYRTIÁ**, an attractive village with the small **Kazantzákis Museum** (Mon, Wed, Sat & Sun 9am–1pm & 4–8pm, Tues & Fri 9am–1pm; €2.95) in a house where the writer's parents once lived. **ARHÁNES**, at the foot of Mount Ioúktas, is a much larger place that was also quite heavily populated in Minoan times. None of the three archeological sites here is open to the public, but **Anemospiliá**, 2km northwest of the town (directions from the archeological museum below), can be visited and has caused huge controversy since its excavation in the 1980s: many traditional views of the Minoans, particularly that of Minoan life as peaceful and idyllic, have had to be rethought in the light of the discovery of an apparent human sacrifice. Close to Arhánes' main square, an excellent new **archeological museum** (daily except Tues 8.30am–3pm; free) displays finds from here and other nearby excavations, including the strange ceremonial dagger seemingly used for human sacrifice. From Arhánes you can also drive (or walk with a couple of hours to spare) to the summit of Mount Ioúktas to see the imposing remains of a Minoan **peak sanctuary** and enjoy spectacular panoramic **views** towards Knossós (with which it was linked) and the northern coast beyond. At **VATHÍPETRO**, south of the mountain, is a **Minoan villa and vineyard** (Mon–Sat 8.30am–2pm; free), which once controlled the rich farmland south of Arhánes. Inside, a remarkable collection of farming implements was found, as well as a unique **wine press** which remains *in situ*. Substantial amounts of the farm buildings remain, and it's still surrounded by fertile vines (Arhánes is one of Crete's major wine-producing zones) three and a half thousand years later – making it probably the oldest still-functioning vineyard in Europe, if not the world.

Southwest from Iráklion: sites and beaches

If you take a **tour** from Iráklion (or one of the resorts), you'll probably visit the **Górtys**, **Festós** and **Ayía Triádha** sites in a day, with a lunchtime swim at **Mátala** thrown in. Doing it by public transport, you'll be forced into a rather more leisurely pace, but there's still no reason why you shouldn't get to all three and reach Mátala within the day; if necessary, it's easy enough to hitch the final stretch. **Bus services** to the Festós site are excellent, with some nine a day to and from Iráklion (fewer run on Sun), five of which continue to or come from Mátala; there are also services direct to Ayía Galíni. If you're arriving in the afternoon, plan to visit Ayía Triádha first, as it closes early.

The route to Áyii Dhéka

The road from Iráklion towards Festós is a pretty good one by the standards of Cretan mountain roads, albeit rather dull. The country you're heading towards is the richest agricultural land on the island, and right from the start the villages en route are large and businesslike. In the biggest of them, **Ayía Varvára**, there's a great rock outcrop known as the **Omphalos** (Navel) of Crete, supposedly the very centre of the island.

Past here, you descend rapidly to the fertile fields of the Messará plain, where the road joins the main route across the south near the village of **ÁYII DHÉKA**. For religious Cretans Áyii Dhéka is something of a place of pilgrimage; its name, "The Ten Saints", refers to ten early Christians martyred here under the Romans. The old Byzantine church in the centre of the village preserves the stone block on which they are supposed to have been decapitated and in a crypt below the modern church on the village's western edge you can see the martyrs' (now empty) tombs. It's an attractive village to wander around, with several places to eat and even some **rooms** along the main road.

Górtys

Within easy walking distance of Áyii Dhéka, either through the fields or along the main road, sprawls the site of **Górtys** (daily 8am–6pm; €2.40), ruined capital of the Roman province that included not only Crete but also much of North Africa. After a look at the plan of the extensive site at the entrance, cutting across the fields to the south of the road will give you some idea of the scale of this city, at its zenith in approximately the third century AD. An enormous variety of remains, including an impressive **theatre**, and a couple of

temples are strewn across your route and more spectacular discoveries are being unearthed by the archeologists who return to dig each summer. Even in Áyii Dhéka you'll see Roman pillars and statues lying around in people's yards or propping up their walls.

There had been a settlement here from the earliest times and evidence of a Minoan site has been enearthed on the acropolis, but the extant ruins date almost entirely from the Roman era. Only now is the site being systematically excavated by the Italian Archeological School. At the main entrance to the **fenced site**, to the north of the road, are the ruins of the still impressive **basilica of Áyios Títos**; the eponymous saint converted the island to Christianity and was its first bishop. Beyond this is the **odeion** which houses the most important discovery on the site, the **Law Code**. These great inscribed blocks of stone were incorporated by the Romans from a much earlier stage of the city's development; they're written in an obscure early Greek-Cretan dialect, and in a style known as *boustrophedon* (ox-ploughed), with the lines reading alternately in opposite directions like the furrows of a ploughed field. At ten metres by three metres, this is reputedly the largest Greek inscription ever found. The laws set forth reflect a strictly hierarchical society: five witnesses were needed to convict a free man of a crime, only one for a slave; raping a free man or woman carried a fine of a hundred staters, violating a serf only five. A small **museum** in a loggia (also within the fenced area) holds a number of large and finely worked sculptures found at Górtys, more evidence of the city's importance.

Míres

Some 20km west of Górtys, **MÍRES** is an important market town and focal point of transport for the fertile Messará plain: if you're switching buses to get from the beaches on the south coast to the archeological sites or the west, this is where you'll do it. There are good facilities including a **bank**, a few **restaurants** and a couple of **rooms**, though there's no particular reason to stay unless you are waiting for a bus or looking for work (it's one of the better places for agricultural jobs). A useful **internet** café, *Net Escape* (Ⓦ www.netescape.gr), near the bus stop will allow you to send a few emails while awaiting onward connections. Heading straight for Festós, there's usually no need to stop.

Festós (Phaestos)

The **Palace of Festós** (daily 8am–6pm; €3.55) was excavated by the Italian, Federico Halbherr (also responsible for the early work at Górtys), at almost exactly the same time as Evans was working at Knossós. The style of the excavations, however, could hardly have been more different. Here, to the approval of most traditional archeologists, reconstruction was kept to an absolute minimum – it's all bare foundations, and walls which rise at most a metre above ground level. This means that despite a magnificent setting overlooking the plain of Messará, the palace at Festós is not as immediately arresting as those at Knossós or Mália. Much of the site is fenced off and, except in the huge central court, it's almost impossible to get any sense of the place as it was; the plan is almost as complex as at Knossós, with none of the reconstruction to bolster the imagination.

It's interesting to speculate why the palace was built halfway up a hill rather than on the plain below – certainly not for defence, for this is in no way a good defensive position. Psychological superiority over the peasants or reasons of health are both possible, but it seems quite likely that it was simply the magnificent view that finally swayed the decision. The site looks over Psilorítis to the north and the huge plain, with the Lasíthi mountains beyond it, to the east. Towards the top of Psilorítis you should be able to make out a small black smudge: the entrance to the Kamáres cave (see p.700).

On the ground closer at hand, you can hardly fail to notice the strong similarities between Festós and the other palaces: the same huge rows of storage jars, the great courtyard with its monumental stairway, and the theatral area. Unique to Festós, however, is the third courtyard, in the middle of which are the remains of a **furnace** used for metalworking. Indeed, this eastern corner of the palace seems to have been home to a number of craftsmen, including potters and carpenters. Oddly enough, Festós was much less ornately decorated than Knossós; there is no evidence, for example, of any of the dramatic Minoan wall-paintings.

The **tourist pavilion** near the entrance serves drinks and **food**, as well as the usual postcards, books and souvenirs. The nearby village of **ÁYIOS IOÁNNIS**, along the road towards Mátala, has economical **rooms**, including some at *Taverna Áyios Ioannis* (☎08920/42 006; ❶), which is also a good place to eat.

Ayía Triádha

Some of the finest artworks in the museum at Iráklion came from **Ayía Triádha** (daily 8.30am–3pm; €1.45), about a 45-minute walk (or a short drive) from Festós. No one is quite sure what this site is, but the most common theory has it as some kind of royal summer villa. It's smaller than the palaces, but if anything even more lavishly appointed and beautifully situated. In any event, it's an attractive place to visit, far less crowded than Festós, with a wealth of interesting little details. Look out in particular for the row of **stores** in front of what

PALACE OF FESTÓS

was apparently a marketplace, although recent thinking tends towards the idea that these were constructed after the villa had declined, possibly in the Mycenaean period. The remains of a **paved road** that probably led down to a harbour on the Gulf of Messará can also be seen running alongside the royal villa. The sea itself looks invitingly close, separated from the base of the hill only by Timbáki airfield (mainly used for motor racing these days), but if you try to drive down there, it's almost impossible to find your way around the unmarked dust tracks. There's a fourteenth-century **church** – dedicated to Áyios Yeóryios – at the site, worth visiting in its own right for the remains of ancient frescoes.

Mátala

MÁTALA has by far the best-known **beach** in Iráklion province, widely promoted and included in tours mainly because of the famous **caves** cut into the cliffs above its beautiful sands. These are believed to be ancient **tombs** first used by Romans or early Christians, but more recently inhabited by a sizeable hippie community. You'll still meet people who will assure you that this is *the* travellers' beach on Crete. Not any more it isn't. Today, the town is full of package tourists and tries hard to present a respectable image. The caves have long since been cleared and cleaned up and these days are a fenced-off **archeological site** (April–Sept daily 10am–4pm; €1.50) and locked up every evening.

A few people still manage to evade the security, or sleep on the beach or in the adjacent campsite, but on the whole the place has changed entirely. The years since the early 1980s have seen the arrival of crowds and the development of hotels, restaurants and even a disco to service them; early afternoon, when the tour buses pull in for their swimming stop, sees the beach packed to overflowing. If you're prepared to accept Mátala for what it is – a resort of some size – you'll find the place more than bearable. The town beach is beautiful, and if the crowds get excessive, you can climb over the rocks in about twenty minutes (past more caves, many of which are inhabited through the summer) to another excellent stretch of sand, known locally as "Red Beach". In the evening, when the trippers have gone, there are waterside bars and restaurants looking out over invariably spectacular sunsets.

The chief problems concern prices and crowds: rooms are both expensive and oversubscribed, and food is good but not cheap. If you want **accommodation**, try looking up the little street to the left as you enter town, just after the *Zafiria* hotel (☎08920/45 112, ℱ45 725;❷), where there are several rooms for rent, such as *Matala View* (☎08920/45 114;❶) and *Pension Nikos* (☎08920/42 375, ℱ 45 120;❷). If these are full, then everywhere closer in is likely to be as well, so head back out on the main road, or try the **campsite**, *Camping of Matala* (☎08920/45 720), next to the beach above the car park; *Kommos Camping* (☎08920/45 596) is a nicer site, but a few kilometres out of Mátala and reached by heading back towards Pítsidia and turning left along a signed track. There are places to **eat and drink** all over the main part of town, and it's worth seeking out the *Skala* fish taverna on the south side of the bay for fresh seafood and a great view. Nightlife is confined to a solitary summer **disco**, *Kandari*, plus a couple of music bars on the main square. On the south side of the bay, *Odysea* and the neighbouring *Sea Horse* are popular drinking haunts. A new **internet** facility has opened inside the stylish *Kafeneío* bar on the main square. Impossible to miss are most other facilities, including stores and a bookshop, currency exchange, car and bike rental, travel agents, post office and a covered market where tourist tat has almost squeezed out the fruit and veg stalls.

Around Mátala: Pitsídhia and Kalamáki

One way to enjoy a bit more peace is to stay at **PITSÍDHIA**, about 5km inland. This has long been a well-used option, so it's not quite as cheap as you might expect, but there are plenty of rooms, lively places to eat and even music bars. If you decide to stay here, the beach at **KALAMÁKI** is an alternative to Mátala. Both beaches are approximately the same distance to walk, though there is a much better chance of a bus or a lift to Mátala. Kalamáki has developed somewhat, with a number of **rooms** – *Psiloritis* (☎08920/45 693, ℱ45 249; ➊) is a good bet – and a couple of tavernas, but it's still a rather unfinished, soulless little place. The beach stretches for miles, surprisingly wild and windswept, lashed by sometimes dangerously rough surf. At the southern end (more easily reached by a path off the Pitsídhia–Mátala road) lies **Kómmos**, once a Minoan port serving Festós and now the site of a major archeological excavation. It's not yet open to the public, but you can peer into the fenced-off area to see what's been revealed so far, which is pretty impressive: dwellings, streets, hefty stonework and even the ship sheds where repairs on the Minoan fleet were carried out.

Iráklion's south coast

South of the Messará plain are two more beach resorts, Kalí Liménes and Léndas, with numerous other little beaches along the coast in between, but nothing spectacular. **Public transport** is very limited indeed; you'll almost always have to travel via Míres (see p.688). If you have your own transport, the roads in these parts are all passable and newly sealed, but most are very slow going; the Kófinas hills, which divide the plain from the coast, are surprisingly precipitous.

Kalí Liménes

While Mátala itself was an important port under the Romans, the chief harbour for Górtys lay on the other side of Cape Líthinon at **KALÍ LIMÉNES**. Nowadays, this is once again a significant port – for oil tankers. This has rather spoiled its chances of becoming a major resort, and there are few proper facilities, but some people like Kalí Liménes: it's certainly off the beaten track and the constant procession of tankers gives you something to look at while beach lounging. There are a couple of places offering **rooms** – the best is the seafront *Taverna Panorama* (☎08920/97 517; ➊) which also has a decent **taverna** attached. The coastline is broken up by spectacular cliffs and, as long as there hasn't been a recent oil spill, the beaches are reasonably clean and totally empty.

Léndas

LÉNDAS, further east along the coast, is far more popular, with a couple of buses daily from Iráklion and a partly justified reputation for being peaceful (sullied by considerable summer crowds). Many people who arrive think they've come to the wrong place, as at first sight the village looks shabby, the beach is small, rocky and dirty, and the rooms are frequently all booked. A number of visitors leave without ever correcting that initial impression, but the attraction of Léndas is not the village at all but on the other (west) side of the headland. Here, there's a vast, excellent sandy beach, part of it usually taken over by nudists, and a number of taverna/bars overlooking it from the roadside. The beach is a couple of kilometres from Léndas, along a rough track; if you're walking, you can save time by cutting across the headland. A considerably more attractive prospect than staying in Léndas itself is **camping** on the beach to the west of the village, or with luck getting a **room** at one of the few beach tavernas – try *Villa Tsapakis* (☎08920/95 378, ℱ95 377; ➊) with seaview rooms and reductions for longer stays. They will also change **money on a credit card** here (a useful service in this part of Crete where banks and cash-machines are nonexistent) and have their own **taverna**, *Odysseas*, nearby. After you've discovered the beach, even Léndas begins to look more welcoming, and at least it has most of the facilities you'll need, including a couple of minimarkets and the friendly Monza travel agency, both of which will change money, a single-screen **internet** café on the main square, and numerous places to **eat and drink**.

Once you've come to terms with the place, you can also explore some less good but quite deserted beaches eastwards, and the scrappy remains of **ancient Lebena** on a hilltop overlooking them. There was an important Asclepion (temple of the god Asclepius) here around some now-diverted warm springs, but only the odd broken column and fragments of mosaic survive in a fenced-off area on the village's northern edge.

East of Iráklion: the package-tour coast

East of Iráklion, the startling pace of **tourist development** in Crete is all too plain to see. The merest hint of a beach is an excuse to build at least one hotel, and these are outnumbered by the concrete shells of resorts-to-be. It's hard to find a room in this monument to the package-tour industry, and it can be expensive if you do.

Goúrnes and Goúves

As a general rule, the further you go, the better things get: when the road detours all too briefly inland, the more alluring Crete of olive groves and stark mountains asserts itself. You certainly won't see much of it at **GOÚRNES**, where an abandoned former US Air Force base is about to be transformed into a **giant sea aquarium** and visitor complex, or at nearby Káto Goúves, where there's a **campsite**, *Camping Creta* (☎08970/41 400), sharing a boundary with the former base. From here, however, you can head inland to the old village of **GOÚVES**, a refreshing contrast, and just beyond to the **Skotinó cave**, one of the largest and most spectacular on the island (about an hour's walk from the coast; open all hours; free).

Not far beyond Goúrnes is the turning for the direct route up to the Lasíthi plateau, and shortly after that you roll into the first of the big resorts, Hersónissos or, more correctly, Límin Hersoníssou; Hersónissos is the village in the hills just behind, also overrun by tourists.

Hersónissos (Límin Hersoníssou)

HERSÓNISSOS was once just a small fishing village; today it's the most popular of Crete's package resorts. If what you want is plenty of bars, tavernas, restaurants and Eurodisco nightlife, then this is the place to come. The resort has numerous small patches of sand beach between rocky outcrops, but a shortage of places to stay in peak season.

Hersonissos' focal main street, the two-kilometre long Odhós Elefthériou Venizélou, is a seemingly endless ribbon of bars, travel agents, tacky jewellery and beachwear shops, amusement arcades and – during the daytime at least – nose-to-tail traffic jams. North of here, along the modern seafront, a solid line of restaurants and bars is broken only by the occasional souvenir shop; in their midst you'll find a small pyramidal Roman **fountain** with broken mosaics of fishing scenes, the only real relic of the ancient town of Chersonesos. Around the headland above the harbour and in odd places along the seafront, you can see remains of Roman harbour installations, mostly submerged.

Beach and clubs excepted, the distractions of Hersónissos comprise **Lychnostatis Open-Air Museum** (Tues–Sun 9.30am–2pm; €3), a surprisingly rewarding "museum" of traditional Crete, on the coast at the eastern edge of the town; a small aquarium, **Aqua World** (April–Oct daily 10am–9pm; €4.40, children and students €2.90), just off the main road at the west end of town, up the road almost opposite the *Hard Rock Cafe*; the watersports paradise **Star Water Park** (daily June–Sept 10am–7pm; April & May 10am–6pm; €12.50 for a full day, or €9.50 half-day, reductions for under-12s) near the beach at the eastern end of the resort; and, a few kilometres inland, the competing **Aqua Splash Water Park** which has similar features and prices.

A short distance inland are the three **hill villages** of Koutoulafári, Piskopianó and "old" Hersónissos, which all have a good selection of tavernas, and are worth searching out for accommodation.

Practicalities

Hersónissos is well provided with all the back-up **services** you need to make a holiday go smoothly. Banks, bike and car rental and post office are all on or just off the main drag, as are the taxi ranks. A number of **internet** cafés have opened along the main street, the cheapest of which is *El Greco Palace*, Venizélou 109, at the eastern end. **Buses** running east and west leave every thirty minutes.

Finding somewhere to stay can verge on the impossible in July and August. Much of the **accommodation** here is allocated to package-tour operators and what remains for casual visitors is among the priciest on the island. To check for availability of accommodation generally, the quickest and best option is to enquire at one of the many travel agencies along the main street, Venizélou, such as Zakros Tours (☎08970/22 317) at no. 46. The town's most reasonably priced (for Hersónissos) central options include the *Nancy*, Ayías Paraskevís 15 (☎08970/22 212; ❸), and *Virginia*, Máchis Krítis 18 (☎ & ℉ 08970/22 455; ❸), but be prepared for a fair amount of noise. One place to try on the western edge as you enter the town is *Hotel Ilios* (☎08970/22 500, ℉22 582; ❹), just back from the main road, which has a rooftop pool. There are two good **campsites**: one at the eastern end of town, *Caravan Camping* (☎08970/22 025), which also has several reed-roofed bungalows, and *Camping Hersonissos* (☎08970/22 902), just to the west of town. The well-run "paleo" (old) **youth hostel** is no longer affiliated to the main organization and charges €8.80 for a bed with use of kitchen; it's sited at the extreme eastern end of Venizélou (☎08970/23 674), a little beyond *Caravan Camping* (see above) and serves meals.

Despite the vast number of **eating places**, there are few in Hersónissos worth recommending, and the tavernas down on the harbourfront should be avoided. One of the few Greek tavernas that stands out is *Kavouri* along Arhéou Theátrou, but it's fairly expensive; a cheaper in-town alternative for some delicious and inexpensive Cretan cooking is *Taverna Creta Giannis*, Kaniadakí 4, just off the south side of Venizélou slightly east of the church. Nearby, and also definitely worth a try, is *Passage to India*, an authentic and extremely good Indian restaurant; it lies on Petrakis, another side street just off the main street near the church. Heading out of town on the Piskopianó road, near the junction to Koutoulafári, the friendly *Fegari* taverna also serves good Greek food at reasonable prices. Sitting at your table overlooking the street below you can view the steady trek of clubbers heading down the hill to the bars and night-clubs of Hersónissos. The hill villages have the greatest selection of tavernas, particularly Koutoulafári, where you can have a relaxed evening amongst the narrow streets and small platías.

Hersónissos is renowned for its **nightlife**, and there's certainly no shortage of it. A night's partying kicks off around the **bars** ringing the harbour, which is packed with promenaders and the overspill from countless noisy music bars from 10pm through to the early hours. After midnight, the larger **disco-clubs** and **pubs** in the streets leading up to and along Elefthériou Venizélou are the places to be seen. Currently the most popular music clubs are *Aria* (open July–Aug only), the island's largest, on the main road at the west end of town, *It After Dark*, also on Venizélou, and *Camelot* and *New York*, both near the harbour. The *Hard Rock Café*, close to *Aria* on Venizélou, has a terrace where clubbers chill out between venues. If you fancy a quiet drink then you've come to the wrong resort, but you could try *Kahluai Beach Cocktail Bar* or *Haris Ouzo & Raki Place* (beneath the *Hotel Virginia*). There is an open-air **cinema** showing original-version films at the *Creta Maris* hotel at the west end of the town and close to the beach.

Stalídha

STALÍDHA is a Cinderella town, sandwiched in between its two louder, brasher and some would say uglier sisters, Mália and Hersónissos, but it is nei-ther quiet or undeveloped. This rapidly expanding beach resort, with more than sixty tavernas and bars and a few discos, can offer the best of both worlds, with a friendlier and more relaxed setting, a better beach (and usual array of watersports) and very easy access to its two livelier neighbours. The town essentially consists of a single, relatively traffic-free street which rings the seafront for more than two miles, before the apartment blocks briefly become fewer and further, until the mass development of Mália begins.

Finding a place to stay can be difficult, since **accommodation** is almost entirely in studio and apartment blocks which are booked by package compa-nies in high season. Out of season, however, you may well be able to negotiate a very reasonable price for a studio apartment complete with swimming pool; ask in the central travel agencies first, as they will know what is available, and expect to pay at least €25 for two. Finding somewhere to **eat** is less difficult as there are plenty of rather ordinary tavernas, the best and most authentic being *Maria's* and the *Hellas Taverna*, both at the western end of the seafront.

Stalídha is completely overshadowed by its neighbours when it comes to **nightlife**, though you can dance at *Bells* disco, on the main coast road, or at *Rhythm*, on the beach; the music bars *Sea Wolf Cocktail Bar* and *Akti Bar* are near each other along the beach.

Mália

Along with the other resorts along this stretch of coast, much of **MÁLIA** is carved up by the package industry, so in peak season finding a place to stay is not always easy. The town's focus is a T-junction (where the **bus** drops you) and from where the Beach Road – a kilometre-long strip lined with bars, clubs, games arcades, tavernas and souvenir shops – heads north to the sea and beach-es. South of this junction the older village presents a slightly saner image of what Mália used to be, but even here rampant commercialism is making inroads.

Within the map:

- Paved Road
- New excavations
- North Court
- Storerooms (pithoi)
- N
- Processional Way
- Pillared Hall
- Lustral Basin
- Royal Apartments
- Archive Room
- Lodge
- West Court
- Storerooms (covered)
- Pillar Crypt
- Storeroom
- Central Court
- Altar
- Entrance
- Storage pits
- South Entrance
- **PALACE OF MÁLIA**
- 0   25 m

The best **accommodation** options, especially if you want any sleep, are among the numerous **rooms** and **pensions** signposted in the old town, such as *Esperia* (℡08970/31 086; ❸), up a side road slightly east of the T-junction. Backtracking from the junction, along the main Iráklion road, there are a number of reasonably priced **pensions** on the left and right including *Hibiscus* (℡08970/31 313, ℻32 042; ❷), which has rooms and studios with kitchenette and fridge around a pool in a garden behind. If you really want to be in the centre of things, try *Kostas* (℡08970/31 485; ❷), a family-run pension incongruously located behind the mini-golf at the end of the Beach Road. Otherwise, on arrival visit one of the travel companies along the main road – such as Stallion Travel, Venizélou 128 (℡08970/33 690) – to enquire about accommodation availability. All the other things you're likely to need – **banks** with cash machines, **post office** and food shops – are strung out along the main street near the junction, but the town's best **internet** access, *Internet Café*, is bang in the middle of the Beach Road madness (about a third of the way down on the right), but no less friendly or efficient for that.

Eating in Mália is unlikely to be a problem as **restaurants** jostle for your custom at every step, especially along the Beach Road. None is particularly good here, and a few are diabolical. The best places for a meal are around Platía Ayíou

Dhimitríou, a pleasant square beside the church in the centre of the old village to the south of the main road. Here, you could try *Kalimera* or *Petros*, or the pleasant *Kalesma* with a delightful terrace, perhaps after an aperitif at *Bar Yiannis* just north of the church or *Ouzeri Elizabeth* alongside it, where they serve local wine from the barrel. A little harder to find, and to the west of the square, *Apolafsi* is a good-quality small family taverna which is slightly less pricey than the others.

The Beach Road comes into its own at night, when the profusion of **bars**, **discos** and **clubs** erupt into a pulsating cacophony. The aptly named *Zoo* is one of the most frenetic, and once past midnight the internal walls part to reveal an even larger dance area. Other popular venues (many British-owned and -run) along the strip include *Cloud*, *Cosmos*, *Midway*, *Zig-Zag* and *Road House*. There are also a clutch of "English pubs" with names like *Newcastle* and *Camden*. Unfortunately, a good night's clubbing is frequently spoiled by groups of drunken youths pouring out of these bars and getting into brawls. At one point the situation got so bad that tour operators threatened to pull out of the resort if action wasn't taken to deal with the hooligans – all rather ironical as it was they who were shipping them in by the plane-load on cut-price packages. Recent years have seen a police clampdown on such activities as drinking on the street, and the situation has considerably improved.

The Palace of Mália

Much less imposing than either Knossós or Festós, the **Palace of Mália** (Tues–Sun 8.30am–3pm; €2.40), 2km east of Mália town, in some ways surpasses both. For a start, it's a great deal emptier and you can wander among the remains in relative peace. While no reconstruction has been attempted, the palace was never reoccupied after its second destruction in the fifteenth-century BC, so the ground plan is virtually intact. It's a great deal easier to comprehend than Knossós and, if you've seen the reconstructions there, it's easy to envisage this seaside palace in its days of glory. There's a real feeling of an ancient civilization with a taste for the good life, basking on the rich agricultural plain between the Lasíthi mountains and the sea.

From this site came the famous **gold pendant** of two bees (which can be seen in the Iráklion museum or on any postcard stand), allegedly part of a horde that was plundered and whose other treasures can now be found in the British Museum in London. The beautiful leopard-head axe, also in the museum at Iráklion, was another of the treasures found here. At the site, look out for the strange indented stone in the central court (which probably held ritual offerings), for the remains of ceremonial stairways and for the giant *pithoi* which stand like sentinels around the palace. To the north and west of the main site, archeological digs are still going on as the **large town** which surrounded the palace comes slowly to light, and part of this can now be viewed via an overhead walkway.

Any passing **bus** should stop at the site, or you could even rent a **bike** for a couple of hours as it's a pleasant, flat ride from Mália town. Leaving the archeological zone and turning immediately right, you can follow the road down to a lovely stretch of clean and relatively peaceful **beach**, backed by fields, scrubland and a single makeshift taverna, which serves good fresh fish. From here you can walk back along the shore to Mália or take a bus (every 30min in either direction) from the stop on the main road.

Sísi and Mílatos

Head **east** from the Palace of Mália, and it's not long before the road leaves the coast, climbing across the hills towards Áyios Nikólaos. If you want to escape the frenetic pace of all that has gone before, try continuing to **SÍSI** or

MÍLATOS. These little shore villages are bypassed by the main road as it cuts inland, and are still very much in the early stages of the tourist industry, though both have several **tavernas** – the seafront *Fisherman's Place* in Sísi is worth a try. The more developed of the two, Sísi, is charmingly situated around a small harbour overlooked by balcony bars and more tavernas. The resort has recently opened its first **disco bar** (*Faros*), a sure sign that more development is on the way, portended by a large holiday complex (*Kalimera Krita*) a couple of kilometres to the east; there's even a **post office**, confirming its resort status. Accommodation in both places is mainly in studios and apartments; it's best to ask in the travel agencies for details of availability. In Sísi there's also a small pension, *Elena* (no phone; ❸) just behind the harbour, and a shady **campsite** with pool and taverna (☎08410/71 247) signposted on the way in.

In quieter Mílatos, rooms can be found in the old village, 2km inland, but the seaside settlement – despite a rather pebbly beach – is more desirable. A number of the seafront tavernas let out rooms and, outside the peak season when there's little chance of a bed, the friendly *Taverna Socrates* (☎08410/81 375; ❶) is worth a try and does decent **food**. Despite their beaches, the resorts make for a refreshing change of pace, and there are some fine, deep aprons of sand in the rocky coves beyond the resort centres.

West of Iráklion: around Psilorítis

Most people heading west from Iráklion speed straight out on the **E75 coastal highway**, nonstop to Réthymnon. If you're in a hurry this is not such a bad plan; the road is fast and spectacular, hacked into the sides of mountains which for the most part drop straight to the sea, though there are no more than a couple of places where you might consider stopping. By contrast, the old roads inland are agonizingly slow, but they do pass through a whole string of **attractive villages** beneath the heights of the Psilorítis range. From here you can set out to explore the **mountains** and even walk across them to emerge in villages with views of the south coast.

The coastal route towards Réthymnon

Leaving the city, the **new highway** runs behind a stretch of highly developed coast, where the hotels compete for shore space with a cement works and power station. As soon as you reach the mountains, though, all this is left behind and there's only the clash of rock and sea to contemplate. As you start to climb, look out for **Paleókastro**, hovering beside a bridge which carries the road over a small cove; the castle is so weathered as to be almost invisible against the brownish face of the cliff.

Ayía Pelayía and Fódhele

Some 3km below the highway, as it rounds the first point, lies the resort of **AYÍA PELAYÍA**. It looks extremely attractive from above but, once there, you're likely to find the narrow, taverna-lined beach packed to full capacity; this is not somewhere to roll up in high season without reserved **accommodation**, although in quieter times *Zorba's Rooms* (☎ & ℗ 0810/256 072; ❷), along the nameless main street behind the beach, should have space. Opposite here, the Pangosmio travel agency (☎0810/811 402, ℗811 424) may be able to come up with something, even at the last minute in high season. Out of season you might find a real bargain apartment and, despite the high-season crowds, the resort maintains a dignity long since lost in Mália and Hersónissos, and even a certain exclusivity; a couple of Crete's most luxurious hotels, including the enormous *Peninsula* (℡0810/811 313, ℻811 219, Ⓦwww.peninsula.gr; Ⓖ), nestle on the headlands just beyond the main town beach. There are plenty of **mini markets** for buying picnic food and **internet** access is available at *Netcafé Atlas*, next door to *Zorba's Rooms*.

Not far beyond Ayía Pelayía, there's a turning inland to the village of **FÓDHELE**, allegedly El Greco's birthplace. A plaque from the University of Valladolid (in Spain) acknowledges the claim and, true or not, the community has built a small tourist industry on that basis. There are a number of craft shops and some pleasant tavernas where you can sit outside along the river. A peaceful 1km walk (or drive) takes you to the spuriously titled (and rarely open) "El Greco's house" and the more worthwhile and picturesque fourteenth-century Byzantine **church of the Panayía** (Mon–Fri 9.30am–5pm; free) with frescoes, opposite. None of this amounts to very much but it is a pleasant, relatively unspoiled village if you simply want to sit in peace for a while. A couple of **buses** a day run here from Iráklion, and there's the odd tour; if you arrive on a direct bus, the walk back down to the highway (about 3km), where you can flag down a passing service, is not too strenuous.

Balí and Pánormos

BALÍ, on the coast approximately halfway between Iráklion and Réthymnon, also used to be tranquil and undeveloped, and by the standards of the north coast it still is in many ways. The village is built around a trio of small coves, some 2km from the highway (a hot walk from the bus), and is similar to Ayía Pelayía except that the beaches are not quite as good and there are no big hotels, just an ever-growing proliferation of studios, apartment buildings, rooms for rent and a number of "modest hotels" (brochure-speak). You'll have plenty of company here and it has to be said that Balí has become a package resort too popular for its own good. The third and best beach, known as "Paradise", no longer really deserves the name; it's a beautiful place to splash about, surrounded by mountains rising straight from the sea, but there's rarely a spare inch on the sand in high season.

Continuing along the coast, the last stop before you emerge on the flat stretch leading to Réthymnon is at **PÁNORMOS**. This makes a good stopover if you're in search of somewhere more peaceful and authentic. The small sandy beach can get crowded when boats bring day-trippers from Réthymnon, but most of the time the attractive village remains relatively unspoiled, and succeeds in clinging to its Cretan identity. There are several decent **tavernas** – try *Taverna Panorama* in the heart of the village – and **rooms** places, one large hotel and the very comfortable *Pension Lucy* (℡08340/51 212, ℻51 434; Ⓞ), which has also sprung a seafront offshoot with balcony studio rooms and apartments.

Inland towards Mount Psilorítis

Of the **inland routes**, the old main road (via Márathos and Dhamásta) is not the most interesting. This, too, was something of a bypass in its day and there are few places of any size or appeal, though it's a very scenic drive. If you want to dawdle, you're better off on the road which cuts up to **Týlissos** and then goes via **Anóyia**. It's a pleasant ride through fertile valleys filled with olive groves and vineyards, a district (the Malevísi) renowned from Venetian times for the strong, sweet Malmsey wine.

Týlissos and Anóyia

TÝLISSOS has a significant archeological site (daily 8.30am–3pm; €1.20) where three Minoan houses were excavated; unfortunately, its reputation is based more on what was found here (many pieces in the Iráklion museum) and on its significance for archeologists than on anything which remains to be seen. Still, it's worth a look, if you're passing, for a glimpse of Minoan life away from the big palaces, and for the tranquillity of the pine-shaded remains.

ANÓYIA is a much more tempting place to stay, especially if the summer heat is becoming oppressive. Spilling prettily down a hillside close below the highest peaks of the mountains, it looks traditional, but closer inspection shows that most of the buildings are actually concrete; the village was destroyed during World War II and the local men rounded up and shot – one of the German reprisals for the abduction of General Kreipe by the Cretan Resistance. The town has a reputation as a **handicrafts** centre (especially for woven and woollen goods), skills acquired both through bitter necessity after most of the men had been killed, and in a conscious attempt to revive the town. At any rate it worked, for the place is thriving today – thanks, it seems, to a buoyant agricultural sector made rich by stockbreeding, and the number of elderly widows keen to subject any visitor to their terrifyingly aggressive sales techniques.

Quite a few people pass through Anóyia during the day, but not many of them stay, even though there are some good pensions and rented rooms in the upper half of the town, including the flower-bedecked *Aris* (☎08340/31 460, ⓕ31 058; ❶) and the nearby *Aristea* (☎08340/31 459; ❷), which has en-suite rooms and spectacular views, and includes breakfast. The town has a very different, more traditional ambience at night, and the only problem is likely to be finding a **place to eat**: although there are plenty of snack bars and so-called tavernas, most have extremely basic menus, more or less limited to spit-barbecued lamb, which is the tasty local speciality served up by the grill places on the lower square. If you can face it, a steep hike to the top of the village will bring you to *Taverna Skalómata* with well-prepared taverna standards and a fine view.

Mount Psilorítis and its caves

Heading for the mountains, a smooth road ascends the 21km from Anóyia to an altitude of 1400m on the **Nídha plateau** at the base of Mount Psilorítis. Here, the *Taverna Nida* (☎08340/31 141; April–Sept daily; Sat & Sun only in winter) serves up hearty taverna standards and has a couple of **rooms** (❶), which makes it a good base for hikes in the surrounding mountains. A short path leads from the taverna to the celebrated **Idhéon Ándhron** (Idean cave), a rival of that on Mount Dhíkti (see p.701) for the title of Zeus's birthplace, and certainly associated from the earliest of times with the cult of Zeus. The remnants of a major archeological dig carried out inside – including a miniature railway used by archeologists to remove tonnes of rock and rubble – still litter the site giving the place a rather unattractive prospect. When you enter the cave down concrete steps into the depths, it turns out to be a rather shallow affair, devoid even of natural wonders. In short, there's not a great deal to see.

The taverna also marks the start of the way to the top of **Mount Psilorítis** (2456m), Crete's highest mountain, a climb that for experienced, properly shod hikers is not at all arduous. The route (now forming a stretch of the E4 Pan-European footpath) is well marked with the usual red dots, and it should be a six- to seven-hour return journey to the **chapel of Tímios Stavrós** ("Holy Cross") at the summit, although in spring, thick snow may slow you down.

If you're prepared to camp on the plateau (it's very cold, but there's plenty of available water) or find rooms at the taverna, you could continue on foot next day down to the southern slopes of the range. It's a beautiful hike and also relatively easy, four hours or so down a fairly clear path to **Vorízia** where there is no food or accommodation, although **KAMÁRES**, 4km west, has both: for **rooms**, the very cheap and basic *Hotel Psiloritis* (☎08920/43 290; ❶) should have a bed, and the best **place to eat** is the *Taverna Bournelis* at the village's western end. If you're still interested in caves, there's a more rewarding one above Kamáres, a climb of some five hours on a good, but aggressively steep path. The start of the route is just to the left of the *Taverna Bournelis* and the proprietors here can advise on the ascent (in Greek and German only). There is at least one daily **bus** from here down to Míres and alternate (more difficult) routes to the peak of Psilorítis if you want to approach from this direction.

Eastern Crete

Eastern Crete is dominated by **Áyios Nikólaos**, and while it is a highly developed resort, by no means all of the east is like this. Far fewer people venture beyond the road south to **Ierápetra** and into the eastern isthmus, where only **Sitía** and the famous beach at **Vái** ever see anything approaching a crowd. Inland, too, there's interest, especially on the extraordinary **Lasíthi** plateau, which is worth a night's stay if only to observe its abidingly rural life.

Inland to the Lasíthi plateau

Leaving the palace at Mália, the highway cuts inland towards **NEÁPOLI**, soon beginning a spectacular climb into the mountains. Set in a high valley, Neápoli is a market town little touched by tourism. There is one excellent **hotel** (*Neapolis*; ☎08410/33 966; ❷), some rooms, a modern church and a folk museum. Beyond the town, it's about twenty minutes before the bus suddenly emerges high above the Gulf of Mirabéllo and Áyios Nikólaos, the island's biggest resort. If you're stopping, Neápoli also marks the second point of access to the **Lasíthi Plateau**.

Scores of bus tours drive up here daily to view the "thousands of white-cloth-sailed windmills" which irrigate the high plain ringed by mountains, and most groups will be disappointed. There are very few working windmills left, and these operate only for limited periods (mainly in June), although most roadside tavernas seem to have adopted many of those made redundant as marketing features. This is not to say the trip is not justified, as it would be for the drive alone, and there are many other compensations. The plain is a fine example of rural Crete at work, every inch devoted to the cultivation of potatoes, apples, pears, figs, olives and a host of other crops; stay in one of the villages for a night or two and you'll see real life return as the tourists leave. There are plenty of easy rambles around the villages as well, through orchards and past the rusting remains of derelict windmills.

You'll find **rooms** in the main village of **TZERMIÁDHO**, where the *Hotel Kourites* (☎08440/22 194; ❷) is to be found on the eastern edge, **ÁYIOS**

YEÓRYIOS – where there's a **folk museum**, and the economical and friendly *Hotel Dias* (☎08440/31 207; ❶) – and **PSYKHRÓ**, where the *Hotel Zeus* (☎08440/31 284; ❷) lies close to the Dhiktean cave.

The Dhiktean cave

Psykhró is much the most visited village on the plateau, as it's the base for visiting Lasíthi's other chief attraction, the birthplace of Zeus, the **Dhiktean cave** (daily 8.30am–7pm, Oct–March closes at 3pm; €2.40). In legend, Zeus's father, the Titan Kronos, was warned that he would be overthrown by a son and accordingly ate all his offspring; however, when Rhea gave birth to Zeus in the cave, she fed Kronos a stone and left the child concealed, protected by the Kouretes, who beat their shields outside to disguise his cries. The rest, as they say, is history (or at least myth). There's an obvious path running up to the cave from Psykhró, near the start of which (beyond the car park) the mule handlers will attempt to persuade you the ascent is better done on one of their steeds (costing a hefty €6). In reality, it's hardly a particularly long or dauntingly steep hike to the cave entrance.

The cave has been made more "visitor friendly" in recent years which has introduced concrete steps in place of slippery stones, and electric lighting instead of flashlamps and candles. Inevitably some of the magic and mystery has been lost and the "guides", who used to make the visit much more interesting with their hilarious and preposterous tales, have now been banned, presumably in the interests of accuracy and decorum. Thus you will now have to pick out for yourself the stalactites and stalagmites formed in the image of the breasts of Rhea where the infant Zeus was suckled, as well as the baby Zeus himself – a feat verging on the impossible for someone lacking a Cretan imagination.

One of the cave guardians, Petros Zarvakis, is also a wildlife expert and leads **guided wild-flower and bird-spotting hikes** (April–Sept) into the mountains surrounding the plain, and also to the summit of Mount Dhíkti; if he is not on duty at the cave entrance, he can be contacted at his home in the village (☎08440/31 316 for details). **Buses** run around the plateau to Psykhró direct from Iráklion and from Áyios Nikólaos via Neápoli. Both roads offer spectacular views, coiling through a succession of passes guarded by lines of ruined windmills.

Áyios Nikólaos and around

ÁYIOS NIKÓLAOS ("Ag Nik" to the majority of its British visitors) is set around a supposedly bottomless **salt lake**, now connected to the sea to form an inner harbour. It is supremely picturesque and has some style and charm, which it exploits to the full. There are no sights as such but the excellent **archeological museum** (Tues–Sun 8.30am–3pm; €1.45) and an interesting **folk museum** (daily except Sat 10am–1.30pm & 7–9.30pm; €0.90) are both worth seeking out. The lake and port are surrounded by restaurants and bars, which charge above the odds, and whilst the resort is still very popular, some tourists are distinctly surprised to find themselves in a place with no decent beach at all.

There are swimming opportunities further north however, where the pleasant low-key resort of **Eloúnda** is the gateway to the mysterious islet of **Spinalónga**, and some great backcountry to the north – perfect to explore on a scooter. Inland from Áyios Nikólaos, **Kritsá** with its famous frescoed church and textile sellers is a tour-bus haven, but just a couple of kilometres away, the imposing ruins of **ancient Lató** are usually deserted.

Áyios Nikólaos practicalities

The **tourist office** (April–Oct daily 8am–9.30pm; ☎08410/22 357, ℉82 534), situated between the lake and the port, is one of the best on the island for information about accommodation. The greatest concentration of **stores** and **travel agents** are on the hill between the bridge and Platía Venizélou (along the streets 25-Martíou, Koundourou and 28-Oktovríou). The main **ferry agent** is Plora Travel (☎08410/26 465 or 23 090) on the corner of 28-Oktovríou and K. Sfakianáki. The **post office** (Mon–Sat 7.30am–2pm) is halfway up the newly pedestrianized 28-Oktovríou on the right. To **hire a motorbike**, **scooter** or **mountain bike** try the reliable Mike Manolis

ÁYIOS NIKÓLAOS

RESTAURANTS & BARS

Auoas	**A**
Café Migomis	**D**
I Pita Tou Ríga	**B**
Itanos	**F**
La Strada	**E**
Ofou To Lo	**G**
Pelagos	**C**
Sarris	**H**

Eloúnda

Iráklion

Archeological Museum

E. STAVROU

STRATIGOU KORITSAS

KORAKA

AKTI S. KOUNDOUROU

Ferry Dock

Tourist Police

PALEOLOGOU

THEOTOKOPOLOU

KORNAROU

SOLOMOU

Folk Museum

(i)

Bottomless Lake

OMIROU

AKTI I. KOUNDOUROU

LASTHENI

PASIFAIS

EVANS

ABIADHNIS

MILOU

PLASTIRA

28 OKTOVRIOU

KOUNDOUROU

M. SFAKIANAKI

ELEFTHERION

25 MARTIOU

ALEXOMANOLI

KITROPLATIA

PLATIA VENIZELOU

OTE

SFAKIANAKI

MODATSOU

Cathedral

KOSTI POLYTEKHNIOU

S. VENIZELOU

KYPROU

KONDOYIANNI

S. MERAMBELLOU

K. TAVLA

KOSIRI

AKTI ATLANTIDHOS

Bus Station

Town beach

Marina

Kritsá & the east

N

0   100 m

ACCOMMODATION

Atlantis	**8**
Eva	**4**
Green House	**6**
Marilena	**1**
Mediterranean	**3**
Rea	**2**
Rooms Mary	**5**
Sgouros	**7**

(℡08410/24 940), who has a pitch along Modatsou, just northeast of the OTE. Good **car rental** deals are available at Club Cars, 28-Oktovríou 24 (℡08410/25 868), near the post office. Various **boat trips** to points around the gulf (such as Spinalónga and Eloúnda; about €7.50) leave from the west side of the harbour. **Internet** cafés *Peripou*, 28-Oktovríou 25 (daily 9.30am–2am; €3 per hour), and *Café du Lac* at no. 17 on the same street are Áyios Nikólaos's most central places to pick up your emails.

Accommodation

The town is no longer packed solid with tourists, so it is much easier to find a place to stay, though in the peak season you won't have so much choice. One thing in your favour is that there are literally thousands of **rooms**, scattered all around town. The tourist office normally has a couple of boards with cards and brochures about hotels and rooms, including their prices. If the prices seem very reasonable it is because many are for the low season. There is no longer a youth hostel, and the nearest **campsite** is *Gournia Moon*, 17km away (see p.706).

Atlantis, Metamorfoseos, one block east of the bus station ℡08410/28 964. Nothing special but handy for early or late buses; there's a snack bar below for breakfast. ❶

Hotel Eva, Stratigoú Kóraka 20 ℡08410/22 587. Decent simple rooms in a misnamed pension close to the centre. ❶

Green House, Modhátsou 15 ℡08410/22 025. Probably the best cheap place to stay in town; clean with shared facilities. ❶

Marilena, Érythrou Stavroú 14 ℡08410/22 681, ℗24 218. Not the bargain it once was, but it's still a pleasant place to stay; some rooms with sea view and balcony. ❸

Rooms Mary, Evans 13 near the Kitroplatía ℡08410/24 384. Very friendly place with en-suite balcony rooms (some with sea view); access to fridge and use of kitchen. Also has some apartments nearby costing slightly more. ❶

Mediterranean, S. Dhávaki 27 ℡08410/23 611. Clean, economical rooms without bath close to the lake. ❶

Hotel Rea, Marathónos 1 ℡08410/82 023, ℗28 324. Charming older hotel with stunning views from pleasant balcony rooms overlooking the Mirabéllo Gulf. ❸

Sgouros, Kitroplatía ℡08410/28 931, ℗25 568. Modern hotel overlooking one of the town's beaches, and close to plenty of tavernas. ❷

Eating

At least when it comes to eating there's no chance of missing out, even if some of the prices are fancier than the restaurants. There are tourist-oriented **tavernas** all around the lake and harbour and little to choose between them, apart from the different perspectives you get on the passing fashion show. Have a drink here perhaps, or a mid-morning coffee, and choose somewhere else to eat. The places around the Kitroplatía are generally fairer value, but again you are paying for the location.

Auoas, Paleológou 44. This taverna serves good, traditional Cretan dishes in and under a plant-covered trellised courtyard, where food and wine prices are among the lowest in town.

Café Migomis, Nikoláou Plastíra 22. Pleasant café high above the bottomless lake with a stunning view. Perfect place for breakfast, afternoon or evening drinks.

I Pita Tou Ríga, Paleológou 24, close to the lake. Excellent Lilliputian snack-bar/restaurant serving imaginative fare – salads, filled pitta breads and some Asian dishes; has a small terrace.

Itanos, Kyprou 1, off the east side of Platía Venizélou. Popular with locals, this taverna serves

Cretan food and wine and has a terrace across the road opposite.

La Strada, Nikoláou Plastíra 5, just below the west side of Platía Venizélou. Authentic and good-value pizza and pasta (although the meat dishes are pricey), should you fancy a change of cuisine.

Ofou To Lo, Kitroplatía. Best of the moderately priced places on the seafront here: the food is consistently good.

Pelagos, on Stratigoú Kóraka, just back off the lake behind the tourist office. A stylish fish taverna with garden, serving excellent food reflected in the prices.

Sarri's, Kíprou 15, off the east side of Platía
Venizélou. Great little economical neighbourhood

café-diner especially good for breakfast fare and
souvláki, all served on a leafy terrace.

Drinking and nightlife

After you've eaten you can get into the one thing which Áyios Nikólaos undeniably does well: **bars and nightlife**. Not that you really need a guide to this
– the bars are hard to avoid, and you can just follow the crowds to the most
popular places centred around the harbour and 25-Martíou. For a more relaxed
drink you could try *Hotel Alexandros* on Paleológou (behind the tourist office),
with a rooftop cocktail bar overlooking the lake, which after dark metamorphoses into a 1960s to 1980s period music bar. A similar pace rules at *Zygos* on
the north side of the lake which serves low-priced cocktails and ices until the
small hours. One curiosity worth a look in the harbour itself is *Armida*, a bar
inside a beautifully restored century-old wooden trading vessel, serving cocktails and simple *mezédhes*.

Quiet drinking, however, is not what it's all about in the **disco bars**. *Lipstick*,
on the east side of the harbour is the only genuine full-blown dance club while
the nearby *Studio* doesn't hit its stride until the small hours when the pubs and
restaurants close. There are raucous music bars to try at the bottom of 25-
Martíou ("Soho Street") where it heads up the hill – *Rififi*, *Royale*, *Tounel* and
Sant Maria all get going at sunset; across the harbour *Aquarius*, *Charlie Chan*,
Lotus, *Cellar* and *Roxy* are also very popular and you'll soon be accosted by
their respective greeters as they each try to persuade you to help swell their
takings.

The coast north of Áyios Nikólaos

North of Áyios Nikólaos, the swankier hotels are strung out along the coast
road, with upmarket restaurants, discos and cocktail bars scattered between
them. **ELOÚNDA**, a resort on a more acceptable scale, is about 8km out along
this road. Buses run regularly, but if you feel like renting a scooter it's a spectacular ride, with impeccable views over a gulf dotted with islands and moored
supertankers. Ask at the bookshop near the post office, on the central square
facing the sea, about the attractive seaview *Delfinia Apartments* (☎08410/41
641, ℻41 515; ❶–❹). Or you could try the friendly *Pension Oasis* (☎08410/41
076, ℻41 128; ❷), which has rooms with kitchenette just off the square, behind
the church; there are quite a few similar places along the same road.
Alternatively, one of the many travel agents around the main square can help
with finding a room or apartment; try the friendly Olous Travel (☎08410/41
324, ℻41 132), which also gives out information and changes money or travellers' cheques. For **eating**, *Britomares*, in a plum spot in the centre of the harbour, is the town's best taverna, and more economical fish and *mezédhes* are to
be had at the simple *Ouzerí Manos*, last in line on the north side of the harbour. **Nightlife** tends to be generally low key, and centres around café terraces
and cocktail bars. The *Hellas* café, on a backroad behind the beach, has live
Greek music at weekends.

Just before the centre of the village, a road (signposted) leads downhill to a
natural causeway leading to the ancient "sunken city" of **Oloús**. There are
restored windmills, a short length of canal, Venetian salt pans and a well-preserved dolphin **mosaic**, inside a former Roman basilica, but of the sunken city
itself no trace beyond a couple of walls in about two feet of water. At any rate
swimming is good, though watch out for sea urchins.

From Eloúnda, kaïkia run half-hourly in high season (about €6 return) to the
fortress-rock of **Spinalónga**. As a bastion of the Venetian defence, this tiny islet

withstood the Turkish invaders for 45 years after the mainland had fallen; in more recent decades, it served as a leper colony. As you watch the boat which brought you disappear to pick up another group, an unnervingly real sense of the desolation of those years descends. **PLÁKA**, back on the mainland, and 5km north of Eloúnda, used to be the colony's supply point; now it is a haven from the crowds, with a small pebble beach and a couple of ramshackle fish **tavernas**, one of which, *Taverna Spinalonga*, can arrange a boat to take you across to Spinalónga for about €4.50. There are boat trips daily from Áyios Nikólaos to Oloús, Eloúnda and Spinalónga (costing around €7.50–9), usually visiting at least one other island along the way.

Inland to Kritsá and Lató

The other excursion everyone takes from Áyios Nikólaos is to **KRITSÁ**, a "traditional" village about 10km inland. Buses run at least every hour from the bus station, and despite the commercialization it's still a good trip: the local **crafts** (weaving, ceramics and embroidery basically, though they sell almost everything here) are fair value, and it's also a welcome break from living in the fast lane at "Ag Nik". In fact, if you're looking for somewhere to stay around here, Kritsá has a number of advantages: chiefly availability of **rooms**, better prices and something at least approaching a genuinely Cretan atmosphere; try *Argyro* (☎08410/51 174; ❶), with pleasant rooms around a courtyard on your way in to the village. The small platía at the centre of the village is the focus of life and there are a number of decent places to eat here, too: *Taverna-Snack Bar Tzortzis*, just uphill from the platía and bus stop, is a good bet, or *Sygonos*, near the bus stop, for a meal or coffee and cake under one of the plane trees.

On the approach road, some 2km before Kritsá, is the lovely Byzantine **church of Panayía Kyrá** (April–Oct daily 8.30am–2.30pm; €2.40), inside which survives perhaps the most complete set of Byzantine frescoes in Crete. The fourteenth- and fifteenth-century works have been much retouched, but they're still worth the visit. Excellent (and expensive) reproductions are sold from a shop alongside. Just beyond the church, a surfaced road leads off for 3km to the archeological site of **Lató** (Tues–Sun 9am–3pm; closed first Sun of the month; free), where the substantial remains of a Doric city are coupled with a grand hilltop setting. The city itself is extensive, but largely neglected, presumably because visitors and archeologists on Crete are more concerned with the Minoan era. Ruins aside, you could come here just for the views: west over Áyios Nikólaos and beyond to the bay and Oloús (which was Lató's port), and inland to the Lasíthi mountains.

The eastern isthmus

The main road south and then east from Áyios Nikólaos is not a wildly exciting one, essentially a drive through barren hills sprinkled with villas and skirting above the occasional sandy cove. Five kilometres beyond a cluster of development at Kaló Hório, a track is indicated on the right for the **Moní Faneroméni**. The track (though partly asphalted) is a rough one and climbs dizzily skywards for 6km, giving spectacular views over the Gulf of Mirabéllo along the way. The **view** from the monastery over the gulf must be among the finest in Crete. To get into the rather bleak-looking monastery buildings, knock loudly. You will be shown up to the chapel, built into a cave sanctuary, and the frescoes – although late – are quite brilliant.

Gourniá, Pahiá Ámmos and Mókhlos

Back on the coast road, it's another 2km to the site of **Gourniá** (Tues–Sun 8.30am–3pm; €1.45), slumped in the saddle between two low peaks. The most completely preserved **Minoan town**, its narrow alleys and stairways intersect a throng of one-roomed houses (of which only the ground-floor walls survive – they would have had at least one upper floor) centred on a main square, and the rather grand house of what may have been a local ruler or governor. Although less impressive than the great palaces, the site is strong on revelations about the lives of the ordinary people – many of the dwellings housed craftsmen in wood, metal and clay, who left behind their tools and materials to be found by the excavators. Its desolation today (you are likely to be alone save for a dozing guard) only serves to heighten the contrast with what must have been a cramped and raucous community 3500 years ago.

It is tempting to cross the road here and take one of the paths through the wild thyme to the sea for a swim. Don't bother – the bay and others along this part of the coastline act as a magnet for every piece of floating detritus dumped off Crete's north coast. There is a larger beach (though with similar problems), and rooms to rent, in the next bay along at **PAHIÁ ÁMMOS**, about twentyminutes' walk, where there is also an excellent fish taverna, *Aiolus*; in the other direction, there's the campsite of *Gournia Moon* (☎08420/93 243), with its own small cove and a swimming pool.

This is the narrowest part of the island, and from here a fast road cuts across the isthmus to Ierápetra (p.708) in the south. In the north though, the route on towards Sitía is one of the most exhilarating in Crete. Carved into cliffs and mountain-sides, the road teeters above the coast before plunging inland at Kavoúsi. Of the beaches you see below, only **MÓKHLOS** is at all accessible, some 5km below the main road. This sleepy seaside village has a few rooms, a hotel or two and a number of **tavernas** – *To Bogázi* is good – squatting along its tiny harbour; if you find yourself needing a **place to stay**, you could try the rooms at the clean and simple *Pension Hermes* (☎08430/97 074; ❶) behind the waterfront, which are the cheapest in the village, or there's *Hotel Sofia* (☎08430/94 738, ⑤94 238; ❷) on the harbour itself for a bit more en-suite luxury. Nearer Sitía the familiar olive groves are interspersed with vineyards used for creating wine and sultanas, and in late summer the grapes, spread to dry in the fields and on rooftops, make an extraordinary sight in the varying stages of their slow change from green to gold to brown.

Sitía

SITÍA is the port and main town of the relatively unexploited eastern edge of Crete. It's a pleasantly scenic if unremarkable place, offering a plethora of waterside restaurants, a long sandy beach and a lazy lifestyle little affected even by the thousands of visitors in peak season. There's an almost Latin feel to the town, reflected in (or perhaps caused by) the number of French and Italian tourists, and it's one of those places that tends to grow on you, perhaps inviting a longer stay than intended. For entertainment there's the **beach**, providing good swimming and windsurfing, and in town a mildly entertaining **folklore museum** (Mon–Sat 9.30am–5pm; €1.45), a Venetian fort and Roman fish tanks to explore, plus an excellent **archeological museum** (July & Aug daily 8.30am–3pm; Sept–June Tues–Sun same hours; €1.45). As part of a government push to increase tourism at this end of the island, a new **international airport** (due to open in 2004) is being constructed on a plateau above the town, and will most likely have a big impact on Sitía itself as well as the surrounding area.

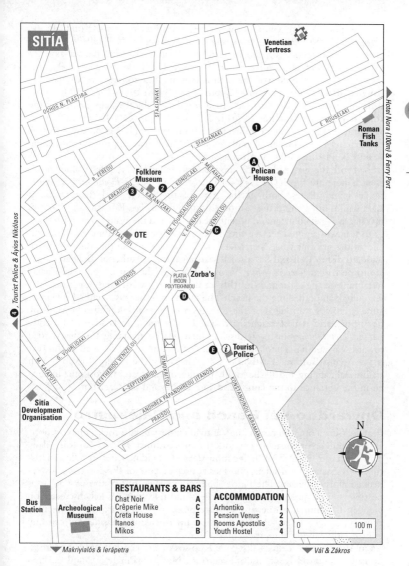

SITÍA

Venetian
Fortress

ODHOS N. PLASTIRA

SFAKIANAKI

I. SFAKIANAKI

❶

Hotel Nora (100m) & Ferry Port

E. ROUSELAKI

Roman
Fish
Tanks

R. TEREOU

Folklore
Museum

Ⓐ
Pelican
House

N. KAZANTZAKI

I. KONDILAKI

METAXAKI

EM. EGLINDALIDHOU

Ⓑ

V. KORNAROU

EL. VENIZELOU

Ⓒ

V. ARKADHIOU

❷

KAPETAN SIFI

❸

OTE

MYSONOS

PLATIA
IROON
POLYTEKHNIOU

Zorba's

Ⓓ

4, Tourist Police & Áyios Nikólaos

Sitía
Development
Organisation

G. VOURLIDAKI

ELEFTHERIOU VENIZELOU

4-SEPTEMVRIOU

ANDHREA PAPANDHREOU (ITANOS)

PRAISOU

DIMOKRITOU

Ⓔ

i Tourist
Police

KONSTANDINOU KARAMANLI

M. KATAPOTI

N

Bus
Station

Archeological
Museum

RESTAURANTS & BARS
Chat Noir   A
Crêperie Mike   C
Creta House   E
Itanos   D
Mikos   B

ACCOMMODATION
Arhontiko   1
Pension Venus   2
Rooms Apostolis   3
Youth Hostel   4

0   100 m

▼ Makriyialós & Ierápetra

▼ Váï & Zákros

Practicalities

The bus drops you at the new **bus station** (actually an office on the street) on the southwest fringe of the centre and close to the town's main **supermarket**, useful for stocking up on provisions. There are plenty of cheap pensions and **rooms** within easy walking distance, especially in the streets around the folklore museum and beyond here towards the ferry port. A good and friendly **youth hostel** (☏08430/22 693; dorm beds €4.40, rooms ❶) on the main road as it enters town from Áyios Nikólaos also has a few private rooms and a garden for tents; there's rarely any problem about sleeping on the beach (though it is worth going a little way out of town to avoid any danger of being roused by the police). For economical rooms, try *Pension Venus*, Kondiláki 60 (℡08430/24 307; **❶**), or *Hotel Arhontiko*, Kondiláki 16 (℡08430/28 172; **❶**); en-suite accommodation is available at *Rooms Apostolis*, Kazantzákis 27 (℡08430/22 993; **❷**), and *Hotel Nora*, Rouseláki 31 (℡08430/23 017; **❷**), near the ferry port. Should you have problems finding somewhere to stay, the **tourist office** (Mon–Fri 9am–2.30pm & 5–8.30pm; ℡08430/23 300) on the seafront at the start of the beach road should be able to help, or there's the **tourist police** at Mysónos 24 (daily 7.30am–2.30pm; ℡08430/24 200), who also provide limited tourist information; both can supply a good town map. A colourful weekly **market** takes place on Tuesdays between 7am and 2pm along Odhós N. Plastira to the northwest of the centre.

For **food**, the waterside places are relatively expensive; the best-value choices near here are the *Itanos Cafe* for mezédhes and *Creta House* serving traditional island dishes, both at the start of the beach road (Konstandínou Karamanlí). Just behind the seafront the popular *Mikos*, Kornárou 117, serves up charcoal-grilled meat and potent local wine, and the waiters run with dishes to a newly aquired terrace fifty metres away on the seafront. At the north end of the seafront *Chat Noir*, Metaxaki 2, is a new arrival that does the usual standard dishes well and has a small seafront terrace. Authentic Belgian crepes are to be had at *Creperie Mike*, Venizélou 162, to the east of the focal *Zorba's* restaurant on the seafront. **Nightlife** centres on a few bars and discos near the ferry dock and out along the beach. The town's monster disco-club, *Planitarion*, attracts crowds from all over the east. It's a couple of kilometres beyond the ferry port, and is best reached by taxi. The in-town alternative is the aptly named *Hot Summer* open-air disco, which lies 800m along the beach road towards Váï, and has a pool and gardens. The one major excitement of the year is the August **Sultana Festival** – a celebration of the big local export, with traditional dancing and all the locally produced wine you can consume included in the entrance to the fairground, located beyond the ferry port.

Onward to Váï Beach and Palékastro

Leaving Sitía along the beach, the Váï road climbs above a rocky, unexceptional coastline before reaching a fork to the **monastery of Toploú** (daily 9am–1pm & 2–6pm; €2.40). The monastery's forbidding exterior reflects a history of resistance to invaders, but doesn't prepare you for the gorgeous flower-decked cloister within. The blue-robed monks keep out of the way as far as possible, but in quieter periods their cells and refectory are left discreetly on view. In the church is one of the masterpieces of Cretan art, the eighteenth-century icon *Lord Thou Art Great* by Ioánnis Kornáros. Outside you can buy enormously expensive reproductions.

Váï Beach itself features alongside Knossós or the Lasíthi plateau on almost every Cretan travel agent's list of excursions. Not surprisingly, it is now covered in sunbeds and umbrellas, though it is still a superb beach. Above all, it is famous for its palm trees, and the sudden appearance of the grove is indeed an exotic shock; lying on the fine sand in the early morning, the illusion is of a Caribbean island – a feature seized upon by countless TV-commercial makers seeking an exotic location on the cheap. As everywhere, notices warn that "camping is forbidden by law", and for once the authorities seem to mean it – most campers climb over the headlands to the south or north. If you do sleep out, watch your belongings, since this seems to be the one place on Crete with crime on any scale. There's a compulsory car park (€1.75), a café and an expensive taverna at the beach, plus toilets and showers. Because of its status as a nature reserve there is **no accommodation** here whatsoever; the nearest place offering a bed for the night is Palékastro (see below). By day you can find a bit more solitude by climbing the rocks or swimming to one of the smaller beaches which surround Váï. **Ítanos**, twenty-minutes' walk north by an obvious trail, has a couple of tiny beaches and some modest ruins from the Classical era.

PALÉKASTRO, an attractive farming village some 9km south, makes a good place to stopover. Although its beaches can't begin to compare with those at Váï, you'll find several modest places with **rooms** – among them *Hotel Hellas* (☏08430/61 240, 🖷61 340, ✉hellas_h@otenet.gr; ❷), which offers en-suite facilities and food, and the good-value *Vai* (☏08430/61 287; ❶), with rooms above a taverna at the west end of the village, on the Sitía road. The extensive **beaches** provide plenty of space to **camp** out without the crowds, but you should respect local sensitivities, keeping away from the main strands and responsibly disposing of any rubbish. Add in a small **folk museum** (May–Oct Tues–Sun 8.30am–1pm; free), a number of reasonable **tavernas**, a few **bars** and even a **dance-club**, *Design*, and the place begins to seem positively throbbing. The sea is a couple of kilometres down a dirt track, effortlessly reached with a scooter hired from Motor Action (☏08430/61 276) next door to the *Hotel Hellas*. Palékastro is also the crossroads for the road south to Zákros and your own transport presents all kinds of beach and exploration possibilities.

Zákros

ÁNO ZÁKROS (Upper Zákros) lies a little under 20km from Palékastro. There are several tavernas and a simple hotel, the *Zakros* (☏08430/43 379, 🖷93 379; ❶), which has some rooms with bath and great views from its rear rooms; it also offers guests a free minibus service to the Minoan palace and beach. The Minoan palace is actually at Káto ("lower") Zákros, 8km further down towards the sea. Most buses run only to the upper village, but in summer, a couple every day do run all the way to the site. Part way along you can, if on foot, take a short cut through an impressive **gorge** (the "Valley of the Dead", named for ancient tombs in its sides) but it's usually not difficult to hitch if your bus does leave you in the village.

The **Palace of Zákros** (Tues–Sun: April–Sept 8am–7pm; Oct–March 8am–3pm; €1.45) was an important find for archeologists; it had been occupied only once (between 1600 and 1450 BC), and was abandoned hurriedly and completely. Later, it was forgotten almost entirely and as a result was never plundered or even discovered by archeologists until very recently. The first major excavation began only in 1960; all sorts of everyday objects (tools, raw materials, food, pottery) were thus discovered intact among the ruins, and a great deal was learned from being able to apply modern techniques (and knowledge of the Minoans) to a major dig from the very beginning. None of this is especially evident when you're at the palace, except perhaps in a particularly simple ground plan, so it's as well that it is also a rewarding visit in terms of the setting. Although the site is set back from the sea, in places it is often marshy and waterlogged – partly the result of eastern Crete's slow subsidence, partly the fault of a spring which once supplied fresh water to a cistern beside the royal apartments, and whose outflow is now silted up. In wetter periods, among the remains of narrow streets and small houses of the town outside the palace and higher up, you can keep your feet dry and get an excellent view down over the central court and royal apartments. If you want a more detailed overview of the remains, buy the guide to the site on sale at the entrance.

The delightful village of **KÁTO ZÁKROS** is little more than a collection of tavernas, some of which rent out rooms around a peaceful beach and minuscule fishing anchorage. It's a wonderfully restful place, but is often unable to cope with the volume of visitors seeking accommodation in high season, and as rooms are rarely to be had on spec you'd be wise to ring ahead. You should also be aware that villagers are far more hostile these days to wild camping after years of problems, and you should be sensitive to their concerns. Reliable rooms can be found at *Poseidon* (☎08430/93 316; ●), which has fine sea views, and the friendly *George Villas* (☎ & ⓕ 08430/93 201; ❷), 600m behind the archeological site along a driveable track. Otherwise ask at the seafront *Poseidon* (☎08430/26 896) taverna which seems to act as an agent for many other room options.

Ierápetra and the southeast coast

From Sitía, the route south is a cross-country roller-coaster ride until it hits the south coast at **MAKRYIALÓS**. This little fishing village has one of the best beaches at this end of Crete, with fine sand which shelves so gently you feel you could walk the 320km to Africa. Unfortunately, since the early 1990s it has been heavily developed, so while still a very pleasant place to stop for a swim or a bite (the outstanding *Porfíra* taverna on the sea is recommended), it's not somewhere you're likely to find cheap **rooms**. Outside of peak season you could try *Irini Rooms* (☎08430/51 422; ❷), on the main road through the village near where the bus drops you.

From here to Ierápetra there's little reason to stop; the few beaches are rocky and the coastal plain submerged under ranks of polythene-covered greenhouses. Beside the road leading into Ierápetra are long but exposed stretches of sand, including the appropriately named "Long Beach", where you'll find a **campsite**, *Camping Koutsounari* (☎08420/61 213), which offers plenty of shade and has a taverna and minimarket.

Ierápetra

IERÁPETRA itself is a bustling modern supply centre for the region's farmers. It also attracts a fair number of package tourists and not a few backpackers looking for work in the prosperous surrounding agricultural zone, especially out of season. The tavernas along the tree-lined seafront are scenic enough and the EU blue-flagged beach stretches a couple miles east. But as a town, most people find it pretty uninspiring, despite an ongoing modernization programme which has cleaned up the centre and revamped the seafront. Although there has been a port here since Roman times, only the **Venetian fort** guarding the harbour and a crumbling Turkish minaret remain as reminders of better days. What little else has been salvaged from the one-room **Archeological Museum** (Tues–Sat 8am–3pm; €1.50) near the post office.

The town hall (*dhimarhío*) on the main square Platía Kanoupáki, or the library next door, should be able to provide a copy of the detailed town map (but not much else) which will help you find your way around. If you want to stay, head up Kazantzákis from the chaotic bus station, and you'll find a friendly welcome and good-value apartment-style **rooms** at *Rooms Popi* at no. 27 (☎08420/24 289; ●), or equal comfort in the nearby *Cretan Villa*, Lakérdha 16 (☎ & ⓕ 08420/28 522, ⓦ www.cretan-villa.com; ❷), a beautiful 180-year-old house. More central and economical is the *Hotel Ersi*, Platía Eleftherías 20

(☎08420/23 208;❶), which will also rent you a seafront apartment nearby for not much more than the cost of a room. The cheapest rooms option is *Rent Rooms Nikos*, Ioannidou 4, in the old town (☎08420/23 208;❶), close to the *Gorgona* taverna. You'll find places to **eat** and **drink** all along the waterfront, the better places such as *Taverna Napoleon* and *Gorgona* being towards the Venetian fort. **Nightlife** centres on a clutch of **clubs**, **bars** and fast-food places along central Kyrba, behind the promenade. Ierápetra's **internet café**, *Orfeas* (€3 per 30min), is at Koundourioútou 25, just north of the museum, and serves good breakfasts.

West from Ierápetra

Heading west from Ierápetra, the first stretch of coast is grey and dusty, the road jammed with trucks and lined with drab ribbon development. There are a number of small resorts along the beach, though little in the way of public transport. If travelling under your own steam, there is a scenic detour worth taking at Gría Liyiá: the road on the right for Anatolí climbs to Máles, a village clinging to the lower slopes of the **Dhíkti range**. Here would be a good starting point for **walking** through some stunning mountain terrain (the E4 Pan-European footpath which crosses the island from east to west passes just 3km north of here). Otherwise, the dirt road back down towards the coast (signposted Míthi) has spectacular views over the Libyan Sea, and eventually follows the Mírtos river valley down to Mírtos itself.

Mírtos and Árvi

MÍRTOS, 18km west of Ierápetra, is the first resort that might actually tempt you to stop, and it's certainly the most accessible, just off the main road with numerous daily **buses** to Ierápetra and a couple direct to Iráklion. Although developed to a degree, it nonetheless remains tranquil and inexpensive, with lots of young travellers (many of whom often sleep on the beach, to the irritation of locals). There are plenty of **rooms** possibilities, amongst which you could try the central *Rooms Angelos* (☎08420/51 106; ❷) and *Nikos House* (☎08420/51 116;❶), or the less expensive *Rooms Despina* (☎08420/51 343; ❶) at the back of the village near the bus stop. A useful travel agent, Magic Tours (☎08420/25 135, ☏28 809) on the central main street is a good source of **information**, **changes money**, rents **cars** and sells boat and plane tickets. Just off the road from Ierápetra a couple of kilometres east of the village (and signed) are a couple of excavated hilltop **Minoan villas** you might want to explore: Néa Mírtos and Pírgos.

After Mírtos the main road turns inland towards Áno Viánnos, then continues across the island towards Iráklion; several places on the coast are reached by a series of rough side-tracks. That hasn't prevented one of them, **ÁRVI**, from becoming a larger resort than Mírtos. The beach hardly justifies it, but it's an interesting little excursion (with at least one bus a day) if only to see the bananas and pineapples grown here and to experience the microclimate – noticeably warmer than neighbouring zones, especially in spring or autumn – that encourages them. For rooms you could try the central *Pension Gorgona* (☎08950/71 211;❶).

Beyond Árvi

Two more villages, Keratókambos and Tsoútsouros, look tempting on the map. **KERATÓKAMBOS** has a rather stony beach and a range of **rooms**, not easy to come by in August. Try the *Morning Star* taverna (☎08950/51 209; ❶) which has rooms with and without bath, or the comparable *Taverna Kriti*

(☎08950/51 231; ➊) next door; the **food** at both places is tasty too. Although popular with Cretan day-trippers, Keratókambos is a great place to escape the tourist grind for a spell.

TSOÚTSOUROS, 10km west as the crow flies and now linked by an asphalted road to the major highway further north, is similar to its neighbour with a line of tavernas, hotels and rooms places arching behind a seafront, to the east and west of which are a couple of decent if pebbly, grey-sand **beaches**. Not as popular as its neighbours, **rooms** may be available here when the other resorts are full. Try *Rooms Mihalis* (☎08910/92 250; ➊) near the centre of the seafront. There are no facilities for changing money at either place, although both have a couple of **supermarkets**, handy for gathering picnic ingredients.

If you hope to continue across the **south** of the island, be warned that there are no buses, despite completion of the road towards Míres after years of work. It's an enjoyable rural drive, but progress can be slow; there's very little traffic if you're trying to hitch.

Réthymnon and around

The relatively low, narrow section of Crete which separates the Psilorítis range from the White Mountains in the west seems at first a nondescript, even dull part of the island. Certainly in scenic terms it has few of the excitements that the west can offer; there are no major archeological sites and many of the villages seem modern and ugly. On the other hand, **Réthymnon** itself is an attractive and lively city, with some excellent beaches nearby. And on the south coast, in particular around **Plakiás**, there are beaches as fine as any Crete can offer, and as you drive towards them the scenery and villages improve by the minute.

Réthymnon

Since the early 1980s, **RÉTHYMNON** has seen a greater influx of tourists than perhaps anywhere else on Crete, with the development of a whole series of large hotels extending almost 10km along the beach to the east. For once, though, the middle of town has been spared, so that at its heart Réthymnon remains one of the most beautiful of Crete's major cities (only Haniá is a serious rival) with an enduringly provincial air. A wide sandy beach and palm-lined promenade border a labyrinthine tangle of Venetian and Turkish houses lining streets where ancient minarets lend an exotic air to the skyline. Dominating everything from the west is the superbly preserved outline of the **fortress** built by the Venetians after a series of pirate raids had devastated the town.

The town

With a **beach** right in the heart of town, it's tempting not to stir at all from the sands, but Réthymnon repays at least some gentle exploration. For a start, you could try checking out the further reaches of the beach itself. The waters protected by the breakwaters in front of town have their disadvantages – notably crowds and dubious hygiene – but less sheltered sands stretch for miles to the east, crowded at first but progressively less so if you're prepared to walk a bit.

Away from the beach, you don't have far to go for the most atmospheric part of town, immediately behind the **inner harbour**. Almost anywhere here, you'll find unexpected old buildings, wall fountains, overhanging wooden balconies, heavy, carved doors and rickety shops, many still with local craftsmen sitting out front, gossiping as they ply their trades. Look out especially for the **Venetian loggia**, which houses a shop selling high quality and expensive reproductions of Classical art; the **Rimóndi fountain**, another of the more elegant Venetian survivals; and the **Nerandzés mosque**, the best preserved in

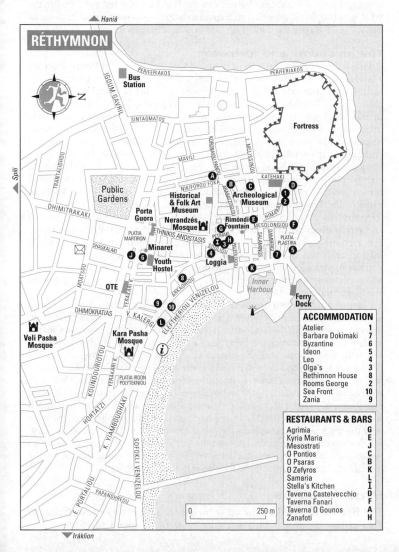

RÉTHYMNON

Haniá
Spíli
Iráklion

Bus Station
Fortress
Public Gardens
Porta Guora
Historical & Folk Art Museum
Archeological Museum
Nerandzés Mosque
Rimóndi Fountain
Minaret
Youth Hostel
Loggia
OTE
Inner Harbour
Ferry Dock
Veli Pasha Mosque
Kara Pasha Mosque

ACCOMMODATION

Atelier	1
Barbara Dokimaki	7
Byzantine	6
Ideon	5
Leo	4
Olga's	3
Rethimnon House	8
Rooms George	2
Sea Front	10
Zania	9

RESTAURANTS & BARS

Agrimia	G
Kyria Maria	E
Mesostrati	J
O Pontios	C
O Psaras	B
O Zefyros	K
Samaria	L
Stella's Kitchen	I
Taverna Castelvecchio	D
Taverna Fanari	F
Taverna O Gounos	A
Zanafoti	H

0   250 m

Réthymnon but currently serving as a music school and closed to the public. When repairs are completed it should again be possible to climb the spiral staircase to the top of the **minaret** for a stunning view over the town. Simply by walking past these three, you'll have seen many of the liveliest parts of Réthymnon. Ethnikís Andistásis, the street leading straight up from the fountain, is also the town's **market** area.

The old city ends at the Porta Guora at the top of Ethnikís Andistásis, the only surviving remnant of the city walls. Almost opposite are the quiet and shady **public gardens**. These are always a soothing place to stroll, and in the latter half of July the **Réthymnon Wine Festival** is staged here. Though touristy, it's a thoroughly enjoyable event, with spectacular local dancing as the evening progresses and the barrels empty. The entrance fee includes all the wine you can drink, though you'll need to bring your own cup or buy one of the souvenir glasses and carafes on sale outside the gardens.

The museums and fortress

A little further up the street from the Nerandzés mosque at M.Vernárdhou 28, a beautifully restored seventeenth-century Venetian mansion is the home of the small but tremendously enjoyable **Historical and Folk Art Museum** (Mon–Fri 9.30am–2pm; €2.95, children and students €1.45). Gathered within four, cool, airy rooms are musical instruments, old photos, basketry, farm implements, an explanation of traditional ceramic and breadmaking techniques, smiths' tools, traditional costumes and jewellery, lace, weaving and embroidery (look out for a traditional-style tapestry made in 1941 depicting German parachutists landing at Máleme), pottery, knives and old wooden chests. It makes for a fascinating insight into a fast disappearing rural (and urban) lifestyle, which had often survived virtually unchanged from Venetian times to the 1960s, and is well worth a look.

Heading in the other direction from the fountain you'll come to the fortress and **Archeological Museum** (Tues–Sun 8.30am–3pm; €1.40), which occupies a building almost directly opposite the entrance to the fortress. This was built by the Turks as an extra defence, and later served as a prison, but it's now entirely modern inside: cool, spacious and airy. Unfortunately, the collection is not particularly exciting, and really only worth seeing if you're going to miss the bigger museums elsewhere on the island.

The massive **Venetian fortress** (Tues–Sun 8am–7pm; reduced hours out of season; €2.40) is a must, however. Said to be the largest Venetian castle ever built, this was a response, in the last quarter of the sixteenth century, to a series of **pirate raids** (by Barbarossa among others) that had devastated the town. Inside is now a vast open space dotted with the remains of all sorts of barracks, arsenals, officers' houses, earthworks and deep shafts, and at the centre a large domed building that was once a church and later a **mosque** (complete with a surviving but sadly defaced *mihrab*). It was designed to be large enough for the entire population to take shelter within the walls, and you can see that it probably was. Although much is ruined, it remains thoroughly atmospheric, and you can look out from the walls over the town and harbour, or in the other direction along the coast to the west. It's also worth walking around the outside of the fortress, preferably at sunset, to get an impression of its fearsome defences, plus great views along the coast and a pleasant resting point around the far side at the *Sunset* taverna.

Practicalities

The **bus station** in Réthymnon is by the sea to the west of town just off Periferiakós, the road which skirts the waterfront around the fortress. The

tourist office (April–Sept Mon–Fri 8am–7pm; ☎08310/56 350) backs onto the main town beach, close to the mobile **post office** (summer only). If you arrive by **ferry**, you'll be more conveniently placed, over at the western edge of the harbour. To access the **internet** and pick up emails head for the *Galero Internet Café* (€4.50 per hr), beside the Rimóndi fountain in the old town or *Café-Bar Internet*, Platía Martiron 4, near the Porta Guora on the south edge of the old town (€1.20 per 15min) or – between the two – User Computer Shop, Ethnikis Andistaseos 83, has similar rates.

Accommodation

There's a great number of places to stay in Réthymnon, and only at the height of the season are you likely to have difficulty finding somewhere, though you may get weary looking. The greatest concentration of **rooms** is in the tangled streets west of the inner harbour, between the Rimóndi fountain and the museums; there are also quite a few places on and around Arkadhíou and Platía Frakidháki.

The nearest **campsite**, *Camping Elizabeth* (☎08310/28 694), lies 4km east of town; take the bus for the hotels (marked *Scaleta/El Greco*) from the long-distance bus station to get there. It's a pleasant, large site on the beach, with all facilities.

Atelier, Himáras 32 ☎08310/24 440. Pleasant rooms close to *Rooms George*, run by a talented potter, who has her studio in the basement and sells her wares in a shop on the other side of the building. ❷

Barbara Dokimaki, Platía Plastíra 14 ☎08310/22 319, ⓕ24 581. Strange warren of a rooms place, with one entrance at the above address, just off the seafront behind the *Ideon*, and another on Dambérgi; ask for the newly refurbished top-floor studio rooms, which have balconies and kitchenette. ❷

Byzantine, Vospórou 26 ☎08310/55 609. Excellent-value rooms in a renovated Byzantine palace. The tranquil patio bar is open to all, and breakfast is included in price. ❷

Rooms George, Makedhonías 32 ☎08310/50 965. Decent en-suite rooms (some with fridge), near the Archeological Museum. ❷

Ideon, Platía Plastíra 10 ☎08310/28 667, ⓕ28 670. High-class hotel with a brilliant position just north of the ferry dock; little chance of space in season, though. ❺

Leo, Vafé 2 ☎08310/26 197. Good hotel with lots of wood and a traditional feel; the price includes breakfast, and there's a bar. ❷

Olga's Pension, Soulíou 57 ☎08310/54 896, ⓕ29 851. The star attraction at this very friendly pension on one of Réthymnon's most touristy streets is the resplendent flower-filled roof garden. ❶

Rethimnon House, V. Kornárou 1 ☎08310/23 923. Very pleasant rooms of a high standard in an old building just off Arkadhíou. Bar downstairs. ❷

Sea Front, Arkádhiou 159 ☎08310/51 981, ⓕ51 062, ⓔelotia@ret.forthnet.gr. Rooms with sea views and balconies in an attractively refurbished mansion with ceiling fans and lots of wood. ❷

Youth hostel, Tombázi 41 ☎08310/22 848. The cheapest beds (€4.50) in town. Large, clean, and very friendly and popular, it has food, showers, clothes-washing facilities and a multilingual library.

Zania, Pávlou Vlástou 3 ☎08310/28 169. Pension right on the corner of Arkadhíou; a well-adapted old house, but only a few rooms. ❶

Eating and drinking

Immediately behind the town beach are arrayed the most touristy **restaurants**, the vast majority being overpriced and of dubious quality. One that maintains some integrity (and reasonable prices) is the *Samaria* taverna, almost opposite the tourist office. Around the inner **harbour** there's a second, rather more expensive, group of tavernas, specializing in fish, though as often as not the intimate atmosphere in these places is spoiled by the stench from the harbour itself; *O Zefyros* is one of the less outrageously pricey and maintains reasonable standards. Not far from here and slightly west of Platía Plastíra, *Taverna Fanari* at Makedhonías 5 is a good-value little restaurant serving up tasty lamb and chicken dishes. Another good option in this zone is *Taverna Castelvecchio*, Himáras 29, a long-established family taverna next to the fortress which has a pleasant terrace with view over the town and offers some vegetarian choices.

The cluster of kafenía and tavernas by the **Rimóndi fountain** and the newer places spreading into the surrounding streets generally offer considerably better value than the inner harbour, and a couple of the old-fashioned kafenía serve magnificent yogurt and honey. Places to try include *Kyria Maria* at Moskhovítou 20, tucked down an alley behind the fountain (after the meal, everyone gets a couple of María's delicious *tyropitákia* with honey on the house); *Agrimia*, a reliable standard on Platía Petiháki, slightly east of the fountain; and the *Zanfoti* kafenío overlooking the fountain which is relatively expensive, but a great place to people-watch over a coffee; and for a slightly cheaper option *O Psaras* (The Fisherman), a simple, friendly taverna by the church on the corner of Nikifórou Foká and Koronéou. A good lunchtime stop close to the Archeological Museum is *O Pontios*, Melissinoú 34, a simple place with tables outside and an enthusiastic female proprietor. Healthy, home-baked lunches can also be had at *Stella's Kitchen*, a simple café linked to *Olga's Pension* at Soulíou 55, where meals can be enjoyed up on the leafy roof garden. Tucked behind the church on Platía Martíron, *Mesostrati* is a pleasant little neighbourhood ouzerí/taverna serving well-prepared Cretan country dishes and has a small terrace. A noisier evening alternative is *Taverna O Gounos*, Koronéou 6 in the old town; the family who run it perform live *lyra* every night, and when things get really lively the dancing starts.

If you want takeaway food, there are numerous **souvláki** stalls, including a couple on Arkadhíou and Paleológou and another at Petikháki 52, or you can buy your own ingredients at the **market** stalls set up daily on Ethnikís Andistásis below the Porta Guora. There are small general stores scattered everywhere, particularly on Paleológou and Arkadhíou; east along the beach road you'll even find a couple of mini supermarkets. The **bakery** I Gaspari on Mesolongíou, just behind the Rimóndi fountain, sells the usual cheese pies, cakes and the like, and it also bakes excellent brown, black and rye bread. There's a good *zaharoplastío*, *N.A. Skartsilakos*, at Paleológou 36, just north of the fountain, and several more small cafés which are good for breakfast or a quick coffee.

Nightlife

Nightlife is concentrated in the same general areas as the tavernas. At the west end of Venizélou, in the streets behind the inner harbour, the overflow from a small cluster of noisy music bars – *Venetsianako*, *Dimman* and *Xtreme* – begins to spill out onto the pavement as partygoers gather for the nightly opening of the *Fortezza Disco* in the inner harbour itself, which is the glitziest in town, flanked by its competitors *Metropolis*, *NYC*, *Nitro* and the nearby *Opera Club* a little way down Salamínos. Heading up this street, a string of more subdued cocktail bars – *Petaloúda*, *Memphis*, *Santan* and *Pasodia* – cater for those in search of a quieter drink, as does *Notas*, at Himeras 27 near the *Fortezza* and facing the *Atelier* pension, which puts on live (acoustic) guitar and song every night. A new bar scene popular with the local student community has recently taken root around Platía Plastira, above the inner harbour, where music bars include *Karma*, *Art*, *Da Cappo* and *Enzzo*, all with expansive terraces.

Around Réthymnon

While some of Crete's most drastic resort development spreads ever eastwards out of Réthymnon, to the west a sandy coastline, not yet greatly exploited, runs all the way to the borders of Haniá province. But of all the short trips that can be made out of Réthymnon, the best known and still the most worthwhile is to the **monastery of Arkádhi**.

Southeast to Arkádhi

The **monastery of Arkádhi** (daily 8am–1.30pm & 3.30–8pm; entry to museum €1.45), some 25km southeast of the city and immaculately situated in the foothills of the Psilorítis range, is also something of a national Cretan shrine. During the 1866 rebellion against the Turks, the monastery became a rebel strongpoint in which, as the Turks gained the upper hand, hundreds of Cretan independence fighters and their families took refuge. Surrounded and, after two days of fighting, on the point of defeat, the defenders ignited a powder magazine just as the Turks entered. Hundreds (some sources claim thousands) were killed, Cretan and Turk alike, and the tragedy did much to promote international sympathy for the cause of Cretan independence. Nowadays, you can peer into the roofless vault where the explosion occurred and wander about the rest of the well-restored grounds. Outside the entrance a modern monument displays the skulls of many of the victims. The sixteenth-century **church** survived, and is one of the finest Venetian structures left on Crete; other buildings house a small **museum** devoted to the exploits of the defenders of the (Orthodox) faith. The monastery is easy to visit by public bus or on a tour.

West to Aryiroúpolis, Yeoryoúpoli and beyond

Leaving Réthymnon to the west, the main road climbs for a while above a rocky coastline before descending (after some 5km) to the sea, where it runs alongside sandy **beaches** for perhaps another 7km. An occasional hotel offers accommodation, but on the whole there's nothing but a line of straggly bushes between the road and the windswept sands. If you have your own vehicle, there are plenty of places you can stop at here for a swim, and rarely anyone else around – but beware of some very strong currents.

One worthwhile detour inland is to **ARYIROÚPOLIS**, a charming village perched above the Mousselás river valley and the seat of ancient Lappa, a Greek and Roman town of some repute. The village is famous for its **springs** which gush dramatically from the hillside and provide most of the city of Réthymnon's water supply. Among a number of **places to stay** try *Rooms Argiroupolis* (☎08310/81 148, ℗81 149; ❷), near the springs, or *Rooms Zografakis* (08310/81 269; ❶) and *Agnantema* (☎08310/81 172; ❶) in the upper village. For **places to eat**, you're spoilt for choice, with five tavernas at the springs and a bar (serving tasty mezédhes) in the upper village together with tavernas at the *Zografakis* and *Agnantema* rooms places, the latter enjoying a spectacular terrace view down the river valley. A shop under the arch in the main square, named Lappa Avocado and selling local products of the region including olive oil and avocado-based skin products, can provide a free **map** detailing a surprising number of churches, caves and ancient remains to see in and around the village, including an outstanding third-century **Roman mosaic**. An interesting **folklore museum** (daily 10am–7pm; free) – signed from the main square – is worth a look for its collection of tapestries, farm implements, photos and ephemera collected by the Zografakis family who have lived here for countless generations. There are numerous fine **walks** to be had in the surrounding hills, on which the proprietor of the Lappa Avocado shop, who speaks English, will advise. Although little over 20km from Réthymnon and easy to get to with your own transport, Aryiroúpolis is also served by **buses** from Réthymnon's bus station (Mon–Fri only) at 11.30am and 2.30pm, and in the reverse direction at 7.30am, 12.30pm and a late afternoon service at 4.45pm (May–Oct) or 3.30pm (rest of year).

Back on the coastal route, if you are looking for a place to relax for a while, probably the best base is **YEORYOÚPOLI** just across the provincial border in Haniá, where the beach is cleaner, wider and further from the road. There's been a distinct acceleration in the pace of development at Yeoryoúpoli over the last few years and it's now very much a resort, packed with rooms to rent, small hotels, apartment buildings, tavernas and travel agencies; there's even a small land train to transport visitors along the seafront and on short excursions. But everything remains on a small scale, and the undeniably attractive setting is untarnished, making it a very pleasant place to pass a few days, as long as you don't expect to find many vestiges of traditional Crete. Most of the better rooms, including *Rent Rooms Stelios* (☎08250/61 308; ❷), *Irene* (☎08250/61 278; ❷) and *Cretan Cactus* (☎08250/61 027; ❶), are away from the main platía along the road down towards the beach. More central possibilities include *Rooms Voula* (☎08250/61 359; ❶) above a gift shop to the east of the platía and the *Paradise Taverna* (☎08250/61 313; ❷) off the southeast corner of the platía, which has rooms and is a good place to eat.

Within walking distance inland – though it can also be visited on the tourist train from Yeoryoúpoli – is **Kournás**, Crete's only freshwater lake, set deep in a bowl of hills and almost constantly changing colour. There are a few tavernas with rooms to rent along the shore here (bring mosquito repellent), or you could try for a bed in the nearby hill village of **MATHÉS** where the *Villa Kapasa* (☎08250/61 050; ❷) has some very pleasant en-suite rooms around a garden. *Taverna Mathes*, the village taverna has great terrace views and good food. A few kilometres uphill from the lake in **KOURNÁS** village, the *Kali Kardia* taverna is another great place to sample the local lamb and sausages.

Beyond Yeoryoúpoli, the main road heads inland, away from a cluster of coastal villages beyond Vámos. It thus misses the Dhrápano peninsula, the setting for the film of *Zorba the Greek*, with some spectacular views over the sapphire Bay of Soúdha and several quiet beaches. **Kókkino Horió**, the movie location, and nearby **Pláka** are indeed postcard-picturesque (more so from a distance), but **Kefalás**, inland, outdoes both of them. On the exposed north coast there are good beaches at **Almyrídha** and **Kalýves**, and off the road between them. Both are fast developing into resorts in their own right; accommodation is mostly in apartments and rooms are scarce, although there are a few mid-range and more upmarket hotels, and a decent pension, *Katrina* (☎08250/31 366; ❶), a short walk uphill from the centre of Almyrídha. With a string of good fish tavernas (try *Dimitri's*) along the beach and a pleasantly refreshing sea breeze, Almyrídha also makes for an enjoyable lunch stop.

South from Réthymnon

There are a couple of alternative routes south from Réthymnon, but the main one heads straight out from the centre of town, an initially featureless road due south across the middle of the island towards **Ayía Galíni**. About 23km out, a turning cuts off to the right for **Plakiás** and **Mýrthios**, following the course of the spectacular Kourtaliótiko ravine.

Plakiás and the south coast

Since the late 1980s, **PLAKIÁS** has undergone a major boom and is no longer the pristine village all too many people arriving here expect. That said, it's still quite low key, and there's a satisfactory beach and a string of good tavernas around the dock. There are hundreds of **rooms**, but at the height of summer you'll need to arrive early if you hope to find one; the last to fill are generally those on the road leading inland, away from the waterside. For rooms try *Christos Taverna* (☎08320/31 472; ❶) or the nearby *Stefanakis Rooms* (☎08320/ 32 027; ❶) on the seafront, or the excellent balcony rooms at *Ippokambos* (☎08320/31 525; ❶) slightly inland on the road to the relaxed **youth hostel** (☎08320/31 306; €3.75 dorms), which is 500m inland and signed from the seafront.

Once you've found a room there's not a lot else to discover here. Every facility you're likely to need is strung out around the waterfront, including a temporary **post office** parked by the harbour, **bike rental**, **money exchange**, **supermarket** and even a **laundry**. Places to eat are plentiful too. The attractive **tavernas** on the waterfront in the centre are a little expensive; you'll eat cheaper further inland – seek out *Taverna Medusa* at the east end of town, reached up the road inland from the Monza Travel agency and then right. On the way to here you'll pass *Nikos Souvlaki* which dishes up the least expensive meals in town, often accompanied by live *bouzoúki* music in the evenings. Just around the corner from the *Christos* taverna (which is a good bet for fish) at the west end of the harbour you'll find a line of waterfront places facing west – *Sunset* and *Glaros* are worth a try.

Mýrthios

For a stay of more than a day or two, **MÝRTHIOS**, in the hills behind Plakiás, also deserves consideration. It's no longer a great deal cheaper, and its once-popular youth hostel which put it on the map with legions of younger travellers over the years sadly closed in 1999. But at least you'll find locals still outnumbering the tourists, and the friendly *Plateia Taverna* – which catered to many of the youth hostel's guests – has had a makeover and still serves up excellent food. They can also advise on places to stay in the village. The Plakiás bus will usually loop back through Mýrthios, but check; otherwise, it's less than five-minutes' walk from the junction. It takes twenty minutes to walk down to the beach at Plakiás, a little longer to Dhamnóni, and if you're prepared to walk for an hour or more, there are some entirely isolated coves to the west – ask for directions at the taverna.

Dhamnóni

Some of the most tempting **beaches** in central Crete hide just to the east of Plakiás, though unfortunately they're now a very poorly kept secret. These three splashes of yellow sand, divided by rocky promontories, are within easy walking distance and together go by the name **Dhamnóni**. At the first, Dhamnóni proper, there's a taverna with showers and a wonderfully long strip of sand, but there's also a lot of new development including a number of nearby rooms for rent and a huge and ugly Swiss-owned holiday village, which has colonized half of the main beach. At the far end, you'll generally find a few people who've dispensed with their clothes, while the little cove which shelters the middle of the three beaches (barely accessible except on foot) is entirely nudist. Beyond this, **Ammoúdhi** beach has another taverna, *Ammoudi* (☎08320/31 355; ❷), with good rooms for rent, and slightly more of a family atmosphere.

Préveli and "Palm Beach"

Next in line comes **PRÉVELI**, some 6km southeast of Lefkóyia. It takes its name from a **monastery** (daily 8am–1.30pm & 3.30–8pm; €2.60) high above the sea which, like every other in Crete, has a proud history of resistance, in this case accentuated by its role in World War II as a shelter for marooned Allied soldiers awaiting evacuation off the south coast. There are fine views and a monument commemorating the rescue operations, but little else to see. The evacuations took place from "**Palm Beach**", a sandy cove with a small date-palm grove and a solitary drink stand where a stream feeds a little oasis. The beach usually attracts a summer camping community and is now also the target of day-trip boats from Plakiás and Ayía Galíni. Sadly, these groups between them deposit heaps of rubbish, often leaving this lovely place filthy, and despite an ongoing clean-up campaign it seems barely worth the effort. The climb down from the monastery is steep, rocky and surprisingly arduous: it's a great deal easier to come here by boat.

Spíli and Ayía Galíni

Back on the main road south, the pleasant country town of **SPÍLI** lies about 30km from Réthymnon. A popular coffee break for coach tours passing this way, Spíli warrants time if you can spare it. Sheltered under a cliff are narrow alleys of ancient houses, all leading up from a platía with a famous 24-spouted **Venetian fountain**. If you have your own transport, it's a worthwhile place to stay, peacefully rural at night but with several good **rooms** for rent. Try the *Green Hotel* (☎08320/22 225; ❶) on the main road or the charming *Rooms Herakles* (☎08320/22 411; ❷; reductions for stays of more than one night) just behind, the eponymous proprietor of which can advise on some superb **walks** in the surrounding hills. *Rooms Herakles* also rents out **mountain bikes**, there are two **banks** along the main street (with cash dispensers) and **internet** access is possible at *Cafe Babis*, close to the Venetian fountain.

The ultimate destination of most people on this road is **AYÍA GALÍNI**. If heading here was your plan, maybe you should think again since this picturesque "fishing village" is so busy in high season that you can't see it for the tour buses, hotel billboards and British package tourists. It also has a beach much too small for the crowds that congregate here. Even so, there are a few saving graces – mainly some excellent restaurants and bars, plenty of rooms and a friendly atmosphere that survives and even thrives on all the visitors. Out of season, it can be quite enjoyable too, and from November to April the mild climate makes it an ideal spot to spend the winter. A lot of long-term travellers do just that, so it's a good place to find work packing tomatoes or polishing cucumbers. If you want somewhere to stay, start looking at the top end of town, around the main road: the economical *Hotel Minos* (☎08320/91 292; ❶), with superb views, is a good place to start, with the nearby *Hotel Hariklia* (☎08320/91 350, ℻91 257; ❷) as a backup, but there are dozens of possibilities, and usually something to be found even at the height of summer.

The coastal plain east of Ayía Galíni, hidden under acres of polythene greenhouses and burgeoning concrete sprawl, must be among the ugliest regions in Crete, and **Timbáki** the dreariest town. Since this is the way to Festós and back to Iráklion, you may have no choice but to grin and bear it.

The Amári Valley

An alternative route south from Réthymnon, and a far less travelled one, is the road which turns off on the eastern fringe of town to run via the **Amári**

Valley. Very few buses go this way, but if you're driving it's well worth the extra time. There's little specifically to see or do (though hidden away are a number of richly frescoed Byzantine churches), but it's an impressive drive under the flanks of the mountains and a reminder of how, in places, rural Crete continues to exist regardless of visitors. The countryside here is delightfully green even in summer, with rich groves of olive and assorted fruit trees, and if you **stay** (there are rooms in Thrónos and Yerákari), you'll find the nights are cool and quiet. It may seem odd that many of the villages along the way are modern: they were systematically destroyed by the German army in reprisal for the 1944 kidnapping of General Kreipe.

Haniá and the west

The substantial attractions of Crete's westernmost quarter are all the more enhanced by its relative lack of visitors, and despite the now-rapid spread of tourist development, the west is likely to remain one of the emptier parts of the island. This is partly because there are no big sandy beaches to accommodate resort hotels, and partly because it's so far from the great archeological sites. But for mountains and empty (if often pebbly) beaches, it's unrivalled.

Haniá itself is an excellent reason to come here and, along with Réthymnon, is one of the two Cretan cities which could be described as enjoyable in itself. The immediately adjacent coast is relatively developed and not overly exciting; if you want beaches head for the south coast. **Paleohóra** is the only place which could really be described as a resort, and even this is on a thoroughly human scale; others are emptier still. **Ayía Rouméli** and **Loutró** can be reached only on foot or by boat; **Hóra Sfakíon** sees hordes passing through but few who stay; **Frangokástello**, nearby, has a beautiful castle and the first stirrings of development. Behind these lie the **Lefká Óri** (White Mountains) and, above all, the famed walk through the **Gorge of Samariá**.

Haniá

HANIÁ, as any of its residents will tell you, is spiritually the capital of Crete, even if the nominal title was passed back (in 1971) to Iráklion. For many, it is also by far the island's most attractive city, especially if you can catch it in spring, when the Lefká Óri's snowcapped peaks seem to hover above the roofs. Although it is for the most part a modern city, you might never know it as a tourist. Surrounding the small outer harbour is a wonderful jumble of half-derelict **Venetian streets** that survived the wartime bombardments, and it is here that life for the visitor is concentrated. Restoration and gentrification, consequences of the tourist boom, have made inroads of late, but it remains an atmospheric place.

Arrival, information and orientation

Large as it is, Haniá is easy to handle once you've reached the centre; you may get lost wandering among the narrow alleys of the old city but that's a rela-

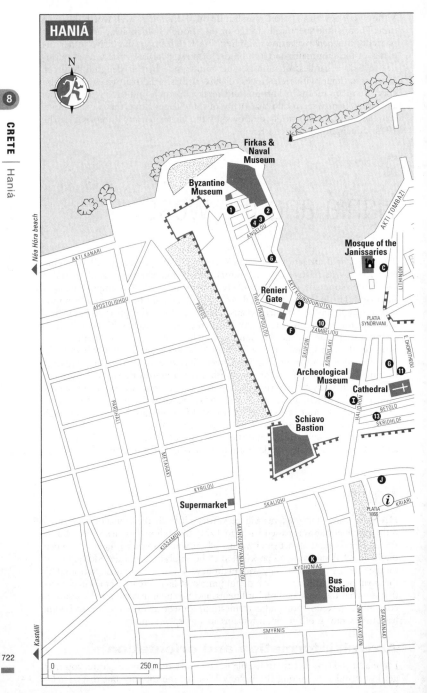

HANIÁ

N

Firkas &
Naval
Museum

Byzantine
Museum

❶
❷
❹❸

ANGELOU

❻

AKTI TOMBAZI

AKTI KANARI

Mosque of the
Janissaries

NONHILITI

ⓒ

APOSTOLIDHOU

AKTI KOUNDOURIOTOU

Renieri
Gate

❾

THEOTOKOPOULOU

PLATIA
SYNDRIVANI

PIREOS

Ⓕ

ZAMBELIOU

❿

E. DHOROTHEOU

SKUFON

KONDILAKI

Ⓖ

⓫

PARDHALI

Archeological
Museum

Ⓗ

Cathedral

✛

HALIDHON

Ⓘ

BETOLO

METAIRAKI

Schiavo
Bastion

⓭

SKRIDHLOF

KYRILOU

Ⓙ

KISSAMOU

Supermarket

SKALIDHI

PLATIA
1866

KRIARI

ⓘ

MANOUSOYANAKIDHOU

ZIMVRAKAKIDHON

Ⓚ

KYDHONIAS

Bus
Station

SMYRNIS

SFAKIANAKI

◄ Néa Hóra beach

◄ Kastélli

0   250 m

ACCOMMODATION

Amphora	6
Fidias	12
Kastelli	7
Lena	1
Lucia	9
Meltemi	2
Monastiri	5
Nikos	8
Rooms George	10
Rooms Stella	4
Thereza	3
To Dhiporto	13
Vranas Studios	11

RESTAURANTS

Anaplous	D
Aroma	C
Dino's	A
Ela	H
Iordanis Boúgatsa	K
Karnayio	B
Nea Vouli	J
Rudi's Bierhaus	E
Tamam	F
Tasty Souvlaki	I
Tholos	G

Inner Harbour

SARPIDHONOS

AKTI ENÓSEOS

PLATIA
KATEHAKI

Arsenali

KALERGON

KASTÉLLI

IKAROU

SIFAKA

SPIÁNTZA

KANEVAROU

SIFAKA

San Rocco

VOURDOUBA

MINOUS

AKTI MIAOULI

Ayios Nikólaos

PLATIA
1821

KARAOLI

DHASKALOYIANNIS

SARPAKI

Anaryíri Minaret

POTIE

DHALIANI

Minaret

TSOUDHERON

NIKIFOROU FOKA

KYPROU

Market

PLATIA
S. VENIZELOU

ELEFTHERIOU VENIZELOU

YIANNARI

National Bank

OTE

Stadium

N. PLASTIRA

VELOUDRAKIDHON

ANDHREA

TRIKOUPI

KOBAI

► Akrotíri

Tourist Police

AGHOHRONIOU

PAPANDHREOU

Public Gardens

TZANAKAKI

► Platía Eleftherías

Olympic Airways

KORNAROU

SFAKIANAKI

► Platía Eleftherías

SOLOMOU

▼ new road, Soúdha, Réthymnon & Iráklion

tively small area, and you're never far from the sea or from some other obvious landmark. The **bus station** is on Kydhonías, within easy walking distance from the centre – turn right out of the station, then left down the side of Platía-1866 and you'll emerge at a major road junction opposite the top of Halídhon, the main street of the old quarter leading straight down to the Venetian harbour. Arriving by **ferry**, you'll anchor about 10km east of Haniá at the port of Soúdha: there are frequent buses from here which will drop you by the **market** on the fringes of the old town, or you can take a taxi (around €4.50). From the city's efficient new **airport** (15km east of town on the Akrotíri peninsula) taxis (around €8.80) will almost certainly be your only option, though it's worth a quick check to see if any sort of bus is meeting your flight. The very helpful **tourist office** is in the new town, just off Platía-1866 at Kriári 40 (Mon–Fri 8am–2.30pm ☎08210/92 624, ℻92 943).

Accommodation

There must be thousands of **rooms** to rent in Haniá and, unusually, quite a few comfortable **hotels**. Though you may face a long search for a bed at the height of the season, eventually everyone does seem to find something. The nearest **campsite** within striking distance is *Camping Hania* (☎08210/31 138), some 4km west of Haniá behind the beach, served by local bus. The site is lovely, if rather basic, and just a short walk from some of the better beaches.

Harbour area

Perhaps the most desirable rooms of all are those overlooking the **harbour**, which are sometimes available at reasonable rates: be warned that this is often because they're very noisy at night. Most are approached not direct from the harbourside itself but from Zambelíou, the alley behind, or from other streets leading off the harbour further around (where you may get more peace). The nicest of the more expensive places are here, too, equally set back but often with views from the upper storeys. In recent years the popularity of this area has led to anyone with a room near the harbour tarting it up and attempting to rent it out at a ridiculously inflated price. You'll often be touted in the street for these and it's wise not to commit yourself until you've made comparisons with some of the more reasonable places listed below.

Amphora, Theotokopoúlou 20 ☎ & ℻ 08210/93 224. Large, traditional hotel in Venetian mansion, and beautifully renovated; worth the expense if you get a view, but probably not for the cheaper rooms without one. ❺

Rooms George, Zambelíou 30 ☎08210/88 715. Old building with steep stairs and eccentric antique furniture; basic rooms vary in price according to position and size. ❶

Lucia, Aktí Koundouriótou ☎08210/90 302, ℻91 834. Harbourfront hotel with balcony rooms; less expensive than you might expect for one of the best views in town. ❷

Pension Lena, Theotokopoúlou 60 ☎ & ℻ 08210/86 860, ✆www.lena@travelling-crete.com. Charming rooms in an old wooden Turkish house

restored by friendly German proprietor. Pleasant breakfast café below. ❷

Meltemi, Angélou 2 ☎08210/92 802. First of a little row of pensions in a great situation on the far side of the harbour; perhaps noisier than its neighbours, but excellent views and a good café downstairs. ❷

Rooms Stella, Angélou 10 ☎08210/73 756. Creaky, eccentric old house above a ceramics shop, close to the *Lucia*, with plain, clean rooms. ❷

Thereza, Angélou 8 ☎ & ℻ 08210/92 798. Beautiful old house in a great position, with stunning views from roof terrace and some of the rooms; classy decor, too. A more expensive pension than its neighbours but deservedly so; unlikely to have room in season unless you book. ❸

The old town: east of Halídhon

In the eastern half of the old town rooms are far more scattered, usually cheaper, and in the height of the season your chances are much better over here. **Kastélli**, immediately east of the harbour, has some lovely places with views from the heights. Take one of the alleys leading left off Kanevárou if you want to try these, but don't be too hopeful since they are popular and often booked up.

To Dhiporto, Betólo 41, one block north of Skridhlóf ☎08210/53 430. A very good-value rooms place with economical doubles and trebles. Recommended. ❶

Fidias, Kalinákou Sarpáki 8 ☎08210/52 494. Signposted from the cathedral, this favourite backpackers' meeting place is rather bizarrely run, but is a friendly pension and has the real advantage of offering single rooms or fixing shares. Its dormitory rooms are the cheapest in town (€5.50). ❶

Kastélli, Kanevárou 39 ☎08210/57 057, ℱ45 314. Not in the prettiest of locations, but a comfortable, modern, reasonably priced pension and very quiet at the back. All rooms come with fans and anti-mosquito machines. The owner is excep-

tionally helpful and also has a few apartments and a beautiful house (for up to five people) to rent. ❷

Monastiri, Ayíou Márkou 18, off Kanevárou ☎08210/54 776. Pleasant rooms, some with a sea view in the restored ruins of a Venetian monastery. ❷

Nikos, Dhaskaloyiánnis 58 ☎08210/54 783. One of a few down here near the inner harbour; good-value, relatively modern rooms, all with shower. Same owner has economical studios nearby with kitchen and fridge. ❷

Vranas Studios, Ayíon Dhéka and Kalinákou Sarpáki, near the cathedral ☎ & ℱ 08210/58 618. Pleasant, spacious studio-style rooms with TV, air-con, fridge and kitchenette. ❹

The City

Haniá has been occupied almost continuously since Neolithic times, so it comes as a surprise that a city of such antiquity should offer little specifically to see or do. It is, however, a place which is fascinating simply to wander around, stumbling upon surviving fragments of city wall, the remains of **ancient Kydonia** which are being excavated, and odd segments of Venetian or Turkish masonry.

Kastélli and the harbour

The **port** area is as ever the place to start, the oldest and the most interesting part of town. It's at its busiest and most attractive at night, when the lights from bars and restaurants reflect in the water and crowds of visitors and locals turn out to promenade. By day, things are quieter. Straight ahead from Platía Syndriváni (also known as Harbour Square) lies the curious domed shape of the **Mosque of the Janissaries**, built in 1645 (though heavily restored since) and the oldest Ottoman building on the island. It has recently reopened as a gallery to house temporary exhibitions.

The little hill that rises behind the mosque is **Kastélli**, site of the earliest habitation and core of the Minoan, Venetian and Turkish towns. There's not a great deal left, but archeologists believe that they may have found the remains of a Minoan palace (logically, there must have been one at this end of the island) in the **excavations** being carried out – and open to view – along Kanevárou. It's also here that you'll find traces of the oldest **walls**; there were two rings, one defending Kastélli alone, a later set encompassing the whole of the medieval city. Beneath the hill, on the inner (eastern) harbour, the arches of sixteenth-century **Venetian arsenals** survive alongside remains of the outer walls; both are currently undergoing restoration.

Following the esplanade around in the other direction leads to a hefty bastion which now houses Crete's **Naval Museum** (daily 9am–4pm; €1.80). The collection is not exactly riveting, although a recently added section on the 1941 **Battle of Crete** with fascinating artefacts, and poignant photos depicting the suffering here under the Nazis, perhaps justifies the entry fee. You might want to wander in anyway for a (free) look at the seaward fortifications and the platform from which the modern Greek flag was first flown on Crete (in 1913). Walk around the back of these restored bulwarks to a street heading inland and you'll find the best-preserved stretch of the outer walls. Just behind the Naval Museum at the top of Theotokopolou lies the new **Byzantine Museum** (Tues–Sun 8.30am–3pm; free) with a small but interesting collection of mosaics, icons and jewellery from the various periods of Byzantine rule.

The old city

Behind the harbour lie the less picturesque but more lively sections of the old city. First, a short way up Halídhon on the right, is Haniá's **Archeological Museum** (Tues–Sun 8.30am–2.30pm; €1.45) housed in the Venetian-built church of San Francesco. Damaged as it is, especially from the outside, this remains a beautiful building and it contains a fine little display, covering the local area from Minoan through to Roman times. In the garden, a huge fountain and the base of a minaret survive from the period when the Turks converted the church into a mosque; around them are scattered various other sculptures and architectural remnants.

The **cathedral**, ordinary and relatively modern, is just a few steps further up Halídhon on the left. Around it are some of the more animated shopping areas, particularly **Odhós Skrídhlof** ("Leather Street"), lined with the shops of traditional leathermakers plying their trade, with streets leading up to the back of the market beyond. In the direction of the Spiántza quarter are ancient alleys with tumbledown Venetian stonework and overhanging wooden balconies; though gentrification is spreading apace, much of the quarter has yet to feel the effect of the city's modern popularity. There are a couple more **minarets** too, one on Dhaliáni, and the other in Platía-1821, which is a fine traditional platía to stop for a coffee.

The new town

Once out of the narrow confines of the maritime district, the broad, traffic-choked streets of the **modern city** have a great deal less to offer. Up Tzanakáki, not far from the market, you'll find the **public gardens**, a park with strolling couples, a few caged animals (including a few *kri-kri* or Cretan ibex) and a café under the trees; there's also an open-air auditorium which occasionally hosts live music or local festivities. Beyond here, you could continue to the **Historical Museum**, Sfakianáki 20 (Mon–Fri 9am–2pm; free), but the effort would be wasted unless you're a Greek-speaking expert on the subject; the place is essentially a very dusty archive with a few photographs on the wall. Perhaps more interesting is the fact that the museum lies on the fringes of Haniá's desirable residential districts. If you continue to the end of Sfakianáki and then go down Iróön Polytekhníou towards the sea, you'll get an insight into how Crete's other half lives. There are several (expensive) garden restaurants down here and a number of fashionable café-bars where you can sit outside.

The beaches

Haniá's beaches all lie to the west of the city. For the packed **city beach**, this means no more than a ten-minute walk following the shoreline from the naval museum, but for good sand you're better off taking the local bus out along the coast road. This leaves from the east side of Platía-1866 and runs along the coast road as far as **Kalamáki beach**. Kalamáki and the previous stop, **Oásis beach**, are again pretty crowded but they're a considerable improvement over the beach in Haniá itself. In between, you'll find emptier stretches if you're prepared to walk: about an hour in all (on sandy beach virtually all the way) from Haniá to Kalamáki, and then perhaps ten minutes from the road to the beach if you get off the bus at the signs to *Aptera Beach* or *Camping Hania*. Further afield there are even finer beaches at **Ayía Marína** to the west, or **Stavrós** (see p.729) out on the Akrotíri peninsula (reached by KTEL buses from the main station).

Eating

You're never far from something to **eat** in Haniá: in a circle around the harbour is one restaurant, taverna or café after another. All have their own character, but there seems little variation in price or what's on offer. Away from the water, there are plenty of slightly cheaper possibilities on Kondhiláki, Kanevárou and most of the streets off Halídhon. For snacks or lighter meals, the cafés around the harbour on the whole serve cocktails and fresh juices at exorbitant prices, though breakfast (especially "English") can be good value. For more-traditional places, try around the market and along Dhaskaloyiánnis (*Synganaki* here is a good traditional bakery serving *tyrópitta* and the like, with a cake shop next door). Fast food is also increasingly widespread, with numerous *souvláki* places on Karaolí; at the end of the outer harbour, near the naval museum; and around the corner of Plastíra and Yiannári, across from the **market** (see "Listings" overleaf, for details of the market and supermarkets).

Anaplous, Sífaka 37. A couple of blocks west of Platía-1821, this is a popular new open-air restaurant inside a stylishly "restored" ruin of a Turkish mansion bombed in the war. Serves both mezédhes and full meals to live guitar music.

Aroma, Aktí Tombázi 4, next to the Mosque of the Janissaries. Pleasant café with great harbour view to savour over lazy breakfasts or late drinks.

Dino's, inner harbour by bottom of Sarpidhónos. One of the best choices for a pricey seafood meal with a harbour view. The nearby *Faka* is also good.

Ela, top of Kondhiláki. Standard taverna food with live Greek music accompaniment to enliven your meal in yet another roofless taverna townhouse.

Iordanis Bougatsa, Kydhonias 96, opposite the bus station. This place serves little except the traditional creamy *bougátsa*, a sugar-coated cheese pie to eat in or take away.

Karnáyio, Platía Kateháki 8. Set back from the inner harbour near the port police. Not right on the water, but one of the best harbour restaurants nonetheless.

Meltemi, Angélou 2. Slow, relaxed terrace bar

beneath the rooms place of the same name; good for breakfast, and where locals (especially expats) sit whiling the day away or playing *tavli*.

Nea Vouli, Yiannári 27, just west of Platía-1866. Excellent and stylish restaurant popular with locals, serving high-quality standards at modest prices. Closed Sun.

Rudi's Bierhaus, Sífaka 24. Haniá's beer shrine: Austrian Rudi Riegler's bar stocks more than a hundred of Europe's finest beers to accompany very tasty mezédhes.

Tamam, Zambelíou just before Renieri Gate. Young, trendy place with adventurous Greek menu including much vegetarian food. Unfortunately only a few cramped tables outside, and inside it can get very hot. Slow service.

Tasty Souvlaki, Halídhon 80. Always packed despite being cramped, which is a testimonial to the quality and value of the *souvláki*. Better to take away.

Tholos, Ayíon Dhéka 36. Slightly north of the cathedral, *Tholos* is another "restaurant in a ruin", this time Venetian/Turkish, with a wide selection of Cretan specialities.

Bars and nightlife

Haniá's **nightlife** has more than enough venues to satisfy the most insomniac night-owls. Most of the clubs and disco bars are gathered in the area around the inner harbour, whilst there are plenty of terrace bars along both harbourfronts, with more scattered throughout the old quarter.

The smartest and newest places to sit out and be seen in the evening are on and around **Sarpidhónos**, in the far corner of the inner harbour, a good example of which is *Ta Dhyo Lux*, one of a line of bars here and the place to try an expensive but sublime lemon *graníta*. The nearby *Fraise* is another popular venue. Heading from here around towards the outer harbour, you'll pass others including the *Four Seasons*, a very popular bar by the port police, and then reach a couple of the older places including *Scorpio* behind the Plaza bar complex on the harbour. To the southeast of the inner harbour running along the **Aktí Miaoúli** seafront just outside the eastern wall are a string of terrace cafés catering almost exclusively to a local under-thirty clientele, and this is currently *the* place to be seen for Haniote late drinkers. At the opposite or **western end of the harbour** *Fagotto*, Angélou 16, is a pleasant, laid-back jazz bar, often with live performers. Other music bars near here are *Mythos* and *Street* on the outer harbour, playing rock and modern Greek sounds until the early hours. **Disco clubs** proper include *Ariadni* on the inner harbour (opens 11.30pm, but busy later), and *Millennium*, a big, bright place on Tsoudherón behind the market, which doesn't really get going until 2am. West of here along Skalídhi (no. 39) *Titanic* is another dance place which is a late starter, and, not far away, tucked down a passage near the Schiavo Bastion (Skalídhi and Halídhon), *N.R.G* is a new place that becomes frenetic after midnight.

A venue offering more traditional entertainment is the *Café Kriti*, Kalergón 22, at the corner of Andhroyíou, basically an old-fashioned kafenío where there's **Greek music** and **dancing** virtually every night. It's also worth checking for events at the open-air auditorium in the public gardens, and for performances in restaurants outside the city, which are the ones the locals will go to. Look for posters, especially in front of the market and in the little platía across the road from there.

For **films**, you should also check the hoardings in front of the market. There are open-air screenings at Attikon, on Venizélou out towards Akrotíri, about 1km from the centre, and occasionally in the public gardens.

Listings

Airlines Olympic, with scheduled daily flights between Haniá and Athens plus frequent flights to Thessaloníki, has an office at Tzanakáki 88 (Mon–Fri 9am–4pm; ☎08210/57 701, 57 702 or 57 703) opposite the public gardens. Other airlines running daily scheduled services to the mainland are Aegean-Cronus, Venizélou 12 (☎08210/51 100) and Axon, Haniá airport (☎08210/20 928). For airport information call ☎08210/63 264.

Banks and exchange The main branch of the National Bank of Greece is directly opposite the market with two cash dispensers. Convenient smaller banks for exchange are next to the bus station, at the bottom of Kanevárou just off Platía Syndriváni, or at the top of Halídhon. There are also a couple of exchange places on Halídhon, open long hours.

Bike and car rental Possibilities everywhere, especially on Halídhon, though these are rarely the best value. For bikes, try Kavroulakis, Halídhon 91 (☎08210/43 342) or Summertime,

Daskaloyiánnis 7, slightly northeast of the market (☎08210/98 918); for cars, two reliable local companies are Hermes, Tzanakáki 52 (☎08210/54 418) or Tellus Rent a Car, Kanevárou 9, east of Platía Syndriváni (☎08210/50 400). Good deals for *Rough Guide* readers are available from El Greco Cars at the *El Greco* hotel (☎08210/91 818, ✉cars@elgreco.gr), where readers showing this guide will receive a 25 percent discount.

Boat trips Various boat trips are offered by travel agents around town, mostly to Soúdha Bay or out to beaches on the Rodhópou peninsula. Stavros Cruises (mobile ☎094/4914045) in the Old Harbour or Domenico's (☎08210/55 019), on Kanevárou, offers some of the best of these. The *Angela* sails daily in summer at 1.30pm from the Old Harbour to the offshore island of Áyii Theódori, for swimming and *kri-kri* (ibex) spotting. The *Evagelos* glass-bottomed boat sails three times daily from the Old Harbour to Theodorou with an extension on Saturdays to the Rodhópou peninsula

(for information call the mobile number
☎094/5874283).

Ferry tickets The ANEK line office is on Venizélou,
right opposite the market (☎08210/27 500).

Internet Haniá has three internet cafés: *Sante* on
the outer harbour at Aktí Koundouriótou 55–56 (€3
per hr); the more tranquil *Vranas* (€1.50; 30min),
just north of the cathedral and beneath *Vranas
Studios* (see "Accommodation"); *E-Café*,
Theotokopólou 53 near *El Greco Cars* (€1.50;
30min) is a relaxed and friendly newcomer.

Laundry There are five laundries, the best of
which is Speedy Laundry (☎08210/88 411;
9am–9pm), junction of Koronéou and Korkidi, just
west of Platía-1866 charging €6 for a load; they
will also collect and deliver. Others are Laundry
Express at Kanevárou 38 (Mon–Sat 9am–10pm)
and Fidias, Sarpaki 6 (next to the pension of the
same name; Mon–Sat 9am–9pm). All do service
washes.

Left luggage The bus station has a left-luggage
office open 6am–8.30pm; €0.90/1.50 per item
per day depending on size.

Market and supermarkets To buy food, head for
the entertaining market which has fresh fruit and
vegetables, meat and fish, bakers, dairy stalls and
general stores for cooked meats, tins, etc. Several
small stores by the harbour platía sell cold drinks
and food, which are expensive but open late. Small
supermarkets can be found on Platía-1866 and the
larger Marinopolos supermarket is at the top of
Pireos, outside the western wall, close to the
Schiavo Bastion.

Post office The main post office is on Tzanakáki
(Mon–Fri 7am–8pm, Sat 8am–2pm).

Taxis The main taxi ranks are in Platía-1866. For
radio taxis try ☎08210/98 700 or 94 300.

Telephones Cardphones (all over town) are the
best bet for overseas calls.

Tourist police Inconveniently located at Iraklíou
23 in the southern suburb of Koubés (☎08210/53
333).

Travel agencies El Greco Travel, on Kidhonías
near the bus station (☎08210/86 015), and
Interkreta, on Platía Eleftherías in the new town
(☎08210/27 222), are both good for inexpensive
bus tickets, flights and standard excursions. For
cheap tickets home try Bassias Travel, Halídhon 69
(☎08210/44 295), very helpful for regular tickets
too. They also deal in standard excursions. Other
travel agents for tours and day-trips are everywhere.

Around Haniá: the Akrotíri and Rodhópou peninsulas

Just north of Haniá, the **Akrotíri peninsula** loops around to protect the Bay
of Soúdha and a NATO military base and missile-testing area. In an ironic
twist, the peninsula's northwestern coastline is fast developing into a luxury
suburb; the beach of Kalathás, near Horafákia, long popular with jaded
Haniotes is surrounded by villas and apartments. **STAVRÓS**, further out, has
not yet suffered this fate, and its **beach** is absolutely superb if you like the calm,
shallow water of an almost completely enclosed lagoon. It's not very large, so
it does get crowded, but rarely overpoweringly so. There's a makeshift taver-
na/*souvláki* stand on the beach, and a couple of tavernas across the road, but for
accommodation you need to search slightly south of here, in the area around
Blue Beach, where there are plenty of apartment buildings but no low budget accommodation in summer whatsoever. On Blue Beach you could try
Zorba's Rooms (attached to a taverna of the same name) which rents out apartments (☎08210/39 010; ②).

Inland are the **monasteries** of **Ayía Triádha** (daily 9am–7pm; €1.20) and
Gouvernétou (daily 7am–2pm & 4–7.30pm; €1.45). The former is much
more accessible and has a beautiful seventeenth-century church inside its pink-
and-ochre cloister, though ongoing renovations – the latest has turned one
building into an olive-oil factory where the monks produce and bottle their
own oil – on occasions make the normally peaceful enclosure more like a
building site. Four kilometres north of Gouvernétou – which is in a far better
state of preservation and where traditional monastic life can still be observed –

you can clamber down a craggy path to the amazing and abandoned ruins of the **monastery of Katholikó**, built into a craggy ravine, and the remains of its narrow (swimmable) harbour.

West to Rodhópou

The coast to the west of Haniá was the scene of most of the fighting during the German invasion in 1941. As you leave town, an aggressive, monumental diving eagle commemorates the slain German parachutists, and at Máleme there's a big German cemetery; the Allied cemetery is in the other direction, on the coast just outside Soúdha. There are also beaches and considerable tourist development along much of this shore. At **Ayía Marína** there's a fine sandy beach and an island offshore said to be a sea monster petrified by Zeus before it could swallow Crete. Seen from the west, its "mouth" still gapes open.

Between **Plataniás** and **Kolymvári** an almost unbroken strand unfurls, by no means all sandy, but deserted for long stretches between villages. The road here runs through mixed groves of calamus reed (Crete's bamboo) and oranges; the windbreaks fashioned from the reeds protect the ripening oranges from the *meltémi*. At Kolymbári, the road to Kastélli cuts across the base of another mountainous peninsula, **Rodhópou**. Just off the main road here is a monastery, **Goniá** (daily 8am–12.30pm & 4–8pm; free; respectable dress required), with a view most luxury hotels would envy. Every monk in Crete can tell tales of his proud ancestry of resistance to invaders, but here the Turkish cannon balls are still lodged in the walls to prove it, a relic of which the good fathers are far more proud than any of the icons.

South to the Samarian Gorge

From Haniá the **Gorge of Samariá** (May–Oct; €3.60 for entry to the national park) can be visited as a day-trip or as part of a longer excursion to the south. At 18km, it's Europe's longest gorge and is startlingly beautiful. In the June to August period (ring Haniá tourist office for other times) **buses** leave Haniá bus station for the top at 6.15am, 7.30am, 8.30am and 1.30pm (this latter service changes to 4.30pm outside school term time), depositing you at the gorge entrance and then collecting you at the port of Hóra Sfakíon for the return trip to Haniá. Should you take the last bus you will need to spend a night at Ayía Rouméli (the end of the gorge) as you will not get through the gorge in time for the last boat. For the three early buses you'll normally be sold a return ticket (valid from Hóra Sfakíon at any time). It's well worth catching the earliest bus to avoid the full heat of the day while walking through the gorge, though be warned that you will not be alone – there are often as many as five coachloads setting off before dawn for the nail-biting climb into the White Mountains. There are also direct early-morning buses from Iráklion and Réthymnon and bus tours from virtually everywhere on the island, adding up to a couple of thousand plus walkers on most days during high season.

Despite all the crowds, the walk *is* hard work, especially in spring when the stream is a roaring torrent. Early and late in the season, there is a danger of **flash floods**, which are not to be taken lightly: in 1993, a number of walkers perished when they were washed out to sea. For this reason the first and last three weeks of the season are entirely dependent on the weather and you will only be allowed into the gorge if the authorities deem it safe. If in doubt (and to save yourself a wasted journey), phone the Haniá Forest Service's **gorge information number** (☎08210/67 140) or the gorge office (☎08210/67 179) for information. Should you arrive after 4pm you will only be allowed into the first couple of kilometres from each end of the gorge and the wardens ensure that no one remains in the gorge overnight, where camping is strictly forbidden.

Omalós

One way to avoid an early start from the north coast would be to stay at **OMALÓS**, in the middle of the mountain plain from which the gorge descends. There are plenty of **tavernas** and some ordinary **rooms** for rent – the friendly no-frills Samaria pension (☎08210/67 168; ❶) is the cheapest – plus a clutch of surprisingly fancy **hotels**; the *Hotel Gingilos* (☎08210/67 181; ❶) is good value and its proprietor will drive you the 5km to the top of the gorge next morning if you stay overnight. However, if you're on foot, since the village is some way from the start of the path, and the first buses arrive as the sun rises, it's almost impossible to get a head start on the crowds. Some people sleep out at the top (where there's a bar-restaurant in the *Tourist Lodge* and kiosks serving drinks and sandwiches), but a night under the stars here can be a bitterly cold experience. The one significant advantage to staying up here would be if you wanted to undertake some other climbs in the White Mountains, in which case there's a **mountain hut** (☎08210/54 560; €6 per person) about ninety-minutes' hike (signed) from Omalós or from the top of the gorge.

The gorge

The **gorge** itself begins at the *xylóskala*, or "wooden staircase", a stepped path plunging steeply down from the southern lip of the Omalós plain. Here, at the head of the track, opposite the sheer rock face of Mount Gíngilos, the crowds pouring out of the buses disperse rapidly as keen walkers march purposefully down while others dally over breakfast, contemplating the sunrise for hours. You descend at first through almost alpine scenery: pine forest, wild flowers and very un-Cretan greenery – a verdant shock in the spring, when the stream is also at its liveliest (and can at times be positively dangerous). Small churches and viewpoints dot the route, and about halfway down you pass the abandoned village of **Samariá**, now home to a wardens' station, with picnic facilities and filthy toilets. Further down, the path levels out and the gorge walls close in until at the narrowest point (the *sidherespórtes* or "iron gates") one can practically touch both tortured rock faces at once, and, looking up, see them rising sheer for almost a thousand feet.

At an average pace, with regular stops, the walk down takes five or six hours, and the upward trek considerably longer. It's strenuous (you'll know all about it next day), the path is rough, and solid shoes are vital. On the way down, there is plenty of water from springs and streams (except some years in Sept and Oct), but nothing to eat. The park that surrounds the gorge is a refuge of the Cretan wild ibex, the *kri-kri*, but don't expect to see one; there are usually far too many people around.

Villages of the southwest coast

When you finally emerge from the gorge, it's not long before you reach the singularly unattractive village of **AYÍA ROUMÉLI**, which is all but abandoned until you reach the beach, a mirage of iced drinks and a cluster of tavernas with **rooms** for rent. If you want to get back to Haniá, buy your boat tickets now, especially if you want an afternoon on the beach; the last boat (connecting with the final 6.30pm bus from Hóra Sfakíon) tends to sell out first. If you plan to stay on the south coast, you should get going as soon as possible for the best chance of finding a room somewhere nicer than Ayía Rouméli.

Loutró

For tranquillity, it's hard to beat **LOUTRÓ**, two-thirds of the way to Hóra Sfakíon, and accessible only by boat or on foot. The chief disadvantage of Loutró is its lack of a real beach; most people swim from the rocks around its small bay. If you're prepared to walk, however, there are **deserted beaches** along the coast to the east which can also be reached by hired **canoe**. Indeed, if you're really into walking there's a **coastal trail** through Loutró which covers the entire distance between Ayía Rouméli and Hóra Sfakíon, or you could take the daunting zigzag path up the cliff behind to the mountain village of **Anópoli**. Loutró itself has a number of **tavernas** and **rooms**, though not always enough of the latter in peak season. Call the *Blue House* (☎08250/91 127, ⓦ www.delftmarkt.nl; ❶) if you want to book ahead; this is also the best place to eat. Slightly more upmarket accommodation is on offer at the nearby *Hotel Porto Loutro* (☎08250/91 433; ❷), which also hires out canoes and runs full-day **cruises** on its own boat to Palm Beach and the island of Gávdhos; prices should be posted outside. There's space to **camp** out on the cape by a ruined fort, but due to a long history of problems, you should be aware that campers are not very popular in the village. If you're determined to camp, head for the **beaches** and coves to the east (such as Sweetwater) and west (Mármara) of the resort which can be reached on foot, or more comfortably by canoe or daily boats from the harbour.

Hóra Sfakíon and beyond

HÓRA SFAKÍON is the more usual terminus for walkers traversing the gorge, with a regular boat service along the coast to and from Ayía Rouméli. Consequently, it's quite an expensive and not an especially welcoming place; there are plenty of **rooms** and some decent **tavernas**, but for a real beach you should jump straight on a bus (currently running at 11am and 6pm April–Sept) going toward Plakiás. Plenty of opportunities for a dip present themselves en route, one of the most memorable at **Frangokástello**, named after a crumbling Venetian attempt to bring law and order to a district that went on to defy both Turks and Germans. The foursquare, crenellated and imposing thirteenth-century **castle**, isolated a few kilometres below a chiselled wall of mountains, looks like it's been spirited out of the High Atlas or Tibet. The place is said to be haunted by ghosts of Greek rebels massacred here in 1829: every May, these *dhrossoulítes* (dewy ones) march at dawn across the coastal plain and disappear into the sea near the fort. The rest of the time Frangokástello is peaceful enough, with a superb beach and a number of tavernas and rooms, but is somewhat stagnant if you're looking for things to do. A new and stylish **pool-bar** *Eiscafe*, a little west and inland from the castle has livened things a little and the proprietors here can advise on **accommodation** possibilities should you want to stopover. Slightly further east, and less influenced by tourism or modern life, are the attractive villages of **Skalotí** and **Rodhákino**, where basic lodging and food can be found in the villages proper or their seafront offshoots a couple of kilometres to the south.

Soúyia

In quite the other direction from Ayía Rouméli, less regular boats also head to **SOÚYIA** and on to Paleohóra. Soúyia, until World War II merely the anchorage for Koustoyérako inland, is low key, with a long, grey pebble beach and mostly modern buildings (except for a church with a sixth-century Byzantine mosaic as the foundation). Since the completion in 1990 of the paved road to Haniá, the village has started to expand; even so, except in the very middle of summer, it continues to make a good fall-back for finding a room or a place to camp, eating cheaply and enjoying the beach when the rest of the island is seething with visitors.

Of the **rooms** places try the seafront *Hotel Santa Irene* (☎08230/51 342, ℻51 182, ✉nanadakis@cha.forthnet.gr; ❷), where en-suite rooms come with view; cheaper en-suite rooms are on offer at the friendly *Lissos* (☎08230/51 244; ❶), reached by turning east along the seafront and then inland. An excellent source of **information** on rooms and lots more is Polifimos Travel (☎ & ℻ 08230/51 022, ✉polifim@otenet.gr) on the main street just in from the seafront; they keep piles of information on everything to do in the area – including **gorge walks** in the beautiful Ayía Iríni gorge and a fine hike to the nearby ancient site of **Lissós**. They can also advise on the latest bus and ferry **timetables**, **change money**, **rent cars** and have a couple of screens for **internet** access. For **food**, the nearby *Rembetiko* has a pleasant garden terrace. At the eastern end of the seafront the German-run *Omikron* taverna has a more northern-European ambience and offers some **vegetarian** choices. Finally, as petrol is scarce in these parts, it's worth noting that there is **no pump station** and a full tank would be a wise precaution.

Kastélli and the western tip

Apart from being Crete's most westerly town, and the end of the main E65 coastal highway, **KASTÉLLI** (Kíssamos, or Kastélli Kissámou as it's variously known) has little obvious attraction. It's a busy town with a rocky central **beach** (although there's an excellent sandy beach to the west) visited mainly by people using the boat that runs twice weekly to the island of Kýthira and the Peloponnese. The very ordinariness of Kastélli, however, can be attractive: life goes on pretty much regardless of outsiders, and there's every facility you might need. The town was important in antiquity and a number of recently excavated **mosaics** are visible around the centre (follow the signs) and finds from these digs and others nearby are to be displayed in the town's new **museum** (due to open in 2002) located in the refurbished former Venetian governor's residence on the main square.

A round trip

If you have transport, a circular drive from Kastélli, taking the coast road in one direction and the inland route through Élos and Topólia, makes for a stunningly scenic circuit. Near the sea, villages cling to the high mountainsides, apparently halted by some miracle in the midst of calamitous seaward slides. Around them, olives ripen on the terraced slopes, the sea glittering far below. Inland, especially at **ÉLOS**, the main crop is the chestnut, whose huge old trees shade the village streets.

South of **TOPÓLIA**, the chapel of Ayía Sofía is sheltered inside a cave which has been used as a shrine since Neolithic times. Cutting south just before Élos, a spectacular paved road continues through the high mountains towards Paleohóra. On a motorbike, with a sense of adventure and plenty of fuel, it's great: the bus doesn't come this way, villagers still stare at the sight of a tourist, and a host of small, seasonal streams cascade beside or under the asphalt.

As regards practicalities, the **ferry agent's office** in Kastélli is one block inland from the main square, Platía Kastellíou (Xirouxákis; ☎08220/22 655). The **ferry dock** lies 2km west of town – a significant walk if you're heavily laden, or an inexpensive taxi ride. For **rooms**, *Vergerakis* (aka *Jimmy's*; ☎08220/22 663; ❶) has clean and simple rooms on the main square, but the more attractive option is the excellent *Hotel Galini Beach* (☎08220/23 288, ℱ23 388, ⓦwww.galinibeach .com; ❷) at the east end of the seafront near the sports stadium, or *Maria Beach* (☎08220/22 610 ℱ23 626; ❷) with some much cheaper rooms which you need to ask for on the town's sandy western beach. Heading north from the main square brings you to the beach promenade where there are a number of **tavernas** – *To Kelari* is worth a try – and late-night drinking and music **bars** popular with the local younger set, particularly at weekends.

Falásarna to Elafonísi

To the west of Kastélli lies some of Crete's loneliest, and, for many visitors, finest coastline. The first place of note is ancient and modern **Falásarna**, which has city ruins meaning little to the non-specialist, but overlooking some of the best beaches on Crete, wide and sandy with clean water. There's a handful of **tavernas** and an increasing number of **rooms** for rent: try the seafront *Sun Set* (☎08220/41 204; ❶) near the archeological site. Otherwise, you may have to sleep out, as many people do; make sure to take any rubbish away with you. This can mean that the main beaches are dirty, but they remain beautiful, and there are plenty of others within walking distance. The nearest real town is **Plátanos**, 5km up a paved road, along which there are a couple of daily buses.

Further south, the western coastline is still less discovered and there's little in the way of official accommodation. **SFINÁRI** has a few houses which rent rooms, and a quiet pebble beach a little way below the village where there's a small **campsite** next to the reliable *Captain Fidias's* taverna. **KÁMBOS** is similar, but even less visited, its beach a considerable walk down a hill. However, **accommodation** is available at the good-value *Rooms Hartzulakis* (☎08220/44 445; ❶) on the edge of a long gorge which also leads down to the sea; the same place has a terrace **taverna** with great views, and the proprietor can advise on **walking** hereabouts. Beyond them both is the **monastery of Khryssoskalítissa** increasingly visited by tours from Haniá and Paleohóra now the road has been sealed, but well worth the effort for its isolation and nearby beaches; the bus gets as far as Váthy, from where the monastery is another two-hours' walk away, although you could try hitching – with a fair chance of success – as many of the tourist cars are bound to be heading for the same destination.

Five kilometres beyond Khryssoskalítissa, another stretch of newly laid asphalt has replaced the former cratered nightmare of a track leading to the coast, opposite the tiny uninhabited islet of **Elafonísi**, marooned in a gloriously scenic turquoise lagoon. It's almost too easy now as you glide effortlessly down to the sea, and the increasing number of visitors and almost total lack of facilities to cater for them when they arrive is proving a major problem which no one seems to want to tackle.

You can easily wade out to the islet with its sandy beaches and rock pools, and the shallow lagoon is warm and crystal clear. It looks magnificent, but daily boat trips from Paleohóra and coach tours from elsewhere on the island have attracted a cluster of beach stalls renting loungers and selling tourist tat, which ensures that, in the middle of the day at least, it's far from deserted. To cope with the resulting sanitary problems, a single and totally inadequate portable toilet has been installed by the authorities next to the beach. If you want to stay, and really appreciate the place, there are a couple of seasonal tavernas, but bring some supplies unless you want to be wholly dependent on them.

Kándanos and Paleohóra

Getting down to Paleohóra by the main road which leaves the north coast at Tavronítis, 22km west of Haniá, is a lot easier, and several daily buses from Haniá make the trip. But although this route also has to wind through the western outriders of the White Mountains, it lacks the excitement of the routes to either side. **KÁNDANOS**, at the 58-kilometre mark, has been entirely rebuilt since it was destroyed by the Germans for its fierce resistance to their occupation. The original sign erected when the deed was done is preserved on the war memorial in the central square: "Here stood Kándanos, destroyed in retribution for the murder of 25 German soldiers, and never to be rebuilt again." The pleasantly easy-going and once again substantial village had the last laugh.

When the beach at **PALEOHÓRA** finally appears below it is a welcome sight. The little town is built across the base of a peninsula, its harbour and a beach known as Pebble Beach on the eastern side, the wide sands ("Sandy Beach") on the other. Above, on the outcrop, Venetian ramparts stand sentinel. These days Paleohóra has developed into a significant resort, but it's still thoroughly enjoyable, with a main street filling with tables at night as diners spill out of the restaurants, and with a pleasantly chaotic social life. You'll find a helpful **tourist office** (Mon & Wed–Sun 10am–1pm & 6–9pm; ☎08230/41 507) in the town hall on Venizélos, the official name of the main street; they have full accommodation lists and a provide a decent **map** which is useful for finding food and accommodation locations.

There are plenty of **places to stay** (though not always many vacancies in high season) – try the basic *Dolphin Rooms* (☎08230/41 703; ❶), below the Venetian fort, or *Castello Rooms* (☎08230/41 143; ❷), at the southern end of Sandy Beach, for a little more en-suite luxury. *Savas Rooms* (☎08230/41 075; ❶), near the bus station at the north end of town, does balcony en-suite rooms with kitchenette, fridge and fan for a very reasonable price. There's also a fair-sized **campsite** 2km north of Pebble Beach; if you are tempted to sleep on the main Sandy Beach – one of the best on the south coast, with showers, trees and acres of sand – be prepared for trouble from police and local residents who are no longer willing to tolerate this; your best bet is to get as far away from the town as possible if you want to be left in peace. When you tire of Paleohóra and the excellent **windsurfing** in the bay (boards for hire from Happy Surf on the beach), there are excursions up the hill to Prodhrómi, for example, or along a five- to six-hour coastal path to Soúyia.

For **eating** and **drinking**, tavernas, bars and cafés are to be found throughout the resort, particularly along the roads behind the two beaches. A good place to try for some imaginative **vegetarian** specials is *The Third Eye*, just out of the centre towards Sandy Beach. Other decent in-town eating places include *Pizzeria Niki*, off the south side of Kontekáki, and *The Wave* at the south end of Pebble Beach, serving good fish on a seaside terrace. As Paleohóra publicizes itself as a "family" resort there's an unwritten curfew around 11pm when the bars lower their sounds, so if you're looking for some untamed nightlife you've definitely come to the wrong place. The only raucous sounds after this hour are at the **dance club** *Palehora Club* at the extreme north end of the Pebble Beach and close to the campsite, where you can boogie beneath the stars on a dance floor overlooked by palms. An open-air **cinema**, Cine Attikon, tucked away in the northern backstreets is also worth knowing about; most of their films are in English and programmes (which change daily) are posted in the tourist office.

Almost everything else you're likely to need is located in the centre of town. **Banks** (with cash dispensers), **travel agents**, a **laundry**, **mountain bike** and **car hire** companies and **internet** access (at PC Corner above the *Alaloom* cocktail bar) are all along Venizélos, while the **post office** is on the road behind Sandy Beach. There are two **pharmacies** on Kontekáke, the road running from east to west at the south end of Venizélou, and there's a **health centre** in the street parallel to Venizélos to the west. **Boats** run from here to Elafonísi, the island of Gávdhos and along the coast to Soúyia and Ayía Rouméli; the travel agency Interkreta Travel (☎08230/41 393, ℱ41 050), close to the junction of Venizélos and Kondekáki, is the best source for information and tickets. They also have information about trips to walk the **Samariá Gorge**, see p.732, from here, with a bus leaving daily at 6am throughout the summer.

Gávdhos

The island of **Gávdhos**, some fifty kilometres of rough sea south of Paleohóra, is the most southerly landmass in Europe. Gávdhos is small (about 10km by 7km) and barren, but it has one major attraction: the enduring **isolation** which its inaccessible position has helped preserve. It is possible to turn up on spec and find a bed, but travel agents in Paleohóra such as Interkreta (see above) will arrange a room if you want one and also provide current ferry information. There's a semi-permanent community of campers and would-be "Robinson Crusoes" resident on the island throughout the summer – in addition to the six indigenous families who live here year round. Largely because water is often difficult to obtain most people choose to base themselves near to one of the three largest beaches and at the most popular of all, **SARAKINÍKO**, there are at least seven beachfront **tavernas** – *Taverna Gerti & Manolis* have **rooms** (☎08230/41 103; ❶) – in addition to a squatters' community spreading a shanty town of unsightly breezeblock summer dwellings behind the beach. Providing you avoid the crowds in August, if all you wanted is a beach to yourself and a taverna to grill your fish, this remains the place for you.

Travel details

Buses

For the latest timetables and complete route and fare information visit KTEL's website at ⊛http://bus-service-crete-ktel.com/timetables2.html
Áyios Nikólaos–Sitía (4 daily 7am–4.30pm; 2hr).
Haniá–Hóra Sfakíon (3 daily 8.30am–2pm; 2hr).
Haniá–Paleohóra (4 daily 8.30am–3.30pm; 2hr).
Haniá–Réthymnon–Iráklion (17 daily, 2 via old road 5.30am–8.30pm; 3hr total).
Iráklion–Ayía Galíni (8 daily 6.30am–6.30pm; 2hr 15min).

Iráklion–Áyios Nikólaos (20 daily 6.15am–8.30pm; 1hr 30min).
Iráklion–Festós (8 daily 7.30am–4.30pm; 1hr 30min).
Iráklion–Ierápetra (8 daily 6.30am–7.30pm; 2hr 30min).
Kastélli–Haniá (14 daily 6am–7pm; 1hr 30min).
Réthymnon–Spíli–Ayía Galíni (3 daily 7am–2.15pm; 45min–1hr 30min).

Ferries

For the latest timetables for domestic and international ferries from and to Crete visit ⊛www.greek-islands.gr or ⊛www.ferries.gr

Áyios Nikólaos and Sitía 5 sailings a week to Pireás (12hr), 4 ferries a week to Kásos, Kárpathos, Hálki and Rhodes; 4 weekly to Mílos.

Haniá 1 or 2 ferries daily to Pireás (9hr).
Hóra Sfakíon 5 ferries daily to Loutró/Ayía
Rouméli; 4 weekly to Gávdhos in season.
Iráklion 2 ferries daily to Pireás (12hr); 1 daily
fast ferry to Pireás (6hr); 2 ferries weekly to
Thessaloníki; 1 daily ferry to Thíra (4hr), also fast
boats and hydrofoils (2hr 30min); daily ferries to
Páros in season; 1–2 weekly to Mýkonos and Íos;

weekly to Náxos, Tínos, Skýros, Skíathos.
Kastélli (Kíssamos) 2 ferries weekly to Pireás
(11hr); 1–4 ferries weekly to Kýthira; 1 ferry weekly
to Yíthio (8hr); 1 ferry weekly to Kalamáta (9hr).
Paleohóra 3 boats a week in season to Gávdhos.
Also daily sailings to Elafonísi and Soúyia.
Réthymnon daily ferries to Pireás (12hr); seasonal
day-trips to Thíra.

Flights

Flights are on Olympic unless otherwise stated.
Haniá–Athens (4 daily on Olympic; 4 daily on
Aegean-Cronus; 2 daily on Axon)
Haniá–Thessaloníki (2 weekly on Olympic; 3
daily on Aegean-Cronus)
Iráklion–Athens (5–7 daily on Olympic; 6 daily on
Aegean-Cronus; 3–4 daily on Axon)

Iráklion–Rhodes (2 weekly, summer only, on
Olympic; 1–2 daily on Aegean-Cronus)
Iráklion–Thessaloníki (2 weekly on Olympic; 3
daily on Aegean-Cronus)
Iráklion–Thíra (2 weekly)
Sitía–Athens (1 weekly, Fri all year)

The Dodecanese

CHAPTER 9 # Highlights

* **Northern Kárpathos** Old walking trails take you between traditional villages. See p.746

* **Ródhos old town** Superbly preserved medieval streets, inextricably linked with the Knights of Saint John. See p.756

* **Lindos Acropolis, Rhodes** A pleasing blend of ancient and medieval culture; also great views over the town, but visit out of season for more atmosphere. See p.763

* **Thárri monastery, Rhodes** Superb Byzantine frescoes in the oldest religious foundation on the island. See p.767

* **Sými** The officially protected harbour and hillside village teem with trippers during the day, but a stay overnight is rewarding. See p.776

* **Volcano on Níssyros** The craters of the dormant volcano still hiccup, though the most recent – producing ash, steam and earthquakes – was in 1933. See p.789

* **Hóra, Astypálea** The windswept island "capital" is perched dramatically above the sea and has a beautiful Venetian *kástro*. See p.803

* **Mount Dhíkeos** The hike up is worthwhile for the views over the Dodecanese. See p.797

* **Brós Thermá, Kós** Relax in the shoreline hot springs, which flow into the sea, protected by a boulder ring. See p.797

* **Hóra, Pátmos** Crowned by the monastery dedicated to Saint John, who wrote the New Testament Book of Revelation on the island. See p.820

The Dodecanese

The furthest Greek island group from the mainland, the **Dodecanese** (Dhodhekánisos) lie close to the Turkish coast – some of the islands, like Kós and Kastellórizo, almost within hailing distance of Anatolia. Because of this position, and their remoteness from Athens, the islands have had a turbulent history: they were the scene of ferocious battles between German and British forces in 1943–44, and were only finally included in the modern Greek state in 1948 after centuries of occupation by Crusaders, Ottomans and Italians. Even now the threat (real or imagined) of invasion from Turkey is very much evident in the form of numerous military bases and smaller watch-points. Despite certain high-level civilian rapprochements which have taken place between Greece and Turkey in recent years, the Greek army and air force clearly prefer to keep their powder dry.

Whatever the rigours of the various occupations, their legacy includes a wonderful blend of architectural styles and of Eastern and Western cultures. Medieval Rhodes is the most famous, but almost every island has some Classical remains, a Crusaders' castle, a clutch of traditional villages and abundant grandiose public buildings. For these last the Italians, who occupied the Dodecanese from 1912 to 1943, are mainly responsible. In their determination to beautify the islands and turn them into a showplace for fascism they undertook public works, excavations and reconstruction on a massive scale; if historical accuracy was often sacrificed in the interests of style, only an expert is likely to complain. A more sinister aspect of the Italian administration was the

---

Accommodation price codes

Throughout the book we've categorized accommodation according to the following **price codes**, which denote the cheapest available double room in high season. All prices are for the room only, except where otherwise indicated. Many hotels, especially those in category ④ and over, include breakfast in the price; you'll need to check this when booking. During low season, rates can drop by more than fifty percent, especially if you are staying for three or more nights. Exceptions are during the Christmas and Easter weeks when you'll pay high-season prices. Single rooms, where available, cost around seventy percent of the price of a double.

① Up to €24	④ €43–58
② €24–33	⑤ €59–72
③ €34–42	⑥ €73 and upwards

Note: Youth hostels and mountain refuges typically charge €7–9 for a dormitory bed. For more accommodation details, see pp.51–54.

attempted forcible Latinization of the populace: spoken Greek and Orthodox observance were banned in public from 1923 to 1943. The most tangible reminder of this policy is the (rapidly dwindling) number of older people who can still converse – and write – more fluently in Italian than in Greek.

Aside from this bilingualism, the Dodecanese themselves display a marked topographic and economic schizophrenia. The dry limestone outcrops of **Kastellórizo**, **Sými**, **Hálki**, **Kássos** and **Kálymnos** have always been forced to rely on the sea for their livelihoods, and the wealth generated by this maritime culture – especially during the nineteenth century – fostered the growth of attractive port towns. The sprawling, relatively fertile giants, **Rhodes**

(Ródhos) and **Kós**, have recently seen their traditional agricultural economies almost totally displaced by a tourist industry grown up around good beaches and nightlife, as well as some of the most exciting historical monuments in the Aegean. **Kárpathos** lies somewhere in between, with a lightly forested north grafted on to a rocky limestone south; **Tílos**, despite its lack of trees, has ample water, though the green volcano-island of **Níssyros** does not. **Léros** shelters softer contours and more amenable terrain than its map outline would suggest, while **Pátmos** and **Astypálea** at the fringes of the archipelago offer architecture and landscapes more typical of the Cyclades.

The largest islands in the group are connected by regular **ferries**, and none (except for Kastellórizo, Astypálea and sometimes Tílos) is hard to reach. Rhodes is the main transport hub, with services to Turkey, Israel and Cyprus, as well as connections with Crete, the northeastern Aegean, the Cyclades and the mainland. Kálymnos and Kós are jointly an important secondary terminus, with a useful ferry based on Kálymnos, hydrofoil services using Kós as a focus and transfer point, and excursion boats based on Kós providing a valuable supplement to larger ferries arriving at uncivil hours.

Kássos

Like Psará islet in the northeast Aegean, **Kássos** contributed its large fleet to the Greek revolutionary war effort, and likewise suffered appalling consequences. In late May 1824, an Ottoman army sent by Ibrahim Pasha, Governor of Egypt, besieged the island; on June 7, aided perhaps by a traitor's tip as to the weak point in Kássos's defences, the invaders descended on the populated north-coastal plain, slaughtered most of the inhabitants and put houses, farms and trees to the torch.

Barren and depopulated since then, Kássos attracts few visitors, despite regular air links with Rhodes and Kárpathos, and being a port of call on ferry lines from those isles to Crete. Numerous sheer gorges slash through lunar terrain, with fenced smallholdings of midget olive trees providing the only permanent relief. Springtime grain crops briefly soften the usually empty terraces, and livestock somehow survives on a thin furze of thornbush. What remains of the population is grouped together in five villages facing Kárpathos, leaving most of the island uninhabited and uncultivated. Until very recently, there was little sign here of the wealth brought into other islands by diaspora Greeks or – since Kássos hasn't much to offer them – tourists; amidst the occasional new concrete monster, crumbling houses and disused hillside terraces poignantly recall better days. A long pattern of serving as roving pilots, or residence in Egypt (Kassiots were instrumental in digging the Suez Canal), has been eclipsed by subsequent emigration to the US. Thus American logo-T-shirts and baseball caps are *de rigueur* summer fashion, and the conversation of vacationing expatriates is spiked with Americanisms.

Kássos can be a nuisance to reach, and matters are unlikely to improve as two companies have gone bust attempting to build a new harbour, with the third contractor looking to follow suit. The existing jetty just west of Boúka fishing port in the capital, Frý (pronounced "free"), is so poor that passing ferries won't stop if any appreciable wind is up. In such cases, you disembark at Kárpathos and fly the remaining distance in a light, nineteen-seater aircraft. The air ticket plus a taxi fare to Kárpathos airport isn't much more than the fare charged by Finíki (Kárpathos)-based excursion boats which can manoeuvre into Boúka in most weathers. The airport lies 1km west of Frý, an easy enough walk, otherwise a cheap (€1.50) ride on one of the island's three taxis. Except in July and August, when a few rental motorbikes and boat excursions are offered, the only method of exploring the island's remoter corners is by hiking along fairly arduous, shadeless paths and roads. Place-name signposting tends to be in Greek only, and in Kassiot dialect at that – clearly the islanders aren't expecting many non-Kassiot visitors.

Frý and Emboriós

Most of the appeal of the capital, **FRÝ**, is confined to the immediate environs of the wedge-shaped fishing port of **Boúka**, protected from the sea by two crab-claws of breakwater and overlooked by the cathedral of Áyios Spyrídhon. Inland, Frý is engagingly unpretentious, even down-at-heel; there are no concessions to tourism, and little attempt has been made to prettify an essentially scruffy little town that's quite desolate out of season. Somewhat overpriced **accommodation** is found at the seafront hotels *Anagenissis* (☎02450/41 495, ℱ41 036, ⓦwww.kassos-island.gr; ❷) and, just behind with fewer views, the less expensive, all-en-suite *Anessis* (☎02450/41 201, ℱ41 730; ❷). The manager of the *Anagenissis* also has a few pricier apartments, and runs the all-in-one travel agency just below (though Olympic has its own premises two doors down). Both hotels tend to be noisy owing to morning bustle on the waterfront – and the phenomenal number of small but lively fast-food joints and café-bars in town, some right underneath. During high season a few **rooms** operate; these tend to be more expensive and mostly located in the suburb of Emboriós, fifteen-minute's walk east.

Outside of peak season, Frý can support only one full-service **taverna**: *O Mylos*, overlooking the intermittent harbour works. Luckily it's excellent and reasonable, with a good variety of daily-special *mayireftá* at lunch and sometimes fish grills by night. From late June to early September you can also try *Iy Oraia Bouka*, perched above Boúka, or *To Meltemi* ouzerí, on the way to Emboriós. In Emboriós itself, only *Ta Tessera Adherfia* by the palm-tree church shows any sign of life outside of summer. Shops in Frý, including two fruit stalls, are fairly well stocked for self-catering.

Local beaches

Frý's town **beach**, if you can call it that, is at **Ammouá** (Ammoudhiá), a thirty-minute walk beyond the airstrip along the coastal track. This sandy cove, just before the landmark chapel of Áyios Konstandínos, is often caked with seaweed and tar, but persevere five minutes more and you'll find much cleaner pea-gravel coves. The determined can swim off the little patch of sand at **Emboriós**, along with the half-dozen resident ducks, and there's a more private pebble stretch off to the right. But having got this far, you may as well continue ten to fifteen minutes along the shore, first along an old track, then on a path past the last house, for a final scramble to the base of the **Gaïdhouropoúli** ravine, where there's another secluded pebble cove. Otherwise, it's worth shelling out for high-season boat excursions to far better beaches on a pair of islets visible to the northwest, **Armathiá** and **Makrá**. There are no amenities (or shade) on either islet, so come prepared.

The interior

At the edges of the agricultural plain just inland from Frý cluster a number of villages, linked to each other by road; all are worth a passing visit, and can be reached by foot in a single day.

Larger in extent and more rural than Frý, **AYÍA MARÍNA**, 1500m inland and uphill, is most attractive seen from the south, arrayed above olive groves; one of its two belfried churches is the focus of the island's liveliest festival, on July 17. Some fifteen minutes beyond the hamlet of Kathístres, a further 500m southwest, the cave of **Ellinokamára** is named for the late Classical, polygonal wall completely blocking the entrance; its ancient function is uncertain, perhaps a cult shrine or tomb complex. To reach it, turn south at the two restored windmills in Ayía Marína, then right (west) at the phone-box junction; carry on, straight and down (not level and left) until you see a red-dirt path going up the hillside to a crude, stone-built pastoral hut. Some modern masonry walls enclose the start of this path, but once at the hut (the cave is more or less underneath it) you're compelled to hop a fence to visit – there are no gates. From Ellinokamára another, fainter path – you'll probably need a guide – continues within ninety minutes in the same direction to the larger, more natural cave of **Seláï**, with impressive stalactites in the rear chamber.

Generally, walking opportunities on Kássos are poor – trails are few, unmarked and in poor condition, with no shade and few reliable water sources. An exception is the forty-minute path from Arvanitohóri to Póli, which is clearly walled in and enjoyable, shortcutting the road effectively – it starts at the base of the village, where two trees occupy planter wells. **PÓLI**, somewhat impoverished and resolutely agricultural, is the site of a badly deteriorated ancient and medieval acropolis – a few stretches of fortification remain – and marks the start of a four-kilometre road leading southeast to **Áyios Mámas**, signposted in dialect as "**Áï Mámas**", one of two important rural monasteries, perched spectacularly overlooking the sea. Alternatively, from Póli you can descend – again on walled-in path for the first twenty minutes, then dirt track – to **PANAYÍA**, famous for its now-neglected mansions – many of Kássos's wealthiest ship captains hailed from here – and for the oldest surviving church on the island, the eighteenth-century **Panayía tou Yióryi**.

Between Ayía Marína and Arvanitohóri, another road, that used to be just a dirt track and was only recently paved over, veers off southwest from the road linking the two villages towards the rural monastery of **Áyios Yeóryios Hadhión**. The pleasure of walking this route, however, has been somewhat diminished by the paving over of the road, so you'll probably want to hire a taxi, rent a bike if available or hitch a lift in at least one direction. At the beginning of the route you skirt the narrows of a fearsome gorge, and from there on you are unlikely to see another living thing aside from goats, sheep or an occasional Eleonora's falcon. After about an hour, the Mediterranean appears to the south, a dull expanse ruffled only by the occasional ship bound for Cyprus and the Middle East. When you finally reach a fork, adopt the upper, right-hand turning, following derelict phone lines towards Áyios Yeóryios Hadhión (signed as "**Áï Yeóryi**"), 12km (3hr on foot) from Frý. This is busiest at its late-April festival time, but during the warmer months there's a resident caretaker who runs a small snack/drinks bar. There are a few open guest cells (ask nicely, donation expected) and cistern water here if you need to fill up canteens; the only other water en route is a well at the route's high point.

From the monastery it's another 3km on dirt track – motorbikes can make it most of the way – to **Hélatros** ("Hélathros" on older maps), a lonely cove at the mouth of one of the larger, more forbidding Kassiot canyons. The sand-and-gravel beach itself is small and mediocre, but the water is pristine and – except for the occasional fishing boat – you'll probably be alone. The lower, left-hand option at the fork is the direct track to Hélatros, but this is only 2km shorter and, following severe 1995 storm damage, impassable to any vehicle and

all but the most energetic hikers; since the paving of the upper road to Áï
Yeóryi, it is likely to have got even worse.

Kárpathos

A long, narrow island marooned between Rhodes and Crete, wild **Kárpathos**
has always been something of an underpopulated backwater, although it is the
third largest of the Dodecanese. An habitually cloud-capped mountainous spine
rises to over 1200m, and divides the more populous, lower-lying south from an
exceptionally rugged north. A magnificent, windswept coastline of cliffs and
promontories has begun to attract significant numbers of Scandinavian and
German package tourists, who arrive on several direct international charters
weekly. Since the 1990s, these clients have more or less monopolized several
resorts in the southern part of the island, pushing independent travellers up to
the remote north of the island. Despite this development, Kárpathos remains
saddled with a deficient road system – only partly paved, unspeakable otherwise
– and expensive taverna food, which offsets reasonable room prices. Most
island-hoppers come here for a glimpse of the traditional village life in the far
north, and for the numerous superb, secluded beaches.

The island's interior isn't the most alluring: the central and northern uplands
were badly scorched by forest fires in the 1980s, and agriculture plays a slighter
role than on any other Greek island of comparable size. The Karpathians are
too well off to bother much with farming; massive emigration to America and
the resulting remittance economy has transformed Kárpathos into one of the
wealthiest Greek islands.

Kárpathos's four Classical cities figure little in ancient chronicles. Alone of the
major Dodecanese, the island was held by the Genoese and Venetians after the
Byzantine collapse and so has no castle of the crusading Knights of St John, nor
any surviving medieval fortresses of consequence. The Ottomans couldn't be
bothered to settle or even garrison it; instead they left a single judge or *kadi* at
the main town, making the Greek population responsible for his safety during
the many pirate attacks.

Pigádhia (Kárpathos Town)

The island capital of **PIGÁDHIA**, often known simply as Kárpathos, nestles
at the south end of scenic **Vróndi Bay**, whose sickle of sand extends 3km
northwest. The town itself, curling around the jetty and quay where ferries and
excursion boats dock, is as drab as its setting is beautiful; an ever-increasing
number of concrete blocks contributes to the air of a vast building site, making the Italian-era port police and county governmental buildings seem like
heirlooms by comparison. Although there's nothing special to see, Pigádhia
does offer just about every facility you might need, albeit with a definite pack-
age-tourism slant.

Getting around

Olympic Airways (book a week minimum in advance – planes to Rhodes have
just nineteen seats) is at the west end of Apodhímon Karpathíon, the "Street of
the Overseas Karpathians", at the corner of Platía 5-Oktovríou. Possi Travel
(☎02450/22 235) are sole agents for LANE, currently the only shipping line
to call at Pigádhia, and also sell air tickets when Olympic is shut. The **post
office** is on Ethnikís Andístasis, while all three **banks** have cash dispensers.

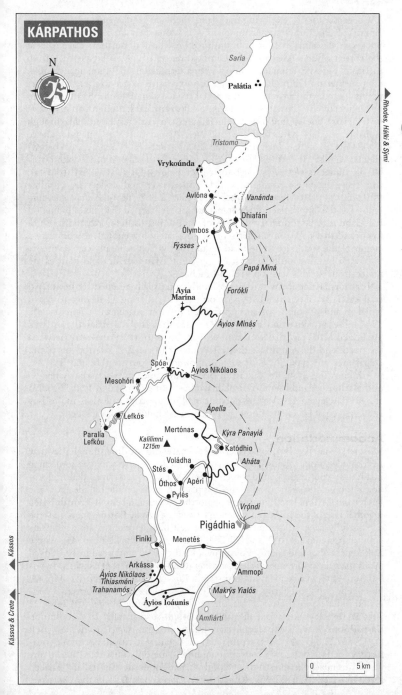

KÁRPATHOS

N

Saría

Palátia ••

Trístomo

Vrykoúnda •••

Avlóna •   *Vanánda*

                    Dhiafáni •

Ólymbos •

Fýsses

                Papá Miná

                Forókli

**Ayía
Marína** •

                Áyios Minás'

Spóa •   Áyios Nikólaos •

Mesohóri •

                Ápella

Lefkós •

Mertónas •   *Kýra Panayiá*

Paralía
Lefkóu •   *Kalilímni
1215m* ▲   Katódhio •

            Voládha •   *Aháta*

Stés •
Óthos • Apéri •

        Pylés •

                Vróndi

                Pigádhia ⚓

Finíki •   Menetés •

Arkássa •

Áyios Nikólaos ••   Ammopí •
Tihiasméni
Trahanamós •

            Makrýs Yialós

    Áyios Ioáunis •

        Amfiárti

                ✈

▶ Rhodes, Hálki & Sými

◀ Kássos

Kássos & Crete ◀

0   5 km

When it comes to exploring the island, there are regular **buses** to Pylés, via Apéri, Voládha, Óthos and Ammopí, as well as one daily (in term time only) to Spóa via Mesohóri; the "station" (just a stop with a destination-placard) is at the corner of 28-Oktovríou and Dhimokratías, a couple of blocks back from the front. Set-rate, unmetered **taxis**, with a terminal in the municipal car park a bit further up Dhimokratías, aren't too expensive to get to these and other points (such as the airport) on the paved road system, but charge a fortune to go anywhere else. Upwards of a dozen outfits **rent cars**, though you may have to try every one to find a free vehicle; rates are vastly over the odds, though available models have improved of late. Agencies to try include Circle (☎02450/22 690), which may give discounts to *Rose Studios* (see below) clients; friendly *Avis* (☎02450/22 702), at the north edge of town, with possible discounts to *Hotel Panorama* guests (see below); Drive (☎02450/61 249); and Trust, based in Ammopí, which will deliver and collect in Pigádhia (☎02450/81 060). Moto Carpathos (☎02450/22 382), near the *dhimarhío*, currently has the largest fleet of scooters for rent. Be warned that the only fuel on the island is to be found at two pairs of stations just to the north and south of town, and that tanks on smaller scooters are barely big enough to complete a circuit of the south, let alone head up north – which is, in any case, expressly forbidden by most outfits. For seagoing jaunts, **windsurfers** and **canoes** are rented from various stalls on Vróndi beach.

Northern Kárpathos is most pleasantly and usually reached **by boat**. Two rival kaïkia are moored side by side on the jetty, offering all-in **day-tours** to Dhiafáni and Ólymbos for around €13.20 (pay on board); the *Chrisovalandou III* is more attractive and stable in heavy sea than the *Karpathos II*. Less well publicized is the fact that you can use these boats to travel **one-way** between the north and the south in either direction – the standard rate for this is €6. Departures are typically 8.30am northbound, 4.30pm southbound. It's also worth knowing about the tiny **mail boat** which once or twice weekly reverses this pattern: southbound from Dhiafáni at 8am, northbound from Pigádhia at 3pm (fare again €6). Various agents can also offer trips to Kássos and to isolated east-coast beaches without facilities (bring lunch if not included).

Accommodation

Most ferries are met by people offering **self-catering studios**, though they may be forbidden from touting on the quay itself. Unless you've arranged something in advance, you might consider such offers – the town is so small that no location is too inconvenient, though the best place to stay is on the hillside above the bus terminal. More luxurious places lie north, towards and behind **Vróndi** beach to either side of the ruined fifth-century basilica of **Ayía Fotiní**, but tend to be occupied by package groups. Three of the best hillside premises are perennially popular *Rose Studios* (☎02450/22 284, ✉reservations@mailgate.gr; ❶), whose well-kept studios and rooms are run by a kindly family and need to be booked in advance; the courteous *Amaryllis Studios* (☎02450/22 375; ❷), slightly downhill and east, with enormous units; and *Elias Rooms* (☎02450/22 446; ❶; June–Sept only) just above the *Hotel Karpathos*, with en-suite rooms in a converted older house. Lower down, the rambling, en-suite *Konaki* (☎02450/22 908; ❶) on 28-Oktovríou, the upper through-road parallel to Apodhímon Karpathíon, is a backpackers' standby, while the *Hotel Karpathos* itself (☎02450/22 347; ❶) is serviceable and in a central location. For more comfort try the following two conventional hotels, the only ones that cater in any way to nonpackage guests: the helpful *Atlantis*, opposite the Italian "palace" (☎02450/22 777, 📠22 780, ✉htatlantis@yahoo.com; ❹) and the *Panorama*, in a quiet inland lane at the start of the Vróndi beach road (☎02450/23 262, ⓕ23 021; ❸).

Eating and drinking

Most of Pigádhia's waterfront **tavernas** are undistinguished – *yíros* and chips reign supreme – and overpriced, though quality and value improves significantly as you head east towards the ferry dock. Towards the end of the strip are clustered three worthy choices: *To Perigiali*, a fairly genuine ouzerí with good bread and home-made desserts; *To Kyma*, good for nonfarmed fish; and the best all-rounder, *Iy Orea Karpathos*, with palatable local bulk wine, *trahanádhes* soup, sausages and great spinach pie. One block inland, the clear winner is *To Ellinikon*, a *mezedhopolío* that caters all year round to a local clientele with hot and cold *orek-tiká*, meat and good desserts. Live **music** can be heard nightly (June–Sept) at the *Kafenio Life of Angels*, one of the few surviving old buildings next to the church on Apodhímon Karpathíon, though the sessions here are not by any means the best on the island. More trendy **bars** such as *Art Café-Bar*, *Rocks* and *Escape* offer taped sounds from perches overlooking the bay. Pigádhia's main **internet café** is *Café Galileo* (ⓦwww.caffegalileo.gr), two doors down from Olympic on Apodhímon Karpathíon. At Vróndi there are two serviceable lunchtime tavernas at the southerly, town end: *To Limanaki* and the *Seaside Snack Bar*.

Southern and western Kárpathos

The southern extremity of Kárpathos, towards the airport, is extraordinarily desolate and windswept. There's a couple of relatively undeveloped sandy beaches – in particular **Makrýs Yialós** – on the southeast coast in the region known as Amfiárti, but they're only really attractive to foreign windsurfers who come to take advantage of the prevailing northwesterlies. Most people go no further in this direction than **AMMOPÍ**, just 7km from Pigádhia. This, together with the development at Vróndi and Arkássa, is the closest thing on Kárpathos to a purpose-built beach resort. The two sand-and-gravel, tree-fringed coves are bordered by half a dozen **tavernas** and increasing numbers of **hotels** and **rooms** – recommendable among these, not dominated by packages, are the *Votsalakia Rooms* (☎02450/22 204; ❷) and the *Sunflower Studios* (☎ & ⓕ 02450/81 019; ❷). West out of Pigádhia the road climbs steeply 9km up to **MENETÉS**, an appealing ridgetop village with handsome old houses, a tiny folklore museum and a spectacularly sited church. There are two **tavernas** here (*Koula* and *Ta Dhyo Adhelfia*) and a World War II memorial with sweeping views north.

Beyond Menetés, you descend to **ARKÁSSA**, on the slopes of a ravine draining to the west coast, with excellent views to Kássos en route. Despite just one good nearby beach interrupting a mostly rocky shore, Arkássa has been heavily developed, with hotels and restaurants sprouting in clusters. Much of the **accommodation** is aimed squarely at the package market, but independent travellers could try the en-suite *Hotel Dimitrios* (☎02450/61 353, ⓕ61 249; ❷ including breakfast), or the *Seaside Studios* (☎02450/61 421; ❷) above **Áyios Nikólaos** beach signposted just south, a 600-metre stretch of sand – rare hereabouts – with a single taverna. Most other **tavernas** lie north of the ravine in the village centre, for example the durable *Petaloudha* on the dead-end access street.

A few hundred metres south of where the ravine meets the sea, a signposted cement side road leads briefly to the whitewashed chapel of **Ayía Sofía**, marooned amidst various remains of Classical and Byzantine Arkessia. These consist of several mosaic floors with geometric patterns, including one running diagonally under the floor of a half-buried chapel, emerging from the walls on either side. The Paleókastro headland beyond was the site of Mycenaean Arkessia; the walk up is again signposted, but scarcely worth it for the sight of a few stretches of polygonal wall and a couple of tumbled columns.

The tiny fishing port of **FINÍKI**, just a couple of kilometres north, offers a minuscule beach, fairly regular excursions to Kássos, half a dozen **tavernas** and several **rooms/studios** establishments. Accommodation includes *Giavasis Studios* (☎02450/61 365; ❷), on the road to the jetty, or for more comfort and value the well-designed and -built *Arhontiko Studios* up on the main bypass road (☎02450/61 473, ℱ61 054; ❸). *Iy Marina* and *To Dhelfini* are currently the most salubrious eateries in Finíki, though there's another well-loved one, *Kostas*, 500m north under two tamarisks at reefy Kamarákia beach.

The west-coast road is asphalted all the way to the turning for the attractive resort of **PARALIÁ LEFKOÚ**, shore annexe of the inland hamlet of Lefkós. Although this is a delightful place for flopping on the beach, only three weekly buses call, and Paralía Lefkoú marks the furthest point you can reach from Pighádhia on a small motorbike and return safely without running out of fuel. However, any effort will be rewarded by the striking topography of cliffs, hills, islets and sandspits surrounding a triple bay. There are now over two dozen places to stay, and perhaps half as many tavernas, but package companies tend to monopolize the better **accommodation** from June to September. Exceptions include the *Akroyiali Studios* (☎02450/71 178; ❶), on a stonier, fourth bay just south off the access road, and the spartan but en-suite *Sunweek Studios* (☎02450/71 025; ❶), above *Zorbas* taverna on the seaward promontory. On the said promontory you'll find the most authentic eating option, the seafood-rich *Steki tou Kalymnou*.

Back on the main road, you climb northeast through one of the few sections of Karpathian pine forest not scarred by fire to **MESOHÓRI**. The village tumbles down towards the sea around narrow, stepped alleys, coming to an abrupt halt at the edge of a flat-topped bluff dotted with three tiny, ancient chapels and separated from the village proper by a vast oasis of orchards. These are nurtured by the fountain (best water on the island) underneath the church of **Panayía Vryssianí**, wedged against the mountainside just east and invisible from the end of the access road. On the stair-street leading to this church is an excellent taverna, the *Dhramoundana*, remarkably reasonable for Kárpathos, and featuring local capers, sausages and marinated "sardines" (really a larger fish, *menoúla*). The paved main road continues over the island's watershed to Spóa, overlooking the east coast (see opposite).

Central Kárpathos

The **centre** of Kárpathos supports a quartet of villages blessed with superb hillside settings, ample running water – and a cool climate, even in August. Nearly everyone here has "done time" in North America, then returned home with their nest eggs. New Jersey, New York and Canadian car plates tell you exactly where repatriated islanders struck it rich – often fabulously so (the area has the highest per capita income in Greece). West-facing **PYLÉS** is the most attractive, set above another spring-fed oasis, while **ÓTHOS**, noted for its red wine and a private ethnographic museum, is the highest (approx 400m) and chilliest, on the flanks of 1215-metre Mount Kalilímni. Among several **tavernas** here, try *Toxotis*, basically a bar with mezédhes and a couple of cooked dishes of the day, plus the excellent bread the village is noted for. On the east side of the ridge you find **VOLÁDHA** with its tiny Venetian citadel and a pair of tavernas. From **APÉRI**, the largest, lowest and wealthiest settlement, you can drive 6km along a very rough road to the dramatic pebble beach of **Aháta**, with just a rather modest snack bar.

Beyond Apéri, the road up the **east coast** is extremely rough in places, passing above beaches most easily accessible by boat trips from Pigádhia. **Kýra Panayiá** is the first encountered, reached via a paved but twisty side road through Katódhio hamlet; there's a surprising number of villas and rooms and a few tavernas in the ravine behind the 150m of fine gravel and sheltered, turquoise water. **Ápella** is the best of the beaches you can reach by road, though there's a final short path from the single taverna-rooms (the only facility) at the road's end to the scenic 300-metre gravel strand. The end of this route is **SPÓA**, high above the shore just east of the island's spine, with a snack bar and more reliable kafenío at the edge of the village which might make better meal stops than the overpriced *Votsalo* down at **Áyios Nikólaos**, 5km below, a small hamlet with an average beach and the overgrown ruins of a Paleo-Christian basilica to explore.

Northern Kárpathos

Although connected by dirt road with Spóa, much the easiest (and usual) way to get to northern Kárpathos is by sea. Inter-island ferries call at Dhiafáni two or three times a week in season, or there are the above-cited smaller tour kaïkia from Pigádhia daily. The journey time on the smaller boats is about ninety minutes, with boats met at Dhiafáni by buses for the eight-kilometre transfer up to the traditional village of Ólymbos, the main attraction in this part of the island.

Ólymbos and around

Originally founded as a pirate-safe refuge in Byzantine times, windswept **ÓLYMBOS** straddles a long ridge below slopes studded with mostly ruined windmills. Two restored ones, beyond the main church, grind wheat and barley during late summer only, though one is kept under sail most of the year. Its basement houses a small ethnographic museum (odd hours; free), while a small shop nearby sells locally produced farm products. The village has long attracted foreign and Greek ethnologists, who treat it as a living museum of peasant dress, crafts, dialect and music long since gone elsewhere in Greece. It's still a very picturesque place, yet traditions are vanishing by the year. Nowadays it's only the older women and those working in the several tourist shops who wear the striking and magnificently colourful traditional dress – an instant photo opportunity in exchange for persistent sales pitches for the trinkets, many of them imported.

After a while you'll notice the prominent role that the women play in daily life: tending gardens, carrying goods on their shoulders or herding goats. Nearly all Ólymbos men emigrate or work outside the village, sending money home and returning only on holidays. The long-isolated villagers also speak a unique dialect, said to maintain traces of its Doric and Phrygian origins – thus "Ólymbos" is pronounced "Élymbos" locally. Live vernacular music is still heard regularly and draws crowds of visitors at festival times, in particular Easter and August 15, when you've little hope of finding a bed.

Among places to **stay**, the friendly *Rooms Restaurant Olymbos* (☎02450/51 252; ❶), near the village entrance, has rooms with baths or unplumbed ones with traditional furnishings, while the *Café-Restaurant Zefiros*, near the centre and run by two sisters, manages the en-suite *Hotel Astro* (☎02450/51 378; ❷).

There are a few other places to **eat**; one of the best and most obvious is *O Mylos*, occupying one of the restored mills and offering locally made wine and home-style specialities.

From the village the superb west-coast beach at **Fýsses** is a sharp 35-minute drop below, first cross-country, later by path. Most **local hikes**, however, head more gently north or east, many of them on waymarked paths, though you'll have to stay overnight in the area to enjoy them. The easiest option is the ninety-minute walk back down to Dhiafáni, beginning just below the two working windmills. The way is well marked, with water en route. It eventually drops to a ravine amidst extensive forest, though the last half-hour is mostly over bulldozed riverbed. You could also tackle the trail north to the ruins and beach at **Vrykoúnda** ("Vrougoúnda" in dialect), via sparsely inhabited **Avlóna**, set on a high upland devoted to grain. *Rooms Olymbos* plans to open an annexe soon at the edge of this hamlet, but it's best to take food and ample water to make a day of it, as it's just under three-hours' walk one way to Vrykoúnda, which offers traces of Hellenistic/Roman Brykous, the remote cave-shrine of John the Baptist on the promontory and good swimming. Trístomo, a Byzantine anchorage in the far northeast of Kárpathos, can also be reached on a magnificent cobbled way beginning above Avlóna; the return is by the same way. There's also a fine ninety-minute marked path from Avlóna down to Vanánda beach (see below).

Dhiafáni

Although its popularity is growing – especially since the 1996 completion of a new dock for large ferries – rooms in **DHIAFÁNI** are still inexpensive, and the pace of life slow outside of August. There are plenty of places at which to stay and eat, shops that will change money and even a small travel agency, Orfanos Travel (℡02450/51 410), which has its own en-suite hotel (❷). The obvious *Mayflower Hotel* (℡02450/51 228; ❷) opposite the quay is to be refurbished for comfort in 2002; otherwise try the non-en-suite *Pansion Delfini* (℡02450/51 391; ❶), up on the southern hillside, though it ain't the same since life-and-soul of the place Kalliopi Lioreisi died in 2000. On the front, the most reliable, year-round **tavernas** are Italian-run *Iy Gorgona/L'Angolo* and the *Mayflower*.

Boat trips are offered to various nearby **beaches**, as well as to the Byzantine site of Palátia on the uninhabited islet of **Saría** or through the narrow strait to Trístomo anchorage and the ruins of Vrykoúnda. There are several places within walking distance. Closest is **Vanánda**, a stony beach with an eccentrically managed campsite-snack bar in the oasis behind. To get there, follow the pleasant signposted path north through the pines, but don't believe the signs that say ten minutes – it's over thirty minutes away, shortcutting the more recent road. **Papá Miná**, with a few trees and cliff-shade, lies an hour's walk away via the cairned trail taking off from the road to the ferry dock.

Rhodes (Ródhos)

It's no accident that **Rhodes** is among the most visited of the Greek islands. Not only is its east coast lined with numerous sandy beaches, but the capital's nucleus is a beautiful and remarkably preserved medieval city, the legacy of the crusading Knights of St John who used the island as their main base from 1309 until 1522. Unfortunately this showpiece is jammed to capacity with over a million tourists in a good year, as against about 111,000 permanent inhabitants (including many foreigners). Of transient visitors, Germans, Brits, Swedes,

RHODES

Italians and Danes predominate in that order, though they tend to arrive in different months of the year.

Blessed with an equable climate and strategic position, Rhodes was important from earliest times despite a lack of good harbours. The best natural port spawned the ancient town of Lindos which, together with the other city-states Kameiros and Ialyssos, united in 408 BC to found the new capital of Rhodes at the northern tip of the island. At various moments the cities allied themselves with Alexander, the Persians, Athenians or Spartans as prevailing conditions suited them, generally escaping retribution for backing the wrong side by a combination of seafaring audacity, sycophancy and burgeoning wealth as a trade centre. Following the failed siege of Demetrios Polyorketes in 305 BC, Rhodes prospered even more, displacing Athens as the major venue for rhetoric and the arts in the east Mediterranean. The town, which lies underneath virtually all of the modern city, was laid out by one Hippodamus in the grid layout much in vogue at the time, with planned residential and commercial quarters. Its perimeter walls totalled nearly 15km, enclosing nearly double the area of the present town, and the Hellenistic population was said to exceed 100,000 – a staggering figure for late antiquity, as against 50,631 at the last modern census.

Decline set in when Rhodes became involved in the Roman civil wars, and Cassius sacked the city; by late imperial times, it was a backwater, a status confirmed by numerous barbarian raids during the Byzantine period. The Byzantines were compelled to cede the island to the Genoese, who in turn surrendered it to the Knights of St John. The second great siege of Rhodes, during 1522–23, saw Ottoman Sultan Süleyman the Magnificent oust the stubborn knights, who retreated to Malta; the town once again lapsed into relative obscurity, though heavily colonized and garrisoned, until its seizure by the Italians in 1912.

Arrival and information

All international and inter-island **ferries** dock at the middle of Rhodes' three ports, the commercial harbour of Kolóna; the only exceptions are local **boats** to and from Sými, all excursion craft, and the **hydrofoils**, which use the yacht harbour of Mandhráki. Its entrance was supposedly once straddled by the Colossus, an ancient statue of Apollo built to celebrate the end of the 305 BC siege; today two columns surmounted by bronze deer are less overpowering replacements.

The **airport** is 13km southwest of town, by the village of Paradhísi; public urban buses bound for Paradhíssi, Kalavárdha, Theológos or Sálakos pass the stop (look for the perspex-and-wood kiosk) on the main road opposite the northerly car-park entrance fairly frequently between 6am and midnight (fare €1.50). A taxi into town will cost €10.30–19.10, plus bags and airport supplement, depending on the time of day. Orange-and-white **buses** for both the west and east coasts of Rhodes leave from two almost adjacent terminals on Papágou and Avérof, just outside the Italian-built New Market (a tourist trap, to miss without regret). Between the lower eastern station and the **taxi** rank at Platía Rimínis there's a fairly useless **municipal tourist office** (June–Sept Mon–Sat 9am–9pm, Sun 9am–3pm), while some way up Papágou on the corner of Makaríou stands the more reliable **EOT office** (Mon–Fri 7.30am–3pm); both dispense bus and ferry schedules, the latter also providing a list of standard taxi fares, complete with complaint form. Rhodes taxi drivers don't have a good reputation – some have been found to take kickbacks from hotels or overcharge passengers.

Ródhos Town

RÓDHOS TOWN divides into two unequal parts: the compact old walled city, and the New Town which sprawls around it in three directions. The latter dates from the Ottoman occupation, when Greek Orthodox natives – forbidden to dwell in the old city – founded several suburb villages or *marásia* in the environs, which have since merged. Commercialization is predictably rampant in the walled town, and in the modern district of Neohóri ("Niohóri" in dialect), west of Mandhráki yacht harbour; the few buildings which aren't hotels are souvenir shops, car-rental or travel agencies and bars – easily sixty to seventy in every category. The pointy bit of Neohóri is surrounded by a continuous **beach**, complete with deckchairs, parasols and showers, particularly on the more sheltered east-facing section called **Élli**. At the northernmost point of the island an **Aquarium** (daily: April–Sept 9am–9pm; Oct–March 9am–4.30pm; €1.75), officially the "Hydrobiological Institute", offers some diversion with its subterranean maze of seawater tanks. Upstairs is a less enthralling collection of half-rotten stuffed sharks, seals and even a whale. Some 200m southeast stand the **Murad Reis mosque**, an atmospherically neglected Muslim cemetery, and the equally dilapidated **Villa Cleobolus**, where Lawrence Durrell lived from 1945 to 1947.

Just a few paces northwest of this, the Italian-built Albergo delle Rose (*Hotel Rodon*) was refurbished and pressed into service in 1999 as the **Casino of Rhodes**, Greece's third largest, and unusually, open to locals as well as visitors. Admission is €15, the minimum age is 23 and ID is required.

Accommodation

Hotels and pensions at all price levels abound in the Old Town, mostly in the quad bounded by Omírou to the south, Sokrátous to the north, Perikléous to the east and Ippodhámou to the west. There are also a few possibilities worth considering in Neohóri, especially if you're bound for the airport or to Sými at an early hour. During crowded seasons, or late at night, it's prudent to either ring ahead or be prepared to accept the offers of proprietors meeting the ferries and change base next day if necessary – as it frequently is, since standards amongst quay-touted premises tend to be low.

Old Town

Andreas, Omírou 28D ☎02410/34 156, ⓕ74 285, ⓦwww.hotelandreas.com. Perennially popular (reservations needed) and under new dynamic management, this is one of the more imaginative old-house restoration-pensions, refurbished in 2000. Rooms in a variety of formats (including family-size) and plumbing arrangements (most en-suite). Terrace view-bar for breakfast and evenings, two-night minimum stay, credit cards accepted, indeed vital for advance booking. Open March 15–Oct 31. ❸

Apollo, Omírou 28C ☎02410/63 894. Basic – cold-water sinks in rooms, baths in halls – but clean and friendly rooms place, under new management since 2001 and lightly refurbished; the self-catering kitchen makes it good for longer stays. ❶

La Luna, Ierokléous 21 ☎ & ⓕ 02410/25 856. Clean, wood-trimmed if plain (no en suites) pension in a converted old Turkish house, complete with still-functioning *hamam* (Turkish bath). Garden bar for breakfast, by the citrus and banana trees. ❹

Marco Polo Mansion, Ayíou Fanouríou 42 ☎ & ⓕ 02410/25 562, ⓦwww.marcopolomansion.web. Superb 1999 conversion of an old Turkish mansion, again with a *hamam* on site, but here all rooms are en suite and exquisitely furnished with antiques

from the nearby eponymous gallery, plus cotton pillows and handmade mattresses. Large buffet breakfasts provided by ebullient manageress Efi, and adjoining café after hours. One-week minimum stay, book ahead; part open in winter, breakfast included. ❻

Niki's, Sofokléous 39 ☎02410/25 115. Some rooms can be on the small side, but almost all are en suite, and upper-storey ones have fine views. There's a washing machine, common terrace and friendly management to round things off. ❸

Pink Elephant/Roz Elefandas, officially Irodhótou 42 but actually on Timahídhas ☎ & ⓕ 02410/22 469. Simple but clean rooms occupying several levels of a modernized old building, near the traditional red-light district; roof deck with sunning and covered sections. Discount for singles. ❸

S. Nikolis, Ippodhámou 61 ☎02410/34 561, ⓕ32 034, ⓦwww.s-nikolis.gr. A variety of premises in the west of the Old Town. Hotel/honeymoon-suite rates of €44 (low) and €147 (high) include breakfast, TV and air-con; the self-catering apartments (€59–88) are among the finest restoration results in the Old Town, and interconnect to accommodate groups/families. Booking essential, and accepted only with credit-card number. Open April–Nov.

Spot, Perikléous 21 ☎ & ⓕ 02410/34 737. Yet another old-town hotel under a new generation of management, this modern building has cheerfully painted en-suite rooms of varying formats with textiles on the walls, and air-con or fans, representing superb value. Internet facilities and free luggage storage. Open March–Nov. ❸

Via-Via, Lysipoú 2, alley off Pythagóra ☎ & ⓕ 02410/77 027, ⓔviavia@rho.forthnet.gr. Efficiently but congenially French-run hotel; most 1–4-person rooms are en suite but two share a

bath, all simply but tastefully furnished, with ongoing improvements. Self-catering kitchen, roof terrace for breakfast with an eyeful of the Ibrahim Pasha mosque opposite. Credit card or giro-cheque required for reservations. Open March to early Jan. ❸

Youth Hostel, Eryíou 12 ☎02410/30 491. Both 3–5-bunk dorms and doubles (€23.50) in this courtyarded house with kitchen facilities; €7.50 for a bunk, but non-YHA-affiliated.

Neohóri

Hotel Capitol, Dhilberáki 65–67 ☎ & ⓕ02410/28 645. Another old house with fairly large, en-suite, terrazo-floored rooms; some family-size quads upstairs. Breakfast served in back garden by young managing couple (Greek/German). ❹

Casa Antica, Amarándou 8 ☎02410/26 206. Double and quad studios in a madeover 150-year-old house, with clean, white-tile decor, courtyard, roof terrace. Near some of the better Neohóri tavernas. ❹

Hotel Esperia, Yeoryíou Gríva 7 ☎02410/23 941, ⓕ23 164, ⓔesperiaesperia-hotels.gr. Well-priced,

well-run B-class hotel in a quiet location overlooking a little plaza. Small-to-medium size, though salubrious and tasteful rooms with showers, not tubs. Open all year. ❹

New Village Inn, Konstandopédhos 10 ☎02410/34 937, ⓔnewvillageinn@rho. forthnet.gr. Whitewashed, somewhat grotto-like en-suite rooms "refreshed" yearly, air conditioning planned. Friendly Greek and American management; singles available at a good rate. Open most of the year. ❸

The Old Town

Simply to catalogue the principal monuments and attractions cannot do full justice to the infinitely more rewarding **medieval city**. There's ample gratification to be derived from slipping through the eleven surviving gates and strolling the streets, under flying archways built for earthquake resistance, past the warm-toned sandstone and limestone walls painted ochre or blue, and over the *hokhláki* (pebble) pavement.

Dominating the northernmost sector of the city's fourteenth-century fortifications is the **Palace of the Grand Masters** (summer Mon 2.30–9pm, Tues–Fri 8.30am–9pm; winter Mon 12.30–3pm, Tues–Sun 8.30am–3pm; €6). Largely destroyed by an ammunition depot explosion set off by lightning in 1856, it was reconstructed by the Italians as a summer home for Mussolini and Victor Emmanuel III ("King of Italy and Albania, Emperor of Ethiopia"), neither of whom ever visited Rhodes. The exterior, based on medieval engravings and accounts, is passably authentic, but inside, free rein was given to Fascist delusions of grandeur: a marble staircase leads up to rooms paved with Hellenistic mosaics from Kós, and the ponderous period furnishings rival many a northern European palace. The ground floor is home to the splendid **Medieval Exhibit** and **Ancient Rhodes, 2400 Years** gallery (same hours and admission ticket), together the best museums in town. The medieval collection highlights the importance of Christian Rhodes as a trade centre, with exotic merchandise placing the island in a trans-Mediterranean context. The Knights are represented with a display on their sugar-refining industry and a gravestone of a Grand Master; precious manuscripts and books precede a wing of post-Byzantine icons, moved here permanently from Panayía Kástrou (see p.758). Across the courtyard in the north wing, "Ancient Rhodes" overshadows the official archeological museum by explaining the everyday life of the ancients, arranged topically (beauty aids, toys, cookware, worship and so on); highlights

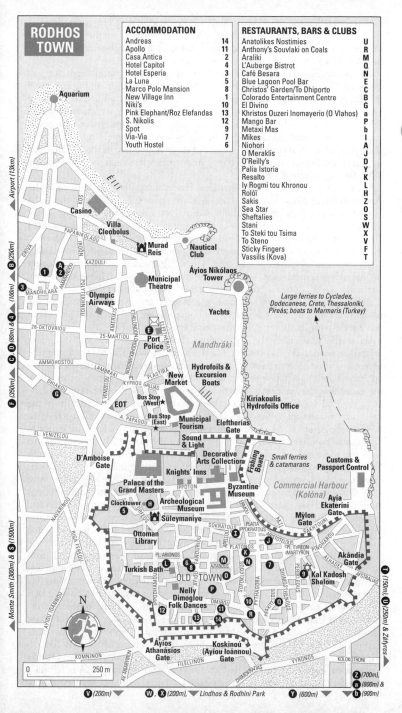

RÓDHOS TOWN

ACCOMMODATION

Andreas	14
Apollo	11
Casa Antica	2
Hotel Capitol	4
Hotel Esperia	3
La Luna	5
Marco Polo Mansion	8
New Village Inn	1
Niki's	10
Pink Elephant/Roz Elefandas	13
S. Nikolis	12
Spot	9
Via-Via	7
Youth Hostel	6

RESTAURANTS, BARS & CLUBS

Anatolikes Nostimies	U
Anthony's Souvlaki on Coals	R
Araliki	M
L'Auberge Bistrot	Q
Café Besara	N
Blue Lagoon Pool Bar	E
Christos' Garden/To Dhiporto	C
Colorado Entertainment Centre	B
El Divino	G
Khristos Ouzeri Inomayerio (O Vlahos)	a
Mango Bar	P
Metaxi Mas	b
Mikes	I
Niohori	A
O Meraklis	J
O'Reilly's	D
Palia Istoria	Y
Resalto	K
Iy Rogmi tou Khronou	L
Roloï	H
Sakis	Z
Sea Star	O
Sheftalies	S
Stani	W
To Steki tou Tsima	X
To Steno	V
Sticky Fingers	F
Vassilis (Kova)	T

9

THE DODECANESE | Ródhos Town

757

include a Hellenistic floor mosaic and a household idol of Hecate, goddess of the occult. On Tuesday and Saturday afternoons, there's a supplementary tour of the **city walls** (one hour starting at 2.45pm; €6), beginning from a gate next to the palace and finishing at the Koskinoú gate.

The heavily restored **Street of the Knights** (Odhós Ippotón) leads due east from the Platía Kleovoúlou in front of the Palace; the "Inns" lining it housed the Knights of St John, according to linguistic and ethnic affiliation, until the Ottoman Turks compelled them to leave for Malta after a six-month siege in which the defenders were outnumbered thirty to one. Today the Inns house various government offices and cultural institutions vaguely appropriate to their past, with occasional exhibitions, but the whole effect of the Italians' renovation is predictably sterile and stagey (indeed, nearby streets were used in the 1987 filming of *Pascali's Island*).

At the bottom of the hill, the Knights' Hospital has been refurbished as the **Archeological Museum** (Tues–Sun 8.30am–3pm; €2.40), though the arches and echoing halls of the building somewhat overshadow the appallingly labelled and presented contents – largely painted pottery dating from the sixth and seventh centuries BC. Behind the second-storey sculpture garden, the Hellenistic statue gallery is more accessible; in a rear corner stands the so-called "Marine Venus", beloved of Lawrence Durrell, but lent a rather sinister aspect by her sea-dissolved face – in contrast to the friendlier *Aphrodite Bathing*. Virtually next door is the **Decorative Arts Collection** (Tues–Sun 8.30am–3pm; €1.50), gleaned from old houses across the Dodecanese; the most compelling artefacts are carved cupboard doors and chest lids painted in naive style with mythological or historical episodes.

Across the way stands the **Byzantine Museum** (Tues–Sun 8.30am–3pm; €1.50), housed in the old cathedral of the Knights, who adapted the Byzantine shrine of Panayía Kástrou for their own needs. Medieval icons and frescoes lifted from crumbling chapels on Rhodes and Hálki, as well as photos of art still *in situ*, constitute the exhibits; it's worth a visit since most of the Byzantine churches in the Old Town and outlying villages are kept locked. The highlight of the collection is a complete fresco cycle from the domes of Thárri monastery (see p.767) dating from 1624, removed in 1967 to reveal much older work beneath.

If instead you head south from the Palace of the Grand Masters, it's hard to miss the most conspicuous Turkish monument in Rhodes, the rust-coloured **Süleymaniye mosque**. Rebuilt in the nineteenth century on foundations three hundred years older, it's currently closed and under scaffolding like most local Ottoman monuments, though it's soon to emerge from its lengthy refit in all its candy-striped glory. The Old Town is in fact well sown with mosques and *mescids* (the Islamic equivalent of a chapel), many of them converted from Byzantine shrines after the 1522 conquest, when the Christians were expelled from the medieval precinct. A couple of these mosques are still used by the sizeable **Turkish-speaking minority** here, some of them descended from Muslims who fled Crete between 1898 and 1913. Their most enduring civic contributions are, opposite the Süleymaniye, the **Ottoman Library** (Mon–Fri 7.30am–2.30pm & 6–9pm, Sat & Sun 8am–noon; tip to custodian), with a rich collection of early medieval manuscripts and Korans, and the imposing, still-functioning **hamam**, or Turkish bath, on Platía Ariónos up in the southwest corner of the medieval city (often shut for "repairs", specimen hours Tues 1–6pm, Wed–Fri 11am–6pm, Sat 8am–6pm; €1.50, but €0.90 Wed & Sat).

Heading downhill from the Süleymaniye mosque, you come to **Odhós Sokrátous**, once the heart of the Ottoman bazaar, and now the "Via Turista", packed with fur and jewellery stores pitched at cruise-ship tourists. Beyond the tiled central fountain in Platía Ippokrátous, Odhós Aristotélous leads into the Platía tón Evréon Martýron (Square of the Jewish Martyrs), named in memory of the large local community that was almost totally annihilated during the summer of 1944. Of the four synagogues which once graced Rhodes, only the ornate, arcaded **Kal Kadosh Shalom** (daily 10am–5pm; donation) on Odhós Simíou just to the south survives. It's maintained essentially as a memorial to the approximately 1800 Jews of Rhodes and Kós sent from here to the concentration camps; plaques in French – the language of educated Ottoman Jews across the east Aegean – commemorate the dead. At the rear of the building, a one-room **museum**, set up by a Los Angeles attorney of Jewish Rhodian descent, features archival photos of the community's life on Rhodes and in its far-flung diaspora in the Americas and Africa.

About 2km southwest of Mandhráki, the sparse, unenclosed remains of **Hellenistic Rhodes** – a restored theatre and stadium, plus a few columns of an Apollo temple – perch atop Monte Smith, the hill of Áyios Stéfanos renamed after a British admiral who used it as a watchpoint during the Napoleonic wars. The wooded site is popular with joggers and strollers, but for summer shade and greenery the best spot is probably **Rodhíni Park**, nearly 2km south of town on the road to Líndhos, and served by city bus route #3. The wooded Zimboúli ravine here, fed by natural springs, is home to ducks, peacocks and (in special pens) the native miniature Rhodian deer. Hellenistic **rock-cut tombs**, signposted via a separate side road at the south end of the park, constitute a final possible diversion.

Eating and drinking

Eating well for a reasonable price in and around Ródhos Town is a challenge, but not an insurmountable one. As a general rule, the remoter and further south you go, the better value you'll find – so touristy, alas, has the Old Town become. Unless otherwise stated, the following restaurants are open all year round.

Old Town

Anthony's Souvlaki on Coals, cnr Omírou and Pythagóra. Exactly as the sign says, superbly executed *souvláki* for a mostly local clientele. A few salads and starters too; supper only; inexpensive.

Araliki, Aristofánous 45. Bohemian expatriates and travellers tired of standard resort grub seek out this old-style *kafenío* on the ground floor of a medieval house. Small plates of exquisitely original *mezédhes* are provided from a perennial menu by Italian proprietors Miriam (the savouries) and Valeria (the sweets), and there are also (often more compelling) daily specials. Reckon on €16.20 per person with drinks, which include Nissyrot *soumádha* or mainland wine. Open March–Dec daily except Sun from 11.30am until late; also closed two random weeks July & Aug.

L'Auberge Bistrot, Praxitélous 21. Genuine, popular, French-run bistro with excellent Frenchified food: allow €17.70 per person for three hefty courses plus wine from a well-selected Greek list, jazz soundtrack included. Summer seating in the courtyard of this restored medieval inn; inside under the arches during cooler months. Open late March to late Dec for supper daily except Mon.

O Meraklis, Aristotélous 30. A *patsatzídhiko* (tripe-soup kitchen) that's only open 3–8am for a motley clientele of post-club lads, Turkish stallholders, nightclub singers and travellers just stumbled off an overnight ferry. Great free entertainment, including famously rude staff, and the soup – the traditional Greek hangover cure – is good too.

Mikes (pronounced "mee-kess"), nameless alley behind Sokrátous 17. Inexpensive (for Rhodes, anyway) hole-in-the-wall, serving only grilled fish, salads and wine.

Sea Star (aka *Pizanias*), Sofokléous 24, cnr of the square ☎02410/22 117. A three-decades-old institution, where Pizanias mans the grill himself. Not only fresh scaly fish – staff show you the pink gills – but shellfish like *kydhónia* (cockles) and *petalídhia* (limpets), grilled octopus and squid. With two bottles of expensive wine, starters and loads of seafood, four can eat for €85–88 – elsewhere in the Old Town it'd be double that. Reservations recommended.

Neohóri

Anatolikes Nostimies, Kapodhistríou 60, Akándia port. The name means "Anatolian Delicacies", and that's what's on offer at this Rhodian Turkish-run grill: Turkish/Middle Eastern dips and starters, plus sixteen variations of kebab. Not much atmosphere, but friendly and reasonable; post-prandial hubble-bubble provided on request. Open 11am–midnight.

Khristos Ouzeri Inomayerio (O Vlahos), Klavdhíou Pépper 165, at the big bend, Zéfyros beach. As the name implies, ouzerí fare – marinated fish or peppers, *gávros*, great *tzatzíki* – accompanying a vast oúzo list, plus vegetable-strong *mayireftá* (cuttlefish with spinach, fish soup, eggplant *imam*) that sell out quickly. Not as cheap (€10.30–11.80) or big-portioned as formerly, but still worth the trek out.

Metaxi Mas, Klavdhíou Pépper 115, Zéfyros beach. No sign or menu in English – look for the elevated boat – at this seafood ouzerí purveying various exotic titbits; count on €32.40–35.30 per couple with booze, slightly cheaper per person in a group – but still 25 percent less than in the Old Town. Daily lunch and supper except Sun, lunch only.

Niohori, Ioánni Kazoúli 29, by the Franciscan monastery. Also known as "Kiki's" after the jolly proprietress, this homey, inexpensive local serves lunch and supper; best for grills, sourced from their own butcher/farm.

Palia Istoria, Mitropóleos 108, cnr Dhendhrínou, Ámmos district ☎02410/32 421. Reckoned to be the best *kultúra* taverna in town, but predictably expensive for such dishes as celery hearts in egg-lemon sauce and scallops with mushrooms and artichokes, washed down by a hundred-strong wine list. Supper only, closed Sun; reservations essential.

Sakis, Ipsilándou 27, Áyios Nikólaos. Genuine tav-

erna with pleasant patio seating, equally popular with Rhodians and savvy expats. Excellent seafood and starters; it's possible to have three courses (including modest fish) and a beer for €11.50. Supper only.

Sheftalies, Tsaldhári 21, south of Monte Smith past Marinopoulos Supermarket. Direct antithesis to *Palia Istoria*, since you can fill up for €7.40. Zero atmosphere, but a genuine charcoal griller featuring the namesake *sheftaliés*, dioxin-free chicken (some find this too peppery) and *kokorétsi*, plus a few daily *mayireftá* plates.

Stani, Ayías Anastasías 28, cnr Paleón Patrón Yermanoú, south of the Koskinoú Gate. Most central outlet of a chain of Rhodian Turkish confectioners, scooping out two dozen flavours of the best ice cream on the island, publicity for rival *Mike's* notwithstanding.

To Steki tou Tsima, Peloponnísou 22, around cnr from preceding. Very reasonable seafood ouzerí, with the stress on aficionados' shellfish titbits (*foúskes, spiniálo*) and small fish not prone to farming. No airs or graces, just patently fresh materials, and open Sun too.

To Steno, Ayíon Anaryíron 29, 400m southwest of the Ayíou Athanasíou Gate. A genuinely welcoming ouzerí, with outdoor seating during the warmer months and limited but superb menu (chickpea soup, courgette croquettes, sausages) at eminently reasonable prices.

Vassilis (Kova), Kolokotróni, 80m east of Kanadhá, south of Akándia commercial port. Another place to go when you're down to your last euro: a friendly working-man's canteen, busiest from noon to 2pm, with several *mayireftá* dishes to choose from and shady glass-conservatory seating between the auto-repair shops. Also opens evenings.

Nightlife

The Old Town formerly had a well-deserved reputation for being tomb-silent at night; this has changed drastically since the late 1990s, with an entire alley (Miltiádhou) off Apéllou given over to a half-dozen loud music bars and clubs, frequented almost exclusively by Greeks. This is just appetizers for the estimated two hundred foreigner-patronized bars and clubs in Neohóri, where theme nights and various other gimmicks predominate. They are found mostly along the streets and alleys bounded by Alexándhrou Dhiákou, Orfanídhou, Lohagoú Fanouráki and Nikifórou Mandhilará.

Sedate by comparison, Ministry of Culture-approved folk dances (June–Oct Mon, Wed, Fri 9.20pm; €10.30) are presented with live accompaniment by the Nelly Dimoglou Company, performed in the landscaped "Old Town Theatre" off Andhroníkou, near Platía Ariónos. More of a technological extravaganza is the **Sound and Light** show, spotlighting sections of the city walls, staged in a garden just off Platía Rimínis. There's English-language narration nightly except Sunday, its screening time varying from 8.15pm to 10.15pm (€3.50).

Thanks to a large contingent from the local university, there are several year-round **cinemas** showing first-run fare indoors or open-air according to season and air-con capabilities. Choose from among the summer-only outdoor cinema by the Rodon Municipal Theatre, next to the town hall in Neohóri; the Metropol multiplex, southeast of the Old Town opposite the stadium, refurbished in 2001; and the nearby Pallas multiplex on Dhimokratías, refurbished in 1999.

Blue Lagoon Pool Bar, 25-Martíou 2, Neohóri. One of the better theme bars, in this case a "desert island" with palm trees, waterfalls, live turtles and parrots, a shipwrecked galleon – and taped music. Open March–Oct 8.30am–3am.

Café Besara, Sofokléous 11–13, Old Town. Congenial breakfast café/low-key boozer run by an Australian lady, with interesting mixed clientele and live music some nights.

Christos' Garden/To Dhiporto, Dhilberáki 59, Neohóri. This combination art-gallery/bar/café occupies a carefully restored old house and courtyard with pebble-mosaic floors throughout. Incongruously classy for the area.

Colorado Entertainment Centre, Orfanídhou 57, cnr Aktí Miaouli, Neohóri. Triple venue: "pub" with live in-house band (rock covers), "club" with taped sounds, and quiet upstairs chill-out bar.

El Divino, Alexándhrou Dhiákou 5, Neohóri. Very classy, Greek-frequented "music bar" with garden seating and the usual range of coffees and alcohol. Open June–Oct.

Mango Bar, Platía Dhoriéos 3, Old Town. Piped music and a variety of drinks at this durable bar on an otherwise quiet plaza; also a good source of breakfast after 8am, served under a plane tree.

O'Reilly's, Apolloníou Rodhíou 61, Neohóri. Irish theme pub which serves Irish draught and claims to have live music nightly.

Resalto, Plátonos 6, opposite the mosque. Live Greek rebétika and laïkó sounds, rather cheaper than nearby rival *Café Chantant*. Weekends only in low season.

Iy Rogmi tou Khronou, Platía Arıónos. Taped music (not house or techno) at a reasonable level and a congenial crowd make this newly opened bar worth a look.

Rolóï, Orféos 1, Old Town. The Baroque clocktower erected by Ahmet Fetih Pasha in 1857 is now the focus of possibly the most exclusive café-bar in the Old Town. Admission charge to climb the tower, and steeply priced drinks, but you are paying for the terrific view.

Sticky Fingers, Anthoúla Zérvou 6, Neohóri. Long-lived music bar with reasonable drinks; live rock several nights weekly from 10pm onwards. Fri & Sat only off-season.

Listings

Airlines Olympic, Iérou Lóhou 9 ☎02410/24 571. Cronus-Aegean Airlines, Ethelondón Dhodhekanisíon 20 ☎02410/24 400 or 25 444.

Bookshop Second Storey Books, Amarándou 24, Neohóri, has a large stock of used English paperbacks; open all year, normal shop hours. For new books, try News Stand at Grigoríou Lambráki 23.

Car rental Prices at non-international chains are fairly standard at €41–44 per day, but can be bargained down to about €32–35 a day, all-inclusive, out of peak season and/or for long periods. More flexible outfits, all in the New Town, include Alamo/National, 28-Oktovríou 18 ☎02410/73 570; Drive, Avrasrlías 2 ☎02410/68 243; Just/Ansa, Mandhilará 70 ☎02410/31 811; Kosmos, Papaloúka 31 ☎02410/74 374; Orion, Yeoryíou Leóndos 36 ☎02410/22 137; and Payless, Íonos Dhragoúmi 29 ☎02410/26 586.

Exchange Most conventional bank branches are near Platía Kýprou in Neohóri, plus there are various exchange bureaux keeping long hours. At other times use the cash dispensers of the Commercial Bank (branch in the Old Town too), Alpha Bank or National Bank (also Old Town branch).

Ferry agents DANE, Avstralías 92 ☎02410/43 150, to Pireás via select Dodecanese; Dodhekanisos Navtiliaki, Avstralías 3, by Shell station ☎02410/70 590, for catamaran to most Dodecanese islands; Inspiration, Aktí Sakhtoúri 4 ☎02410/24 294 (base of main ferry dock), for most G&A boats to Dodecanese and Cyclades, plus DANE sailings; Kyriakoulis Maritime, Neoríon dock ☎02410/78 052, for hydrofoils to Kós and all intervening islands; Kouros, Karpáthou ☎02410/24 377, and Kydon, Ethelondón Dhodhekanisíon 14 ☎02410/23 000, between them act for both companies plying routes to Cyprus; LANE, Alexándhrou Dhiákou 38 ☎02410/33 607, to Crete via Hálki, Kárpathos, Kássos. Weekly tourist office departure-schedule handouts are deeply unreliable, and even get the addresses shown above wrong; authoritative sailing information is available at the *limenarhío* (port police), on Mandhráki esplanade near the post office.

Internet cafés The most central and competitive of several are *Rock Style*, Dhimokratías 7, opposite the stadium ⓦ www.rockstyle.gr, and *Mango Bar* (see "Nightlife" overleaf) ⓔ karelas@rho. forthnet.gr.

Laundries House of Laundry, Erythroú Stavroú 2, Neohóri; Star, Kostí Palamá 4–6, behind New Market; Wash & Go, Plátonos 33, Old Town.

Motorbike rental Low-volume scooters will make little impact on Rhodes; sturdier Yamaha 125s, suitable for two people, start at about €20 a day. In the Old Town, Mandar Moto at Dhimosthénous 2, cnr Platía Evréon Martýron, has a large stable of medium-sized scooters suitable for short jaunts. Recommended outlets in Neohóri include Margaritis, Ioánni Kazoúli 23, with a wide range of late models up to 500cc, plus mountain bikes; or (to roll out in style) Rent a Harley at 28-Oktovríou

80 – classic models for two riders start at a whopping €97 per day.

Post office Main branch with outgoing mail and poste restante on Mandhráki harbour; open Mon–Fri 7.30am–8pm.

Scuba diving Waterhoppers, Trident and Dive Med all tout for business at Mandhráki quay; however, days out are expensive (€39.70 for boat transfer and one dive, €20.60 for second dive) and you're restricted to one small site at Thérmes Kallithéas.

Travel agencies Recommended in the Old Town is Castellania, Evripídhou 1–3, cnr Platía Ippokrátous ☎ 02410/75 860, which can arrange all domestic air tickets, both domestic and international ferries, and also discount scheduled and charter flights abroad. In Neohóri, Visa Travel Club at Grigóri Lambráki 54 ☎ 02410/33 282, ⓦ www.visatravelclub.gr, and Contours at Ammohóstou 9 ☎ 02410/36 001 are also worth contacting. There is no central outlet for hydrofoil tickets to Marmaris in Turkey – comparison shopping is recommended.

The east coast

Heading down the coast from the capital you have to go some way before you escape the crowds from local beach hotels, their numbers swollen by visitors using the regular buses from town or on boat tours out of Mandhráki. You might look in at the decayed, abandoned spa of **Thérmes Kallithéas**, a prize example of enjoyable mock-orientalia dating from the Italian period. Located 3km south of Kallithéa resort proper, down a paved track through pines, the buildings are set in a palm grove, though an EU-funded restoration begun in 1999 proceeds at a snail's pace. Nearby are several secluded coves framed by rock formations which often interpose themselves between the water and the sand, the latter furnished with sunbeds and (in most cases) snack bars. The former fishing village of **FALIRÁKI**, which primarily draws a youngish package clientele, is all too much in the mould of a Spanish *costa* resort, while the scenery just inland – arid, scrubby sandhills at the best of times – has been made that much bleaker by late 1980s fire damage that stretches way beyond Líndhos. The cape to the south, **Ladhikó** (45-minute path from Faliráki), shelters the more scenic bay of "Anthony Quinn", named in honour of the late actor whom Greeks took to their hearts following his roles in *Zorba the Greek* and *The Guns of Navarone* (the latter filmed locally).

The enormous mass of **Tsambíka**, 26km south of town, is the first place at which most nonpackage visitors will seriously consider stopping. Actually the very eroded flank of a once much-larger mountain, this promontory has a monastery on top offering unrivalled views along some 50km of coastline. From the main highway, a steep, 1500-metre cement drive leads to a small car park and a snack bar, from which steps take you to the summit. The little monastery here is unremarkable except for its September 8 festival: childless women climb up – sometimes on their hands and knees – to be relieved of their barrenness, and any children born afterwards are dedicated to the Virgin with the names Tsambikos or Tsambika, which are particular to the Dodecanese. From the top you can survey **Kolýmbia** just to the north, a small beach to one side of a tiny, rock-girt cove, backed by a dozen, low-rise hotels. Shallow **Tsambíka** Bay on the south side of the headland warms up early in the spring, and the excellent beach, though protected by the forest service from development – all it has is a taverna and a half-dozen *kantína* caravans – teems with people all summer.

The next beach south is gravelly **Stegná** with its mix of summer cottages for locals and accommodation for Germans. It has at least two **tavernas** (*Kozas* and *Pitropos*) which attract a Greek clientele. Stegná is reached by a steep road east from the less rewarding village of **ARHÁNGELOS**, just inland and over-looked by a crumbling castle. Though you can disappear into the warren of alleys between the main road and the citadel, the place is now firmly caught up in package tourism, with a full complement of banks, tavernas, minimarts and jewellery stores. Another overnight base on this stretch of coast, English-dominated this time, is **HARÁKI**, a pleasant if undistinguished two-street fishing port with mostly self-catering accommodation (generally ❸) overlooked by the stubby ruins of **Feraklós castle**, the last stronghold of the Knights to fall to the Turks. You can swim off the town beach if you don't mind an audience from the handful of waterfront cafés and tavernas, but most people head west out of town, then north 800m along a marked dirt track to the secluded **Agáthi beach**. The (marginally) best taverna near Haráki is *Efterpi*, 200m south at so-called Massári beach.

Líndhos

LÍNDHOS, the island's second-ranking tourist attraction, erupts from barren surroundings 12km south of Haráki. Like Ródhos Old Town, its charm is heavily undermined by commercialism and crowds: up to half a million visitors in a typical year. At midday dozens of coaches park nose-to-tail on the narrow southerly access road, with even more on the drives down to the beaches. Back in the village itself, those few vernacular houses not snapped up by package operators have, since the 1960s, been bought up and refurbished by wealthy British, Germans and Italians. The old agora or serpentine high street presents a mass of fairly indistinguishable bars, creperies, mediocre restaurants and travel agents. Although high-rise hotels and all vehicular traffic have been prohibited inside the municipal boundaries, the result is a relentlessly commercialized theme park – hot and airless in August, but deserted and quite ghostly in winter.

Nonetheless, if you arrive before or after peak season, when the pebble-paved streets between the immaculately whitewashed houses are relatively empty of both people and droppings from the donkeys shuttling up to the acropolis (see below), you can still appreciate the beautiful, atmospheric setting of Líndhos. The most imposing fifteenth-to eighteenth-century **captains' residences** are built around *hokhláki* courtyards, their monumental doorways often fringed by intricate stonework, with the number of braids or cables supposedly corresponding to the number of ships owned. A few are open to the public, most notably the **Papakonstandis Mansion**, the most elaborate and now home to an unofficial museum; entrance to the "open" mansions is free but some pressure will probably be exerted on you to buy something, especially lace and embroidery.

On the bluff looming above the town, the ancient acropolis with its Doric **Temple of Athena** (restorations ongoing) and imposing **Hellenistic stoa** is found inside the Knights' **castle** (summer Tues–Sun 8am–7pm, Mon 12.30–7pm; rest of year Tues–Sun 8.30am–3pm; €6) – a surprisingly felicitous blend of ancient and medieval culture. Though the ancient city of Lindos and its original temple dated from at least 1100 BC, the present structure was begun by local ruler Kleoboulos in the sixth century BC after a fourth-century fire.

Líndhos's north beach, once the main ancient harbour, is overcrowded and occasionally polluted; if you do base yourself here, cleaner, quieter **beaches** are to be found one cove beyond at Pállas beach (with a nudist annexe around the headland), or 5km north at **Vlyhá Bay**. South of the acropolis huddles the small, perfectly sheltered **St Paul's harbour**, where the apostle is said to have landed in 58 AD on a mission to evangelize the island.

Practicalities

It used to be tempting fate to just turn up and hope for **accommodation** vacancies on spec, but since certain British tour companies pulled out of Líndhos in the late 1990s, it's something of a buyers' market. If you're not met at the bus stop under the giant fig tree by proprietors touting rooms, Pallas Travel (☎02440/31 494, ☎31 595) can arrange a room or even a whole villa for a small fee. The oft-cited backpackers' standbys, 1970s-vintage *Pension Electra* (☎02440/31 226; ❷) and *Pension Katholiki* (☎02440/31 445; ❷), next door to each other on the way to the north beaches, are both low standard (shared baths) and overpriced.

Local **restaurants** tend to be exploitive and serve bland fare; one of the better ones, *Agostino's*, by the southerly car park, has the important virtues of bulk Émbonas wine and real country sausages (not imported hot dogs), but goes and spoils it by serving tinned veg as accompaniment. You may as well push the boat out at *Mavrikos* on the fig-tree square, founded in 1933 and in the same family ever since. Mezédhes like *manoúri* cheese with basil and pine-nuts are accomplished, as are quasi-French main courses like cuttlefish in wine sauce; dipping into the excellent (and expensive) Greek wine list as well will add €17.50 a bottle to the typical food charge of €20.50–23.50 per person. If your wallet won't stretch that far, try the *Panorama* up on the main road, 2km towards Vlyhá, which does good fish, though – like *Agostino's* – it's not hugely less expensive than *Mavrikos* these days. For snacks and desserts, try *Il Forno*, an Italian-run bakery, and *Gelo Blu*, still the best of several gelaterie here despite the departure of its Italian founders. There are currently three **internet cafés** operating in Líndhos. Local **car-rental** rates tend to be cheaper than in Ródhos Town, though you've less choice in models, and vehicles may be less roadworthy. There are two proper **banks**, working normal hours, each with cash dispensers. And finally, Lindos Suntours (☎02440/31 333) has metred phones (call boxes tend to have huge queues) and a nice line in unclaimed one-way charter seats back to Britain, as does Village Holidays (☎02410/31 486).

The west coast

Rhodes' west coast is the windward flank of the island, so it's damper, more fertile and more forested; most beaches, however, are exposed and decidedly rocky. None of this has deterred development, and as in the east the first few kilometres of the busy shore road down from the capital have been surrendered entirely to tourism. From Neohóri's aquarium down to the airport, the shore is fringed by an almost uninterrupted line of Miami-Beach-style hotels, though such places as Triánda, Kremastí and Paradhísi are still nominally villages, with real centres. This was the first part of the island to be favoured by the package operators, and tends to be frequented by a decidedly sedate, middle-aged/family clientele that doesn't stir much from the poolside.

There's not much inducement to stop until you reach the important archeological site of **KAMEIROS**, which together with Líndhos and Ialyssos was one of the three Dorian powers that united during the fifth century BC to found the powerful city-state of Rhodes. Soon eclipsed by the new capital, Kameiros was abandoned and only rediscovered in 1859. As a result it is a particularly well-preserved Doric townscape, doubly worth visiting for its beautiful hillside site (summer Tues–Sun 8am–7pm, winter 8.30am–3pm; €3). While none of the individual remains is spectacular, you can make out the foundations of two small temples, the re-erected pillars of a Hellenistic house, a Classical fountain, and the stoa of the upper agora, complete with a water cistern. Because of the gentle slope of the site, there were no fortifications, nor was there an acropolis. On the beach below Kameiros there are several tavernas, highly commercialized but acceptable while waiting for one of the two daily buses back to town (if you're willing to walk 4km back to Kalavárdha you'll have a better choice of service).

At the tiny anchorage of **KÁMIROS SKÁLA** (aka Skála Kamírou) 15km south, there are five more-touristy restaurants, which somewhat inexplicably have become the target of coach tours. Less heralded is the daily **kaïki** which leaves for the island of **Hálki** at 2.30pm, weather permitting, returning early the next morning; on Wednesdays and Sundays there are day-trips departing at 9am and returning at 4pm. For a better **meal**, skip the circus here and proceed 400m southwest to off-puttingly named **Paralía Kopriá** ("Manure Beach"), where *Psarotaverna Johnny's* has good non-farmed fish and *orektiká*, especially on Sundays when own-made *dolmádhes* and (seasonally) squash blossoms may be on the menu with the usual standards; it's been "discovered" and so is pricier than it used to be, but still worth a stop.

A couple of kilometres south of Skála, the "Kastello", signposted as **Kástro Kritinías**, is from afar the most impressive of the Knights' rural strongholds, and the paved access road is too narrow and steep for tour buses. Close up it proves to be no more than a shell, but a glorious shell, with fine views west to assorted islets and Hálki. You make a "donation" to the formidable old woman at the car park in exchange for fizzy drinks, seasonal fruit or flowers.

Beyond Kritinía itself, a quiet hillside village with a few rooms and tavernas, the main road winds south through the dense forests below mounts Akramýtis and Atávyros to **SIÁNNA**, the most attractive mountain settlement on the island, famous for its aromatic pine-sage honey and *soúma*, a grape-residue distillate similar to Italian *grappa* but far smoother. The tiered, flat-roofed farmhouses of **MONÓLITHOS**, 4km southwest at the end of the public bus line, are scant justification for the long trip out here, and food at the four **tavernas** is indifferent owing to the tour-group trade, but the view over the bay is striking and you could use the village as a base by staying in rooms or at the *Hotel Thomas* (☎02410/22 741 or 02460/61 291; €26.50), which has fair-sized rooms belying a grim exterior, and due for a refit in 2002. Diversions in the area include yet another **Knights' castle** 2km west of town, photogenically perched on its own pinnacle but enclosing even less inside than Kástro Kritinías, and the sand-and-gravel beaches (no facilities) at **Foúrni**, five paved but curvy kilometres below the castle. In the headland between the first and second beaches are some caves that were hollowed out by early Christians fleeing persecution.

The interior

Inland Rhodes is hilly, and the northern two-thirds still mostly wooded, despite the depredations of arsonists. You'll need a vehicle to see its highlights, especially as enjoyment resides in getting away from it all; no single site justifies the tremendous expense of a taxi or the inconvenience of trying to make the best of sparse bus schedules.

Ialyssos and the Valley of the Butterflies

Starting from the west-coast highway, turn inland at the central junction in Tríanda for the five-kilometre uphill ride to the scanty acropolis of ancient **Ialyssos** (Tues–Sun 8am–7pm; €3) on flat-topped, strategic Filérimos hill; from its Byzantine castle Süleyman the Magnificent directed the 1522 siege of Rhodes. Filérimos means "lover of solitude", after the tenth-century settlement here by Byzantine hermits. The existing **Filérimos monastery**, restored successively by Italians and British, is the most substantial structure here. As a concession to the Rhodian faithful, the church alone is usually open to pilgrims after the stated hours. Directly in front of the church sprawl the foundations of third-century **temples to Zeus and Athena**, built atop a far older Phoenician shrine. Below this, further towards the car park, lies the partly subterranean church of **Aï-Yeórgis Hostós**, a simple, barrel-vaulted structure with fourteenth- and fifteenth-century frescoes, not as vivid or well preserved as those at Thárri or Asklipió (see p.769). A little way southeast of the parking area, a hillside **Doric fountain** with a columned facade was only revealed by subsidence in 1926 – and is now off-limits owing to another landslip which has covered it again. Southwest of the monastery and archeological zone, a "Way of the Cross", with the fourteen stations marked out in copper plaques during the Italian era, leads to an enormous concrete crucifix, a recent replacement of an Italian-built one; you're allowed to climb out onto the cross-arms for a supplement to the already amazing view. Illuminated at night, the crucifix is clearly visible from the island of Sými and – perhaps more pertinently – infidel Turkey across the way.

The only highly publicized tourist "attraction" in the island's interior, **Petaloúdhes** or the **Butterfly Valley** (May–Sept daily 8.30am–sunset; spring/autumn €1.50, June 15–Sept 15 €2.20), reached by a seven-kilometre paved side road bearing inland from the west-coast highway between Paradhíssi and Theológos, is actually a rest stop for Jersey tiger moths (*Panaxia quadripunctaria*). Only in summer do these creatures congregate here, attracted for unknown reasons by the abundant *Liquidambar orientalis* trees. In season, the moths roost in droves on the tree trunks; they cannot eat during this final phase of their life cycle, must rest to conserve energy and die of starvation soon after mating. When sitting in the trees, the moths are a well-camouflaged black and yellow, but flash cherry-red overwings in flight.

There's a popular **taverna** partway up the valley, by the roadside, but for even better fare continue up the road to the edge of **PSÍNTHOS** village, where the friendly *Piyi Fasouli* serves excellent grills and appetizers at seating overlooking plane trees and the namesake spring.

Eptá Piyés to Profítis Ilías

Heading inland from Kolýmbia junction on the main east-coast highway, you've a four-kilometre walk or drive to **Eptá Piyés** (Seven Springs), a superb oasis with a tiny dam created by the Italians for irrigation. A shaded streamside **taverna**, immensely popular at weekends with islanders and visitors alike, serves hearty grills at fairly normal prices, though a recent refit suggests changes in style. A trail, or a rather claustrophobic Italian aqueduct-tunnel, both lead from the vicinity of the springs to the reservoir.

Continuing inland, you reach the Italian governor's crumbling, Art Deco summer residence at Eleoússa after another 9km, in the shade of the dense forest at the east end of Profítis Ilías ridge. Two other undisturbed villages, Platánia and Apóllona, nestle on the south slopes of the mountain overlooking the start of an area bereft of trees, but most people keep straight on 3km further from Eleoússa to the late Byzantine church of **Áyios Nikólaos Foundoúkli** (St Nicholas of the Hazelnuts). The partly shaded site has a fine view north over cultivated valleys, and locals descend in force for picnics on weekends. The frescoes inside, dating from the thirteenth to the fifteenth centuries, could do with a good clean, but various scenes from the life of Christ are recognizable.

Heading west from the church along mostly paved roads gets you finally to **Profítis Ilías**, where the Italian-vintage chalet-hotels *Elafos* and *Elafina* (now hosting childrens' summer camps) hide in deep woods just north of the 798-metre peak, Rhodes' third-highest point but out of bounds as a military area. However, there's good, gentle strolling below and around the summit, and a snack bar on the through road is generally open in season.

Atávyros villages

All tracks and roads west across Profítis Ilías converge on the main road from Kalavárdha bound for **ÉMBONA(S)**, a large and architecturally nondescript village backed up against the north slope of 1215-metre **Mount Atávyros**. Émbona, with its two *dhomátia* places and half-dozen meat-oriented **tavernas** (try *Savvas*), is more geared to handling tourists than you might expect, since it's the venue for summer "folk-dance tours" from Ródhos Town. The village also lies at the heart of the island's most important wine-producing districts, and CAÏR – the Italian-founded vintners' co-operative – produces a choice of acceptable mid-range varieties. However, products of the smaller, family-run Emery winery (☎02460/41 208; daily 9am–4.30pm for tasting tours) at the northern outskirts are more esteemed. To get some idea what Émbona would be like without tourists, carry on clockwise around the peak past the Artamíti monastery, to less celebrated **ÁYIOS ISÍDHOROS**, with nearly as many vines and tavernas, a more open feel, and the **trailhead** for the five-hour return ascent of Atávyros. This path, beginning at the northeast edge of the village at a wooden placard and well-marked with paint splodges, is the safest and easiest way up the mountain, which has extensive foundations of a Zeus temple on top.

Thárri monastery

The road from Áyios Isídhoros to Siánna is paved; not so the perennially rough one that curves for 12km east to Láerma, but it's worth enduring if you've any interest in Byzantine monuments. The **monastery of Thárri**, lost in pine forests 5km south, is the oldest religious foundation on the island, re-established as a living community of half a dozen monks in 1990 by the charismatic abbot Amfilohios. The striking *katholikón* (open daily, all day) consists of a long nave and short transept surmounted by barrel vaulting. Various recent cleanings have restored damp-smudged frescoes dating from 1300 to 1450 to their former exquisite glory. The most distinct, in the transept, depict the Evangelists Mark and Matthew, plus the Archangel Gabriel, while the nave boasts various acts of Christ, including such scenes as the *Storm on the Sea of Galilee*, *Meeting the Samaritan Woman at the Well* and *Healing the Cripple*.

The far south

South of a line connecting Monólithos and Lárdhos, you could easily begin to think you had strayed onto another island. Gone are most of the five-star hotels and roads to match, and with them the bulk of the crowds. Gone too are most other tourist facilities and public transport. Only one or two daily buses (in season) serve the depopulated villages here (except for Yennádhi), approaching

△ Painting in shop, Rhodes

along the east coast; tavernas grace the more popular stretches of sand, but aside from the growing package enclaves of Lárdhos, Péfki and Kiotári, there are few places to stay.

Despite the shelving of plans for a second island airport in the area, new beachfront development mushrooms to either side of **LÁRDHOS**, itself solidly on the tourist circuit despite an inland position between Láerma and the peninsula culminating in Líndhos. The beach 2km away is gravelly and dull, so it's best to continue 3km to **Glýstra** cove, a small but delightful crescent, with umbrellas and a snack bar. Four kilometres east of Lárdhos, **PÉFKI** (Péfkos on some maps) began life as the garden annexe and overflow for Líndhos, but is now a burgeoning package resort in its own right; the sea is clearer than at Lárdhos, with small, well-hidden beaches which are getting harder to find with all the new development on the clifftop.

Asklipió

Nine kilometres beyond Lárdhos, a paved side road heads 3.5km inland to **ASKLIPIÓ**, a sleepy village guarded by a crumbling castle and graced by the Byzantine church of **Kímisis Theotókou** (daily 9am–6pm; free). The building dates from 1060, with a ground plan nearly identical to Thárri's, except that two subsidiary apses were added during the eighteenth century, supposedly to conceal a secret school in a subterranean crypt. The frescoes within are in better condition than those at Thárri owing to the drier local climate; they are also a bit later, though some claim that the final work at Thárri and the earliest here were executed by the same hand, a master from Híos.

The format and subject matter of the frescoes are equally rare in Greece: didactic "cartoon strips" which extend completely around the church in some cases, featuring extensive Old Testament stories in addition to the more usual lives of Christ and the Virgin. There's a complete sequence from Genesis, from the Creation to the Expulsion from Eden; note the comically menacing octopus among the fishes in the panel of the Fifth Day, and Eve subsequently being fashioned from Adam's rib. A *Revelation of John the Divine* takes up most of the east transept; pebble-mosaic flooring decorates both the interior and the vast courtyard. Two adjacent buildings house separate museums: an ecclesiastical exhibit (donation requested) and a more interesting folklore gallery full of rural craft tools.

To the southern tip

Back on the coast road, the beachfront hamlet of **KIOTÁRI** has mushroomed as a package venue for Germans and Italians since the mid-1990s, when the Orthodox Church elected to sell up its vast holdings here. You could sample the **tavernas** *Il Ponte* and *Lighthouse*, at opposite ends of the developed strip, and have a swim. But there's little local character remaining, so you'll most likely choose to continue 4km to **YENNÁDHI**, the only sizeable settlement on this coast, served by up to six buses daily. The older village core inland offers various amenities including **car rental**, a **post office**, some rooms (try *Betty Studios* by the pharmacy; ☎02440/43 020; ④) and a few **tavernas**; best of these is *Klimis*, one of three behind the seemingly endless sand-and-gravel beach, with good house wine, *mayireftá* and occasional fish grills.

Some 10km south of Yennádhi, and 2km inland, **LAHANIÁ** village with its eponymous **hotel** (☎02440/43 089; ②) and smattering of private rooms makes another possible base. Abandoned after a postwar earthquake, since the 1980s its older houses have been mostly occupied and renovated by Germans on long-term lease agreements. On the main platía at the lower, eastern end of the village, the *Platanos* taverna has decent food and seating between the church and two wonderful fountains, one with an Ottoman inscription.

You can go directly from Lahaniá to **Plimýri**, an attractive sandy bay backed by dunes heaped up by strong afternoon winds; so far the only facility is the **taverna** *Plimirri Beach* with mostly farmed fish on the menu, next to the church of Zoödhóhou Piyís which has ancient columns upholding its vaulted porch. Beyond Plimýri the road curves inland to **KATTAVIÁ**, over 100km from the capital, marooned amidst grain fields; the village, like so many in the south, is three-quarters deserted, the owners of the closed-up houses off working in Australia or North America.

There are a few **rooms** to rent, a vital **filling station** and several **tavernas** at the junction that doubles as the platía – most interesting of these are the brightly coloured *Martine's Bakaliko/Mayeriko* (closed Thurs), run by folk from Lahanía, which has some vegetarian dishes and attempts to use local organic ingredients when possible.

From Kattaviá a paved road leads on to **Prassoníssi**, Rhodes' southernmost extremity and a mecca for European **windsurfers**. The sandspit which tethers Prassoníssi ("Leek Island") to Rhodes was partially washed away by storms early in 1998, but enough remains to create flat water on the east side and up to two-metre waves on the west, ideal for different ability levels. Of the two windsurfing centres operating here, Swiss-run Procenter (April–Oct; ☎02440/91 045, ✉procenter.prasonisi@EUnet.at) is the more professional, with hourly rates from €13.50, and a ten-hour card (valid over several days) from €112. They're geared for one-week packages, including jeeps and lodged in rooms above the *Lighthouse Restaurant*, one of a half-dozen food and accommodation outfits here; the UK agent is Sportif (☎012730/844919, ✉Sportif@compuserve.com).

The far southwest

From Lahaniá it's also possible to head 9km northwest along a narrow paved road to the picturesque hilltop village of **MESANAGRÓS**. This already existed in some form by the fifth century AD, if foundations of a ruined basilica at the village outskirts are anything to go by. A smaller thirteenth-century chapel squats amidst mosaic-floor patches of the larger, earlier church, with a *hokhláki* floor and stone barrel arches (key from the nearby kafenío).

The onward road to Skiádhi monastery, 6km distant, is shown incorrectly on most maps. Take the Kataviá-bound road initially, then bear right onto an unsigned dirt track after about 2km; the last 4km are quite badly surfaced. Known formally as Panayía Skiadhení, **Skiádhi monastery** – despite its undistinguished modern buildings – was founded in the thirteenth century to house a miraculous icon of the Virgin; in the fifteenth century a heretic stabbed the painting, and blood flowed from the wound in the Mother of God's cheek. The offending hand was, needless to say, instantly paralyzed; the fissure, and intriguing brown stains around it, are still visible. The immediate surroundings of the monastery are rather dreary since a fire in 1992, but the views west are stunning. Tiny Khténia islet is said to be a petrified pirate ship, rendered into stone by the Virgin in answer to prayers from desperate locals. Except on September 7–8, the festival of the icon, you can stay the night by arrangement with the caretaker.

West of Kataviá, the completely paved island loop road emerges onto the deserted, sandy southwest coast; Skiádhi can also be reached from this side as well, by another dirt road. Only strong swimmers should venture far offshore here, as it's exposed and tricky currents are the rule.

The nearest village is nondescript, agricultural **APOLAKKIÁ**, 7km north of the Skiádhi turning and equipped with a bona fide **hotel**, **tavernas**, popular with bike-tourers, and shops. Northwest, the road leads to Monólithos, while the northeasterly bearing leads quickly and pleasantly back to Yennádhi via Váti. Due north, just below an irrigation reservoir, the tiny frescoed chapel of **Áyios Yeóryios Várdhas** (unlocked) is worth the short detour if you have your own transport.

Hálki

Hálki, a tiny (20 square kilometres), waterless, limestone speck west of Rhodes, is a fully fledged member of the Dodecanese, though all but about three hundred of the former population of three thousand emigrated (mostly to Rhodes or to Florida) in the wake of a devastating sponge blight during the early 1900s. Despite a renaissance through tourism in recent years, the island is tranquil compared with its big neighbour, with a slightly weird, hushed atmosphere owing to foreigners in their villas vastly outnumbering locals for much of the year. The big event of the day is the arrival of the regular afternoon kaïki from Kámiros Skála on Rhodes.

Hálki first attracted outside attention in 1983, when UNESCO designated it the "isle of peace and friendship" and the seat of regular international youth conferences. Some 150 crumbling houses were to be restored at UNESCO's expense as accommodation for delegates, but by 1987 just one hotel had been completed, and the only sign of "peace and friendship" was a stream of UNESCO and Athenian bureaucrats staging musical binges under the rubric of "ecological seminars". Confronted with an apparent scam, the islanders sent UNESCO packing and contracted two UK package operators to complete restorations and bring in paying guests. There is now in fact a third tour company present, and most of the ruins have been refurbished.

Emborió

The skyline of **EMBORIÓ**, the island's port and only habitation, is pierced by the tallest freestanding clocktower in the Dodecanese and, a bit further north, the belfry of Áyios Nikólaos church. Emborió's restored houses are pretty much block-booked from April to October by the tour companies mentioned; independent travellers will be lucky to find anything at all on spec, even early or late in the season. Non-package **accommodation**, all requiring advance reservations, includes the delightful, en-suite *Captain's House* (☎02460/45 201; ❷), which has the feel of an old French country hotel and whose English manageress Christine can point you in likely directions if she's full; *Pension Keanthi* (☎02460/45 334; ❷) near the school, offering bland, pine-furnished rooms with high ceilings plus a few galleried studios (❸); and the municipally-owned *Hotel Halki* (☎02460/49 390; ❸) in the old sponge factory on the south side of the bay, indifferently managed and beset by creeping damp, but likely to have a vacancy. Of the half-dozen **tavernas** along the field-stoned, pedestrianized waterfront, *Remezzo* (aka *Takis*) is excellent for *mayireftá* and pizzas, *Maria* behind the post office has good grills, while *Houvardas*, near the north end of the quay has proven reliable for *mayireftá* over the years. Amongst a similar number of bars and cafés, the standout has to be *Soula's* (aka "The Parrot Bar" after resident birds), near the base of the jetty, with puddings and own-made ice cream to die for. There's a **post office**, four well-stocked stores, two good bakeries cranking out a range of bread and pies, plus two **travel agencies** which sell boat tickets and change money (there's no bank); one of them, Zifos Travel (☎02460/45 028, ✉zifos-travel@rho.forthnet.gr) often has a few vacancies amongst studios which they hold back from the UK companies.

The rest of the island

Three kilometres west lies the old pirate-safe village of **HORIÓ**, abandoned in the 1950s but still crowned by the Knights' castle. Except during the major August 14–15 festival, the church here is kept securely locked to protect its frescoes. Across the valley, the little monastery of **Stavrós** is the venue for the other big island bash on September 14. There's little else to see or do inland, though you can spend three hours **walking** across the island on the 1998-vintage dirt track, the extension of the cement "Tarpon Springs Boulevard" donated by the expatriate community in Florida. At the end of the road (best arrange a ride out, and walk back) you'll come to the monastery of **Ayíou Ioánnou Prodhrómou**; the caretaker there can put you up in a cell (except around August 29, the other big festival date), but you'll need to bring supplies. The terrain en route is monotonous, but compensated by views over half the Dodecanese and Turkey.

Longish but narrow **Póndamos**, fifteen-minutes' walk west of Emborió, is the only sandy beach on Hálki, and even this has had to be artificially supplemented. The sole facility is the somewhat pricey *Nick's Pondamos Taverna*, serving lunch daily, plus supper four evenings weekly. Small and pebbly **Yialí**, west of and considerably below Horió via a jeep track, lies an hour's hike away from Póndamos. A thirty-minute walk north of Emborió lies **Kánia**, with a rocky foreshore and a rather industrial ambience from both power lines and the island's only petrol pump to one side.

Since these three coves are no great shakes, it's worth signing on at Emborió quay for **boat excursions** to more remote beaches. More or less at the centre of Hálki's southern shore, directly below Horió's castle, **Trahiá** consists of two coves to either side of an isthmus; you can (just) reach this overland by rough path from Yialí, and this trail is scheduled to be bulldozed into a track soon. North-coast beaches figuring as excursion-boat destinations include the pretty fjord of **Aréta**, **Áyios Yeóryios** just beyond, and the remote double bay of **Dhýo Yialí**. Of these, Aréta is the most attractive, and the only one accessible overland (in ninety minutes one-way) by experienced hillwalkers equipped with the *Chalki, Island of Peace and Friendship* map based on the old Italian topographical survey products.

Alimniá (Alimiá) islet

One of the more promoted local boat excursions visits **Alimniá (Alimiá) islet**, roughly halfway between Hálki and Rhodes. Despite more well-water and greenery and a better harbour than Hálki's, the deserted village here, overlooked by a few palm trees and yet another Knights' castle, was completely abandoned by the 1960s. The locals were initially deported during World War II after they admitted to assisting British commandos sent in April 1944 to sabotage the enemy submarines who used the deep harbour here. The seven commandos themselves were captured on the spot by the Nazis, bundled off first to Rhodes, then to Thessaloníki, where six were summarily executed as spies rather than regular prisoners of war; future Austrian premier and UN Secretary General Kurt Waldheim allegedly countersigned their death sentences.

Interesting history acknowledged, Alimniá is probably not a place you'd want to be stuck for an entire day. Excursions on offer are pricey (about €20.50, picnic lunch included), beach space very limited, the castle a hot, 45-minute walk up (the best thing to do here) and the crumbling village behind its salt marsh unedifying. If you snorkel in the outer bay beyond little Áyios Mínas monastery, you might glimpse outlines of the Italian-built submarine pens to one side of the deep bay. The former inhabitants only show up to graze livestock, or on the date of the annual festival (Áyios Yeóryios).

Kastellórizo (Meyísti)

Kastellórizo's official name, Meyísti (biggest), seems more an act of defiance than a statement of fact. While the largest of a tiny group of islands, it is actually the smallest of the Dodecanese, over seventy nautical miles from its nearest Greek neighbour (Rhodes) but barely more than a nautical mile off the Turkish coast at the narrowest straits. At night its lights are quite outnumbered by those of the Turkish town of Kaş, which lies across the bay and with whom Kastellórizo generally has excellent relations.

Until the early 1900s there were almost 14,000 people here, supported by a fleet of schooners that transported goods, mostly timber, from the Greek towns of Kalamaki (now Kalkan) and Andifelos (Kaş) on the Anatolian mainland opposite. But the withdrawal of island autonomy after the 1908 "Young Turk" revolution, the Italian seizure of the other Dodecanese in 1912 and an inconclusive 1913–1915 revolt against the Turks sent the island into decline. A French occupation of 1915–21 prompted destructive shelling from the Ottoman-held mainland, a harbinger of worse to come (see below). Shipowners failed to modernize their fleets upon the advent of steam power, preferring to sell ships to the British for the Dardanelles campaign, and the new frontier between the island and republican Turkey, combined with the expulsion of all Anatolian Greeks in 1923, deprived any remaining vessels of their trade. During the 1930s the island enjoyed a brief renaissance when it became a major stopover point for French and Italian seaplanes, but events at the close of World War II put an end to any hopes of the island's continued viability.

When Italy capitulated to the Allies in the autumn of 1943, a few hundred Commonwealth commandos occupied Kastellórizo, departing of their own accord in spring 1944 – leaving the island deserted and vulnerable to the attentions of pirates. In early July, a harbour fuel dump caught (or was set on) fire and an adjacent arsenal exploded, taking with it more than half of the two thousand houses on Kastellórizo. Even before these events most of the population had left for Rhodes, Athens, Australia (especially Perth) and North America. Today there are just 342 official residents here by the last census (with only 250 actually living permanently on Kastellórizo), largely maintained by remittances from over 30,000 emigrants and by subsidies from the Greek government, which fears that the island will revert to Turkey should their numbers diminish any further.

Yet Kastellórizo has a future of sorts, thanks to expat "Kassies" who have begun renovating their crumbling ancestral houses as retirement or holiday homes. Each summer, the population is swelled by returnees of Kassie ancestry. Occasionally they celebrate traditional weddings in the **Áyios Konstandínos** cathedral at Horáfia, which incorporates ancient columns from Patara in Asia Minor. Access has also improved since the late 1980s: an airport (domestic flights only) was completed, and the harbour dredged to accommodate larger ferries, though the island has yet to be designated an official port of entry to Greece, which causes problems for both yachties and conventional travellers crossing from Turkey.

You will either love Kastellórizo and stay a week, or crave escape after a day; its detractors dismiss the island as a human zoo maintained by the Greek government for the edification of nationalists, while partisans celebrate an atmospheric, barely commercialized outpost of Hellenism.

Kastellórizo Town

The current population is concentrated in the northern town of **KASTELLÓRIZO** – supposedly the finest natural harbour between Beirut and Fethiye on the Turkish coast – and its little "suburb" of **Mandhráki**, just over the fire-blasted hill with its half-ruined Knights' castle. Its outer bulwark now houses the worthwhile local **museum** (Tues–Sun 7am–2.30pm; free), with displays including plates from a Byzantine shipwreck, frescoes rescued from decaying rural churches and a reconstruction of an ancient basilica on the site of today's gaudy Ayíou Yeoryíou Santrapé church at Horáfia. Just below and beyond the museum, in the cliff-face opposite Psorádhia islet, is Greece's only **Lycian house-tomb**; it's well signposted from the shoreline walkway, up some steps beside the first wooden lamp standard.

Most of the town's surviving mansions are ranged along the waterfront, their tiled roofs, wooden balconies and blue or green shutters on long, narrow windows having obvious counterparts in the originally Greek-built houses of Kalkan and Kaş just across the water. Just one or two streets back, however, many properties are derelict – abandonment having succeeded where the World War I shelling, a 1926 earthquake and the 1944 explosions failed; sepia-toned posters and black-and-white postcards on sale of the town in its prime are poignant evidence of its later decline.

Practicalities

Kastellórizo is not really geared up for large numbers of visitors, though **pensions** in the old houses have been upgraded to en-suite status, and prices have climbed in recent years. If you're not met off the boat, the best budget en-suite options include the large-roomed *Pension Caretta* (☎ & ⓕ02460/49 028, ⓦwww.kastellorizo.de; ❷), which also has a fine restored apartment (❹); the nearly adjacent *Kristallo* (☎02460/41 209; ❷); and the *Pension Asimina*, behind the arcaded market (☎02460/49 361; ❷). More luxury is available at the recently-built, air-conditioned *Kastellorizo Hotel Apartments* (☎02460/49 044, ⓕ49 279, ⓦwww.kastellorizohotel.gr; ❺–❻), on the opposite side of the bay from the ferry jetty, offering quality-fitted studios or galleried maisonettes, some with sea view.

Apart from fish, goat meat and wild-fig preserves, plus whatever can be smuggled over from Kaş, Kastellórizo has to import foodstuffs and drinking water from Rhodes; prices when eating out can consequently be higher than usual, with the further pretext of the island's celebrity status. It's best to continue past the two most conspicuous waterfront **tavernas**, which do average fare only, and continue a few steps to *To Mikro Parisi* for reliably fresh and affordable seafood and meat grills. Other good quayside choices include *Iy Ipomoni* (supper only), two doors left from the arcaded market, featuring simple but wholesome grills and unusual dishes like sea-snails; *Kaz-Bar*, to the right of the Italian market, where chef Colin and his mother serve up fine grills, vegetable dishes and cold mezédhes nightly except perhaps Thursday in off-season; and the inexpensive but savoury *Akrothalassi*, purveying decent grills and salads near the west end of the quay, by the church. Two to recommend inland are *Iy Orea Meyisti* and *Ta Platania* (June–Sept), opposite Áyios Konstandínos in Horáfia, good for daily-changing *mayireftá* and desserts, often home-made. There are more puddings, and good breakfasts at *Zaharoplastio Iy Meyisti*, back on the waterfront. **Nightlife** spills out of the half-dozen *barákia* lining the quay.

A single **bank**, with handy cash dispenser, stands on the east quay; the **post office** is found on the far side of the bay. Better of the town's two travel agencies is Papoutsis (☎02410/70 830), which represents all boats calling here, and sells Olympic tickets. A public transfer van shuttles between town and airstrip at flight times; Damian Mavrothalassitis of *Pension Caretta* is the airport agent and can also sell tickets in a pinch.

It is possible to arrange a ride over **to Turkey** on one of four local boats, most reliably on Monday or Friday. The standard day-return fee is €14.70 (one-way €11.80), and you have to leave your passport with the authorities the day before. Although Kastellórizo is not yet a legal port of entry to Greece – it lacks a proper Schengen database computer, and customs stamps – police here cannot legally deny disembarkation to EU nationals arriving **from Kaş**, which is an official entry–exit point for Turkey.

The rest of the island

Kastellórizo's austere hinterland is predominantly bare rock, flecked with stunted vegetation; incredibly, two or three generations ago much of the countryside was carefully tended, producing wine of some quality and in quantity. A rudimentary paved road system links points between Mandhráki and the airport, but there aren't many specific places on it to visit and no scooters for rent. Karstic cliffs drop sheer to the sea, offering no anchorage for boats except at the main town, Mandhráki and Návlakas fjord (see overleaf).

Rural monasteries and ruins

Heat permitting, you can hike up the obvious, zigzag stair-path, then south through desolate fire-charred scrub to the rural **monastery of Áyios Yeóryios toú Vounioú**, 35 minutes away. The sixteenth- to eighteenth-century church boasts fine rib-vaulting and a carved *témblon*, but its highlight is a crypt, with the frescoed, subterranean chapel of **Áyios Harálambos** off to one side; access is via a steep, narrow passage descending from the church floor – bring a torch and grubby clothes, and get the key first from Kostas the keeper, who lives behind the *Little Paris* taverna. Alternatively, a fifteen-minute track-walk west of the port leads to the peaceful monastery of **Ayías Triádhas**, perched on the saddle marked by the OTE tower, and an army base (off-limits) – one of many strongpoints which have sprouted here since the Ímia crisis (see p.1017).

The onward path arrives after twenty minutes at the ancient citadel of **Paleókastro**, where you'll find masonry from Classical to medieval times, a warren of vaulted chambers, tunnels, cisterns plus another little monastery with a *hokhláki* courtyard. From any of the heights above town there are tremendous views north over sixty kilometres of Anatolian coast.

The shoreline and Rhó

Swimming is complicated by a total absence of decent beaches and an abundance of sea urchins and razor-sharp limestone reefs; the safest entry near town lies beyond the graveyard at Mandhráki, or people just dive from the lidos on the northwest quay (incidentally, it's illegal to swim across the harbour mouth).

Once away from the shore, you're rewarded by clear waters with a rich variety of marine life. From Áyios Yeóryios toú Vounioú, you can continue 45 minutes further on foot, first on a useless new bulldozer track, then on the original, French-built *kalderími*, to the multi-lobed fjord of **Návlakas**, a favourite mooring spot for yachts and fishing boats. The French built this cobbled way to facilitate offloading supplies here during World War I, safe from Ottoman artillery. Uniquely on Kastellórizo, this bay is sea-urchin-free, with freshwater seeps keeping the temperature brisk; there's superb snorkelling to 25-metre depths off the south wall.

Over on the southeast coast, accessible only by a 45-minute boat ride from town, the grotto of **Perastá** (Galázia Spiliá) deserves a look for its stalactites and strange blue-light effects; the low entrance, negotiable only by inflatable raft, gives little hint of the enormous chamber within, with monk seals occasionally nesting in another adjacent cave. Ninety-minute rubber-raft trips (€6 minimum per person) visit only the cave, or for a minimum of €15 on a larger kaïki, you can take it in as part of a five-hour tour that includes Rhó islet.

Should you make the trip out to **Rhó**, the tomb of *Iý Kyrá tís Rhó* (**The Lady of Rhó**), aka Dhespina Akhladhiotis (1898?–1982) – who resolutely hoisted the Greek flag each day on that islet in defiance of the Turks on the mainland – is the first thing you see when you dock at the sandy, northwestern harbour. From here a path heads southeast for 25 minutes to the islet's southerly port, past the side trail up to the intact Hellenistic fortress on the very summit. The islet has no facilities – just a few soldiers to prevent Turkish military landings or poachings of the hundreds of goats – so bring your own food and water.

Sými

Sými's most pressing problem, lack of fresh water, is in many ways also its saving grace. As with so many dry, rocky Dodecanese islands, water must be imported at great expense from Rhodes, pending completion of a reservoir in the distant future. Consequently, the island can't hope to support more than a handful of large hotels; instead, hundreds of people are shipped in daily during the season from Rhodes, relieved of their money and sent back. This arrangement suits both the Symiots and those visitors lucky enough to stay longer; many foreigners return regularly, or even own houses here.

Once beyond the inhabited areas, you'll find a surprisingly attractive island that has retained some of its original forest cover of junipers, valonea oaks and even a few pines – ideal walking country in spring or autumn (though not midsummer, when temperatures are among the highest in Greece). Another prominent feature of the landscape are dozens of tiny monasteries, usually locked except on their patron saint's day, though their cisterns with a can on a string for fetching water are usually accessible.

Sými Town

SÝMI, the island's capital and only proper town, consists of **Yialós**, the excellent natural port, and **Horió**, on the hillside above. Incredibly, less than a hundred years ago the place was richer and more populous (25,000) than Ródhos Town, its wealth generated by shipbuilding and sponge-diving, skills nurtured since pre-Classical times. Under the Ottomans, Sými, like most of the smaller Dodecanese, enjoyed considerable autonomy in exchange for a yearly tribute in sponges to the sultan; but the Italian-imposed frontier, the 1919–22 Greco-

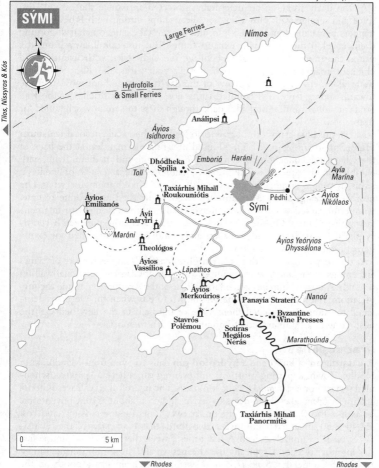

Within the map:

SÝMI

N

Datça (Turkey) ▲

Large Ferries

Nímos

Hydrofoils
& Small Ferries

Análipsi

Áyios
Isídhoros

Dhódheka
Spília

Emborió   Haráni

Ayía
Marína

Toli

Taxiárhis Miháïl
Roukouniótis

Pédhi

Áyios
Nikólaos

Sými

Áyios
Emilianós

Áyii
Anáryiri

Maróni

Theológos

Áyios Yeóryios
Dhyssálona

Áyios
Vassílios

Lápathos

Áyios
Merkoúrios

Panayía Stateri

Nanoú

Byzantine
Wine Presses

Stavrós
Polémou

Sotíras
Megálos
Nerás

Marathoúnda

Taxiárhis Miháïl
Panormítis

0   5 km

Tilos, Nísyros & Kós

▼ Rhodes

Rhodes ▼

Right margin:

9

THE DODECANESE | Sými

Turkish war, the advent of synthetic sponges and the gradual replacement of
the crews by Kalymniots spelt doom for the local economy. Vestiges of past
nautical glories remain in still-active boatyards at Pédhi and Haráni, but today
the souvenir-shop sponges come entirely from overseas and, the recent boom
notwithstanding, a significant fraction of the magnificent nineteenth-century
mansions stands roofless and empty.

The approximately twenty-five hundred remaining Symiots are scattered fairly evenly throughout the mixture of Neoclassical and more typical island
dwellings; despite the surplus of properties, many outsiders have preferred to
build anew, rather than restore derelict shells accessible only by donkey or on
foot. As on Kastellórizo, a wartime ammunition blast – this time set off by the
retreating Germans – levelled hundreds of houses up in Horió. Shortly afterwards, the official Axis surrender of the Dodecanese to the Allies was signed
here on May 8, 1945: a plaque marks the spot at the present-day *Restaurant Les
Catherinettes*.

777

At the lively **port**, an architecturally protected area since the early 1970s, spice and sponge stalls plus a few jewellery shops throng with Rhodes-based trippers between 11am and 3.30pm, and the several excursion craft disgorging them envelop the quay with exhaust fumes. But just uphill, away from the water, the more peaceful pace of village life takes over, with livestock and chickens roaming free-range. Two massive stair-paths, the Kalí Stráta and Katarráktes, effectively deter many of the day-trippers and are most dramatic towards sunset; large, owl-haunted ruins along the lower reaches of the Kalí Stráta are lonely and sinister after dark, though these too are now scheduled for restoration.

A series of blue arrows through Horió leads to the excellent local **museum** (Tues–Sun 10am–2pm; €1.50). Housed in a fine old mansion at the back of the village, the collection concentrates on Byzantine and medieval Sými, with exhibits on frescoes in isolated, locked churches and a gallery of medieval icons, as well as antiquarian maps and the inevitable ethnographic wing. The nearby **Hatziagapitos Mansion** has been refurbished as an annexe; here, wonderful carved wooden chests are the main exhibits, along with fragmentary wall-paintings. On the way back to central Horió, the nineteenth-century pharmacy, with its apothecary jars and wooden drawers labelled for exotic herbal remedies, is worth a look.

At the very pinnacle of things, a **Knights' castle** occupies the site of Sými's ancient acropolis, and you can glimpse a stretch of Classical polygonal wall on one side. A dozen churches grace Horió; that of the Assumption, inside the fortifications, is a replacement of the one blown to bits when the Germans detonated the munitions cached there. One of the bells in the new belfry is the nose-cone of a thousand-pound bomb, hung as a memorial.

Practicalities

A **catamaran**, a **kaïki** and a **hydrofoil** run daily to Sými from Mandhráki in Ródhos Town, departing morning and evening on either an *epivatikó* (scheduled service) or *ekdhromikó* (excursion) basis. The hydrofoil *Aigli* leaves Rhodes at 9am or 6pm, takes 55 minutes to arrive, and costs about €10. Conventional boats like the *Symi I* require just under two hours for the crossing, and cost €7.40–8.80 on an excursion ticket, two-thirds that as an *epivatikó*; the catamaran Symi II is similarly priced. A few times a week there are also mainline ferries in either direction, typically the cheapest of all (1hr 40min journey time). ANES, the outlet for *Symi I/Symi II/Aigli* tickets, maintains a booth on the quay and an office in the marketplace lanes (☎02460/71 444). Among **ferry** agents, Sunny Land, also in the market, is the agent for ANEK (the *Nissos Kalymnos*), while DANE Lines and the Dodecanese Express catamaran is handled by Symi Tours nearby (☎02460/71 307).

There's no official tourism bureau, but the island's English-language advertiser-newsletter, *The Symi Visitor* (free; Ⓦwww.symivisitor.com), is literate and has current island gossip with informative features. The **post office** in the official Italian "palace" is open standard hours; of the two **banks**, the Alpha/Ionian is more efficient and has a cash dispenser. During the season a small green bus (€0.60 flat fare) shuttles between Yialós and Pédhi via Horió on the hour (returning at the half-hour) until 11pm. There are also six **taxis** (allow €3 Yialós–Horió with baggage), and one or two pricey outlets for **motor-scooter rental** (€20.50 and up daily), though this is a perfect island for boat and walking excursions. A **laundry** operates in the grid of market lanes, resorted to by those whose hosts forbid clothes-washing in rooms.

Accommodation

Accommodation for independent travellers is somewhat limited and proprietors tend not to meet arriving boats, though the situation isn't nearly so bad as on Hálki. Studios, rather than simple rooms, predominate, and package operators control most of these, though curiously you may have an easier time finding spots in July/August than during spring/autumn, considered the most pleasant season here. Despite asphyxiating summer heat, air conditioning and ceiling fans are rarely found – go for north-facing and/or balconied units when possible. If you're planning in advance, the Symi Visitor website (see opposite) is worth consulting.

Albatros, marketplace ☎02460/71 707 or 71 829. Partial sea views from this exquisite, small hotel; pleasant second-floor breakfast salon, air-con. ❹

Aliki, Haráni quay ☎02460/71 665, ⓕ71 655, ⓦwww.simi-hotelaliki.gr. A complete overhaul of an 1895 mansion, and Sými's poshest hotel: tasteful rooms with wood floors and some antique furnishings, and large bathrooms, though only some have sea views. Breakfast included in price. ❻

Anastasia, behind the post office ☎02460/71 364. Pleasantly set hotel, though with limited harbour views, this has parquet-floored rooms plus a couple of studios, with some package allotment however. ❸

Egli Rooms, base of the Kalí Stráta ☎02460/71 392. Basic (non-en-suite), but clean enough rooms, and usually has vacancies when everyone else is full. ❷

Fiona, at the top of the Kalí Stráta ☎02460/72 088. Mock-traditional hotel building whose large airy rooms have double beds and stunning views; breakfast in mid-air on common balcony. ❹

Jean Manship, c/o *Jean & Tonic Bar* ☎ & ⓕ02460/71 819 8pm–1am Greek time. Jean manages two traditional houses in Horió, both suitable for couples and with stunning views. ❸–❹

Katerina Tsakiris Rooms Horió ☎02460/71 813. Just a handful of very plain en-suite rooms with shared kitchen and grandstand view; reserva-

tions essential. ❷–❹

Les Catherinettes, above eponymous restaurant, north quay ☎02460/72 698, ⓔmarina-epe@rho.forthnet.gr. Creaky but spotless en-suite pension in a historic building with painted ceilings and seaview balconies for most rooms. ❸

Symi Visitor Accommodation ☎02460/72 755, ⓔsymi-vis@otenet.gr. Managed by affable returned Greek–Australian Nikos Halkitis and partner Wendy Wilcox, who offer a variety of houses restored as double-occupancy studios in prime locations of Horió. Rates range from €35.30 at *The Cottages* to €103 at *The Mule House*, by way of €53 at *The Windmills*; they also have pricier units suitable for 4–5 persons.

Taxiarhis Apartments, edge of Horió overlooking Pédhi ☎02460/72 012, ⓕ72 013. Secluded, well-designed row of studios and one-bedroom apartments with common areas and balconies, though some package groups. Breakfast on request. ❹–❺

Titika Rooms, rear of platía Yialós (enquire at sponge shop left of National Bank, or ☎02460/71 501). No views, but quiet and well-equipped rooms with fridge and air-con; tiny common kitchen and shared terrace with tables. ❷–❹

Villa Symeria up the Kalí Stráta (contact *Albatros Hotel*). Restored mansion comprising two apartments with either air-con or fans, suitable for up to four and six persons respectively. ❻

Eating and drinking

You're best off avoiding most **eateries** on the north and west quays of the port, where menus, ingredients, prices and attitudes have been terminally warped by the day-trip trade. Away from these areas, you've a fair range of choice among *kultúra* tavernas, old-style *mayireftá* places, a few genuine ouzerís and even a traditional kafenío or two.

To Amoni, inland side of main platía, Yialós. An excellent, inexpensive, authentic ouzerí, where big helpings of liver, sausage and seafood titbits accompany the usual fried vegetarian starters and mainland bulk wine. Open most of the year, though supper only low season; seating indoors and out.

Dhimitris, south quay, on the way out of town. Excellent, family-run seafood-stressing ouzerí with

exotic items such as *hokhlióalo* (sea snails), *foúskes* (mock oysters), *spinóalo* (pinna-shell flesh) and the indigenous miniature shrimps, along with the more usual dishes and lots of vegetarian starters.

Ellinikon, south side main platía, Yialós. The most prominent of the *kultúra* tavernas, where host Nikos Psarros will escort you to the cooled wine cellar to choose from among 140 varieties of top Greek wine. Food portions aren't huge, but recipes – squid-ink pasta, seafood moussakás, roasts, ice cream with mulberry sauce – are rich. Budget €25 per head plus the cost of wine.

O Ilios, west quay. British-run, with "English" or healthy full breakfasts, plus vegetarian meals and own-made cakes. Also does picnic hampers for beach outings – notify them the previous day. Open 8am–10.30pm.

To Kantirimi, north side main square, Yialós. A good source of pancake or waffle breakfasts under the trees; becomes a snack café/bar later in the day.

O Meraklis, rear of the bazaar. Polite service and fair portions of well-priced *mayireftá* and mezédhes make this a reliable bet April–Dec. Sample meal: beans, beets, dips, and roast lamb with potatoes as a tender main course. Allow €13–14 each.

Mythos, south quay between bus/taxi stop, Yialós. Superb, supper-only ouzerí that's reckoned among the best, and best-value, cooking on the island. There is a menu, but why not let chef Stavros hit you with his Frenchified medley which includes salad, seafood starters (squid in basil sauce), duck with juniper berries, lamb slices, and own-made desserts. Budget €20.50 a head before dipping into the decent wine list. Roof terrace annexe opening soon.

Pahos, west quay, beside *O Ilios* (no sign). The old-boys' kafenío, in operation since World War II, and still a classic spot for a sundown oúzo and people-watching.

Yiorgos, near top of Kalí Stráta in Horió. Jolly, much-loved institution maintaining consistent food quality since 1977, with summer seating on a pebble-mosaic courtyard. Service can be slipshod, but perennial recipes include feta-stuffed peppers, spinach-rice, chicken in mushroom-wine sauce, and grilled fish when available. Open random lunchtimes in season, supper only indoors in winter.

Nightlife

Nightlife continues into the early hours and is sometimes abusively loud, with a number of bars owned by expatriates. Up in Horió, convivial *Jean & Tonic* is the heart and soul of the bar scene, catering to a mixed clientele (visitors and expats until 3am, Greek restaurateurs 3am until dawn) most of the year; a short way down the Kalí Stráta, *Kali Strata* is a low-key place with unbeatable views and excellent, wide-ranging music. Down at Yialós, the *Harani Club* has the nicest interior and a mix of Greek and international music depending on the crowd, until 2am; its neighbours in the noisy alley nicknamed "the Gaza strip" have lapsed into high-volume aural assaults aimed at empty tables. Elsewhere, *Katoi* on the south quay is a no-touts, no-hassle bar favoured by locals, whilst *The Club* on the platía functions between midnight and dawn, and has a pool table.

Around the island

Sými has no big sandy beaches, but there are plenty of pebbly stretches at the heads of the deep, protected bays which indent the coastline. **PÉDHI**, a 45-minute walk from Yialós, retains some of its former identity as a fishing hamlet, with enough water in the plain behind – the island's largest – to support a few vegetable gardens. The beach is poor, though, and patronage from yachts and the giant, overpriced *Pedhi Beach* hotel (☎02460/71 981, ℱ71 982; ◎) has considerably bumped up prices at several local **tavernas**, of which the most reasonably priced and authentic is *Iy Kamares* at the far south end. Many will opt for another twenty minutes of walking via a rough but obvious path along the south shore of the almost landlocked bay to **Áyios Nikólaos**. The only all-sand beach on Sými, this offers sheltered swimming, tamarisks for shade and a mediocre taverna. Alternatively, a paint-splodge-marked path on the north side of the inlet leads in just over half an hour to **Ayía Marína**, where there's a minuscule beach, a shingle lido with sunbeds, another snack bar and a monastery-capped islet to which you can easily swim.

Around Yialós, you'll find tiny **NOS (Navtikós Ómilos Sýmis)** "beach" ten minutes past the boatyards at Haráni, but there's sun here only until lunchtime and it's usually packed with day-trippers. You can continue along the cement-paved coast road, or cut inland from the Yialós platía past the abandoned desalination plant, to appealing **Emborió** (Nimborió) Bay, with a poor **taverna** (*Metapontis*) and an artificially sand-strewn beach a bit beyond. Inland from this are Byzantine mosaic fragments under a protective shelter, and, nearby, a catacomb complex known locally as **Dhódheka Spília**.

Plenty of other, more secluded coves are accessible by energetic walkers with sturdy footwear, or those prepared to pay a modest sum for the taxi-boats (daily in season 10am–1pm, returning 4–5pm; one-way fares available to the nearer bays cited above). These are the best method of reaching the southern bays of **Marathoúnda** and **Nanoú**, and the only method of getting to the spectacular fjord of **Áyios Yeóryios Dhyssálona**. Dhyssálona lacks a taverna and lies in shade after 1pm, while unalluring Marathoúnda is fringed by coarse, slimy pebbles, making Nanoú the most popular destination for day-trips. The 200-metre beach there consists of gravel, sand and small pebbles, with a scenic backdrop of pines and a reasonable taverna (menu of squid, chips and salad) behind. It's also possible to reach Nanoú overland, via Panayía Strateří chapel up on the main trans-island road, descending a scenic, forested gorge for some 45 minutes; most of the old path from Horió to Panayía Strateří still exists, making a marvellous traverse of about three hours in total, leaving time for a meal and swim at Nanoú before the boat trip back to Yialós.

For more hiking adventures, you can cross the island from Horió in ninety minutes to **Áyios Vassílios**, the most scenic of the gulfs with its Lápathos beach; in about the same time to **Tolí**, a deserted, west-facing cove, also accessible from Emborió; or in three hours, partly through forest, from Yialós to **Áyios Emilianós** at the island's extreme west end, where a little monastery is tethered to the body of Sými by a causeway. On the way to the latter you should look in at the monastery of **Taxiárhis Mihaïl Roukouniótis** (daily 9am–2pm & 4–8pm), Sými's oldest, with naive eighteenth-century frescoes and a peculiar ground plan: the current *katholikón* is actually superimposed on a lower, thirteenth-century structure abandoned after being burnt and pillaged by pirates during the 1400s, though a fine fresco of St Lawrence (Áyios Lavréntios) survives behind the altar screen. Resident, trilingual Father Amfilohios will gladly tell you anything else you might possibly wish to know about the place.

The Archangel is also honoured at the huge monastery of **Taxiárhis Mihaïl Panormítis** near the southern tip of the island, Sými's biggest rural attraction and generally the first port of call for the excursion boats from Rhodes (confirm the itinerary if you wish to proceed direct to Yialós – some craft do). These allow only a quick thirty-minute tour; if you want more time, you'll have to come by scooter from Yialós (though the still-unpaved road down from the central escarpment is terrible, with nine hairpin bends), or arrange to stay the night (€9 minimum donation) in the **xenónas** (inn) set aside for pilgrims. There are large numbers of these in summer, as Mihaïl has been adopted as the patron of sailors in the Dodecanese.

Like many of Sými's monasteries, Panormítis is of recent (eighteenth-century) vintage and was thoroughly pillaged during World War II, so don't expect too much of the building or its treasures. An appealing pebble-mosaic court surrounds the central *katholikón*, tended by the monk Gabriel and lit by an improbable number of oil lamps. It's also graced by a fine *témblon*, though the frescoes are recent and mediocre. One of the two small museums (€1.50 admits to both) contains a strange mix of precious antiques, exotic junk (stuffed crocodiles and koalas, elephant tusks), votive offerings, models of ships and a chair piled with messages-in-bottles brought here by Aegean currents – the idea being that if the bottle or toy boat arrived, the sender got their prayer answered. There's a small beach, a shop/kafenío, a bakery and a **taverna** (*Panormio*) popular with passengers of the many yachts calling in. Near the taverna stands a memorial commemorating three Greeks, including the monastery's abbot, executed in February 1944 by the Germans for aiding British commandos.

Tílos

The small, blissfully quiet island of **Tílos**, with an official population of about five hundred (dwindling to eighty in winter), is one of the least frequented and worst connected of the Dodecanese, though it can (in theory) be visited on a day-trip by hydrofoil or catamaran once or twice a week. Why anyone would want to come for just a few hours is unclear: while it's a great place to rest on the beach or go walking, there is nothing very striking at first glance. After a few days, however, you may have stumbled on several of the seven small castles of the Knights of St John which stud the crags, or found some of the inconspicuous medieval chapels clinging to the hillsides.

Tílos shares the characteristics of its closest neighbours: limestone mountains resembling those of Hálki, plus volcanic lowlands, pumice beds and red-lava sand as on Níssyros. Though rugged and scrubby on its heights, the island has ample water – from springs or pumped up from the agricultural plains – and clusters of oak and terebinth near the cultivated areas. From many points on the island you've startling views across to Kós, Sými, Turkey, Níssyros, Hálki, Rhodes and even (weather permitting) Kárpathos.

Since the mid-1990s, however, development on Tílos has threatened to reverse the conditions which many visitors have historically come to enjoy; besides the Dodge City atmosphere of Livádhia (see below), a hyperactive bull-dozing programme has scarred virtually every mountain in the east of the island. A 1998-vintage road from the telecom-tower hill, heading east along the summit ridge, is intended to facilitate a proposed fish farm at Áyios Séryios, which will finish that cove as a leisure beach.

Tílos's main road, widened and repaved in 1999–2000, runs 7km from Livádhia, the port village, to Megálo Horió, the capital and only other significant habitation. A public **minibus** links the two, and services are theoretically scheduled to coincide with ferry arrivals; at other times the bus makes up to six runs daily along the Livádhia–Éristos stretch. There are also two **taxis**, or you can rent a **car** from two outlets in Livádhia (Stefanakis Travel and Tilos Travel). Stefanakis currently has a monopoly on ferry tickets; Tilos Travel is arguably the more helpful, however (☎ & ⓕ 02460/44 294, ⓦ www.tilostrav-el.co.uk), offering a full accommodation booking service, money exchange, boat excursions all season – providing there are sufficient passenger numbers – and scooter rental. The island's single filling station lies between Livádhia and Megálo Horió.

Many visitors come specifically to **walk**, assisted by the extremely accurate **map** prepared by Baz "Paris" Ward and sold locally – or by certified walking **guides** Iain and Lyn Fulton (☎ 02460/44 128 or 094/6054593, ⓔ fulton@otenet.gr), who may take you on unusual itineraries not described or mapped in existing literature. A half-dozen critical sections of deteriorating trail or *kalderími* have been surveyed in preparation for cleaning and rebuilding in the near future, so quality walking opportunities may have stabilized and should improve in the future.

Livádhia

With its unpaved streets, unfinished building sites and higgledy-piggledy lay-out, **LIVÁDHIA** makes a poor introduction to the island, but it remains the better equipped of the two settlements to deal with tourists, and is closer to the majority of remaining path-hikes. There are generally enough beds in the various **rooms** and **hotels** to go around, but in peak season it's certainly worth phoning ahead. Budget options include a few adjacent outfits on the shore just beyond the Italian "palace", for example *Paradise* (aka *Stamatia's*; ☎ 02410/44 341; ❶) or two studios next door at *Galini* (aka *Paraskevi* ☎ 02410/44 280; ❷). Further along the bay are some newer, better-appointed options: *Anastasia* (☎ 02460/44 111; ❶), just behind the *Armenon* taverna, where a usual willing-ness to bargain offsets slightly small rooms, or *Pavlos and Nina* (☎ 02460/44 011; ❷), overlooking the sea near the friendly *Eleni Beach Hotel* about halfway around the bay (☎ 02460/44 062, ⓕ 44 063; ❹), with large airy rooms requir-ing advance booking. The *Faros Hotel* (☎ 02460/44 068; ❸) at the extreme end of the bay is widely praised for calm and its hospitable managing family, and also has a decent restaurant.

Inland, go for the well-appointed *Studios Irinna* (☎ 02410/44 366; ❷), alias *Kula's*, above the ironmonger's which runs it; the *Hotel Irini* (☎ 02410/44 293, ⓕ 44 238; ❹), 200m inland from mid-beach, with a pool, all mod cons and generally a few on-spec vacancies in amongst the Laskarina package clients here; or, tops on the island and only really available outside peak season, the B-class *Hotel Tilos Mare* (☎ 02460/44 100, ⓕ 44 105; ❸).

There must be a dozen-plus **tavernas** operating around Livádhia in peak sea-son, of which perhaps half merit consideration. Among the more authentic spots for a no-nonsense Greek feed are *Irina* (alias *Stefanos and Maria*), doling out inexpensive *mayireftá* right on the shore near the church; *Psistaria Kritikos* in the village centre, well regarded by carnivores for its goat chops, sausages and chicken; *To Armenon* (alias Nikos') on the shore road, an excellent and salubrious beach-taverna-cum-ouzerí, with octopus salad, white beans and the like; and inland on the way to *Armenon*, the *Pantelis Souvla Maria's Pizza* (sic), doing just those things superbly, despite zero atmosphere courtesy of plastic chairs and a purple bug-zapper. The best place for reliably fresh grilled fish with mezédhes is *Blue Sky*, an unmissable eyrie perched above the ferry dock.

For **breakfast** (plus evening pizzas and home-made desserts), Anglo-Italian *Joanna's Café*, just inland from *Kritikos*, is hard to beat, also with a long list of strong cocktails. *Iy Omonia*, under trees strung with light bulbs, near the post office, is the enduringly popular "traditional" alternative for a sundowner, breakfast or while waiting for a ferry, and also does inexpensive, savoury mezédhes. Livelier, organized **nightlife** in or near Livádhia is limited to three bars: *Cafe Ino* on the shore near *Irina* for the trendy set, the *Bozi* at the far east end of the bay (nightly in summer, weekends otherwise) and a durable music pub in Mikró Horió (see below).

There's a **post office**, but as yet no bank or cash dispenser, so come with sufficient Greek cash or apply to either travel agency (Tilos Travel will do cash advances on plastic for a small commission). A **bakery** and several well-stocked **supermarkets** round out the roster of amenities.

Around the island

From Livádhia you can walk an hour north along the obvious trail to the pebble bay of **Lethrá**, or in about the same time south on separate itineraries to the secluded coves of **Stavrós** or **Thólos**. The track to the former begins between the *Tilos Mare Hotel* and the *Castellania Apartments*, becoming a trail at the highest new house in the village; once up to the saddle with its new road, you've a sharp drop to the beach – ignore over-eager cairning in the bed of the descending ravine, the true path is up on the right bank, indicated by red-paint surveyor's marks. The route to Thólos begins by the cemetery and the chapel of **Áyios Pandelímon** with its Byzantine *hokhláki* court, then curls around under the seemingly impregnable castle of **Agriosykiá**; from the saddle overlooking the descent to Thólos (again, surveyed in preparation for refurbishment), a route marked with cairns leads northwest to the citadel in twenty minutes. It's less than an hour's walk west, with some surviving path sections shortcutting the road curves, up to the ghost village of **Mikró Horió**, whose 1200 inhabitants left for Livádhia during the 1950s. The only intact structures are the church (locked except for the August 15 festival) and an old house which has been restored as a small-hours **music pub** and operates only during July and August, with a variable formula of Greek/foreign music, and a shuttle van laid on from the port.

Megálo Horió and Éristos

The rest of Tílos's inhabitants live in or near **MEGÁLO HORIÓ**, which has an enviable perspective over the vast agricultural *kámbos* stretching down to Éristos (see opposite), and is overlooked in turn by the vast castle of the Knights, which encloses a sixteenth-century chapel. The castle was built on the site of ancient Tílos – with recycled masonry evident – and is reached by a stiff, thirty-minute climb that begins on the lane behind the Ikonomou supermarket before threading its way through a vast jumble of cisterns, house foundations and derelict chapels – the remains of the much-larger medieval Megálo Horió. Two more flanking fortresses stare out across the plain: the easterly one of **Messariá** help-fully marks the location of the **Harkadhió** cave (closed for ongoing excava-tions), where Pleiocene midget-elephant bones were discovered in 1971. A sign-posted 500-metre track goes there from the road, ending near a spring and mod-ern amphitheatre (to be used in a new summer festival) just below the cave-mouth, which was hidden for centuries until a World War II artillery barrage exposed it. The bones themselves have been transferred to a tiny, not very com-pelling **museum** in Megálo Horió, on the ground floor of the town hall (open Mon–Fri 8am–2.30pm on application upstairs to the warden).

Your choices for **accommodation** in the village are the *Pension Sevasti* (☎02410/44 237; ❶) at the lower end of town, the central *Milios Apartments* (☎02410/44 204; ❷) or, best of the lot, *Studios Ta Elefandakia* (☎02410/44 213; ❷), set among attractive gardens by the car park. Of the two **tavernas**, the *Kali Kardhia*, next to the *Pension Sevasti*, is more reliably open and has the best view; there's a traditional **kafenío** by historic Taxiárhis church, and fur-ther up, the Athenian-run *Kafenio Ilakati* (late May to Sept only), with cakes and drinks.

South of and below Megálo Horió, signs direct you towards the three-kilo-metre paved side road to the long, pink-grey-sand **Éristos** beach, allegedly the island's best, though summer rubbish piles from campers can be disconcerting, and a reefy zone must be crossed entering the water. The far south end, where the reef recedes, is also a designated nudist zone, as are the two secluded, attrac-tive coves at Kavliáris south beyond the headland (accessible by path only). About halfway down the road on the right amongst the orchards is *Taverna-Rooms Tropikana* (☎02410/44 020; ❶), nothing special in either respect, but the most reliable all-season venue for a snack near the beach. For more comfort, there's the 1998-built *Eristos Beach Hotel* (☎02460/44 024; ❷) – the rooms are good value, though the management can be less than welcoming.

The far northwest

The main road beyond Megálo Horió hits the coast again at dreary **Áyios Andónios**, whose one bright spot is a single **taverna**, the *Dhelfíni*, open much of the time for the benefit of local fishermen. At low tide on the exposed, aver-age beach you can find more lava-trapped skeletons strung out in a row – human this time, presumably tide-washed victims of a Nissyrian eruption in 600 BC, and discovered by the same archeologists who found the miniature pachyderms.

There's better swimming at isolated **Pláka** beach, 2km west of Áyios Andónios, where people camp rough despite a total lack of facilities. The paved road finally ends 8km west of Megálo Hório at the fortified **monastery of Ayíou Pandelímona**, founded in the fifteenth century for the sake of its miraculous spring. The settlement hosts the island's major festival from July 25 to 27, and lately a friendly Serbian family has been in residence, acting as care-takers and operating a small snack/drinks *kantína*. The monastery's tower-gate and oasis setting, more than two hundred forbidding metres above the west coast, are the most memorable features, though an eminently photogenic inner courtyard boasts a *hokhláki* surface, and the church a fine marble floor. On the *katholikón* wall, an early eighteenth-century fresco shows the founder-builder holding a model of the monastery, while behind the ornate altar screen hides another fresco of the Holy Trinity.

The public minibus calls in here perhaps once or twice a day. To vary the **return to Megálo Horió**, you can walk back much of the way on a sign-posted path; it's shown correctly on Baz Ward's map, and ends at the minor monastery of Panayía Kamariani near Áyios Andónios. Committed and experienced hill-walkers can tackle the challenging path which curls around the southwest flank of Profítis Ilías, Tílos's highest mountain, finishing three hours later at **Éristos**. This begins, as signposted, beside the monastery; it's a well-surveyed route, with no real exposure or sharp drops, but there's only one spring along the way, rather disheartening scree at the start, and the wild feel of a remote traverse on a much larger island.

Níssyros

Volcanic **Níssyros** is noticeably greener than its southern neighbours Tílos and Hálki, and unlike them has proven wealthy enough to retain over eight hundred of its population year-round (down, though, from 10,000 in 1900). While remittances from abroad (particularly Astoria, New York) are significant, most of the island's income is derived from the offshore islet of Yialí, where a vast lump of **pumice** is slowly being quarried away by Lava Ltd. The concession fee collected from Lava by the municipality has engendered a huge public payroll and vast per-capita sums available to spend, making Níssyros something of a mini-Kuwait. Under the circumstances, the Nissyrians bother little with agriculture other than keeping cows and pigs; the hillside terraces meticulously carved out for grain and grapes lie fallow, and wine is no longer made locally.

The main island's peculiar geology is potentially a source of other benefits: DEI, the Greek power company, spent the years between 1988 and 1992 sinking exploratory **geothermal** wells and attempting to convince the islanders of the benefits of cheap electricity. In 1993, a local referendum went massively against the project, and DEI, together with its Italian contractor, took the hint and packed up. The desalination plant, reliant on an expensive fuel-oil generator, scarcely provides enough fresh water to spur a massive growth in package tourism. The relatively few tourists (mostly German) who stay the night, as opposed to the day-trippers from Kós, still find peaceful villages with a minimum of concrete eyesores and a friendly if rather tight-knit population.

Níssyros also offers good **walking** opportunities through a countryside planted with oak and terebinth, on a network of trails fitfully marked and maintained with EU money; wherever you stroll you'll hear the contented grunting of pigs as they gorge themselves on acorns from the many oak trees. Autumn is a wonderful time, especially when the landscape has perked up after the first rains, though the late-January almond-blossoming no longer occurs, as the trees have unhappily died out.

Mandhráki

MANDHRÁKI is the deceptively large port and island capital, with blue patches of sea visible at the end of narrow streets lined with tightly-packed houses, whose brightly painted balconies and shutters are mandated by law. Except for the tattier fringes near the ferry dock, where multiple souvenir shops and bad tavernas pitched at day-trippers leave a poor first impression, the bulk of the place is cheerful and villagey, arrayed around the community orchard or *kámbos* and overlooked by two ancient fortresses.

Into a corner of the nearer of these, the fourteenth-century Knights' castle, is wedged the little monastery of **Panayía Spilianí**, built on this spot in accordance with instructions from the Virgin, who appeared in a vision to one of the first Christian islanders. The monastery's prestige grew after raiding Saracens failed to discover the vast quantities of silver secreted here in the form of a rich collection of Byzantine icons. During 1996–97, the Langadháki area just below was rocked by a series of earthquakes, damaging a score of venerable houses (mostly repaired now), and rendering the small folklore museum homeless, though it was never really worth the admission fee for a couple of mannequins in traditional dress. A new combination archeological-ethno-graphical-historical museum has been built on the *kámbos* with money donated by the Nissyrian founder of the Vitex paint company, and should be ready for visitors by the end of 2001.

As a defensive bastion, the seventh-century BC Doric **Paleókastro** (unrestric-ted access), twenty-minutes' well-signposted walk out of the Langadháki district, is infinitely more impressive than the Knights' castle, and ranks as one of the more underrated ancient sites in Greece. You can clamber up onto the massive, polygonal-block walls by means of a broad staircase beside the still-intact gateway.

Practicalities

You'll see a handful of port **hotels** on your left as you disembark; cheapest of these is the waterfront *Three Brothers* (☎02420/31 344; ❶) and the *Romantzo* (☎02420/31 340; ❶) across the way, with partial sea views, and fridges in the simple but well-kept rooms; they also run the *Studios Volcano* (❸) in town. For slightly more comfort, try the municipally run *Xenon Polyvotis* (☎02420/31 011, ℉31 204; ❷) just beyond, whose biggish, neutral-decor rooms have fans and (mostly) knockout sea views. In the town proper, the main budget option is the small, very simple, hillside *Hotel Ypapandi* (☎02420/31 485 or visit *Taverna Panorama*; ❶), near Mandhráki's most comfortable accommodation, the *Hotel Porfyris* (☎02420/31 376, ⓕ31 176; ❹), also overlooking the sea and *kámbos*, with gardens and a large swimming pool. There's little actually on the shore aside from *Studios Sunset-Iliovasilema* (☎02420/31 159 or 097/2141344; ❸), adequate and quiet, near the converted windmill.

Culinary **specialities** include pickled caper greens, honey, *pittiá* (chickpea croquettes) and *soumádha*, an almond-syrup drink widely sold in recycled wine bottles, though it's now made from imported almonds and must be consumed within three months of purchase. When eating out, it's best to give all of the commercialized, shoddy shoreline **tavernas** a miss – simple, old-fashioned *Manolis Papatsou* is the honourable exception, often with fresh fish – in favour of more genuine haunts inland. Top of the heap is evening-only, musical ouzerí *Iy Fabrika* (closed Thurs), with indoor/outdoor tables by season and family recipes from founder Patti preserved by second owner Manolis, also the miners' chef on Yialí. On their days off, the staff here go to eat at resolutely simple *Panayiotis* (no sign) in Langadháki, open on summer evenings only, and serving lovingly prepared home-style dishes at a half-dozen outside tables. Pricier runners-up include *Panorama*, with bean and mushroom salad and suckling pig on offer, or *Irini* on lively, ficus-shaded Platía Ilikioméni, with more involved *mayireftá* unavailable elsewhere. Finally, little *Taverna Nissiros*, the oldest eatery in town, is always busy despite predictably average grill quality. Focuses of **nightlife** are Platía Ilikioméni and a string of *barákia* on the shore at Lefkándio district west of *Manolis*, the most popular of these being the *Enallax*.

The most useful of Mandhráki's three **travel agencies** is Dhiakomihalis, which acts as a representative for most ferries and hydrofoils, rents cars and exchanges money. Kentris, near the town hall, does G&A ferries and Olympic Airways tickets. There's a **post office** at the port and a single **bank** in town, but it has no cash dispenser and levies stiff commissions, as does Dhiakomihalis. At the base of the jetty is the **bus stop**, with (theoretically) up to four daily departures to the hill villages and five to Pálli; otherwise, there are two set-rate **taxis** and three outlets for **scooter rental**, among which Alfa and John and John (branch also in Pálli) provide the best service – rates begin at €10.30 per day.

Beaches and Pálli

Beaches on Níssyros are in even shorter supply than water, so much so that tour agencies here occasionally peddle excursions to a sandy cove on **Áyios Andónios** islet, opposite the Yialí mines. Closer at hand, the short, black-rock beach of **Hokhláki**, behind the Knights' castle, is unusable if the wind is up, and the town "beach" of **Miramáre** at the eastern edge of the harbour is merely a lido filled with sand in high season, a last resort in any weather. It's best to head east along the main road, passing the refurbished spa of **Loutrá** (hot mineral water only by doctor's referral) and the smallish "**White Beach**" (properly Yialiskári), 2km along and dwarfed by an ugly hotel. The Loutrá spa, though itself sporadically shut for restoration, is well worth a stop for its "snack bar" at the far end of the building, really an **ouzerí** with generous portions of reasonably priced salads, fried appetizers, seafood and meat.

A kilometre or so further, 4km in total from Mandhráki, the fishing village of **PÁLLI** makes an excellent hangout at lunchtime, when the port fills with trippers. Tavernas are multiplying, but stick with the two long-term favourites: the less expensive *Ellinis*, with spit-roasted meat by night, grilled fish in season and simple rooms upstairs (☎02420/31 453; ❷), or the adjacent *Afroditi* (aka *Nikos &*

Tsambika), with big portions of grills and *mayireftá*, Cretan bulk wine and excellent own-made desserts. They've also a house to rent, all or in part (☎02420/31 242; €41 for the entire house). The scooter-rental outlet, an excellent bakery cranking out brown bread and fine pies (branch in Mandhráki), and modest nightlife make Pálli also worth considering as a base. A tamarisk-shaded, dark-sand **beach**, kept well groomed of late, extends east of Pálli, to the abandoned Pantelídhi spa, behind which the little grotto-chapel of **Panayía Thermianí** is tucked inside the vaulted remains of a Roman baths complex. To reach Níssyros's best beaches, continue in this direction for an hour on foot (or twenty minutes by bike along the road), past an initially discouraging seaweed- and cowpat-littered shoreline, to the delightful cove of **Liés**, with a snack bar, *Oasis* (June 15–Sept 15). Just beyond here the now-dirt road ends at a car park. Walking a further fifteen minutes along a trail over the headland brings you to the idyllic, 300-metre expanse of **Pahiá Ámmos**, with grey-pink sand heaped in dunes, limited shade at the far end and a large colony of "freelance" campers in summer.

The interior

Níssyros's central, dormant **volcano** gives the island its special character and fosters the growth of the abundant vegetation – and no stay would be complete without a visit. When excursion boats arrive from Kós, several agency coaches and usually one of the public buses are pressed into service to take customers into the interior. These tours tend to monopolize the crater floor between 11am and 2pm, so if you want solitude, use early-morning or late-afternoon scheduled buses to Nikiá (three daily continue to the crater floor), a scooter or your own two feet to get there.

The road up from Pálli winds first past the virtually abandoned village of **EMBORIÓS**, where pigs and free-ranging cattle (a major driving hazard) far outnumber people, though the place is slowly being bought up and restored by Athenians and foreigners. New owners are often surprised to discover natural saunas, heated by volcano steam, in the basements of the crumbling houses; at the outskirts of the village there's a signposted public **steam bath** in a grotto, its entrance outlined in white paint. If you're descending to Pálli from here, an old cobbled way starting at the sharp bend below the sauna offers an attractive short cut of the four-kilometre road, while another *kalderími* drops from behind *To Balkoni tou Emboriou* **taverna** (sporadically May–Sept, limited menu) to within a quarter-hour's walk of the craters.

NIKIÁ, the large village on the east side of the volcano's caldera, is, with seventy inhabitants, more of a going concern, and its spectacular situation 14km from Mandhráki offers views out to Tílos as well as across the volcanic caldera. There are three places to **drink** (and, modestly, **eat**) here: *Porta* (summer eves only) and *Platia* on or near the engagingly round *hokhláki* plaza, or *Nikia*, at the entrance to the village. By the bus turnaround area, signs point to the 45-minute **trail** descending to the crater floor; a few minutes downhill, you can detour briefly to the eyrie-like **monastery of Áyios Ioánnis Theológos**, which only comes to life at the September 25 festival. To **drive** directly to the volcanic area you must use the road which veers off just past Emboriós.

However you approach the **volcano**, a sulphurous stench drifts out to meet you as fields and scrub gradually give way to lifeless, caked powder. The sunken main crater of **Stéfanos** is extraordinary, a moonscape of grey, brown and sickly yellow; there is another, less-visited double crater (dubbed **Polyvótis**) to the west, equally dramatic, with a clear trail leading up to it from the access road. The perimeters of both are pocked with tiny blowholes from which jets of steam puff constantly and around which form little pincushions of pure sulphur crystals. The whole floor of the larger crater seems to hiss, and standing in the middle you can hear something akin to a huge cauldron bubbling away below you. According to legend this is the groaning of Polyvotis, a Titan crushed here by Poseidon under a huge rock torn from Kós. When there are tour groups around, a small, tree-shaded snack bar operates in the centre of the wasteland, and a booth on the access road sporadically charges admission (€1.50) to the volcanic zone.

Since the 1991 destruction of the old direct *kalderími* between the volcano and Mandhráki, finding pleasant options for **walking** back to town requires a bit of imagination and possession of Beate and Jürgen Franke's locally available, GPS-drawn topographical map (free). First choice involves backtracking along the main crater access road for about 1km from the admission booth to find the start of a clear, crudely marked path which passes the volcanic gulch of **Káto Lákki** and the monastery of **Evangelístra** on its two-hour-plus course back to the port. You can lengthen the trip by detouring from Evangelístra south to **Profítis Ilías**, the island's summit, a two-hour round-trip – the route is well marked with cairns or white paint and was cleaned in 1998. An alternative approach to Evangelístra requires returning to Emboriós and leaving from the top of the village, near the cemetery and small castle, on a 45-minute course to the monastery – an enjoyable link, despite haphazard marking and cleaning. From Evangelístra, the onward route to Mandhráki briefly follows the now mostly paved road down before the marked path resumes, handily shortcutting hairpin bends.

Kós

After Rhodes, **Kós** is the second largest and most popular island in the Dodecanese, and there are superficial similarities between the two. Here also the harbour is guarded by an imposing castle of the Knights of St John; the streets are lined with grandiose Italian public buildings; and minarets and palm trees punctuate extensive Hellenistic and Roman remains. Although its hinterland for the most part lacks the wild beauty of Rhodes' interior, acre for acre Kós is the most fertile of the Dodecanese, blessed with rich soil and abundant ground water.

Mass tourism has largely displaced the old agrarian economy amongst the population of just over 28,000, and outside the main town and Kardhámena this is very much a family-holiday isle, where you can turn the kids loose on pushbikes. Except for Kós Town and Mastihári, there aren't many independent travellers, and from early July to early September you'll be lucky to find any sort of room at all without reservations far in advance, or a prebooked package. The tourist industry is juxtaposed rather bizarrely with cows munching amidst baled hay, and Greek Army tanks exercising in the volcanic badlands around the airport. All these peculiarities acknowledged, Kós is still definitely worth a few days' time while island-hopping: its handful of mountain villages are appealing, the tourist infrastructure excellent (including such amenities as regular city buses and cycle paths) and swimming opportunities are limitless – virtually the entire coast is fringed by beaches of various sizes, colours and consistencies.

Kós Town

The town of **KÓS**, home to over half of the island's population, spreads in all directions from the harbour, with most of its charm residing in scattered ancient and medieval antiquities. Apart from the Knights' castle, the first thing you see on arrival, there's a wealth of Hellenistic and Roman remains, many of which

KÓS & PSÉRIMOS

Bodrum (Turkey)

Léros

Kálymnos & Léros

Kálymnos

Marathoúnda
Avlákia
Vathý
Grafiótissa
Platý

Psérimos

Límniónas
Cape Dhrépano

Áyios Theológos
Áyios Ioánnis Thymianós
Panayía Palatianí
Astypaliá
Kéfalos
Kamári
Kastrí
Láira 428m
Zíni 362m
Aspri Pétra
Cape Krikéllo

Áyios Stéfanos
"Kamíla "Camel"
"Paradise
"Banana
Psitós Grémos "Sunny
Polémi "Magic

N
0   5 km

9

THE DODECANESE | Kós

791

Cape Skandhári
Kós Town
Lámbi
Selvéri
Zipári
Tingáki
Marmári

Alykí
Linopótis

Áyios Ioánnis
Mastihári
Troúlos
Pláka
Andimáhia

Knights' Castle
Kardhámena

Amanioú
Pylí
Harmýlio
Lagoúdhi
Paleó Pylí
Tólari

Evangelístria
Asómati
Ziá
Áyios Dhimítrios
A S F E N D H I O Ú
D Í K E O S
Khristós 846m

Asklepíon
Platáni
(Kermetés)
Áyios Gavríil
Ambávris

Brós Thermá

Áyios Fokás

Cape Psalídhi
Cape Áyios Fokás

Rhodes

Níssyros & Tílos

Níssyros

KÓS TOWN

(200m), Capmsite (1500m), Psalídhi, Áyios Fokás & Brós Thermá

PLATÍAS

Ayías Paraskevís — D
Dhiagóras — F
'Dolphin' — A
Eleftherías — C
Kazoúli — B
K. Paleológou — E

RESTAURANTS, CAFÉS & BARS

Café Aenaos — H
Australia-Sydney — K
Beach Boys — B
Blues Brothers — G
Central Café — I
Four Roses — J
Fresko Gelateria-Kafe — M
Koakon — E
Café del Mare — F
Nikos O Psaras — D
Noufara — A
Pote tin Kyriaki — L
Taurus — C
Taverna Ambavris — N

ACCOMMODATION

Afendoulis — 5
Alexis — 1
Kamelia — 3
M. Tselepi — 4
Phaethon — 2
Theodhorou Beach — 6

Yacht Marina

Summer Cinema

ITALIAN QUARTER

Hydrofoil Jetty

Ferry & Catamaran Dock

Knights' Castle

Hippocrates' Plane Tree

Turkish Bath (Hamam Bar)

Loggia

Agora

Old Synagogue

Pórta toú Fórou

Deftardar

Market

Winter Cinema

Museum

Excursion Boats

Port Police

Hippocrates Park

Hellenistic Baths

Ancient Stadium

Atik

Turkish Fountain

KTEL

Olympic Airways

Casa Romana

Roman Odeíon

Western Excavations

Catholic Cemetery

Lámbi (2km)

(100m) & B

Ambávris & Plataní

Villages & Askleípion

were only revealed by an earthquake in 1933, and excavated subsequently by the Italians, who also planned and laid out the "garden suburb" extending east of the central grid. Elsewhere, vast areas of open space alternate with a hotchpotch of Ottoman monuments and later mock-medieval or Art Deco buildings.

The **castle** (Tues–Sun 8am–2.30pm; €2.40) is reached via a causeway over its former moat, now filled in and planted with palms (hence the avenue's Greek name, Finíkon). The existing double citadel, which was built in stages between 1450 and 1514, replaced an original fourteenth-century fort deemed not capable of withstanding advances in medieval artillery. A fair proportion of ancient Koan masonry has been recycled into the walls, where the escutcheons of several Grand Masters of the Knights of St John can also be seen.

Immediately opposite the castle entrance stands the riven trunk of Hippocrates' plane tree, its branches now propped up by scaffolding instead of the ancient columns of yore; at seven hundred years of age, it's not really elderly enough to have seen the great healer, though it has a fair claim to being one of the oldest trees in Europe. Adjacent are two Ottoman fountains (a dry hexagonal one and a working one in an ancient sarcophagus) and the eighteenth-century **mosque of Hassan Pasha**, also known as the Loggia Mosque after the portico on one side; its ground floor – like that of the **Defterdar mosque** on Platía Eleftherías – is taken up by rows of shops.

Opposite the latter stands the Italian-built **Archeological Museum** (Tues–Sun 8am–2.30pm; €2.40), with a predictable Latin bias in the choice of exhibits. Four rooms of statuary are arrayed around an atrium with a mosaic of Hippocrates welcoming Asklepios to Kós; the most famous item, purportedly a statue of Hippocrates, is indeed Hellenistic, but most of the other highly regarded works (such as Hermes seated with a lamb) are Roman.

The largest single section of ancient Kós is the **agora**, a sunken, free-access zone containing a confusing jumble of ruins, owing to repeated earthquakes between the second and sixth centuries AD. More comprehensible are the so-called western excavations, lent definition by two intersecting marble-paved streets and the **Xystos** or restored colonnade of a covered running track. In the same area lie several floor mosaics, such as the famous one of Europa being carried off by Zeus in the form of a bull, though these tend to be off-limits or hidden under protective gravel. To the south, across Grigoríou toú Pémptou, are a garishly restored Roman-era odeion and the **Casa Romana** (Tues–Sun 8.30am–3pm; €1.50), a third-century-AD house built around three atria with surviving patches of mosaic floors showing panthers and tigers, plus assorted sea creatures.

Kós also retains a thoroughly commercialized **old town**, lining the pedestrianized street running from behind the market hall on Platía Eleftherías as far as Platía Dhiagóras and the isolated minaret overlooking the western archeological zone. One of the few areas of town to survive the 1933 earthquake, today it's crammed with expensive tourist boutiques, cafés and snack bars. About the only genuinely old thing remaining here is a capped **Turkish fountain** with a calligraphic inscription, found where the walkway cobbles cross Odhós Venizélou.

Practicalities

Large **ferries and catamarans** anchor just outside the harbour at a special jetty by one corner of the castle; **excursion boats** to neighbouring islands sail right in and dock all along Aktí Koundouriótou. **Hydrofoils** tie up south of the castle at their own berth, on Aktí Miaoúli. Virtually all ferry and excursion boat agents sit within 50m of each other at the intersection of pedestrianized Vassiléos Pávlou and the waterfront. Among the more helpful and genuinely representative of ferries and hydrofoils, not just expensive excursions, are Adris

Nissia at Vassiléos Pávlou 2, and Exas at Andóni Ioannídhi 4 (☎02420/29 900). If you just want to clear out, Aeolos Travel at Annéttas Laoumtzí 8 (☎02420/ 26 203) often has stray one-way charter seats back to the UK.

The **airport** is 24km southwest of Kós Town in the centre of the island; an Olympic Airways shuttle bus (€3) meets Olympic flights for a transfer to the town terminal, but if you arrive on any other flight you'll have to either take a taxi or head towards the giant roundabout outside the airport gate and find an orange-and-cream-coloured KTEL bus – they run from here to Mastihári, Kardhámena and Kéfalos as well as Kós Town. The **KTEL terminal** in town is a series of stops around a triangular park 400m back from the water, with an info booth adjacent at Kleopátras 7 (tickets on the bus). The municipality also runs a frequent **local bus** service, DEAS, through the beach suburbs and up to the Asklepion, with a ticket and information office at Aktí Koundouriótou 7. Push- or **mountain-bike** rental are popular options for getting around, given the island's relative flatness; if you want a **motor scooter**, try Moto Harley at Kanari, corner Neomartýrou Khrístou, while Autorent/Helen's at Apostólou Pávlou 31 (☎02420/28 882 or 094/4450062) or in Psalídhi suburb, at both the *Ramira* and *Okeanis* hotels, has a reputation for good-condition **cars**, as does Marion at Vasiléos Yeoryíou 1 (☎02420/26 293).

The municipal **tourist office** at Vassiléos Yeoryíou 3 (July & Aug daily 8am–9pm; May & June, Sept & Oct Mon–Fri 9am–8pm, Sat 8am–3pm; Nov–April Mon–Fri 8am–3pm) keeps stocks of local maps, bus timetables and ferry schedules (the latter not to be trusted implicitly). For more involved information, head for the News Stand book store and newsagent just behind the archeological museum on Platía Kazoúli. No fewer than six **banks** have cash dispensers, while the **post office** is at Vassiléos Pávlou 14. **Internet cafés** include *Café del Mare* at Megálou Alexándhrou 4 (the best equipped), or *Taurus* at Mandhilará 9. **Laundries** include Happy Wash at Mitropóleos 20, Laundry Center on Mandhilará 56 and Laundromat Center at Alikarnassoú 124.

Accommodation

If you're just in transit, you're virtually obliged to **stay** in Kós Town, and even if you plan a few days on the island, it still makes a sensible base, as it is the public transport hub and has the greatest concentration of vehicle rental and nightlife. Be wary of the touts which besiege most arriving sea-craft – their rooms are apt to be unlicensed, inconveniently remote and of dubious cleanliness.

Good, licensed, budget choices in the centre include the deservedly popular *Pension Alexis* (☎02420/25 594; ❷; March–Nov), Irodhótou 9 at the corner of Omírou, across from the Roman agora, with wood-floored, non-en-suite rooms and a self-catering kitchen; the same welcoming family runs the *Hotel Afendoulis* (☎02420/25 321; ❸; April–Nov), about 600m south at Evripýlou 1, with large, balconied en-suite rooms and breakfast available. If they're full, try the nearby *Hotel Kamelia* at Artemisías 3 (☎02420/28 983, ℗27 391; ❸), claimed open all year, with winter heating; the rear rooms have an orchard view. Other quiet possibilities include the air-conditioned *Hotel Phaethon* at Venizélou 75 (☎02420/228 901; ❹) and the self-catering rooms let by Moustafa Tselepi (☎02420/28 896; ❸) at Metsóvou 8 (enquire at Venizélou 35). For more comfort and a small private beach, the *Hotel Theodhorou Beach*, 1200m from the centre at the end of town towards Psalídhi (☎02420/22 280, ℗23 526; ❹) has generous-sized rooms not completely monopolized by packages and attractive common areas. The well-appointed **campsite** (☎02420/23 275; May to early Oct) lies another 1300m out towards Cape Psalídhi, and can be reached by either the DEAS bus service or its own minibus (which meets ferrries).

Eating, drinking and nightlife

Despite an overwhelming first impression of Euro-bland cuisine, it's easy to **eat** well and even reasonably in Kós Town, as long as you search inland, away from the harbour. The *Australia-Sydney* on Vassiléos Pávlou opposite the post office is a cheap and cheerful hole-in-the wall with a limited menu of daily dishes where two can eat for under €15; the *Koakon*, on Ieroú Lóhou, at the corner of Amerikís, offers *mayireftá* in a more salubrious environment without the usual multinational flags and photo-menus; while *Noufara* at Kanári 67 is carnivore heaven with roast chicken, *kondosoúvli* and the like. Moving up in the world, the nearby *Nikolaos O Psaras*, on the corner of Alikarnassoú and Avérof, is the most genuine fish taverna in town, with good *orektiká* preceding mildly pricey seafood. Kos's sole real ouzerí is tiny *Pote tin Kyriakí* at Pissándhrou 9 (closed Sun, as the name says), which neither wants nor gets many tourists – there's only a Greek sign out, and no menu per se – proprietor Angelos recites the day's fare. Equal to any of these is *Ambavris* (May–Oct), 800m south out of town by the road from near Casa Romana, in the eponymous village. To order from their English-only à la carte menu is to miss the point of the place; take the hint about "Mezedes" and let the house bring on their best – this changes seasonally but won't much exceed €19 for six plates, drinks extra.

For **breakfast**, the *Central/Kentriko Cafe* on Platía Ayía Paraskevís behind the market hall does American pancakes with fresh fruit juices, while you can join the largely Greek crowd at *Café Aenaos*, right under the Defterdar mosque, and people-watch while refilling your Greek coffee from the traditional *bríki* used to brew it up. For **snacks** or **dessert**, *Fresko Gelateria-Café*, on the corner of Kleopátras and Ioannídhi, serves crepes and waffles in the morning, sticky cakes or decadent own-made ice cream later on. For a convivial **drink** on the water, try long-lived *Blues Brothers* on Aktí Koundouriótou, near the port police; equally durable music bars with dance floors include *Four Roses* on the corner of Arseníou and Vassiléos Yeoryíou, and *Beach Boys* at Kanári 57. If you prefer loud techno and house, look no further than the "Pub Lanes", officially Nafklírou and Dhiákou; every address is a bar, whose identity tends to change each season, so just choose according to the crowd and the noise level. Otherwise there is one active **cinema**, the Orfeas, with summer and winter (Oct–May) premises as shown on the map; the indoor premises also hosts concerts and other special events.

The Asklepion and Platáni

Native son **Hippocrates** is justly celebrated on Kós; not only does he have a tree, a street, a park, a statue and an international medical institute named after him, but the **Asklepion** (summer Tues–Sun 8am–7pm, earlier closure winter; €2.35) 4km south of town, one of just three in Greece, is a major tourist attraction. DEAS buses run to the site via Platáni 8am–6pm and to Platáni only 7–11.45pm; otherwise it's a 45-minute walk. There is a small snack bar at the Asklepion, or pause for lunch in Platáni (see overleaf) en route.

The Asklepion was actually founded just after the death of Hippocrates, but it's safe to assume that the methods used and taught here were his. Both a temple to Asklepios (god of medicine, son of Apollo) and a renowned curative centre, its magnificent setting on three artificial hillside terraces overlooking Anatolia reflects early recognition of the importance of the therapeutic environment. Until recently, two fountains provided the site with a constant supply of clean, fresh water, and extensive stretches of clay piping are still visible, embedded in the ground.

Hippocrates (c. 460–370 BC) is generally regarded as the father of scientific medicine, though the Hippocratic oath probably has nothing to do with him and is in any case much altered from its original form. Hippocrates was certainly born on Kós, probably at Astypalia near present-day Kéfalos, but otherwise details of his life are few and disputed; what seems beyond doubt is that he was a great physician who travelled throughout the Classical Greek world, but spent at least part of his career teaching and practising at the Asklepion on his native island. A vast number of medical writings have been attributed to Hippocrates, only a few of which he could have actually written; *Airs, Waters and Places*, a treatise on the importance of environment on health, is widely thought to be his, but others were probably a compilation from a medical library kept on Kós, which later appeared in Alexandria during the second century BC. This emphasis on good air and water, and the holistic approach of ancient Greek medicine, now seems positively contemporary.

Today very little remains standing above ground, owing to the chronic earthquakes and the Knights' use of the site as a quarry. The lower terrace in fact never had many structures, being instead the venue for the observance of the *Asklepieia* – quadrennial celebrations and athletic/musical competitions in honour of the healing god. Sacrifices to Asklepios were conducted at an **altar**, the oldest structure on the site, whose foundations can still be seen near the middle of the second terrace. Just to its east, the Corinthian columns of a second-century AD **Roman temple** were partially re-erected by nationalistically minded Italians. A monumental **staircase** leads from the altar to the second-century BC Doric temple of Asklepios on the topmost terrace, the last and grandest of a succession of the deity's shrines at this site.

About halfway to the Asklepion, the village of **PLATÁNI** (also Kermetés, from the Turkish name *Germe*) is, along with Kós Town, the remaining place of residence for the island's dwindling community of ethnic Turks. Until 1964 there were nearly three thousand of them, but successive Cyprus crises and the worsening of relations between Greece and Turkey prompted mass emigration to Anatolia, and a drop in the Muslim population to currently under a thousand. Several excellent, Turkish-run tavernas are to be found at and around the main crossroads junction, with a working Ottoman fountain: *Arap* (summer only), the slightly less touristy *Asklipios* and *Sherif* across the way (summer only) and *Gin's Palace* (all year), each offering Anatolian-style mezédhes (fried vegetables with yogurt, *bourekákia*, and so on) and kebabs better than most in Kós Town.

Just outside Platáni on the road back to the port, the island's neglected **Jewish cemetery** lies in a dark conifer grove, 300m beyond the well-kept Muslim graveyard. Dates on the Hebrew-Italian-script headstones stop after 1940, after which none of the local Jews were allowed the luxury of a natural death prior to their deportation in summer 1944. Their former synagogue, a wonderfully orientalized Art Deco specimen at Alexándhrou Dhiákou 4, was refurbished in 1991 as a municipal events hall.

Eastern Kós

If you're looking for anything resembling a deserted **beach** near the capital, you'll need to make use of the DEAS bus line connecting the various resorts to either side of town, or else rent a vehicle; pedal-bikes can take advantage of the cycle paths extending as far east as Cape Psalídhi. Closest is **Lámbi**, 3km north towards Cape Skandhári with its military watchpoint, the last vestige of a vast army camp which has deferred to the demands of tourism – and supposed intra-NATO amity.

The bus line usually terminates at Áyios Fokás, 8km southeast of Kós Town, but sometimes continues an extra 4km to unusual and remote **Brós Thermá** (last service around 6pm); if you make the trip with your own transport be prepared to negotiate a rough dirt track for the final kilometre. Brós Thermá is known for its **hot springs** – best experienced at sunset or after – which issue from a grotto and flow through a trench into a shoreline pool protected by boulders, heating the seawater to an enjoyable temperature. Winter storms typically disperse the boulder wall, rebuilt every April, so that the pool changes from year to year. Just adjacent, the long-running *Psarotaverna Therma* does affordable seafood – especially parrotfish, swordfish and tuna, though the rest of the menu is unmemorable.

Tingáki and Marmári

The two neighbouring beach resorts of Tingáki and Marmári are separated from each other by the salt marsh of **Alykí**, which retains water until June after a wet winter. Between January and April Alykí is host to hundreds of migratory birds, and most of the time you'll find tame terrapins to feed near the outlet to the warm, shallow sea, though the drought of recent years means you're unlikely to see any of this until the next rainy winter. There's almost always a breeze along this coast, which means plenty of windsurfers for hire at either resort. The profiles of Kálymnos, Psérimos and Turkey's Bodrum peninsula all make for spectacular scenery. If you're aiming for either of these resorts from town, especially on a bike of any sort, it's safest and most pleasant to go by the obvious **minor road** which takes off from the southwest corner of town; the entire way to Tingáki is paved, and involves the same distance as using the main trunk road and marked turn-off. Similarly, a grid of paved rural lanes links the inland portions of Tingáki and Marmári.

TINGÁKI, a busy beachside resort popular with Brits, lies 12km west of the harbour. Oddly, there's very little accommodation near the beach in the dozen or so medium-sized hotels and more numerous studios; most of these are scattered inland through fields and cow pastures. One of the better hotels, if heavily subscribed to by packages, is the family-oriented *Hotel Constantinos Ilios* (☎02420/69 411; ❺), a well-designed bungalow complex. The best local taverna here is *Ambeli* (supper only), well signposted 2.5km east of the main beachfront crossroads. Among car-rental outfits, Sevi (☎02420/69 076) can be recommended, and will even deliver vehicles on request to Kós Town. The beach itself is white sand, long and narrow – it improves, and veers further away from the traffic of the frontage road, as you head southwest.

MARMÁRI, 15km from town, has a smaller built-up area than Tingáki, and the beach itself is broader, especially to the west where it forms little dunes. Most hotels here are monopolized by German tour groups, but you might hit on an on-spec vacancy at the B-class, 1997-built *Esperia* on the main access road down from the island trunk road (☎02420/42 010, ⊜42 012; ❹), in grassy surroundings. Just inland on the same street stands a pair of adjacent noteworthy **tavernas**: *Apostolis* and the currently superior *Dimitris*, offering *mezedhákia*, seafood and meat grills at reasonable prices and usually also open weekends November to April.

The Asfendhioú villages

The main interest of inland Kós resides in the villages on **Mount Dhíkeos**, a handful of settlements collectively referred to as **Asfendhioú**, nestled amidst the island's only natural forest. Together they give a good idea of what Kós looked like before tourism and ready-mix concrete arrived, and all are now severely depopulated by the mad rush to the coast. They are accessible via the curvy side road from Zipári, 8km from Kós Town; a badly marked but paved minor road to Lagoúdhi; or by the shorter access road for Pylí.

The first Asfendhioú village you reach up the Zipári road is Evangelístria, where a major crossroads by the parish church leads to Lagoúdhi and Amanioú (west), Asómati (east) and Ziá (uphill). **ZIÁ**'s spectacular sunsets make it the target of up to six evening tour buses daily, though the village has barely a dozen families still resident, and its daytime tattiness seems to increase each tourist season. Best of the dozen **tavernas** here is the *Olympia*, at the start of the pedestrian walkway up to the church, open all year with such dishes as chickpeas, bulgur pilaf, *spédzofaï* (sausage and pepper stew), dark bread and good bulk wine; there's a good *pikilía* of mezédhes "off-menu", especially at weekends when a local clientele predominates. Ziá is also the trailhead for the ascent of 846-metre Dhíkeos peak, a two-and-a-half-hour round-trip, initially on track but mostly by path. The route is fairly obvious, and the views from the pillbox-like summit chapel of Metamórfosis are ample reward for the effort. Up top, you can also ponder the esoteric symbolism of a giant crucifix fashioned out of PVC sewer pipe and filled with concrete.

East of Ziá or Evangelístria, roads converge at **ASÓMATI**, home to about thirty villagers and numbers of outsiders restoring abandoned houses; the evening view from the church of Arhángelos with its pebble mosaic rivals that of Zía, though there are no reliable facilities here. **ÁYIOS DHIMÍTRIOS**, 2km beyond along a fairly rough track, is marked by its old name of Haïhoúdhes on some maps, and is today completely abandoned except for a single house next to the attractive church; you can continue from here on 3.5km of more rough road to the junction with the paved road linking Platáni with the municipal rubbish tip.

Pylí

PYLÍ can be reached via the paved road through Lagoúdhi and Amanioú, or from the duck-patrolled Linopótis pond on the main island trunk road. In the upper of its two neighbourhoods, 100m west of the partly pedestrianized square and church, the simple *Iy Palia Piyi* taverna serves inexpensive but appetizing grills and mezédhes in a superb setting, beside a giant cistern-fountain (*piyí*), decorated with carved lion-head spouts. Pylí's other attraction is the so-called **Harmýlio** (Tomb of Harmylos), signposted near the top of the village as "Heroon of Charmylos". This consists of a subterranean, niched vault (fenced off), probably a Hellenistic family tomb; immediately above, traces of an ancient temple have been incorporated into the medieval chapel of Stavrós.

Paleó (medieval) **Pylí**, roughly 3km southeast of its modern descendant, was the Byzantine capital of Kós. Head there via Amanioú, keeping straight at the junction where signs point left to Ziá and Lagoúdhi. In any case, the castle should be obvious on its rock, straight ahead; the deteriorating road ends next to a spring, opposite which a stair-path leads within fifteen minutes to the roof of the fort. En route you pass the remains of the abandoned town tumbling southwards down the slope, as well as three fourteenth-century chapels with fresco fragments within; the first one encountered, Arhángelos, has the best-preserved scenes, though the third church (Ipapandí) is the most architecturally interesting.

Western Kós

Near the arid, desolate centre of the island, well sown with military installations, a pair of giant, adjacent roundabouts by the airport funnels traffic northwest towards Mastihári, northeast back towards town, southwest towards Kéfalos, and southeast to Kardhámena.

Mastihári and Andimáhia

The least developed, least "packaged" and least expensive of the northern shore resorts, **MASTIHÁRI** has a shortish, broad beach extending west, and a less attractive one at **Troúlos** 1.5km east. At the end of the westerly beach, inside a partly fenced enclosure, lie remains of the fifth-century basilica of **Áyios Ioánnis**, one of several on the island. If you want to **stay**, try quieter digs overlooking the west beach such as the simple *Hotel Kyma* (☎02420/59 045; ❶) or the *Hotel Fenareti* (☎02420/59 024) further up the grade, with rooms (❶) and studios (❷) in a peaceful garden environment. *O Makis*, one street inland from the quay, and *Kali Kardia*, at the base of the jetty, are the best of a half-dozen tavernas, both well regarded for fresh fish, mezédhes and (at *Kali Kardia*) *mayireftá*. Mastihári is also the port for small ro-ro **ferries** to Kálymnos; there are three well-spaced departures in each direction most of the year, timed more or less to coincide with Olympic Airways' flight schedules – though KTEL buses to or from Kós Town don't (perhaps deliberately) always dovetail well.

The workaday village of **ANDIMÁHIA**, 5km southeast of Mastihári, straggles over several ridges; the only concession to tourism is a much-photographed windmill on the main street, operating as a working museum (typically 8.30am–6pm) with its unfurled sails. If open, for a token fee you can climb up to the mast loft and observe its workings – which incidentally point downwind, not into the wind as popularly imagined. East of Andimáhia, reached via a marked, three-kilometre side road, an enormous, triangular **Knights' castle** overlooks the straits to Níssyros. Once through the imposing north gateway (unrestricted access), you can follow the well-preserved west parapet, and visit two interior chapels: one with a fresco of Áyios Khristóforos (St Christopher) carrying the Christ Child, the other with fine rib-vaulting. Work is underway to provide electricity and unsafe masonry is being consolidated with an eye to using the castle grounds for nocturnal spectacles, so you can expect opening hours and an admission fee in the future.

Kardhámena

KARDHÁMENA, on the southeast coast 31km from Kós Town, is the island's largest package resort after the capital itself, with locals outnumbered twenty to one in season by visitors (mostly young Brits) intent on getting as drunk as possible as cheaply as possible. Runaway local development has banished whatever redeeming qualities the place may once have had, reducing it to a seething mass of bottle-shops, bars, trinket shops and excursion agencies. Pubs named the *Black Swan* or *Slug and Lettuce* dispense imported beer, and you can even find fish and chips. A hefty sand beach stretches to either side of the town, hemmed in to the east with ill-concealed military bunkers and a road as far as Tolári, home to the massive *Norida Beach* all-inclusive complex.

Kardhámena is most worth knowing about as a place to catch a **boat to Níssyros**. There are supposedly two daily sailings in season: the morning tourist excursion kaïki at either 9am or 9.30am, and another, less expensive, barely publicized one – the *Chrissula* – at 2.30pm, but in practice the afternoon departure (typically Mon, Wed, Thurs & Fri) can occur any time between 1.30pm and 6.30pm, depending on when the Nissyrians have finished their shopping.

Outside high season, there are generally a few **rooms** not taken by tour companies, and prices are not outrageous. For more comfort, the *Hotel Rio* (☎02420/91 627; ❹) gets good reviews, and like most accommodation here is underpriced for its class. **Tavernas** are not very numerous, and predictably poor, though the longest-lived and most reasonable one is *Andreas*, right of the jetty as you face the sea.

South-coast beaches

The thinly populated portion of Kós southwest of the airport and Andimáhia boasts the most scenic and secluded beaches on the island, plus a number of minor ancient sites. Though given fanciful English names and shown as separate extents on tourist maps, the south-facing **beaches** form essentially one long stretch at the base of a cliff, most with sunbeds and a jet-ski franchise. **Magic**, officially Polémi, is the longest, broadest and wildest. **Sunny/Markso**, signposted as Psilós Gremós and easily walkable from Magic, has a taverna. **Langádha** is the cleanest and most picturesque, with junipers tumbling off its dunes. **Paradise**, often dubbed "Bubble Beach" because of volcanic gas vents in the tidal zone, is small and oversubscribed, with wall-to-wall sunbeds. **Camel** (Kamíla) is the smallest and loneliest, protected somewhat by the steep drive in.

Uninterrupted beach resumes at **Áyios Stéfanos**, overshadowed by a huge Club Med complex, and extends 5km west to Kamári (see below). A marked public access road leads down to the beach just west of a small peninsula, crowned with the exquisite remains of two triple-aisled, sixth-century basilicas. Though the best preserved on the island, several columns have been toppled since the 1980s, and wonderful bird mosaics languish under a permanent layer of "protective" gravel. The basilicas overlook tiny but striking Kastrí islet with its little chapel; in theory it's an easy swim (sometimes wading) across from the westerly beach, with some of the best snorkelling on Kós around the rock formations, but you must run the gauntlet of boats from the local water-ski school.

The far west

Essentially the shore annexe of Kéfalos (see below), **KAMÁRI** is a sprawling package resort of rapidly multiplying breeze-blocks, pitched a few notches above Kardhámena; it's a major watersports centre and an alternative departure point for Níssyros (up to five days weekly in season). *Stamatia*, near the main roundabout, is the oldest and (relatively) most authentic **taverna** hereabouts; one independent **hotel** that can be recommended is the simple *Maria* (☎02420/71 308; ❷), on the seafront west of the main road up to **KÉFALOS**, 43km from Kós Town. Squatting on a bluff looking down the length of the island, this is the end of the line for buses: a dull village but worth knowing about for its post office and as a staging point for expeditions into the rugged peninsula terminating dramatically at Cape Kríkello.

Main highlights of a half-day tour here, beginning along the widened ridge road south, are: a Byzantine church incorporating an ancient temple, 1km beyond the village; the late Classical theatre (unrestricted access), with two rows of seats remaining, and Hellenistic temple of **ancient Astypalia**, 500m further at the side-path signposted "Palatia"; and the cave of **Asprí Pétra** (inhabited during the Neolithic period), marked rather vaguely off the ridge road and requiring a half-hour walk to reach. A paved road west from just after Astypalia leads to an often windy beach and small chapel at **Áyios Theológos**, 7km from Kéfalos; the *Sunset Wave* taverna is a reliable option for a home-made sweet and coffee, though the fare in recent years has tended towards the hamburger-and-chips variety. Keeping to the main paved road until the end of the line brings you to the appealing (but usually locked) monastery of **Áyios Ioánnis Thymianós**, also 7km from the village.

About 1.5km north of Kéfalos on the road tracing the island's summit ridge, a paved side road covers the 2.7km to **Limniónas**, the only north-facing beach and fishing anchorage on this part of Kós. Of the two fish **tavernas** here, higher, hillside *Miltos* is preferable for excellent *orektiká*, home-made bread, and very fresh fish. Two compact sandy beaches sit either side of the peninsula.

Psérimos

Psérimos could be an idyllic little island were it not so close to Kós and Kálymnos. Throughout the season, both of these larger neighbours dispatch daily excursion boats, which compete strenuously to dock at the small harbour village of **AVLÁKIA**. In midsummer, day-trippers blanket the main sandy beach which curves around the bay in front of Avlákia's thirty-odd houses and huge communal olive grove; even during May or late September you're guaranteed at least a hundred outsiders daily (versus a permanent population of 25). There's a couple of other, somewhat less-attractive beaches to hide away on during the day: clean **Vathý** (sand and gravel), a well-marked, thirty-minute path-walk east, starting from behind the *Taverna Iy Pserimos*, or grubbier **Marathoúnda** (pebble), a 45-minute walk north on the main trans-island track. Nowhere on Psérimos, including the monastery of Grafiótissa (big festival Aug 15), is much more than an hour's walk away.

Even during the season there won't be too many other overnighters, since there's a limited number of beds available, and your reception at some of the more put-upon snack bars may become warmer once it's clear that you're **staying**. Pick of the several small pensions is *Tripolitis* (☎02430/23 196; ❶), over English-speaking *Nick and Anna's* café-snack bar, or the rooms above *Taverna Manola* on the opposite end of the beach (☎02430/51 540; ❶), who also keep the plusher *Studios Kalliston* next door (❷). There's just one small, limited-stock **store**, since most of the island's supplies are brought in daily from Kálymnos. Eating out however, won't break the bank, and there's often fresh fish in the handful of **tavernas**; many of these have contracts with the tour boats, but *Taverna Manola* doesn't, and despite modest appearances proves very adept at ouzerí fare and seafood.

Nearly all the **boats** based on Kós and Kálymnos harbour operate triangle tours (approximately €17.50), which involve departure between 9.30am and 10am, followed by a stop for swimming on either Platý islet or adjacent Psérimos, lunch in Avlákia, or Póthia, the port of Kálymnos (or even on board), and another swimming stop at whichever islet wasn't visited in the morning. If you want to spend the entire day on Psérimos, you're much better off departing Póthia at 9.30am daily on the tiny *Nissos Pserimos*, returning at 4pm (€6 round-trip). The islanders themselves use this boat to visit Kálymnos for shopping and administrative business; with just a bare handful of children, there is no longer a school on the island.

Astypálea

Geographically, historically and architecturally, **Astypálea** (alias Astropália) would be more at home among the Cyclades – on a clear day you can see Anáfi or Amorgós (to the southwest and northwest respectively) far more easily than any of the other Dodecanese. Moreover, Astypálea's inhabitants are descendants of medieval colonists from the Cyclades, and the island looks and feels more like these than its neighbours to the east.

Despite an evocative butterfly shape, Astypálea does not immediately impress you as the most beautiful of islands. The heights, which offer modest walking opportunities, are windswept and covered in thornbush or dwarf juniper. Yet the herb *alisfakiá*, brewed as a tea, flourishes too, and hundreds of sheep and goats manage to survive – as opposed to snakes, which are (uniquely in the Aegean) entirely absent. Lush citrus groves and vegetable patches in the valleys signal a relative abundance of water, hoarded in a reservoir. The various beaches along the bleak, heavily indented coastline often have reef underfoot and suffer periodic dumpings of seaweed.

In antiquity the island's most famous citizen was Kleomedes, a boxer disqualified from an early Olympic Games for causing the death of his opponent. He came home so enraged that he demolished the local school, killing all its pupils. Things have calmed down a bit in the intervening 2500 years, and today Astypálea is renowned mainly for its honey, fish and lobster (which finds its way into the local dish of *astakomakaronádha*); the abundant local catch has only been shipped to Athens since the late 1980s, a reflection of the traditionally poor ferry links in every direction. These have improved recently with the introduction of extra services towards Piréas via select Cyclades, and high-season links with Rhodes via a few intervening islets, but outside July or August you still risk being marooned here for a day or two longer than intended. There is, curiously, no conventional package tourism here since Laskarina Holidays deleted the island from their list in 1995, frustrated by chronically unreliable connections to Kós and its airport.

Despite this relative isolation, plenty of people find their way to Astypálea during the short, intense midsummer season (mid-July to the first Sept Sun before school starts), when the 1500 permanent inhabitants are all but over-run by upwards of 7000 guests a day. Most arrivals are Athenians, French or Italians, supplemented by large numbers of yachties and foreign owners of holiday homes in the understandably popular Hóra. At such times you won't find a bed without reserving well in advance, and camping rough is expressly frowned upon.

Skála and Hóra

The main harbour of **SKÁLA** or Péra Yialós dates from the Italian era (Astypálea was the first island the Italians occupied in the Dodecanese) and most of the settlement between the quay and the line of nine windmills is even more recent. Its only real bright spot is a 1998-inaugurated **archeological museum** (June–Sept Tues–Sun 8am–2pm & 6pm–midnight, Oct–May Tues–Sun 8am–2pm; free), a single well-lit room crammed with the best local finds spanning all historical periods from the Bronze Age to medieval times.

As you climb up beyond the port towards **HÓRA**, however, the neighbour-hoods get progressively older and more attractive, their steep streets enlivened by the photogenic *poúndia*, or colourful wooden balconies-with-stairways of the whitewashed houses, which owe much to the building styles of Mýkonos and Tínos, the origins of the colonists brought to repopulate the island in 1413. The whole culminates in the thirteenth-century **kástro**, one of the finest in the Aegean, erected not by the Knights but by the Venetian Quirini clan and sub-sequently modified by the Ottomans after 1537. Until well into the twentieth century over three hundred people lived inside the *kástro*, but depopulation and a severe 1956 earthquake combined to leave only a desolate shell today. The fine rib vaulting over the main west gate supports the church of Evangelístria Kastrianí, one of two intact here, the other being Áyios Yeóryios (both usually locked). Currently the *kástro* grounds are in the throes of a consolidation and restoration project undertaken by the Byzantine antiquities authority, designed to keep the perimeter fortifications from crumbling further.

Skála, and to a lesser extent Hóra, have **accommodation** ranging from spar-tan, 1970s-vintage rooms to new luxury studios; proprietors tend not to meet ferries unless arrangements have been made, even if they have vacancies. Owing to high-season harbour noise – particularly the sound of ferries drop-ping anchor at 3am – you might prefer more atmospheric restored studios or entire houses (€73.50 for 2 peak season, but just €29.40 low) up in Hóra if uninterrupted sleep is a priority; enquire at Kostas Vaïkousis' antique shop on the quay or reserve in advance on ☎02430/61 430. Rather plusher are the 2000-built *Kilindra Studios* on the quiet west slope of Hóra (☎02430/61 966, ℱ61 131, ﹢http://astypalea.com/kilindra; open all year), offering luxury amenities including a swimming pool – units accommodate two to four peo-ple, with the smallest at €88 (€59 low season).

Otherwise, the obvious, bog-standard port **hotels** are the 1993-refurbished *Astynea* (☎02430/61 040, ℱ61 209; ❸) and the elderly but fairly well-kept *Paradisos* (☎02430/61 224, ℱ61 450; ❸), both en-suite with sea views. Of two backpackers' standbys on the east shore of the bay, *Akti Rooms* (☎02430/61

281; ❹) are much better equipped and maintained than the misnamed *Karlos Studios* (☎02460/61 330; ❸), actually large rooms which are only worth it if you get a seaview unit. A small, basic, seasonal **campsite** operates amongst calamus reeds and tamarisks behind Dhéftero Marmári Bay (see opposite), about 4km along the road to Análipsi, but it can be mosquito-plagued any year after a wet winter (an increasingly rare occurrence).

During August, upwards of 25 **tavernas** and beach snack-bars operate across the island, few of them memorable and many concerned primarily with turning a quick profit. Among the more reliable Skála options, *Iy Monaxia* (aka *Viki's*), one block inland from the ferry jetty by the old power plant, has excellent home-style cooking and is open all year round. The *Astropalia* (closes end Sept) on the hillside above the street up to Hóra, does good, if somewhat pricey, fish and not much else; there's even better seafood, and superbly prepared own-grown vegetable dishes, at the homey *Australia* (open all year), just inland from the head of the bay. Behind the *Hotel Paradhisos*, you'll find more careful cooking, polished presentation (and much higher prices) at *Aitherio* and *Maïstrali* (both open into Oct); it's pot-luck as to which is better any given night. Under the *Astynea* you'll find two more worthy options: *To Steki* for grills, and the *Dapia Café*, for full breakfasts, midday crepes and homemade ice cream.

Most **nightlife** happens up in more atmospheric Hóra, where the esplanade between the windmills and the base of the *kástro* seems to be one solid café-bar. Of these, the favourites are the unsigned *Tou Nikola* (*Iy Myli*) on the corner, with the island's characters in residence, and the all-purpose *Aigaion* on the opposite side, which does snacks in season. All these are joined in season by music bars such as long-lived *Kastro*, best for conversation-level music, and the newer *Panorama* where the island's youth hang out until dawn. The **post office** and most shops are here, though the island's only **bank** (Emboriki/Commercial), complete with cash dispenser, is down in Skála by the port police.

Two **buses** run along the paved road between Hóra, Skála, Livádhia and Analípsi, frequently in July and August from 8am until 11pm, much less regularly out of season. There are only two official **taxis**, far too few to cope with passenger numbers in season; several places rent out **scooters**, the most reliable being Lakis and Manolis (☎02430/61 263), with branches at Hóra and Skála dock, and also renting out a few cars and jeeps. The island **map** sold locally is grossly inaccurate, even by lenient Greek-island standards, though in compensation rural junctions are adequately signposted.

Around the island

A twenty-minute walk (or a short bus journey) from Hóra brings you to **LIVÁDHIA**, a fertile valley with a popular, good beach with a variable collection of restaurants and cafés immediately behind. You can rent a **room or studio** just inland – for example at *Studios O Manganas* (☎02430/61 68; ❺), on the frontage road, representing the highest standard here, or *Venetos Studios & Bungalows* (☎02430/61 490; ❹), on the westerly hillside. Among the half-dozen **tavernas**, *To Yerani* is about the most consistently open (until Oct) and renowned for its excellent *mayireftá*; they also keep simple rooms adjacent (☎02430/61 484; ❸).

If the busy beach here doesn't suit, continue southwest fifteen minutes on foot to three small single coves at **Tzanáki**, packed out with naturists in midsummer. The third large bay beyond Livádhia, more easily reached by motorbike, is **Áyios Konstandínos**, a partly shaded, sand-and-gravel cove with a good seasonal taverna. Around the headland, the lonely beaches of **Vátses** and **Kaminákia** are more usually visited by excursion boat from Skála, subject to weather and captain's whim. By land, Vátses has the easier dirt road in, some twenty minutes by scooter from Livádhia; it's one of the sandier island beaches but prone to wind. The track to Kaminákia is atrocious in its final moments, but the sheltered, clean scenic cove makes the effort worthwhile; like Vátses it has a simple *kantína*, staying open into September.

A favourite outing in the west of the island is the two-hour walk or half-hour motorbike trip from Hóra to the oasis of **Áyios Ioánnis**, just under 10km distant. Proceed northwest along the signposted paved road beginning from the windmills, then keep left when a side-track goes right to Panayía Flevariotíssas monastery. Beyond this point the main track, briefly dampened by a spring seeping across the road surface, curls north towards farming cottages at Messariá before reaching a junction with gates across each option. Take the left-hand one, and soon the walled orchards of the uninhabited farm-monastery of Áyios Ioánnis come into view. From the balcony of the church, a steep, faint path leads down to the base of a ten-metre waterfall, though alas, after several dry years, the bathing pools here have dried up.

Northeast of the harbour are three coves known as **Próto** (First), **Dhéftero** (Second) and **Tríto** (Third) **Mármari**, and marked as **Marmári A'**, **B'** and **C'** respectively on some maps. The first is home to the power plant and boat-yards; the next hosts the campsite (see opposite); while the third, reasonably attractive, also marks the start of the path east to the perfectly decent coves of unfortunately named **Mamoúni** ("Bug" or "Critter" in Greek). Beyond Tríto Marmári, the middle beach at **Stenó** ("narrow", after the isthmus here), with sandy shore and shallows, a few tamarisks and a seasonal *kantína*, is the best.

ANÁLIPSI, widely known as **Maltezána** after medieval Maltese pirates, is a ten-kilometre bus trip or taxi ride from town. Although the second-largest settlement on Astypálea, there's surprisingly little for outsiders save a narrow, sea-urchin-speckled beach (there are better ones east of the main bay) and a nice view south to some islets. Despite this, blocks of **rooms** (open only July & Aug) sprout in ranks well back from the sea, spurred by the proximity of the airport, 700m away. Among a handful of tavernas, the most reliably open (Feb–Christmas) is *Analipsi* (aka *Irini's*, after the proprietress) by the jetty, which doubles as the kafenío for the local fishermen and seemingly every passing worker on the island. The food – fish fry-ups, or *kakaviá* (fish soup) for those willing to wait – is simple but excellent and normally priced. At a somewhat higher mark-up, but also high-quality, is *Ovelix* a few hundred yards inland, where you have to pre-order your fish (℡02430/61 260; closes mid-Sept). Behind calamus reeds and eucalyptus near the fishing jetty lie the best-preserved mosaic floors on the island: those of the Byzantine **Tallarás baths**, with somewhat crude figures of zodiacal signs, the seasons personified, and a central androgynous figure (Time or Fortune) holding the cosmic orb.

The motorable dirt track ends 23km from Hóra at **Mésa Vathý** (invariably and erroneously shown on most maps as Éxo Vathý), a sleepy fishing village with a single **taverna** (*Iy Galíni*) and superb small-craft anchorage in what's an almost landlocked inlet. Frankly, though, it's not really worth the long, bumpy trip out unless you're a yachtie, and to rub salt in the wound, the fish on the menu is usually frozen (if local). Following several accidents, this is no longer the **backup ferry port** in winter, when Skála is buffeted by the prevailing southerlies; foot passengers (but no vehicles) are transferred ashore to the unlit quay at **Áyios Andhréas**, just west of Tríto Marmári.

Kálymnos

Most of the 17,000-strong population of **Kálymnos** lives in or around the large port of Póthia, a wealthy but not conventionally beautiful town, famed for its sponge industry. Unfortunately, almost all of the eastern Mediterranean's sponges were devastated by a mysterious disease in 1986, related to freak warm currents, and only three or four of the fleet of thirty-odd boats are still in use. In response to this catastrophe (and a smaller repeat outbreak in 1999), the island established a tourist industry – confined to one string of beach resorts – and also retro-fitted most of its sponge boats for deep-sea fishing. Warehouses behind the harbour still process and sell sponges all year round, though most of these are imported from Asia and the Caribbean. There are also still numbers of elderly gentlemen about who rely on two canes, walking frames or even wheelchairs, stark evidence of the havoc wrought in their youth by nitrogen embolism (the "bends"), long before divers understood its crippling effects. The departure of the remaining sponge fleet, usually just after Easter, is preceded by a festive week known as *Yprogrós*, with food, drink and music; the fleet's return, approximately six months later, has historically also been the occasion for more uproarious, male-oriented celebration in the port's bars.

Kálymnos essentially consists of two cultivated and inhabited valleys sandwiched between three limestone ridges, harsh in the full glare of noon but magically tinted towards dusk. The climate, especially in winter, is alleged to be drier and healthier than that of neighbouring Kós or Léros, since the quick-draining limestone strata, riddled with many caves, doesn't retain as much moisture. The rock does, however, admit seawater, which has tainted Póthia's wells; drinking water must be brought in by tanker truck from the Vathýs valley, and there are also potable springs at Dhámos, Potamí district of Póthia and Hóra.

Since Kálymnos is the home port of the very useful local namesake ferry (see p.808), a minor hub for Kyriakoulis Maritime hydrofoils, and moreover where the long-distance ferry lines from the Cyclades and Astypálea join up with the main Dodecanesian routes, many travellers arrive unintentionally, and are initially most concerned with how to move on quickly. Yet Kálymnos has sufficient attractions to justify a stay of several days while island-hopping – or even longer, as the package industry at the western beaches suggests.

Póthia

PÓTHIA (sometimes pronounced Pothiá), without being obviously picturesque, is colourful and authentically Greek, its houses marching up the valley inland or arrayed in tiers up the sides of the mountains framing it. Your first and overwhelming impression will be of the phenomenal amount of noise engendered by motorbike traffic and the cranked-up sound systems of the half-dozen waterfront cafés. This is not entirely surprising, since with nearly 16,000 inhabitants, Póthia recently overtook Kós Town as the second-largest municipality in the Dodecanese, after Ródhos Town.

Perhaps the most rewarding way to acquaint yourself with Póthia is by wandering the backstreets, where elegant Neoclassical houses are surrounded by surprisingly large gardens, and craftsmen ply their trade in a genuine workaday bazaar. The Pothians particularly excel in iron-working, and all but the humblest dwellings in the eastern Evangelístria district are adorned by superbly ornate banisters, balcony railings and fanlights. During the Italian occupation, many local houses were painted blue and white to irritate the colonial overlords, and though the custom has all but died out, the Greek national colours still appear amongst more traditional pink and ochre buildings.

Of the two local museums, priority should be given to the **Municipal Nautical and Folklore Museum** (Mon–Fri 8am–1.30pm, Sat–Sun 10am–12.30pm; €1.50), on the seaward side of Khristós cathedral. A large photo in the foyer shows Póthia as it was in the 1880s, with no quay, jetty, roads or sumptuous mansions, and with most of the population still up in Hóra, while other photos document sponge-fishing and the Allied liberation of 1945. Three-dimensional exhibits include horribly primitive divers' breathing apparatuses, and "cages" designed to keep propellers from cutting air lines, a constant fear. The local **archeological museum** (Tues–Sun 10am–2pm; free guided tours only) is installed in a grand former residence of the Vouvallis family of sponge magnates. A rather eclectic collection, including a kitsch-furnished Second Empire parlour and small troves from the island's several caves, it's not exactly required viewing.

Practicalities

Accommodation is rarely a problem, since *dhomátia* proprietors usually meet the ferries (though many of the premises touted are substandard, unlicensed or remote, often all three). The town's best, and quietest **hotel**, near the Vouvalis museum, is the garden-set *Villa Themelina* (☎02430/22 682, ℉23 920, ⓦwww.griechenland.com/io2/reisen/302.html; ❸; open all year but no breakfast Oct–Easter), housed in an early-twentieth-century mansion (another Vouvalis property) plus modern studio annexes (❹), with breakfast patio and a large swimming pool. The high-ceiling, bug-screened, wood-floored rooms in the main house make this Kálymnos's most elegant accommodation. Next niche down, on the west quay but fairly quiet, is occupied by the *Arhondiko* (☎02430/24 051, ℉24 149; ❸), another refurbished mansion whose somewhat plain rooms have TV and fridge; some also have balconies, though promised heating/air-con has not materialized. Two places in Amoudhára district (west of the harbour) are worth contacting in advance: the en-suite *Pension Greek House* (☎02430/29 559; ❶; open most of year) with volubly friendly management and kitsch decor; and considerably above this, the well-signposted, well-kept *Hotel Panorama* (☎02430/22 917, ℉23 138; April–Oct; ❸), which has balconied rooms with views and a pleasant breakfast salon; studios are planned in the future.

The best place for **eating out** used to be the line of fish tavernas northeast along the waterfront past the Italian-built municipal "palace", but standards here have dipped recently. Currently far and away the best seafood and Kalymnian specialties are found at *Taverna Pandelis*, tucked inconspicuously into a cul-de-sac behind the waterfront *Olympic Hotel*; this features daily, fresh-gathered shellfish like *foúskes* and *kalógnomes* and wild scaly fish at reasonable prices. Other alternatives include *mayireftá* at *Xefteris*, well signposted inland from Khristós cathedral, with courtyard seating, or excellent wood-fired pizzas at *Porto Kalymnos* and *Imia*, near each other at mid-quay. Sticky-cake fans will want to attend the traditional *Zaharoplastiki O Mihalaras* back on restaurant row, while four paces west from here, just before the municipal "palace", *Apothiki* is an old warehouse operating reliably as a musical bar for some years now. Back by *Taverna Pandelis*, *Nefeli* is the better equipped of two **internet cafés**, while adjacent *Escape* functions as another music pub. A summer **cinema**, Cine Oasis, operates behind the traditional, column-facaded café-tearoom *Ai Musai*, on the front.

All **boat** and **hydrofoil** agents, including the headquarters of the *Nissos Kalymnos*, plus a municipal **tourist information** booth (sporadic Mon–Fri hours), line the waterfront as you bear right out of the pier-area gate. Olympic Airways has an office at Patriárhou Maxímou 12, 200m inland from the quay, and the new airport near Árgos village is supposed to commence operations in late 2002 (flights to/from Athens only). Finally, four **banks** on or just behind the waterfront (Ethniki, Alpha, Emboriki, Agrotiki) have cash dispensers.

Around the island

Buses run as far as Emborió in the northwest and Vathý in the east, from a stop beside the municipal "palace", with schedules helpfully posted near many stops, and departures in season fairly frequent. Tickets must be bought beforehand from authorized kiosks, and cancelled on board. Otherwise, you can use shared **taxis** from Platía Kýprou (more than KTEL rates, less costly than a normal taxi), or rent a **scooter** from reputable Scootermania (☎02430/51 780), just back from the waterfront, near where it bends south. **Car rental** is also available (eg an Avis franchise, ☎02430/28 990), though the island's compact enough that only families would need one.

The castles and basilicas

Just over 1km northwest of Póthia, in the suburb of Mýli, is a castle of the Knights of Saint John, **Kástro Khryssoheriás** (unrestricted access). From the whitewashed battlements there are wonderful views southeast over town to Kós, and north towards Hóra and Péra Kástro. The former Kalymnian capital of **HÓRA** (aka Horió), 1.5km further along the main road, is still a village of nearly three thousand inhabitants, and guards a critical pass in local geography, focus of settlement in every era. Steep steps lead up from its eastern edge to the Byzantine citadel-town of **Péra Kástro** (daily May–Oct 10am–2pm; tip to guide), appropriated by the Knights of Saint John and inhabited until late in the eighteenth century. Inside the imposing gate the former heaps of rubble are slowly being re-pieced together; a guided tour by the warden visits five well-maintained, whitewashed chapels, containing late medieval fresco fragments.

Some 200m past the turning for Árgos en route to the northwest coast from Horió, you can detour briefly left to visit two early Byzantine basilicas which are fairly representative, and among the easiest to find, of a vast number on Kálymnos. The more impressive of the two, accessed by whitewashed steps on the left just as the highway begins to descend, is that of **Khristós tís Ierousalím**, probably dating from the late fourth century, with its apse fully preserved; the three-aisled **Limniótissa** church in an adjacent field is larger but considerably less intact.

West coast resorts

From the basilicas, the road dips into a tree-shaded valley leading to the consecutive **beach resorts** of Kandoúni, Myrtiés and Massoúri, collectively referred to as "Brostá" by islanders. **KANDOÚNI**, some 200m of brown, hard-packed sand favoured by the locals, is the shore annexe of the rich agricultural valley-village of **Pánormos** (aka Eliés). Accommodation closest to the water here is monopolized by tour companies, and for both bathing and staying you're better off at **Linária**, the north end of the same bay. A smaller cove set apart from Kandoúni proper by a rock outcrop, this has better sand and the possibility of **staying** at *Skopellos Studios* (☏02430/47 155; ❸), on the slope below the church. For **eating**, the best option is *Ouzeri Giannis/Ta Linaria* on the shore, with leisurely service but abundant portions of grills and seafood.

The next beach north, **Platý-Yialós**, though again a bit shorter than Kandoúni, is arguably the best on the island: cleaner than its southern neighbours, more secluded, and placed scenically at the base of a cliff, opposite Ayía Kyriakí islet. A lone **taverna** (*Kyma*), right behind the sand at road's end, will do for lunch (closes at sunset). Among a handful of choices for **staying** on spec, long-time favourite is the Vavoulas family's *Pension Plati Gialos* (☏02430/47 029, ⊛www.pension-plati-gialos.de), actually overlooking Linária, recently improved with extended balconies, mosquito nets and a breakfast terrace; choose between rooms (❷) or two apartments for four (€44).

The main road climbs from Pánormos up to a pass, where the *Hotel Kamari* (☏02430/47 278, ⓕ48 130; ❷) is another non-packaged possibility, with views from most rooms, before descending in zigzags to meet the sea again 8km from Póthia at **MYRTIÉS**. Together with **MASSOÚRI** (1km north) and **ARMEÓS** (2km north and end of the line for most buses), it sees the lion's share of Kálymnos tourism: all too many neon-lit music bars, "special menus", souvenir shops and the other accoutrements of the package trade. The beach at Myrtiés is narrow, pebbly and cramped by development, though it does improve as you approach Massoúri. The closest all-sand beach to Myrtiés lies 500m south, at **Melitsahás** cove (Melitsáhas in dialect), which also has the only locally patronized **taverna** at its fishing anchorage, *Iy Dhrossia* (all year), best for oysters, lobster and shrimp as well as scaly fish at affordable rates. Most local **accommodation** is block-booked by overseas companies; remote exceptions enjoying spectacular views include the largish *Maria's Studios* (☎02430/48 135 or 28 528; ❷), above Melitsahás, or *Studios Niki's* (☎02430/47 201; ❷), up on the higher one-way bypass road between Myrtiés and Massoúri. Possibly this coast's most appealing feature is its position opposite the evocatively shaped islet of Télendhos (see below), which frames some of the most dramatic sunsets in Greece. It's also possible to go from Myrtiés directly to Xirókambos on Léros aboard the daily early-afternoon **kaïki**.

Some 5km beyond Massoúri, **ARYINÓNDA** has a clean pebble beach backed by a single **rooms** outfit (*Arginonta Beach* ☎02430/40 000; ❶), with a friendly proprietor, and a few beach **tavernas**. It is also the trailhead for the spectacular two-and-a-half-hour walk inland and over two gentle passes to Metóhi in the Vathý valley. From the bus-stop and gravelled car-park area and small spring, head southeast on a path between rock walls which soon climbs the south flank of the ravine here, sporadically marked by paint dots. Don't believe sources which show the route emerging at Styménia, and be aware that in the future the municipality intends to bulldoze a road from just above the *Arginonta Beach* to Styménia, which may disrupt the first half-hour or so of the trail. You'll need a sun hat, stout shoes and a litre or so of water, as the next source is in Plátanos hamlet, beyond Metóhi.

The end of the bus line, **EMBORIÓS**, 20km from the port, offers a gravel-and-sand beach, which improves as you head west, **accommodation** (much of it taken up by Laskarina Holidays) and a number of **tavernas**, including the long-running *Harry's Paradise*, with attached, air-conditioned garden apartments (☎02430/40 061; ❹) in bland white-and-pine decor, and *Kapetan Kostas*, closer to the sea. If the twice-daily bus service fails you, there is usually a shuttle boat back to Myrtiés at 4pm (leaving the latter at 10am).

Télendhos

The trip across the strait to the striking, volcanic-plug islet of **TÉLENDHOS** is arguably the best reason to come to Myrtiés; little boats shuttle to and fro constantly throughout the day and late into the night. According to local legend, Télendhos is a petrified princess, gazing out to sea after her errant lover; the woman's-head profile is most evident at dusk. The hardly less pedestrian geological explanation has the islet sundered from Kálymnos by a cataclysmic earthquake in 554 AD; traces of a submerged town are said to lie at the bottom of the straits.

Home to about fifteen permanent inhabitants, Télendhos is car-free and blissfully tranquil, though even here package tourism has arrived in a fairly big way. For cultural edification you'll find the ruined thirteenth-century **monastery of Áyios Vassílios** and an enormous, 1997-excavated **basilica of Ayía Triádha** up on the ridge, part way along the flagstoned, ten-minute path to **Hokhlakás** pebble beach, which is small but very scenic, with sunbeds for rent.

There are about eight places to **eat** and a roughly equal number of **accommodation** establishments, most (but not all) linked to the tavernas. Establishments that get uniformly positive reviews include *Barba Stathis* taverna en route to Hokhlakás; *Pension Studios Rita* (☎02430/47 914, ✆47 927; ❷), rooms and renovated-house studios managed by the namesake snack-bar/café; the simple but en-suite rooms above the worthy *Zorba's* (☎02430/48 660; ❶) or, north beyond Áyios Vassílios, the Greek-Australian-run *On the Rocks*. This combines the functions of superbly appointed rooms with double glazing, mosquito nets and so on

(☏02430/48 260, ℱ48 261, ⓦwww.telendos.com/otr; ❹), full-service taverna with lovely home-made desserts, and a bar that's the heart and soul of local **nightlife** (including Mon & Fri "Greek Nights"). At one corner of the premises you can visit yet another Byzantine monument, the chapel of Áyios Harálambos, occupying a former bathhouse. If you want more (relative) luxury on Télendhos, you'll have to squeeze in between packages at the *Hotel Porto Potha* (☏02430/47 321, ℱ48 108, ⓔportopotha@klm.forthnet.gr; ❷), set rather bleakly at the very edge of things but with a large pool and friendly managing family.

Vathýs

The first four kilometres east from Póthia seem vastly unpromising (power plant, rubbish tip, multiple gasworks and quarries), until you round a bend and the ten-kilometre ride ends dramatically at **VATHÝS**, a long, fertile valley, carpeted with orange and tangerine groves, whose colour provides a startling contrast to the mineral greys and oranges higher up on Kálymnos. At the simple fjord port of **RÍNA**, more ruined basilicas flank the bay; near the southerly one is the best accommodation option, the helpful *Rooms Manolis* (☏02430/41 300; ❶). Some of the five tavernas are pricier than you'd expect, owing to patronage from the numerous yachts which call here; currently the best choice, with shambolic service but good grilled fish, is *The Harbor*, first place on the right at road's end.

The steep-sided inlet has no beach to speak of, so people swim off the artificial lido on the far right; the closest pebble-coves reachable overland are **Aktí**, about 3km back towards Póthia, a functional pebble strand with sunbeds and a single snack bar, and **Pezónda**, a little further north, reached by steep track (and then a 45-minute walk northwest) starting from Metóhi hamlet. At track's end another path heads east in fifteen minutes to the amazingly set little **monastery of Kyrá Psilí**, frequented only on August 15.

Boat excursions sometimes visit the stalactite cave of **Dhaskalió**, inhabited in Neolithic times, out towards the fjord mouth on its north flank, and the remoter, tiny beaches of **Almyrés** and **Dhrasónda**, accessible only by sea.

It's possible to **walk** back to Póthia along the old direct *kalderími* which existed before the coastal highway – a two-hour jaunt which begins in Plátanos hamlet. The route is tricky to find in this direction, however, so most people start in Póthia, at the church of Ayía Triádha behind the *Villa Themelina* hotel – the way is marked initially by red paint splodges.

The southwest

Some 6km southwest of Póthia, the small bay of **Vlyhádhia** is reached via a narrow ravine draining from the nondescript village of Vothýni. The sand-and-pebble beach here isn't really worth a special trip, since the bay is apt to be sumpy and at least some of the locals (who have blotted out all Roman-alphabet road signs) are resentful of foreigners. If you're interested in **scuba diving**, the Vlyhádhia area is one of the limited number of legal diving areas in Greece. Stavros Valsamidhes, the local divemaster, has also assembled an impressive **Museum of Submarine Finds** (Mon–Sat 9am–7pm, Sun 10am–2pm; free), which in addition to masses of sponges and shells offers a reconstructed ancient wreck with amphorae and World War II debris. Depending on your ability, dives (arrange in advance on ☏02430/50 662; €30 for one dive, €53 for two) may visit ancient wrecks *in situ*, as well as seal caves.

Póthia-based kaïkia make well-publicized excursions to the cave of **Kefála** just west of Vlyhádhia, the most impressive of half a dozen caverns around the island. You have to walk thirty minutes from where the boats dock, but the vividly coloured formations repay the effort; the cave was inhabited before recorded history, and later served as a sanctuary of Zeus (who is fancifully identified with a particularly imposing stalagmite in the biggest of six chambers).

Léros

Léros is so indented with deep, sheltered anchorages that during World War II it harboured, in turn, the entire Italian, German and British Mediterranean fleets. Unfortunately, many of these magnificent fjords and bays seem to absorb rather than reflect light, and the island's relative fertility can seem scraggly and unkempt when compared with the crisp lines of its more barren neighbours. These characteristics, plus the island's lack of spectacularly good beaches, meant that until the late 1980s just a few thousand foreigners (mostly Italians who grew up on the island), and not many more Greeks, came to visit each year, mostly in August.

Such a pattern is now history, with German, Dutch, Danish and British package operators at the vanguard of those "discovering" Léros and the company of islanders unjaded by mass tourism. Foreign-visitor numbers have, however, levelled off since the late 1990s, with matters unlikely to change until and unless the tiny airport is expanded to accommodate jets.

Not that Léros needs, or strenuously encourages, mass tourism; various **prisons and sanatoriums** have dominated the Lerian economy since the 1950s, directly or indirectly employing about a third of the population. During the junta era, the island hosted a notorious detention centre at Parthéni, and today the mental hospital on Léros remains the repository for many of Greece's more intractable psychiatric cases; another asylum is home to hundreds of mentally handicapped children. The island's domestic image problem is compounded by its name, the butt of jokes by mainlanders who pounce on its similarity to the word *lerá*, connoting rascality and unsavouriness.

In 1989, a major scandal emerged concerning the administration of the various asylums, with EU maintenance and development funds found to have been embezzled by administrators and staff, and the inmates kept in degrading and inhumane conditions. Since then, an influx of EU inspectors, foreign psychiatrists and extra funding have resulted in drastic improvements in patient treatment, including the establishment of halfway houses across the island.

More obvious is the legacy of the **Battle of Léros** on November 12–16, 1943, when overwhelming German forces displaced a Commonwealth division which had landed on the island following the Italian capitulation. Bomb nose-cones and shell casings still turn up as gaily painted garden ornaments in the courtyards of churches and tavernas, or have been pressed into service as gateposts. Each year for three days following September 26, memorial services and a naval festival commemorate the sinking of the Greek battleships *Queen Olga* and *Intrepid* during the German attack.

Unusually for a small island, Léros has abundant ground water, channelled into potable cisterns at several points. These, plus low-lying ground staked with the avenues of eucalyptus trees planted by the Italians, make for an unusually active mosquito contingent, so come prepared. The island is compact enough to walk around, with sufficient hills to give mountain-bikers a good work-out. There is a reasonable bus service, plus several scooter- and bicycle-rental outfits, of which Motoland (branches at Álynda and Pandélli) have proven the most reliable.

Lakkí and Xirókambos

All large **ferries** arrive at the main port of **LAKKÍ**, once the headquarters of a bustling, purpose-built Italian naval base. Boulevards far too wide for today's paltry amount of traffic are lined with some marvellous Art Deco edifices, including the round-fronted cinema (closed since 1985), the primary and secondary schools, a shopping centre with a round atrium and the defunct *Leros Palace Hotel*.

Buses don't meet the ferries – instead there's a taxi squadron that charges set fares to standard destinations. Few people stay willingly at any of the handful of moribund hotels in Lakkí, preferring to head straight for the resorts of Pandélli, Álynda or Vromólithos (see overleaf). There's just one bona fide **taverna**, *To Petrino*, inland next to the **post office**, two cash dispensers attached to the National/Ethniki and Commercial/Emboriki **banks**, Kastis, the DANE agent, and Gribelos, the island's sole G&A Ferries agent. The nearest approximation of a **beach** is at sand-and-gravel **Kouloúki**, 500m west, where there's a seasonal taverna and some pines for shade, though it's too close to the ferry jetty for most tastes. You can carry on another kilometre or so to **Merikiá**, which is a slight improvement and also has a taverna.

XIRÓKAMBOS, nearly 5km from Lakkí in the far south of the island, is the point of arrival for the afternoon kaïki from Myrtiés on Kálymnos (it goes back very early the following morning). Though billed as a resort, it's essentially a fishing port where folk also happen to swim – the beach here is poor to mediocre, improving as you head west. **Accommodation** is available at *Villa Maria* (✆02470/22 827; ❷) on the beach or, for a higher standard, the *Hotel Efstathia* (✆02470/24 099; ❹), actually studio apartments with huge, well-furnished doubles as well as family fourplexes, plus a large pool. **Meals** can be had at *Taverna Tzitzifies*, just by the jujube trees at the east end of things, where the road hits the shore. The island's **campsite** (✆02470/23 367), with an in-house scuba-diving centre, is in an olive grove at the village of **LEPÍDHA**, 750m back up the road to Lakkí. Just north of the site, an access drive on the far side of the road leads up a tiny acropolis with stretches of ancient masonry and sparse patches of early Christian mosaics.

Pandélli and Vromólithos

Just less than 3km north of Lakkí, Pandélli and Vromólithos together form the fastest-growing resort on the island – and are certainly two of the more attractive and scenic places to stay, if not eat.

PANDÉLLI is still very much a working port, the cement jetty benefiting local fishermen as well as an increasing number of yachts which call here. A negligible beach is compensated for by a relative abundance of non-package **accommodation**, such as the *Pension Happiness* (✆02470/23 498; ❷) where the road down from Plátanos meets the sea, or, for a higher standard, the *Niki Studios* (✆02470/25 600; ❸) at the base of the road to the castle, airy, Aussie-run and with partial sea views. Up on the ridge dividing Pandélli from Vromólithos, the *Pension Fanari* (✆02470/23 152; ❷) would seem a good choice for its calm setting below the road and views across to the castle, though hot-water provision was defective at our last stay. Further south along the ridge road, the en suite *Hotel Rodon* (✆02470/23 524; ❷) is another possibility, though a potentially noisy (but recommended; see below) restaurant operates right next door, as does the musical *Beach Bar*, perched on a rock terrace below, facing Vromólithos. The other long-lived local **bar** is the civilized *Savana*, at the opposite end of Pandélli, beyond the row of waterfront **tavernas** which, alas, have in recent years mostly become tourist traps of the first order. Exceptions include *Psaropoula*, with good fish and *mayireftá*; *Kafenio tou Tzamma*, a seafood ouzerí; and the taverna adjacent to *Hotel Rodon*, the *Dimitris*, which scores highly for its stuffed squash blossoms (in autumn) and chunky, herby Lerian sausages.

VROMÓLITHOS boasts the best easily accessible **beach** on the island, car-free and hemmed in by hills studded with massive oaks. The shoreline is gravel and coarse sand, and the sea here is clean, but as so often on Léros you have to cross a nasty, sharp reef at most points before reaching deeper water. Two **tavernas** behind the beach trade more on their location than their cuisine, but the standard of **accommodation** here is higher than at Pandélli, with the result that much of it tends to be monopolized by package companies.

Plátanos and Ayía Marína

The Neoclassical and vernacular houses of **PLÁTANOS**, the island capital 1km west of Pandélli, are draped gracefully along a saddle between two hills, one of them crowned by the inevitable Knights' castle. Known locally as the **Kástro**, this is reached either by a paved but potholed road peeling off the

Pandélli road, or via a more scenic stair-path from the central square; the battlements, and the views from them, are dramatic, especially near sunrise or sunset. The medieval church of **Panayía tou Kástrou** inside the gate houses a small museum (daily 8am–1pm & 4–7.30pm; €1.50), though its carved *témblon* and naive oratory are more remarkable than the sparse exhibits, which are mostly icons and other liturgical items.

Except for *Hotel Eleftheria* (☎02470/23 550; ❷), with a peaceful hillside location, Plátanos is not really a place to stay or eat, although it's well sown with **shops** and **services**. The latter include Olympic Airways, south of the turning for Pandélli, a **post office**, down the road towards Ayía Marína, and two **banks** (one with a cash dispenser). The single **bus** (schedule posted at the stop, opposite the island's main **taxi** rank) plies four to six times daily between Parthéni in the north and Xirókambos in the south.

Plátanos merges seamlessly with **AYÍA MARÍNA**, 1km north on the shore of a fine bay, still graced by a small, Italian-built public market building. If you're travelling to Léros on an excursion boat, catamaran or hydrofoil, this will be your port of entry. Although accommodation here is very limited, it's arguably the best place to **eat** on the island. Just west of the police station, on the water, *Mezedhopolio tou Kapaniri* is a good, reasonable ouzerí, at its best after dark, featuring plenty of fried vegetable first courses. Just inland opposite the *Agrotiki Trapeza* in a little alley, the *Kapetan Mihalis* ouzerí claims to be open all day and offers a range of inexpensive local specialities, including various fish marinated in salt (*pastós*). Further west, there's the *Ouzeri Neromylos*, out by the marooned windmill, serving a wide variety of dishes. A semblance of **nightlife** is provided by a half-dozen bars, such as *Enallaktiko*, with a few **internet** terminals, and *Harama* on the quay. Kastis Travel nearby (☎02470/22 140) is about the most useful travel agency on the island, plus there's a stand-alone **cash dispenser** on the quay.

Álynda and the north

ÁLYNDA, 3km northwest of Ayía Marína, ranks as the longest-established resort on Léros, with development just across the road from a long, narrow strip of pea-gravel beach. It's also the first area for accommodation to open in spring, and the last to shut in autumn. Many of the half-dozen **hotels** and **pensions** here are block-booked by tour companies, but you may have better luck at two outfits overlooking the war cemetery: *Hotel Gianna* (☎02470/23 153; ❸), with fridge-equipped rooms plus a few studios, or the nearby *Studios Diamantis* (☎02470/23 213; ❸) just inland, with large balconied units, though not the pleasantest management. At Krithóni, 1.5km south, more comfort is available at the island's top-flight accommodation: the *Crithoni Paradise* (☎02470/25 120, ☏24 680; ❻), a mock-traditional low-rise complex with buffet breakfast, a large pool and all mod cons in the rooms. **Restaurant** options aren't brilliant, except for *To Steki* next to the war cemetery, open year round with good grills and rich mezédhes attracting a local clientele.

The **Allied War Graves Cemetery**, mostly containing casualties of the November 1943 battle, occupies a walled enclosure at the south end of the beach; immaculately maintained, it serves as a moving counterpoint to the holiday hubbub outside. The other principal sight at Álynda is the privately run **Historical and Ethnographic Museum** (May–Sept only, daily 10am–1pm & 6–9pm; €3), housed in the unmistakable castle-like mansion of Paris Bellinis (1871–1957). Most of the top floor is devoted to the Battle of Léros: relics from the sunken *Queen Olga*, a wheel from a Junkers bomber, a stove made from a bomb casing. There's also a rather grisly mock-up clinic (mostly gynecological tools) and assorted rural impedimenta, costumes and antiques.

Alternative beaches near Álynda include **Panayiés**, a series of gravel coves (one naturist) at the far northeast of the bay, and **Goúrna**, the turning for which lies 1km or so off the trans-island road. The latter, Léros's longest sandy beach, is hard-packed and gently shelving; it's also wind-buffeted, bereft of any nearby facilities, and permanently fringed by an impromptu car park and dumped construction rubble. A separate road beyond the Goúrna turning leads to **Kokálli**, no great improvement beach-wise, but flanked to one side by the scenic islet of **Áyios Isídhoros**, which is tethered to the mainland by a causeway, its eponymous chapel perched on top.

Seven kilometres from Álynda along the main route north, a marked sidetrack leads left to the purported **Temple of Artemis**, on a slight rise just west of the airport runway. In ancient times, Léros was sacred to the goddess, and the temple here was supposedly inhabited by guinea fowl – the grief-stricken sisters of Meleager, metamorphosed thus by Artemis following their brother's death. All that remains now are some jumbled, knee-high walls, which may in fact have been an ancient fortress, but the view is superb. The onward road skims the shores of sumpy, reed-fringed Parthéni Bay, with its dreary army base (formerly the political prison), until the paved road ends 11km along at **Blefoútis**, a rather more inspiring sight with its huge, virtually landlocked bay. The beach (the rough Lerian norm) has tamarisks to shelter under and an adequate taverna, *Iy Thea Artemi*, for *kalamári*-and-chips-type lunch.

Pátmos

Arguably the most beautiful and certainly the best known of the smaller Dodecanese, **Pátmos** has a distinctive, immediately palpable atmosphere. It was in a cave here that St John the Divine (in Greek, *O Theológos* or "The Theologian"), received the New Testament's Book of Revelation and unwittingly shaped the island's destiny. The monastery honouring him, founded here in 1088 by the Blessed Khristodhoulos (1021–93), dominates Pátmos both physically – its fortified bulk towering high above everything else – and, to a considerable extent, politically. While the monks inside no longer run the island as they did for more than six centuries, their influence has nonetheless stopped Pátmos going the way of Rhodes or Kós.

Despite vast numbers of visitors and the island's firm presence on the cruise, hydrofoil and yacht circuits, tourism has not been allowed to take Pátmos over completely. While there is a number of clubs and even one disco around Skála, drunken rowdiness is virtually unknown, and this is one island where you do risk being ticked off for nudism on all but the most isolated beaches. Package clients have only since the 1990s begun to outnumber independent visitors, and are pretty much confined to Gríkou and a handful of larger hotels at Skála and Kámbos. Day-trippers still exceed overnighters, and Pátmos seems an altogether different place once the last cruise ship has gone at sunset. Away from Skála, development is appealingly subdued if not deliberately retarded, thanks to the absence of an airport.

Skála and around

SKÁLA, with most of the island's population of about three thousand, seems initially to contradict any solemn, otherworldly image of Pátmos. The water-

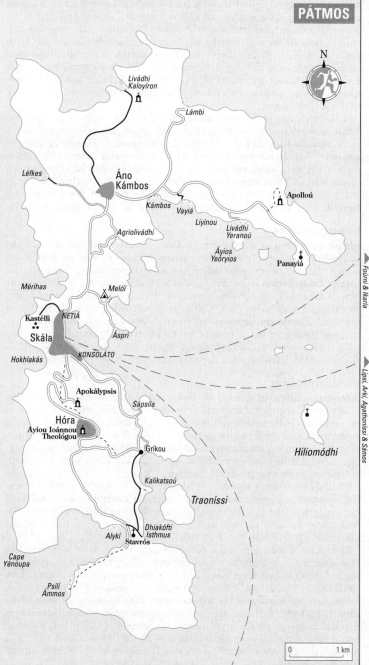

PÁTMOS

N

Livádhi
Kaloyíron

Lámbi

Léfkes

Áno
Kámbos

Apolloú

Kámbos   Vayiá

Liyínou

Agriolivádhi

Livádhi
Yeranoú

Áyios
Yeóryios

Panayiá

Mérihas

Melóï

Kastélli   NETIÁ

Skála

Áspri

Hokhlakás   KONSOLÁTO

Apokálypsis

Sápsila

Hóra
Ayíou Ioánnou
Theológou

Hiliomódhi

Gríkou

Kalikatsoú

Traoníssi

Cape
Yénoupa

Dhiakófti
Isthmus

Alykí   Stavrós

Psilí
Ámmos

0   1 km

side, with its ritzy cafés and clientele, is a bit too sophisticated for such a small town, and some of the service staff a bit world-weary. During peak season, the quay and commercial district swarm by day with hydrofoil and cruise-ship passengers souvenir-hunting or being shepherded onto coaches for the ride up to the monastery; after dark there's still a considerable traffic in well-dressed cliques of visitors on furlough from the cruise ships which weigh anchor after midnight. In winter (which here means by Oct 10), Skála assumes a ghost-town air as most shops and restaurants close, and their owners and staff go back to Rhodes or Athens.

Melóï beach, one of the most convenient and popular coves on the island, lies 1.5km to the north (see opposite); Hóra, a bus or taxi ride up the mountain, is a more attractive base, but has few rooms. Yet given time – especially in spring or autumn – Skála reveals some more enticing corners in the residential fringes to the east and west, where vernacular mansions hem in pedestrian lanes creeping up the hillsides. The modern town dates only from the 1820s, when the Aegean had largely been cleared of pirates, but at the summit of the westerly rise, **Kastélli**, you can see the extensive foundations of the island's ancient acropolis.

Practicalities

Almost everything of interest can be found within, or within sight of, the Italian-built municipal "palace": large ferries anchor opposite, the port police occupy the east end, the **post office** one of its corners, though the municipal **tourist information** office in the rear of the building was not operating at the time of research, and never was of much use anyway. **Motorbike rental** outfits are common, with lowish rates (€10 a day or less) owing to the modest size of the island. **Excursion boats** to Psilí Ámmos, Lipsí and Arkí/Maráthi all leave at about 10am from just in front of Astoria Travel and Apollon Travel, the two most reliable places handling hydrofoil tickets. G&A Ferries and the *Nissos Kalymnos*/DANE have separate agencies on, or just off, the central square.

Accommodation

Accommodation touts meet all ferries and hydrofoils, and their offerings tend to be a long walk distant and/or inland – not necessarily a bad thing, as no location is really remote, and anywhere near the waterfront, which doubles as the main road between Gríkou and Kámbos, will be noisy. Pátmos vernacular architecture is quite distinctive, but you wouldn't know it from most lodgings, bland if inoffensive rooms thrown up during the 1980s, with institutional (one might even say monastic) furnishings.

Establishments worth reserving in advance (they'll often then send a van to fetch you) are scattered across several districts. In **central Skála**, good hotel choices include the 1970s-vintage but quiet *Dhiethnes* (☎02470/31 357; ❸), back in the fields, or the welcoming *Galini*, in a secluded cul-de-sac off the Hóra road (☎02470/31 240, ℉31 705; ❹).

Konsoláto district, east of the centre near the fishing anchorage, has more high-quality digs, though the worst noise from fishing boats and cruisers coming and going at 4am. Here you'll find the slightly overpriced *Captain's House* (☎02470/31 793, ℉32 277; ❺), with friendly management, above-average furnishings and car rental available, and the better-value *Byzance* a few steps inland (☎02470/31 052, ℉31 663, ✉byzance@hol.gr; ❹), with premises spread over two buildings – go for the larger rooms with balconies looking onto a garden. Some 150m further towards Gríkou, the *Blue Bay* (☎02470/31 165, ℉32 303, ✉bluebayhotel@yahoo.com; ❺) is not as well appointed, but has calm, unbeatable sea views.

Netiá, the unglamorous area northwest between the power plant and Mérihas cove, is actually a good choice as a base. Various members of a Greek-Australian family run clustered establishments: the *Hotel Australis* (☎02470/31 576; ④), with full breakfast for the price and myriad small kindnesses that guarantee repeat clientele; and the adjacent *Villa Knossos* (☎02470/32 189, ⓕ32 284; ④), whose rooms all have attractive terraces, or the simpler *Pension Sydney* (☎02470/31 139; ③). But the best standard in this area is provided by the *Hotel Asteri* (☎02470/32 465, ⓕ31 347, ⓔpasca@otenet.gr; ④), unimprovably set on a knoll overlooking the bay, in a well-landscaped environment that's also a working farm – guests have own-produced honey, eggs and tomatoes at breakfast.

Pebbly **Hokhlakás** Bay, just a ten-minute walk southwest of the central market street, is perhaps the quietest district, with wonderful sunset views. Comfortable options here include the hillside *Summer* (☎02470/31 769, ⓕ31 170; ⑤); the *Maria* down in the flatlands (☎02470/31 201, ⓕ32 018; ⑤), where air conditioning and big seaview balconies make up for tiny bathrooms; the budget en-suite rooms, right on the water, above the *Cactus Restaurant* (☎02470/33 059; ②); and Skála's top accommodation, the *Romeos* (☎02470/31 962, ⓕ31 070, ⓔromeos@w12.gr; ⑥) on the southerly slope, with a pool, large common areas, and sizeable units numerous enough that there's usually a vacancy. Hokhlakás isn't very swimmable; if you're keen to stay nearer a proper beach, head for the well-run, pleasantly set **campsite** (*Stefanos-Flowers*) at **MELÓÏ**, just down the slope from Pátmos's most exclusive digs: the *Porto Scoutari Hotel* (☎02470/33 124, ⓕ33 175; ⑥), a self-catering bungalow complex open all year, furnished with mock antiques and original art, and arrayed around a pool and enjoying sea views.

Eating and drinking

Restaurant options are surprisingly limited in Skála; there are altogether too many *souvláki/ yíros* joints and not enough good-value, sit-down places. Easily the town's best and most distinctive is seafood-only *Ouzeri To Hiliomodhi*, just off the start of the Hóra road, with its vegetarian *mezédhes* and delicacies such as limpets (served live, be warned), grilled octopus and salted anchovies. Honourable mentions go to *Pandelis*, one lane inland behind Astoria Travel, where a wide-ranging menu of reliably good *mayireftá* make up for famously dour, if efficient, service, and *Cactus* on the beach at Hokhlakás, doing *nouvelle-minceur* Italian snacks (don't show up too hungry) accompanied by Italian wines and aperitifs.

Aside from that, you're best off heading a bit out of town. Melóï has an excellent *mayireftá* taverna, *Melloi* (alias *Stefanos*), reasonably priced and open early or late in the season; just over the hill at **Áspri** cove are two summer-only fish tavernas, *Aspri* and *Kyma* with in-your-face views of the Hóra; the former is reckoned better, pricier and opens at lunch too. At Sápsila Bay, 2km southeast of Skála, *Benetos* (June–Sept; reserve on ☎02470/33 089) has since 1998 established a reputation as one of the best spots on the island for seafood and generic Mediterranean dishes. Back in town, the most reliable **breakfast** venue is the second, smaller platía beyond the main one, where *La Frianderie* serves hot drinks and croissants under medieval arches, and the adjacent bakery turns out terrific turnovers. The biggest and most durable **café-bar** is the wood-panelled, barn-like *Café Arion* on the waterside, where local youth play cards; others include open-air *Kafe Aman* in Konsoláto, with music and snacks, and the livelier, indoor *Consolato* late night disco, almost next door. Skála has two **internet cafés**: one inside the *Blue Bay Hotel*, the other – *Millennium* – on the main lane to Hokhlakás cove.

The monasteries and Hóra

Top of your sightseeing agenda is likely to be the monastery of Ayíou Ioánnou Theológou (St John), sheltered behind massive defences in the hilltop capital of Hóra. There is a regular KTEL bus up, or you can do a forty-minute walk by a beautiful old cobbled path. To find its start, proceed through Skála towards Hokhlakás, and once past the telecoms building and the *Millennium Internet Café* bear left onto a lane starting opposite an ironmonger's; follow this uphill to its end on the main road – immediately opposite you'll see the cobbled path. Just over halfway, you might pause at the **monastery of Apokálypsis** (Mon, Wed, Fri & Sat 8am–1pm, Tues & Thurs 8am–1pm & 4–6pm, Sun 8am–noon & 4–6pm; free) built around the cave where St John heard the voice of God issuing from a cleft in the rock, and where he sat dictating his words to a disciple. In the cave wall, the presumed nightly resting place of the saint's head is fenced off and outlined in beaten silver.

This is merely a foretaste of the monastery of **Ayíou Ioánnou Theológou** (same hours and admission as Apokálypsis). In 1088, the soldier-cleric Ioannis "The Blessed" Khristodhoulos was granted title to Pátmos by Byzantine Emperor Alexios Komnenos; within three years he and his followers had completed the essentials of the existing monastery, the threats of piracy and the Selçuk Turks dictating a heavily fortified style. A warren of interconnecting courtyards, chapels, stairways, arcades, galleries and roof terraces, it offers a rare glimpse of a Patmian interior; hidden in the walls are fragments of an ancient Artemis temple which stood here before being destroyed by Khristodhoulos. Off to one side, the **treasury** (same hours; €3.50) justifies its hefty entrance fee with its magnificent array of religious treasure, mostly medieval icons of the Cretan school, but pride of place goes to an unusual mosaic icon of Áyios Nikólaos, and the eleventh-century parchment chrysobull (edict) of Emperor Alexios Komnenos, granting the island to Khristodhoulos.

Hóra

The promise of security afforded by St John's stout walls spurred the growth of **HÓRA** immediately outside the fortifications. It remains architecturally homogeneous, with cobbled lanes sheltering dozens of shipowners' mansions from the island's seventeenth- to eighteenth-century heyday. High, windowless walls and imposing wooden doors betray nothing of the opulence within: painted ceilings, pebble-mosaic terraces, flagstoned kitchens, and carved furniture. Inevitably, touristic tattiness disfigures the main approaches to the monastery gate, but away from the principal thoroughfares are lanes that rarely see traffic, and by night, when the monastery ramparts are floodlit to startling effect, it's hard to think of a more beautiful Dodecanesian village. Neither should you miss the **view** from Platía Lódza (named after the remnant of an adjacent Venetian *loggia*), particularly at dawn or dusk. Landmasses to the north, going clockwise, include Ikaría, Thýmena, Foúrni, Sámos with its brooding mass of Mount Kérkis, Arkí, and the double-humped Samsun Dağ (ancient Mount Mykale) in Turkey.

Among several tavernas in Hóra, *Vangelis* on the inner square has a wonderful old jukebox, friendly service and view seating on various levels, but alas the cooking has declined since the late 1990s; you'll probably eat better at *Balkoni* near the monastery. Again on the square, *Kafeteria Stoa* is minimally touristy despite its showcase interior, still functioning as the village kafenío. There are, however, very few places to **stay**; foreigners here are mostly long-term occupants, who have bought up and restored almost a third of the crumbling mansions since the 1960s. Getting a short-term room can be a pretty thankless task, even in spring or autumn; the best strategy is to contact *Vangelis* taverna early in the day, or phone ahead for reservations to Yeoryia Triandafyllou (☎02470/31 963; ❸) or Marouso Kouva (☎02470/31 026; ❸).

The rest of the island

Pátmos, as a locally published guide once memorably proclaimed, "is immense for those who know how to wander in space and time". Lesser mortals may find it easier to get around on foot, or by bus. There's still scope for **walking** despite a dwindling network of paths; otherwise a single **bus** offers surprisingly reliable service between Skála, Hóra, Kámbos and Gríkou – the main stop, with a posted timetable, is right in front of the main ferry dock.

After its extraordinary atmosphere and magnificent scenery, **beaches** are Patmos's principal attraction. From Hóra, a paved road (partly shortcut by a path) winds east to the sandiest part of rather overdeveloped and cheerless **GRÍKOU**, the main venue for Patmian package tourism – and shut tight as a drum come late September. The beach itself, far from the island's best, forms a narrow strip of hard-packed sand giving way to large pebbles towards the south. En route you pass the hillside *Flisvos* (aka *Floros*) taverna, going since the 1960s with a limited choice of inexpensive, savoury *mayireftá*, served on the terrace; they also have simple rooms (❶) and fancier apartments (❹) – reserve on ☎02470/31 380, ☻32 094. Another good **accommodation** option here, open late in the year and not monopolized by packages, is the hillside *Hotel Golden Sun* (☎02470/32 318, ☻34 019; ❺), with most rooms facing the water.

From Hóra, you can ride a scooter over as far as the Dhiakoftí isthmus, beyond which a thirty-minute walk southwest leads to **Psilí Ámmos** beach. This is the only pure-sand cove on the island, with shade lent by tamarisks, nudism galore at the far south end and a good lunchtime **taverna** that occasionally does roast goat, freshly shot on the surrounding hills. There's also a summer kaïki service here from Skála, departing by 10am and returning at 5pm.

More good beaches are to be found in the north of the island, tucked into the startling eastern shoreline (west-facing bays are uniformly unusable owing to wind and washed-up debris); most are accessible from side roads off the main route north from Skála. **Melóï** is handy and quite appealing, with tamarisks behind the slender belt of sand, and good snorkelling offshore. The first beach beyond Méloï, **Agriolivádhi (Agriolívadho)**, has mostly sand at its broad centre, kayak rental, and two tavernas: one at mid-beach, the other (*O Glaros*, doing fish) on the south hillside. Hilltop Kámbos is the only other real village on the island, the focus of scattered farms in little oases all around; **Kámbos** beach, 600m downhill, is popular with Greeks, and the most developed remote resort on the island, with seasonal watersports facilities and tavernas (best of these *Ta Kavourakia*), though its appeal is diminished by the road just inland and a rock shelf in the shallows.

East of Kámbos are several less-frequented coves, including pebble **Vayiá**, nudist **Liyínou** and sand-and-gravel **Livádhi Yeranoú**, the latter with more tamarisks, an excellent namesake taverna doing simple but clean grills and salads, and an islet to swim out to. From lower Kámbos you can also journey north to the bay of **Lámbi**, best for swimming when the prevailing wind is from the south, and renowned for an abundance of multicoloured volcanic stones – as well as one of the best beach **tavernas** on the island, *Lambi-Leonidas*, open May to October, with a wide range of fish, mezédhes and grilled meat.

Lipsí

Of the various islets to the north and east of Pátmos, **LIPSÍ** is the largest, most interesting and most populated, and the one that has the most significant summer tourist trade. The presence of a British package company, on-spec French and Italian travellers, and the island's appearance on both main-line and off-line ferry routes, mean that it's unwise to show up in peak season without a reservation (though rooms proprietors meet arrivals at other times).

During quieter months, however, Lipsí still makes an idyllic halt, its sleepy pace making plausible a purported link between the island's name and that of Calypso, the nymph who legendarily held Odysseus in thrall. Deep wells provide water for many small farms, but there is only one flowing spring, and pastoral appearances are deceptive – four times the relatively impoverished full-time population of about seven hundred live overseas (many in Tasmania, for some reason). Most of those who remain cluster around the fine harbour, as does the majority of food and lodging.

A prime **accommodation** choice in all senses is Nikos' and Anna's welcoming *Apartments Galini* (☎02470/41 212, ℗41 012; ⑤), the first building you see above the ferry jetty; Nikos may take guests for fishing trips on request. Equally sought after, though less airy, are the *Studios Kalymnos* in a garden on the road north out of "town" (☎02470/41 141, ℗41 343, ℮studios_kalymnos@lipsi-island.gr; ②), run by Laid Back Holidays (see below). Other good options not monopolized by package clients include *Rena's Rooms* (☎02470/41 363 or 41 120; ②), overlooking Liendoú beach, the *Flisvos Pension* at the east end of the port (☎02470/41 261; ②); the *Glaros* (☎02470/41 360; ②) on the hillside behind the *Kalypso Hotel/Restaurant*; and *Studios Paradise* (☎02470/41 125; ③), up on the ridge north of the *Dhelfini* restaurant which manages it. Top of the heap is the 1997-built *Aphrodite Hotel* (☎02470/41 000 or 41 394; ⑤), a studio-bungalow complex designed to accommodate package clients, though they're not adverse to walk-ins at slow times.

Among eight or so **tavernas**, mostly on or just behind the quay, *To Dhelfini* next to the police station and *O Yiannis* next to the eponymous rooms are the best all-rounders, with a good range of grilled items, appetizers and often local bulk wine (white or rosé). Salubrious *Tholari*, at the east end of the bay, opens all year; while *Theologos Fish Restaurant* on the quay is reliably fresh – he only opens when he's caught something. On the waterfront to either side of the *Kalypso*, kafenía and ouzerís with idiosyncratic decor (especially *Asprakis*) offer mezédhes outdoors – an atmospheric and almost obligatory pre-supper ritual, where an ouzo and octopus chunk runs to €1.20. Later on, *The Rock* is the clear winner amongst a handful of **bars** for a congenial crowd and good taped music. Two licensed **travel agents** (Paradhisis ☎02470/41 120 and Laid Back; phone as above) organize excursions and change money, though there's a free-standing Emboriki/Commercial **cash dispenser** near the former. The **post office** is up a stairway on the attractive cathedral platía, opposite a hilariously indiscriminate **ecclesiastical museum** (theoretically Mon–Fri 9.30am–1.30pm & 4–8pm, Sat/Sun 10am–2pm, best chances of admission 10am–1pm daily; free) featuring such "relics" as oil from the sanctuary on Mount Tabor and water from the Jordan River, as well as archeological finds and two letters from Greek revolutionary hero Admiral Miaoulis.

The island's **beaches** are rather scattered, though none is more than an hour's walk distant. Closest to town, and sandiest, are **Liendoú** and **Kámbos**, but many visitors prefer the attractive duo of **Katsadhiá** and **Papandhriá**, adjacent sand-and-pebble coves 2km south of the port, with an extremely basic taverna,

Andonis (May–Sept), just inland from a musical snack-café-bar run by Andonis' son, *Dilaila* (June–Sept), which dominates the main bay here and runs an informal pine-grove campsite (free but you must buy a meal from them daily).

An hour's walk along the paved road leading west from town brings you to protected **Platýs Yialós**, a small, shallow, sandy bay with a single taverna (mid-June to late Sept only). During these periods a pair of adapted transit vans provides a **minibus** service from the port to all the points cited above; otherwise you can rent a **scooter** from one of two outlets and point them towards isolated east-coast beaches. Of these, **Hokhlakoúra** consists of rather grubby shingle with no facilities, though nearby **Turkómnima** is better. A final ten-minute path scramble gets you from a rough track's end to **Monodhéndhri**, on the northeast coast, notable only for its lone juniper tree and nudist practice – though there's a superior, nameless cove just to the right.

A growing network of roads, paved or otherwise, rather limit opportunities for genuine path-**walks** through the undulating countryside, dotted with blue-domed churches. The most challenging route heads west from the pass between Kámbos and Platýs Yialós to the bay of **Kímisi** (3hr round-trip), where Filippos the octogenarian religious hermit used to dwell in a tiny monastery above the shore, next to the single island spring. A particularly ugly road has been bulldozed in from the north to disturb his solitude, and paved; Filippos is ill now and living back in town.

Arkí, Maráthi and Agathónissi

About two-thirds the size of Lipsí, **Arkí** is considerably more primitive, lacking drinking water, dynamo electricity (there are solar panels), ferry anchorage or much in the way of a village centre. Just 45 permanent inhabitants eke out a living here, mostly engaged in fishing, though catering for yacht parties attracted here by the superb anchorage is increasingly important. Arkí is an elective, once-weekly stop on the *Nissos Kalymnos* and Miniotis Lines routes: if you want to disembark here, you must warn the captain well in advance, so he can radio for the shuttle service from the island. Most visitors arrive by the more reliable supply boat from Pátmos, which actually docks at the quay. Of the three tavernas on the round harbourside platía, the better two – *Nikolas* (☎02470/32 477) and *O Trypas* (☎02470/32 230) – each control a handful of rooms (❷), but avoid August when Italians and Greeks snap up every vacancy in advance. *Nikolas* is more food-oriented, with homemade puddings, while *O Trypas* doubles as the happening music pub, courtesy of the owner's enormous collection of CDs and tapes.

You can swim at the "Blue Lagoon" of **Tiganákia** at the southeast tip of the island – excursions from Lipsí stop there – but there are no real beaches to speak of on Arkí. The nearest sandy, tamarisk-shaded one is just offshore on the islet of **Maráthi**, where another pair of **tavernas** caters to day-trippers who come at least several times a week from Pátmos or Lipsí. *Marathi* (☎02470/31 580; ❶), run by the engaging Mihalis Kavouras, is the more traditional, cosy outfit, with waterside seating and simple, adequate rooms; *Pantelis* (☎02470/32 609; ❷) is plusher but more commercially minded, and only open June to October.

The small, steep-sided, waterless islet of **Agathónissi (Gaïdharo)** is too remote – much closer to Turkey than Pátmos, in fact – to be a target of day-excursions, though a few are advertised on Sámos. Intrepid German and Italian backpackers (some of whom return annually) form its main clientele, along with a steady trickle of yachts. Even though hydrofoil connections dovetail fairly well with appearances of the *Nissos Kalymnos* or a Miniotis Line boat, you should count on staying for three days, especially if the wind's up. Despite the lack of springs (cisterns are ubiquitous, topped up by tanker shipments from Rhodes), the island is greener and more fertile than apparent from the sea; mastic, carob and scrub oak on the heights overlook two arable plains in the west. Just 146 people live here, down from several hundred before World War II, but those who've opted to stay seem determined to make a go of raising goats or fishing (more accurately, fish-farming), and there are virtually no abandoned or neglected dwellings.

Most of the population lives in the hamlet of **MEGÁLO HORIÓ**, just visible on the ridge above the harbour of **ÁYIOS YEÓRYIOS**, and level with tiny **Mikró Horió**. Except for two café-restaurants (*Dhekatria Adherfia* being the more reliable) and the *Katsoulieri Pension* (☎02470/29 035; ②) in Megálo Horió, all amenities are in the port. Here the choice is between *Rooms Theoloyia Yiameou* (☎02470/29 005; ①), the vine-patioed *Hotel Maria Kamitsi* (☎02470/29 003; ①), *George's Rooms* behind and inland (☎02470/29 064; ①), or the 1999-built *Yiannis Rooms* (☎02470/29 062; ②), of a slightly higher standard. Worthy **eating/drinking** options in Áyios Yeóryios include *George's* (he of the rooms) near the jetty, local hangout *Limanaki*, with fish grills, and *Glaros*, perhaps the best all-rounder.

With no wheeled transport for rent, exploring involves **walking** along the cement- or dirt-road network, or following a limited number of tracks and paths. If you don't swim at the port, which has the largest beach, you can walk twenty minutes southwest along a track to shingle-gravel **Spiliás**, or continue another quarter-hour along a faint path over the ridge to **Gaïdhourávlakos**, where nudists enjoy a gravel-and-sand cove. Bays in the east of the island, all served by the paved road system (occasionally shortcut by trails), tend to be dominated by fish farms; **Pálli** is the most pristine of these, though usually visited by boat trip. At **Thóli** in the far southeast, an hour-plus trek away, you can see an arcaded Byzantine structure, probably a combination granary and trading post, and by far the most venerable sight on Agathoníssi.

Travel details

To simplify the lists below, several companies/boats have been left out. DANE provides a once-weekly link between Rhodes, Kós, Sámos and Thessaloníki in each direction, while NEL also plies once weekly (north, then south) between Rhodes, Kós, Sámos, Híos, Lésvos, Límnos and Alexandhroúpoli.

Nissos Kalymnos

The small, slow but reliable Nissos Kalymnos (cars carried) is the most regular lifeline of the smaller islands (aside from Kárpathos and Kássos) – it visits them all twice a week between mid-March and mid-Jan. This ship can be poorly publicized on islands other than its home port; if you encounter difficulties obtaining information, you should phone the central agency on Kálymnos (☎02430/29 612). Specimen schedules, observed for some years now, are as follows:

Mid-March to April and mid-Sept to mid-Jan Mon and Fri 7am, leaves Kálymnos for Kós,

Níssyros, Tílos, Sými, Rhodes; out to Kastellórizo late afternoon, turns around at midnight. Tues and Sat 9am, departs Rhodes for Sými, Tílos, Níssyros, Kós, Kálymnos, with a Tues evening return trip to Astypálea. Wed and Sun departs Kálymnos 7am for Léros, Lipsí, Pátmos, Arkí (Wed only), Agathónissi, Pythagório (Sámos), returning from Sámos at 2.30pm bound for Kálymnos via the same islands. Thurs 7am from Kálymnos to Astypálea, returns immediately.

May to mid-June Mon and Fri 7am, leaves Kálymnos for Kós, Níssyros, Tílos, Sými, Rhodes;

out to Kastellórizo late afternoon, turns around at midnight. Tues and Sat 9am, departs Rhodes for Sými, Tílos, Níssyros, Kós, Kálymnos, with an evening return trip both days to Astypálea. Wed and Sun departs Kálymnos 7am for Léros, Lipsí, Pátmos, Arkí (Wed only), Agathónissi, Pythagório (Sámos), returning from Sámos at 2.30pm bound for Kálymnos via the same islands. Thurs, idle. Mid-June to mid-Sept Mon and Thurs 7am, leaves Kálymnos for Kós, Níssyros, Tílos, Sými,

Rhodes; out to Kastellórizo late afternoon, turns around at midnight. Tues and Fri 9am, departs Rhodes for Sými, Tílos, Níssyros, Kós, Kálymnos, with an evening return trip both days to Astypálea. Wed and Sun departs Kálymnos 7am for Léros, Lipsí, Pátmos, Arkí (Wed only), Agathónissi, Pythagório (Sámos), returning from Sámos at 2.30pm bound for Kálymnos via the same islands. Sat, 7am from Kálymnos to Astypálea, returning immediately,

Large ferries

Note that the following frequencies are only valid for the period mid-June to mid-Sept; in spring or autumn some of the more esoteric links, such as Astypálea to Níssyros, or Foúrni to Kós, do not operate.

Agathoníssi 1 weekly on Miniotis Lines to Arkí, Lipsí, Pátmos, Sámos (Pythagório).

Astypálea 3–5 weekly to Amorgós, Náxos, Páros and Pireás, 1 weekly to Sýros, on one of two companies; 1–2 weekly to Kós, Kálymnos, Rhodes and Níssyros on DANE or G&A.

Hálki 2 weekly to Ródhos Town, Kárpathos (both ports), Kássos, Crete and Mílos on LANE, all subject to cancellation in bad weather. Once-daily kaïki (6am) to Rhodes (Kámiros Skála).

Kálymnos Similar ferry service to Kós, plus 3 daily ro-ro ferries, well-spaced, to Mastihári; daily morning kaïki to Psérimos; and a daily kaïki (1pm) from Myrtiés to Xirókambos on Léros.

Kárpathos (both ports) and **Kássos** 2–3 weekly with each other, Crete (Áyios Nikólaos and/or Sitía), Mílos and Ródhos Town, on LANE; 1–2 weekly to Hálki on LANE.

Kastellórizo (Méyisti) 1 weekly to Rhodes, then Pireás indirectly, via select Dodecanese and Cyclades.

Kós 7–14 weekly to Rhodes, Kálymnos, Léros, Pátmos and Pireás on G&A or DANE; 3 weekly to Ikaría (Áyios Kírykos) on G&A; 1–2 weekly to Foúrni and Lipsí on G&A; 1 weekly to Tílos, Níssyros, Astypálea and Sými on DANE and G&A; 1 weekly to Náxos, Páros, Sýros on G&A; 3 daily ro-ro ferries year-round from Mastihári to Kálymnos; 4–7 weekly excursion kaïkia to Níssyros; 4 weekly islanders' kaïkia from Kardhámena to Níssyros.

Léros 7–14 weekly to Pireás, Pátmos, Kálymnos,

Kós and Rhodes on G&A or DANE; 3 weekly to Ikaría (Áyios Kírykos); 2 weekly to Foúrni; 1 weekly to Sými, Tílos on DANE; 1 weekly to Lipsí on G&A; seasonal daily excursion boats from Ayía Marína to Lipsí and Pátmos (2pm), and from Xirókambos to Myrtiés on Kálymnos (7.30am).

Lipsí 1 weekly to Léros, Kós, Pátmos, Ikaría (Áyios Kírykos), Tílos, Níssyros on G&A; 1 weekly to Sámos (Vathý) on Hellas Ferries.

Níssyros and Tílos Same as for Sými, plus excursion boats between Níssyros and Kós as follows: to Kardhámena nearly daily at 3.30–4pm; 4–7 weekly to Kós Town (all of these are seasonal). The islanders' somewhat less expensive "shopping" kaïki, the *Chrissula*, leaves 4–5 times weekly at 7am. Unless you're bound for the airport it's not really cheaper to use Kardhámena services when you consider the bus to Kós Town – €7.50 to Kardhámena on an excursion boat, versus €9 to Kós.

Pátmos Similar ferry service to Léros, with the addition of 1 weekly to Sámos (Vathý) on Hellas Ferries, 1 weekly to Arkí, seasonal tourist boats to Sámos (Pythagório), Lipsí, Arkí and Maráthi on a daily basis; Mon–Thurs only to Arkí in low season.

Rhodes 7–14 weekly to Kós, Kálymnos and Pireás on G&A or DANE; at least 1 daily to Léros and Pátmos on G&A or DANE; 2 weekly to Kárpathos, Kássos, Hálki, Crete (Sitía or Áyios Nikólaos), Mílos on LANE; 2 weekly to Foúrni and Ikaría (Áyios Kírykos) on G&A; 1–2 weekly to Sými, Lipsí, Tílos, Níssyros, Astypálea on G&A or DANE; 1 weekly to Náxos, Páros, Sýros.

Sými 1–2 weekly to Rhodes, Tílos, Níssyros, Kós, Kálymnos, Léros, Pátmos and Pireás on G&A Ferries or DANE; at least daily catamaran or hydrofoil run by ANES to Rhodes.

Catamarans

Two high-speed catamarans ply the Dodecanese: The *Dodecanese Express*, also known as *O Spanos* after the supermarket chain which owns it, and the *Sea Star*. The *Dodecanese Express*, based on Rhodes, can carry 4–5 cars and a slightly larger

number of two-wheelers; it's a sleek, new, Norwegian-built craft, with a limited amount of deck space (but no deck chairs). The *Sea Star* does not carry vehicles, and is the much less reliable of the two, fitfully serving the line

Tílos–Rhodes with occasionally other nearby islands thrown in.

2001 was the *Dodecanese Express*'s second season, and departure patterns seem to have settled down as follows: daily 8.30am departure from Rhodes to Kós, Kálymnos, Léros and Pátmos, calling at Lipsí 4 days weekly (usually northbound) and Tílos and Níssyros once weekly, both inbound and outbound, usually Wed; returns from Pátmos shortly after 1pm, arrives Rhodes 6.30–7.30pm. In spring or autumn it may call at Lipsí just once or twice weekly, serving Sými and Kastellórizo instead twice weekly. It has never called at Astypálea, Agathoníssi, Hálki, Kárpathos or Sámos (Pythagório) and is unlikely to in the future.

Hydrofoils

Two hydrofoil companies, Kyriakoulis Maritime and Laoumtzis Flying Dolphins, serve the Dodecanese between mid-May and mid-Oct, operating out of Rhodes, Kálymnos and Sámos (Kyriakoulis only), plus Kós (both companies). Kyriakoulis Maritime has ten craft in theory, inherited from the amalgamation of previously existing companies Samos Hydrofoils and Dodecanese Hydrofoils, but only about six of these are active at any given time. Schedules are complicated but fairly predictable. In peak season, there is a daily link Rhodes–Kós and back, north in the morning and south in the evening; on successive weekend days it may detour via Sými or Níssyros. Another craft leaves Kálymnos between 7 and 11am for Kós and a selection of islands north to Pythagório on Sámos, returning between 12.30 and 2pm; while the third craft, based in Pythagório, leaves Kós between 1 and 2pm, returning to Sámos via Kálymnos, Léros, Lipsí and Pátmos. Several days a week, this craft calls at Foúrni as well, and twice a week Agathoníssi is served. Still another craft based on Kálymnos leaves at dawn for Rhodes via Kós, returning between 4 and 6pm; once or twice a week it will call at Hálki and Tílos either direction. There is also a nominal Saturday service from Kálymnos to Astypálea, but owing to weather conditions and lack of passenger demand this tends to run at most three times in any summer. Some of the unusual runs to the smaller islands can get completely booked by transfers of package-tour groups. For current routes and schedules, phone ☎02420/25 920 (Kós), ☎02410/78 052 (Rhodes) or ☎02730/80 620 (Sámos).

Laoumtzis Flying Dolphins, based in Kós, has two craft with a fairly set pattern. One craft always leaves Kós at around 8am for Rhodes, returning shortly after 5pm. Twice weekly there are diversions via Sými in each direction, and on Sat there's the "milk run" via Níssyros, Tílos and Hálki, designed to get package patrons to/from their weekend charters. Twice a week the other craft provides an express run up to Pátmos in the morning, returning in the late afternoon. For exact details ring ☎02420/26 388.

International ferries

Kós 2–14 weekly to Bodrum, Turkey (45min). Greek boat or Laoumtzis hydrofoil leaves 9am, returns 4pm; €29.50 return, Greek tax inclusive; no cheap day-return or one-ways, no Turkish port tax. Identically priced Turkish boat (*Fahri Kaptan*) or hydrofoil, departs Bodrum 9am or so, leaves Kós 4.30pm; this provides the only service in winter.

Rhodes Daily in summer to Marmaris, Turkey (1hr) by Greek hydrofoil; €29.40 one-way, €41.20 return, plus $10 Turkish port tax. There is no longer a regularly scheduled Turkish car ferry; this must be arranged specially and will work out expensive, so drivers may be better off going to Kós and using the *Fahri Kaptan* to Bodrum. Also 2–3 weekly to Limassol, Cyprus (18hr) and Haifa, Israel (39hr).

Flights

Note: All are on Olympic Aviation/Olympic Airways unless stated otherwise.

Kárpathos 1–2 daily to Rhodes; 3 weekly to Kássos; 3–5 weekly to Athens.
Kássos 3 weekly to Kárpathos; 5 weekly to Rhodes.
Kastellórizo (Meyísti) 1 daily to Rhodes June–Sept, 3 weekly otherwise.

Kós 3 daily to Athens.
Léros 4–6 weekly to Athens.
Rhodes On Olympic, 5 daily to Athens; 2 weekly to Iráklion (April–Oct); 2–5 weekly to Thíra; 3 weekly to Thessaloníki; 2 weekly to Mýkonos (June–Sept). On Aegean-Cronus, 5 daily to Athens; 1–2 daily to Iráklion; 1 daily to Thessaloníki.

10

The East and North Aegean

CHAPTER 10

Highlights

✳ **Vathý, Sámos** The two-wing archeological museum is among the best in the islands; the star is the huge kouros from the local shrine of Hera. See p.834

✳ **Ikaría** Western Ikaría has superb beaches and an idio-syncratic life-style. See p.848

✳ **Southern Híos** The architec-turally unique *mastihohoriá* (mastic villages) were laid out by the Genoese and have a Middle Eastern feel. See p.858

✳ **Néa Moní, Híos** Particularly fine Byzantine mosaics in a monastery which survived earthquake, massacre and fire. See p.860

✳ **Thermal baths, Lésvos** Those at Loutrá Yéras are especially well-kept and ideal for relaxing after a lengthy journey. See p.872

✳ **Mólyvos, northern Lésvos** This castle-crowned resort village is arguably the most beautiful on the island. See p.878

✳ **Mýrina, Límnos** A character-ful port town with a fine cas-tle. See p.884

✳ **Samothráki** The spiritual focus of the north Agean, remote Samothráki's Sanctuary of the Great Gods is surrounded by natural grandeur. See p.891

✳ **Alykí, Thássos** A beautifully situated beach with ancient and Byzantine archeological sites. See p.899

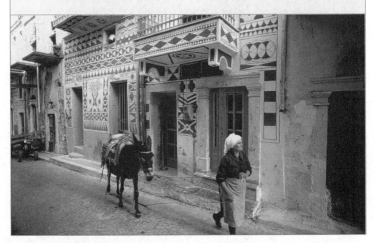

10

The East and North Aegean

T he seven substantial islands and four minor islets scattered off the north Aegean coast of Asia Minor and northeastern Greece form a rather arbitrary archipelago. Although there are some passing simi- larities in architecture and landscape, the strong individual character of each island is far more striking. Despite their proximity to modern Turkey, members of the group bear few signs of an Ottoman heritage, espe- cially when compared with Rhodes and Kós. There's the occasional mosque, often shorn of its minaret, but by and large the enduring Greekness of these islands is testimony to the four-millennium-long Hellenic presence in Asia Minor, which ended only in 1923. This heritage is regularly referred to by the Greek government in an intermittent prop- aganda war with Turkey over the sovereignty of these far-flung outposts. Tensions here have often been worse than in the Dodecanese, aggravated by potential undersea oil deposits in the straits between the islands and the Anatolian mainland. The Turks have also persistently demanded that Límnos, astride the sea lanes to and from the Dardanelles, be demilitarized, but so far Greece has shown no signs of giving in.

Accommodation price codes

Throughout the book we've categorized accommodation according to the following **price codes**, which denote the cheapest available double room in high season. All prices are for the room only, except where otherwise indicated. Many hotels, espe- cially those in category ❹ and over, include breakfast in the price; you'll need to check this when booking. During low season, rates can drop by more than fifty per- cent, especially if you are staying for three or more nights. Exceptions are during the Christmas and Easter weeks when you'll pay high-season prices. Single rooms, where available, cost around seventy percent of the price of a double.

❶ Up to €24	❹ €43–58
❷ €24–33	❺ €59–72
❸ €34–42	❻ €73 and upwards

Note: Youth hostels and mountain refuges typically charge €7–9 for a dormitory bed. For more accommodation details, see pp.51–54.

The heavy military presence can be disconcerting, and despite the growth of tourism, large tracts of land remain off-limits as army or air force bases. But as in the Dodecanese, local tour operators do a thriving business shuttling passengers for inflated tariffs between the easternmost islands and the Turkish coast with its amazing archeological sites and busy resorts. Most of these islands' main ports and towns are not quaint, picturesque spots, but urbanized administrative, military and commercial centres. In most cases you should suppress any initial impulse to take the next boat out, and press on into the interiors.

Sámos ranks as the most visited island of the group, but if you can leave the crowds behind, is still arguably the most verdant and beautiful, even after a devastating July 2000 fire. **Ikaría** to the west remains relatively unspoiled, if a minority taste, and nearby **Foúrni** is a haven for determined solitaries, as are the Híos satellites **Psará** and **Inoússes**, neither of which have any package tourism. **Híos** proper offers far more cultural interest than any neighbours to the south, but its natural beauty has been ravaged by fires, and the development of tourism was until the late 1980s deliberately retarded. **Lésvos** may not impress initially, though once you get a feel for its old-fashioned, Anatolian ambience, you may find it hard to leave. By contrast virtually no foreigners and few Greeks visit **Áyios Efstrátios**, and with good reason. **Límnos** to the north is much livelier, but its appeal is confined mostly to the area immediately around the attractive port town. To the north, Samothráki and Thássos are totally isolated from the others, except via the mainland ports of Kavála or Alexandhroúpoli, and remain easier to visit from northern Greece, which administers them. **Samothráki** (officially in Thrace) has one of the most dramatic seaward approaches of any Greek island, and one of the more important ancient sites. **Thássos** (technically belonging to eastern Macedonia) is more varied, with sandy beaches, mountain villages and minor archeological sites.

Sámos

The lush and seductive island of Sámos was formerly joined to Asia Minor, until sundered from Mount Mykale opposite by Ice Age cataclysms; the resulting 2500-metre strait is now the narrowest distance between Greece and Turkey in the Aegean, except at Kastellórizo. There's little tangible evidence of it today, but Sámos was also once the **wealthiest island** in the Aegean and, under the patronage of the tyrant Polykrates, home to a thriving intellectual community: Epicurus, Pythagoras, Aristarchus and Aesop were among the residents. Decline set in as the star of Classical Athens was in the ascendant, though Sámos's status was improved somewhat in early Byzantine times when it constituted its own *theme* (imperial administrative district). Towards the end of the fifteenth century, the Genoese abandoned the island to the mercies of pirates; following their attacks, Sámos remained **almost uninhabited** until 1562, when an Ottoman admiral received permission from the sultan to repopulate it with Greek Orthodox settlers recruited from various corners of the empire.

The heterogeneous descent of today's islanders largely explains an enduring identity crisis and a rather thin topsoil of indigenous culture. Most of the village names are either clan surnames, or adjectives indicating origins elsewhere – constant reminders of **refugee descent**. Consequently there is no genuine Samiote music, dance or dress, and little that's original in the way of cuisine and architecture. The Samiotes compensated somewhat for this deracination by fighting fiercely for independence during the 1820s, but despite their accomplishments in sinking a Turkish fleet in the narrow strait and annihilating a landing army, the Great Powers handed the island back to the Ottomans in 1830, with the consoling proviso that it be **semi-autonomous**, ruled by an appointed Christian prince. This period, referred to as the *Iyimonía* (Hegemony), was marked by a mild renaissance in fortunes, courtesy of the hemp and (especially) tobacco trades. However, union with Greece in 1912, the ravages of a bitter World War II occupation and mass emigration effectively reversed the recovery until tourism appeared on the horizon during the 1980s.

Today the Samian economy is increasingly dependent on package **tourism**, far too much of it in places; the eastern half of the island, and a large part of the south coast, has pretty much surrendered to the onslaught of holiday-makers, although the more rugged northwestern part has retained some of its undeveloped grandeur. The clientele is rather sedate and couples-oriented; the absence of an official campsite on such a large island, tame nightlife a world away from that in the Cyclades, and phalanxes of self-catering villas hint at the sort of custom expected.

The heavily developed areas have unsurprisingly been the most afflicted by **repeated wildfires**, in particular one which lasted a week in July 2000, destroying twenty percent of the island's forest and orchards, and over ninety dwellings. If you mention Sámos to other Greeks, they say "Ah, tó nisí poú kaíke" ("Oh, the island that burned"), and if you take into account other areas that had been torched since 1987, Sámos is indeed about half-scorched. The trees will be a half-century in returning, and the tourist market a good few years in overcoming this stigma. Volunteer fire-lookouts have now sprouted at critical points, but it does seem a case of locking the stable after the horse has bolted.

Getting there and getting around

Sámos **airport** lies 14km southwest of Vathý and 3km west of Pythagório; an ambitious terminal expansion should be complete by 2003. There are no fewer than three **ferry ports**: Karlóvassi in the west, plus Vathý and Pythagório in the east, making the island a major hub for travel in every direction, though traditional sailing routes seem to have been altered slightly by the wreck of the *Express Samina* (see p.42). All ferries between Pireás, Sýros, Mýkonos, Ikaría and Sámos call at both Karlóvassi and Vathý (except for the high-speed catamaran which serves only Vathý), as do the smaller Miniotis Line ferries linking the island with Híos and, at high season, Foúrni and Ikaría. There was, however, no reliable link with Páros and Náxos for most of summer 2001, and this situation may continue in future years. Vathý also receives the weekly NEL sailing between northern Greece and the Dodecanese, via most intervening islands, the weekly DANE ferry between Thessaloníki and Rhodes, plus small boats from Kuşadası. Pythagório siphons off a bit of the Turkey shipping in high season, and additionally sees two regular weekly ferry connections from as far south as Kós in the Dodecanese, plus a seasonal Miniotis service to Lipsí, Foúrni and Agathoníssi. Both ports host **hydrofoil services** (Kyriakoulis Maritime): Vathý is the start-point base of pretty-undependable hydrofoils to Híos, northern Ikaría and Lésvos, while Pythagório has the lion's share of traffic, with more reliable services to all the Dodecanese down to Kós, plus forays over to Foúrni and southern Ikaría.

The **bus terminals** in Pythagório and Vathý lie within walking distance of the ferry dock; at Karlóvassi, you must make your own way the 3km into town from the port. There is no airport bus service; **taxi** fares to various points are stipulated on prominent placards, and in high season taxis to the airport or docks must be booked several hours in advance. The KTEL service itself is

SÁMOS

Kuşadası (Turkey)

Kuşadası (Turkey)

TURKEY

Nissi

Kalámi

Ayía
Paraskeví

Vathý

Áno Vathý

Kamára

Ayía Zóni

Zoödhóhou
Piyís

Paleókastro

Kérveli

Posidhónio

Kadúna

Psilí
Ámmos

Mykáli

Kokkári

Tsamadoú

Lemonákia

Avlákia

Tzaboú

Platanákia

Áyios Konstandínos

Pnáka

Vourliótes

Vrondianís

Mt. Ámbelos
1153m

Manolátes

Ámbelos

Stavrinídhes

Idhroússa

Kondakéïka

Piáki

Áyios Nikólaos

Karlóvassi

Pándhrossos

Mavratzéi

Mytilíni

Timíou
Stavroú

Hóra

Glyfádha

Efpalínio
Tunnel

Pythagório

Roman
Baths

Potokáki

Heraion

Iréon

Petrokáravo

Megális
Panayías

Myíi

Koumaradhéi

Pagóndas

Kyriakoú

Tsópela

Pyrgos

Neohóri

Koútsi

Plátanos

Spatharéi

Kouméïka

Bállos

Órmos
Marathókambou

Voútsalákia

Psilí Ámmos

Limniónas

Meséo

Metamórfosis

Lékka

Kosmadhéi

Kastaniá

Marathókambos

Evangelístrias

Limáni
Paleó

Potámi

Mikró Seïtáni

Megálo Seïtáni

Dhrakéi

Ayía
Triádha

Mt. Kérkis
1437m

Panayía
Makriní

Kallithéa

Vársamo

N

5 km

0

Híos & Lésvos

Ikaría & Foúrni

Foúrni

Fourni

Pátmos & Foúrni

Arkí, Lípsi & Agathoníssi

excellent along the Pythagório–Vathý and Vathý–Kokkári–Karlóvassi routes, but poor otherwise; with numerous car- and motorbike-rental outlets, it's easy to find a good deal outside July or August and, with tourist numbers down lately twenty percent, perhaps all year round.

Vathý

Lining the steep northeastern shore of a deep bay, beachless **VATHÝ** (often confusingly referred to as **SÁMOS**, like the island) is a busy provincial town which grew from a minor anchorage after 1830, when it replaced Hóra as the island's capital. It's an unlikely, somewhat ungraceful resort, which has seen several hotel bankruptcies since the late 1990s, and is minimally interesting for the most part – although the pedestrianized bazaar, tiers of surviving Neoclassical houses and the hill suburb of **ÁNO VATHÝ**, a separate community of tottering, tile-roofed houses have some attraction – and the only real highlight is the excellent **archeological museum** (Tues–Sun 8.30am–2.30pm; €2.40), set behind the small central park beside the restored Neoclassical town hall. One of the best provincial collections in Greece is housed in both the old Paskhallion building and a modern wing across the way, specially constructed to house the star exhibit: a majestic, five-metre-tall *kouros*, discovered out at the Heraion sanctuary. The *kouros*, the largest free-standing effigy to survive from ancient Greece, was dedicated to Apollo, but found together with a devotional mirror to Mut (the Egyptian equivalent of Hera) from a Nile workshop, one of only two discovered in Greece to date.

In the compelling **small-objects collection** of the Paskhallion, more votive offerings of Egyptian design prove trade and pilgrimage links between Sámos and the Nile valley going back to the eighth century BC. The Mesopotamian and Anatolian origins of other artwork confirm the exotic trend, most tellingly in a case full of ivory miniatures: Perseus and Medusa in relief, a kneeling, perfectly formed mini-*kouros*, a pouncing lion and a drinking horn ending in a bull's head. The most famous local artefacts are the dozen or so bronze griffin-heads, for which Sámos was the major centre of production in the seventh century BC; mounted on the edge of bronze cauldrons, they were believed to ward off evil spirits.

Practicalities

From the **ferry dock** the shore boulevard – Themistoklí Sofoúli – describes a 1300-metre arc around the bay. About 400m along is pedestrianized Platía Pythagóra, distinguished by its lion statue and some ugly concrete-barricade "sculpture"; about 800m along there's a major turning inland to the **KTEL** terminal, a chaos of buses at a perennially cluttered intersection by the ticket office. The minimally useful **tourist information** office is at 25-Martíou 4 (May–Oct Mon–Fri 9am–2pm; winter sporadic hours), worth a stop, if only for its comprehensive bus schedules and accommodation listings. If you've arrived with your own vehicle, beware of the pay-and-display **parking** scheme (strip tickets from kiosks €0.30 per hour) in effect along most of the waterfront.

The most useful waterfront **ferry/travel agent** for independent travellers is By Ship, with two branches: one at the base of the jetty (℡02730/80 445), primarily handling ships and hydrofoils, and one about 300m southeast (℡02730/25 065); between them they sell tickets for most ferry lines (DANE, NEL, Hellas Ferries, G&A), as well as air tickets on both Olympic and Axon. At present Miniotis Lines representation is restricted to Nautica near the *Samos Hotel*, and Kyriakoulis Maritime hydrofoil tickets are sold almost everywhere. Vathý is chock-

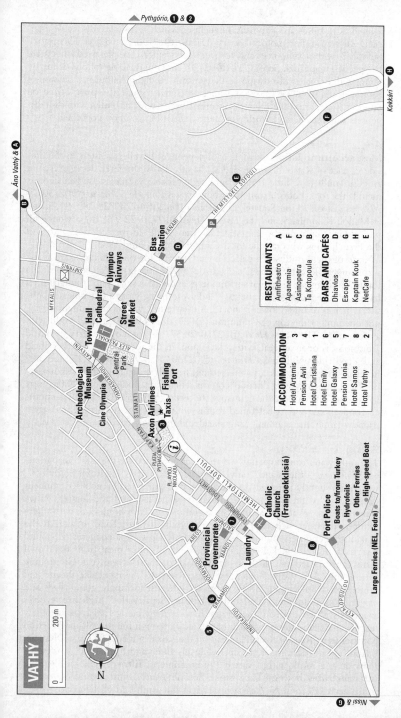

VATHÝ

0 — 200 m

N

▲ Pythgório, **1** & **2**

Ⓐ Áno Vathý & Ⓐ

Ⓑ

Ⓗ Kokkári ▶

MYKÁLIS

SMÝRNIS

Ⓕ

Ⓔ THEMISTOKLI SOFOULI

KANÁRI

P

Ⓓ

Bus Station

Olympic Airways

Town Hall

Cathedral

Street Market

ALEX PASHÁLI

KAPETÁN

Archeological Museum

Central Park

YIANNIS SARHOÚ

KATÉVENI

Cine Olympia

STAMÁTI

Fishing Port

Ⓒ

P

P

Axon Airlines

Taxis

★ **3**

ℹ

PLATÍA PYTHAGÓRA

PL. AVÍOU NIKOLÁOU

THEMISTOKLÍ SOFOÚLI

LOGOTHÉTI

KAPETÁN

4

AREOS

NEOMÁRON

6

Provincial Governorate

MANÓLI

KEFALOPÓULOU

LYKOÚRGOU

GRÁMMOU

ENDIMÁTOU

Laundry

7

Catholic Church (Frangoekklisía)

5

8

Port Police

Boats to/from Turkey

Hydrofoils

Other Ferries

High-speed Boat

Large Ferries (NEL, Fedra)

KEFALOPÓULOU

▼ Níssi & Ⓖ

ACCOMMODATION

Hotel Artemis	3
Pension Avli	4
Hotel Christiana	1
Hotel Emily	6
Hotel Galaxy	5
Pension Ionia	7
Hotel Samos	8
Hotel Vathy	2

RESTAURANTS

Amfitheatro	A
Apanemia	F
Asimopetra	C
Ta Kotopoula	B

BARS AND CAFÉS

Dhiavlos	D
Escape	G
Kaptain Kouk	H
NetCafe	E

a-block with **bike-** and **car-rental** franchises, which keeps rates reasonable, especially off-season. For motorbikes, try Aramis (☎02730/22 682) at Themistoklí Sofoúli 5, with a large fleet and recovery service; for cars, preferred outlets are Budget at Themistoklí Sofoúli 31 (☎02730/28 856), Reliable (phone as for By Ship), with branches islandwide, or the similarly far-flung Autoplan, a division of Samina Tours (☎02730/23 555). Other amenities include the **post office** on Smýrnis, inland from the Olympic terminal, five waterfront **banks** with cash dispensers and a self-serve **laundry** on pedestrianized Lykoúrgou Logothéti.

Accommodation

Most **accommodation** available to independent travellers clusters in the hillside district of Katsoúni, more or less directly above the ferry dock; except in August, you'll have little trouble finding affordable vacancies. Budget choices include the rock-bottom, somewhat noisy waterfront *Hotel Artemis* (☎02730/27 792; ●) just off "Lion Square"; the *Pension Ionia* (☎02730/28 782; ●), inland at Manoli Kalomíri 5; and the *Pension Avli* (☎02730/22 939; ●), a wonderful period piece up a nearby stair-street at Áreos 2, the former convent school of the French nuns who ran the local Catholic church until 1973.

None of these outfits is a palace by any means; for more luxury start at the surprisingly affordable *Hotel Galaxy* (☎02730/22 665; ●), at Angéou 1 near the top of Katsoúni, set in garden surroundings and with a small pool, though you'll have to dodge package allotments – and avoid being sent to the annexe opposite, which is of much lower standard. If they're full, try the sympathetic *Emily*, just downhill at the top of Grámmou (☎02730/24 691; ●), a small outfit with a roof garden. The *Samos Hotel* (☎02730/28 377; ●) right by the ferry dock and a bit noisy, is open all year, with a little pool in the roof garden. Further afield and a taxi ride uphill, the *Christiana* (☎02730/27 149 or 23 084; ●), the only hotel in Áno Vathý, has a ravine setting, friendly management, an enormous pool and a tie-in, giving discounts on car rental with Budget. Some 400m away in Neápoli district near the cemetery, the *Vathy* (☎02730/28 124; ●) is another good choice for its balconied rooms with bay view, small pool and again friendly family management; ring ahead and they may fetch you in their van.

Eating and drinking

The only waterfront **tavernas** worth a second glance are the 2001-inaugurated *Asimopetra* – the island's only *kultúra* taverna – at Themistoklí Sofoúli 97, which has slightly bumped-up prices but well-presented Frenchified minceur dishes, novelty breads and an impressive wine list; and the less expensive *Apanemia Ouzeri*, at the far southwest end of the shore boulevard, with interesting and rather rich recipes, so starve yourself beforehand. Inland, at the Plátanos junction en route to Áno Vathý, *Ta Kotopoula* is a congenial all-round taverna featuring chicken (as in the name) and other meat from their own farms, plus *mezédhes*. All three are open all or most of the year. Continuing further into Áno Vathý, *Amfitheatro* – right next to the namesake theatre and double medieval church of Aï Yiannáki – does surprisingly good salads and *mayireftá* dishes (dinner only, late June to early Sept). Vathý's **nightlife** revolves around its waterfront bars, the longest lived of these being *Escape*, on a seaview terrace at Kefalopoúlou 9 (north of the jetty), though the real till-dawn action is currently at *Kaptain Kook*, 2km out on the Kokkári road. The Cine Olympia, inland on Yimnasiárhou Katevéni, is plushly fitted and operates all year (summers on the roof), with a variable programme of **films**. There are also two **internet cafés**, both on Themistoklí Sofoúli: *Dhiavlos* just around the corner from the KTEL, and *NetCafe* at no. 175, at the south end of the front.

Around Vathý

The immediate environs of Vathý offer some modest beaches and small hamlets, though you'll usually need your own transport to visit them. Two kilometres east and uphill spreads the vast inland plateau of **Vlamarí**, devoted to vineyards and supporting the hamlets of Ayía Zóni and Kamára (plus an increasing number of bad-taste modern villas); from Kamára you can climb up a partly cobbled path to the clifftop **monastery of Zoödhóhou Piyís**, for superb views across the end of the island to Turkey.

Heading north out of Vathý, the narrow road ends after 7km at the pebble bay and fishing port of **AYÍA PARASKEVÍ** (or Nissí), with good swimming. There are, alas, no longer any reliable facilities here other than a fitfully working snack-bar, *Aquarius* (typically July & Aug only).

As you head southeast from Vathý along the main island loop road, the triple chapel at **Trís Ekklisíes** marks an important junction, with another fork 100m along the left-hand turning. Bearing left twice takes you through the hilltop village of Paleókastro, 3km beyond which is another junction. Forking left yet again, after another 3km you reach the quiet, striking bay of **Kérveli**, with a small beach, a pair of tavernas (the friendly *Sea and Dolphins* has good mezédhes and *soúma*, the local spirit, but mains have declined in quality and climbed in price lately) by the water and another characterful favourite with simple grills only, *Iy Kryfi Folia*, about 500m uphill along the access road. Taking the right fork leads to **Posidhónio**, with an even smaller beach and another pair of tavernas: the right-hand one, *Kerkezos*, takes its cooking more seriously, though it's expensive. A right turn at the junction before Paleókastro leads to the beaches of Mykáli and Psilí Ámmos, the only spots in this section with a bus service. **Mykáli**, a kilometre of windswept sand and gravel, has been encumbered with three package hotels; the best place to try on spec here is *Villa Barbara* (☎02730/25 192; ❹), which has apartments behind the *Sirenes Beach* hotel. Far and away the best **eating** on this coast is at *Kalypso*, which has excellent and well-priced *mayireftá* and is reached by its own dead-end access road off the main Mykáli-bound route. **Psilí Ámmos**, further east around the headland, is a crowded, sandy cove backed by several commercialized tavernas, none worth recommending; if you swim to the islet beware of strong currents which sweep through the narrow straits.

Pythagório and around

Most traffic south of Vathý heads for **PYTHAGÓRIO**, the island's premier resort, renamed in 1955 to honour native son Pythagoras, ancient mathematician, philosopher and mystic. Until then it was known as Tigáni (Frying Pan) – in midsummer you'll learn why. The sixth-century BC tyrant Polykrates had his capital here, now subject to sporadic excavations which have forced modern Pythagório to expand northeast and uphill. The village core of cobbled lanes and thick-walled mansions abuts a small **harbour**, fitting almost perfectly into the confines of Polykrates' ancient port, but today devoted almost entirely to pleasure craft and overpriced cocktail bars.

Sámos's most complete **castle**, the nineteenth-century *pýrgos* of local chieftain Lykourgos Logothetis, overlooks both the town and the shoreline. Logothetis, together with a certain "Kapetan Stamatis" and Admiral Kanaris, chalked up decisive victories over the Turks in the summer of 1824. The final battle was won on Transfiguration Day (August 6), and accordingly the church inside the castle precinct is dedicated to this festival. More antiquities include the fairly dull **Roman baths**, signposted as "Thermai", 400m west of town

(Tues–Sun 8.30am–2.30pm; free) and a minuscule **archeological collection** in the town hall on Platía Irínis (Tues–Thurs & Sun 9am–2pm, Fri & Sat 10am–2pm; free). Considerably more interesting is the **Efpalínio tunnel** (Tues–Sun 8.30am–2.30pm; €1.50), a 1040-metre aqueduct bored through the mountain just north of Pythagório at the behest of Polykrates. To get there, take the signposted path from the shore boulevard at the west end of town, which meets the vehicle access road toward the end of a twenty-minute walk.

Further subterranean experience can be had at the monastery of **Panayía Spilianí**, high on the hillside over town. Though most of this has been insensitively restored and touristified, behind the courtyard lies a cool, hundred-metre-long grotto, at one end of which is a shrine to the Virgin (open daylight hours; free). This was the presumed residence of the ancient oracular priestess Fyto, and a pirate-safe hideout in medieval times.

Practicalities

If there are any **accommodation** vacancies – more likely of late, with local package tourism down twenty percent – rooms proprietors meet all incoming ferries and hydrofoils. The **tourist information booth** (June–Sept daily 8am–10pm; ☎02730/62 274), on the main thoroughfare, Lykoúrgou Logothéti, can help in finding rooms and sells tickets for the *Nissos Kalymnos* ferryboat. Quietly located at the seaward end of Odhós Pythagóra, south of Lykoúrgou Logothéti, the modest *Tsambika* (☎02730/61 642; ❷) or the more comfortable *Dora*, a block west (☎02730/61 456; ❸), are two pensions worth considering. Some 50m inland from the north side of the harbour past the customs house, *Lambis Rooms* on Odhós Íras (☎02730/61 396; ❷) is another backpackers' transit stop. Another peaceful area is the hillside north of Platía Irínis, where *Studios Galini* (☎02730/61 167 or 010/98 42 248 in winter; ❹) has high-quality self-catering units with ceiling fans, balconies and kind English-speaking management. The *Evelin* (☎02730/61 124, ℱ61 077; ❸) isn't brilliantly located out by the traffic lights – convenient only for the airport – but it's comfortable, good value and friendly and has a swimming pool, double glazing against noise and on-site motorbike rental.

Eating out can be frustrating in Pythagório, with value for money often a completely alien concept. For waterside dining, you're best off at the far east end of the quay, beyond the shut-down hotel, where the *Remataki* (open all year) features vegetarian dishes such as *angináres ala políta* (stewed artichokes with veg), and the adjacent *Psaropoula* (April–Oct) offers reliably fresh and affordable fish as well as *orektiká* – these are the only two spots the locals themselves will be seen in. Night-owls gather at the *Mythos Club* on Platía Irínis, while all-year **Cine Rex** in Mytiliní village, 7km northwest, screens standard first-run fare.

Buses serving the local area leave from the **stop** that lies just west of the intersection of Lykoúrgou Logothéti and the road to Vathý. Two **banks** (both with cash dispensers) and the **post office** are also on Lykoúrgou Logothéti. The flattish country to the west is ideal for cycling, a popular activity, and if you want to rent a **motorbike** several outfits on Logothéti will oblige you.

Around Pythagório

The main local beach stretches for several kilometres west of the Logothetis "castle", punctuated about halfway along by the end of the airport runway, and the cluster of nondescript hotels known as **POTOKÁKI**. Just before the turn-off to the heart of the beach sprawls the ultra-luxurious *Doryssa Bay* complex (☎02730/61 360, ℱ61 463, ❻www.doryssabay.gr; ❻), which includes a meticulously concocted fake village, guaranteed to confound archeologists of future eras. No two of the units, joined by named lanes, are alike, and there's even a platía with a café. Although you'll have to contend with the hotel crowds and low-flying jets, the sand-and-pebble **beach** here is well groomed and the water clean; for more seclusion you'll have to head out to the end of the road.

The Potokáki access road is a dead end, with the main island loop road pressing on past the turn-off for the airport and Iréon hamlet. Under layers of alluvial mud, plus today's runway, lies the processional Sacred Way joining the ancient city with the **Heraion**, the massive shrine of the Mother Goddess (Tues–Sun 8.30am–2.30pm; €2.40). Much touted in tourist literature, this assumes humbler dimensions – one surviving column and assorted foundations – upon approach. Yet once inside the precinct you sense the former grandeur of the temple, never completed owing to Polykrates' untimely death at the hands of the Persians. The site chosen, near the mouth of the still-active Imvrassós stream, was Hera's legendary birthplace and site of her trysts with Zeus; in the far corner of the fenced-in zone you glimpse a large, exposed patch of the paved Sacred Way.

The modern resort of **IRÉON** nearby is a nondescript grid of dusty streets behind a coarse-shingle beach, attracting a slightly younger and more active clientele than Pythagório. Here you'll find more nonpackage rooms and a small **hotel**, *Venetia* (📞02730/95 295; ❸) within sight of the water. The oldest and most authentic **taverna** is the *Ireon*, at the far west end by the fishing harbour, also with namesake, basic rooms upstairs (📞02730/95 361; ❷).

Southern Sámos

Since the circumisland bus only passes through or near the places below once or twice daily, you really need your own vehicle to explore them. Some 5km west of Hóra, a well-marked side road leads up and right to **MAVRATZÉÏ**, one of two Samian "pottery villages", which lost 49 houses to the fire in 2000. The few surviving local potteries specialize in the *Koúpa tou Pythagóra* or "Pythagorean cup", supposedly designed by the sage to leak over the user's lap if they are overfilled. Slightly more practical wares can be found in **KOUMARADHÉÏ**, back on the main road, another 2km along.

From here you can descend a paved road to the sixteenth-century monastery of **Megális Panayías** (theoretically daily 9am–noon & 5–7pm), containing the finest frescoes on the island. This route continues to **MÝLI**, submerged in citrus groves and also accessible from Iréon. Four kilometres above Mýli sprawls **PAGÓNDAS**, a large hillside community with a splendid main square and an unusual communal fountain house on the south hillside. From here, a scenic paved road curls 9km around the hill to **SPATHARÉÏ** – its surroundings sadly devastated by repeated fires – set on a natural balcony offering the best sea views this side of the island. From Spatharéï, the road loops back 6km to **PÝRGOS**, at the head of a ravine draining southwest and the centre of Samian honey production; the most reliable local **taverna** (June–Oct) lies 3km west, in the plane-shaded Koútsi ravine which just escaped the July 2000 blaze.

The rugged and beautiful coast south of the Pagóndas–Pýrgos route is largely inaccessible, glimpsed by most visitors for the first and last time from the descending plane bringing them to Sámos. **Tsópela**, a highly scenic sand-and-gravel cove at a gorge mouth, is the only beach here with marked track access and a good seasonal taverna; you'll need a sturdy motorcycle (not a scooter) or jeep to get down there. The western reaches of this shoreline, which suffered comprehensive fire damage in 1994, are approached via the small village of **KOUMÉÏKA**, with a massive inscribed marble fountain and a pair of kafenía on its square. Below extends the long, pebble bay at **BÁLLOS**, with sand, a cave and naturists at the far east end. Bállos itself is merely a sleepy collection of summer houses, several simple places to stay and a few tavernas, all on the shore road. The best **accommodation** for walk-ins is the *Hotel Amfilisos* (☎02730/31 669, ℉31 668; ❷), while far and away the finest **dining** is found at *Akrogiali* nearby, with an honourable mention for humbler *Iy Paralia* off to the east. Returning to Kouméïka, the dubious-looking side road just before the village marked "Velanidhiá" is in fact partly paved and usable by any vehicle – a very useful short cut if you're travelling towards the beaches beyond Órmos Marathokámbou (see p.843).

Kokkári and around

Leaving Vathý on the north coastal section of the island loop road, you've little to stop for until **KOKKÁRI**, Sámos's third major tourist centre after Pythagório and the capital. Sadly, while lower Vathý and Pythagório had little beauty to sacrifice, much has been irrevocably lost here. The town's profile, covering two knolls behind twin headlands, remains unaltered, and one or two families still doggedly untangle their fishnets on the quay, but in general its identity has been altered beyond recognition, with constant inland expansion over vineyards and the abandoned fields of boiling onions that gave the place its name. Since the exposed, rocky beaches here are buffeted by near-constant winds, the promoters have made a virtue of necessity by developing the place as a successful windsurfing resort.

Practicalities

As in Vathý and Pythagório, a fair proportion of Kokkári's **accommodation** is block-booked by tour companies; establishments not completely devoted to such trade include *Lemos* (☎02730/92 250; ❹), near the north end of the west beach, and the more modest *Vicky* (☎02730/92 231; ❸), facing the same strand. For a guaranteed view of the fishing port, try the *Pension Alkyonis* (☎02730/92 225; ❷) or the *Pension Angela* (☎02730/92 052; ❷). Otherwise Yiorgos Mihelios has a range of rooms and flats to rent (☎02730/92 456; ❷–❹), including the *Pension Green Hill*. If you get stuck, seek assistance from the seasonal **EOT post** (☎02730/92 217), housed in a Portakabin near the main church. If money's no object, then it has to be the A-class *Arion* (☎02370/92 020, ℉92 006, ⓦwww.diavlos.gr/samos/arion/arion1.html; ❻), a well-designed bungalow complex on an unburnt patch of hillside 2km west.

Most **tavernas** line the north waterfront, and charge above the norm, though they're steadily losing ground to breakfast or cocktail bars. At the far east end of things, *Ta Adhelfia/The Brothers* is a good-value place strong on grilled fish and meat, but with a few oven dishes daily; adjacent and further west, *To Avgo tou Kokora* is another good (if pricier) all-rounder, while *Piccolo Porto* still further west does excellent Italian dishes, including wood-fired pizzas. The co-managed *Barino*, also here at mid-strip, is the best breakfast place, with various fresh-squeezed juices, waffles and crepes. Most (noisy) **bars** ring the little square just west of where the concreted stream (with its family of ducks) meets the sea, but there's also the more elaborate and well-established disco, *Cabana Beach Club*, on the west beach, drawing clubbers from across the island.

Other amenities include an Emboriki/Commercial Bank **cash dispenser** on the through road, a **post office** in a Portakabin on a seaward lane and next door, a long-hours, self-service **laundry**; there are also branches of the major Vathý **travel agents**, and a newsstand.

West of Kokkári: the coast

The closest sheltered beaches are thirty- to forty-minutes' walk away to the west, all with sunbeds and permanently anchored umbrellas. The first, **Lemonákia**, is a bit too close to the road, with an obtrusive café, though many *Arion* patrons like it; 1km beyond, the graceful crescent of **Tzamadhoú** figures in virtually every EOT poster of the island. With path-only access, it's a bit less spoiled, and each end of the beach (saucer-shaped pebbles) is by tacit consent a nudist/gay zone. There's one more pebble bay, 7km west beyond Avlákia, called **Tzaboú**, but it's not worth a special detour when the prevailing northwest wind is up.

The next spot of any interest along the coast road is **Platanákia**, essentially a handful of tavernas and rooms for rent at a bridge by the turning for Manolátes (see p.842); best of the tavernas is *Iy Apolavsis*, with a limited choice of very good *mayireftá*. Platanákia is actually the eastern suburb of **ÁYIOS KONSTANDÍNOS**, whose surf-pounded esplanade has been prettified. However, there are no usable beaches within walking distance, so the collection of warm-toned stone buildings, with few modern intrusions, constitutes a peaceful alternative to Kokkári. In addition to modest 1970s-vintage **rooms**, such as the *Four Seasons* (☎02730/94 287; ❷) or the *Atlantis* (☎02730/94 329; ❶) just above the highway, there's a new generation of more modern rooms below the road, such as *Maria's* (☎02730/94 460; ❸). **Eating** out, you're spoilt for choice; besides *Iy Apolavsis*, there's *To Kyma* at the east end of the quay, with good bulk wine and *mayireftá*; *To Akroyiali* at mid-quay, where the food's cheaper and better than the plastic menu–photos suggest; or (best of all) the *Aeolos* at the far west end of the esplanade (June–Sept), with terrific fish or grilled meat and a few well-chosen baked dishes.

Once past "Áyios", as it's locally abbreviated, the mountains hem the road in against the sea, and the terrain doesn't relent until **Kondakéïka**; its diminutive shore annexe of **Áyios Nikólaos** has an excellent venue for fish meals in *Iy Psaradhes* (☎02730/32 489; Easter–Oct), with a terrace lapped by the waves – booking in season is mandatory as it's appeared (deservedly) in so many guides. There's also the reasonable beach of **Piáki**, ten-minutes' walk east past the last studio units, evidence of a mild explosion in package development here since 1995.

Hill villages

Inland between Kokkári and Kondakéïka, an idyllic landscape of pine, cypress and orchards is overawed by dramatic mountains; except for some streaks of damage reaching the sea between Lemonákia and Tzaboú, it miraculously escaped the July 2000 fire. Despite destructive nibblings by bulldozers, some of the trail system linking the various **hill villages** is still intact, and walkers can return to the main highway to catch a bus home. Failing that, most of the communities can provide a bed at short notice.

The monastery of **Vrondianís** (Vrónda), directly above Kokkári, was once a popular destination, but between severe fire damage in 2000 and the army's use of it as a barracks, the place only really comes alive during its annual festival (Sept 7–8). **VOURLIÓTES**, 2km west of the monastery, has beaked chimneys and brightly painted shutters sprouting from its typical tile-roofed houses. Restaurateur greed has ruined the formerly photogenic central square, by cutting down two ancient mulberries, and it's best to pass over the tavernas here in favour of *Iy Pera Vrysi*, at the village entrance, or (even better) the *Piyi Pnaka* taverna, in the idyllic eponymous hamlet just off the ascending Vourliótes road.

MANOLÁTES, further uphill and an hour-plus walk away via a deep river canyon, also has several simple tavernas (the pick of these being *Iy Filia* near the village entrance), and is the most popular trailhead for the five-hour round-trip up **Mount Ámbelos** (Karvoúnis), the island's second-highest summit. From Manolátes you can no longer easily continue on foot to Stavrinídhes, the next village, but should plunge straight down, partly on a cobbled path, through the shady valley known as **Aïdhónia** (Nightingales), towards Platanákia. Manolátes has accommodation with *Studios Angela* at the edge of town (☎02730/94 478; ❸), but by far the most characterful base in the area is down in Aïdhónia at the *Hotel Aidonokastro* (☎02730/94 686, ☏94 404; ❹). Here the kindly, English-speaking Yannis Pamoukis has renovated half the abandoned hamlet of **Valeondátes** as a unique cottage-hotel, each former house comprising a pair of two- or four-person units with traditional touches.

Karlóvassi

KARLÓVASSI, 35km west of Vathý and the second town of Sámos, is decidedly sleepier and more old-fashioned than the capital, despite having roughly the same population. Though lacking in distinction, it's popular as a base for exploring western Sámos's excellent beaches and walking opportunities. The name, despite a vehement denial of Ottoman legacy elsewhere on Sámos, appears to be a corruption of the Turkish for "snowy plain" – the plain in question being the conspicuous saddle of Mount Kérkis overhead. The town divides into four straggly neighbourhoods: Néo, well inland, whose untidy growth was spurred by the influx of post-1923 refugees; Meséo, across the usually dry riverbed, tilting appealingly off a knoll towards the shore; and postcardworthy Paleó (or Áno), above Limáni, the small harbour district.

Most tourists stay at or near **Limáni**, the part of town with most of the tourist facilities. Hotels tend to have road noise and not much view; **rooms**, all on the inland pedestrian lane behind the through road, are quieter – try those of Vangelis Feloukatzis (☎02730/33 293; ❷). The port itself is an appealing place with a working boatyard at the west end and all the **ferry-ticket agencies** grouped at the middle; a shuttle-bus service operates from Néo Karlóvassi, timed to coincide with boat arrivals and departures. Tavernas and bars are abundant on the quay, though the only remarkable ones are *Rementzo* (April–Oct), tellingly the locals' hangout, with good fish in season plus *mayireftá*, and the more touristy *Boussoulas* next door, which stays open year-round, with consistent quality. The local university contingent (a maths and computer science faculty is based here) keeps **nightlife** surprisingly lively; try *Popcorn* on the quay.

Immediately overhead is the partly hidden hamlet of **Paleó**, its hundred or so houses draped on either side of a leafy ravine, but no reliable tourist facilities. **Meséo**, just east, is a conceivable alternative base to Limáni, with the *Hotel Aspasia* (☎02730/31 201; ❹), well sited 100m west of the wood-fired bakery, with a pool and air-conditioning. Following the street linking the central square to the waterfront, you pass one of the improbably huge, early twentieth-century churches, topped with twin belfries and a blue-and-white dome, which dot the coastal plain here. Just at the intersection with the shore road you'll find the friendly, good-value, sunset-view *To Kyma* ouzerí (April–Oct), where the Sudanese proprietress adds a welcome Middle Eastern touch to the broad variety of dishes – most days you'll fight for a table.

Néo has little to recommend it besides a wilderness of derelict stone-built warehouses and mansions down near the river mouth, reminders of the long-vanished leather industry which flourished here during the first half of the twentieth centry. However, if you're staying at Limáni, you'll almost certainly visit one of the three **banks** (with cash dispensers), the **post office** or the **bus stop** on the main lower square. There are virtually no **eateries** except the popular, year-round *Dionysos Psistaria*, on the west side of town at the start of the Marathókambos road.

Western Sámos

Visitors tolerate dull Karlóvassi for the sake of western Sámos's excellent **beaches**. Closest of these is **Potámi**, forty-minutes' walk away via the coast road from Limáni or an hour by a more scenic, high trail from Paleó. This broad arc of sand and pebbles gets crowded at summer weekends, when virtually the entire population of Karlóvassi descends on the place. Near the end of the trail from Paleó stands *To Iliovasilema*, a friendly if oversubscribed *psistariá* with fish and meat; there are also a very few **rooms** signposted locally, and many folk camp rough along the lower reaches of the river which gives the beach its name.

A streamside path leads twenty minutes inland, past the eleventh-century church of **Metamórfosis** – the oldest on Sámos – to a point where the river disappears into a small gorge (a new, guardrailed but still vertiginous stairway takes you up and left here). Otherwise, you must swim and wade 100m in heart-stoppingly cold water through a sequence of fern-tufted rock pools before reaching a low but vigorous waterfall; bring shoes with good tread and perhaps even rope if you want to explore above the first cascade. You probably won't be alone until you dive in, since the canyon is well known to locals and tour agencies. Just above the Metamórfosis church, a clear if precipitous path leads up to a small, contemporaneous **Byzantine fortress**. There's little to see inside other than a subterranean cistern and badly crumbled lower curtain wall, but the views out to sea and up the canyon are terrific, while in October the place is carpeted with pink autumn crocuses.

The coast beyond Potámi ranks among the most beautiful and unspoiled on Sámos; since the early 1980s it has served as a protected refuge for the rare monk seal. The dirt track at the west end of Potámi bay ends after twenty minutes on foot, from which you backtrack 100m or so to find the well-cairned side trail running parallel to the water. After twenty minutes along this you'll arrive at **Mikró Seïtáni**, a small pebble cove guarded by sculpted rock walls. A full hour's walk from the trailhead, through partly fire-damaged olive terraces, brings you to **Megálo Seïtáni**, the island's finest beach, at the mouth of the intimidating Kakopérato gorge. You'll have to bring food and water, though not necessarily a swimsuit – there's no dress code at either of the Seïtáni bays.

Southwestern beach resorts

The first place you reach on the island loop road south of Karlóvassi is **MARATHÓKAMBOS**, a pretty, amphitheatrical village overlooking the eponymous gulf; there's a taverna or two, but no short-term accommodation. Its port, **ÓRMOS MARATHOKÁMBOU**, 18km from Karlóvassi, has recently emerged as a tourist resort, though some character still peeks through in its backstreets. The port has been improved, with kaïkia offering day-trips to Foúrni and the nearby islet of Samiopoúla, while the pedestrianized quay has become the focus of attention, home to several **tavernas** – best of these, by a nod, *Kyra Katína*, with a good range of seafood. Among the few nonpackaged **accommodation** outfits, try *Studios Avra* (☏ 02730/37 221; ❸), unimprovably perched above the jetty.

The beach immediately east from Órmos is hardly the best; for better ones continue 2km west to **VOTSALÁKIA** (officially signposted as "Kámbos"), Sámos's fastest-growing resort, straggling a further 2km behind the island's longest (if not its most beautiful) beach. But for most, Votsalákia is still a vast improvement on the Pythagório area, and the mass of 1437-metre Mount Kérkis overhead rarely fails to impress (see below). As for **accommodation**, Emmanuil Dhespotakis (☎02730/31 258; ❸) has numerous premises towards the quieter, more scenic western end of things. Also in this vicinity is *Loukoullos*, an unusual *kultúra* **taverna** overlooking the sea where all fare is prepared in a wood oven. Other facilities include branches of nearly all the main Vathý travel agencies, offering **vehicle rental** (necessary, as only two daily buses call here) and money exchange.

If Votsalákia doesn't suit, you can continue 3km past to the 600-metre beach of **Psilí Ámmos**, more aesthetic and not to be confused with its namesake beach in the southeast corner of Sámos. The sea shelves very gently here, and cliffs shelter clusters of naturists at the east end. Surprisingly there is still little development: just three small studio complexes in the pines at mid-beach, and two tavernas back up on the road as you approach, either of these fine for a simple lunch. Access to **Limniónas**, a smaller cove 2km further west, passes the *Limnionas Bay Hotel* (☎02730/37 057; ❻), much the highest-standard accommodation locally with its tiered units arrayed around a garden and pool. Yachts and pleasure kaïkia occasionally call at the protected bay, which offers decent swimming away from a rock shelf at mid-strand, especially at the east end where there's a simple **taverna**.

Mount Kérkis and around

Gazing up from a supine seaside position, you may be inspired to climb **Mount Kérkis**. The classic route begins at the west end of the Votsalákia strip, along the bumpy jeep track leading inland towards Evangelistrías convent. After thirty minutes on the track system, through fire-damaged olive groves and past charcoal pits (a major local industry), the path begins, more or less following power lines up to the convent. A friendly nun may proffer an oúzo in welcome and point you up the paint-marked trail, continuing even more steeply up to the peak. The views are tremendous, though the climb itself is humdrum once you're out of the trees. About an hour before the top there's a chapel with an attached cottage for sheltering in emergencies, and just beyond, a welcome spring. All told, it's a seven-hour outing from Votsalákia and back, not counting rest stops.

Less ambitious walkers might want to circle the flanks of the mountain, first by vehicle and then by foot. The road beyond Limniónas to Kallithéa and Dhrakéï, truly back-of-beyond villages with views across to Ikaría, is paved most of the way to Dhrakéï, making it possible to venture out here on an ordinary motorbike. The bus service is better during the school year, when a vehicle leaves Karlóvassi (Mon–Fri 1pm) bound for these remote spots; during summer it only operates two days a week at best (typically Mon & Fri).

From **DHRAKÉÏ**, the end of the line with just a pair of very simple kafenía to its credit, a lovely trail, minimally damaged by a track, descends ninety minutes through forest to Megálo Seïtáni, from where it's easy enough to continue on to Karlóvassi within another two-and-a-half hours. People attempting to reverse this itinerary often discover to their cost that the bus (if any) returns from Dhrakéï early in the day, at about 2.30pm, compelling them to stay at one of two unofficial **rooms** establishments (summer only) in Dhrakéi, and dine at one of four taverna-kafenía. In **KALLITHÉA**, there's only a simple *psistariá* on the square. From Kallithéa, a newer track (from beside the cemetery) and an older trail both lead up within 45 minutes to a spring, rural chapel and plane tree on the west flank of Kérkis, with path-only continuation for another thirty minutes to a pair of cave-churches. **Panayía Makriní** stands detached at the mouth of a high, wide but shallow grotto, whose balcony affords terrific views of Sámos's west tip. By contrast, **Ayía Triádha**, a ten-minute scramble overhead, has most of its structure made up of cave wall; just adjacent, another long, narrow, volcanic cavern can be explored with a torch some hundred metres into the mountain.

After these subterranean exertions, the closest spot for a swim is **Vársamo** (Válsamo) cove, 4km below Kallithéa and reached via a well-signposted dirt road. The beach here consists of multicoloured volcanic pebbles, with two caves to shelter in and a single very friendly **taverna** just inland, run by three generations of women.

Ikaría

Ikaría, a narrow, windswept landmass between Sámos and Mýkonos, is little visited and invariably underestimated. The name supposedly derives from the legendary Icarus, who fell into the sea just offshore after the wax bindings on his wings melted. For years the only substantial tourism was generated by a few **hot springs** on the south coast, some reputed to cure rheumatism and arthritis, some to make women fertile, though others are so highly radioactive that they've been closed for decades.

Ikaría, along with Thessaly on the mainland and Lésvos, has traditionally been one of the Greek Left's strongholds. This tendency dates from the long decades of right-wing domination in Greece, when (as in past ages) the island was used as a place of **exile** for political dissidents. Apparently the strategy backfired, with the Communist transportees favourably impressing and proselytizing their hosts; at the same time, many Ikarians emigrated to North America, and ironically their regular capitalist remittances help keep the island going. It can be a bizarre experience to be treated to a monologue on the evils of US imperialism, delivered by a retiree in perfect Alabama English. Of late, the Ikarians tend to embrace any vaguely Left cause; posters urge you variously to attend rallies on behalf of Turkish political prisoners or contribute to funding a Zapatista teacher-training school in Chiapas. Athens has historically reacted to this contrarian stance with long periods of punitive neglect, which has only made the islanders even more profoundly self-sufficient and idiosyncratic, and supportive (or at least tolerant) of the same in others. Local pride dictates that outside opinion matters not a bit, and until very recently Ikarians seemed to have little idea what "modern tourists" expected. A lack of obsequiousness, and a studied eccentricity, are often mistaken for hostility.

These are not the only Ikarian quirks, and for many the place is an acquired taste, contrasting strongly (for better or worse) with Sámos. Except for forested portions in the northwest (now much fire-denuded near the shore to clear land for hotels), it's not a strikingly beautiful island, with most of the terrain consisting of scrub-covered schist put to good use as building material. The mostly desolate south coast is overawed by steep cliffs, while the north face is less sheer but nonetheless furrowed by deep canyons creating hairpin bends extreme even by Greek-island standards. Neither are there many postcard-picturesque villages, since the rural schist-roofed houses are generally scattered so as to be next to their famous apricot orchards, vineyards and fields.

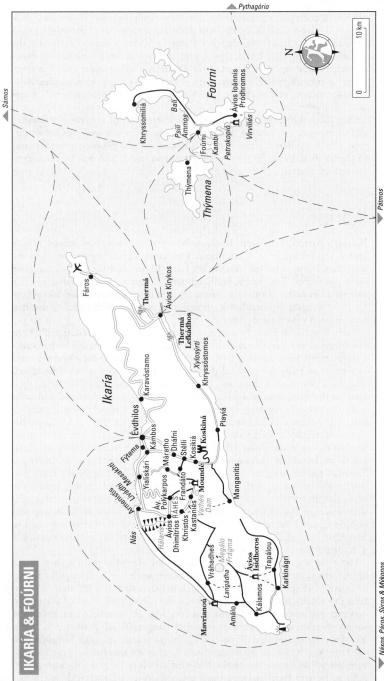

IKARÍA & FOÚRNI

Until the mid-1990s, the Ikarians resisted most attempts to develop their island for conventional tourism; charter flights still don't land here, as the northeastern airport can't accommodate jets. Since then, however, there's been a slow but steady increase in the quantity and quality of tourist facilities in and around Armenistís, the only resort of consequence.

Áyios Kírykos and around

Passing ferries on the Páros–Náxos–Foúrni–Dodecanese line call at the south-coast port and capital of **ÁYIOS KÍRYKOS**, about 1km southwest of the island's main thermal resort. Because of the spa trade, beds are at a premium in town; arriving in the evening from Sámos, accept any reasonable offers of rooms at the jetty, or – if in a group – proposals of a taxi ride to the north coast, which shouldn't cost more than €22 per vehicle to Armenistís. A cream-and-green **bus** sets out across the island from the main square (summer Mon–Fri only at noon) to Évdhilos, usually changing vehicles there at 1.30pm, for the onward trip to Armenistís.

The baths (daily 8am–1pm) in **Thérma** are rather old-fashioned stone tubs, with preference given to those under medical care. A better bet for a less formal soak are the more natural, shoreline hot springs at **Thérma Lefkádhos**, 3km southwest of Áyios Kírykos, below a cluster of villas. Here the seaside spa is derelict, leaving the water to boil up right in the shallows, mixing with the sea between giant volcanic boulders to a pleasant temperature.

A more conventional beach – the largest on the south coast – is found at **Fáros**, 10km northeast of Áyios Kírykos along a good paved road (which also serves the airport). A considerable colony of summer cottages shelters under tamarisks fringing the mixed sand-and-gravel strand, with a reefy zone to cross before deep water; this rather end-of-the-world place looks across to Foúrni and Thýmena, whose beaches (and landscape) it strongly resembles. But the best reason to make the trip out is an excellent, inexpensive and quick-serving **fish taverna**, *Leonidas*, with grilled or fried seafood plus bulk wine (excellent, as it usually is on Ikaría), better than anything in Áyios itself and accordingly popular.

Practicalities

Hydrofoils, the small Miniotis Lines ferries and kaïkia for Foúrni use the small east jetty; large ferries and catamarans dock at the main west pier. There are several **hotels**, such as the *Isabella* (☏02750/22 839; ❷–❸) above the National Bank, or the friendly, basic but spotless *Akti* (☏02750/22 694; ❶–❸), on a knoll east of the hydrofoil and kaïki quay, with views of Foúrni from the garden; both have rooms with and without bathrooms. Otherwise, **pensions** and **rooms** are not especially cheap. Directly behind the base of the ferry jetty and a little to the west there's the well-appointed *Pension Maria-Elena* (☏02750/22 835, Ⓕ22 223; ❸), with sea views. All in a row to the east and suffering some noise from the several kafenía and snack bars below are the *Pension Ikaria* (☏02750/22 804; ❷), the studios above the *Snack Bar Dedalos* (☏02750/22 276; ❸) and the clean *dhomátia* run by Ioannis Proestos (☏02750/23 176; ❷).

Eating out, you've even less choice than in lodging. It's best to give the obvious quayside eateries a miss in favour of the grilled dishes served up at the *Estiatorio Tzívaeri*, just inland from Ioannis Proestos's rooms, or *Iy Klimataria* just around the corner for less distinguished but year-round *mayireftá*. The front is more glitzy, with *Casino* the last remaining traditional kafenío; for further entertainment there's a **summer cinema**, the Rex, with first-run fare. Three **banks** with cash dispensers, a **post office** on the road out of town and three ferry/hydrofoil **agents** round up the list of essentials. You can **rent** motorbikes and cars here, too, but both are typically cheaper in Armenistís.

Évdhilos and around

The twisting, 41-kilometre road from Áyios Kírykos to Évdhilos is one of the most hair-raising on any Greek island (especially as a taxi passenger), and the long ridge extending the length of Ikaría often wears a streamer of cloud, even when the rest of the Aegean is clear. Karavóstamo, with its tiny, scruffy port, is the first substantial north-coast place, beyond which a series of three beaches leads up to **ÉVDHILOS**. Although this is the island's second town and a daily ferry stop on the Sámos–Mýkonos–Sýros line, it's far less equipped to deal with visitors than Áyios Kírykos. Évdhilos offers just two **hotels** – the *Evdoxia* on the slope southwest of the harbour (☎02750/31 502; ⑤) and the low-lying *Atheras* (☎02750/31 434, ℗31 926; ④) with a small pool – plus a few **rooms**, the best of which are run by Apostolos Stenos (☎02750/31 365; ①) just west of town. A **post office** up towards the *Evdoxia*, a pair of **cashpoints**, and two good **beaches** just to the east, are also worth knowing about, though the nearer beach will be blighted in the coming years by a new, much-needed harbour jetty. Among several waterfront **restaurants**, the wood-signed "*Kafestiatório*" between *O Flisvos* and the Blue Nice **boat-ticket agency** is the most reliable and reasonable option, but for more interesting fare head 1km west of the harbour to **Fýtema** hamlet, where just on the roadside *To Inomayerio tis Popis,* alias *To Fytema* (Easter–Sept), has lots of options for vegetarians, excellent local wine, low prices and pleasant terrace seating, though portions are on the small side.

KÁMBOS, 1.5km west of Fýtema, offers a small hilltop museum with finds from nearby **ancient Oinoe**; the twelfth-century church of Ayía Iríni lies just below, with the remains of a fourth-century Byzantine basilica serving as the entry courtyard. Lower down still are the sparse ruins of a Byzantine palace (just above the road) used to house exiled nobles, as well as a 250-metre-long sandy beach with a musical drinks *kantína*. *Rooms Dhionysos* are available from the store run by Vassilis Kambouris (☎02750/31 300 or 31 688; ②), who also acts as the unofficial and enthusiastic tourism officer for this part of Ikaría, keeping the keys for the church and museum.

By following the road heading inland from the large church in Évdhilos, you can also visit the Byzantine **castle of Koskiná** (Nikariás), just over 15km south. The road signposted for Manganítis is paved through Kosikiá, just over 9km away, and for 2km more to the marked side track. You can get a bike or jeep along this to within a short walk of the tenth-century castle, perched on a distinctive conical hill, with an arched gateway and a fine vaulted chapel.

Beyond this turning, the road creeps over the island watershed and drops precipitously in hairpins towards the south coast; most of this is paved, and with your own vehicle offers an alternative (and much less curvy) way back to Áyios Kírykos in much the same time as via Karavóstomo.

Armenistís and around

Most people carry on to **ARMENISTÍS**, 57km from Áyios Kírykos, and with good reason: this little resort lies below Ikaría's finest (if much diminished) forest, with two enormous, sandy beaches battered by near-constant surf – **Livádhi** and **Mesakhtí** – five- and fifteen-minutes' walk to the east respectively. The waves, which attract Athenian surfers, are complicated by strong lateral currents (as signs warn), and regular summer drownings have prompted the institution of that Greek rarity, lifeguard service. Armenistís itself is spectacularly set, looking

10

northeast along the length of Ikaría towards sun- and moonrise, with Mount Kérkis on Sámos closing off the horizon on a clear day. A dwindling proportion of older, schist-roofed buildings, plus fishing boats hauled up in a sandy cove, lend Armenistís the air of a Cornish fishing village. Despite gradual growth it remains a manageable place, reminiscent of similar youth-oriented, slightly "alternative" spots in southern Crete, though gentrification (and a strong package presence) has definitely set in, and the islanders' tolerance doesn't extend to nude bathing. The long-running, semi-official campsite behind Livádhi beach closed in 2001 – a sign of the times – and probably won't reopen; a few freelance tents still sprout in the rivermouth greenery behind Mesakthí. Several "music bars", often with live Greek gigs, operate seasonally behind Livádhi and at the quay's north end, but for most visitors **nightlife** takes the form of extended sessions in the tavernas and cafés overlooking the anchorage, or the *zaharoplastía* (especially *En Plo*) at the village entrance.

Practicalities

There are easily a score of rooms establishments in the Armenistís area, as well as four bona fide **hotels**. Among the latter, the 1999-built *Erofili Beach*, right at the entrance to "town" (☎02750/71 058, ℱ71 483, ⓦwww.erofili.gr; ⑥) is considered the best on the island and has a small pool perched dramatically over Livádhi beach. Runners-up include the *Messakhti Village* complex (☎02750/71 331, ℱ71 330, ⓦwww.messakti-village.gr; ⑥) just above Mesakhtí beach, with a larger pool, its common areas and private terraces making up for the slightly minimalist self-catering units suitable for families of three to six, or – on the western edge of Armenistís – the *Daidalos* (☎02750/71 390, ℱ71 393, ⓔdaidalos@aegean-exodus.gr; ⑤), the less impersonal and less package-dominated of two adjacent hotels, with another eyrie-pool, unusually appointed rooms and a shady breakfast terrace. If your budget doesn't run to the *Erofili Beach*, the adjacent *Kirki Rooms* (☎02750/71 254, ℱ71 083; ②) are spartan but en suite, with large private balconies and sea views; on the opposite side of the road, but at the top of the hill, the similar-decor *Armena Inn* (☎02750/71 320; ③) has private parking, seclusion, unobstructed views and cooking facilities in the rooms. Along the shore lane, the *Paskhalia* **rooms** (☎0275/71 302 or 010/24 71 411 in winter; ①) are on the small side but are en suite and good value, with great views east, while at the far end of Livádhi beach, the *Atsahas Apartments* (☎ & ℱ 02750/71 226; ③) offer the best standard and setting outside of the hotels.

Discounting the *zaharoplastía* and *souvláki* stalls (a pair each), there are five full-service **tavernas** in Armenistís, of which three have a consistently good reputation. *Dhelfíni*, its terrace hovering right above the fishing cove, is the cheap-and-cheerful favourite – come early or very late for a table, and a mix of grills or *mayireftá*. *Paskhalia* (aka *Vlahos* after the helpful managing family) also serves similar fare at its seaview terrace up the hill, and is the most reliable venue for both breakfast and off-season travellers, open until mid-October. Down on the quay itself, *Symposio* is pricier but well worth it for its creative recipes and rich ingredients reflecting the German co-management and chef. Further afield, the *Atsahas*, attached to the namesake apartments, is pretty good as a beach taverna, with generous portions but occasionally undercooked and over-oiled fare. Just east of Mesakthí in the fishing settlement of **Yialiskári**, looking out past pines to a picturesque church on the jetty, there's another cluster of tavernas overlooking the boat-launching slips, of which *Tramountana* and *Kelari* are the most popular, the former purveying superb parrotfish fry-ups if you strike lucky. Yialiskári is also home to the area's only **internet café**, *Ic@rian-Sea*.

There are now at least four **scooter/mountain-bike rental** agencies in Armenistís; among a like number of **car-rental** outlets, Aventura (☎02750/71 117) is the most prominent, with a branch in Évdhilos which could be handy for ferry departures at an ungodly hour (typically 4am), when the buses aren't yet running. Indeed getting away when you need to is the main drawback to staying in Armenistís, since both taxis and buses can be elusive, though predictability has improved slightly over the years. Theoretically, **buses** head for Évdhilos three times daily mid-June to mid-September, fairly well spaced (typically 7.15am, noon & 7pm, returning an hour or so later) and designed to coincide with ferries; Áyios Kírykos has only one through service year-round at 7.15am, though this can be full with school kids in term-time. If you've a ferry to catch, it's far easier on the nerves to prebook a **taxi**: ring Kostas Stroupas (☎02750/41 132), or Yiannis Tsantiris (☎02750/41 322).

Ráhes

Armenistís is actually the shore annexe of four inland hamlets – Áyios Dhimítrios, Áyios Polýkarpos, Kastaniés and Khristós – collectively known as **RÁHES**. Despite the modern, mostly paved access roads through the pines (trails shortcut them), the settlements retain a certain Shangri-La quality, with the older residents speaking a positively Homeric dialect. On an island not short of foibles, Khristós (Khristós Rahón in full) is particularly strange inasmuch as the locals sleep until 11am or so, shop and educate their kids until about 4pm, then have another nap until 9pm, whereupon they rise and spend the entire night shopping, eating and drinking until almost dawn. In fact most of the villages west of Évdhilos adhere to this schedule, defying central government efforts to bring them in line with the rest of Greece.

Near the pedestrianized *agorá* of Khristós, paved in schist and studded with gateways fashioned from the same rock, there's a **post office** and a **hotel/restaurant** (☎02750/71 269; ❸), but in accordance with the above diurnal schedule, lunchtime can offer pretty slim pickings. The most reliable venue (strictly after 1pm) are the unmarked premises of Vassilis Yiakas, at the far southeast end of the pedestrian way – you'll know it from the enormous Victrola and the bare wood floors. The slightly spaced-out demeanour of those serving – plus numbers of old boys shambling around in dirty clothes, with their flies unzipped – may be attributable to overindulgence in the excellent home-brewed **wine** which everyone west of Évdhilos makes. The local festival is August 6, though better ones take place further southwest in the woods at the Langádha valley (August 14–15) or at the Áyios Isídhoros monastery (May 14).

Since the early 1990s, **walking** between Ráhes and the coastal resorts has rocketed in popularity, and there are finally locally produced, accurate if somewhat chatty map-guides widely available. The black-and-white *Road & Hiking Map of Western Ikaria* (€1.20) shows most asphalt roads, tracks and trails in the west-centre of the island; the more closely focused, colour *Round of Rahes on Foot* (€3) details a loop hike taking in the best the Ráhes villages have to offer. The route sticks mostly to surviving paths, and is well marked; the authors suggest a full day for the circuit, with ample rests, though total walking time won't be more than six hours. More advanced outings involve descending the Hálaris canyon, with its historic bridge, to Nás, or crossing the island to Manganítis via Ráhes.

Nás

By tacit consent, Greek or foreign hippies and beachside naturists have been allowed to shift 3km west of Armenistís by paved road to **Nás**, a tree-clogged river canyon ending in a small but deceptively sheltered sand-and-pebble beach. This little bay is almost completely enclosed by weirdly sculpted rock formations, but for the same reasons as at Mesakhtí it's unwise to swim outside the cove's natural limits. The crumbling foundations of the fifth-century temple of **Artemis Tavropoleio** (Patroness of Bulls) overlook the permanent deep pool at the mouth of the river. If you continue inland along this past colonies of freelance campers defying prohibition signs, you'll find secluded rock pools for freshwater dips. Back at the top of the stairs leading down to the beach from the road are six tavernas, most of them offering rooms. Among the **tavernas**, *O Nas* doesn't abuse its prime position, operating Easter to October, with a good range of lunchtime *mayireftá*; among **rooms**, the *Artemis* (☎02750/71 485; ❸) overlooks the river canyon, while *Thea* (☎02750/71 491; ❸) faces out to sea, both places halving the rates out of season.

Satellite islands: Thýmena and Foúrni

The straits between Sámos and Ikaría are speckled with a mini-archipelago of three islets, of which the inhabited ones are Thýmena and Foúrni. More westerly **Thýmena** has one tiny hillside settlement; a regular kaïki calls at the quay below on its way between Ikaría and Foúrni, but there are no tourist facilities, and casual visits are explicitly discouraged. Foúrni is home to a huge fishing fleet and one of the more thriving boatyards in the Aegean; thanks to these, and the improvement of the jetty to receive car ferries, its population is stable, unlike so many small Greek islands. The islets were once the lair of Maltese pirates, and indeed many of the islanders have a distinctly North African appearance.

The aforementioned **kaïki** leaves Ikaría at about 1pm several days weekly, stays overnight at Foúrni and returns the next morning; another twice-weekly kaïki from Karlóvassi, and the larger car ferries which appear every few days, are likewise not tourist excursion boats but exist for the benefit of the islanders. The only practical way to visit Foúrni on a day-trip is by using the tourist kaïki *Ayios Nikolaos*, which leaves Áyios Kírykos daily in season at 10am, and returns from Foúrni at 5pm, or on one of the summer morning **hydrofoils** out of Sámos (Vathý or Pythagório).

Foúrni

Apart from the remote hamlet of **Khryssomiliá** in the north, where the island's longest (and often roughest) road goes, most of Foúrni's inhabitants are concentrated in the **port** and Kambí hamlet just to the south. The harbour community is larger than it seems from the sea, with a friendly ambience reminiscent of 1970s Greece. Among several **rooms** establishments, the most popular are the various premises run by Manolis and Patra Markakis (☎02750/51 268), immediately to your left as you disembark; there are simple rooms, some with balconies (❶), and superb hilltop studios (❷). If they're full you can head inland to the modern block of Evtyhia Amoryianou (☎02750/51 364; ❶), whose father Nikos Kondylas meets all boats and is a mine of information about the island.

There are two full-service waterfront **tavernas**: local favourite *Rementzo*, better known as *Nikos'*, where, if you're lucky, the local *astakós* or Aegean lobster may be on the menu until mid-August; or the cheaper, less polished *Miltos*, also with good seafood. For breakfast and desserts, repair to the tamarisk terrace at the Markakis family's *To Arhondiko tis Kyras Kokonas*, under their inn. There's surprisingly lively **nightlife** at a half-dozen music bars, clubs and ouzerís, often until 5am.

The central "high street", fieldstoned and mulberry-shaded, ends well inland at a little platía with more traditional kafenía under each of two plane trees;

between them stands a Hellenistic sarcophagus found in a nearby field, and overhead is a conical hill, site of the ancient acropolis. There's a **post office**, plus several surprisingly well-stocked shops, but at the time of writing no functioning cash machine or other money-changing facilities, so come prepared.

A fifteen-minute trail-walk south from the school, skirting the cemetery and then slipping over the windmill ridge, brings you to **KAMBÍ**, a scattered community overlooking a pair of sandy, tamarisk-shaded coves which you may share with chickens and hauled-up fishing boats. There are two cheap, comparable and sustaining **tavernas**: the *Kambi* with tables on the sand, and *O Yiorgos* clinging to the side of a valley inland. A path continues to the next bay south which, like Kambí cove, is a preferred anchorage for wandering yachts.

Heading north from the harbour via steps, then a trail, you'll find another **beach**: **Psilí Ámmos** in front of a derelict fish-processing plant, with shade at one end. At the extreme north of the island, remote **KHRYSSOMILIÁ** is still best approached by the taxi-boat *Evangelistria* rather than the atrocious eighteen-kilometre road. The village, split into a shore district and a hillside settlement, has a decent beach flanked by better but less accessible ones. Simple **rooms** and **meals** can be arranged on the spot, though the locals can be less than forthcoming with outsiders. The hamlet and monastery of **Áyios Ioánnis Pródhromos** in the far south of Foúrni is probably a better day-trip target on foot, taxi-boat or by scooter (available for rent), with some good, secluded beaches just below.

Híos

"Craggy Híos", as **Homer** aptly described his putative birthplace, has a turbulent history and a strong identity. It has always been relatively prosperous: in medieval times through the export of mastic **resin** – a trade controlled by Genoese overlords between 1346 and 1566 – and later by the **Ottomans**, who dubbed the place Sakız Adası ("Resin Island"). Since union with Greece in 1912, several shipping dynasties have emerged here, continuing the pattern of wealth. Participation in the maritime way of life is widespread, with someone in almost every family spending time in the merchant navy.

The more powerful ship-owning families and the military authorities did not encourage tourism until the late 1980s, but the worldwide shipping crisis and the saturation of other, more obviously "marketable" islands eroded their resistance. Increasing numbers of foreigners are discovering a Híos beyond its rather daunting port capital: fascinating villages, important Byzantine monuments and a respectable, if remote, complement of beaches. While unlikely ever to be dominated by tourism, the local scene has a distinctly modern flavour – courtesy of numerous returned Greek-Americans and Greek–Canadians – and English is widely spoken.

Unfortunately, the island has suffered more than its fair share of **catastrophes** during the past two centuries. The Turks perpetrated their most infamous, if not their worst, anti-revolutionary atrocity here in March 1822, massacring 30,000 Hiots and enslaving or exiling even more. In 1881, much of Híos was destroyed by a violent **earthquake**, and throughout the 1980s the natural beauty of the island was markedly diminished by devastating forest fires, compounding the effect of generations of tree-felling by boat-builders. Nearly two-thirds of the majestic pines are now gone, with substantial patches of woods persisting only in the far northeast and the centre of Híos.

In 1988 the first charters from northern Europe were instituted, signalling potentially momentous changes for the island. But there are still fewer than four thousand guest beds on Híos, the vast majority of them in the capital or the nearby beach resorts of Karfás and Ayía Ermióni. Further expansion, however, is hampered by the lack of direct flights from most countries (including Britain), and the refusal of property owners to part with land for the extension of the airport runway.

Híos Town

HÍOS, the harbour and main town, will come as a shock after modest island capitals elsewhere; it's a bustling, concrete-laced commercial centre, with little predating the 1881 quake. Yet in many ways it is the most satisfactory of the east Aegean ports; time spent exploring is rewarded with a large and fascinating marketplace, several museums and some good, authentic tavernas. Although it's a sprawling town of about 30,000, most things of interest to visitors lie within a hundred or so metres of the water, fringed by Leofóros Egéou.

South and east of the main platía, officially Plastíra but known universally as Vounakíou, extends the marvellously lively tradesmen's **bazaar**, where you can find everything from parrots to cast-iron woodstoves. Opposite the Vounakíou **taxi rank**, the grandiosely titled "**Byzantine Museum**", occupying the old **Mecidiye Mosque** (Tues–Sun 10am–1pm; free), is little more than an archeological warehouse, with Turkish, Jewish and Armenian marble gravestones in the courtyard testifying to the island's varied population in past centuries.

Until the 1881 earthquake, the Byzantine–Genoese **Kástro** was completely intact; thereafter developers razed the seaward walls, filled in much of the moat to the south and made a fortune selling off the real estate thus created around present-day Platía Vounakíou. Today the most satisfying entry to the citadel is via Porta Maggiora behind the town hall. The top floor of a medieval mansion just inside is home to the **Justiniani Museum** (Tues–Sun 9am–3pm, in summer may open daily 9am–7pm; €1.50, Sun €0.90), with a satisfying (and periodically changing) collection of unusual icons and mosaics rescued from local church-

HÍOS TOWN

0 ——— 100 m

Ⓐ (700m), ▲ Volissós & Vrondádhos

◄ Néa Moní

KÁSTRO

Baynakli Mosque Ⓑ

ⒸⒸ

ANDHIAKOS

MARTYROU

HIONIS

Dry Moat

ÁYIO YERÍOU

PROKIOU

Port Police

Ⓒ Miniotis Ferry Berth

NEORION

Turkish Cemetery

Justiniani Museum

Hydrofoil Berth

Pireás-Lésvos-Sámos Ferry Berth

Wholesale Fish Market

Central Park

Town Hall

KÁSTRO

DHIMOKRATIAS

Blue (City) Bus Station

Cine Kipos

POLYTEKHNIOU

Porta Maggiora

LADHIS

Inoússes Kaïki

Ferry to Turkey

Customs & Passport Control

OmirioCentre

Byzantine Museum Ⓜ

Taxi Rank

PLATIA VOUNAKÍOU

ⓘ

KANARI

ⒹⒹ 2

Day Excursion Boats

N

KTEL Bus Station

BAZAAR

SKANAVI

DHAMALA

VOUPALOU

ROÏ DHOU

SGOUTA

KALOPLITOU

DHIMOYERONDIAS

E. ARGENTI

PILOTARIAS

Ⓔ

Olympic Airways

KANALA

LEOFÓROS EGÉOU

OMIROU

RODHOKANAKI

RESTAURANTS

Ta Dhyo Adherfia | I
O Hotzas | K
Ino. Iakovos | B
Kronos | F
Ta Mylarakia | A
Taverna tou Tassou | J
Theodosiou | C

PSIHARI

F. ARYENDI

Ⓕ Cathedral ✝

VENIZELOU

N. VAMVA

KORAÏ

Maritime Museum

STEFANOU TSOURI

Argenti Museum

Cine Diana

Miniotis Ferry Berths

CAFÉS & BARS

Enter | H
Ivískos | D
To Loukoumi | E
Metropol | G

LEOFÓROS EGÉOU

ⒼⒼ Ⓗ

SOURI

MIHAIL

PORFIRA

LIVANOU

ⓘ

Ⓖ

E. HANDHRI

Ⓖ

KOKALLI

STAVROU LIVANOU

DELAGRAMMATIKA

KOUNDOURIOTOU

FAVIÉROU

DHAMIANOU

PIPINOU

MOUSSON

MIHALON

Archeological Museum

▼ Ⓚ (100m)   ▼ Mastic Villages   Airport & Karfás ▼

ACCOMMODATION

Alex Rooms | 5
Fedra | 4
Kyma | 7
Pelineon Rooms | 3
Rodhon | 1
Villa Maro | 2
Hios Rooms | 6

es. The small dungeon adjacent briefly held 75 Hiot hostages before their execution by the Ottomans in 1822. The old residential quarter inside the surviving castle walls, formerly the Muslim and Jewish neighbourhoods, is well worth a wander; among the wood and plaster houses you'll find assorted Ottoman monuments in various states of decay: a Muslim cemetery, a small minaretless mosque, a ruined *hamam* (Turkish bath) and several inscribed fountains.

Further afield, three other museums beckon. The **Maritime Museum** at Stefánou Tsoúri 20 (Mon–Sat 10am–1pm; free) consists principally of model ships and oil paintings of various craft, Greek and foreign, all rather overshadowed by the mansion containing them. In the foyer are enshrined the knife and glass-globe grenade of Admiral Kanaris, who partly avenged the 1822 massacre by ramming and sinking the Ottoman fleet's flagship. In the centre of town, the **Argenti Folklore Museum** (Mon–Thurs 8am–2pm, Fri 8am–2pm & 5–7.30pm, Sat 8am–12.30pm; €1.50), on the top floor of the Koraï Library at Koraï 2, features ponderous genealogical portraits of the endowing family, an adjoining wing of costumes and rural impedimenta, plus multiple replicas of Delacroix's *Massacre at Híos*, a painting which did much to arouse sympathy for the cause of Greek independence.

The **Archeological Museum** on Mihálon (June–Sept daily 8am–7pm; Oct–May Tues–Sun 8am–2.30pm; €1.50) finally reopened in late 1999 after an eight-year overhaul. The wide-ranging and well-lit collection, arranged both thematically and chronologically from Neolithic to Roman times, demands at least an hour or so of one's attention. Highlights include limestone column bases from the Apollo temple at Faná in the shape of lion's claws; numerous statuettes and reliefs of Cybele (the Asiatic goddess was especially honoured here); Archaic faïence miniatures from Emborió in the shape of a cat, a hawk and a flautist; terracottas from various eras of a dwarf riding a boar; and figurines (some with articulated limbs) of *hierodouloi* or sacred prostitutes, presumably from an Aphrodite shrine. Most famous of all is an inscribed edict of Alexander the Great from 322 BC, commanding local political changes and setting out relations between himself and the Hiots.

Arrival, information and services

Ferries large and small, plus the infrequent **hydrofoil**, dock at various points as shown on the town map. The **airport** lies 4km south along the coast at Kondári, a €3.50 taxi-ride away; otherwise any blue urban bus labelled "Kondári Karfás" departing from the terminal on the north side of the park passes the airport gate, opposite which is a conspicuous stop with shelter. **Ferry** agents cluster to either side of the customs building, towards the north end of the waterfront Egéou and its continuation Neoríon: NEL (℡02710/23 971) is a few paces south of customs, while Miniotis Lines, at Neoríon 21–23 (℡02710/24 670) or Egéou 11 (℡02710/21 463), operates small, slow ferries to many neighbouring islands. Hiona Travel at Neoríon 13 is the central agent for Hellas Ferries, though Hellas (and the few weekly hydrofoils to Lésvos or Sámos, plus air tickets) are also handled by competent Serafim Travel at Kanári 24 (℡02710/23 558). The Turkish evening ferry to Çeşme as well as the most regular boat to Inoússes, is represented by Faros Travel at Egéou 18 (℡02710/27 240). The helpful municipal **tourist office** (May–Sept daily 7am–10pm; Oct–April Mon–Fri 7am–3pm; ℡02710/44 389) is at Kanári 18, near the Alpha Bank.

The standard green-and-cream **KTEL buses** leave from a parking area beside their ticket office on the south side of the park, behind the Omirio Cultural Centre. While services to the south of Híos are adequate, those to the centre and northwest of the island are almost nonexistent, and to explore there you'll need to rent a powerful **motorbike** or a car, or share a **taxi** (which are bright red here, not grey as in most of Greece). Three independent or small-chain **car-rental** agencies sit in a row at Evyenías Handhrí 5–7, behind the eyesore *Chandris Hotel*; of these, Vassilakis/Reliable Rent a Car (☎02710/29 300 or 094/4334898), with a branch at Mégas Limniónas, is particularly recommended. The **post office** is on Omírou, while numerous **banks** all have cash dispensers. A final Hiot idiosyncrasy is afternoon **shopping hours** limited to Monday and Thursday in summer.

Accommodation

Híos Town has a fair bit of affordable **accommodation**, rarely completely full. Most places line the water or the perpendicular alleys and parallel streets behind, and almost all are plagued by traffic noise to some degree – listed are the more peaceful establishments.

Alex Rooms, Mihaïl Livanoú 29 ☎02710/26 054. The friendly proprietor often meets late-arriving ferries; otherwise ring the bell. There's a roof garden above the well-furnished rooms, some en-suite. ❶

Fedra, Mihaïl Livanoú 13 ☎02710/41 130, ⓕ41 128. Well-appointed pension in an old mansion, with stone arches in the downstairs winter bar; in summer the bar operates outside, so ask for a rear room to avoid nocturnal noise. ❹

Hios Rooms, Kokáli 1, cnr Egéou ☎02710/20 198 or 097/2833841. Wood-floored, high-ceilinged rooms, mostly with shared bath but relatively quiet for a seafront location, lovingly restored by proprietors Don (New Zealander) and Dina (Greek), who live on-site. ❶

Kyma, east end of Evyenías Handhrí ☎02710/44 500, ⓕ44 600, ⓦhttp://chios.proodos.gr/kyma. En-suite hotel rooms in a Neoclassical mansion or a modern extension, with TV, huge terraces on the sea-facing side and jacuzzis in some rooms. Splendid service and big breakfasts really make

the place. The old wing saw a critical moment in modern Greek history in September 1922, when Colonel Nikolaos Plastiras commandeered it as his HQ after the Greek defeat in Asia Minor, and announced the deposition of King Constantine I. ❺ Aug, ❸ otherwise.

Pelineon Rooms, Omírou 9, cnr Egéou ☎02710/28 030. Choose between light, airy and noisy seaview rooms (most en suite), or quiet, pokey ones at the back, though these are affected by cooking fumes from the *souvláki* bar below. ❷

Rodhon, Platéon 10 ☎02710/24 335. The owners can be awkward, and the rooms are not en suite, but it's just about the only place inside the *kástro*, and pretty quiet. ❸

Villa Maro, Roïdhou 15 ☎02710/27 003. Modern pension tucked onto a tiny plaza just inland from the water; rear rooms unfortunately overlook the public toilets, but all are en-suite, tile-floored and well equipped, plus there's a pleasant breakfast/snack bar on the ground floor. ❹

Eating

Eating out in Híos Town can be more pleasurable than the fast-food joints, touristy tavernas and multiple *barákia* on the waterfront (and American-style pizza parlours inland) would suggest; it is also usually a lot cheaper than on neighbouring Sámos or Lésvos.

Ta Dhyo Adherfia, cnr Mihalón and Mihaïl Livanoú. No-nonsense, competent *mayireftá* and grills, served in the garden during warmer months. Open Sun too.

O Hotzas, Yeoryíou Kondhýli 3, cnr Stefánou Tsoúri, off map. Oldest (and arguably best) taverna in town, with chef Ioannis Linos, the fourth generation of his family, presiding. Menu varies seasonally, but expect a mix of vegetarian dishes (*mavromátika*, cauliflower, stuffed red peppers), and sausages, baby fish and *mydhopílafo* (rice and mussels) washed down by own-brand oúzo or retsina. Allow €12 each. Dinner only, garden in summer; closed Sun.

Inomayerio Iakovos, Ayíou Yeoryíou Frouríou 20, Kástro. A good balance of well-executed fishy dishes, grilled titbits, cheese-based recipes and vegetables; local white bulk wine or oúzo. Atmospheric garden seating in a vine-cloaked ruin opposite, or inside during winter. Budget €10–12 each. Closed Sun, and no lunch Sept–June.

Kronos, Filíppou Aryéndi 2, cnr Aplotariás. The island's best, and own-made ice cream, purveyed since 1929; limited seating or take away.

Ta Mylarakia, by three restored windmills in Tambákika district, on the road to Vrondádhos (☎02710/40 412). A large, well-priced seafood selection, every kind of Hiot oúzo and limited waterside seating make reservations advisable in summer. Dinner all year, lunch also Oct–April.

Tavernaki tou Tassou Stávrou Livanoú 8, Bella Vista district. Superb all-rounder with creative salads, better-than-average bean dishes, dolmádhes, snails, properly done chips, and a strong line in seafood; a bit pricier than usual – allow €15 each – but Tassos' and Tsambika's cooking is worth it.

Good barrel wine; open lunch and supper most of the year, with seaview garden seating during warmer months.

Theodhosiou Ouzeri Neoríon 33. The genuine article, with a large, reasonable menu, moved in 2001 to large, quieter, arcaded premises from its old spot opposite the main ferry berth. Dinner only; closed Sun.

Drinking, nightlife and entertainment

The 1400 or so students at the local technical schools and economics/business management faculties of the University of the Aegean help keep things lively, especially along the portion of the waterfront between the two "kinks" in Egéou.

Cine Kipos in central park from June to mid-Sept only. Quality/art-house first-run fare, two screenings nightly; watch for flyers around town or enquire at *Pension Fedra*. During winter, the action shifts to *Cine Diana* under the eponymous hotel.

Enter seaward from the *Faidra* hotel. The best-equipped internet café with ten or so terminals upstairs.

Iviskos about halfway along Egéou. This tasteful café is the most popular daytime hangout on the quay, with a range of juices, coffees and alcoholic drinks.

To Loukoumi alley off Aplotariás 27/c. Old warehouse refitted as a café (8am–2pm), ouzerí (7pm–2am) and occasional events centre. Well executed and worth checking out, but closes May–Oct & Sun.

Metropol Egéou. The longest-lived and most civilized of the music bars on this stretch of the front.

Omirio south side of the central park. Cultural centre and events hall with frequently changing exhibitions; foreign musicians often come here after Athens concerts to perform in the large auditorium.

Beaches near Híos Town

Híos Town itself has no beaches worth mentioning; the closest decent one is at **KARFÁS**, 7km south beyond the airport and served by frequent blue buses. Once there you can **rent cars** at MG (℡02710/32 222) or bikes from Rabbit Moto (℡02710/32 501) both uphill from the bus stop. Most large Hiot package hotels are planted here, to the considerable detriment of the 500-metre-long beach itself, sandy only at the south end, where all watersports are offered. The main bright spot is a unique **pension**, *Markos' Place* (℡02710/31 990, Ⓦwww.marcos-place.gr; ❶–❷; April–Nov), installed in the disestablished **monastery of Áyios Yeóryios and Áyios Pandelímon**, on the hillside south of the bay. Markos Kostalas, who leases the premises from Thymianá municipality, has created a uniquely peaceful, leafy environment much loved by special-activity groups. Guests are lodged in the former pilgrims' cells, with a kitchen available; individuals are more than welcome (there are several single "cells"), though advance reservations are advisable and a minimum stay of four days is required. Visitors should also like cats (there are usually about twenty in residence).

Shoreline **eating** quality has declined so much that it's better to strike inland. *Ouzeri To Apomero* (open daily), in hillside Spiládhia district west of the airport (go around the runway and follow the many luminous green signs) has lovely terrace seating, live music a few nights weekly in summer, and such delights as pancetta with cumin, *garídhes saganáki* and *sheftalyés* (Cypriot-style meat rissoles). Inland, between Thymianá and Neohóri, *Fakiris Taverna* (open all year but weekends only in winter) offers home-marinated aubergine and artichokes, goat baked in tomato sauce and excellent wood-fired pizzas along with well-executed seafood and pork-based *bekrí mezé* in big portions. Until a sign is put up, the easiest way to find it is to head south on the road to Kalimassiá and then turn west onto Ayíou Trýfonos road, just before Neohóri, and proceed about a kilometre.

Some 2km further along the coast from Karfás, **AYÍA ERMIÓNI** is not a beach but a fishing anchorage surrounded by a handful of tavernas (again, none standing out) and apartments to rent. The nearest beach is at **Mégas Limniónas**, a few hundred metres further, smaller than Karfás but more scenic where low cliffs provide a backdrop. Both Ayía Ermióni and Mégas Limniónas are served by extensions of the blue-bus route to either Karfás or Thymianá, the nearest inland village. The coast road loops up to Thymianá, from where you can (with your own transport only) continue 3km south towards Kalimassiá to the turning for **Ayía Fotiní**, a 700-metre pebble beach with exceptionally clean water. There's no shade, however, unless you count shadows from the numerous blocks of rooms contracted out to Scandinavian tour operators; a few tavernas cluster around the point where the side road meets the sea, but there's better eating at the south end of the strand, in the **restaurant** operating in the grounds of **Áyios Emilianós monastery**.

Southern Híos

Besides olive groves, the gently rolling countryside in the south of the island is also home to the **mastic bush** (*Pistacia lentisca*), found across much of Aegean Greece but only here producing an aromatic resin of any quality or quantity. For centuries it was used as a base for paints, cosmetics and the chewable jelly beans, which became a somewhat addictive staple in the Ottoman harems. Indeed, the interruption of the flow of mastic from Híos to Istanbul by the revolt of spring 1822 was one of the root causes of the brutal Ottoman reaction.

The wealth engendered by the mastic trade supported twenty *mastihohoriá* (mastic villages) from the time the Genoese set up a monopoly in the substance during the fourteenth and fifteenth centuries, but the end of imperial Turkey and the development of petroleum-based products knocked the bottom out of the mastic market. Now it's just a curiosity, to be chewed – try the sweetened Elma-brand gum – or drunk as a liqueur called *mastíha*, though it has had medicinal applications since ancient times. These days, however, the *mastihohoriá* live mainly off their tangerines, apricots and olives.

The towns themselves, the only settlements on Híos spared by the Ottomans in 1822, are architecturally unique, laid out by the Genoese but retaining a distinct Middle Eastern feel. The basic plan consists of a rectangular warren of tall houses, with the outer row doubling as the town's perimeter fortification, and breached by a limited number of arched gateways.

The mastic villages

ARMÓLIA, 20km from town, is the smallest and least imposing of the mastic villages. Its main virtue is its pottery industry; the best workshop, selling useful kitchenware as well as the usual kitsch souvenirs, is Yeoryios Sfikakis, the third outfit on the right as you head southwest. **PYRGÍ**, 5km further south, is the most colourful of these communities, its houses elaborately embossed with *xystá*, geometric patterns cut into whitewash, revealing a layer of black volcanic sand underneath; strings of sun-drying tomatoes add a further splash of colour in autumn. On the northeast corner of the central square the twelfth-century Byzantine church of **Áyii Apóstoli** (Tues–Thurs & Sat 10am–1pm), embellished with much later frescoes, is tucked under an arcade. Of late, vast numbers of postcard racks and boutiques have sprung up on every main thoroughfare, detracting somewhat from the atmosphere. Pyrgí has a handful of **rooms**, many of them bookable through the Women's Agricultural and Tourist Cooperative (℡02710/72 496; ❷) – the office is on the left as you walk up from the bus stop. In the medieval core you'll find a **bank** (with cashpoint), a **post office** and a few *souvláki* grills, but no real tavernas. **OLÝMBI**, 7km further west along the bus route serving Armólia and Pyrgí, is the least visited of the mastic villages, but not devoid of interest. The characteristic tower-keep, which at Pyrgí stands half-inhabited away from the modernized main square, here looms bang in the middle of the platía, its ground floor occupied by the community kafenío on one side, and *Estiatorio Pyrgos* on the other, with more elaborate main dishes.

Sombre, monochrome **MESTÁ**, 4km west of Olýmbi, is considered the finest example of the genre; despite more snack bars and trinket shops than strictly necessary on the outskirts, Mestá remains just the right side of twee as most people here still work the land. From its main square, dominated by the **church of the Taxiárhis** (the largest on the island), a bewildering maze of cool, shady lanes with anti-seismic buttressing and tunnels, leads off in all directions. Most streets end in blind alleys, except those leading to the six gates; the northeast one still has its original iron grate. If you'd like to stay, there are half a dozen **rooms** in restored traditional dwellings managed by Dhimitris Pipidhis (℡02710/76 319; ❸) and Dhespina Karambela (℡02710/76 065 or 22 068, or ask at *O Morias sta Mesta* taverna, below; ❸). Alternatively, three separate premises managed by Anna Floradhi (℡02710/76 455; ❸) are somewhat more modernized, and like the other two outfits are open year-round, with heating. Of the two **tavernas** on the main platía, *O Morias sta Mesta* is renowned for tasty rural specialities like pickled *krítamo* (rock samphire) and locally produced raisin wine, which is heavy, semi-sweet and sherry-like. However, portions have shrunk of late, and *Mesaionas* – whose tables share the square – is better value and has perhaps the more helpful proprietor (she also has rooms: ℡02710/76 494; ❸).

The south coast

One drawback to staying in Mestá is a lack of good beaches nearby; the closest candidate is surf-battered, facility-less **Merikoúnda**, 4km west of Mestá by dirt track. Reached by a seven-kilometre side road starting just west of Pyrgí, the little cove of **Káto Faná** is also bereft of amenities (save for a spring), but more sheltered; by the roadside 400m above the shore, the fragmentary remains of an Apollo temple surround a medieval chapel.

Pyrgí is actually closest to the two major beach resorts in this corner of the island. The nearest, 6km distant, is **EMBORIÓS**, an almost landlocked harbour with four passable **tavernas** (*Porto Emborios* has the edge with homemade desserts and *atherína*-and-onion fry-up); there's a scanty, British-excavated acropolis on the hill to the northeast, vaguely signposted 1km along the road to Kómi – all finds are displayed in Híos Town's archeological museum. For swimming, follow the road to its end at an oversubscribed car park and the beach of **Mávros Yialós** (Mávra Vólia), then continue by flagstoned walkway over the headland to another, more dramatic pebble strand (part nudist) of purpley-grey volcanic stones, twice as long and backed by impressive cliffs.

If you want sand you'll have to go to **KÓMI**, 3km northeast, also accessible from Armólia via Kalamotí; there are just a few tavernas (most reliably open of these are *Nostalgia* and *Bella Mare*), café-bars and summer apartments behind the pedestrianized beachfront. The bus service is fairly good in season, often following a loop route through Pyrgí and Emboriós.

Central Híos

The portion of Híos extending west and southwest from Híos Town matches the south in terms of interesting monuments, and good roads (being improved still further with EU funding) make touring under your own power an easy matter. There are also several beaches on the far shore of the island which, though not necessarily the best on Híos, are fine for a dip at the middle or end of the day.

The Kámbos

The **Kámbos**, a vast fertile plain carpeted with citrus groves, extends southwest from Híos Town almost as far as the village of Halkió. The district was originally settled by the Genoese during the fourteenth century, and remained a preserve of the local aristocracy until 1822. Exploring it by bicycle or motorbike is less frustrating than going by car, since the web of narrow, poorly marked lanes sandwiched between high walls guarantee disorientation and frequent backtracking. Behind the walls you catch fleeting glimpses of ornate old mansions built from locally quarried sandstone; courtyards are paved in pebbles or alternating light and dark tiles, and most still contain a pergola-shaded irrigation pond filled by a *mánganos* or donkey-powered water-wheel, used before the age of electric pumps to draw water up from wells up to 30m deep.

Many of the sumptuous three-storey dwellings, constructed in a hybrid Italo-Turco-Greek style, have languished derelict since 1881, but an increasing number are being converted for use as private estates or unique **accommodation**. The best and most consistently attended of these is *Mavrokordatiko* (☎02710/32 900, ℱ32 902, ⓦwww.mavrokordatiko.com; ❹–❻), about 1.5km south of the airport, with enormous heated, wood-panelled rooms and breakfast (included) served by the *mánganos* courtyard.

Not strictly speaking in Kámbos, but most easily reached from it en route to the *mastihohoriá*, is an outstanding rural Byzantine monument. The thirteenth-century **church of Panayía Krína**, isolated amidst orchards and woods, is well worth the challenge of negotiating a maze of paved but poorly marked lanes beyond Vavýli village, 9km from town. It's currently closed indefinitely for snail's-pace restoration, but a peek through the apse window will give you a fair idea of the finely frescoed interior, sufficiently lit by a twelve-windowed drum. All of the late medieval frescoes which overlay the Byzantine work have been removed, and are sometimes displayed in Híos Town's Byzantine and Justiniani museums (see p.854). The alternating brick and stonework of the exterior alone justifies the trip here, though architectural harmony is marred by the later addition of a clumsy lantern over the narthex, and the visibly unsound structure is kept from collapse by cable-binding at the roofline.

Néa Moní

Almost exactly in the middle of the island, the **monastery of Néa Moní** was founded by the Byzantine Emperor Constantine Monomahos ("The Dueller") IX in 1042 on the spot where a wonder-working icon had been discovered. It ranks among the most beautiful and important monuments on any of the Greek islands; the mosaics, together with those of Dháfni and Ósios Loukás on the mainland, are among the finest surviving art of their age in Greece, and the setting – high up in still partly forested mountains 15km west of the port – is no less memorable.

Once a powerful and independent community of six hundred monks, Néa Moní was pillaged in 1822 and most of its residents (including 3500 civilians sheltering here) put to the sword; since then many of its outbuildings have languished in ruins, though a recent EU grant has prompted massive restoration work. The 1881 tremor caused comprehensive damage, while exactly a century later a forest fire threatened to engulf the place until the resident icon was paraded along the perimeter wall, miraculously repelling the flames. Today the monastery, with its giant refectory and vaulted water cisterns, is inhabited by just a couple of lay workers.

Bus excursions (around €12) are provided by the KTEL on Tuesday and Friday mornings, continuing to Anávatos, Lithí and Armólia; otherwise come by motorbike, or walk from Karyés, 7km northeast, to which there is a regular blue-bus service. **Taxis** from town, however, are not prohibitive, at about €15 round-trip per carload, including a wait while you look around.

Just inside the main gate (daily 8am–1pm & 4–8pm) stands a **chapel/ossuary** containing some of the bones of those who met their death here in 1822; axe-clefts in children's skulls attest to the savagery of the attackers. The **katholikón**, with the cupola resting on an octagonal drum, is of a design seen elsewhere only in Cyprus; the frescoes in the exonarthex are badly damaged by holes allegedly left by Turkish bullets, but the **mosaics** are another matter. The narthex contains portrayals of the various saints of Híos sandwiched between *Christ Washing the Disciples' Feet* and the *Betrayal of Christ*, in which Judas's kiss has unfortunately been obliterated, but Peter is clearly visible lopping off the ear of the high priest's servant. In the dome of the sanctuary (currently hidden by scaffolding), which once contained a complete life-cycle of Christ, only the *Baptism*, part of the *Crucifixion*, the *Descent from the Cross*, the *Resurrection* and the Evangelists *Mark* and *John* survived the earthquake.

The west coast

With your own transport, you can proceed 5km west of Néa Moní to **AVGÓNYMA**, a cluster of dwellings on a knoll overlooking the coast; the name means "Clutch of Eggs", an apt description when it's viewed from the ridge above. Since the 1980s, the place has been almost totally restored as a summer haven by descendants of the original villagers, though the permanent population is just seven. A returned Greek-American family runs a reasonable, simple-fare **taverna**, *O Pyrgos* (open all year), in an arcaded mansion on the main square; co-managed *To Arhondiko* and *To Asteria* at the outskirts have far less reliable cooking and opening hours. The classiest **accommodation** option here is *Spitakia*, a cluster of small restored houses for up to five people (☎02710/20 513 or 094/5569787, ℱ02710/43 052, ✉missetzi@otenet.gr; ◐).

A paved side road continues another 4km north to **ANÁVATOS**, whose empty, dun-coloured dwellings, soaring above pistachio orchards, are almost indistinguishable from the 300-metre-high bluff on which they're built. During the 1822 insurrection, some four hundred inhabitants and refugees threw themselves over this cliff rather than surrender to the besieging Ottomans, and it's still a preferred suicide leap. Anávatos can now only muster two permanent inhabitants, and given a lack of accommodation, plus an eerie, traumatized atmosphere, it's no place to be stranded at dusk – though there's a very good **taverna**, *Anavatos*, at the village entrance (open for lunch most of the year, plus dinner in summer).

West of Avgónyma, the main road descends 6km to the sea in well-graded loops. Turning right (north) at the junction leads first to the beach at **Elínda**, alluring from afar but rocky and murky up close; it's better to continue towards more secluded, mixed sand-and-gravel coves to either side of Metóhi (best of these are **Tigáni** and **Makriá Ámmos**, the latter nudist), or to **SIDHI-**

ROÚNDA, the only village hereabouts (with a summer taverna), which enjoys a spectacular hilltop setting overlooking the coast.

All along this coast, as far southwest as Liménas Mestón, are round **watch-towers** erected by the Genoese to look out for pirates – the first swimmable cove you reach by turning left from the junction has the name **Kastélla** (officially Trahíli), again mixed sand and gravel. A sparse weekday-only bus service resumes 9km south of the junction at **LITHÍ**, a friendly village of whitewashed buildings perched on a wooded ledge overlooking the sea. There are tavernas and kafenía near the bus turnaround area, but most visitors head 2km downhill to **Paralía Lithíou**, a popular weekend target of Hiot townies for the sake of its large but hard-packed, windswept beach. The better of two tavernas here is *Ta Tria Adherfia*; the other, *Kyra Despina*, has a few rooms (☎02710/73 373; ③).

Some 5km south of Lithí, the valley-bottom village of **VÉSSA** is an unsung gem, more open and less casbah-like than Mestá or Pyrgí, but still homogeneous. Its honey-coloured buildings are arrayed in a vast grid punctuated by numerous belfries; there's a simple taverna (*Snack Bar Evanemos*) installed in a tower-mansion on the main through road.

Northern Híos

Northern Híos never really recovered from the 1822 massacre, and the desolation left by fires in 1981 and 1987 will further dampen inquisitive spirits. Since the early 1900s the villages have languished all but deserted much of the year, which means correspondingly sparse bus services. About one-third of the former population now lives in Híos Town, venturing out here only during major festivals or to tend smallholdings; others, based in Athens or the US, visit their ancestral homes for just a few intense weeks in midsummer, when marriages are arranged between local families.

The road to Kardhámyla

Blue city buses run north from Híos Town up to **VRONDÁDHOS**, an elongated coastal suburb that's a favourite residence of the island's many seafarers. Homer is reputed to have lived and taught here, and in the terraced parkland just above the little fishing port and pebble beach you can visit his purported lectern, more probably an ancient altar of Cybele. Accordingly many of the buses out here are labelled "Dhaskalópetra", the Teacher's Rock.

Some 15km out of town, just past the tiny bayside hamlet of Pandoukiós, a side road leads to stony **Áyios Isídhoros** cove, home to the rather inconveniently located (and sporadically open – ring first to check) island **campsite**, *Chios Camping* (☎02710/74 111), though the site itself is shaded and faces Inoússes islet across the water. **LANGÁDHA**, just beyond, is probably the first point on the eastern coast road where you'd be tempted to stop, though there is no proper beach nearby. Set at the mouth of a deep valley, this attractive little harbour settlement looks across its bay to a pine grove, and beyond to Turkey. There are a couple of **rooms** outfits, but most evening visitors come for the sustaining seafood at two adjacent **tavernas** on the quay: *Tou Kopelou*, better known as *Stelios'*, and second-choice *Paradhisos*.

Just beyond Langádha an important side road leads 5km up and inland to **PITYÓS**, an oasis in a mountain pass presided over by a tower-keep; people come here from some distance to **dine** at *Makellos* on the west edge of the village, a shrine of local cuisine (June–Sept daily; Oct–May Fri–Sun evenings only). Continuing 4km more brings you to a junction allowing quick access to the west of the island and the Volissós area (see opposite).

Kardhámyla and around

Most traffic proceeds to **ÁNO KARDHÁMYLA** and **KÁTO KARDHÁMYLA**, the latter 37km out of the main town. Positioned at opposite edges of a fertile plain rimmed by mountains, they initially come as welcome relief from Homer's crags. Káto, better known as **MÁRMARO**, is larger, indeed the island's second town, with a bank, post office and filling station. However, there is little to attract a casual visitor other than some Neoclassical architecture; the port, mercilessly exposed to the *meltémi*, is strictly businesslike, and there are few tourist facilities. An exception is *Hotel Kardamyla* (☎02720/23 353; ❻ Aug, ❹ otherwise), co-managed with Híos Town's *Hotel Kyma*. It has the bay's only pebble beach, and its restaurant is a reliable source of lunch (July & Aug) if you're touring. Worthwhile independent **tavernas** include *"Snack Bar" Irini Tsirigou*, by the port authority, or *Iy Vlyhadha*, facing the eponymous bay west over the headland, with locally produced suckling pig and squid.

For better swimming head west 5km to **Nagós**, a gravel-shore bay at the foot of an oasis, which is where the summertime bus service sometimes terminates. Lush greenery is nourished by active springs up at a bend in the road, enclosed in a sort of grotto overhung by tall cliffs. The place name is a corruption of *naos*, after a large Poseidon temple that once stood near the springs, but centuries of orchard-tending, antiquities-pilfering and organized excavations after 1912 mean that nothing remains visible. Down at the shore the swimming is good, if a bit chilly; there are two mediocre **tavernas** and a few **rooms** to rent. Your only chance of relative solitude in July or August lies 1km west at **Yióssonas**; this is a much longer beach, but less sheltered, rockier and with no facilities.

Volissós and around

VOLISSÓS, 42km from Híos Town by the most direct road (44km via the much easier Avgónyma route), was once the market town for a dozen remote hill villages beyond, and its old stone houses still curl appealingly beneath the crumbling hilltop Byzantine fort. The towers were improved by the Genoese, from whose era also dates the utterly spurious "House of Homer" signposted near the top of town. Volissós can seem depressing at first, with the bulk of its 250 mostly elderly permanent inhabitants living in newer buildings around the main square, but opinions improve with longer acquaintance. The upper quarters are in the grip of a restoration mania, most of it done in admirable taste, with ruins changing hands for stratospheric prices.

Grouped around the platía you'll find a **post office**, a **bank** with cashpoint, two well-stocked shops and three mediocre **tavernas**; there's a better one up in Pýrgos district by the castle car-park, the vegetarian *Kafenio E* (April–Sept), run by Nikos Koungoulios; reservations (☎02740/21 480) are advised. A filling station operates 2.5km out of town, the only one hereabouts; you should plan on overnighting since the bus only comes out here on Sundays on a day-trip basis, or on Monday, Wednesday and Friday in the early afternoon (unless you care to travel at 4am). This should cause no dismay, since the area has the best beaches and some of the most interesting **accommodation** on Híos. The most reliably available and staffed of a few restoration projects are sixteen old houses, mostly in Pýrgos district, available through Omiros Travel (☎02740/21 413, ℉21 521; ❸). Units usually accommodate two people – all have terraces, fully equipped kitchens and features such as tree trunks upholding sleeping lofts.

LIMNIÁ, (sometimes Limiá), the port of Volissós, lies 2km south, with a small ferry coming from and going to Psará (theoretically Mon, Wed & Fri most of the year). The most consistent **tavernas** here are the long-established

Ta Limniá on the jetty for *mayireftá*, or summer-only *To Limanáki* at the rear of the cove, best for fish. At Limniá you're not far from the fabled beaches either. A 1.5-kilometre walk southeast over the headland brings you to **Managrós**, a seemingly endless sand-and-pebble beach. More intimate, sandy **Lefkáthia** lies just a ten-minute stroll along the cement drive threading over the headland north of the harbour; amenities are limited to a seasonal snack shack on the sand, and Ioannis Zorbas's apartments (☎02740/21 436, ℗21 720; ❸), beautifully set in a garden where the concrete track joins an asphalt road down from Volissós. This is bound for **Límnos** (not to be confused with Limniá), the next protected cove, 400m east of Lefkáthia, where *Taverna Akroyiali* provides salubrious food and professional service, and the spruce *Latini Apartments* (☎02740/21 461, ℗21 871; ❹) are graced with multiple stone terraces.

Ayía Markélla, 5km further northwest of Límnos, stars in many local postcards: a long, stunning beach fronting the monastery of Híos's patron saint, the latter not especially interesting or useful for outsiders, since its cells are reserved for Greek pilgrims. In an interesting variation on the expulsion of the money-changers from the temple, only religious souvenirs are allowed to be sold in the holy precincts, while all manner of plastic junk is on offer just outside. There's a single, rather indifferent taverna to hand as well, and around July 22 – the local saint's **festival** and biggest island bash – the "No Camping" signs are doubtless unenforced.

The dirt road past the monastery grounds is passable to any vehicle, with care, and emerges up on the paved road running high above the northwest coast. Turn left and proceed to the remote village of **ÁYIO GÁLA**, whose claim to fame is a **grotto–church** complex, built into a stream-lapped palisade at the bottom of the village. Signs ("Panayía Ayiogaloúsena") point to a lane crossing the water, but for access, except at the festival on August 23, you'll need to find the key-keeper (ask at the central kafenío), and descend via a flight of stairs starting beside a eucalyptus tree. Of the two churches inside the cavern, the larger one near the mouth of the grotto dates from the fifteenth century but seems newer owing to a 1993 external renovation. Inside, however, a fantastically intricate *témblon* vies for your attention with a tinier, older chapel, built entirely within the rear of the cavern. Its frescoes are badly smudged, except for a wonderfully mysterious and mournful Virgin, surely the saddest in Christendom, holding a knowing Child.

Satellite islands: Psará and Inoússes

There's a single settlement, with beaches and an isolated rural monastery, on both of Híos's satellite isles, but each is surprisingly different from the other, and of course from their large neighbour. Inoússes, the nearer and smaller islet, has a daily kaïki or hydrofoil service from Híos Town in season; Psará has less regular services subject to weather conditions (in theory daily from either Híos or Limniá), and is too remote to be done justice on a day-trip.

Psará

The birthplace of revolutionary war hero Admiral Kanaris, **Psará** devoted its merchant fleets – the third largest in 1820s Greece after those of Ídhra and Spétses – to the cause of independence, and paid dearly for it. Vexed beyond endurance, the Turks landed overwhelming forces in 1824 to stamp out this nest of resistance. Perhaps 3000 of the 30,000 inhabitants escaped in small boats which were rescued by a French fleet, but the majority retreated to a hilltop powder magazine and blew it (and themselves) up rather than surrender. The nationalist poet Dhionysios Solomos immortalized the incident in famous stanzas:

On the Black Ridge of Psará,
Glory walks alone.
She meditates on her heroes
And wears in her hair a wreath
Made from a few dry weeds
Left on the barren ground.

Today, it's a sad, stark place fully living up to its name ("the grey things" in Greek), which never really recovered from the holocaust. The Turks burned whatever houses and vegetation the blast had missed, and the permanent population barely exceeds four hundred. The only positive recent development was a 1980s revitalization project instigated by a French-Greek descendant of Kanaris and a Greek team. The port was improved, mains electricity and pure water provided, a secondary school opened, and cultural links between France and the island established, though so far this has not been reflected in increased tourist numbers.

Arrival can be something of an ordeal: the regular small ferry from Híos Town can take up to four hours to cover the 57 nautical miles of habitually rough sea. Use the port of Limniá to sail in at least one direction if you can; this crossing takes just over an hour at just over half the price.

Since few buildings in the east-facing harbour community predate the twentieth century, it's a strange hotchpotch of ecclesiastical and secular architecture that greets the eye on disembarking. There's a distinctly southern feel, more like the Dodecanese or the Cyclades, and some peculiar churches of which no two are alike in style.

If you **stay overnight**, there's a choice between a handful of fairly basic rooms and three more professional outfits: *Psara Studios* (☎02740/61 233; ❹) and *Apartments Restalia* (☎02740/61 000, ℱ61 201; ❺ August, ❸ otherwise), both a bit stark but with balconies and kitchens, or the EOT *xenónas* (☎02740/61 293; ❶) in a restored prison. For **eating**, the best and cheapest place is the EOT-run *Spitalia*, housed in a renovated medieval hospital at the north edge of the port. A **post office**, bakery and shop complete the list of amenities; there is no full-service bank.

Psará's **beaches** are decent, improving the further northeast you walk from the port. You quickly pass Káto Yialós, Katsoúni and Lazarétta with its off-putting power station, before reaching **Lákka** ("narrow ravine"), fifteen minutes along, apparently named after its grooved rock formations in which you may have to shelter – much of this coast is windswept, with a heavy swell offshore. **Límnos**, 25 minutes from the port along the coastal path, is big and attractive, but there's no reliable taverna here, or indeed at any of the other beaches. The only other thing to do on Psará is to walk north across the island – the old track there has now been paved – to the **monastery of the Kímisis (Assumption)**; uninhabited since the 1970s, this comes to life only in the first week of August, when its revered icon is carried in ceremonial procession to town and back on the eve of August 5.

Inoússes

Inoússes has a permanent population of about three hundred – less than half its prewar figure – and a very different history from Psará. For generations this medium-sized islet has provided the Aegean with many of her wealthiest shipping families: various members of the Livanos, Lemos and Pateras clans (with every street or square named after the last-named family) were born here. This helps explain the large villas and visiting summer yachts in an otherwise sleepy Greek backwater – as well as a **maritime museum** (daily 10am–1pm; €1.20) near the quay, endowed by various shipping magnates. At the west end of the quay, the bigwigs have also funded a large nautical academy, which trains future members of the merchant navy.

On Sundays in season can you make an inexpensive **day-trip** to Inoússes from Híos with the locals' ferry *Inousses*; on most other days of the week this arrives at 3pm, returning early the next morning. One or two days weekly in summer there's an unreliable hydrofoil service as well, leaving Híos at about 9.30am, and returning from Inoússes at about 3pm. Otherwise, during the tourist season you must participate in the pricier excursions offered from Híos, typically on the *Maria*, with return tickets running up to three times the cost of the regular ferry.

Two church-tipped islets, each privately owned, guard the unusually well-protected harbour (whose jetty is currently being expanded); the **town** of Inoússes is surprisingly large, draped over hillsides enclosing a ravine. Despite a wealthy reputation, its appearance is unpretentious, the houses displaying a mix of vernacular and modest Neoclassical style. There is just one, fairly comfort-able **hotel**, the *Thalassoporos* (T02720/51 475; ❷), on the main easterly hill-side lane, but no licensed pensions or rooms. **Eating out** is similarly limited; every season a few simple ouzerís off towards the nautical academy try their luck, but the most reliable option is the simple good-value *Taverna Pateronissia*, conspicuous at the base of the disembarkation jetty. Otherwise, be prepared to patronize one of the three shops (one on the waterfront, two up the hill). Beside the museum is a **post office** and a **bank**.

The rest of this tranquil island, at least the southern slope, is surprisingly green and well tended; there are no springs, so water comes from a mix of fresh and brackish wells, as well as a reservoir. The sea is extremely clean and calm on the sheltered southerly shore; among its beaches, choose from **Zepánga**, **Biláli** or **Kástro**, respectively five-, twenty- and thirty-minutes' walk west of the port. More secluded **Fourkeró** (Farkeró in dialect) lies 25 minutes east: first along a cement drive ending at a seaside chapel, then by path past pine groves and over a ridge. As on Psará, there are no reliable facilities at any of the beaches.

At the end of the westerly road, beyond Kástro, stands the somewhat macabre convent of **Evangelismoú**, endowed by a branch of the Pateras family. Inside reposes the mummified body of the lately canonized daughter, Irini, whose prayers to die of cancer in place of her terminally ill father Panagos were answered early in the 1960s on account of her virtue and piety; he's entombed here also, having outlived Irini by some years. The abbess, presiding over about twenty nuns, is none other than the widowed Mrs Pateras; only women are allowed admission, and even then casual visits are not encouraged.

Lésvos (Mytilíni)

Lésvos, the third-largest Greek island after Crete and Évvia, is not only the birthplace of Sappho, but also of Aesop, Arion and – more recently – the Greek primitive artist Theophilos, the Nobel laureate poet Odysseus Elytis and the novelist Stratis Myrivilis. Despite these artistic associations, Lésvos may not at first strike the visitor as particularly beautiful or interesting; much of the land-scape is rocky, volcanic terrain, dotted with thermal springs and alternating

LÉSVOS

with vast grain fields, salt pans or even near-desert. But there are also oak and pine forests as well as vast olive groves, some of these over five hundred years old. With its balmy climate and suggestive contours, the island tends to grow on you with prolonged acquaintance.

Lovers of medieval and Ottoman **architecture** certainly won't be disappointed. Castles survive at the main town of Mytilíni, at Mólyvos, Eressós and near Ándissa; most of these date from the late fourteenth century, when Lésvos was given as a dowry to a Genoese prince of the Gateluzzi clan following his marriage to the niece of one of the last Byzantine emperors. Apart from Crete and Évvia, Lésvos was the only Greek island where Turks settled significantly in rural villages (they usually stuck to the safety of towns), which explains the odd Ottoman bridge, shed-like mosque or crumbling minaret often found in the middle of nowhere. Again unusually for the Aegean islands, Ottoman reforms of the eighteenth century encouraged the emergence of a Greek Orthodox land- and industry-owning aristocracy, who built rambling mansions and tower-houses, a few of which survive. More common are the bourgeois townhouses of the worthies in Mytilíni town, built early in the twentieth century to French Second Empire models; many of these have often been pressed into service as government buildings or even restored as hotels.

Social and economic idiosyncrasies persist: anyone who has attended one of the extended village *paniyíria*, with hours of music and tables in the streets groaning with food and drink, will not be surprised to learn that Lésvos has the highest alcoholism rate in Greece. Breeding livestock, especially horses, is disproportionately important, and traffic jams caused by mounts instead of parked cars are not unheard of – signs reading "Forbidden to Tether Animals Here" are still common, as are herds of apparently unattended donkeys wandering about. Much of the acreage in olives is still inaccessible to vehicles, and the harvest can only be hauled out by those donkeys – who are duly loaded en masse onto the back of trucks to be transported to the point where the road fizzles out.

Historically, the olive plantations, oúzo distilleries, animal husbandry and fishing industry supported those who chose not to emigrate, but with these enterprises relatively stagnant, mass-market tourism has made visible inroads. However, it still accounts for just five percent of the local economy: there are still few large hotels outside the capital, Skála Kalloní or Mólyvos; self-catering villas barely outnumber rooms, and the first official campsites only opened in 1990. Foreign tourist numbers have in fact levelled out since 1996, the result of stalled plans to expand the airport, unrealistic hotel pricing and the dropping of the island from several German and Dutch tour operators' programmes.

Public **buses** tends to radiate out from the harbour for the benefit of working locals, not day-tripping tourists. Carrying out such excursions from Mytilíni is next to impossible anyway, owing to the size of the island – about 70km by 45km at its widest points – and the last few appalling roads (most others have been improved, along with their signposting). Moreover, the topography is complicated by the two deeply indented gulfs of Kalloní and Yéra, with no bridges across their mouths, which means that going from A to B involves an obligatory change of bus at either Mytilíni, on the east shore, or the town of Kalloní, in the middle of the island. It's best to decide on a base and stay there for a few days, exploring its immediate surroundings on foot or by rented vehicle.

Mytilíni Town

MYTILÍNI, the port and capital, sprawls between and around two bays divided by a fortified promontory, and in Greek fashion often doubles as the name

▲ *Mandamádhos*

MYTILÍNI

0 ___ 200 m

RESTAURANTS		CAFÉS & NIGHTLIFE	
Averoff	C	Flame	D
Ermis	A	Hott Spott	E
Paradhosiako-Kalderimi	B	Liquid	F
Stratos	G	Marush	E
		Papagallino	D

Epáno Skála

Mólyvos & Yéra Baths ◄

Ancient Excavations ● 1

Fortress (Kástro)

Yéni Tzamí

Hamam

● 2

● 3

Ancient Theatre

● 4

Áyios Theodhóros Cathedral

Tsamákia Beach

New Museum

● 5 ● B

City Bus Station

● C ● D ● E Old Museum

Ay. Therápon ● 6 NEL Shipping Office

Byzantine Art Museum

Summer Festival Box Office

✉ Summer Cinema

Port Police

● F

Customs

Ferry Boat Quay

FANARI

● G

KTEL Bus Station

P

Olympic Airways

P

Blue City Bus Marquees

N

Stadium

● 7

Loutrá ◄

ACCOMMODATION	
Arion	6
New Life	5
Pelayia Koumniotou	3
Salina's Garden Rooms/ Thalia Rooms	2
Vetsikas Dhiethnes	4
Villa 1900	7
Zoumboulis Rooms	1

▼ *Airport & Variá*

of the island. Many visitors are put off by the combination of urban bustle and (in the traditionally humbler northern districts) slight seediness, and contrive to leave as soon as possible; the town returns the compliment by being a fairly impractical and occasionally expensive place to base yourself.

Nonetheless, Mytilíni has enough to justify a layover of a few hours. On the promontory sits the Byzantine-Genoese-Ottoman **fortress** (Tues–Sun 8am–2.30pm; €1.50), comprising ruined structures from all these eras and an Ottoman inscription above a Byzantine double-headed eagle at the south gate. Further inland, the town skyline is dominated in turn by the Germanic-Gothic belfry spire of **Áyios Theodhóros** and the mammary dome of **Áyios Therápon**, both expressions of the post-Baroque taste of the nineteenth-century Ottoman Greek bourgeoisie. They stand more or less at opposite ends of the bazaar, whose main street, Ermoú, links the town centre with the little-used north harbour of Páno Skála. On its way there Ermoú passes several expensive but rather picked-over antique shops near the roofless, derelict **Yéni Tzamí** at the heart of the old Muslim quarter, just a few steps east of a superb Turkish **hamam**, currently being restored to its former glory and due to function again as a bathhouse by late 2002. Between Ermoú and the castle lies a maze of atmospheric lanes lined with grandiose Belle Époque mansions and elderly vernacular houses, though most of the ornate townhouses are to be found in the southerly districts of Sourádha and Kióski, on the way to the airport.

Mytilíni's excellent **archeological collection** is housed in **two separate galleries** (May–Sept daily 8am–7pm; Oct–April Tues–Sun 8.30am–3pm; €1.50), a few hundred metres apart. The newer, upper museum, at the base of 8-Noemvríou, is devoted to finds from wealthy Roman Mytilene, in particular three rooms of well-displayed mosaics from second/third-century AD villas – highlights are a crude but engaging scene of Orpheus charming all manner of beasts, and two fishermen surrounded by clearly recognizable (and edible) sea creatures. Earlier eras are represented in the older wing (Tues–Sun 8.30am–3pm; same ticket as Roman wing), housed in a former mansion just behind the ferry dock. The ground floor has Neolithic finds from Áyios Vartholoméos cave and Bronze Age Thermí, but the star, late-Classical exhibits upstairs include minutely detailed terracotta figurines: a pair of acrobats, two *kourotrophoi* figures (goddesses suckling infants, predecessors of all Byzantine Galaktotrofoússa icons), children playing with a ball or dogs, and Aphrodite riding a dolphin. A specially built annexe at the rear contains stone-cut inscriptions of various edicts and treaties, plus a Roman sculpture of a drunken satyr asleep on a wineskin.

There's also a worthwhile **Byzantine Art Museum** (no regular hours at present; apply to church office adjacent Mon–Fri 9am–noon) just behind Áyios Therápon, containing various icons rescued from rural churches, plus a canvas of the *Assumption* by Theophilos (see p.872).

Practicalities

There's no bus link with the **airport**, so a shared taxi for the 7km into Mytilíni Town is the usual shuttle method; Olympic Airways is southwest of the main harbour at Kavétsou 44. As on Híos, there are two **bus stations**: the *iperastykó* (standard KTEL) buses leave from a small station near Platía Konstandinopóleos at the southern end of the harbour, while the *astykó* (blue bus) service departing from one corner of the enormous free public **car park** nearby (which you should use if driving, as there are no other easily available spaces in the centre). If you're intent on getting over to Ayvalık in Turkey on the Turkish **boats** *Cunda Express* or *Jalehan*, book tickets through either Dimakis Tours at Koundouriótou 73 (☎02510/27 865) or Picolo Travel at no. 73a (☎02510/27 000). NEL Ferries has its own agency at Koundouriótou 47 (☎02510/28 480), though tickets (including the high-speed service) are also sold through Dimakis Tours, while Hellas Ferries and the occasional hydrofoil south are handled by Picolo Travel.

Car rental is best arranged through reputable local-chain franchises like Payless/Auto Moto at Koundouriótou 49 (☎02510/43 555, ⓔautomoto@otenet.gr), Budget next door (☎02510/29 600), Egeon at Híou 2 (☎02510/29 820), Just at no. 47 (☎02510/43 080) or Alpha in the alley off Koundouriótou 83 (☎02510/26 113) – though it's often cheaper to rent at the resort of your choice. Other amenities include the **post office** on Vournázon, behind the central park, and at least five **banks** along Koundouriótou with cash dispensers, plus a free-standing booth on the quay. Before leaving town, you might visit the **EOT** regional headquarters at James Aristárhou 6

(Mon–Fri 8am–2.30pm) to get hold of their excellent town and island maps, plus other brochures.

Accommodation

Finding **accommodation** can be initially daunting: the waterfront hotels are noisy and exorbitantly priced, with few single rooms to speak of. If you need to stay, it's preferable to hunt down better-value rooms in the backstreets, especially between the castle and Ermoú, with supply usually exceeding demand. Yeoryíou Tertséti street in particular has two possibilities: the friendly if basic *Pelayia Koumniotou* at no. 6 (☏02510/20 643; ❶), or the fancier, en-suite *Vetsikas/Dhiethnes* at no. 1 (☏02510/24 968; ❷). Two other quiet establishments sit between the north harbour and fortress: *Salina's Garden Rooms*, behind the Yéni Tzamí at Fokéas 7 (☏02510/42 073; ❶), co-managed with the *Thalia Rooms* across the street (☏02510/24 640; ❶). Moving slightly upmarket, *Zoumbouli Rooms*, facing the water on Navmahías Ellís (☏02510/29 081; ❸), are en-suite and air conditioned, but may get more noise from traffic and the ouzerí below. *New Life* at the end of Olýmbou, a cul-de-sac off Ermoú (☏02510/42 650 or 093/2279057; ❸), offers wood-floored, en-suite rooms in an old mansion, or similarly priced ones, but with bizarre modern murals, in the co-managed *Arion* down the street at Árionos 4. *Villa 1900*, another restored mansion in the south of town at P. Vostáni 24 (☏02510/23 448, ⓕ28 034; ❹), has en-suite, variable-sized units with fridges, air conditioning and sometimes traditional ceiling murals.

Eating, drinking and nightlife

Dining options in Mytilíni have improved since a late-1990s nadir, when several of the more characterful old-style ouzerís and tavernas shut down in favour of fast-food joints. The obvious, if blatantly touristy, venue for a seafood blowout is the cluster of tavernas on the southerly quay known as Fanári; *Stratos* at the far end is marginally the best, and the only one that doesn't tout aggressively. For *mayireftá* (including early-morning *patsás*), look no further than the *Averoff* on the west quay, a popular place for lunch before an afternoon ferry departure. Finally, there are two recently refurbished, traditional ouzerís at opposite ends of the bazaar. *Paradhosiako-Kalderimi* (closed Sun) occupies two premises around Thássou 2, with seating under the shade of vines; the fare is large-portioned if a bit plainly presented for about €12 per head. For the same or even less (and with friendlier service), you might be better off at the *Ermis* (open daily), best of a cluster of ouzerís up at Páno Skála; a recent refit hasn't much affected its century-old decor (panelled ceiling, giant mirrors, faded oil paintings), or its claimed two centuries of purveying titbits to a jolly, mixed crowd in the pleasant courtyard.

For **snacks**, **breakfast and drinks**, try either *Liquid*, Koundouriótou 79, which does omelettes, or *Papagallino* nearby at no. 59, which offers crepes and pricey smoothies, and a magnificent interior atrium occasionally hosting exhibits. With an important university in residence, Mytilíni can offer decent **nightlife and entertainment**, especially along the northeast quay, which the student contingent have claimed as their own. Here, all in a row between Budget car rental and the NEL agency, you'll find *Flame* (with bowling upstairs), *Papagallino* (see above), *Marush* (with video games) and the durable *Hott Spott*. Formal live events constitute the *Lesviakó Kalokéri*, held in the castle or other venues from mid-July to late August, while the summer cinema Pallas is between the post office and the park on Vournázon.

Around Mytilíni

Beyond the airport and Krátigos village, the paved road loops around to **Haramídha**, 14km from town and the closest decent (pebble) beach (the fee-entry town "beach" at Tsamákia is mediocre); the eastern bay has several taver-nas. The double cove at **Áyios Ermoyénis**, 3km west, is more scenic and sandy but small and crowded at weekends, with no full-service taverna, just a snack bar. The latter is more directly accessible from Mytilíni via Loutrá village. For other pleasant immersions near Mytilíni, make for **Loutrá Yéras**, 8km along the main road to Kallóní. These public baths (daily: June–Sept 7am–7pm; April–May & Oct 8am–6pm; Nov–March 9am–5pm; €2) are just the thing if you've spent a sleepless night on a ferry, with ornate spouts that feed 38°C water to marble-lined pools in vaulted chambers; there are separate facilities for men and women.

The Variá museums

The most rewarding single targets near Mytilíni are a pair of museums at **VARIÁ**, 5km south of town (half-hourly buses). The **Theophilos Museum** (May–Sept Tues–Sun 9am–2pm & 6–8pm; Oct–April may open 9am–2pm only; €1.50 includes key-catalogue) honours the painter, born here in 1873, with four rooms of wonderful, little-known compositions specifically commissioned by his patron Thériade (see below) during the years leading up to Theophilos' death in 1934. A wealth of detail is evident in elegiac scenes of fishing, reaping, olive-picking and baking from the pastoral Lésvos which Theophilos obviously knew best; there are droll touches also, such as a cat slinking off with a fish in *The Fishmongers*. In classical scenes – *Sappho and Alkaeos*, a landscape series of Egypt, Asia Minor and the Holy Land, and episodes from wars historical and contemporary – Theophilos was clearly on shakier ground. In *Abyssinians Hunting an Italian Horseman*, the subject has been conflated with New World Indians chasing down a conquistador.

The adjacent, imposing **Thériade Museum** (Tues–Sun 9am–2pm & 5–8pm; €1.50) is the brainchild of another native son, Stratis Eleftheriades (1897–1983). Leaving the island at an early age for Paris, he gallicized his name to Thériade and went on to become a renowned avant-garde art publisher, convincing some of the leading artists of the twentieth century to participate in his ventures. The displays – slightly depleted by a recent burglary – consist of lithographs, engravings, wood-block prints and watercolours by the likes of Miró, Chagall, Picasso, Matisse, Le Corbusier, Léger, Rouault and Villon, either annotated by the painters themselves or commissioned as illustrations for the works of prominent poets and authors – an astonishing collection for a relatively remote Aegean island.

Southern Lésvos

The southernmost portion of the island is indented by two great inlets, the gulfs of **Kallóní** and **Yéra**, the first curving in a northeasterly direction, the latter northwesterly, creating a fan-shaped peninsula at the heart of which looms 967-metre Mount Ólymbos. Both shallow gulfs are almost landlocked by virtue of very narrow outlets to the open sea, which don't have – and probably never will have – bridges spaning them. This is the most verdant and productive olive-producing territory on Lésvos, and the stacks of pressing-mills stab the skyline.

With its disused industrial warehouses, **PÉRAMA** is one of the larger places on the Gulf of Yéra, and has a regular **kaïki-ferry** service (no cars) linking it with Koundoroudhiá and blue city buses to/from Mytilíni on the far side. A more likely reason to show up is to patronize one of the better **taverna-ouzerís** in the region: *Balouhanas*, northernmost of a line of eateries on the front, with a wooden, cane-roofed balcony jutting out over the water. The name's a corruption of *balıkhane* or "fish-market" in Turkish, and seafood is a strong point, whether grilled or made into croquettes, as are regional starters like *giouzlemés* (cheese-stuffed fried crepe) and own-made desserts. They're open all year (lunch & dinner); count on €15 per head.

Plomári and around

Due south of Mount Ólymbos, at the edge of the "fan", **PLOMÁRI** is the only sizeable coastal settlement in the south, and indeed the second largest municipality on Lésvos. It presents an unlikely juxtaposition of scenic appeal and its famous oúzo industry, courtesy of several local distilleries. Despite a resounding lack of good beaches within walking distance, it's besieged in summer by hordes of Scandinavian tourists, but you can usually find a **room** (they are prominently signposted) at the edge of the old, charmingly dilapidated town, or (better) 1km west in **Ammoudhélli** suburb, which has a small pea-gravel beach. Your best bet for an on-spec vacancy is the welcoming *Pension Lida* above the inland Platía Beniamín (☎ & ℉ 02520/32 507; ❷), a fine restoration inn occupying adjacent old mansions, with seaview balconies for most units. Rustling up a decent meal presents more difficulties, with the dinner-only *Platanos* taverna at the central plane tree often unbearably busy, and nothing special at that. Better to stick to the east end of the harbour park-square, where *Bacchus* is reliable and long-established. Ammoudhélli can offer shambolic but friendly *To Ammoudhelli*, perched unimprovably over the beach and open at lunch too; skip the touristy printed menu and ask for the dishes of the day (which can be anything from *ambelofásola* to sardines) and *orektiká* like *tyrokafterí* and grilled octopus – budget €9 each.

Áyios Isídhoros, 3km east, is where most tourists actually stay; pick of the hotels here, not completely overrun with package tours, is the *Pebble Beach* (☎02520/31 651, ℉31 566; ❹), with most of the large rooms overlooking a slightly reefy section of beach. Eating out here, try *Iy Mouria*, where the road turns inland to cross the creek draining to the long, popular pebble beach, or (1km inland from this) *Tou Panaï*, with seating in an olive grove.

Melínda, another 700-metre sand-and-shingle beach at the mouth of a canyon, lies 6km west of Plomári by a mostly paved road. Here you'll find three inexpensive **taverna-rooms** outfits, of which *Maria's* (☎02520/93 239; ❶) is an endearingly ramshackle place with simple but reasonably priced food and lodging, with *Paradhisos* (☎02520/93 220; ❶) of similar standard; *Melinda* (aka Dhimitris Psaros; ☎02520/93 234; ❶) at the west end of the strand has a more elaborate menu and en-suite rooms. Even more unspoiled (thanks to a formerly dreadful ten-kilometre side road in, now sixty percent paved), **Tárti**, some 22km in total from Plomári, is a 400-metre-wide cove where Lésvos hoteliers and restaurant owners take *their* holidays. There are three beachfront **tavernas**, plus **rooms** lining the final stretch of road should you want to stay.

The **bus** into Plomári travels via the attractive villages of Paleókipos and Skópelos (as well as Áyios Isídhoros); the road north from Plomári to Ayiássos has paving and public transport only as far as Megalohóri.

Ayiássos and Mylélia

AYIÁSSOS, nestled in a remote, wooded valley under the crest of Mount Ólymbos, is the most beautiful hill town on Lésvos, its narrow cobbled streets lined by ranks of tiled-roof houses. On the usual, northerly approach, there's no clue of the enormous village until you see huge knots of parked cars at the southern edge of town (where the bus leaves you after the 26-kilometre run from Mytilíni).

Don't be put off by endless ranks of kitsch wooden and ceramic souvenirs or carved "Byzantine" furniture, aimed mostly at Greeks, but continue past the central **church of the Panayía Vrefokratoússa**, originally built in the twelfth century to house an icon supposedly painted by the Evangelist Luke, to the **old bazaar**, with its kafenía, yogurt shops and butchers' stalls. With such a venerable icon as a focus, the local August 15 *paniyíri* is one of the liveliest in Greece, let alone Lésvos. Ayiássos also takes Carnival very seriously; there's a club dedicated to organizing it, opposite the post office. The best **restaurants** are *Dhouladhelli*, on your left as you enter the village from the extreme south (bus stop) end, or the idiosyncratic nocturnal ouzerí *To Stavrí*, at the extreme north end of the village in Stavrí district. At either of these spots you can eat for a fraction of the prices asked at the coastal resorts.

If you're headed for Ayiássos with your own transport, you might visit the **Mylélia water mill**, whose inconspicuously signposted access track takes off 1km west of the turning for Ípios village. The name means "place of the mills", and there were once several hereabouts, powered by a spring, up-valley at Karíni. The last survivor (open daily 9am–6pm), restored to working order, has not been made twee in the least; the keeper will show you the millrace and paddle-wheel, as well as the flour making its spasmodic exit, after which you're free to buy gourmet pastas at the adjacent shop.

Vaterá, Skála Polikhnítou – and spas en route

A different bus route from Mytilíni leads to Vaterá beach via the inland villages of Polikhnítos and Vríssa. **VRÍSSA** itself has just opened a new **natural history museum** (daily 9.30am–7pm; €0.90) dedicated to local paleontological finds – it's not exactly required viewing at present, but a new, more extensive gallery is promised. Until 20,000 years ago, Lésvos (like all other east Aegean islands) was joined to the Asian mainland, the gulf of Vaterá was a subtropical lake, and all manner of creatures flourished here, their fossilized bones constituting the star exhibits.

If you're after a hot bath, head for the small, vaulted **spa-house** 1.5km east of Polikhnítos, well restored by an EU programme (daily: July–Aug 6–11am & 3–6pm; spring/autumn 7–11am & 4–6pm; €1.50); there are separate, pink-tinted chambers for each sex. Alternatively there are more **hot springs** at **Áyios Ioánnis**, signposted 3km below the village of Lisvóri. On the far side of the stream here are two pools housed in whitewashed, vaulted chambers (€1.50 fee payable when adjacent snack bar attended); the left-hand one's nicer, and there's no gender segregation or dress code.

VATERÁ, 9km south of Polikhnítos, is a huge, seven-kilometre-long sand beach, backed by vegetated hills; the sea here is delightfully calm and clean, the strand itself rated as one of the best in Greece. If you intend to stay here you'll probably want your own transport (there's **car rental** locally through Alpha, ☎02520/61 132), as the closest well-stocked shops are 4km away at Vríssa, and the bus appears only a few times daily. Development straggles for several kilometres to either side of the central T-junction, consisting mostly of seasonal villas and apartments for locals; at the west end of the strip is one of the very few consistently attended and professionally run hotels, the Greek- and American-owned *Vatera Beach* (☎02520/61 212, ℱ61 164, ☻www.our-lesvos.com; ⑤), whose rooms have air-con and fridges. It also has a good attached restaurant with own-grown produce and shoreline tables from where you can gaze on the cape of **Áyios Fokás** 3km to the west, where only foundations remain of a temple of Dionysos and a superimposed early Christian basilica. The little tamarisk-shaded anchorage here has an acceptable fish **taverna**, *Akrotiri/Agelerou*; it's better than most eateries east of the T-junction at Vaterá, many of which only operate July and August, but not so good as the half-dozen tavernas at **SKÁLA POLIKHNÍTOU**, 4km northwest of Polikhnítos itself, where *T'Asteria* and *Exohiko Kendro Tzitzifies* can both be recommended, staying open most of the year. Skála itself is pleasantly workaday, with only a short, narrow beach but one unusual accommodation option, "Soft Tourism" run by Lefteris and Erika (☎02520/42 678 or 093/7925435; ❷), who also have the concession to run the Polikhnítos spa. They generally host special-interest groups April to June and September, but welcome independent travellers during July and August.

East from Vaterá, a partly paved road leads via Stavrós, and then Akrássi (this stretch will be the last to be improved) to either Ayiássos or Plomári within ninety minutes. When leaving the area going north towards Kallóní, use the short cut via the naval base and seashore hamlet at Akhladherí – it's completely paved, despite appearing otherwise on obsolete maps.

Western Lésvos

The main road west of Loutrá Yéras is surprisingly devoid of settlement, with little to stop for before Kallóní other than the traces of an ancient **Aphrodite temple** at **Mésa** (Méson), 1km north of the main road, and signposted just east of the Akhladherí turn-off. At the **site** (Tues–Sun 8am–2.30pm; free) just eleventh-century BC foundations and a few column stumps remain, plus the ruins of a fourteenth-century Genoese-built basilica wedged inside; it was once virtually on the sea but a nearby stream has silted things up in the intervening millennia. All told, it's not worth a special trip, but certainly make the short detour if passing by. With more time and your own transport, you can turn northeast towards **Ayía Paraskeví** village, midway between two more important monuments from diverse eras: the Paleo-Christian **basilica of Halinádhou**, and the large **medieval bridge** of Kremastí.

KALLONÍ itself is an unembellished agricultural and market town more or less in the middle of the island, with various shops and services (including pharmacies, a post office and three banks with cash dispensers). Some 3km south lies **SKÁLA KALLONÍS**, a somewhat unlikely package resort backing a long but coarse-sand beach on the lake-like gulf. It's mainly distinguished as a bird-watching centre, attracting hundreds of twitchers for the March–May nesting season in the adjacent salt marshes. Pick of a half-dozen **hotels** is the human-scale bungalow complex *Malemi* (☎02530/22 594, ℗22 838, ⓦwww.hit360.com/malemi; ❺), with a variety of units from doubles to family suites, attractive grounds, tennis court and a large pool. **Tavernas** lining the quay with its fishing fleet are generally indistinguishable – though most offer the gulf's celebrated *sardhélles pastés*, or salt-cured sardines; the locals themselves tend to favour *Mimi's*, on the square just inland.

Inland monasteries and villages

West of Kallóní, the road winds 4km uphill to the **monastery of Limónos**, founded in 1527 by the monk Ignatios, whose actual cell is maintained in the surviving medieval north wing. It's a huge, rambling complex, with just a handful of monks and lay workers to maintain three storeys of cells around a vast, plant-filled courtyard. The *katholikón*, with its ornate carved-wood ceiling and archways, is built in Asia Minor style and is traditionally off-limits to women; a sacred spring flows from below the south foundation wall. A former abbot established a **museum** (daily 9.30am–6.30pm, may close 3pm off-season; €1.50) on two floors of the west wing; the ground-floor ecclesiastical collection is, alas, the only wing open as of writing, with the more interesting upstairs ethnographic gallery off-limits indefinitely. Content yourself with an overflow of farm implements stashed in a corner storeroom below, next to a chamber where giant *pithária* (urns) for grain and olive oil are embedded in the floor.

The main road beyond passes through **VATOÚSSA**, a landlocked and beautiful settlement in the heart of Lésvos's westernmost landmass. Besides unspoilt architecture it can offer two sterling examples of the endangered traditional oúzo-mezédhes kafenío in the upper platía: *Tryfon* and *Mihalis*.

Some 8km beyond Vatoússa, a short track leads down to the sixteenth-century **monastery of Perivolís** (daily 8am–1hr before sunset; donation, no photos), built in the midst of a riverside orchard (*perivóli*). Feeble electric light is available to view the narthex's fine if damp-damaged frescoes. In an apocalyptic panel worthy of Bosch (*The Earth and Sea Yield up their Dead*) the Whore of Babylon rides her chimera and assorted sea-monsters disgorge their victims; just to the right, towards the main door, the Three Magi approach the Virgin enthroned with the Christ Child. On the north side you see a highly unusual iconography of *Abraham, the Virgin, and the Penitent Thief of Calvary in Paradise*, with the Four Rivers of Paradise gushing forth under their feet; just right are assembled the Hebrew kings of the Old Testament.

ÁNDISSA, 3km further on, nestles under the arid west's only pine grove; at the edge of the village a sign implores you to "Come Visit Our Square", not a bad idea for the sake of several kafenía sheltering under three enormous plane trees. For more substantial fare, however, follow the paved road from directly below Ándissa 6km north to **GAVATHÁS**, a fishing hamlet with a narrow, partly protected beach (there's a bigger, surf-buffeted one at Kámbos just to the east) and a few places to eat and stay – among these are *Rooms Restaurant Paradise* (☎02530/56 376; ❷), serving good fish and locally grown vegetables.

Just west of Ándissa there's an important junction. Keeping straight leads you past the still-functioning **monastery of Ipsiloú**, founded in 1101 atop an outrider of the extinct volcano of Órdhymnos. The *katholikón*, tucked in one corner of a large, irregular courtyard, has a fine wood-lattice ceiling but had its frescoes repainted to detrimental effect in 1992; more intriguing are portions of Iznik tile stuck in the facade, and the handsome double gateway. Upstairs you can visit a fairly rich **museum** of ecclesiastical treasure (sporadically open; small donation). Ipsiloú's patron saint is John the Theologian, a frequent dedication for monasteries overlooking apocalyptic landscapes like the surrounding parched, boulder-strewn hills.

Signposted just west is the paved, five-kilometre side road to the main concentration of Lésvos's rather overrated **petrified forest** (daily 8am–sunset; €1.50), a fenced-in "reserve" which is toured along 3km of walkways. For once, contemporary Greek arsonists cannot be blamed for the state of the trees, created by the combined action of volcanic ash from Órdhymnos and hot springs some fifteen to twenty million years ago. The mostly horizontal sequoia trunks average a metre or less in length, save for a few poster-worthy exceptions; another more accessible (and free) cluster is found south of Sígri (see opposite), plus there is a fair number of petrified logs strewn about the courtyard of Ipsiloú.

Sígri

SÍGRI, near the western tip of Lésvos, has an appropriately end-of-the-line feel; the bay here is guarded both by an Ottoman castle, and the long island of Nissiopí, which protects the place somewhat from prevailing winds. Accordingly it's an important NATO naval base, with one or two weekly NEL **ferries** to Rafina, Psará, Áyios Efstrátios and Límnos obliged to dodge numbers of battleships often anchored here. The eighteenth-century **castle** (built atop the ruins of an earlier one) sports the sultan's monogram over the entrance, something rarely seen outside Istanbul, and a token of the high regard in which this productive island was held. The vaguely Turkish-looking **church of Ayía Triádha** is in fact a converted mosque, while the town itself presents a drab mix of vernacular and cement dwellings. The town beach, south of the castle headland, is narrow and hemmed in by the road; there are much better beaches at **Faneroméni**, 3.5km north by coastal dirt track from the northern outskirts of town, plus another 2km south, just below the fifteen-kilometre dirt track to Eressós; neither beach has any facilities.

Most **accommodation** is monopolized by British tour company Direct Greece, but you might try *Nelly's Rooms and Apartments* (☎02530/54 230; ❸), overlooking the castle, or the nearby *Rainbow Studios* (☎02530/54 310; ❸). Among several **tavernas**, the best all-rounder, just inland, is Italian-run, ultra-hygienic *Una Fatsa Una Ratsa*, with lovely grilled garlicky vegetables, pizza, pasta, grills and an Italian wine list; *Remezzo* further back is good for lobster. *Kavo Doro* opposite the jetty gets first pick of the fishermen's catch, but is no longer nearly as cheap as it was.

Skála Eressoú

Most visitors to western Lésvos park themselves at the resort of **SKÁLA ERESSOÚ**, accessible via the southerly turning between Ándissa and Ipsiloú. The three-kilometre beach here runs a close second in quality to Vaterá's, and consequently the place rivals Plomári and Mólyvos for numbers of visitors, who form an odd mix of Brits, Germans, Scandinavians, Greek families, neo-hippies and lesbians. Behind stretches the largest and most attractive agricultural plain on Lésvos, a welcome green contrast to the volcanic ridges above.

There's not much to Skála – just a roughly rectangular grid of perhaps five streets by eight, angling up to the oldest cottages on the slope of **Vígla hill**. The waterfront pedestrian zone (officially Papanikolí) is divided by a café-lined round platía midway along dominated by a bust of **Theophrastos**, the renowned botanist who hailed from ancient Eressós. This was not, as you might suppose, on the site of the modern inland village, but atop Vígla hill at the east end of the beach; some of the remaining citadel wall is still visible from a distance. On top, the ruins prove scanty, but it's worth the scramble up for the views – you can discern the ancient jetty submerged beyond the modern fishing anchorage.

Another famous reputed native of ancient Eressós was **Sappho** (c. 615–562 BC), the ancient poetess and reputed lesbian. There are usually appreciable numbers of gay women here paying homage, particularly at the two hotels devoted to their exclusive use (see overleaf), and in the clothing-optional zone of the beach west of the river mouth. Ancient Eressós endured into the Byzantine era, the main legacy of which is the **basilica of Áyios Andhréas** behind the modern church, merely foundations and an unhappily covered floor mosaic; the adjacent museum of local odds and ends is even less compelling.

Skála has countless **rooms and apartments**, but ones near the sea fill early in the day or are block-booked by tour companies; in peak season often the best and quietest you can hope for is something inland overlooking a garden or fields. Even following a recent decline in tourist numbers (Direct Greece has dropped the resort, citing a lack of commitment to "family values"), it's wise to entrust the search to Sappho Travel (☎02530/52 140, ☏52 000). Jo and Joanna are switched-on and helpful, also serving as the local Budget car-rental station, ferry agent and air-ticket source; they are happy to place walk-ins in accommodation (❷–❹), but suggest you consult their UK-based website, ⓦwww.lesvos.co.uk, in advance. Otherwise, there are just three bona fide **hotels** in the village, and two of these – the remote *Antiopi* (☎02530/53 311; ❶ rooms, ❸ studios) and the seafront *Sappho the Eressia* (☎02530/53 495, ☏53 174, ⓔSappho_sarani@hotmail.com; ❸) – are run exclusively by and for lesbians. The alternative is the central, air-conditioned *Galini* (☎02530/53 138, ☏53 137; ❹), slightly inland.

Most **tavernas**, with elevated wooden dining platforms, crowd the beach; none is utterly awful – they wouldn't survive the intense competition for falling tourist numbers – but some stand out. The *Blue Sardine* at the far west end of the front is an excellent seafood ouzerí with good bread, clearly identified frozen items, unusual salads and extra touches to the fish. By contrast, adjacent, grossly overpriced *Adonis* is best avoided in favour of *Soulatsos* a couple of doors further east, a good full-on taverna with meat and fish dishes. East of the platía, *Zephyros* makes a good account of itself for grills, while Canadian-run *Yamas* is the place for pancake breakfasts, veggie burgers, wholemeal bread and decadent chocolate desserts. The gay-women's contingent favours *Dhekati Mousa/Tenth Muse*, on the Theophrastos platía, though everyone is made welcome; a summer **cinema** further inland rounds up the nightlife. Skála has a **post office** and a coin-op **laundry** near the church, but **no bank** or cash dispenser; come prepared or pay travel agency commissions.

If you're returning to the main island crossroads at Kallóni, you can complete a loop from Eressós along the western shore of the Gulf of Kallóni via the hill villages of Mesótopos and Ágra; this route is now entirely paved, despite obsolete maps showing it as a track.

Northern Lésvos

The main road north of Kallóni winds up a piney ridge and then down the other side into increasingly attractive country, stippled with poplars and blanketed by olive groves. Long before you can discern any other architectural detail, the cockscomb silhouette of **Mólyvos castle** indicates your approach to the oldest established tourist spot on Lésvos.

Mólyvos (Míthymna)

MÓLYVOS (officially Míthymna), 61km from Mytilíni, is arguably the most beautiful village on Lésvos. Tiers of sturdy, red-tiled houses, some standing defensively with their rear walls to the sea, mount the slopes between the picturesque harbour and the **Genoese castle** (Tues–Sun 8am–2.30pm; €1.50), which provides interesting rambles around its perimeter walls and views of Turkey across the straits. Closer examination reveals a score of weathered Turkish fountains along flower-fragrant, cobbled alleyways, a reflection of the fact that before 1923 Muslims constituted over a third of the local population and owned most of the finest dwellings. You can try to gain admission to the **Krallis and Yiannakos mansions**, or the **municipal art gallery** occupying the former residence of local author Argyris Eftaliotis, which hosts temporary exhibitions. The small **archeological museum** (Tues–Sun 8am–2.30pm;

free), in the basement of the town hall, features finds from the ancient town, including blue Roman beads to ward off the evil eye (belief in this affliction is age-old and pan-Mediterranean). Archival photos depict the Greek conquest of the island in November–December 1912, with Ottoman POWs being dispatched afterwards from Mólyvos port to Anatolia. Barely excavated **ancient Mithymna** to the northwest is of essentially specialist interest, though a necropolis has been unearthed next to the bus stop.

Modern dwellings and hotels have been banned from the municipal core, but this hasn't stopped a steady drain of all the authentic life from the upper bazaar; just one lonely tailor still plies his trade amongst souvenir shops vastly surplus to requirements, and the last traditional locals' ouzerí shut in 1989. Cast as an upmarket resort in the early 1980s, Mólyvos is now firmly middle of the road, with the usual silly T-shirts and other shoddy souvenirs carpeting every vertical surface of yet another, however intrinsically attractive, stage-set for mass tourism.

Practicalities

The **town beach** is mediocre, improving somewhat as you head towards the southern end and a clothing-optional zone. Advertised **boat excursions** to bays as remote as Ánaxos and Tsónia (see overleaf) seem a frank admission of this failing; there are also five to seven daily minibus shuttles in season, linking all points to Ánaxos and Eftaloú.

The main sea-level thoroughfare, straight past the tourist office, heads towards the harbour; along or just below it stand a number of bona fide **hotels** or **pensions** not completely taken over by packages. These include the *Hermes* very near the beach (☎02530/71 250; ❹), with large airy rooms; the *Molyvos I* next door (☎02530/71 496, ℱ71 640; ❺); the humble *Poseidon* just down from the tourist office (☎02530/71 981; ❸); and the *Adonis* inland and northwest of these (☎02530/71 866, ℱ71 636; ❺), which has heating and is thus the only all-year hotel here. For rooms, seek out the modern studio units of Khryssi Bourdhadonaki (☎02530/72 193; ❸), towards Ayía Kyriakí; those of Panayiotis Baxevanellis (☎02530/71 558 or call at the *El Greco* cake shop; ❶), with a preponderance of double beds and a communal kitchen; *Studios Voula* below the castle car park (☎02530/72 017 or 71 305), which has studios (❸) or a restored four-person house (❹), both with knockout views; and the quiet, exceedingly simple rooms of Varvara Kelesi (☎02530/71 460; ❷), way up by the castle. Otherwise, rooms can be reserved through the municipal **tourist office** by the bus stop (daily: summer theoretically 8am–3pm & 6.30–8.30pm; spring and autumn 8.30am–3pm; ☎02530/71 347). The official **campsite**, *Camping Methymna*, lies 2km northeast of town on the Eftaloú road.

The sea-view **tavernas** on the lower market lane of 17-Noemvríou are all much of a muchness, where you pay primarily for the view; it's far better to either head for outlying villages (see overleaf) or descend to the fishing port, where *The Captain's Table* (with green chairs) combines the virtues of fresh seafood, meat grills and vegetarian mezédhes, while *To Khtapodhi*, in the old customs house by the port entrance, has fairly consistent quality and treats such as *sardhélles pastés*. Many consider the five-kilometre trip east to Vafiós worth it to patronize either *To Petrino*, *Taverna Vafios* or *Taverna Ilias*, especially the last of them with its wonderful bread and bulk wine – but avoid deep-fried dishes at any of these places. Also highly recommended, and open all year, is *Iy Eftalou*, 4km northeast near the eponymous spa (see p.881), where the food (mostly grills) and tree-shaded setting are splendid. For dessert, try the pudding and cake shop *El Greco* on the lower market lane, where proprietor Panayiotis is a wonderful raconteur (in several languages).

THE EAST AND NORTH AEGEAN | Northern Lésvos

10

Midsummer sees a short **festival of music and theatre** up in the castle, and there's also a well-regarded summer **cinema** next to the taxi rank. Night-owls are well catered for with a selection of music bars: *Music Bazaar* near the harbour for loud, danceable sounds; *Skala* just up the hill from the port, with live music three nights weekly; the disco and young-things' hangout *Congas Bar* (shuts mid-Sept) below the shore road; and the all-season *Gatelousi Piano Bar* near the *Olive Press Hotel*, a more genteel branch of state-of-the-art outdoor disco *Gatelousi*, 3km towards Pétra, the place to be seen on a Saturday night (June–Aug only). Around the tourist office you'll find two **bank** autotellers, plus numerous **motorbike and car rental** places, including Kosmos (☎02530/71 650). The main **post office** is near the top of the upper commercial street, with a seasonal branch on the shore road Mihaïl Goútou.

Pétra and Ánaxos

Since there are political and practical limits to the expansion of Mólyvos, many package companies have shifted emphasis to **PÉTRA**, 5km due south. The place has sprawled untidily behind its broad sand beach and seafront square, but the core of old stone houses, many with Levantine-style balconies overhanging the street, remains. Pétra takes its name from the giant **rock monolith** located some distance inland and enhanced by the eighteenth-century **church of the Panayía Glykofiloússa**, reached via 103 rock-hewn steps. Other local attractions include the sixteenth-century **church of Áyios Nikólaos**, with three phases of well-preserved frescoes, and the intricately decorated **Vareltzídhena mansion** (Tues–Sun 8.30am–7pm, may close earlier off-season; free), with naive wall paintings of courting couples and a stylized view of a naval engagement at Constantinople.

Most small hotels and studios are block-booked, so on-spec arrivals should make a beeline for the Women's Agricultural Tourism Cooperative on the south side of the seafront square (☎02530/41 238, ℱ41 309, ℮womes@otenet.gr), formed by Pétra's women in 1984 to offer something more unusual for visitors. In addition to operating an excellent, inexpensive restaurant on the square, with both grills and *mayireftá* served at rooftop seating, they arrange rooms or studios (❶–❷) in a number of scattered premises. Aside from the co-operative's eatery, most tavernas lack distinction, though some people like *Iy Dhrosia* and *To Khrysso Petalo* behind the beach. You're probably better off out of town – either at the *Taverna Petri* in the *Petri* village 3km inland, with superb home-recipe *mayireftá* and a view terrace, or at Avláki, 1.5km southwest en route to Ánaxos, where there's a competent, signposted eponymous taverna/ouzerí behind a tiny beach.

ÁNAXOS, 3km south of Pétra, is a higgledy-piggledy package resort fringing by far the cleanest beach in the area: a kilometre of sand cluttered with sunbeds, pedalos and a handful of tavernas that are an improvement on the unmemorable snack bars of yore. From anywhere along here you enjoy beautiful sunsets between and beyond three offshore islets.

Around Mount Lepétymnos

East of Mólyvos, the villages of 968-metre **Mount Lepétymnos**, marked by tufts of poplars, provide a day's rewarding exploration. The first stop, though not exactly up the hill, might be **Loutrá Eftaloú**, some thermal baths 5km along the road passing the campsite. Insist on patronizing the hot pool under the Ottoman-era domed structure, not the sterile modern tub-rooms (daily 8am–noon & 2–6pm; €2.40). Nearby, there is a considerable number of fancy hotels and bungalow complexes, friendliest and best value (though tour-dominated like the others) being the *Eftalou* (☎02530/71 584; ❹), with a pool, well-tended garden and loyal repeat clientele.

The main road around the mountain first heads 6km east to **VAFIÓS**, with its three aforementioned tavernas (see p.879), before curling north around the base of the peaks. This route is entirely paved, but the twice-daily bus service back towards Mytilíni does not resume until Áryennos, 6km before the exquisite hill village of **SYKAMINIÁ** (**Sykamiá**), birthplace of the novelist Stratis Myrivilis. Below the "Plaza of the Workers' First of May", with its two traditional kafenía and views north to Turkey, one of the imposing basalt-built houses is marked as his childhood home. A marked trail shortcuts the twisting road down to **SKÁLA SYKAMINIÁS**, easily the most picturesque fishing port on Lésvos. Myrivilis used it as the setting for his best-known work, *The Mermaid Madonna*, and the tiny rock-top chapel at the end of the jetty will be instantly recognizable to anyone who has read the book.

On a practical level, Skála has a few pensions, such as the central *Gorgona* (☎02530/55 301; ❷), and four **tavernas**. The most durable of these is *Iy Skamnia* (aka *Iy Mouria*), with seating under the mulberry tree in which Myrivilis used to sleep on hot summer nights, though newer *Anemoessa* (closest to the chapel) has overtaken it quality-wise. The only local beach is the extremely stony one of **Kayiá** 1.5km east, where *Psarotaverna Kayia* near its east end does lots of dishes besides fish.

Continuing east from upper Sykaminiá, you soon come to **KLIÓ**, whose single main street (marked "kentrikí agorá") leads down to a platía with a plane tree, fountain, kafenía and more views across to Turkey. The village is set attractively on a slope, down which a six-kilometre dirt road, marked in English or Greek and passable with care in an ordinary car, descends to **Tsónia beach**, 600m of beautiful pink volcanic sand.

South of Klió, the route forks at Kápi, from where you can complete a loop of the mountain by bearing west along a road completely paved except for a few hundred metres before Stýpsi. **PELÓPI** is the ancestral village of unsuccessful 1988 US presidential candidate Michael Dukakis (who finally visited the island in 2000), and sports a former mosque, now used as a warehouse, on the main square. **IPSILOMÉTOPO**, 5km further along, is punctuated by a minaret (but no mosque) and hosts revels on July 17, the feast of Ayía Marína. By the time you reach sprawling **STÝPSI**, you're just 4km shy of the main Kalloní–Mólyvos road; it's also not a bad start-point for rambles along Lepétymnos's steadily dwindling network of trails (a locally sold guide by Mike Maunder, *17 Walks Around Pétra and Mólyvos*, details some).

Mandamádhos and Taxiárhis monastery

The main highway south from Klió and Kápi leads back to the capital through **MANDAMÁDHOS**. This attractive inland village is famous for its pottery, including the Ali Baba-style *pithária* (olive oil urns) seen throughout Lésvos, but more so for the "black" icon of the Archangel Michael, whose enormous **monastery of Taxiárhis** (daily: summer 6am–10pm; winter 6.30am–7pm), in a valley just northeast, is the powerful focus of a thriving cult. The image – supposedly made from a mixture of mud and the blood of monks slaughtered in a massacre – is really more idol than icon, both in its lumpy three-dimensionality and in the former rather pagan manner of veneration. First there was the custom of the coin-wish, whereby you pressed a coin to the Archangel's forehead – if it stuck, your wish would be granted. Owing to wear and tear on the image, the practice is now forbidden, with supplicants referred to an alternative icon by the main entrance.

It's further believed that while carrying out his various errands on behalf of the faithful, the Archangel gets through more footwear than Imelda Marcos. Accordingly the icon used to be surrounded not by the usual *támmata* (votive medallions) but by piles of miniature gold and silver shoes. The ecclesiastical authorities, embarrassed by such "primitive" practices, removed all the little shoes in 1986. Since then, a token substitute has reappeared: several pairs of tin slippers which can be filled with money and left in front of the icon. Just why his devotees should want to encourage these perpetual peripatetics is unclear, since in Greek folklore the Archangel Michael is also the one who fetches the souls of the dying, and modern Greek attitudes towards death are as bleak as those of their pagan ancestors.

Límnos

Límnos is a sizeable agricultural and garrison island whose remoteness and peculiar ferry schedules have until recently protected it from the worst excesses of the holiday trade. Most summer visitors are Greek, particularly from Thessaloníki, though the locals are becoming increasingly used to numbers of German and British visitors. Accommodation tends to be comfortable if a bit overpriced, with a strong bias towards self-catering units, and **backpackers** are explicitly **discouraged**. The bucolic island has been getting trendy of late: there are upscale souvenir shops, village houses restored by Thessalonians as weekend retreats, some sort of noon-to-small-hours musical bar at every beach, and a fairly significant gay scene.

Límnos's traditional role is as an army posting. Its **military presence** ran to 25,000 soldiers at the nadir of Greco-Turkish relations in the late 1980s, though it is now down to about 10,000; conventional tourism was slow in coming because the islanders made a reliable living off the soldiers and family members coming to visit them. Since the 1960s, the island has been the focus of periodic disputes between the Greek and Turkish governments; Turkey has a long-standing demand that Límnos should be demilitarized, and Turkish aircraft regularly intrude Greek air space overhead, prompting immediate responses from the Greek Air Force squadron here.

The bays of **Bourniá** and **Moúdhros**, the latter one of the largest natural harbours in the Aegean, almost divide Límnos in two. The west of the island is dramatically bare and hilly, with abundant basalt put to good use as street cobbles and house masonry. Like most volcanic islands, Límnos produces excellent wine from westerly vineyards – good dry whites, rosés and excellent retsina – plus oúzo at Kondiás. The east is low-lying and speckled with marshes popular with duck-hunters, where it's not occupied by cattle, combine harvesters and vast corn fields.

Despite off-islander slander to that effect, Límnos is not flat, barren or tree-less; much of the countryside consists of rolling hills, well vegetated except on their heights, and with substantial clumps of almond, jujube, myrtle, oak, poplar and mulberry trees. The island is, however, extremely dry, with irrigation water pumped from deep wells, and a limited number of potable springs. Yet various terrapin-haunted creeks bring sand to several long, **sandy beaches** around the coast, where it's easy to find a stretch to yourself – though there's no escaping the stingless jellyfish which occasionally pour out of the Dardanelles and die here in the shallows (they've fortunately decreased in recent years). On the plus side, beaches shelve gently, making them ideal for children and quick to warm up in early summer, with no cool currents except near the river mouths.

LÍMNOS

N

0   5 km

Bourniá
Bay

Kótsinas

Salt Marsh

Kéros

Piáka

Panayiá

Áyios Sózon

Kavírio
(Kabireío)

Ifestía
(Hephaestia)

Kondopoúli

Kalliópi

Pokyókhni
(Polyochni)

Fyssíni

Kamínia

Roussopoúli

Skandháli

Repanídhi

Romanoú

Lýkhna

Allied War
Cemetery

Város

Atsikí

Moúdhros
Bay

Karpássi

Livadhohóri

Kallithéa

Néa
Koútali

Moúdhros

Dháfni

Áyios Dhimítrios

Angariónes

Pedhinó

Tsimándhria

Dhapóri

Havoúli

Katálakos

Allied War
Cemetery

Portianoú

Thermá

Sardhés

Kornós

Kaspakás

Kondiás

Thános

Evgátis
(Áyios Pávlos)

Áyios Ioánnis

Avlónas

Ríha Nerá

Mýrina (Kástro)

Platý

Paralía
Platý

Paralía
Thánous

Playós
Mólos

Mýrina

MÝRINA (Kástro), the capital and port on the west coast, has the atmosphere of a provincial market town rather than of a resort. With about five thousand inhabitants, it's pleasantly low-key, if not especially picturesque, apart from a core neighbourhood of old stone houses dating from the Ottoman occupation, and the ornate Neoclassical mansions at Romeïkós Yialós. Few explicitly Turkish monuments have survived, though a fountain at the harbour end of Kýdha retains its calligraphic inscription and is still highly prized for its drinking water. Most other things of interest line Kydhá/Karatzá, the main shopping street stretching from the harbour to Romeïkós Yialós, the beach and esplanade to the north of the castle, or Garoufalídhou, its perpendicular offshoot, roughly halfway along.

The originally Byzantine **castle** (access unrestricted), on a headland between the ferry dock and Romeïkós Yialós, is quite ruined despite later additions by the Genoese and Ottomans, but warrants a climb at sunset for views over the town, the entire west coast and – in exceptional conditions – over to Mount Athos, 35 nautical miles west (which can also be glimpsed from any suitable height east of town).

The **Archeological Museum** (daily 8am–7pm; €1) occupies an Ottoman mansion behind Romeïkós Yialós, not far from the site of Bronze Age Myrina in the suburb of Rihá Nerá. Finds are assiduously labelled in Greek, Italian and English, and the entire premises are exemplary in terms of presentation – the obvious drawback being that many of the best items have been spirited away to Athens, leaving a collection that's essentially of specialist interest. The south ground-floor gallery is mainly devoted to pottery from Polyókhni (Polychni); the north wing contains more of the same, plus items from ancient Myrina; upstairs features galleries of post-Bronze Age artefacts from Kavírio (Kabireio) and Ifestía (Hephaestia). The star upper-storey exhibits are votive lamps in the shape of sirens, found in an Archaic sanctuary at Hephaestia, much imitated in modern local jewellery. Rather less vicious than Homer's creatures, they are identified more invitingly as the "muses of the underworld, creatures of super-human wisdom, incarnations of nostalgia for paradise". Another entire room is devoted to metalwork, of which the most impressive items are gold jewellery and bronze objects, both practical (cheese graters, door-knockers) and whimsical-naturalistic (a snail, a vulture).

Practicalities

The sleek new civilian **airport** is 19km east of Mýrina, almost at the exact geographic centre of the island, sharing a runway with an enormous air-force base; there's an Olympic-run shuttle bus between town and airport – consult the Olympic office for departure times (☏02540/22 078). **Ferries** dock at the southern end of the town, in the shadow of the castle; there are separate agencies for the sailings of NEL boats (☏02540/22 460) and the *Saos II* (☏02540/29 571).

The **bus station** is on Platía Eleftheríou Venizélou, at the north end of Kydhá. One look at the sparse schedules (only a single daily afternoon departure to most points, slightly more frequently to Kondiás and Moúdhros) will convince you of the need to rent a vehicle. **Cars**, **motorbikes** and **bicycles** can be had from Myrina Rent a Car (☏02540/24 476 or 24 100), Petridou Tours (☏02540/22 039), Holiday (☏02540/24 357), Best (☏02540/22 127) or Auto Europe (☏02540/23 777); rates for bikes are only slightly above the island norm, but cars are expensive. A motorbike (most obviously from Moto

Lemnos, ☎02540/25 002) is generally enough to explore the coast and the interior, as there are few steep gradients but many perilously narrow village streets.

All five **banks** have cash dispensers; the **post office** and Olympic airlines terminal are adjacent to each other on Garoufalídhou, with a **laundry** across the way by the Hotel Paris. There are **internet** facilities at *Excite Club*, just behind the port roundabout, and at *Joy*, by the post office.

Accommodation

Despite Límnos's steady gentrification, you may still be met off the boat with offers of a **room**; there are officially a couple dozen licensed establishments. The most durable budget establishment is the welcoming *Apollo Pavillion*, hidden away in a peaceful cul-de-sac off Frýnis (☎02540/24 315, ℗23 712, @apollo47@otenet.gr), with multibed rooms in the basement (€26.50 for a standard double) and more comfortable self-catering units upstairs (●). Otherwise, try the *Hotel Lemnos* (☎02540/22 153, ℗23 329; ●), by the harbour, with air-con, fridges and balconies offsetting small-hours ferry noise, or the quiet *Hotel Ifestos* in Andhróni district (☎02540/24 960, ℗23 623; ●), with similar amenities but a mix of sea and mountain views, a pleasant bar-lounge and professional service (something of a rarity in town).

Romeïkós Yialós has a few **pensions and small hotels** housed in its restored houses, though all are affected by evening noise from the bars below. Best value is *Blue Waters* (☎02540/24 403, ℗25 004, @bwkon@otenet.gr; ●), with smallish but decently appointed rooms; one block inland at Sakhtoúri 7, *Pension Romeïkos Yíalos* (☎02540/23 787; ●) in a stone mansion may be quieter. Just north of Romeïkós Yialós, the areas of Rihá Nerá and Áyios Pandelímonas are likely bets for self-catering units. Finally, the *Akti Myrina* (☎02540/22 681, ℗22 947, @www.ventaglio-com) is a self-contained **luxury** complex of wood-and-stone bungalows (avoid the awful modern annexe) at the north end of Romeïkós Yialós, with all conceivable diversions and comforts. It is run by, and mainly caters for Italians, and is off-limits from late June through August, but during low season (May/Sept) you can squeeze in for €235 per couple per night, all meals and sports facilities included.

There's **no official campsite** on Límnos; Greek caravanners and campers have been banished from the north end of Platý beach, though a few tents still sprout furtively at Paralía Thánous and at Kéros (see p.887).

Eating and drinking

About halfway along Kydhá, *O Platanos* serves traditional *mayireftá* to big crowds on an atmospheric little square under two plane trees; for affordable seaside dining, look no further than *Ostria* at the town of Toúrkikos Yialós beach, which offers a mix of grills, fish and ouzomezédhes from noon until late. Seafood is excellent on Límnos owing to its proximity to the Dardanelles and seasonal fish migrations; accordingly there are no fewer than five tavernas arrayed around the little fishing port. There's little to distinguish their prices or menus, though *O Glaros* at the far end is considered the best – and works out slightly more expensive.

Not too surprisingly given the twee setting, the restaurants and bars on Romeïkós Yialós are pretty poor value, except for a drink in sight of the castle. The tree-shaded tables of *Iy Tzitzifies* on Rihá Nerá, the next bay north, are a far better option; most of the extensive menu of fish, mezédhes and *mayireftá* is likely to be available on any given day.

Western Límnos

As town **beaches** go, Romeïkós Yialós and Toúrkikos Yialós are not at all bad; Rihá Nerá is even better, with watersports craft on offer. But if you're looking for more pristine conditions, head 3km north past the *Akti Myrina* to Avlónas, unspoiled except for the *Porto Marina Palace* luxury complex flanking it on the south. Some 6km from town you work your way through **KÁSPAKAS**, its north-facing houses in pretty, tiled tiers, before plunging down to **Áyios Ioánnis**. Here, the island's most unusual taverna (late June to Aug) features seating in the shade of piled-up volcanic boulders, with a serviceably sandy beach just north of the fishing anchorage. If it's shut, *Taverna Iliovasilemata* to the south is welcoming, with good (if slightly pricey) fish.

PLATÝ, 2km southeast of Mýrina, has had its profile spoiled by the kind of modern villa construction that is blighting many Limnian villages latterly, but it does have two nocturnally popular **tavernas**. By far the better of these is *O Sozos*, just off the main platía, where you'll have to show up early for a table (groups should reserve on ☏02540/25 085). Fine *orektiká*, lamb chops, steamed mussels, grilled *biftéki*, *tsípouro* and local bulk wine are strong points; the bill shouldn't exceed €9. The long sandy beach, 700m below, is popular and usually jellyfish-free, with watersports available; except for the unsightly Mark Warner compound at the south end, the area is still pretty rural, with sheep parading to and fro at dawn and dusk. The single **hotel**, low-rise *Plati Beach* (☏02540/23 583 or 094/4965189; ❷), has an enviable position in the middle of the beach, but get a room towards the back if you don't fancy noise from the ground-floor bar/restaurant; there are more basic **rooms**, though with fridges and proper showers, available through *Tzimis Taverna* (☏02540/24 142; ❶), which divides the lunchtime trade with its neighbour *Grigoris* near the south end of the beach, though both lose out in the evenings to the village-centre tavernas. The highest standard of **studios** in the area, if not the island, is the tastefully landscaped *Villa Afroditi* (☏02540/23 141, ℉25 031, winter ☏01/96 33 488; ❹), with a pleasant pool bar, weekly barbecue nights for guests, and one of the best buffet breakfasts in Greece. The South African management also offers a lovely restored house in Kondiás village, which sleeps four – €73.50 per night for a week's stay.

THÁNOS, 2km further southeast, seems a bigger, more architecturally characterful version of Platý village, with a well-regarded central-platía taverna (evenings only) and high-standard mock-trad bungalows at the east edge (☏02540/23 162; ❹). **Paralía Thánous**, 1.5km on a paved road below the village, is perhaps the most scenic of the southwestern beaches, flanked by weird volcanic crags and with views on a clear afternoon out to Áyios Efstrátios island. Of two tavernas, one, *O Nikos* (☏02540/22 787; ❶), rents a handful of basic rooms. Beyond Thános, the road curls over to the enormous beach at **Evgátis** (Áyios Pávlos), reckoned to be the island's best, with more igneous pinnacles on the west. Despite this rating, there's so far just the regulation music bar/*kantína* on the sand, and a full-service taverna across the road.

Some 3km further along (11km from Mýrina), **KONDIÁS** is the island's third largest settlement, cradled between two hills tufted with Limnos's only pine forest. Stone-built, red-tiled houses combine with the setting to make Kondiás the most attractive inland village, a fact not lost on the urban Greeks restoring old houses with varying degrees of taste. Short-term facilities are limited, and aren't much better at the shore annexe of **Dhiapóri**, 2km east. The beach is unappealing (and backed by a huge, fenced-off minefield), the tavernas listless, with the main interest lent by the narrow isthmus dividing the bays of Kondiás and Moúdhros.

Eastern Límnos

The shores of **Moúdhros Bay**, glimpsed south of the trans-island road, are muddy and best avoided unless you're a clam-digger. The bay itself enjoyed considerable importance during World War I, culminating in the Ottoman surrender aboard the British warship HMS *Agamemnon* here on October 30, 1918. The port of **MOÚDHROS**, the second-largest town on Límnos, is a dreary place, with only a wonderfully kitsch, two-belfried church to recommend it. The closest decent beach is at **Havoúli**, 4km south by dirt track and still far from the open sea. Despite this, there are three hotels here; best of these, if overpriced, is *Kyma* (℡02540/71 333, ℻71 484; ❹), whose more reasonable restaurant is well placed for a lunch break if you're visiting the archeological sites and beaches of eastern Límnos.

About 800m along the Roussopoúli road, you pass an **Allied military cemetery** (unlocked) maintained by the Commonwealth War Graves Commission; its neat (if rather dry) lawns and rows of white headstones seem incongruous in such parched surroundings. In 1915, Moúdhros Bay was the principal staging area for the disastrous Gallipoli campaign. Of the roughly 36,000 Allied dead, 887 – mainly battle casualties who died after having been evacuated to the base hospital at Moúdhros – are buried here, with 348 more at another signposted graveyard behind the church in Portianoú.

Indications of the most advanced Neolithic civilization in the Aegean have been unearthed at **Polyókhni** (**Polyochni**), 3km from the gully-hidden village of Kamínia (7km east of Moúdhros). The site occupies a bluff overlooking a long, narrow rock-and-sand beach flanked by stream valleys. Since the 1930s, Italian excavations have uncovered five layers of settlement, the oldest from late in the fourth millennium BC, predating Troy on the Turkish coast opposite. The town met a sudden, violent end from war or earthquake in about 2100 BC. The actual **ruins** (daily 8am–7pm; free) are of essentially specialist interest, though a *bouleuterion* (assembly hall) with bench seating, a mansion and the landward fortifications are labelled. During August and September the Italian excavators are about, and may be free to show you around the place; at other times you should obtain the useful TAP brochure from the Mýrina museum to make any sense of the place.

Ifestía and Kavírio, the other significant **ancient sites** on Límnos, are reached via the village of Kondopoúli, 7km northeast of Moúdhros. Both sites are rather remote, and only reachable with your own transport. **Ifestía** (**Hephaestia**), 4km from Kondopoúli by rough, signposted track, has little to offer nonspecialists. **Kavírio** (**Kabireio**), on the opposite shore of Tigáni Bay and accessed by the same road built to serve the now-bankrupt and derelict Kaviria Palace luxury complex, is more evocative. The **ruins** (daily 8am–7pm; free) are those of a sanctuary connected with the cult of the Samothracian Kabiroi (see p.891), though the site here is probably older. Little survives other than the ground plan, but the setting is undeniably impressive. Eleven column stumps stake out a stoa, behind eight spots marked as column bases in the *telestirio* or shrine where the cult mysteries took place. More engaging, perhaps, is a nearby sea grotto identified as the Homeric **Spiliá toú Filoktíti**, where the Trojan war hero Philoctetes was abandoned by his comrades-in-arms until his stinking, gangrenous leg had healed. Landward access to the cave is via steps leading down from the caretaker's shelter, though final access (from a little passage on the right as you face the sea) involves some wading.

The beach at **Kéros**, 2.5km by dirt road below **KALLIÓPI** (which has two snack bar/**tavernas**, and smart **rooms** at the edge of town – ℡02540/41 730,

3), is the best in this part of the island. A 1500-metre stretch of sand with dunes and a small pine grove, plus shallow water, it attracts a number of Greek tourists and foreigners with camper vans and windsurfers; a small snack *kantína* operates near the parking area during July and August only.

On the other side of Kondopoúli, reached via Repanídhi village, the often dirty, hard-packed beach of **Kótsinas** is set in the protected western limb of Bourniá Bay. The nearby anchorage (follow signs to "Kótsinas Fortress") offers a pair of **tavernas**; the better of these is *Tò Koráli* by the water, which is reliably open at lunch, with a wide range of mezédhes and affordable fish. Up on a knoll overlooking the jetty, there's a corroded, sword-brandishing statue of Maroula, a Genoese-era heroine who delayed the Ottoman conquest by a few years, and a large **church of Zoödhóhou Piyís** (the Life-Giving Spring). This is nothing extraordinary, but beside it 63 steps lead down through an illuminated tunnel in the rock to the potable (if slightly mineral) spring in question, oozing into a cool, vaulted chamber.

Áyios Efstrátios (Aï Strátis)

Áyios Efstrátios is without doubt one of the quietest and loneliest islands in the Aegean. Historically, the only outsiders to stay here were compelled to do so – it served as a place of exile for political prisoners under both the Metaxas regime of the 1930s and the various right-wing governments that followed the civil war. It's still unusual for foreign travellers to visit the island, and, if you do, you might be asked why you've shown up.

You may initially ask yourself the same question, for **ÁYIOS EFSTRÁTIOS** village – the only habitation on the island – must be one of the ugliest in Greece. Devastation caused by an earthquake in February 1968, which killed half the population, was compounded by the reconstruction plan: the contract went to a company with junta connections, who prevented the survivors from returning to their old homes and used army bulldozers to raze even those structures that could have been repaired. From the hillside, some two dozen surviving houses of the old village overlook its replacement, whose grim rows of prefabs constitute a sad monument to the corruption of the junta years. If you're curious, there's a pre-earthquake photograph of the village in the kafenío by the port.

Architecture apart, Áyios Efstrátios still functions as a traditional fishing and farming community, with the prefabs set at the mouth of a wooded stream valley draining to the sandy harbour beach. Tourist amenities consist of just two basic **tavernas** (a third may open in midsummer), plus a total of three **pensions**. Best of these, in one of the surviving old houses, is the *Xenonas Aï-Stratis* (☎02540/93 329; ③); Andonis Paneras (☎02540/93 209; ③) and Apostolos Paneras (☎02540/93 343; ③) have more conventional rooms in the prefabs. These relatively stiff prices for such an out-of-the-way place reflect Aï Strátis' increasing popularity with Greeks, and you may have to ring all three spots for a vacancy in season.

As you walk away from the village – there are few cars and no real roads – things improve rapidly. The landscape, dry hills and valleys scattered with a surprising number of oak trees, is deserted apart from wild rabbits, sheep, an occasional shepherd, and some good beaches where you can camp in seclusion. **Alonítsi**, on the north coast – a ninety-minute walk from the village following a track up the north side of the valley – is a two-kilometre stretch of sand with rolling breakers and views across to Límnos.

South of the village, there's a series of greyish sand beaches, most with wells and drinkable water, although with few real paths in this part of the island, getting to them can be something of a scramble. **Lidharío**, at the end of an attractive wooded valley, is the first worthwhile beach, but again it's a ninety-minute walk, unless you can persuade a fisherman to take you by boat. Some of the caves around the coast are home to the rare Mediterranean monk seal, but you're unlikely to see one.

Ferries on the Kavála-Límnos-Rafína line call at Áyios Efstrátios twice weekly most of the year; in summer a small Límnos-based ferry, the *Aiolis*, sails every weekday (Mon–Fri) at 3pm from Límnos, returning the next morning. Despite recent harbour improvements, this is still a very exposed anchorage, and in bad weather you could end up stranded here far longer than you bargained for. If an indefinite stay does not appeal, it's best to visit from Límnos on the day-trip offered by the *Aiolis* (usually on Sun).

Samothráki (Samothrace)

Samothráki has one of the most dramatic profiles of all the Greek islands, second only to Thíra's: its dark mass of granite rises abruptly from the sea, culminating in the 1611-metre **Mount Fengári**. Seafarers have always been guided by its imposing outline, clearly visible from the mainland, and in legend its summit provided a vantage point for Poseidon to watch over the siege of Troy. The mostly forbidding coastline provides no natural anchorage, but in ancient times the island was colonized by settlers from Thrace, with more recent migrations from Anatolia and Lésvos swelling the population. Landing is still very much subject to the vagaries of the notoriously unpredictable weather, but it did not deter pilgrims who, for hundreds of years, journeyed to the island to visit the **Sanctuary of the Great Gods** and were initiated into its mysteries. The Sanctuary remains the main archeological attraction of the island which, too remote for most tourists, combines earthy simplicity with natural grandeur. The tourist season is relatively short-lived – essentially (late) July and August – but you will find some facilities open as early as Easter and one or two all year round.

Kamariótissa

All ferries and hydrofoils dock at the dull village of **KAMARIÓTISSA**, where you're unlikely to want to spend much time. That said it could be your most convenient base, since some of Samothráki's best **hotels** lie along or just behind the tree-lined seafront and various **rooms** for rent, many them more than acceptable, can be found in the maze of streets behind; owners often meet incoming vessels. As on most islands with a short season, accommodation can be pricey for what you get, and bargaining is not always productive, especially in midsummer. Along the shore, some way east of your point of arrival, is the recently refurbished *Kyma* (☎05510/41 263; ❸); be aware that rooms overlooking the pebbly beach can get noise from the string of *barákia* which constitutes Samothráki's main nightlife, and avoid the hotel restaurant – the taverna (see below) is much better. Calmer, but somewhat pricier, is the *Niki Beach* (☎05510/41 561; ❹) beyond the far north end of the quay. Above, occupying a bluff and visible from out to sea, is the slightly impersonal *Aeolos* (☎05510/41 595, ℉41 810; ❺); with a large pool and quiet, spacious rooms, it's the island's most comfortable accommodation and offers good half-board deals out of season. Bars and cafés on the harbourfront serve snacks and breakfasts, but the only commendable **taverna** is the *Limanaki*, at the southern end, beyond the docks: excellent Limniot wine from the barrel is perfect with the fish and seafood on offer, which you can virtually watch being unloaded by local fishermen as you order.

Motorbikes and **cars** are in short supply, so it's worth grabbing one immediately on disembarkation – or even reserving a bike in advance from Hanou Brothers (☎05510/41 511) or a car from Niki Tours (☎05510/41 465), which sells plane tickets as well; also try Kyrkos car rental (☎097/4371122). For information about and tickets for **ferries and hydrofoils**, a converted container opposite the docks acts as offices. A fairly reliable timetable for island **buses** is also posted here; these travel up to eight times daily in season (but only twice weekly in deepest winter) along the north coast to Loutrá (Thermá) via Paleópoli (near the site of the Sanctuary) or Karyótes, or directly inland seven times daily to the largest village, Hóra. As with lodging, rented transport is more expensive than on most islands, but if you've the means go for a car as Samothracian roads are often dangerously windswept for bikes. Note that there is currently only one fuel pump on the entire island, 1km above the port, en route to Hóra. Kamariótissa also has a **bank** with a cash dispenser, but no post office.

Hóra

HÓRA, also known as **Samothráki**, is the island's capital. Far larger than implied by the portion visible from out at sea, it's an attractive town of Thracian-style stone houses, some of them whitewashed, clustered around a hollow in the western flanks of Mount Fengári. It is dominated by the Genoese Gateluzzi fort, of which little survives other than the gateway. Half an hour or so can be whiled away at the charming **folklore museum**, which is free, but the opening hours are erratic; it contains a motley collection of clothing, domestic items and miscellany.

Hóra has no reliable short-term accommodation, though asking for unadvertised rooms in the various kafenía along the winding commercial street can be productive. On the atmospheric, irregularly shaped platía, a couple of **tavernas**, *Iy Platia* and the more down-to-earth *To Kastro*, provide the best suppers on the island, with such delicacies as stuffed squid and *mýdhia saganáki* (mussels with cheese). There have been mutterings of moving the administrative capital down to Kamariótissa, but until further notice the island's **post office** is here.

The Sanctuary of the Great Gods

From Hóra it is 3km to the hamlet of Paleópoli (see below) and, in a stony but thickly wooded ravine between it and the plunging northwestern ridge of Mount Fengári, lie the remains of the **Sanctuary of the Great Gods**. Buses from Kamariótissa stop nearby, opposite a small car park on the seashore. From the late Bronze Age until the early Byzantine era, the mysteries and sacrifices of the cult of the Great Gods were performed on Samothráki, indeed in ancient Thracian dialect until the second century BC. The island was the spiritual focus of the northern Aegean, and its importance in the ancient world was comparable (although certainly secondary) to that of the Mysteries of Eleusis.

The religion of the Great Gods revolved around a hierarchy of ancient Thracian fertility figures: the Great Mother Axieros, a subordinate male deity known as Kadmilos, and the potent and ominous twin demons the *Kabiroi*, originally the local heroes Dardanos and Aeton. When the Aeolian colonists arrived (traditionally c.700 BC) they simply syncretized the resident deities with their own – the Great Mother became Cybele, her consort Hermes and the *Kabiroi* were fused interchangeably with the *Dioskouroi* Castor and Pollux, patrons of seafarers. Around the nucleus of a sacred precinct the newcomers made the beginnings of what is now the Sanctuary.

Despite their long observance, the mysteries of the cult were never explicitly recorded, since ancient writers feared incurring the wrath of the *Kabiroi* (who could brew up sudden, deadly storms), but it has been established that two levels of initiation were involved. Both ceremonies, in direct opposition to the elitism of Eleusis, were open to all, including women and slaves. The lower level of initiation, or *myesis*, may, as is speculated at Eleusis, have involved a ritual simulation of the life, death and rebirth cycle; in any case, it's known that it ended with joyous feasting, and it can be conjectured, since so many clay torches have been found, that it took place at night. The higher level of initiation, or *epopteia*, carried the unusual requirement of a moral standard (the connection of theology with morality, so strong in the later Judeo-Christian tradition, was rarely made by the early Greeks). This second level involved a full confession followed by absolution and baptism in bull's blood.

The only **accommodation** near the Sanctuary is in the tiny hamlet of **PALEÓPOLI**, where the old and basic *Xenia Hotel* (☎05510/41 166 or 41 230; ❹) offers a downmarket alternative to the smart but overpriced *Kastro Hotel* (☎05510/89 400, ℱ41 001, ⓦwww.kastro.hotel.gr; ❻), which comes with pool, restaurant and sea views; there are also some basic but en-suite rooms (❺) down on the seashore below the *kastro*.

The site

The **site** (Tues–Sun 8.30am–8.30pm, or dusk if earlier; €1.50 combined ticket with museum but no charge for site when museum is closed) is well labelled, simple to grasp and strongly evokes its proud past, while commanding views of the mountains and the sea. You might like to visit the **archeological museum** first (Tues–Sun 8.30am–3pm), and its exhibits spanning all eras of habita-

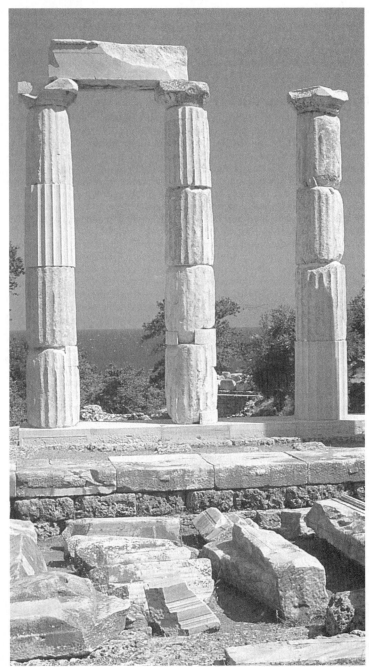

△ Sanctuary of the Great Gods, Samothráki

tion, from the Archaic to the Byzantine, since it explains the significance of the Sanctuary. Highlights include a **frieze** of dancing girls from the propylon of the Temenos, entablatures from different buildings, and Roman votive offerings such as coloured glass vials from the necropolis of the ancient town east of the Sanctuary. You can also see a reproduction of the exquisitely sculpted marble statue, the *Winged Victory of Samothrace*, which once stood breasting the wind at the prow of a marble ship in the Nymphaeum (see below). Discovered in 1863 by a French diplomat to the Sublime Porte it was carried off to the Louvre, where it is a major draw, and the well-crafted copy, visible here, was graciously donated to this museum a mere century later.

The **Anaktoron**, or hall of initiation for the first level of the mysteries, dates in its present form from Roman times. Its inner sanctum was marked by a warning stele, now in the museum, and at the southeast corner you can make out the **Priestly Quarters**, an antechamber where candidates for initiation donned white gowns. Next to it is the **Arsinoeion**, the largest circular ancient building known in Greece, used for libations and sacrifices. Within its rotunda are the fourth-century BC walls of a double precinct where a rock altar, the earliest preserved ruin on the site, has been uncovered. A little further south, on the same side of the path, you come to the **Temenos**, a rectangular area open to the sky where the feasting probably took place, and, edging its rear corner, the conspicuous **Hieron**, the site's most immediately impressive structure. Five columns and an architrave of the facade of this large Doric edifice, which hosted the higher level of initiation, have been re-erected; dating in part from the fourth century BC, it was heavily restored in Roman times. The stone steps have been replaced by modern blocks, but Roman benches for spectators remain *in situ*, along with the sacred stones where confession was heard. To the west of the path you can just discern the outline of the theatre, while just above it, tucked under the ridge is the **Nymphaeum (Fountain) of Nike**, which the *Winged Victory* used to preside over (see above). West of the theatre, occupying a high terrace, are remains of the main stoa; immediately north of this is an elaborate medieval fortification made entirely of antique material.

The north coast

With its running streams, giant plane trees and namesake hot springs, **LOUTRÁ** (aka **THERMÁ**), 6km east of Paleópoli, is a pleasant place to stay, although less so when it's packed in late July and August, mainly with an incongruous mixture of foreign hippies and elderly Greeks, here to take the sulphurous waters. You have a Hobson's choice of three facilities: the sterile, junta-era main baths (in theory, daily 8am–1pm & 5–7pm; often closed out of season; €1.50), the *psarováthres* or "fish ponds" – a trio of pleasantly rustic open-air pools with a wooden sun-shade, and a ramshackle hut with a very hot pool (keys from the warden of the main baths). These last two are free with no fixed opening hours, and they're reached by a dirt road starting above and to the right as you face the "improved" spa. For a cold-water but far more appealing contrast, the low waterfalls and rock pools of **Gría Váthra** are signposted 1.5km up the paved side road leading east from the main Thermá access drive.

Loutrá is also the prime base for the tough, six-hour climb up the 1611-metre **Mount Fengári** (known to the ancients as **Sáos**, a name found on some maps to this day), the highest peak in the Aegean islands; the path starts at the top of the village, beside a concrete water tank and a huge open-boled plane tree. Tell your accommodation proprietors that you're going, but no one else, as the police may try to stop you – army teams have been summoned on occasion to rescue ill-prepared climbers on what can be an unforgiving mountain. Fengári is Greek for "moon" and, according to legend, if you reach the top on the night of a full moon your wish will come true – most of those foolhardy enough to attempt this will just hope to get back down safely.

Loutrá is a rather dispersed place, with its winding dead-end streets, all ghostly quiet in winter, and its white-elephant miniharbour – built as an alternative to Kamariótissa, but never used. **Accommodation** includes the *Kaviros Hotel* (☎05510/98 277; ❹), just east of the "centre", and, further downhill, 700m from the beach, the *Mariva Bungalows* (☎05510/98 258; ❹). None of the tavernas is very inspired, a possible result (or cause) of a predominance in self-catering rooms; *Paradhisos* has the best setting, up under the trees, and charges accordingly. About halfway along the track to Gría Váthra, *Safki*, a summer-only café-bar, occupies the delightful old schoolhouse.

Beyond Loutrá and a ford, on the wooded coastline and reached by a road initially signposted "military camp", are two municipal **campsites**: the first, 1.5km from the village, although large, has no facilities except toilets, while the second, 3km from the village, is more expensive but has hot water, electricity, a small shop, restaurant and bar. The Loutrá bus sometimes goes to either site if you ask nicely.

Beaches on Samothráki's north shore are mostly clean but uniformly pebbly and exposed, but it's still worth continuing along the road east from Loutrá for the views and one or two minor sights. At **Cape Foniás** there's a ruined Gateluzzi watchtower and, 45-minutes' walk inland along the stream, there are **waterfalls** and cold pools much more impressive than those at Gría Váthra, though the signposted description of "canyon" is exaggerated. Some 15km from Loutrá along a fine corniche road is **Kípos beach**, a long strand facing the Turkish-held island of Gökçeada (Ímvros to the Greeks) and backed by open pasture and picturesque crags. The water is clean and there's a rock overhang for shelter at one end, a spring, shower and seasonal drinks *kantína*, but no food available.

The south coast

From the warmer south flank of the island, with its fertile farmland dotted with olive-groves, there are fine views out to sea – as far as Gökçeada on a clear day. Up to three daily buses go from Kamariótissa via the sleepy village of Lákoma as far as **PROFÍTIS ILÍAS**, an attractive hill village with a number of good **tavernas** – the best being *Paradhisos*, with a wonderful terrace – but no accommodation to speak of, except for some basic **rooms** (❷–❸). From Lákoma it is 8km east to aptly named **Pahiá Ámmos** ("coarse sand"), a long, clean beach with a taverna-rooms place (☎05510/94 235; ❸) at the west end. The nearest (meagre) supplies are in Lákoma, but this doesn't deter big summer crowds who also arrive by excursion kaïkia. These also continue east to **Vátos**, a secluded and sometimes nudist beach also accessible by land, the **Kremastá Nerá** coastal waterfalls, and finally round to Kípos beach (see above).

Thássos

Just 12km from the mainland, **Thássos** has long been a popular resort island for northern Greeks, and since the early 1990s has also attracted a cosmopolitan variety of tourists, in particular Romanians, Serbs, Bulgarians and Hungarians holidaying a tank or so of petrol away from home, plus plenty of the usual Germans and Brits on packages. Far from unspoiled – vast numbers of rural *bouzoúkia* (music halls) and tavernas lay on music at weekends with cheerful vulgarity – it has, however, some areas of outstanding natural beauty and the island's ordinary rural industries have somehow managed to survive.

Thássos still makes a substantial living from the pure-white marble which constitutes two-thirds of the landmass, found only here and quarried at dozens of sites (legal and unlicensed) in the hills between Liménas and Panayía. Olives, honey, fruit and nuts (often sold candied) are also important products. The spirit *tsípouro*, rather than wine, is the main local tipple; pear extract, onions or spices like cinnamon and anise are added to home-made batches.

Inhabited since the Stone Age, Thássos was settled by Parians in the seventh century BC, attracted by gold deposits between modern Liménas and Kínyra. Buoyed by revenues from these, and from silver mines under Thassian control on the mainland opposite, the ancient city-state here became the seat of a medium-sized seafaring empire. Commercial acumen did not spell military invincibility however; the Persians under Darius swept the Thassian fleets from the seas in 492 BC, and in 462 BC Athens permanently deprived Thássos of its autonomy after a three-year siege. The main port continued to thrive into Roman times, but lapsed into Byzantine and medieval obscurity.

Sadly, the salient fact of more recent history has been a series of devastating, deliberately set **fires** in the 1980s and 1990s; the worst one, in 1989, began near

Rahóni and burned for three days as far as Mariés. Only the northeastern quadrant of the island, plus the area around Astrís and Alykí, escaped, though the surviving forest is still home to numerous pine martens.

Thássos is just small enough to circumnavigate in one full day on a rented motorbike or car. The KTEL will do the driving for you – albeit with little chance for stopping – some four times daily. **Car rental** is dominated by Potos Car Rental (☎05930/23 969), with branches in all main resorts, or Rent-a-Car Thassos (☎05930/22 535), also widely represented, as are most of the major international chains, such as Budget at Theagénous 2 in Liménas (☎05930/23 050). Vigorous bargaining with the local one-off outfits is often productive of 35-percent discounts on official rates – particularly in early June or mid-September. On the other hand, don't bother showing up in Thássos much before or after these dates, as most facilities will be shut, and the weather can be dodgy in any case. Most hotels are closed between October and the end of April, so call ahead to check.

Liménas

LIMÉNAS (also signposted as Limín or Thássos) is the island's capital, though not the only port. Kavála-based ferries stop down the coast at Skála Prínou, with a KTEL bus always on hand to meet arrivals. The town, though largely modern, is partly redeemed by its picturesque fishing harbour and the sub-

THÁSSOS TOWN (LIMÉNAS)

RESTAURANTS AND BARS
Full Moon   D
Marina's Bar   G
To Perastikon   F
Iy Piyi   H
Platanos   C
Platia Café   E
Simi   B
Syrtaki   A

ACCOMMODATION
Akropolis Hotel   7
Alkyon Hotel   3
Amfipolis Hotel   1
Athanasia Hotel   6
Filoxenia Inn   2
Kipos Studios   4
Lena Hotel   5
Mironi & Victoria Hotels   8

N

Town Beach
ROOMS
Ancient Theatre
Ancient Port (Limenáki)
RO-RO Ferry Dock
Hydrofoil Berth
Taxi Stand
Museum (shut)
Temple of Dionysos
Artemis Shrine
Byzantine Basilica
MAIN PLATIA
Agora
Castle & Apollo Temple
ACROPOLIS
Natural Spring
Temple of Athena Polyouhos
ROOMS
Irakleio
Shrine of Pan
Gate of Zeus & Hera
0   200 m
Gate of Hercules
Gate of Silenos
Gate of Parmenon
Skála Prínou
Panayía & Alykí

stantial remains of the ancient city which appear above and below the streets.

With its mineral wealth and safe harbour, **ancient Thassos** prospered from Classical to Roman times. The largest excavated area is the agora, a little way back from the fishing harbour. The site (free) is fenced but not always locked, and is most enjoyably seen towards dusk. Two Roman stoas are prominent, but you can also make out shops, monuments, passageways and sanctuaries from the remodelled Classical city. At the far end of the site (away from the sea) a fifth-century BC passageway leads through to an elaborate sanctuary of Artemis, a substantial stretch of Roman road and a few seats of the odeion. The nearby archeological museum is closed indefinitely for extensive expansion.

From a **temple of Dionysos** behind the fishing port, a path curls up to a **Hellenistic theatre**, fabulously positioned above a broad sweep of sea. It's currently open, but is a chaos of excavation, with summer-festival performances set to resume in the distant future. On the same corner of the headland as the theatre, you can still see the old-fashioned kaïkia being built, and gaze across to the uninhabited islet of Thasopoúla. It's possible to rent boats from the fishing harbour, self-skippered or not, to take you there and elsewhere.

From just before the theatre, the trail winds on to the **acropolis**, where a Venetian-Byzantine-Genoese fort arose between the thirteenth and fifteenth centuries, constructed from recycled masonry of an Apollo temple which stood here. You can continue, following the remains of a massive circuit of fifth-century walls to a high terrace supporting the foundations of the Athena Polyouhos (Athena Patroness of the City) temple, with Cyclopean walls. An artificial cavity in the rock outcrop just beyond was a shrine of Pan, shown in faint relief playing his pipes. From behind the summit, a rock-hewn stairway provided a discreet escape route to the Gate of Parmenon, the only gate in the fortifications to have retained its lintel; it's named from an ancient inscription ("Parmenon Made Me") on a nearby wall slab. From here a track, then a paved lane descend through the southerly neighbourhoods of the modern town, for a satisfying one-hour circuit.

Practicalities

Given the cheap-and-cheerful-package ethos, cuisine is not Liménas's strong point, and eateries are generally overpriced. The picturesque **tavernas** around the old harbour are predictably touristy – sophisticated *Simi* is marginally the best, and serves memorably good wine. Another good option is *Syrtaki*, at the far eastern end of the overly popular town beach. In the town centre, greasy fast food is all too abundant, though a dependable favourite for *mayireftá* is *Iy Piyi*, up at the south corner of the main square, next to the natural sunken spring of the name. *Platanos*, with a pleasant terrace opposite the ferry docks, is the place to head for breakfast, be it English style or ambrosia-like yogurt and honey, and its coffee is highly drinkable. Finally, *To Perastikon* at the northwest corner of the square near *Iy Piyi*, serves the best ice cream on the island. By contrast, there's plenty of choice in local **bars**: *Full Moon* near the *Hotel Amfipolis* is the main Anglophile watering-hole, and comes with a paperback-swap library. *Platia Cafe Bar* on yet another corner of the basilica square, has good music, while *Marina's Bar* near the *Hotel Alkyon* is the best waterfront nightspot, attracting a mainly Greek clientele.

Mountain and motorbikes can be rented from Billy's Bikes (☎05930/22 490), Thomai Tsipou (☎05930/22 815) or Babis (☎05930/22 129). The KTEL office is on the front, virtually opposite the ferry mooring; the service is good, with several daily **buses** to Panayía and Skála Potamiás, Limenária via Potós, Theológos, Kínyra and Alykí. The **taxi** rank is just in front of the bus stop. Thassos Tours (☎05930/23 250), at the east end of the waterfront, is the principal airline agent (the closest airport is Kavála's Alexander the Great, 14km from Keramotí on the mainland, see p.533). Several **banks** have cash dispensers.

Accommodation

At first glance Liménas – plagued with vehicle traffic and often noisy bars – seems an unlikely resort, with many **hotels** enjoying little in the way of calm or views. Despite this, there are some worthy finds; if none from the list below suits, there are also areas in the southwest of town, and some relatively quiet rooms (❷–❸) just behind the town beach. Note that most of the town hotels are shut from October to early May. The closest **campsite** to town is at Nystéri cove, 2.5km west; the beach is OK, and its snack bar has tables out on a lawn, but the site is small, basic and on hard ground.

Akropolis ☎05930/22 488, ⓕ22 441. Occupying a fine traditional house with flagstone floors and a rear garden-bar, though it can get traffic noise; worth a try now that package companies don't use it. ❷

Alkyon ☎05930/22 148, ⓕ23 662. Certainly the most pleasant of the harbour hotels; English tea and breakfast, plus friendly, voluble management make it a home from home for independent British travellers. Open most of the year; ask also about their cottage in Sotíras and beach villa at Astris. ❸

Amfipolis ☎05930/23 101, ⓕ22 110. Housed in a folly, this atmospheric hotel is the town's most exclusive accommodation outfit – and you pay dearly for the privilege; some package commitment. ❺

Athanasia ☎05930/23 247. Giant and eccentrically furnished rooms with balconies; take the lane inland from behind the *Xenia Hotel* to reach it. Run by a friendly fisherman, this place takes the overflow from the *Alkyon*. ❷

Filoxenia Inn ☎05930/23 331, ⓕ22 231. Quietly situated behind the archeological museum, this has immaculate new rooms with fridges, designated breakfast areas and a garden with a small pool. ❸

Kipos Studios ☎05930/22 469. In a quiet cul-de-sac near *Iy Piyi* taverna, this has cool lower-ground-floor doubles (❸) and four-person galleried apartments of a fair standard (❹); a pool has been installed in the garden, ostensibly to make the premises attractive to package companies.

Lena ☎05930/23 565. Good-value hotel, lightly refurbished in 1998, near the post office, with English-speaking management; no packages. ❸

Myroni ☎05930/23 256, ⓕ22 132. Excellent value, well run and allergic to package companies. It's co-managed with the more modest *Victoria* (☎05930/23 556; ❸) next door, with which it shares a common breakfast room. ❹

Around the coast

Whether you plan to circumnavigate the island clockwise, or in the opposite direction, plan on a lunch stop at **Alykí**, roughly a third of the way along in the circuit described below, and the most photogenic spot along the coast.

Panayía, Potamiá and Mount Ipsárion

The first beach east of Liménas, **Makrýammos**, is a purpose-built, controlled-access compound for package tourists, so carry on to **PANAYÍA**, the attractive hillside village overlooking Potamiá Bay. It's a large, thriving place where life revolves around the central square with its large plane trees, multispouted fountain and slate-roofed houses. Top **accommodation** choice in both senses is the *Hotel Thassos Inn* (☎05930/61 612, ⓕ61 027; ❹), up in the Trís Piyés district near the Kímisis church, with fine views over the rooftops. Second choice, slightly lower down, is the vine-shrouded *Hotel Theo* (☎05930/61 284; ❸), more old-fashioned but with a nice ground-floor bar. Down on the main road, beside the municipal car park, the newish, clean *Pension Stathmos* (☎05930/61 666; ❹) is the quietest of several nearby, with stunning views out the back; there are also high-standard rooms (☎05930/61 981; ❸) below the school basketball courts. Some readers have complained about high-pressure touting tactics from the hotly competing tavernas on the square; for a more low-key approach, try *Iy Thea*, a view-terrace *psistariá* at the southeast edge of town en route to Potamiá.

POTAMIÁ, much lower down in the river valley, is far less prepossessing – with modern red tiles instead of slates on the roofs – and thus little visited, though it has a lively winter carnival. It also offers the **Polygnotos Vayis Museum** (Tues–Sat 9.30am–12.30pm, summer also 6–9pm, Sun 10am–1pm; free), devoted to the locally born sculptor; though Vayis emigrated to America when young, he bequeathed most of his works to the Greek state. Potamiá also marks the start of the commonest route up to the 1204-metre summit of **Mount Ipsárion**. Follow the bulldozer track to the big spring near the head of the valley extending west of the village (last water here), where you'll see the first red-painted arrows on trees. Beyond this point, cairns mark the correct turnings in a modern track system; forty minutes above the spring, take an older, wide track, which ends ten minutes later at a narrow ravine with a stream and the current trailhead. The path is steep, strenuous and unmaintained, and you'll be dependent on cairns and painted arrows. Go early in the day or season, and allow four hours up from Potamiá, and nearly as much for the descent.

Skála Potamiás and Khryssí Ammoudhiá

The onward road from Potamiá is lined with *dhomátia*- and apartment-type accommodation, popular with Germans. A side road some 12km from Liménas takes you down to **SKÁLA POTAMIÁS**, at the southern end of the bay, where some fairly uninspired **tavernas** line the harbour front; a road off to the left brings you to sand dunes extending all the way to the far northern end of the bay. An honourable exception amongst the tavernas is *Flor International* (no sign), at the corner where the bus (hourly 7am–8pm to Liménas) turns around; the *Afrodite*, a short way along, is also acceptable for *mayireftá*. Worth a mention also is *Eric's Bar* on the approach road, where one Stratos Papafilippou has made a career of his uncanny resemblance to footballer Eric Cantona; full English breakfast (of course) available. The best places to **stay** are either above the plane-shaded traffic turnaround area by the port, beyond the tavernas – where the *Hera* (☎05930/61 467; ❶), just on the left looking inland, or the *Delfini* (☎05930/61 275; ❶), 200m straight back, are peaceful but basic – or, if you're prepared to pay rather more, there's the *Miramare* (☎05930/77 209; ❻), which has a swimming pool among well-manicured gardens, further up the same lane. Alternatively, head north along the shore towards the sandy beach, for **rooms**, to either side of the *Arion* (☎05930/61 486; ❸) and *Anna* (☎05930/61 070; ❷) hotels, which represent the best value hereabouts. The north end of this beach is called **Khryssí Ammoudhiá** ("golden sands"), merely another cluster of tavernas, hotels and a campsite; a direct road (no bus service) spirals the 5km down from Panayía. Once there, you can choose between the self-catering *Villa Emerald* (☎05930/61 979; ❺) or the *Golden Sand* (☎05930/61 771 or 61 209; ❹), nearer the sands. The *Golden Beach* campsite (☎05930/61 472) is the only official one on this side of the island.

Kínyra and Alykí

The dispersed hamlet of **KÍNYRA**, some 24km south of Liménas, marks the start of the burnt zone which overlooks it, though incipient greenery suggests that recovery is underway; it's endowed with a poor beach, a couple of grocery stores and several small hotels. Those not block-booked include *Villa Athina* (☎05930/41 214; ❷) at the north end of things, whose top-floor rooms see the water over the olive trees, and the welcoming *Pension Marina* (☎05930/31 384; ❷). The *Faros* is about the only independent taverna here. Kínyra is convenient for the superior **beaches** of Loutroú (1km south) and partly nudist Paradise (3km along) – officially called Makrýammos Kinýron – both of which can be reached down poorly signposted dirt tracks. The latter ranks as most scenic of all Thassian beaches, with still-forested cliffs inland and a namesake islet offshore beyond the extensive shallows, with much cleaner water than at Khryssí Ammoudhiá, though a couple of ugly buildings have sprung up over the past year or so. So far the only place for food and drink is a mediocre snack bar that exploits its monopoly.

The south-facing coast of Thássos has the balance of the island's best beaches. **ALYKÍ** hamlet, 35km from Liménas and just below the main road, faces a perfect double bay which almost pinches off a headland. Alone of Thassian seaside settlements, it retains its original whitewashed, slate-roofed architecture, because the presence of extensive antiquities here has led to a ban on any modern construction. The ruins include an ancient temple to an unknown deity, and two exquisite early-Christian basilicas out on the headland, with a few columns re-erected. The sand-and-pebble west bay gets oversubscribed in peak season, though you can always stalk off to the less crowded, rocky east cove, or snorkel in the crystal-clear waters off the marble formations on the headland's far side. A row of water-edge **tavernas** compete for your custom, with *To Limanaki/The Little Mole* winning, if only for its varied menu. Ask around for **rooms** (❸).

Arhangélou Mihaïl to Potós

Some 5km west of Alykí, the **convent of Arhangélou Mihaïl** (open reasonable daylight hours) clings spectacularly to a cliff on the seaward side of the road. Though founded in the twelfth century above the spot where a spring had gushed forth, it has been hideously renovated by the nuns, resident here since 1974. A dependency of Filothéou on Mount Áthos (see p.523), its prize relic is a purported nail from the Crucifixion.

At the extreme south tip of Thássos, 9km further west, **ASTRÍS** (Astrídha) can muster two uninspiring medium-sized hotels, a few rooms and a good beach. Just 1km west is another better but crowded beach, Psilí Ámmos, with watersports on offer. A few kilometres further, **POTÓS** is the island's prime Germanophone package venue, its centre claustrophobically dense, with the few non-block-booked rooms overlooking cramped alleys. However, the kilometre-long beach is still unspoiled. For a less touristy place to eat, the **taverna** *Iy Mouria* remains one of the cheaper and better places and is tucked away at the southern end of the seafront, in a semi-pedestrianized street; next door, *Michael's Place* has great ice cream and breakfasts. Along the harbourfront a string of varyingly trendy **bars and cafés** offer viable alternatives. There are plenty of rental outlets for **cars**, scooters and mountain bikes, including the headquarters of Potos Rent a Car. **Pefkári** with its manicured beach and namesake pine-grove, 1km west, is essentially an annexe of Potós, with a few mid-range **accommodation** options such as *Prasino Veloudho* (☎05930/52 001, ℱ51 232; ❸) and the rather more upmarket *Thassos* (☎05930/51 596, ℱ51 794; ❻). The **campsite**, the *Pefkari* (☎05930/51 190; June–Sept), with its attractive wooded location and clean facilities, is one of the best on Thássos.

Limenária and the west coast

LIMENÁRIA, the island's second town, was built to house German mining executives brought in by the Ottomans at the turn of the 19th/20th centuries. Their remaining mansions, scattered on the slopes above the harbour, lend some character, but despite attempts at prettifying the waterfront, it's not the most attractive place on Thássos though it is handy for its **banks** and cash dispensers, **post office** and seasonal hydrofoil connections. The best **accommodation**, should you take a shine to the place is the hotel *George* (T05930/51 413, F52 530; 4), a relative newcomer with bright and modern rooms at the lower end of the main street leading down to the harbourfront. At the east end of the quay, in some 1960s blocks, are a cluster of very basic hotels such as the *Sgouridis* (T05930/51 241; 3) and the towering *Papayioryiou* (T05930/51 205; 2–3), with mostly Greek clientele. There are also plenty of **rooms** on offer (1–3). For eating and drinking, choose from among half-a-dozen each of bars and eateries along the front.

The closest good beach is **Trypití**, a couple of kilometres west – turn left into the pines at the start of a curve right. All development – mostly package villas – is well inland from the broad, 800-metre long strand, although there are umbrellas and sun loungers for rent. The cleft which the name refers to (literally "pierced" in Greek), is a slender tunnel through the headland at the west end of the beach, leading to a tiny three-boat anchorage.

Continuing clockwise from Limenária to Thássos Town, there's progressively less to stop off for as the western coast is the most exposed and scenically least impressive. The various *skáles* such as Skála Kaliráhis and Skála Sotíros – stop-offs for ferries – are bleak, straggly and windy. **Skála Marión**, 13km from Limenária, is the exception that proves the rule: an attractive little bay, with fishing boats hauled up on the sandy foreshore, and the admittedly modern low-rise village arrayed in a U-shape all around. There are **rooms** available (2–3), a few tavernas, and, most importantly, two fine beaches on either side. **Skála Prínou** has little to recommend it, other than ferry connections to Kavála. Buses are usually timed to coincide with the ferries, but if you want to stay, there are several hotels, numerous rooms, quayside tavernas and an EOT **campsite** (T05930/71 171; June–Sept) 1km south of the ferry dock. **Skála Rahoníou**, between here and Limenás, has more accommodation (including the *Perseus* campsite) and fish restaurants, as well as proximity to **Pahýs beach**, 9km short of Limenás, by far the best strand on the northwest coast. Narrow dirt tracks lead past various tavernas through surviving pines to the sand, partly shaded in the morning.

The interior

Few people get around to exploring inland Thássos – with the post-fire scrub still barely waist-high, it's not always rewarding – but there are several worthwhile excursions to or around the **hill villages**, besides the aforementioned trek up Mount Ipsárion from Potamiá (see p.901).

From Potós you can head 10km along a well-surfaced but poorly signposted road to **THEOLÓGOS**, founded in the sixteenth century by refugees from Constantinople and the island's capital under the Ottomans (the last Muslims only departed after 1923). Its houses, most with oversized chimneys and slate roofs, straggle in long tiers to either side of the main street, surrounded by generous kitchen gardens or walled courtyards. A stroll along the single high street, with its couple of kafenía, a soldiers' bar, sandalmaker and traditional bakery, is rewarding and quickly dispels the off-putting effect of vigorous advertising at the outskirts for "Greek Nights" at local tavernas. Two that eschew musical gimmicks and rely on their good fare are the long-running *Psistaria Lambiris*, near the edge of town, and *Kleoniki/Tou Iatrou*, in the very centre, on the right-hand side past the bus stop and police station. They're at their best in the evening when the *soúvles* loaded with goat and suckling pig start turning.

Despite its proximity as the crow flies, there's no straightforward way from Theológos to **KÁSTRO**, the most naturally protected of the anti-pirate redoubts; especially with a car, it's best to descend to Potós before heading up a rough, seventeen-kilometre dirt track from Limenária. Thirty ancient houses and a church surround a rocky pinnacle, fortified by the Byzantines and the Genoese, which has a sheer drop on three sides. Summer occupation by shepherds is becoming the norm after total abandonment in the nineteenth century, when mining jobs at Limenária proved irresistible. There's only one kafenío on the ground floor of the former school, one telephone therein, no mains electricity and far more sheep than people.

From Skála Marión an unmarked but paved road (slipping under the main highway bridge to the north) proceeds 11km inland through gnarled, old olive-trees, to well-preserved **MARIÉS** at the top of a wooded stream valley; of two tavernas here, the well-signed one to the right, *Bethel*, is more of a going concern. From Skála Sotíros, a very steep road heads 3.5km up to **SOTÍRAS**, the only interior village with an unobstructed view of sunset over the Aegean and thus popular with foreigners who've bought up about half of the houses for restoration. On the ridge opposite are exploratory shafts left by the miners, whose ruined lodge looms above the church. On the plane-shaded square below the old fountain, *O Platanos* taverna is congenially run by Maria and Manolis, who offer grills plus one *mayireftá* dish-of-the-day, good bulk wine and sometimes their potent, home-made *tsípouro*.

From Prínos (Kalýves) on the coast road, you've a six-kilometre journey inland to the Kazavíti villages, shrouded in greenery that escaped the fires; they're (poorly) signposted and mapped officially as Megálo and Mikró Prínos but still universally known by their Ottoman name. **MIKRÓ KAZAVÍTI** marks the start of the track south for the convent of Ayíou Pandelímona, and **MEGÁLO KAZAVÍTI**, 1km beyond, was once the architectural showcase of the island, a fact apparently lost on many of the outsiders who bought holiday homes here and proceeded to carry out appallingly vandalistic renovations, though thankfully some have been done tastefully. On the magnificent platía, arguably the prettiest spot on the whole island, are a couple of decent, normal-priced **tavernas**, while *Vassilis*, below in a beautifully restored house, is regarded as a cut above. Some 4km up from its *skála*, **RAHÓNI** is well set at the head of its denuded valley, paired with the small village of Áyios Yeóryios across the way. The road up to the square has plenty of simple tavernas, for example *Iy Dhrosia*.

Travel details

To simplify the lists that follow we've excluded two regular sailings in a generally north-to-south direction. These are the weekly DANE sailing between Rhodes, Kós, Sámos and Thessaloníki (23hr for the full run, usually over the weekend), and the NEL sailing linking Alexandhroúpoli with Límnos, Lésvos, Híos, Sámos, Kós and Rhodes (one-way trip through all ports, total 30hr).

We've also omitted the more convoluted long-distance schedules kept by the small ferries of Miniotis Lines, based on Híos. These slow and often tardy craft link Híos with Sámos (both northern ports) twice a week year-round, usually Sun & Thurs evening, returning Tues & Fri evening. Twice weekly (usually Mon & Fri), they venture from Sámos (Karlóvassi and Pythagório respectively) to Foúrni and Ikaría (Áyios Kírykos) and back, and twice weekly (typically Tues & Fri am) there's an out-and-back run from Pythagório to Agathoníssi, Arkí, Lipsí and Pátmos – these additional services are reliably available June to Oct, though year-round departures are foreseen as of late 2001.

Áyios Efstrátios 2 weekly on NEL Lines to Límnos, Rafína and Kavála; 5 weekly by small local ferry to Límnos; 1 weekly to Lésvos (Sígri) and Psará.

Foúrni 2–3 weekly ferries to Sámos (northern ports), Náxos, Páros and Pireás; 2–3 weekly to Pátmos, Kós, Rhodes; morning kaïki to Ikaría on Mon, Wed, Fri; twice weekly (usually Mon & Thurs) morning kaïki to Karlóvassi (Sámos).

Híos 11 weekly on NEL Lines to Pireás (10hr slow ferry, 4hr high-speed) and Lésvos (3hr 30min/1hr 30min); 4 weekly to Pireás and Lésvos on Hellas Ferries; 1–2 weekly to Límnos on NEL, usually with a long layover at Mytilíni; 1 weekly to Lésvos, Sámos, Sýros on Hellas Ferries. Daily 2pm kaïki to Inoússes except Sun morning, and Tues in off-season; 4 weekly on Miniotis Lines – usually Tues, Thurs, Sat & Sun – from Híos Town to Psará (3hr 30min), 3 weekly on Miniotis from Limniá to Psará, usually Mon, Wed, Fri pm (1hr 30min).

Ikaría At least daily from either Áyios Kírykos or Évdhilos to Sámos (both northern ports) and Pireás, on Hellas Ferries, G&A or NEL's catamaran; 3 weekly to Rhodes, Kós, Pátmos, Foúrni, Náxos and Páros from Áyios Kírykos; 5–6 weekly to Mýkonos from Évdhilos; 3 weekly to Sýros from Évdhilos; 3 weekly to Mýkonos and Sýros, from Áyios Kírykos; daily kaïki from Áyios Kírykos to Foúrni; 3 weekly kaïkia, usually Mon, Wed, Fri am, from Manganítis to Áyios Kírykos.

Lésvos 10–12 weekly on NEL Lines from Mytilíni to Pireás (11hr direct, 13hr 30min via Híos, 7hr 30min on high-speed craft; 16hr 30min via Mýkonos/Sýros); 9–11 weekly to Híos (3hr 30min, or 1hr 30min high-speed); 4 weekly to Híos and Pireás on Hellas Ferries; 3–4 weekly to Límnos (6hr from Mytilíni, 5hr from Sígri); 2 weekly to Thessaloníki (14hr); 1–3 weekly to Kavála on NEL (12hr from Mytilíni, 10hr from Sígri); 1 weekly to Rafína on NEL (8hr, from Sígri only); 1 weekly to Áyios Efstrátios on NEL (4hr, from Sígri only); 1 weekly to Psará on NEL (4hr, from Sígri only); 1 weekly to Mýkonos and Sýros on NEL; 1 weekly to Sámos and Sýros on Hellas Ferries.

Límnos 5–6 weekly on NEL Lines to Lésvos (Mytilíni or Sígri); 4 weekly to Kavála, 2 weekly to Lávrio, and 1 weekly to Thessaloníki, Samothráki direct on the Saos II; 3 weekly to Kavála and Rafína on NEL; 2 weekly to Thessaloníki, Pireás and Híos on NEL.

Psará 1 weekly on NEL Lines to Lésvos (Sígri) Áyios Efstrátios, Límnos, Kavála; 1 weekly direct to Pireás (8hr).

Sámos (Karlóvassi) As for Vathý, but no NEL catamaran service; also 2 weekly kaïki departures, usually early Mon and Thurs afternoon, to Foúrni.

Sámos (Pythagório) 2 weekly (Wed and Sun afternoon) with the Nissos Kalymnos to Agathoníssi, Lipsí, Pátmos, Léros and Kálymnos, with onward connections to all other Dodecanese (see p.824 for the full schedule).

Sámos (Vathý) 1–2 daily, on G&A or Hellas Ferries, to Ikaría (Áyios Kírykos or Évdhilos) and Pireás (13–14hr); 5 weekly to Pireás by NEL high-speed boat (6hr); 4–6 weekly to Mýkonos and Sýros; 2 weekly to Foúrni, Páros and Náxos on G&A; 1 weekly to Pátmos and Lipsí on Hellas Ferries.

Samothráki 2–3 daily ferries to/from Alexandhroúpoli (2hr 30min) in season, dropping to 5–6 weekly out of season. Also 2 weekly late spring and early autumn, up to 4 weekly in peak season, to Kavála (and thence other north Aegean islands). During July & Aug, 1 weekly (usually Fri) direct to Límnos; 4 other days there is tedious indirect service via Kavála.

Thássos 8–10 ferries daily, in summer months only (1 daily Oct–May), between Kavála and Skála Prínou (1hr 15min; 7am–10pm, 6am–9pm to Kavála from the island); 10 daily all year round between Keramotí and Liménas (40min; 7am–10pm, 6am–8.30pm from Thássos).

Hydrofoils

Just one company, Kyriakoulis Maritime, operates in the east Aegean. Based on Sámos and Kós, this offers (late May to late Sept) nearly daily early morning and early afternoon service from Pythagório to Pátmos, Lipsí, Léros, Kálymnos and Kós (in the Dodecanese), returning from Kós in the late afternoon, and conversely morning service from Kós through the same ports, returning from Pythagório at mid-afternoon. Ikaría and Foúrni are called at 5–6 times weekly (sometimes from Vathý instead), with Agathónissi served twice weekly. In 2001 there were also 3 weekly nominal high-season links between Sámos (Vathý), Híos, Inoússes and Lésvos, departing in the morning and returning early afternoon, but these are deeply unreliable

owing to weather and typically run once weekly at best. From Easter to mid-May, and late Sept to late Oct, official frequencies fall to 4–5 weekly to the Dodecanese cited (but 2 to Lipsí, 1 to Agathoníssi); 2 weekly to Foúrni/Ikaría; and 1 weekly to Híos/Inoússes/Lésvos.

Samothráki is served by hydrofoil from Alexandhroúpoli April–Nov 4–7 times weekly, usually at 8am (1hr); mid-June to mid-Sept there are 1–2 extra daily departures at 1 and/or 5pm. Two to four times weekly the morning or early afternoon sailing may continue on to Límnos, but don't rely on this.

Thássos (Liménas) used to be served all year by hydrofoils from Kavála, but the service is now limited to the summer: 8–15 times daily, 7am–9pm

(6am–8pm from Thássos); in the high season there may also be 2–3 daily departures from

Kavála to the west-coast resorts of Skála Kaliráhon, Skála Marión and Limenária.

International ferries

Híos–Çeşme (Turkey) 2–13 boats weekly, depending on season. Spring/autumn, about 7 weekly; Thurs evening (Turkish boat) and Sat morning (Greek boat) services tend to run year-round. Passenger fares on the Greek boat (*Psara*, Miniotis Lines) are €47 one-way, €59 open return (no day-return fare), including Greek taxes; no Turkish taxes. These are the "rack rates", which can often be beaten by comparison shopping and bargaining; it's also about twenty percent less expensive to travel *from* Turkey. Turkish boat (typically *Ertürk II*) is usually cheaper going from Híos, at €33 one-way, €44 return, Greek taxes inclusive. Small cars €73.50 each way, taken on either morning or evening boats. Journey time 45min.

Mytilíni (Lésvos)–Ayvalık (Turkey) 4–8 weekly May–Oct; winter link unreliable. One of two Turkish craft, the *Cunda Express* and the *Jalehan*, departs Mytilíni 8am most days; the *Jalehan* (carries two cars) may also do an evening trip Tues, Thurs, Sat. Passenger rates €38 one-way, €47 round trip, all taxes inclusive. Small cars €58 each way. Journey time 1hr 40min.

Vathý (Sámos)–Kuşadası (Turkey) At least 1 daily, late April to late Oct; otherwise a small Turkish boat only by demand in winter, usually Fri or Sat. Morning Greek boat, 4–5 weekly (passengers only); afternoon Turkish boats (usually 2 daily in season taking two cars apiece). Rates are €38 one-way including taxes on both the Greek and Turkish sides, €43 open return; no day-return rate. Small cars €50 one-way. Journey time 1hr 30min. Also occasional (2–3 weekly) services in season from Pythagório, passengers only (journey time 2hr 15min).

Flights

NB All flights on Olympic Airways/Aviation unless otherwise specified. Frequencies are for the period May–Oct only.

Híos–Athens (4–5 daily on Olympic; 1hr)
Híos–Thessaloníki (3 weekly, 1 via Lésvos; 1hr 30min–2hr)
Lésvos–Athens (4–5 daily on Olympic; 55min; 3 daily on Aegean-Cronus; 45min)
Lésvos–Híos (1 weekly; 30min)

Lésvos–Thessaloníki (6–8 weekly on Olympic, 1 daily on Aegean-Cronus; 1hr 10min–2hr)
Límnos–Athens (3–4 daily; 1hr)
Límnos–Lésvos (4 weekly; 40min)
Límnos–Thessaloníki (6 weekly; 45min)
Sámos–Athens (4–5 daily on Olympic; 1hr; 2 daily on Axon; 40min)
Sámos–Thessaloníki (3 weekly on Olympic; 1hr 20min

11

The Sporades and
Évvia

CHAPTER 11 **Highlights**

✳ **Laláría beach, Skiáthos** A
beautiful beach covered with
smooth white stones, with
steep cliffs rising behind it.
See p.913

✳ **Glóssa** An unspoiled,
authentic Greek town, set
high above the port of
Loutráki. See p.914

✳ **Skópelos Town** One of the
prettiest towns in the
Sporades. See p.914

✳ **Sky*ros** Only recently "discovered" by tourism, this is
one of the most traditional
islands in the Aegean. See
p.921

✳ **The goat dance** One of
Greece's liveliest and most
outrageous festivals. See
p.922

✳ **The convent of Ayíou
Nikoláou Galatáki** Superbly
set on the wooded slopes of
Mount Kandhíli and decorated with vivid sixteenth-
century frescoes. See p.934

✳ **Loutrá Edhipsoú** Greece's
biggest spa town, with plenty of Belle Époque hotels
(many well restored) to marvel at. See p.936

11

The Sporades and Évvia

The three northern **Sporades**, Skiáthos, Skópelos and Alónissos, are scattered (as their Greek name suggests) just off the mainland, their mountainous terrain betraying their origin as extensions of Mount Pílio in Thessaly. They are archetypal holiday islands, with a wide selection of good beaches, transparent waters and thick pine forests. All are very busy in season, with Skiáthos attracting by far the most package tours.

Skiáthos has the best beaches, and is still the busiest island in the group, though these days **Skópelos** gets very crowded, too. **Alónissos** is the quietest of the three, and has the wildest scenery, so it's really more for nature lovers than night-owls. **Skýros**, further southeast, retains more of its traditional culture than the other three islands, though development is now well under way. The main town doesn't yet feel like a resort, but its main street is not without its fast-food and souvenir shops. Unlike on the other three islands, the best beaches are those closest to the main town. To the south, the huge island of **Évvia** (or Euboea) runs for 150km alongside the mainland. It is one of the most attractive Greek islands, with a forested mountain spine and long stretches of rugged, largely undeveloped coast. Perhaps because it lacks any impressive ruins or real

Accommodation price codes

Throughout the book we've categorized accommodation according to the following **price codes**, which denote the cheapest available double room in high season. All prices are for the room only, except where otherwise indicated. Many hotels, especially those in category ❹ and over, include breakfast in the price; you'll need to check this when booking. During low season, rates can drop by more than fifty percent, especially if you are staying for three or more nights. Exceptions are during the Christmas and Easter weeks when you'll pay high-season prices. Single rooms, where available, cost around seventy percent of the price of a double.

❶ Up to €24	❹ €43–58
❷ €24–33	❺ €59–72
❸ €34–42	❻ €73 and upwards

Note: Youth hostels and mountain refuges typically charge €7–9 for a dormitory bed. For more accommodation details, see pp.51–54.

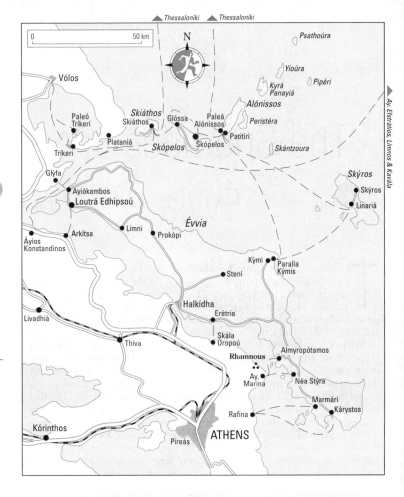

island feel owing to its proximity to the mainland, Évvia is explored by few foreign tourists, though Athenians and Thessalians visit the island in force and have erected holiday homes around half a dozen of its major resorts.

The Sporades are well connected by **bus** and **ferry** with Athens (via Áyios Konstandínos or Kými), Thessaloníki and Vólos, and it's easy to island-hop in the northern group. The only ferry connection to Skýros is from Kými, plus a Flying Dolphin hydrofoil service in summer from Vólos via the other Sporades. Évvia is linked to the mainland by a bridge at its capital Halkídha, and by a series of shuttle ferries. Both Skiáthos and Skýros have airports.

Skiáthos

The commercialization of **Skiáthos** is legendary among foreigners and Greeks: it's a close fourth to that of Corfu, Mýkonos and Rhodes. But if you've some time to spare, or a gregarious nature, you might still break your journey here to sample the best, if most overcrowded, **beaches** in the Sporades. Along the south and southeast coasts, the road serves an almost unbroken line of villas, hotels and restaurants, and although this doesn't take away the island's natural beauty, it makes it difficult to find anything unspoiled or particularly Greek about it all. As almost the entire population lives in Skiáthos Town, a little walking soon pays off. However, camping outside official sites is strongly discouraged, since summer turns the dry pine-needles to tinder.

Skiáthos Town

Skiáthos Town, where the ferries dock, looks great from a distance, but as you approach, tourist development becomes very apparent, especially to the east side of the port and around Alexándhrou Papadhiamándi, where most of the services, the tackier shops, "English" pubs and eateries are located. But tucked into the alleys on the western, older side of town, it is still possible to find some pockets of charm: older houses, gardens and flowers galore. Skiáthos boasts some good restaurants and nightclubs, and can be fun, in a crowded, boisterous way.

The few sights comprise the **Papadhiamándi museum** (Tues–Sun 9.30am–1pm & 5–8pm; free) – housed in the nineteenth-century home of one of Greece's best-known novelists – and two antique shops, Archipelago two blocks in from the waterfront, and the enduring Galerie Varsakis (open usual shop hours), on Platía Trión Ierarhón near the fishing port. The latter has one of the best **folklore displays** in Greece, and many of the older items would do the Benaki Museum proud; the proprietor neither expects, nor wants, to sell the more expensive of these, which include antique textiles, handicrafts and jewellery.

Arrival, transport and other facilities

Buses and **taxis** ply from the area around the **ferry harbour**. To Koukounariés, the bus is the cheapest option (€0.80); it runs at least hourly in summer (every fifteen minutes at peak times), the last bus returning at 1am.

A large number of competing **rental outlets** in town, most on the front behind the ferry harbour, offer bicycles, motorbikes, cars and motorboats. For bikes, good rates can be had from Makis Dimas, whose workshop is signposted at the far end of Papadhiamándi. The cheapest, smallest cars go for around €45 a day, as do motorboats. Several travel agents organize "round-the-island" **mule trips** (€18 a day), and there's **horseriding** at the Pinewood Riding Club (no phone) at Koukounariés. Most other facilities are on Alexándhrou Papadhiamándi, including the **post office**, **banks** and a branch of American Express.

Accommodation

Much of the island's accommodation is in Skiáthos Town. The few reasonably priced **hotels** or **pensions** are heavily booked in season, though you can usually find a room, albeit at a slightly more elevated price than on most islands. At other times, supply exceeds demand and you can find very cheap **rooms** with a little bargaining. Try for locations in the older quarters to the west; avoid lodgings in the flatlands to the north, as they tend to be noisy. There is a room-owners' association kiosk on the quay that opens fitfully in high season, but at other times bookings can be made through several tourist agencies. For an honest and helpful approach, try the Mare Nostrum at Papadhiamándi 21 (☏04270/21 463) or the efficient Heliotropio (☏04270/22 430, ☏21 952) on the seafront. A more direct option is Adonis Stamelos's rooms just outside town at Megáli Ámmos (☏04270/22 962; ❸). Good, small hotels include the *Bourtzi* (☏04270/22 694; ❺) and *Pothos* (☏04270/21 304; ❺), both immaculate with delightful gardens, and the *Orsa* (℡04270/22 430; ❻), a remodelled house overlooking the sea on the west side of the port which can be booked through Heliotropio. Other fine options are the *Alkyon Hotel*, on the seafront at the commercial port end (℡04270/22 981; ❻), or the *Meltemi Hotel*, on the front near the taxi rank (℡04270/22 493; ❻).

The island has three official **campsites**. Koukounariés and Asélinos are fairly decent with standard facilities. Xanémos beach is 3km northeast of Skiáthos Town, right next to the airport runway, and, apart from being within walking distance of the town, has little to recommend it.

Eating, drinking and nightlife

You're spoiled for choice for **eating places**, but nothing is particularly cheap apart from the few burger/*yíros* joints. One of the best of the cheaper tavernas is *Zorba's*, opposite the taxi rank, while *Mesogeia*, above and to the west of Plátia Trión Ierarkhón, has excellent moussaka and home-cooked dishes. *Ellinikon*, up in the backstreets above the west seafront, also has home-style cooking and good wine in a secluded garden, while *Cuba*, set in a leafy square east of Papadhiamándi, has a huge range of grilled meat, fish and starters. For more elegant dining, head for *Agnantio*, at the start of the road to Evangelístria, for superlative Greek cuisine and views; *The Windmill* at the top of the hill above Áyios Nikólaos, for nouvelle cuisine and views; and *Calypso*, on the east waterfront, for genuine Italian food. Back on the west side, above the flat rocks where people sunbathe, *Tarsanas* is a converted boatbuilders' yard with a picturesque veranda – the best place in town for an evening drink as the harbour lights come on.

Nightlife centres on the clubs on or near Polytekhníou. The best places are *Borzoi*, the oldest club on the island, *Stones* and the *Apothiki Music Hall* for Greek music and a good atmosphere, while on the seafront *BBC* pulses till dawn. In the bars in the backstreets around Polytekhníou you can hear a wider range of music; places like the *Banana* are pop-oriented and popular with British beer-drinkers, the old and much-loved *Kentavros* plays jazz and blues, *Adagio* has classical music in the evenings, and *Blue Chips* is a stylish, upmarket place. On the east shore, the chic *Remezzo* with its maritime motifs is a perennial favourite, while *Kavos* and *Kalua* rival it for pumping out the loudest disco sounds.

Skiáthos's outdoor **cinema**, *Refresh Paradiso*, on the ring road, shows new releases in their original language. Another source of entertainment is the little offshore Boúrtzi fortress, transformed into an outdoor **theatre** and home to occasional plays and musical performances during the summer.

Around the island

Other than using the buses or the various rental outlets in town, you could also get your bearings on a **boat trip** around the island. These cost about €15 per person and leave at around 10am. Or try a boat trip to the islet of **Tsougriá** (opposite Skiáthos Town), where there's a good beach and a taverna. Boats leave from the fishing harbour beyond the Boúrtzi, and not the yacht anchorage to the north of the ferry harbour; east-coast boats leave from the quay area in front of the bus station.

If you're interested in seeing more of Skiáthos on foot, the locally produced guide to **walks** (by Rita and Dietrich Harkort; available in larger tourist shops) has detailed instructions and maps for trails all over the island.

The monasteries and Kástro

The **Evangelístria monastery** (daily 8am–noon & 4–8pm) is more than an hour on foot out of Skiáthos Town. Founded in the late eighteenth century, it is exceptionally beautiful, even beyond the grandeur of isolation you find in all Greek monasteries. The Greek flag was raised here in 1807, and heroes of the War of Independence such as Kolokotronis pledged their oaths to fight for freedom here. To reach the monastery, walk 500m out of the centre of town on the road towards the airport until, at the point where the asphalt veers to the right, you take a prominently signposted paved side road that veers left; be careful to stick to this and not to wander off onto the dirt roads.

Beyond Evangelístria, a mule track continues to the abandoned **Áyios Harálambos monastery**, from where it's possible to walk across the island to the ruined capital of Kástro along another dirt road; this takes about two hours. To reach Kástro from Skiáthos Town, it's quicker to take the direct paved road towards it on a motorbike, or take a kaïki ride round the island and get off at the beach below Kástro.

Just over halfway between Evangelístria and Kástro, a well-used dirt track (signposted) turns left and heads towards the abandoned fifteenth-century monastery of **Panayía tís Kekhriás**, three-hours' walk from town. It's said to be the oldest on the island and has a colony of bats inside. It's a beautiful walk (or organized donkey-ride), and there are two pebbly beaches below, one with a welcoming stream that provides a cool shower. Back on the paved road, you can continue to within a thirty-minute walk of **Kástro** – a spectacular spot, built on a windswept headland. In the past, the entrance was only accessible by a drawbridge, which has been replaced by a flight of steps. The village was built in the sixteenth century, when the people of the island moved here for security from pirate raids. It was abandoned three hundred years later in 1830, following independence from Turkey, when the population moved back to build the modern town on the site of ancient Skiáthos. The ruins are largely over-grown, and only three churches survive intact, the largest still retaining some original frescoes. From outside the gates, a path leads down the rocks to a good pebble **beach**; with a stream running down from the hills and a daytime café (with slightly overpriced food and drinks), it makes a good place to camp. For an apparently inaccessible spot though, it does attract a surprising number of people. All the island excursion boats call here, and even when they've gone, there's little chance of having the ruins or beach to yourself.

Finally, the seventeenth-century **Kounístra monastery** can be reached by turning right off the paved road that runs north across the island from Tróulos to Asélinos. It's a very pretty spot, with a beautiful carved icon screen, splendid icons, a grape arbour and a taverna.

The beaches

The real business of Skiáthos is **beaches**. There are reputed to be more than sixty of them, but that's hardly enough to soak up the hordes of summer vis-itors: at the height of the season, the local population of four thousand can be swamped by up to fifty thousand visitors. The beaches on the northeast coast aren't easily accessible unless you pay for an excursion kaïki: reaching them on foot requires treks more arduous than those described above. The bus, though, runs along the entire south coast, and from strategic points along the way you can easily reach a good number of beaches. The prevailing sum-mer *meltémi* wind blows from the north, so the beaches on the south coast are usually better protected. Most of the popular beaches have at least a drinks/snacks stall; those at Vromólimnos, Asélinos and Tróulos have proper tavernas.

The beaches before the **Kalamáki peninsula** (where English and rich Greeks have their villas) are unexciting, but on the promontory itself are the highly rated **Ayía Paraskeví** and **Vromólimnos beaches**, close to Koliós hamlet; Vromólimnos offers windsurfing and waterskiing. For scuba enthusi-asts, there is the Dolphin Diving Centre (☎04270/22 599) at the *Nostos* hotel, on the eastern side of the Kalamáki peninsula by Kanapiítsa hamlet.

Just before Tróulos beach, the last on the south coast before Koukounariés, you can turn right up a paved road, which runs 4km north to **Mégas Asélinos**, a very good beach with a campsite, beach bar and a reasonable tav-erna. A daily bus and excursion boats call here, so it's crowded in season. A fork in the paved road leads to Kounístra monastery (see above) and continues to **Mikrós Asélinos**, just east of its larger neighbour and somewhat quieter.

The bus only goes as far as **KOUKOUNARIÉS**, a busy resort with wood-en walkways traversing the sand to a series of *kantínas* selling drinks and light snacks, though the three beaches are excellent if you don't mind the crowds. There's a majestic sandy bay of clear, gradually deepening water, backed by acres of pines, which despite its popularity merits at least one visit if only to assess the claim that it's the best beach in Greece. The road runs behind a small lake at the back of the pine trees, and features a string of **hotels**, **rooms** and **restaurants**, as well as a good campsite. Here, the *Strofilia* apartments which sleep four (☎04270/49 251, ℱ49 585, ℮strophilia@n-skiathos.gr; ❻) are par-ticularly nicely furnished. The smart *Limni Hotel*, right opposite the lake itself, is also decent value (☎04270/49 362; ❹). Jet-skis, motorboats, windsurfing and waterskiing are all available off the beach.

"**Banana beach**" (also known as Krassá), the third cove on the far side of Poúnda headland, is one of the trendiest beaches with watersports, a couple of bars and tolerance of nude bathing. For the less adventurous, the turning for

Ayía Eléni, 1km from the road, leads to a pleasant beach with a drinks kiosk. Further north, **Mandhráki** and **Eliá** beaches have similar facilities, and are accessible by scooter along dirt tracks.

The famed **Laláia beach**, almost at the northernmost point of Skiáthos, can be reached by taxi-boats from the town. Covered with smooth white stones, it's beautiful, with steep cliffs rising behind it; the swimming is excellent, but beware of the undertow. The island's three natural grottoes – Skotiní, Galázia and Halkiní – are nearby, and are included in many of the "round-the-island" trips. East of Evangelístria are the greyish sands of **Mégas Yialós**, one of the less crowded beaches, and **Xánemos**, another nudist beach; both suffer from airport noise.

Skópelos

Bigger, more rugged and better cultivated than Skiáthos, **Skópelos** is almost as busy, but its concessions to tourism are lower key and in better taste than in Skiáthos. Most of the larger beaches have sunbeds, umbrellas and some watersports, though smaller, secluded coves do exist. Inland, the island is a well-watered place, growing olives, plums, pears and almonds. **Glóssa** and **Skópelos**, its two main towns, are also among the prettiest in the Sporades, clambering uphill along paved steps, their houses distinguished by attractive wooden balconies and grey slate roofs. A number of **nationalities** have occupied the island at various stages of its history, among them the Romans, Persians, Venetians, French and, of course, the Ottomans. The Ottoman pirate-admiral Barbarossa (Redbeard) – actually a Greek renegade from Lésvos – had the entire population of the island slaughtered in the sixteenth century.

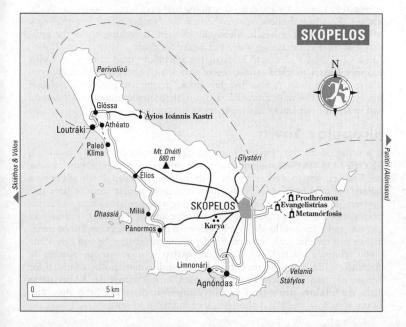

Loutráki, Glóssa and the west

Most boats and hydrofoils call at both ends of Skópelos, stopping first at the small port of **LOUTRÁKI** ("Glóssa" on schedules) with its narrow pebble beach, small hotels and rooms for rent. The village has been spoiled a little by development at either end, but it's not a bad place to stay if you're after peace and quiet; try *O Stelios* (☎04240/33 412; ❸), a simple pension above the *Vrahos* taverna, the *Avra* (☎04240/33 550; ❹) or any of the rooms advertised just in from the seafront. Though most of the quayside tavernas don't offer value for money, there are exceptions: the *Orea Ellas* taverna by the harbour is shaded by beautiful chestnut trees and sells a highly recommended, home-made retsina, while the *Flisvos* is a friendly place with decent pasta dishes.

High above Loutráki, **GLÓSSA** would be perhaps a preferable base if it had more places to stay. It is a sizeable and quite beautiful, totally Greek town, with several kafenía, a taverna and a few rooms to let, some of which are hot and musty, with erratic water pressure. *Kostas and Nina's* place (☎04240/33 686; ❸) has simple, clean rooms, some with a view; they also rent out studios longer term, or you could stay at the *Selinounda Apartments* (☎04240/33 570; ❹) on the road between Loutráki and Glóssa. The one central taverna, popular *To Agnandi*, serves excellent, innovative food and has a roof terrace with wonderful views, while *Iy Kali Kardhia*, east of town on the road out towards Élios, also serves good food in a pleasant setting. Incidentally, it's a good idea to accept offers of a taxi ride up to Glóssa from Loutráki; it's a stiff walk up even if you know the path shortcuts, and taxi drivers will know if there are any vacancies. If it's really high season, though, and even Glóssa is packed, two nearby villages, **Athéato** and **Paleó Klíma**, have rooms, while Élios on the coast below has two big hotels, bungalows and rooms.

Ninety-minutes' walk from Glóssa, up to the north coast, will bring you to the **beach** called **Perivolioú**. The walk itself is worthwhile, passing a **monastery** next to a stone cairn containing masses of human bones and skulls. There's also a huge hollow oak tree here, in the heart of which is a small tank of drinking water. The beach, when you get there, is nothing out of the ordinary, but there's pure spring water and a cave for shade.

East of Glóssa, a dirt road leads to the splendidly sited church of **Áyios Ioánnis Kastrí**, perched on the top of a rock high above a small sandy cove where you can swim. A new unsightly house nearby has spoiled the isolation somewhat, but the walk from Glóssa (again, about ninety minutes) is beautiful and peaceful, with hawks and nightingales for company.

Skópelos Town

If you stay on the ferry beyond Loutráki – probably the best plan – you reach **SKÓPELOS TOWN**, sloping down one corner of a huge, almost circular bay. The best way to arrive is by sea, with the town revealed slowly as the boat rounds the final headland. Though more and more people seem to have discovered Skópelos Town, the locals are making a tremendous effort to keep it from going the way of Skiáthos. The harbour area is practically wall-to-wall tavernas and cafés, but the shops and eateries in the back alleys tend to be imaginative and tasteful, with wooden, hand-painted name signs. Spread below the oddly whitewashed ruins of a Venetian **kástro** is an enormous number of churches – 123 reputedly, though some are small enough to be mistaken for houses and most are locked except for their annual festival day. Other sights include a **folklore museum** (Wed–Fri 10am–2pm & 6–8pm, Sat 6–9pm, Sun 11am–1pm & 6–9pm) and photography exhibitions in summer.

Outside town, perched on the slopes opposite the quay, are two convents, worth visiting for their seclusion and views: **Evangelístrias** (daily 8am–1pm & 4–7pm), which is within view of the town, and **Pródhromou** (daily 8am–1pm & 5–8pm). The monastery of **Metamórfosis**, also on this promontory, was abandoned in 1980, but is now being restored by the monks and is open to visitors. Access is simplest by following an old road behind the line of hotels along the bay to Evangelístria (an hour's walk). From there it's an extra half-hour's scramble over mule tracks to Pródhromos, the remotest and most beautiful of the three. Ignore the new road that goes part way – it's longer, and misses most of the beauty of the walk.

Practicalities

The **ferry quay** is at the western end of a long promenade, lined with an array of boutiques, bars, stores and restaurants. The local hydrofoil agency is Skopelos Shipping (℡04240/22 767). To get to the **bus station**, turn left where the quay meets the main road, and follow the sea until you pass the children's swings and the second *períptero*, at the point where the road divides around a car park. Opposite the bus station entrance, a short road leads into a maze of lanes and signposts to the **post office**. There are **banks** (with cash dispensers) about 50m from the quay. Among the several **motorbike rental** outlets, friendly service can be had at Panos Bikes (℡04240/23 696), near the start of the road towards Glóssa. For around €15, day-long **boat cruises** offer to take you around the island or to Alónissos and the marine park.

In the main part of the town there are dozens of **rooms** for rent. These can be arranged through the Association of Room Owners office (℡ & ℗ 04240/24 567; daily 9am–noon & 6–8pm), on the seafront 100m from the ferry dock. Alternatively, there are a few pleasant small hotels such as *Andromache* (℡04240/22 940, or enquire at Madro Travel by the quay ℡04240/22 145; ❹), in a quiet old house near the post office, and the relaxed and casual *Kyr Sotos* (℡04240/22 549, ℗23 668; ❹) nearby. The old-style *Georgios* (℡04240/22 308; ❹), right by the quay, is a fair standby and the gaily painted *Adonis* (℡04240/22 231, ℗23 239; ❺), just above the mid-seafront is also good though noisy. For larger, more **expensive hotels** with pools higher up from the port, you're unlikely to find a space without having booked through a tour operator, but if you fancy the likes of the cosy *Elli* (℡04240/22 943, ℗23 284; ❻) on the east side of town, the modern *Aperitton* (℡04240/22 256, ℗22 976; ❻) on the ring road above the town, or the first-rate, neo-rustic *Dionyssos* (℡04240/23 210, ℗22 954; ❻), also on the ring road – ask about vacancies at Madro Travel on the quay.

There's a wide variety of **places to eat**, ranging from the acceptable to the truly excellent. Those at the near end of the harbour, like *Angelos-Ta Kymata, Molos* and *Klimataria*, all offer decent meals, as does *To Aktaion*, with exceptionally pleasant staff and large, delicious and reasonably priced portions. At the far end of the front *Stergios* has tasty dishes like chicken in white-wine sauce. A little way inland, two *souvláki* places, both named *O Platanos*, compete for the distinction of having the best *yíros*; the one with blue chairs also has a much wider menu. If you're sick of Greek food, then *Perivoli*, above the two *souvladzídhika* at the east end of town, is the place for an "international-cuisine" gourmet blowout – fairly affordable at about €19 apiece.

Nightlife in Skópelos is on the increase, but is more of the late-night bar than the nightclub variety, apart from the *Cocos* disco out of town. That said, *Metro, Ano Kato* and *Panselinos,* which form a cluster on Dhoulídhis, are pretty jumping on a hot summer evening. Among bars, look out for the classy *Vengera*, in a restored house that compares favourably with the town's folk art museum, and the small, atmospheric *Nemesis*. The *bouzoúki* joint *Meintani* is housed in an old olive press near Souvlaki Square, while the *Skopelitissa* and *Anatoli* on top of the *kástro* play Greek music till the early hours.

Around the rest of the island

Buses cover the island's main paved road between Skópelos Town and Loutráki via Glóssa (around 6–8 times daily 7am–10.30pm), stopping at the paths to all the main beaches and villages. **Stáfylos**, 4km south of town, is the closest beach, though rather small and rocky. It's getting increasingly crowded, but the *Terpsis* taverna, just inland at a spot shaded by a vast pine tree, is famous for its quality grilled meat (especially chicken). Among the new room ventures, *Mando* (℡04240/23 917; ❺) is friendly and quiet.

When Stáfylos gets too busy, it's better to go to **Velanió** beach, a short walk east along the coast, to have a chance of escaping the crowds. Nudity is acceptable and although the official campsite has long since closed, you shouldn't be hassled if you stay a night or two. There's spring water and a *kantína* too.

Further around the coast to the west, the tiny horseshoe-shaped harbour of **AGNÓNDAS** (with its three fish tavernas and rooms) is the start of a fifteen-minute path (2km by road) or half-hourly kaïki trip to **LIMNONÁRI**, 300m of fine sand set in a closed, rocky bay. The *Limnonari Beach* restaurant serves delicious spiral-shaped local *tyrópittes* and rents rooms (℡04240/23 046; ❹).

PÁNORMOS is very much a full-blown, commercial resort, with rooms, tavernas, a campsite, yacht anchorage and watersports. The beach here is gravelly and steeply shelving, but there are small secluded bays close by. The thirty-room *Panormos Beach Hotel* (℡04240/22 711, ℻23 366; ❻) has a beautiful garden and fine views, and is lovingly looked after; beyond it, the *Adrina Beach* (℡04240/23 373; ❻) is one of the most attractive and most expensive hotels in the Sporades. Slightly further on at **MILIÁ**, there is a tremendous, 1500m sweep of tiny pebbles beneath a bank of pines, facing the islet of Dhassía. There's one taverna and the *Milia Apartments* (℡04240/23 998; ❹) in this languid setting; nudist swimming is possible at a lovely five-hundred-metre-long beach a little way north. The shore beyond is indented with many tiny coves, ranging from individual- to family-size.

Further north, **ÉLIOS**, 9km short of Glóssa, is a medium-sized, fairly new resort settled by residents of the earthquake-damaged villages above it, with nothing special to offer besides a pleasant beach. If you want to stay, try the *Hotel Apartments Zanneta* (℡04240/33 140, ℻33 717; ❻). Beyond here, the renovated village of Paleó Klíma marks the start of a beautiful forty-minute **trail** to Glóssa, via the empty hamlet of Áyii Anáryiri and the oldest village on the island, **Athéato** (Mahalás).

West of Skópelos Town, various jeep tracks and old paths wind through olive and plum groves towards **Mount Dhélfi** and the Vathiá forest, or skirt the base of the mountain northeast to Revýthi hill with its fountains and churches, and the site of **Karyá**, with its *sendoúkia:* ancient rock-cut tombs which may be early Christian. To the northwest of Skópelos Town, **Glystéri** is a small pebble beach with no shade, whose taverna is much frequented by locals on Sundays. A fork off the Glystéri and Mount Dhélfi tracks can – in theory – be followed across the island to Pánormos within ninety minutes; it's a pleasant walk, though the route isn't always obvious.

Alónissos and some minor islets

The most remote of the Sporades, **Alónissos** is also, at first sight, the least attractive, owing to an unfortunate recent history. The vineyards were wiped out by disease in 1950, and the *hóra* was damaged by an earthquake in 1965. Although its houses were mostly repairable, lack of water, combined with corruption and the social control policies of the new junta, were instrumental in the transfer of virtually the entire population down to the previously unimportant anchorage of Patitíri. The result is a little soulless, but what charm may be lacking in the built environment on the coast is made up for by the hospitality of the islanders.

Patitíri and the old town

PATITÍRI is not a good introduction to the island, though it's trying hard to rectify that. The port, a pretty cove flanked by pine trees, is marred by rows of flat-roofed concrete buildings rising up behind it. Nevertheless, the line of near-identical bars and restaurants that runs along the waterfront is pleasant enough. Alónissos attracts fewer visitors than Skíathos or Skópelos; most of those who do come stay in Patitíri, and from mid-July to the end of August it can get very crowded. It's easy, though, to pick up connections here for beaches and the old town, and there are several good hotels to choose from. The most interesting place to visit is the **Monk Seal Information Centre** (daily 10am–1pm & 7–10pm) on the first floor of a building halfway along the seafront. The displays include models, photos, video and slide shows.

   PALEÁ ALÓNISSOS is a fine but steep fifty-minute walk via the traditional *kalderími* – signposted on the left just outside Patitíri. Alternatively, there's a frequent bus service in the mornings and afternoons. Although some houses are still derelict, much of the village has been painstakingly restored, mainly by the English and Germans who bought the properties at knock-down rates. Only a few local families continue to live here, which gives the village a rather odd and un-Greek atmosphere, but it is picturesque, and the views make the trip worthwhile.

Practicalities

All the important facilities are in Patitíri; **buses** and **taxis** have adjacent terminals. The **post office** is on the Hóra road, while kaïkia leave from the quay beside the *Pension Flisvos*. You can rent a scooter or larger motorbike at Dhyo Trohi or even a car (check with Ikos Travel, overleaf) at reasonable prices. The roads between Patitíri, Stení Vála and the northernmost point on the island are paved, and the dirt roads down to the beaches are in good condition: not half as dangerous as the twisting, busy roads on Skíathos and Skópelos. A couple of the rental places on the waterfront also rent out motorboats and dinghies.

   Rooms are easy to find here, as you'll probably be approached with offers as you get off the ferry, sometimes by older women wearing traditional blue-and-white costumes. The local room-owners' association (☎ & ℗ 04240/65 577), on the front, can also find you a room (mostly ❸) in Patitíri or nearby Vótsi. Other options include the *Ioulieta* pension (☎04240/65 463; ❸), *Haravyi* (☎04240/65 090, ℗65 189; ❺) and *Pantheon* (☎04240/65 139; ❹). Best in the higher price range are *Liadromia* (☎04240/65 521, ℗65 096, ⓔliadromia@alonisso.com; ❺), above the port, *Niirides* (☎04240/65 643; ❺),

ALÓNISSOS

N

Koupelousáko
● Yérakas

Alónissos

Áyios
Dhimítrios
● Mourteró
Kalamákia
● Stení Vála
● Livádhia

Peristéra

Megáli
Ammos
● Miliá   Kokkinókastro

Vrysítsa
Khryssí Miliá
Vótsi
Paleá Alónissos ●   ● Roussoúm Yialós
Megálos   PATITÍRI
Mourtiás
Výthisma ● Marpoúnda

Peristéra ●

0   5 km

comprising studio apartments with pool, and *Paradise* (☎04240/65 160; ❺), on the promontory east of the port with a pool overlooking the sea. Ikos Travel, the hydrofoil agent (☎04240/65 320), can do bookings for a limited number of rooms and apartments in the old town, though accommodation here is in short supply, so expect to pay well over the odds, particularly in season. Otherwise, ask around; few people put up "room for rent" signs, but try the simple and clean *Fadasia House* (☎04240/65 186; ❸), at the entrance to Hóra.

The **restaurants** on the front of Patitíri are reasonably priced, but for the most part the food is nothing special. One exception is the *Pleiades*, its tables set in a peaceful courtyard, and with well-executed dishes from a limited menu. Recommended ouzerís include *To Kamaki*, two blocks up towards the post office from the waterfront, with an amazing selection of seafood. Two other ouzerís worth a try on the same road are *Kala Krassa* and *Kapetan Spyros*. The *Tzimakis* grill has good food in a splendid setting on the promontory. Up in the old town, *Astrofengia* has breathtaking terrace seating, a German take on Greek recipes, and decadent desserts.

Nightlife is low-key. The best of the seafront bars is *Pub Dennis*, whose ice-cream concoctions are divine, though both *En Plo* and *La Vie* are popular. Club-wise, *Borio* and *Enigma* are fairly European, while *Rembetika*, on the road to the old town, specializes in Greek music.

The island's beaches

Alónissos has some of the cleanest water in the Aegean, but it's lacking in sandy beaches. There's only two really – Výthisma and Vrysítsa. The rest vary from rough to fine pebbles. There's a very limited bus service along the Hóra–Patitíri–Stení Vala route, but kaïkia run half-hourly from Patitíri north to Khryssí, Miliá, Kokkinókastro, Stení Vála, Kalamákia and Áyios Dhimítrios, and south around the coast to Marpoúnda, Výthisma and Megálos Mourtiás. Kaïkia also sail occasionally to Livádhia and Peristéra islet.

At Patitíri there's decent swimming from the rocks around the promontory to the north; pick your way along a hewn-out path past the hotels and you're there (ladder provided). To the north, above the headlands, Patitíri merges into two adjoining settlements, **Roussoúm Yialós** and **Vótsi**. For better beaches, you'll have to get in a boat or on a bike.

Khryssí Miliá, the first good beach, has pine trees behind the sand and a taverna; there's a couple of new hotels on the hillside above, such as the posh *Milia Bay* (☎04240/66 035, ℻66 037, ✉milia-bay@forthnet.gr; ●), and it

The Mediterranean monk seal

The **Mediterranean monk seal** has the dubious distinction of being the European mammal most in danger of extinction. Fewer than eight hundred survive worldwide, the majority around the Portuguese Atlantic island of Madeira. A large colony off the coast of the West African state of Mauritania was decimated early in 1997: an estimated two hundred seals died, possibly poisoned by algae. Small numbers survive in the Ionian and Aegean seas; the largest population here, of around thirty seals, lives around the deserted islands north of Alónissos.

Monk seals can travel up to 200km a day in search of food, but they usually return to the same places to rear their **pups**. They have one pup every two years, and the small population is very vulnerable to disturbance. Originally, the pups would have been reared in the open, but with increasing disturbance by man, they have retreated to isolated sea caves, with partly submerged entrances, particularly around the coast of the remote islet of Pipéri.

Unfortunately, the seals compete with fishermen for limited stocks of fish, and, in the overfished Aegean, often destroy nets full of fish. Until recently it was common for seals to be killed by fishermen. This occasionally still happens, but in an attempt to protect the seals, the seas around the northern Sporades have been declared a **marine wildlife reserve**: fishing is restricted in the area north of Alónissos and prohibited within 5km of Pipéri. On Alónissos, the conservation effort and reserve have won a great deal of local support, mainly through the efforts of the Hellenic Society for the Protection of the Monk Seal (HSPMS), based at Stení Vála. The measures have been particularly popular with local fishermen, as tight restrictions on larger, industrial-scale fishing boats from other parts of Greece should help restore local stocks, and eventually benefit the fishermen financially.

Despite this, the government has made no serious efforts to enforce the restrictions, and boats from outside the area continue to fish around Pipéri. There are also government plans to reduce the prohibited area around Pipéri to 500m. On a more positive note, the HSPMS, in collaboration with the Pieterburen Seal Creche in Holland, has reared several abandoned seal pups, all of which have been successfully released in the seas north of Alónissos.

For the moment, your chances of actually seeing a seal are remote, unless you plan to spend a few weeks on a boat in the area. It's recommended that you shouldn't visit Pipéri – this is officially prohibited in any case – or approach sea caves on other islands which might be used by seals, or try to persuade boat-owners to do so.

can get crowded in summer. At **Kokkinókastro**, over the hill to the north, excavations have revealed the site of ancient Ikos and evidence of the oldest known prehistoric habitation in the Aegean. There's nothing much to see, but it's a beautiful spot with a good red-pebble beach, and, in July and August, a daytime bar.

STENÍ VÁLA, opposite the island of Peristéra, a haven for the yachts and flotillas that comb the Sporades, has almost become a proper village, with two shops, several houses, a bar, rooms and five tavernas, one of which stays open more or less throughout the year. The Monk Seal Treatment and Rehabilitation Centre, housed in a small hut on the beach, can provide information and insight into the HSPMS's work. There's an unofficial campsite (☎04240/65 258) in an olive grove by the harbour, a long pebble beach – Glýfa, where boats are repaired – and some stony beaches within reasonable walking distance in either direction. **KALAMÁKIA**, to the north, also has a couple of tavernas and a few rooms.

If you want real solitude, **Áyios Dhimítrios**, **Megáli Ámmos**, and **Yérakas** (an old shepherds' village at the northernmost point of Alónissos) are possibilities. However, before committing yourself to a Robinson Crusoe existence, check it out by scooter or take one of the round-the-island trips available, and return the next day with enough food for your stay: there are no stores outside the port and Stení Vála. West of Patitíri, **Marpoúnda** features a large hotel and bungalow complex and a rather small beach. It's better to turn left after the campsite towards **Megálos Mourtiás**, a pebble beach with several tavernas linked by dirt track with Paleá Alónissos, 200m above. **Výthisma**, the lovely beach just before Megálos Mourtiás, can only be reached by boat, the path here having been washed out. Further north, visible from Paleá Alónissos, **Vrysítsa** is tucked into its own finger-like inlet. There's sand and a taverna, but little else.

Beyond Alónissos: some minor islets

Northeast of Alónissos, half a dozen tiny **islets** speckle the Aegean. Virtually none of these has any permanent population, or a ferry service, and the only way you can reach them – at least Peristéra, Kyrá Panayía and Yioúra – is by excursion kaïki (ask at Ikos Travel), weather permitting. No boats are allowed to take you to the other, more remote islets, as they are protected areas within the Sporades National Marine Park. But though it is possible to be left for a night or more on any of the closer islands, be sure to bring more supplies than you need: if the weather worsens you'll be marooned until such time as small craft can reach you.

Peristéra is the closest islet to Alónissos, to which it was once actually joined, but subsidence (a common phenomenon in the area) created the narrow straits between the two. It is graced with some sandy beaches and there is rarely anyone around, though some Alonissans do come over for short periods to tend the olive groves, and in season there are regular evening "barbecue boats" from the main island. As on Alónissos, a few unofficial campers are tolerated, but there is only one spot, known locally as "Barbecue Bay", where campfires are allowed.

Kyrá Panayiá (also known as Pelagós) is the next islet out and is equally fertile. It's owned by the Meyístis Lávras monastery of Mount Athos and there are two monasteries here, one still inhabited. Boats call at a beach on the south shore, one of many such sandy stretches and coves around the island. There's no other permanent population besides wild goats.

Nearby **Yioúra** boasts a stalactite cave reputed to be the previous abode of Polyphemus, the Cyclops who imprisoned Odysseus, but you won't be able to check its credentials. No one is allowed within 500m of the island, since, like Pipéri, it lies inside the restricted zone of the Marine Park.

Pipéri, near Yioúra, is a seabird and monk-seal refuge, and permission from a ministry of the environment representative (in Alónissos) is required for visits by specialists; nonscientists are not allowed. Tiny, northernmost **Psathoúra** is dominated by its powerful modern lighthouse, the tallest in the Aegean, although here, as around many of these islands, there's a submerged ancient town, brought low by the endemic subsidence. Roughly halfway between Alónissos and Skýros, green **Skántzoura**, with a single empty monastery and a few seasonal shepherds, is a smaller version of Kyrá Panayiá.

Skýros

Despite its proximity to Athens, **Skýros** remained a very traditional and idiosyncratic island until recently. Any impetus for change had been neutralized by the lack of economic opportunity (and even secondary schooling), forcing the younger Skyrians to live in Athens and leaving behind a conservative gerontocracy. A high school was finally provided in the mid-1980s, and the island has

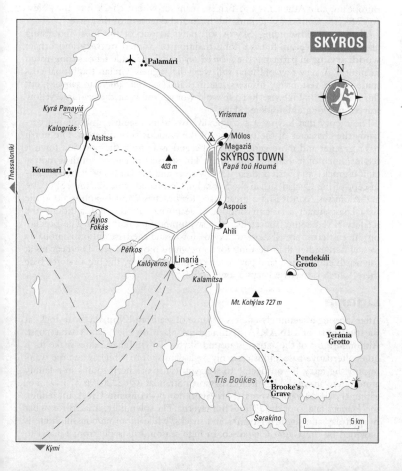

SKÝROS

N

Palamári

Kyrá Panayiá

Yirísmata

Kalogriás

Atsítsa

Mólos

Magaziá

SKÝROS TOWN

Papá toú Houmá

Thessaloníki

403 m

Koumari

Aspoús

Áyios Fokás

Ahíli

Péfkos

Kalóyeros

Linariá

Pendekáli Grotto

Kalamítsa

Mt. Kohýlas 727 m

Yeránia Grotto

Trís Boúkes

Brooke's Grave

Sarakíno

0   5 km

Kými

Goat dances and wild ponies

Skýros has some particularly lively, even outrageous, festivals. The *Apokriátika* (pre-Lenten) Carnival here is structured around the famous **goat dance**, performed by masked revellers in the village streets. The foremost character in this is the Yéros, a menacing figure concealed by a goatskin mask and weighed down by garlands of sheep bells. Accompanying him are Korélles and Kyriés ("Maidens" and "Ladies" – who are transvestites, as only the men participate) and Frangi (maskers in "Western" garb). For further details, read Joy Koulentianou's *The Goat Dance of Skyros*, available in Athens and occasionally on the island.

The other big annual event takes place near Magaziá beach on August 15, when children race domesticated members of the **wild pony** herd, native to Skýros and said to be related to the Shetland pony (if so, it must be very distantly). They are thought, perhaps, to be the diminutive horses depicted in the Parthenon frieze, and at any time of the year you might find some of the tame individuals tethered and grazing near Skýros Town.

---

been somewhat "discovered" since that time. It's now the haunt of continental Europeans, chic Athenians and British, many of whom check into the "New Age" Skýros Centre, to "rethink the form and direction of their lives".

All this notwithstanding, Skýros still ranks as one of the most interesting places in the Aegean. It has a long tradition of painted **pottery** and ornate **woodcarving**, in particular the *salonáki skyrianó* (handmade set of sitting-room furniture). A very few old men still wear the vaguely Cretan traditional costume of cap, vest, baggy trousers, leggings and *trohádhia* (Skýrian sandals), but this is dying out. Likewise, just a few old women still wear the favoured yellow scarves and long embroidered skirts.

The theory that Skýros was originally two islands seems doubtful, but certainly the character of the two parts of the island is very different. The north has a greener and more gentle landscape, and away from the port and town it retains much of its original pine forest. The sparsely inhabited south is mountainous, rocky and barren; there are few trees and the landscape is more reminiscent of the Cyclades than the Sporades. Compared with Skiáthos, Skópelos and Alónissos, Skýros isn't a great place for beaches. Most **beaches** along the west coast attract a certain amount of seaborne rubbish, and, although the scenery is sometimes spectacular, the swimming isn't that good. The beaches on the east coast are all close to Skýros Town, and the best option is probably to stay here rather than heading for somewhere more isolated. The beaches at the north end of the island have been commandeered by the big air-force base there, which otherwise keeps a low profile.

Linariá

After crossing a seemingly endless expanse of sea from Kými, the boat docks at the tiny port of **LINARIÁ**, a functional place on the island's west coast. Although most of the action is around Skýros Town, Linariá does make for a quiet alternative base and is certainly a pleasant spot to while away time waiting for the ferry. If you decide to stay, you can rent cheap rooms in a family atmosphere above the bay from Khrysoula Strandzi (☎02220/96 378; ❷). For eating try the *Almyra* taverna (May–Sept), for no-nonsense Greek mezédhes, the *Psariotis* ouzerí or the *Filippos* fish taverna. The splendidly situated *Kavos* bar is open day and night for drinks and snacks, while more raucous nightlife is provided by the *Castro Club* disco. In high season, kaïka ply from Linariá to the Pentekáli and Yeránia **grottoes**, and to the islet of **Sarakíno**, which has a cave and a very few Skyrian wild ponies – almost extinct in the wild. There's a reasonable sandy **beach** called **Kalóyeros** a few minutes' walk along the main road from Linariá, where you can camp.

An asphalt road connects Linariá to Skýros Town, 10km away, and then continues round past the airport to Atsítsa, where the Skyros Centre has its main branch; **buses** to **Skýros Town** and **Magaziá**, on the coast below, leave from the quay. Midway up the Linariá–Skýros Town route, a paved side road goes to Ahíli and Kalamítsa. Most other roads are passable by scooter, apart from the direct track between Skýros Town and Atsítsa.

Skýros Town

SKÝROS TOWN (also known as Horió), with its decidedly Cycladic architecture, sits on the landward side of a high rock rising precipitously from the coast. According to legend, King Lycomedes pushed Theseus to his death from its summit. The town doesn't feel like a resort, with its workaday atmosphere, but away from the tattier outskirts is decidedly picturesque. The older and more intriguing parts of town are higher up, climbing towards the **kástro**, a mainly Byzantine building, built on the site of the ancient **acropolis**. There are few traces of the acropolis, although remains of the Classical city walls survive below on the seaward side of the rock. The *kástro* is open to visitors; to reach its upper parts you pass through a rather private-looking gateway into the monastery, then through an attractive shaded courtyard and up a whitewashed tunnel. There's little to see at the top, apart from a few churches in various states of ruin, but there are great views over the town and the island, and the climb up takes you through the quieter and more traditional part of town, with glimpses into traditionally decorated houses. With their gleaming copper pots, porcelain plates and antique embroideries decorating the hearth, these dwellings are a matter of intense pride among the islanders, who are often found seated in their doorways on tiny carved chairs.

At the northern end of town is the striking and splendidly incongruous **memorial to Rupert Brooke**. It takes the form of a bronze statue of "Immortal Poetry" and its nakedness caused a scandal among the townspeople when it was first erected. Brooke, who visited the south of the island very briefly in April 1915, died shortly afterwards of blood poisoning on a French hospital ship anchored offshore and was buried in an olive grove above the bay of Trís Boúkes. (The site can be reached on foot from Kalamítsa, by kaïki, or, less romantically, by taxi.) Brooke, who became something of a local hero, despite his limited acquaintance with Skýros, was adopted as the paragon of patriotic youth by Kitchener and later Churchill, who conveniently overlooked his forthright socialist and internationalist views.

Just below the Brooke statue are two museums. The **Archeological Museum** (Tues–Sun 8am–2pm; €1.50) has a modest collection of pottery and statues from excavations on the island, and a reconstruction of a traditional Skýros house interior. The privately run **Faltaïts Museum** (daily 10am–1pm & 5.30–8pm/6–9pm in summer; free), in a nineteenth-century house built over one of the bastions of the ancient walls, is more interesting, with a collection of domestic items, costumes, embroideries, porcelain and rare books.

Practicalities

The **bus** from Linariá leaves you by the school, 200m below the main platía; in season, schedules are guaranteed to meet the ferries, but otherwise it can be

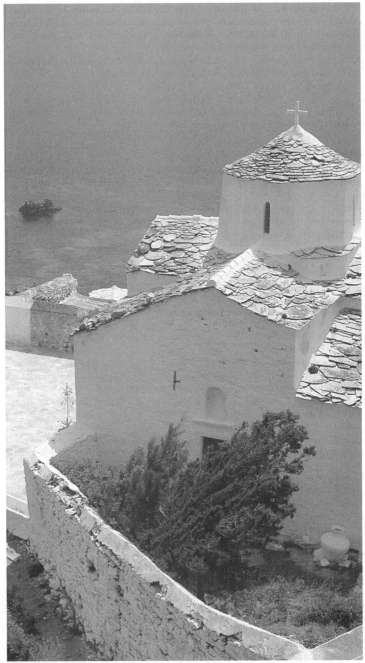

△ Skópelos Town

limited, in which case you might be better off getting a taxi. The **post office** and **bank** are both near the platía. Skýros Travel (☎02220/91 600 or 91 123), on the main street above the platía, can provide **information** or advice, and can find a room or hotel; in high season it's a good idea to telephone them in advance. Of the **motorbike and bicycle** rental places in the area around the platía, the most prominent and efficient is Trahanas (☎02220/92 032).

You'll probably be met off the bus with offers of **rooms**, which it's as well to accept. If you'd like to stay in a traditional Skyrian house, those of Anna Stergiou (☎02220/91 657; ❸) and Maria Mavroyiorgi (☎02220/91 440; ❸) are both clean and cosy. Or you could try the pleasant, if rather overpriced, *Nefeli* hotel (☎02220/91 964, Ⓕ92 061; ❻) on the main road before the platía. A more basic option is the *Elena* (☎02220/91 738; ❷) next to the post office, which has very cheap singles with shared bath. There's a picturesque **campsite** nearer the beach, at the bottom of the steps below the archeological museum, with basic amenities but a good bar and friendly management.

The platía and the main street running by it are the centre of village life, with a few noisy pubs and a wide choice of kafenía, tavernas and fast-food places. There are just a few outstanding **places to eat**: most are overpriced, or serve undistinguished fare. *Maryetis* has the best grilled fish and stewed goat, *O Papous ki Ego* is Hóra's best ouzerí, with a mix of fried plates and grilled cuttlefish, while the *Sweets Workshop* does some wonderful cakes. For a special occasion, try *Kristina's* restaurant below the taxi rank (signposted); its Australian owner has an imaginative menu featuring great desserts. The *Panorama*, in the lower town, towards Magaziá, is also good for its home cooking with a view.

The town's **nightlife** is mostly bar-based until very late, when the few clubs get going. The most popular **bars** are the trendy *Kalypso* which plays jazz and blues, dance-oriented *Kata Lathos* and the rockier *Iroön* and *Rodon*. Later on, *Iy Stasis* is one of the most popular places. The best clubs include the *Skyropoula*, *Mylos* and the *Stone Club*. Some bars also serve good breakfasts; here the favourite is *Anemos*, followed by *Kalypso*, which has tasty Danish pastries. Another fine supper-only wine-bar with an extensive range of generic Mediterranean snacks is *Anatolikos Anemos*, near the museum, with sweeping views across the bay.

Magaziá and Mólos and nearby beaches

A path leads down past the archeological museum towards the small coastal village of **MAGAZIÁ**, coming out by the official campsite. From Magaziá, an 800-metre-long sandy beach stretches to the adjacent village of **MÓLOS**. In recent years, a sprawl of new development between the road and the beach has more or less joined the two villages together. Despite this, the beach is still good, and there are lots of **rooms** down here for the young crowd that uses the beach's watersports and volleyball facilities. *Stamatis Marmaris* (☎02220/91 672; ❸) beyond Mólos, and *Manolis Balotis* (☎02220/91 386; ❸) near the campsite, are both excellent choices. More upmarket hotels include the *Paliopyrgos* (☎02220/91 014, Ⓕ92 185; ❹), halfway between the beach and town, with a wonderful view, and the *Angela* (☎02220/91 764; ❺), garden-set bungalows in Mólos. The beachfront **tavernas** often compare favourably with those in town: on the Magaziá side *Stefanos* taverna is reliable, while the *Koufari* ouzerí near the *Xenia Hotel* has excellent food for higher prices. At Mólos try *Tou Thoma To Magazi,* the *Maryetis* garden restaurant and the ouzerí at *Balabani's Mill*, all at the end of the beach. It's worth sampling lobster in Skýros: it's a local speciality, often served flaked into pasta as *astakomakaronádha*.

For quieter beaches, carry on past Mólos, or try the excellent and undeveloped (unofficial nudist) beach, **Papa tou Houma**, directly below the *kástro*. The path down to the beach starts 150m beyond the *Skyropoula* disco, and isn't obvious from above. However, further along the road south of here, the beaches are disappointing until **Aspoús**, which has a couple of tavernas and rooms to rent, as well as the smart *Ahillion* hotel (℡02220/93 300, ℗93 303; ❶). Further south, **Ahíli**, had one of the best beaches on the island until the construction of its new marina. Southeast of Ahíli, the coast is rocky and inaccessible, although you can take a kaïki trip down to the bay of **Trís Boúkes**, passing some picturesque sea caves on the way.

Around the rest of the island

In summer, the whimsical bus service visits the more popular beaches. But if you want to branch out on your own, rent a scooter. Tracks and footpaths diverge from the main circle road, leading inward and seaward. Among the most interesting places to head for is **Palamári**, the neglected site of an early Bronze Age settlement and a spectacular beach. Turn right after the road has begun to descend to the airport plain.

For a taste of the wooded interior, a hike on the dirt track from Skýros Town to **ATSÍTSA** is well worth the effort; it takes three to four hours, and is too rough for a scooter. Atsítsa is an attractive bay with pine trees down to the sea (tapped by the Skyrian retsina industry), a very good fish **taverna** (*O Andonis*) and an increasing number of rooms, in addition to the Skyros Centre buildings. The beach here is rocky and isn't great for swimming, but there are small sandy beaches fifteen- and twenty-minutes' walk to the north at **Kalogriás** and **Kyrá Panayiá**, with its eponymous taverna, though they are nothing out of the ordinary.

Elsewhere in the coniferous north, **Áyios Fokás** and **Péfkos** bays are easiest reached by a turning from the paved road near Linariá, while access from Atsítsa is via a reasonable dirt road. Both are in the process of being discovered by villa companies, but they have few rooms. Though quite primitive, Áyios Fokás has a very basic, excellent taverna; Péfkos has two, of which *Barba Mitsos* is the more appealing (these are only open in high season, as are all the other tavernas away from Linariá, Skýros Town, Magaziá and Mólos). The bay is beautiful, and the beach reasonable but not that clean – the beaches around Skýros Town are much better for swimming.

As for exploring the great southern mountain of **Kohýlas**, this is best attempted only if you have a four-wheel-drive vehicle, as the tracks are poor away from the main west-coast road via Kalamítsa to the naval base at Trís Boúkes (where Rupert Brooke is buried). **Kalamítsa** beach, just east of Linariá but tricky to get to from there, lacks character, but the *Mouries* taverna between it and Linariá is worth a stop, as is the remote beach halfway to Trís Boúkes, which has no facilities.

Évvia (Euboea)

Évvia is the second-largest Greek island (after Crete), and seems more like an extension of the mainland to which it was in fact once joined. At **Halkídha**, the gateway to the island, the curious old drawbridge has only a forty-metre channel to span, the island reputedly having been split from Attica and Thessaly by a blow from Poseidon's trident (earthquakes and subsidence being the more

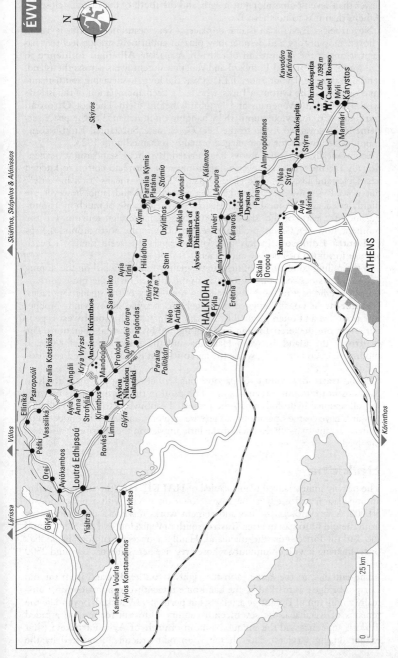

ÉVVIA

N

Skíathos, Skópelos & Alónissos

Skýros

Vólos

Lárissa

Glýfa
Yiáltra
Oreí
Péfki
Vassiliká
Ayiókambos
Loutrá Edhipsoú
Elliniká
Psaropoúli
Paralía Kotsikiás
Angáli
Ayía Anna
Strofyliá
Krýa Vrýssi **Ancient Kírinthos**
Kírinthos
Limni
Rovies
Glýfa
Ayíou Nikoláou Galatáki
Dhervéni Gorge
Mandoúdhi
Prokópi
Sarakíniko
Néo Artáki
Ayía Iríni
Hiliádhou
Steni
Dhírfys 1743 m
Paralía Politikón
Pagóndas

Kaména Voúrla
Áyios Konstandínos
Arkítsa

Kórinthos

ATHENS

Kými
Paralía Kými
Platána
Stómio
Oxýlithos
Avlonári
Ayía Thékla
Basílica of Áyios Dhimítrios
Aliéri
Amárynthos
Káravos
Skála Oropoú
Erétria
Fýlla
HALKÍDHA
Ramnous
Ayía Marína
Néa Stýra
Panayía
Almyropótamos
Stýra
Dhrakóspita
Marmári
Néa Stýra
Ancient Dystos
Lépoura
Kálamos

Kavodóro (Kafiréas)
Dhrakóspita
Óhi, 1399 m
Castel Rosso
Mýli
Kárystos

0   25 km

pedestrian explanations). Besides the newer suspension bridge bypassing Halkídha and also linking Évvia to the mainland, there are ferry crossings at no fewer than seven points along its length, and the south of the island is closer to Athens than it is to northern Évvia.

Nevertheless, Évvia *is* an island, in places a very beautiful one. But it has an idiosyncratic history and demography, plus an enduringly strange feel that has kept it out of the mainstream of tourism. A marked **Albanian influence** in the south, and scattered Lombard and Venetian watchtowers acrosss the island, lend a distinctive flavour. Indeed, Évvia was the longest-surviving south-mainland outpost of the Ottoman Turks, who had a keen appreciation of the island's wealth, as did the Venetians and Lombards before them. The last **Ottoman garrison** was not evicted until 1833, hanging on in defiance of the peace settlement that awarded Évvia to the new Greek state. Substantial Turkish communities, renowned for their alleged brutality, remained until 1923.

Economically, Évvia has always been prized. By Greek standards, it's exceptionally **fertile**, producing everything from grain, corn and cotton to kitchen vegetables and livestock. The classical name "Euboea" means "rich in cattle", but nowadays cows are few and far between; its kid and lamb, however, are highly rated, as is the local retsina. Because of the collapse of much of its mining industry, parts of the island are actively seeking foreign tourism. For the moment, however, Greeks predominate, especially in the north around the spa of **Loutrá Edhipsoú**. In July and August, Évvia can seem merely a beach annexe for much of Thessaly and Athens.

In the rolling countryside of the **north**, grain combines whirl on the sloping hay meadows between olive groves and pine forest. This is the most conventionally scenic part of the island, echoing the beauty of the smaller Sporades. The **northeast coast** is rugged and largely inaccessible, its few sandy beaches surf-pounded and often plagued by flotsam and jetsam; the **southwest** is gentler and more sheltered, though much disfigured by industrial operations. The **centre** of the island, between Halkídha and the easterly port of Kými, is mountainous and dramatic, while the far **southeast** is mostly dry and very isolated.

Public **transport** consists of passable bus services along the main roads to Kárystos in the southeast, and Loutrá Edhipsoú in the northwest. As of writing, all seasonal hydrofoils along the protected southwest coast from Halkídha upwards have ceased operations. Otherwise, explorations are best conducted by rented car; any two-wheeler will make little impact on the enormous distances involved.

Halkídha

The heavily industrialized island-capital of **HALKÍDHA** (the ancient *Chalkis*, an appellation still used) is the largest town on Évvia, with a population of 50,000. A shipyard, rail sidings and cement works make it a dire place, apart from the old Ottoman quarter, **Kástro**, south of Venizélou, and the area around the Turkish fortress on the mainland. Hardly a trace remains of Halkídha's once-thriving Jewish community, whose presence here dates back around 2500 years.

The entrance to the *kástro* – on the right as you head inland from the old Euripos bridge – is marked by the handsome fifteenth-century **mosque**, nominally a museum of Byzantine artefacts, but permanently locked. Beyond lie the remains of Karababa, the seventeenth-century Ottoman fortress, an arcaded Turkish aqueduct and the unique basilican **church of Ayía Paraskeví** (shut except during services). The church is an odd structure, converted by the

Crusaders during the fourteenth century into a Gothic cathedral. In the opposite direction, in the new town, an **archeological museum** at Venizélou 13 (Tues–Sun 8am–2.30pm; €1.50) has a good display of prehistoric, Hellenic and Roman finds from all over the island. The waterside overlooks the **Évripos**, the narrow channel dividing Évvia from the mainland, whose strange currents have baffled scientists for centuries. You can stand on the bridge that spans the narrowest point and watch the water swirling by like a river. Every few hours the current changes and the "tide" reverses. Aristotle is said to have thrown himself into the waters in despair at his inability to understand what was happening, so if you're puzzled you're in good company; there is still no entirely satisfactory explanation.

Practicalities

For most visitors, though, such activities are strictly time-fillers, with much the best view of the place to be had from the bus or train on the way out. **Trains** arrive on the mainland side of the channel, beneath the old fortress; given numerous, quick rail links with Athens, there's little reason to stay overnight. Should you want to, the basic *Kentrikon* hotel (☎02210/22 375; ❸) is a far better deal than the huge waterfront establishments it backs onto. Most other services of interest lie within sight of the old Évripos bridge. The **bus station** is 400m from the bridge along Kótsou, then 50m right; you should get a connection for any corner of the island as long as you show up by 2pm, later for Kými or Límni.

Halkídha is noted for its superior seafood and ouzerís; the waterfront **restaurants** are popular at weekends with Athenians but not necessarily the best-value options. Two to try are *Ta Pende Fi* at Evvías 61, a classic fish taverna in a peaceful setting, or the more central, long-running *Ouzeri Tsaf* at Papanastasíou 3, off Platía Agorás, again strong on seafood titbits. For the truly impecunious or time-pressured, there's also a handful of acceptable grills serving adequate lunches in the immediate vicinity of the bus station.

Halkídha to Kými

The coast road heading east out of Halkídha is an exceptionally misleading introduction to the interior of Évvia. The industrial zone gives way to nondescript hamlets, which are succeeded between Erétria and Amárynthos by sequestered colonies of Athenian second homes, rather bleak beaches and large hotels frequented by British and German package-tour companies. There are some intriguing **Frankish towers** at **Fýlla**, worth a detour inland from Vasilikó if you have a car, but little else.

Modern **ERÉTRIA** is a rather dreary resort laid out on a grid plan; for non-package travellers its main asset is a well-advertised ferry service across to Skála Oropoú in Attica. The site of **ancient Eretria** is more distinguished, though much of it lies under the town. A few scanty remains are dotted around the town centre, most conspicuously an **agora** and a **temple of Apollo**, but more interesting are the excavations in the northwest corner, behind the excellent small museum (Tues–Sun 8am–2.30pm; €1.50), opened in 1991 in collaboration with the Swiss School of Archeology. Here a **theatre** has been uncovered; steps from the orchestra descend to an underground vault used for sudden entrances and exits. Beyond the theatre are the ruins of a **gymnasium** and a **sanctuary**. The museum guard will be happy to unlock the fourth-century BC **House of Mosaics**, five-minutes' walk from the museum. Of the dozen or so hotels in town one of the more affordable and interesting options is the municipal tourist complex *Dreams Island* (☎02290/61 224, ℱ61 268; ❹), which occupies a tiny offshore island, linked by causeway to the end of the bay. For a beachside, self-contained complex, try the B-class, 1998-renovated *Grand Bleu* (☎02290/61 012, ℱ61 090; ❹), 2km from the centre.

Nine kilometres further along, **AMÁRYNTHOS** is a smaller and more pleasant resort to stay in. Though the town boasts nothing of particular interest, the seafront square is picturesque enough and there is an ample selection of good eateries, such as *Stefanos* fish taverna right by the square and *To Limenaki* a few minutes west of it. Two good accommodation options are *Iliaktidhes Hotel Apartments* (☎02290/37 605; ❹), just off the main road, and the B-class *Stefania Hotel* (☎02290/38 382, ℱ38 384; ❺), right on the beach.

Just before **Aliveri**, an enormous modern power plant and a virtually intact medieval castle seem incongruously juxtaposed, and more Frankish towers look down from nearby hills. Though Aliveri itself is dreary, the nearby fishing harbour of **Káravos** has several pleasant watering holes, among them the *Vlahos* taverna. Thereafter, the route heads inland. Beyond Lépoura, where the road branches north and south, the scenery improves drastically. Take the north fork towards Kými, and cross some of the most peaceful countryside in Greece. With your own vehicle you can detour east after 5km at Neohóri to the excellent beaches at **Kálamos** and **Korasídha**. There is a growing selection of rooms and tavernas at Kálamos.

Twelve kilometres north of Lépoura, at Háni Avlonaríou, stands the Romanesque thirteenth- or fourteenth-century **basilica of Áyios Dhimítrios**, Évvia's largest and finest (ask for the key at the café next door). **AVLONÁRI** proper, 2km east, is dominated by a hill that commands most of the island's centre. At its crown is a huge Lombard or Venetian tower, rearing above the Neoclassical and vernacular houses that tier the lower slopes. There's a single taverna below the platía, though no accommodation.

This part of Évvia is particularly well endowed with Byzantine chapels, since Avlonári was an archiepiscopal see from the sixth century onwards. Back on the road to Kými, a left fork just north of Háni Avlonaríou (the bus goes this way) leads past the hamlet of **Ayía Thékla**, where a small, shed-like **chapel** of that saint, probably slightly later than Áyios Dhimítrios, hides in a lush vale below the modern church. Inside, enough fresco fragments remain with their large-eyed faces to suggest what has been lost over time. The right fork leads towards the coast and takes you past Oxýlithos, with its somewhat more elaborate chapels of **Áyios Nikólaos** and **Ayía Ánna**, both at least a hundred years older than Áyios Dhimítrios.

The road hits the coast at the fine beach of **Stómio** (known also as just Paralía, or "Beach"), some 1500m of sand closing off the mouth of a river, which is deep, swimmable and often cleaner than the sea. To the north and east you glimpse the capes enclosing the broad bay of Kými. Up on the road, there are a couple of cafés and a small pension; most facilities, however, are further round the coast at **PLATÁNA**, where another river is flanked by a line of older houses, many with rooms or flats to rent.

Despite its name, the extremely functional port of **PARALÍA KÝMIS** has no real beach, and is not a particularly congenial place to be stuck overnight waiting for a ferry to Skýros. The most substantial and traditional **taverna** is *Spanos/To Egeo*, at the south end of the front, while *To Valanti* is also reasonable and the sweet little *Rock Club* plays eclectic sounds; there are just two **hotels**, *Coralli* (☎02220/22 212, ℱ23 355; ❹) and *Beis* (☎02220/22 604, ℱ22 870; ❹).

Most travellers get to **KÝMI** (the main ferry port to Skýros) by bus, which takes the inland route via Ayía Thékla. The upper part of town is built on a green ridge overlooking both the sea and Paralía Kými, 4km below. Note that all buses deposit you in the upper town except for the one or two daily that connect with the ferry. At the bottom of the town, on the harbour-bound road, you can visit the **Folklore Museum**, which has an improbably large collection of costumes, household and agricultural implements and old photos recording the doings of Kymians both locally and in the US, where there's a huge community. Among the emigrants was Dr George Papanikolaou, deviser of the "Pap" cervical smear test, and there's a statue honouring him up in the upper-town platía, where you might ask about **rooms**. There are some good **tavernas** like *To Balkoni*, on the main road towards the shore, with its superb view, where you can sample the products of the local vineyards.

To get up into the rugged country west of Kými, you must negotiate jeep tracks through the forest, or return to Halkídha for the bus service up to **STENÍ**, a large and beautiful village at the foot of Mount Dhírfys. The village has a few cheap *psistariés* and two **hotels**, the *Dirfys* (☎02280/51 217; ❸) and the *Steni* (☎02280/51 221; ❸). It's a good area for hiking, most notably up the peaks of Dhírfys and Xirovoúni, and beyond to the isolated beach hamlets of Hiliádhou and Ayía Iríni, though you'll need a specialist hiking guide to do this (see "Books", p.1077).

Southeast Évvia

The extension of Évvia southeast of Lépoura, so narrow that you can sometimes glimpse the sea on both sides, has a flavour very distinct from the rest of the island. Often bleak and windswept, it forms a geological unit with neighbouring Ándhros, with shared slates and marble. Ethnically, the south also has much in common with that northernmost Cyclade: both were heavily settled by Albanian immigrants from the early fifteenth century onwards, and Arvanítika – a **medieval dialect** of Albanian – was until recently the first language of the remoter villages here. Even non-Arvanítika speakers often betray their ancestry by their startlingly fair colouring and aquiline features. For a place so close to Athens, the south is often surprisingly untouched by modernity; some of the houses have yet to lose their original slate roofs. Others still lack electricity, and the few fields on the steep slopes are far more often worked by donkeys and horses than by farm machinery.

Immediately southeast of Lépoura, most maps persist in showing the lake of Dhýstos in bright blue. In fact, the lake area has been almost totally drained and reclaimed as rich farmland, much to the detriment of the migratory birds who used to stop off here, and to the annoyance of Greek and foreign environmentalists who would prefer that they still did so. Atop the almost perfectly conical hill in the centre of the flat basin are the sparse fifth-century BC ruins of **ancient Dystos** and a subsequent medieval citadel, hard to explore because the surroundings are so swampy.

Beyond the Dhýstos plain, the main road continues along the mountainous spine of the island to Kárystos at the southern end of the paved road system and bus line. If you have your own transport, it's worth stopping off at **STÝRA**, above which are a cluster of **Dhrakóspita** (Dragon Houses), signposted at the north edge of the village and reached by track, then trail. They are so named because only mythological beings were thought capable of shifting into place their enormous masonry blocks. Their origins and uses have yet to be definitively established. The most convincing theory suggests that they are sixth-century BC temples built by immigrants or slaves from Asia Minor working in the nearby marble and slate quarries.

The shore annexe of **NÉA STÝRA**, 5km downhill from the hill village, is a fairly standard package resort, worth knowing about only for its handy ferry connection to Ayía Marína (which gives access to ancient Ramnous) on the Attic peninsula. Much the same can be said for **MARMÁRI**, 19km south, except in this case the ferry link is with Rafina. Here the smart *Hotel Delfini* (☎02240/31 296, ⓕ32 300; ❸) is surprisingly good value and there are a few decent places to eat; try the *Zygos mezedhopolío*, which serves cheap fish in a nice atmosphere. The road between Marmári and Kárystos is now more or less finished, completing the "superhighway" and allowing you to enjoy the nether reaches of the island as you cruise down to its last major settlement.

Kárystos and around

At first sight **KÁRYSTOS** is a rather boring grid (courtesy of nineteenth-century Bavarian town-planners), which ends abruptly to east and west and is studded with modern buildings. King Otho liked the site so much that he contemplated transferring the Greek capital here, and there are still some graceful Neoclassical buildings dating from that period. Kárystos improves with prolonged acquaintance, though you're unlikely to stay for more than a few days. What it can offer is the superb (if often windy) beach to the west, the smaller, sandier **Psilí Ámmos** ten-minutes' walk to the east and a lively, genuine working-port atmosphere. Only one plot of fenced-in foundations, in the central bazaar, bears out the town's ancient provenance, and the oldest obvious structure is the fourteenth-century Venetian **Bourtzi** (locked except for occasional summer-evening art exhibitions) on the waterfront. This small tower is all that remains of once-extensive fortifications. Every evening the shore road is blocked with a gate at this point to allow an undisturbed promenade by the locals. There is a small but interesting **archeological museum** (Tues–Sun 8am–3pm; €1.50) inside the Cultural Centre opposite the Bourtzi, displaying finds from the local area – mostly statues and temple carvings, plus a few smaller votive objects.

Practicalities

Rafina-based **ferries** and **hydrofoils** also serve Kárystos, though services via Marmári are more frequent; **buses** arrive inland, above the central platía and below the National Bank, near a tiny combination grill/ticket office labelled KTEL. This has information on the extremely infrequent (once daily at best) departures to the remote villages of the Kavodóro (Kafiréas) cape to the east. Information on the August wine festival and sightseeing in the region, including walking routes, is provided by the friendly tourist office in a kiosk near the quay.

Finding affordable **accommodation** is not a big problem. The most central is the *Als* (☎02240/22 202, ⓕ25 002; ❸), right opposite the quay, although it may get noisy in high season. Other options are the big *Galaxy* (☎02240/22 600, ⓕ22 463; ❹) on the west side of the waterfront, the plush *Apollon Suite* (☎02240/22 045, ⓕ22 049, ⓔapollon-suite@yahoo.com; ❻) on Psilí Ámmos beach, and the excellent *Karystion* (☎02240/22 391, ⓕ22 727; ❹), which does mouthwatering breakfasts and is situated in the park beyond the Bourtzi on the shore road. Another strategy is to follow up signs in restaurant windows advertising **rooms** inland.

You're also spoilt for choice when **eating out**, as Kárystos must have more restaurants than the rest of Évvia put together. Good choices include the *Kavo Doro*, a friendly and reasonable taverna on Párodos Sakhtoúri one block west of the square, serving *mayireftá*; *Ta Kalamia*, at the west end of the esplanade by the start of the beach, a cheap, filling and popular lunchtime option; and English-speaking *Ta Ovreïka*, in the old Jewish quarter at Sakhtoúri 114, with both Greek and "international" cuisine as well as breakfasts. On the road running up from the *Als* there are several fine *psistariés*, serving the local lamb and goat for which Kárystos is renowned.

Mount Óhi

The obvious excursion from Kárystos is inland towards **Mount Óhi** (1399m) Évvia's highest peak after Dhírfys and Xirovoúni. **MÝLI**, a fair-sized village around a spring-fed oasis, 3km straight inland, makes a good first stop, with its few tavernas. Otherwise, the medieval castle of **Castel Rosso** beckons above, a twenty-minute climb up from the main church (longer in the frequent, howling gales). Inside, the castle is a total ruin, except for an Orthodox **chapel of Profítis Ilías** built over the Venetians' water cistern, but the sweeping views over the sea and the town make the trip worthwhile.

Behind, the ridges of Óhi are as lunar and inhospitable as the broad plain around Kárystos is fertile. From Mýli, it's a three-hour-plus hike up the largely bare slopes, mostly by a path cutting across the new road, strewn with unfinished granite columns, abandoned almost two thousand years ago. The path passes a little-used alpine club shelter (fed by spring water) and yet another *dhrakóspito*, even more impressive than the three smaller ones at Stýra. Built of enormous schist slabs, seemingly sprouting from the mountain, this one is popularly supposed to be haunted.

From Halkídha to Límni

The main road due north from Halkídha crosses a few kilometres of flat farmland and salt marsh on either side of the refugee settlement of Néa Artáki, after which it climbs steeply through forested hills and the **Dhervéni gorge**, gateway to the north of Évvia. With your own transport, you can take a pleasant detour along the road left before Psákhna to the long pebbly beach of **Paralía Politikón**, dotted with places to stay or eat.

The village of **PROKÓPI** lies beyond the narrows, in a valley defined by the rich and beautiful woods that make it famous. A counterpoint, in the village itself, is the ugly 1960s pilgrimage church of **Saint John the Russian**, which holds the saint's relics. The "Russian" was actually a Ukrainian soldier, captured by the Ottomans in the early eighteenth century and taken to Turkey where he died. According to locals, his mummified body began to promote miracles, and the saint's relics were brought here by Orthodox Greeks from Cappadocian Prokópi (today Ürgüp) in the 1923 population exchange – Évvian Prokópi is still referred to by the locals as Akhmétaga, the name of the old Turkish fiefdom here that was bought by an English nobleman, Edward Noel, a cousin of Lord Byron's, right after the War of Independence. His descendants the Noel-Bakers now run summer courses in various crafts, based in the manor house.

Following a shady, stream-fed glen for the 8km north of Prokópi, you suddenly emerge at **Mandoúdhi**, much the biggest village in the north of the island, though now squarely in the doldrums following the collapse of the local magnesite industry; ignore signs or depictions on certain maps of a beach at Paralía Mandoúdhi, which is nothing more than abandoned quarries and crushing plants. The closest serviceable beach is at **Paralía Kírinthos**, better known as **Krýa Výssi** (take a right-hand turning off the main road, 3km beyond Mandoúdhi). At the coast, a river and an inlet bracket a small beach, with the headland south of the river supporting the extremely sparse remains of **ancient Kirinthos**. The hamlet of Kírinthos, just past Mandoúdhi, has some visitors, owing to the craft school there.

Back on the main road, a fork at Strofyliá, 8km north of Mandoúdhi, offers a choice of routes: continue north to the coastal resorts that curl round the end of the island (see opposite), east to Pýli and then south to some unspoiled beaches on the way to Cape Sarakíniko, or head west for Límni.

Límni

If you're hunting for a place to stay, **LÍMNI**, on the west coast 19km from Strofiliá, is by far the most practical and attractive base north of Halkídha. The largely Neoclassical, tile-roofed town, built from the wealth engendered by nineteenth-century shipping prowess, is the most appealing on the island, with serviceable beaches and a famous convent nearby. A small **folk art museum** features pottery, coins and sculpture fragments, as well as local costumes, fabrics and furniture.

Buses from Halkídha stop at the north side of the quay. Límni has a **post office** and **two banks**, all inland just off the main through-road into town from Strofiliá.

As yet, Límni gets few package tours, and **accommodation** is usually available in its rooms or hotels, except during August. At the extreme southern, quieter, end of the waterfront, the *Límni* (☎02270/31 316; ❷) is good value, with singles and doubles; the *Plaza* (☎02270/31 235; ❷), beside the bus stop, is very similar, but has no singles and gets some noise from nocturnal revels outside. Smarter rooms with TV can be rented at *Livaditis* (☎02270/31 640; ❹), above *Pyrofanis*, an ouzerí beyond the *Plaza*. The best **place to eat** in terms of setting, menu and popularity is *O Platanos* (under the enormous quayside plane tree) with the adjacent *Avra* not far behind. Other local favourites are *Kallitsis* inland from the waterfront, and *Lambros* and *O David* on the way to Katoúnia beach to the south of town.

Around Límni

There are no recommendable beaches in Límni itself, though if you continue 2.5km northwest from the town you reach the gravel strand of **Kohýli**, with a basic but leafy **campsite** out on the cape, 500m beyond mid-beach. Here there are some congenial places to stay, most notably *Denis House* (☎02270/31 787; ❺) and the more luxurious *Ostria* (☎02270/32 247; ❺), which has a pool and includes breakfast.

ROVIÉS, some 14km west of Límni, doesn't really stand out, but with its medieval tower, rooms, hotels, grid of weekenders' apartments and services, it's the last place of any sort along the scenic coast road to Loutrá Edhipsoú.

The outstanding excursion from Límni is 7km south (under your own steam) to the **convent of Ayíou Nikoláou Galatáki**, superbly set on the wooded slopes of Mount Kandhíli, overlooking the north Evvian Gulf. To get there, veer up and left at the unsigned fork off the coast road; there's no formal scheme for visiting, but don't show up in the early afternoon or around sunset as the gates will be shut. Though much rebuilt since its original Byzantine foundation atop a Poseidon temple, the convent retains a thirteenth-century tower built to guard against pirates, and a crypt. One of a dozen or so nuns will show you frescoes in the *katholikón* dating from the principal sixteenth-century renovation. Especially vivid, on the right of the narthex, is the *Entry of the Righteous into Paradise*: the righteous ascend a perilous ladder to be crowned by angels and received by Christ, while the wicked miss the rungs and fall into the maw of Leviathan.

Below Ayíou Nikoláou Galatáki, and easily combined with it to make a full half-day outing, are the pebble-and-sand beaches of **Glýfa**, arguably the best on this part of Évvia's southwest-facing coast. There are several in succession, leading up to the very base of Mount Kandhíli, some reachable by paths, the last few only by boat. The shore is remarkably clean, considering the number of summer campers who pitch tents here for weeks on end; a single roadside spring, 2km before the coast, is the only facility in the whole zone.

Northern coastal resorts

Returning to the junction at Strofiliá, take the main road north for 8km to **AYÍA ÁNNA** (locally and universally elided to *Ayiánna*), which has long enjoyed the unofficial status of Évvia's most **folkloric village**, by virtue of traditional costumes worn by the older women and an assiduous local ethnographer, Dimitris Settas, who died in 1989. The place itself is nothing extraordinary, and most passers-by are interested in the prominently marked turn-off for **Angáli beach**, 5km east. This is billed as the area's best, and it's sandy enough, the low hills behind lending a little drama, but like this entire coast it's exposed and can gather rubbish. A frontage road, set back 200m or so, is lined by a few kilometres of anonymous villas and apartments, with the "village" at the north end. The *Agali Hotel* (☎02270/97 104, ℻97 067; ❺) is a congenial place to stay, and there is also a campsite. Horseriding on the beach is a well-advertised and popular diversion.

Ten kilometres north of Ayía Ánna, a side road heads downhill for 6km, past the village of Kotsikiá, to **Paralía Kotsikiás**. The small cove with its taverna and rooms serves primarily as a fishing-boat anchorage, and its tiny, seaweed-strewn beach is of little interest. **Psaropoúli beach**, 2km below Vassiliká village (13km north of the Kotsikiá turn-off), is more useable in its three-kilometre length, but like Ayía Ánna it is scruffy and shadeless, with a smattering of rooms, self-catering units and tavernas not imparting much sense of community. If you choose to stay, you can't do much better than *Motel Canadiana* (☎02260/43 274; ❷), where the road down meets the seafront. **Elliniká**, the next signposted beach, lies just 800m below its namesake village inland; it's far smaller than Angáli or Psaropoúli, but cleaner and certainly the most picturesque spot on this coast, with a church-capped islet offshore as a target to swim to. The approach driveway has a very limited number of facilities: a minimarket, one taverna and a few studios. *Motel Aigaio* (☎02260/42 262; ❸) is as good as any for a stay.

Beyond Elliniká, the road (and bus line) skirts the northern tip of Évvia to curl southwest towards **PÉFKI**, a seaside resort mobbed with Greeks in summer, which straggles for some 2km along a mediocre beach. The best **restaurants**, near the north end of this strip, include *Ouzeri Ta Thalassina* and *Psitopolio O Thomas*, while *Zaharoplastio O Peristeras* proffers decadent desserts. **Accommodation** is the usual Évvian mix of self-catering units and a few seaside hotels such as *Galini* (☎02260/41 208, ℻41 650; ❹) and *Myrtia* (☎02260/41 202; ❸), all resolutely pitched at mainlanders; the **campsite**, *Camping Pefki*, is 2km north of town behind the beach, rather pricey and geared to people with caravans. Hydrofoils for the Sporades depart from here at most once daily in the morning during summer only.

The next resort (14km southwest), **OREÍ**, is a low-key fishing village, whose cafés are favoured by those in the know as the best places to watch the sunset. It has a fine statue of a Hellenistic bull, hauled up from the sea in 1965. Nearby Néos Pýrgos beach has a selection of rooms and restaurants. Some 7km further along the coast, **AYIÓKAMBOS** has a frequent ferry connection to Glýfa on the mainland opposite, from where there are buses to Vólos. Ayiókambos is surprisingly pleasant considering its port function, with a patch of beach, two or three tavernas and a few rooms for rent.

The trans-island bus route ends 14km south of Ayiókambos at **LOUTRÁ EDHIPSOÚ**, which attracts older Greeks, who come to bathe at the **spas** renowned since antiquity for curing everything from gallstones to depression. The spas themselves are cheap (€1 for 20min) and quite an experience. The vast number of hotels, some old and creaky, which service the summer influx means good deals can be had off-season. The classy 1920s-vintage *Egli* (T02260/22 215, F22 886; ❸) on the seafront is a good choice, while you can really push the boat out at the 1897-built *Thermae Sylla* (T02260/60 100, F22 055, Wwww.thermaesylla.gr; ❻), a French-style monument atop what's claimed to be the best thermal spring in Greece, thoroughly overhauled in 1998. More affordable options in the side streets near the port are *Valar's* (T02260/22 278, F23 419; ❸) and the more modern *Lito* (T02260/22 081; ❸). There is an abundance of tavernas strung along the front; try the leafy restaurant of the *Egli* or the traditional *To Fagadhiko tou Barous*, which offers a wide selection of mezédhes.

There are less-regimented **hot springs** at **Yiáltra**, 15km west around the head of Edhipsós bay, where the water boils up on the rocky beach, warming the shallows to comfortable bath temperature. From Loutrá Edhipsoú, the coast road heads southeast to Límni.

Travel details

Following the recent shake-ups in the Greek sea-transport industry, all ferry services out of Vólos and Áyios Konstandínos to the northern Sporades, as well as hydrofoils, are run solely by Hellenic (Minoan) Flying Dolphins or its subsidiaries. Hydrofoils – and the catamaran between Áyios Konstandínos and Thessaloníki, via the islands – only run reliably between early June and mid-September. These craft are, as ever, pricier than the ferries, but cut journey times virtually in half. Kými-to-Skýros is another, over-priced monopoly sailing served by a single ferry.

Skiáthos, Skópelos and Alónissos

Ferries
NB Departure frequencies given are for the June-to-mid-Sept period, and are valid in reverse sense.
Áyios Konstandínos to: Skiáthos (2–3 daily; 3hr); Skópelos (1–2 daily; 5hr); Alónissos (1 daily, 6hr).

Vólos to: Skiáthos (3–4 daily; 3hr); Skópelos (2–3 daily; 4hr); Alónissos (1–2 daily; 5hr).
NB This is the most consistent service out of sea-son, and always the cheapest.

Catamaran
Daily from July to mid-Sept, and 5 times weekly in June, there's a catamaran which typically leaves Thessaloníki at 1.45pm, calls at Alónissos, Skópelos and Skiáthos between 4.20 and 5.20pm,

doubling back from Áyios Konstandínos at 6.30pm through all these islands in reverse, arriving back in Thessaloníki just before midnight. This is a small "Flying Cat" and no vehicles are carried.

Hydrofoils
Áyios Konstandínos to: Skiáthos, Glóssa, Skópelos and Alónissos (1 daily at 10am; sets off from Alónissos same day at 6.30am).
Tríkeri (Pílion) to: Vólos, Skiáthos, Skópelos (both ports) and Alónissos (1–2 daily).

Paleó Tríkeri Island to: Vólos, Skiathos, Skópelos (both ports) and Alónissos (1 daily)
Vólos to: Skiáthos, Skópelos Town (4–5 daily); Glóssa, Alónissos (2–3 daily).

Flights
Athens to: Skiáthos (mid-June to mid-Sept 1

daily, otherwise 3 weekly; 50min).

Skýros

Ferries

Skýros is served from Kými (2hr) by conventional ferry, the *Lykomidis*. Services are at least twice daily mid-June to mid-Sept (usually at around 11am and 5–6pm), once daily (6–7pm) the rest of the year; there may be an additional 9pm boat at summer weekends – ☎02220/22 522 for current information. There is a connecting bus service for the late-afternoon boat, from the Liossíon 260 ter-minal in Athens (departs 10am & 2.45pm). Once or twice a week in July and Aug only, there is a rather useful long-haul ferry connecting Skýros with Skiáthos and Thessaloníki to the north, and Iráklio (Crete) to the far south, via Sýros, Páros, Mýkonos and Thíra in the Cyclades; this is typically run by G&A Ferries.

Flights

Athens to: Skýros (mid-June to mid-Sept 2 week-ly; 40min).

Évvia

Buses

Athens (Liossíon 260 terminal) to: Halkídha (every 30min 5.30am–9.30pm; 1hr 30min); Kými (5 daily; 3hr 15min).

Halkídha to: Kárystos (2 daily; 3hr); Kými (8 daily; 1hr 45min); Límni (5 daily; 1hr 30min); Loutrá Edhipsoú (4 daily; 3hr).

Trains

Athens (Laríssis station) to: Halkídha (19 daily; 1hr 30min).

Ferries

Arkítsa to: Loutrá Edhipsoú (at least hourly July–Sept 15, every 1–2hr otherwise, last at 10–11pm/8–9pm; 45min).
Ayía Marína to: Néa Stýra (summer 12–14 daily; 45min); Alymyropótamos dock (summer 1 daily; 45min).

Glýfa to: Ayiókambos (8–11 daily summer, 4 in winter; last sailing at 8.30pm/5pm; 30min).
Rafína to: Kárystos (Mon–Fri 1 daily in evening, Sat & Sun 2 daily; 1hr 15min); Marmári (8–9 daily; 45min).
Skála Oropoú to: Erétria (March–Oct every 30min 6.45am–7.45pm, then hourly to 11pm; 30min).

Hydrofoils

Péfki to: Skiáthos, Skópelos and Alónissos (June 4 weekly, July to mid-Sept 1 daily, in the evening).
NB Connecting buses from Athens run to Rafína (every 30min; 1hr), Ayía Marína (5 daily; 1hr 15min) and Skála Oropoú (hourly; 1hr 30min) all from the Mavromatéon terminal, and to Arkítsa and Glýfa from the Liossíon 260 terminal.

The Ionian Islands

* **Kérkyra (Corfu) Town**
  Venetian fortresses, beautiful
  churches, fine museums and
  appealing architecture,
  Corfu's capital is the cultural
  heart of the Ionians. See
  p.943

* **Perouládhes, Corfu** This
  beach, shaded till early afternoon and backed by sheer
  vertical cliffs, is an excellent
  hang-out, especially off season. See p.954

* **Andípaxi** Some of the
  Ionian's best swimming and
  snorkelling can be had at the
  exquisite beaches of Paxi's
  little sister on a day-trip from
  Gaïos. See p.964

* **Lefkádha's west coast** The
  archipelago's finest beaches
  run from Ai Nikítas via
  Káthisma, Yialós and
  Egremní down to Pórto
  Katsíki. See p.969

* **Mount Énos, Kefalloniá** The
  highest point in the Ionians
  boasts its own species of fir
  and has stunning vistas of sea
  and distant land. See p.971

* **Melissáni Cave, Kefalloniá**
  See dappled sunlight on the
  water amid rock formations
  on a boat trip inside this
  once-enclosed underwater
  cave. See p.974

* **Itháki's Homeric sites**
  Relive the myths on
  Odysseus's island by visiting
  the Arethoússa Spring, the
  cave of Eumaeus and the
  Nymphs, Alalkomenae and
  Pelikáta Hill. See p.981

* **Boat tour round Zákynthos**
  The best way to see the
  impressive coastline, including
  the Blue Caves and Shipwreck
  Bay, is by daily cruise from
  Zákynthos Town. See p.986

12

The Ionian Islands

The six **Ionian** islands, shepherding their satellites down the west coast of the mainland, float on the haze of the Adriatic, their green, even lush, silhouettes coming as a shock to those more used to the stark outlines of the Aegean. The fertility of the land is a direct result of the heavy rains that sweep over the archipelago – and especially Corfu – from October to March, so if you visit at this time, come prepared.

The islands were the Homeric realm of Odysseus, centred on Ithaca (modern Itháki) and here alone of all modern Greek territory (except for Lefkádha) the Ottomans never held sway. After the fall of Byzantium, possession passed to the **Venetians** and the islands became a keystone in Venice's maritime empire from 1386 until its collapse in 1797. Most of the population must have remained immune to the establishment of Italian as the official language and the arrival of Roman Catholicism, but Venetian influence remains evident in the architecture of the island capitals, despite damage from a series of earthquakes.

On Corfu, the Venetian legacy is mixed with that of the **British**, who imposed a military "protectorate" over the Ionian islands at the close of the Napoleonic Wars, before ceding the archipelago to Greece in 1864. There is, however, no question of the islanders' essential Greekness: the poet Dhionyssios Solomos, author of the national anthem, hailed from the Ionians, as did Nikos Mantzelos, who provided the music, and the first Greek president, Ioannis Kapodhistrias.

Accommodation price codes

Throughout the book we've categorized accommodation according to the following **price codes**, which denote the cheapest available double room in high season. All prices are for the room only, except where otherwise indicated. Many hotels, especially those in category ❹ and over, include breakfast in the price; you'll need to check this when booking. During low season, rates can drop by more than fifty percent, especially if you are staying for three or more nights. Exceptions are during the Christmas and Easter weeks when you'll pay high-season prices. Single rooms, where available, cost around seventy percent of the price of a double.

❶ Up to €24	❹ €43–58
❷ €24–33	❺ €59–72
❸ €34–42	❻ €73 and upwards

Note: Youth hostels and mountain refuges typically charge €7–9 for a dormitory bed. For more accommodation details, see pp.51–54.

Today, **tourism** is the dominating influence, especially on **Corfu** (Kérkyra), which was one of the first Greek islands established on the package-holiday circuit. Parts of its coastline are among the few stretches in Greece with development to match the Spanish *costas*, and in summer even its distinguished old capital, Kérkyra Town, wilts beneath the onslaught. However, the island is large enough to retain many of its charms and is perhaps the most scenically beautiful of the group. Parts of **Zákynthos** (Zante) – which with Corfu has the Ionians' most oversubscribed beaches – have also gone down the same tourist path, but elsewhere the island's pace and scale of development is a lot less intense. Little **Páxi** is rather tricky to reach and lacks the water to support

The islands of **Kýthira** and **Andikýthira**, isolated at the foot of the Peloponnese, are historically part of the Ionian islands. However, at some 200km from the nearest other Ionians, and with no ferry connections to the northerly Ionians, they are most easily reached from **Yíthio** or **Neápoli** and are thus covered in Chapter Two. Similarly, the island of **Kálamos**, Lefkádha's most distant satellite, is inaccessible from the Ionian group and covered therefore in Chapter Four.

large-scale hotels, but still gets surprisingly packed in August, while **Lefkádha** – which is connected to the mainland by a causeway and "boat bridge" – has, so far at least, quite a low-key straggle of tourist centres and only two major resorts, despite boasting some excellent beaches. Perhaps the most rewarding duo for island-hopping are **Kefaloniá** and **Itháki**, the former with a series of "real towns" and a life in large part independent of tourism, the latter, Odysseus's rugged capital, protected by an absence of sand. The Ionian islands' claims to Homeric significance are manifested in the countless bars, restaurants and streets named after characters in the *Odyssey,* including the "nimble-witted" hero himself, Penelope, Nausicaa, Calypso and Cyclops.

Corfu (Kérkyra)

Between the heel of Italy and the west coast of mainland Greece, green, mountainous **Corfu (Kérkyra)** was one of the first Greek islands to attract mass tourism in the 1960s. Indiscriminate exploitation turned parts into eyesores, but much of the island still consists of olive groves, mountain or woodland. The majority of package holidays are based in the most developed resorts, but unspoiled terrain is often only a few minutes' walk away.

Corfu is thought to have been the model for Prospero's and Miranda's place of exile in Shakespeare's *The Tempest,* and was certainly known to writers like Spenser and Milton and – more recently – Lear and Miller, plus Gerald and Lawrence Durrell. Lawrence Durrell's *Prospero's Cell* evokes the island's "delectable landscape", still evident in some of the best beaches of the whole archipelago.

The staggering amount of accommodation (over 5000 places) on the island means that competition keeps prices down even in high season, at least in many resorts outside of Kérkyra Town. Prices at restaurants and in shops also tend to be a little lower than average for the Ionians.

Kérkyra (Corfu) Town

The capital, **KÉRKYRA (CORFU) TOWN**, was renovated for an EU summit in 1994, and is now one of the most elegant island capitals in the whole of Greece. Although many of its finest buildings were destroyed by Nazi bombers in World War II, its two massive forts, the sixteenth-century church of Áyios Spyrídhon and buildings dating from French and British administrations remain intact. As the island's major port of entry by ferry or plane, Kérkyra Town is packed in summer.

Arrivals, information and services

Ferries and hydrofoils to and from Italy, the mainland (Igoumenítsa and Pátra) and Paxí dock at the New Port (Néo Limáni) west of the Néo Froúrio (New Fort). The Old Port (Paleó Limáni), east of the New Port, is used for day-excursions. Most of the ferry offices are on the main road opposite the New Port;

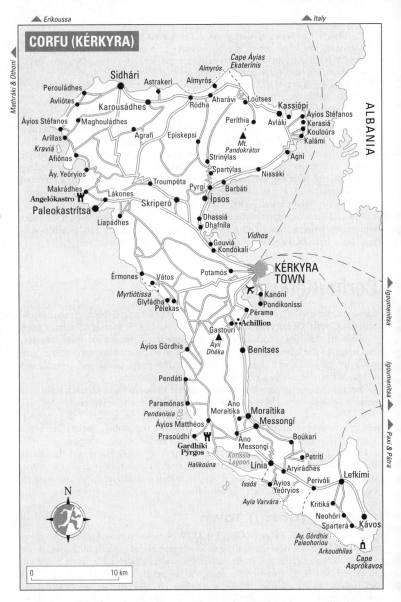

CORFU (KÉRKYRA)

ferries to Italy or south towards Pátra become very busy in summer and book-ing is advisable. The port authority (☎06610/32 655) can advise on services.

The **airport** is 2km south of the city centre. There are no airport buses, although local **blue buses** #5 and #6 can be flagged at the junction where the airport approach meets the main road (500m). It's a thirty-minute walk on flat terrain into town (follow the road running beside the *Hotel Bretagne* opposite the junction for the shortest route or turn right then follow the sea road).

Taxis charge around €6 (but agree the fare in advance) or phone ☎06610/33 811 for a radio cab.

The **tourist office** (Mon–Fri 8am–2pm; ☎06610/37 520) on the corner of Vouleftón and Mantzárou has accommodation and transport details. The **post office** is on the corner of Alexándhras and Zafiropoúlou (Mon–Fri 7.30am–8pm). Of the town's several internet cafés, the best value are *Recorder*, P. Konstandá 1 (Mon–Sat 9am–2pm & 6–11pm; ☎06610/46 549), just off Platía San Rocco, and *Hobby Net*, Solomoú 32 (daily 10am–11pm; ☎06610/44 475), near the Old Port.

Getting around

Corfu's **bus** service radiates from the capital. There are **two** terminals: the islandwide green bus service is based on Avramíou, and the suburban blue bus system, which also serves nearby resorts such as Benítses and Dhassiá, is based in Platía San Rocco (Platía G. Theotóki). Islandwide services stop between 6 and 8pm, suburban ones at around 10pm. Printed English timetables are available for both and can be picked up at the tourist office. Avramíou also serves Athens and Thessaloníki, and sells combined bus-and-ferry tickets. Major **ferry** lines have franchises on Ethnikís Andistásis opposite the New Port: Minoan (☎06610/25 000, ℱ46 555), Strintzis (☎06610/81 222, ℱ26 660), ANEK (☎06610/24 504, ℱ36 935), Fragline (☎06610/38 089, ℱ35 416), Ventouris (☎06610/32 664) and Adriatica (☎06610/38 089). The Petrakis agency (☎06610/38 690, ℱ26 555) runs the **hydrofoil** service to Paxí and Igoumenítsa, as well as tours to Albania, Párga and other Ionian islands, which it sells at much cheaper rates than the travel agents in the resorts.

Cars can also be rented from international agencies at the airport or in town; try Avis, Ethnikís Andistásis 42 (☎06610/24 404), Budget, Venízelou 22 (☎06610/49 100; airport ☎06610/44 017) or Hertz (☎06610/33 547). Among local companies, Sunrise, Ethnikís Andistásis 14 (☎06610/44 325) rents out cars, and **bikes** can be rented from Easy Rider, I. Theotóki 128 (☎06610/43 026), both in the New Port.

Accommodation

Accommodation in Kérkyra Town is busy all year round, and fairly expensive. Room owners often meet mainland and international ferries, or you can try the Room Owners' Association, near the tourist office at Polylá 24 (Mon–Fri 9am–1.30pm & 6–8pm; ☎06610/26 133, ℱ23 403). Budget travellers might best head straight for the nearest **campsite** at Dhassiá (see p.949).

Arcadion, Kapodhistríou 44 ☎06610/37 670, ℱ45 087, ℮arcadion@otenet.gr. Has moved upmarket after renovation. In a central setting so street noise can be a problem. ❻

Astron, Dónzelot 15 ☎06610/39 505, ℱ33 708, ℮hotel_astron@hol.gr. Tastefully renovated hotel in the Old Port. Good deals available outside the short peak season. All rooms with fan and optional air-con. ❻

Atlantis, Xenofóndos Stratigoú 48 ☎06610/35 560, ℱ46 480, ℮atlanker@mail.otenet.gr. Large and spacious air-conditioned hotel but rather lacking in character. ❻

Bella Venezia, Zambéli 4 ☎06610/46 500, ℱ20 708, ℮belven@hol.gr. Smart, yellow Neoclassical

building just behind the *Cavalieri*, with all the *Cavalieri*'s comforts, but cheaper. ❺

Cavalieri, Kapodhistríou 4 ☎06610/39 041, ℱ39 283. Smart and friendly, with all mod cons, great views and a roof bar open to the public. ❻

Europa, Yitsiáli 10 ☎06610/39 304. Small family hotel one block back from the New Port. One of the best deals around. Some rooms have TV. ❸

Hermes, Markorá 14 ☎06610/39 268. An old favourite in a busy part of town. The cheapest rooms have shared bathrooms. Overlooks the noisy market. ❸

Ionion, Xenofóndos Stratigoú 46 ☎06610/39 915, ℱ44 690. Conveniently located in the New Port, this is a large, functional, friendly and very

reasonably priced hotel. Ceiling fans in all rooms. ④
Phoenix, Khryssostómou Smýrnis 2, Garítsa

☎06610/42 290, ⊕42 990. Small, stylish hotel between the airport and the seafront. Good value, with complimentary breakfast. ④

The Town

Kérkyra Town comprises a number of distinct areas. The **Historic Centre**, the area enclosed by the Old Port and the two forts, consists of several smaller districts: **Campiello**, the oldest, sits on the hill above the harbour; **Kofinéta** stretches towards the Spianádha (Esplanade); **Áyii Apóstoli** runs west of the Mitrópolis (orthodox) cathedral; while tucked in beside the Néo Froúrio are **Ténedos** and what remains of the old **Jewish quarter**. These districts form the core of the old town, and their tall, narrow alleys conceal some of Corfu's most beautiful architecture. **Mandoúki**, beyond the Old Port, is the commercial and dormitory area for the port, and is worth exploring as a living quarter of the city, away from the tourism racket. The town's **commercial area** lies inland from the Spianádha, roughly between Yeoryíou Theotóki, Alexándhras and Kapodhistríou streets, with shops and boutiques around Voulgaréos and Yeoryíou Theotóki and off Platía Theotóki. Tucked behind Platía San Rocco and Odhós Theotóki is the old morning **market** which sells fish and farm produce.

The most obvious sights are the forts, the **Paleó Froúrio** and **Néo Froúrio**, whose designations (*paleó* – "old", *néo* – "new") are a little misleading, since what you see of the older structure was begun by the Byzantines in the midtwelfth century, just a hundred years before the Venetians began work on the newer citadel. They have both been damaged and modified by various occupiers and besiegers, the last contribution being the Neoclassical shrine of **Saint George**, built by the British in the middle of Paleó Froúrio during the 1840s. Looming above the Old Port, the Néo Froúrio (daily 9am–10pm; €1.50) is the more interesting of the two architecturally. The entrance, at the back of the fort, gives onto cellars, dungeons and battlements, with excellent views over the town and bay; there's a small gallery and café at the summit. The Paleó Froúrio (daily 9am–7pm; €2.40) is not as well preserved and contains some incongruous modern structures, but has an interesting Byzantine museum just inside the gate, and even more stunning views from the central Land Tower. It also hosts daily son et lumière shows.

Just west of the Paleó Froúrio, the **Listón**, an arcaded street built during the French occupation by the architect of the Rue de Rivoli in Paris, and the green **Spianádha** (Esplanade) it overlooks, are the focus of town life. The cricket pitch, still in use at the northern end of the Spianádha, is another British legacy, while at the southern end the **Maitland Rotunda** was built to honour the first British High Commissioner of Corfu and the Ionian islands. The neighbouring statue of Ioannis Kapodhistrias celebrates the local hero and statesman (1776–1831) who led the diplomatic efforts for independence and was made Greece's first president in 1827. At the far northern end of the Listón, the nineteenth-century **Palace of SS Michael and George**, a solidly British edifice built as the residence of their High Commissioner (one of the last of whom was the future British prime minister William Gladstone), and later used as a palace by the Greek monarchy. The former state rooms house the **Asiatic Museum** (Tues–Sun 8.30am–3pm; free) which is a must for aficionados of Oriental culture, although it's currently undergoing some reorganization. Amassed by Corfiot diplomat Gregorios Manos (1850–1929) and others, it includes Noh theatre masks, woodcuts, wood and brass statuettes, samurai weapons and art works from Thailand, Korea and Tibet. Opened in 1996, the adjoining **Modern Art**

Museum (daily 9am–9pm; €1.50) holds a small collection of contemporary Greek art. It's an interesting diversion, as are the gardens and café-bar secreted behind the palace.

In a nearby backstreet off Arseníou, five minutes from the palace, is the museum dedicated to modern Greece's most famous nineteenth-century poet, **Dhionysios Solomos** (Mon–Fri 5–8pm; €0.60). Born on Zákynthos, Solomos was author of the poem *Ímnos stín Eleftheria* (*Hymn to Liberty*), which was to become the Greek national anthem. He studied at Corfu's Ionian Academy, and lived in a house on this site for much of his life.

Up a short flight of steps on Arseníou, the **Byzantine Museum** (Tues–Sun 9am–3pm; €1.50) is housed in the restored church of the Panayía Andivouniótissa. It houses church frescoes and sculptures and sections of mosaic floors from the ancient site of Paleópolis, just south of Kérkyra Town. There are also some pre-Christian artefacts, and a collection of icons dating from the fifteenth to nineteenth centuries.

▲ *Vídhos*

Paleokastrítsa, the north, **2** , **3** , **4 & B** ◄

◄ *Airport, Achíllion & the south*

KÉRKYRA (CORFU) TOWN

0   200 m

N

ACCOMMODATION

Arcadion	5
Astron	1
Atlantis	2
Bella Venezia	8
Cavalieri	7
Europa	3
Hermes	6
Ionion	4
Phoenix	9

RESTAURANTS

Aleko's Beach	C
Mourayia	A
Orestes	B
Papiris	E
To Paradosiakou	F
Rex	H
Tenedos	G
Venetian Well Bistro	D
Yioyias	I

9 ▼   ▼ *Mon Repos Estate & Kanóni*

△ Stairs in Kérkyra (Corfu) old town

A block behind the Listón, down Spyrídhonos, is the sixteenth-century **church of Áyios Spyrídhon**, whose maroon-domed campanile dominates the town. Here you will find the silver-encrusted coffin of the island's patron saint, **Spyrídhon** – Spyros in the diminutive – after whom about half the male population is named. Four times a year (Palm Sunday and the following Sat, Aug 11 and the first Sun in Nov), to the accompaniment of much celebration and feasting, the relics are paraded through the streets of Kérkyra Town. Each of the days commemorates a miraculous deliverance of the island credited to the saint – twice from plague during the seventeenth century, from a famine of the sixteenth century and (a more blessed release than either of those for any Greek) from the Turks in the eighteenth century.

The next most important of the town's many churches, the **Mitrópolis** (orthodox cathedral), perched at the top of its own square opposite the Old Port, also houses the remains of a saint, in this case Saint Theodora, the ninth-century wife of Emperor Theophilus. The building dates from 1577 and the plain exterior conceals a splendid iconostasis, as well as some fine icons, including a fine sixteenth-century image of *Saint George Slaying the Dragon* by the Cretan artist Mihail Dhamaskinos, and three dark, atmospheric Italianate paintings.

Kérkyra Town's **Archeological Museum** (Tues–Sun 8.30am–3pm; €2.35), just south round the coast, is the best in the archipelago. The most impressive exhibit is a massive (17m) gorgon pediment excavated from the Doric temple of Artemis at Paleópolis, just south of Kérkyra Town ; this dominates an entire room, the gorgon flanked by panthers and mythical battle scenes. The museum also has fragments of Neolithic weapons and cookware, and coins and pots from the period when the island was a colony of ancient Corinth.

Just south of Platía San Rocco and signposted on the corner of Methodhíou and Kolokotróni, the well-maintained **British cemetery** features some elaborate civic and military memorials. It's a quiet green space away from the madness of San Rocco, and in spring and early summer is alive with dozens of species of orchids and other exotic blooms.

The outskirts

Each of the following sights on the outskirts of the city is easily seen in a morning or afternoon, and best visited from the town rather than outlying resorts.

Around the bay from the Rotunda and Archeological Museum, tucked behind Mon Repos beach, the **Mon Repos** estate (8am–7pm; free) contains the most accessible archeological remains on the island. Thick woodland conceals two **Doric temples**, dedicated to Hera and Artemis. The Neoclassical Mon Repos **villa**, built by British High Commissioner Frederic Adam in 1824 and handed over to Greece in 1864, is the birthplace of Britain's Prince Philip and was finally opened fully to the public in summer 2001 (daily 9am–3pm; €1.50).

The most famous excursion from Kérkyra Town is to the islets of **Vlahérna** and **Pondikoníssi**, 2km south of town below the hill of Kanóni, named after the single cannon trained out to sea atop it. A dedicated bus (#2) leaves San Rocco square every half-hour, or it's a pleasant walk of under an hour. Reached by a short causeway, the tiny white convent of Vlahérna is one of the most photographed images on Corfu. Pondikoníssi ("Mouse Island") can be reached by a short boat trip from the dock at Vlahérna (€1.50 return). Tufted with greenery and a small chapel, Vlahérna is identified in legend with a ship from Odysseus's fleet, petrified by Poseidon in revenge for the blinding of his son Polyphemus, the Homeric echoes somewhat marred by the thronging masses and low-flying aircraft from the nearby runway. A quieter destination is

Vídhos, the wooded island visible from the Old Port, reached from there by an hourly shuttle kaïki (€0.90 return).

Four kilometres further to the south, past the resort sprawl of Pérama, is a rather more bizarre attraction: the **Achillion** (daily 9am–3pm; €2.35), a palace built in a (fortunately) unique blend of Teutonic and Neoclassical styles in 1890 by Elizabeth, Empress of Austria. Henry Miller considered it "the worst piece of gimcrackery" that he'd ever laid eyes on and thought it "would make an excellent museum for surrealistic art". The house is predictably grandiose, but the gardens are pleasant to walk around and afford splendid views in all directions.

Eating and drinking

Although there are the inevitable tourist traps, Kérkyra Town offers some excellent, quality restaurants. As well as those listed below, there are several decent *psarotavérnes* on the Garítsa seafront, though you need to be careful of the fish prices.

Aleko's Beach, Faliráki jetty. Set in the tiny harbour below the palace with great views, this place offers simple, mostly grilled meat and fish dishes at good prices.

Mourayia, Arseníou 15–17. This unassuming, good-value ouzerí near the Byzantine Museum does a range of tasty mezédhes, including sausage and seafood such as mussels and shrimp. One of the best seafront establishments.

Orestes, Xenophóndos Stratigóu, in Mandoúki. Probably the best fish and seafood restaurant in town, and better priced than the central or Garítsa equivalents.

Papiris, Ayías Theodóras 25. A well-concealed Campiello restaurant serving fine family cooking such as meats in rich sauces. Justifiably popular with locals.

To Paradosiakon, Solomoú 20. Behind the Old Port, this friendly place serves good fresh food, especially home-style oven dishes like *stifádho* and *kokkinistó*.

Rex, Zavitsiánou behind the Listón. Pricey owing to its location, but some of the best food in the centre, mixing Greek with north European.

Tenedos, 1st Párodhos Solomoú 1, Spiliá. At the foot of the steps to the Néo Froúrio, this place offers an excellent range of mezédhes, eg courgette fritters and *yígandes* plus succulent meat dishes to the accompaniment of subtle live guitar music.

Venetian Well Bistro, Platía Kremásti. A well-kept secret, tucked away in a tiny square a few alleys to the south of the cathedral, this is the nearest you're likely to get to Greek *nouvelle cuisine*, with large portions, and exotica such as wild boar in red wine sauce and Albanian calves' livers done in oúzo. Very expensive.

Yioyias, Guildford St. The best all-round-value taverna in town, set in an atmospheric pedestrianized road. Wonderful range of mezédhes, meat – try the *sofrito* – and fish dishes, all washed down with fine (and cheap) barrelled wine.

Nightlife

Kérkyra Town has plenty to offer in the way of **bars** and nightlife. On the Listón, avoid the mark-ups at the *Magnet* and follow the locals to *Aegli*, *Europa* or *Olympia*, or drink in one of the hotels; the *Cavalieri* rooftop bar can be heaven at night and stays open till the wee hours. For local atmosphere, try *Dirty Dick's*, on the corner of Arseníou and Zavitsiánou, or the expat hangout *Mermaid*, on Ayíon Pandón off the Listón, which will give you a different spin on island culture.

Corfu's self-proclaimed **disco** strip lies a couple of kilometres north of town, past the New Port. Here, at nightclubs like *Symplegma*, the *Hippodrome* (the town's biggest disco, with its own pool), and the bizarrely decorated *Apokalypsis* and *Coca*, party animals dress up for wild and fairly expensive nights out. In some clubs, women travelling without male partners should beware of *kamákia* – slang for Greek males "spearfishing" for foreign women. Somewhat calmer and smaller watering holes on the same strip include *Ethnik* and *Pagoda*. Kérkyra Town's two **cinemas** – the winter Orfeus on the corner of Akadhimías and Aspióti and the open-air summer Phoenix down the side street opposite – both show mostly English-language films.

The northeast and the north coast

The northeast, at least beyond the immediate suburbs, is the most typically Greek part of Corfu – it's mountainous, with a rocky coastline chopped into pebbly bays and coves, above wonderfully clear seas. Green **buses** between Kérkyra Town and Kassiópi serve all resorts, along with some blue suburban buses as far as Dhassiá.

Kérkyra Town to Ípsos

The landscape just north of Kérkyra Town is an industrial wasteland, and things don't improve much at the first village you come to, **KONDÓKALI**, overrun by holiday developments. The old town consists of a short street with a number of bars and traditional *psistariés*, the best of which are *Gerekos* and *Takis*, an international restaurant, *Flags*, and the pricey *Lithari* fish taverna.

Neighbouring **GOUVIÁ** is also Corfu's largest yachting marina. The village boasts a couple of small **hotels**, notably the *Hotel Aspa* (℡06610/91 409; ❸) and great-value *Gouvia View* by the beach (℡06610/91 167). For **rooms**, try Maria Lignou (℡06610/91 348; ❸) or Karoukas Travel (℡06610/91 596, ℻91 943, ✆karoukas@otenet.gr). There's a number of decent **restaurants**, including *The Captain's* taverna and *Steki psistariá*, and a couple of pizzerias, *La Bonita* and *Palladium*. The very narrow shingle **beach**, barely 5m wide in parts, shelves into sand; given the sea traffic, the water quality is doubtful.

Two kilometres beyond Goúvia the coastline begins to improve at **DHAFNÍLA** and **DHASSIÁ**, set in wooded bays with pebbly beaches. Two large and expensive **hotels**, the *Dassia Chandris* and *Corfu Chandris* (both ℡06610/97 100–3, ℻93 458, ✆chandris@ker.forthnet.gr; ❻), dominate Dhassiá, with extensive grounds, pools and beach facilities. The more reasonable *Hotel Amalia* (℡06610/93 523; ❹) has pleasant en-suite rooms and its own pool and garden. **Rooms** are scarce, although Spyros Rengis's minimarket in Dhassiá has a few (℡06610/90 282; ❸) and the Dafnilas supermarket has some of the cheapest going (℡06610/90 282; ❶). Dhafníla does, however, have the best **campsite** on the island, *Dionysus Camping Village* (℡06610/91 417, ℻91 760); tents are pitched under terraced olive trees. *Dionysus* also has simple bungalow huts, a pool, shop, bar and restaurant, and the friendly, multilingual owners offer a ten-percent discount to Rough Guide readers.

ÍPSOS, 2km north of Dhassiá, can't really be recommended to anyone but hardened bar-hoppers. There is hardly room to swing a cat on the thin pebble beach, right beside the busy coast road, and the resort is pretty tacky. Most **accommodation** is prebooked by package companies, although Premier/Ípsos Travel (℡06610/93 661, ℻93 637) can offer rooms. *Corfu Camping Ípsos* (℡06610/93 579, ℻93 741) has a bar and restaurant, and offers standing tents. Ípsos is also home to one of the island's major **diving centres**, Waterhoppers (℡06610/93 867, ✆diverclub@hotmail.com). **Eating** on the main drag is dominated by fast food, though a more traditional meal and a quieter setting can be found in the *Akrogiali* and *Asteria* tavernas, by the marina to the south of the strip. The northern end is largely devoted to competing bars and discos.

North to Áyios Stéfanos

Ípsos has now engulfed the neighbouring hamlet of Pyrgí, which is the main point of access for the villages and routes leading up to **Mount Pandokrátor**; the road, signposted Spartílas, is 200km beyond the junction in Pyrgí. A popular base for walkers is the village of **STRINÝLAS**, 16km from Pyrgí. Accommodation is basic but easy to come by: the *Elm Tree Taverna*, a long-time favourite with walkers, can direct you to rooms. In summer the main routes are busy, but there are quieter walks taking in the handsome Venetian village of Epískepsi, 5km northwest of Strinýlas – anyone interested in walking the Pandokrátor paths is advised to get the **map** of the mountain by island-based cartographer Stephan Jaskulowski or Hilary Whitton-Paipeti's walking book, both available locally.

The coast road beyond Ípsos mounts the slopes of Pandokrátor towards **BARBÁTI**, 4km further on. Here you'll find the best beach on this coast, though its charm has been somewhat diminished recently by the initial construction of the gargantuan *Riviera Barbati* complex. The beach is a favourite with families, and much **accommodation** is prebooked in advance. However, there are some rooms available on spec – *Paradise* (☎06630/91 320, ⓕ91 479; ❸) and *Roula Geranou* (☎06630/92 397; ❷), both on the main road.

The mountainside becomes steeper and the road higher beyond Barbáti, and the population thins drastically. **NISSÁKI** is a sprawling roadside settlement rather than a village, with a number of coves, the first and last accessible by road, the rest only by track – the furthest dominated by the gigantic, expensive and rather soulless *Nissaki Beach Hotel* (☎06630/91 232, ⓕ22 079, ⓔnissaki@otenet.gr; ❺ half-board). There's a couple of shops and a bakery, and a few travel and **accommodation agencies**. The British-owned Falcon Travel (☎06630/91 318, ⓕ91 070, ⓔfalcontr@otenet.gr; ❸) rents out apartments above the first beach, a tiny, white-pebble cove with a trio of fine tavernas – try the quayside *Mitsos*. The *Nissaki Holidays Center* (☎06630/91 166, ⓕ91 206), up by the junction, may have some cheaper rooms.

Three pebbly coves no one visiting this coast should miss are Agní, not far past the *Nissaki Beach Hotel*, Kalámi and neighbouring Kouloúra: the first for its trio of fine tavernas, the second for its Durrell connection, the third for its exquisite bay. Crowds flock to **AGNÍ** for the fine eating – *Nicolas* is the oldest taverna and just pips *Toula* and *Agni* for quality. **KALÁMI** is on the way to being spoiled, but the village is still small and you can imagine how it would have looked in the year Lawrence Durrell spent here on the eve of World War II. The **White House**, where Durrell wrote *Prospero's Cell*, is now split in two: the ground floor is an excellent taverna; the upper floor is let through CV Travel (see basics). Sunshine Travel (☎06630/91 170, ⓕ91 572, ⓔinfo@sunshineclub.gr) and Kalami Tourist Services (☎06630/91 062, ⓕ91 369, ⓔkalamits@otenet.gr) both have a range of rooms on their books, or ask at *Matella's* restaurant (☎06630/91 371; ❷). The **restaurant** at the White House is recommended, as is *Matella's*, the *Kalami Beach Taverna* and *Pepe's*, all on the beach. Two cocktail bars compete for the happy-hour trade.

The tiny harbour of **KOULOÚRA** has managed to keep its charm intact, set at the edge of an unspoiled bay with nothing to distract from the pine trees and kaïkia. The fine **taverna** here has to be the most idyllic setting for a meal in the whole of Corfu.

Around the coast to Aharávi

Two kilometres beyond Kouloúra down a shady lane, the large pebble cove of **Kerasiá** shelters the family-run *Kerasia Taverna*. The most attractive resort on this stretch of coast, however, 3km down a lane from Agnitsíni on the main road, is **ÁYIOS STÉFANOS**. Most **accommodation** here is of the upmarket prebooked villa sort, and the village has yet to succumb to any serious development; so far only the *Kochili* taverna has independent rooms and apartments (☎06630/81 522; ❸). Recommended are the *Galini* and *Kaparelli* **tavernas**, and the pricier *Eucalyptus* over by the village's small beach. The *Waves* café and *Damianos* cocktail bar are the main spots to idle with a drink.

A thirty-minute walk from the coastguard station above Áyios Stéfanos, along a newly surfaced road, stretches the beach of **Avláki**, a pebble bay that provides lively conditions for the **windsurfers** who visit the beach's windsurf club. There are two **tavernas**, the *Barbaro* and *Avlaki*, and some **rooms** a few hundred yards back from the beach – *Mortzoukos* (℡06630/81 196; ❸), and *Tsirimiagos* (℡06630/81 522; ❸).

Further round the coast is **KASSIÓPI**, a fishing village that's been transformed into a major party resort. The Roman emperor Tiberius had a villa here, and the village's sixteenth-century church is said to stand on the site of a temple of Zeus once visited by Nero. Little evidence of Kassiópi's past survives, apart from an abandoned Angevin *kástro* on the headland – many visitors come for the nightlife and the five pebbly beaches. Most **accommodation** in Kassiópi is through village agencies; the largest, Travel Corner (℡06630/81 220, ℻81 108, ✉info@kassiopi.com), on the main road near the square, is a good place to start. An independent alternative, the smart *Kastro* café-pension, overlooks the beach behind the castle (℡06630/81 045; ❺), and Elli Tsiliani (℡06630/81 483; ❸) offers bargain rooms behind Kalamíonas beach. International cuisine dominates **eating** in Kassiópi – try the tasty Italian at *Little Italy*, the Tex-Mex at *Poco loco* or the *Sze Chuan* Chinese – but for something more traditional, head for the *Three Brothers* taverna on the harbour, or the neighbouring *Porto* fish restaurant. At night, Kassiópi rocks to the cacophony of its music and video bars: the flashiest is the gleaming hi-tech *Eclipse*, which also shows DVDs, closely followed by the *Baron*, *Angelos* and *Jasmine*, all within falling-over distance of the small town square. The *Axis Club* boasts imported British DJs, and frolics sometimes extend onto the beach until dawn. The village is also home to one of the most reliable diving operations, Corfu Divers (℡06630/81 218, ✉corfudivers@yahoo.com), which is partly British-run. Internet facilities are available at the *Pallace* bar (℡06630/81 719), off the main road.

The coastline beyond Kassiópi is overgrown and marshy until you get to little-used **Almyrós beach**, one of the longest on the island. It is also the least-developed beach, with only a few apartment buildings under construction at the hamlet of **Almyrós**. For a peaceful stay you could try *Villa Maria* (℡06630/63 359; ❸) and eat at *Liberty's* grill a little further along the beach. The Andinióti lagoon, smaller than Korissía on Kéa, but still a haven for birds and twitchers, backs Cape Áyias Ekaterínis to the east. With its wide main road, **AHARÁVI**, the next stop west on the main coast road, resembles an American Midwest truck stop, but the village proper is tucked behind this in a quiet crescent of old tavernas, bars and shops. Aharávi makes a quieter beach alternative to the southerly strands, and should also be considered by those seeking alternative routes up onto **Mount Pandokrátor**. Roads to small hamlets such as Áyios Martínos and Láfki continue onto the mountain, and even a stroll up from the back of Aharávi will find you on the upper slopes in under an hour.

Accommodation isn't easy to find, but a good place to start is Castaway Travel (℡06630/63 541, ℻63 376, ✉castaway@otenet.gr) or HN Travel (℡06630/63 458, ℻63 454). One independent hotel is *Dandolo* (℡06630/63 557, ℻63 457; ❹), set in lush grounds towards the old village. There's a number of **restaurants** on Aharávi's main drag; go for the *Pump House* steak and pasta joint, the traditional tavernas *Chris's* and *George's*, or the *Young Tree*, which specializes in Corfiot dishes such as *sofríto* (veal stew with vinegar seasoning) and *pastitsádha* (a variation on *pastítsio*). The bar-restaurants tend to get quite rowdy at night, although the light and airy *Captain Aris* is a pleasant watering hole. For a quieter evening, head for the excellent *Theritas* taverna, the friendly *Mitsouras* kafenío or the cosy *Hole in the Wall* pub, all in the old village.

Ródha, Sidhári and Avliótes

Just to the west, **RÓDHA** has tipped over into overdevelopment, and can't be wholeheartedly recommended for those after a quiet time. Its central crossroads have all the charm of a service station, and the beach is rocky in parts and swampy to the west. "Old Ródha" is a small warren of alleys between the main road and the seafront, where you'll find the best **restaurants** and **bars**: the *Taverna Agra* is the oldest in Ródha and the best place for fish, and the *Rodha Star Taverna* and *New Port* are also good. For bars, try *Big Ben* or *Five Roses*, both with Sky Sports, or the trendier bar-club *Skouna*. For **accommodation**, the friendly seafront *Roda Inn* (☎06630/63 358; ❸) has decently priced en-suite rooms. Both the Anglo-Greek NSK UK Travel (☎06630/63 471, ☻63 274) on the main drag and Nostos Travel on the seafront (☎06630/64 602, ☻64 601) rent rooms and handle car rental. The smart *Roda Beach Camping* (☎06630/93 120) is a little way east of the resort, while even pleasanter *Karoussades Camping* (☎ & ☻ 06630/31 415) is to the west towards Sidhári. Myron's good-rate motorbike rental (☎06630/63 477) and Kostas horse-riding are also based in Ródha. Several kilometres inland from Ródha, just east of Agrafí, the Angonari *mezedhopolío* serves an excellent range of dishes and great barrelled wine in a relaxed garden with subtle live music.

The next notable resort, **SIDHÁRI**, is expanding rapidly and is totally dominated by British-package tourists; it has a small but pretty town square, with a bandstand set in a small garden, but this is lost in a welter of bars, boutiques and snack joints. The beach is sandy but not terribly clean, and many people tend to head just west to the curious coves, walled by wind-carved sandstone cliffs, around the vaunted Canal d'Amour. The best sources of **rooms** are Maria Fakiola (☎06630/95 369; ❷) and Nikolaos Korakianitis's minimarket on the main road (☎06630/95 058; ❷). The biggest accommodation agency is run by young tycoon Philip Vlasseros, whose Vlasseros Travel (☎06630/95 695, ☻95 969) also handles car rental, horse-riding and excursions, including a once-weekly trip to the Dhiapóndia islands (see p.958). Sidhári's **campsite**, *Dolphin Camping* (☎06630/31 846), is some way inland from the junction at the western end of town. Most **restaurants** are pitched at those looking for a great night out rather than a quiet meal in a taverna. The pricey *Olympic* is the oldest taverna here; also recommended are the *Diamond* and *Sea Breeze* tavernas or *Kavvadias* on the eastern stretch of beach. Ethnic cuisine and cheap full-on English breakfasts are also readily available. There are no quiet bars in Sidhári, and two **nightclubs** vie for late custom, the *Remezzo* and *Caesar's*. Sidhári also has its own waterpark with free entry, a good place to keep the kids happy.

The Sidhári bus usually continues to **AVLIÓTES**, a handsome hill town with several bars and tavernas but few concessions to tourism. The town is noteworthy for two reasons: its accessibility to the stunning beach, bordered by vertical cliffs and shady in the mornings, below the quiet village of Perouládhes, just over 1km away, and the fact that **Áyios Stéfanos** (see p.954) is under thirty-minutes' walk from here, downhill through lovely olive groves.

Paleokastrítsa and the northwest coast

The northwest conceals some of the island's most dramatic coastal scenery, the violent interior mountainscapes jutting out of the verdant countryside. The area's honeypot attraction, **Paleokastrítsa**, is the single most picturesque resort on Corfu, but is suffering from its popularity. Further down the west coast, the terrain opens out to reveal long sandy beaches, such as delightful **Myrtiótissa** and the backpackers' haven of **Áyios Górdhis**. Public **transport** along the west coast is difficult: virtually all buses ply routes from Kérkyra Town to single destinations, and rarely link resorts.

Paleokastrítsa

PALEOKASTRÍTSA, a small village surrounded by dramatic hills and cliffs, has been identified as the Homeric city of Scheria, where Odysseus was washed ashore and escorted by Nausicaa to the palace of her father Alcinous, king of the Phaeacians. It's a stunning site, as you would expect, though one that's long been engulfed by tourism. The focal point of the village is the car park on the seafront, which backs onto the largest and least attractive of three **beaches**, home to sea taxis and kaïkia. The second beach, to the right and signed by flags for Mike's Ski Club, is stony with clear water, and the best of the three is a small unspoiled strand reached along the path by the *Astakos Taverna*. Protected by cliffs, it's undeveloped apart from the German-run Korfu-Diving Centre (☎06630/41 604) at the end of the cove. From the beach in front of the main car park, you can get a **boat trip** to some nearby seawater caves, known as the "blue grottoes" (€5.85 for a half-hour trip, €8.80 for drop-off and later pick-up), a trip worth taking for the spectacular coastal views. Boats also serve as a taxi service to three neighbouring beaches, Áyia Triánda, Platákia and Alípa, which all have snack bars.

On the rocky bluff above the village, the **Theotókou monastery** (7am–1pm & 3–8pm; free, although donations invited) is believed to have been established in the thirteenth century. There's also a museum, resplendent with icons, jewelled Bibles and other impedimenta of Greek Orthodox ritual, though the highlight is the gardens, with spectacular coastal views. Paleokastrítsa's ruined castle, the **Angelókastro**, is around 6km up the coast; only approachable by path from the hamlet of Kríni, it has stunning, almost circular views of the surrounding sea and land. For a drink or snack with tremendous views, it's worth stopping at either the *Bella Vista* or *Golden Fox* tavernas on the way up, between Lákones and Makrádhes.

Unfortunately, perhaps owing to the pressure of commerce in such a small space, there's a rather mercenary air about tourism here. **Accommodation** is at a premium, and you may be expected to commit yourself for three to seven days in some places. A good **hotel** is the family-run *Odysseus* (☎06630/41 209, ℱ41 342; ❺), on the road into town, while the nearby modern *Akrotiri Beach* (☎06630/41 237, ℱ41 277, ✉belvenht@hol.gr; ❻) is friendly and unpretentious. There are good-value **rooms** for rent above Alípa beach on the road down into Paleokastrítsa: try at the *Dolphin Snackbar* (☎06630/41 035; ❹), the *Green House* (☎06630/41 311; ❸) or Michalas tourist bureau (☎06630/41 113, ℱ41 298, ✉michalastravel@ker.forthnet.gr). Above the village, past Nikos' Bikes, the friendly Korina family also have rooms (☎06630/44 064; ❸). *Paleokastritsa Camping* (☎06630/41 204, ℱ41 104) is just off the main road into town, a ten-minute walk from the centre.

There isn't a huge choice of **restaurants** in the centre of Paleokastrítsa. The *Astakos Taverna* and *Corner Grill* are two traditional places, while *Il Pirata* offers a variety of Italian and Greek dishes, including local fish and seafood, and the seafront *Smurfs* has a good seafood menu despite the name. Also recommended are the very smart *St Georges on the Rock*, and the shady *Calm*, which has internet facilities. **Nightlife** hangouts include the restaurant-bars in the centre, and those straggling up the hill towards Lákones. By the Lákones turning is Paleokastrítsa's one nightclub, *The Paleo Club*, a small disco-bar with a garden.

Áyios Yeóryios and Áyios Stéfanos

Like many of the west-coast resorts, **ÁYIOS YEÓRYIOS**, 6km north of Paleokastrítsa, isn't actually based around a village. The resort has developed in response to the popularity of its large sandy bay, and it's a major **windsurfing** centre, busy even in low season. There is one particularly good-value **hotel**, the *Alkyon Beach* (℡06630/56 204, ℻96 206; ❸), some rooms at the Arista supermarket (℡06630/96 350; ❶) or *Studio Eleana* (℡ & ℻ 06630/96 366; ❸) and the *San George* campsite (℡06630/51 759), nearly 1km back from the beach towards Kavvadhádhes. On the way north towards Áyios Stéfanos, the pleasant sandy beach of **Aríllas** has given rise to gradual development, including several tavernas – try *Kostas on the Beach*. Accommodation can be arranged through Arillas Travel (℡06630/51 280, ℻51 381, ✉arillast@otenet.gr) or there is the smart *Akti Arilla* hotel (℡06630/51 201, ℻51 221, ✉aktiaril@otenet.gr; ❹ half-board).

The northernmost of the west-coast's resorts, **ÁYIOS STÉFANOS** is low-key, popular with families and a quiet base from which to explore the northwest and the Dhiapóndia islands, visible on the horizon. Day-trips to Mathráki, Othoní and Eríkoussa (see p.958) run every Thursday in season, and range from €14.65 to €23.50 per person. Áyios Stéfanos's oldest **hotel**, the *Nafsika* (℡06630/51 051, ℻51 112; ❸), has a large restaurant, a favourite with villagers, and gardens with a pool and bar. In recent years it has been joined by the upmarket *Thomas Bay* (℡06630/51 767, ℻51 913; ❺) and *Hotel San Stefano* (℡06630/51 053, ℻51 202; ❸), attached to the *Golden Beach* taverna. For those on a budget, Pelis and Maria's gift shop offers bargain **rooms** (℡06630/51 424; ❷) and the *Restaurant Evinos* (℡ & ℻ 06630/51 766; ❷) has apartments above the village. A number of travel agencies handle accommodation, among them San Stefanos (℡06630/51 910, ℻51 771, ✉steftrav@otenet.gr) in the centre. Besides the above-mentioned hotels, good options for **eating** include the *Waves* and very reasonable *Mistral* tavernas above the beach, while *O Manthos* taverna serves Corfiot specialities like *sofríto* and *pastitsádha*. For **nightlife**, there's a couple of lively music bars, *Magnet* and *Athens*, plus the small *Enigma* nightclub.

Central and southern Corfu

Two natural features divide the centre and south of Corfu. The first is the **plain of Rópa**, whose fertile landscape backs on to some of the best beaches on this coast. Settlements and development stop a little to the south of Paleokastrítsa and only resume around **Érmones** and **Pélekas** – a quick bus ride across the island from Kérkyra Town. Down to the south, a second dividing point is the **Korissía lagoon**, the sandy plains and dunes that skirt this natural feature being great places for botanists and ornithologists. Beyond, a single road trails the interior, with sporadic side roads to resorts on either coast. The landscape here is flat, an undistinguished backdrop for a series of increasingly developed beaches and, in the far south, **Kávos**, Corfu's big youth resort.

Érmones to the Korissía lagoon: the west coast

ÉRMONES, south of Paleokastrítsa, is one of the busiest resorts on the island, its lush green bay backed by the mountains above the Rópa River. The resort is dominated by the upmarket *Ermones Beach* **hotel** (℡06610/94 241, ℻94 248; ❻ half-board), which provides guests with a funicular railway down to the beach. More reasonably-priced accommodation can be found at the *Pension Katerina* (℡06610/94 615; ❷) and *Georgio's Villas* (℡06610/94 950; ❸), on the hillside above the road that leads to the beach. Both the *Maria* and *Nafsica* **tav-**

ernas above the beach provide good, filling mezédhes and main dishes. Just inland is the Corfu Golf and Country Club (☎06610/94 220), the only golf club in the archipelago, and said to be the finest in the Mediterranean.

The nearby small village of **VÁTOS** has a couple of tavernas, a disco and rooms, and is on the Glyfádha bus route from Kérkyra Town. Spyros Kousounis, owner of the *Olympic Restaurant and Grill* (☎06610/94 318; ❸) on the main road has rooms and apartments, as does Prokopios Himarios (☎06610/94 503; ❸), next to the Doukakis café-minimarket up in the village. The Myrtiótissa **path** is signposted just beyond the extremely handy, if basic, *Vatos Camping* (☎06610/94 393).

Far preferable to the gravelly sand of Érmones are the sandy beaches just south of the resort, at Myrtiótissa and Glyfádha. In *Prospero's Cell*, Lawrence Durrell described **Myrtiótissa** as "perhaps the loveliest beach in the world"; it was until recently a well-guarded secret but now gets very busy in the summer and supports three *kantínas*, so it's best visited either at the end of the day or out of high season. Above the beach is the tiny whitewashed **Myrtiótissa monastery**, dedicated to Our Lady of the Myrtles.

The sandy bay of **GLYFÁDHA**, walled in by cliffs, is dominated by the *Louis Grand* hotel. There's a far better **accommodation** option at the extreme north end of the beach, the *Glifada Beach* (☎06610/94 258; ❹), whose owners, the Megas family, also have a fine taverna. The resort's other accommodation is likely to be block-booked, though the *Gorgona* pool bar and *Restaurant Michaelis* might have rooms. Nightlife centres on two music bars, the *Kikiriko* and *Aloha*, which pump out heavy-duty sounds all day, as the beach is popular with young Greek and Italian trendies.

PÉLEKAS, inland and 2km south of Glyfádha, has long been popular for its views – the **Kaiser's Throne** viewing tower, along the road to Glyfádha, was Wilhelm II's favourite spot on the island. New developments are beginning to swamp the town, but there are some good **room** deals here, including the friendly *Pension Paradise* (☎06610/94 530; ❸) on the way in from Vátos, and the *Alexandros* taverna (☎06610/94 215, ☎94 833, ☻axel@hol.gr; ❸) and *Thomas* (☎06610/94 491; ❸) both on the way towards Kaiser's Throne. Agatha's Tours (☎06610/94 283, ☎94 602) may have some even cheaper rooms. Among the **tavernas**, the *Alexandros* and *Roula's Grill House* are highly recommended. The colourful *Zanzibar* is a pleasant spot for a drink by the diminutive square, whose Odhigitria church, renovated in 1884, is worth a peek. Pélekas's sandy **beach** is reached down a short path. Here you'll find *Maria's Place*, an excellent family-run **taverna/rooms** place (☎06610/94 601; ❸), with fish caught daily by the owner's husband. Sadly, the beach has been rather spoilt by the monstrous *Pelekas Beach* hotel that now looms over it.

Around 7km south of Pélekas, **ÁYIOS GÓRDHIS** is one of the key play beaches on the island, largely because of the activities organized by the startling **Pink Palace** complex (☎06610/53 103, ☎53 025, ☻Pink-Palace@ker.forth-net.gr) which dominates the resort. It has pools, games courts, restaurants, a shop and a disco. Backpackers cram into communal rooms for up to ten (smaller rooms and singles are also available) for €23.50 a night, including breakfast and evening meal. Other accommodation is available on the beach, notably at the quieter *Michael's Place* taverna (☎06610/53 041; ❸); the neighbouring *Alex-in-the-Garden* **restaurant** is also a favourite.

Inland from the resort is the south's largest prominence, the humpback of **Áyii Dhéka** (576m), reached by path from the hamlet of Áno Garoúna; it is the island's second-largest mountain after Pandokrátor. The lower slopes are wooded, and it's possible to glimpse buzzards wheeling on thermals over the higher slopes.

Around 5km south by road from Áyios Górdhis, the fishing hamlet of **PENDÁTI** is still untouched by tourism. There is no accommodation here, but *Angela's* café and minimarket and the *Strofi* grill cater to villagers and the few tourists who wander in. Another 4km on, **PARAMÓNAS** affords excellent views over the coastline, and, being rather low-key, offers some of the best **accommodation** deals on the island: the panoramic *Sunset* (☎06610/75 149, ⓕ75 686; ❶), right above the beach, and the *Paramonas Bridge* restaurant (☎06610/75 711; ❶), a little further inland, are both extremely good value, as is the *Areti Studios* (☎06610/75 838; ❷), on the road in from Pendáti.

The town of **ÁYIOS MATTHÉOS**, 3km inland, is still chiefly an agricultural centre, although a number of kafenía and tavernas offer a warm if bemused welcome to passers-by: head for the *Mouria* snack bar-grill, or the modern *Steki*, which can rustle up tasty mezédhes. On the other side of Mount Áyios Matthéos, 2km by road, is the **Gardhíki Pýrgos**, the ruins of a thirteenth-century castle built in this unlikely lowland setting by the despots of Epirus. The road continues on to the northernmost tip of splendid and deserted **Halikoúna** beach on the sea edge of the **Korissía lagoon**, which, if you don't have your own transport, is most easily reached by walking from the village of Línia (on the Kávos bus route) via Íssos beach; other, longer routes trail around the north end of the lagoon from Áno Messongí and Khlomotianá. Over 5km long and 1km wide at its centre, Korissía is home to turtles, tortoises, lizards and numerous indigenous and migratory birds. For one of the quietest stays on the island, try *Marin Christel Apartments* (☎06610/75 947; ❹), just north of Halikoúna beach, or *Logara Apartments* (☎06610/76 477; ❹), 500m inland.

Benítses to Petríti: the east coast

South of Kérkyra Town, there's nothing to recommend before **BENÍTSES**, a once notorious bonking-and-boozing resort, whose old town at the north end is now reverting to a quiet bougainvillea-splashed Greek village. There's really little to see here, beyond the ruins of a Roman bathhouse at the back of the village, and the tiny **Shell Museum**, part-exhibit, part-shop. **Rooms** are plentiful: try Best Travel (☎06610/72 037, ⓕ71 036; ❸) and All Tourist (☎06610/72 223; ❸). Visitor numbers have picked up again after a serious decline, and some hotels can offer good deals. The *Corfu Maris* (☎06610/72 035; ❹), on the beach at the southern end of town, has modern en-suite rooms with balconies and views, while the friendly *Hotel Benitsa* and neighbouring *Agis* in the centre (both ☎06610/39 269; ❷) offer quiet rooms set back from the main road. Benítses has its fair share of decent if not particularly cheap **tavernas**, notably *La Mer de Corfu* and the Corfiot specialist *Spiros*, as well as the plush *Marabou*. The **bars** at the southern end of town like *Happy Dog* and *Tribal Club* are fairly lively, despite new rules controlling all-night partying, and the *Stadium* **nightclub** is still going strong. If you're looking for a quiet drink head for the north end of the village, away from the traffic.

MORAÏTIKA's main street is an ugly strip of bars, restaurants and shops, but its beach is the best between Kérkyra Town and Kávos. Reasonable beach-side **hotels** include the *Margarita Beach* (☎ & ⓕ 06610/76 267; ❹) and the *Three Stars* (☎06610/75 862; ❹). The Budget Ways agency (☎06610/76 768, ⓕ75 664; ❸) offers a range of accommodation and there are **rooms** between the main road and beach, and up above the main road: try Alekos Bostis (☎06610/75 637; ❸) or Kostas Vlahos (☎06610/55 350; ❷). Much of the main drag is dominated by souvenir shops and minimarkets, as well as a range of **bars**, including the village's oldest, *Charlie's*, which opened in 1939, and the lively *Very Coco* nightclub. The *Rose Garden* **restaurant** is just off the main road and has a fair mix of vegetarian, Greek and international food, as does the unfortunately named beach restaurant *Crabs*, where the seafood and special salads are excellent. The village proper, **ÁNO MORAÏTIKA**, is signposted a few minutes' hike up the steep lanes inland, and is virtually unspoiled. Its tiny houses and alleys are practically drowning in bougainvillea, among which you'll find two **tavernas**: the *Village Taverna* and the *Bella Vista*, which has a basic menu but justifies its name with a lovely garden, sea views and breezes.

Barely a hundred metres on from the Moraïtika seafront, **MESSONGÍ** continues this stretch of package-tour-oriented coast. The sandy beach is dominated by the vast *Messonghi Beach* **hotel** complex (☎06610/76 684, ℱ75 334; ⑥), plush but impersonal and rather disorganized. Both the *Hotel Gemini* (☎06610/75 221, ℱ 75 213; ⑥ half-board) and great-value *Pantheon Hall* (☎06610/75 802, ℱ75 801; ②) have pools and gardens, and en-suite rooms with balconies. Messongí has a number of good **restaurants**: notably the *Memories* taverna, which specializes in Corfiot dishes and serves its own barrel wine, and the upmarket *Castello*. An alternative is to head for the beachside *Bacchus* and *Spanos* tavernas a short walk south on the road to Boúkari. Try the *Dimensions* bar for a relaxed seaside drink.

The quiet road from Messongí to **BOÚKARI** follows the seashore for about 3km, often only a few feet above it. Boukári itself comprises little more than a handful of tavernas, a shop and a few small, family-run hotels; the *Boukari Beach* is the best of the **tavernas**, offering fresh fish and live lobster. The very friendly Vlahopoulos family who run the taverna also manage two small hotels nearby, the *Penelopi* and newer *Villa Alexandra* (☎06620/51 269, ℱ51 792; ③), as well as good rooms (②) attached to the taverna. Boukári is out of the way, but an idyllic little strip of unspoiled coast for anyone fleeing the crowds elsewhere on the island, and inland from here is the unspoiled wooded region around **Aryirádhes**, rarely visited by tourists and a perfect place for quiet walks.

Back on the coastline, the village of **PETRITÍ** fronts onto a small but busy dirt-track harbour, but is mercifully free of noise and commerce; its beach is rock, mud and sand, set among low olive-covered hills. The *Pension Egrypos* (☎06620/51 949; ③) has **rooms** and a **taverna**. At the harbour, three tavernas serve the trickle of sea traffic: the smart *Limnopoula* guarded by caged parrots, and the more basic but friendly *Dimitris* and *Stamatis*. Back from the village, near the hamlet of Vassilátika, is the elegant *Regina* **hotel**, with gardens and pool (☎06620/52 132, ℱ52 135; ④).

Southern Corfu

Across the island on the west coast, the beach at **ÁYIOS YEÓRYIOS** spreads as far south as Ayía Varvára, and north to encircle the edge of the Korissía lagoon, around 12km of uninterrupted sand. The village itself, however, is an unprepossessing sprawl. British package operators have arrived in force, with bars competing to present bingo, quizzes and video nights. The smart *Golden Sands* (☎06620/51 225, ℱ51 140; ④) has a pool, open-air restaurant and gardens, but the best **hotel** bargain is the smaller *Blue Sea* (☎06620/51 624, ℱ51 172, ℮bluesea@otenet.gr; ③); both are situated midway along the seafront road. The easiest place to look for good **rooms** is at Stork Tours (☎ & ℱ 06620/51 168; ②), halfway along the seafront. Áyios Yeóryios has a number of good **restaurants** on the seafront: *La Perla's* which serves Greek and north European food in a walled garden; the *Napoleon psistariá*; and the *Dario* Italian joint. **Nightlife** centres around music and pool bars like the *Gold Hart* and *Traxx*, although the best bar in Áyios Yeóryios is the sea-edge *Panorama*, which has views as far south as Paxí.

A few minutes' walk north of Áyios Yeóryios, **Íssos** is a far better and quieter beach; the dunes north of Íssos are an unofficial nude-bathing area. Facilities around Íssos are sparse: one **taverna**, the *Rousellis Grill* (which sometimes has rooms), a few hundred metres from the beach on the lane leading to Línia on the main road, and the *Friends* snack bar in Línia itself. An English-run **windsurfing school** operates on the beach.

Anyone interested in how a Greek town works away from the bustle of tourism shouldn't miss **LEFKÍMI**, on the island's east coast. The second-largest town after Corfu, it's the administrative centre of the south of the island as well as the alternative ferry port to/from Igoumenítsa, with half a dozen daily crossings in summer, and has some fine architecture, including two striking churches: **Áyios Theódoros**, on a mound above a small square, and **Áyios Arsénios**, with a vast orange dome that can be seen for miles. There are some **rooms** at the *Cheeky Face* taverna (☎06620/22 627; ❷), by the bridge over the canal that carries the Himáros River through town, and the *Maria Madalena* apartments (☎06620/22 386; ❸) further up. A few **bars** and **restaurants** sit on the edge of the canal – try the home cooking at *Maria*. Away from the centre, the *Hermes* bar has a leafy garden, and there's a number of other good local places where tourists are rare enough to guarantee you a friendly welcome, including the *Mersedes* and *Pacific* bars, and, notably, the *Kavouras* and *Fontana* tavernas.

There are no ambiguities in **KÁVOS**, directly south of Lefkími: either you like 24-hour drinking, clubbing, bungee-jumping, go-karts, video bars named after British sitcoms and chips with almost everything, or you should avoid the resort altogether. Kávos stretches over 2km of decent sandy beach, with watersports galore. This is very much package-tour territory; if you want independent **accommodation**, try Pandis Travel (☎06620/61 400, ℉61 401) or Island Holidays (☎06620/61 357, ℉61 426), and the nearest to genuine Greek **food** you'll find is at the *Two Brothers psistariá*, at the south end of town. Fast food and British-style ethnic cuisine are much easier to come by. *Future* is the biggest **club**, with imported north European DJs, followed by *Whispers*, *42nd St* and *Buzz*. Favourite **bars** include *JCs*, *Jungle*, *The Face*, *Fire* and *Bonkers*, and at night the main drag is one unbroken crowd of young revellers.

Beyond the limits of Kávos, where few visitors stray, a path leaving the road south to the hamlet of Sparterá heads through unspoiled countryside; after around thirty minutes of walking it reaches the cliffs of **Cape Asprókavos** and the crumbling **monastery of Arkoudhílas**. The cape looks out over the straits to Paxí, and down over deserted **Arkoudhílas beach**, which can be reached from Sparterá, 5km by road but only 3km by the signed path from Kávos. Even wilder is **Áyios Górdhis Paleohoríou beach**, 3km further on from Sparterá, one of the least visited on the island and not to be confused with the eponymous beach further north.

Corfu's satellite islands

Corfu's three inhabited satellite islands, **Eríkoussa**, **Othoní** and **Mathráki**, in the quintet of **Dhiapóndia islands**, are scattered up to 20km off the northwest coast. Some travel agencies in the northern resorts offer **day-trips** to Eríkoussa only, often with a barbecue thrown in – fine if you're happy to spend the day on the beach. A trip taking in all three islands from Sidhári or Áyios Stéfanos is excellent value: they are between thirty and sixty minutes apart by boat, and most trips allow you an hour on each (longer on sandy Eríkoussa).

Locals use day-trip boats between the islands, so it's possible to pay your way between them. There is also a thrice-weekly **ferry** from Kérkyra Town, the *Alexandros II*, which brings cars and goods to the islands, but given that it has to sail halfway round Corfu first, it's the slowest way to proceed.

Mathráki

Hilly, densely forested and with a long empty beach, beautiful **Mathráki** has the fewest inhabitants of the three islands. Portelo beach begins at the edge of the tiny harbour, and extends south for 3km of fine, dark-red sand, a nesting site for the endangered **loggerhead turtle** (see box on p.987). It's important therefore not to camp anywhere near the beach – and not to make any noise there at night.

A single road rises from the harbour into the interior and the scattered village of **KÁTO MATHRÁKI**, where just one friendly taverna-kafenío-shop overlooks the beach and Corfu. The views are magnificent, as is the sense of isolation. However, Mathráki is gradually gearing up towards visitors, and islander Tassos Kassimis (☎06630/71 700; ❸) already rents **rooms**. The road continues to the village of **Áno Mathráki**, with its single, old-fashioned kafenío next to the church, but this is beyond walking distance on a day-visit.

Othoní

Six kilometres north, **Othoní** is the largest, and at first sight the least inviting of Corfu's satellite islands. The island has a handful of good tavernas and rooms for rent in its port, **ÁMMOS**, but the reception from islanders who aren't in the tourism trade is rather cool. Ámmos has two beaches, both pebbly, one in its harbour. The village kafenío serves as a very basic shop, and there's one smart **restaurant**, *La Locanda dei Sogni*, which also has **rooms** (☎06630/71 640; ❸) – though these tend to be prebooked by Italian visitors. Three tavernas, *New York*, *Mikros* and tiny *Rainbow*, offer decent but fairly limited menus; the owner of the *New York* also offers rooms for rent (☎06630/71 581; ❸). The island's interior is dramatic, and a path up out of the village leads through rocky, tree-covered hills to the central hamlet, **Horió**, after a thirty-minute walk. Horió, like other inland villages, is heavily depopulated – only about sixty people still live on the island through the winter – but it's very attractive, and the architecture is completely traditional.

Eríkoussa

East of Othoní, **Eríkoussa** is the most popular destination for day-trippers. It's invariably hyped as a "desert island" trip, although this is a desert island with a medium-sized hotel, rooms, tavernas and a year-round community. In high season, it gets very busy: Eríkoussa has a large diaspora living in America and elsewhere who return to family homes in their droves in summer, so you may find your *yiá soú* or *kaliméra* returned in a Brooklyn accent.

Eríkoussa has an excellent golden sandy beach right by the harbour, with great swimming, and another, quieter, beach reached by a path across the wooded island interior. The island's cult following keeps its one **hotel**, the *Erikoussa* (☎06630/71 110, ☎71 555; ❹), busy through the season; rooms are en suite with balconies and views. Simpler rooms are available from the *Anemomilos* **taverna** (☎06630/71 647; ❸). If you're hoping to stay, phoning ahead is essential, as is taking anything you might not be able to buy – the only shop is a snack bar selling basic groceries.

Paxí (Paxos) and Andípaxi

Verdant, hilly and still largely unspoiled, **Paxí (Paxos)** is the smallest of the main Ionian islands. Barely 12km by 4km, it has no sandy beaches, no historical sites, only two hotels and a serious water shortage, yet is so popular it is best avoided in high season. It's a particular favourite of yachting flotillas, whose spending

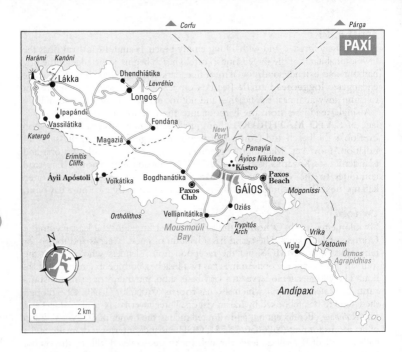

PAXÍ

▲ Corfu   ▲ Párga

Harámi   Kanóni
         Lákka   Dhendhiátika
                              Levréhio
                          Longós
     Ipapándi
   Vassilátika   Fondána
Katergó   Magaziá   New
                                  Port
    Erimítis   Panayía
    Cliffs   Áyios Nikólaos
 Áyii Apóstoli   Voïkátika   Bogdhanátika Kástro   Paxos
                              Paxos   GÁÏOS   Beach
                              Club   Mogoníssi
                                   Oziás
        Orthólithos   Vellianitátika
                                    Trypitós
     Mousmoúli   Arch
        Bay   Vríka
                                   Vígla Vatoúmi
                                              Órmos
                                           Agrapidhiás

                           Andípaxi

0   2 km

habits have brought the island an upmarket reputation, making it just about the most expensive place to visit in the Ionian islands and lending it a rather cliquey air. Pockets of unauthorized camping, however, are tolerated after the closure of the official site. Most accommodation is block-booked by travel companies, though there are local tour operators whose holiday deals are often a fraction of the price. The capital, **Gáïos**, is quite cosmopolitan, with delis and boutiques, but northerly **Lákka** and tiny **Longós** are where hardcore Paxophiles head.

Gáïos

Most visitors arrive at the New Port 1km north of **GÁÏOS**, a pleasant town built around a small square on the seafront overlooking two islands, Áyios Nikólaos and Panayía. Room owners often meet ferries, although it's advisable to phone ahead: try Gaïos Travel (☎06620/32 033, ℱ32 175, ℮gaiostrv@ otenet.gr) or Bouas Tours (☎06620/32 401, ℱ32 610, ℮info@bouastours.gr), both situated on the seafront. Paxí's two seasonal **hotels** are both near Gáïos: the *Paxos Beach Hotel* (☎06620/31 211, ℱ32 695, ℮zerbas1@otenet.gr; ❻ half-board) which has smart en-suite bungalows on a hillside above a pebbly beach 2km south of town, and the fairly luxurious *Paxos Club Hotel* (☎06620/32 450, ℱ32 097; ❻), 2km inland from Gáïos.

Gáïos boasts a number of decent **tavernas**, most of which are on the pricey side. One exception is the friendly family-run *Acropol*, on a side street off the square, which serves wholesome meat, fish and veg dishes at very reasonable rates. Also recommended are *Dodo's*, set in a garden inland from the Anemoyiannis statue; the *Volcano*, which is the best of those on the square; and *Vassilis*, which has the best selection and prices of the trio to the left of the road up towards the bus stop. *The Cellar* at the top of the square is the best place for a tasty *souvláki*. Other options include the *Blue Grotto*, in an alleyway off the

THE IONIAN ISLANDS | Gáïos

12

962

square, or *Carcoleggio's*, 1.5km out of town towards Bogdhanátika, popular with locals for its grills. The two kafenía, the *Gonia* by the old ferry ramp and the unnamed one opposite the *Acropol* are the traditional places for a coffee or drink. Trendier bars include *Carnayo* near the square and *Deep Blue* round the quay towards the new port. The *Phoenix* disco out by the new port opens sporadically after midnight and has a terrace for sublunar fun, while the inland *Tango*, beyond the bus stop, is a more regular disco.

Inland are some of the island's oldest settlements, such as Oziás and Vellianitátika, in prime walking country, but with few if any facilities. Noel Rochford's book, *Landscapes of Paxos* (Sunflower), lists dozens of walks, and cartographers Elizabeth and Ian Bleasdale's *Paxos Walking Map* is on sale in most travel agencies.

The rest of the island

Paxí's one main road runs along the spine of the island, with a turning at the former capital Magaziá, leading down to the tiny port of Longós. The main road continues to Lákka, the island's funkiest resort, set in a breathtaking horseshoe bay. Two buses ply the road between Gáios and Lákka six times a day, most diverting to swing through Longós. The Gáios–Lákka bus (30min) affords panoramic views, and the route is an excellent walk of under three hours (one-way). A taxi between the two costs around €8–9.

Approached from the south, **LÁKKA** is an unprepossessing jumble of buildings, but once in its maze of alleys and neo-Venetian buildings, or on the quay with views of distant Corfu, you do get a sense of its charm. Lákka's two **beaches**, Harámi and Kanóni, are the best on the island, although there have been complaints in high season of pollution from the yachts that cram the bay. The terraced olive grove behind Kanóni is a favourite with campers but has no facilities. **Accommodation** is plentiful (except in high season) from the island's two biggest agencies: Planos Holidays (☎06620/31 744, ℻31 010, ✉planos@ otenet.gr) or Routsis (☎06620/31 807, ℻31 161, ✉routis-holidays@ ker.forthnet.gr), both on the seafront. The latter runs two bargain rooming houses, *Ilios* and *Lefcothea* (both ❷). There's an embarrassment of good tavernas, such as the friendly *Nionios* and its new neighbour *Pounendes*, or the more upmarket *Pergola* and exotic *Rosa di Paxos*. There's a similar wealth of bars: the seafront *Romantica* cocktail bar, *Serano* in the square, or the friendly *To Ariston* kafenío – the hub of village life. Lákka is also well situated for **walking**: up onto either promontory, to the lighthouse or Vassilátika, or to Longós and beyond. One of the finest walks – if combined with a bus or taxi back – is an early evening visit to the **Erimítis cliffs**, near the hamlet of Voïkátika: on clear afternoons, the cliffs change colour at twilight like a seagoing Uluru (Ayers Rock).

LONGÓS is the prettiest village on the island, and perfectly sited for morning sun and idyllic alfresco breakfasts. The village is dominated by the upmarket villa crowd, but the Planos office here (☎ & ℻ 06620/31 530) is the best place to look for accommodation. Longós has some of the island's best restaurants: the seafront *Vassilis*, which does terrific fish dishes, *Kakarantzas*, with a wide variety of fish and seafood, and *Iy Gonia*, a much simpler and cheaper *psistariá*. *To Taxidhi* on the quay is a nice spot for coffee or an early drink, while *Four Seasons* and *Ores* pander to the night-owls.

Longós has a small, scruffy beach, with sulphur springs favoured by local grannies, but most people swim off Levréhio beach in the next bay south, which gets the occasional camper. (Islanders are touchy about camping for fear of fires; it's politic to ask at the beach taverna if it's acceptable to camp.) Longós is at the bottom of a steep winding hill, making **walking** a chore, but the short circle around neighbouring **Dhendhiátika** provides excellent views, and the walk to **Fondána** and **Magaziá** can be done to coincide with a bus back to Longós.

Andípaxi

A mile south, Paxí's tiny sibling **Andípaxi** has scarcely any accommodation and no facilities beyond several beach tavernas open during the day in season. It is most easily reached by the frequent shuttle kaïkia from Gáïos (€3–4). The sandy, blue-water coves have been compared with the Caribbean, but you'll have to share them with kaïkia and sea taxis from all three villages, plus larger craft from Corfu (boats from Paxí may also take you to its sea stacks and caves, the most dramatic in the Ionian islands).

Boats basically deposit you either at the sandy **Vríka beach** or the longer pebble beach of **Vatoúmi**. Vríka has a taverna at each end, of which *Spiros* (☎06620/31 172) has good food and can arrange self-catering accommodation up in **Vígla**, the island's hilltop settlement, on a weekly basis. Vatoúmi's only facility is the justifiably named *Bella Vista*, perched on a cliff high above the beach, although a taverna was under construction behind the beach at the time of writing.

For a swim in quieter surroundings the trick is to head south away from the pleasure-craft moorings, although path widening has made even the quieter bays more accessible. Paths also lead inland to connect the handful of homes and the southerly lighthouse, but there are no beaches of any size on Andípaxi's western coastline and thick thorny scrub makes it difficult to approach. In low season, there's also the risk of bad weather keeping pleasure craft in port and stranding you on the island.

Lefkádha (Lefkas)

Lefkádha is an oddity. Connected to the mainland by a long causeway through lagoons, it barely feels like an island, at least on the busier eastern side – and historically in fact it isn't. It is separated from the mainland by a canal cut by Corinthian colonists in the seventh century BC, which has been re-dredged (after silting up) on various occasions since, and today is spanned by a thirty-metre boat-drawbridge built in 1986. Lefkádha was long an important strategic base, and approaching the causeway you pass a series of fortresses, climaxing in the fourteenth-century castle of **Santa Maura** – the Venetian name for the island. These defences were too close to the mainland to avoid an Ottoman tenure, which began in 1479, but the Venetians wrested back control a couple of centuries later. They were in turn overthrown by Napoleon in 1797 and then the British took over as Ionian protectors in 1810. It wasn't until 1864 that Lefkádha, like the rest of the Ionian archipelago, was reunited with Greece.

At first glance Lefkádha is not overwhelmingly attractive, although it is a substantial improvement on the mainland just opposite. The whiteness of its rock strata – *lefkás* has the same root as *lefkós*, "white" – is often brutally exposed by road cuts and quarries, and the highest ridge is bare except for ugly military and telecom installations. With the marshes and sumpy inlets on the east coast, mosquitoes can be a midsummer problem. On the other hand, the island is a fertile place, supporting cypresses, olive groves and vineyards, particularly on the western slopes, and life in the mountain villages remains relatively untouched, with the older women still wearing traditional local dress – two skirts (one forming a bustle), a dark headscarf and a rigid bodice.

Lefkádha has been the home of various literati, including two prominent Greek poets, Angelos Sikelianos and Aristotelis Valaoritis, and the British writer Lafcadio Hearn. Support for the arts continues in the form of a well-attended international **festival** of theatre and folk-dancing, now extended throughout the summer, with most events staged in the Santa Maura castle. On a smaller scale, frequent village celebrations accompanied by *bouzoúki* and clarinet ensure that the strong local wine flows well into the early hours.

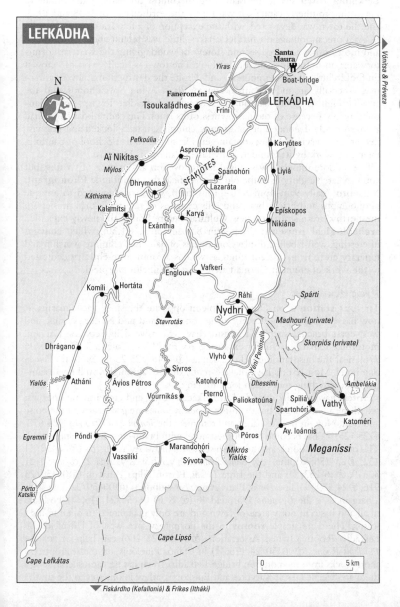

Lefkádha remains relatively undeveloped, with just two major resorts: **Vassilikí**, in its vast bay in the south, claims to be Europe's biggest windsurf centre; **Nydhrí**, on the east coast, overlooks the island's picturesque archipelago, and is the launching point for the barely inhabited island of **Meganíssi**.

Lefkádha Town and around

Lefkádha Town sits at the island's northernmost tip, hard by the causeway. Like other southerly capitals, it was hit by the earthquakes of 1948 and 1953, and the town was devastated, with the exception of a few **Italianate churches**. As a precaution against further quakes, little was rebuilt above two storeys, and most houses acquired second storeys of wood, giving the western dormitory area an unintentionally quaint look. The town is small – you can cross it on foot in little over ten minutes – and despite the destruction, still very attractive, especially around the main square, Platía Ayíou Spyridhónos, and the arcaded high street of Ioánnou Méla. Much of Lefkádha Town is pedestrian-only, mainly because of the narrowness of its lanes. The centre boasts over half a dozen richly decorated private family churches, usually locked and best visited around services. Many contain gems from the Ionian School of painting, including work by its founder, Zakynthian Panayiotis Doxaras.

The folklore museum was closed for renovation at the time of writing, but you can catch a glimpse of the old way of life at the quaint little **Phonograph Museum** (daily 9am–1pm & 6–11pm; free), which is dedicated to antique phonographs and bric-a-brac, and sells cassettes of rare traditional music. On the northwestern seafront a new Cultural Centre houses the newly expanded **archeological museum** (Tues–Sun 8.30am–3pm; €1.50), which contains interesting, well-labelled displays on aspects of daily life, religious worship and funerary customs in ancient times, as well as a room on prehistory dedicated to the work of eminent German archeologist Wilhelm Dörpfeld.

Practicalities

The **bus station** is on Dhimítri Golémi opposite the small yacht marina. It now has services to almost every village on the island, and Nydhrí, Vassilikí and west-coast beaches such as Káthisma have extensive daily services. Car and motorbike rental is useful for exploring; try EuroHire, Golémi 5 (☎06450/26 776), near the bus station or I Love Santas (☎06450/25 250) next to the *Ionian Star* hotel. Most resorts have bicycle-rental outlets, although you'll need stamina to do anything more than local touring.

Hotels have actually dwindled in Lefkádha Town, and currently number just six. All are in busy areas, but the more expensive ones are glazed against the noise and heat. Now in private hands and renamed, the *Ionian Star* (☎06450/24 672, ℉25 125; ❻) has become the plushest hotel with brand-new fittings and a pool. The other smart hotels are the stylish seafront *Nirikos*, Ayías Mávras (☎06450/24 132, ℉23 756; ❻), the cosy *Santa Maura*, Spyridhónos Viánda 2 (☎06450/21 308–9, ℉26 253; ❹) and the large *Lefkas*, Pétrou Filípa Panáyou (☎06450/23 916, ℉24 579; ❻). The *Patras*, Platía Áyiou Spyridhónos (☎06450/22 359; ❷) is a bargain, as is the *Byzantio*, Dörpfeld 40 (☎ & ℉ 06450/21 315; ❷); both are small and basic, in noisy areas of town and are only guaranteed to open in high season. There are simple **rooms** in the dormitory area west of Dörpfeld: the Lefkádha Room Owners Association (☎06450/21 266) can help, or try the *Pinelopis Rooms* (☎06450/24 175; ❷) in Odhós Pinelópis, off the seafront two short blocks from the pontoon bridge. Lefkádha Town has no campsite, although there are decent sites at Karyótes and Epískopos, a few kilometres to the south.

The best **restaurants** are hidden in the backstreets: the *Regantos* taverna, on Dhimárhou Venióti is the local favourite, but opening hours can be erratic. If it's closed, head for the *Lighthouse*, in its own small garden on Filarmonikís. The *Romantika* on Mitropóleos has nightly performances of Lefkadhan *kantádhes*, while the smartest place in town is the *Adriatica*, Faneroménis and Merarhías, where people tend to dress up to eat.

Of the **bars** in the main square, the *Serano* ouzerí/café is the cheapest, with occasional evening entertainment from buskers, jugglers and even fire-eaters. Further from the action the best is the *Cafe Karfakis*, on Ioánnou Melá, an old-style kafenío with splendid *mezédhes*, or the real local hangout *Theofilos* further along. The trendiest bars such as *Excess* and *Il Posto* line the seafront west of the bridge. The town's outdoor **cinema**, Eleni, on Faneroménis, has two showings and programmes change daily.

Around Lefkádha Town

The town has a decent and fairly large shingle beach west of the lagoon at **Yíras**, a forty-minute walk from the centre. In season there's also a bus (hourly 10am–2pm) from the bus station. Roughly 4km long, the beach is often virtually deserted even in high season; there's a **taverna** at either end, and at the western end a couple of **bars** in the renovated windmills, as well as the trendy *Club Milos*.

The uninhabited **Faneroméni monastery** (daily 8am–2pm & 4–8pm; free) is reached by any of the west-coast buses, or by a steep hike on foot from town (30min) through the hamlet of Fríni. There's a small museum and chapel, and an ox's yoke and hammer, used when Nazi occupiers forbade the use of bells. There are wonderful views over the town and lagoon from the Fríni road.

The island's **interior**, best reached by bus or car from Lefkádha Town, offers imposing mountainscapes and excellent walking between villages only a few kilometres apart. **KARYÁ** is its centre, with a hotel, the *Karia Village Hotel* (☎06450/41 004; ④), tucked away above the village, and some rooms: try the Kakiousis family (☎06450/61 136; ②), Olga Lazari (☎06450/61 547; ②) or Michael Halikias (☎06450/61 026; ①). The leafy town square has a popular taverna, *Iy Klimataria*, just off the platía and two *psistariés* on it, *Ta Platania*, and the smarter *O Rousos*. Karyá is the centre of the island's lace and weaving industry, with a fascinating small **museum** set in a lacemaker's home. The historic and scenic villages of **Vafkerí** and **Englouví** are within striking distance, with the west-coast hamlets of **Dhrymónas** and **Exánthia** a hike over the hills.

The east coast to Vassilikí

Lefkádha's east coast is the most accessible and the most developed part of the island. Apart from the campsites at Karyótes (*Kariotes Beach*, ☎ & ⑤ 06450/71 103) and Epískopos (*Episcopos Beach*, ☎06450/71 388), there's little point stopping before the small fishing ports of **LIYIÁ**, which has some rooms and the hotel *Konaki* (☎06450/71 127, ⑤71 125; ⑥), or **NIKIÁNA**, where you'll find the hotel *Pegasus* (☎06450/71 766, ⑤25 290; ⑥) and the smarter but considerably cheaper *Ionion* (☎06450/71 721, ⑤71 852; ⑤), as well as the *Porto Fino* pension (☎06450/71 389; ③). In addition, Nikiána has a selection of fine tavernas, notably the *Pantazis*, which also has rooms to let, and the *Lefko Akroyiali*, a good fish restaurant further south. Beaches here tend to be pebbly and small.

Most package travellers will find themselves in **NYDHRÍ**, the coast's biggest resort, with ferry connections to Meganíssi and myriad **boat trips** around the nearby satellite islands. The German archeologist Wilhelm Dörpfeld believed

Nydhrí, rather than Itháki, to be the site of Odysseus's capital, and did indeed find Bronze Age tombs on the plain nearby. His theory identifying ancient Ithaca with Lefkádha fell into disfavour after his death in 1940, although his obsessive attempts to give the island some status over its neighbour are honoured by a statue on Nydhrí's quay. Dörpfeld's tomb is tucked away at Ayía Kyriakí on the opposite side of the bay, near the house in which he once lived, visible just above the chapel and lighthouse on the far side of the water.

Nydhrí is an average resort, with some good pebble beaches and a lovely setting, but the centre is an ugly strip with heavy traffic. The best place to stay is the *Hotel Gorgona* (℡06450/92 197, ℻92 268; ❸), set in a lush garden away from the traffic a minute along the Ráhi road, which leads to Nydhrí's very own **waterfall**, a 45-minute walk inland. There are also rooms in the centre – try Emilios Gazis (℡06450/92 703; ❷) and Athanasios Konidharis (℡06450/92 749; ❸). The town's focus is the Aktí Aristotéli Onássi quay, where most of the rather ritzy **restaurants** and **bars** are found. The *Barrel* and *Il Sappore* restaurants are pricey but recommended, as is the *Agra* on the beach, slightly less so *George's*. However, eating is better value on the noisy main drag – try *Agrabeli* or *Ta Kalamia*. Nightlife centres around bars like *No Name* and *Byblos*, and the late-night *Status* or *Tropicana*.

Nydhrí sits at the mouth of a deep inlet stretching to the next village, somnolent **VLYHÓ**, with a few good tavernas and mooring for yachts. Over the Yéni peninsula across the inlet is the large **Dhessími Bay**, home to two campsites: *Santa Maura Camping* (℡06450/95 007, ℻95 493), and *Dessimi Beach Camping* (℡06450/95 374, ℻95 190), one at each end of the beach but often packed with outsized mobile homes. The *Pirofani* beach taverna in between them is excellent.

The coast road beyond Vlyhó turns inland and climbs the foothills of Mount Stavrotás, through the hamlets of Katohóri and Paliokatoúna to **Póros**, a quiet village with few facilities. Just south of here is the increasingly busy beach resort of **MIKRÓS YIALÓS**, boasting a handful of **tavernas**, a few rooms at *Oceanis Studios* (℡ & ℻ 06450/95 095; ❹), plus the posh *Poros Beach Camping* (℡06450/95 452, ℻95 152), which has bungalows (❹), shops and a pool. For food, try the *Rouda Bay* taverna opposite the beach, which also has rooms (℡ & ℻ 06450/95 634, ✉manolitsis@otenet.gr; ❺).

A panoramic detour off the main road to quiet **Vournikás** and **Sývros** is recommended to walkers and drivers (the Lefkádha–Vassilíki bus also visits); both places have tavernas and some private rooms. It's around 14km to the next resort, the fjord-like inlet of **SÝVOTA**, 2km down a steep hill (bus twice daily). There's no beach except for a remote cove, but some fine fish tavernas: the *Ionion* is the most popular, but the *Delfinia* and *Kavos* are also good. Ask at the *Delfinia* or the adjacent Yiannis supermarket for **rooms** (℡06450/31 180, ℻31 050; ❸), or there's a basic unofficial campsite by the bus stop at the edge of the village.

Beyond the Sývota turning, the mountain road dips down towards Kondárena, almost a suburb of **VASSILIKÍ**, the island's premier watersports resort. Winds in the huge bay draw vast numbers of windsurfers, with light morning breezes for learners and tough afternoon blasts for advanced surfers. Booking your **accommodation** ahead is mandatory in high season. Hotels are not cheap: *Pension Hollidays* (℡06450/31 011; ❹), round the corner from the ferry dock, is a reasonable option with air conditioning and TV in all rooms. Also good value for its rating is slightly more upmarket *Hotel Apollo* (℡06450/31 122, ℻31 142; ❹) nearby. In the centre of town, the two main hotels are the smart and reasonably priced *Vassiliki Bay Hotel* (℡06450/21 567,

23 567; ④) and the *Hotel Lefkatas* (☎06450/31 801, ⓕ31 804; ⑤), a large, modern building overlooking the busiest road in town. Rooms and apartments are available along the beach road to Póndi: *Billy's House* (☎06450/31 418; ③) and *Christina Politi's Rooms* (☎06450/31 440; ③) are smart and purpose-built or ask at the central Samba Tours (☎06450/31 520). The largest of the three beach windsurf centres, *Club Vassiliki*, offers all-in **windsurf tuition** and accommodation deals. Vassilikí's only **campsite**, the large *Camping Vassiliki Beach* (☎06450/31 308, ⓕ31 458), is about 500m along the beach road; it has its own restaurant, bar and shop.

Vassilikí's pretty quayside is lined with **tavernas** and bars, notably the *Dolphin Psistaria*, the glitzier *Restaurant Miramare*, specializing in fish, the *Penguin* and *Alexander*, which has pizza, as well as the *Jasmine Garden* Chinese. The best place for a **drink** is *Livanakis* kafenío (next to the bakery), now modernized but still genuine and cheap.

The beach at Vassilikí is stony and poor, but improves 1km on at tiny **PÓNDI**; most non-windsurfers, however, use the daily kaïki trips to nearby Ayiófili or around Cape Lefkátas to the superior beaches at Pórto Katsíki and Egremní on the sandy west coast. There's a gradually increasing number of places to stay at Póndi, some with great views of the bay and plain behind, particularly from the terrace of the *Ponti Beach Hotel* (☎06450/31 572, ⓕ31 576; ⑤), which is very popular with holidaying Greeks, and has a decent restaurant and bar. The *Nefeli* (☎06450/31 515; ③), right on the beach, is much better value though.

The west coast

Tsoukaládhes, just 6km from Lefkádha, is developing a roadside tourism business, but better beaches lie a short distance to the south, so there's very little reason to stay here. Four kilometres on, the road plunges down to the sand-and-pebble **Pefkoúlia beach**, one of the longest on the island, with two tavernas at the north end, one of which, *Mesoyios*, has rooms (☎06450/97 070, ⓕ97 170; ④) and unofficial camping down at the other end, about 2km away.

Jammed into a gorge between Pefkoúlia and the next beach, Mýlos, is **AÏ NIKÍTAS**, the prettiest resort on Lefkádha, a jumble of lanes and small wooden buildings. The back of the village is a dust-blown car park, which detracts from the appeal of the pleasant, if basic, *O Aï Nikitas* **campsite** (☎06450/97 301, ⓕ21 173), set in terraced olive groves. The most attractive **accommodation** is in the *Pension Ostria* (☎06450/97 483, ⓕ97 300; ④), a beautiful blue-and-white building above the village decorated in a mix of beachcomber and ecclesiastical styles. The *Villa Milia* (☎06450/97 475; ③), by the junction, or the *Elena patisserie* (☎06450/97 385; ③) offer better rates than most. Other options are in the alleys that run off the main drag; the best bets are the small *Hotel Selene* (☎06450/97 369; ④) and quieter *Olive Tree* (☎06450/97 453, ⓕ97 153; ④), which is also signposted from the main route. The best tavernas include the *Sapfo* fish taverna by the sea and the *T'Agnantia*, just above the main street, which serves excellent traditional cuisine. *Captain's Corner* near the beach is the liveliest drinking venue.

Sea taxis (€1.50 one-way) ply between Aï Nikitás and **Mýlos** beach, or it's a 45-minute walk (or bus ride) to the most popular beach on the coast, **Káthisma**, a shadeless kilometre of fine sand, which becomes nudist and a lot less crowded beyond the large jutting rocks halfway along. There are two tavernas on the beach: the barn-like *Kathisma Beach* (☎06450/97 050, ⓕ97 335; ⑤), with smart apartments, and the expensive and unfriendly *Akroyiali*. Above the beach the *Sunset* has **rooms** (☎06450/97 488; ❹) and the *Balkoni* restaurant commands fine views. Beyond Káthisma, hairpin bends climb the flank of Mount Méga towards the small village of **KALAMÍTSI**, a much cheaper base for this area: Spyros Karelis (☎06450/99 214; ❷) and Spyros Veryinis (☎06450/99 411; ❷) have rooms. *Hermes* (☎06450/99 417; ❷), the *Blue and White House* (☎06450/99 413; ❸) and *Pansion Nontas* (☎06450/99 451; ❸) have larger rooms and apartments. There are also three good tavernas: the *Paradeisos* in its own garden with fountain, the more basic *Ionio* and, just north of the village, the aptly titled *Panoramic View*. Three kilometres down a newly paved road is the village's quiet sandy beach.

South of Kalamítsi, past the hamlets of Hortáta, which boasts the excellent *Lygos* taverna with rooms (☎06450/33 395; ❷), and Komíli, the landscape becomes almost primeval. At 38km from Lefkádha Town, **ATHÁNI** is Lefkádha's most remote spot to stay, with a couple of good tavernas which both have great-value rooms: the *Panorama* (☎06450/33 291, ⓕ33 476; ❷) and *O Alekos* (☎06560/33 484; ❷), the latter only open in high season. Three of the Ionian's choicest **beaches**, each with basic refreshment facilities, are accessible from Atháni: the nearest, reached by a 4km paved road is **Yialós**, followed by **Egremní**, down a steep incline unpaved for the last 2km. Further south an asphalted road leads to the dramatic and popular twin beach of **Pórto Katsíki**, where there are several better-stocked *kantínas* on the cliff above.

Keeping to the main road for 14km from Atháni will bring you to barren **Cape Lefkátas**, which drops abruptly 75m into the sea. Byron's Childe Harold sailed past this point, and "saw the evening star above, Leucadia's far projecting rock of woe: And hail'd the last resort of fruitless love". The fruitless love is a reference to Sappho, who in accordance with the ancient legend that you could cure yourself of unrequited love by leaping into these waters, leapt – and died. In her honour the locals termed the place *Kávos tís Kyrás* ("Lady's Cape"), and her act was imitated by the lovelorn youths of Lefkádha for centuries afterwards. And not just by the lovelorn, for the act (known as *katapondismós*) was performed annually by scapegoats – always a criminal or a lunatic – selected by priests from the Apollo temple whose sparse ruins lie close by. Feathers and even live birds were attached to the victims to slow their descent and boats waiting below took the chosen one, dead or alive, away to some place where the evil banished with them could do no further harm. The rite continued into the Roman era, when it degenerated into little more than a fashionable stunt by decadent youth. These days, in a more controlled modern re-enactment, Greek hang-gliders hold a tournament from the cliffs every July.

Lefkádha's satellites

Lefkádha has four satellite islands clustered off its east coast, although only one, **Meganíssi**, the largest and most interesting, is accessible. **Skorpiós**, owned by the Onassis family, fields armed guards to deter visitors. **Madhouri**, owned by the family of poet Nanos Valaoritis, is private and similarly off-limits, while tiny **Spárti** is a large scrub-covered rock. Day-trips from Nydhrí skirt all three islands, and some stop to allow swimming in coves.

Meganíssi

Meganíssi, twenty minutes by frequent daily ferries from Nydhrí, is a large island with limited facilities but a magical, if bleak landscape. Ferries stop first at **Spiliá**, below **SPARTOHÓRI**, an immaculate village with whitewashed buildings and an abundance of bougainvillea. The locals – many returned émigrés from Australia – live from farming and fishing and are genuinely welcoming. You arrive at a jetty on a pebble beach with a few tavernas and a primitive but free (for a night or two only) campsite behind the excellent *Star Taverna*. The village proper boasts three restaurants: a pizza place called the *Tropicana*, which can direct you to **rooms** (℡ 06450/51 486; ❶–❸), the *Gakias* and the traditional taverna *Lakis*. Further west round the coast at Áyios Yiánnis there is a good beach with the *Il Paradiso* taverna and a makeshift campsite, a great spot to unwind in.

The attractive inland village of **KATOMÉRI** is an hour's walk through magnificent country. It has the island's one **hotel**, the *Meganissi*, a comfortable place with a restaurant and pool (℡ 06450/51 240, ℻ 51 639; ❹), and a few café-bars. Ten-minutes' walk downhill is the main port of **VATHÝ**, with some accommodation (*Different Studios:* ℡ 06450/22 170; ❸) and several highly-rated restaurants, notably the waterside taverna, *Porto Vathi*, which Lefkádhans flock to on ferries for Sunday lunch, and the *Rose Garden*. After the high-season madness of Nydhrí, Meganíssi's unspoiled landscape is a tonic, and it's easy to organize a **day-trip** from Nydhrí, getting off at Spiliá, walking via Spartohóri to Katoméri for lunch at the *Meganissi* or down at Vathý, from where you can catch the ferry back. Paths lead from Katoméri to remote beaches, including popular **Ambelákia**, but these aren't realistic on a day-trip.

Kefalloniá

Kefalloniá is the largest of the Ionian islands – a place that has real towns as well as resorts. Like its neighbours, Kefalloniá was overrun by Italians and Germans in World War II; the "handover" after Italy's capitulation in 1943 led to the massacre of over five thousand Italian troops on the island by invading German forces. These events form a key episode in Louis de Bernières' novel, *Captain Corelli's Mandolin*, a tragicomic epic of life on the island, which takes place mostly during the occupation and whose film version was made on the island in 2000.

Until the late 1980s, the island paid scant regard to tourism; perhaps this was partly due to a feeling that Kefalloniá could not easily be marketed. Virtually all of its towns and villages were levelled in the 1953 earthquake, and these masterpieces of Venetian architecture had been the one touch of elegance in a severe, mountainous landscape. A more likely explanation, however, for the island's late emergence on the Greek tourist scene is the Kefallonians' legendary reputation for insular pride and stubbornness, and a good measure of eccentricity.

Having decided on the advantages of an easily exploitable industry, however, Kefalloniá is at present in the midst of a tourism boom. Long favoured by Italians, it has begun attracting British package companies, for whom an airport terminal was constructed in the mid-Nineties, while virtually every decent beach has been endowed with restaurants. There are definite attractions here, with some **beaches** as good as any in the Ionian islands, and a fine (if pricey) local wine, the dry white *Rombola*. Mercifully, the anticipated Corelli factor has not so far led to the island becoming either oversubscribed or overexpensive. Moreover, the island seems able to soak up a lot of people without feeling at all crowded, and the magnificent scenery speaks for itself, the escarpments culminating in the 1632-metre bulk of **Mount Énos**, declared a national park to protect the fir trees (*Abies cephalonica*) named after the island.

KEFALLONIÁ AND ITHÁKI

N

Astakós

Astakós & Pátra

Ithíki

Saratíniko
Bay

Lipá

Arethoússa
Spring

VATHÝ

Perahóri

Ayíou Andhréou
Bay

Paleohóra

Moní
Taxiarhón

Skhínos
Bay

Loúisa

Cave
of the
Nymphs

Dhéxa

Mólos
Gulf

Mount
Etós

Alalkomenae

Kióni

Pelikáta
Hill

Moní
Katharón

Anoyí

Mount
Nírito

Afáles
Bay

Fríkes

Ayios Ioánnis

Léfki

Exoyí

Platríthiás

Homeric
school

Stavrós

Palis
Bay

Psaetós Bay

Neohóri

Émblisi

Fiskárdho

Fókis

Kondharáta

Evretí

Vassilikiádhes

Dhivaráta

Ayía Efimía

Mánganos

Mazoukáta

Halikerí

Ayía Ierousalím

Áyia
Kyriakí

Ássos

Mýrtos

Angónas

Zóla

Ayios
Spyrídhonas

Athéras

▲ *Kyllíni*

Póros

Tzanáta

Skála

Ratzakli

Markópoulo

Pástra

Káto
Kateliós

**Monastery
of Sissiá**

Vlaháta

Lourdháta

Moussáta

*Mount Énos
1628m* ▲

Áyios
Eleftérios

Trapezáki

Pessádha

Spartiá

Koriána

Ávythos

Kourkomeláta

Keramiés

Metaxáta

Peratáta

Lakíthra

**Áyios
Yeóryios
Fortress**

Ándisami

SÁMI

Melissáni Cave

Karavómylos

Dhrogaráti Cave

Áyios
Yerásimos

Frangáta

*Mount
Evmorfía
846m* ▲

Dhilináta

Dhavgáta

Fársa

ARGOSTÓLI

Dhrápano
Causeway

Lássi

*Makrýs
Yialós*

*Platýs
Yialós*

Katavóthres

Lixoúri

Lipedha

*Mégas
Lákkos*

Mantzavináta

Xi

*Cape
Akrotíri*

Koúnopetra

**Monastery
of Kipouréon**

Ayía Thékli

Petaní

▼ *Áyios Nikólaos (Zákynthos)*

▼ *Kyllíni*

5 km

0

973

For **airport** arrival see the Argostóli section on p.975. Kefaloniá's **bus** system is basic but expanding, and with a little legwork it can be used to get you almost anywhere on the island. Key routes connect Argostóli with the main tourist centres of **Sámi**, **Fiskárdho**, **Skála** and **Póros**. There's a useful connection from Sámi to the tiny resort of **Ayía Efimía**, which also attracts many package travellers. If you're using a motorbike, take care, as the terrain is very rough in places – although an increasing number of roads are being surfaced – and the gradients can sometimes be a bit challenging for underpowered machines. The island has a plethora of **ferry** connections, principally from Fiskárdho to Lefkádha and Itháki, and from Sámi to Itháki, Pátra and Italy, as well as links from Argostóli and Póros to Kyllíni and Pessádha to Zákynthos.

Sámi and around

Most boats dock at the large and functional port town of **SÁMI**, built and later rebuilt near the south end of the Itháki straits, more or less on the site of ancient Sami. This was the capital of the island in Homeric times, when Kefaloniá was part of Ithaca's maritime kingdom: today the administrative hierarchy is reversed, Itháki being considered the backwater. With the only ferry link to Pátra, frequent connections to Itháki and direct links to Italy, the town is clearly preparing itself for a burgeoning future. The long sandy beach that stretches round the bay is quite adequate; 2km beyond ancient Sami, lies a fine pebble beach, **Andísami**.

The town has three big **hotels**: the *Sami Beach* (☎06740/22 802, ⓕ22 846, ⓔsamibeach@otenet.gr; ❾) and friendly *Athina Beach* (☎06740/23 066, ⓕ23 040; ❾), both actually situated at the far end of the beach in Karavómylos, and the *Pericles* (☎06740/22 780, ⓕ22 787; ❾), over 1km along the Argostóli road, which has extensive grounds, two pools and sports facilities. The best mid-range bet is the *Ionion* (☎06740/22 035; ❸), followed by the *Melissani* (☎ & ⓕ 06740/22 464; ❹), both behind the seafront; on the front itself the *Kastro* (☎06740/22 282, ⓕ23 004; ❹) is very comfortable. Both *períptera* on the quay offer rooms, as do a variety of private homes a few blocks back from the front. Sámi's **campsite**, *Camping Karavomilos Beach* (☎06740/22 480, ⓕ22 932), has over 300 well-shaded spaces, a taverna, shop and bar, and opens onto the beach. It is by far the better of the island's two official sites.

Sámi doesn't have a great many **tavernas** beyond those on the seafront; visitors tend to go to the slightly touristic *Adonis* or the *Dolphins*, but cheaper and more genuine choices are *Gorgona* and *O Faros*, both with a good selection of veg and meat dishes, including the famous local meat pie. Better still, head further towards the beach to the *Akroyiali*, where you can sample fresh seafood, succulent meat dishes and good local wine. The *Riviera* and *Aqua Marina* are the favourite **bars** in the evenings, while the best place for a snack breakfast or ice cream is *Captain Jimmy's*. The seafront Sami Center (☎06740/22 254) rents out **motorbikes** at fair rates.

The Dhrogaráti and Melissáni caves

Another good reason to stay in Sámi is its proximity to the Drogharáti and Melissáni caves; the former is 5km out of town towards Argostóli, the latter 3km north towards Ayía Efimía. A very impressive stalagmite-bedecked chamber, **Dhrogaráti** (April–Oct daily 8am–9pm; €3) is occasionally used for concerts thanks to its marvellous acoustics – Maria Callas once sang here. **Melissáni** (8am–sunset; €4.70) is partly submerged in brackish water, which,

THE IONIAN ISLANDS | Sámi and around

amazingly, emerges from an underground fault which leads the whole way under the island to a point near Argostóli. At that point, known as Katavóthres, the sea gushes endlessly into a subterranean channel – and, until the 1953 earthquake disrupted it – the current was used to drive sea mills. That the water, now as then, still ends up in the cave has been shown with fluorescent tracer dye. The beautiful textures and shades created by the light pouring through the collapsed roof of the cave make it a must.

Ayía Efimía

AYÍA EFIMÍA, 9km north of Sámi, is a friendly little fishing harbour popular with package operators, yet with no major developments. Its two drawbacks are its beaches – the largest, Paradise beach, is around 20m of shingle, although there are other coves to the south – and its poor transport connections (only two daily buses to Sámi and Fiskárdho). **Accommodation** here is good at two small, smart **hotels**: *Pyllaros* (℡06740/61 800, ℻61 801; ❺) and the better-value *Moustakis* (℡ & ℻ 06740/61 030; ❹) or the apartments of Yerasimos Raftopoulos (℡06740/61 233, ℻61 216; ❹). The *Dendrinos* **taverna**, round the headland past the harbour, is the place for island cuisine; the *Pergola* also has a wide range of island specialities and standard Greek dishes. Predictably, the café-bar where the film crew and actors used to hang out has been renamed *Captain Corelli's*. The town's nightclub is *Paranoia*, 700m out of town towards Fiskárdho. The *Strawberry zaharoplastío* is the place for a filling breakfast.

Southeast Kefalloniá

Travel **southeast from Sámi** has been made a lot easier by the completion of the asphalt road to **Póros** and the consequent addition of a twice-daily bus route between the two. Another route links Póros to **Skála** along the recently paved coastal road.

Póros

PÓROS was one of the island's earliest developed resorts, and definitely gives the impression of having seen better days. The town's small huddle of hotels and apartment blocks is almost unique on Kefalloniá, and not enhanced by a scruffy seafront and thin, pebbly beach.

Póros does, however, have a regular ferry link to **Kyllíni** on the mainland, a viable alternative to Sámi–Pátra. Póros is actually made up of two bays: the first, where most tourists are based, and the actual harbour, a few minutes over the headland. There's plenty of rooms, apartments and a few **hotels**. The best deal is at the cosy *Santa Irina* (℡06740/72 017, ℻72 117, ✉maki@otenet.gr; ❸), by the crossroads inland, while the nearby *Odysseus Palace* (℡06740/72 036, ℻72 148; ❺) often gives good discounts. The *Kefalos* (℡06740/72 139; ❹) has en-suite rooms on the seafront. Among **travel agents**, Poros Travel by the ferry dock (℡06740/72 476, ℻72 069) offers a range of accommodation, as well as services such as car rental and ferry bookings. The main seafront has the majority of the **restaurants** and **bars**. The *Fotis Family* taverna serves good food in a pleasant setting and the *Mythos* café has internet access. At night, however, the old port is quieter and has more atmosphere, with tavernas such as *Tzivas* and the *Dionysus*, which are strong on local seafood.

The aforementioned road twists 12km around the rocky coastline from Póros to Skála at the southern extremity of the island. It's a lovely, isolated route, with scarcely a building on the way, save for a small chapel, 3km short of Skála, next to the ruins of a **Roman temple**.

Skála

In total contrast to Póros, the resort of **SKÁLA** is a low-rise development set among handsome pines above a few kilometres of good sandy beach. A **Roman villa** and some mosaics were excavated here in the 1950s, near the site of the *Golden Beach Palace* rooms, and are open daily to the public.

Its faithful return crowd keep Skála busy until well after Póros has closed for the season, and accommodation can be hard to find. There are studios and apartments at *Dionysus Rooms* (☎06710/83 283; ❸), a block south of the high street, and rooms can be found at the *Golden Beach Palace* (☎06710/83 327; ❹) above the beach or through Etam Travel Service (☎06710/83 101, ℗83 142). The more upmarket *Tara Beach Hotel* (☎06710/83 250, ℗83 344, ℮tarabeach@tarabeach.gr; ❻) has rooms and individual bungalows in lush gardens on the edge of the beach. Skála boasts a number of good **restaurants**: the *Pines*, the *Flamingo*, and, on the beach, the *Paspalis* and *Sunset*. Drinkers head for *The Loft* cocktail **bar** and the beachside *Pikiona* pool-bar.

Skála to Lourdháta

Some of the finest sandy beaches on the island are just beyond Skála below the village of Ratzákli, and around the growing microresort of **KÁTO KATELIÓS**, which already has a couple of hotels: the smart *Odyssia* (☎06710/81 615, ℗81 614; ❻) and the *Galini Resort* (☎06710/81 582, ℮niko-P-@hotmail.com; ❺), which has good deals on **apartments** for four. There are also some rooms and apartments available through the *Lighthouse* taverna (☎06710/81 355; ❷) and *Jimmy's* (☎06710/81 363; ❹). Of the half a dozen restaurants and cafés at the seafront, the *Blue Sea* taverna is renowned for the freshness and quality of its fish, the *Arbouro* offers a wide selection of dishes, while the *Cozy* bar is the prime drinking location. The coast around Káto Kateliós is also Kefaloniá's key breeding ground for the loggerhead **turtle** (see box, p.987). Camping on the nearby beaches is discouraged.

The inland village of **MARKÓPOULO**, claimed by some to be the birthplace of homophonous explorer Marco Polo, witnesses a bizarre snakehandling ritual every year on August 15, the **Assumption of the Virgin festival**. The church where this ritual is enacted stands on the site of an old convent. The story goes that when the convent was attacked by pirates, the nuns prayed to be transformed into snakes to avoid being taken prisoner. Their prayers were supposedly answered, and each year the "return" of a swarm of small, harmless snakes is meant to bring the villagers good luck. As Mother Nature is unlikely to keep to such a schedule, some discreet snake-breeding on the part of the village priests must be suspected.

The coastline is largely inaccessible until the village of **VLAHÁTA**, which has some rooms and restaurants, but there's little point in staying up here, when you can turn 2km down to **LOURDHÁTA**, which has a kilometre-long shingle beach, mixed with imported sand. *Adonis* (☎06710/31 206; ❹) and *Ramona* (☎06710/31 032; ❸) have **rooms** just outside the village on the approach road, while the one **hotel**, the *Lara* (☎06710/31 157, ℗31 156, ℮larab@hol.gr; ❺), towards the beach, has en-suite rooms with sea views and a pool. There's a couple of **tavernas** on the tiny plane-shaded village square – *Alexia's* and the *Diamond* – as well as the smarter *Spiros* steak and grill house above and *Dionysus*, closer to Vlaháta, while at the beach itself *Mangas* is good, if a little costly. The beachside *Astrabar* is friendly and plays a good mix of English and Greek music into the wee hours. Another fine beach, reached by a turning from Moussáta, west of Vlaháta, is **Trapezáki**, an attractive strand with just one restaurant by the small jetty.

Argostóli and around

ARGOSTÓLI, Kefalloniá's capital, is a large and thriving town, virtually a city, with a marvellous site on a bay within a bay. The stone bridge, connecting the two sides of the inner bay, was initially constructed by the British in 1813. A small obelisk remains, but the plaque commemorating "the glory of the British Empire" has disappeared. The town was totally rebuilt after the earthquake, but has an enjoyable streetlife that remains defiantly Greek, especially during the evening *vólta* around **Platía Metaxá** – the nerve centre of town – and along the pedestrianized Lithóstrotou, which runs parallel to the seafront.

The **Korgialenio History and Folklore Museum** (Mon–Sat 9am–2pm; €3), on Ilía Zervoú behind the Municipal Theatre, has a rich collection of local religious and cultural artefacts, including photographs taken before and after the 1953 quakes. Insight into how the island's nobility used to live can be gained from a visit to the new **Focas-Cosmetatos Foundation**, on Valianoú opposite the provincial government building. It contains elegant furniture and a collection of lithographs and paintings, including works by nineteenth-century British artists Joseph Cartwright and Edward Lear. The newly refurbished **Archeological Museum** (Tues–Sun 8.30am–3pm; €1.50), on nearby R. Vergóti, has a sizeable collection of pottery, jewellery, funerary relics and statuary from prehistoric, through Mycenaean to late Classical times. It is well laid out and labelled, rivalling Kérkyra Town's (see p.947) as the best such museum in the Ionians.

Practicalities

Argostóli's shiny new **Kefalloniá airport** lies 7km south of town. There are no airport buses, and suburban bus services are so infrequent or don't go close enough that a taxi (at an inflated flat rate of around €10) is the only dependable connection. Those arriving in Argostóli by bus from Sámi or elsewhere will wind up at the KTEL **bus station**, a minute from the Dhrápano causeway and ten-minutes' walk south of the main square, Platía Metaxá. Argostóli's friendly **tourist office** (summer Mon–Fri 7.30am–2.30pm & 5–10pm, Sat 9am–1pm; rest of year Mon–Fri 7.30am–2.30pm; ℡06710/22 248, ℻24 466), on Andoníou Trítsi at the north end of the seafront, next to the port authority, has information about rooms, piles of brochures and trail guides, and can advise on transport, sites and all resorts around the island. The islandwide Sunbird agency (℡06710/23 723, ℻25 484) is a reliable outlet for car or motorbike rental. Excelixis (℡06710/25 530) at Minoos 3, behind the church on Lithóstrotou, has internet facilities.

Hotels around Platía Metaxá stay open all year, but tend to be pricey: the best bet here is the *Ionian Plaza* (℡06710/25 581, ℻25 585; ❺). A good mid-range option away from the square is the *Fokas*, Yeroulánou 1–3 (℡06710/22 566, ℻23 109; ❹), while the partly British-run *Mouikis*, Výronos 3 (℡06710/23 454, ℻24 528, ✉hotel@mouikis.com; ❻) is classy but not cheap; one of the best deals going, if you don't mind sharing a bathroom, is the friendly *Chara* (℡06710/22 427; ❶), set in a lovely shady courtyard at the corner of G.Vergóti and Dhevossétou near Dhrápano bridge. The newly upgraded pension attached to the *Tsima Cavo* cafeteria (℡06710/23 941; ❸), opposite the Lixoúri ferry ramp, is good value, with TV in all the air-conditioned rooms. In a working town with a large permanent population, **private rooms** aren't too plentiful, but you can call the Roomowners Association (℡06710/29 109) to see what's on offer. Some of the best bargains can be found through waterfront tavernas, such as the *Kalafatis* (℡06710/22 627; ❷–❹), not far from the Dhrápano bridge on the Metaxá waterfront or the *Tzivras* (℡06710/24 259; ❶–❷), on Vandórou, just off the centre of the waterfront. A number of travel agencies also offer rooms, apartments and villas: try Ainos Travel (☎06710/22 333, ⓕ24 608), opposite the Archeological Museum, or Myrtos at A. Trítsi 117 (☎06710/25 895, ⓕ24 230, ⓔMyrtostr@compulink.gr; ❸–❺). The town's **campsite**, *Argostóli Camping* (☎06710/23 487), lies 2km north of the centre, just beyond the Katovóthres sea mills; there's only an infrequent bus service in high season, so you'll probably have to walk and it's rather basic and limited in shade.

The aforementioned *Tzivras Estiatório* (only open until 5pm) is one of the best places to try Kefallonian cuisine; the upmarket *Captain's Table* **taverna** just off the main square is worth a splurge for its live *kantádhes*, though they can just about as easily be heard from the far more reasonable *To Steki* next door. Of the seafront eateries, the *Maistrato* ouzerí near the square has a good selection of seafood and mezédhes and also features gentle live music. For a change of diet, try the *Queen Vic*, 50m towards the front from the square, a non-tacky British pub, serving excellent Indian food in the garden. Local posers hang out at *Central* café-bar and the *Flonitiko* café, both on the square, and the nearby *My Way* club-bar; the *Space Girls* bar, round the corner from *My Way*, is rather more esoteric and *Cinema* is a late-night indoor disco by the museum. The quay bars, particularly the *Aristofanis* kafenío by the Dhrápano bridge, are quiet, cheap and have the best views.

South of Argostóli: beaches and Áyios Yeóryios

Many package travellers will find themselves staying in **LÁSSI**, a short bus ride or twenty-minute walk from town. Lássi sprawls unattractively along a busy main road, but it does have good sandy beaches, particularly at **Makrýs Yialós** and **Platýs Yialós**, although they're right under the airport flight path. **Beaches** such as **Ávythos** are well worth seeking out, although if you're walking beyond **Kourkomeláta** there is a real if occasional risk of being attacked by farm dogs, particularly during the hunting season (Sept 25–Feb 28). There is very little accommodation in the region, and precious few shops or bars. **Pessádha** has a twice-daily ferry link with Zákynthos in summer, but little else, and be warned that the pathetic bus service from Argostóli is no good for connecting with the boats. You'll have to hitch or take an expensive taxi in most cases.

With a scooter, the best inland excursion is to **ÁYIOS YEÓRYIOS**, the medieval Venetian capital of the island. The old town here supported a population of 15,000 until its destruction by an earthquake in the seventeenth century: substantial ruins of its **castle** (Tues–Sat 8am–8pm, Sun 8am–2pm; €1.50), now reopened after extensive renovations, churches and houses can be visited on the hill above the modern village of Peratáta. Byron lived for a few months in the nearby village of Metaxáta and was impressed by the view from the summit in 1823; sadly, as at Messolóngi, the house where he stayed no longer exists. Two kilometres south of Áyios Yeóryios is a fine collection of religious icons and frescoes kept in a restored church that was part of the nunnery of Áyios Andhréas.

Mount Énos

At 15km from a point halfway along the Argostóli–Sámi road, **Mount Énos** isn't really a walking option, but roads nearly reach the official 1632-metre summit. The mountain has been declared a national park, to protect the *Abies cephalonica* firs (named after the island) which clothe the slopes. There are absolutely no facilities on or up the mountain, but the views from the highest point in the Ionian islands out over its neighbours and the mainland are wonderful. In low season, watch the weather, which can deteriorate with terrifying speed. Not far before the mountain turning, taking a detour towards Frangáta is doubly rewarded by the huge and lively **Áyios Yerásimos**

monastery, which hosts two of the island's most important festivals (Aug 15 and Oct 20), and right behind it the **Robola winery** (8am–8pm in summer), which offers a free self-guided tour and generous wine-tasting.

Lixoúri

Half-hourly ferries (hourly in winter) ply between the capital and **LIXOÚRI** throughout the day until midnight. The town was flattened by earthquakes, and hasn't risen much above two storeys since. It's a little drab, but has good restaurants, quiet hotels and is favoured by those who want to explore the eerie quakescapes left in the south and the barren north of the peninsula. **Hotels** are not especially plentiful or cheap, but two comfortable air-conditioned options are the *La Cité* (☎06710/92 701, ℱ92 702; ❹), four blocks back from the front, and a beach hotel just south of town, *Summery* (☎06710/91 771, ℱ91 062; ❹). Two agencies offer cheaper accommodation in town: A. D. Travel (☎06710/93 142, ℱ92 663; from ❶) on the main road through town, and Perdikis Travel (☎06710/91 097, ℱ92 503; from ❸) on the quay. Among the tavernas, *Akrogiali* on the seafront is excellent and cheap, drawing admirers from all over the island. *Iy Avli*, on the block behind, serves a variety of dishes in a leafy garden, while *Adonis* is a good basic *psistariá* at the back of the square. *Adagio* is the trendy place to drink on the square, but the seafront has a couple of much more genuine *kafenía*.

Lixoúri's nearest beach is **Lípedha**, a two-kilometre walk south. Like the **Xí** and **Mégas Lákkos** beaches (served by bus from Lixoúri and both with restaurants and accommodation), it has rich-red sand and is backed by low cliffs. Those with transport can also strike out for the monastery at **Kipouréon**, and north to the spectacular beach at **Petaní**, where there are two reasonable restaurants, the further of which, *Xougras*, should have rooms by 2002, courtesy of Greek-American Dina (☎06710/97 128; ❸), and should make a tremendous place for a relaxed stay.

The west coast and the road north

The journey between Argostóli and Fiskárdho, by regular bus or rented vehicle, is the most spectacular ride in the archipelago. Leaving town, the road rises into the Evmorfía foothills and, beyond Agónas, clings to near-sheer cliffs as it heads for Dhiваráta, which has a smattering of rooms and is the stop for **Mýrtos beach**. It's a four-kilometre hike down on foot (you can also drive down), with just one taverna on the beach, but from above or below this is the most dramatic beach in the Ionian islands – a splendid strip of pure-white sand and pebbles. Sadly, it's shadeless and gets mighty crowded in high season.

Six kilometres on is the turning for the atmospheric village of **ÁSSOS**, clinging to a small isthmus between the island and a huge hill crowned by a ruined fort. Accommodation is scarce – villagers invariably send you to Andhreas Rokos' rooms (☎06740/51 523; ❶) on the approach road, which are great value, or you can opt for the posher *Kanakis Apartments* opposite (☎06740/51 631, ℱ51 660; ❺). Ássos has a small pebble beach, and three tavernas, notably the *Nefeli* and the *Platanos Grill*, on a plane-shaded village square backed by mansions, mostly now restored after being ruined in the quake. It can get a little claustrophobic, but there's nowhere else like it in the Ionian islands.

Fiskárdho

FISKÁRDHO, on the northernmost tip of the island, sits on a bed of limestone that buffered it against the worst of the quakes. Two **lighthouses**, Venetian and Victorian, guard the bay, and the ruins on the headland are believed to be from a twelfth-century chapel begun by Norman invader

Robert Guiscard, who gave the place his name. The nineteenth-century harbour frontage is intact, nowadays occupied by smart restaurants and chic boutiques. There is a small new **Environmental and Nautical Museum**, with free entry but erratic opening hours, near the quay.

The island's premier resort, Fiskárdho is very busy through to the end of October, with accommodation at a premium. The cheapest rooms are those of Sotiria Tselenti (☎06740/41 204; ❸), 50m back from the tiny square, followed by *Regina's* (☎06740/41 125; ❸) with its own café at the back of the village, next to the car park. *Theodora's Café Bar* has rooms in whitewashed houses on the quay (☎06740/41 297; ❸), and another reasonable option is the small *Erissos* pension (☎06740/41 327; ❹), just off the seafront. Pama Travel (☎06740/41 033, ☎41 032), on the seafront furthest away from the ferry quay, is another source of rooms and costlier apartments. There's a wealth of good restaurants. Two to try on the seafront are the *Tassia,* which has a vast range of seafood, and the *Captain's Table,* serving succulent Greek and Kefallonian fare. On the sqaure, *Alexis* serves pizzas and pastas, while *Lagoudera,* just off the square, specializes in tasty oven food. *Sirenes,* on the seafront, near the square, is the favoured bar, although the seafront kafenío's mezédhes are the finest to be had anywhere. The dance spot is *Kastro Club* up at the back of the village. There are two good pebble beaches – **Émblisi** 1km back out of town and **Fókis** just to the south – and a nature trail on the northern headland. Daily **ferries** connect Fiskárdho to Itháki and Lefkádha in season.

Itháki

Rugged **Itháki**, Odysseus's legendary homeland, has yielded no substantial archeological discoveries, but it fits Homer's description to perfection: "There are no tracks, nor grasslands . . . it is a rocky severe island, unsuited for horses, but not so wretched, despite its small size. It is good for goats." In Constantine Cavafy's splendid poem *Ithaca*, the island is symbolized as a journey to life:

> *When you set out on the voyage to Ithaca*
> *Pray that your journey may be long*
> *Full of adventures, full of knowledge.*

Despite the romance of its name, and its proximity to Kefalloniá, very little tourist development has arrived to spoil the place. This is doubtless accounted for in part by a dearth of beaches, though the island is good walking country, with a handful of small fishing villages and various pebbly coves to swim from. In the north, apart from the ubiquitous drone of scooters, the most common sounds are sheep bells jangling and cocks (a symbol of Odysseus) crowing.

Its beaches are minor, mainly pebbly with sandy seabeds, but relatively clean and safe; the real attractions are the interior and sites from the **Odyssey**. Some package travellers will find themselves flying into Kefalloniá and being bused to Fiskárdho (sit on the left for the bus ride of your life), for a short ferry crossing to **Fríkes** or the premier resort **Kióni**. Most visitors, however, will arrive at **Vathý**, the capital.

Vathý

Ferries from Pátra, Astakós and a minority of those from Kefalloniá land at the main port and capital of **VATHÝ** (Itháki Town), a bay within a bay so deep that few realize the mountains out "at sea" are actually the north of the island. This snug town is compact, relatively traffic-free and boasts the most idyllic seafront setting of all the Ionian capitals. Like its southerly neighbours, it was damaged by the 1953 earthquake, but some fine examples of pre-quake architecture remain here and in the northern port of **Kióni**. Vathý has a small **archeological museum** on Odhós Kalliníkou (Tues–Sun 8am–2.30pm; free), a short block back from the quay. There are banks, a post office, police and a medical centre in town.

Vathý now has three **hotels**: the old but air-conditioned *Mentor* (℡06740/32 433, ℻32 293; ❺) at the left end of the seafront, the newer *Omirikon* (℡06740/33 598, ℻33 596; ❻) further on round the bay, and much better-value *Captain Yiannis* (℡06740/33 173, ℻32 849; ❹), complete with pool. Room owners meet ferries until the end of the season, but you can also call ahead to Vassiliki Vlassopoulou (℡06740/32 119; ❸), whose rooms are in pleasant gardens by the church above the quay. The town's two main quayside travel agents, Polyctor Tours (℡06740/33 120, ℻33 130, ✉polyctor@otenet.gr) and Delas Tours (℡06740/32 104, ℻33 031, ✉delas@otenet.gr) both offer a range of accommodation throughout the island.

Even though it's tiny, Vathý has a wealth of **tavernas** and **bars**. Many locals head off south around the bay towards *Gregory's*, popular for its lamb and fish, and the more traditional *Tziribis* and *O Vrachos*. In town, the excellent *O Nikos* fills early, while *To Kohili* is the best of the half-dozen harbourside tavernas. The *Sirenes Ithaki Yacht Club* is upmarket with a nautical theme, but as usual the town's ancient kafenío one street back from the front is the spot for a quiet and inexpensive tipple with the locals.

There are two reasonable pebble **beaches** within fifteen-minutes' walk of Vathý: **Dhéxa**, over the hill above the ferry quay, and tiny **Loútsa**, opposite it around the bay. Better beaches at **Sarakíniko** and **Skhinós** to the south are an hour's trek along recently improved roads leaving the opposite side of the bay. In season, daily kaïkia ply between the quay and remote coves.

Odysseus sights

Three of the main **Odysseus** sights are just within walking distance of Vathý: the Arethoússa Spring, the Cave of the Nymphs and ancient Alalkomenae, although the last is best approached by **bus** or **taxi** (no more than €12 round-trip).

The Arethóussa Spring

The walk to the **Arethóussa Spring** – allegedly the place where Eumaeus, Odysseus's faithful swineherd, brought his pigs to drink – is a three-hour round trip along a track signposted next to the seafront OTE. The unspoiled landscape and sea views are magnificent, but the walk crosses slippery inclines and might best be avoided if you're nervous of heights. The route is shadeless, so take a hat and plenty of water.

Near the top of the lane leading to the spring path, a signpost points up to what is said to have been the **Cave of Eumaeus**. The route to the spring continues for a few hundred metres, and then branches off onto a narrow footpath through gorse-covered steep cliffs. Parts of the final downhill track involve scrambling across rock fields (follow the splashes of green paint), and care should be taken around the small but vertiginous ravine that houses the **spring**. The spring is sited at the head of a small ravine below a crag known as **Korax** (the raven), which matches Homer's description of the meeting between Odysseus and Eumaeus. In summer it's just a dribble of water.

The spring is a dead end – the only way out is back the way you came. If weather and time allow, you might swim in a small cove a short scramble down from the spring. If you're uneasy about the gradients involved, it's still worth continuing along the track that runs above it, which loops round and heads back into the village of **Perahóri** above Vathý, which has views as far as Lefkádha to the north. On the way, you'll pass **Paleóhora**, the ruined medieval capital abandoned centuries ago, but with vestiges of houses fortified against pirate attacks and some churches still with Byzantine frescoes.

The Cave of the Nymphs

The **Cave of the Nymphs** (Marmarospíli) is about 2.5km up a rough but navigable road signposted on the brow of the hill above Dhéxa beach. The cave is atmospheric, but it's underwhelming compared to the caverns of neighbouring Kefalloniá, and these days is illuminated by coloured lights. The claim that this is the *Odyssey*'s Cave of the Nymphs, where the returning Odysseus concealed the gifts given to him by King Alcinous, is enhanced by the proximity of Dhéxa beach, although there is some evidence that the "true" cave was just above the beach, and was unwittingly demolished during quarrying many years ago.

Alalkomenae and Pisaetós

Alalkomenae, Heinrich Schliemann's much-vaunted "Castle of Odysseus", is signposted on the Vathý–Pisaetós road, on the saddle between Dhéxa and Pisaetós, with views over both sides of the island. The actual site, however, some 300m uphill, is little more than foundations spread about in the gorse. Schliemann's excavations unearthed a Mycenaean burial chamber and domestic items such as vases, figurines and utensils (displayed in the archeological museum), but the ruins actually date from three centuries after Homer. In fact, the most likely contender for the site of Odysseus's castle is above the village of Stavrós (see below).

The road (though not buses) continues to the harbour of **Pisaetós**, about 2km below, with a large pebble beach that's good for swimming and popular with local rod-and-line fishermen. There is just one *kantína* here serving the regular ferries from Sámi on Kefalloniá.

Northern Ithàki

The main road out of Váthy continues across the isthmus and takes a spectacular route to the northern half of Ithàki, serving the villages of **Léfki**, **Stavrós**, **Fríkes** and **Kióni**. There are only two daily **buses**, though the north of Ithàki is excellent scooter country; the close proximity of the settlements, small coves and Homeric interest also make it good rambling country. Once a day a kaïki also visits the last two of those communities – a cheap and scenic ride used by locals and tourists alike to meet the mainline ferries in Vathý. As with the rest of Ithàki there is only a limited amount of accommodation.

Stavrós and around

STAVRÓS, the second-largest town on the island, discounting Perahóri, is a steep two kilometres above the nearest beach (Pólis Bay). It's a pleasant enough town nonetheless, with kafenía edging a small square dominated by a rather fierce statue of Odysseus. There is even a tiny **museum** (Tues–Sun 9.30am–2.30pm; free) off the road to Platrithiás, displaying local archeological finds. Stavrós's Homeric site is on the side of **Pelikáta Hill**, where remains of roads, walls and other structures have been suggested as the possible site of Odysseus's castle. Stavrós is useful as a base if both Fríkes and Kióni are full up, and is an obvious stopping-off point for exploring the northern hamlets and the road up to the medieval village of Anoyí (see below). Both Polyctor and Delas handle **accommodation** in Stavrós; the traditional *Petra* taverna (℡06740/31 596; ❸) offers rooms, or there's the *Porto Thiaki* pension (℡06740/31 245, ℻31 638;❸) above the pizzeria. The oldest and best taverna is *Fatouros*, and the *Margarita zaharoplastío* is a good place for a drink or to sample the local sweet *rovaní* (syrupy rice cakes).

A scenic mountain road leads 5km southeast from Stavrós to **ANOYÍ**, which translates roughly as "upper ground". Once the second-most important settlement on the island, it is almost deserted today. The centre of the village is dominated by a free-standing Venetian campanile, built to serve the (usually locked) church of the **Panayía**, which comes alive for the annual *paniyíri* on August 14, the eve of the Virgin's Assumption; at other times enquire at the kafenío about access to the church, the Byzantine frescoes of which have been heavily restored following centuries of earthquake damage. On the outskirts of the village are the foundations of a ruined **medieval prison**, and in the surrounding countryside are some extremely strange rock formations, the biggest being the eight-metre-high Iraklís (Hercules) rock, just east of the village. The **monastery of Katharón**, 3km further south along the road, has stunning views down over Vathý and the south of the island, and houses an icon of the *Panayía* discovered by peasants clearing scrubland in the area. Byron is said to have stayed here in 1823, during his final voyage to Messolóngi. The monastery celebrates its festival on September 8 with services, processions and music.

Two roads push north of Stavrós: one, to the right, heads 2km down to Fríkes, while the main road, to the left, loops below the hill village of **Exoyí**, and on to **Platrithiás**. Just off the start of the road up to Exoyí a signpost points about 1km along a rough track to the supposed **School of Homer**, where excavations still in progress have revealed extensive foundations, a well and ancient steps. The site is unfenced and well worth a detour for its views of **Afáles Bay** as much as the remains. On the outskirts of Platrithiás a track leads down to Afáles, the largest bay on the entire island, with an unspoiled and little-visited pebble beach. The landscape around here, thickly forested in parts and dotted with vineyards, is excellent walking terrain.

Fríkes

At first sight, tiny **FRÍKES** doesn't appear to have much going for it. Wedged in a valley between two steep hills, it was only settled in the sixteenth century, and emigration in the nineteenth century almost emptied the place – as few as two hundred people live here today – but the protected harbour is a natural year-round port. Consequently, Fríkes stays open for tourism far later in the season than neighbouring Kióni, and has a better range of tavernas. There are no beaches in the village, but plenty of good, if small, pebble strands a short walk away towards Kióni. When the ferries and their cargoes have departed, Fríkes falls quiet and this is its real charm: a downbeat but cool place to lie low.

Fríkes' one **hotel** is the smart but pricey *Nostos* (℡06740/31 644, ℻31 716; ❺) or you can try the equally comfy *Aristotelis Apartments* (℡06740/31 079, ℻31 179; ❸). Kiki Travel (℡ & ℻06740/31 387; from ❷) has **rooms** and other accommodation, as do the adjacent souvenir shop (℡06740/31 735;❷) and *Ulysses* taverna (℡06740/31733; ❸). Phoning ahead is advisable and in peak season chances are slim. Fríkes has a quartet of good seafront **tavernas**: the *Symposium*, the *Rementzo*, the *Penelope* and aforementioned *Ulysses*. Tucked in the corner of the harbour, *Café Bemenis* often springs into life late at night as the north's main meeting place for youngsters.

Kióni

KIÓNI sits at a dead end 5km southeast of Fríkes. On the same geological base as the northern tip of Kefalloniá, it avoided the very worst of the 1953 earthquakes, and so retains some fine examples of pre-twentieth-century architecture. It's an extremely pretty village, wrapped around a tiny harbour, and tourism here is dominated by British blue-chip travel companies and visiting yachts.

The bay has a small **beach**, 1km along its south side, a sand and pebble strand below a summer-only snack bar. Better pebble beaches can be found within walking distance towards Fríkes. While the best **accommodation** has been snaffled by the Brits, some local businesses have rooms and apartments to let, among them *Captain's Apartments* (☎06740/31 481, ℱ31 090; ❹), K. Raftopulos (☎06740/31 654; ❸) and *Kioni Vacations* (☎06740/31 668; ❸). A quieter option, a short walk uphill on the main road in the hamlet of Ráhi, are the rooms and studios run by Captain Theofilos Karatzis and his family (☎06740/31 679; ❸), which have panoramic views.

Kióni's **restaurants** are dotted around the picturesque harbour, but compare unfavourably with those in Fríkes; *Mythos* has a wide selection and is the best of the bunch, the *Avra* fish taverna and *Kioni* pizzeria are adequate, while the upmarket *Calypso* taverna has interesting dishes but is overpriced. Village facilities stretch to two well-stocked shops, a post office and a couple of bars and cafés.

Zákynthos (Zante)

Zákynthos, southernmost of the six core Ionian islands, currently teeters between underdevelopment and indiscriminate commercialization. Much of the island is still green and unspoiled, but the development in some resorts is threatening to spill over into the quieter parts.

The island has three distinct zones: the barren, mountainous northwest; the fertile central plain; and the eastern and southern coasts which house the resorts. The big resort – rivalling the biggest on Corfu – is **Laganás**, on Laganás Bay in the south, a 24-hour party venue that doesn't give up from Easter until the last flight home in October. There are smaller, quieter resorts north and south of the capital, and the southerly Vassilikós peninsula has the best countryside and beaches, including exquisite **Yérakas**.

Although half-built apartment blocks are spreading through the central plain, this is where the quieter island begins: farms and vineyards, ancient villages and the ruins of Venetian buildings levelled in the 1948 and 1953 earthquakes. The island still produces fine wines, such as the white Popolaro, as well as sugar-shock-inducing *mandoláto* nougat, whose honey-sweetened form is best. Zákynthos is also the birthplace of *kantádhes*, the hybrid of Cretan folk song and Italian opera ballad that can be heard in tavernas in Zákynthos Town and elsewhere. It also harbours one of the key breeding sites of the endangered **loggerhead sea turtle** at Laganás Bay. The loggerhead (see box on p.987) is the subject of a continuing dispute between tourism businesses and environmentalists, which has caused an international political scandal and even provoked a bomb attack against the environmentalists.

Zákynthos Town

The town, like the island, is known as both **ZÁKYNTHOS** and Zante. This former "Venice of the East" (*Zante, Fior di Levante*, "Flower of the Levant", in

ZÁKYNTHOS

Shipwreck Bay

Anafonítria
Anafonítria
Volímes
Mount
Astéri
583m
Cape Skinári

Blue
Caves

Áyios
Nikólaos

Skinári
Makrýs
Yialós

Xyngiá

Stenítis
Bay
Mariés

Alykés

Alykón Bay

N

Kambí
Éxo Hóra
Mount
Vrahiónas
756m
Katastári

Alikanás

Dhrossiá

Yerakári
Ayía
Marína
Tragáki
Pahiá Ámmos

Áyios Léon

Limniónas

Kilioméno
Mount
Athéras
Maherádho

Tsiliví

Plános

Vanáto

Bóhali

ZÁKYNTHOS

Megálo
Vounó

Limní
Kerioú
Laganás
Argássi

Kerí
Kalamáki
Mount
Kakavakia
413m
Mount
Skopós
492m

Marathiá
Caves

Marathoníssi

Dháfni
Pórto Zóro

Áno Vassilikós
Banana
Peloúzo
Áyios
Nikólaos
Yérakas
Pórto Róma

0   5 km

Pessádha (Kefalloniá)

Kyllíni

an Italian jingle), rebuilt on the old plan, has bravely tried to re-create some of its style, though reinforced concrete can only do so much.

The town stretches beyond the length of the wide and busy harbour, its main section bookended by the grand **Platía Solomoú** at the north, and the church of **Áyios Dhionýsios**, patron saint of the island, at the south. The church is well worth a visit for the dazzling giltwork and fine modern murals inside, and a new **museum**, which has some fine paintings and icons (daily 8.30am–11pm; €0.90). The vestments of Saint Dhionýsios are kept in the restored church of Áyios Nikólaos tou Mólou on Platía Solomoú. The square is named after the island's most famous son, the poet Dhionysios Solomos, the father of modernism in Greek literature, who was responsible for establishing demotic Greek (as opposed to the elitist *katharévousa* form) as a literary idiom. He is also the author of the lyrics to the national anthem, an excerpt from which adorns the statue of Liberty in the square. There's an impressive **museum** (daily 9am–2pm; €2.35) devoted to the life and work of Solomos and other Zakynthian luminaries in nearby Platía Ayíou Márkou. It shares its collection with the museum on Corfu (see p.945), where Solomos spent most of his life. Another local man of letters, who had a museum dedicated to him by the town council in 1998, is novelist and playwright **Grigorios Xenopoulos**. His eponymous museum (Mon–Fri 9am–2pm; free), which occupies the small house he inhabited in Gaïta street, not far from Áyios Dhionýsios church, displays a modest collection of manuscripts, books and photographs, as well as the house's original furniture.

Platía Solomoú is home to the town's **library**, which has a small collection of pre- and post-quake photography, and the massive **Zákynthos Museum** (Tues–Sun 8am–2.30pm; €2.35), sometimes referred to as the Byzantine Museum, most notable for its collection of artworks from the Ionian School, the region's post-Renaissance art movement, spearheaded by Zakynthian painter Panayiotis Doxaras. The movement was given impetus by Cretan refugees, unable to practise under Turkish rule. It also houses some secular painting and a fine model of the town before the earthquake.

Zákynthos's other main attraction is its massive **kástro**, brooding over the hamlet of Bóhali on its bluff above the town. The ruined Venetian fort (daily 8am–7.30pm in summer, 8am–2pm in winter; €1.50) has vestiges of dungeons, armouries and fortifications, plus stunning views in all directions. Its shady carpet of fallen pine needles makes it a great spot to relax or picnic. Below the *kástro* walls, **Bóhali** has a couple of good though expensive tavernas, some hosting nightly *kantádhes*, although Zakynthian driving habits make the thirty-minute walk from town a risky business after dark. The ugly new **amphitheatre** on the road up from town sometimes hosts concerts. Further towards the *kástro* the **Maritime Museum** (daily 9.30am–2.30pm & 6.30–10.30pm; €2.35) contains plenty of naval paraphernalia and presents an interesting chronological history of Hellenic seafaring.

⑫

Boat trips from Zákynthos

At least ten pleasure craft offer **day-trips** around the island from the quay in Zákynthos town for €9–15. All take in sights such as the **Blue Caves** at Cape Skinári, and moor in **Tó Naváyio (Shipwreck Bay)** and the **Cape Kerí** caves. You might want to shop around for the trip with the most stops, as eight hours bobbing round the coast can become a bore. Check also that the operators actually take you into the caves.

Practicalities

Zákynthos is a working town with limited concessions to tourism, although there are hotels and restaurants aplenty, and it's the only place to stay if you want to see the island by public transport. The **bus** station is one block back from the seafront, about halfway along it. On the front nearby, the **tourist police** have a fairly welcoming office (daily 7.30am–9.30pm; ☎06950/27 367) in the main police station, which can supply basic information and help people find accommodation. The Roomowners Association (☎06950/49 498) can also be contacted for accommodation around town and all over the island. Of the central **hotels**, the *Egli*, on Loútzi (☎06950/28 317; ❸) is the bargain, tucked in beside the gargantuan and more expensive *Strada Marina* (☎06950/42 761, ℉28 733; ❺). There are quieter hotels in the Répara district beyond Platía Solomoú: try either the *Plaza* (☎06950/48 909, ℉45 733; ❺) or the classy *Palatino*, Kolokotróni 10 (☎06950/27 780, ℉45 400, ✉palatzak@otenet.gr; ❻), both near the municipal lido. Cheaper options at the back of town include the functional *Apollo*, Tertséti 30 (☎06950/42 838; ❸), opposite the post office, and the cosier *Haravyi* pension, Xanthopoúlou 4 (☎06950/23 629; ❷) further south. Most of the **restaurants** and bars on the seafront and Platía Ayíou Márkou are bedevilled by traffic, although the seafront *Psaropoula* does fine meat and fish, and the pricey but elegant *Komis*, across the quay from Áyios Dhionýsios, serves unusual seafood dishes and is far enough away from the bustle. First stop though, should be the friendly *Arekia* beyond the lido, which offers succulent taverna staples and nightly *kantádhes*. The neighbouring *Alivizos* also specializes in island cuisine and music, and the *Green Boat* further along serves up quality fare at a snip. When the bored teens get off their bikes, they go **clubbing** to bars like *Base* on Ayíou Márkou, which plays anything from Miles Davis to Philip Glass, or the *Jazz Café*, on Tertséti which, despite plundering the London jazz club's logo, is actually a techno bar with DJ and token cover charge.

The south and west

The road heading southeast from Zákynthos passes through **ARGÁSSI**, the busiest resort on this coast, but with a beach barely a few feet wide in parts. Although independent travellers would be better off basing themselves at one of the places further down, it could be used as a jumping-off point for the Vassilikós peninsula; there are rooms at the *Pension Vaso* (☎06950/44 599; ❸) and *Soula* (☎06950/44 864; ❸) just off the main road entering the village, and the seafront boasts some smart hotels, among them the *Locanda* (☎06950/45 386, ℉23 769; ❹) and the joint *Chryssi Akti/Paradise Beach* (☎06950/28 679, ℉28 699; ❺). Beyond a few indigenous tavernas – try *Three Brothers* or *The Big Plate* restaurant – culture is mainly low-brow with set-piece "Greek nights", one notable exception being the *Venetsiana*, which accompanies traditional food with nightly *kantádhes*. Argássi is also home to some of the island's biggest and most popular discos on the town side, such as *Vivlos* and *Barrage*, and a host of cheap and cheerful bars in the village.

The Vassilikós peninsula

The peninsula that stretches southeast of Argássi is one of the most attractive parts of the island, with a happy blend of development and natural beauty. Various maps vaguely identify different inland spots as **Vassilikós** villages, but the real interest lies in the series of small beach resorts, mainly situated on the east coast. The first two are recently developed **Kamínia**, with the comfortable *Levantino* rooms (☎ & ☎ 06950/35 366; ❹), and the more established **Pórto Zóro**, a better strand with the good-value eponymous hotel (☎06950/35 304, ☎35 087; ❹) and restaurant. The only real facilities away from the coast are to be found at the sprawling village of **Áno Vassilikós**, which serves the nearby beaches of **Iónio** and **Banana**. Among accommodation possibilities are the *Vassilikos Apartments* (☎06950/35 280; ❹), on the main road, and *Angelika* (☎06950/35 201; ❸), by the church just off it. Among the **tavernas**, on the main road, *O Adherfos tou Kosta* is well worth a try, as is the *Logos Rock Club*. Isolated **Áyios Nikólaos** has a good beach and lures day-trippers from Argássi, Kalamáki and Laganás with a **free bus** service in season; its expanding *Vasilikos Beach* (☎06950/35 325, ☎35 327, ✉stnicks@otenet.gr; ❺) complex is the focal point of a fast-emerging hamlet with a few restaurants and rooms – the neat white *Christina's* (☎06950/39 474; ❷) is one of the best deals on the island.

At the very tip of the peninsula is its star: **Yérakas**, a sublime crescent of golden sand. It's also a key loggerhead turtle breeding ground, and is therefore off-limits between dusk and dawn; the excellent open-air **Turtle Info Centre** provides interesting background on these and other sea creatures. Otherwise, there's little here beyond two tavernas back from the beach and some pleasant, if remote, cabin accommodation at *Liuba Apartments* (☎06950/35 372; ❸). The beach does draw crowds, but the 6am bus out of Zákynthos Town should secure you a few hours of Yérakas to yourself. Compared with Yérakas, **Pórto Róma**, back on the east coast, is a disappointment, a small sand-and-pebble bay with a taverna and bar, some rooms on the approach road and occasional hardy campers, although there is a more genuinely Greek flavour to it. Beaches on the west coast, like **Dháfni**, require your own transport and have few facilities, but are worth a visit, especially in the quieter months.

Laganás and Kalamáki

The majority of the 400,000 people or so who visit Zákynthos each year find themselves in **LAGANÁS**. The nine-kilometre beach in the bay is good, if trampled, and there are entertainments from watersports to ballooning, and even an occasional funfair. Beachfront bars and restaurants stretch for well over a kilometre, the bars and restaurants on the main drag another kilometre inland. Some stay open around the clock; others just play music at deafening volume until dawn. The competing video and music bars can make Laganás at night resemble the set of *Bladerunner*, but that's how its predominantly English visitors like it. If this is your bag, there's no place better; if it isn't, flee. **Accommodation** is mostly block-booked by package companies. There's a basic campsite on the southern edge of town, where there are also quietish private rooms, or you can contact the Union of Room Owners (daily 8.30am–2pm & 5–8pm; ☎06950/51 590). As for hotels, try the old-fashioned *Byzantio* (☎06950/51 136; ❸), near the crossroads, *Pension Tasoula* (☎06950/51 560; ❹), between the beach and the campsite, or the larger *Ionis* (☎06950/51 141, ☎51 601, ✉ionishtl@otenet.gr; ❺), on the main drag towards the beach. *Nefeli* and *Zougras* are among the more authentic **tavernas**, the former hosting nightly *kantádhes*, and respectable Chinese/Indian food can be had at *Bee Garden* or *Taj Mahal*. Favourite **bars** include *Kamikazi*, *Must*, *Potters Bar* and *Zeros* nightclub.

Neighbouring **KALAMÁKI** has a better beach than Laganás, and is altogether quieter, although both resorts suffer from airport noise. There are several sizeable, mostly package-oriented hotels, but the upmarket *Crystal Beach*

Loggerhead turtles

The Ionian islands harbour the Mediterranean's main concentration of **loggerhead sea turtles** (*Caretta caretta*). These creatures, which lay their eggs at night on sandy coves, are under direct threat from the tourist industry in Greece. Each year, many turtles are injured by motorboats, their nests are destroyed by bikes ridden on the beaches, and the newly hatched young die entangled in deckchairs and umbrellas left out at night on the sand. The turtles are easily frightened by noise and lights, too, which makes them uneasy cohabitants with freelance campers and late-night discos.

The Greek government has passed laws designed to protect the loggerheads, including restrictions on camping at some beaches, but local economic interests tend to prefer a beach full of bodies to a sea full of turtles.

On Laganás, nesting grounds are concentrated around the fourteen-kilometre bay, but Greek marine zoologists striving to protect and study the turtles are in angry dispute with locals and the burgeoning tourist industry. Other important locations include the turtles' nesting ground just west of Skála on Kefalloniá, although numbers have dwindled to half their former strength in recent years, and now only about 800 remain. Ultimately, the turtles' main hope of survival may rest in their being appreciated as a unique tourist attraction in their own right.

While capitalists and environmentalists are still at, well, loggerheads, the **World Wildlife Fund** has issued guidelines for visitors:

1. Don't use the beaches of Laganás and Yérakas between sunset and sunrise.
2. Don't stick umbrellas in the sand in the marked nesting zones.
3. Take your rubbish away with you – it can obstruct the turtles.
4. Don't use lights near the beach at night – they can disturb the turtles, sometimes with fatal consequences.
5. Don't take any vehicle onto the protected beaches.
6. Don't dig up turtle nests – it's illegal.
7. Don't pick up the hatchlings or carry them to the water, as it's vital to their development that they reach the sea on their own.
8. Don't use speedboats in Laganás Bay – a 9kph speed limit is in force for vessels in the bay.

(☎06950/42 788, ℱ42 917; ❻) keeps some rooms aside and the islandwide Spring Tours agency (☎06950/43 795) can also arrange accommodation. The two *Stanis* tavernas have extensive menus of Greek and international dishes, although the beachside version is geared more to lunches and its sibling more to evening meals. Alternatives include *Afrodite* and *Merlis* or the *Guru* curry house. **Nightlife** centres around bars like *Harvest* and *Down Under* on the Laganás road, and the *Cave Club* or *Vyzantio* discos on the hillside above the village, which play foreign and Greek dance music respectively.

Kerí

The village of **KERÍ** is hidden in a fold above the cliffs at the island's southernmost tip. The village retains a number of pre-quake, Venetian buildings, including the church of the **Panayía Kerioú**; the Virgin is said to have saved the island from marauding pirates by hiding it in a sea mist. Kerí is also famous for a geological quirk, a series of small tar pools mentioned by both Pliny and Herodotus, but these have mysteriously dried up in recent years. A rough path leaving the southern end of the village leads 1km on to the lighthouse, with spectacular views of the sea, rock arches and stacks and a taverna. The beach next to **Límni Kerioú** at the southwestern end of Laganás Bay has developed into a laid-back and picturesque resort and is home to the Turtle Beach Diving Centre (☎ & ℱ 06950/48 768). **Rooms** can be found at the friendly *Pension*

Limni (📞06950/48 716; ❸) or through the local Roomowners Association (📞 & 🅕 06950/45 105). For **food** there is the *Pirates of Kastello* overlooking the bay from the far end and the *Keri* restaurant, which has good daily specials.

Maherádho, Kilioméno and Kambí

The bus system does not reach the wild western side of the island, but a rental car or sturdy motorbike will get you there. **MAHERÁDHO** boasts impressive pre-earthquake architecture set in beautiful arable uplands, surrounded by olive and fruit groves. The church of **Ayía Mávra** has an impressive free-standing campanile, and inside a splendid carved iconostasis and icons by Zakynthian painter Nikolaos Latsis. The town's major festival – one of the biggest on the island – is the saint's day, which falls on the first Sunday in June. The other notable church in town, that of the Panayía, commands breathtaking views over the central plain.

KILIOMÉNO is the best place to see surviving pre-earthquake domestic architecture, in the form of the island's traditional two-storey houses. The town was originally named after its church, **Áyios Nikólaos**, whose impressive campanile, begun over a hundred years ago, still lacks a capped roof. The *Alitzerini* taverna still occupies a cave-like house that dates from 1630. The road from Kilioméno passes through the nondescript village of Áyios Léon, from where two turnings lead through fertile land and down a newly-paved loop road to the impressive rocky coast at **Limniónas**, where there is a tiny bay and a taverna.

Further along the main road another turning leads to the tiny clifftop hamlet of **KAMBÍ**, popular with day-trippers, who come to catch the sunset over the sea. And indeed, there are extraordinary views to be had of the 300-metre-high cliffs and western horizon from Kambí's three clifftop **tavernas**. The best of the three is named after the imposing concrete **cross** above the village, constructed in memory of islanders killed here during the 1940s, either by nationalist soldiers or Nazis. The tiny village of **Mariés**, 5km to the north and set in a wooded green valley, has the only other coastal access on this side of Zákynthos, a seven-kilometre track leading down to the rocky inlet of **Stenítis Bay**, where there's a taverna and yacht dock, and another road to the uninspiring **Vrómi Bay**, from where speedboats run trips to Shipwreck Bay (see below).

The north

North and inland from Zákynthos Town, the roads thread their way through luxuriantly fertile farmland, punctuated with tumulus-like hills. **Tsiliví**, 5km north of the capital, is the first beach resort here, which has now effectively merged with the hamlet of **PLÁNOS** and matches Argássi for development. Unfortunately, this part of the coastline suffers from occasional oil pollution, with nothing but the winter storms to clear it. There's a good, basic **campsite**, *Zante Camping* (📞06950/61 710), beyond Plános, and, for a prime package-tour location, a surprising variety of accommodation – try the beachside *Anetis Hotel* (📞06950/44 590, 🅕28 758; ❹), which has air-conditioning and TV in all rooms; *Gregory's* rooms (📞06950/61 853; ❸); or contact Tsilivi Travel (📞06950/44 194, 🅕22 655), on the inland road in from town. *The Olive Tree* taverna is the best of a touristy bunch, while the *Mandarin* Chinese is fairly authentic. Pubs such as *The Local* and *Red Lion* tend to be Brit-oriented.

The beaches further along this stretch of coast become progressively quieter and pleasanter, and they all have at least a smattering of accommodation and restaurants to choose from. Good choices include **Pahiá Ámmos**, with the

THE IONIAN ISLANDS | The north

Pension Petra (☎06950/61 175; ❸) and *Porto Roulis* fish taverna. Also recommended is **Dhrossiá**, where you can find the *Avouris* (☎06950/61 716; ❸) and *Drosia* apartments (☎06950/62 256; ❹) and eat at another popular fish taverna, *Andreas*.

Alykés and its bay

Ormós Alykón, 12km north of Tsiliví, is a large sandy bay with lively surf and two of the area's largest resorts. The first, **ALIKANÁS**, is a small but expanding village, much of its accommodation being overseas villa rentals; the second, **ALYKÉS**, named after the spooky salt pans behind the village, has the best beach north of the capital. There are **rooms** near the beach and a number of **hotels** set back from it, but with sea views – try the *Ionian Star* (☎06950/83 416, ☏83 173; ❹) or the *Montreal* (☎06950/83 241, ☏83 342, ✉montreal@montreal.gr; ❺), although the best deal is off the crossroads at the *Picadilly* (☎06950/83 606; ❷). There are many eating joints, among the best the *Anatolikos*, *Fantasia* and *Golden Dolphin* tavernas. Alykés is the last true resort on this coast, and the one where the bus service largely gives out. **Xyngiá** beach, 4km north, has sulphur springs flowing into the sea – follow the smell – which provide the odd sensation of swimming in a mix of cool and warm water. The next small beach of **Makrýs Yialós**, which has a good taverna, makeshift campsite and a diving school, also makes for an extremely pleasant break on a tour of the north.

Áyios Nikólaos, 6km on, is a small working port serving daily ferries to and from Pessádha on Kefalloniá. From here another good trip is a ride by **kaïki** (around €6) to the extreme northern tip of the island, where the **Blue Caves** are some of the more realistically named of the many contenders in Greece. They're terrific for snorkelling, and when you go for a dip here your skin will appear bright blue. The road snakes onwards through a landscape of gorse bushes and dry-stone walls until it ends at the lighthouse of **Cape Skinári**. With only a taverna and a cafeteria, and a view of the mountainous expanse of Kefalloniá, it's a good spot for unofficial camping, or you could stay in the unique setting of the converted windmill rented out by *Tò Faros* taverna (☎06950/31 132; ❹).

Katastári, Ayía Marína and Volímes

The northern towns and villages are accessible only to those with cars or sturdy motorbikes, and although there are guided coach tours from the resorts, none is really geared to tourism. Two kilometres inland from Alykés, **KATASTÁRI** is the largest settlement after the capital. Precisely because it's not geared towards tourism, it's the best place to see Zákynthian life as it's lived away from the usual racket. Its most impressive edifice is the huge rectangular church of Iperáyia Theotókos, with a twin belfry and small new amphitheatre for festival performances.

AYÍA MARÍNA, a few kilometres south of Katastári, has a church with an impressive Baroque altar screen, and a belfry that's being rebuilt from the remnants left after the 1953 earthquake. As in most Zákynthos churches, the bell tower is detached, in Venetian fashion. Just above Ayía Marína is the *Parthenonas* taverna, rightly boasting one of the best views on the island. From here you can see the whole of the central plain from beyond Alykés in the north to Laganás Bay in the south.

VOLÍMES is the centre of the island's embroidery industry – with your own transport, you could make it to the **Anafonítria monastery**, 3km south, thought to have been the cell of the island's patron saint, Dhionysios, whose festivals are celebrated on August 24 and December 17. A newly paved road leads on to the cliffs overlooking **Shipwreck Bay** (Tó Naváyio), with hair-raising views down to the shipwreck (a cargo ship which ran aground in the Sixties) and a taverna to recover your composure in.

Travel details

Corfu (Kérkyra)

There are 4 or 5 daily flights between Corfu and Athens (1hr), and 3 weekly except Sun to Thessaloníki (1hr). Several ferries (Port Authority ☎06610/32 655) per hour (5.15am–10pm) run between Corfu and Igoumenítsa (1hr 15min) in high season. Also 6 daily between Igoumenítsa and Lefkími (40min). Additionally, many ferries between Italy (Brindisi, Bari, Ancona and Venice) and Pátra stop at Corfu; stopover is free if specified in advance and there is no problem buying Corfu–Pátra tickets. Although there is only a twice-weekly ferry to Paxí, there are up to 5 hydrofoils daily in season, either direct (1hr) or via Igoumenítsa (1hr 30min). The twice-weekly (Wed & Sat) tour hydrofoil does sometimes take one-way passengers to Kefaloniá. Buses to Athens via the Igoumenítsa ferry depart 3 or 4 times daily, twice daily to Thessaloníki.

Eríkoussa, Mathráki and Othoní

A car ferry, the *Alexandros II*, runs from Kérkyra Town to all the islands 3 times weekly (Tues & Thurs 7.30am; Sun 9am) and to Othoní only on Sat (4pm). The ferry leaves from near the BP station on the seafront, midway between the Old and New Ports, although it involves sailing halfway round the island. Quicker access, favoured by islanders without vehicles, is via daily excursions from Sidhári or Áyios Stéfanos run by Nearchos Seacruises (☎06630/95 248).

Itháki (Ithaca)

Seasonal ferries from Fríkes to: Fiskárdho (Kefaloniá; 1 daily; 1hr); Nydhrí (Lefkádha; 1 daily; 1hr 45min). Pisaetós to: Sámi (Kefaloniá; 3 daily; 45min). Váthý to: Astakós (1 daily; 2hr 30min); Pátra (2 daily; 5hr); Sámi (Kefaloniá; 2 daily; 1hr). Off-season, there is 1 daily service on each route, weather permitting – check with Port Authority (☎06740/32 909).

Kefaloniá

1–2 daily flights to and from Athens (1hr). Ferries in season from Sámi to: Astakós (1 daily;

4hr); Pátra (4 daily;1hr 40min–2hr 30min); Pisaetós (Itháki; 3 daily; 45min); Vathý, (Itháki; 2 daily; 1hr). Also ferries from Póros to Kyllíni (3 daily; 1hr 15min). Fiskárdho to: Fríkes (Itháki; 1 daily; 1hr); Nydhrí (Lefkádha; 1 daily; 2hr 45min); Vassilikí (Lefkádha; 3 daily; 1hr 15min). Argostóli to: Kyllíni (2 daily; 2hr 30min); Lixoúri (every 30min; 20min). Pessádha to: Áyios Nikólaos (Zákynthos; 2 daily; 1hr 30min). Most routes maintain 1 daily service in winter – check with Port Authorities (Argostóli ☎06710/22 224; Sámi ☎06740/22 031; Póros ☎06740/72 460). The twice-weekly tour hydrofoils from Sámi to Corfu will usually take one-way passengers.
5 daily buses from Argostóli to Athens (6–7hr). 1 daily from Lixoúri, Póros and Sámi.

Lefkádha

5 buses daily to and from Athens (6–7hr), and 5 buses daily to the Áktio ferry (30min) for Préveza, passing Áktio airport (25min). 7 ferries daily in season from Nydhrí to Meganíssi; daily connections (several in summer and 1 all year) from Nydhrí or Vassilikí to Kefaloniá (Fiskárdho) and Itháki (Fríkes). The weekly cruise boat *Ikaros* will take one-way passengers to Párga or Paxí.

Paxí

Ferry connections to Paxí (Port Authority ☎06620/32 259) have stabilized in the last couple of years. To Corfu, there is a twice-weekly service throughout the year, plus up to 5 hydrofoils daily. There are 1–3 daily ferries to/from Igoumenítsa. In summer 2 kaïkia connect daily with Párga.

Zákynthos

Zákynthos Town to: Kyllíni (5 daily all year, up to 8 in season; 1hr 30min). Áyios Nikoláos to: Pessádha (Kefaloniá; 2 daily May–Sept; 1hr 30min).
Buses from Zákynthos Town to Athens (3–8 daily, according to season; 6hr).
Flight (on Olympic) from Zákynthos Town to Athens (1–2 daily; 1hr).

contexts

contexts

CONTEXTS

The historical framework

This section is intended to lend some perspective to travels in Greece, and is heavily weighted towards the era of the modern, post-independence nation. More detailed accounts of particular periods are to be found in relevant sections of the guide.

Neolithic, Minoan and Mycenaean ages

Other than the solitary discovery of a fossilized Neanderthal skull near Thessaloníki, the earliest evidence of **human settlement** in Greece is to be found at Néa Nikomedhía, near Véria. Here, traces of large, rectangular houses dated to around 6000 BC have been excavated.

It seems that people originally came to this eastern Mediterranean territory in fits and starts, predominantly from Anatolia. These pre-**Hellenes** settled in essentially peaceful farming communities, made pottery and worshipped earth/fertility goddesses – clay statuettes of which are still found on the sites of old settlements. This simple way of life eventually disappeared, as people started to tap the land's resources for profit and to compete and trade.

Minoans and Mycenaeans

The years between around **2000** and **1100** BC were a period of fluctuating regional dominance, based at first upon sea power, with vast **royal palaces** serving as centres of administration. Particularly important were those at **Knossos** on Crete, and **Mycenae**, **Tiryns** and **Pylos** in the Peloponnese.

Crete monopolized the eastern Mediterranean trade routes during an era subsequently called the **Minoan Age**, with the palace at Knossos surviving two earthquakes and a massive volcanic eruption on the island of Thíra (Santoríni) at some indefinite point between 1500 and 1450 BC. The most obvious examples of Minoan culture can be seen in frescoes, in jewellery and in pottery, the distinctive red-and-white design on a dark background marking the peak period of Minoan achievement. When Knossos finally succumbed to disaster, natural or otherwise, around 1400 BC, it was the flourishing centre of Mycenae that assumed the leading role (and gave its name to the civilization of this period), until it in turn collapsed around 1200 BC.

This is a period whose history and remains are bound up with its **legends**, recounted most famously by Homer and his disciples. Knossos was the home of King Minos, while the palaces of Mycenae and Pylos were the respective bases of Agamemnon and Nestor; Menelaos and Odysseus hailed from Sparta and Ithaca. The Homeric and other legends relating to them almost certainly reflect the growing prevalence of violence, revenge and war, instigated and aggravated by trade rivalry. The increasing scale of conflict and militarization is exemplified by the massive Mycenaean fortifications of the Peloponnese and central mainland that were built around many of the palaces and dubbed Cyclopean by later ages, after the only beings thought capable of hefting the huge stones.

The Greece of these years was by no means a united nation – as the Homeric legend reflects – and its people were divided into what were in effect a series of splinter groups, defined in large part by sea and mountain barriers and by access to **pasture**. Settlements flourished according to their proximity to and prowess on the sea, as well as the fertility of their land; most were self-sufficient, specializing in the production of particular items for **trade**. Olives, for example, were associated with the region of Attica, and minerals with the island of Mílos.

The Dorian and Classical eras

The Mycenaean-era Greek states had also to cope with and assimilate periodic influxes of new peoples and trade. The traditional view of the collapse of the Mycenaean civilization has it that a northern "barbarian" tribe, the **Dorians**, "invaded" from the north, devastating the existing palace culture and inaugurating a "dark age"; a competing theory has the so-called "Sea Peoples", probably based in southwestern Anatolia, conducting a series of raids over several decades. These days, archeologists see the influx more in terms of shifting trade patterns, though undoubtedly there was major disruption of the palace cultures and their sea power during the eleventh century BC.

Two other trends are salient to the period: the almost total supplanting of the mother goddesses by **male deities** (a process begun under the Mycenaeans) and the appearance of an **alphabet** still recognizable by modern Greeks, which replaced the so-called "Linear A" and "Linear B" Minoan/Mycenaean scripts.

City-states: Sparta and Athens

The ninth century BC ushered in the beginnings of the Greek **city-state** (polis). Citizens – rather than just kings or aristocrats – became involved in government and took part in community activities and organized industry and leisure. Colonial ventures increased, as did commercial dealings, and a consequent rise in the import trade was gradually to create a new class of manufacturers.

The city-state was the life of the people who dwelt within it and each state retained both its independence and a distinctive style, with the result that the sporadic attempts to unite in a league against an external enemy were always pragmatic and temporary. The two most powerful states to emerge were Athens and Sparta, who were to exercise rivalry over the next five centuries.

Sparta was associated with the Dorians, who had settled in large numbers on the fertile Eurotas (Évrotas) river plain. The society of Sparta and its environs was based on a highly militaristic, hierarchical ethos, accentuated by the need to defend the exposed and fertile land on which it stood. Rather than build intricate fortifications, the people of Sparta relied upon military prowess and a system of laws decreed by the (semi-legendary) **Lycurgus**. Males were subjected to military instruction between the ages of seven and thirty. Weak babies were known periodically to "disappear"; the majority of the population, the helots, existed in a state of serfdom as they worked to support the elite. Girls too had to perform athletic feats of sprinting and wrestling, and even dwellings were more like barracks than houses.

Athens, the fulcrum of the state of Attica, was dynamic and exciting by contrast, though here too slavery and its variants were vital to the economy. Home to the administrations of Solon and **Pericles**, the dramatic talents of Sophocles and Aristophanes, the oratory of the historian Thucydides and Demosthenes, and the philosophical power of Socrates and Plato, it made up in cultural achievement what it lacked in Spartan virtue. Yet Sparta did not deserve all the military glory. The Athens of the sixth and fifth centuries BC, the so-called **Classical period** in Greek history, played the major part in repelling the armies of the Persian king Xerxes at Marathon (490 BC) and Salamis (480 BC), campaigns later described by Aeschylus in *The Persians*.

Athens also gave rise to a tradition of democracy (*demokratia*), literally "control by the people" – although at this stage "the people" did not include either women or slaves. In Athens there were three organs of government. The Areopagus, composed of the city elders, had a steadily decreasing authority and eventually dealt solely with murder cases. Then there was the Council of Five Hundred (men), elected annually by ballot to prepare the business of the Assembly and to attend to matters of urgency. The Assembly gave every free man a political voice; it had sole responsibility for law-making and provided an arena for the discussion of important issues. It was a genuinely enfranchised council of citizens.

This was a period of intense creativity, particularly in Athens, whose actions and pretensions were fast becoming imperial in all but name. Each city-state had its **acropolis**, or high town, where religious activity was focused. In Athens, Pericles endowed the acropolis with a complex of buildings, whose climax was the temple of the Parthenon. Meanwhile, the era saw the tragedies of Sophocles performed, and the philosophies of Socrates and Plato expounded.

Religion at this stage was polytheistic, ordering the eleven other main Olympian gods under the aegis of Zeus. Urban temples tended to be dedicated to Zeus, Athena or Poseidon. In the countryside the proliferation of names and of sanctuary finds suggests a preference for Apollo, Hera, Dionysos and Artemis.

The Peloponnesian War

The power struggles between Athens and Sparta, allied with various networks of city-states, eventually culminated in the Peloponnesian War of 431–404 BC. After these conflicts, superbly recorded by Thucydides and nominally won by Sparta, the city-state ceased to function so effectively.

This was in part due to drained resources and political apathy, but to a greater degree a consequence of the increasingly commercial and complex pressures on everyday life. Trade, originally spurred by the invention of **coinage** in the sixth century BC, continued to expand; a revitalized Athens, for example, was exporting wine, oil and manufactured goods, getting corn in return from the Black Sea and Egypt.

The amount of time each man had to devote to the affairs of government decreased, and a position in political life became a professional job rather than a natural assumption. Democracy had changed, while in philosophy there was a shift from the idealists and mystics of the sixth and fifth centuries BC to the Cynics, Stoics and Epicureans – followers, respectively, of Diogenes, Zeno and Epicurus.

Hellenistic and Roman Greece

The most important factor in the decline of the city-states was meanwhile developing outside their sphere, in the kingdom of Macedonia.

The Macedonian Empire

Ruling from the Macedonian capital of Pella, **Philip II** (reigned 359–336 BC) was forging a strong military and unitary force, extending his territories into Thrace and finally establishing control over Athens and southern Greece. His son, **Alexander the Great**, in a brief but glorious thirteen-year reign, extended these gains into Persia and Egypt and parts of modern India and Afghanistan.

This unwieldy empire splintered almost immediately upon Alexander's death in 323 BC, to be divided into the three Macedonian dynasties of **Hellenistic Greece**: the Antigonids in Macedonia, the Seleucids in Syria and Persia and the Ptolemies in Egypt. Each was in turn conquered and absorbed by the new Roman empire, the Ptolemies – under their queen Cleopatra – last of all.

Roman Greece

Mainland Greece was subdued by the Romans over some seventy years of campaigns, from 215 to 146 BC. Once in control, however, **Rome** allowed considerable autonomy to the old territories of the city-states. Greek remained the official language of the eastern Mediterranean, and its traditions and culture coexisted fairly peacefully with that of the overlords during the next three centuries.

In central Greece both **Athens** and **Corinth** remained important cities, but the emphasis was shifting north – particularly to towns, such as **Salonica** (Thessaloníki), along the new Via Egnatia, a military and civil road engineered between Rome and Byzantium via the port of Brundisium (modern Brindisi in Italy). Among the **islands**, Rhodes had declined since Hellenistic times, but Kós, Lésvos, Thássos and Gortys on Crete remained important centres.

The Byzantine empire and Medieval Greece

The shift of emphasis northwards was given even greater impetus by the decline of the Roman empire and its apportioning into eastern and western empires. In 330 AD Emperor Constantine moved his capital to the Greek city of Byzantium, and here emerged Constantinople (modern Istanbul), the "new Rome" and spiritual and political capital of the Byzantine empire.

While the last western Roman emperor was deposed by barbarian Goths in 476, this eastern portion was to be the dominant Mediterranean power for some seven hundred years; only in 1453 did it collapse completely.

Christianity

Christianity had been introduced under Constantine, and by the end of the fourth century it was the official state religion, its liturgies (still in use in the Greek Orthodox Church), creed and New Testament all written in Greek. However, a distinction must be drawn between perceptions of Greek as a language and culture and as a concept. The Byzantine empire styled itself Roman, or *Romios*, rather than Hellenic, and moved to eradicate all remaining symbols of pagan Greece. The Delphic Oracle was forcibly closed, and the Olympic Games discontinued, by the emperor Theodosius I at the end of the fourth century. Schools of philosophy, especially neo-Platonic ones, did however survive until 529.

The seventh century saw **Constantinople** besieged by Persians, and later Arabs, but the Byzantine empire survived, losing only Egypt, the least "Greek" of its territories. From the ninth to the early eleventh centuries it enjoyed an archetypal "golden age" in culture, confidence and security. Bound up with the Orthodox Byzantine faith was a sense of spiritual superiority, and the emperors saw Constantinople as a "new Jerusalem" for their "chosen people". It was the beginning of a diplomatic and ecclesiastical conflict with the Catholic West that was to have disastrous consequences over the next five centuries. In the meantime the eastern and western patriarchs mutually excommunicated each other.

From the seventh until the eleventh centuries **Byzantine Greece**, certainly in the south and centre, became something of a provincial backwater. Administration was absurdly top-heavy and imperial taxation led to semi-autonomous provinces ruled by military generals, whose lands were usually acquired from bankrupted peasants. This alienation of the poor provided a force for change, with a disaffected populace ready to turn to or co-operate with the empire's enemies if the terms offered were an improvement.

Waves of **Slavic raiders** needed no encouragement to sweep down from the north Balkans throughout this period. At the same time other tribal groups moved down more peaceably from **central Europe** and were absorbed with little difficulty. According to one theory, the nomadic **Vlachs** from Romania eventually settled in the Píndhos Mountains, and later, from the thirteenth century onwards, immigrants from **Albania** repopulated the islands of Spétses, Ídhra, Angístri, Salamína, Ándhros and Évvia, as well as parts of Attica and the Peloponnese.

The Crusades: Frankish and Venetian rule

From the early years of the eleventh century, less welcome and less assimilable Western forces began to appear. The **Normans** landed first at Corfu in 1085, and returned again to the mainland with papal sanction a decade later on their way to liberate Jerusalem.

These were only a precursor, though, for the forces that were to descend en route for the **Fourth Crusade** of 1204, when Venetians, Franks and Germans turned their armies directly on Byzantium to sack and occupy Constantinople. These Latin princes and their followers, intent on new lands and kingdoms, settled in to divide up the best part of the empire. All that remained of Byzantium were four small peripheral kingdoms or **despotates**: the most powerful in Nicaea in Asia Minor, less significant ones at Trebizond on the Black Sea, and (in present-day Greece) in Epirus and around Mystra in the Peloponnese (known in these times as the Morea).

There followed two extraordinarily involved centuries of manipulation and struggle between Franks, Venetians, Genoese, Catalans and Turks. The Paleologos dynasty at Nicaea recovered the city of Constantinople in 1261, but little of its former territory and power. Instead, the focus of Byzantium shifted to the Peloponnese, where the autonomous **despotate of Mystra**, ruled by members of the imperial family, eventually succeeded in wresting most of the peninsula from Frankish hands. At the same time this despotate underwent an intense cultural renaissance, strongly evoked in the churches and shells of cities still visible at Mystra and Monemvasiá.

Ottoman occupation

CONTEXTS | The historical framework

Within a generation of driving out the Franks, the Byzantine Greeks faced a much stronger threat in the expanding empire of the **Ottomans**. "Turks" is the common term used for them in Greece, but the Ottomans were in fact a motley, assimilative crew, who included large numbers of Albanian, Arab and Kurdish Muslims, as well as Christian renegades from Venice, Hungary and the territory of Greece. Torn apart by internal struggles between their own ruling dynasties, the Palaeologi and Cantacuzenes, and unaided by the Catholic West, the Byzantine Greeks were to prove no match for the Ottomans. On Tuesday, May 29, 1453, a date still solemnly commemorated by the Orthodox Church, Constantinople fell to the besieging sultan Mehmet II.

Mystra was to follow within seven years, and Trebizond within nine, by which time virtually all of the old Byzantine empire lay under Ottoman domination. Only the **Ionian islands**, **Crete** and the **Cyclades**, which remained Venetian for two more centuries (or longer), and a few scattered and remote enclaves – like the Máni in the Peloponnese and Soúli in Epirus – were able to resist the "Turkish" advance.

Ottoman rule

Under what Greeks refer to as the *turkokratía* or era of **Ottoman rule**, the lands of present-day Greece passed into rural provincialism, taking refuge in a self-protective mode of village life that was only substantially disrupted by World War II. Taxes and discipline, sporadically backed up by the massacre of dissenting communities, were inflicted by Istanbul (as Constantinople was renamed), but large areas passed into the hands of local chieftains who often had considerable independence.

Greek identity, meanwhile, was preserved through the offices of the **Orthodox Church** which, despite instances of enforced conversion, the sultans allowed to continue. The **monasteries**, sometimes secretly, organized schools and became the trustees of Byzantine culture, though this had gone into stagnation after the fall of Constantinople and Mystra, whose scholars and artists emigrated west, adding impetus to the Renaissance.

As Ottoman administration became progressively more decentralized and inefficient, individual Greeks rose to local positions of considerable influence, and a number of communities achieved a degree of autonomy. Ambelákia village in Thessaly, for example, established an industrial co-operative system to export dyed cloth to Europe, paying only direct taxes to the sultan. And on the Albanian-repopulated islands of Ídhra and Spétses, as well as Kássos and Psará, a Greek merchant fleet came into being in the eighteenth century, permitted to trade throughout the Mediterranean. Greeks, too, were becoming organized overseas in the sizeable expatriate colonies of central Europe, which often had affiliations with the semi-autonomous village clusters of Zagóri (in Epirus) and Mount Pílion.

The struggle for independence

Despite these privileges, by the eighteenth century opposition to Ottoman rule was becoming widespread, exemplified most obviously by the **klephts** (brigands) of the mountains. It was not until the nineteenth century, however, that a resistance movement could muster sufficient support and firepower to prove a real challenge to the Ottomans. In 1770 a Russian-backed uprising had been easily and brutally suppressed, but fifty years later the situation was different.

In Epirus the Ottomans were overextended in subduing the expansionist campaigns of local ruler Ali Pasha. The French Revolution had given impetus to "freedom movements", and the Greek fighters were provided with financial and ideological underpinnings by the Filikí Etería, or "Friendly Society", a secret group recruited among the exiled merchants and intellectuals of central Europe.

This somewhat motley coalition of klephts and theorists launched their insurrection at the monastery of **Ayía Lávra** near Kalávryta in the Peloponnese, where on March 25, 1821, the Greek banner was openly raised by the local bishop, Yermanos.

The War of Independence

To describe in detail the course of the **War of Independence** is to provoke unnecessary confusion, since much of the rebellion consisted of local and fragmentary guerrilla campaigns. What is important to understand is that Greeks, though fighting for liberation from the Ottomans, were not fighting as and for a nation. Motives differed enormously: landowners assumed their role was to lead, and sought to retain and reinforce their traditional privileges, while the peasantry saw the struggle as a means towards land redistribution.

Outside Greece, the prestige of and publicity for the insurrection were promoted by the arrival of a thousand or so European **Philhellenes**, almost half of them German, though the most important was the English poet, **Lord Byron**, who died while training Greek forces at Mesolóngi in April 1824.

Though it was the Greek guerrilla leaders, above all **Theodhoros Kolokotronis**, "the old man of the Morea", who brought about the most significant military victories of the war, the death of Byron had an immensely important effect on public opinion in the West. Aid for the Greek struggle had come neither from Orthodox Russia, nor from the Western powers of France and Britain, both still ravaged by the Napoleonic Wars. But by 1827, when Mesolóngi fell again to the Ottomans, these three "Great Powers" finally agreed to seek autonomy for certain parts of Greece, and they sent a combined fleet to put pressure on the sultan's Egyptian army, then ransacking and massacring in the Peloponnese. Events took over, and an accidental naval battle in **Navarino Bay** resulted in the destruction of almost the entire

Turkish–Egyptian fleet. The following spring, Russia itself declared war on the Ottomans, and the Sultan Mahmud II was forced to accept the existence of an autonomous Greece.

At a series of conferences from 1830 to 1832, Greek independence was confirmed by the Western powers, and borders were drawn in 1832. These included just 800,000 of the six million Greeks living within the Ottoman empire, and territories which were for the most part the poorest of the Classical and Byzantine lands: Attica, the Peloponnese and the islands of the Argo-Saronic, Sporades and Cyclades. The rich agricultural belt of Thessaly, Epirus in the west and Macedonia in the north remained in Ottoman hands. Meanwhile, the Ionian islands were controlled by a British protectorate and the Dodecanese by the Ottomans (and after 1913 by recently unified Italy).

The emerging state

Modern Greece began as a republic, and **Ioannis Kapodistrias**, its first president, concentrated his efforts on building a viable central authority and government in the face of diverse protagonists from the independence struggle. Almost inevitably he was assassinated – in 1831, by two chieftains from the ever-disruptive Máni – and perhaps equally inevitably the three powers stepped in. They created a monarchy, gave limited aid and set on the throne a Bavarian prince, **Otho (Otto)**.

The new king proved an autocratic and insensitive ruler, bringing in fellow Germans to fill official posts and ignoring all claims by the landless peasantry for redistribution of the old estates. In 1862 he was forced from the country by a popular revolt, and the Europeans produced a new prince, this time from Denmark, who requested that Britain cede the Ionian islands as a condition of accession. **George I**, in fact, proved more capable: he had the first railways and roads built, introduced limited land reforms in the Peloponnese and oversaw the first expansion of the Greek borders.

The Megáli Idhéa and expansionist wars

From the very beginning, the unquestioned motive force of Greek foreign policy was the **Megáli Idhéa** (Great Idea) of liberating Greek populations outside the country and incorporating the old territories of Byzantium into the kingdom. In 1878 **Thessaly**, along with southern Epirus up to Árta, was ceded to Greece by the Ottomans.

Less illustriously, the Greeks failed in 1897 to achieve *énosis* (union) with Crete by attacking Ottoman forces on the mainland, and in the process virtually bankrupted the state. The island was, however, placed under a high commissioner, appointed by the Great Powers, and in 1913 did become a part of Greece.

It was from Crete, also, that the most distinguished modern Greek statesman emerged. **Eleftherios Venizelos**, having led a civilian campaign for his island's liberation, was elected as Greek prime minister in 1910. Two years later he organized an alliance of Balkan powers to fight the **Balkan Wars** (1912–13), campaigns that saw the Ottomans virtually driven from Europe. With Greek borders extended to include the northeast Aegean islands, northern Thessaly, central Epirus and parts of Macedonia, the Megáli Idhéa was approaching reality. At the same time Venizelos proved himself a shrewd manipulator of domestic public opinion by revising the constitution and introducing a series of liberal social reforms.

Division, however, was to appear with the outbreak of **World War I**. Venizelos urged Greek entry on the Allied side, seeing in the conflict possibilities for the "liberation" of Greeks in Thrace and Asia Minor, but the new king, Constantine I, who was married to a sister of the German Kaiser, imposed a policy of neutrality. Eventually Venizelos set up a revolutionary government in Thessaloníki, polarizing the country into a state of civil war along Venezelist–Royalist lines, but in 1917 Greek troops entered the war to join the French, British and Serbians in the **Macedonian campaign**. Upon the capitulation of Bulgaria and Ottoman Turkey, the Greeks occupied **Thrace** (both western and eastern), and Venizelos presented demands at Versailles for the predominantly Greek region of Smyrna on the Asia Minor coast.

The Katastrofí and its aftermath

This was the beginning of one of the most disastrous episodes in modern Greek history, the so-called **Katastrofí** ("Catastrophe"). Venizelos was authorized to move forces into Smyrna in 1919, but in Turkey itself a new nationalist movement was taking power under Mustafa Kemal, or **Atatürk** as he came to be known. In 1920 Venizelos lost the elections and monarchist factions took over, their aspirations unmitigated by the Cretan's skill in foreign diplomacy. Despite Allied support for such ventures now having completely evaporated, Greek forces were ordered to advance upon Ankara in an attempt to bring Atatürk to terms.

This so-called **Anatolian campaign** ignominiously collapsed in summer 1922 when Turkish troops forced the Greeks back to the coast and a hurried evacuation from **Smyrna**. As they left Smyrna, the Turks moved in and systematically massacred much of the Armenian and Greek population before burning most of the city to the ground.

Although an entire Greek army remained intact in eastern Thrace, Britain, hitherto Greece's only backer, let it be known that Greece would be wisest to accept Atatürk's own terms, formalized by the Treaty of Lausanne in 1923, which ordered the **exchange of religious minorities** in each country – in effect, the first large-scale regulated ethnic cleansing. Turkey was to accept 390,000 Muslims resident on Greek soil. Greece, mobilized almost continuously for the last decade and with a population of under five million, was faced with the resettlement of over 1,400,000 Christian refugees. Many of these had already read the writing on the wall after 1918 and arrived of their own accord – from Bulgaria and revolutionary Russia as well as Asia Minor; significant numbers were settled on Thássos, Límnos, Lésvos, Híos, Sámos, Évvia and Crete, as well as around Athens and in the northern mainland. The Megáli Idhéa had ceased to be a viable blueprint.

Changes, inevitably, were intense and far-reaching. The last great agricultural estates of Thessaly were finally redistributed, both to Greek tenants and refugee farmers, and huge shanty towns grew into new quarters around Athens, Pireás and other cities, a spur to the country's then almost nonexistent industry.

Politically, too, reaction was even swifter. By September 1922, a group of Venezelist army officers under Colonel Nikolaos Plastiras assembled after the retreat from Smyrna, "invited" King Constantine to abdicate and executed six of his ministers held most responsible for the debacle. Democracy was nominally restored with the proclamation of a republic, but for much of the next decade changes in government were brought about by factions within the armed forces. Meanwhile, among the urban refugee population, unions were being formed and the Greek Communist Party (KKE) was established.

Venizelos's last gasp – and the rise of Metaxas

Elections in 1928 **returned Venizelos** to power, but his freedom to manoeuvre was restricted by the Great Crash of the following year. He had borrowed heavily abroad and was unable to renegotiate loan terms in 1931. Late 1932 saw a local crash caused by England's abandonment of the gold standard, with Greek currency heavily devalued and Venizelos forced from office. His supporters under Plastiras tried to forcibly reinstate him in March 1933, but their coup was quashed and Venizelos fled to Paris, where he died three years later.

By 1936 the Communist Party had enough electoral support to hold the balance of power in parliament, and would have done so had not the army and the by-then restored king decided otherwise. **King George II** had been returned by a plebiscite held – and almost certainly manipulated – the previous year, and so presided over an increasingly factionalized parliament. In April 1936 George II appointed **General John Metaxas** as prime minister, despite the latter's being supported by only six elected deputies. Immediately a series of KKE-organized strikes broke out and the king, ignoring attempts to form a broad liberal coalition, dissolved parliament without setting a date for new elections. It was a blatantly unconstitutional move and opened the way for five years of ruthless and at times absurd dictatorship.

Metaxas averted a general strike with military force and proceeded to set up a state based on **fascist** models of the era. Left-wing and trade-union opponents were imprisoned or forced into exile, a state youth movement and secret police set up and rigid censorship, extending even to passages of Thucydides, imposed. But it was at least a Greek dictatorship, and though Metaxas was sympathetic to Nazi organizational methods and economics, he completely opposed German or Italian domination.

World War II and the Greek civil war

Using a submarine based on Léros in the Dodecanese, the Italians tried to provoke the Greeks into prematurely entering **World War II** by surreptitiously torpedoing the Greek cruiser *Elli* in Tínos harbour on August 15, 1940, but they met with no immediate response. However, when Mussolini occupied Albania and sent an ultimatum on October 28, 1940, demanding passage for his troops through Greece, Metaxas responded to the Italian foreign minister with the apocryphal one-word answer "óhi" (no). (In fact, his response, in the mutually understood French, was "C'est la guerre.") The date marked the entry of Greece into the war, and the gesture is still celebrated as a national holiday.

Galvanized into brief unity by the crisis, the Greeks drove Italian forces from the country and moreover managed to take control of the long-coveted and predominantly Greek-populated northern Epirus (southern Albania). However, the Greek army subsequently frittered away its strength in the snowy mountains of northern Epirus rather than consolidating its gains or defending the Macedonian frontier, and proposed co-ordination with the British never materialized.

Occupation and resistance

In April of the following year Nazi mechanized columns swept through Yugoslavia and across the Greek mainland, effectively reversing the only Axis defeat to date, and by late May 1941, airborne and seaborne **German invasion** forces had completed the occupation of Crete and the other islands. Metaxas had died before their arrival, while King George and his new self-appointed ministers fled into exile in Cairo; few Greeks, of any political persuasion, were sad to see them go.

The joint Italian-German-Bulgarian Axis occupation of Greece was among the bitterest experiences of the European war. Nearly half a million Greek civilians starved to death over the winter of 1941–42, as all available food was requisitioned, principally by the Germans, to feed occupying armies. In addition, entire villages throughout the mainland, but especially on Crete, were burned at the least hint of resistance activity and nearly 130,000 civilians slaughtered. In their northern sector, which included Thássos and Samothráki, the Bulgarians desecrated ancient sites and churches to support a future bid to annexe "Slavic" Macedonia.

Primarily in the north, too, the Nazis supervised during 1944 the deportation to concentration camps of virtually the entire Greek–Jewish population of nearly 80,000. Thessaloníki – where the former UN secretary-general and Austrian president Kurt Waldheim worked for Nazi intelligence – contained 57,000, the largest Jewish population of any Balkan city, and there were significant populations in all the Greek mainland towns and on many of the islands. After the Italians capitulated in September 1943, the Jewish communities in Rhodes, Kós, Crete, Corfu, Vólos, Évvia and Zákynthos in particular were exposed to the full force of Nazi racial doctrine, though in the last three places co-operation between courageous church or municipal authorities and the budding Resistance (see below), ensured that most local Jews survived.

With a quisling government in Athens – and an unpopular, discredited royalist government-in-exile in Cairo – the focus of Greek political and military action over the next four years passed largely to the **EAM**, or National Liberation Front. By 1943 it was in virtual control of most areas of the country, working with the British on tactical operations, with its own army (ELAS), navy and both civil and secret police forces. Initially it commanded widespread popular support and appeared to offer an obvious framework for the resumption of postwar government.

However, most of its highest-ranking members were communists, and the British prime minister, **Winston Churchill**, was determined to reinstate the monarchy. Even with two years of the war to run, it became obvious that there could be no peaceable post-liberation regime other than a republic. Accordingly, in August 1943, representatives from each of the main resistance movements (including two noncommunist groups) flew clandestinely to Cairo to request that the king not return unless a plebiscite had first voted in his favour. Both the Greek and British authorities refused to consider the proposal, and the best possibility of averting civil war was lost.

The EAM contingent returned divided, as perhaps the British had intended, and a conflict broke out between those who favoured taking peaceful control of any government imposed after liberation, and the hard-line Stalinist ideologues, who forbade Popular-Front-type participation in any "bourgeois" regime.

In October 1943, with fears of an imminent British landing force and takeover, ELAS launched a full-scale attack upon its Greek rivals; by the following April, they had wiped out all but the EDES, their most right-wing rival, suspected of collaboration with the Germans. ELAS's ferocity was spurred by the failure of the Egyptian conference and by half-true reports that British and American agents were being infiltrated into Greece to prevent the establishment of a communist government when the Germans began withdrawing their forces.

Liberation and civil war

In fact, as the Germans began to leave in October 1944, most of the EAM leadership agreed to join a British-sponsored "official" **interim government**. It quickly proved a tactical error, however. With almost ninety percent of the provinces under their control, the communists were eventually given only one-third representation in Athens, and a new regular army began to form, based on the extreme-right-wing Mountain Brigade, the Sacred Band and even the fascist Security Battalions, rather than the ELAS officer corps. The king showed no sign of renouncing his claims, and, in November, Allied forces under British general Ronald Scobie ordered ELAS to disarm. On December 3 all pretences of civility or neutrality were dropped; the police fired on an EAM demonstration in Athens, killing at least sixteen, and fighting broke out between ELAS and British troops, in the so-called **Dhekemvrianá** events. Though ELAS quickly quashed all opposition in the countryside, they failed to drive the British and right-wing Greeks from Athens, thus losing their best chance of seizing power. In their fury at being thwarted, ELAS rounded up their most influential and wealthiest opponents in the largest towns, and marched them out to rural areas in conditions that guaranteed their death.

A truce of sorts was negotiated at Várkiza the following February, but the agreement was never implemented. The army, police and civil service remained in right-wing hands and while collaborationists were often allowed to retain their positions, left-wing sympathizers, many of whom were merely Venizelist Republicans and not communists, were systematically excluded. The elections of March 1946 were won by the right-wing parties (the Left, perhaps unwisely, boycotted them), followed by yet another rigged plebiscite in favour of the king's return. By 1947 guerrilla activity had again reached the scale of a full **civil war**, with ELAS reorganized into the Democratic Army of Greece (**DSE** in Greek).

In the interim, King George had died and been succeeded by his brother Paul (with his consort Frederika), while the **Americans** had taken over the British role, and begun implementing the Cold War **Truman doctrine**. In March 1947 they took virtual control of Greece, their first significant postwar experiment in anti-communist intervention. Massive economic and military aid was given to a client Greek government, with official decrees that had to be countersigned by the American Mission chief in order to become valid.

In the mountains US military advisers trained the initially woeful Nationalist army for **campaigns against the DSE**, and in the cities there were mass arrests, court-martials and imprisonments – a kind of "White Terror" – lasting until 1951. Over three thousand government executions were recorded, including (for their pacifist stance and refusal to swear loyalty oaths) a number of Jehovah's Witnesses, "a sect proved to be under communist domination", according to US Ambassador Grady. To deny the DSE local support, over 700,000 civilians were forcibly evacuated from mountain villages and dumped in squalid internment camps near towns, a move which helped destroy any hope of postwar rural existence.

In the autumn of 1949, with the Yugoslav–Greek border closed after Tito's rift with Stalin, the last DSE guerrillas finally admitted defeat, retreating into Albania from their strongholds on Mount Grámmos. Atrocities had been committed on both sides, including, from the Left, considerably more than three thousand executions, widescale vandalization of monasteries and the dubious evacuation of children from "combat areas" (as told in Nicholas Gage's virulently anti-communist book *Eleni*). Such errors, as well as the high percentage of openly separatist Slavophones amongst their ranks, and the hopelessness of 30,000 lightly armed guerrillas fighting an American-backed army, undoubtedly doomed the DSE's efforts from the start.

Reconstruction American style 1950–67

After a decade of war that had shattered much of Greece's infrastructure (supposedly not one bridge was left standing by 1948), it was a demoralized, shattered country that emerged into the Western political orbit of the 1950s. Greece was also perforce American-dominated, enlisted into the Korean War in 1950 and NATO the following year. In domestic politics, the US embassy – still giving the orders – foisted upon the Greeks a winner-take-all electoral system, which was to ensure victory for the Right over the next twelve years. Overt leftist activity was banned (though a "cover" party for communists was soon founded); those individuals who were not herded into political "re-education" camps or dispatched by firing squads, legal or vigilante, went into exile throughout Eastern Europe, to return only after 1974. The 1950s also saw wholesale depopulation of remote villages as migrants sought work in Australia, America and western Europe, or the larger Greek cities.

The American-backed, highly conservative "**Greek Rally**" party, led by General Papagos, won the first decisive post-civil-war elections in 1952. After the general's death, the party's leadership was taken over – and to an extent liberalized – by **Constantine Karamanlis**. Under his rule, stability of a kind was established and some economic advances registered, particularly after the revival of Greece's traditional German markets. Health and life expectancy improved dramatically as the age-old scourges of tuberculosis and malaria were finally confronted with American-supplied food and pesticides. Less commendable was Karamanlis's encouragement of the law of **andiparohí**, whereby owners of small refugee shanties or Neoclassical mansions alike could offer the site of their property to apartment-block developers in exchange for two flats (out of eight to ten) in the finished building. This effectively ripped the heart out of most Greek towns, and explains their baleful aesthetics a half-century on.

The main crisis in foreign policy throughout this period was **Cyprus**, where a long terrorist campaign was waged by Greek–Cypriots opposing British rule, and there were sporadic threats of a new Greco-Turkish war. An ultimately unworkable compromise solution was forced on the island by Britain in 1960, granting independence without the possibility of "self-determination" (ie union with Greece). Much of the traditional Greek–British goodwill was destroyed by the issue, with Britain seen to be acting with regard primarily for its two military bases (over which, incidentally, it still retains sovereignty).

By 1961, unemployment, the Cyprus issue and the imposition of US nuclear bases on Greek soil were changing the political climate, and when Karamanlis was again elected there was strong suspicion of a fraud arranged by the king and army. Strikes became frequent in industry and even agriculture, while King Paul and autocratic, fascist-inclined Queen Frederika were openly attacked in parliament and at protest demonstrations. The far Right grew uneasy about "**communist resurgence**" and, losing confidence in their own electoral influence, arranged the assassination of left-wing deputy **Grigoris Lambrakis** in Thessaloníki in May 1963. (The murder, and its subsequent cover-up, is the subject of Vassilis Vassilikos's thriller *Z*, filmed by Costa-Gavras.) It was against this volatile background that Karamanlis dissolved parliament, lost the subsequent elections and left the country.

The new government – the first controlled from outside the Right since 1935 – was formed by **George Papandreou's Centre Union Party**, and had a decisive majority of nearly fifty seats. It was to last, however, for under two years as conservative forces conspired to thwart its progress. In this the chief protagonists were army officers and their constitutional commander-in-chief, the new king, 23-year-old Constantine II.

Since power in Greece depended on a pliant military as well as a network of political appointees, Papandreou's most urgent task in order to govern securely and effectively was to reform the armed forces. His first minister of defence proved incapable of the task and, while he was investigating the right-wing plot suspected of rigging the 1961 election, "evidence" was produced of a leftist conspiracy connected with Papandreou's son Andreas (also a minister in the government). When the allegations grew to a crisis, George Papandreou assumed the defence portfolio himself, a move which the king refused to sanction. He then resigned in order to gain a fresh mandate at the polls, but the king would not order new elections, instead persuading members of the Centre Union – chief among them Constantine Mitsotakis – to defect and organize a coalition government. Punctuated by strikes, resignations and mass demonstrations, this lasted for a year and a half until new elections were eventually set for May 28, 1967. They failed to take place.

The colonels' junta 1967–74

It was a foregone conclusion that Papandreou's party would win the polls against the discredited coalition partners. And it was equally certain that there would be some anti-democratic action to prevent it from reassuming power. Disturbed by the party's leftward shift, King Constantine was said to have briefed senior generals for a coup d'état, to take place ten days before the elections. However, he was caught by surprise, as was nearly everyone else, by the **coup** of April 21, 1967, staged by a group of "unknown" colonels. It was, to quote Andreas Papandreou, "the first successful CIA military putsch on the European continent".

The **colonels' junta**, having taken control of the means of power, was sworn in by the king and survived the half-hearted counter-coup which he subsequently attempted to organize. It was an ostensibly **fascist regime**, absurdly styling itself as the true "Revival of Greek Orthodoxy" against Western "corrupting influences", though in reality its ideology was nothing more than warmed-up dogma from the Metaxas era mixed with ultranationalism.

All **political activity was banned**, independent trade unions were forbidden to recruit or meet, the press was so heavily censored that many papers stopped printing and thousands of "communists" were arrested, imprisoned and often tortured. Among the persecuted were both Papandreou, the composer Mikis Theodorakis (deemed "unfit to stand trial" after three months in custody) and Amalia Fleming (widow of Alexander Fleming). While relatively few people were killed outright, thousands were permanently maimed physically and psychologically in the junta's torture chambers. The best-known Greek actress, Melina Mercouri, was stripped of her citizenship in absentia, and thousands of prominent Greeks joined her in exile.

Culturally, the colonels put an end to popular music (closing down most of the live rebétika and *néo kýma* clubs) and inflicted ludicrous censorship on literature and the theatre, including (as under Metaxas) a ban on production of the Classical tragedies. By contrast, chief colonel Papadopoulos's rambling, illiterate speeches became a byword for bad grammar, obfuscation and Orwellian Newspeak.

The colonels lasted for seven years, opposed (especially after the first two years) by the majority of the Greek people, officially excluded from the Council of Europe, but propped up and given massive aid by US presidents **Lyndon Johnson** and **Richard Nixon**. To them and the CIA the junta's Greece was an ideal client state: human rights considerations were then considered trivial; orders were placed for sophisticated military technology; and foreign investment on terms highly unfavourable to Greece was made available to multinational corporations. This exploitation of an underdeveloped nation was a fairly routine scenario played out in a number of other places at the time.

Opposition was voiced from the beginning by exiled Greeks in London, the United States and western Europe, but only in 1973 did demonstrations break out openly in Greece – the colonels' secret police had done too thorough a job of infiltrating domestic resistance groups and terrifying everyone else into docility. On November 17 the students of **Athens Polytechnic** began an occupation of their buildings. The ruling clique lost its nerve; armoured vehicles stormed the Polytechnic gates and a still-undetermined number of students (estimates range from 34 to three hundred) were killed. Martial law was tightened and junta chief Colonel Papadopoulos was replaced by the even more noxious and reactionary General Ioannides, head of the secret police.

The return to civilian rule 1975–81

The end of the ordeal, however, came within a year as the dictatorship embarked on a disastrous political adventure in **Cyprus**, essentially the last playing of the Megáli Idhéa card. By attempting to topple the Makarios government and impose *énosis* (union with Greece) on the island, they provoked a Turkish invasion and occupation of forty percent of Cypriot territory. The army finally mutinied and **Constantine Karamanlis** was invited to return from Paris to again take office. He swiftly negotiated a ceasefire (but no durable solution) in Cyprus, withdrew temporarily from NATO and warned that US bases would have to be removed except where they specifically served Greek interest.

In November 1974 Karamanlis and his **Néa Dhimokratía (New Democracy) party** were rewarded by a sizeable majority in **elections**, with a centrist and socialist opposition. The latter was the **Panhellenic Socialist Movement (PASOK)**, a new party led by Andreas Papandreou.

The election of Néa Dhimokratía was in every sense a safe conservative option, but to Karamanlis's enduring credit it oversaw an effective and firm return to democratic stability, even legitimizing the KKE (Communist Party) for the first time in its history. Karamanlis also held a **referendum on the monarchy**; 59 percent of Greeks rejected the return of Constantine II, so he instituted in its place a French-style presidency, which he himself occupied from 1980 to 1985, and again from 1990 to 1995. Economically there were limited advances, although these were more than offset by inflationary defence spending (the result of renewed tension with Turkey), the hastily negotiated entrance into the EC and the decision to let the drachma float after decades of its being artificially fixed at thirty to the US dollar.

Most crucially, Karamanlis failed to deliver vital reforms in bureaucracy, social welfare and education; and while the worst figures of the junta were brought to trial and jailed indefinitely, the face of Greek political life and administration was little changed. By 1981 inflation was hovering around 25 percent, and it was estimated that tax evasion was depriving the state of one-third of its annual budget. In foreign policy the US bases remained and it was felt that Greece, back in NATO, was still acting as little more than an American satellite. The traditional Right had proved demonstrably inadequate to the task at hand.

PASOK 1981–89

"Change" (*Allayí*) and "Out with the Right" (*Ná Fíyi íy Dhexiá*) were the slogans of the election campaign that swept **PASOK** and Andreas Papandreou to power on October 18, 1981. This victory meant a chance for Papandreou to form the first socialist government in Greek history and break a half-century monopoly of authoritarian right-wing rule. With so much at stake, the campaign had been passionate even by Greek standards, and PASOK's victory was greeted with euphoria both by the generation whose political voice had been silenced in the civil war and by a large proportion of the young. Their hopes ran naively and perhaps dangerously high.

The electoral margin, at least, was conclusive. PASOK won 174 of the 300 parliamentary seats and the Communist KKE – though not a part of the new government – returned another thirteen deputies, one of them composer Mikis Theodorakis, while Néa Dhimokratía moved into unaccustomed opposition. There appeared to be no obstacle to the implementation of a **radical programme**: devolution of power to local authorities, the effective nationalization of heavy industry, improvement of the woefully skeletal social services, a purge of bureaucratic inefficiency and malpractice, the end of bribery and corruption as a way of life, an independent and dignified foreign policy following expulsion of US bases and finally withdrawal from NATO and the European Community.

A change of style was promised, too, replacing the country's long traditions of authoritarianism and bureaucracy with openness and dialogue. Even more radically, given that Greek political parties had long been the personal followings of charismatic leaders, PASOK was to be a party of ideology and principle, dependent on no single individual member. Or so, at least, thought some of the youthful PASOK cadres.

The new era started with a bang. ELAS was officially recognized; hitherto they hadn't been allowed to take part in any celebrations, wreath-layings or other ceremonies commemorating the wartime Resistance. Peasant women were granted pensions for the first time – 3000 drachmas a month (about $55 in 1982), the same as their outraged husbands – and wages were indexed to the cost of living. In addition, civil marriage was introduced, family law was reformed in favour of wives and mothers, and equal rights legislation was put on the statute book.

These quick, low-cost and popular reformist moves seemed to mark a break with the past, and the atmosphere had indeed changed. Greeks no longer lowered their voices to discuss politics in public places or wrapped their opposition newspaper in the respectably conservative *Kathimerini*. At first there were real fears that the climate would be too much for the military who would once again intervene to choke a dangerous experiment in democracy, especially when Andreas Papandreou, imitating his father, briefly assumed the defence portfolio himself. But he went out of his way to soothe military susceptibilities, increasing their salaries, buying new weaponry and being fastidious in his attendance at military functions.

The end of the honeymoon

Papandreou promised a bonanza which he must have known, as an academically trained economist, he could not deliver. As a result he pleased nobody. He could not fairly be blamed for the inherited lack of investment, low productivity, deficiency in managerial and labour skills and other chronic problems besetting the Greek economy. However, he certainly aggravated the situation early in his first term by allowing his supporters to indulge in violently anticapitalist rhetoric, which frightened off potential investors, and by the prosecution and humiliation of the Tsatsos family, owners of one of Greece's few competitive businesses (Hercules Cement) for the illegal export of capital, something of which every Greek with any savings was guilty. These were cheap victories, not backed by any rational programme of public investment, and the only nationalizations were of hopelessly lame-duck companies.

Faced with this sluggish economy and burdened with the additional charges of (marginally) improved social benefits and wage indexing, Papandreou's government also had to cope with the effects of world recession. **Shipping**, the country's main foreign-currency earner, was devastated. Remittances from émigré workers fell off as they became unemployed in their host countries, and tourism diminished under the dual impact of the recession and US President Ronald Reagan's warning to Americans to stay away from allegedly terrorist-vulnerable Athens airport.

With huge quantities of imported goods continuing to be sucked into the country in the absence of significant domestic production, the **foreign debt** topped £10 billion in 1986, while inflation remained at 25 percent and the balance of payments deficit approached £1 billion. Greece also began to experience the social strains of unemployment for the first time. Not that it didn't exist before, but it had always been concealed as underemployment because of numerous family-run businesses and the rural/seasonal nature of the economy – as well as by the absence of reliable statistics.

The second term

A modest spending spree transparently intended to buy votes, continued satisfaction at the discomfiture of the Right, plus the popularity of his Greece-for-the-Greeks foreign policy gave Papandreou a second term with a June 1985 electoral victory scarcely less decisive than the first. But his complacent and, frankly, dishonest slogan was "Vote PASOK for Even Better Days". By October PASOK had imposed a two-year wage freeze and import restrictions, abolished the wage-indexing scheme and devalued the drachma by fifteen percent. Papandreou's fat was pulled out of the fire by none other than his *bête noire*, the European Community, which offered a huge two-part loan on condition that an IMF-style **austerity programme** was maintained.

The political price of such classic monetarist strategies, accompanied by shameless soliciting for foreign investment, was the alienation of the communists and most of PASOK's own core constituency. Increasingly autocratic (ironic, given his earlier pledges of openness), Papandreou's response to **dissent** was to fire recalcitrant trade union leaders and expel some three hundred members of his own party. Assailed by strikes, the government stumbled badly, losing much ground in the municipal elections of October 1986 to Néa Dhimokratía, including the mayoralties of the three major cities – Athens, Thessaloníki and Pátra – the first two retained by them ever since. Papandreou assured the nation that he had taken the message to heart, but all that followed were two successive cabinet reshuffles, which saw the departure of most remaining PASOK veterans; the new cabinet was so unsocialist that even the right-wing press called it "centrist".

Women's rights in Greece

Women's right to vote wasn't universally achieved in Greece until 1956 and, until the mid-1970s, adultery was still a punishable offence. The socialist party, PASOK, had a strong theoretical programme for **women's rights**, and their women's council review committees, set up in the early, heady days, effected a landmark reform with the 1983 **Family Law**. This prohibited requiring dowry (though custom still demands it) and stipulated equal legal status and shared property rights between husband and wife.

Subsequently however, the PASOK governments did little to follow through on **practical issues**, like improved child care, health and family planning. Contraception is not available as part of the skeletal Greek public health service, leaving many women to fall back on abortion as the preferred method of birth control – still running (as for many years past) to an estimated 70–80,000 a year.

By far the largest women's rights organization is the **Union of Greek Women**. Founded in 1976, this espouses an independent feminist line and is responsible for numerous consciousness-raising activities across the country, though it remains too closely linked to PASOK for the comfort of many. Indeed, Margaret Papandreou felt compelled to resign from the Union following her well-publicized divorce from Andreas, leaving it without her effective and vocal leadership. Other, more autonomous groups have been responsible for setting up advice and support networks, highlighting women's issues within trade unions and campaigning for changes in media representation.

None of this is easy in a country as socially variable as Greece. In many rural areas women rely heavily on traditional extended families for security, and are unlikely to be much affected by legislative reforms or city politics. Yet Greek men of all classes and backgrounds are slowly becoming used to the notion of women in positions of power and responsibility and are taking a substantial share in child-rearing – both postures utterly unthinkable two decades ago, and arguably one of the few positive legacies with which PASOK can at least in part be credited.

Similar about-faces took place in foreign policy. The first-term anti-US, anti-NATO and anti-EC rhetoric had been immensely popular, and understandable for a people shamelessly bullied by bigger powers since 1830. There was some high-profile nose-thumbing, like refusing to join EC partners in condemning Jaruzelski's Polish regime or the Soviet downing of a Korean airliner. The "realistic" policies that Papandreou increasingly pursued during his second term were far more conciliatory towards his big Western brothers. Not least was the fact that **US bases** remained in Greece until 1994, largely owing to the fear that snubbing NATO would lead to Greece being exposed to Turkish aggression, still the only issue that unites the main parties to any degree. As for the once-reviled **European Community** (soon to be the European Union), Greece had by now become an established beneficiary, and its leader was hardly about to bite the hand that feeds.

Scandal

Even as late as **mid-1988**, despite the many betrayals and failings of Papandreou, it seemed unlikely that PASOK would be toppled in the following year's elections. This was due mainly to the lack of a credible alternative. Constantine Mitsotakis, a bitter personal enemy of Papandreou's since 1965, when his defection had brought down his father's government and set in motion the events that culminated in the junta, was an unconvincing and unlikeable character at the helm of Néa Dhimokratía. Meanwhile, the liberal centrist parties had disappeared, and the main communist party, the KKE, seemed trapped in a Stalinist timewarp under the leadership of Harilaos Florakis. Only the **Ellenikí Aristerá (Greek Left)** or Euro-Communist party spun off from the KKE, seemed to offer any sensible alternative, but they had a precariously small following.

However, a combination of spectacular blunders, plus perhaps a general shift to the Right influenced by the cataclysmic events in Eastern Europe, conspired against PASOK. First came the extraordinary **cavortings of the prime minister** himself. Late in 1988, seventy-year-old Papandreou was flown to Britain for open-heart surgery. He took the occasion, with fear of death presumably rocking his judgement, to make public a year-long liaison with a 34-year-old Olympic Airways hostess, **Dimitra "Mimi" Liani**. Widespread media images of an old man shuffling about after a young, large-chested blonde, to the public humiliation of Margaret, his American-born wife, and his family, were not helpful (Papandreou soon divorced Margaret and married Mimi). His integrity was further dented when he missed important public engagements in order to relive his youth in flashy nightspots with Mimi.

The real damage, however, was done by a series of **economic scandals**, ranging from illegal arms deals to fraudulent farm-produce sales by assorted ministers. The most serious of these involved a self-made, Greek-American con-man, **Yiorgos Koskotas**, director of the Bank of Crete, who embezzled £120m (US$190m) of deposits and, worse still, slipped through the authorities' fingers on a private jet back to the US, where he had begun his career as a housepainter. Certain PASOK ministers and even Papandreou himself were implicated in this scandal.

United in disgust at this corruption, the other left-wing parties – KKE and Ellinikí Aristerá – formed a coalition, **Synaspismós**, siphoning off still more support from PASOK.

Three bites at the cherry

In this climate, an inconclusive result to the **June 1989 election** was unsurprising. Less predictable, however, was the formation of a bizarre "**kathársis**"

(purgative) coalition of conservatives and communists, expressly to cleanse PASOK's Augean stables.

Synaspismós would have formed a government with PASOK, but set an impossible condition for doing so – that Papandreou step down as prime minister. In the deal finally cobbled together between the Left and Néa Dhimokratía, Mitsotakis was denied the premiership, too, in favour of **Ioannis Tzanetakis**, a popular former naval officer who had led a mutiny against the junta.

During the three months that the coalition lasted, *kathársis* turned out to be largely a matter of burying the knife as deeply as possible into the ailing body of PASOK. Andreas Papandreou and three other ministers were officially indicted of involvement in the Koskotas affair – though there was no time to try them before the Greek people returned once again to the polls. In any case, the chief witness and protagonist, Koskotas himself, was still imprisoned in America, awaiting extradition proceedings.

Contrary to the Right's hope that publicly accusing Papandreou and his cohorts of criminal behaviour would pave the way for a Néa Dhimokratía victory, PASOK actually recovered slightly in the **November 1989 elections**, though the result was again inconclusive. This time the Left refused to do deals with anyone, resulting in a caretaker government under the neutral aegis of Xenophon Zolotas, reluctantly dragged into the prime minister's office from the rectorship of Athens University. His only mandate was to keep the country on the rails while preparations were made for yet another election.

These took place in **April 1990** with the same party leaders *in situ*, and with Synaspismós having completed its about-turn to the extent that in the five single-seat constituencies (the other 295 seats are drawn from multiple-seat constituencies in a complex system of reinforced proportional representation), they supported independent candidates jointly with PASOK. Greek communists are good at about-turns, though; after all, composer Mikis Theodorakis, musical torch-bearer of the Left during the dark junta years, and formerly a KKE MP, was now standing for Néa Dhimokratía, prior to his resignation from politics altogether.

On the night, Néa Dhimokratía scraped home with a majority of one, later doubled with the defection of a centrist, and Mitsotakis finally realized his long-cherished dream of becoming prime minister. The only other memorable feature of the election was the first parliamentary representation for an independent member of the Turkish minority in Thrace, and for the Greens in Attica – a focus for many disaffected PASOK voters.

A return to the right: Premier Mitsotakis

On assuming power, Mitsotakis prescribed a course of **austerity measures** to revive the chronically ill economy. Little headway was made, though given the world recession that was hardly surprising. Greek inflation was still approaching twenty percent annually, and at nearly ten percent, unemployment remained chronic. Other measures introduced by Mitsotakis included laws to combat strikes and **terrorism**. The latter had been a perennial source of worry for Greeks since the appearance in 1974 of a group called **Dhekaeftá Novemvríou** ("November 17", the date of the colonels' attack on the Polytechnic in 1973). Since 1974 they (and one or two copycat groups) have killed 24 industrialists, politicians and NATO military personnel and have attacked buildings of foreign corporations in Athens; the lack of any significant arrests to date fuels continued speculation that they were a rogue faction from within PASOK itself. It hardly seemed likely that Mitsotakis's laws, however, were the solution. They stipulated that the typically long-winded, ideologically contorted statements of the group could no longer be published, which led to one or two newspaper editors being jailed for a few days for defiance – much to everyone's embarrassment. The **anti-strike laws** threatened severe penalties but were equally ineffectual, as breakdowns in public transport, electricity and rubbish collection all too frequently illustrated.

As for the Koskotas scandal, the man himself was eventually extradited and gave evidence for the prosecution against Papandreou and various of his ministers. The trial was televised and proved as popular as any soap opera, given its twists of high drama – which included one of the defendants, Agamemnon "Menios" Koutsoyiorgas, dying in court of a heart attack in front of the cameras. The case against Papandreou gradually ran out of steam and he was officially acquitted (by a margin of one vote on the tribunal panel) in early 1992. The two other surviving ex-ministers, Tsovolas and Petsos, were convicted, given jail sentences (bought off with a heavy fine) and barred from public office for a time.

The great showcase trial thus went out with a whimper and did nothing to enhance Mitsotakis's position. If anything, it served to increase sympathy for Papandreou, who was felt to have been unfairly victimized. The indisputable villain of the piece, Koskotas, was eventually convicted of major fraud and is serving a lengthy sentence at the high-security Korýdhallos prison.

The Macedonian question

The last thing the increasingly unpopular Mitsotakis needed was a major foreign policy headache. That is exactly what he got when, in 1991, one of the breakaway republics of the former Yugoslavia named itself **Macedonia**, thereby injuring Greek national pride and sparking off vehement protests at home and abroad. Diplomatically, the Greeks fought tooth and nail against anyone's recognizing the breakaway state, let alone its use of the name "Macedonia", but their position became increasingly isolated, and by 1993 the new country had gained official recognition from both the EU and the UN – albeit under the provisional title of the Former Yugoslav Republic of Macedonia (FYROM), in Greek.

Salt was rubbed into Greek wounds when the FYROM started using the "Star of Vergina" (and of the ancient Macedonian kings) as a national symbol on their new flag, allegedly printed a banknote portraying the White Tower of Thessaloníki (Solun in Macedonian) and retained passages in its constitution referring to "unredeemed" Aegean territories. Greece still refuses to call its neighbour Macedonia, instead referring to it as Proín Yugoslaviki Dhimokratía Makedhonás, or *Tá Skópia* after the capital – and for quite some time you couldn't go anywhere in Greece without coming across officially placed stickers proclaiming that "Macedonia was, is and always will be Greek and only Greek!"

The ongoing argument for legitimacy hinges mostly on whether the ancient Macedonian kings were pure-bred Hellenes (the Greek position), Hellenized barbarians (the neutral conclusion) or proto-Slavs (the Macedonian claim).

The pendulum swings back

The Macedonian problem effectively led to Mitsotakis's political **demise**. Mitsotakis had also been plagued for many months by accusations of phone-tapping and theft of antiquities to stock his large private collection in Crete, plus links with a complicated contracts scandal focused on the national cement company. In the early summer of 1993 his ambitious and disaffected foreign minister, **Andonis Samaras**, jumped on the bandwagon of resurgent Greek nationalism to set up his own party, **Politikí Ánixi (Political Spring)**. His platform, still right-wing, was largely based on action over Macedonia, and during the summer of 1993 more **Néa Dhimokratía** (ND) MPs defected, making Politikí Ánixi a force to be reckoned with. When parliament reconvened in September to approve severe new budget proposals, it became clear that the government lacked sufficient support, and early **elections** were called for **October 1993**.

On October 11, Papandreou romped to election victory; ND lost in 85 percent of the constituencies and the Synaspismós was replaced as the third party in parliament by Samaras's Politikí Ánixi and the unreconstructed communists, now under Aleka Papariga. The youthful Miltiades Evert, ex-mayor of Athens, replaced Mitsotakis as head of Néa Dhimokratía, so that – along with ex-KKE head Florakis – two of the dinosaurs of post-junta politics had passed from the scene.

The morning after

And so a frail-looking Papandreou, now well into his seventies, became prime minister for the third time. He soon realized that he was not going to have nearly so easy a ride as in the 1980s.

PASOK immediately fulfilled two of its pre-election promises by removing restrictions on the reporting of terrorists' communiques and deprivatizing the Athens city bus company. The new government also set about improving the health system, and began proceedings for Mitsotakis to be tried for his purported misdemeanours, though all charges were mysteriously dropped in January 1995, prompting allegations of an under-the-table deal between Papandreou and his old nemesis.

The root of popular dissatisfaction remained **the economy**, still in dire straits. Nor could PASOK claim to have won any diplomatic battles over Macedonia, despite a lot of tough posturing. The only concrete move was the imposition in October 1993 of a **trade embargo** on the FYROM, which merely landed the Greeks in trouble with the European Court of Justice – and succeeded in virtually shutting down the port of Thessaloníki. By contrast, alone among NATO members, Greece was conspicuous for its open **support of Serbia** in the wars wracking ex-Yugoslavia, ostentatiously breaking that particular embargo with supply trucks to Belgrade via Bulgaria.

In autumn 1994, for the first time ever in a PASOK-sponsored reform, provincial governors were directly elected in regional elections, rather than appointed from Athens. The following spring, **presidential elections** were held in parliament to designate a successor to the 88-year-old Karamanlis, who enjoyed just three years of well-deserved retirement before his death in spring 1998. The winner, supported by Politikí Ánixi and PASOK, was Kostis Stefanopoulos, ex-head of the dissolved party **DIANA** (Democratic Renewal). Untainted by scandal, if a bit of a nonentity, he had been nominated by Samaras and accepted by Papandreou in a deal that would allow PASOK to see out its term without ructions.

The prime recurring scandal for 1995 had to do with the high-security **prison of Korýdhallos**, home to Koskotas, the former junta figures – and Colombian-style rackets. Two mass breakout attempts bracketed the discovery of an extensive drug-dealing ring controlled from inside; a call girl was detected in Koskotas's cell, as were large quantities of guns, ammunition and narcotics in the office of the head warden (subsequently arrested). The prison remains a hellhole to this day, largely controlled by Albanian and Romanian prisoners.

In November, Greece lifted its embargo on "Macedonia", opening the borders for tourism and trade in return for FYROM suitably editing its constitution and removing the offending emblem from their flag. Relations, in fact, were instantly almost normalized, with only the name still a moot point; perennial possibilities include "New Macedonia" or "Upper Macedonia", though as of writing the place was still being referred to as FYROM (the Former Yugoslav Republic of Macedonia) by most outsiders.

The end of an era

However, the emerging critical issue was the 76-year-old Papandreou's obstinate clinging to power despite obvious signs of dotage. Numerous senior members of PASOK became increasingly bold and vocal in their criticism, no longer fearing expulsion or the sack as in the past.

By late 1995, Papandreou was desperately ill in intensive care at the Onassis hospital, dependent on life-support machinery. As there was no constitutional provision for replacing an infirm (but alive) prime minister, the country was essentially rudderless for two months, until the barely conscious old demagogue finally faced up to his own mortality and signed a letter **resigning** as prime minister (though not as party leader) in January 1996. The "palace clique" of Mimi Liani and cohorts was beaten off in the parliamentary replacement vote in favour of the allegedly colourless but widely respected technocrat **Kostas Simitis**, who seemed to be just what the country needed after years of incompetent flamboyance.

Upon assuming office, Simitis indicated that he wouldn't necessarily play to the gallery as Papandreou had with (for a Greek politician) this remarkable statement:

"Greece's intransigent nationalism is an expression of the wretchedness that exists in our society. It is the root cause of the problems we have had with our Balkan neighbours and our difficult relations with Europe."

These beliefs were immediately put to the test by a tense armed face-off with Turkey over the uninhabited Dodecanese double-islet of Ímia, which very nearly degenerated into a shooting war. Simitis eventually bowed to US and UN pressure and ordered a withdrawal of Greek naval forces, conceding "disputed" status to the tiny goat-grazed outcrops – in hindsight a wise decision, but one for which at the time he was roundly criticized in parliament by fire-eating ND MPs and the media.

Andreas finally succumbed to his illness on June 22, 1996, prompting a moving display of national mourning; it was genuinely the end of an era, with only Karamanlis (who died less than two years later) and junta colonel Papadopoulos (who died, still incarcerated, in June 1999) as the last remaining "dinosaurs" of postwar Greek politics. Already his canonization process proceeds apace, with a spate of streets renamed to honour him in provincial towns where he was always revered, but the long-term **verdict of history** is likely to be harsher. Papandreou the Younger valued sycophancy over ability, and in his declining years was completely manipulated by the "Palace Clique" around "Mimi" (styled as the Empress Theodora reincarnated by many observers). Alleged Bank of Crete transactions aside, he also enjoyed indubitable success as a "common cheat" (as described by Karamanlis in his tart memoirs), dying with a huge fortune which he could not possibly have amassed on a public servant's salary.

Simitis two, ND nil

Papandreou's demise was promptly followed by PASOK's summer conference, where Simitis ensured his survival as party leader by co-opting his main internal foe, Papandreou's former head of staff, Akis Tsohadzopoulos, with a promise of future high office (minister of defence at the time of writing). Following the summer congress, Simitis cleverly rode the wave of pro-PASOK sympathy caused by Papandreou's death and called **general elections** a year early in **September 1996**.

The **results** were as hoped for: 162 seats for PASOK versus 108 for Néa Dhimokratía despite a margin of only three percentage points, the winner's strength artificially inflated by a convoluted electoral law. Given that the two main parties' agendas were virtually indistinguishable, the core issues boiled down to which was better poised to deliver results – and whether voters would be swayed by ND chief Evert's strident Slav- and Turk-baiting nationalism (they weren't). The biggest surprise was the collapse of Samaras's Politikí Ánixi, which failed to clear the three-percent nationwide hurdle for parliamentary representation, but three leftist splinter parties did well: eleven seats and just over five percent for Papariga's KKE, ten seats (including one Thracian Muslim deputy) with about the same tally for the Synaspismós under new chief Nikos Konstantopoulos, and nine seats at just under five percent for the Democratic Social Movement (DIKKI), founded early in the year by rehabilitated ex-minister Tsovolas to push for 1980s-vintage leftist policies. Evert resigned as ND leader, and was succeeded by Karamanlis's nephew Kostas. Néa Dhimokratía was down but by no means out; in the **June 1999** Euro-elections the party finished first nationwide and sent forty percent of Greece's Euro MPs to Strasbourg.

Simitis's first-term problems arose mainly from the economic squeeze caused by continuing **austerity measures**. In December 1996, protesting farmers closed off the country's main road and rail arteries for several weeks, before dismantling the blockades in time for people to travel for the Christmas holidays. Much of 1997 saw teachers or students (or both) on strike over proposed educational reforms – essentially about imposing some discipline on the notoriously lax school regimens. September 1997 also saw a timely boost to national morale and economic prospects with the awarding of the 2004 **Olympic Games** to Athens. Simitis sensibly warned against people treating it as an excuse merely for unbridled money-making projects, and hopefully more substantial and long-lasting benefits will accrue. The new airport at Spáta and (after a fashion) the Athens metro have been completed but, worryingly, much of the infrastructure for the Games has yet to materialize.

Simitis, by nature far more pro-European than his maverick predecessor, devoted himself to the unenviable task of getting the Greek economy in sufficiently good shape to meet the criteria for **monetary union**. The *Eforía* or Greek Inland Revenue has made some highly publicized headway in curbing the largest **black economy** in the EU, by requiring meticulous documentation of transactions and by publicly "outing" the more flagrant tax-dodgers.

After some initial success with his "hard drachma" policy (often propping it up by dumping foreign currency reserves), Simitis was obliged to devalue it upon Greece's **entry to the ERM** in March 1998; however, with other internationally traded currencies badly exposed in the Far East economic crises, the drachma regained prior levels by October 1998. The fact that inflation is staying consistently down in single figures for the first time in decades is testament to Simitis' ability as an accountant; indeed his nickname, amongst both foes and supporteers, is *o loyistís* or "the book-keeper". Simitis has also had the sense to delegate to the capable, and refrain from meddling, such that his Finance Minister Yannos Papantoniou has had an unprecedented six years on the job.

Increasingly amicable relations with its Balkan neighbours – Greece is the principal foreign investor in Bulgaria and the FYROM, for example – promise to generate jobs and trim unemployment, currently just over nine percent officially (though among recent graduates it is more like twenty percent). But the most dramatic **improvement in international relations** has occurred with old nemesis Turkey, brought about by the severe **earthquake** which struck northern Athens on September 7, 1999, killing scores, rendering almost one hundred thousand homeless. It came less than a month after the devastating tremor in northwest Turkey, and ironically proved to be the spur for a thaw between the two historical rivals. Greeks donated massive amounts of blood and foodstuffs to the Turkish victims, and were the earliest foreign rescue teams on hand in Turkey; in turn they saw Turkish disaster-relief squads among the first on the scene in Athens. Soon afterwards, **Foreign Minister George Papandreou** (son of Andreas) announced that Greece had dropped its longtime opposition to EU financial aid to Turkey in the absence of a solution to the outstanding Cyprus and Aegean disputes, and further indicated that Greece would not at present oppose Turkish candidacy for accession to the EU.

With his handling of the Turkish détente and progress towards EMU the main campaign issues, Simitis called **elections** five months earlier than required, on **April 9, 2000**. In the event, PASOK squeaked into office for an unprecedented third consecutive term by a single percentage point, 43.7 to ND's 42.7, with 158 seats against 125. The crucial factor that swung the cliffhanger – not decided until 1am the day after – was voters' mistrust of Karamanlis the Younger's manifest inexperience. The KKE held steady at just over five percent and eleven seats, but Synaspismós barely cleared the three-percent hurdle for its six seats, while DIKKI didn't.

Simitis capped his narrow victory by announcing Greece's official **entry into the euro-currency zone** on June 20, at an EU summit in Portugal. He needed this bit of good news, as the country's international reputation had again taken a battering on June 8, when the terror group November 17 emerged from a couple of years' quiescence by assassinating **Brigadier Stephen Saunders**, the UK military attache, while his car was stalled in Athens traffic. There were various mutterings abroad (again, especially in the US) that adequate security could not be guaranteed for the forthcoming, Greece-hosted Olympics. In July, the Orthodox Church mounted a last-ditch attack on the **new-style national identity cards**, which omitted to state the bearer's religion; government spokesmen proclaimed that the old-style cards were illegal under EU regulations, and an ND-sponsored bill to allow for optional citation of religious faith was defeated in parliament.

Tourism, the most important foreign-exchange earner for the country, had had a pretty good year in 1999 (after a rocky spring occasioned by the Kosovo war, roundly condemned by most, traditionally pro-Serbian Greeks), but a well-publicized spate of forest fires during an unusually hot summer, plus the *Express Samina* shipwreck (see box, p.42) conspired to make 2000 an *annus horribilis* for tourist arrival numbers. 2001 was another bad season, ending on the double sour notes of the September 11 US terror incidents (which means no significant American arrivals for the foreseeable future) and Virgin Atlantic's announcement that it was abandoning its London–Athens routes as of October 28.

In the run-up to the Olympics, Greece has mounted a renewed public relations campaign for the return of the **Elgin marbles** from the British Museum.

A new museum for the Parthenon relics is finally being built south of the Acropolis, with a large wing pointedly reserved for the eventual return of the marbles, which, as Greece broadly hints, it would be a nice gesture to have back in time for the Games. The long-standing British argument that the Greeks were incompetent barbarians not fit to curate the precious friezes was rather undercut by the 1999 revelation that heavy-handed "cleaning" in 1937–38, with wire brushes and harsh solvents, had damaged the sculptures irreparably. Foreign Minister Papandreou travelled to London in June 2000 to state the Greek case and was heard sympathetically by Labour and Lib–Dem MPs (the Tories walked out), but was ultimately rebuffed by Tony Blair's announcement that the UK had no intention of budging on the issue.

Greek society today

The following summary concentrates on recent, salient events and can only give a flavour of the massive, ground-level changes which have occurred in Greece since the late 1980s. First and foremost, it's a conspicuously wealthier, more **consumerist society** than before, with vast disparities in income, imbued with rampant Thatcherism (in particular a mania for privatizing), long after that ideology has largely subsided in its homeland. Athens, Thessaloníki and most large towns have their legions of **yuppies**, addicted to gourmet wines, properly-made cappuccinos, designer accessories, fast cars and **travel**; even small-town agencies promote junkets to Thailand and Cuba (the current trendy favourites). Greek domestic tourism is also heavily marketed, in particular weekend breaks to "name" islands like Corfu, Thíra, and Rhodes, or outdoor expeditions to the mountains; there are numerous Greek-language travel magazines, Sunday supplements and bound guides, advising the yuppies where to spend their cash.

Mobile phones are ubiquitous – along with Italy and Cyprus, Greece has the highest per-capita use in Europe – and the success of the two private networks has forced partly privatized OTE to offer its own mobile network at reasonable prices, and in general sharpen up. You can walk into an OTE phone shop and get any high-tech device or network service more or less instantly, unlike the bad old days – as recently as 1994 – when OTE was a national disgrace and provision of a simple analogue line could take years.

In tandem with this increased materialism, the **Orthodox Church** has declined from "guardian of the nation" to something of a national embarrassment. Rather than address the pressing social problems and hidden poverty occasioned by Greece's immigrant crisis (see opposite), its version of moral leadership has been to organize demos against the new secularized ID cards (as above), and (more understandably) to extract from Pope John Paul II, during his May 2001 visit, an apology for the 1204 sacking of Constantinople. But the Church's medieval mindset has really come to the fore in its continuing ban on cremation, and near-hysteria on the subject of bar codes. Greece is the only EU country where cremation is forbidden; every summer there's a malodorous backlog of corpses to be interred at the overcrowded cemeteries, whilst others relatively surreptitiously cart their relatives' remains to be burnt in more accommodating Bulgaria or Romania, under threat of excommunication – Orthodox doctrine is adamant that immolation would compromise the Resurrection, and that the bones of a saint (still revered as relics) might inadvertently be destroyed. But it's bar codes on ID cards and hand- or forehead-stamping for casino patrons and bank employees that have really excercised the Athonite monks in particular (and made them something of a laughing-stock). They, and a considerable number of the lay faithful, see this as a Jewish–Masonic conspiracy, fulfilling *Revelations* 13:16–17 and 14:9, verses which relate to the Mark of the Beast; vast stacks of printed leaflets are distributed on the subject.

The clergy's rantings notwithstanding, bar-coded Greece is now firmly locked into the **global economy**, and not just in the matter of cross-border shipment of the dead. International franchises such as *McDonalds*, Next, Häagen Dazs and The Body Shop proliferate in most larger towns; consumer interest rates have plunged, the Athens stock exchange has burgeoned (before crashing spectacularly, prompting a wave of suicides by those who lost their savings), and foreign or multinational companies have flocked to invest. It is they who are funding and carrying out massive infrastructure improvements designed to long outlast the 2004 Olympics: the airport at Spáta, metros in Athens and Thessaloníki, the Río-Andírrio bridge over the Gulf of Corinth and the Via Egnatia expressway across Epirus, Macedonia and Thrace. **Overseas companies** are also quietly **acquiring** more (or less) productive elements of the Greek economy; Britain's Blue Circle, for example, in 1998 purchased Hercules Cement from Italian interests, while Cyprus Airways and an Australian holding group were among contenders to buy out troubled flag-carrier Olympic Airways (as of writing, it seems that Axon Airlines, one of several private airlines to emerge since air travel was deregulated in 1994, will get the nod). The 2003 end of cabotage – whereby only Greek companies have been allowed to provide ferry services within Greece – should weed out the flakier shipping companies and have the others pulling their socks up, under threat of possibly being challenged by the likes of P&O or Fred Olsen. Matters can only get better since the *Express Samina* sinking, which fully exposed the weaknesses in safety, pricing and personnel training of Greek Aegean transport – and most of all the oligopolies which have resulted from domestic companies following overseas examples and engaging in extensive **corporate takeovers**. Minoan (now Hellas) Flying Dolphins, the responsible party in the shipwreck, had acquired Ceres Hydrofoils, several smaller steamship outfits and a majority interest in an airline, to become the largest domestic transport company; Alpha Bank absorbed the troubled Ionian/Ioniki Bank in early 1999 and instantly became the second largest banking/insurance group in the country.

It used to be that a lifetime sinecure with the civil service was the goal for most graduates, but no longer – now young people crave a **career** in the private sector, with unlimited salary prospects, and will initially work for low pay which older, less-qualified professionals with families – who often must cobble together part-time jobs – simply can't live on. Yet most Greeks have now become too grand for menial jobs; the late Andreas once grumbled that Greece shouldn't remain "a nation of waiters", though it seems he needn't have worried.

Greece may continue to occupy the EU's economic cellar with Portugal, but it's still infinitely wealthier (and more stable) than any of its neighbours, and this has acted as a magnet for **a permanent underclass of immigrants**. Since 1990 they have arrived in numbers estimated variously at 800,000 to over a million, a huge burden for a not especially rich country of just over ten million (it would be the equivalent of Britain having six million refugees rather than a few hundred thousand). These days your waiter, hotel desk clerk or cleaning lady is most likely to be Albanian, Ukrainian or Bulgarian, to cite the three largest groups of arrivals. There are also significant communities of Russians, Poles, Filipinos, Romanians, Sudanis, Kurds, equatorial Africans and Georgians (not to mention ethnic Greeks from the Caucasus) – a striking change in what had hitherto been a homogeneous, parochial culture.

The **Greek response** to this has been decidedly mixed; the Albanians, making up roughly half the influx, are almost universally detested (except for the ethnic-Greek northern Epirots), and blamed for all manner of social ills. They have also prompted the first anti-immigration measures with teeth in a country whose population is more used to being on the other side of such laws – Greece is a member of the Schengen visa scheme and sees itself, as in past ages, as the first line of defence against the barbarian hordes from the Orient. All of the east Aegean islands regularly receive boatloads of people fleeing from every country in Asia, and the country's few refugee camps (near Athens) are grossly inadequate. In June 2001, as an attempt to cope, legal residence was offered to the estimated half-a-million illegals who could demonstrate two-years' presence in Greece, and pay a hefty amount for retroactive social security contributions; yet when this **amnesty period** ended in early September, fewer than 350,000 of these individuals had applied to be "regularized", leaving the remainder still subject to arrest and deportation.

On a positive note, these diverse groups, increased travel abroad by the Greeks themselves, touring bands and dance companies and programmes on the private television channels have created a taste for **exotic music and foods**. One doesn't always have to wait for the summer festivals to see name jazz, blues or soul acts in Thessaloníki or Athens, and there are now decent foreign-cuisine restaurants there as well as in many of the major resorts. All of these factors, however, have had the effect of making Greece less identifiably Greek and, it must be said, of making the native Greeks themselves rather less welcoming and more self-absorbed than formerly.

The Greek minorities

The principal Greek minorities – Vlachs, Sarakatsáni, Turks, Jews, Slavo-phones, Catholics and Gypsies – are little known, even within Greece. Indeed, to meet Vlachs or Sarakatsáni who remain true to their roots you'll have to get to some fairly remote parts of Epirus. Greco-Turks are another matter, with a sizeable (and recently problematic) community living, as they have done for centuries, in Thrace, Rhodes and Kós. The Jews of Greece, as so often, tell the saddest history, having been annihilated by the Nazi occupiers during the latter stages of World War II. Slavophones are officially a taboo subject, and the Catholics largely restricted to the Cyclades, while the Gypsies are admired – from a distance – only for their musicality.

The Vlachs and Sarakatsáni

The **Vlachs'** homeland is in the remote vastness of the Píndhos mountains in **northwestern Greece** near the Albanian frontier. Traditionally they were transhumant shepherds, although some have long led a more settled existence in Métsovo and a score of villages around. As the town grew in prosperity, the Vlachs traded their sheep products further and further afield. Local merchants established themselves in Constantinople, Vienna, Venice and elsewhere, expanding into other lines of business: Vlachs played a major role in Balkan mule-back haulage and the hotel trade – specifically caravanserais where mule convoys halted.

They are an ancient, close-knit community with a strong sense of identity, like their rival shepherd clan, the Sarakatsáni (see overleaf), whom they despise as "tent-dwellers" and who, in turn, just as passionately despise them for living in houses. Unlike the Sarakatsáni, however, their mother tongue is not Greek, but Vlach, a Romance language, which even today is full of words that anyone with a little Latin can easily recognize: *loop* for wolf, *mulier* for women, *pene* for bread. When the Italians invaded Greece in World War II, Vlach soldiers in the Greek army were often used as interpreters, though there were very few instances of later collaboration. Incidentally, the Vlachs prefer to call themselves *Roumaní* (Arouman) and their language *Roumaniká*; the word *vláhos* in Greek often means "yokel" or "bumpkin".

It used to be thought that the Vlachs were descendants of Roman legionaries stationed in the provinces of Illyria and Dacia, who over the centuries had wandered up and down through the Balkans in search of grazing land for their sheep. Those who finally settled in northern Greece were trapped there by the creation of modern frontiers upon the disintegration of the Austro-Hungarian and Ottoman empires. Because of these supposed Romanian connections and enduring official anxieties about the separatist tendencies of northern Greek minorities, the Vlachs have been objects of suspicion to the modern state. To their chagrin many villages with Slavic or Vlach names were officially renamed during the Metaxas dictatorship of the 1930s, and Vlach schoolchildren for-bidden to use their mother tongue.

There is, however, a more recent, better-supported theory about their origins, which argues that the Greek Vlachs at least are of Greek descent and have always inhabited these same regions of the Píndhos mountains; during Roman times the Romans found it convenient to train local people as highway guards for the high passes on the old Roman road, the Via Egnatia, which connected Constantinople with the Adriatic. Thus the Vlachs learned Latin through their association with the Romans and preserved it in distorted form because of the isolation of their homeland and the exclusive nature of their pastoral way of life.

Sadly, though probably inevitably, the Vlachs' unique traditions are in danger of extinction. Until World War II, a prosperous Vlach family might have 10,000 sheep, and when they set off on the annual migration from their lowland winter pastures to the mountains it was like a small army on the march: two or three complete generations, together with all their animals and belongings. Nowadays few flocks number more than 250 ewes, and the annual migration takes place in lorries – though a few veterans still do it on foot. Hundreds of Vlachs have sold their flocks, and moved to the towns or emigrated. There are depressingly few young men among the remaining shepherds. The hardships of their life are too many and the economic returns too small.

The **Sarakatsáni**, celebrated in Patrick Leigh Fermor's *Roumeli* (see p.1078) and J. K. Campbell's **Honour, Family and Patronage** (see p.1087), by contrast appear to be indisputably indigenous, and speak an archaic form of Greek. The distinctive costumes and reed tents which Leigh Fermor described are now a thing of the past, to be pulled out only for feast days and ethnographic theme parks, but traces of their former lifestyle persist. Until a few decades ago they were true transhumants, moving between winter quarters well below the snowline and summer pastures in the mountains. After World War II the government required them to establish permanent winter dwellings, but they still return each summer to the heights, where they pasture their sheep on land rented from the village councils – often composed of their hereditary adversaries, the Vlachs.

Jews and Turks

Jews and **Turks** in Greece are, for historical reasons, conveniently considered together. Since the decline of the Ottoman empire, these two minorities have often suffered similar fates as isolated groups in a nonassimilating culture. Yet it seems that enclaves of each will endure for the foreseeable future.

Origins and settlements

The **Greek Jewish community** is one of the oldest established in Europe, dating back to the early Hellenistic period when Greek-speaking Jews were already settled at Rhodes, Corinth, Athens, Thebes, Salonika, Véria, Delos, Crete and Sparta. During the Roman and Byzantine eras, these Jews were termed Romaniot, and urban colonies flourished throughout the Balkans. In Greece these additionally included, by the twelfth to fourteenth centuries, Corfu, Zákynthos, Pátra, Halkídha, Lárissa and, most importantly, Ioánnina.

The most numerically significant Jewish communities in Greece, however, date back to shortly after the taking of Constantinople by the **Ottomans**. In 1493 Sultan Beyazit II invited Spanish and Portuguese Jews expelled from those countries to settle in the Ottoman empire. This great influx of **Sephardim** (Ladino-speaking Jews) soon swamped many of the original Romaniot centres, particularly at Kós, Rhodes, Véria and Salonika, and within two centuries, Ladino – officially Judeo-Spanish, a mix of medieval Spanish and Portuguese with Turkish, Hebrew and Arabic augments – had largely supplanted Greek as the lingua franca of Balkan Jewry, with Italian and Hungarian refugee Jews nearly as numerous as the Romaniots. However, *Ladinismo* (the medieval Iberian Jewish culture) never penetrated the Romaniot enclaves of Ioánnina and Halkídha, which remain proudly Greek-speaking to this day. Moreover, the Greek- and non-Greek-speaking Jews differed in religious observance as well as language, resulting in numerous small synagogues being founded in each town for each group – and little intermarriage between the sects.

Ottoman officials and their families fanned out across the Balkans to consolidate imperial administration, thus sowing the seeds of the numerous **Muslim communities** in present-day Bulgaria, Albania, former Yugoslavia and Greece. The Ottoman authorities often appointed Jews as civil servants and tax collectors; one, Joseph Nasi, became governor of the Cyclades in 1566, but dared not show his face there, ruling instead through a representative.

As a result of this and other episodes, especially on Crete, Jews became identified with the ruling hierarchy in the eyes of the Orthodox Christian population, and at the 1821 outset of the **War of Independence** inhabitants of the Jewish quarters of Pátra, Trípoli, Athens and virtually all others within the confines of the nascent Greek state, were put to the sword along with the Muslim population. Survivors of the various massacres fled north, to territories that remained under Ottoman control. Within the new Greek kingdom, a small community of Ashkenazi Jews arrived in Athens, along with the Bavarian king Otho, during the 1830s.

Under the Greek state

The **expansion** of the Greek nation thereafter resulted in the decline of both the Greco-Jewish and Greco-Turkish populations. New annexations or conquests (Thessaly in 1878, Epirus, Macedonia, the northeast Aegean and Crete in 1913) provoked a wave of forced or nervous Judeo-Turkish migration to the other side of the receding Ottoman frontier. Although Jews were never forbidden to stay in newly occupied territory, rarely were they explicitly welcome, although the Romaniot communities in Ioánnina and Halkídha were understandably pro-Greek. During the latter half of the nineteenth century – long after such incidents had peaked in western Europe – there were repeated outbreaks of anti-Semitic riots whenever Jewish communities were falsely accused of murdering Christian children in order to obtain blood thought necessary for ritual use.

The Turks – or more correctly, **Muslims**, since "Turk" was a generic term for any Muslim, including Albanians, and ethnic Greeks who had converted to Islam for economic advantage – were subject to various expulsion orders. Between 1913 and 1923 the Muslims of **Crete**, mostly converted islanders, were forced to choose between apostasy to Christianity or exile, if they hadn't emigrated voluntarily between 1898 and 1913. (The newly Orthodox can today often be distinguished by their ostentatiously Christian surnames, such as Stavroulakis, Khristakis, and so on.) Those who opted to stand by their faith were summarily deposited in the closest Turkish-Muslim settlements on Greek islands just over the Ottoman border; Kós Town, the nearby village of Platáni, and Ródhos Town were three of the more convenient ones.

When the Italians formally annexed the **Dodecanese** after World War I, the Muslims were allowed to remain and were thus rendered exempt from any of the provisions of the 1923 Treaty of Lausanne (stipulating the wholesale exchange of "Turk" and "Greek" populations in the wake of the Asia Minor war). Additionally, the Jewish communities of Kós and Rhodes flourished, as there was little or no anti-Semitism under Italian Fascist rule until the mid-1930s. In Rhodes there had been a long tradition of co-operation between the Muslim and the Jewish communities. In Ottoman days Jews were the only *millet* (subject ethnic group) allowed out after the city gates were closed at dusk, and since 1948 Muslim and Jewish leaders have consulted on how best to counter government strategies to deprive each of their rights and property. The dilapidated refugee village of Kritiká ("the Cretans") still huddles by the seaside on the way to the airport, and walking through Ródhos' old town it's easy to spot dwindling numbers of Turkish names on the signboards of various jewellers, tinsmiths and kafenía. Those Turks who live in the old town itself, moreover, have in some cases been there since the sixteenth century and will proudly tell you that they have every right to be considered native Rhodians. This notwithstanding, numbers diminish through emigration to Turkey every year, with (until 1997) those leaving – even to third countries like Australia – denied any right of return.

In **Kós**, Cretan Muslims settled both in the port town – where they remain economically active – and at Platáni, which still has a mixed Greek Orthodox and "Turkish" population. However, since the first major Cyprus crisis of 1964, numbers have dropped by two-thirds, and the Turkish-language primary school has been forcibly closed.

During the early 1900s, the same era as the Cretan deportations, the status of mainland Jews and Turks in the path of Greek nationalism was more ambiguous. Even after the respective 1878 and 1913 acquisitions of **Thessaly**, **Epirus** and **Macedonia**, Muslim villages continued to exist in these regions. The **Tsamídhes**, an Albanian-speaking, nominally Muslim tribe localized in Epirus and Thesprotía, were left alone until World War II, when they made the grievous error of siding with the invading Italian army; after 1944 they were massacred or expelled, first by the National Army and later by guerrilla bands.

Thessaloníki in the late nineteenth and early twentieth century was one of the largest Jewish towns in the world. Jews made up roughly half the population, and dominated the sailing, shipping and chandlery trades, such that the harbour ceased operations on Saturday, but functioned on Sunday. In addition there were numerous **Dönme**, or more properly **Ma'min**, Jews who had chosen to follow the "false messiah" Sabbatai Zvi into Islam in the 1670s, but maintained certain aspects of Jewish worship in secret. As provided for by the Treaty of Lausanne, the authorities insisted on the departure of the Dönme along with other Turkic Muslims. The 20,000 Dönme (Turkish for "renegades", after Zvi's conversion to Islam) insisted that they were "really" Jews, but to no avail. Indeed as early as 1913, with a rapid influx of Greek Orthodox into the conquered city, Thessaloníki had already begun to lose its strong Hebraic character; the fire of 1917, emigration to Palestine, the arrival of Greek Orthodox refugees from Anatolia after 1923 and the tenure of the Nazis effectively brought an era to a close.

The same period, around the time of World War I, also saw the end of Muslim (and minute Jewish) enclaves on the islands of **Thássos**, **Samothráki**, **Límnos**, **Lésvos** and **Híos**, where it is claimed the "Turks" themselves destroyed the fine *hamam* before departing. On **Sámos** there is a special, tiny Jewish cemetery with the graves of two brothers, who helped start the wine co-op in 1935; otherwise there had not been a significant Jewish community here since Byzantine times, and Muslims were (uniquely in the east Aegean) forbidden to settle here after the seventeenth century.

Western Thrace, the area between the Néstos and Évros rivers, was always home to large numbers of **Muslims**, and it remained their last bastion after the 1919–22 Asia Minor War. The **Treaty of Lausanne** (1923) confirmed the right of this minority to remain *in situ*, in return for a continued Greek Orthodox presence in Istanbul (still known to Greeks as Konstandinoúpoli), the Princes' Islands and on the islands of Ténedhos and Ímvros.

Over the years, the Turks have repeatedly abrogated the terms of the pact by repressive measures and reduced the Turkish Greek Orthodox population to two percent of pre-1923 levels. The Greeks have acted comparatively leniently, and today Muslims still make up a third of the population of Greek Thrace, being highly visible in the main towns of **Alexandhroúpoli**, **Komotiní** and **Xánthi**. Muslims control much of the tobacco culture hereabouts, and baggy-trousered, head-scarved women tending young plants can frequently be glimpsed from the trains which pass through their fields.

The loyalty of these Thracian "Turks" to the Greek state was amply demonstrated during **World War II**, when they resisted the invading Bulgarians and Nazis side-by-side with their Christian compatriots. In return the two occupying forces harassed and deported to death camps many local Muslims. During the 1946–49 civil war Thracian Muslims again suffered at the hands of ELAS, who found the deep-seated conservatism of these villagers exasperating and laboured under the misconception that all local Muslims were traitors.

Only the **Pomaks**, a non-Turkic Muslim group of about 40,000 distributed across the Rodhópi ranges north of Xánthi and Komotiní, collaborated to any extent with the Bulgarians, probably on the basis of ethnic affinity. The Pomaks as a group were probably Slavic Bogomil heretics forcibly converted to Islam in the sixteenth century; they speak a degenerate dialect of Bulgarian with generous mixtures of Greek and Turkish. The authorities still keep them on a tight rein; until the early 1990s Pomaks required a travel permit to leave their immediate area of residence, and visitors in turn required a permit to visit certain of their villages near Ehínos. The main reward of a trip into their Rodhópi homeland is some magnificent scenery; there's not much arable land amidst the wild, pine-forested hills, and what there is – down in the river valleys – is devoted entirely to hand-tilled tobacco. Pomaks are occasionally found living outside Thrace, particularly near certain mines in Viotía, the mainland region opposite Évvia, where their skills as sappers and tunnellers are required.

Until recently, the Orthodox and "Turkish" Thracian communities lived in a fairly easy (if distant) relationship with each other, but during the early 1990s a series of ugly intercommunal incidents and official prosecution of Turkish political leaders cast doubt on the carefully cultivated international image of Greece's toleration of its minorities. It has, in fact, always been true that treatment of these Muslims functions as a barometer of relations at a more general level between Greece and Turkey, and as a quid pro quo for perceived maltreatment of the remaining Greek Orthodox in Turkey.

But it is the **Jews** rather than the Muslims who have suffered the greatest catastrophes during and since **World War II**. Jews who chanced to live in the Italian zone of occupation were initially no worse off than their compatriots, but after Italy's capitulation in September 1943 and the German assumption of control, conditions deteriorated rapidly. Eighty-five percent of a Jewish population of around 80,000 was rounded up by the Nazis in the spring and summer of 1944, never to return. The Bulgarian occupation forces tended to substitute Greek Jews for Bulgarian ones on the death trains as part of their "Bulgarization" programme, thus earning an unjustified reputation for clemency.

Greek Christians often went to extraordinary lengths to protect their persecuted countrymen, overshadowing the few instances of sordid betrayal; in this respect the Greek record is rather better than many western European countries, France for example. The mayor and bishop of Zákynthos and the bishop of Halkídha put themselves at risk to save the local Jewish communities, virtually ordering their Christian neighbours to hide and feed them; as a result nearly all of them survived. In Athens, the police chief and the archbishop arranged for the issue of false identity cards and baptismal certificates, which again saved huge numbers of Jews. In Athens, Tríkala, Lárissa and Vólos especially, where the rabbi was active in the resistance to occupation, most Jews were warned in good time of what fate the Germans had in store for them, and took to the hills to join the partisans. Romaniot Jews, indistinguishable from their Orthodox neighbours in appearance and tongue, fared best, but the Ladino-speaking Jews of northern Greece, with their distinctive surnames and customs, were easy targets for the Nazis. It must also be said that certain portions of the Greek business community in **Thessaloníki** benefited greatly from the expulsion of the Jews, and needed little encouragement to help themselves to the contents of the abandoned Jewish shops. Jewish sensibilities were further offended in the postwar era when the German desecration of the huge Jewish cemetery was completed by the construction of the University of Thessaloníki and expansion of the fairgrounds.

The paltry number of **survivors** returning from the death camps to Greece was insufficient to form the nucleus of a revival in most provincial towns, and moving to Athens or **emigration** to Israel was often a preferable alternative to living with ghosts. Currently barely six thousand Jews remain in Greece. In Thessaloníki there are around a thousand Sephardim, who generally keep a low profile aside from the Molho family's famous bookstore. Lárissa retains about three hundred Sephardim, who are still disproportionately important in the clothing trade. However, young Jewish women outnumber their male counterparts, so intermarriage with Orthodox men has long been a pattern. Small Romaniot communities of a hundred persons or less continue to exist in Halkídha, Ioánnina, Corfu, Tríkala and Vólos. The Kós, Haniá and Rhodes congregations were virtually wiped out, and today only about 35 Jews – many of these from the mainland – live in Ródhos town. Here, the Platía ton Evreón Martýron (Square of the Jewish Martyrs), at the edge of the former Jewish quarter, commemorates over 1800 Jews of Kós and Rhodes deported by the Germans. About 3000 of today's Greek Jews live in Athens, which is also home to the **Jewish Museum of Greece**.

Slavophones

Despite a population exchange between Greece and Bulgaria in 1918, and the flight of many **Slavophones** abroad after 1948, there remain approximately 40,000 individuals in Greece whose at-home language is some approximation of Macedonian. They dwell in a ribbon along the northern frontier, from Préspa to the internal border with Thrace at the Néstos River. If Greeks can seem unreasonable on the question of "Turks", they become positively apoplectic at the mention of any Slavic minority; successive governments of whatever political stripe have indicated that any official recognition of such is out of the question, and counter any activism to the contrary with arrests or unofficial harassment. This position becomes slightly more understandable when such a population is viewed as a potential fifth column for a theoretically expansionist FYROM (Former Yugoslav Republic of Macedonia). Slavophones in Greece did not have their position in Greece made any more tenable during World War II and the civil war, when at various times – until such were suppressed by ELAS as an expression of "bourgeois nationalism" – communist statements contained references to "self-determination for Macedonian peoples", which could be construed to mean dismembering northern Greece and joining parts of it to a hypothetical Macedonian state. In the event, the victorious central government leaned hard on everybody unlucky enough to be dwelling in a northern border zone, regardless of political hue; in some places villages were evacuated, in others Greek-speaking colonists of "healthy national character" were imported to dilute the Slavophone population, along with other discriminatory measures. These had their desired effect, inasmuch as many Slavophones emigrated to Yugoslavia, Canada, America and Australia, where some have become part of the increasingly vocal pro-Macedonian lobby. Since the 1980s there has been some improvement in terms of increased material prosperity, but don't look for Slavic-language schools or public song performances any time soon.

Catholics

The **Catholics** of the Cyclades, numbering no more than 12,000, are a legacy of Venetian settlement in the Aegean following the piratical Fourth Crusade in 1204. Today they live principally on the islands of Sýros and Tínos, with much tinier enclaves on Thíra, Náxos, Sámos, Rhodes and certain provincial towns such as Pátra. Often Italianate last names (Dellaroka) or given names (Leonardhos, Frangiskos) distinguish them from their neighbours. Descended from once-powerful feudal lords, they are today insignificant in civic as well as numerical terms, though they have always attracted suspicion as being less than "one-hundred percent Greek"; in 1994 a civil servant on Náxos was promoted out of harm's way after making an outrageous public pronouncement about "Papist fifth-columnists in our midst". The Catholic Church hierarchy, for its part, has made periodic complaints about a certain legal disability; like all other non-Orthodox denominations, it is classified as a *xénon dhógma* (foreign creed), and as such its schools (unlike Orthodox academies) are ineligible for state subsidies.

The visit of Pope John Paul II to Greece in June 2001, the first ever by a pontiff, sparked a furore. It was opposed by significant numbers of the Orthodox clergy, who heaped public abuse on Catholic belief as heresy, and the pope as the chief heretic; John Paul was eventually compelled to issue a grovelling apology to assembled Orthodox for past Catholic behaviour, in particular the 1204 sack of Constantinople. Most of the crowds which assembled to greet the pope were Filipinos and Poles – as most resident Catholics are in Greece these days.

Gypsies

The **Gypsies** first came to the Balkans in about the eleventh century, probably a low-ranking caste from Rajasthan on the Indian subcontinent, and were soon well enough established to figure in Byzantine chronicles of the 1300s. Nazi policy towards them was simlar to that adopted towards the Jews; most were sent directly to extermination facilities, reckoned not even worth a month of slave labour. Given their elusive, anti-authoritarian nature, no one knows exactly how many Gypsies there are in Greece at present; 150,000, of which ninety percent are nominally Greek Orthodox and the rest Muslim, seems a good guess. They are concentrated on the mainland, especially Thessaly and Étolo-Akarnanía, and in the Athenian neighbourhoods of Kolonós and Ayía Varvára, though they maintain a transient presence on all of the larger islands, and large families are a common sight on the ferry-boats. Driving outsized trucks fitted with loud-hailers, Gypsy vendors fan out across the country, peddling plastic garden furniture, cheap carpets, house plants, basketry, watermelons and other produce – rather a come-down from their traditional livelihoods of metal-smithing, bear-training, shadow-puppeteering and horse-dealing, which it seems their Rajasthani ancestors also engaged in. Marginalized by centuries of nationalism and industrial advance, they are in Greece – as elsewhere in central Europe – undereducated, increasingly reliant on begging and generally despised by the majority population.

But an echo of the past survives in events such as the **zoöemboropaniyíri** (animal-trading festival), a moveable feast which begins at Peloponnesian Stymfalía around September 14 (the Exaltation of the Cross) and drifts west in stages to meet another party coming from Káto Ahaïa; these then travel jointly to Nafpaktós, where the festival finishes on October 26, the day of Áyios Dhimítrios. Rural tools and spit-roasted meat amongst tatty synthetic goods characterize this as a harvest fair, with Gypsies figuring prominently both as livestock-dealers and evening musicians.

Gypsies are finally (if often grudgingly) being properly credited with disproportionate prominence in the ranks of Greek mainland instrumental **musicians**, among them the *sandoúri* player Aristidhis Moskhos, the late clarinettist Vassilis Soukas, the late crooner Manolis Angelopoulos, the protest guitarist Kostas Hatzis and the *laïkó* star Eleni Vitali. Indeed virtually all of the now-settled clans of mainland clarinettists were originally of Gypsy origin, and for every personality like Vitali who makes no bones about their background, there is another who still feels he or she must conceal it. Incidentally, it is worth emphasizing that Gypsies are not necessarily more talented musically than their host culture; it's just that for many centuries, excluded from bazaar guilds or even fixed residence, they had few other choices of profession. Until recently in many northern towns, there was a designated kafenío in the marketplace which acted as an "employment exchange" for Gypsy musicians between engagements. For more on Greek music in general, see p.1057.

Buried treasures – the story of Greek archeology

Archeology until the second half of the nineteenth century was a very hit-and-miss affair. The early students of antiquity went to Greece to draw and make plaster casts of the great masterpieces of Classical sculpture. Unfortunately, a number soon found it more convenient or more profitable to remove objects wholesale, and might be better described as looters than scholars or archeologists.

Early excavations

The **British Society of Dilettanti** was one of the earliest promoters of Greek culture, financing expeditions to draw and publish antiquities. Founded in the 1730s as a club for young aristocrats who had completed the Grand Tour and fancied themselves arbiters of taste, the Society's main qualification for membership (according to most critics) was habitual drunkenness. Its leading spirit was Sir Francis Dashwood, a notorious rake who founded the infamous Hellfire Club. Nevertheless, the society was the first body organized to sponsor systematic research into Greek antiquities, though it was initially most interested in Italy. Greece, then a backwater of the Ottoman empire, was not a regular part of the Grand Tour and only the most intrepid adventurers undertook so hazardous a trip.

In the 1740s, two young artists, James Stuart and Nicholas Revett, formed a plan to produce a scholarly record of ancient Greek buildings. With the support of the society they spent three years in Greece, principally around Athens, drawing and measuring the surviving antiquities. The first volume of *The Antiquities of Athens* appeared in 1762, becoming an instant success. The publication of their exquisite illustrations gave an enormous fillip to the study of Greek sculpture and architecture, which became the fashionable craze among the educated classes; many European Neoclassical town and country houses date from this period.

The Dilettanti financed a number of further expeditions to study Greek antiquities, including one to Asia Minor in 1812. The expedition was to be based in Smyrna, but while waiting in Athens for a ship to Turkey, the party employed themselves in excavations at Eleusis, where they uncovered the Temple of Demeter. It was the first archeological excavation made on behalf of the society, and one of the first in Greece. After extensive explorations in Asia Minor, the participants returned via Attica, where they excavated the Temple of Nemesis at Rhamnous and examined the Temple of Apollo at Sounion.

Several other antiquarians of the age were less interested in discoveries for their own sake. A French count, Choiseul-Gouffier, removed part of the Parthenon frieze in 1787 and his example prompted **Lord Elgin** to detach much of the rest in 1801. These were essentially acts of looting – "Bonaparte has not got such things from all his thefts in Italy", boasted Elgin – and their legality was suspect even at the time.

Other discoveries of the period were more ambiguous. In 1811, a party of English and German travellers, including the architect C.R. Cockerell, uncovered the Temple of Aphaia on Égina and shipped away the pediments. They auctioned off the marbles for £6000 to Prince Ludwig of Bavaria, and, inspired by this success, returned to Greece for further finds. This time they struck lucky with 23 slabs from the Temple of Apollo Epikourios at Bassae, for which the British Museum laid out a further £15,000. These were huge sums for the time and highly profitable exercises, but they were also pioneering archeology for the period. Besides, removing the finds was hardly surprising: Greece, after all, was not yet a state and had no public museum; antiquities discovered were sold by their finders – if they recognized their value.

The new nation

The Greek **War of Independence** (1821–28) and the establishment of a modern Greek nation changed all of this – and provided a major impetus to archeology. Nationhood brought an increased pride in Greece's Classical heritage, nowhere more so than in Athens, which succeeded Náfplio as the nation's capital in 1834 largely on the basis of its ancient monuments and past.

As a result of the selection of Prince Otto of Bavaria as the first king of modern Greece in 1832, the Germans, whose education system laid great stress on Classical learning, were in the forefront of archeological activity.

One of the dominant Teutonic figures during the early years of the new state was **Ludwig Ross**. Arriving in Greece as a student in 1832, he was on hand to show the new king around the antiquities of Athens when Otto was considering making the town his capital. Ross was appointed deputy keeper of antiquities to the court, and in 1834 began supervising the excavation and restoration of the Acropolis. The work of dismantling the accretion of Byzantine, Frankish and Turkish fortifications began the following year. The graceful Temple of Athena Nike, which had furnished many of the blocks for the fortifications, was rebuilt, and Ross's architect, Leo von Klenze, began the reconstruction of the Parthenon.

The Greeks themselves had begun to focus on their ancient past when the first stirrings of the independence movement were felt. In 1813 the Philomuse Society was formed, which aimed to uncover and collect antiquities, publish books and assist students and foreign philhellenes. In 1829 an orphanage on the island of Égina, built by Kapodistrias, the first president of Greece, became the first Greek archeological museum.

In 1837 the **Greek Archeological Society** was founded "for the discovery, recovery and restoration of antiquities in Greece". Its moving spirit was Kyriakos Pittakis, a remarkable figure who during the War of Independence had used his knowledge of ancient literature to discover the Klepsydra spring on the Acropolis – solving the problem of lack of water during the Turkish siege. In the first four years of its existence, the Archeological Society sponsored excavations in Athens at the Theatre of Dionysos, the Tower of the Winds, the Propylaia and the Erechtheion. Pittakis also played a major role in the attempt to convince Greeks of the importance of their heritage; antiquities were still being looted or burned for lime.

The great Germans: Curtius and Schliemann

Although King Otto was deposed in 1862 in favour of a Danish prince, Germans remained in the forefront of Greek archeology in the 1870s. Two men dominated the scene: Heinrich Schliemann and Ernst Curtius.

Ernst Curtius was a traditional Classical scholar. He had come to Athens originally as tutor to King Otto's family and in 1874 returned to Greece to secure permission for conducting the **excavations at Olympia**, one of the richest of Greek sanctuaries and site of the most famous of the ancient pan-hellenic games. The reigning Kaiser Wilhelm I intended that the excavation would proclaim to the world the cultural and intellectual pre-eminence of his empire. Curtius took steps to set up a **German Archeological Institute** in Athens and negotiated the **Olympia Convention**, under the terms of which the Germans were to pay for and have total control of the dig; all finds were to remain in Greece, though the excavators could make copies and casts; and all finds were to be published simultaneously in Greek and German.

This was an enormously important agreement, which almost certainly prevented the treasure of Olympia and Mycenae following that of Troy to a German museum. But other Europeans were still in very acquisitive mode: French consuls, for example, had been instructed to purchase any "available" local antiquities in Greece and Asia Minor, and had picked up the Louvre's great treasures, the *Venus de Milo* and *Winged Victory* of Samothrace, in 1820 and 1863 respectively.

At **Olympia**, digging began in 1875 on a site buried beneath many feet of river mud, silt and sand. Only one corner of the Temple of Zeus was initially visible, but within months the excavators had turned up statues from the east pediment. Over forty magnificent sculptures, as well as terracottas, statue bases and a rich collection of bronzes, were uncovered, together with more than four hundred inscriptions. The laying bare of this huge complex was a triumph for official German archeology.

While Curtius was digging at Olympia, a man who represented everything that was anathema to orthodox Classical scholarship was standing archeology on its head. **Heinrich Schliemann**'s beginnings were not auspicious for one who aspired to hunt for ancient cities. The son of a drunken German pastor, he left school at fourteen and spent the next five years as a grocer's assistant. En route to seeking his fortune in Venezuela, he was left for dead on the Dutch coast after a shipwreck; later, working as a book-keeper in Amsterdam, he began to study languages. His phenomenal memory enabled him to master four by the age of 21. Following a six-week study of Russian, Schliemann was sent to St Petersburg as a trading agent and had amassed a fortune by the time he was 30. In 1851 he visited California, opened a bank during the Gold Rush and made another fortune.

His financial position secure for life, Schliemann was almost ready to tackle his life's ambition – the search for **Troy** and the vindication of his lifelong belief in the truth of Homer's tales of prehistoric cities and heroes. By this time he spoke no fewer than seventeen languages, and had excavated on the island of **Ithaca**, writing a book which earned him a doctorate from the University of Rostock.

Although most of the archeological establishment, led by Curtius, was unremittingly hostile to the millionaire amateur, Schliemann sunk his first trench at the hill called Hisarlik, in northwest Turkey, in 1870; excavation proper began in 1871. In his haste to find the city of Priam and Hector and to convince the world of his success, Schliemann dug a huge trench straight through the mound, destroying a mass of important evidence, but he was able nevertheless to identify nine cities, one atop the next. In May 1873 he discovered the so-called **Treasure of Priam**, a stash of gold and precious jewellery and vessels. It convinced many that the German had indeed found Troy, although others contended that Schliemann, desperate for academic recognition, assembled it from other sources. The finds disappeared from Berlin at the end of World War II, but in 1994 archeologists discovered that artefacts held by some museums in Russia originated in Troy; most of these are currently on display in the Pushkin Museum in Moscow, with a few items also in the Hermitage collection in St Petersburg. The Germans have requested their return but as the Russian government has since linked this matter to the vexed question of reparations for the damage done to their land and property by the German army, it seems that they are destined to remain in Russia for the foreseeable future.

Three years later Schliemann turned his attentions to **Mycenae**, again inspired by Homer, and once more following a hunch. Alone among contemporary scholars, he sought and found the legendary graves of Mycenaean kings inside the existing Cyclopean wall of the citadel rather than outside, unearthing in the process the magnificent treasures that today form the basis of the Bronze Age collection in the National Archeological Museum in Athens.

He dug again at Troy in 1882, assisted by a young architect, Wilhelm Dörpfeld, who was destined to become one of the great archeologists of the next century (though his claim that Lefkádha was ancient Ithaca never found popular acceptance). In 1884 Schliemann returned to Greece to excavate another famous prehistoric citadel, this time at **Tiryns**.

Almost single-handedly, and in the face of continuing academic obstruction, Schliemann had revolutionized archeology and pushed back the knowledge of Greek history and civilization a thousand years. Although some of his results have been shown to have been deliberately falsified in the sacrifice of truth to beauty, his achievement remains enormous.

The last two decades of the nineteenth century saw the discovery of other important Classical sites. Excavation began at **Epidaurus** in 1881 under the Greek archeologist **Panayotis Kavvadias**, who made it his life's work. Meanwhile at **Delphi**, the French, after gaining permission to transfer the inhabitants of the village to a new site and demolishing the now-vacant village, began digging at the sanctuary of Apollo. Their excavations began in 1892, proved fruitful and continued nonstop for the next eleven years; they have gone on sporadically ever since.

Evans and Knossós

The beginning of the twentieth century saw the domination of Greek archeology by an Englishman, **Sir Arthur Evans**. An egotistical maverick like Schliemann, he too was independently wealthy, with a brilliantly successful career behind him when he started his great work and recovered another millennium for Greek history. Evans excavated the **Palace of Minos** at **Knossós** on Crete, discovering one of the oldest and most sophisticated of Mediterranean societies.

The son of a distinguished antiquarian and collector, Evans read history at Oxford, failed to get a fellowship and began to travel. His chief interest was in the Balkans, where he was special correspondent for the *Manchester Guardian* during the 1877 uprising in Bosnia. He took enormous risks in the war-torn country, filing brilliant dispatches and still finding time for exploration and excavation.

In 1884, at the age of 33, Evans was appointed curator of the Ashmolean Museum in Oxford. He travelled whenever he could, and it was in 1893, while in Athens, that his attention was drawn to **Crete**. Evans, though very short-sighted, had almost microscopic close vision. In a vendor's stall he came upon some small drilled stones with tiny engravings in a hitherto unknown language; he was told they came from Crete. He had seen Schliemann's finds from Mycenae and had been fascinated by this prehistoric culture. Crete, the crossroads of the Mediterranean, seemed a good place to look for more.

Evans visited Crete in 1894 and headed for the legendary site of **Knossós**, which had earlier attracted the attention of Schliemann (who had been unable to agree a price with the Turkish owners of the land) and where a Cretan had already done some impromptu digging, revealing massive walls and a storeroom filled with jars. Evans bought a share of the site and five years later, after the Turks had been forced off the island, returned to purchase the rest of the land. Excavations began in March 1899 and within a few days evidence of a great complex building was revealed, along with artefacts which indicated an astonishing cultural sophistication. The huge team of excavation workers unearthed elegant courtyards and verandas, colourful wall-paintings, pottery, jewellery and sealstones – the wealth of a civilization which dominated the eastern Mediterranean 3500 years ago.

Evans continued to excavate at Knossós for the next thirty years, during which time he established, on the basis of changes in the pottery styles, the system of dating that remains in use today for classifying Greek prehistory: Early, Middle and Late Minoan (Mycenaean on the mainland). He published his account of the excavation in a massive six-volume work, *The Palace of Minos*, which was published between 1921 and 1936. Like Schliemann, Evans attracted criticism and controversy for his methods – most notably his decision to speculatively reconstruct parts of the palace – and for many of his interpretations of what he found. Nevertheless, his discoveries and his dedication put him near to the pinnacle of Greek archeology.

Into the twentieth century: the foreign institutes

In 1924 Evans gave to the **British School of Archeology** the site of Knossós along with his on-site residence, the Villa Ariadne, and all other lands within his possession on Crete (it was only in 1952 that Knossós became the property of the Greek government). At the time the British School was one of several foreign archeological institutes in Greece; founded in 1886, it had been preceded by the **French School**, the **German Institute** and the **American School**.

Greek archeology owes much to the work and relative wealth of these foreign schools and others that would follow. They have been responsible for the excavation of many of the most famous sites in Greece: the **Heraion on Sámos** (German); the sacred island of **Delos** (French); sites on **Kós** and in southern Crete (Italian); **Corinth**, **Samothráki** and the **Athenian Agora** (American), to name but a few. Life as a resident foreigner in Greece at the beginning of the century was not for the weak-spirited – one unfortunate member of the American School was shot and killed by bandits while on a trip to visit sites in the Peloponnese – but there were compensations in unlimited access to antiquities in an unspoiled countryside.

The years between the two world wars saw an expansion of excavation and scholarship, most markedly concerning the **prehistoric civilizations**. Having been shown by Schliemann and Evans what to look for, a new generation of archeologists was uncovering numerous prehistoric sites on the mainland and Crete, and its members were spending proportionately more time studying and interpreting their finds. Digs in the 1920s and 1930s had much smaller labour forces (there were just 55 workmen under Wace at Mycenae, as compared with hundreds in the early days of Schliemann's or Evans's excavations) and they were supervised by higher numbers of trained archeologists. Though perhaps not as spectacular as their predecessors, these scholars would prove just as pioneering as they established the history and clarified the chronology of the newly discovered civilizations.

One of the giants of this generation was **Alan Wace**, who while director of the British School of Archeology from 1913 to 1923 conducted excavations at Mycenae and established a chronological sequence from the nine great **thólos** tombs on the site. This led Wace to propose a new chronology for prehistoric Greece, which put him in direct conflict with Arthur Evans. Evans believed that the mainland citadels had been ruled by Cretan overlords, whereas Wace was convinced of an independent Mycenaean cultural and political development. Evans was by now a powerful member of the British School managing committee, and his published attacks on Wace's claims, combined with the younger archeologist's less than tactful reactions to Evans's dominating personality, resulted in the abrupt halt of the British excavations at Mycenae in 1923 and the no less sudden termination of Wace's job. Wace was pressured to leave Greece, and it was not until 1939 that he returned. In the interval his theories gained growing support from the archeological community, and are today universally accepted.

Classical archeology was not forgotten in the flush of excitement over the Mycenaeans and Minoans. The period between the wars saw the continuation of excavation at most established sites, and many new discoveries, among them the sanctuary of Asclepius and its elegant Roman buildings on **Kós**, excavated by the Italians from 1935 to 1943, and the Classical Greek city of **Olynthos**, in northern Greece, which was dug by the American School from 1928 to 1934. After the wholesale removal of houses and apartment blocks that had occupied the site, the American School also began excavations in the **Athenian Agora**, the ancient marketplace, in 1931, culminating in the complete restoration of the Stoa of Attalos.

The advent of **World War II** and the invasion of Greece first by the Italians and then the Germans called a halt to most archeological work, although the Germans set to work again at **Olympia**, supposedly due to Hitler's personal interest. A few Allied-nation archeologists also remained in Greece, principal among them **Gorham Stevens** and **Eugene Vanderpool**, of the American School, both of whom did charitable work. Back in America and Britain, meanwhile, archeologists were in demand for the intelligence arm of the war effort, both for their intimate knowledge of the Greek terrain and their linguistic abilities, which proved invaluable in decoding enemy messages.

More recent excavations

Archeological work was greatly restricted in the years after World War II, and in the shadow of the Greek civil war. A few monuments and museums were restored and reopened but it was not until 1948 that excavations were resumed with a Greek clearance of the Sanctuary of Artemis at **Brauron** in Attica. In 1952 the American School resumed its activities with a dig at the Neolithic and Bronze Age site of **Lerna** in the Peloponnese. Greek archeologists began work at the Macedonian site of **Pella**, the capital of ancient Macedonia, the **Necromanteion of Ephyra** in Epirus and, in a joint venture with the French, at the Minoan site of **Káto Zákros** on Crete. These and many other excavations – including renewed work on the major sites – were relatively minor operations in comparison to earlier digs. This reflected a modified approach to archeology, which laid less stress on discoveries rather than on documentation. Instead of digging large tracts of a site, archeologists concentrated on small sections, establishing chronologies through meticulous **analysis** of data. Which is not to say that there were no **finds**. At Mycenae, in 1951, a second circle of graves was unearthed; at Pireás (Piraeus), a burst sewer in 1959 revealed four superb Classical bronzes; and a dig at the Kerameikos cemetery site in Athens in 1966 found four thousand potsherds used as ballots for ostracism. Important work has also been undertaken on **restorations** – in particular the **theatres** at the Athens Acropolis, Dodona and Epidaurus, which are used in summer festivals.

A number of postwar excavations have been as exciting as any in the past. In 1961 the fourth great Minoan palace (following those unearthed at Knossós, Féstos and Mália) was discovered at the extreme eastern tip of the island of Crete at **Zákros** by Cretan archeologist **Nikólaos Pláton**. Its harbour is now thought to have been the Minoan's main gateway port to and from the Orient, and many of the artefacts unearthed in the palace storerooms – bronze ingots from Cyprus, elephants' tusks from Syria, stone vases from Egypt – seem to confirm this. At **Akrotíri** on the island of Thíra (Santoríni), **Spyros Marinatos** revealed, in 1967, a Minoan-era site that had been buried by volcanic explosion around 1550 BC. Its buildings were two or three storeys high, and superbly frescoed. Marinatos was later tragically killed while at work on the site when a wall fell on him, and is now buried there. A decade later came an even more dramatic find at **Vergina** (ancient Aegae), in northern Greece, the early capital of the Macedonian kingdom and which later became its necropolis. Here, **Manolis Andronikos** found a series of royal tombs dating from the fourth century BC. Unusually, these had escaped plundering by ancient grave robbers and contained an astonishing hoard of exquisite gold treasures. Piecing together clues – the haste of the tomb's construction, an ivory effigy head, gilded leg armour – Andronikos showed this to have been the **tomb of Philip II of Macedon**, father of **Alexander the Great**. Subsequent forensic examination of the body's remains supported historical accounts of Philip's limp and blindness. It was an astonishing and highly emotive find, as the artefacts and frescoed walls showed the sophistication and Hellenism of ancient Macedonian culture. With the background of an emerging, self-styled Slavo-Macedonian state on Greece's northern border, archeology had come head-to-head with politics.

At the beginning of the new century the various foreign schools along with Greek universities and the 25 ephorates of Prehistoric and Classical

Antiquities are still at work in the field, although the emphasis today is equally concerned with the task of conserving and protecting what has been revealed as well as unearthing new finds. All too often newly discovered sites have been inadequately fenced off or protected, and a combination of the elements and malicious trespassers – sometimes both – have caused much damage and deterioration. The **American School** continues its work on the agora at Athens and also in excavating Roman Corinth; the **British School** is engaged in excavating the acropolis at Sparta and in ongoing work at the Minoan site of Palékastro in eastern Crete. In Crete too, the **French School** is carrying out further excavations which are uncovering the town surrounding the Minoan palace at Mália; they are also continuing restoration work on the Sanctuary of Apollo on the island of Delos. Meanwhile, and in the footsteps of Curtius, the **German Institute** continues its long-standing association with excavations at Olympia and the Kerameikos cemetery in Athens and is still at work on the Heraion, the mammoth sanctuary dedicated to the goddess Hera, on the island of Samos. The **Italian School** is based mainly in Crete where, among other sites, the impressive forum of the island's Roman capital at Gortys is being revealed. Since World War II Greek archeologists have also played a leading role and the **Greek Archeological Society** is involved in excavation and conservation work in all parts of Greece including Marathon, Epidaurus, Dodona as well as at Akrotíri, where more of the remarkable buried Minoan site with paintings and multistorey buildings is slowly and spectacularly being excavated and protected.

Mythology, an A to Z

While all ancient cultures had their **myths**, those of ancient Greece have had the greatest influence on Western civilization. The Trojan War, the wanderings of Odysseus, the adventures of Herakles – these and many other stories have inspired some of the finest literature, music and art.

Homer and his followers were the first bards to codify some of the stories in around 800 BC, but they had existed in the oral tradition for many years, and it was another few centuries before Homeric epics were actually written down and other legends set forth in **Hesiod's** *Theogeny*. With the ritual enactment of the myths in their religious festivals and ceremonies, along with their representation in designs on their pots and the performances of the stories at theatre and drama competitions, Greek myth and culture became inextricably blended.

Many versions of the myths exist, some of which are contradictory and confusing. Below is a summary of the principal **gods** and **heroes**. For further reading Pierre Grimal's *Dictionary of Classical Mythology* is a good reference, but perhaps the best starting point and a way into feeling how the myths might have been told is to read Homer's epics *The Iliad* and *The Odyssey*.

Agamemnon see Atreus, or Trojan War.

Aphrodite When Kronos castrated Ouranos and threw his testicles into the sea off Cyprus, the water spumed and produced Aphrodite, which means "born from sea foam". Her most famous shrines were at Paphos (Cyprus), Knidos on the Anatolian coast and on Lésvos. Aphrodite's magic girdle made people fall in love with the wearer, but her famed adultery with Ares ended badly when she became ensnared in the nets that Hephaistos, her husband, had made to expose her infidelity. She restored her virginity, but later had an affair with Hermes which produced a double-sexed offspring – Hermaphroditos. She particularly favoured the mortal Paris, instigator of the Trojan War.

Apollo, the illegitimate son of Zeus and the nymph Leto, was god of the sun, of plagues and, conversely, of healing. He killed the Python snake that terrorized the land around Delphi, a location with which he subsequently had great associations (his other two main precincts were on the islet of Delos, his purported birthplace, and Letoön in Asia Minor). His shrine at Delphi was, with Olympia, considered one of the centres of the Hellenic world, and through the priestess of the oracle here, the god gave prophecies to pilgrims. Outstandingly beautiful Apollo represented music and poetry, and was usually depicted with either a bow and arrow or a lyre, which was a gift to him from Hermes. He was not generally unlucky in love, but was famously spurned by Daphne.

Ares, the god of war and the only legitimate son of Zeus and Hera, had few associations with myths or temples – not surprisingly, given Zeus's famous utterance that Ares was the most hateful of all his offspring. Usually attended by his demon henchmen Deimos (Terror) and Phobos (Fear), Ares was not, however, uniformly victorious – in *The Iliad* he was more than once outwitted by Athena.

Argonauts, see Jason and the Argonauts.

Ariadne, see Theseus, Ariadne and the Minotaur.

Artemis, Apollo's twin sister, was the goddess of hunting, the moon, unmarried maidens and indeed all of nature beyond the city. Her epithet was "Mistress of the Animals" and she was typically attended by trains of nymphs and lions. Artemis was always described as a virgin endowed with perpetual youth; she also had a dark aspect that involved human sacrifice at some of her rites. Furthermore, she killed the huntsman Orion who tried to rape her, and instigated the death of Actaeon who had seen her bathe naked by changing him into a stag and setting his own hounds upon him. Her most important shrines were at Brauron in Attica, at Sparta and at Ephesos in Asia Minor.

Athena did not have a conventional birth – she sprang fully formed out of the head of Zeus ready for battle with armour, helmet and spear. Hephaistos had split Zeus's forehead for the "birth" to occur, and then attempted to ravish her; she remained a virgin, but some of his semen which he flicked off her thigh fell to earth, where it grew up as her son Ericthonius-Erechteus, legendary first king of Athens. She was accordingly the protectress and namesake of that city and by extension all others, and was regarded as the goddess of both war and certain more peaceable crafts and trades vital to civilized life: olive culture, wool-gathering, spinning, ship-building, chariots and horse tackle. Her many temples are typically on city acropoles or centres; she was ever ready to intervene on behalf of favourite mortals, particularly Odysseus and Herakles.

Atlas, see Herakles.

Atreus, House of A dynasty haunted by revenge, murder, incest and tragedy. Atreus hated his younger brother Thyestes, and when their separate claims for the kingship of Mycenae were voiced, the gods promoted Atreus. Atreus banished Thyestes, but learning that his wife had had an affair with him, Atreus feigned forgiveness and recalled him from exile. He then had Thyestes' sons murdered, cut up, cooked and fed to Thyestes. When Thyestes had finished eating, Atreus showed him the heads of his children, clarifying the true nature of the meal. He again banished Thyestes, who took refuge at Sikyon and, sanctioned by the gods, fathered Aegisthus by his daughter, Pelopia. Pelopia then married Atreus, her uncle, and Aegisthus (who did not know who his real father was) was brought up and cared for by Atreus. When Aegisthus came of age, Atreus instructed him to kill Thyestes, but Aegisthus found out the truth, returned to Mycenae and killed Atreus. Atreus's two sons were Agamemnon and Menelaos. Agamemnon paid for his father's crimes by dying at the hands of his wife Clytemnestra (who had committed adultery with Aegisthus while Agamemnon was fighting at Troy). She ensnared him in a net while he took a bath and stabbed him to death. She in turn was killed by her son Orestes, who was pursued by the Furies before being absolved of matricide by Athena.

Bacchus, see Dionysos.

Centaurs and Lapiths The centaurs were monstrous beings with the heads and torsos of men and the lower bodies of horses. They lived a debauched life, feeding on raw flesh and enjoying the pleasures of wine, but were also considered particularly skilled in sorcery and herbal healing. There are tales of centaurs battling with Herakles on his quest to complete the Twelve Labours, but the most famous story is of the fight that broke out between them and the Lapiths, a race of heroes and warriors who were the descendants of the river god Pineos (the Piniós still flows near Mount Olympus). Pirithous, a Lapith of partial centaurean descent, invited them all to his wedding. At the feast the latter tried to abduct all the women, including the bride. A bloody brawl followed, of which the Lapiths were the victors; it is depicted on the pediment reliefs at Olympia, as a metaphor for the triumph of reason over barbarism.

Daphne The nymph Daphne was one of the daughters of the river god

Pineos. Apollo took a fancy to her and chased her through the woods, but just as he caught up with her, she prayed to her father to save her. He took pity and turned her into a laurel tree, and she became rooted to the spot. Apollo loved her even as a tree and made the laurel sacred, dedicating wreaths of its leaves as a sign of honour. Her name, to this day, is the Greek word for the laurel tree.

Demeter was the goddess of agriculture, in particular corn, grain and pigs, as well as of death and regeneration. Both her origins and rites were shadowy, though we do know that women were her particular devotees. She exercised her power by making the whole Earth sterile after her daughter Persephone's abduction by Hades. The mother-and-daughter duo were usually revered together, particularly at their major sanctuary at Eleusis.

Dionysos, also known as Bacchus, was the god of wine and mystic ecstasy. He was the son of Zeus by Semele, who during conception was consumed by the god in the form of a lightning-bolt; Zeus rescued the unborn child and sewed him up in his thigh for the full gestation period. On birth, he was conveyed by Hermes to a far-off realm to be reared by the nymphs, and as a small boy he was disguised as a girl to hide him from Hera. As a youth, he was abducted by pirates; Dionysos caused the ship to be overgrown with ivy and vines (henceforth his symbols) and in panic the pirates dived overboard to become the first dolphins. Thus at his festivals a commemorative miniature ship was carried or propelled on wheels, suitably decorated. In art he is often shown riding in a chariot drawn by panthers, and followed by a coterie of satyrs, sileni and mortal followers brandishing *thyrsoi* (wands topped with pine cones). Dionysos' semi-mythical women followers, the maenads, roamed the countryside at certain seasons in a state of madness; more usually, he was revered in the form of a bearded mask on a column, the antecedent of the comic and tragic masks of theatre. He rescued Ariadne from Náxos following her abandonment there by Theseus.

Eurydice, see Orpheus and Eurydice.

Golden Fleece, see Jason and the Argonauts.

Hades was the brother of Zeus and Poseidon, and when the cosmos was divided between them he was allotted the underworld. His name means "the invisible", because in the battle with Kronos and the Titans he concealed himself by wearing a magic helmet given to him by the Cyclops. To refer to him as Hades was thought to bring about his awesome anger, so the Greeks called him by his surname Pluto, which means "the rich" and alludes to the wealth that lies hidden underground. His wife was Demeter's daughter, Persephone. Rather than temples, he had suitably mysterious oracles, most notably at Ephyra in Epirus and that of Trophonios at Levadia.

Helen was the daughter of Zeus, who appeared in the form of a swan to her mother Leda. She was believed to be the most beautiful woman in the world. Her husband Menelaos, king of Sparta, entertained the Trojans Paris and Aeneas and was foolish enough to leave them alone with her; Paris abducted her. Some sources say she went willingly, impressed by his beauty and wealth; others say she was raped. In either event her departure from Sparta was the cause of the Trojan War.

Hephaistos was the god of fire and a master craftsman. In his workshop on volcanic Límnos, where he was especially revered, he fashioned everything from jewellery to armour. Elsewhere his cult was less elaborated, except at Athens, where he had a sumptuous temple in honour of his role in siring Erechtheus (see Athena). He was made lame, and there are two conflicting versions of how he sustained his injuries: either they were inflicted when Zeus threw him from Olympus because he had defended Hera in a quarrel, or alternatively when Hera, who bore him, tossed him down to Límnos in disappointment at his ugliness. Clever as well as unprepossessing, he was married to Aphrodite, the most beautiful of the goddesses.

Hera was Zeus's sister, wife and the most powerful of the goddesses – she wreaked her vengeance and jealousy on anyone whom Zeus seduced and the offspring of most of his encounters. Zeus punished her heavily for her anger against Herakles by suspending her from her wrists from Mount Olympus, weighing her ankles down with anvils, and whipping her. Despite her vindictive and irascible Homeric portrayal, she was the protecting deity of wives and marriage. Her totems and sacrificial animals were the cow, the cuckoo and the peacock; her principal temples were on Sámos, near Argos, at modern Perahóra and at Olympia.

Herakles (Hercules) was the superhero of the ancient world. A mighty hunter and sacrificer, Herakles appealed to young men in particular. His mother was the mortal Alcmene, and his father Zeus. Jealous Hera sent two snakes to kill Herakles while he was still in his cradle, which he duly strangled, all good preparation for his Twelve Labours.

These were commanded by King Eurystheus of the Argolid, who was under the thrall of Hera. These tasks took him to the fringes of the known world, even involving his supporting it on his shoulders while Atlas took a break to lend him a hand in his final task. The Labours were: to kill the Nemean lion; to slay the many-headed Hydra monster at Lerna; to bring back the wild boar of Erymanthus alive; to hunt the Keryneian hind that was sacred to Artemis; to kill the man-eating birds at the lake of Stymphaleia; to clean the stables of King Augeas; to bring back the untameable Cretan bull alive; to capture the flesh-eating horses of Diomedes; to fetch the girdle of the Amazon warrior queen; to fetch the herds of Geryon from beyond the edge of the ocean; to capture Cerberus the guard dog of the underworld gates; and finally to fetch the golden apples from the garden of the Hesperides.

Curiously for such a macho figure, Herakles spent a certain amount of time as a slave, or in drag, or both. During a fit of madness sent by Hera, he slew his wife and children at Thebes; in atonement he passed some years dressed as a woman in the court of Queen Omphale of Lydia.

His death was as dramatic as his life. Deianeira, his second wife, gave him a garment that she thought had magic powers and would prevent him from being unfaithful to her. When he put it on, it burned into his flesh; the cloak had, it seemed, been steeped in the blood of the centaur Nessos, who had been slain by Herakles in the act of attempting to rape Deianeira. (With his dying breath, Nessos got posthumous revenge by telling Deianeira that his blood was a love-philtre rather than poisonous.) Unable to bear the pain, Herakles built a funeral pyre and immolated himself. He was fully deified by Zeus – the only mortal or demigod to be so honoured.

Hermes was the son of Zeus and Maia, the daughter of Atlas. He was born in the Kyllene mountains of Arcadia, where his only major temple existed at Pheneos. A trickster figure, Hermes showed his mettle by inventing the lyre on the day of his birth, then stealing Apollo's sacred cattle, denying the deed to his brother. Zeus effected a reconciliation, and Hermes gave Apollo the lyre in exchange for the cattle and a golden staff.

Hermes was the god of commerce, thievery, herdsmen, travel and boundaries; rather than shrines he had herms, stone cairns or boundary-markers. In his role as Conductor of Souls, Hermes regularly crossed between the living and underworld. He was often depicted wearing winged shoes, a wide-brimmed hat and carrying the herald's staff which showed his position as the divine messenger.

Hippolytos and Phaedra Hippolytos, son of the hero Theseus and the Amazon Hippolyta, was an accomplished hunter who revered Artemis and scorned Aphrodite. Aphrodite sought to teach him a lesson and conspired for Phaedra, the new wife of Theseus, to fall in love with the young man. When she was spurned by Hippolytos she feared he might reveal her advances and so accused him of rape. When Theseus heard this, he called upon Poseidon to kill his son; Hippolytos was then flung from his chariot and torn apart by his horses. Phaedra in shame and remorse hanged herself.

Io, a priestess of Hera at Argos, was only one of the many mortals who caught Zeus's eye, but before he could get to know her better, Hera got wind of his interest and Zeus hastily transformed Io into a cow. Hera demanded her as a present, and placed her under the guard of Argos, the hundred-eyed monster. Hera then proceeded to torment poor Io the cow by sending a stinging gadfly to goad her on her travels. She made for the sea, first to the Ionian Sea, which was named after her, and then crossed the straits into Asia at the Bosporus (literally, the "Cow Ford"). Before settling in Egypt, she wandered all over Asia, even bumping into Prometheus, who was chained for a few centuries to the Caucasus mountain range.

Jason and the Argonauts Jason, a Greek hero from Iolkos (present-day Vólos), was the legitimate heir to the Thessalian throne, which had been usurped by his uncle Pelias. The latter received a prophecy that he would die at the hands of a one-sandalled man. When Jason appeared in his court, shod accordingly, the frightened Pelias attempted to get rid of him by sending him on what he hoped would be a fatal quest to the remote Black Sea kingdom of Colchis for the Golden Fleece. He assembled his crew, assorted heroes of the ancient Greek world, and commissioned a ship, called the *Argo* after its maker Argos, and built with the help of Athena and Hera – its prow had the remarkable gift of speech and prophecy. A long, incident-filled journey followed, including landfall at Límnos where the crew repopulated the island, the local women having previously murdered their menfolk. Some of the crew didn't complete the voyage, including Herakles who missed the boat because he was searching for his favourite, Hylas, a beautiful boy who had been abducted by the nymphs. Hera instructed the sea-nereids to carry the *Argo* past the dangerous Wandering Rocks, which would otherwise have smashed the ship. When Jason and his crew finally arrived in Colchis, King Aeëtes would not hand over the Golden Fleece unless Jason completed various labours. The king's daughter, the sorceress Medea (see overleaf), fell in love with Jason and undertook to help him; they stole the fleece and fled, pursued by Aeëtes. Medea slowed down their pursuers by tearing up her brother Apsyrtus and casting his body parts into the sea, obliging Aeëtes to collect the pieces. Zeus was greatly angered by this heinous crime and the *Argo* spoke to the crew, telling them that they would have to purify themselves at Circe's island. After more wanderings through treacherous seas, the crew arrived at Iolkos, where Medea fulfilled the prophecy by doing away with Pelias, and then proceeded to Corinth where Jason dedicated the Golden Fleece to Poseidon.

Judgement of Paris The goddess Eris (Strife) began a quarrel between Athena, Hera and Aphrodite by throwing a golden apple between them and saying that it belonged to whichever goddess was the most beautiful. All the gods were too frightened to judge the contest, so Hermes took the goddesses to the top of Mount Ida for Paris, the son of Priam of Troy, to decide. Each used bribery to win his favour: Athena offered him wisdom and victory in combat, Hera the kingdom of Asia, but Aphrodite, the winner of the contest, offered him the love of Helen of Sparta.

Kronos The Titan Kronos was the youngest son of the pre-Olympian deities Gaia and Ouranos, who seized power in the heavens by castrating his father. Once on the throne, Kronos lived in perpetual fear of the prediction that one of his offspring would one day overthrow him, and so he swallowed all of his children except Zeus – Zeus's mother Rhea had substituted a stone for the bundle that Kronos thought was his baby. Kronos and his Titan brothers were defeated in a cosmic battle by Zeus and his Olympian supporters.

Lapiths, see Centaurs and Lapiths.

Maenads The maenads were the possessed or intoxicated female followers of Dionysos. They wore scanty clothes, had wreaths of ivy around their heads and played upon tambourines or flutes in their processions. They had power over wild animals, and in their frenzy they believed they drank milk or honey from freshwater springs. In their orgiastic ecstasies they tore limb from limb those who offended them, did not believe or who spied upon their rites – including Orpheus.

Medea exacted gruesome revenge on any who stood against her. She persuaded the daughters of Pelias (see Jason and the Argonauts) to cut their father up and put him in a boiling cauldron, having convinced them that if they did so she could rejuvenate him. To their extreme disappointment, his body parts did not come back together. Akastos, Pelias's son, banished her and Jason as a punishment; they went together to Corinth, where Jason abandoned her to marry Kreusa the daughter of the local king Kreon. In revenge, Medea orchestrated a gruesome death for Kreusa by sending her a tunic which burst into flames when donned, and then murdered her own two young sons by Jason.

Minotaur, see Theseus, Ariadne and the Minotaur.

Mount Olympus, see Zeus.

Muses The Muses were the result of nine nights of lovemaking between Mnemosyne (Memory) and Zeus. They were primarily singers and the inspiration for music (to which they gave their name), but also had power over thought in all its forms: persuasion, eloquence, knowledge, history, mathematics and astronomy. Apollo conducted their singing around the Hippocrene fountain on Mount Helikon, or on Mount Olympus itself.

Nymphs There were various subspecies of nymph: meliads were the nymphs of the ash trees; nereids lived in the springs and streams; naïads in the ocean; dryads were individual tree nymphs; oreads were the mountain nymphs; and the alseids lived in the groves. They were thought to be the daughters of Zeus and attended certain deities, particularly Artemis and Poseidon.

Odysseus Our word "odyssey" derives from Odysseus's ten-year journey home, which was no less fraught with danger, adventure and grief than the ten-year war against the Trojans which preceded it. Shipwrecked, tormented by the gods, held against his will by bewitching women, almost lured to his death by the hypnotic Sirens, witnessing his comrades devoured by the giant one-eyed Cyclops Polyphemos and all the time missing and desiring his faithful wife Penelope, Odysseus proved himself to be a great and scheming hero. At the end of his arduous journey he arrived in disguise at his palace on Ithaca to find suitors pestering his wife. He contrived a cunning trap and killed them all with a bow which only he could flex.

Oedipus was a man profoundly cursed. The Delphic Oracle said that Laius, king of Thebes, should not father any children, for if he did one would kill him. When Oedipus was born Laius abandoned the baby, piercing his ankles with a nail and tying them together: hence the name, which means "swollen foot". But the baby was discovered and brought up at the court of the neighbouring king, Polybos, at Corinth. The same oracle revealed to the adult Oedipus that he would kill his father and marry his mother. When he heard this news he resolved not to return home to Corinth, but east of Delphi he met with Laius, who was heading west to consult the oracle as to how to rid Thebes of the Sphinx. Because the road was narrow, Laius ordered Oedipus to get out of the way, and when one of the guards pushed him, Oedipus drew his sword in anger and, not knowing that Laius was his father, killed him and most of his entourage. He then made his way to Thebes, where Laius had been king, and solved the riddle of the Sphinx. As a reward and in thanks, he was crowned king and offered Laius's widow Iocaste (his mother) in marriage. Plague then fell upon Thebes, because of the crimes of patricide and incest at the heart of the city. The Delphic Oracle instructed Oedipus to expel the murderer of Laius, and in his ignorance he ordered the guilty party cursed and banished. The seer and prophet Teiresias then revealed the full nature of the crime to Iocaste and Oedipus; she hanged herself and he put out his own eyes. He left the city as a vagabond accompanied by his daughter Antigone, and only at his death was granted peace. Attica, the country that received his dead body, became blessed.

Orpheus and Eurydice Orpheus was a great musician who received his lyre from Apollo himself. He played and sang so beautifully that wild beasts were charmed, trees would uproot themselves to come closer, and even the very rocks were moved. He enlisted in the crew of Argonauts and sang for them to row their oars in time. On his return from the *Argo*'s voyage he married the nymph Eurydice. She was bitten by a snake on the banks of the river Pineos and died, and Orpheus was so distraught that he went to the underworld to bring her back to life. His wish was granted by Hades on condition that during the return journey he would not look back at her. As the couple approached daylight, however, his mind became consumed with doubt and, turning around to see if she was behind him, he lost her forever. He preached that Apollo was the greatest god, much to the anger of Dionysos, who set the maenads on him. They tore him apart and cast his head, still singing, into the Thracian river Hebrus; it was finally washed up on the shores of the island of Lésvos, supposedly conferring great musical gifts on the local population.

Ouranos was the personification of the sky and by his union with Gaia (Earth) fathered many children, including Kronos (see opposite) and the Titans (see below). Gaia became so exhausted by her husband's continual advances that she sought protection from her sons. Kronos was the only one to assist; he cut off Ouranos's testicles with a sickle and threw them into the sea, giving rise to Aphrodite.

Pan The patron of shepherds and flocks, Pan was the son of Hermes and a nymph and, with his beard, horns, hairy body and cloven hooves, was said to be so ugly that his own mother ran from him in fear. He had an insatiable libido, energetically pursuing both sexes. Apollo learned the art of prophecy from Pan, and hunters looked to him for guidance. He enjoyed the cool woodland shade and streams of Arcadia and relished his afternoon naps so much that he wreaked havoc if he was disturbed.

Pandora, see Prometheus.

Pegasus, see Poseidon.

Penelope, see Odysseus.

Persephone, also known as Kore (the Maiden), was out picking flowers one day when the Earth opened up and swallowed her; she had been abducted by Hades riding his chariot. Her mother Demeter was distraught and when she found out the truth, she left Olympus in protest and made the Earth sterile so that it produced no crops. Zeus ordered Hades to return Persephone, but because she had eaten pomegranate seeds in the underworld she was bound to him. As a compromise, she would be allowed to return to Earth for two-thirds of the year and had to reside with Hades for the remaining third. Thus Demeter divided the year into seasons, so that while Persephone was with Hades the Earth would be wintry and sterile, and while she was on Earth the ground would be fertile for spring, summer and autumn.

Perseus A son of Zeus, and believed to be a direct ancestor of Herakles, Perseus was cast out to sea in a trunk with his mother Danae, because his grandfather feared a prophecy that Perseus would one day kill him. Danae and Perseus were washed up on Sérifos island, where they were discovered by a fisherman who looked after them. When Perseus came of age, the king of Sérifos demanded that he bring back the head of Medusa the gorgon, whose gaze could turn people to stone. Perseus acquired some special aids from Hermes and Athena to perform the task, including a helmet which made him invisible, and winged sandals to fly through the air. He cut off Medusa's head while looking at her reflection in Athena's polished shield. On his return flight he saw and fell in love with Andromeda, who was being offered as a sacrifice to a sea-monster. He rescued her and returned home to find his mother had been raped by the king. He held up the gorgon's head, turned the king to stone and then presented the head as a gift to Athena, who placed it in the middle of her shield. Perseus went on to participate in the king of Larissa's celebratory games; he competed in the discus-throwing competition, but his throw went off course and killed his grandfather, who was a spectator, thus fulfilling the prophecy.

Phaedra, see Hippolytos and Phaedra.

Poseidon was the god of the sea, earthquakes and storms, and patron of fishermen. In the battle with Kronos and the Titans, Poseidon, the brother of Zeus, wielded the trident which he later used to shake both sea and land. After the victory he was awarded, by lot, the realm of the ocean, where he dwelt in the depths. He produced some strange offspring, including the Cyclops Polyphemos who had it in for Odysseus, and mated with the gorgon Medusa – which resulted in the winged horse Pegasus. He quarrelled frequently with the other gods, competing with them for power over some of the major cities including Athens, Corinth and Argos. Although he helped destroy Troy, as recounted in *The Iliad*, he also persecuted Odysseus mercilessly on his return home. Among his numerous temples, the most important were those at Isthmía, Soúnio and Póros near Athens; Mykale in Asia Minor; and an oracle at Cape Ténaro.

Prometheus For someone whose name means "forethought", Prometheus showed a distinct lack of it. In his desire to help mankind, he stole fire from the heavens and was immediately punished by Zeus, who bound him in chains, tied him to the Caucasus mountains and then sent an eagle to peck perpetually at his liver. Zeus then dealt with mankind by sending Pandora to Prometheus' brother Epimetheus, whose name means "afterthought". Her curiosity about the contents of his box got the better of her and, peeping inside, she unleashed all the evils and one good (hope) on the world. Prometheus gave some useful advice to Herakles when he passed by on one of his labours and Herakles rewarded him by setting him free.

Theseus, Ariadne and the Minotaur Theseus's father, Aegeus of Athens, sent him as a child away from Athens for his own safety. At sixteen the hero returned, in full strength and with the weapons that his father had set aside for him. Theseus was destined for a life of action, and his greatest adventure was to kill the Minotaur on Crete. As tribute from Athens, King Minos demanded six men and six women every nine years for sacrifice to the Minotaur – a gruesome beast, half-man half-bull, born from the bestial copulation of the queen Pasiphae with the huge bull sent by Poseidon. The Minotaur was kept in the labyrinth at Crete. Ariadne, Minos's daughter, had fallen in love with Theseus and contrived to help him kill the Minotaur. She gave him a ball of thread so that he would not lose his way in the labyrinth and then accompanied him in his flight from the island, only to be abandoned later on the island of Náxos. Dionysos saw her disconsolate on the shore, took pity on her and married her. Theseus, meanwhile, on his return to Athens forgot to change the black sails to white as a signal to his father that he was alive, and Aegeus – thinking that his son had been killed by the Minotaur – threw himself into the sea which took his name: the Aegean.

Titans The Titans were the six male children of Ouranos and Gaia. Their six sisters, who helped them father numerous gods, were called the Titanides. Kronos was the youngest Titan, and after he had overthrown his father he helped his brothers to power. The Titans lost their grip when they were toppled by the upstart Olympians, led by Zeus, in the cataclysmic battle called the Titanomachia.

Trojan War When Menelaos of Sparta realized that the Trojan Paris had made off with his wife Helen, he called on his brother Agamemnon of Mycenae. Together they roused the might of Greece to get her back. With just about every hero (Ajax, Achilles, Troilus, Hector, Paris, Odysseus, Priam, Diomedes, Aeneas) making an appearance in this epic, the story of the Trojan War is arguably the greatest tale from the ancient world. Homer's *Iliad* dealt with only one aspect of it, the wrath of Achilles. The ten-year war, fought over a woman and which sent many heroes' souls down to Hades, was finally won by the trickery of the Greeks, who used a huge wooden horse left ostensibly as a gift to the Trojans to smuggle an armed platoon inside the city walls. The cunning plan was thought to be the work of Odysseus, who, like many of the surviving heroes, had a less-than-easy journey home.

Zeus was the supreme deity, king of gods and men, but did not get to this position without a struggle. His father, the Titan Kronos, seized power in the heavens by castrating Ouranos the sky god, and in turn lived in fear that one of his own offspring would one day overthrow him. So he swallowed all of his children except Zeus, whose mother, Rhea, came to the rescue and hid him in a cave on the island of Crete, where the warrior Kouretes concealed his cries by smashing their swords and shields together. When he came of age, Zeus poisoned Kronos so that he vomited up all Zeus's siblings; with their help, and the assistance of the Cyclops, he cast Kronos and the Titans from Mount Olympus, the home of the gods. The Cyclops gave Zeus the thunderbolt as a weapon to use in the battle and it became his symbol of power, and emblem of his role as deity of weather and rain. Zeus used his position to maintain cosmic order, control the other gods and men and to get his way with whomever he fancied. Numerous myths tell of his metamorphoses to mate with a variety of mortals out of sight of his jealous wife Hera; all of his liaisons resulted in offspring, which included Herakles, Perseus and Helen.

Wildlife

For anyone who has first seen Greece at the height of summer with its brown parched hillsides and desert-like ambience, the richness of the wildlife – in particular the flora – may come as a surprise. As winter changes to spring, the countryside (and urban waste ground) transforms itself from green to a mosaic of coloured flowers, which attract a plethora of insect life, followed by birds. Isolated areas, whether true islands or remote mountains such as Olympus, have had many thousands of years to develop their own individual species. Overall, Greece has around six thousand species of native flowering plants, nearly four times that of Britain but in the same land area. Many are unique to Greece, and make up about one-third of Europe's endemic plants.

Some background

In early antiquity Greece was thickly forested: Aleppo and Calabrian pines grew in coastal regions, giving way to fir or black pine up in the hills and low mountains. But this **native woodland** contracted rapidly as human activities expanded. By Classical times, a pattern had been set of forest clearance, followed by agriculture, abandonment to scrub and then a resumption of cultivation or grazing. Huge quantities of timber were consumed in the production of charcoal, pottery and smelted metal, and for ships and construction work. Small patches of virgin woodland have remained, mostly in the north and northeast, but even these are under threat from loggers and arsonists.

Greek **farming** often lacks the rigid efficiency of northern European agriculture. Many peasant farmers still cultivate little patches of land, and even city-dwellers travel at weekends to collect food plants from the countryside. Wild greens under the generic term *hórta* are gathered to be cooked like spinach, and grape hyacinth bulbs are boiled as a vegetable. The buds and young shoots of capers, and the fruit of wild figs, carobs, plums, strawberry trees, cherries and sweet chestnuts are harvested. Emergent snails and mushrooms are collected after wet weather. The more resilient forms of wildlife can coexist with these uses, but for many Greeks only those species that have practical uses are regarded as having any value. Now however, increasing access to heavier earth-moving machinery means farmers can sweep away an ancient meadow full of orchids in an easy morning's work – often to produce a field that is used for forage for a year or two and then abandoned to coarse thistles. Increasingly, the pale scars of dirt tracks crisscross once intact hill- and mountainsides, allowing short-termist agricultural destruction of previously undisturbed upland habitats.

During the 1950s there was a policy of draining **wetlands** in order to increase agriculture, and many important areas were lost to wildlife completely. Those lakes, lagoons and deltas that remain are, in theory, now protected for their fragile biodiversity and their environmental and scientific value – but industrial and sewage pollution, disturbance, and misuse are unchecked. Visit, for example, the Yiálova lagoon reserve – one of Greece's most stunningly beautiful wetlands – in the southwest Peloponnese, to see the wildlife, and to understand the problems of many protected areas. Local 4WD vehicles and noisy motorbikes race through the dunes destroying the surface stability and decimating the nesting chameleons; Greek military planes practice low-flying over flocks of flamingos; rows of illegally overnighting camper vans disfigure the beaches; and locals drive out here to dump unwanted televisions and fridges. On Lésvos, one of the island's main tourist attractions, the Kallóni salt-pans, once beloved by rare birds, are being poisoned by sewage. In the main-land interior, the increasing demand for power brings huge hydroelectric schemes to remote rivers and gorges with little chance for opposition to be heard.

The **church**, whose lands once often provided wildlife with a refuge from hunters, now looks to capitalize on their value for major tourist developments, with plans to develop mass tourism and golf courses around the Toploú Monastery in eastern Crete, already one of Greece's most water-deficient areas. In the north, the forests of sacred Mount Áthos are being surrendered to com-mercial logging.

Since the 1970s, **tourist developments** have ribboned out along coastlines, sweeping away both agricultural plots and wildlife havens as they do so. These expanding resorts increase local employment, often attracting inland workers to the coast; the generation that would have been shepherds on remote hill-sides now works in tourist bars and tavernas. Consequently, the pressure of domestic animal grazing, particularly in the larger islands, has been significant-ly reduced, allowing the regeneration of tree seedlings. Crete, for example, now has more woodland than at any time in the last five centuries, but forest fires remain a threat everywhere. Fires since 1980 have destroyed much of the tree cover in Thássos, southern Rhodes, Kárpathos, Híos and, in 2000, Sámos; the trees may well regenerate eventually, but by then the complex shade-depend-ent ecology is irrecoverably lost.

Despite an often negative attitude to wildlife, Greece was probably the first place in the world where it was an object of study. Theophrastos (372–287 BC) was the first recorded **botanist** and a systematic collector of general informa-tion on plants, while his contemporary, Aristotle, studied the animal world. During the first century AD the distinguished physician Dioscorides compiled a herbal that remained a standard work for over a thousand years.

Flowers

Whereas in temperate northern Europe plants flower from spring until autumn, the arid summers of Greece confine the main **flowering period** to the spring, to a climatic window when the days are bright, the temperatures are not too high and the groundwater supply still adequate. **Spring** starts in the southeast, in Rhodes, in early March, and then travels progressively west-wards and northwards. Rhodes, Kárpathos and eastern Crete are at their best in March, western Crete in early April, the Peloponnese and eastern Aegean mid-April to late April, and the Ionian islands in early May, though a cold dry win-ter can cause several-weeks' delay. In the higher mountains the floral spring is held back until the chronological summer, with the alpine zones of central and western Crete in full flower in June, while mainland mountain blooms emerge in July.

The delicate flowers of early spring – orchids, fritillaries, anemones, cycla-men, tulips and small bulbs – are replaced as the season progresses by more robust shrubs, tall perennials and abundant annuals, but many of these close down completely for the fierce **summer**. A few tough plants, like shrubby thyme and savory, continue to flower through the heat and act as magnets for butterflies.

Once the worst heat is over, and the first showers of **autumn** arrive, so does a second "spring", on a much smaller scale but no less welcome after the brown drabness of summer. Squills, autumn cyclamen, crocus in varying shades, pink or lilac colchicum, yellow sternbergia and other small bulbs all come into bloom, while the seeds start to germinate for the following year's crop of annuals. By the new year, early-spring bulbs and orchids are flowering in the south.

Seashore

Plants on the **beach** tend to be hardy species growing in a difficult environment where fresh water is scarce. Feathery tamarisk trees are adept at surviving this habitat, and consequently are often planted to provide shade. On hot days or nights you may see or feel them "sweating" away surplus saltwater from their foliage.

Sand dunes in the southern and eastern islands may support the low gnarled trees of the prickly **juniper**. These provide shelter for a variety of colourful small plants, while the flat sandy areas or "slacks" behind the dunes can be home to a variety of plants, where they have not been illegally ploughed for short-term forage crops. Open stretches of beach sand usually have fewer plants, particularly nowadays in resort areas where the bulldozed "spring cleaning" of the beach removes the local flora along with the winter's rubbish.

Watercourses

Large areas of **freshwater** are naturally scarce, particularly in the warmer south. Many watercourses dry up completely in the hot season, and what seem to be dry river courses are often simply flood-beds which fill irregularly at times of torrential rain. Consequently, there are few true aquatic plants compared with much of Europe. However, species that survive periodic drying-out can flourish, such as the giant reed or **calamus**, a bamboo-like grass reaching up to 6m in height and often cut for use as canes. It frequently grows in company with the shrubby, pink- or white-flowered and very poisonous **oleander**.

Cultivated land

Arable fields can be rich with colourful weeds: scarlet poppies, blue bugloss, yellow or white daisies, wild peas, gladioli, tulips and grape hyacinths. Small **meadows** can be equally colourful, with slower-growing plants such as orchids in extraordinary quantities. In the absence of herbicides, olive groves can have an extensive underflora. In the presence of herbicides there is usually a yellow carpet of the introduced, weedkiller-resistant Oxalis pes-caprae, which now occurs in sufficient quantity to show up in satellite photographs.

Lower hillsides

The rocky earth makes cultivation on some hillsides difficult and impractical. Agriculture is often abandoned and areas regenerate to a rich mixture of shrubs and perennials – known as **garigue**. With time, a few good wet winters, and in the absence of grazing, some shrubs develop into small trees, intermixed with tough climbers – the much denser **maquis** vegetation. The colour yellow often predominates in early spring, with brooms, gorse, Jerusalem sage and the three-metre giant fennel followed by the pink and white of large rockroses (*Cistus spp.*). An abundance of the latter is often indicative of an earlier fire, since they flourish in the cleared areas.

A third vegetation type is **phrygana** – smaller, frequently aromatic or spiny shrubs, often with a narrow strip of bare ground between each hedgehog-like bush. Many **aromatic herbs** such as lavender, rosemary, savory, sage and thyme are native to these areas, intermixed with other less tasty plants such as the toxic euphorbias and the spiny burnet or wire-netting bush.

Nearly 160 species of **orchid** are believed to occur in Greece; their complexity blurs species' boundaries and keeps botanists in a state of taxonomic flux. In particular, the Ophrys bee and spider orchids have adapted themselves, through subtleties of lip colour and false scents, to seduce small male wasps. These insects mistake the flowers for a potential mate, and unintentionally assist the plant's pollination. Other orchids mimic the colours and scents of nectar-producing plants, to lure bees. Though all species are officially protected, many are still picked for decoration – in particular the giant Barlia orchid – and fill vases in homes, cafés, tavernas and even on graves.

Mountains and gorges

The higher **mountains** of Greece have winter snow cover, and cooler weather for much of the year, so flowering is consequently later than at lower altitudes. The **limestone peaks** of the mainland, and of islands such as Corfu, Kefal-loniá, Crete, Rhodes, Sámos and Thássos, hold rich collections of attractive rock plants, flowers whose nearest relatives may be from the Balkan Alps or from the Turkish mountains. Gorges are another spectacular habitat, particularly rich in Crete. Their inaccessible cliffs act as refuges for plants that cannot survive the grazing, competition or more extreme climates of open areas. Many of Greece's endemic plants are confined to cliffs, gorges or mountains.

Much of the surviving **original woodland** is in mountain areas. In the south, the woodland includes cypress, Greek fir and several species of pine, with oak and flowering ash. The cypress is native to the south and east Aegean, but in its columnar form it has been planted everywhere with a Mediterranean climate. Further north there are also juniper and yew, with beech, hornbeam, maple, chestnut and poplar. The cooler shade of woodland provides a haven for plants which cannot survive full exposure to the Greek summer. Such species include wonderful red, pink or white peonies and the scarlet martagon lily, along with helleborine and bird's-nest orchids, and numerous ferns.

With altitude, the forest thins out to scattered individual conifers and hermes oak, before finally reaching a limit at around 1500–2000m on the mainland – much lower on the islands. Above this treeline are summer meadows, and then bare rock. If not severely grazed, these habitats are home to many low-growing, gnarled, but often splendidly floriferous plants.

Birds

Migratory species which have wintered in East Africa move north in spring through the eastern Mediterranean from mid-March to mid-May, or later, depending on the season and the weather. Some stop to breed in Greece; others move on into the rest of Europe. The southern islands can be the first land-fall after a long sea-crossing, and smaller birds recuperate for a few days before moving on north. Larger birds such as storks and ibis often fly very high, and binoculars are needed to spot them as they pass over. In autumn the birds return, but usually in more scattered numbers. Although some species such as quail and turtle dove are shot, there is nothing like the wholesale slaughter that takes place in some other Mediterranean countries.

Swallows, and their relatives the martins, are constantly swooping through the air to catch insects, as are the larger and noisier swifts. Warblers are numerous, with the Sardinian warbler often conspicuous because of its black head, bright red eye and bold habits; the Rüppell's warbler is considerably rarer, and confined to thicker woodland. Other small insect-eaters include stonechats, fly-catchers and woodchat shrikes.

At **night**, the tiny Scops owl has a very distinct, repeated single-note call, very like the sonar beep of a submarine; the equally diminutive little owl is by contrast also visible by day, particularly on ruined houses, and has a strange repertoire of cries, chortles and a throaty hiss. Certainly the most evocative nocturnal bird is the nightingale, which requires wooded stream valleys and is most audible around midnight in May, its mating season.

Larger **raptors** occur in remoter areas, particularly around mountain gorges and cliffs. Buzzards are perhaps the most abundant, and mistaken by optimistic birdwatchers for the rarer, shyer eagles. Griffon vultures are unmistakable, soaring on broad, straight-edged wings, whereas the lammergeier is a state-of-the-art flying machine with narrow, swept wings, seen over mountain tops by the lucky few. Lesser kestrels are brighter, noisier versions of the common kestrel, and often appear undisturbed by the presence of humans. Also to be seen in the mountains are ravens, and smaller, colourful birds such as alpine choughs, common choughs, black and white wheatears, wallcreepers and the blue rock thrush.

In lowland areas, hoopoes are a startling combination of pink, black and white, particularly obvious when they fly; they're about the only natural predator of the processionary caterpillar, a major pest in pine forests. The much shyer golden oriole has an attractive song but is rarely seen for more than a few moments before hiding its brilliant colours among the olive trees. Rollers are bright blue and chestnut. Multicoloured flocks of slim and elegant bee-eaters fill the air with their soft calls as they hunt insects. Brightest of all is the king-fisher, more commonly seen sea-fishing than in northern Europe.

In those areas of **wetland** that remain undrained and undisturbed, birds flourish. In saltmarshes, coastal lagoons, estuaries and freshwater ponds, herons and egrets, ducks, osprey, glossy ibis and spoonbills, black storks, white storks, pelicans and many waders can be seen feeding. Cormorants roost on and dive from coastal cliffs from late summer onwards, while greater flamingos sometimes occur, as lone individuals or small flocks, particularly in salt pans in the eastern Aegean.

Mammals

Greece's small **mammal** population ranges from small rodents and shrews to hedgehogs, hares and squirrels (a very dark form of the red). Rats are particularly common on Corfu and Sámos. Medium-sized mammals include badgers and foxes, but one of the commonest is the fast-moving, ferret-like, stone (or beech) marten, named for its habit of decorating stones with its droppings to mark territory.

In the mainland mountains, mostly in the north, are found the shy chamois and wild boar, with even shyer predators like lynx, wolves and brown bear. In the White Mountains of Crete an endemic ibex, known to Cretan hunters as the *agrími* or *krí-krí*, is occasionally seen running wild but more often penned as a zoo attraction. When formerly in danger of extinction, a colony of them was established on the offshore islet of Dhía, where they managed in turn to exterminate the rare local flora.

The extremely rare Mediterranean **monk seal** also breeds on some stretches of remote coast in the east Aegean and Sporades; the small world population is now highly endangered since losing many individuals – and most of its main breeding ground – to a toxic algal bloom off Morocco. If spotted, these seals should be treated with deference; they cannot tolerate human disturbance, and on present trends are unlikely to survive much into the new millennium.

Reptiles and amphibians

Reptiles flourish in the hot dry summers of Greece and there are many species, the commonest being **lizards**. Most of these are small, slim, agile and wary, rarely staying around for closer inspection. They're usually brown to grey, with subtle patterns of spots, streaks and stripes, though in adult males the undersides are sometimes brilliant orange, green or blue. The more robust green lizards, with long whip-like tails, can be 50cm or more in length, but equally shy and fast-moving unless distracted by territorial disputes with each other.

On some islands, mainly in the central and eastern Aegean, lives the angular, iguana-like **agama**, sometimes called the Rhodes dragon. Occasionally reaching a robust 30cm in length, their skin is rough and grey to brown with indistinct patterning. Unlike other lizards, they will often stop to study you, before finally disappearing into a wall or under a rock.

Geckos are large-eyed nocturnal lizards, up to 15cm long, with short tails and often rough skins. Their spreading toes have claws and ingenious adhesive pads, allowing them to walk up house walls and onto ceilings in their search for insects. Groups of them lie in wait near bright lights that attract their prey, and small ones living indoors can have very pale, translucent skins. Not always popular locally – one Greek name for them, *miaró*, means "defiler" after their outsized faeces – they should be left alone to eat mosquitoes and other bugs. The **chameleon** is a rare, slow-moving and swivel-eyed inhabitant of eastern Crete, Yiálova and some eastern Aegean islands such as Sámos. Although essentially green, it has the ability to adjust its coloration to match the surroundings.

Once collected for the pet trade, **tortoises** can be found on much of the mainland, and some islands, though not on Crete. Usually it is their noisy progress through vegetation on sunny or wooded hills that first signals their presence. They spend their often long lives grazing the vegetation and can reach lengths of 30cm. Closely related **terrapins** are more streamlined, freshwater tortoises which love to bask on waterside mud by streams or ponds, including on many islands. Shy and nervous, they are usually only seen as they disappear under water. They are scavengers and will eat anything, including fingers if handled.

Sea turtles occur mostly in the Ionian Sea, but also in the Aegean. The least rare are the loggerhead turtles (*Caretta caretta*), which nest on Zákynthos and Kefalloniá, and occasionally in Crete. Their nesting grounds are disappearing under tourist resorts, although they are a protected endangered species (see the box on p.989).

Snakes are abundant in Greece and many islands; most are shy and non-venomous. Several species, including the Ottoman and nose-horned **vipers**, do have a poisonous bite, though they are not usually aggressive. They are adder-like and often have a very distinct, dark zigzag stripe down the back. They are only likely to bite if a hand is put in the crevice of a wall or a rock-face where one of them is resting, or if they are attacked. Unfortunately, the locals in some areas attempt to kill any snake they see, and thus greatly increase the probability of their being bitten. Leave them alone, and they will do the same for you (but if worst comes to worst, see the advice on p.29). Most snakes are not only completely harmless to humans, but beneficial in that they keep down populations of pests such as rats and mice. There are also three species of legless lizards – slow-worm, glass lizard and legless skink – all equally harmless, which suffer because they are mistaken for snakes.

Frogs and **toads** are the commonest and most obvious amphibians in most of Greece, particularly during the spring breeding season. The green toad has green marbling over a pinkish or mud-coloured background, and a cricket-like trill. Frogs prefer the wettest places, and the robust marsh frog particularly revels in artificial water-storage ponds, whose concrete sides magnify their croaking impressively. Tree frogs are tiny jewels, usually emerald green, with huge and strident voices at night. They rest by day in trees and shrubs, and can sometimes be found in quantity plastered onto the leaves of water-side oleanders.

Newts, complete with lacy external gills, can be seen in a few alpine tarns of the north mainland. Search for **salamanders** in ponds at breeding time, under stones and in moist crevices outside the breeding season. The orange-on-black fire salamander is often found promenading in the mountains after rain.

Insects

Greece teems with **insects.** Some pester, like flies and mosquitoes, but most are harmless to humans. The huge, slow-flying, glossy black carpenter bee may cause alarm by its size and noise, but is rarely a problem.

detailed maps, plus an annotated species-by-species bird list with much useful information. Contact the author directly at ©email@richard-brooks.co.uk.

George Handrinos and T. Akriotis *Birds of Greece* (A&C Black, UK). A comprehensive guide that includes island birdlife.

Heinzel, Fitter and Parslow *Collins Guide to the Birds of Britain and Europe;* **Petersen, Mountfort and Hollom** *Field Guide to the Birds of Britain and Europe* (Collins, UK; Stephen Green Press, US). Though not specific to Greece, these two field guides have the best coverage of Greek birds outside of Lésvos.

Mammals

Corbet and Ovenden *Collins Guide to the Mammals of Europe* (Collins, UK; Stephen Green Press, US). The best field guide on its subject.

Reptiles

Arnold, Burton and Ovenden *Collins Guide to the Reptiles and Amphibians of Britain and Europe* (Collins, UK; Stephen Green Press, US). A useful guide, though it excludes the Dodecanese and east Aegean islands.

Jiri Cihar *Amphibians and Reptiles* (Conran Octopus, UK; o/p). Selective coverage, but includes most endemic species of the Dodecanese and east Aegean isles.

Insects

Michael Chinery *Collins Guide to the Insects of Britain and Western Europe* (Collins, UK; Stephen Green Press, US). Although Greece is outside the geographical scope of the guide, it will provide genus identifications for most insects seen.

Lionel Higgins and Norman Riley *A Field Guide to the Butterflies of Britain and Europe* (Collins, UK; Stephen Green Press, US). A thorough and detailed field guide that illustrates nearly all species seen in Greece.

Marine life

B. Luther and K. Fiedler *A Field Guide to the Mediterranean* (HarperCollins, UK; o/p). Very thorough; includes most Greek shallow-water species.

CONTEXTS | Wildlife

Grasshoppers and **crickets** swarm through open areas of vegetation in summer, with several larger species that are carnivorous on the smaller and can bite strongly if handled. Larger still is the grey-brown locust, which flies noisily before crash-landing into trees and shrubs. The high-pitched and endlessly repeated chirp of house crickets can drive one to distraction, as can the summer whirring of cicadas on the trunks of trees. The latter insects are giant relatives of the aphids that cluster on roses.

From spring through to autumn Greece is full of **butterflies**, particularly during late spring and early summer. There are three swallowtail species, named for the drawn-out corners of the hind-wings, in shades of cream and yellow, with black and blue markings. Their smaller relatives, the festoons, lack the tails, but add red spots to the palette. The rarer, robust brown-and-orange pasha is unrelated but is Europe's largest butterfly. In autumn the black-and-orange plain tiger or African monarch may appear, sometimes in large quantities. In areas of deciduous woodland, look high up and you may see fast-flying large tortoiseshells, while lower down, southern white admirals skim and glide through clearings between the trees. Some of the smallest but most beautiful butterflies are the blues. Their subtle, camouflaging grey and black undersides make them vanish from view when they land and fold their wings.

Some of the Greek **hawkmoths** are equally spectacular, particularly the green-and-pink oleander hawkmoth. Their large caterpillars can be recognized by their tail horn. The hummingbird hawkmoth, like its namesake, hovers at flowers to feed, supported by a blur of fast-moving wings. Tiger moths, with their black-and-white forewings and startling bright orange hindwings, are the "butterflies" that occur in huge quantity in sheltered sites of islands such as Rhodes and Páros. The giant peacock moth is Europe's largest, up to 15cm across. A mixture of grey, black and brown, with big eye-spots, it is usually only seen during the day while resting on tree trunks.

Other insects include the camouflaged praying mantis, holding their power-ful forelegs in a position of supplication until another insect comes within reach. The females are voracious, and notorious for eating the males during mating. Ant-lion adults resemble a fluttery dragonfly, but their young are huge-jawed and build pits in the sand to trap ants. Hemispherical carob beetles col-lect balls of dung and push them around with their back legs, while the huge longhorn beetles of the southern Ionian islands munch their way through tree trunks. Longhorns are named for their absurdly extended, whip-like antennae. Cockroaches of varying species live in buildings, particularly hotels, restaurants and bakeries, attracted by warmth and food scraps.

Corfu is famous for its extraordinary **fireflies**, which flutter in quantities across meadows and marshes on May nights, speckling the darkness with bursts of cold light to attract partners. The Epirot mainland opposite also has its fair share of these creatures; look carefully in nearby hedges, and you may spot the less flashy, more sedentary glow-worm.

Centipedes are not often seen, but the fast-moving twenty-centimetre scol-ipendra should be treated with respect since they can give very painful bites. Other non-vertebrates of interest include the land crabs, which are found in the south and east. They need water to breed, but can cause surprise when found walking on remote hillsides. There are plenty of genuine marine crea-tures to be seen, particularly in shallow seawater sheltered by rocks – sea cucumbers, sea butterflies, octopus, marine worms, starfish and sea urchins.

Music

Music is central to Greek culture; even the most indifferent visitor will be aware of its ubiquitous presence in ferries, tavernas and other public spaces. Like most aspects of Greece, it's an amalgamation of native and Anatolian styles, with occasional contributions from the West. In fact, Western music made little impression until recent decades, when aesthetic disputes arose between adherents of folk- or *laïkí*-derived styles and those spurning ethnic roots in favour of jazz, symphonic and rock idioms – a reflection of the modernizing-versus-traditionalism debates raging in the nation at large.

Many older songs, invariably in Eastern-flavoured minor scales (or more correctly, modes), have direct antecedents in the forms and styles of both **Byzantine religious chant** and that of the **Ottoman empire**, though the more nationalistically minded musicologists claim their original descent from the now-lost melodies of ancient Greece. Almost all native Greek instruments are near-duplicates of ones used throughout the Islamic world, though it's an open question as to whether the Byzantines, Arabs or Persians first constructed particular instruments. To this broadly Middle Eastern base Slavs, Albanians and Italians have added their share, resulting in an extraordinarily varied repertoire of traditional and modern pieces.

Byzantine sacred music

Sacred **Byzantine chant** forms the bedrock from which much later Greek secular music sprang. Despite its canonical constancy, and prohibition on

Discographies

Each of the following sections is accompanied by a discography. The ◗ symbol denotes a disc available on CD; * tags a particularly recommended recording. Serial numbers are given for LPs and CDs when known; unless UK or US is stated, all are Greek labels. Cassette pressing has been mostly discontinued in Greece.

For suggestions on disc hunting in Greece, see the Athens shopping section (p.154). In the UK the best source is Trehantiri, 367 Green Lanes, London N4; (☎020/8802 6530, 🖰www.trehantiri.com), which also operates a worldwide mail-order service. In North America, try Down Home Music, 10341 San Pablo Ave, El Cerrito, CA 94530 (☎510/525-2129). Heritage discs, pressed by Interstate Music in East Sussex, are uniformly excellent, but can occasionally be difficult to find in shops; if necessary get them mail-order through Swift Record Distributors, 3 Wilton Rd, Bexhill-on-Sea, East Sussex TN40 1HY (☎01424/220028, 🖷213440). When in Greece, consider investing in a copy of the monthly music magazine *Dhifono* (€6), which includes a covermount CD. It's strictly potluck what you get – it can be lousy new Greek rock or wonderful archival rebétika or folk, but at the price you lose little; instructions in the back (in Greek) tell you where to get back issues – Aristoníkou 1–3, second floor, Mets, Athens; Mon–Fri 9am–3pm (though some of the better ones are sold out).

instrumentation, it is by no means a museum tradition. Some of the finest liturgical chanting can be heard on Mount Athos in northern Greece, but only men can visit, by special arrangement (see chapter five). More conveniently, tenor Lycourgos Angelopoulos and his excellent choir – the best group currently active – used to chant every Sunday at Ayía Iríni church in Athens' flower market, and still do so on occasion now that its restoration is complete. Greeks get tetchy with foreign critics who fail to give Byzantine music its due, but they are partly to blame themselves; there are a lot of mediocre Greek-originated recordings about, while quality musicians go unrecorded. The great Constantinopolitan psáltis (chanter) Thrasyvoulos Stanitsas, who moved to Athens in 1964, has no extant discography, while all of the Angelopoulos recordings in print have been brought out on French labels. Overseas record stores, unsure of whether to class Byzantine music as "ethnic", "classical" or "sacred", often end up not stocking it at all, or only by special order.

Regional folk music

The most promising times to hear regional folk music live are at the numerous summer *paniyíria* (saints'-day festivals) – or more tourist-oriented cultural programmes – when musicians normally based in Athens or city clubs during winter tour the islands and villages. However, it's as well to know that a marked decline in this type of music began during the 1960s – a trend accelerated by the 1967–74 junta – so that traditional instrumentation is now often replaced by something more appropriate to rock concerts, aggravated by pick-ups for plucked-string instruments not tolerant of amplification, and excessive reverb. Younger musicians, who have been deprived of (or actively scorn) the oral transmission of technique from older master players, are not always what they could be. Furthermore, on the islands at least, most musicians are semi-professionals, required to supplement their income with another trade. All this makes recent re-releases on CD of old archival material more precious, and an increasing number of revival groups are attempting to recapture the musicianship, if not the ethos, of the old-timers.

Crete, Kássos, Hálki and Kárpathos

This arc of southern islands is one of the most promising areas in Greece for hearing live music at any season of the year. The dominant instrument here is the lýra, a three-stringed fiddle directly related to the Turkish kemençe. This is played not on the shoulder but balanced on the thigh, with (in the Dodecanese only) tiny bells attached to the bow, which the musician can jiggle for rhythmical accent. The strings are metal, and since the centre string is just a drone, the player improvises only on the outer two with a convex bow, changing pitch by pressing the fingernails on the fretless neck. The contemporary Cretan lýra, a product of the 1930s, is larger, tuned lower, lacks a drone string but has a fingerboard, and is played with a straighter bow. Usually the lýra is backed up by one or more **laoúta**, similar to the Turkish/Arab oud but more closely resembling a mandolin, with a long fretted neck and four sets of double strings. These are rarely used to their full potential – a *laoúto* solo is an uncommon treat – but a good player will coax a pleasing, chime-like tone from the instrument.

In several places in the south Aegean, notably northern Kárpathos, a primitive bagpipe, the **askomandoúra** or *tsamboúna*, joins the lýra and *laoúto*. During the colonels' dictatorship the playing of the bagpipe in the Cyclades was banned lest tourists think the Greeks "too primitive" – though hopefully all concerned have recovered from any sense of cultural inferiority. If you remember Kazantzakis's classic novel (or the movie), his hero Zorba played a *sandoúri*, or hammer dulcimer, for recreation, but it was actually little known or used until after 1923 on most islands, being introduced by Asia Minor refugees. Today, accomplished players are few, and in *kritikí* (Cretan music), *nisiótika* (island songs) and rebétika (see p.1063), the instrument has been relegated to a supporting role. On older Cretan recordings you may hear solos on the *voúlgari*, a stringed instrument, essentially a small *saz* (Turkish long-necked, fretted lute), which has now all but died out. Modern Cretan artists to look out for on recordings include Kostas Moundakis, the late acknowledged lýra master, the late Nikos Xylouris, justifiably dubbed "the nightingale of Crete" for his soaring voice, and his younger, lýra-playing brother Andonis who performs under the name Psarandonis.

Other Aegean islands

On most of the Aegean islands, and particularly the Cyclades, you'll find the lýra replaced by a more familiar-looking **violí**, essentially a Western violin. Accompaniment was provided until recently by *laoúto* or *sandoúri*, though these days you're more likely to be confronted (or affronted) by a bass-guitar and drum rhythm section. The *tsamboúna* is also popular in the Cyclades (and Ikaría and Sámos), when it's played in conjunction with a two-headed, shoulder-strung drum called the **toumbáki**.

Unlike on Crete, where you can often catch the best music in special clubs or *kéndra*, Aegean-island performances tend to be spontaneous and less specialized; festivals and saints' days in village squares offer the most promising opportunities. The melodies, like much folk music the world over, rely heavily on the pentatonic scale. Lyrics, especially on the smaller islands of the central Aegean, touch on the perils of the sea, exile and – in a society where long periods of separation and arranged marriage were the norm – thwarted love. Though since the 1960s the prolific **Konitopoulos clan** from Náxos has become virtually synonymous with *nisiótika*, older stars like **Anna and Emilia Hatzidhaki**, **Effi Sarri** and **Anna Karabesini** – all from the Dodecanese archipelago – offer a warmer, more innocent delivery. Amongst violinists, **Yiannis Zevgolis** and **Stathis Koukoularis**, both from Náxos, stand out.

Lésvos occupies a special place in terms of island music; before the turbulent decade of 1912–22, its "mainland" was Asia Minor rather than Greece, its urban poles Smyrna and Constantinople rather than Athens. Accordingly, its music is far more varied and sophisticated than the Aegean norm, having absorbed

*❍ Songs of… (Society for the Dissemination of National Music, Greece). A thirty-disc-plus series of field recordings from the 1950s to the 1970s, each covering traditional music of one region or type. All LPs contain lyrics in English and recordings are easily available in Athens in LP, cassette or CD form, especially at the Museum of Greek Popular Musical Instruments, p.123. Best to date are Thrace 1 (SDNM 106); Epirus 1 (SDNM 111); Peloponnese (SDNM 113); Mytilene and Chios (SDNM 110); Mytilene and Asia Minor (SDNM 125); Rhodes, Chalki and Symi (SDNM 104); Amorgos, Kythnos and Sifnos (SDNM 105); and Kassos and Karpathos (SDNM 103).

*❍ Various *Anthology of Greek Folk Songs, 1929–1940, vol 1* (FM Records 666). Lots of Yiorgos Papadsiheris and Mihalis Kallergis on vocals, clarinet by Nikos Tzaras and Nikos Karakostas, plus a host of rebétika greats "moonlighting", and demonstrating the porosity of boundaries between Greek song types. *Vol 4* (FM Records 671) of the same set emphasises Epirus more, and is equally worthy.

❍ Various *Avthentika Nisiotika tou Peninda* (Lyra 0168). Good Cretan and Pontic material from the 1950s, with the Dodecanese also represented, from the collection of the late Ted Petrides, musician and dance master.

❍ Various *Dhimotiki Paradhosi: Morias* (Minos 7 24383 49042 4). Good, inexpensive anthology of Peloponnese standards with Yiorgos Papasidheris on many tracks.

*❍ Various *Kritiki Mousiki Paradhosi, Iy Protomastores 1920–1953* (Aerakis, ten CDs). For many visitors, Cretan music consists of monotonous sawing on the lýra and verses in impenetrable dialect; this is the perfect antidote. The whole set's prohibitively pricey, but fortunately discs are available individually; go for no. 1 (Baxevanis, lýra and small orchestra); no. 4 (Stelios Foustalieris, the last master of the *voúlgari*, knowledge of which died with him); no. 5 (Yiannis Demirtzoyiannis, guitarist and epic singer); and no. 6 (Yiorgis Koutsourelis, on melodic *laoúto*).

❍ Various *Paniyiria sta Horia mas* (CD, Minos 7 24348 00112 2). Another good general anthology of non-electrified, pre-1960s material.

*❍ Various *Seryiani sta Nisia Mas, vol 1* (CD, MBI 10371). Excellent retrospective of various *nisiótika* hits and artists, mostly from the 1950s; the easiest way to hear the vintage stars listed under "Other Aegean islands".

*❍ Various *Songs and Melodies of Patmos* (CD, Politistikon Idhryma Dhodhekanisou 201). Live 1995 field recordings of pieces as raw but compelling as you'd hear them at an old-time festival.

❍ Various *Takoutsia, Musiciens de Zagori: Inédit – Grèce – Epiré* (Inédit/Auvidis, France). Drinking songs, dance tunes and dirges performed by one of the last working clans of Epirot Gypsy musicians. Lots of fine fiddle and clarinet, with an all-acoustic *koumpanía* providing support.

*❍ Khronis Aïdhonidhis *T'Aïdhonia tis Anatolis: Songs of Thrace and Asia Minor* (Minos 847/848, Greece). One of the best and most accessible collections available, featuring the top singer of material from Thrace and western Asia Minor, plus an orchestra directed by Ross Daly and solos on four tracks by versatile Yiorgos Dalaras. Aïdhonidis sings alone on the equally good *Tragoudhia keh Skopi tis Thrakis/Songs and Tunes of Thrace* (Crete UP 7/8).

*❍ Banda tis Florinas (Ano Kato-Rei 2008, Thessaloníki). Wonderfully twisted brass-band music unique to western Macedonia, edging into ethnic-jazz territory with a nudge from guest saxophonist Floros Floridhis, one of the foremost personalities on Greece's avant-garde/improvisational scene. Recommended for demolishing stereotypes about Greek music.

❍ Roza Eskenazi and Rita Ambatzi *Se Dhimotika Tragoudhia/In Folk Songs* (Minos 4 802167 29). Mainland standards interpreted with incredible verve, showing the versatility of these two normally associated with rebétika.

❍ Tassos Halkias (EMI 74321 318232). #4 of the long out-of-print "Great Solos" series, this re-release of a 1977 session features the master clarinetist at his most heartfelt.

◑**Emilia Hatzidhaki** *Thalassina Tragoudhia* (LP: Panvox 16311, reissued as CD by MBI). The sole easily available collection dedicated to this artist, who otherwise appears only on *nisiótika* anthologies.

*◑**Petros Loukas Halkias** *Dhromi tis Psykhis* (CD, Papingo/BMG-Ariola 74321 318232) and *Miroloyia ke Yirismata* (Lyra 4717). Technically impeccable updating of the clarinet tradition, but with traditional backing *koumpanía* of *laoúto*, *violí* and percussion; purists prefer *Miroloyia*, but the more orchestrated Papingo disc may be easier to find. However, even better is *Petro-Loukas Chalkias (sic) & Kompania* (World Network 46), wonderful improvisations and dialogues in a four-member group.

◑**Anna Karabessini & Effi Sarri** CD reissues from old LP's: *Yialo Yialo Piyeno* (Lyra 0102067); *Tis Thalassas* (Lyra 10777) and *Ena Glendi* (Lyra; 10717). Two singing sisters from the island of Kós, who were for the Dodecanese what the Konitopoulos family (see below) was for the Cyclades; the fact that they performed only for private gatherings added to their status.

◑**Xanthippi Karathanasi** *Tragoudhia ke Skopi tis Makedhonias/Songs and Tunes of Macedonia* (CD, University Press of Crete). High quality, like all UP Crete releases; the only quibble is that the sidemen are so good that they threaten to overshadow Xanthippi's vocals.

Irini Konitopoulou-Legaki ◑*Athanata Nisiotika 1* (Tzina-Astir 1020). A 1978 warhorse, beloved of bus drivers across the islands. *◑*Anefala Thalassina* (Lyra 4693) from 1993 is far less commercial and one of the finest recordings from Náxos, featuring fellow Naxian *lautiéris* Dhimitris Fyroyenis and Yiannis Zevgolis, one of the last old-style island violinists. Aged 61, Irini sings her heart out in a richer, deeper voice than she was known for on club stages.

◑**Yiorgos Konitopoulos & Clan** *Sto Diava tou Egeou* (Minos EMI 77) and *Yiorgos ke Irini Konitopoulou-Legaki: Apo Limani se Limani* (EMI 107243480859231). CD reissues of early recordings made by violinist Yiorgos with sister Irini (as above), of a famous (and numerous) Náxos family musically active for the past four decades.

*◑**Yiorgos Koros** *Ta Organika tis Smyrnis* (Lyra 3405). Master fiddler Koros lets rip, with Aristidhis Moskhos backing on *sandoúri*.

*◑**Lesvos Aiolis** *Tragoudhia ke Hori tis Lesvou/Songs & Dances of Lesvos* (University Press of Crete, double CD 9/10). Two decades' worth (1974–96) of field recordings of the last traditional music extant on the island, a labour of love supervised by musicologist Nikos Dhionysopoulos. Pricey, but the quality and uniqueness of the instrumental pieces especially, and the huge illustrated booklet, merit the expense.

*◑**Lesvos: Mousika Stavrodhromia sto Egeo/Musical Crossroads of the Aegean** (University of the Aegean five-CD set with an enormous book accompanying it (with photos). Everything from Asia Minor music played in Lésvos to carols and wedding songs. Very pricey but worth it.

Psarandonis *Palio Krasi in'iy Skepsi Mou* (Lyra/Musurgia Graeca 4775), *Idheon Antron* (Musurgia Graeca 4948). Wonderful outings by a musican ostracized by his fellows for his idiosyncratic style; daugher Niki sings two gorgeous cuts on *Idheon Antron*.

*◑**Thalassa Thymisou/Sea of Memories: Tragoudhia ke Skopi apo tis Inousses** (Navtiko Mousio Inousson-En Khordais CD 1801/1802). The result of a "field trip" by the En Khordais traditional music school of Thessaloníki to Inoússes, a small islet northeast of Híos, to rescue vanishing traditional material; the result's superb, a mix of live sessions in Inoussan tavernas and some studio recordings. Thorough and intelligent notes, but no lyrics translations.

◑**Tragoudhia tou Pondou** *Songs of Pontos* (CD, En Khordais 1910). Songs of the dominant refugee group around Thessaloníki, re-released from the 1960s archives of Macedonian public radio. Pontic music is an acquired taste, but this is the best batch we've sampled.

*◑**Nikos Xylouris** *O Arkhangelos tis Kritis, 1958–1968* (CD, MBI 10376); *Ta Khronia stin Kriti* (2CD, MBI10677/78). These are the best two retrospectives, with copious notes; the first covers his initial decade of recordings, previously unavailable, with self-accompaniment on the *lýra*.

melodies and instrumentation from the various groups who lived in neighbouring Anatolia; for example, Lésvos is the only island with a vital tradition of brass bands, and virtually every Greek dance rhythm is represented in local music.

Ionian islands

By way of complete contrast, the Ionian islands – except for Lefkádha – alone of all modern Greek territory never saw Turkish occupation and have a predominantly Western musical tradition. The indigenous song-form is Italian both in name (**kantádhes**) and instrumentation (guitar and mandolin); it's most often heard these days on **Lefkádha** and **Zákynthos**.

The Peloponnese, Central Greece and Epirus

Many of the folk lyrics of the Peloponnese, central and western Greece hark back to the years of Ottoman occupation and to the War of Independence; others, in a lighter tone, refer to aspects of pastoral life. All these are classified as *dhimotiká tragoúdhia* or folk-songs. The essential instrumentation consists of the **klaríno** (clarinet), which reached Greece during the 1830s, introduced either by Gypsies or by members of King Otto's Bavarian entourage. Backing was traditionally provided by a *koumpanía* consisting of *kithára* (guitar), *laoúto*, *laoutokithára* (a hybrid in stringing and tuning) and *violí*, with *toumberléki* (lap drum) or *défi* (tambourine) for rhythm. Many mainland tunes are danceable, divided by rhythm into such categories as *kalamatianó* (a line dance), *tsámiko*, *hasaposérviko* or *syrtó*, the quintessential circle dance of Greece. Those that are not include the slow, stately *kléftiko,* similar to the *rizítiko* of Crete, both of which relate, baldly or in metaphor, incidents or attitudes from the years of the Ottomans and the rebellions for freedom.

Stalwart vocalists to look for on old recordings include **Yiorgos Papasidheris** and **Yioryia Mittaki**, the latter actually of Arvanitic (Albanian-speaking) origin, as well as **Roza Eskenazi** and **Rita Abatzi** (see under "Rebétika", opposite). Among instrumentalists, the violinist **Yiorgos Koros**, and clarinetists **Yiannis Saleas**, **Manos Achalinotopoulos** and the late Vassilis Soukas are especially remarkable, good examples of the (mostly) Gypsy or Gypsy-descended musicians who virtually dominate instrumental music on mainland Greece (curiously, Gypsies rarely sing *dhimotiká*, preferring laïkó).

The music of **Epirus** (Ípiros) still exhibits strong connections with that of northern Epirus (now falling within neighbouring Albania) and the Former Yugoslav Republic of Macedonia, particularly in the polyphonic pieces sung by both men and women. They tend to fall into three basic categories, which are also found further south: *mirolóyia* or laments (the instrumental counterpart is called a *skáros*); drinking songs or *epitrapézia*; and various danceable melodies as noted above, common to the entire mainland and many of the islands. Most famous of the Epirot clarinetists are members of the numerous Halkias clan, including the late, great **Tassos Halkias** and the younger, unrelated **Petros Loukas Halkias**.

Since the *paleá dhimotiká* are strongly associated with national identity, it's not surprising that they were for many years pressed into political service. During election campaigns each party's local store-front headquarters or sound trucks blasted out continuous *paleá dhimotiká* (plus *andártika* – see p.1068 – by the Left), interspersed with political harangues. Since 1989, however, this practice has been (officially) banned.

Macedonia and Thrace

Thrace and **Macedonia** remained Ottoman territory until early in the twentieth century, with a bewilderingly mixed population, so music here can sound more generically Balkan. Meriting a special mention are the brass bands, introduced in the nineteenth century by Ottoman military musicians, peculiar to western Macedonia. Owing to the huge influx of Anatolian refugees after 1923, northern Greece has also remained a rich treasure-trove for collectors and ethnomusicologists seeking to document the fast-vanishing old music of Asia Minor. *Kálanda* (Christmas carols), carnival dances, wedding processionals and table songs abound. Noteworthy singers – both still alive and active – include **Xanthippi Karathanassi** and **Khronis Aïdhonidhis**. Incidentally, amongst the Pomaks and other local Muslims, the main festival and wedding season in Thrace runs from autumn through spring, the opposite of elsewhere; summer is reserved for tending the precious local tobacco crop.

The Thracian **kaváli**, or end-blown flute, is identical to the Turkish and Bulgarian article; so too is the northern bagpipe, or *gáïda*. The *zournás*, a screechy, double-reed oboe similar to the Islamic world's shenai, is much in evidence at weddings or festivals, together with the deep-toned *daoúli* drum, as a typically Muslim or Orthodox Gypsy ensemble. Other percussion instruments like the *daïrés* or tambourine and the *darboúka*, the local version of the *toumberléki*, make for some sharply demarcated dance rhythms such as the *zonarádhikos*. The *klaríno* is present here as well, as are two types of lýras, but perhaps the most characteristic melodic instrument of Thrace is the *oúti* or oud, whose popularity received a boost after refugee players arrived.

Rebétika

Rebétika began as the music of the Greek urban dispossessed – criminals, refugees, drug-users, defiers of social norms. It had existed in some form in Greece and Constantinople since at least the beginning of the twentieth century. But it is as difficult to define or get to the origins of as jazz or blues, with which spurious comparisons are often made; although rebétika shares marked similarities in spirit with those American styles, there's none whatsoever in origins or in musical form. The themes of the earlier songs – illicit or frustrated love, drug addiction, police oppression, disease and death – and the tone of the delivery – resignation to the singer's lot, coupled with defiance of authority – will be familiar to Westerners. But even the word "rebétika" is of uncertain derivation, most likely from **harabati**, an old Turkish word meaning, variously, "a shanty town", "a privileged drunkard" and "unconventionally dressed bohemian" – all certainly aspects of rebétika culture. Accordingly, searches for the birth of rebétika must be conducted in the Asia Minor of the last years of the Ottoman empire as well as in Greece proper.

Most outsiders equate Greek music with the **bouzoúki**, a long-necked, fretted, three-stringed lute derived, like the Turkish *saz* and *baglamás*, from the Byzantine *tambourás*. Early in the twentieth century, however, only a small proportion of Greek mainland musicians used it. At the same time, across the Aegean in Smyrna and Constantinople, musical cafés, owned and staffed almost entirely by Greeks, Jews, Armenians and even a few Gypsies, had become popular. Groups typically featured a violinist, a *sandoúri* player and a female vocalist, who usually jingled castanets and danced on stage. The metrically free, improvisational singing style was known as *café-aman* or just **amanés** (plural *amanédhes*), after both the setting and the frequent repetition of the exclamation *aman aman* (Turkish for "alas, alas"), used both for its sense and to fill time while the performers searched their imaginations for more explicit lyrics.

Despite the sparse instrumentation, this was an elegant, riveting performance style requiring considerable skill, harking back to similar vocalization in central Asia. Some of its greatest practitioners included **Andonis "Dalgas"** (Wave) **Dhiamandidhis**, so nicknamed for the undulations in his voice; **Roza Eskenazi**, a Greek Jew who grew up in Constantinople; her contemporary **Rita Abatzi**, from Smyrna; **Marika Papagika**, from the island of Kós, who emigrated to America where she made her career; **Agapios Tomboulis**, a tanbur and oud player of Armenian background; and **Dhimitris "Salonikiyé" Semsis**, a master fiddler from northern Macedonia. The spectrum of origins of these performers gives a good idea of the range of cosmopolitan influences in the years immediately preceding the emergence of "real" rebétika.

The 1919–22 Greco-Turkish war and the resulting 1923 **exchange of populations** were key events in the history of rebétika, resulting in the influx to Greece of over a million Asia Minor Greeks, many of whom settled in shanty towns around Athens, Pireás and Thessaloníki. The *café-aman* musicians, like most of the other refugees, were in comparison to the Greeks of the host country extremely sophisticated; many were highly educated, could read and compose music and had even been unionized in the towns of Asia Minor. Typical of these were **Panayiotis Toundas**, a Smyrniote composer, who after arrival in Athens eventually became head of the Greek division of first Odeon and then Columbia Records, succeeding Semsis in that capacity, and **Vangelis Papazoglou**, another composer who failed to survive World War II. It was galling for the less lucky refugees to live initially on the periphery of the new society in poverty and degradation; most had lost all they had in the hasty evacuation, and many, from inland Anatolia, could initially speak only Turkish. In their misery they sought relief in another long-standing Ottoman institution, the *tekés* or hashish den.

In the **tekédhes** of Pireás, Athens and Thessaloníki, a few men would sit around a charcoal brazier, passing around a *nargilés* (hookah) filled with hashish. One of them might improvise a tune on the *baglamás* or the *bouzoúki* and begin to sing. The words, either his own or those of the other dervíses ("dervishes" – several rebetic terms were a burlesque of those of mystical Islamic tradition), would be heavily laced with insiders' argot, in the manner of the Harlem jive of the same era. As the *taxími* (long, studied introduction) was completed, one of the smokers might rise and begin to dance a **zeïbékiko**, named after the zeybeks, a warrior caste of western Anatolia. It would be a slow, intense, introverted performance following an unusual metre (9/8), not for the benefit of others but for himself.

By the early 1930s, several important male musicians had emerged from the *tekés* culture: the beguilingly-voiced **Stratos Payioumtzis**, **Anestis Delias** (aka **Artemis**), who was to die during the World War II occupation, the only rebétis to actually succumb to drug addiction; Yiorgos Tsoros, better known as **Batis**, an indifferent musician but generous and engaging; and **Markos Vamvakaris**, the most famous of this quartet, a Catholic from Sýros who had run away to Pireás aged fifteen. Though an indisputable master of the *bouzoúki*, he protested to his friends that his voice, ruined perhaps from too much hash-smoking, was no good for singing. But he soon bowed to their encour agement and his gravelly, unmistakable sound set the standard for male vocals over the next decade. His only close peer as an instrumentalist was **Ioannis Papaïoannou**, with whom he occasionally played; Papaïoannou's some-time vocalist Rena Dalia recorded a few famous cuts singing **in Turkish** – a practice which stopped altogether after the late 1950s, with the dying off of the audience that understood such lyrics, and anti-Turkish sentiment arising from the first Cyprus crises.

Songs about getting stoned, or **mastoúriaka**, were a natural outgrowth of the *tekédhes*. One of the most famous, composed and first recorded in the mid-1930s, included the following lines:

> On the sly I went out in a boat
> And arrived at the Dhrákou Cave
> Where I saw three men stoned on hash
> Stretched out on the sand.
> It was Batis, and Artemis,
> And Stratos the Lazy.
> Hey you, Strato! Yeah you, Strato!
> Fix us a terrific nargilé,
> So old Batis can have a smoke...

It is interesting to observe that the most commonly heard version of this song, from the 1950s, bowdlerizes the lyrics, substituting "Play us a fine bit of bouzoúki" for "Fix us a fine nargilé", and so forth.

This "Golden Age" of rebétika – as indeed it was, despite the unhappy lives of many performers, and necessarily limited audience – was short lived. The association of the music with a drug-laced underworld would prove its undoing. After the imposition of the Metaxas dictatorship in 1936, harder-core musicians with uncompromising lyrics and lifestyles, were blackballed by the recording industry; anti-hashish laws were systematically enforced, and police harassment of the *tekédhes* was stepped up. Even possession of a *bouzoúki* or *baglamás* became a criminal offence, and several of the big names did time in jail. Others went to Thessaloníki, where the police chief Vassilis Mouskoundis was a big fan of the music and allowed its practitioners to smoke in private.

For a while, such persecution – and the official encouragement of tangos and frothy Italianate love songs, which always had a much wider public – failed to dim the enthusiasm of the *mánges* (roughly translatable as "wide boys" or "hep cats") who frequented the hash dens. Beatings or prison terms were taken in their stride; time behind bars could be used, as it always had been around the Aegean, to make *skaptó* (dug-out) instruments. A *baglamás* could easily be fashioned from a gourd cut in half or even a tortoise shell (the sound box), a piece of wood (the neck), catgut (frets) and wire for strings, and the result would be small enough to hide from the guards. Jail songs were composed and became popular in the underworld. The lyrics below, with some literal translation from the 1930s argot, are from a typical, much-recorded song:

> *Iy Lahanádhes (The Pickpockets)*
> Down in Lemonádhika there was a ruckus
> They caught two pickpockets who acted innocent
> They took 'em to the slammer in handcuffs
> They'll get a beating if they don't cough up the loot.
> Don't beat us, Mr. Copper, you know very well
> This is our job, and don't expect a cut.

Early rebétika – anthologies

*❶ **Authentic USA Rembetika, vols 1–4** (Lyra 4644 and 4635-4637). The title is a wild misnomer, unless original 78s were released first in the US, as these feature all the usual suspects, already well established in Greece. Volume 4 is devoted to songs about tuberculosis, the scourge of Greece until the 1950s.

❶ **Amanedhes** (Minos 724383443529). Includes some early cuts made in Istanbul, with Gypsy clarinetists appearing on several tracks.

❶ **Cafe Rembetika: The Birth of the Greek Blues** (Nascente NSCD 064) Despite the dumbed-down title and sketchy liner notes, a well-remastered retrospective.

❶ **The Greek Archives** (CD, FM Records, Greece). Luxuriously packaged (though skeletal notes in English), this multidisc series, uneven but generally worthy, manages usually not to duplicate earlier releases. Discs are arranged in two batches, each title devoted to a theme or particular artist. From the first, twelve-volume series, choose from among no. 1 (*Rembetico Song in America 1920–1940*, FM 627); no. 6 (*Women of the Rembetico Song*, FM 632); no. 7 (*Unknown Smyrna 1922–1940*, FM 633); no. 8 (*Armenians, Jews, Turks & Gipsies* [NB, as portrayed, not performing] FM 634) and no. 9 (*Constantinople in Old Recordings*, FM 635). From the second batch, *Anthology of Rémbetiko* [sic] *Songs 1933–1940* (FM 654), *Anthology of Smyrnean Songs 1920–1938* (FM 658) and *Songs of the Sea* (FM 661) are wonderful.

*❶ **Greek Orientale: Smyrneic-Rembetic Songs and Dances** (Polylyric 9033, US). Superb collection spanning the 1920s to early 1930s, with Roza, Rita, Marika Papagika and Dhimitris Semsis. Good sleeve notes and lyric translations.

❶ **Greek Orientale Rebétika 1911–37** (Arhoolie, US). A worthwhile compilation, with Roza Eskenazi, Andonis Dalgas and many more. Includes Roza's "Why I Smoke Cocaine".

*❶ **Historic Urban Folk Songs from Greece** (Rounder CD 1079, US/Direct Distribution, UK). The above-cited artists, plus many more on terrific selections, mostly from the 1930s; complements *Greek Orientale* well, with no duplications.

*❶ **Lost Homelands: The Smyrneic Song in Greece, 1928–35** (Heritage HT 27). Lots of Dalgas, the great rivals Rita Abatzi and Roza Eskenazi, plus instrumental improvisations; as usual for this label, top sound quality and intelligent notes.

❶ **Iy Megali tou Rembetikou** (LP, Margo/CD, Minos; Greece). A collection of over twenty albums, but only the first ten are worth it, and available on CD. The best are *no. 1 (Early Performers, CD Minos 4 80193 25), no. 3 (Vassilis Tsitsanis, LP/CD Margo 8150), no. 4 (Ioannis Papaioannou, LP/CD Margo 8152), *no. 7 (Stratos Payoumtzis, LP/CD Margo 8217), no. 8 (Kostas Roukounas, CD Minos 4 80267 29) and *no. 9 (Spyros Peristeris composer, Markos Vamvakris playing/singing, LP/CD Margo 8219).

❶ **Mourmourika – Songs of the Greek Underworld, 1930–55** (Rounder/Direct 1120). Songs of the *mourmourídhes* or street toughs; rare tracks, many censored after 1937, by relatively unknown artists. Decent sound quality, good liner notes.

*❶ **Rebétika in Pireaus 1933–37 Vol 1 & 2** (Heritage HT 26 and 30). The gang that played – and smoked – together, in top form: Markos, Batis, Stratos and Artemis.

Iy Rembetiki Istoria (LP, EMI Regal 14C 034 70364-70380/CD, Minos). Six-volume series which was among the first material reissued after the junta fell, and still a good start to a collection. Nos. 1 and 4 are mostly Smyrneic/Asia Minor songs; no. 2 is mostly from the 1930s; while nos. 3 and 6 are mixed, stressing Tsitsanis and other 1950s material. No. 5 is the runt of the litter.

❶ **Smyrneïka 1927–35** (MBI 10557). Duplicates parts of the Polylyric and Rounder discs; worth snagging in Greece only if you can't find the other two.

Early rebétika – single artists

*❶ **Rita Abatzi 1933–1938** (Heritage HT 36). With outstanding accompanists, sound quality and notes, this has the edge on *Rita Ambatzi I* (Minos 7 24348 040923 3), part of the Arheio series in Greece. The only discs so far devoted exclusively to this refugee Smyrnean, with a huskier, more textured voice than her peer Roza Eskenazi.

*❶ **Dalgas Andonios Dhiamandidhis 1928–33** (Heritage HT 34). The best disc devoted entirely to the gifted *amanés* artist.

❶ **Anestis Dhelias 1912–1944** (Lyra 4642, Greece). Mostly *mastoúriaka* (hash songs) by the man known as Artemis, performed by the "Gang of Four".

*❶ **Roza Eskenazi 1933–1936** (Heritage HT35). Superb renditions with her usual sidemen Semsis, Tomboulis, plus Lambros on *kanonáki*; extremely varied selection of standards and rare gems make this the best of several collections available.

❶ **Marika Papagika** *Greek Popular and Rebetic Music in New York 1918–29* (Alma Criolla, Berkeley, California, ACCD802). Her best work, with husband Gus backing on *sandoúri*; includes a superb, rare duet with Marika Kastrouni.

❶ **Vangelis Papazoglou 1897–1943** (Lyra 4713-14). Double album of his compositions from the 1920s and 1930s, sung by most of the top stars of the era, including Stellakis, Roza Eskenazi, Kostas Roukounas and Rita Abatzi. Marred by poor sound quality, but several versions of his classic *Iy Lahanadhes.*

❶ **Markos Vamvakaris** *Bouzouki Pioneer 1932–1940* (Rounder, US/Direct, UK 1139). Excellent sound quality, good notes and unusual material – not a trace of his hackneyed and over-covered "Frangosyriani" – make this a top choice. *Afthentika Rembetika tis Amerikis no.2* (Lyra 4635) is mostly Markos, and wonderful; the title's a wild misnomer, as Vamvakaris never went to America, though some 78s may have been simultaneously issued there and Greece.

Later and contemporary rebétika

*❶ **Elliniki Apolavsis** *Apagorevemena Rembetika* (BMG-Falirea 74321/444182). One of the better revival groups from the mid-1980s, with meaty instrumentation (including *cura*, oud and *laoúto*) and material from the late 1920s to early 1930s.

*❶ **Sotiria Bellou 1946–56** (Minos 4 80217 24; no. 5 in Iy Megali tou Rembetikou series). Virtually the only disc under her name without the electric backing of later years; here she performs mostly with Tsitsanis. Includes the original of the classic "Ta Kavourakia".

Marika Ninou *Stou Tzimi tou Hondrou/At Jimmy the Fat's* (LP, Venus-Tzina1053). Poor sound quality since it was a clandestine wire recording, but still a classic. Ninou performs live with Tsitsanis at their habitual club in 1955, Ninou giving it her all; includes two cuts in Turkish. Well worth rooting out.

*❶ **Marika Ninou/Vassilis Tsitsanis** (Philips 6483004). Not as soulful as the Venus disc, but a far better sound and more than adequate renditions of their favourites, including "Synnefiasmeni Kyriaki" and the gut-wrenching "Yennithika".

Vassilis Tsitsanis *Yia Panta 1937–40 vols 1 & 2* (LP, EMI-HMV 401026/401027 Greece); *1938–55 vols 1 & 2* (LP, EMI 70193). First and best vinyl discs of two multivolume series; mostly Stratos on vocals on 1937–40, joined by Ninou and Bellou on 1938–55. May have been reissued in a condensed CD by now.

*❶ **Vassilis Tsitsanis 1936–1946** (Rounder 1124, US/Direct UK). A fine first disc to begin a Tsitsanis collection; again mostly male singers, but includes his reputed first recording, a *mastoúriaka* with Yeoryia Mittaki, and good notes.

*❶ **Stavros Xarhakos** *Rembetiko* CBS 70245). Soundtrack to the namesake film, available as a double LP or, in edited form, on one CD. Virtually the only "original" rebétika to be composed in the last fifty years, with lyrics by poet Nikos Gatsos.

❶ **Ioanna Yiorgakopoulou** *Iy Rembetissa* (EMI 4 80014 29). First and best of four identically titled albums featuring this unjustly neglected singer-composer.

We "eat cabbages" and pinch "slippers" so we can
Have a regular rest in jail.
Death don't scare us, it's only hunger we mind,
That's why we nick "cabbage" and get along fine.
Vangelis Papazoglou (1934)

Moreover, the *rebétes* suffered from the disapproval of the puritanical left as well as the puritanical right; the growing Communist Party of the 1930s considered the music and its habitués hopelessly decadent and politically unevolved. When Vamvakaris was about to join the leftist resistance army ELAS in 1943, he was admonished not to sing his own material "lest it corrupt the heroic proletariat". The Left preferred *andártika* (Soviet-style revolutionary anthems), though Sotiria Bellou, a *rebétissa* (female rebetic musician) and active communist whose career began late in the 1940s, was a conspicuous exception.

Bellou was one of several important female vocalists to accompany **Vassilis Tsitsanis**, the most significant composer and *bouzoúki* player to emerge after Vamvakaris; the others were **Marika Ninou** and **Ioanna Yiorgakopoulou**, the latter also a composer in her own right. From Tríkala in Thessaly, Tsitsanis abandoned law studies to cut his first record in 1936 for Odeon, directed by rebetic composer **Spyros Peristeris**. The war interrupted his — and everyone else's — recording career from late 1940 until late 1945, a period which Tsitsanis spent running a musical taverna in Thessaloníki; when World War II, and the civil war that followed, ended, a huge backlog of songs composed during the occupation awaited the studios. The traumatic decade between 1939 and 1948 had erased the fashion for *mastoúriaka*; more than ever, audiences instead craved vaguely Neapolitan melodies and words about love. Tsitsanis was happy to oblige, and for the first time rebétika enjoyed something like a mass following, but his love lyrics were anything but insipid, and the demoralization of the war years prompted him to also compose darker works, most famous of these "Synnefiasmeni Kyriaki":

Cloudy Sunday, you seem like my heart
Which is always overcast, Christ and Holy Virgin!
You're a day like the one I lost my joy.
Cloudy Sunday, you make my heart bleed.
When I see you rainy, I can't rest easy for a moment;
You blacken my life and I sigh deeply.
(composed 1943, first recorded 1948)

Although Tsitsanis performed almost up to his death in 1984 – his funeral in Athens was attended by nearly a quarter of a million people – 1953 effectively marked the end of the original rebetic style. In that year, **Manolis Hiotis** added a fourth string to the *bouzoúki*, allowing it to be tuned tonally rather than modally; electrical amplification to reach larger audiences, maudlin lyrics and over-orchestration were not long in following. Performances in huge, barnlike clubs, also called *bouzoúkia*, became debased and vulgarized. Virtuoso *bouzoúki* players, assisted by kewpie-doll-type female vocalists, became immensely rich – the so-called *arhondorembétes* like Hiotis and **Yiorgos Zambetas**. The clubs themselves were clip-joints where Athenians paid large sums to break plates and watch dancing whose flashy steps and gyrations were a travesty of the simple dignity and precise, synchronized footwork of the old-time *zeïbékiko*.

Ironically, the original rebétika material was rescued from oblivion by the colonels' junta of 1967–74. Along with dozens of other features of Greek culture, rebétika verses were banned. The younger generation coming of age under the dictatorship took a closer look at the forbidden fruit and derived solace, and deeper meanings, from the nominally apolitical lyrics.

When the junta fell in 1974 – and even a little before – there was an outpouring of reissued recordings of the old masters. Initially these were merely 33rpm pressings of the original 78s, with no re-editing or liner notes, but the industry – prompted in part by growing demand from foreigners – has lately resorted to higher production values, though little in the way of startlingly new finds.

Over the next decade live rebétika also enjoyed a revival, beginning with a clandestine 1979 club near the old Fix brewery in Athens, whose street credentials were validated when it was raided and closed by the police. These smoky attempts to recapture prewar atmosphere, and eventually larger venues, saw performances by revival groups such as **Ta Pedhia apo tin Patra**, **Iy Rembetiki Kompania** and **Iy Opisthodhromiki Kompania** and (from Thessaloníki) **"Hondronakos"** (Stefanos Kiouproulis), **"Maryo"** (Maria Konstandinidhou) and Agathonas Iakovidhis with his **Rembetika Synkrotima Thessalonikis**. A feature film by Kostas Ferris, *Rembetiko* (1983), attempted to trace the music from Asia Minor of the 1920s to Greece of the 1950s, and garnered wide acclaim in Greece and abroad. Today, however, the fashion has long since peaked, and hardly any clubs and bands remain from the dozens which made their appearance between 1978 and 1986.

The éntekhno revolution

The "Westernization" of rebétika that had begun with Tsitsanis and been completed by the *arhondorembétes* paved the way for the *éntekhno* music which emerged during the late 1950s. **Éntekhno**, literally "artistic" or "sophisticated", encompassed an orchestral genre where folk instruments and melodies, where present, would be interwoven into a much larger symphonic fabric.

Its first, and most famous, practitioners were exact contemporaries **Manos Hatzidhakis** and **Mikis Theodhorakis**, both classically trained musicians and admirers of rebétika. Already in 1948, Hatzidhakis had defended rebétika in a lecture, suggesting that Greek composers be inspired by it, rather than bow to the prevailing left-wing/middle-class prejudice against it; in a period when most Greek tunes imitated Western light popular music, he had transcribed rebétika for piano and orchestra, keeping only the spirit and nostalgic mood of the original. Theodhorakis, a disciple of Tsitsanis, included *zeïbékiko* and *hasápika* on his earliest albums, with Grigoris Bithikotsis or Stelios Kazantzidhis on vocals and Manolis Hiotis as *bouzoúki* soloist. Other engagingly accessible work was his 1966 sessions with the Horódhia Trikálon (the Trikala Choir). His international reputation became distorted by his overplayed and over-covered 1965 soundtrack for *Zorba the Greek*; indeed soon after this he shunned Byzantine/folk/rebetic influence completely in favour of quasiclassical, overtly political symphonic works and film soundtracks dictated by his communist affiliation.

❍**Manos Hatzidhakis** *Matomenos Gamos: Paramythi horis Onoma* (Columbia GCX107). Nikos Gatsos-translated lyrics, with Lakis Pappas singing.

*❍**Yannis Markopoulos** *Thiteia* ((LP/CD, EMI 14C062 70123). With lyrics by Manos Eleftheriou, many consider this – including hits like "Malamatenia Logia" – Markopoulos's best effort, but *Anexartita* (CD, Minos EMI 7243 834897 25) is also a strong contender, with an incredible range of talent and the original live version of the bitter "ly Ellada", recorded just after the junta fell.

❍**Mikis Theodhorakis** **Epitafios* (EMI Columbia) and **To Axion Esti* (EMI Columbia). These are his most influential, reputation-justifying works. The four sessions with the Horodhia Trikalon may still be around on CD (Olympic 1099–1102). If you want to be sure of touching all bases, a recent five-CD set (EMI 14C 045 1702572) includes the best recordings of his best-loved songs, organized roughly chronologically and by type (one disc is entirely soundtracks, another theatre pieces and so forth).

*❍**Stavros Xarhakos/Nikos Xylouris Sylloyi** (Minos 701242). Lyrics by Nikos Gatsos, Xylouris's crystalline voice and orchestra conducted by Khristodhoulos Halaris have made this a landmark 1973 recording; the funky electric guitar licks actually work, the wistful Track 8, "Itane mia Fora", is still much loved and played.

The *éntekhno* of Theodhorakis and Hatzidhakis combined not only rebetic and Byzantine influences with quasiclassical orchestral arrangements, but also fused Greek music with the country's rich **poetic tradition**. Among Theodhorakis's first albums was his 1963 *Epitafios/Epifaneia*, based on poems by Yiannis Ritsos and George Seferis, and its 1964 successor, *To Axion Esti*, a folk-flavoured oratorio incorporating poetry by Nobel laureate Odysseas Elytis. Hatzidhakis countered in 1965 with *Matomenos Gamos*, a version of Garcia Lorca's *Blood Wedding* translated into Greek by poet-lyricist Nikos Gatsos, and also tried his hand at rendering Elytis in song. Together, these early works changed Greek perceptions of *bouzoúki*-based music, popularized Greek poetry for a mass audience and elevated lyricists such as Gatsos and Manos Eleftheriou to the status of bards.

The down side of this increased sophistication was an inevitable distancing from indigenous roots, in particular the modal scale. The new genre, with its catchy tunes, seemed almost a natural for elevator music and film soundtracks. Like Theodhorakis, Hatzidhakis was haunted by soundtracks composed for various movies starring Melina Mercouri, most notably *Never on Sunday* (1960). Hatzidhakis (died 1994), mostly steered clear of political statements; instead he launched, during the 1980s, his own record label, Seirios, to provide a forum for nonmainstream musicians.

Whatever their shortcomings, Theodhorakis and Hatzidhakis paved the way for successors, less classical and more folk-leaning, such as **Stavros Xarhakos**, most famous abroad for his soundtrack to the films *Ta Kokkina Fanaria* (The Red Lanterns) and *Rembetiko*. Xarkhakos's exact contemporary, Yiannis Markopoulos, also did the all-but-obligatory soundtrack (*Who Pays the Ferryman*, 1978) but otherwise is perhaps the most interesting and consistently Greek-sounding of these four composers to emerge from the 1960s. His best work dates from the early-to-mid-1970s – in retrospect, the Indian summer of *éntekhno*.

Laïkó: son of rebétika

Diametrically opposed to *éntekhno* was the authentic **laïkó** or "popular" music of the 1950s and 1960s, its gritty, tough style a direct heir to rebétika, undiluted by Western influences. Laïkó used not only *zeïbékiko* and *hasápika* time signatures but also the *tsiftetéli*, another rhythm from Asia Minor mistakenly known as "belly-dance" music overseas. Once again, "debased" oriental influences dominated Greek pop, much to the chagrin of those who objected to the apolitical, decadent, escapist song content. This orientalizing reached its high – or low – point during the brief mid-1960s craze for *indoyíftika*, Indian film music lifted straight from Bollywood and reset to Greek lyrics; chief culprit was the Gypsy singer Manolis Angelopoulos.

The most notable "straight" laïkó performer was **Stelios Kazantzidhis** (1931–2001), a man whose volcanic, mournful style was often imitated but never matched. His work, frequently in duets with "Marinella" (Kyriaki Papadhopoulou) and Yiota Lidhia, immortalized the joys and sorrows of the Greek working class which emerged from the 1940s faced with a choice of life under the restrictive regimes of the time, or emigration. Disgusted with the atmosphere in the *bouzoúkia* clubs, he quit performing live in 1966, but after a brief hiatus returned to the studio under the aegis of Khristos Nikolopoulos and Akis Panou, two of the most influential laïkó songwriters. It is difficult to encapsulate the love and loyalty "Stellaras" (as he was nicknamed) inspired in his fans over a fifty-year career; Umm Kalthum's role in the Arab world is about as close as you'll get. Truck-drivers emblazoned their cabs with a single word, "Iparho" (the name of his biggest hit); on the day he died, almost every CD player in the land played Kazantzidhis songs in tribute, and his funeral in gritty Elefsína was thronged by thousands.

Any summary of laïko singers would be incomplete without **Yiorgos (George) Dalaras**, a musical phenomenon in Greece since he made his 1968 vinyl debut with the composer Manos Loïzos. Born in 1952, the son of a Pireás rebétika player, Dalaras has featured on nearly a hundred records, spanning the range of Greek music from rebétika and *dhimotiká* material, the works of Theodhorakis, Hatzidhakis and Markopoulos, and – more recently – collaborations with the flamenco guitarist Paco de Lucia and American blues star Al Di Meola. Something of a national institution, Dalaras has always – even during the junta years – remained a fierce supporter of popular struggles, with benefit concerts for various worthy causes. In his commitment to quality musicianship he has scrupulously avoided the banalities of the *bouzoúki* scene.

Amongst notable laïkó composers and lyricists, **Apostolos Kaldharas** was the most prolific during the 1950s and 1960s; he gave singer Yiannis Parios, considered second only to Yiorgos Dalaras, his start, and introduced laïkó star **Haris Alexiou** with his landmark 1972 album *Mikra Asia*. **Khristos Nikolopoulos** was a young *bouzoúki* virtuoso who emerged during the 1970s as a composer; his above-noted collaboration with Kazantzidhes peaked in 1975 with the album Yparho, and he has since gone on to mega-selling co-efforts with Dalaras and Alexiou – and a spectacular public attack by Kazantzidhis in 1998 over alleged plagiarism. **Akis Panou** (died 1999) was less prolific and commercially successful – taking time out to be a painter and copper-engraver – but he too produced noteworthy albums with Dalaras, Bithikotsis and Stratos Dhionysiou as well as Kazantzidhes.

Laïkó discography

*❶ **Haris Alexiou** From a huge discography, start with *Ta Tragoudhia tis Haroulas* (LP/CD, Minos 349) with lyrics by Manolis Rasoulis and Manos Loizos, which secured her position as the queen of laïkó for the 1980s, or *Dhodheka Laïka Tragoúdhia* (CD, Minos). Of recent output, go for *Odhos Nefelis* (Philips 5426740).

❶ **Yiorgos Dalaras** Latin (Minos 671/672). A 1987 team-up with Al Di Meola, Glykeria and others, plus Latin rhythms and instrumentalists. Dalaras taught himself enough Spanish to sing passably; nearly half a million copies sold. *A Portrait: George Dalaras* (CD, EMI) is a "best-of" sampler with both live and studio work spanning his entire career, easily found outside Greece.

❶ **Glykeria** (Kotsoula) *Me ti Glykeria stin Omorfi Nhykhta* (Lyra 3367). Enduringly popular disc showcases this versatile laïko singer and rebétika/nisiótika revivalist most active in the 1980s.

❶ **Kostas Hatzis and Haris Alexiou** *Iy Alexiou Tragoudhaei Hadzis* (Minos 1002/1003). Hatzis by himself is disappointing; but with Alexiou, singing in Greek or (on two cuts) Romany, it's Greek flamenco.

*❶ **Apostolos Kaldharas** *Mikra Asia* (Minos 4800962) marked Haris Alexiou's 1972 debut and helped spark the rebétika revival of the mid-1970s; *Vyzantinos Esperinos* (Minos 8014122), with more of Haris and less of Dalaras, is also worth pursuing.

❶ **Stelios Kazantzidhes** *Kazantzidhis 3, 1959–1962* (EMI-Regal). The quintessential early laïkó classic that made him a national institution; and of course there's *Iparho* (Minos), the 1975 anthem-album. *Ena Glendi me ton Stelara* (MBI 10596/7 or MBI 10648) is a recent, intimate acoustic session, essentially celebrating his birthday at a taverna.

*❶ **Akis Panou** *Ta Megala Tragoudhia* (3LP/2CD, EMI 478938) 1993. Retrospective that's one of the best starts to a laïkó collection, and specifically the work of this versatile composer, lyricist and bouzoúki virtuoso.

Although laïkó and *éntekhno* represented opposite poles, these extremes sometimes met, with *éntekhno* composers – especially Yiannis Markopoulos – often hiring laïkó singers for dates, or trying their hand at writing in laïkó style. These syntheses became increasingly exceptional (after the success of *Epitafios/Epifaneia* and *Axion Estí*) as Greek record labels tried to marginalize laïkó; this trend accelerated under the junta, a disaster for many types of music. Not only was the greater portion of laïkó banned from the radio as being too "oriental" and "defeatist", but folk music – already disparaged as old-fashioned by a generation coming of age with the Beatles – increasingly fell into disrepute through its use for propaganda purposes. In these conditions, only *elafrolaïkó* (literally "light popular) and *éntekhno*, with its minority audience and potential for coded messages within oblique lyrics, flourished. The dulcet voices of Dalaras and others were soon preferred to the penetrating sound of Kazantzidhes, but the stage was set for the emergence of singer-songwriters – many of them guitarists from Thessaloníki – and groups of folk-rockers, who together wrested back control of Greek music from the purveyors of anodyne pap.

Singer-songwriters and folk-rock

The first significant musician to break out of the *bouzoúki* mould was Thessalonian **Dhionysis Savvopoulos**, who burst on the scene in 1966 with a maniacal, rasping voice and angst-ridden lyrics, his persona rounded out by shoulder-length hair and outsized glasses. Initially linked with the short-lived *néo kýma* movement – a blend of watered-down *éntekhno* and French *chanson* performed in Athenian *boîtes* soon closed down by the colonels – Savvopoulos's work soon became impossible to pigeonhole: equal parts twisted Macedonian folk, Bob Dylan and Frank Zappa at his jazziest is a useful approximation. Though briefly detained and tortured, he was able to continue performing, and became

Singer-songwriters and contemporary music discography

*❍ **Eleftheria Arvanitaki** *Ta Kormia ke ta Mahairia* (CD, Polydor 527059). Best-selling venture of compositions by Lina Nikolakopoulou with lyrics by Mihala Ganas, meatier than her much-publicized work with Ara Dinkjian; *Tragoudhia yia tous Mines* (Polygram 537 057 2) is more upbeat and laïko-based. In *Ektos Programmatos* (Mercury 538659-2) Eleftheria returns to her roots in these rollicking sessions at Athens and Thessaloníki clubs: a gallop through musical Greece of the last fifty years.

*❍ **Himerini Kolymvites** (self-produced, 1981). First and arguably best of four discs, with surreal lyrics, laïko and rebétiko influences, plus rich, drunken melodies, which has acquired enduring cult status in the years since its 1981 release. *Ohi Lathi Panda Lathi* (Lyra 4886), a live 1997 album shared with Banda tis Florinas, seems a welcome return to form after disappointing efforts in the interim.

❍ **Stamatis Kraounakis and Lina Nikolakopoulou** *Kykloforo keh Oploforo* (Polydor 827589). First and most successful of their several collaborations.

*❍ **Sokratis Malamas** *Kyklos* (LP, Lyra 4744). Embodies his latest style; the earlier *Tis Meras ke tis Nykhtas* (LP, Lyra 4654) is more in the mode of Papazoglou.

Notis Mavroudhis and Nikos Houliaras *Ekdhromi* (LP, Zodiac 88002). Rare, guitar–voice duo: one side contains haunting versions of Epirot folk-songs, the other original pieces. Worth scouring the flea market for.

❍ **Thanos Mikroutsikos, Lina Nikolakopoulou, Haris Alexiou** *Krataei Khronia Avti iy Kolonia* (Minos 852). Uneven 1990 effort, but Haris is wonderful as ever; the hit single "Mia Pista apo Fosforo" caught on across the Aegean, with a Turkish cover version by Sezen Aksu.

❍ **Nikos Papazoglou** *Haratsi* (Musurgia Graeca ML 0013). Alternates introspective ballads with hard-driving electric rock. The 1990 offering *Synerga* (Lyra 4559, Greece) is gentler, even mystical, more in the mould of later Xydhakis. His more recent *Otan Kindhynevis Paixe tin Pouroudha* (Lyra 4798) is also in a similar vein.

❍ **Dhionysis Savvopoulos** Though not his first disc, the radical 1970 *Ballos* (Lyra 3573), a Balkan folk release that set off the brief folk-rock movement, established his position irrevocably; *Dheka Khronia Kommatia* (Lyra 3715/0081) is a retrospective anthology of the artist's first (some say best) decade; yet *Trapezakia Exo* (Lyra 3360/0041), more digestibly folky, is a personal favourite.

Nena Venetsanou This France-based singer and occasional composer has a deep, earthy voice which lends itself to a number of genres. *Ikones* (Musrugia Graeca MA 008) reworks everything from Hatzidhakis to *nisiótika* to *chanson*; *Zeïbekika* (MBI MMB 10816) is a suprisingly successful attempt to recast this rebétiko style as "profane prayers", song in chamber format in various French chapels.

*❍ **Nikos Xydhakis and Friends** *Konda sti Dhoxa mia Stigmi* (Lyra 0039). One of the best Greek discs of the late 1980s, with haunting Xydhakis arrangements and compositions; their 1991 follow-up *Tenedos* (Lyra 4590) was less even, but had the wonderful single "Tsigaro Ego sto Stoma mou dhen Evala Oute Ena".

*❍ **Nikos Xydhakis, Nikos Papazoglou, Manolis Rasoulis** *Iy Ekdhikisi tis Yiftias* (Lyra 0019). Ground-breaking recording of the late 1970s, still much loved in Greece; its follow-up *Ta Dhithen* (Lyra 0019) with Manolis Rasoulis is nearly its equal, containing the single "Iy Manges Dhen Yparhoun Pia", covered by Haris Alexiou.

something of a consolation and password to the generation coming of age under the junta.

Out of Savvopoulos's "Balkan rock" experiments sprang a short-lived movement whose artists alternated electric versions of traditional songs with original material. Few left much trace in discography or longevity of performance except for folk "updater" **Mariza Koch**, the Gypsy protest guitarist-singer **Kostas Hatzis**, and folk/*éntekhno* performer **Arletta**, all still active to various degrees.

Despite a modest discography compared to the *éntekhno* composers, it's difficult to overestimate Savvopoulos's effect on subsequent artists. Credit (or blame) for much Greek rock and fusion jazz can be laid at his door; during his brief tenure as head of Lyra records, and later as an independent producer, Savvopoulos gave breaks to numerous younger artists, many of them also from northern Greece. Among Savvopoulos's protégés and spiritual heirs were **Nikos Xydhakis** and **Manolis Rasoulis**, whose landmark 1978 pressing, Iy *Ekdhikisi tis Yiftias* (*The Revenge of Gypsydom*) actually embodied the backlash of laïkó culture (laïkó, in Greek, means "common" or "low-class" as well as "popular") against the pretentiousness of 1960s and 1970s *éntekhno* and other "politically correct" music. Its spirited, defiant lyrics and *tsiftetéli* rhythms were both homage to and send-up of the music beloved by Greek truck-drivers, Gypsy or otherwise.

As with mainland folk instrumental music, real **Gypsies** have been disproportionately important in laïkó, both as performers and composers, though many go to considerable length to conceal the fact; however, for every "assimilated" personality there are others, such as **Eleni Vitali**, **Makis Khristodhoulopoulos** and **Vassilis Païteris** who make no bones about their identity.

Contemporary music: 1980 to the present

After an equally successful 1979 reprise (*Ta Dhithen*) with more or less the same personnel, Xydhakis and Papazoglou in particular went on to pursue successful independent careers, Xydhakis in the style that hard-core laïkó fans dismiss as *koultouriárika* (high-brow stuff). His most successful venture in this vein was the 1987 *Konda sti Dhoxa mia Stigmi* with **Eleftheria Arvanitaki** guesting on vocals. Arvanitaki, who began her career on a Savvopoulos album, and next with the rebétika revival group Opisthodhromiki Kompania, went on to participate in a host of *éntekhno* and laïkó sessions, and is currently considered Greece's hottest popular vocalist, though of late she's veered off into the world-crossover category. A Thessalonian like Savvopoulous, **Nikos Papazoglou** is a more varied songwriter than Xydhakis; his material, also based on laïkó and folk, often has a harder electric-rock edge, though his 1990 *Synerga* can match Xydhakis for introspection and orientalism. Other performers to emerge from the "Salonica Scene" after 1981 included Himerini Kolymvites, a group of architects led by Aryiris Bakirtzis, the laïkó composer **Yiorgos Zikas** and most recently Papazoglou disciple **Sokratis Malamas**.

*❶**Manos Achalinotopoulos** *Yakinthos/Hyacinth* (CD, Sony SK60243). Up-and-coming clarinetist joins forces with other young traditional musicians in original compositions encompassing styles from Byzantine chant to Thracian *zournádhes*. Atmospheric and a largely successful experiment.

*❶**Ross Daly** *Selected Works* (BMG Ariola 70205 or Oriente 01, Germany). The best place to start, a compilation from many earlier, out-of-print albums (a chronic problem with Daly's work). Other goodies, still occasionally available, include *Ross Daly* (LP, RCA-BMG 70184) and *An-Ki* (RCA-BMG 27021), at his most eastern, with Iranian percussionist Jamshid Chemirani. *Mitos* (World Network 8) consists of 1991 concert recordings with Spyridhoula Toutoudhaki singing; one of the best documents of Daly's musical workshop "Labyrinth".

*❶**Haïnidhes** *Haïnidhes* (MBI 10492) and *Kosmos ki Oneiro ine Ena* (MBI 10576) are their first two, and best, albums, with folk-influenced original compositions taking precedence over old standards.

***Khristodhoulos Halaris** *Dhrossoulites* (Minos 7243 480179 25). Still his most riveting and worthy work, with lyrics by Nikos Gatsos and vocals by Khrysanthos and Dhimitra Galani.

❶**Loudhovikos Ton Anoyion** (Yiorgos Dhramoundanis) *O Erotas stin Kriti ine Melangolikos* (Seirios 88010) and *O Haïnis* (Seirios 90005). His second and third albums 1988–1990, which helped restore the Cretan mandolin to its rightful place. *Pyli tis Ammou* (Mylos 009, Thessaloníki) exemplifies his later evolution in a larger group, with guest appearances by Malamas, Papazoglou and Nena Venetsanou.

David Saltiel *Jewish–Spanish Songs of Thessaloniki* (Oriente CD14). Fourteen Ladino songs, mostly from the late nineteenth century, hauntingly revived and sung by a Nazi death-camp survivor; a precious document of a culture that has all but vanished.

❶**Domna Samiou** *Seryiani me tin Domna Samiou* (Minos 7243 4 89781 27). Good 1986 session with the inveterate collector, singer and revivalist – arguably her best work since the 1973 *Ehe Yia Panayia* (EMI Columbia 14C 062 70115).

Vosporos *Greek Composers of Constantinople* (LP/CD, EMI 064 1701421). First, 1987 exploration of the medieval Constantinopolitan dimension of Greek music; also notable is *Live at the Palas Theatre* (LP, Lyra-Om 51/52). Since 1994, balanced vocals in Greek and Turkish have become pre-eminent, without a loss of instrumental virtuosity and innovation; it's hard to choose between *Ellinika ke Asikika* (CD, MBI 10608-2) and *Valkania Oneira/Balkan Dreams* (CD, MBI 10645).

❶**Savina Yiannatou** *Anixi sti Saloniki/Spring in Salonika* (LP/CD, Lyra/Musurgia Graeca 4765). Re-creations of Ladino Sephardic songs, the latest of several such efforts, with Middle Eastern instrumental backing; Savina's voice can take some getting used to, however. The CD has four extra cuts and full notes. Her more recent *Songs of the Mediterranean* (Musurgia Graeca 4900) are superb interpretations of songs from Spain to Cyprus, with her trademark vibrato in check and crisp accompaniment from an orchestra led by Kostas Vomvolos.

***Ziyia** *From the Mountains to the Islands* (AgaRhythm, self-produced, 1993, USA) and *Travels with Karagiozis* (Aga Rhythm, self-produced, 1995, USA). Folk and rebetic material by a five-member, bicoastal American group who are better instrumentalists than many current Greek practitioners – typical of how rebétika has caught on overseas long after the craze for it has subsided in Greece.

Back in Athens, *éntekhno* and other Westernizing trends took longer to relax their grip, under the aegis of composers such as classically trained **Thanos Mikroutsikos**, briefly Minister of Culture after Melina Mercouri's death, who despite his high-brow leanings has worked with Alexiou, Dalaras and top laïkó *éntekhno* vocalist Dhimitra Galani. **Lina Nikolakopoulou** also made a splash with a number of thoughtful, if somewhat slick, albums stretching into the 1990s, exploring the boundaries between rock, jazz-cabaret and *éntekhno*.

Byzantine, Anatolian and folk revival groups

An offshoot of *éntekhno* during the late 1970s and early 1980s involved combining folk and Byzantine traditions. Long before his unfortunate ventures into speculative Byzantine song, musicologist and arranger Khristodhoulos Halaris followed up a version of the Cretan epic *Erotokritos*, showcasing Nikos Xylouris and Tania Tsanaklidou, with the riveting *Dhrossoulites*, which featured Khrysanthos, a high-voiced male singer of Pontic descent, on alternate tracks with Dhimitra Galani.

Ottoman rather than Byzantine Constantinople was the inspiration for **Vosporos**, a group co-ordinated in Istanbul from 1986 to 1992 by psáltis (church chanter) and kanonáki-player Nikiforos Metaxas to explore Ottoman classical, devotional and popular music. Since then the group has reformed as Fanari tis Anatolis, with Greek and Turkish singers alternating a variety of Greek folk material with Anatolian songs or mystical Alevi ballads.

Ross Daly, whose interests and style overlap slightly with Vosporos, also merits catching on disc, live in Athens clubs or touring abroad. English-born but Irish by background, Daly plays a dozen traditional instruments and has absorbed influences not only from Crete, where he was long resident, but from throughout the Near East. Alone or with a group, he has recorded strikingly contemporary interpretations of traditional pieces, as well as original compositions.

Occasionally this eclecticism has gone a bit too far, but with lapses of taste reined in, updating of folk material can be manifestly successful, as with two "exports" from Crete: mandolinist **Loudhovikos ton Anoyeion**, originally one of Hatzidhakis's finds at Seirios, and the six-member, all-acoustic group **Haïnidhes**. To foreign ears either sounds more accessible and exciting than more orthodox, scholarly revivalists such as **Domna Samiou**, who has performed both well-known and obscure material from every corner of the Greek world. Newer, crossover performers attempting (again with mixed success) to explore neighbouring influences on Greek music include **Notios Ihos**, led by Ahilleas Persidhis, and **Night Ark**, featuring Armenian performer/composers Haig Yagdjian and Ara Dinkjian.

Marc Dubin and George Pissalides

Books

Where separate editions exist in the UK and US, publishers are detailed below in the form UK publisher; US publisher, unless the publisher is the same in both countries. Where books are published in one country – or Athens – only, this follows the publisher's name.

An out-of-print but still highly recommended book is indicated by the abbreviation "o/p"; the recommended Greek-specialist book dealers often have large back-stocks of these. University Press is abbreviated as UP.

Books marked ★ are particularly recommended, many of them part of a "Modern Greek Writers" series, numbering over thirty titles, issued by the Athenian company Kedros Publishers.

Travel and general accounts

Modern accounts

★ **Kevin Andrews** *The Flight of Ikaros* (Penguin, o/p). An intense and compelling account of an educated, sensitive archeologist loose in the backcountry during the civil war. Half a century on, this is still one of the best books on Greece as it was before "development".

★ **Gillian Bouras** *A Foreign Wife* (Penguin, Australia). In which a woman who married a Greek-Australian during the 1960s consents to return permanently to the mother country in 1980. An excellent chronicle of cross-cultural/continental angst and the migrant experience in both directions, with penetrating insights into child-rearing, comparative views of leisure, local medicine and general expectations tempered by the grinding Messinian poverty of only a few decades ago. It inaugurates a series of several works: *A Fair Exchange*, the sequel; *Aphrodite and the Others*, in which Bouras explores her always-difficult relations with her formidable mother-in-law; the autobiographical novel *A Stranger Here*, in which the widespread ambivalence

of being in Greece – never content there, yet not being able to keep away – is teased out still more exquisitely; and *Starting Again* (all Penguin, Australia).

Robert Carver *The Accursed Mountains: Journeys in Albania* (Flamingo, UK). It's not usual to include a book on a neighbouring country, but this one's essential to understand why nearly a million Albanians have fled the place for Greece. Carver also succinctly captures Greek attitudes towards Albanians (and vice versa), and includes a pithy vignette about the Prespa basin. It's as well to know, however, that the book has come under attack by Albanian scholars and the British diplomatic corps for gross inaccuracies and alleged plagiarism, as well as abuse of hospitality and confidentiality.

Gerald Durrell *My Family and Other Animals* (Penguin, UK). Sparkling, funny anecdotes of Durrell's childhood on Corfu during the 1930s – and his passion for the island's fauna: toads, tortoises, bats, scorpions, the lot.

Lawrence Durrell *Prospero's Cell* (Faber & Faber; Penguin, o/p); *Reflections on a Marine Venus* (Faber & Faber; Penguin); *The Greek Islands* (Faber & Faber, o/p; Penguin, o/p). The elder Durrell lived before World War II with Gerald and the family on Corfu, the subject of *Prospero's Cell*. *Marine Venus* recounts Lawrence's 1945–47 experiences and impressions of Rhodes and other Dodecanese islands.

⭐ **Yorgos Ioannou** *Refugee Capital* (Kedros, Athens; Central Books, UK). Brilliant essays on the city by a native of Thessaloníki; especially good on the reasons for its political power-lessness, the grip of the Orthodox Church and the deportation of the Jews, by way of praise for its flow-ering shade trees and cruising opportunities at its old cinemas (Ioannou was gay).

⭐ **Sheelagh Kanneli** *Earth and Water: A Marriage in Kalamata* (Efstathiadhis, Athens). A classic account of that rare thing – a foreign woman integrating successfully into provincial Greek society. Rich in period detail of pre-tourism and pre-earthquake Kalamáta.

Katherine Kizilos *The Olive Grove: Travels in Greece* (Lonely Planet Journeys, UK). Returned, ambivalent Greek-Australian's musings on the country, and Istanbul, with an excel-lent final section on how the civil war tore apart her father's natal vil-lage in the Peloponnese.

⭐ **Patrick Leigh Fermor** *Roumeli* (Penguin, UK); *Mani* (Penguin; Peter Smith). Leigh Fermor is an aficionado of rural Greece's vanishing minorities and disappearing customs. These two books, written in the late 1950s and early 1960s respectively, are not so much travelogues as scholarly works interspersed with strange and hilari-ous yarns. Though overwritten in parts, they remain among the best

books on any aspect of modern Greece.

Peter Levi *The Hill of Kronos* (Harvill, o/p; Dutton, o/p). Beautifully observed landscape, mon-uments and also politics as Levi describes how he is drawn into resistance to the colonels' junta. *A Bottle in the Shade: Journeys in the Peloponnese* (Sinclair Stevenson, UK) describes his return, thirty years later, to his old haunts, but proves far less engaged and more ruminant.

⭐ **Willard Manus** *This Way to Paradise: Dancing on the Tables* (Lycabettus Press, Athens). An American expatriate's memoir of nearly four decades in Líndhos, Rhodes, beginning long before its descent into mass-tourist tattiness. Wonderful period detail, including hippie/bohemian excesses and often hilarious cameos by the likes of S.J. Perelman, Germaine Greer and Martha Gellhorn.

⭐ **Henry Miller** *The Colossus of Maroussi* (Minerva, o/p; New Directions). Corfu, Crete, Athens and the soul of Greece in 1939, with Miller, completely in his element, at his most inspired.

James Pettifer *The Greeks: the Land and People* since the War (Penguin; Viking). A useful, if spottily edited and now slightly dated (1994) intro-duction to contemporary Greece – and its recent past. Pettifer charts the state of the nation's politics, food, family life, religion and tourism.

Dilys Powell *An Affair of the Heart* (Souvenir Press, UK). A welcome reissue of a classic account of Greece from the 1930s to the 1950s. Powell accompanied archeologist husband Humfry Payne on a dig of the Hera sanctuary at Perahóra, Korinthía, and forged a lifelong bond with the vil-lagers there. After Payne's sudden death in 1936, she travelled across the country from Epirus to Crete, journeys described in *The Traveller's Journey is Done* (Hodder & Stoughton, o/p) and the *Villa*

Ariadne (Efstathiadis, Athens; Libri Publications, UK). Powell is generally let down by her poor facility in Greek, occasionally cloying sentimentality and political naïveté (the *Villa Ariadne* is probably the most clear-eyed work), but this acknowledged, her books have stood the test of time.

★ **Tim Salmon** *The Unwritten Places* (Lycabettus Press, Athens). Veteran Hellenophile describes his love affair with the Greek mountains, and the Vlach communities of the Píndhos, in particular following the last clan and their flocks to make the autumn migration (*dhiáva*) to the flatlands on foot.

★ **Patricia Storace** *Dinner with Persephone* (Granta; Pantheon). A New York poet, resident for a year in Athens (with forays to the provinces) puts the country's psyche on the couch, while avoiding the same position with various predatory males. Storace has a sly sense of humour, and in showing how permeated – and imprisoned – Greece is by its imagined past, gets it right ninety percent of the time.

Sarah Wheeler *An Island Apart* (Abacus, o/p). An entertaining chronicle of a five-month ramble through Évvia, one of the least-visited islands. Wheeler has a sure touch with Greek culture and an open approach to nuns, goatherds and academics; the main quibble is her success in making Évvia seem more interesting than it really is.

Older accounts

★ **James Theodore Bent** *Aegean Islands: The Cyclades, or Life Among the Insular Greeks* (Argonaut, US, o/p, but available in A4 format from Ⓦwww.hebesweb.com/hguides/bent.htm). Originally published in 1881, this remains the best account of island customs and folklore; it's also a highly readable, droll account of a year's Aegean travel.

Robert Byron *The Station* (Century, UK, o/p). Travels on Mount Athos in the 1930s, by one of the pioneering scholars of Byzantine art and architecture.

Nikos Kazantzakis *Travels in Greece: Journey to the Morea* (Bruno Cassirer, UK, o/p). Slightly stilted translation of the Cretan novelist's journey around the Peloponnese, and his increasing alienation from 1930s Greece.

Edward Lear *Journals of a Landscape Painter in Greece and Albania* (Century, UK, o/p). Highly entertaining journals of two journeys through Greece and Albania in autumn 1848 and spring 1849, by the famous landscape painter and author of *The Book of Nonsense*. Further doses of Lear, *The Corfu Years* and *The Cretan Journal*, have been published by Denise Harvey in Límni, Évvia (Greece).

★ **Sidney Loch** *Athos, The Holy Mountain* (Molho, Thessaloníki, Greece). A resident of Ouranópoli from 1924 to 1954, Loch recounts the legends surrounding the various monasteries of Mount Athos, as gleaned from his years of walking through the monastic republic. Inevitably nostalgic, as the Athos he knew has been utterly swept away since the 1980s.

Terence Spencer *Fair Greece, Sad Relic: Literary Philhellenism from Shakespeare to Byron* (Denise Harvey, Athens, available in UK; Scholarly Press). Masterfully traces how the scribblings of poets steeped in the classics, culminating in Byron, and the accounts of early travellers to what's now Greece, gradually fuelled European support for the 1821 Revolution – despite the misgivings of many of them about the contemporary Greeks themselves. Also demonstrates just how old the Zorba stereotype is (the feckless, "merrie Greke" is already described in the 1500s).

Richard Stoneman, ed *A Literary Companion to Travel in Greece* (Getty Centre for the History of Art and the Humanities, US). Ancient and medieval authors, plus Grand Tourists – good for dipping into.

The classics

Many of the classics make excellent companion reading for a trip around Greece – especially the historians Thucydides and Herodotus. Reading Homer's *Odyssey* when you're battling with or resigning yourself to the vagaries of island ferries puts your own plight into perspective. One slightly less well-known source, especially recommended for travels around the Peloponnese, is Pausanias's fourth-century AD *Guide to Greece*, annotated by Peter Levi in its Penguin edition with notes on modern identifications of sites mentioned.

Most of the standard undergraduate staples are part of the Penguin Classics paperback series. Routledge and Duckworth both also have a huge, steadily expanding backlist of Classical Studies, though many titles are expensive and quite specialized.

Herodotus *The Histories* (Penguin), or A.D. Godley, tr (Cambridge UP). Revered as the father of systematic history and anthropology, this fifth-century BC Anatolian writer chronicled both the causes and campaigns of the Persian Wars, as well as the contemporary, assorted tribes and nations inhabiting Asia Minor.

Homer *The Iliad; The Odyssey*. The first concerns itself, semi-factually, with the late Bronze Age war of the Achaeans against Troy in Asia Minor; the second recounts the hero Odysseus's long journey home, via seemingly every corner of the Mediterranean. For a verse rendition, ★Richmond Lattimore's translation (University of Chicago, *Iliad*; HarperCollins, *Odyssey*) has yet to be bettered. For a prose rendition, ★Martin Hammond's *Iliad* (Penguin) and *Odyssey* (Duckworth, UK) currently edge out second-best choices by the father-and-son team of E.V. Rieu (*Iliad*, Penguin) and D.C.H. Rieu (*Odyssey*, Penguin).

Ovid *The Metamorphoses*, A.D.

Melville, tr (Oxford UP). Though collected by a first-century AD Roman poet, this remains one of the most accessible renditions of the more piquant Greek myths, involving transformations as divine blessing or curse.

Pausanias *The Guide to Greece* (Penguin, 2 vols, Vol. 2 currently o/p). Essentially the first-ever guidebook, intended for Roman pilgrims to the holy sites of the Greek mainland; invaluable for later archeologists in assessing damage or change to temples over the intervening centuries, or (in some cases) locating them at all.

Plutarch *The Age of Alexander; On Sparta; The Rise and Fall of Athens* (Penguin). Another ancient author, writing perhaps with the benefit of hindsight, but with the disadvantage of unreliable sources and much conjecture.

⊠ **Thucydides** *History of the Peloponnesian War* (Penguin). Bleak month-by-month account of the conflict, by a cashiered Athenian officer whose affiliation and dim view of human nature didn't usually obscure his objectivity; see George Cawkwell's book (below) for a revisionist view.

Xenophon *The History of My Times* (Penguin). Thucydides' account of the Peloponnesian War stops in 411 BC; this work continues events until 362 BC.

Ancient history and interpretation of the classics

Mary Beard and John Henderson *The Classics: a Very Short Introduction* (Oxford UP). As it says; an excellent overview.

A.R. Burn *History of Greece* (Penguin). Probably the best general introduction to ancient Greece, though for fuller analysis you'll do better with one or other of the following more specialized titles.

Paul Cartlege *Cambridge Illustrated History of Ancient Greece* (Cambridge UP). Large-format, pricey volume packed with information useful for both novices and experts.

George Cawkwell *Thucydides and the Peloponnesian War* (Routledge). Recent, revisionist overview of Thucydides' work and relations with main personalities of the war, challenging previous assumptions of his infallibility.

M.I. Finley *The World of Odysseus* (Pimlico, UK). The latest reprint of a 1954 warhorse, pioneering in its investigation of the historicity (or otherwise) of the events and society related by Homer. Breezily readable and stimulating, with prejudices apparent rather than subtle.

Michael Grant and John Hazel *Who's Who in Classical Mythology* (Routledge). A gazetteer of over 1200 mythological personalities, together with historical and geographical background.

Pierre Grimal, ed *Dictionary of Classical Mythology* (Penguin). Though translated from the French, still considered to have the edge on

the more recent Grant/Hazel title.

Simon Hornblower *The Greek World 479–323 BC* (Routledge). An erudite survey of ancient Greece at its zenith, from the end of the Persian Wars to the death of Alexander; now a standard university paperback text.

John Kenyon Davies *Democracy and Classical Greece* (Fontana; Harvard UP). An established and accessible account of the Classical period and its political developments.

Robin Lane Fox *Alexander the Great* (Penguin). An absorbing study, which mixes historical scholarship with imaginative psychological detail.

Oswyn Murray *Early Greece* (Fontana; Harvard UP). The Greek story from the Mycenaeans and Minoans through to the beginning of the Classical period.

Robin Osborne *Greece in the Making 1200–479 BC* (Routledge). A well-illustrated paperback on the rise of the city-state.

John Purkis *Teach Yourself Classical Civilisation* (Teach Yourself Books). A nice, succinct introduction to the subject.

Tony Spawforth *Greece, an Oxford Archaeological Guide* (Oxford UP). An interpretive guide, by the co-author, with Simon Hornblower, of the also-recommended *Oxford Classical Dictionary* (Oxford UP).

F.W. Walbank *The Hellenistic World* (Fontana; Harvard UP). Greece under the sway of the Macedonian and Roman empires.

Ancient religion

Harry Brewster *River Gods of Greece* (I.B. Tauris; St Martin's). Most ancient rivers had a deity associated with them; here are the cults and legends.

★ **Walter Burkert** *Greek Religion: Archaic and Classical* (Blackwell). A superb overview of deities and their attributes and antecedents, rites, the protocol of sacrifice and the symbolism of major festivals; especially good on relating Greek worship to its predecessors in the Middle East.

Matthew Dillon *Pilgrims and Pilgrimage in Ancient Greece* (Routledge). A pricey hardback exploring not only the main sanctuaries such as Delphi, but also minor oracles, the role of women and children and the secular festivities attending the rites.

Nano Marinatos and Robin Hagg *Greek Sanctuaries: New Approaches* (Routledge). The form and function of the temples, in the light of recent scholarship.

R. Gordon Wasson, Albert Hoffmann, Carl Ruck *The Road to Eleusis: Unveiling the Secret of the Mysteries* (Harcourt Brace, US, o/p). A well-argued monograph expounding the theory that the Eleusinian mysteries were at least in part a psychedelic trip, courtesy of grain-ergot fungus. Guaranteed to outrage mainstream classicists, though even Burkert (see above) admits they may have a case.

Food and wine

Rosemary Barron *Flavours of Greece* (Grub Street, UK). Probably the leading cookbook among many contenders, by an internationally recognized authority on Greek cuisine. Contains over 250 recipes.

Andrew Dalby *Siren Feasts* (Routledge). Subtitled *A History of Food and Gastronomy in Greece*, this analysis of ancient texts demonstrates just how little Greek cuisine has changed in three millennia; also excellent on the introduction and etymology of common vegetables and herbs.

★ **Alan Davidson** *Mediterranean Seafood* (Penguin, o/p). A 1972 classic, periodically reprinted, this amazingly erudite and witty book catalogues (almost) all known edible species, complete with legends, anecdotes, habits, local names and a suggested recipe or two for each.

★ **James Davidson** *Courtesans and Fishcakes* (HarperCollins, UK). The politics, class characteristics and etiquette of consumption and consummation – with wine, women, boys and seafood – in ancient Athens, with their bearing on both historical events and modern attitudes.

★ **Nico Manessis** *The Illustrated Greek Wine Book* (Olive Press Publications, Corfu; available at select retailers in Greece or through Ⓦwww.greekwineguide.gr). Covers almost all the wineries, from mass-market to micro, with very reliable ratings; also fascinating features on grape varieties, traditional retsina-making, and even how Greeks were instrumental in introducing vines to the New World. Pricey but worth it.

Nikos Stavroulakis *Cookbook of the Jews of Greece* (Lycabettus Press, Athens; Cadmus Press, US). Tasty recipes interspersed with their relation to the Jewish liturgical year, plus potted histories of the communities which produced them. There have been murmurings, however, that many of the recipes emanate from one subgroup – the ex-Jewish Ma'min of Thessaloníki.

300 Traditional Greek Recipes (Grecocard, Greece). As it says; the best of a huge pile of glossy pictorial cookbooks pitched at the tourist market.

Archeology and art

John Beckwith *Early Christian and Byzantine Art* (Yale UP). Illustrated study placing Byzantine art within a wider context.

William R. Biers *Archeology of Greece: An Introduction* (Cornell UP, US). A 1990s-revised and excellent standard text.

★ **John Boardman** *Greek Art* (Thames & Hudson, UK). A very good concise introduction: part of the "World of Art" series.

Reynold Higgins *Minoan and Mycenaean Art* (Thames & Hudson). A clear, well-illustrated round-up.

Sinclair Hood *The Arts in Prehistoric Greece* (Penguin; Yale UP). A sound introduction to the subject.

Roger Ling *Classical Greece* (Phaidon, UK). Another useful illustrated introduction.

Colin Renfrew *The Cycladic Spirit* (Thames & Hudson; Abrams). A fine, illustrated study of the meaning and purpose of Cycladic artefacts.

Gisela Richter *A Handbook of Greek Art* (Phaidon; Da Capo). An exhaustive survey of the visual arts of ancient Greece.

★ **William St Clair** *Lord Elgin and the Marbles* (Oxford UP). The latest word on the vicissitudes of the statues whose ownership remains hotly disputed.

R.R.R. Smith *Hellenistic Sculpture* (Thames & Hudson). A modern reappraisal of the art of Greece under Alexander and his successors.

★ **David Talbot Rice** *Art of the Byzantine Era* (Thames & Hudson). Talbot Rice was, with Robert Byron, one of the pioneering scholars in the "rediscovery" of Byzantine art; this is an accessible illustrated study.

Peter Warren *The Aegean Civilizations* (Phaidon, o/p; P. Bedrick Books, o/p). An illustrated account of the Minoan and Mycenaean cultures.

"Coffee-table" books

William Abramowicz *The Greek File: Images of a Mythic Land* (Rizzoli). An obstinately nostalgic black-and-white look at the country in the 1980s, by this veteran Condé Nast photographer; the main complaint is it fails to take on board the vast changes that had swept through Greece since Manos's pioneering work (see below).

Costis Copsides *The Jews of Thessaloniki through the Postcards (sic) 1886–1917* (self-published,

Thessaloníki). Jewish personalities, business and monuments, and the pre-fire city in general, as seen by Jewish postcard publishers.

★ **Chris Hellier** *Monasteries of Greece* (Tauris Parke; St Martin's Press). A magnificently photographed survey of the surviving, active monasteries and their treasures, with insightful accompanying essays.

★ **Constantine Manos** *A Greek Portfolio* (W.W. Norton). A long-awaited, reasonably priced reissue of a

1972 classic: the fruits of a gifted Greek-American photographer's three-year odyssey in the early Sixties through a country on the edge of modernization, still essentially unchanged from the 1930s. The quality and insight you'd expect from a member of the Magnum co-operative, in elegiac black-and-white photos.

Mark Ottaway *The Most Beautiful Villages of Greece* (Thames & Hudson, UK). Not exhaustively inclusive, but easily available and with good photos by Hugh Palmer.

Clay Perry *Vanishing Greece* (Conran Octopus; Abbeville Press, both o/p). Well-captioned photos depict the threatened landscapes and relict ways of life in rural Greece; now in paperback.

Suzanne Slesin et al *Greek Style* (Thames & Hudson; Crown). Stunning (if sometimes contrived) designer-tweaked interiors from Corfu, Rhodes and Sérifos, among other spots.

Janine Trotereau *Greece from the Air* (Thames & Hudson). A translation of a French-issued work, with photos by Yann Arthus.

Byzantine, medieval and Ottoman history

Averil Cameron *The Mediterranean World in Late Antiquity, AD 395–600* (Routledge). Essentially the early Byzantine years.

Nicholas Cheetham *Medieval Greece* (Yale UP, o/p in US). A general survey of the period and its infinite convolutions in Greece, with Frankish, Catalan, Venetian, Byzantine and Ottoman struggles for power.

John Julius Norwich *Byzantium: The Early Centuries*; *Byzantium: the Apogee* and *Byzantium: The Decline* (all Penguin; Viking-Knopf). Perhaps the main surprise for first-time travellers to Greece is the fascination of Byzantine monuments, above all at Mystrás. This is an astonishingly detailed yet readable trilogy, also available in one fat volume as ★*A Short History of Byzantium* (Penguin).

🔲 **Vangelis Pavlidis** *Rhodes 1306–1522: A Story* (Rodos Image, Rhodes). A caricature-illustrated history of the Knights of St John's occupation of Rhodes, by one of Greece's leading political cartoon-

ists, but this isn't tourist pap – rigorous research and witty text illuminate a little-known era in the Dodecanese.

Michael Psellus *Fourteen Byzantine Rulers* (Penguin). A fascinating contemporary source on the stormy but brilliant period from 976 to 1078.

Steven Runciman ★*The Fall of Constantinople, 1453* (Canto-Cambridge UP) is the standard account of the event; *The Great Church in Captivity* (Cambridge UP) follows the vicissitudes of the Orthodox Patriarchate in Constantinople up to the War of Independence. *Byzantine Style and Civilization* (Penguin, o/p in US) and *Mistra* (Thames & Hudson, o/p in US) are more slanted towards art, culture and monuments.

🔲 **Archbishop Kallistos (Timothy) Ware** *The Orthodox Church* (Penguin). A good introduction to what is effectively the established religion of Greece, by the Orthodox archbishop resident in Oxford.

Modern Greece

Timothy Boatswain and Colin Nicolson *A Traveller's History of Greece* (Windrush Press; Interlink). Dated (coverage ceases in early 1990s) but well-written overview of the important Greek periods and personalities.

David Brewer *The Flame of Freedom: The Greek War of Independence 1821–1833* (John Murray, UK). A newish history with just a few black-and-white illustrations.

☆ **Richard Clogg** *A Concise History of Greece* (Cambridge UP). A remarkably clear and well-illustrated account of Greece, from the decline of Byzantium to 1992, with the emphasis on recent decades; there are numerous maps and lengthy feature captions to the artwork.

Douglas Dakin *The Unification of Greece, 1770–1923* (Ernest Benn; St Martin's, both o/p). A benchmark account of the foundation of the Greek state and the struggle to extend its boundaries.

☆ **Oriana Fallaci** *A Man* (Arrow; Pocket Books, o/p). A gripping account of the junta years, relating the author's involvement with Alekos Panagoulis, the army officer who attempted to assassinate Colonel Papadopoulos in 1968. Issued ostensibly as a "novel" in response to threats by those who were implicated in Panagoulis's own murder in 1975.

George Kassimeris *Europe's Last Red Terrorists: The Revolutionary Organization 17 November (17N)* (C. Hurst & Co, UK). The latest word on Europe's most elusive urban terror group, though when it comes to unravelling the mystery of just who they are, Kassimeris comes little closer than anyone else.

☆ **H.A. Lidderdale**, trs and ed *The Memoirs of General Makriyannis, 1797–1864* (Oxford UP, o/p). The "Peasant General", one of the few honest and self-sacrificing protagonists of the Greek uprising, taught himself to write at age 32 to set down this apologia of his conduct, in vivid demotic Greek. It's heartbreaking in its portrayal of the incipient schisms, linguistic and otherwise, that tore the country apart until recently.

☆ **Michael Llewellyn Smith** *Ionian Vision, Greece in Asia Minor, 1919–22* (C. Hurst; University of Michigan). A standard work, by the former UK ambassador to Greece, on the disastrous Anatolian campaign, which led to the exchange of populations between Greece and Turkey. His account evinces considerable sympathy for the post-1920 royalist government pursuing an unwanted, inherited war they know is unwinnable.

Yiannis Roubatis *Tangled Webs: The US in Greece 1947–67* (Pella Publishing, US). Chronicles growing American involvement in Greece during the lead-up to the military coup.

Peter Varoulakis *The Greek War of Independence* (Hellenic International Press). A nice counterweight to the Brewer work, with lots of colour reproductions of famous scenes, with far less text.

C.M. Woodhouse *Modern Greece, A Short History* (Faber & Faber). Woodhouse was active in the Greek Resistance during World War II. Writing from a more right-wing perspective than Clogg, this history (from the foundation of Constantinople in 324 to the 1980s), is briefer and a bit drier, but scrupulous with facts. *The Rise and Fall of the Greek Colonels* (Granada, o/p; Watts) recounts the (horror) story of the dictatorship.

World War II and its aftermath

David H. Close *The Origins of the Greek Civil War* (Longman, o/p). An excellent, readable study that focuses on the social conditions in 1920s and 1930s Greece that made the country so ripe for conflict. Draws on primary sources, slays a few sacred cows along the way, and is relatively objective (though he's no great fan of the Left).

Nicholas Gage *Eleni* (Collins Harvill; Ballantine). A controversial account by a Greek-born *New York Times* correspondent who returns to Epirus to avenge the death of his mother, condemned by an ELAS tribunal in 1948. Good descriptions of village life, but somewhat blinkered political "history". The book inspired a response by a left-wing writer, Vassilis Kavathas, whose family had been decimated by the Right, entitled *Iy Alli Eleni* (*The Other Eleni*), not as yet translated into English.

Iakovos Kambanellis *Mauthausen* (Kedros, Athens; Central Books, UK). Kambanellis was active in the Resistance, caught by the Germans, and sent to Mauthausen, the concentration camp reserved for those politicians or partisans who had opposed the Nazis' rise to power. Harrowing atrocities in flashback there are aplenty, but the main thrust of the book is post-liberation, describing the author's awkward romance with a Lithuanian Jew, and how the idealist inmates are slowly disillusioned as they see that the "New World Order" will be scarcely different from the old. The basis of a play, and the Theodhorakis oratorio of the same name.

Mark Mazower *Inside Hitler's Greece: The Experience of Occupation* 1941–44 (Yale UP). Somewhat choppily organized, but the standard of scholarship is high and the photos alone justify the price. Demonstrates how the complete demoralization of the country and the incompetence of conventional politicians led to the rise of ELAS and the onset of civil war. The sequel to this is *After the War was Over: Reconstructing the Family and State in Greece, 1943–1960* (Princeton UP), consisting of scholarly articles on various aspects of Greece in the period specified.

Eddie Myers *Greek Entanglement* (Alan Sutton, UK, o/p). The inside story of the Gorgopotamos viaduct sabotage operation by the British brigadier who led it, and lots else about co-ordinating the Resistance from 1942 to 1944. Myers comes across as under no illusions as to the qualities of the various Greeks he had to deal with.

Marion Sarafis and Martin Eve *Background to Contemporary Greece, vols 1 & 2* (Merlin, UK). Useful, not overly academic essays on a wide variety of subjects, from the death of katharévoussa to (especially) the civil war; a mild left-wing bias, not surprising since Sarafis is the (English) widow of DSE commander Stefanos Sarafis.

Adrian Seligman *War in the Islands* (Allan Sutton, UK). Collected oral histories of a little-known Allied unit: a flotilla of kaïkia organized to raid the Axis-held Aegean islands. Boy's Own stuff, with service-jargon-laced prose, but lots of fine period photos and detail.

Michael Ward *Greek Assignments: SOE 1943–UNSCOB 1948* (Lycabettus Press, Athens). The author, British consul in Thessaloníki from 1971 to 1983, parachuted into the Píndhos as a guerrilla and walked the width of the country; most amazing is how the Germans controlled only the towns, leaving the countryside to the Resistance. While assigned to discourage other British servicemen from doing so, he married a Greek and later returned to observe the civil war. **C.M. Woodhouse** *The Struggle for Greece, 1941–49* (Hart-Davis, o/p;

Beekman). A masterly and by no means uncritical account of this crucial decade, explaining how Greece emerged without a communist government.

Ethnography

☆ **Juliet du Boulay** *Portrait of a Greek Mountain Village* (Oxford UP, o/p; Denise Harvey, Límni, Évvia). An account of the village of Ambéli, on Évvia, during the 1960s. The habits and customs of an all-but-vanished way of life are observed and evoked in an absorbing narrative.

John K. Campbell *Honour, Family and Patronage* (Oxford UP). A classic study of a Sarakatsáni community in the Píndhos mountains, with much wider applicability to rural Greece.

Rae Dalven *The Jews of Ioannina* (Lycabettus Press, Greece, available in the UK/US). The history and culture of the thriving pre-Holocaust community, related by a poet and translator of Cavafy (see "Modern Greek Poetry", p.1090), herself an Epirot Jew.

☆ **Loring Danforth and Alexander Tsiaras** *The Death Rituals of Rural Greece* (Princeton UP). Many visitors find Greek funeral customs – the wailing, the open-casket vigils, the disinterment after three years – the most disturbing aspect of the culture; this book helps make sense of them.

☆ **Renée Hirschon** *Heirs of the Greek Catastrophe: the Social Life of Asia Minor Refugees in Piraeus* (Berghahn Books, New York/Oxford). A classic 1981 study now reissued in a revised edition. It shows how this community in Kokkinia maintained a separate identity three generations after 1923, and is also a pioneering study of how the spatial characteristics of the emergency housing dictated kinship and friendship. It's inevitably nostal-

gic, as increasing wealth has largely dissolved the community, but still of vital importance to understanding why Athens is so higgledy-piggledy.

☆ **Gail Holst-Warhaft** *Road to Rembétika: Songs of Love, Sorrow and Hashish* (Denise Harvey, Límni, Évvia; available in the UK). The most intriguing Greek urban musical style of the past century, evocatively traced by a Cornell University professor; useful discography has been updated to the mid-1990s.

☆ **Anastasia Karakasidou** *Fields of Wheat, Hills of Blood* (University of Chicago, US). An excellent if controversial work on the recent formation of Greek national consciousness in Macedonia (see box pp.456–457), declined for publication by Cambridge UP.

☆ **John Cuthbert Lawson** *Modern Greek Folklore and Ancient Greek Religion: A Study in Survivals* (University Books, New York; o/p). Exactly as the title states, and still highly applicable a century after its writing; well worth scouring libraries and antiquarian dealers for.

Peter Mackridge and Eleni Yannakakis, eds *Ourselves and Others: Development of a Greek Macedonian Identity Since 1912* (Berg, UK). A collection of essays by experts of several nationalities, covering much the same ground as Karakasidou, examined from the historical, linguistic and anthropoligical perspectives.

Nikos Stavroulakis *Salonika: Jews and Dervishes* (Talos Press, Athens, available in the US). Monograph by the former curator of the Jewish

Museum of Greece, lavishly illustrated with old photos, of two of Thessaloníki's most distinctive communities – which only vanished in the 1920s and 1940s respectively. **T.J. Winnifrith** *The Vlachs: The*

History of a Balkan People (Duckworth; St Martin's Press). A rather heavy-going hotchpotch on the existing Vlach communities in Greece and the Balkans, but the only study easily available.

Modern Greek fiction

Roderick Beaton *An Introduction to Modern Greek Literature* (Oxford UP). A chronological survey of fiction and poetry from Independence to the early 1990s, with a useful discussion on the "Language Question".

⭐ **Maro Douka** *Fool's Gold* (Kedros, Athens; Central Books, UK). Describes an upper-class young woman's involvement, and subsequent disillusionment, with the clandestine resistance to the junta.

⭐ **Apostolos Doxiades** *Uncle Petros and the Goldbach Conjecture* (Faber & Faber, UK). Self-translated from the Greek; an excellent read despite the mathematical puzzle at the heart of the novel.

Eugenia Fakinou *The Seventh Garment* (Serpent's Tail). Greek history, from the War of Independence to the colonels' junta, told through the life stories (interspersed in counterpoint) of three generations of women.

⭐ **Andreas Franghias** *The Courtyard* (Kedros, Athens; Central Books, UK). This well-observed but relentlessly depressing tale follows the struggling (and just plain scheming) inhabitants of a working-class Athens shanty town during the early 1950s.

⭐ **Stratis Haviaras** *When the Tree Sings* (Picador; Simon & Schuster, both o/p) and *The Heroic Age* (Penguin, o/p). A two-part, lightly fictionalized autobiography about coming of age in Greece in the 1940s, by the former poetry curator of Harvard University library. Written in English because

Haviaris felt his experiences too keenly to set them down in Greek.

Nikos Kazantzakis Whether in intricate Greek or translated into inadequate English, Kazantzakis can be hard-going, yet the power of his writing still shines through. *Zorba the Greek* is a surprisingly dark, nihilistic work, worlds away from the two-dimensional characters of the film. On the other hand, the movie version of *The Last Temptation of Christ* provoked riots amongst Orthodox fanatics in Athens in 1989. *Christ Recrucified* (published in the US as *The Greek Passion*) resets the Easter drama against the backdrop of Christian/Muslim relations on nineteenth-century Crete, while *Freedom or Death* (published in the US as *Captain Michalis*) chronicles the rebellions of late nineteenth-century Crete. The *Fratricides* portrays a family riven by the civil war, while *Report to Greco* – perhaps the most accessible of his works – is an autobiographical exploration of his Cretanness/Greekness (all Faber & Faber; Touchstone).

⭐ **Artemis Leontis**, ed *Greece: A Traveller's Literary Companion* (Whereabouts Press, San Francisco, US). An overdue idea, brilliantly executed: various regions of the country as portrayed in (very) short fiction or essays by modern Greek writers. A recommended antidote to the often condescending Grand Tourist accounts.

⭐ **Kostas Mourselas** *Red Dyed Hair* (Kedros, Athens; Central Books, UK). A politically incorrect picaresque epic – imagine *Zorba* crossed with *Last Exit to Brooklyn* – of a particularly dysfunctional Pireás paréa (the group you hang out with from youth till middle age). At its centre stands anti-hero Emmanuel Retsinas (aka Louis), mad, bad and very dangerous to know. A particularly good translation of a Greek original that's still selling well, and formed the basis of a popular TV series.

Stratis Myrivilis ★*Life in the Tomb* (Quartet; New England UP). A harrowing and unorthodox war memoir, based on the author's experience on the Macedonian front during 1917–18, well translated by Peter Bien. Completing a kind of trilogy are two later novels, set on the north coast of Lésvos, Myrivilis's homeland: *The Mermaid Madonna* and *The Schoolmistress with the Golden Eyes* (Efstathiadis, Athens). Translations of these are not so good, and tend to be heavily abridged.

Alexandhros Papadiamantis *The Murderess* (Writers & Readers). A landmark novel set on the island of Skiáthos at the beginning of the nineteenth century, in which an old woman, appalled by the fate that awaits them in adulthood, concludes that little girls are better off dead. Also available is a collection of short stories, *Tales from a Greek Island* (Johns Hopkins UP).

★ **Nick Papandreou** *Father Dancing* (Penguin). Thinly veiled roman à clef by the late Andreas's younger son. Papandreou Senior, not too surprisingly, comes across as a gasbag and petty domestic tyrant.

Yannis Ritsos *Iconostasis of Anonymous Saints* (Kedros, Athens; Central Books, London). The first three instalments of a projected nine-volume autobiographical novel. The "anonymous saints" are the characters of these vaguely sequential vignettes. Book 1, *Ariostos the Observant*, written during World War II, is, depending on your view, either a surrealist masterpiece or self-indulgent rubbish; Book 2, *Such Strange Things*, and Book 3, *With a Nudge of the Elbow*, are more straightforwardly based on Ritsos' peers and life events.

★ **Dido Sotiriou** *Farewell Anatolia* (Kedros, Athens; Central Books, London). A perennial favourite since its initial appearance in 1962, this epic chronicles the traumatic end of Greek life in Asia Minor, from World War I to the catastrophe of 1922, as narrated by a fictionalized version of the author's father.

★ **Stratis Tsirkas** *Drifting Cities* (Kedros, Athens; Central Books, London). Set by turns in the Jerusalem, Cairo and Alexandria of World War II, this unflinchingly honest and humane epic of a Greek army hero secretly working for the Leftist Resistance got the author expelled from the Communist Party.

Vassilis Vassilikos *Z* (Four Walls Eight Windows). A novel based closely enough on events – the 1963 political assassination of Gregoris Lambrakis in Thessaloníki – to be banned under the colonels' junta, and brilliantly filmed by Costa-Gavras in 1968.

★ **Alki Zei** *Achilles' Fiancée* (Kedros, Athens; Central Books, London). An often moving portrait of the friendships and intrigues amongst a collection of communist exiles floating between Athens, Rome, Moscow, Paris and Tashkent in the years between the civil war and the colonels' junta. Largely autobiographical, it captures the flavour of the illusions, nostalgia and partyline schisms endemic in this community.

Greece in foreign fiction

Louis de Bernières *Captain Corelli's Mandolin* (Minerva; Random House). Set on Kefalloniá during the World War II occupation, this accomplished 1994 tragicomedy quickly acquired cult, then word-of-mouth bestseller status, but has lately become a *succès de scandale*. When the islanders, Greek Left intellectuals and surviving Italian partisans woke up to its virulent anti-communism and disparaging portrayal of ELAS, there was a furore, with de Bernières eventually obliged to eat large quantities of humble pie in the UK press. It also seems the novel is closely based on the experiences of still-alive-and-kicking Amos Pampaloni, an artillery captain on Kefalloniá in 1942–44 who later joined ELAS, and accuses de Bernières of distorting the roles of both Italians and ELAS on the island. The Greek translation has been suitably abridged to avoid causing offence, and the Big Movie (starring Nicholas Cage and Penelope Cruz), watered down to a pallid love story as a condition for filming on the island, sank without trace after a few weeks in 2001.

John Fowles *The Magus* (Vintage; Dell). Fowles' biggest and best novel: a tale of mystery and manipulation – plus Greek island life – inspired by his stay on Spétses as a teacher, in the 1950s.

Olivia Manning *The Balkan Trilogy, vol 3: Friends and Heroes* (Mandarin,
UK). In which Guy and Harriet Pringle escape from Bucharest to Athens, in the last months before the invasion of 1941. Wonderfully observed and moving.

Mary Renault *The King Must Die*; *The Last of the Wine*; *The Masks of Apollo* (Sceptre; Random House) and others (all Penguin). Mary Renault's imaginative reconstructions are more than the adolescent's reading they're often taken for, with impeccable research and tight writing. The trio above retell, respectively, the myth of Theseus, the life of a pupil of Socrates and that of a fourth-century BC actor. The life of Alexander the Great is told in *Fire from Heaven*, *The Persian Boy* and *Funeral Games*, available separately or in one economical volume.

Catherine Temma Davidson *The Priest Fainted* (The Women's Press, UK). An autobiographical novel in which a Greek-Jewish-American woman tries to find her level in 1980s Athens, and the countryside, and also uncovers what made her mother flee the country three decades before. Lyrical, and a sense of humour not dissimilar to fellow-poet Storace's.

Evelyn Waugh *Officers and Gentleman* (Penguin). This volume of the wartime trilogy includes an account of the Battle of Crete and subsequent evacuation.

Modern Greek poetry

With two Nobel laureates in recent years – George Seferis and Odysseus Elytis – modern Greece has an extraordinarily intense and dynamic poetic tradition. Translations of all of the following are excellent.

C.P. Cavafy *Collected Poems* (Chatto
& Windus; Princeton UP). The complete works, translated by Edmund Keeley and Philip Sherrard, of perhaps the most accessible modern Greek poet, resident for most of his life in Alexandria. For some, *The Complete Poems of*

Cavafy (Harcourt Brace Jovanovich), translated by Rae Dalven, or *The Poems of C. P. Cavafy* by John Mavrogordato (Chatto & Windus, UK) are superior versions.

Odysseus Elytis *The Axion Esti* (Anvil Press; Pittsburgh UP); *Selected Poems* (Anvil Press; Viking Penguin, o/p); *The Sovereign Sun* (Bloodaxe Books; Temple UP, o/p). The major works in good English versions. Easier to find is *Collected Poems* (Johns Hopkins UP), which includes virtually everything except *The Axion Esti*.

Modern Greek Poetry (Efstathiadis, Athens). Despite the publisher's reputation for shoddy work, this in fact is a decent anthology of translations, predominantly of Seferis and Elytis.

Yannis Ritsos *Exile and Return, Selected Poems 1967–1974* (Anvil Press; Ecco Press). A fine volume of Greece's foremost Leftist poet, from the junta era when he was internally exiled on Sámos.

George Seferis *Collected Poems, 1924–1955* (Anvil Press, o/p; Princeton UP, o/p). Virtually the complete works of the Nobel laureate, with Greek and English verses on facing pages. More recent, but lacking the parallel Greek text, is *Complete Poems* (Anvil Press; Princeton UP).

Specific guides

Archeology

☆ **A.R. and Mary Burn** *The Living Past of Greece: A Time Traveller's Tour of Historic and Prehistoric Places* (Herbert Press; HarperCollins). Unusual in extent, this covers sites from Minoan through to Byzantine and Frankish, with good clear plans and lively text.

☆ **Paul Hetherington** *Byzantine and Medieval Greece: Churches, Castles and Art* (John Murray). A gazetteer of all major mainland sites – readable, authoritative and with useful plans. For the islands see his more recent *The Greek Islands: Guide to Byzantine and Medieval Buildings and their Art* (Quiller, UK), equally good and with more illustrations.

Evi Melas, ed *Temples and Sanctuaries of Ancient Greece: A Companion Guide* (Thames & Hudson, o/p). An excellent collection of essays on the main sites, written by archeologists who have worked at them.

Alexander Paradissis *Fortresses and Castles of Greece* (Efstathiadis, Athens). Three exhaustive and extremely prolix volumes, widely available in Greek bookshops.

Hiking

☆ **Lance Chilton** Various walking pamphlets (Marengo Publications, UK). Small but thorough guides to the best walks at various mainland and island charter resorts, accompanied by three-colour maps. Areas covered to date include: Áyios Yeóryios, Corfu; Yeoryioúpolis and Plakiás, Crete; Stoúpa,

Peloponnese; the central Pelion peninsula; the Párga area; Líndhos, Rhodes; Kokkári, Sámos; and Sými. In specialist UK shops or by mail order; catalogue from 17 Bernard Crescent, Hunstanton PE36 6ER (☎ & Ⓕ 01485/532710, Ⓔmarengo@supanet.com).

Marc Dubin *Trekking in Greece*

(Lonely Planet; o/p). Though many sections are showing their age (and the depredations of bulldozers), still an excellent walkers' guide, expanding on the hikes covered in this book. Includes day-hikes and longer treks, both around the mainland and on the islands, plus extensive preparatory and background information.

Andonis Kaloyirou *Walking Routes on Parnitha* (Road Editions, Athens). Small, pocket-sized booklet, packaged with an encased topo map, enables you to get the best out of the nearest mountain escape from Athens.

Tim Salmon *The Mountains of Greece: A Walker's Guide* (Cicerone Press; Hunter). The emphasis in this practical walkers' handbook, updated in 1993, is more specifically on the mainland mountains. Its core is a superb traverse, roughly following the E4 trail along the Píndhos crest, from Delphi to Albania, though there have been complaints that some of the estimated walking times are impossibly fast.

★ **Loraine Wilson** *The White Mountains of Crete* (Cicerone Press; Hunter). Nearly sixty walks and treks from easy to gruelling by the doyenne of foreign trekking guides in Crete; implicitly trustworthy directions and prudent warnings. The book's marred only by the rudimentary maps (buy the Harms series) and rather bizarre transliterations of Greek phrases.

Regional guides

★ **Johan de Bakker** *Across Crete* (World Discovery Guide Books, Netherlands). A superb first volume (central Crete) of three-part coverage of Crete, assessing the modern sites in comparison with the accounts of eighteenth- and nineteenth-century travellers. Vols. 2/3, East/West Crete, due late 2002.

Marc Dubin *The Rough Guide to the Dodecanese and the East Aegean* (Penguin). Exhaustive coverage of the islands described in Chapters Nine and Ten of this book, by a part-time resident of Sámos.

John Fisher and Geoff Garvey *The Rough Guide to Crete* (Penguin). An expanded and practical guide to the island by two Cretophiles, who contributed the Crete chapter to this book.

Peter Greenhalgh and Edward Eliopoulos *Deep Into Mani* (Faber & Faber, o/p). A former member of the wartime Resistance revisits the Máni forty years after first hiding there, and 25 years after Patrick Leigh Fermor's work, in the company of a British scholar. The result is a superb guide to the region and excellent armchair reading.

Lycabettus Press Guides (Athens, Greece). This series takes in many of the more popular islands and certain mainland highlights; most, despite decade-long intervals between revisions, pay their way both in interest and usefulness – in particular those on Páros, Kós, Pátmos, Náfplio, Ídhra and the travels of Saint Paul.

★ **Oliver Rackham and Jennifer Moody** *The Making of the Cretan Landscape* (Manchester UP; St Martin's Press). It's hard to classify this academic-press product written for the casual visitor. As the title says, but much more, taking in geology, natural history, agricultural practices, place names, architecture and demography, all arranged by topic. Not error-free – nothing this ambitious could be – but impressive.

Nikos Stavroulakis *Jewish Sites and Synagogues of Greece* (Talos Press, Athens). A lavishly illustrated alphabetical gazetteer of all Jewish monuments in Greece, with town plans and full histories of the communities that created them. A few have been demolished since publication, however.

Bookshops

Athens has a number of excellent bookshops, at which many of the recommendations above should be available (at fifty percent mark-up for foreign-published titles): see p.155 for addresses. In London, the Hellenic Bookservice, 91 Fortess Rd, Kentish Town, London NW5 1AG (☎020/7267 9499, ⨍7267 9498, �🌐www.hellenic-bookservice.com), is the UK's premier walk-in Greek bookshop: knowledgeable and well-stocked specialist dealers in new, secondhand and out-of-print books. Rivals Zeno's have premises at 57A Nether St, North Finchley, London N12 7NP (☎020/8446 1985, �🌐www.thegreekbookstore.com).

Yachting

H.M. Denham *The Aegean; The Ionian Islands to the Anatolian Coast* (John Murray, UK, o/p). Long the standard references if you were out yachting; still found in secondhand bookshops, but a bit obsolete.

Rod Heikell *Greek Waters Pilot* (Imray, Laurie, Norrie and Wilson, UK). Rather better than the preceding, which it has superseded.

CONTEXTS | Books

language

language

Language

S o many Greeks have lived or worked abroad in North America, Australia and, to a much lesser extent, Britain, that you will find someone who speaks English in the tiniest island village. Add to that the thousands attending language schools or working in the tourist industry – English is the lingua franca of most resorts, with German second – and it is easy to see how so many visitors come back having learned only half a dozen restaurant words.

You can certainly get by this way, but it isn't very satisfying, and the willingness and ability to say even a few words will transform your status from that of dumb *tourístas* to the more honourable one of *xénos/xéni*, a word which can mean foreigner, traveller and guest all rolled into one.

Learning basic Greek

Greek is not an easy language for English-speakers – translators' unions in the UK rate it as harder than German, slightly less complex than Russian – but it is a very beautiful one, and even a brief acquaintance will give you some idea of the debt owed to it by Western European languages.

Language-learning materials

Teach-yourself Greek courses

Breakthrough Greek (Pan Macmillan; book and four cassettes). Excellent, basic teach-yourself course; no Greek lettering, but good for classicists who need to unlearn bad habits.
Greek Language and People (BBC Publications, UK; book and two cassettes available). More limited in scope but good for acquiring the essentials, and the confidence to try them.
Anne Farmakides *A Manual of Modern Greek* (Yale UP; McGill UP; three vols). If you have the discipline and motivation, this is one of the best for learning proper, grammatical Greek; indeed, mastery of just the first volume will get you a long way.
Hara Garoufalia *Teach Yourself Holiday Greek* (Hodder & Stoughton, UK; book and cassette available). Unlike many quickie courses, this provides a good grammatical foundation, but you'll need a dictionary (see overleaf) to supplement the scanty vocabulary lists.
Niki Watts *Greek in Three Months* (Hugo, Dorling Kindersley; book and four cassettes). Delivers as promised; equals or exceeds *Breakthrough Greek*.

Phrasebooks

Greek, a Rough Guide Phrasebook (Penguin, UK & US). Up-to-date and accurate pocket phrasebook not full of "*plume de ma tante*"-type expressions. The English-to-Greek section is sensibly transliterated, though the Greek-to-English part requires basic mastery of the Greek alphabet. Feature boxes fill you in on cultural know-how.

The Oxford Dictionary of Modern Greek (Oxford UP, UK & US). A bit bulky in its wide format, but generally considered the best Greek–English, English–Greek paperback dictionary.

Collins Pocket Greek Dictionary (HarperCollins, UK & US). Very nearly as complete as the Oxford and probably better value for money. The inexpensive *Collins Gem Greek Dictionary* (UK only) is palm-sized but exactly the same in contents – the best day-pack choice.

Oxford Greek–English, English–Greek Learner's Dictionary (Oxford UP, UK & US). If you're planning a prolonged stay, this pricey, hardbound, two-volume set is unbeatable for usage and vocabulary. There's also a more portable one-volume *Learner's Pocket Dictionary*.

The Greek alphabet: transliteration

Set out below is the Greek alphabet, the system of transliteration used in this book, and a brief aid to pronunciation.

Greek	Transliteration	Pronounced
Α, α	a	a as in father
Β, β	v	v as in vet
Γ, γ	y/g	y as in yes except before consonants or a, o or oi when it's a breathy g, approximately as in gap
Δ, δ	dh	th as in then
Ε, ε	e	e as in get
Ζ, ζ	z	z sound
Η, η	i	i as in ski
Θ, θ	th	th as in theme
Ι, ι	i	i as in ski
Κ, κ	k	k sound
Λ, λ	l	l sound
Μ, μ	m	m sound
Ν, ν	n	n sound
Ξ, ξ	x	x sound, never z
Ο, ο	o	o as in toad
Π, π	p	p sound
Ρ, ρ	r	r sound
Σ, σ, ς	s	s sound, except z before m or g; note that single sigma has the same phonic value as double sigma
Τ, τ	t	t sound
Υ, υ	y	y as in barely
Φ, φ	f	f sound
Χ, χ	h before vowels, kh before consonants	harsh h sound, like ch in loch
Ψ, ψ	ps	ps as in lips
Ω, ω	o	o as in toad, indistinguishable from o

Combinations and diphthongs

ΑΙ, αι	e	e as in hey
ΑΥ, αυ	av/af	av or af depending on following consonant
ΕΙ, ει	i	long i, exactly like i or h
ΕΥ, ευ	ev/ef	ev or ef, depending on following consonant
ΟΙ, οι	i	long i, exactly like i or h
ΟΥ, ου	ou	ou as in tourist
ΓΓ, γγ	ng	ng as in angle; always medial
ΓΚ, γκ	g/ng	g as in goat at the beginning of a word, ng in the middle
ΜΠ, μπ	b/mb	b at the beginning of a word, mb in the middle
ΝΤ, ντ	d/nd	d at the beginning of a word, nd in the middle
ΤΣ, τσ	ts	ts as in hits
ΤΖ, τζ	tz	dg as in judge, j as in jam in some dialects

Note on diereses

The dieresis is used in Greek over the second of two adjacent vowels to change the pronunciation that you would expect from the preceding table; often in this book it can function as the primary stress. In the word *kaïki* (caique), the presence of the dieresis changes the pronunciation from "cake-key" to "ka-ee-key" and additionally the middle "i" carries the primary stress. In the word *païdhákia* (lamb chops), the dieresis again changes the sound of the first syllable from "pay" to "pah-ee", but in this case the primary stress is on the third syllable. It is also, uniquely among Greek accents, used on capital letters in signs and personal-name spellings in Greece, and we have followed this practice on our maps.

On top of the usual difficulties of learning a new language, Greek presents the additional problem of an entirely separate **alphabet**. Despite initial appearances, this is in practice fairly easily mastered – a skill that will help enormously if you are going to get around independently (see the alphabet box opposite). In addition, certain combinations of letters have unexpected results. This book's transliteration system should help you make intelligible noises, but you have to remember that the correct **stress** (marked throughout the book with an acute accent or sometimes dieresis) is crucial. With the right sounds but the wrong stress people will either fail to understand you, or else understand something quite different from what you intended – there are numerous pairs of words with the same spelling and phonemes, distinguished only by their stress (the classic, naughty example is *gámo*, "a wedding", versus *gamó*, "I fuck").

Greek words and phrases

Essentials

Yes – **Né**
Certainly – **Málista**
No – **Óhi**
Please – **Parakaló**
OK, agreed – **Endáxi**
Thank you (very much) – **Efharistó (polý)**
I (don't) understand – **(Dhén) Katalavéno**
Excuse me – **Parakaló, mípos**
Do you speak English? – **miláte angliká?**
Sorry/excuse me – **Signómi**
Today – **Símera**
Tomorrow – **Ávrio**
Yesterday – **Khthés**
Now – **Tóra**
Later – **Argótera**
Open – **Anikhtó**
Closed – **Klistó**
Day – **Méra**
Night – **Níkhta**
In the morning – **Tó proï**
In the afternoon – **Tó apóyevma**
In the evening – **Tó vrádhi**

Here – **Edhó**
There – **Ekí**
This one – **Aftó**
That one – **Ekíno**
Good – **Kaló**
Bad – **Kakó**
Big – **Megálo**
Small – **Mikró**
More – **Perisótero**
Less – **Ligótero**
A little – **Lígo**
A lot – **Polý**
Cheap – **Ftinó**
Expensive – **Akrivó**
Hot – **Zestó**
Cold – **Krýo**
With (together) – **Mazí (mé)**
Without – **Horís**
Quickly – **Grígora**
Slowly – **Sigá**
Mr/Mrs – **Kýrios/Kyría**
Miss – **Dhespinís**

Other needs

To eat/drink - **Trógo/píno**
Bakery - **Foúrnos, psomádhiko**
Pharmacy - **Farmakío**
Post office - **Tahydhromío**
Stamps - **Gramatóssima**
Petrol station - **Venzinádhiko**

Bank - **Trápeza**
Money - **Leftá/Khrímata**
Toilet - **Toualéta**
Police - **Astynomía**
Doctor - **Yiatrós**
Hospital - **Nosokomío**

Requests and questions

To ask a question, it's simplest to start with *parakaló*, then name the thing you want in an interrogative tone.

Where is the bakery? - **Parakaló, o foúrnos?**
Can you show me the road to . . . ? - **Parakaló, ó dhrómos yiá . . . ?**
We'd like a room for two - **Parakaló, éna dhomátio yiá dhýo átoma**
May I have a kilo of oranges? - **Parakaló, éna kiló portokália?**
Where? - **Poú?**
How? - **Pós?**

How many? - **Póssi, pósses or póssa?**
How much? - **Póso?**
When? - **Póte?**
Why? - **Yiatí?**
At what time . . . ? - **Tí óra . . . ?**
What is/Which is . . . ? - **Tí ine/Pió íne . . . ?**
How much (does it cost)? - **Póso kání?**
What time does it open? - **Tí óra aníyí?**
What time does it close? - **Tí óra klíni?**

Talking to people

Greek makes the distinction between the informal (*essý*) and formal (*essís*) second person, as French does with "tu" and "vous". Young people, older people and country people often use *essý* even with total strangers, though if you greet someone familiarly and they respond formally, it's best to adopt their usage as the conversation continues, to avoid offence. By far the most common greeting, on meeting and parting, is *yiá sou/yiá sas* – literally "health to you". Incidentally, as across most of the Mediterranean, the approaching party utters the first greeting, not those seated at sidewalk kafenío tables or doorsteps – thus the silent staring as you enter a village.

Hello - **Hérete**
Good morning - **Kalí méra**
Good evening - **Kalí spéra**
Good night - **Kalí níkhta**
Goodbye - **Adío**
How are you? - **Tí kánis/Tí kánete?**
I'm fine - **Kalá íme**
And you? - **Ké essís?**
What's your name? - **Pós se léne?**
My name is . . . - **Mé léne . . .**

Speak slower, please - **Parakaló, miláte pió sigá**
How do you say it in Greek? - **Pós léyete stá Elliniká?**
I don't know - **Dhén xéro**
See you tomorrow - **Thá sé dhó ávrio**
See you soon - **Kalí andhámosi**
Let's go - **Páme**
Please help me - **Parakaló, ná mé voithíste**

Greek's Greek

There are numerous words and phrases which you will hear constantly, even if you rarely have the chance to use them. These are a few of the most common.

Éla! - Come (literally) but also Speak to me! You don't say! etc.
Oríste! - Literally, "Indicate!"; in effect, "What can I do for you?"

Embrós! or **Léyete!** - Standard phone responses
Tí néa? - What's new?
Tí yínete? - What's going on (here)?

Étsi k'étsi – So-so
Ópa! – Whoops! Watch it!
Po-po-po! – Expression of dismay or concern, like French "O là là!"
Pedhí moú – My boy/girl, sonny, friend, etc.

Maláka(s) – Literally "wanker", but often used (don't try it!) as an informal term of address.
Sigá sigá – Take your time, slow down
Kaló taxídhi – Bon voyage

Accommodation

Hotel – Xenodhohío
Inn – Xenón(as)
Youth hostel – Xenónas neótitos
A room . . . – Éna dhomátio . . .
for one/two/three people – yiá éna/dhýo/Tría átoma
for one/two/three nights – yiá mía/dhýo/trís vradhiés
with a double bed – mé megálo kreváti
with a shower – mé doús

Hot water – Zestó neró
Cold water – Krýo neró
Air conditioning – Klimatismós
Fan – Anamistíra
Can I see it? – Boró ná tó dhó?
Can we camp here? – Boroúme na váloume ti skiní edhó?
Campsite – Kámping/Kataskínosi
Tent – Skiní

On the move

Aeroplane – Aeropláno
Bus, coach – Leoforío, púlman
Car – Aftokínito, amáxi
Motorbike, scooter – Mihanáki, papáki
Taxi – Taxí
Ship – Plío/vapóri/karávi
High-speed catamaran – Tahýplio
Hydrofoil – Dhelfíni
Train – Tréno
Train station – Sidhirodhromikós stathmós
Bicycle – Podhílato
Hitching – Otostóp
On foot – Mé tá pódhia
Trail – Monopáti
Bus station – Praktorío leoforíon, KTEL
Bus stop – Stássi
Harbour – Limáni
What time does it leave? – Ti óra févyi?
What time does it arrive? – Ti óra ftháni?
How many kilometres? – Póssa hiliómetra?

How many hours? – Pósses óres?
Where are you going? – Poú pás?
I'm going to . . . – Páo stó . . .
I want to get off at . . . – Thélo ná katévo stó . . .
The road to . . . – O dhrómos yiá . . .
Near – Kondá
Far – Makriá
Left – Aristerá
Right – Dhexiá
Straight ahead – Katefthía, ísia
A ticket to . . . – Éna isitírio yiá . . .
A return ticket – Éna isitírio mé epistrofí
Beach – Paralía
Cave – Spiliá
Centre (of town) – Kéndro
Church – Ekklissía
Sea – Thálassa
Village – Horió

Numbers

1 – énas/éna/mía
2 – dhýo
3 – trís/tría
4 – tésseres/téssera
5 – pénde
6 – éxi
7 – eftá
8 – okhtó
9 – ennéa (or more slangy, enyá)
10 – dhéka
11 – éndheka

12 – dhódheka
13 – dhekatrís
14 – dhekatésseres
20 – íkossi
21 – íkossi éna – (all compounds written separately thus)
30 – triánda
40 – saránda
50 – penínda
60 – exínda
70 – evdhominda

80 - ogdhónda	1000 - hílies/hília
90 - enenínda	2000 - dhýo hiliádhes
100 - ekató	1,000,000 - éna ekatomírio
150 - ekatón penínda	first - próto
200 - dhiakóssies/dhiakóssia	second - dhéftero
500 - pendakóssies/pendakóssia	third - tríto

The time and days of the week

Sunday - Kyriakí	One/two/three o'clock - Mía óra, dhýo/trís
Monday - Dheftéra	(óres)
Tuesday - Tríti	Twenty minutes to four - Tésseres pará
Wednesday - Tetárti	íkossi
Thursday - Pémpti	Five minutes past seven - Eftá ké pénde
Friday - Paraskeví	Half past eleven - Éndheka ké misí
Saturday - Sávato	In half an hour - Sé misí óra
What time is it? - Tí óra íne?	In a quarter-hour - S'éna tétarto

Months and seasonal terms

NB You may see *katharévoussa*, or hybrid, forms of the months written on schedules or street signs; these are the spoken demotic forms.

January - Yennáris	August - Ávgoustos
February - Fleváris	September - Septémvris
March - Mártis	October - Októvrios
April - Aprílis	November - Noémvris
May - Maïos	December - Dhekémvris
June - Ioúnios	Summer schedule - Therinó dhromolóyio
July - Ioúlios	Winter schedule - Himerinó dhromolóyio

A food and drink glossary

Basics

Aláti - Salt	Neró - Water
Avgá - Eggs	Psári(a) - Fish
(Horís) ládhi - (Without) oil	Psomí - Bread
Hortofágos - Vegetarian	Olikís - Wholemeal bread
Katálogo/lísta - Menu	Sikalísio - Rye bread
Kréas - Meat	Thalassiná - Seafood
Lahaniká - Vegetables	Tyrí - Cheese
O logariasmós - The bill	Yiaoúrti - Yogurt
Méli - Honey	Záhari - Sugar

Cooking terms

Akhnistó - Steamed	Sti soúvla - Spit-roasted
Pastó - Marinated in salt	Stó foúrno - Baked
Psitó - Roasted	Tiganitó - Pan-fried
Saganáki - Cheese-based red sauce; also	Tís óras - Grilled/fried to order
any fried cheese	Yakhní - Stewed in oil and tomato sauce
Skáras - Grilled	Yemistá - Stuffed (squid, vegetables, etc)

Soups and starters

Avgolémono – Egg and lemon soup
Dolmádhes – Stuffed vine leaves
Fasoládha – Bean soup
Florínes – Canned red sweet Macedonian peppers
Hortópita – Turnover or pie stuffed with wild greens
Kafterí – Cheese dip with chili added
Kápari – Pickled caper leaves
Kopanistí, khtypití – Pungent, fermented cheese purée
Krítamo – Rock samphire

Mavromátika – Black-eyed peas
Melitzanosaláta – Aubergine/eggplant dip
Revythokeftédhes – Chickpea (garbanzo) patties
Skordhaliá – Garlic dip
Soúpa – Soup
Taramosaláta – Cod roe paté
Tyrokafterí – Cheese dip with chilli, different from kopanistí
Tzatzíki – Yogurt and cucumber dip
Tzirosaláta – cured mackerel dip

Vegetables

Angináres – Artichokes
Angoúri – Cucumber
Ánitho – Dill
Bámies – Okra, ladies' fingers
Bouréki, bourekákia – Courgette/zucchini, potato and cheese pie
Briám – Ratatouille
Domátes – Tomatoes
Fakés – Lentils
Fasolákia – French (green) beans
Horiátiki (saláta) – Greek salad (with olives, feta etc)
Hórta – Greens (usually wild), steamed
Kolokythákia – Courgette/zucchini
Koukiá – Broad fava beans

Maroúli – Lettuce
Melitzánes imám – Aubergine/eggplant slices baked with onion, garlic and copious olive oil
Patátes – Potatoes
Piperiés – Peppers
Pligoúri, pinigoúri – Bulgur wheat
Radhíkia – Wild chicory – a common hórta
Rýzi/Piláfi – Rice (usually with sáltsa – sauce)
Rókka – Rocket greens
Saláta – Salad
Spanáki – Spinach
Vlíta Notchweed – another common hórta
Yígandes – White haricot beans

Fish and seafood

Astakós – Aegean lobster
Atherína – Sand smelt
Bakaliáros – Cod
Barbóuni – Red mullet
Fangrí – Common bream
Galéos – Dogfish, hound shark
Garídhes – Shrimp, prawns
Gávros – Mild anchovy
Glóssa – Sole
Gópa – Bogue
Kalamarákia – Baby squid
Kalamária – Squid
Karavídhes – Crayfish
Kefalás – Axillary bream
Koliós – Chub mackerel
Koutsomoúra – Goatfish (small red mullet)
Kydhónia – Cockles
Lakérdha – Light-fleshed bonito, marinated

Marídhes – Picarel
Melanoúri – Saddled bream
Ménoula Sprat
Mýdhia – Mussels
Okhtapódhi – Octopus
Pandelís – Corvina; also called sykiós
Platý – Skate, ray
Sardhélles – Sardines
Sargós – White bream
Seláhi – Skate, ray
Skathári – Black bream
Skoumbrí – Atlantic mackerel
Soupiá – Cuttlefish
Synagrídha – Dentex
Tsipoúra – Gilt-head bream
Vátos – Skate, ray
Xifías – Swordfish
Yermanós – Leatherback

Meat and meat-based dishes

Arní – Lamb
Biftéki – Hamburger
Brizóla – Pork or beef chop
Hirinó – Pork
Keftédhes – Meatballs
Kokorétsi – Liver/offal roulade, spit-roasted
Kopsídha – (Lamb) shoulder chops
Kotópoulo – Chicken
Kounélli – Rabbit
Loukánika – Spicy home-made sausages
Moskhári – Veal
Moussakás – Aubergine, potato and lamb-mince casserole with bechamel topping
Païdhákia – Rib chops, lamb or goat

Papoutsákia – Stuffed aubergine/eggplant "shoes" – like moussakás without bechamel
Pastítsio – Macaroni "pie" baked with minced meat
Patsás – Tripe and trotter soup
Salingária – Garden snails
Soutzoukákia – Minced meat rissoles/beef patties
Stifádho – Meat stew with tomato and boiling onions
Sykóti – Liver
Tzigeros armás Lamb's liver in cabbage
Youvétsi – Baked clay casserole of meat and kritharáki (short pasta)

Sweets and dessert

Baklavás – Honey and nut pastry
Bougátsa – Salt or sweet cream pie served warm with sugar and cinammon
Galaktobóureko – Custard pie
Halvás – Sweetmeat of sesame or semolina
Karydhópita – Walnut cake
Kréma – Custard

Loukoumádhes – Dough fritters in honey syrup and sesame seeds
Pagotó – Ice cream
Pastélli – Sesame and honey bar
Ravaní – Spongecake, lightly syruped
Ryzógalo – Rice pudding

Fruit and nuts

Akhládhia – Big pears
Aktinídha – Kiwis
Fistíkia – Pistachio nuts
Fráoules – Strawberries
Karpoúzi – Watermelon
Kerásia – Cherries
Krystália – Miniature pears
Kydhóni – Quince

Lemónia – Lemons
Míla – Apples
Pepóni – Melon
Portokália – Oranges
Rodhákino – Peach
Sýka – Figs
Stafýlia – Grapes

Cheese

Ayeladhinó – Cow's-milk cheese
Féta – Salty, white cheese
Graviéra – Gruyère-type hard cheese
Katsikísio – Goat cheese

Kasséri – Medium-sharp cheese
Myzíthra – Sweet cream cheese
Próvio – Sheep cheese

Drinks

Alisfakiá Island sage tea
Boukáli – Bottle
Býra – Beer
Gála – Milk
Galakakáo – Chocolate milk
Gazóza – Generic fizzy drink
Kafés – Coffee
Krasí – Wine
  áspro – white

kokkinélli/ rozé – rosé
kókkino/ mávro – red
Limonádha – Lemonade
Metalikó neró – Mineral water
Portokaládha – Orangeade
Potíri – Glass
Stinyássas! – Cheers!
Tsáï – Tea
Tsáï vounoú – "Mountain" (mainland sage) tea

Greek **grammar** is more complicated still: nouns are divided into three genders, all with different case endings in the singular and in the plural, and all adjectives and articles have to agree with these in gender, number and case. (All adjectives are arbitrarily cited in the neuter form in the boxed lists.) Verbs are even more complex; they come in two conjugations, in both active and passive voices, with passively constructed verbs often having transitive sense. To begin with at least, the best thing is simply to say what you know the way you know it, and never mind the niceties. "Eat meat hungry" should get a result, however grammatically incorrect. If you worry about your mistakes, you'll never say anything.

Katharévoussa, dhimotikí and dialects

Greek may seem complicated enough in itself, but problems are multiplied when you consider that since the early 1800s there has been an ongoing dispute between two versions of the language: **katharévoussa** and **dhimotikí**.

When Greece first achieved independence in the nineteenth century, its people were almost universally illiterate, and the language they spoke – *dhimotikí*, "demotic" or "popular" Greek – had undergone enormous change since the days of the Byzantine empire and Classical times. The vocabulary had assimilated countless borrowings from the languages of the various invaders and conquerors, such as the Turks, Venetians and Slavs.

The finance and inspiration for the new Greek state, as well as its early leaders, came largely from the diaspora – Greek families who had been living in the sophisticated cities of central and eastern Europe, in Constantinople or in Russia. With their European notions about the grandeur of Greece's past, and lofty conception of Hellenism, they set about obliterating the memory of subjugation to foreigners in every possible field. And what better way to start than by purging the language of its foreign accretions and reviving its Classical purity?

They accordingly set about creating what was in effect a new form of the language, *katharévoussa* (literally "cleansed" Greek). The complexities of Classical grammar and syntax were reinstated, and Classical words, long out of use, were reintroduced. To the country's great detriment, *katharévoussa* became the language of the schools and the prestigious professions, government, business, the law, newspapers and academia. Everyone aspiring to membership in the elite strove to master it, and to speak it – even though there was no consensus on how many of the words should be pronounced.

The *katharévoussa/dhimotikí* debate remained a highly contentious issue until the early 1980s. Writers – from Solomos and Makriyiannis in the nineteenth century to Seferis, Kazantzakis and Ritsos in the twentieth – have all championed the demotic, or some approximation of it, in their literature. Advocacy of demotic became increasingly linked to left-wing politics, while crackpot right-wing governments forcibly (re)instated *katharévoussa* at every opportunity. Most recently, the **colonels' junta** (1967–1974) reversed a decision of the previous government to use *dhimotikí* as the medium of instruction in schools, bringing back *katharévoussa*, even on sweet wrappers, as part of their ragbag of notions about racial purity and heroic ages.

Dhimiotikí returned once more after the fall of the colonels and now seems here to stay; perhaps the final blow to the classicizers was the official decision, in 1981, to do away with breath marks (which in fact no longer signified anything) and abolish the three different stress accents in favour of a **single accute accent** (though there are still plenty of leftover road-signs displaying the older system). *Dhimotikí* is used in schools, on radio and TV, and after a fashion in newspapers (with the exception of the extreme right-wing *Estia*). The only institutions which refuse to bring themselves up to date are the Church and the legal professions – so beware rental contracts and official documents.

This is not to suggest that there is now any less confusion. The Metaxas dictatorship of the 1930s changed scores of village names from Slavic to Classical forms, and these official **place names** still hold sway on most road signs and maps – even though the local people may use the *dhimotikí* form. Thus you will see "Leonídhio(n)" or "Spétsai" written, while everyone actually says "Leonídhi" or "Spétses".

Dialects and minority languages

If the lack of any standard Greek were not enough, Greece still offers a rich field of linguistic diversity, both in its regional dialects and minority languages. Ancient **dialects** are alive and well in many a remote area, and some of them are quite incomprehensible to outsiders. The dialect of Sfákia in Crete is one such; Tsakónika (spoken in the east-central Peloponnese) is another, while the dialect of the Sarakatsáni shepherds is said to be the oldest, a direct descendant of the language of the Dorian settlers.

The language of the Sarakatsáni's traditional rivals, the **Vlachs**, on the other hand, is not Greek at all, but a derivative of early Latin, with strong affinities to Romanian. In the ex-Yugoslav and Bulgarian frontier regions you can still hear **Slavic Macedonian** spoken, while small numbers of Sephardic Jews in the north and on Rhodes speak **Ladino**, a medieval form of Spanish. Until a few decades ago **Arvanítika** – a dialect of medieval Albanian – was the first language of many villages of inland Attica, southern Évvia, northern Ándhros, and much of the Argo-Saronic area; it is still spoken (and sung) by the oldest generation. Lately the clock has been turned back, so to speak, as throngs of Albanian immigrants circulate in Athens and other parts of the country. In Thrace there is also a substantial **Turkish-speaking** population, as well as some speakers of **Pomak** (a relative of Bulgarian with a large Greco-Turkish vocabulary).

A glossary of words and terms

Acropolis – Ancient, fortified hilltop.

Agora – Market and meeting place of an ancient Greek city; also the "high street" of a modern village (**Agorá** in modern Greek).

Amphora – Tall, narrow-necked jar for oil or wine.

Áno – Upper; common prefix element of village names.

Archaic period – Late Iron Age period, from around 750 BC to the start of the Classical period in the fifth century BC.

Architrave – Horizontal masonry atop temple columns; same as **Entablature**.

Arhondikó – A lordly stone mansion, as in Kastoriá or Pílion.

Astykó – (Intra) city, municipal, local; adjective applied to phone calls and bus services.

Áyios/Ayía/Áyii Saint or holy (m/f/plural). Common place-name prefix (abbreviated Ag or Ay), often spelled **Agios** or **Aghios**.

Basilica – Colonnaded, "hall-" or "barn-" type church adapted from Roman models, most common in northern Greece.

Bema – Rostrum for oratory (and later the chancel) of a church.

Bouleuterion – Auditorium for meetings of an ancient town's deliberative council.

Capital – The flared top, often ornamented, of a column.

Cella – Sacred room of a temple, housing the cult image.

Classical period – Essentially from the end of the Persian Wars in the fifth century BC until the unification of Greece under Philip II of Macedon (338 BC).

Corinthian – Decorative columns, festooned with acanthus florettes; a temple built in this order.

Dhimarhío – Town hall.

Dhomátia – Rooms for rent in purpose-built blocks or (seldomly these days) private houses.

Dorian – Northern civilization that displaced and succeeded the Mycenaeans and Minoans through most of Greece around 1100 BC.

Doric – Minimalist, unadorned columns, dating from the Dorian period; a temple built in this order.

Drum – Cylindrical or faceted vertical section, usually pierced by an even number of narrow windows, upholding a church cupola.

Entablature – The horizontal linking structure atop the columns of an ancient temple.

Eparhía – Greek Orthodox diocese, also the smallest subdivision of a modern province, analogous to a county.

Exedra – Display niche for statuary.

Exonarthex – The outer vestibule or entrance hall of a church, when a true **Narthex** is present.

Forum – Market and meeting place of a Roman-era city.

Frieze – Band of sculptures around a temple. Doric friezes consist of various tableaux of figures (**Metopes**) interspersed with grooved panels (**Triglyphs**); Ionic ones have continuous bands of figures.

Froúrio – Medieval castle; nowadays, usually means a modern military headquarters.

Garsoniéra/es – Studio villa/s, self-catering apartment/s.

Geometric period – Post-Mycenaean Iron Age era named for the style of its pottery; begins in the early eleventh century BC with the arrival of Dorian peoples. By the eighth century BC, with the development of representational

styles, it becomes known as the **Archaic** period.

Hellenistic period – The last and most unified "Greek empire", created in the wake of Alexander the Great's Macedonian empire and finally collapsing with the fall of Corinth to the Romans in 146 BC.

Heroön – Shrine or sanctuary, usually of a demigod or mortal; war memorials in modern Greece.

Hokhláki – Mosaic of coloured pebbles, found in church or house courtyards of the Dodecanese and Spétses.

Hóra – Main town of an island or region; literally it means "the place". An island *hóra* is often known by the same name as the island.

Ierón – Literally, "sacred" – the space between the altar screen and the apse of a church, reserved for priestly activities.

Ikonostási – Screen between the nave of a church and the altar, supporting at least three icons.

Ionic – Elaborate, decorative development of the older **Doric** order; Ionic temple columns are slimmer, with deeper "fluted" edges, spiral-shaped capitals and ornamental bases.

Iperastykó – Long-distance – as in phone calls and bus services.

Kafenío – Coffee house or café; in a small village the centre of communal life and probably serving as the bus stop, too.

Kaïki (plural **Kaïkia**) – Caique, or medium-sized boat, traditionally wooden and used for transporting cargo and passengers; now refers mainly to island excursion boats.

Kalderími – A cobbled mule-track or footpath.

Kámbos – Fertile agricultural plain, usually near a river mouth.

Kantína – Shack, caravan or even a disused bus on the beach, serving drinks and perhaps sandwiches or quick snacks.

Kástro – Any fortified hill (or a castle), but most often the oldest, highest, walled-in part of an island **Hóra**.

Katholikón – Central chapel of a monastery.

Káto – Lower; common prefix element of village names.

Kendrikí platía – Central square.

Kouros – Nude Archaic statue of an idealized young man, usually portrayed with one foot slightly forward of the other.

Megaron – Principal hall or throne room of a Mycenaean palace.

LANGUAGE | Glossary

Meltémi – North wind that blows across the Aegean in summer, starting softly from near the mainland and hitting the Cyclades, the Dodecanese and Crete full on.

Metope see **Frieze**.

Minoan – Crete's great Bronze Age civilization, which dominated the Aegean from about 2500 to 1400 BC.

Moní – Formal term for a monastery or convent.

Moreás – Medieval term for the Peloponnese; the outline of the peninsula was likened to the leaf of a mulberry tree, *moreá* in Greek.

Mycenaean – Mainland civilization centred on Mycenae and the Argolid from about 1700 to 1100 BC.

Naos – The inner sanctum of an ancient temple; also, any Orthodox Christian shrine.

Narthex – Western vestibule of a church, reserved for catechumens and the unbaptized; typically frescoed with scenes of the Last Judgement.

Neolithic – Earliest era of settlement in Greece, characterized by the use of stone tools and weapons together with basic agriculture. Divided arbitrarily into Early (c.6000 BC), Middle (c.5000 BC) and Late (c.3000 BC).

Néos, Néa, Néo – "New" – a common prefix to a town or village name.

Nomós – Modern Greek province – there are more than fifty of them. Village bus services are organized according to their borders.

Odeion – Small theatre, used for musical performances, minor dramatic productions or councils.

Orchestra – Circular area in a theatre where the chorus would sing and dance.

Palaestra – Gymnasium for athletics and wrestling practice.

Paleós, Paleá, Paleó – "Old" – again a common prefix in town and village names.

Panayía – Virgin Mary.

Pandokrátor – Literally "The Almighty"; generally refers to the stern portrayal of Christ in Majesty frescoed or in mosaic in the dome of many Byzantine churches.

Paniyíri – Festival or feast – the local celebration of a holy day.

Paralía – Beach or seafront promenade.

Pediment – Triangular, sculpted gable below the roof of a temple.

Pendentive – Any of four triangular sections of vaulting with concave sides, positioned at a corner of a rectangular space to support a circular or polygonal dome; in churches, often adorned with frescoes of the four Evangelists.

Períptero – Street kiosk.

Peristereónes – Pigeon towers, in the Cyclades.

Peristyle – Gallery of columns around a temple or other building.

Pinakothíki – Picture gallery, ancient or modern.

Pithos (plural **Pithoi**) – Large ceramic jar for storing oil, grain, etc. Very common in Minoan palaces and used in almost identical form in modern Greek homes.

Platía – Square, plaza.

Polygonal masonry – Wall-building technique of the Classical and Hellenistic period, which used unmortared, closely joined stones; often called "Lesvian polygonal" after the island where the method supposedly originated. The much-(ab)used term "**Cyclopean**" refers only to Mycenean/Bronze Age mainland sites such as Tiryns and Mycenae itself.

Propylaion – Monumental columned gateway of an ancient building; often used in the plural, propylaia.

Pýrgos – Tower or bastion; also tower-mansions found in the Máni or on Lésvos.

Skála – The port of an inland island settlement, nowadays often larger and more important than its namesake, but always younger since built after the disappearance of piracy.

Squinch – Small concavity across a corner of a columnless interior space, which supports a superstructure such as a dome.

Stele – Upright stone slab or column, usually inscribed with an edict; also an ancient tombstone, with a relief scene.

Stoa – Colonnaded walkway in Classical-era marketplace.

Témblon – Wooden altar screen of an Orthodox church, usually ornately carved and painted and studded with icons; more or less interchangeable with **Ikonostási**.

Temenos – Sacred precinct, often used to refer to the sanctuary itself.

Theatral area – Open area found in most of the Minoan palaces with seat-like steps around. Probably a type of theatre or ritual area.

Tholos – Conical or beehive-shaped building, eg a Mycenaean tomb.

Triglyph – see **Frieze**.

Tympanum – The recessed space, flat or carved in relief, inside a pediment.

Acronyms

ANEK - Anónymi Navtiliakí Etería Krítis (Shipping Co of Crete, Ltd), which runs most ferries between Pireás and Crete, plus many to Italy.

DANE - Dhodhekanisiakí Anónymi Navtiliakí Etería (Dodecanesian Shipping Company Ltd), which runs many ferries between Rhodes and Pireás via intervening islands.

DIKKI - Democrat Social Movement, a more left-leaning spinoff from PASOK.

EAM - National Liberation Front, the political force behind ELAS.

ELAS - Popular Liberation Army, the main Resistance group during World War II and the basis of the Communist army during the civil war.

ELTA - Postal service.

EOS - Greek Mountaineering Federation, based in Athens.

EOT - Ellinikós Organismós Tourismoú, National Tourist Organization.

FYROM - Former Yugoslav Republic of Macedonia.

KKE - Communist Party, unreconstructed.

KTEL - National syndicate of bus companies. The term also refers to individual bus stations.

LANE - Lasithiakí Anónymi Navtiliakí Etería (Lasithian Shipping Company Ltd), based in eastern Crete.

ND - Conservative (Néa Dhimokratía) party.

NEL - Navtiliakí Etería Lésvou (Lesvian Shipping Co).

OSE - Railway corporation.

OTE - Telephone company.

PASOK - Socialist party (Pan-Hellenic Socialist Movement).

SEO - Greek Mountaineering Club, based in Thessaloníki.

index

and small print

Index

Map entries are in colour

A

B

Ⓘ

INDEX

Ⓘ

INDEX

1119

Ⓘ

INDEX

O

INDEX

INDEX

①

INDEX

INDEX

1129

I

Twenty Years of Rough Guides

In the summer of 1981, Mark Ellingham, Rough Guides' founder, knocked out the first guide on a typewriter, with a group of friends. Mark had been travelling in Greece after university, and couldn't find a guidebook that really answered his needs. There were heavyweight cultural guides on the one hand – good on museums and classical sites but not on beaches and tavernas – and on the other hand student manuals that were so caught up with how to save money that they lost sight of the country's significance beyond its role as a place for a cool vacation. None of the guides began to address Greece as a country, with its natural and human environment, its politics and its contemporary life.

Having no urgent reason to return home, Mark decided to write his own guide. It was a guide to Greece that tried to combine some erudition and insight with a thoroughly practical approach to travellers' needs. Scrupulously researched listings of places to stay, eat and drink were matched by careful attention to detail on everything from Homer to Greek music, from classical sites to national parks and from nude beaches to monasteries. Back in London, Mark and his friends got their Rough Guide accepted by a farsighted commissioning editor at the publisher Routledge and it came out in 1982.

The Rough Guide to Greece was a student scheme that became a publishing phenomenon. The immediate success of the book – shortlisted for the Thomas Cook award – spawned a series that rapidly covered dozens of countries. The Rough Guides found a ready market among backpackers and budget travellers, but soon acquired a much broader readership that included older and less impecunious visitors. Readers relished the guides' wit and inquisitiveness as much as the enthusiastic, critical approach that acknowledges everyone wants value for money – but not at any price.

Rough Guides soon began supplementing the "rougher" information – the hostel and low-budget listings – with the kind of detail that independent-minded travellers on any budget might expect. These days, the guides – distributed worldwide by the Penguin group – include recommendations spanning the range from shoestring to luxury, and cover more than 200 destinations around the globe. Our growing team of authors, many of whom come to Rough Guides initially as outstandingly good letter-writers telling us about their travels, are spread all over the world, particularly in Europe, the USA and Australia. As well as the travel guides, Rough Guides publishes a series of dictionary phrasebooks covering two dozen major languages, an acclaimed series of music guides running the gamut from Classical to World Music, a series of music CDs in association with World Music Network, and a range of reference books on topics as diverse as the internet, pregnancy and unexplained phenomena. Visit www.roughguides.com to see what's cooking.

Rough Guide credits

Text editors: Ruth Blackmore and Alison Murchie
Series editor: Mark Ellingham
Editorial: Martin Dunford, Jonathan Buckley, Jo Mead, Kate Berens, Ann-Marie Shaw, Helena Smith, Judith Bamber, Orla Duane, Olivia Eccleshall, Geoff Howard, Claire Saunders, Gavin Thomas, Alexander Mark Rogers, Polly Thomas, Joe Staines, Richard Lim, Duncan Clark, Peter Buckley, Lucy Ratcliffe, Clifton Wilkinson, Matthew Teller (UK); Andrew Rosenberg, Stephen Timblin, Yuki Takagaki, Richard Koss (US)
Production: Susanne Hillen, Andy Hilliard, Link Hall, Helen Prior, Julia Bovis, Michelle Draycott, Katie Pringle, Mike Hancock, Zoë Nobes, Rachel Holmes, Andy Turner

Cartography: Melissa Baker, Maxine Repath, Ed Wright, Katie Lloyd-Jones
Picture research: Louise Boulton, Sharon Martins, Mark Thomas
Online: Kelly Cross, Anja Mutic-Blessing, Jennifer Gold, Audra Epstein, Suzanne Welles, Cree Lawson (US)
Finance: John Fisher, Gary Singh, Edward Downey, Mark Hall, Tim Bill
Marketing and Publicity: Richard Trillo, Niki Smith, David Wearn, Chloë Roberts, Claire Southern, Demelza Dallow (UK); Simon Carloss, David Wechsler, Kathleen Rushforth (US)
Administration: Tania Hummel, Julie Sanderson (UK); Hunter Slaton (US)

Publishing information

This ninth edition published February 2002 by Rough Guides Ltd,
62–70 Shorts Gardens, London WC2H 9AH
4th Floor, 345 Hudson St, New York, NY 10014

Distributed by the Penguin Group
Penguin Books Ltd,
80 Strand, London WC2R ORL
Penguin Putnam, Inc.
345 Hudson Street, NY 10014, USA
Penguin Books Australia Ltd,
487 Maroondah Highway, PO Box 257,
Ringwood, Victoria 3134, Australia
Penguin Books Canada Ltd,
10 Alcorn Avenue, Toronto, Ontario,
Canada M4V 1E4
Penguin Books (NZ) Ltd,
182–190 Wairau Road, Auckland 10,
New Zealand
Typeset in Bembo and Helvetica to an original design by Henry Iles.
Printed in Italy by LegoPrint S.p.A

1160pp – Includes index
A catalogue record for this book is available from the British Library

ISBN 1-85828-866-5

The publishers and authors have done their best to ensure the accuracy and currency of all the information in The Rough Guide to Greece, however, they can accept no responsibility for any loss, injury, or inconvenience sustained by any traveler as a result of information or advice contained in the guide.

Help us update

We've gone to a lot of effort to ensure that the ninth edition of The Rough Guide to Greece is accurate and up to date. However, things change – places get "discovered", opening hours can change, restaurants and rooms increase prices or lower standards. If you feel we've got it wrong or left something out, we'd like to know, and if you can remember the address, the price, the time, the phone number, so much the better.

We'll credit all contributions, and send a copy of the next edition (or any other

Rough Guide if you prefer) for the best letters. Everyone who writes to us and isn't already a subscriber will receive a copy of our full-colour thrice-yearly newsletter. Please mark letters: "Rough Guide Greece Update" and send to: Rough Guides, 62–70 Shorts Gardens, London WC2H 9AH, or Rough Guides, 4th Floor, 345 Hudson St, New York, NY 10014. Or send an email to: mail@roughguides.co.uk or mail@roughguides.com

Acknowledgements

Andrew Benson thanks Peter Mackridge in Oxford for his invaluable advice on just about everything; Peter Bowen and everyone on the Akrotíri for Easter festivities and hospitality; Denise and the boys for May Day fun, serious discussions and Athonite wisdom; Brian Donovan for a special insight into the Olympian pantheon, all kinds of insider information and ice-cold beers; Dimitris Nikolaïdhis for his exceptional Thessaloníki expertise; and the management of hotel Le Palace. At Rough Guides, Kate Berens for her continuing confidence, and editor Ruth Blackmore for keeping very calm – congratulations to her, too!

John Bozman thanks Kostas Zissis, Nansy, Thanos, Christos, Suzanna, Sakis, Kostas, Maria and George in Athens; Dimitris and Soula Ghikas on Páros; Despina Kítini and Stavros on Náxos; Artemis on Amorgós; Aris and Loucas Ziras, Markos Karvounis and Sharen Treutel on Thíra; Nik Panou on Agístri; Michael Journtos on Ídhra; David Ewens and Bunny on Ándhros; Sharon Turner on Tínos; John and Koula Kladis on Íos; John van Lerberghe and Maria Paoula on Mýkonos; Aphrodite Depasta, Apostolos Dimopoulos and Apostolis Diareme on Sífnos; Kostas Krinas and Stavros on Sérifos; Sharon Mathiodakis on Milos; Apostolis on Kímolos; Adonis on Kýthnos; Alkestis on Égina; George on the Express Dionyssos; Shirley Watson in Dallas; Kyle McCarthy in New York; Marc Dubin, Ruth Blackmore and Carolyn in London.

Lance Chilton thanks wife Hilary; Chris and Dave Windell in Pyrgiótika; Yiannis Katranis in Spárti; Julia Tzanidou-Zuberer of Porfyra Travel in Kýthira; Babis Doufexis and Nicola Dyas of Doufexis Travel in Stoúpa; Barbara Byrne in Messinía; Chrissy Papavasilopoulos in Iráklion, and Sue Carr in Bury St Edmunds.

Marc Dubin thanks Thanos, Nancy and Susanna in Athens, Roy and Effi Hounsell in Koukouli, the Khristodoulis family in Papingo, George and Barbara Ballis, and George and Effi Kapsalis on Lésvos; Markos Kostalas, and Theodhore and Güher Spordhilis on Híos; Alexis and Dhionysia Zikas on Kós; David, Iain, Lynn, Joanna and Andrea on Tílos, plus Nigel Gardner for the loan of his lovely house; Paul and Stella, plus Efi, Spyros, Sotiris and Marianne (again) on Rhodes; Nikos, Wendy and Jean on Sými; Christine and Alex Sakellaridis on Hálki; Nikos and Anna on Lipsí, Bruno in Galaxídhi; Kostas and Marianthi Pappas in Lykiádhes; Thanasis and Toula Nakas in Kastráki; Nick Gekas in Kalambáka for that vital map; Jill Sleeman in Moúressi; Panayiotis and Aphrodite Papasotiriou on Límnos; Mark and Clovis for the necessary "time out" on Paxí; and last but not least to Pamela for over-eating once again for science, minding the farm in London and cheerfully island-hopping from Ikaría to Kós when we were supposed to be on Lésvos.

Nick Edwards would like to thank the following: the staff of the Corfu and Kefallonia OTE offices; Yiorgia and Catherine and the Zoupanos clan for hospitality in Corfu; Spyros Hytiris for advice and musical sustenance in Corfu; Panayiotis Vandoros for filoxenía, friendship and constant kafedhákia in Argostóli; June Kalogeratou for the homely nest in Zákynthos; Steve and Yiota for the Patra overnight; Steve T, Yiannis K and Klaes K for good times in various spots; and finally Maria for continuing support.

In addition, the editors would like to thank all those involved in producing this book, in particular Link Hall for his expert typesetting and lay-out, Katie Lloyd-Jones for an excellent job with the maps, Sharon Martins for picture research and Russell Walton for proofreading.

Readers' letters

Our thanks to readers of the previous edition who sent in comments and suggestions. In particular:

Regina Whelan Richardson, Laura Davison, Andrea Edwards, Barbara Davies and Bryn Jones, Howard Thompson, Carola Scupham, Ted Frankel, Bev Freeman, Nita Bennett, Alan Singer, Joyce Yamamoto, Helen Griffiths, Brendan Kitchen, Chloe Britton, Ian Gates, Lars Gavelin, Ron Tennant, Oded Shimshon, Brian Donovan, Max Patrick, Ian Shaw, Amanda Lawson, Carola Scupham, Andrew Clarke, David Voas, Laura Davison, Judy Berry, Andrew Land and Sue Carr, Gale Mead, Julia Newell and David Piper, Giuliana Grande, Liz Fogarty, Ian Gates, Gavin Breeze, Ceri Bygrave, Daniel Brook, Phil Davis, Jeff Evans, Anne Galos, Betty Garscia, Letta Gassiou, Eirik Gjonnes, Peter Harmston, Dylan Harris, Andy Kirk, David Lee, Charles Manton, Peter Marsh, Jutta Mistelbacher, Kevin Mitchell, Espen Naevestad, Anne Parker, Joy Rawlin, Ruth A. Cookson, Chris Peeler, Chris Hardy, Teresa P. Reed, Tamara Duker and George Khalaf, Dick and June Elliott, Revd. Mike Strange, Barbara Goulden, Maurice Fenn, Peter Van de Velde and Siska Germonpré, Rebecca Oliver, Stuart and Sally Rolfe, Simon Bridges, David Burt, J H Martin, Wilma Aarts, Anne Parker, Peter Marsh, Mariksa, Andrea Edwards, J. Hofman, Chris Hardy, Richard Teague, Rafal Kowalski, Marc Belgardt, Pamela Marriott, Phillip Stevens, Katherine Allen, Sue Seagroatt, Hugh Bayley, Dylan Harris and Ceri Bygrave, John Dowding.

SMALL PRINT

Photo credits

NO FLIES ON YOU!

The ideas expressed in this code were developed by and for independent travellers.

Learn About The Country You're Visiting

Start enjoying your travels before you leave by tapping into as many sources of information as you can.

The Cost Of Your Holiday

Think about where your money goes - be fair and realistic about how cheaply you travel. Try and put money into local peoples' hands; drink local beer or fruit juice rather than imported brands and stay in locally owned accommodation. Haggle with humour and not aggressively. Pay what something is worth to you and remember how wealthy you are compared to local people.

Embrace The Local Culture

Open your mind to new cultures and traditions - it will transform your experience. Think carefully about what's appropriate in terms of your clothes and the way you behave. You'll earn respect and be more readily welcomed by local people. Respect local laws and attitudes towards drugs and alcohol that vary in different countries and communities. Think about the impact you could have on them.

Exploring The World – The Travellers' Code

Being sensitive to these ideas means getting more out of your travels - and giving more back to the people you meet and the places you visit.

Minimise Your Environmental Impact

Think about what happens to your rubbish - take biodegradable products and a water filter bottle. Be sensitive to limited resources like water, fuel and electricity. Help preserve local wildlife and habitats by respecting local rules and regulations, such as sticking to footpaths and not standing on coral.

Don't Rely On Guidebooks

Use your guidebook as a starting point, not the only source of information. Talk to local people, then discover your own adventure!

Be Discreet With Photography

Don't treat people as part of the landscape, they may not want their picture taken. Ask first and respect their wishes.

We work with people the world over to promote tourism that benefits their communities, but we can only carry on our work with the support of people like you. For membership details or to find out how to make your travels work for local people and the environment, visit our website.

www.tourismconcern.org.uk

Tourism Concer
Campaigning for Ethical and Fairly Traded Tou